PENNIES FROM HEAVEN
The American Popular Music Business in the Twentieth Century

PENNIES FROM HEAVEN

The American Popular Music Business
in the Twentieth Century

RUSSELL SANJEK
Updated by DAVID SANJEK

DA CAPO PRESS • NEW YORK

Library of Congress Cataloging in Publication Data

Sanjek, Russell.
  Pennies from heaven: the American popular music business in the twentieth
century / Russell Sanjek; updated by David Sanjek.
     p.   cm.
  Rev. ed. of: American popular music and its business. v. 3, From 1900 to
1984. 1988.
  Includes bibliographical references and index.
  ISBN 0-306-80706-8 (alk. paper)
  1. Popular music—United States—History and criticism. 2. Music
trade—United States. I. Sanjek, David. II. Sanjek, Russell. American popular
music and its business. III. Title.
ML3477.S2 1996
338.4'778164'09730904—dc20

.ML 3477
S2 1996

96-23223
CIP
MN

•

First Da Capo Press edition 1996

This Da Capo Press paperback edition of *Pennies from Heaven* is an
unabridged republication of Russell Sanjek's *American Popular Music and
Its Business, Volume III: From 1900 to 1984*, first published in New York
in 1988, with the addition of a new preface (most of which originally
appeared as the preface to *American Popular Music Business in the
20th Century* by Russell Sanjek and David Sanjek), two new chapters,
and additions to the bibliography and index, all written by David Sanjek.
It is published by arrangement with Oxford University Press.

Published by Da Capo Press, Inc.
A Subsidiary of Plenum Publishing Corporation
233 Spring Street, New York, N.Y. 10013

Preface

This book is an expansion and updating of the third volume of
American Popular Music and Its Business—The First Four Hun-
dred Years by Russell Sanjek, my late father, published by Oxford University Press in 1989. It covers the years 1900 to 1996,
a rich and provocative period in the history of American entertainment, one marked by persistent technological innovation, an
expansion of markets, the refinement of techniques of commercial exploitation, and the ongoing democratization of American
culture. The invention of motion picture film, radio, and television as well as the current range of reproduction technologies,
from audio cassettes to the compact disc and other digital audio
technology, has broadened the avenues through which popular
music can reach the public. Publishers and record company executives in turn have utilized each of these media to market
their products while the body of writers and performers has increasingly represented a broader range of American society. The
creation of such diverse musical forms as blues, jazz, rhythm and
blues, country, latin, salsa, and rap music, to name but a few,
reflects the diversity of our cultural landscape. These many developments have also necessitated the rewriting of the Copyright
Act, as new rights and privileges of composers and performers
have arisen in response to expanding markets and novel technologies. Today American culture is one of this nation's major
growth industries and our second principal export (following
aerospace) to the world at large.

The present edition incorporates the entire contents of the third volume of my father's work along with a final section that summarizes the major events in the music business between 1985 and 1996. The remainder of this preface summarizes noteworthy material from the second volume of my father's study so as to provide an appropriate context for the main body of the book. Several themes guide the anecdotal record this volume provides and—as much as the many individuals, inventions, recordings, and legal wrangles—drives its narrative. They are, first, the many technological innovations that have permitted the transmission of music through a wide range of media. Corporate, creative, and scientific interests have worked together to create, market, and utilize those media to bring music to the public's attention. Second, each of these inventions has also been utilized by commercial interests to profit from the work of musical artists. The progress of the twentieth century has shown that the control of the entertainment marketplace increasingly rests in a small body of conglomerates. It has also illustrated that on occasion less than legal means have been used to permit music to reach the public through manipulation of the marketplace. Third, the course of the twentieth century has seen the forms of popular music broaden and, in effect, become ever more democratic. The musical canvas has become richer and more diverse as the work of marginalized members of American society has entered the mainstream. Without this diversity, American culture would constitute a narrow tradition. Finally, technological evolution has in turn necessitated that the laws respecting copyright undergo a similar transformation, although it is inescapable that the law will always lag behind the laboratory. (One legal scholar has proposed an average fifteen-year gap between the invention of a technology and the full legal protection of its uses.) Each time an invention increases the variety of means whereby composers or performers might earn royalties for their work, the courts have had to determine how these royalties might be calculated and how that technology affects the concept of intellectual property.

In turning to the material germane to the central discussion of this book, we must first explore the principal technological innovations of the latter half of the nineteenth century that had an important impact upon the music industry: the phonograph and the pianola, otherwise known as the player piano. Both were a boon to music publishers and composers as well as the public. They made it possible not to have to be physically present at a performance to sample many forms of music and opened new avenues of profit.

Thomas Alva Edison lays claim to the invention of the phonograph although several individuals helped to perfect it. Edison began experimenting with a speaking machine in 1877 in an attempt to capitalize upon Alexander Graham Bell's telephone, which had been publicly unveiled the year before. It was his hope that a talking machine might be marketed as a stenographic aid and a benefit to the deaf. He had stumbled upon the principle behind the phonograph when an embossing needle he was using to capture vibrations on paraffin paper accidentally pricked his finger. No one knows what epithet or expletive Edison might have uttered, but soon thereafter his agent was marketing a turntable and cylinder recording apparatus as a "talking machine," one of whose possible uses was illustrated when Edison recorded himself singing "Mary Had a Little Lamb."

In 1878 the Edison Speaking Phonograph Company was founded. Initial public response was great, and some exhibitors made as much as $1800 a week demonstrating the invention by making on-the-spot recordings. Interest waned, however, when the technology proved too frail. Into the breach stepped Alexander Graham Bell, who with two partners—Chichester A. Bell, an English-born cousin, and Charles Sumner Tainter, an American acoustic engineer—sought to create a more dependable recording system than Edison's fragile tin foil-covered cylinder. In 1884 they came up with a wax-coated cardboard cylinder, an improved diaphragm, a fluctuating stylus guided by the recording grooves, and an electric battery-powered motor instead of the original, unsteady hand-cranked device. Edison, recognizing the superiority of Bell's innovations, sought to pool patents and establish a joint enterprise, but Bell struck out on his own. Bell demonstrated the new "graphophone" in 1887 and established the American Graphophone Company.

To regain a competitive edge, Edison attracted public attention by bringing musical performers to his Menlo Park, New Jersey, laboratories to make recordings. While the recordings were initially for publicity's sake alone, their popularity led to the manufacture of coin-operated machines on which disks could be played. By 1889 Edison started to offer his recordings for sale, although he complained that other entrepreneurs were stealing his patents. He was unable to exert a monopoly, however, and other companies began to spring up, including the Columbia Phonograph Company, which was founded by some of Graphophone's original investors. They and others advertised their cylinders for home use or on coin-operated machines in record parlors. These predecessors to the present-day jukebox soon caught the public's attention and emptied its pockets. One dealer reported that in only six months five of his machines brought in over $3,000.

Despite such receipts, Edison stubbornly resisted commercial recordings, while Columbia, soon to be the largest and most successful holder of an Edison patent release, concentrated on the coin-operated automatic players. A market clearly existed for a home phonograph machine, but a disk was needed to replace the cumbersome cylinders. It was invented by the German-born Emile Berliner. In 1888, after having created vital transmitters for Bell Telephone, he conceived of engraving sound vibrations on a metal disk by a chemical action and using a hand-cranked machine on which to play them. His business, however, the Gramophone Company, remained a modest endeavor, and his technological innovation lacked adequate marketing, particularly as a result of the uncertainty of turntable speed produced by manual operation. Edison re-entered the scene and formed the National Phonograph Company. He soon developed a hand-wound spring-driven home phonograph as well as a system to mass produce records, five masters at a time. Columbia at the same time still ruled the cylinder market and had begun to sign well-known performers to exclusive recording contracts, the first said to be the U.S. Marine Band under the baton of the celebrated composer John Philip Sousa.

The hand-cranked machine perfected by Berliner remained inefficient but was the only available technology until 1896, when mechanical genius Eldridge Reeve Johnson, in conjunction with Berliner's company, invented the Victrola. It had a motor-powered drive and an improved sound box. Its new seven-inch recordings were made of celluloid, rather than vulcanized rubber, and their louder sound was an advantage over cylinders. Disgruntled competitors attempted to remove Berliner's firm as a serious competitor by campaigning against Johnson's innovations. His company withstood the opposition, expanded its operations internationally, and opened the first record factory in Hanover, Germany, in 1898. Soon thereafter Berliner and Johnson began to quarrel over patents, and Johnson separated from his employer. In 1900 Johnson set up his own firm, the Consolidated Talking Machine Company, and started to sell records and a player under the name Gramophone. Columbia sued Johnson and sought to have him forbidden to use the Gramophone name. The courts agreed with Columbia's demand, and Johnson replaced the name with one of his own: Victor. Desirous of regaining his association with Johnson, Berliner horse-traded a set of agreements with the inventor, and they formed the Victor Talking Machine Company in 1901.

While debates over patent rights continued, a structured phonographic marketplace was established. Three giants dominated the commercial arena with varied products: Edison, cylinder only; Victor, disks only; and Columbia, both. Production of recorded music multiplied many times in a decade, from 3,750,000 to 27,500,000 in 1909, with a cylinder-to-disk ratio of two to one at the start, and one to nine in 1914, several years after Columbia adopted a disks-only policy. The number of cylinder and record players grew in proportion, from an estimated near million produced in 1904. Victor alone produced 250,000 talking machines in the next five years.

Distribution of both recordings and phonographs was initially handled by mail order and outlet chains, but soon they could be purchased anywhere, from bicycle shops to department stores. Victor and Columbia fixed prices and offered a 15 percent discount on all merchandise. Edison, on the other hand, catered to a mid-American market of rural and small-town consumers. Victor soon dominated the market and benefited from international marketing agreements, particularly those with British Gramophone, who contributed the now famous "Little Nipper" logo, the dog listening to "his master's voice," which began to appear on all Victor records in 1902. British Gramophone that year also inaugurated Victor's higher priced, culturally auspicious Red Seal line, which catered to sophisticated tastes by making some of the world's greatest concert artists available. The Real Seal line began with recordings of Russia's Imperial Opera and soon added the work of opera's Enrico Caruso to their roster. Caruso would become one of Victor's biggest sellers and help the label to dominate the concert field for years.

Victor also initiated royalty payments to artists for recordings. Caruso's earnings illustrate not only how quickly the recording industry had become a major commercial market but also the potential earnings that performers stood to make. When Caruso signed his Victor contract in 1904, he was paid $4,000 for the first ten sides and forty cents per disk, plus an advance on royalties of $10,000 for the coming ten years. His income from recordings over his lifetime was reckoned to be from two to five million dollars.

The other major technological innovation of the second half of the nineteenth century was the pianola, or mechanical piano, first demonstrated at the Philadelphia Exposition in 1876. Its substantial popularity must be examined in the context of the American public's fascination with keyboards and home entertainment. It is estimated that by 1887 some 800,000 pianos had been purchased and more than half a million students studied the instrument. In 1902, another survey found that 92,000 musicians and music teachers were employed in this country, twice as many as in England, a society supposedly more cultured than that of the rough and tumble United States.

In 1850 piano mechanic John McTammany, whose tombstone reads "Inventor of the Player Piano," was granted a series of patents on the mechanical piano. It operated when one pumped a small bellows, which provided air to activate organ reeds and simultaneously worked a perforated paper roll. While McTammany had the wherewithal to design the pianola, he lacked the means to market it, and in 1888 he sold his patents to William B. Tremaine, who merchandised them as he did the products of the Aeolian Organ Company, which he owned as well. Later in 1899 Tremaine introduced the "Aeriola," a self-playing piano perfected by inventor Edwin Scott Votey. It was a pedal-operated machine which, when attached to a piano, enabled one to play the instrument mechanically while using a piano roll. Eventually 75,000 player pianos and a million music rolls were sold. Companies other than Tremaine's

Aeolian benefited from consumer interest. In 1898, the Wurlitzer Company of Cincinnati, Ohio, marketed the first successful coin-operated player piano, and piano parlors sprang up around the country. Enthusiasm for the mechanical keyboard peaked in the early 1920s by which time it had become a $10 million business. In 1921, of the 341,652 keyboards sold, 208,541 were mechanically powered.

The popular music of the day played on victrolas or placed upon piano rolls largely came from the commercial publishers and composers we have come to identify with Tin Pan Alley. That name came into being when the publisher M. Witmark and Sons relocated their offices at 49–51 West 28th Street. It is said, perhaps apocryphally, to have been coined by writer Monroe H. Rosenfeld to describe the firm's piano, which had been fixed to produce the tinkling syncopation of a current popular form of music by interweaving paper strips between its strings.

While American music publishing has a long and illustrious history, it was advances in the marketing and publicizing of catalogues that typified its activities in the second half of the nineteenth century. Practices were developed that allowed material to reach the broadest range of consumers through the widest possible means. Stress was put upon using popular performers to advertise the publishers' wares in return for various forms of financial remuneration—what came to be identified as "pay for play" and later as "payola." "Advance" or "professional" copies of sheet music were given to performers, often featuring their pictures on the cover. This might also involve giving them the "exclusive" rights to perform a particular composition. Often a popular artist would interpolate such an "exclusive" piece into a performance, stopping the program and thereby giving the publisher publicity. Another strategy was to have performance instigated by a "plant" in the audience. Publishers also employed individuals who came to be known as "song pluggers," often the writers of the very material they promoted, who demonstrated compositions before performers or theatrical managers or music sellers in order to entice them to feature the material. Orchestra and dance band leaders were provided with sheet music free of charge, often accompanied by large-sized folders to hold musicians' music on the back of which was displayed the publisher's name in three-inch letters. Innovative forms of marketing were employed as new technologies opened up novel agencies for publicity. One was the projection of stereoptican slides with illustrated song lyrics at theaters, which led to the birth of the "sing along." This was first used to promote Robert Lowry's sentimental classic "Where Is My Wandering Boy Tonight?," and soon songs were being written specifically for stereoptican projection.

Costs for promotion rose quickly and began to eat into publisher's profits. By the middle of the 1890s it was estimated to cost $1300 to launch a song: $250 for 10,000 professional copies; $50 to print a star's picture on the cover of regular copies; $500 for advertising in the trade papers; an initial payment of $500 to a performer guaranteeing to feature the song professionally. Understandably, the odds against success rose equally with the potential profit margin. Only one out of 200 songs made a substantial profit. Fewer than half made back the initial $1300 promotion investment.

At the turn of the century publishers' interest focused particularly upon "production music"—that which was written for musical comedies and four-act plays. It was from this repertoire that most orchestras in large hotels, plush restaurants, and vaudeville houses drew their selections. The attention paid to this branch of entertainment indicated that as much as the publishers of Tin Pan Alley controlled most popular music, a small body of theatrical producers monopolized what appeared on the stages not only of Broadway but also across the country. By 1906 the American theater was a $200-million enterprise employing over 100,000 people, principally under the control of the Klaw-Erlanger organization and newcomers like the Shubert brothers. Klaw-Erlanger, together with several other booking agents, formed a theatrical trust, "the Syndicate," in 1896 which controlled more than 700 theaters nation-wide. Other producers and theater managers trusted their judgment, but whether they did or not "the Syndicate" forced them to accept what it offered, regardless of quality. Its virtual stranglehold over popular entertainment held fast until 1916.

The most illustrious popular composers of the late nineteenth and early twentieth century were Victor Herbert, John Philip Sousa, and George M. Cohan. Herbert was perhaps the first popular American composer to realize the potential monetary gains *writers* might make from their work. In the past composers too often sold their material outright or failed to maximize the possible avenues of exploitation. Herbert insisted that no less than 5 percent of box office receipts be paid to him and his collaborators; that no songs or music by other writers be interpolated into performances of his work; and that he must control the final libretto. His string of hits—35 successful musicals over 30 years—illustrates the degree to which his music appealed to the public. Herbert was also among the first to institutionalize the collection of royalties through his participation in the founding of the American Society of Composers and Publishers (ASCAP).

John Philip Sousa, like Herbert, hit a responsive chord with his many marches and, although a less effective businessman than Herbert, managed to become one of the highest paid composers of his day. Originally intending to be, like Herbert, an operetta composer, Sousa instead became the bandmaster of the U.S. Marine Band, and it was the marches he composed especially for that ensemble that gained him international fame. He resigned that post in 1892 and soon thereafter signed a contract with the John Church Company, of Cincinnati, giving him royalties that eventually rose to 15 percent of the retail price from sheet music sales. In the period July to September 1894 three marches alone brought in $6,588.94. Later he would also profit from the new technology of phonograph recording as performances by his ensemble were among the top sellers of the day.

George M. Cohan proved very popular on the stage with musicals that featured down-to-earth vernacular dialogue and show-stopping tunes at a time when most stage musicals were European-influenced and British musical comedies predominated. The multi-talented Cohen, who wrote the book, music, and lyrics in addition to starring in his shows, appealed to the patriotic spirit of the American public. Such classics as "Yankee Doodle Dandy," "You're a Grand Old Flag," and "Over There" helped to earn him a Congressional medal, the first such honor awarded to an American songwriter. In 1910, when the prolific writer/performer had six hit shows running on Broadway and concurrently on tour, his friend Marc Klaw of the theatrical firm Klaw-Erlanger said Cohan represented "the spirit and energy of the twentieth century—a concentrated essence, four-cylinder power—a protest against and apology for the elimination of the palmy days of the drama . . . This youngster struck a universal chord in his songs and plays, and that is why we know and love him."

While individuals like Herbert, Sousa, and Cohan represented the mainstream tastes of the period, American popular music was beginning to be diversified if not in substance at least in the ranks of those who produced and profited from it. While the Civil War and the period of Reconstruction had modified the legal status of black Americans, racism was far from eradicated even if avenues for black advancement, including in the music business, did begin to appear. Admittedly, the genre to which they were connected had the unappetizing appelation of "coon music," a none too substantial advancement over the prior "darky music." The term applied to all songs sung in black dialect or in some way involving a black person—although it must be remembered that most "coon songs" were performed by whites. Nonetheless, black performers did gain fame, one of the earliest of whom was Ernest Hogan, author of "All Coons Look Alike to Me." This song was one of the era's greatest hits, both as a vocal performance and in a band arrangement by white musician Max Hoffman. Hogan went on to write and appear in a number of musicals and, up to his death in 1907, was said to be the greatest performer ever seen in the American black theater. When pressed about the racial nature of the song that made him famous, Hogan stated he felt it was composed at a time when music needed a new direction, and its success made the path easier for other black artists to follow. Those included Irving Jones, author of "Ballin' the Jack" (1911); Gussie L. Davis, best known for waltzes; Bob Cole, and the brothers James Weldon and J. Rosamund Johnson, who, in addition to several successful musical comedies and comic operas, penned "Lift Every Voice and Sing," which became the National Association for the Advancement of Colored People's official song. Most successful, perhaps, was the stage performer Bert Williams, who, along with his partner George Walker, introduced the cakewalk to the American dance tradition and starred in several popular musicals. Upon Walker's death in 1911 Williams went on to even greater fame as the only black performer in Florenz Ziegfeld's *Follies* in 1910 and he appeared in each subsequent edition until his death. Also, Williams had started recording for the Victor Talking Machine Company in 1901 and was the first black artist to have a sustained career in the recording business.

The musical landscape was most memorably transformed by black writers during this period through the introduction of ragtime, which took embellished or syncopated melody lines and played them off against the "slow drag" of parade music. One of the predecessors of American jazz, ragtime first appeared on the scene in 1896 when Max Hoffman, who served the same function for Ernest Hogan, transcribed performer Ben Harney's "Mr. Johnson Turn Me Loose." The rhythmic eccentricities of Harney's style began the ragtime vogue and produced a number of million sellers in the form of sheet music, recordings, and piano rolls. The greatest ragtime composer certainly was Scott Joplin. His best-selling composition "Maple Leaf Rag" (1906) was recorded by the U.S. Marine Band and sold over a million copies in sheet music. Between 1899 and his death in 1917, Joplin published over fifty pieces, many of which are among the classic ragtime compositions. Joplin, however, had higher aims, although his publisher, John Stark, did not care for some of his more inventive works. This caused Joplin to abandon the popular music business and devote himself to the completion of his opera *Treemonisha,* a 230-page vocal-piano score with twenty-seven interpolated songs, first printed in 1911. During Joplin's lifetime it was performed but once, and under rough-hewn conditions, in 1915 to an invited audience, with Joplin on piano as the sole accompanist. Long after his death the innovative nature of the score was recognized and *Treemonisha* received a full-scale production.

For all ragtime's success, however, its acceptance was far from complete as the racial origin of its principal composers generated virulent prejudice. At its national meeting in 1901 the American Federation of Musicians sought to ban ragtime and all other manifestations of "the negro school." Battle cries were mounted against the purported debasement of musical taste and threat to public morality that black music was said to represent. Such efforts indicated that while the business of American music was being democratized and the body of composers now represented a wider range of the populace, the taint of prejudice was no less evident in the entertainment world than in society at large.

If the music industry did not regulate the racism in American society, it did cooperate with efforts to legislate protection of foreign authors' and composers' rights through the Copyright Act of 1891 and its subsequent revisions in 1897 and 1909. Before 1891, there was no regulation of the works of foreigners, and publishers were free to issue whatever works by foreigners they wished with no legal liabilities or payments to the writer. Creators pressed for some form of protection. The European artistic community had already enacted a binding system of protection. It had been initiated by France's Société des Autuers, Compositeurs et Editeurs de Musique (SACEM), founded in 1851, which was an impetus to other European countries to convene the Berne Convention in 1886. This agreement did not account for mechanical reproduction of music but did assert that any writer who complied with the copyright law of his own country enjoyed full protection against pirated editions or, in the case of printed literature, unauthorized translations in all signatory nations, which, at that time, did not include the United States. When publishing works by foreigners, publishers in the United States were operating under a gentlemen's agreement known to members of the U.S. Board of Trade as "courtesy of the trade." It implied that once a publisher publicly staked out an initial claim to a particular foreign work, it could be expected that others would not initiate an edition of their own.

The supervision of the registration of American copyrights had been entrusted to the Library of Congress and its librarian in 1860. Five years later, a penalty of twenty-five dollars for each failure to make a proper deposit was enacted. A recording fee of fifty cents for each transaction was instituted in 1870, as was a penalty on one dollar for every sheet of printed material found that had been manufactured without the copyright owner's written permission, half of the collected sum to go "to the use of the United States." These regulations doubled the fines incorporated in the first federal Copyright Act signed in 1790. The policing and collection function for the 1865 and 1870 regulations were left to the copyright owner, who had to apply to civil courts for redress.

However, despite these changes, it was recognized that the system was makeshift and not altogether dependable. New calls were issued for further reforms and led to the foundation of the American Publishers' Copyright League in 1887. Their efforts met with success in 1891 when the first major revision since 1790 of the U.S. Copyright Act was made. Known at the Chace Act, its provisions extended copyright protection to twenty-eight years for both resident and nonresident authors if reciprocal copyright relations existed between the two nations involved; books, chromos, and lithographs had to be manufactured in the United States to obtain copyright; foreign copyrighted books could be imported, subject to duty.

Despite the substantial changes wrought by the 1891 Chace Act, music publishing only fully came of age, insofar as the legislative process involving copyright was concerned, in 1895 with the formation of the new Music Publishers Association of the United States. The seventeen members aimed to elevate the tone and character of their business by correcting evident abuses and most of all by achieving adequate revision of the copyright system so that their enterprise was more fully protected. Their efforts resulted in the 1897 revision of the Copyright

Act. It inaugurated a government-supported Copyright Office, increased penalties, and strengthened law against piracy. Most important, it added the words *"and musical"* to the statute enacted in 1856 extending protection to dramatists against unlicensed public performance of their work. This change specifically covered the kind of dramatic performances— operas, farces, extravaganzas, and other forms of musical theater—popular in the period.

Technological developments led in 1906 to a further revision of the Copyright Act, starting with legislative discussion in the Senate and House Patent Committees. The question at hand was whether or not mechanical reproduction of music in the form of piano rolls constituted an infringement. The government argued that the rolls were in effect "writing" and within the scope of the present law. Yet it was two additional provisions unconnected to the piano roll debate that would have a lasting effect on the future of music publishing: protection against unlicensed public performance for profit and compulsory licensing with a two-cent royalty fee on all sheet music. The final hearings in 1908 took into account a recent Supreme Court decision in *White, Smith, vs Apollo* that copyright protection must be extended to cover mechanically recorded music, a provision that, with the growth of the record industry, was to have enormous influence. So too would the final version of the new Copyright Act, signed by President Theodore Roosevelt before he left office in 1909. It included a provision that guaranteed the *exclusive* right "to perform the copyrighted work publicly for profit if it be a musical composition and for the purpose of public performance for profit." Although few in the music industry paid much heed to this new legislation, not too far ahead income from this right would provide the major portion of financial returns from copyrighted music.

Larchmont, New York   D. S.

Contents

Abbreviations, xix

Part One   1900–1920

1. Thomas Edison's Wonderful Kinetoscope Machine, 3
2. Big Time, Small Time, and E. F. Albee, 16
3. The Victrola and the Pianola, 22
4. Inside the Popular-Music Business, 32

Part Two   1921–1930

5. Popular Songs and the Movie Business, 47
6. The Decline and Fall of the House of Albee, 57
7. The Mechanical Music Business, 62
8. A Simple Radio Music Box, 74
9. A Glut of Movie Music, 91

Part Three   1931–1940

10. The Fall and Rise of the Record Business, 117
11. Music in Motion Pictures, 147
12. Popular Music and Radio, 159
13. ASCAP versus the Broadcasters, 184

Part Four   1941–1953

14. On the Road to New Technology and an Expanded Industry, 215
15. Mass Entertainment and the Music Business, 251
16. ASCAP and BMI Face the Reality of Television, 291

Part Five   1954–1966

17. From Monaural to Stereophonic Sound, 333
18. Growth to a Four-Billion-Dollar Business, 367
19. ASCAP versus BMI, 396
20. Payola Problems and Rate Wars, 439

Part Six   1967–1970

21. Copyright Revision or Not?, 493
22. The Music-Licensing Wars, 498
23. Big Money Invades the Music Business, 507
24. FM and Top 40 Radio, 518

Part Seven   1971–1976

25. Continued Fighting over Licensing, 523
26. Industry Associations Play Their Part, 528
27. "The Seven Dirty Words" Case and MOR Music, 543
28. Configurations, Payola, and Soul Music, 549
29. A New Copyright Bill at Last, 563

Part Eight   1977–1980

30. The U.S. Supreme Court and Licensing, 573
31. The Copyright Royalty Tribunal, 581
32. Other Copyright Problems, 588
33. Seesawing Sales and New Ideas in the Record Business, 594

Part Nine   1981–1984

34. Television Music Licensing, 617
35. Rates and Piracy—Unsolved Problems, 624
36. Continuing Difficulties for Music Publishers, 627
37. Tight Control of a Prosperous Record Business, 634

Part Ten   1985–1996

38. Anxious "Indies" in an Aggressive Marketplace, 657
39. Desperately Seeking Synergy, 670

Bibliography, 685
Index, 725

Abbreviations

ACA	American Composers Alliance
AFM	American Federation of Musicians
AGAC	American Guild of Authors and Composers
AIR	American Independent Radio
AMP	Associated Music Publishers
AOR	Album Oriented Rock
ARMADA	American Record Manufacturers and Distributors Association
ASCAP	American Society of Composers and Publishers
BMG	Bertelsman Music Group
BMI	Broadcast Music Incorporated
CEMA	Capitol EMI America
CATV	Cable Television
CGA	Composers Guild of America
CHR	Contemporary Hits Radio
CISAC	Confédération Internationale des Sociétés d'Auteurs et Compositeurs
CLGA	Composers and Lyricists Guild
CMA	Country Music Association
CMDJA	Country Music Disk Jockey Association
CMJ	College Music Journal
CRT	Copyright Royalty Tribunal
CWC	Current Writers Committee
EMI	Electrical & Musical Industries
ERPI	Electrical Research Products Incorporated
HMV	His Majesty's Voice
IFPMP	International Federation of Popular Music Publishers
IRNA	Independent Radio Network Associates
KAO	Keith-Albee-Orpheum
MCA	Music Corporation of America

MDS	Music Dealers Service
MGA	Musicians Guild of America
MICC	Music Industries Chamber of Commerce
MOA	Music Operators of America
MPA	Music Publishers Association
MPCE	Music Publishers Contact Employees
MPHC	Music Publishers Holding Corporation
MPPA	Music Publishers Protection Association
MPPC	Motion Picture Patents Company
NAB	National Association of Broadcasters
NAPA	National Association of Performing Artists
NARM	National Association of Record Merchandisers
NARTB	National Association of Radio and Television Broadcasters
NCRA	National Commission for the Recording Arts
NMPA	National Music Publishers Association
NVA	National Vaudeville Artists
PMA	Publishers and Managers Association
PMRC	Parents Music Resource Council
PRS	British Performing Rights Society
RIAA	Recording Industry Association of America
RPF	Radio Program Foundation
SACEM	Société des Auteurs, Compositeurs et Editeurs de Musique
SARA	Society of American Recordings Artists
SCA	Screen Composers Association
SESAC	Society of European Stage Authors and Composers
SOA	Songwriters of America
SPA	Songwriters Protective Association
UBO	United Booking Office
UCC	Universal Copyright Convention
VMA	Vaudeville Managers Association
VMPA	Vaudeville Managers Protective Association
WEA	Warner Electra Asylum

PART ONE

1900–1920

CHAPTER 1

Thomas Edison's Wonderful Kinetoscope Machine

Two years after Koster & Bial's luxurious Concert Hall in New York presented "living pictures" of a half-clad Diana and her court awaiting the dawn in a program the *New York Times* hailed as "what they now call 'vaudeville' seen at its best'', Thomas Edison's new invention, the Vitascope, projected moving hand-colored pictures of more than life-sized women dancers from the theater's second balcony onto a twenty-foot stereopticon screen. The moving-picture industry came to life on April 23, 1896, following the end of the nation's most serious economic depression up to that time.

During the mid-1880s, feeling that a machine that would do for the eye what his talking machine was doing for the ear was feasible. Edison had put a young laboratory assistant, William K. L. Dickson, to work on the project. The "wizard with a thousand ideas" had in mind an apparatus that would permit viewing through a magnifying lens of continuous pictures, mounted on a cylinder like the one used in his phonograph. Yet, once his patent application for the Kinetoscope, or "moving views," was filed, in late 1888, Edison abandoned the cylinder design. He had seen the work of George Eastman's new Kodak camera, which had a roll of flexible film of 100 separate pictures, and he called on the inventor for assistance. Eastman obliged with a fifty-foot strip of improved thin blank film, and Dickson went to work on a new tack. In August 1891, Edison's new Apparatus for Exhibiting Photographs of Moving Objects was ready for a patent application. Dickson pepped up the first demonstration for Edison of his new invention by appearing on screen to greet his employer with words simultaneously reproduced by a phonograph cylinder synchronized with the filmed action. It was the first talking moving picture. Only the magnifying lens remained of Edison's original concept, now mounted in a wooden cabinet at which a single person could view back-lighted 150-foot-long strips of film rolling through a bank of spools at about forty-five pictures a second.

Because he was then in the midst of an expensive fight with the Columbia Phonograph Company for control of the talking-machine business, Edison believed the $150 for foreign patent applications too much and left his discovery free for unlicensed development in England and on the Continent. When conditions improved in 1893, he built the first motion-picture studio, near his West Orange, New Jersey, laboratories, at a cost of $637.67. Known as the "Black Maria," because of its resemblance to the hooded police truck, it was a fully covered stage suspended from a center pivoting-pole. This allowed following the sunlight, without which early moving pictures could not be made.

In 1894, two agents for Edison's Kinetoscope Company, sole vendor of the device and territorial exhibition rights, purchased the first ten viewing machines to come out of the factory and installed them in a Kinetoscope Parlor at 1155 Broadway, in New York. Entrepreneurs and speculators soon opened exhibition rooms in large cities, generally in connection with a penny arcade, in which a single row of Kinetoscopes stood amid banks of other coin-in-the-slot devices. For a penny or a nickel, patrons could view twenty to fifty feet of film showing trained animals, pretty young dancers from the latest musical comedies, a tooth extraction, Buffalo Bill in a rifle-shooting exhibition, slapstick comedy scenes, the spectacle of a man caught in the act of sneezing, a couple kissing, and other similar wonders. Most of these were filmed under Dickson's direction in the Black Maria, and copies were sold outright to exhibitors for $12.50 to $15.00 each.

Edison believed that his peep-show machine was a money-making novelty whose appeal would soon end, so he neglected to develop it further. There were others, however, who saw the Kinetoscope as a medium for enlarged images, to be thrown on an acceptable large surface. Among them was Major Woodville Latham, of Nashville, Tennessee, who financed the development of a modified Edison machine with an arc lamp behind the film and a projecting lens in front. With Dickson's assistance, he staged a four-minute prize fight in daylight and began to display a crudely filmed version of it to the public in May 1895. New York newspapers reported that his machine outclassed Edison's. Production of it was begun, together with a series of four-minute films made specifically for what he called "the Pantoptikon."

That same year, a young Washingtonian with a bent for tinkering, Thomas Armat, working in the basement of his real estate office developed an improved projector, which he patented as the Vitascope. Recognizing that the chief defect in Latham's projector was its jerky, jumping pictures, he created a "beater mechanism" to provide smoother feeding of the film across the lens. Unable to commercialize his machine, Armat took it to Norman C. Raff, who was in charge of Edison's motion-picture business. He arranged a demonstration. Edison found little new except the feeding process, but he was persuaded by Raff to manufacture it under his own name and thus be the first to market a practical projection machine. With Edison in the box of honor at Koster & Bial's on April 23, 1896, Armat, who had been convinced that participation by the great inventor was essential in order to merchandise the projector successfully, operated his version of the Vitascope. He did this for a week at the Concert Hall.

A number of Edison's original machines had been shipped to London and the Continent, where other improvements were made. Manufacture of cameras, projection machines, and other equipment based on Edison's original patents was also started. The first important competitor to the Kinetoscope came from France, a product of this legal but clandestine development. The original Armat-Edison machine was still in use at Koster & Bial's, and Raff was beginning to sell Kinetoscopes at from $1,500 to $5,000 each, when B. F. Keith's man in New York imported an early Cinématographe, manufactured in Paris. As a result, in the summer of 1896 two Keith theaters in New York were showing moving pictures in connection with their programs of refined vaudeville, using either an Edison or an imported machine. In most other cities and on the western Orpheum Circuit, the Edison monopoly prevailed until a new group, the American Biograph Company, moved into vaudeville houses with projectors and movies of its own manufacture, to which only projectionists in its employ had access. The industry had reached a plateau of development and an exhibition policy that prevailed for several years. Neither Edison nor Biograph sold their cameras, in order to maintain control of film making. During this time, the big-city middle-class audience who patronized refined vaudeville became the first mass market for moving pictures. They were attracted by filmed news events, which often were captured by the camera as they occurred. As competition for the attention of this audience grew hotter, leading to the presentation of a greater variety of expensive live talent, and the movies tended to bore, because they showed the same old subjects, managers instituted the policy of showing moving pictures only in order to clear their houses between live presentations. For the urban poor and the vast masses of less fortunate amusement seekers, the peep show and the phonograph parlor were still among the few inexpensive popular family entertainments.

In 1902, Thomas Talley, the operator of a Phonograph and Kinetoscope Palace in Los Angeles, addressed himself to these multitudes by opening the High Class Electric Theater. There, ladies and children were particularly welcome, to watch a "vaudeville of motion pictures lasting one hour," for which he charged ten cents, matinees for children a nickel. Talley, too, soon found the supply of compelling movies running out. Only after the appearance of the first American "story picture," *The Great Train Robbery,* in 1903 did the first "screen theater" become a viable piece of real estate that could afford to pay as much as $100 for each one-reel fourteen-minute story film.

The Great Train Robbery was made in the wilds of New Jersey, near Edison's manufacturing and laboratory complex, and its exciting action and simple story won Americans over to the new medium. Production of feature films speeded up in makeshift studios indoors in New York and Chicago or, when weather permitted, under the sun. The first true movie theater opened in 1905 in McKeesport, Pennsylvania, where two exhibitor entre-preneurs remodeled a street-level store to resemble a theater, installed a piano, and began to show twenty minutes of movies continuously from eight in the morning until midnight. They called it a "Nickelodeon." Within two years, 5,000 similar places were thriving throughout the nation. These "family theaters" catered to people of all ages by offering a hodgepodge of story pictures and short features: melodramas, comedies, travel pictures, news events, circus performers, dancers, exotic foreigners on their native heath, and, always, hand-illustrated slides flashing a picture-story and the words of a popular song on the screen. Illustrated song-slides, a device introduced in the early 1890s by music publishers to plug their products, had become lavish, expensive undertakings, often employing several dozen individual photographs to depict the story of a ballad. Slide presentations of coon songs, then at the height of their popularity and a substantial por-tion of Tin Pan Alley's production in the early 1900s, served to strengthen the stereotype of American blacks as shiftless no-accounts who feasted on watermelon, fought with razors, and were promiscuous sexual adventurers. Most white minorities in the great American melting pot were treated more kindly, out of fear of offending ticket and sheet-music purchasers.

In slum quarters and shopping areas for the poor, where nickelodeons were concentrated, the flickering images of well-dressed people in luxurious settings, filmed for such people as Charles K. Harris and the Witmarks, excited new Americans with visions of what might be attained in the land of the free. When patrons joined to sing the new songs, the vocabulary of American popular music became their common language, its catch phrases and turns of speech their colloquialisms, and its melodies the folk music of their new country. In the city of Chicago alone, 100,000 persons a day visited a moving-picture house in 1907, one of either 116 nickelodeons or eighteen ten-cent penny arcades with peep shows, films, and coin-operated phonographs. America's appetite for the movies was becoming insatiable. The program in a nickelodeon consisted of three to five reels and was changed almost daily, leading to a demand for new films that only a relative handful of companies were supplying.

Inevitably, as happened in all branches of entertainment, those who owned and monopolized patents, production, and distribution dealing with motion pictures formed a trust. For almost a decade, Edison's legal staff had been engaged in litigation with rival companies over patent misappropriation.

From this chaos, in 1908, the Motion Picture Patents Company emerged, a combination of Edison, American Biograph, Kalem, Lubin, Selig, the Essanay Company, and two foreign concerns, Pathé Frères and George Melies et Cie of Paris. The last two had entered the American market chiefly to foil illegal duplication of their artistically ambitious productions, a common practice of the one-reel film makers, and then began to do business in movie hardware. The MPPC trust licensed motion-picture theaters, taxed each two dollars per week to use officially approved equipment, and rented films for from $15 to $125 per day. The trust also waged a vicious war on unlicensed exhibitors, raided theaters, smashed projectors, and destroyed "outlaw" films made by independent companies. Within eighteen months, 5,281 of the country's 9,490 screen theaters in operation in 1910 had been brought into line. The MPPC's next step was the formation of the General Film Exchange, a syndicate of more than half the 100 sources of supply of moving pictures. The earliest of these had been formed during the 1890s, for exhibitors to trade in or exchange moving pictures they had purchased for an average of ten cents a foot. With member producers no longer selling their wares outright to theaters, these middle-men jobbers cornered local markets by buying large quantities for rental to exhibitors, and profited as never before.

Among the outlaw independents who began to defy the MPPC by making movies of more than one reel were some who played important roles in the popular-music business: the furrier Adolph Zukor; the one-time cloth sponger for a garment house William Fox; and the nickelodeon and exchange owners Harry and Jack Warner. It did not take them or other independents long to become aware that the moving picture was blessed with a unique and still unrecognized capability: it could tell a story whose action spanned several reels without losing an audience's attention. As a consequence, they began vigorously competing to sign performers blessed with the charismatic on-screen personality that attracted ticket buyers. The MPPC had made anonymous economic peons of its human talent, paying low wages and never identifying, on screen, actors or directors; when fans wrote asking the names of certain players they were ignored. Mary Pickford, who was known to her audiences only as "Little Mary," because of the roles she played, was making five dollars a day working for Biograph in California in 1910. Later that year, she was stolen away with an offer of $175 a week. A few months later, it was $1,500 a month and the promise of credit on the screen.

William Fox, the most recalcitrant of the independents and owner of the only rental company that had failed to join the General Film Exchange, began a prolonged legal battle with the movie trust in 1912. His license to deal in any MPPC product was canceled, compelling him to obtain an injunction. Simultaneously, he made use of his strong contacts with New York's powerful Tammany Hall political organization to get the government to institute antitrust action. The combine was forced to do business with him as a result, though the case dragged through the lower courts before it finally was heard by the Supreme Court in 1915.

Adolph Zukor became a sudden new power in the independent movement in 1912, a time when admission prices were doubling to a dime, with little complaint. Leaving his job as treasurer for Marcus Loew's expanding chain of small-time vaudeville and screen theaters, he purchased, for $18,000, the American rights to a French-made two-reeler starring the aging trage-dienne Sarah Bernhardt. Firmly convinced that the time had come for the industry to offer multiple-reel productions of stage-quality picture-stories starring great players in great plays, he by-passed the MPPC and showed *Queen Elizabeth* in midsummer of 1912 in a New York legitimate theater. He charged one dollar for admission, a price never asked before for a movie. Territorial rights were auctioned independently for $80,000, producing an immediate profit of 300 percent. This was surpassed in 1913 by George Kleine, of Kalem, one of the original founders of the movie combine, with the eight-reel *Quo Vadis,* which had been filmed on location in Italy. It played in a legitimate Broadway theater at a dollar a head for twenty-two weeks, and then went on the road to large theaters in major cities, bringing even greater grosses. David Wark Griffith, who had started in the business as a director for five dollars a day, filmed the first long American feature, *Judith of Bethulia,* on four reels. Its receipts, which eventually rose to $200,000, boosted the asking price for his services to more than $50,000 a year.

Such impressive returns from feature films attracted the legitimate-theater syndicates, which controlled a national business estimated in 1910 to pro-duce $100 million annually. Klaw & Erlanger, the earliest of these monop-olies, whose 400 theaters employed 60,000 persons touring in 700 plays and musical attractions, arranged for film distribution through Biograph. The company filmed several features, but exhibitors found their fifty-dollar-a-day rental fee too steep for "New York movies." Abbreviated versions were offered at standard prices instead. Two were made with the black entertainer Bert Williams, who had become an international favorite after his Ziegfeld's *Follies.* Rampant racial prejudice, however, led to riots wherever the films were show, forcing their withdrawal from the market.

The Shubert brothers were more fortunate in their moving-picture ven-tures. One of the leading independent movie makers, Carl Laemmle, found himself with ten reels of negatives made by a production unit assigned to film a two-reel movie on prostitution. With $5,700 already invested, he was loath to risk more, so he sold a one-third interest and all exploitation rights to the Shuberts for $33,000. The final, six-reel, version, advertised as a "$200,000 spectacle in 700 scenes with 800 players . . . showing the traps laid for young girls by vice agents, based on the Rockefeller White Slave Report," went on view in twenty-eight Shubert theaters in the New York area. Four or five showings were given daily, with seats anywhere in the house for thirty-five cents. The Shuberts grossed $440,000. Some of this profit went into World Special Films, to produce films of Broadway plays with the original casts. This in time became part of Zukor's Famous Players–Paramount, the company that paid Mary Pickford one million dollars a year.

William Randolph Hearst, the newspaper tycoon who revolutionized that field with his brand of yellow journalism, had built circulation for his mammoth Sunday editions by publishing the complete words and music of current popular-song hits. Working with the Edison studios in 1912, the Hearst management engaged next in a circulation-building scheme for one of its women's magazines. It ran, monthly, unfinished stories, to which readers were invited to supply endings. These were considered for production by the film makers. Out of this came the first filmed serial story, *The Adventures of Kathlyn*, made in Chicago by the Selig Company, an MPPC member, in conjunction with the *Daily Tribune*. This coalition was forged by Max Annenberg, a former Heast executive who was circulation manager for the paper. The weekly serial pushed the paper's readership up by 10 percent, as it did for other news publications through national syndication. Enraged by his chief competitor's success, Hearst tied up Selig's future production with an agreement for a weekly news film, the *Hearst-Selig Newsreel*, a short-subject attraction that provided a new ingredient to screen-theater programs.

The advent of the first two-dollar movie, *The Birth of a Nation*, in New York City on March 3, 1915, ended the desperate hope held by out-of-work vaudeville troupers that the enormous popularity of moving pictures would soon abate. It was, motion-picture historians agree, a movie seen by more people than had read any book in the history of man other than the *Bible*. It reaped a profit of $50 million in less than forty years.

For his elaborate epic, which cost as much as ten regular features, D.W. Griffith chose a novel about the South during the Civil War, *The Clansman*, by Thomas Dixon. In a review following the film's premiere, the *New York Times* deplored the nasty spirit running through the film, particularly "the unhappy chapter of the Reconstruction and concerning the sorry services rendered by plucking at old wounds." Another review, more direct, pointed to it as a "deliberate attempt to humiliate 10,000,000 American citizens and portray them as nothing but beasts." Indeed, the film evoked a wicked strain of racism in many Americans and led to a revival of interest in the Ku Klux Klan, which the movie glorified.

Technically, *The Birth of a Nation* was a most innovative production. Brilliant camera action went from great battle scenes taken in panorama, to stunning close-ups, even of bit players, to the list of performers' names in the opening credits. It was, at the *Times* observed, an "impressive new illustration of the scope of the motion picture camera," and it brought the moving-picture business to maturity.

Using the legitimate theater's multiple road-presentation method, Zukor's Paramount distribution wing sent out twelve companies. Each was supplied with a 151-page piano score and all orchestral parts of the first important American score of accompanying film music. It was played by as many as sixty musicians in the large theaters where the picture was shown. Working with an unimportant composer of art and operatic music, Joseph Carl Breil, Griffith had chosen appropriate selections from Wagner, Grieg, Beethoven, Schubert, Schumann, Rossini, and other European masters. Most of their music had not yet been heard by the majority of middle-class and poor Americans, and thus was a great novelty. Breil also composed some original music, including a "love strain," which was called "The Perfect Song" when published with words. It later served as theme music for "Amos 'n' Andy," a blackface-comedy radio program that began in the late 1920s. Though the music was mostly what are regarded today as ancient warhorses, it was *The Birth of a Nation*'s introduction to the rousing strains of the *"William Tell* Overture" or the "Ride of the Valkyries" that made them such.

In 1894, when the Edison Kinetoscope Company began the first mass production of short moving pictures for the peep-show machines, it also offered appropriate cylinder recordings for nearly all the films available. A Kineto-Phone phonograph, with earphones, was available for $350 to provide a sort of synchronization of music and filmed action. In the ensuing years, many inventors worked on a process that would truly synchronize music and singing with motion pictures.

The well-financed Camerophone Company introduced its record player coupled with three separate projectors as part of a Brooklyn vaudeville show in 1909. A number of leading Broadway singing actresses had been filmed, and disk recordings of their most popular songs were made simultaneously. Eva Tanguay, the "I don't care girl," received $2,500 for doing the song that brought her that soubriquet; Blanche Ring sang her "Bells on Her Fingers, Rings on Her Toes"; Trixie Friganza and the British music-hall star performer Maria Lloyd were paid at least $1,500 for making disks. The chief technical problem was how to achieve volume sufficient to fill a large theater. That caused the venture to fail.

Pianos were first installed in nickelodeons in order to cover the whirring of the projection machines, and it was left to the pianist to select appropriate music. Exhibitors, however, became concerned about the quality of music and demanded appropriate popular songs or "good" music, "Träumerei," "The Pilgrims' Chorus," "Melody in F," and Louis Moreau Gottschalk's ubiquitous "Dying Poet" and "Last Hope." In the mid-1900s, the Edison Company first programmed suitable instrumental music to be used with its releases, publishing lists in monthly bulletins sent to exchanges, jobbers, and exhibitors. In 1909, the Vitagraph Company of Brooklyn introduced printed and arranged piano scores for its new films.

The insistence by many theater managers that pianists fit the music to the picture led *Moving Picture World* to compliment them for their concern, pointing out in March 1909 that ''a pleasant variation from the eternal ragtime was a refined deliverance of classical music corresponding to the character of the picture, including Schumann's 'Träumerei' and Beethoven's 'Moonlight Sonata', the first time indeed we have ever heard Beethoven in a five-cent theater.'' The writer thought that half the pianists playing in local theaters ''deserve to lose their jobs, for if they can play, they either won't or don't. The pianos should be burnt or put into tune or replaced with better ones.'' The following year, Vitagraph began to issue ''music cue'' sheets for piano and the three-piece orchestras that were being installed in the city's best houses. A Cleveland music publisher, Sam Fox, was the first regularly to issue collections of selected ''mood'' music, beginning in 1913. The compiler and composer of music in the *Sam Fox Moving Picture Music* series was an American-born musician, J. S. Zamecnik, who had studied with Dvořák and played violin with the Pittsburgh Symphony Orchestra under Victor Herbert before becoming music director for a Cleveland theater.

The first original musical score written expressly for a moving picture was composed in 1907 by Camille Saint-Saëns for a ten-minute French production, *L'Assassinat du Duc de Guise*. Max Steiner believes that he himself was the first to conduct a large orchestra in an American screen theater, playing music written by him for a feature movie, *The Bondman*, shown in William Fox's Riverside Theatre in Manhattan in 1915. Recently arrived from Austria, where he had studied composition with Mahler and others, and already the writer of music performed by the Vienna Philharmonic, seventeen-year-old Steiner went to work for Fox, then owner of the biggest independent eastern movie exchange and a string of large theaters. Steiner suggested that *The Bondman* needed something special to entice ticket buyers, and offered an original score for a hundred-piece orchestra, to be played behind the feature movie. Fox agreed, and musicians were recruited from various Fox theaters, where a ten-piece group of several fiddles, trombone, trumpets, piano, banjo, and drums was usual. Steiner could find only one cello player. The assembled group was predominantly brass, he recalled, and when a love scene was played, ''you never heard so many trumpets in your life.'' Griffith's flawed masterpiece was responsible for many changes in film making, but it was the success of *The Birth of a Nation*'s elaborate score that made Fox take a chance on Steiner and his music.

Acoustics were a major concern in building Mitchell B. Mark's new Strand Theatre on New York's Broadway, the first ''movie palace.'' It dwarfed its neighbor, the Liberty, where *The Birth of a Nation* was still running; it had seats for 3,500 on two levels, a thirty-piece orchestra to play for the films, and a large organ to relieve the musicians and give concerts between showings. The top price was twenty-five cents. A million dollars had gone into construction and fittings. After witnessing its great success, other exhibitors spent even more for equally opulent picture houses in New York and other major cities.

According to figures then released by the Committee on Education of the U.S. House of Representatives, 16 million people daily were going to the movies in 1914, and they sparked a building boom that brought the total of U.S. screen theaters to 30,000, 85 percent of them seating 600 or less. For the large houses, admission prices rose to $1.50 in two years, the result of inflation set off by the war in Europe as well as staggering increases in production costs at home. These had escalated ten times for the average feature film, topped by the astounding $100,000 spent for making *The Birth of a Nation.*

The independents' war with the MPPC was wreaking its own toll. Exorbitant salary offers had lured major Broadway and vaudeville luminaries to California, but, finding the work tedious, most of them returned to the stage. Those who stayed were, like William Farnum, unable to resist contracts offering as much as $10,000 a week for their services. Hitherto unknown performers who became screen idols almost overnight flitted from company to company, responding to bidding wars for their services. An obscure British music-hall and variety-show slapstick comic, Charlie Chaplin, quickly caught up with Mary Pickford's record-breaking million-dollar income after one of his first two-reelers, *The Floorwalker,* made that same amount for the Essanay Company. The attorney who thereafter negotiated business deals for Chaplin was Nathan Burkan, one of New York's leading entertainment-business lawyers and chief counsel for the new American Society of Composers, Authors and Publishers.

Wartime shortages of basic materials added to expenses. German carbon, the principal ingredient of raw film, was cut off by the submarine war on Atlantic shipping, as were the cheaper-made European movies that provided nickelodeons with many of their programs. The American movie business was forced to buy only American for the first time.

The attraction of Southern California's benign weather, its nonexistent tax structure, and a semiofficial attitude against union labor had drawn the industry west. Seventy production companies were soon in business there, and their annual budget approached $25 million. It was star power that made a rental fee of $150 possible for a feature film, bringing in average returns of $375,000 for a new movie. This changing economic balance and the new business practices it spawned were leading to the inevitable demise of the once all-powerful movie trust, the Motion Picture Patents Company. New giants were abroad in the land, ready to do battle to the death with the monopoly.

After building his chain to 800 theaters and his fortune to many millions, Fox moved to California to make movies. Through the art of make-up, newspaper publicity, a good portrait photographer, and her certain small talent for evoking unbridled lust, a young actress named Theodosia Goodman was manufactured by Fox into Theda Bara. In three years, she made forty films for him, which built the foundation for one of the 1920s' major independent companies.

Jesse Lasky, a musician who had parlayed his management of the cornet virtuoso B. A. Rolfe into the relative fortune of $150,000, wagered and lost that sum on New York's first dinner-cabaret, the Folies Bergere. Undaunted, in late 1912, with his brother-in-law, the Polish-born glove manufacturer Samuel Goldfish (later Goldwyn), and a young playwright-director, Cecil B. De Mille, he formed Lasky Feature Play Company, in California. Made on a shoestring, their first project, a box-office-hit version of the successful stage drama *The Squaw Man,* led to a partnership in Zukor's Famous Players–Paramount Corporation.

Goldfish was eased out and, with the million dollars paid for his share, formed an independent production unit. Backing from the giant Du Pont munitions and chemical interests supported him as he began to build a reputation for the high quality of his releases, and also learned he could get newspaper space for his malapropisms. De Mille, on the other hand, remained a valuable asset to Paramount, making a series of lavish million-dollar epics that combined portions of the Bible and other history with the pursuit of highly sanitized sex. The latter was always embodied in alluring females, all garbed in daring costumes, which for forty years introduced new fashion trends to the world. Until his death, De Mille was one of the most influential producer-directors, the man who made the word *colossal* a cliché.

The years after 1916 were golden ones for the movie business. New production companies sprouted up overnight both on the West Coast and in eastern cities, where the industry was born. Thirty-five million Americans were going to screen theaters at least once a week, and it appeared to be impossible to lose money on a new feature. Wall Street brokers and other speculators begged for the chance to share in the profits. There was, for example, the Massachusetts small-bank president who ventured $120,000 on the first film starring Lon Chaney, a vaudeville pantomimist, and grossed three million dollars from *The Miracle Worker.* The international banking house of Kuhn, Loeb underwrote $10 million of an issue of Famous Players–Paramount preferred stock, and the forty films then made cleared $21 million. Almost any moviemaker with a record of success had to fight off war-material millionaires who dangled their fortunes before him.

It remained for the child of a theatrical family, Thomas Ince, who turned to the movies when times were bad, to reshape the structure of movie making into the production-line system that prevailed for four decades before television broadcasting absorbed it. In 1914, Zukor, Lasky, and others still thought of their function as that of a theatrical producer: responsibility for financing, choice of story and actors, and hiring of a director and placing responsibility for the finished product on him. To keep affiliated exhibitors supplied with a new feature movie each week, fifty-two a year, was a difficult schedule to maintain. A genius such as Griffith could spend months or more, a million dollars or more, creating a masterpiece, and it could take years to recoup the original investment.

After getting his start as a five-dollar-a-day screen villain, Thomas Ince worked his way up. He acquired the reputation of a man who made "box-office" movies rather than artistic triumphs. In 1915, he, with Griffith and Mack Sennett, a Canadian with a genius for making one-reel slapstick-comedy films, joined the new Triangle Film Corporation. Their leading contract players included Douglas Fairbanks and William S. Hart, and other Broadway players hired to star in two-dollar features. While Griffith was at work on a nearly two-million-dollar production, *Intolerance,* intended to expiate the sins of *The Birth of a Nation,* and Sennett was recruiting the newest of those bathing beauties and Keystone Kops to whom he is inextricable bound in motion-picture history, Ince was forced to assume general control of all production. Unrealistic shooting schedules and mounting costs were restrained by Ince's appointment of supervisors over all aspects of individual features, who were in turn required to report each day's progress. By coordinating activities on the lot, thus reducing costs of shooting time, camera crews, and lighting operators, he built a prospering operation, whose efficiency was much admired and imitated.

While the Hollywood-based companies were taking control of American feature movie making, attrition and legal action brought about the demise of the MPPC. The antitrust lawsuit for which William Fox had lobbied was finally settled by a Supreme Court decision that warned all still-living defendants to desist from further "unlawful acts" or suffer the wrath of a government dedicated to fighting monopoly. A patent-infringement suit brought by the movie trust, in hopes of sustaining the combine's structure, concluded with a decision that negated many of its patents, among them those back to Edison's original peep-show boxes.

Prosperity now began to grow at the expense of independent exhibitors, whose rental fees threatened to rise even higher because of the block-booking policies introduced by Adolph Zukor. In order to get a Pickford film or one with another leading star, it was necessary to buy Zukor's entire output for a season. A second rebellion ensued, directed by Thomas Talley, the fiercely independent Westerner who had opened America's first movie house fifteen years before. Feeling that exhibitors could by-pass the producers and deal directly with the major stars, Talley formed the First National Exhibitors' Circuit in 1917, a combination of twenty-seven theater owners, which made a contract with Charlie Chaplin for him to produce eight two-reel comedies for one million dollars and all production costs. Next to join Talley and First National was Mary Pickford, the reigning queen of the screen. Determined never to be second to Chaplin in money matters, she accepted an offer of $1.05 million for three pictures. During the bidding, Ince was hired away from Triangle, and the new company became serious competition for Zukor and part of the Big Three that dominated Hollywood until the advent of talking pictures. The third element, Metro Pictures Corporation (later Metro-Goldwyn-Mayer), became part of the group in early 1919, after Marcus Loew purchased the floundering company for $3 million, almost a fire-sale price. The one-time newsboy was seeking to assure first-run quality pictures for his nationwide chain of picture and vaudeville houses. Beginning with *The Four Horsemen,* starring the first male Latin screen idol, Rudolph Valentino, Loew turned out top-ranking films.

First National's success indicated to Zukor that he must build up a chain of company-owned screen theaters in order to compete on all levels. A number of intricate real estate and business deals across the country culminated in a new chain of several hundred first-run houses. A new moving-picture monopoly was now in place; it controlled most of the world's total movie production, the distribution systems, and a substantial portion of America's theaters. The antiquated Motion Picture Patents combine had been replaced, by means of modern business methods and native shrewdness, by the Big Three. The only enemy challenging the Big Three's hold on American popular entertainment, E. F. Albee's vaudeville monopoly, was about to join in battle for supreme control.

CHAPTER 2

Big Time, Small Time, and E. F. Albee

Even before modern vaudeville came of age in 1900, the variety stage had been a principal ally of popular-music publishers, by promoting their sheet music. The strategy of paying for play had been formalized in England during the 1860s. The songs sung for pay were, in the main, four-square parlor ballads and waltz songs aimed at the upper middle class, whose principal home entertainment was playing the piano and singing around it.

Beginning in the early 1880s, some American publishers, discerning a growing appetite among the nation's lower classes for music of their own, used the same system, paying variety artists and concert-room singers to "plug" their songs. The sheet-music business prospered, census figures revealed, growing from the small group of music houses in the late 1890s that constituted Tin Pan Alley, on West 28th Street in Manhattan, to forty-five companies, capitalized at $1.6 million and with a value of $2.2 million in 1904. That year, Victor Herbert earned $75,000 from royalties, much more than the $20,000 from the sale of printed music that he averaged annually throughout his lifetime.

Around the turn of the century, the Pianola and the Victrola made inroads into music publishers' profits. After years of political maneuvering and lackadaisical lobbying by the music business, these new users of Tin Pan Alley's products became responsible for paying a royalty when they selected music copyrighted after July 1, 1909. A fee of two cents for each record side or paper music roll was mandatory, although lower rates were eventually negotiated.

The fees paid to vaudevillians for their help in popularizing new songs had become important even to the best-paid variety artists, and whether they appeared in "big-time" or "small-time" vaudeville. The former was staged twice a day, whereas the latter offered three to six performances daily, usually in "pic-vaude" houses, where moving pictures and live variety had become the standard bill of fare by 1912. Neither form of vaudeville offered exorbitant compensation to headline artists, who were, moreover, subservient to a monopoly that grew stronger each year. Eventually, it became the personal fiefdom of a single man: E. F. Albee, who assumed control of the Keith-Albee circuit in 1917 and immediately reorganized it, with a capitalization of $50 million.

The grandson of a Minute Man who stood his ground at Lexington and Concord in 1775, Edward Franklin Albee was born in Maine in 1857. After only a scant education, he went off to join a circus-wagon show, feeding its single elephant and taking care of the mangy lions for seven years. He was seventeen when Benjamin Franklin Keith gave him a job as boy of all work at his Boston variety theater. Gilbert and Sullivan's *Mikado* was all the rage in America that year, and young Albee proposed a production of the comic operetta for twenty-five cents a seat; other Boston theaters were asking $1.50. Crowds stormed Keith's box office each night, and the local constabulary was called out to contain them. The profits paid for building the Bijou Theatre, where Keith and Albee opened the first continuous vaudeville show on July 6, 1885. It ran from ten in the morning to nearly midnight, at ten cents for standing room, a chair for five cents more.

Boston's Bijou was the first of some 700 Keith theaters, whose permanent slogan was: "Cleanliness, courtesy and comfort." The first of these being paramount, performers were allowed not even a polite "oh, heck" on stage.

The first Keith-Albee "temple of the arts," an oversized Boston theater on which half a million dollars was spent for trappings and amenities, opened in 1893 and remained the flagship operation until vaudeville died at the hands of radio some forty years later. New York was invaded simultaneously by a magnificent theater on Union Square. In the next seven years, vaudeville became a big business, with its own monopolistic apparatus, two interlocking coast-to-coast circuits—controlled by Keith in the east and by Martin Beck's Orpheum from Chicago to the Pacific.

During the 1890s, most variety artists had secured their bookings through a dozen agents located in New York and Chicago, who received 10 percent for working on the performers' behalf with theater managers. Led by Pat Casey, the operator of a New England theater, in 1900 some 100 vaudeville managers, representing the majority of America's sixty-seven leading variety houses and many smaller venues, organized the Vaudeville Managers Association. To centralize all bookings and control salaries, a satellite hiring organization, called the United Booking Office, was formed and given the power to offer performers willing to cooperate with VMA a longer working season and better-organized jumps between bookings.

The new organization was fought by means of a strike by the White Rats ("star" spelled backward), a group of the most militant variety artists, led by headline performers. Having been foremost among those who broke the strike, Keith and Albee took control of VMA, whose powers grew and profits increased, but only for cooperative theater manager members. When the newest economic debacle seriously affected ticket sales in late 1906, a theatrical monopoly owned by the producers Marc Klaw and Abe Erlanger joined their most important legitimate-theater competitors, the Shubert brothers, to build and operate a competing national circuit of "advanced" all-star vaudeville. Once it appeared that this venture might succeed, secret negotiations conducted by Albee, as Keith's right-hand man, scuttled it, in return for one million dollars in cash. Klaw and Erlanger and the Shuberts agreed that they would not go into vaudeville during the next ten years. Albee went back to swallowing up all competitors, and successfully accommodated the Keith-Albee circuit to the challenge of Edison's moving pictures while building up a chain of owned, leased, or operated theaters.

There were some performers who attempted to fight the system Keith and Albee had imposed, but only a few of them succeeded to any extent and then only superstars of the magnitude of a Nora Bayes. The White Rats, whose membership had fallen off, attained their first victory in 1910. A new law in New York State putting a ceiling of five percent on an agent's commission roused many performers to action against the UBO, which demanded ten. By the end of that year, a new actors' organization, with 11,000 members, became affiliated with the American Federation of Labor under the name White Rats Actors Union of America.

The following year, New York's state commissioner of licenses reported that 104,000 vaudeville contracts had been approved by his office. They gave an average salary of $80 for vocal performers, $115 for teams, and $250 for acts with four or more members. The only source of employment was some 1,000 theaters giving bit-time, or "class," entertainment on a two-a-day-basis, and about 4,000 small-time houses, many of them pic-vaude theaters. Some performers attempted to evade the power of the UBO and the VMA by playing the latter theaters during the regular twelve-week layoff period between bookings. If caught, however, they faced barring for life from any VMA theater.

Competing vaudeville impresarios were not immune from Keith's vengeance. When Martin Beck moved his Orpheum circuit headquarters to New York in 1905, he booked only through the UBO and respected all territorial rights invoked by the VMA and Keith. Ostensibly with Albee's permission, in 1913 he built the Palace Theatre in New York, as a showplace to exhibit vaudeville's greatest talents. Immediately, he had trouble securing their services. Albee had secretly purchased a 51 percent controlling interest in the Orpheum circuit and forced Beck to surrender ownership of the Palace. It became the apex of the Keith circuit, the stage to which all performers aspired. Albee then made it a "cut" house, where artists were required to give up a quarter of their salary in order to appear.

Such an abuse was only one of many against the artists by UBO, VMA, and Keith's. Because of New York State's five percent limitation on booking commissions, the fiction of "personal representatives," who collected an additional five percent, was created. These so-called managers kicked back at least half of their commissions to a Keith collection agency for the privilege of dealing with the UBO. Variety artists were also asked to pay all traveling expenses, as well as any stage costs, such as special scenery, an extra stagehand who traveled with them when required by Keith regulations, and all musical arrangements. The growing inequities were responsible in great measure for the rising price of "pay for play," about which many music publishers began to complain openly.

The trade paper *Variety* was their chief sounding board in connection with the gratuity system. Founded in 1905 by Sime Silverman, a banker's stage-struck son, the publication became temporarily the chief advocate for the White Rats and the vaudevillians' cause. In retribution, Albee subsidized a rival journal and instituted a boycott of Silverman's paper. Performers who advertised in it were refused UBO bookings. Publishers who advertised new songs there found their entire catalogues barred from VMA theaters. Silverman persevered, however, and when poor times in 1913 brought industrywide booking cuts, he opened his pages to the White Rats.

B. F. Keith died in 1914, leaving half his fifteen-million-dollar estate to his son A. Paul Keith and the balance to Albee. However, the elder Keith had long since pursued charitable affairs exclusively, leaving direction of the empire to Albee and a new general manager, John J. Murdock. A Scottish-born entrepreneur, Murdock had operated vaudeville houses in the Midwest before joining Albee and quickly gaining the respect of New York's show-business world. He was also familiar with the movie business, having been the owner of a Chicago-based film-exhibition concern and an overseas buyer. In 1911, he had been named general manager of a color-film operation, the Kinemacolor Company, reorganized by a New York financial house after it acquired American rights from its British parent company. Murdock set up studios in New York and on the West Coast, where 700-foot reels of color movies were made, starring musical-comedy performers. When hostilities in Europe ended all laboratory work and film processing abroad, he joined the Keith organization.

With full power in his hands, Albee plotted to destroy all opposition from vaudeville performers. Under Murdock's command, a blacklist of all known White Rats was prepared, so that none would ever be employed on the Keith or Orpheum circuit, and the doors of the UBO would forever be closed to them and their agents. Backed with Keith's money, a new union was formed, the National Vaudeville Artists. Pat Casey was promoted from his place as executive secretary for the VMA to be head of the new Vaudeville Managers Protective Association, whose task it was to enforce the blacklist. On Murdock's orders, a new clause was inserted into standard

UBO contracts: it warranted that each performer seeking to do business with the UBO was a member of NVA. If earlier White Rats affiliation was ever discovered, it would mean explusion for life.

A White Rat strike broke out in the Midwest in 1916, in support of stagehands. It was handled with such dispatch by Edwin Claude Mills, the manager of two Oklahoma City vaudeville houses, that he was summoned to the VMPA's New York office to work with Casey and Murdock. Born in 1882, Mills had run away from home at the age of fourteen, to ship as cabin boy aboard a freighter bound for the Argentine. There he jumped ship, and, three years later, reached his hometown, San Antonio. He became a schoolteacher and then worked in a wide-open Texas gambling house. After such more mundane jobs as typewriter salesman, trainmaster, and accounts examiner for three years in the Panama Canal Zone, the lure of carnival tanbark and circus sawdust seduced him. It as an easy step to vaudeville and the movie business.

A number of other White Rat strikes broke out following that in Oklahoma City, chiefly in the Keith headquarters cities of Boston and New York. Mills again demonstrated his abilities in this bitter union-busting war. The White Rats went into bankruptcy, and their headquarters building in New York was bought for Albee's company union, the National Vaudeville Artists.

The price of victory was an action by the Federal Trade Commission, in May 1918, charging that the Vaudeville Managers Protective Association was an illegal combination operating in restraint of trade, dominating the big-time vaudeville business, collecting excessive fees from performers, and using a blacklist to punish union members. Also named in the complaint were the National Vaudeville Artists, United Booking Office, and the Keith Vaudeville Collection Agency, to which professional representatives paid back a share of their commissions. In all of these, Murdock and Casey were officers.

With his control of regional Famous Players and Universal Pictures franchises and distributing agencies, Marcus Loew had become too powerful for Murdock to deal with. Many of the larger Keith theaters ran one or more Loew-controlled pictures as part of their bill, so that, with Loew's local monopolies, it appeared to the government that he was a co-conspirator. Silverman was named in the action because, after Keith's death, he had made peace with Albee and Murdock. As a result only *Variety* salesmen were permitted to go backstage and speak with artists, a privilege long denied them. The publication's special anniversary editions became filled with several hundred pages of advertising, paid for at the rate of $125 a page by NVA members and theaters allied with the VMPA. The White Rats alleged that these ads were placed only because of Keith-Albee pressure.

Pat Casey was the principal Albee spokesman during hearings held by the FTC. He claimed that the association actually benefited performers and managers. Asserting that the VMPA controlled fewer than half of the 907 vaudeville houses in the country, which was patently untrue, he said that in the course of a year Keith's circuit presented some 6,000 acts, giving employment to 8,000 or 9,000 actors. He omitted to mention that they represented only a third of available performers. Yet, at the conclusion of the hearings, the VMPA agreed to mend its ways and remove the clause warranting membership in the NVA to get bookings.

Nevertheless, an extensive hunt for former White Rats continued for years. More subtle means were exerted to bring variety actors to heel, one of them an arbitration clause to deal with disputes. The NVA's Board of Arbitration consisted of three Albee employees, with Casey as chairman.

Given a clean bill of health, the VMPA and other Albee interests prospered. Following young Paul Keith's death in 1918, Albee changed the name of his vaudeville empire to the B. F. Keith Exchange. His profits, estimated conservatively, remained over $10 million annually through 1921. The Orpheum circuit, which had become an Albee subsidiary, showed net profits in 1920 of nearly $4 million, and those of Loew's independent small-time circuit were slightly more for nine months of that year.

With three performers for every job, however, variety artists continued to face long periods of unemployment.

CHAPTER 3

The Victrola and the Pianola

The revised Copyright Act governing popular music, among other intellectual properties, that had become law in mid-1909, created a new right for publishers, composers, authors, and songwriters. It dealt with the mechanical reproduction of music, mandating a royalty of two cents for each cylinder, recording, or paper music roll manufactured. It was a compromise provision, forced on music copyright owners in order to frame legislation acceptable to the White House.

In 1907, President Theodore Roosevelt had learned that a "giant music monopoly," controlling the majority of new works, had granted exclusive piano-roll recording rights to a single manufacturer for a period of thirty-five years. James F. Bowers, president since its inception in 1895 of the Music Publishers Association, had been instrumental in creating that arrangement with the Aeolian Company. Its Pianola and the Victrola were effecting a major change in the way Americans heard music. Anticipating new legislation that would cover the mechanical reproduction of music, Bowers had persuaded eighty-seven publisher members of the association to sign agreements with Aeolian giving it exclusive rights to cut piano rolls of their copyrighted music in return for a royalty of 10 percent of retail price. Exposure of the scheme brought Roosevelt's intervention and the full fury of Aeolian's competitors and the talking-machine business, all crying, "Monopoly!"

During early Congressional hearings, Bowers had been an ineffectual witness for the music trade. In spite of efforts by the Witmark music firm, Leo Feist, Victor Herbert, John Philip Sousa, and attorney Nathan Burkan, the unfavorable (to them) legislation was passed. For the first time in U.S. history, the peacetime bargaining process between supplier and user was to be regulated by the government. The fixed two-cent royalty and a compulsory-licensing provision were to guard against any future music-copyright monopoly.

Aeolian actually benefited from the legislation it had inspired. Instead of having to pay the 10 percent royalty it had promised, a fee of only two cents per reproduction was required. Thus the company continued to dominate the piano-roll business. It enjoyed a major share of sales, which grew from 45,414 units in 1909 to a peak in 1919, when 208,541 player pianos of all types, including its own patented Pianola, were sold.

The compulsory-licensing requirement was punishment visited on the eighty-seven publishers (who owned 381,598 compositions) who had been party to the Aeolian plan and equally on the 117 music firms (controlling 503,597 pieces) which had not. Among the latter were many Tin Pan Alley houses, newcomers to the business, who had brought new promotion techniques that were raising sheet-music sales and profits to new heights, chiefly because of song-plugging exploitation.

With popular sheet music selling for from twenty-five to sixty cents a copy, the wholesale value of printed music reported to the government had more than tripled between 1890 and 1909, rising from $1.7 million to $5.5 million. In 1909, more than 27 million phonograph records and cylinders were manufactured, having a wholesale value of nearly $12 million. More than 25,000 songs were entered for copyright registration, complementing the parallel growth of piano sales to a new high of 365,000 instruments. Twenty years before, the Music Teachers National Association had announced that half a million pre-adults were getting keyboard instruction from its members. These pupils had grown up, as had uncounted thousands of others who had also learned to play the instrument. Moreover, anybody could "play" the Pianola or the Victrola.

Even with the modest two-cent music royalty, piano-roll and phonograph-record manufacturers did not turn immediately to new songs for a substantial part of their output. In the first quarter of the nineteenth-century, only 10 percent of all printed music was of American origin. By the century's end, that figure had risen to 70 percent. One reason for the earlier percentage was the general music trade attitude, shared by its best customers of the "cultured class," that most American music was inferior and not worth either reproducing or purchasing. A practical reason for this attitude was that European music had remained until 1891 in the public domain, free for the taking, because of a biased provision in the original Copyright Act of 1790 that denied protection to all foreign printed materials. American publishers in the post–Civil War period could reproduce any of this noncopyrighted music for as little as two and a half cents for an eight-page edition and make a profit of several hundred percent from each copy. The handful of large publishing houses became, in the main, wholesale-retailers, who had no regard for promoting their own catalogues and no interest in publishing the new kind of raggedy-time popular music the masses of the 1880s and 1890s took to their hearts.

Prior to the outbreak of war in Europe, the major companies devoted a principal portion of their production to vernacular music and novelty recordings, but put major emphasis in their advertising and publicity on music that was good for their general image and also attracted customers of the "better kind." The Victor Talking Machine Company's $1.5 million advertising campaign in 1912 concentrated on its Red Seal line—one-side-only disks, three and a half minutes long at most, of grand-opera selections, familiar old songs, and classical instrumental music. Victor's best seller was the Italian tenor Enrico Caruso, the first performer to be signed to an exclusive contract and a royalty arrangement by an American firm. The thirty-six recordings Caruso cut before 1912 became the cornerstone of that year's Victor Red Seal catalogue of 600 selections, many of them recorded by several performers. Because of its premium prices, ranging from two dollars to seven dollars, depending on the number of artists involved (Victor's popular records cost seventy-five cents), the Red Seal line enjoyed far greater acclaim. Red Seal's first million-copy seller was Alma Gluck's concert-hall version of the Stephen Foster song "Old Folks at Home."

With an ambitious, but inferior grand-opera catalogue, the Columbia Phonograph Company was a poor second to Victor. And Thomas Edison retired from that highfalutin business in 1911, when he abandoned his Amberol opera line, after making 115 cylinders. His best customers were, and remained, those who preferred ragtime, coon songs, Sousa, Herbert, monologues, and sentimental ballads, on which the Edison output was based until its demise in 1929.

Even the most cautious recording executives became convinced of the musical theater's power to create popular hit songs that also appealed to high-class customers after the success in 1907 of Franz Lehar's *Merry Widow* and its lilting waltz duet "I Love You So." Public demand from all classes became so great that F. W. Woolworth restored a sheet-music counter to his growing chain of five-and-ten-cent stores. The economic consequences reshaped the structure of music publishing. Many ballad singers who were carrying on the white minstrel-show tradition, vaudeville comedians, singers of coon songs, and concert bands were among the first to record for all three major companies, performing theater music as well as old favorites going back to Stephen Foster's time. Once the technology had improved sufficiently to capture the higher tones of women's voices, Broadway soubrettes and female vaudeville singers became frequent visitors to recording studios.

The Gramophone Company, with which Victor exchanged pooled patents, had put over the talking machine in England with early recordings of London's music-hall and stage favorites. Now Victor imitated its partner and embarked on a program of recording the best-known American singing stage entertainers, paying them to duplicate the songs with which they were most identified. George M. Cohan cut ten of his show-stopping numbers and boasted to cronies that he had gotten more than Caruso's $4,000 for the session. Columbia and Edison followed suit, and family parlors around America resounded to the voices of Nora Bayes, Raymond Hitchcock, Nat M. Wills, Helen Trix, Blossom Seeley, Irene Franklin, Anna Chandler, Sophie Tucker, Al Jolson, Stella Mayhew, and dozens of other coon shouters, ballad singers, comedians, and leading men and women. Where once they could be seen in the flesh only when entertainment "direct from Broadway" appeared at the local opera house or vaudeville theater, now these luminaries were always on hand, by way of recordings. Musical accompaniments on records were those used on the stage, where they were played by a vaudeville or musical-comedy pit band. Because of recording limitations, some substitutions were made, but the basic ensemble was two cornets, two clarinets, trombone, oboe, flute, tuba, and set of percussion, with two amplified Stroh violins and a similarly equiped viola. Occasionally, a piano was added. The placing of instruments depended on the recording supervisor or musical director. At Columbia, this was Charles Adams Prince. A former cornet player in Sousa's band, Walter B. Rogers, had joined Victor, where he remained in charge of strictly popular recording until 1916.

Not until a dance craze overwhelmed upper-class Americans, and then the world, after 1911, bringing with it a new kind of music, which shifted natural accents to offbeats, did the record manufacturers end their reliance on military bands for all dance-music records. Victor's first house band, the Metropolitan Orchestra, Charles Prince's musicians, the military concert bands directed by Sousa and Arthur Pryor, and one or two others provided all recorded musical accompaniment for the two-step, cakewalk, and other slow-time steps. Then came the turkey trot and other hurry-up dances inspired by Afro-American theatrical and sporting figures, which freed ragtime couples from the strait jacket of the nineteenth century's figure and set dances. Irving Berlin's "Everybody's Doin' It," "Snooky Ookums," and "Alexander's Ragtime Band," Wolfie Gilbert and Lewis Muir's "Waiting for the Robert E. Lee," and other Tin Pan Alley hits in this new manner set feet to moving, even in the world's finest social circles. People danced to lose weight or to be rejuvenated, and some of the best medical minds believed that dancing aided digestion. Best of all, dancing made people, whatever their origins, feel the equal of anyone in high society.

Many people blamed the new feminism, with its crusades for women's rights and access to the ballot box, for the dancing mania that took possession of New York and other major cities around 1912. In a sense, the women's movement was in part the culprit, for it produced Irene Castle, of the dancing Castles, a couple who danced like demons or angels, as the rhythm demanded. A free spirit, who served as the embodiment of the liberated woman, Irene smoked cigarettes, was among the first to have her hair bobbed, and set fashion for the World War I era. Vernon, an Englishman, married the American-born Irene in 1911 and took her to Paris, where they showed the habitués of the exclusive Café de Paris the Texas Tommy, the turkey trot, and other American dances that had apparently moved east from San Francisco's Barbary Coast. The music of Irving Berlin was ideal for these steps, and the Castles introduced both to Europe and the world. The new dances they popularized after their return to New York in 1912 were speedy, simple, and rhythmic, with much shoulder-shaking and arm-waving, but they were performed by the Castles with a grace that few of their pupils could ever emulate.

The Castles operated a number of schools—Temples of Terpsichore—the most popular and glamorous being their Castles in the Air, where young instructors of both sexes taught new steps that Irene said had to be "considerably toned down before they could be used in the drawing room." Among the new dances were the walk, rag, rock, Maxixe, tango, lame duck, and half-in-half. The Syncopated Society Orchestra of black and Puerto Rican musicians usually accompanied the Castles. Its violins, banjo-mandolins, cornet, trombone, cello, bass violin, piano, and drums were directed by James Reese Europe, an extraordinary man. Born in Alabama in 1881, he got his formal music training as a child in Washington, D.C., and then moved to New York around 1906 to become director of several all-black stage productions. He then dedicated himself to the task of presenting Afro-American musicians as capable of playing for any audience and as creators of a vital music that blended their own past with that of white Americans. After he was elected head of the Clef Club, formed by the city's best-known black musicians and singers, Europe produced a number of ambitious concerts of Negro music, which culminated on Carnegie Hall's stage in May 1912. An orchestra of 145 musicians, among them thirty pianists, offered a program of church songs and dance, comedy, and ragtime popular music, calculated, Europe said, to show that black Americans had created "a kind of symphony music that . . . is different and distinctive."

The destiny that brought the Castles back to America put them together with James Europe. He began to conduct the music for all their public appearances and served as musical director for their string of dancing salons. He also wrote the music for most of the dances. When Europe persuaded Vernon Castle to slow down his dancing, to move to tempos that stressed the back beat, as in black music, he introduced the dancer to the one-step. The Castles added it to their repertoire, and with it another Europe improvisation, a variation on the schottische that was called the "fox trot." America's dancing styles were then fixed for several decades.

Record companies were eager to obtain the Castles as phonograph artists. In frantic bidding, Victor won and began a line of dance records that remained profitable until singing stars displaced them after World War II. The first black band to be signed by a recording company, James Europe's fourteen-piece Syncopated Society Orchestra, was added to the roster, alongside the Victor Military Band, which specialized in the hesitation waltz and less exacting steps in a line of $1.25, twelve-inch, five-minute Victor Dance Records. Vernon and Irene Castle supervised all sessions and were featured, with Europe, on the cover of an illustrated Victor *Modern Dance* brochure. Edison and Columbia had their own dance series, the latter's made by an expert who danced the new steps to the music of a studio orchestra while speaking instructions into the recording horn.

World War I ended Victor's partnership with the Castles. Vernon answered his country's call and joined the Royal Flying Corps; he died in a plane crash in 1918. James Europe, whose association with the Castles had led to the almost complete displacement of the omnipresent prewar gypsy-music ensembles from hotels and eating places by his orchestra and by other black musicians, enlisted in the New York Negro Regiment, for which he formed a military band of first-class black and Puerto Rican players. The group was sent to France, where they became known as the "Hellfighters." After their return to the United States at war's end, they were about to embark on a national tour, to promote records they had made for Pathé, when Europe was killed by a member of his orchestra.

In a continuing profitable position as the world's largest record company, Victor was able to maintain its lead over its two major competitors, taken early in the century. In 1914, the company produced a bit more than half of the total of 27 million recorded units. The Edison company, which continued to make cylinders until the late 1920s, issued almost all of the four million produced that year, Columbia having given up their manufacture to concentrate on disks. As the original talking-machine patents began to expire, around 1914, Columbia found itself sharing sales with new companies formed to take advantage of a fading technological monopoly of pooled patents. There were sixty of these by 1916. The most prominent was Aeolian-Vocalion, formed by the player-piano company, and Brunswick-Balke-Collender, an Iowa piano manufacturing company that went into the record business when it found on its hands a surplus of cabinets ordered by the Edison company. Concentrating on the Midwest market, Brunswick made both popular and classical music "personality" records.

Classical-music recording had not progressed beyond the small ensemble stage, though the German Odeon Company had made the first noncut symphony disks in 1911. Columbia got the masters for its serious instrumental music from a British sister company, Columbia Graphophone, which was headed by an American, Louis Sterling. Born in a tenement on New York's lower East Side in 1879, he had become a British citizen and was later knighted for his contributions to music and the theater. Among his pioneering ventures was the first recording of a "complete" original-cast musical revue, *Business as Usual,* in 1915, made in response to requests for music from the show for portable players in the trenches.

Despite growing competition at home, Victor was still ahead of the field in record sales in 1916 and doubled production to 31 million records three years later. When the war curtailed all recording of classical music in Europe, Calvin G. Child, director of Victor's Artists Bureau, looked to America for Red Seal talent. A veteran record man, who had started with Emile Berliner in the 1890s, Child made the bureau more and more an expression of his own tastes. Red Seal sales symbolized Victor's prestige in the business, but they never showed a sales ratio of more than 20 percent of the popular black-label product. Sales went from 2.1 million in 1914 to 9.5 million six years later, when the total value of American phonograph-record production jumped to 106 million.

In 1917, Child signed a contract that remained in force, with modification, until 1940 and brought Victor the Philadelphia Symphony Orchestra and its dynamic director, Leopold Stokowski. The conductor's acoustic sense and the special sound qualities of a church in Camden, New Jersey, acquired by Child as a studio for large instrumental groups made the Philadelphia's releases Victor's most honored products.

The black-label division tended to follow popular taste rather than lead it. Its releases were supervised by a group of classically trained musicians. Rosario Bourdon, a Canadian composer and conductor, joined the company as staff cellist in 1911. Josef Pasternack was trained in Russian Poland, where he mastered almost all instruments before coming to the United States to play viola in the Metropolitan Opera Orchestra. He had been director of the Philadelphia Orchestra and the Boston "Pops" before Victor employed him as musical director in 1916. Nathaniel Shilkret, an American whose tastes ran to popular music, had played with the Victor Herbert orchestra and the Sousa and Pryor bands before being named Victor's director of light music in 1915, at the age of twenty-one. These three had a common aim: to protect the company's reputation for quality and to ensure that the best sound possible was reproduced on surfaces that were shinier and smoother than those of any other company.

The superior Victor product, along with Aeolian's player-piano rolls, enjoyed the majority of all retail sales, leaving competitors to seek ways to cut into their profits. The introduction, after 1910, of coin-operated automatic pianos in penny arcades, billiard parlors, and other public places had quickly displaced the nickel-in-the-slot phonographs and peep-show machines there and significantly increased Aeolian's hold on the family market. This grew larger in 1916, with the first real innovation in the player piano's history—the "word-roll," on whose margin the lyrics of popular songs were printed. Selling at a premium price of seventy-five cents, and more for higher-quality music, the word-rolls offered a new source of music-publishing income. The two-cent royalty mandated in the 1909 Copyright Act was regularly paid, but publishers held that the use of lyrics was not mechanical reproduction, only duplication of protected material not covered by federal law and therefore not subject to the two-cent royalty requirement. That position was twice upheld by the Supreme Court, and royalties from word-rolls soon rose to twelve and sixteen cents. The six leading popular-music houses—Irving Berlin; Leo Feist; T. B. Harms with Francis, Day & Hunter; Shapiro, Bernstein; Waterson, Berlin & Snyder; M. Witmark & Sons—formed the Consolidated Music Corporation to handle their piano-roll licensing. Because the participants controlled a majority of the best-selling songs, Consolidated could insist on a minimum twelve-cent word-roll royalty in addition to the two-cent mechanical rate. It also demanded the production of two additional music rolls from each partner's catalogue before permission would be given to use one of his major hit songs. The first recorded antitrust action involving music publishers was instituted in August 1920 by the United States government, against Consolidated and its owners. This was followed by quick dissolution of the alleged trust. Licensing of piano rolls was eventually assigned to the Music Publishers Protective Association. Even after the courts called for that action, publishers continued to ask for premium royalties for word-rolls of their best-known songs, thus making up in part the losses from the declining business in sheet music. Piano-roll sales boomed during the early 1920s, with most of the two million plus player pianos that had been sold since the Pianola's introduction in the 1890s still, in varying degrees, playable. In 1920, annual sales of the instrument leveled off to around 200,000 units a year, more than half of all pianos being produced.

The Victor Talking Machine Company was not the first to record a jass, or jazz, band, but it did make the first great profits from a new American musical form, whose roots lay deep in the black South. Several authentic jazz bands had appeared in New York theaters and vaudeville houses, where they won favorable press notices and audience plaudits, but little attention from record companies. Two were from New Orleans: Tom Brown's Five Rubes comedy-musical group and the black That Creole Band. Another was the locally based Tennessee Ten. The Tempo Club Orchestra appeared in Ziegfeld's first *Midnight Frolics*. These introduced New Yorkers to music that was fast enough for those frisky steps being featured by the Castles. It was the Original Dixie Land Jazz Band, however, that sold a million records for the Victor Company. This group of five white musicians from New Orleans scored an instant triumph when it played at a restaurant, Reisenweber's on Columbus Circle, in New York, in January 1917. The comic effects it added to a fast kind of New Orleans ensemble playing were a special favorite. The men had already recorded two sides for Columbia, which received little response from the public. A Victor session in February 1917, on the other hand, produced one of the company's earliest million-seller Black Label records: "The Livery Stable Blues," coupled with "Original Dixie Land One-Step." Jazz mania was wedded to the dancing craze, and owners of the city's best cabarets and restaurants scurried around looking for musicians capable of sounding like the Original Dixie Land Jazz

Band, a search that produced the new slap-bass, saxophone music everybody called "jazz." The record industry was already wedded to the imitation of anything that sold, and New York studios worked overtime to capture the new sound. Calvin Child brought Paul Whitman's nine-piece
Ambassador Orchestra into the Camden recording studio. Pianist-arranger
Ferde Grofé's carefully crafted orchestrations of "Whispering," backed by
"Japanese Sandman," were responsible for the sale of millions of disks
and for Whiteman's climb to the throne of jazz, where he ruled as a press
agent–annointed king.

The fast-dance mania and new jazz music were shaped by Afro-American
culture, a fact completely disregarded by those who capitalized on their
union. For years, the record industry had shown little interest in a potential
market of 11 million people, the black Americans who represented nearly
one tenth of the entire population. The purchasing power of this large block
was discovered by pure chance in 1920, when the first recording of music
written by a black songwriter and performed by black talent was consumed
by black record buyers. The "blues"—in its purest form, a three-line AAB
stanza pattern—first came to the attention of most whites with William C.
Handy's "Memphis Blues" (1912) and "St. Louis Blues" (1914). Both
were "vaudeville blues" and not in the traditional form. They were the
latest form in the evolution of popular song from the blackface songs of the
1820s, through Stephen Foster's pre–Civil War "Ethiopian business," the
postwar "plantation songs," and the coon songs of the 1890s' first ragtime
era.

Handy did make records for Columbia in 1917, but he failed to include
either of his two blues hits. The first authentic blues was recorded for the
same label in 1916 by a white man. "Nigger Blues," written by a black
minstrel-show performer in 1912 and published before either of Handy's
pieces, was recorded for Columbia four years later by a Washington attorney, lobbyist, and gifted mimic, George O'Connor, who served the White
House as a blackface entertainer from President McKinley to President Truman.

Like many competing whites, most black professional songwriters preferred the work in the more elastic vaudeville blues form, not as strict as
the traditional blues, which rejected the former as reeking of a better-forgotten
dark heritage. Among those who used both forms was Perry Bradford, a
successful black vaudeville performer and agent, songwriter, and manager
of the young black contralto Mamie Smith, who sang in a stage show he
had written and produced. Reaching New York from Mississippi by way of
Georgia, Bradford was at first regarded by record executives as a "striver,"
one who often came in with worthwhile material. When he played some
new songs for Fred Hager, musical director for OKeh Records, named for
its founder, Otto Heinemann, a session was arranged for Smith to record
two of Bradford's vaudeville blues. Response was favorable to the record,

released in July 1920 without any identification of the singer's color. In November 1920, OKeh released his "Crazy Blues," backed by "It's Right Here for You." Mamie Smith sang, with a black orchestra supervised by Hager and a young assistant, Ralph Peer. Within a month, 75,000 copies were sold, mostly to black buyers. This first record to find a chiefly black audience opened other studios to the new stream of music, which eventually conjoined with a body of white music also from the South to produce the best-selling recorded popular music ever created.

Whether or not out of deference to those black leaders of the postwar period who saw themselves and their brothers and sisters as "the Race," Peer listed the new Mamie Smith titles and other blues recordings as "race records." It was by this name that they continued to be known throughout the 1920s, when black Americans bought as many as 10 million blues and black gospel records in a single year, and the 1930s, when those sales slumped with the failing economy. In the more socially aware time that followed, the designation "rhythm and blues" became general.

CHAPTER 4

Inside the Popular-Music Business

By 1910, Tin Pan Alley's "popular song factories," as the *New York Times* characterized them, had brought the annual aggregate sales of sheet music to 30 million copies, with the assistance of such spectacular hits as "Meet Me Tonight in Dreamland" and "Let Me Call You Sweetheart," which together accounted for a sixth of the entire output. Mail orders from the home were still the important sales medium they had been for more than half a century. In many cities, songwriter-pianists in the employ of local music houses were assigned to large department stores to plug new songs and answer requests for old ones. Some publishers owned the stores' sheet-music departments and controlled what was played or displayed on counters, thus effectively thwarting any promotion of their rivals' music. In syndicate and ten-cent stores, piano-playing clerks pounded out music from noon till after dark as young females in droves made their way to forty-foot sheet-music counters, calculatedly located in the rear of stores. These women, in search of music they had just heard or found advertised on the back cover of music they owned, were the music trade's best customers. Enlarged reproductions of sentimental and scenic sheet-music cover illustrations dominated the departments, placed there through exclusive arrangements for their display. Color art and hand-painted photographs, owned by the music publishers, were also featured there, as they were in illustrated song-slide shows used by nickelodeon operators to fill the time between the three or four reels of a movie showing.

Tin Pan Alley's major contribution to the merchandising and promotion of printed popular music was the implementation of some of John Henry Patterson's basic precepts of salesmanship. That genius of the American Cash Register Company looked for men who could be trained to sell. He emphasized that familiarity with the product must be inculcated in potential customers. New music men therefore drilled their salesmen in the art of publicizing a song through constant repetition. For years before and after World War I, song pluggers were paid twenty dollars a week. Early in the game, Tin Pan Alley learned that the best song pluggers were often the songwriters who created the products, and hired them as both writers and pluggers, paying twenty dollars for plugging and thirty dollars for songs. Under the writer-for-hire arrangement, songs became the exclusive property of the employer. Court rulings in the late 1930s validated this provision in the 1909 Copyright Act. As a result, Fred Fisher, a plugger for Leo Feist, and Ernest Ball, who was on the Witmark payroll, and others lost all rights to some of the best-selling pre-1930 hit songs.

Until the phonograph recordings, radio, and the talking picture supplanted them, live performers were crucial to the process of making the public familiar with new songs. Vaudeville provided the music trade for many years with its chief means of exploitation, through forty-week engagements of headliner music stars across the nation, who constantly performed songs they had been paid to feature. Music publishers also began to pay for the musical arrangements that concert-saloon and variety-hall performers were required to supply, and followed this by giving copies of new songs, exclusive performing rights, food and drink, and, finally, hard cash. When the Keith-Albee circuit's control of vaudeville and its performers extended to the extraction of sizable portions of a week's salary for commissions, kickbacks, trade-paper advertising, and company-union dues, both headliners and small-time acts looked to the music publisher to reward them for making their music popular. The process had become symbiotic, and Tin Pan Alley was obliged to pay higher gratuities than ever for services rendered.

The major companies opened branch offices in important cities along the vaudeville circuits, to make certain that sheet music for the songs being plugged was available in all local stores; to handle the chaotic Monday-morning rehearsals; and to locate missing baggage, get the portable scenery and stage costumes cleaned, and in general make life easier for their "plugs." The branch-office staff was also required to make certain that artists lived up to the letter of their arrangements with publishers and pay the guaranteed weekly sum.

As the system became an ever-greater economic drain, understandings were reached among the major publishers to curtail the "primary evil of our industry." Yet these were violated in the interest of promoting a new hit. The price for popularizing a song by live performance soon ranged from $25,000 to $75,000, due to the frantic bidding competition for the services of top headliners. The importance of cabarets during the dance-craze years, as another place where the new ragtime songs could be promoted, added new candidates—the bandleaders and featured dancers—for this bribery.

Ten-cent popular-song sheet music was selling in greater quantities than ever, but profits began to decrease when Tin Pan Alley's most important distributor of sheet music, the five-and-ten-cent stores, demanded, and received, a 40 percent discount.

The first five-cent counter in a retail store was installed around 1875 in Michigan, where a traveling salesman disposed of his surplus stock of handkerchiefs after promising to take back any that were unsold if the storekeeper would offer them for five cents each. This was far below their usual retail price of twenty-five cents, but it did give the salesman a commission and his jobber-employer a profit. Two years later, Frank W. Woolworth went to clerk in a Watertown, New York, dry-goods store, where a sign advertised "Any item on this table: 5 cents." Impressed by the crowds who came to buy five-cent soap, tin pans, stationery, packets of pins or needles, pen nibs, pencils, buttons, basins, and harmonicas, he opened his own five-cent store, in Lancaster, Pennsylvania, in 1879. Success spawned expansion, and by 1886, his small chain was doing an annual trade of $10,000. Having discovered that jobbers banded together to keep the price of low-cost merchandise high, he eventually broke through this middleman's barrier by paying cash for such large quantities that factories sold directly to him, at the true wholesale price or lower.

In 1911, Woolworth merged his stores with those of some leading competitors and formed a corporation capitalized at $65 million. His new chain of 600 five-and-ten-cent stores in the United States, Canada, and Europe had a total sales volume of $60 million in the first year. Each new store was opened on the traditional Saturday downtown shopping day, after a special preview the previous evening at which invited guests were entertained by a large orchestra, in whose library reposed the "F. W. Woolworth March." A pipe organ played classical and sentimental music in the "largest ten-cent store in the world" on Fifth Avenue and 40th Street, in New York, where a dime remained the highest price until 1935.

Back in 1890, Woolworth, who loved music but played it ineptly on flute and fiddle, had witnessed a dramatic demonstration of the power popular music had to bring customers into his stores. They poured in to buy balloons bearing an image of McGinty, who went "down to the bottom of the sea" in a best-selling song. Fascinated by this hero, the customers also depleted the supply of McGinty watches, which has been bought wholesale for $8.50 a gross. Over the protests of his local managers, Woolworth started selling sheet music. When it did not sell at a profit, he shut down all the music counters. Later, when people started asking for the sheet music of "The Merry Widow Waltz," a new counter was added to every store. By 1913, the chain was selling 150 million pieces of music a year and had succeeded in hammering down the wholesale price to six cents. In January 1918, when the one thousandth store was opened, Woolworth's was selling 200 million copies, and one dime had become the standard price for all popular music other than production and high-class music. Woolworth's competition—Kress, Kresge, Newberry, Kraft, McCrory, Metropolitan Stores and others—was not far behind, profiting from the publishers' readiness to give deep cuts for large sales. It was a time of extraordinary sales for sentimental songs: "Till We Meet Again," 3.5 million; "I'm Forever Blowing Bubbles," 2.6 million; "Joan of Arc, They Are Calling You," 2 million. Yet, because of the ten-cent price, those writers who were favored with a royalty shared only a penny or less.

George M. Cohan's artfully simple "Over There," with its syncopated paraphrase of five notes from "Johnny Get Your Gun," sold two million copies in sheet music and one million records. Written the morning the United States declared war, it was purchased from a Cohan-backed music company for $25,000 by Leo Feist, last of the major publishers to join in the pay-for-play practice. A dedicated exponent of modern business methods, Feist had left a prospering career in the corset trade when his part-time publishing venture began to produce profits. He built it into one of the largest American popular-music companies. Learning that jobbers and retailers ordered music only after a song was successful, he spent nearly $100,000 annually for advertising in general magazines and newspapers to convince the family trade that, as the company's slogan had it, "You can't go wrong with any Feist song!" When the wartime paper shortage confronted him, he sold his fellow publishers on reducing the size of sheet music and discarding the usual single-page insert. He pointed out that it was a nuisance to players, who did not like to have to turn pages. It also saved thousands of dollars in paper and printing costs and reduced shipping charges by one third. Rather than have his headquarters staff alone judge which songs to promote, he held an annual meeting of all branch managers and key personnel, for whom thirty to fifty songs were demonstrated. Buoyed by this participation in company affairs, Feist employees passed on their enthusiasm to local retail outlets, and the company had more million-copy sellers than all its competition combined.

In this period when ten-cent sheet-music ruled, only one man's popular songs maintained the former thirty-cent price: those of Irving Berlin, who was correctly judged by history as the greatest writer of American popular songs. Berlin turned the skill with words and music that produced such pre-1911 vaudeville novelty hits as "My Wife's Gone to the Country," "Yiddle on Your Fiddle Play a Ragtime Tune," "That Ragtime Violin," and "That Mesmerizing Mendelssohn Tune" into the genuine talent that could write complete scores for the London and Broadway stage. He also sang these hits to packed vaudeville audiences. Born in Russia and educated in New York, young Izzy Baline got his first job in the music business at the age of sixteen. In 1909, he went to work for Ted Snyder as song plugger and lyric writer. In its first month, his "Alexander's Ragtime Band" reportedly sold half a million copies, two million by the end of 1911. He became Irving Berlin the Ragtime King, the Hit Maker. To capitalize on this commercial talent, Henry Waterson, Snyder's manager and a man whose canny business sense and shrewdness matched Berlin's genius, organized the firm of Waterson, Berlin & Snyder, with Berlin as president. A transposing piano was made available for the exclusive use of the songwriter, who never learned to play in more than one key. With the instrument's help, he turned out an incredible string of hit songs over the next half century. The vast majority of these were eventually controlled by Irving Berlin, Inc., and its successors. Formed in late 1918, it was owned equally by Berlin, Max Winslow, and Saul Bornstein, formerly business manager for one of the publishing Von Tilzer family firms. The partners each got $500 weekly, and Berlin was also paid a six-cent royalty on popular songs and eight cents on production numbers.

Known as "the man who discovered Irving Berlin," Winslow had assisted him in writing many of the songs that made him famous. As Berlin played on the transposing piano, with one finger, Winslow made suggestions for lyric or metrical changes that would enhance the song's commercial appeal. At his suggestion, when Berlin began to complain about the royalties Waterson paid, the pair left Waterson, Berlin & Snyder in 1918 to form their own company. Almost immediately, Berlin's royalties tripled. Recognized as one of the best vocal coaches in Tin Pan Alley, Winslow imparted an individual style to variety's singing ladies, one that made his pupils known throughout show business as "Winslow's Singles," and made great hits of the Berlin songs they sang. Still a partner, with a one-third share of the business, Winslow left New York in 1933 to join his brother-in-law, Harry Cohn, in Hollywood, there to take charge of Columbia Pictures' music department. Cohn, Columbia Pictures president, had been a Waterson song plugger in the days of Berlin's first success.

Berlin's sudden rise to international fame in the prewar years was not unique. There were a few others who enjoyed acclaim and success from a knack for catching public attention with stories of love that had a strain of sentimentality in the words as well as a certain plaintive touch in the melodies, and from novelty pieces inspired by contemporary life and written to the new shoulder-shaking syncopation. In spite of any inherent appeal or merit, such songs became hits because their nationwide exposure in vaudeville was subsidized by music publishers. Only a concerted industrywide effort to change this system could save music publishing.

The single business association in a position to marshal such cooperation was the Music Publishers Association, approaching a second decade of activity. It was an offshoot of the original Board of Music Trade, a trust in the classic sense formed in 1855 to sustain a uniform standard price for music and to fight music teachers as middlemen. For most of the nineteenth century, the Board had acted in restraint of trade by assigning to members rights in the valuable noncopyrighted foreign music on which 70 percent of the printed music business was then based. It had also opposed any reciprocal international copyright, which would have terminated its members' monopoly of all printed music.

Finding that the MPA's primary interest lay in continuing protection only for the high-class standard music for which a market separate from that for popular songs was developing, a group of leading Tin Pan Alley houses left it in 1907. But once Witmark, Stern and Marks, Feist, and other popular firms diverted income to acquire standard-music catalogues, they resumed membership. In 1914, they again found their interests diverging, over the advancement of standard and educational music and the extinction of a gratuity system affecting their popular catalogues.

Several significant developments affecting this situation had taken place late in the preceding year. When his business fell off due to Keith's boycott of songs publicized in *Variety,* Sime Silverman began to write about the system in detail. He reported that leading publishers had met in secret to find a way to end payments to singers and to present a united front in raising wholesale prices of sheet music to ten cents, which would add an additional $40,000 profit from the sale of a million copies. In October 1913, a group of production songwriters and authors—Victor Herbert, Glen McDonaugh, Gustave Kerker, Louis Hirsch, Silvio Hein, Raymond Hubbell—and their principal publisher, Isidore Witmark, with his attorney, Nathan Burkan, and George Maxwell, the Scottish-born New York representative for G. Ricordi, had met to discuss the formation of an American songwriters' and publishers' society. Legend notwithstanding, it had not been necessary for the Italian opera composer Giacomo Puccini to guide those present through the maze of public-performance licensing. Burkan and Maxwell were knowledgeable, from regular trips to Europe, where state-blessed copyright monopolies collected for the public use of music.

The 1909 Copyright Act included a provision giving an exclusive right to license performance of a copyrighted work "publicly for profit if it be a musical composition and for the purpose of a public performance for profit." Recovery damages for infringement were fixed at not less than $250 or more than $5,000. In 1897, at the behest of Arthur Tams, owner of a music rental library, the words *and musical* had been added to statutes adopted earlier requiring the permission of the owner of a stage work in order to give a public performance, with penalties for failure to do so. In the following twelve years, only three actions involving public performance of musical compositions were brought, all dealing with its use in the professional theater. The 1909 provision mentioned both dramatic and musical performing rights, but no effort was made to license the public performance for profit of music in America until 1911.

That year, the world's first performing-rights society, the French Société des Auteurs, Compositeurs et Editeurs de Musique, again opened offices in New York, for the purpose of collecting five percent of gross receipts from concert managers and theatrical producers when French compositions registered in the United States were played in public. Among those who joined SACEM were Irving Berlin and some American composers of classical music. In 1912, one of these, Blair Fairchild, told a reporter for the *New York Times* some astounding facts about his connection with the society. He cited inequitable distribution of money collected and complained about his inability to resign from SACEM. In the following days, letters supporting his position appeared in newspapers, as did reports of pending action by SACEM against performers and concert managers.

Burkan offered as a model to the six writers and their publishers who gathered in October 1913 SACEM's Articles of Association, which included a stipulation that performance income be divided equally among the writer of the music, of the words, and their publisher. Four months later, another meeting was held, at which, the *Times* reported, "ragtime writers joined hands with publishers of chamber music . . . when composers of every kind and condition of music and every big music publishing concern" met to form the American Society of Composers, Authors and Publishers, for a term of ninety-nine years. Victor Herbert, the most prestigious of the writers, refused the presidency, and George Maxwell was elected. He told the press that ASCAP intended to prevent the playing of all copyrighted music at any public function unless a royalty was paid. Theater orchestras, cabarets, and the phonograph records would, he said, provide the tolls and many millions of dollars would pour into the society's coffers from around the country, at least one million from New York City alone.

With Nathan Burkan as acting counsel, in July 1914, fourteen New York publishers formed a new Music Publishers' Board of Trade and approved a charter that included a fine of $5,000 for direct or indirect payment to performers for purposes of song-boosting. Leo Feist did not participate, saying that he had been the last to fall in line and pay singers and that he would be the last to cease. *Variety* took up the new board's cause at once, with a series of full-page articles, which pointed out to singers that the payment system was detrimental to their careers, restricting, as it did, all performances of those great songs of the past certain to please audiences, merely for the commercial advantage of publishers. Yet it referred to proposed license fees as "tribute" and the move to collect them as "demands," which would bring reprisal from music users.

When announced, ASCAP's rates proved to be more modest than Maxwell had projected. They ranged from five dollars to fifteen dollars monthly, depending on the type of music used, the size of the establishment, and its gross receipts. A few hotels and cabarets signed contracts, but others took to adapting old melodies for the new trot and rag dances. The more militant hotel and restaurant owners prodded the president of the American Federation of Labor's strongest affiliate, the musicians' union, to tell his members not to play any music bearing the imprint of an ASCAP-affiliated publisher.

Mass resignations from ASCAP followed, and *Variety*'s pages began to fill with advertisements of "tax free" music, which could be played without fear of legal action by the society.

Burkan brought some infringers to court, with results that generally proved to be unfavorable to the publishers on appeal. The most productive of these suits was filed in the spring of 1915. It charged that Victor Herbert and his collaborators and their publisher, G. Schirmer (not an ASCAP member), had "heard" an unlicensed performance of their song "Sweethearts," from the operetta of the same name, in a cabaret show at Shanley's Broadway Restaurant on April 1, 1915. Burkan based the action on the dramatic-work licensing provision of the copyright law, rather than on that concerning public performance for profit. In reversing an adverse lower court finding, the Supreme Court ruled for Victor Herbert and the other plaintiffs, Justice Oliver Wendell Holmes writing in the majority opinion:

> If the rights under the copyright law are infringed only by a performance where money is taken at the door, they are very improperly protected. Performances not different in kind from those of the defendants could be given that might compete with and even destroy the success of the monopoly that the law intends the plaintiffs to have. It is enough to say that there is no need to construe the statute so narrowly. The defendants' performances are not eleemosynary. They are part of a total for which the public pays, and the fact that the price of the whole is attributed to a particular item which those present are expected to order is not important. It is true that the music is not the sole object, but neither is the food, which probably could be got cheaper elsewhere. The object is a repast in surroundings that to people having limited powers of conversation or disliking the rival noise give a luxurious pleasure not to be had from eating a silent meal. If music did not pay, it would be given up. If it pays, it pays out of the public's pocket. Whether it pays or not, the purpose of employing it is for profit, and that is enough.

The following several years were clouded by self-serving accounts of progress, but an interesting story can be pieced together from several sources: *Variety* from 1915 to 1929; Raymond Hubbell's typescript memoirs, "From Nothing to Five Million a Year: The Story of ASCAP by a Founder"; letters written by Isidore Witmark while assistant treasurer of ASCAP to his Chicago branch manager, entered into the public record during hearings before the Senate Committee on Patents, April 9, 1924; and a statement by Edwin Claude Mills, taken September 21, 1956, and part of the record in *Schwartz* v. *BMI*.

Variety's revenues from music publishers' advertisements were declining in the summer of 1916, and the new Music Board of Trade appeared to be falling apart, with some members going back to the gratuity system. Shapiro, Bernstein, for instance, purchased publication rights to all songs introduced at the Shuberts' Winter Garden by the star there, Al Jolson, who was "cut in" on the copyrights to assure their performance. Silverman turned the matter over to John J. O'Connor, then in charge of advertising. To replace the impotent board, O'Connor sought to gain the support of the New York publishing fraternity in a new effort to curb the subsidization of performers. Three publishers showed no interest—Feist, Remick, and Max Dreyfus, of T. B. Harms, who published production music almost exclusively and restricted all performances of his music except in the productions of which they were a part and put a notice to that effect on all printed copies.

O'Connor moved next to get the vaudeville monopoly's support and the full backing of both the Vaudeville Managers Association and the United Booking Office to enforce a ban on music owned by Feist and Remick. During the preceding year, the board's activities had been viewed by the publishers Murdock and Casey as a nuisance, which, if successful, would bring requests for increased pay from performers. Having effectively destroyed the White Rats union, and in the process of reducing salaries and blacklisting the rebels, Murdock saw here an opportunity to extend control over vaudeville artists.

To demonstrate Feist's command of song boosting in an Albee house, O'Connor had taken Murdock to a local theater, where the publisher's current best seller, "I Didn't Raise My Boy to Be a Soldier," received a dozen plugs onstage in the course of the program. On being summoned to his office, where they were told by Murdock that the system must be changed or their songs would be banned from all UBO and VMPA theaters, twenty-four music publishers joined the new Music Publishers Protective Association early in 1917, and paid a $1,000 initiation fee. Leo Feist and all other holdouts were persuaded to join after their music was boycotted in Keith houses. Meetings of the MPPA were held in VMPA's headquarters office, and Maurice Goodman, attorney for Keith and his satellite groups, headed a three-man executive committee on which Pat Casey and Claude Mills but no music men served.

The gratuity system was thus brought under control. Whenever a member wavered, he was punished through pressure applied by the VMPA. For instance, Feist's new hit songs were restricted in March 1918 by the UBO, and sheet music for two of them, "It'll Be a Hot Time for the Old Boys When the Young Men Go to War" and "I Don't Want to Get Well, I'm in Love with a Beautiful Nurse," was seized from the counters of Woolworth, Kresge, and other Chicago stores by men representing themselves as federal officers.

ASCAP progress was less satisfactory. Rates for motion-picture houses were fixed in May 1917 at an average of ten cents a seat, and opposition immediately rose from theater-owner groups that predicted this tribute would rise to a million dollars annually. Injunctions against ASCAP collections were obtained, and heavy use was made of the tax-free music offered by publishers who had resigned from the society. Monthly income leveled off around $3,000. Tin Pan Alley was looking for a breakup of the society when rumors flew that additional publishers would leave to ensure the use of their music in picture-vaudeville houses and in hotels, cabarets, and restaurants.

After a series of defeats in the lower courts, ASCAP's victory in the Supreme Court that gave them a federally backed license to operate indicated to Albee and Murdock that in time vaudeville, too, would be a target for taxation. With the MPPA under control, the financially beleaguered society, whose members by then were predominantly production-music authors and composers and a few loyal publishers, was ready for seduction. Bearing a proposal from Murdock, Casey in December 1917 offered AS-CAP his services to ensure regular collections from music users and to obtain licenses from the pic-vaud houses and all non-VMPA-affiliated theaters. In return, the VMPA members would be free to use ASCAP music without payment, and 50 percent of all gross receipts collected by Casey in the first two years would be passed on to Murdock, one third in the following three. After months of negotiation, the terms were agreed to, but when the government's antitrust suit against the vaudeville combine was filed in May 1918, an unsigned document between the parties became a vague "gentlemen's understanding." During the 1924 hearings, Murdock and Casey each filed an affidavit denying any arrangement to favor VMPA houses. However, *Variety* continued to allude to ASCAP's failure to collect from the Albee interests, "through the intervention of the Music Publishers Protective Association." It would appear that a significant sum, amounting to several million dollars at least, remained in the vaudeville trust's coffers and was never paid into the ASCAP treasury during a time when it would have added immeasurably to the society's growth and stability.

In these troubled times for the popular-song business, other elements of the music trade, chiefly those dealing with "high class" music and manufacturers or vendors of musical instruments, pianos, player pianos, and music rolls, phonographs, and recordings, representing an annual business at retail in excess of $250 million, banded together in the autumn of 1918 to form the Music Industries Chamber of Commerce. Paul Brown Klugh, president of the Autopiano Company of New York, a leading competitor to the Aeolian piano interests, with which he had formerly been associated, drew up a blueprint for the new organization. During the next decade of hearings in Washington on copyright revision, the MICC usually appeared in opposition to the MPPA and ASCAP. The printed music trade's only representative in the MICC was the Music Publishers Association, whose sole interest lay in fixing and maintaining a higher price for standard and art music.

It was *Variety*'s judgment in May 1919 that, having survived the war and now coping with higher paper and printing costs, a prospering industry owed much to the MPPA. New members were regularly approved for admission, the payment system appeared to be only a memory, and mechanical royalties were in better shape than ever. The annual production of printed music had increased to 30,000 titles, the majority of them production and popular songs. Although the ten-cent and syndicate stores' strangle hold on wholesale prices continued to cut into profits, these were growing as royalty income from mechanical reproduction on paper rolls and recordings rose. A new standard contract had been drafted by the MPPA that raised the ceiling on piano-roll royalties to twelve and a half cents, with seven and a half the minimum. The five publishers who produced the majority of current hit songs (Berlin; Feist; Waterson, Berlin & Snyder; T. B. Harms with Francis, Day & Hunter; and Shapiro, Bernstein) were using the Consolidated Music Corporation to make deals with the piano-roll manufacturers giving them a rate higher than the MPPA's. With the Remick firm, they collected most of the $1.194 million paid in record royalties, which rose to $2.776 million in 1920, more than 500 times the $54,000 paid in 1910. Nearly four million dollars went to these six for printed popular-music sales, the remaining amount, some five million, being distributed among 154 lesser firms.

Mechanical royalties principally sustained the business during the sudden and unexpected nationwide printers' strike in late 1919–1920, which was finally settled with an across-the-board 50 percent wage increase. Also affected by postwar inflation, the record manufacturers disregarded the federal law's stipulation that royalties be paid monthly and began to issue thirty-to-ninety-day notes in lieu of checks. Heavy winter storms tied up pulp paper supplies. This plus the possibility of immediate bankruptcy for many smaller firms, caused them to raise popular sheet-music prices 300 percent, to thirty cents retail. Instead of advertising long lists of songs, publishers began to concentrate on a half-dozen new numbers and printed sheet music only after demand had been created by plugging in vaudeville theaters, restaurants, and cabarets or by talking machines and player pianos. The buyers for ten-cent stores, in order to stock the hits, began to purchase old music at a few cents a copy and then to offer combination sales, a hit and two old favorites for thirty cents.

The Woolworth Company made one final grandiose effort to prove to Tin Pan Alley that the chain's merchandising and display of ten-cent songs had been chiefly responsible for the million-copy sales. C. V. Nutting, vice president in charge of buying, guaranteed an order for five million copies, at six and a half cents each, of the new song "Afghanistan," published by a small firm owned by the songwriting vaudevillians L. Wolfe Gilbert and Anatole Friedland. The pair placed an initial print order for 400,000 copies, hired an office staff, and waited for the profits to pour in. Giant banners displayed the song in all Woolworth stores, and salesgirls were instructed to push only "Afghanistan." Yet copies piled up on counters and in storerooms, and when local managers returned them, Gilbert and Friedland went bankrupt. Four years earlier, Shapiro, Bernstein had also learned that it took song plugging and hard work to produce results, that advertising and merchandising gimmicks alone did not sell sheet music. In order to prove that he could push a song to the top by featuring it in his coast-to-coast chain of newspapers, William Randolph Hearst had made a one-year contract in 1916 for the exclusive use of Shapiro, Bernstein copyrights. None of the songs he printed sold more than 50,000 copies, and Louis Bernstein took to announcing that public performances were the best sales tool, that "songs must be heard by the people who buy them."

Relations between songwriters and most publishers were still in the state they had been in during Stephen Foster's time; there was little concern for sharing income with those who provided the basic product. Because so many once-leading authors and composers were depending on the charity of colleagues, Irving Berlin, with the help of his dead first wife's brother, the songwriter E. Ray Goetz, formed a benevolent group in April 1919, the Lyric Writers and Composers Protective League. It began to work for an improved and standard songwriters' contract.

In early 1920, it was Leo Feist, Charles K. Harris, Louis Bernstein, and Isidore Witmark, music publishers affiliated with both MPPA and ASCAP —rather than Pat Casey, who represented Keith and Murdock—who served as heralds of a new day. Casey remained in charge of the MPPA, but when labor disputes took more of his time, E. Claude Mills had been brought in as his assistant. With considerable business ability and a personality that charmed a number of important music men, this one-legged Texan, who had lost the limb in a railroad accident, was moved up to the post of chairman of the executive committee, replacing Albee's lawyer, Maurice Goodman. Some publishers began to point out to ASCAP officials that Mills had brought the MPPA to maturity with a uniform word and music roll licensing contract, a bureau whose purpose was to educate dealers to pay their bills on time, and a censoring service to guard against publication of blue lyrics. Mills's fluency in Spanish had helped effect registration in Cuba of copyrights owned by MPPA members that were being reproduced there without permission for sale in Florida and the South. His ability could be available without charge to ASCAP, because the MPPA would continue to pay his $20,000 salary when the two organizations moved under the same roof. The publishers insisted that Mills was the man for them both, that without him there could be no effective merger to present a united front on the question of collecting license fees from picture houses, theaters, hotels, restaurants, and other music users, many of whom had organized trade associations to fight the society.

A major problem had arisen, meanwhile, one that Nathan Burkan and ASCAP officials wished to keep from public attention. The standard form of agreement between composers and authors and their publishers conveyed all rights to the publisher, including the right to renew the copyright. Under it, the writers had no power to grant public-performance rights to ASCAP.

There were many nonmember publishers who controlled important catalogues, and in order to bring them into the society, with their performing rights, and make ASCAP a truly important organization in licensing most popular music, some compromise had to be made. The softening of ASCAP directors and officials on behalf of Mills, and the acceptance of important tax-free catalogues owned by MPPA members led to an agreement, drawn up by Mills and Burkan along lines demanded by the publishers. Each organization would have half of the members of a new twenty-four-man board of directors. ASCAP income, during a period when general license fees were in excess of $10,000 each month, had reposed in the treasury against contingencies. The publishers insisted on its distribution, half to them, the balance to authors and composers.

Twenty-four of ASCAP's six publisher and 150 songwriter members voted for the new plan in December 1920. Louis Hirsch, a Broadway production writer and the youngest of ASCAP's founders, managed to get a special clause written into the new Articles of Association: a two-thirds majority was required in order to affirm any action. It proved a providential defense for songwriters during the years of internal wrangling that lay ahead.

PART TWO

1921–1930

CHAPTER 5

Popular Songs and the Movie Business

The value of a new popular song in promoting a moving picture was demonstrated to the industry in the 1918–19 season by the popularity of "Mickey (Pretty Mickey)," composed on order from the director Marshall Neilan for his movie of the same name. Written under the pseudonym Neil Moret by the Kansas City ragtime songwriter Charles N. Daniels, and published by his own house, the song enjoyed an unexpected success. Many copies of the printed music, which bore a photograph of the picture's star, Mabel Normand, and trumpeted her association with the movie, were sold. Only the presence of the young American Society of Composers, Authors and Publishers, which sought to collect an anticipated $1.5 million annually from movie-house owners and exhibitors, prevented the use of Tin Pan Alley hit songs to attract people to box offices.

The play-what-he-pleased nickelodeon pianist and the automatic player piano operated by the house manager were both going the way of the primitive theater that had spawned them. Live musicians—sometimes as many as 100 in the grand movie palaces—were taking their place. In many new theaters there could also be found a "part one-man band, part symphony orchestra, part sound-effects department," the Rudolph Wurlitzer Company's Orchestra Unit Piano, "the ultimate choice of the world's greatest exhibitors of high-class Motion Pictures." This revolutionary instrument, with electro-pneumatic action and console, was invented by the Briton Robert Hope-Jones in the 1890s. He had come to America in 1903 and begun to manufacture his substitute for a live orchestra. Financial difficulties by 1910 led to the closing of his factory; all patents were turned over to the Wurlitzer Company. From that point on, the superior merchandising facilities of its new owner made the mass-produced "mighty Wurlitzer" the major source of music for films, until the triumph of talking pictures and the Hammond electric organ.

After ASCAP filed actions against screen-theater owners for the use of copyrighted music, they began to use nontaxable music with silent films. Production companies came to their aid by sending cue sheets of public-domain selections with the cans containing each new release. Some of the non-ASCAP standard-music publishers also printed collections of thematic music appropriate for use in movie houses. Film audiences became so familiar with this limited repertory, however, that in 1921 the revival of *The Birth of a Nation* was sent on the road with a newly written accompanying score.

Individual music directors charged with providing film scores in the large theaters found themselves turning more and more to completely unfamiliar selections or to new and original music. Production heads in Hollywood had already recognized that even an inferior picture was made more appealing by the addition of a high-quality musical background that did not intrude on the action. But it took the return of many popular-song publishers to ASCAP to move them to seek original and new tax-free music they could control. Beginning in 1921, classically trained composers with broad experience in the largest film theaters were sought out to provide music that could be sent out in full score and in parts to major theater orchestras and in transcriptions for the smaller theaters' piano or organ. Among the most in demand were: Louis Moreau Gottschalk's youngest brother, Louis Ferdinand, a veteran of the Broadway musical theater before he moved to Hollywood (Orphans of the Storm, *Broken Blossoms, The Four Horsemen of the Apocalypse*); Viennese-trained Hugo Riesenfeld, who was musical director for New York's three largest film theaters and who commanded $1,000 for a complete score (*The Covered Wagon, Sunrise*); American-born violinist and music educator Mortimer Wilson, who studied composition with Max Reger (*Thief of Bagdad, Don Q, The Black Pirate*); the Italian composer Cesare Sodero, who also served Thomas Edison as leader of his recording-studio orchestras; Leo Kempinski, a German-born Pole, composer, conductor, and organist (*Greed*); William Axt, who was conductor for Emma Trentini during World War I, first director of music at the Capitol Theatre in New York, and organizer of the East Coast MGM music department during the advent of talking pictures (*The Big Parade, Ben Hur, Merry Widow, Don Juan*); his frequent collaborator David Mendoza, violinist and conductor at the Capitol Theatre, and concertmaster for the Victor Talking Machine Company; the Dutch composer and conductor David Broekman, who became first musical director for Electrical Research Products; Max Winkler, founder of Belwin Music Company; Erno Rapee, born in Hungary, trained in Germany, who conducted in Europe and South America before becoming director of the first symphonic orchestra in a motion-picture house (New York's Rivoli), and then was musical director at Radio City Music Hall, from its opening until his death in 1945 (*The Iron Horse*, *The Big Parade*, *What Price Glory*? *Seventh Heaven*); Maurice Baron, a Frenchman and Rapee's frequent associate in scoring; and Domenico Savino, graduate of the conservatory at Naples, musical director for Pathé Records, and then on the staff at MGM.

Owning to a large thumb-indexed volume, *Motion Picture Moods for Pianists and Organists,* brought out by G. Schirmer, the largest publisher of silent-picture music, Rapee became the most performed composer for the screen. His 674-page collection of original music for the fifty-two moods and situations generally perceived to be standard in motion pictures and his other, similar, publications served as the chief reference works for moviehouse musicians.

The sudden withdrawal of major catalogues of unlicensed music following ASCAP's reorganization affected motion-picture exhibitors and theater operators almost at once. They faced a stepped-up drive to collect fees from them. Lists of tax-free music that had been prepared for use by members of the new Motion Picture Theater Owners Association, about 13,000 of the businessmen owners of 16,000 movie houses, were rendered obsolete overnight. The destruction of ASCAP became for them an immediate objective. The resolve to accomplish this was strengthened, for some 5,000 owners who had taken out ASCAP licenses and for others who had not, when another depression and a nationwide buyers' strike against all luxury items sharply reduced theater attendance.

Five years of boomtime in Hollywood came to a sudden end and shook out the grafters and the weak of heart, as well as many successful independents. Production, distribution, and exhibition were centralized by the established Big Three and a few major studio heads. Directors whose names assured long lines at the box office were required to give up their independence or leave the business. An increase in industry-owned theaters made block booking universal. Independent exhibitors were thus forced to contract for pictures well in advance of production, before their quality and appeal could be ascertained. The combine of giants—Paramount, MGM, and First National—into which United Artists and Universal were shouldering their way, demonstrated their faith in the future by putting up permanent buildings to replace the temporary ramshackle sprawl of film making's adolescence.

Coincident with an infusion of new blood into the top levels of production, the public resumed its romance with the movies when business improved nationwide, unemployment dropped, and wages went up. Weekly attendance jumped to 50 million, paying $520 million annually, or $68.37 for the average seat on which ASCAP levied a dime.

Because of well-publicized sexual and narcotics problems, a few of Hollywood's most glittering stars began having problems with middle-class Americans, who were enacting laws at state and local levels that called for censorship of new films. Looking for help and improved public relations, the movie moguls found Postmaster General Will S. Hays in 1923. Hired at a salary of $150,000 to be head of the new Motion Picture Producers and Distributors of America, Hays was endowed with absolute power to bar actors for misconduct, and to censor all scripts, using Midwestern prejudices as a guide. The specter of local blacklisting was exorcised.

Hays made it clear to the Motion's Picture Theater Owners Association that their ASCAP problem was not his employer's concern. Soon those most active in the fight against organized music publishers and songwriters found themselves dragged into court by the society, at its own considerable expense, where they generally were found guilty of violating the Copyright Act. Theater owners began to use their connections with local political figures to get anti-music-trust legislation, and they began a well-financed attack on copyright. A major setback occurred when an appeal to the Federal Trade Commission proved fruitless in 1923; that body expressed its regrets for having found no actionable grounds against ASCAP.

Representatives of the theater owners and persons speaking for the new radio business became frequent witnesses in Washington during anti-ASCAP performing-rights licensing hearings held from 1923 to 1926. Both groups tried, unsuccessfully, to survive with a new catalogue of tax-free music offered in 1923 by the defection from ASCAP of several major standard and classical-music publishers, and by all members of the Music Publishers Association. The trade alliance provided its catalogues without charge at a time when the society was urging members to keep music off the radio and out of the hands of unlicensed theater owners and motion-picture companies. With many hotel, cabaret, restaurant, dance-hall, and other trade associations, the theater owners became active supporters of the new National Association of Broadcasters, formed in 1923 to fight ASCAP by creating a plentiful supply of music on which no tax would be collected. Peace came in 1926. As part of the fourth-largest American industry, with sales of 90 million tickets a week, 11,000 exhibitors became ASCAP licensees and paid $525,000, which represented more than half ASCAP's income that year.

The members of the Motion Picture Theater Owners Association could no longer compete effectively with the prosperous theater chains, owned by Wall Street men who also owned major Hollywood interests. These powers were apathetic to any notion of making pictures speak. The talking picture was nothing new, however. It went back to Edison, and its leading developer, an industry outsider, and radio pioneer, Lee De Forest, had as early as 1906, experimented with sound on film. His interest was revived in the early 1920s, after the Radio Corporation of America had purchased most rights to his vacuum tube, which was at the heart of commercial broadcasting. The inventor next acquired a partial interest in the sound-on-film process owned by Theodore E. Case. After improving loudspeakers and recording techniques of the Case system, he formed the Phonofilm Corporation, financed by public offering in 1925. With the larger theaters closed to him, he began to send out talking-movie road shows to small independent theaters. Phonofilm programs were completely self-contained; live musicians were not required to accompany Eddie Cantor, Weber & Fields, the team of Noble Sissle and Eubie Blake, the Ben Bernie, Roger Wolfe Kahn, Ray Miller, and Paul Specht orchestras, the complete *Chauve Souris* theatrical presentation, and the incomparable Al Jolson, who was paid $10,000 to "can" two songs. Inadequate financing plus opposition from the major film companies and protests by projectionists and stagehands' unions put the enterprise out of business.

Throughout the period De Forest was working on his Phonofilm project, the Western Electric Division of American Telephone & Telegraph had secretly been at work on similar experiments. These involved a sound-on-disk process that synchronized action with music and speech by employing twenty-inch phonograph recordings, whose surfaces were far superior to the commercial product. Millions were spent, and when the demonstration of a talking picture starring Maude Adams as made in 1924 and elicited little enthusiasm from Hollywood, Western Electric sold exclusive exploitation rights to the Wall Street broker Walter Rich. While looking for a production company willing to gamble on a major revolution in movie making, he stumbled across the Warner brothers, four Pennsylvanians who had started with a nickelodeon and reached Hollywood eighteen years later, ready to do battle with the Big Five. Although perilously close to bankruptcy, in 1925 they used borrowed capital to buy a half-interest from Rich, including the right to sublease to other companies. The Vitaphone Company was formed, in association with Rich, and production was started in the Warners' East Coast studios. Short popular- and classical-music and comedy movies were made and leased to accompany full-length silent Warner features.

Harry Warner was president of the family film company. Like other movie makers, he had not been impressed by De Forest's experiments and had looked to the infant radio business to promote new movies. Sam Warner was put in charge of equipping KFWB, a Los Angeles station, and became fascinated by the electronic medium. On a trip to New York, he saw the latest Bell Laboratories sound-on-disk movie process and was impressed. Harry, however, resisted any suggestion that Warners go into talking pictures, and it was necessary to trick him into witnessing a Bell demonstration. As he was about to leave the room, an orchestra appeared on the screen. It played with such fidelity that he walked behind the screen to make certain that no live musicians were hiding there. Though convinced by this of the feasibility of synchronizing sound with pictures, he saw the process as ideal only for music, not for speech, and wanted to concentrate on production of musical features only, to bring the world's finest classical music to every city in the nation. Therefore, the movie *Don Juan,* which starred John Barrymore, had only music, and no dialogue.

The first feature movie with music was shown in August 1926, after a year during which the Vitaphone process was refined. The Warners introduced it in New York, along with talking short features produced in the Brooklyn Vitaphone studio. An accompanying score, written for 100 musicians by William Axt and David Mendoza, was performed and recorded by the New York Philharmonic Orchestra. The audience response was ecstatic, but the industry was passive. The Warners were forced to wire theaters in key cities at their own expense, paying between $16,000 and $25,000 to show *Don Juan.*

Except for the 1918 "Mickey," motion-picture "theme songs" usually attracted dust on sheet-music counters. The astonishing success in 1926 of the theme song for *What Price Glory?,* "Charmaine," promised to revive multimillion-copy sales of sheet music. Tin Pan Alley therefore looked with new interest across the river to Brooklyn and the production there of short musical two-reelers.

William Fox, producer of *What Price Glory?,* whose *Seventh Heaven* featured Erno Rapee's second million-selling hit, "Diane," had been an outspoken opponent of adding sound to films. He now saw it as a way to reduce expenses entailed in employing large orchestras for his movie-house chain. After securing a sublicense from Vitaphone, he also obtained rights from Theodore Case to the sound-on-film process and began production of the Fox-Case Movietone Newsreel and one-reel travelogues. Sensing the revival of interest, and with new markets to exploit, Western Electric recovered its bargain-price exploitation rights from the Warners and Case in 1927 and created Electrical Research Products, Inc., to license and service the process to which it held all basic patents.

More than 100 first-run movie houses around the country were now wired, paid for with money advanced by the Warners against future earnings. In the summer of 1927, *The Jazz Singer,* a silent feature with songs, chosen and recorded by Al Jolson, and some recorded dialogue were added, opened in New York and in selected theaters elsewhere. Produced for a half-million dollars, the film starred Jolson, who got a share of the profits rather than a weekly salary. As additional theaters were prepared to accept Vitaphone pictures, a tremendous press campaign built up national interest in this latest miracle of movie making, which actually was only a silent film accompanied by phonograph recordings, and marked no great improvement over the basic technology used in 1910.

A second industrial giant now entered the lists, the General Electric Company, parent of RCA. The latter was owner and operator of the most successful broadcasting operation, the Red and Blue networks, headed by David Sarnoff. During the war, Sarnoff had told his superiors at GE that the technology he predicted would make commercial broadcasting feasible could also effect an improvement in talking and moving pictures. Unlike Western Electric, GE committed its research to photographing sound on film, and demonstrated the first results in 1922. With RCA's interest focused on the creation of a coast-to-coast radio network, progress on talking pictures lagged, however. Then Paramount executives, who were reluctant to fund any Warner Brothers' investment, committed themselves to the GE-RCA Photophone process for a single picture, the aviation epic *Wings,* in 1927. The sound for it was supplied by a film run separately and in synchronization with the silent picture's reels. The movie was a box-office success, but ERPI and Vitaphone had in the meantime stolen a march on their competitors by concluding contracts with seventy-five first-run screen theaters and all five major production companies. They charged $1,000 a reel, and a maximum of $10,000 for a feature movie.

In order to obtain control of a film company that would demonstrate the capacities of GE-RCA's process, Sarnoff purchased for RCA an interest in Joseph P. Kennedy's Film Booking Offices of America for $400,000. The young Massachusetts millionaire had purchased that failing operation from its debt-ridden English owners, solely with money advanced by investors, for a fraction of its original seven-million-dollar capitalization. Although a midget in comparison to Paramount or MGM, with Kennedy in charge, FBO made fifty films in 1926. The most profitable were Western shoot-'em-ups starring Fred Thompson, a Ph.D. from Princeton who was paid $15,000 a week; others featured Tom Mix, who was paid $5,000 more.

With FBO under the corporate umbrella, Sarnoff organized a new unit, RCA Photophone, in March 1928. Kennedy proved to be an invaluable ally, particularly when not required to venture his own money, and Sarnoff used the banker's near-genius for finance to borrow sufficient capital from major investment houses to merge all of RCA's picture interests and buy stock in the Keith-Albee-Orpheum vaudeville–picture-house chain. In possession of agreements with FBO and other small independents responsible for ten percent of Hollywood's total production, and also 200 KAO theaters where Photophone could be immediately installed, Sarnoff and Kennedy ousted E. A. Albee and created Radio-Keith-Orpheum (RKO). The new corporation, with gross assets in excess of $71 million, controlled about 12 percent of all first-run outlets.

While these complicated maneuvers were taking place, Wall Street made another serious move into the movie business and, in 1928, supplied three million dollars to the industry for the retooling of studios and theaters. Vitaphone's technical limitations continued to play havoc with the voices of silent-picture stars and those with impeccable diction and suitable speaking talent imported from Broadway, but it was kind to music and singers. Thus, an increasing portion of talking-picture output depended on interpolated songs or on old Broadway musical comedies and new ones written expressly for the screen. *Variety* began to hammer on the dictum that popular music provided half the appeal of a movie.

Once committed to Western Electric's sound-on-record system, the Warners believed that, like the recording companies, they were entitled to the compulsory mechanical-licensing provision of copyright law and its two-cents-per-side royalty. The Music Publishers Protective Association protested, pointing out that commercial recordings were made for home use only, and threatening, if an appropriate new arrangement was not made, to pull out of ASCAP. In such an event, every theater showing a Warner product would violate the law, and Vitaphone might be strangled in its cradle. The Warners were obliged to accept an agreement, and they signed a contract in late 1926 to pay a minimum $100,000 annual royalty against recorded or synchronized music rights.

After Western Electric pressed the Warner-Rich Vitaphone Company to return its initial license, and ERPI was formed in 1928, the MPPA forged a new agreement with it, again licensing synchronization rights at a rate higher than that called for by the law. These were passed along in turn, to other film makers under their licenses from ERPI. Acting as an agent for MPPA members and as chairman of their board, Claude Mills concluded an arrangement for sixty-three music houses, which were guaranteed total minimum royalties of $100,000 for the first year, $125,000 for the second, graduating upward through the remaining three years. The income was based on a sliding-scale fee of from two and a half to five cents a seat annually from a maximum of two million theaters in which ERPI equipment was installed, in addition to the usual ten-cent-per-seat payment to ASCAP. RCA Photophone and the East Coast Sonoraphone Company, which made short musical movies, were required to sign contracts with similar terms. Mills announced to both the trade and the public that at least one million dollars would be paid annually to both the MPPA and ASCAP. He neglected to mention that a tenth of the publishers' income was due him under terms of his contract with their association.

When ERPI and its licensees became aware in 1929 that the agreement did not include world rights for talking-picture distribution and exhibition, the contract was modified. Higher new fees were set for the use of each individual song. With the MPPA in a temporarily moribund state, publishers received the payment directly.

Within the space of a year, talking pictures had become the principal means for plugging popular music. In late 1928, the world's greatest songwriter, Irving Berlin, agreed to write new material for Universal Pictures in return only for the international promotion offered. Al Jolson's recording of "Sonny Boy," backed with "Rainbow Round My Shoulder," both featured in his second Warner talkie, *The Singing Fool*, which was the first moving picture to ask for a top admission of three dollars, had matched the million-copy sale of Gene Austin's recent pace-setting disk of "My Blue

Heaven.'' It also sold a million copies of sheet music in less than a year. Jolson had been cut in on both copyrights. These and other shining prospects for the music business prompted Louis B. Mayer, head of production at MGM, to get a 51 percent interest in the hustling Robbins Music Corp., of New York City. With assets that rose from $18 million in 1928 to $230 million a year later, in part from their recently acquired control of First National Pictures, Warner Brothers was no longer the poor company publishers had thought it in 1926. It had become obvious to Warner, as to others, that the film industry must get control of a sufficient number of music copyrights to make it totally independent of any combine of music publishers, songwriters, or copyright owners. The ERPI contracts with the MPPA were to expire in a few years, and in order to raise the price of their product by freeing exhibitors from the obligation to pay ASCAP and the publishers, a giant tax-free library of music must be assembled.

No longer dealing in pennies, Warner bought the original Tin Pan Alley music house, formed in 1885, M. Witmark & Sons, for $900,000. No cash was involved in their next transaction, which was floated by listing $8.5 million worth of additional shares of stock. In May 1929, the Dreyfus music interests, involving a dozen firms, the most profitable music operation extant, became Warner Brothers' property. With them came contracts for the exclusive services of the pick of the country's best songwriters and first call on the scores of Broadway's most important musical comedies and operettas. Considerable profits were anticipated from the Dreyfus operation, the Chappell-Harms firms alone accounting for an annual surplus of $500,000 in good years. With Warner owning a majority interest in Remick (in which Dreyfus had a 50 percent interest), Harms and T. B. Harms, New World Music, DeSylva, Brown & Henderson, and several other music houses, there was also the possibility of controlling a major portion of the music publishers' vote in ASCAP policy making and the distribution of its revenues.

By buying control of copyrights, Warner was unique in the rush by movie companies to purchase music houses. Most were interested only in acquiring for hire the services of experienced songwriters, for which they were then paying sums far greater than the average annual income of most of them. Warner looked to the day when it might be freed of onerous and increasingly exorbitant synchronization fees.

Crying doom in the night, *Variety* continued, with little effect, to remind New York publishers that motion-picture-company control would lead to the disappearance of the major share of ASCAP income—fees based on the number of theater seats.

By the summer of 1930 the Great Depression had made the West Coast no longer the Gold Coast. Sound was by then installed in 83 percent of all theaters, but box-office receipts were beginning to fall because of high ticket prices. Hollywood was being forced to reduce the salaries of its top executives and to cut expenses further by firing lesser employees. In the cost-cutting imposed by their Wall Street backers and accountants, film companies began to ease songwriters out of their contracts and send them back to New York, where sheet-music sales had fallen by half, record sales by at least 40 percent.

The overproduction of songs that remained in demand only as long as the movie in which they were featured continued in circulation had effectively blocked from exposure most of those popular songs that used to be written to match the changing tempo and spirit of the times. The moving-picture factories having drained the journeyman talent of most, many songwriters were making their way back to a business that had changed, back to face a new and cruel but important user of their wares: radio.

CHAPTER 6

The Decline and Fall of the House of Albee

Having broken the White Rats union of variety performers and replaced it with his own National Vaudeville Artists as the only accepted representative of organized performers, E. F. Albee was in the van of the fight by legitimate-theater managers in 1919 to smash the Actors' Equity Association. He served during its four-week-long walkout as second vice president of the United Managers Protective Association, and after the actors won became an even more ruthless antilabor man. Whenever it was necessary to post backstage notices cutting salaries or canceling bookings, he took great pleasure in signing them personally.

Bad times forced a drastic change in vaudeville. One quarter of all theaters dropped variety completely or replaced it with one-reel movies. More than two thirds of the 30,000 artists were unemployed. Those who vied for the 5,000 jobs available took whatever Albee and others offered.

Once the government's antitrust action against the vaudeville managers was terminated, with little more than a slap on the hand and a promise to be good, Albee and his general manager, John Murdock, undertook to reorganize the Keith-Albee empire. They purchased additional theaters and, as soon as times improved, increased prices to one dollar, two dollars at the Palace, crown jewel of Albee's treasures. The new Albee theaters included the Hippodrome, in Manhattan, the largest vaudeville house in the world, where the weekly take could be as large as $50,000. The strongest competition came from Marcus Loew, whose chain of small-time or continuous vaudeville theaters, owned by Loew's Enterprises, had a fifty-cent top. The company was reorganized into Loews, Inc., a vaudeville and motion-picture-production company, with a capitalization of $100 million, twice that of Keith-Albee.

Observing the successful solidification of Albee's control of two thirds of all big-time variety, the Shubert brothers decided once again to challenge the monopoly. The agreement not to enter vaudeville for a decade, after they lost a challenge to Keith, was nearing its end. So the Shuberts prepared a new Advanced Vaudeville Circuit, which opened in the autumn of 1922. It offered a thirty-five-week season of unit shows, abridged revues, and musical comedies direct from Broadway at a one-dollar top. Some of Albee's biggest attractions were lured away with promises of roles in forthcoming Shubert Broadway productions and higher salaries, and did for a time attract ticket buyers. Albee, determined to weather the desertions and have his revenge, offered, for the first time in his career, long-term contracts and special considerations to those who remained loyal. When the Shubert incursion came to an end, with a $1.5-million loss, Albee welcomed back the unfaithful only after they confessed their transgressions with paid advertising in the pages of *Variety*.

Once radio changed from a hobbyist's plaything into a potentially profitable medium, with one million sets in use by mid-1922, Keith-Albee added a clause to all contracts banning any appearance on wireless broadcasts. An offer in early 1924 for a weekly broadcast featuring performers at the Palace was rejected, and notices appeared backstage barring songs being featured on radio programs. Only the recognition by broadcasters that talent should receive some payment, and the growth of remote sending facilities in hotels where dance orchestras played, succeeded in thwarting Albee's efforts to keep his chief attractions off the air.

Loew had a different attitude toward broadcasting. He saw it as not only a medium to promote his vaudeville and motion-picture interests but also a source of income. So he went on the air with station WHN, which broadcast from his State Theatre building in New York City. All-night programming was provided by acts booked into the State Theatre and by dance bands playing in local night clubs, over wires for which the management paid in order to get time on the air. In early 1925, after protestations by WHN that it was operating only for good will, an investigation, reported in the *New York Times,* found that the station had an annual income of $300,000 from fees for indirect advertising.

Despite the success on Broadway of all-Negro shows, beginning with *Shuffle Along* in 1921, and the acclaim for hot black jazz bands, many of whom were heard over WHN, the artists whose blues and dance music were discovered on records had little opportunity to display their talents onstage in vaudeville theaters. There were only-black variety and legitimate theaters that catered to black audiences in large urban centers, to which persons in search of exotica sometimes ventured. In the South and Midwest, there was the Theatre Owners Booking Association, through which the best-selling blues artists found all-black audiences. Formed in 1920 by white and black operators, the TOBA was funded with an initial purchase of $300 in capital stock that entitled each to a lifetime franchise to operate. This circuit, of between thirty and forty-five theaters, offered a flat $1,200 weekly for a complete company of twenty performers headed by a recording star, dancer, or variety artist. After deductions for advertising, transportation, and other expenses, the average pay per person was about twenty dollars for a week's work.

Big-time white vaudeville was entering the last years of its life when E. F. Albee declared the year 1926 its one-hundredth anniversary and let loose his underlings and the managers of most of his 600 Keith-Albee houses to celebrate that occasion by going on a five-a-day schedule. It was hardly the time for cheering. Ninety-seven percent of the country's 21,000 theaters were by then film houses, 3,000 of them first-run places, of which 100 charged more than eighty-five cents for admission. The remainder was made up of 500 legitimate theaters, many burlesque houses, and a dozen two-a-day variety-only palaces that charged from $1.25 to $3.30 a person. The movie industry had also made serious inroads into theater real estate. Despite the Federal Trade Commission's injunction that the Big Five divest themselves of such holdings and stick to making movies, Paramount was cementing its control of the country's first-run houses. Universal was in the process of floating a $50-million stock issue in order to finance and operate its own chain of 1,000 theaters.

Further competition was being readied for vaudeville and its remaining dozen two-a-day houses by the approaching completion in several large cities of magnificent new "cathedrals of the motion-picture," which were to present feature movies and vaudeville. The first of these ornately ambitious edifices was Paramount's Broadway theater on the former site of the Shanley restaurant, where "Sweethearts" was performed without permission, resulting in ASCAP's first important legal victory. Gross profit for the opening week, in 1926, was a record-breaking $80,000; a million dollars for the first year of operation. The following summer, two more five-presentations-a-day houses opened: Grauman's Chinese Theatre, in Hollywood, and the world's largest, the Roxy, in New York. Seating 2,200 and built at the cost of a million dollars, Grauman's opened with the Pathé–De Mille production of *The King of Kings,* a silent film to which a Photophone sound track had been added. Grander, the Roxy, with 6,250 seats, represented an eight-million-dollar investment, and it cost $50,000 a week for its large symphony orchestra, corps de ballet, other dancers, chorines, solo singers, and other talent. During opening week, the musical director, Erno Rapee, conducted an augmented orchestra to accompany a silent feature and the lavish stage show, for which opening-night tickets cost eleven dollars. The Paramount's million-dollar income paled in comparison with the Roxy's $5.5 million.

By then one of the world's most hated men, Albee was blissfully unaware of the approaching end of his power and basking in the glory of *Variety*'s report that he was the seventh most prosperous man in show business, with holdings of $25 million. His closest associate and trusted confidant Murdock was twelfth, with $10 million.

In the face of life-threatening competition from talking pictures and network radio, Albee was persuaded to approve long-term contracts with an annual salary increase for the 300 headline acts that his United Booking Office forced on many of the country's independent theaters. The average annual income of the 6,000 performers who continued to work behind footlights had shrunk to $2,000, and there was no longer any prospect of money from music publishers. Tin Pan Alley was learning that the talking picture and radio provided the plugging that made hits and sold sheet music.

Murdock's experience in the picture business dated back to his days as head of America's first color-movie company, and he was at home negotiating the purchase by Keith-Albee of an important interest in Pathé–De Mille Pictures, whose president's chair he immediately occupied. It was generally believed that this public friendship with Joseph Kennedy was in connection with a merger of FBO and Pathé. But both had other fish to fry. The long-secret business collusion between Keith-Albee and the dominant western Orpheum circuit was made public by the official merger that created Keith-Albee-Orpheum.

In May 1928, a meeting was held by Kennedy and the vaudeville magnate, during which an offer to buy 200,000 shares of KAO stock for $4.2 million was declined. Only after Murdock pointed out that the bid represented five dollars above the sixteen-dollar-price quoted on the Curb Exchange did Albee agree to sell. The syndicate of Wall Street houses for which Kennedy acted gave him a bonus of $150,000, elected him chairman of the board, and approved an option to buy 75,000 shares of KAO at the prevailing price of twenty-one dollars. Immediately, a purge of Albee's favorites was initiated; only Pat Casey and Murdock emerged apparently unscatched and still loyal.

Murdock and Kennedy announced a few months later that Pathé and FBO had signed contracts with RCA Photophone. The latter would install its equipment in 200 KAO theaters. In October, FBO and KAO merged with RCA Photophone to create RKO from whose title all reference to Albee was deliberately omitted. Kennedy was named chairman, with Murdock as his leading associate.

The mounting deficit being built by vaudeville's decline, however, as well as the general ineptitude of the new management brought in hard-eyed A T & T financial men to run the corporation. Kennedy resigned, as did Murdock. When RKO stock reached fifty dollars, Kennedy exercised his option and realized a profit of some two million, approximately the same amount he made from the sale of his FBO holdings. The following March Edward F. Albee was dead of a heart attack.

No one could save vaudeville. Only four theaters in the country offered variety entertainment exclusively. With its holdings in picture and sound equipment and the licensing business at stake, RKO offered units of four acts on a fifty-week basis to theaters, at the top price of $3,000 for the entire company. Loew's, Inc., whose management was generally a step ahead of competitors, dropped all live entertainment, and most independents closed their doors. The Vaudeville Managers Protective Association, once so powerful it manipulated music publishers and songwriters, was bankrupt. The "I don't care" lady, Eva Tanguay, who had been the highest-paid star in the business, accepted $150 for a three-day run in a Brooklyn theater. The National Vaudeville Artists union discontinued payment of the traditional $1,000 death benefit, which had been Albee's pride, even though the dead usually had paid twice that to the fund.

Having held on until their deadliest enemy was dead and buried, the White Rats bowed to the inevitable and surrendered the American Federation of Labor charter granted twenty years earlier. The Palace Theatre, once the seventh heaven of every vaudevillian, was already wired for sound pictures. Soon, the only true vaudeville in the old tradition being sent out by RKO was its *Varieties* unit, whose biggest-drawing attractions generally were people from the movies.

CHAPTER 7

The Mechanical Music Business

With 200 companies manufacturing talking machines of various sizes and prices, the record business reached peak sales at retail in 1921 of $106.5 million ($47.8 million wholesale), a figure that was not exceeded for twenty-six years. The industry was so important a factor in the music business that *Variety* added a monthly best-selling records chart in July 1920. Two of the industry's original three giants, Edison and Victor, were in good financial shape in 1921, the former with its best sales year yet, $26 million, and Eldridge Johnson's Camden-based company with $55 million from the sale of 51 million disks. The death in mid-1921 of Victor's best-selling operatic artist, Enrico Caruso—an occasion marked by publication of "They Needed a Songbird in Heaven (So They Took Caruso Away)"—stimulated sales of $2.5 million of the star's Red Seal recordings. Buying back, for nine million dollars in cash, a half-interest in Victor's British associate, the Gramophone Company–His Master's Voice, which he had sold years before for $50 million, put Johnson and his stockholders in a financial position envied by all rivals and gave them major access to the entire world's phonograph market.

Columbia was not faring well. Control had fallen into the hands of Wall Street speculators, whose pursuit of dividends raised the price of Columbia stock out of all proportion to its assets. The overproduction of disks and phonograph machines, to pay the interest on loans, and the depression of 1921 speeded the company to involuntary bankruptcy and receivership.

Shorn of all financial manipulation, the industry's fundamental economics in 1921 were easy to comprehend. A single disk cost twenty cents to make, including any royalty owed to copyright owners. The sale of 5,000 recordings, whose prices could range from seventy-five cents to the seven dollars being paid for Caruso's version, with other singers, of the sextet from *Lucia,* effectively wiped out all production costs and made further sales mostly profit. This equation attracted get-rich-quick operators and spurred the formation of 150 companies looking for a mass market for which a fifty-cent ten-inch record was attractive. The market was there, as music publishers learned from the declining sales of their thirty-five-cent sheet music to buyers who could get two hits or two pieces of jazz music for a half-dollar or less.

This increased supply of the same new material on cheaper labels brought about abandonment of the traditional release-date policy forced on Columbia, Victor, Edison, and the piano-roll makers in exchange for a 10 percent "breakage" discount. The first release of a new copyrighted piece had always been withheld from the public until the publisher felt that all initial sheet-music sales were squeezed out. He then informed the manufacturer that the time had come to release the disk, after which other companies could duplicate it. Because of heavy competition, the old-line record makers began to release a new recording whenever they chose to, but, regarding it as sacrosanct, continued to take advantage of the breakage discount.

The growing popularity of radio broadcasts, as represented by an increase in receiver sales, and the improved records and phonograph machines being brought out by the independents further upset the normal balance of power. In 1922, Columbia introduced a silent record surface developed by technicians in its British branch, which was about to be sold to Louis Sterling and some European investors in the interests of building an American cash reserve. Born in the United States, and with twenty years of experience in the international business, Sterling, fiercely aggressive, was readier to accept new technology than his debt-ridden U.S. counterparts. Meanwhile, as sales began to drop, Victor improved its own surfaces and brought out the first double-faced Red Seals. It deleted from its catalogue thousands of old selections whose masters did not lend themselves to the advancing technology. The world's largest record company was not as quick to respond to the new "flat-top" cabinet, combination record machines and radio receivers introduced by smaller companies to compete with the Victrola. The original of that machine, a raised-lid cabinet, had never been redesigned, with the result that Victrola sales dropped by 20 percent, and Victor dealers added other, more modern, lines. Emerson Records, one of the largest and most successful of the postwar independents, similarly found itself unable to keep pace and sold its assets to a group of creditors for $50,000. Eddie Cantor, the Shubert brothers' singing star, had been signed by Emerson, but after its sale he jumped that contract to join Brunswick, for a guarantee over five years of $220,000.

Some years before, David Sarnoff had attempted, without success, to persuade Victor officials that radio's time was fast approaching. The men in charge at Camden continued to be skeptical. Sarnoff therefore turned to the new second-largest American record company, Brunswick, and sold

$1.5 million worth of receiving equipment for installation in a new line of Radiola models, merchandised by RCA. The Radiola's loudspeaker displaced earphones, and a new piece of furniture moved into the country's living rooms. Victor relented in time, meeting the challenge with a new console model containing space into which a radio set could be placed by the owner.

In the hands of creditors, who sought to recoup whatever was feasible, Columbia joined the competition and began to issue blues recordings and other minority-interest music. During the next fourteen years, many of the most brilliant and influential vaudeville and country blues and jazz recordings appeared on the Columbia label. OKeh's pioneering venture in 1920 into recording black women singers and black music had been surprisingly successful from the start, and it had brought about the introduction of "race records" by most other labels. Brunswick, instead, initiated a jazz-dance series with all-white orchestras. Immediately successful, it began with the 1921 recording of "Wabash Blues" by the Isham Jones band, whose cornetist used a "wah-wah" mute to create the sounds of a sobbing woman that were responsible for its large sales.

Black musicians, songwriters, and publishers played a key role in the production of race records, from signing performers to the final selection of material to be recorded. Whether written by the artist or by the black talent scout–producer, race songs initially were assigned to a publishing company owned by the latter, to which royalties were paid. Talent was paid by the piece, from the twenty-five dollar to fifty dollars per side that prevailed for many years to the $200 a song Columbia paid Bessie Smith in 1924. That was after recordings by this "Empress of the Blues" had continued to sell many more than the 5,000 copies that paid back expenses. Most blues records did not, and artists preferred a flat fee in lieu of royalty. Although unfair to those performers whose recordings were popular, the system served to cover the costs of failures and eventually became "what everybody did." In fact, a payment of twenty-five dollars was more than that from half the standard mechanical royalty of 1.8 cents for the sale of 25,000 records. The appropriation of original material by a publishing company owned by the record producer did lead to the formation of several major music companies, some of which were owned in conjunction with the manufacturer.

The production of "hillbilly" music, which accounted for as much as a quarter of all popular sales by 1930, began as an accommodation to an Atlanta record distributor and dealer, Polk Brockman, who handled the OKeh line for that territory. He had been hearing the old-time fiddle music of a local favorite, Fiddlin' John Carson, played regularly over radio station WSB, a property of the city's newspaper, the *Constitution*. Convinced that a large Southern market for the music existed, Brockman suggested to OKeh that Carson be recorded in the city where he was most comfortable, and offered to buy a large quantity of the pressings. Ralph Peer, assistant to

Fred Hager, chief of OKeh production, was presented with the proposition and consulted with the company's chief engineer, Charles Hibbard, on the feasibility of recording on location, something that had not, to anybody's knowledge, been attempted since the days of portable cylinder machines. The son of an early Columbia franchise-holder in Missouri, Peer had worked for the label's Kansas City branch office in his teens and learned the business side. After service in the Navy during World War I, he went to New York to work for OKeh Records in sales, merchandising, and production. There, he was responsible for labeling the music intended for black buyers as "race" and that in the old-time field as "hillbilly."

The June 14, 1923, recording session with Fiddlin' John Carson was "terrible," in the estimation of all involved, but Brockman had faith in Carson's old-time versions of two songs, one of them a Will Shakespeare Hays black-dialect plantation number of the 1870s, "Little Old Log Cabin Down the Lane." It had assumed the mantle of high-class music after it had been recorded by the Metropolitan Opera diva Alma Gluck, for a Red Seal version, which sold well. Brockman's faith was justified when sales of the first release covered costs and more, and OKeh embarked on assembling the industry's first hillbilly record catalogue, for which music was often recorded by Ralph Peer on portable equipment during sessions that sometimes embraced only race music.

In taped interviews made in 1959, cited in Nolan Porterfield's *Jimmie Rodgers,* Peer described the royalty and artist-payment system he evolved, which became standard for both hillbilly and race music and later spilled over into popular songs. His basic principle became never to record an established selection. He insisted on getting artists who could write their own music. For this he created what became one of two standard contracts offered to recording artists for original music. It assigned all rights to OKeh for a twenty-five dollar talent fee per side and gave a guaranteed royalty to the composer-artist of .005 cents per side sold. That figure became standard for all selections whose rights were assigned to the recording company. The balance was retained by the manufacturer-publisher.

Operators of the cheaper labels, which sold for twenty-five to thirty-nine cents, established another method to create royalty-free recordings. Denied the 10 percent breakage allowance and finding it prohibitive to pay four cents to publishers, the smaller companies backed up hit songs, for which they paid, with royalty-free material. Songwriters were solicited for, usually second-rate, material they had not been able to sell and were paid $50 to $150 for all mechanical rights only. They were free to assign all remaining rights to a music publisher. Many of the jazz groups that recorded for Plaza Music Company, which made and distributed four different labels (Banner, Regal, Domino, and Oriole), sold their original instrumental numbers to publishers, thus sacrificing what often was the only source of royalty income for the publicity that would be engendered by sales to the public.

With sound quality that was sometimes superior to the scratchy, tinny reproduction of the original old Victrola and other talking machines, radio had a serious impact on the sale of high-price records, as did the competing, often fly-by-night operations that produced inexpensive disks for the syndicate and ten-cent chain stores. Hoping to increase sales and stem their losses, the new Big Three, Victor, Brunswick, and Columbia, rushed to make large offers to dance-band leaders and vocalists who might move records in large quantities. Brunswick stole Al Jolson from Columbia with the offer of $10,000 per usable side, a one third increase over his previous contract. Victor's policy of ten weekly releases, twenty sides, and that of other companies of regularly bringing out new issues twice a month, which were duplicated immediately by the cheap record companies, proved to be self-defeating. Before record retailers or music publishers had the opportunity to advertise and exploit numbers from the current supply, they were asked to place orders or select material for promotion from the new releases that would inundate them in a few days. Victor failed to persuade new investors that the industry whose sales had fallen by nearly half in a few years could hope for a return to prosperity. To offset losses, the company was obliged to enter into serious negotiations with Sarnoff for the manufacture, in its modern cabinet factory at Camden, of combination RCA radio-phonographs. Agreement was reached in May 1925, shortly after Victor had obtained the license for an electric recording process.

The introduction of improved technology, heralded by the installation of electric recording microphones and equipment in the Victor and Columbia studios, again proved to be the phonograph and record makers' salvation. The demands during the 1918 war for the widest possible international communication had brought about the development of quality amplification devices and microphones to improve wireless telephony. Sarnoff's continued insistence on the wedding of a radio and a talking machine in a single enclosure was based on his knowledge of the progress of experiments being carried on after the war in the A T & T Bell Laboratories. Great strides were made in the production of an electromagnetic recording head and a reproducing machine to turn the imprisoned vibrations into current that could be amplified to any desired volume by use of the same vacuum tubes that made radio possible. The result was a more lifelike sound, with increased frequency response. This was created in great measure by new developments that allowed the use of spacious recording facilities in which small groups were no longer required to huddle around a single recording horn. In the prevailing acoustic recording, large ensembles could not be handled, and the so-called symphonic orchestras were never more than a third of their true grand selves. Experiments with larger horns had failed to help, and even Edison's immense 200-foot-long sheet-brass recording device had proved incapable of dealing with an augmented ensemble. Usually it took half a day or longer to rehearse and record each individual selection, and additional sessions were often needed to provide a performance that a music committee would approve. Once technicians learned to cope with the new electric process, however, a single day's work might result in as many as a half-dozen acceptable renditions.

One element in Sarnoff's grand plan to establish the world's largest radio manufacturing and broadcasting empire called for the acquisition of Victor's furniture-making facilities. In spite of sagging income, that company was still in a favorable cash position, and therefore not ready to talk of merger or sale. Representatives of Western Electric, A T & T's licensing division, in late 1924 demonstrated the new electric recording process for Victor executives and offered to license its exclusive use. When no decision was forthcoming, Western Electric was free to enter into negotiations with American Columbia. In London, Louis Sterling had been greatly impressed by test pressings surreptitiously dispatched to him, and in early 1925 he rushed to New York to effect an agreement with Western Electric. With $2.2 million lent by J. P. Morgan interests, he purchased American Columbia from its debt-holders and incorporated the business into his European operation. A nonexclusive contract was negotiated with Western Electric for $50,000 and a share in future profits. A similar arrangement was made by Victor in March, and both companies worked furiously to master the new miracle. Secrecy was the keyword at Camden, so the public would not learn that existing machines and disks would be rendered antiques by the new electrical recording process. Nationwide cut-rate sales were organized to dispose of stock on hand, and in the autumn of 1925 Columbia and Victor put out their first electrically recorded disks. At the same time, Victor introduced a full line of new Orthophonic Victrolas. General reaction was skeptical at first. Many dance-music lovers remained faithful to the acoustic interpretations of hot music and hit songs that sold three for a dollar. Columbia succeeded in attracting more serious music lovers by means of a remarkable demonstration of electric recording's capabilities. Using a microphone suspended over the Metropolitan Opera House stage, its engineers recorded the British hunting song "Do You Ken John Peel," by 850 members of fifteen metropolitan-area clubs, gathered there for a concert by the Associated Glee Clubs of America. "Adeste Fideles," sung by the entire group—4,850 singers, according to the company's magazine advertising—was issued jointly with "John Peel" on a twelve-inch Columbia record in June. Public response was commensurate with the company's enthusiasm.

With superior manufacturing and merchandising, Victor was off on its second era of vast profits as sales of its Orthophonic recordings continued to increase. Americans had already spent more than two billion dollars on talking machines and assorted supplies since the 1890s, and seemed ready to pour out more in the interest of better-sounding music. Victor's skill at stimulating customer response by means of lavish magazine advertising and a six-million-dollar campaign restored the company to its long-held supremacy. It received $20 million in advance orders in the first week. Because of Victor's aggressive sales department, Columbia's new Viva-Tonal and Brunswick's Improved Panatrope, an all-electric machine developed in association with General Electric, were effectively blocked from real competition.

Recording techniques had undergone a major change, but, slow to move, industry practices did not swerve from those developed in the preceding quarter century. Records were no longer a by-product in the manufacture of phonographs, but executives still relied on music publishers' enthusiasm and their promises to work on proffered advance copies or lead sheets of music chosen by the studios selection committees. Hoping to ensure good treatment, some publishers formed close relationships with key record men to make certain that their "weak sister" tunes went on the back of "sure-fire" hits. When any bribery was exposed, the resulting scandal was as only a one-day wonder in an industry that had grown up on the gratuity system.

The average sale of individual releases soon tumbled, and a scatter-shot policy of picking material became the custom. Believing that the combined sales of more releases would exceed those of the past, when merchandising concentrated on a few major artists, the leading record makers spent six million dollars for talent. A small group of artists who enjoyed regular and steady sales were signed to long-term contracts with a built-in royalty. Most bandleaders and singers were happy to make records on any terms, since they were the best source of getting attention and providing live audiences, their major source of income. This led to signing too many unknown bands and too many unknown singers to record too many unknown songs. At Victor, where conscientious quality control still rejected one of every five records pressed, distributors were allowed a 50 to 55 percent discount, and then sold to dealers and retailers at 40 percent off. The manufacturer shared equally all costs for local advertising but left the matter of promotion, including cooperation with touring artists, and other exploitation in the hands of the distributor or retailer.

In heralding a broadcast by its contract artists, Victor completely disregarded Brunswick's programs, a few weeks earlier, which offered art and concert music performed by talent appearing on its label. Instead, the first true demonstration of the power of promotion over a group of radio stations took place January 1, 1925, after Victor made an arrangement with A T & T to waive the customary advertising fees of its eight eastern station affiliates in return for an hour of the "world's best music." Lucrezia Bori, John McCormack, the popular Shannon Male Quartet, and an orchestra under the direction of Nathaniel Shilkret, who was the only talent to be compensated, performed their most recently recorded music, copies of which were available at Victor dealers throughout the listening area. An audience estimated at eight million heard McCormack encore spontaneously a performance of Irving Berlin's "All Alone," which he had recently recorded but which was not yet released. Within the month, orders poured in for a quartermillion copies of the recording, and eventually "All Alone" sold 1.225 million records in all versions, a million copies of sheet music, and 160,000 player-piano rolls.

With total retail sales of $69.9 million in 1927, $72.6 million the following year, and $75.1 million in 1929, the record business was returning to the prosperity of the postwar period. Victor was, as usual, in the forefront, with profits stimulated by the improving quality of both players and disks, to which advances in the continued development of radio receivers contributed significantly. In 1926, twice as many homes—450 of 1,000—owned phonographs as owned radios—220 of 1,000. The ratio rapidly changed in favor of broadcasting when the price of sets powered by regular house current fell, and battery-operated receivers went the way of crystal sets and their earpiece.

Wall Street introduced David Sarnoff to a challenger to his ambition to own the Victor company. It was the combination of the Speyer and J & W Seligman investment houses, which offered $40 million for the business. Negotiations were concluded in December 1926, and the new owners celebrated a year-end prediction that sales for the past year would almost equal those in the boom year of 1921. The Texas-born singer Gene Austin, a veteran of the three-for-a-dollar studios, provided the Seligmans with almost immediate joy. His 1927 recording on the Victor black label of "My Blue Heaven" sold in the millions, an all-time seller that was topped for the first time by Bing Crosby's wartime hit of the Irving Berlin "golden oldie" from the movie *Holiday Hotel,* "White Christmas."

Ralph Peer was now associated with Victor, in charge of race and hillbilly recording. He did not receive any salary; instead, he was given control of any music he recorded on field trips to the South and in the New York and Camden studios. Fearful that he would destroy the company's reputation for paying artists the highest amounts, Victor executives insisted that Peer double the twenty-five dollars a side he had been paying performers at OKeh in addition to a .005 royalty for assignment of the copyright. In the first year under this understanding, Victor paid Peer $250,000 in a single quarter for his publisher's seventy-five percent of mechanical royalties.

The most important talent contributing to his income was a tuberculer white ex-railroad man from Mississippi, Jimmie Rodgers. Peer first recorded the singer-guitarist in August 1927 in a hotel room. The recording equipment he used on his trips was a handmade portable, folding version of Western Electric's finest machines. According to the best estimates, slightly more than 100 songs were recorded by the Singing Brakeman in the next three years, and were published, in print, by Peer, properly copyrighted, only after Rodgers became a best-selling record artist and stage performer.

Alarmed by rumors that a merger of Victor with the RCA interests was a possibility, and would give his major rival an over-the-air promotion monopoly through the National Broadcasting Company, Sterling made a bold move to save his American Columbia holdings. United Independent Broadcasters, an improvised network of about a dozen stations on the verge of dissolution, could provide a ready-made outlet for advertising and promoting Columbia, its artists, and new releases. Sterling offered to pay a bonus of $165,000 to a reorganized Columbia Phonograph Broadcasting Company, of which he and a few selected investors would hold control, and would receive in return ten hours a week on the air at night. Shortly before the contract was signed, in August 1927, the Federal Radio Commission, formed to regulate broadcasting, made an early ruling that failure to inform listeners when music mechanically reproduced on piano rolls and phonograph records was used constituted a fraud. This raised some question about the use of radio for effective promotion, but the Sterling deal was made, and Columbia began to hunt for advertisers to buy time on its nightly broadcasts. Only one was ready to be identified with a record manufacturer, particularly now that NBC's Red, White, and Blue networks were ready to provide nationwide facilities for sponsored broadcasts. Sterling recognized that his investment was ill-advised and announced his intention to pull out of the operation as soon as new financing could be found. The money came from Philadelphia, provided by a group that included William Paley, the young heir to a large cigar-manufacturing company, who found radio the most effective medium to sell his products. Sterling was bought out, and the network name was changed to the Columbia Broadcasting System, eliminating any connection with the phonograph business. In the twenty-seven-year-old Paley, broadcasting got a new and daring innovator, whose contribution would match that of David Sarnoff in many areas. He also became a ruthless, imaginative record man, from whom the industry heard much.

More than one third of all nonclassical music recorded by Victor in 1928 was controlled by Ralph Peer under terms of his agreement with the company; of this, 22.9 percent was hillbilly and 21.7 percent black. Eighty percent of the latter was actually released for sale. In order to conceal his steadily rising royalty income from Victor, Peer formed a number of music firms. The most important was the Southern Music Publishing Company, which was started with an investment of $1,000. Despite the precaution, Victor's treasurer noticed the large size of Peer's returns, and in late 1928 Peer was obliged to turn over the operation of Southern Music to the record company, although he still shared control of all material already copyrighted and could add to his catalogue any new publisher-free popular works recorded by the company's orchestras and vocalists.

The great American middle class, of all social and racial backgrounds, had become the chief target for advertising and promotion of popular music, which was becoming increasingly homogenized in character. Victor backed its new release of "In a Little Spanish Town," by its top-selling bandleader, Paul Whiteman, with the first of a series of streetcar advertisements in big cities. Aimed at a potential 1.2 million passengers a month, the campaign was expected to stimulate at least a one-out-of-100 sales response. Merchandising and promotion of a similar type by Victor's competitors were crucial in making best sellers of other syncopated dance music: by bandleaders George Olsen, Leo Reisman, Jean Goldkette, Fred Waring, and vocalists Ruth Etting, Nick Lucas, Whispering Art Gillham, Seger Ellis, Vaughn De Leath, Kate Smith, Annette Henshaw, and Little Jack Little, all of whose disks were purchased by both white and black customers in northern metropolitan markets.

Sarnoff's master plan approached realization in January 1929 when the board of RCA, of which he was now vice-president, approved his proposal to acquire a first-class furniture factory to make cabinets for RCA receivers and land and facilities for the manufacture of RCA sets, RCA tubes, and allied RCA products. The Victor Talking Machine Company, with total assets of about $69 million, was purchased by the transfer of $150 million worth of RCA common stock in exchange for a seven-eighths interest in the record company, which was divided among RCA, General Electric, and Westinghouse. It took months of corporate fighting and intrigue for Sarnoff to get control, then reorganize and consolidate the combined RCA Victor company, of which he became president.

Developments of a lesser consequence were taking place at Columbia, Brunswick, and the American Record Company. The last was chief manufacturer of three-for-one-dollar records for department and variety stores and mail-order houses. Sterling temporarily revitalized his American Columbia company with a number of flamboyant business moves, among them the capture of Paul Whiteman from Victor with a guarantee of $175,000 a year. Labels of new releases by the King of Jazz bore a caricature of the bandleader in five colors. When RCA Victor first reduced Red Seal production—one of a number of decisions made by the new management to tighten the operation—Sterling filled the gap by importing masters made by Europe's most famous concert artists. Yet, in spite of the major commitment of its facilities to the manufacture of RCA radio phonographs, Camden beat Sterling and all others, producing 34.5 million of the 65 million disks sold in 1929.

"Wall Street Lays an Egg," *Variety* headlined on page one of its October 30, 1929, issue to announce the collapse of America's financial markets. Two days later, the Edison company terminated all manufacture of cylinders, disks, and phonographs, retaining only the production of radios and dictating machines. RCA stock fell from 114 to 20 in the next few weeks. With the Great Depression, unemployment figures soared, and record sales began to fall, by 39 percent in 1930 alone.

The race market was the first to evaporate; only the hot dance bands— those of Duke Ellington, Fletcher Henderson, King Oliver, all on Victor— and certain white Red Nichols units issued among the race disks managed to hold on for a time, principally due to large demand by college students. Surprising everybody but Peer and a few other talent scouts and field-recording supervisors, hillbilly records, generally unadvertised by the manufacturers, who left such exploitation to the artists themselves, enjoyed a 25 percent share of all popular-record sales. Jimmie Rodger's "Blue Yodel Number 1," the first of his series of old-time versions of black race blues, had outsold all of Victor's popular releases. There was now so much demand for hillbilly records that some New York companies, who found only a few suitable local artists available, used as many as a dozen different names for a single performer. But as the Depression deepened, hillbilly record sales began to slide as well.

Despite the unexpected large sale of the two double-faced, twelve-inch records of Maurice Ravel's *Bolero* made by Serge Koussevitzky and the Boston Orchestra, Victor's Red Seal series was slowly phased out. Most artists' contracts were not renewed; instead, recordings by small ensembles or soloists became the order of the day. Special sales emphasis was put on albums of classically influenced and artistically arranged versions of songs and instrumental music by Stephen Foster, Rudolf Friml, Victor Herbert, and other "great American composers."

Devastating new competition came from the once-a-week, fifteen-cent, single-faced Durium records, available only on newsstands. With an average sale of 500,000, Durium soon seemed to be taking the straight Tin Pan Alley popular-song market away from everybody.

To get control of popular music, an important ingredient in talking pictures, Hollywood had been buying up the New York popular-music business. Warner Brothers, which had recently acquired a dozen major music houses, looked to ensure the public exploitation of those catalogues and their singing-star personalities, and so purchased the failing Brunswick business. With a veteran record man, Jack Kapp, in charge, Brunswick then recorded all the songs from each of its new talking picture, performed as they were on screen. It was hoped that at least one would be a hit and stimulate additional ticket sales.

In May 1930, Sarnoff was celebrating his first month as president of the Radio Corporation of America when word came that the Justice Department had filed a giant antitrust action. The government was seeking to dissolve the giant complex of pooled patents, manufacturing facilities, and ownership of broadcasting, vaudeville, motion picture, and electronic properties, which Sarnoff had so laboriously assembled. Undaunted, he presided over ceremonies in September at Camden, by then the Radio Center of the World, where work benches and assembly lines that had once produced the Victrola were turning out radio receivers in wooden cabinets of all sizes, in only a fraction of which was record-playing equipment installed.

The world, many said, was about to witness the final fall of its most popular means of musical entertainment.

CHAPTER 8

A Simple Radio Music Box

Many of the days popular "genteel" melodies had been performed on the first broadcast over wire lines, from Philadelphia, and were heard, with great difficulty because of stormy weather, by an audience in New York's Steinway Hall, in April 1877. The occasion was a demonstration of his telephone by Elisha Gray, an unsuccessful litigant against Alexander Graham Bell's claim to the initial patent for "transmitting vocal and other sounds telegraphically." Bell's backers and promoters regarded his invention primarily as a business machine, and the development of broadcasting over it was proceeding with far greater speed in Europe than in the United States. The most advanced system there in 1893 provided twelve hours of music and news a day to clients in Budapest. A few hundred miles to the southwest, a young Italo-Irish student, Guglielmo Marconi, was at work on a wireless device that could harness Herzian waves and send electric signals over distances of at least a few miles. The ensuing "most wonderful scientific development of recent times," as the press called it, was demonstrated to the world in December 1901 when Marconi's wireless sent the prearranged letter *S* from England to an experimental station in Newfoundland. The manufacture and installation of wireless-transmission receiving units for communication between ships at sea and land bases became a principal function of the British-owned Marconi Telegraph Companies, operating in England and the United States. Marconi became a wealthy man. Years later, the United States Supreme Court overturned his patent, because it had been proved to them beyond reasonable doubt that an eccentric genius Nikola Tesla, had demonstrated a radio-controlled model boat and had begun experiments to transmit electrical power across the Atlantic some years before Marconi's broadcast.

Many competent experimenters were simultaneously applying current

technology in the United States, often without regard for patent law, adding
to their findings by communication through the ether with one another and
with a growing band of hobbyists equally smitten by the mysteries of wireless telegraphy. One of the most innovative was Lee De Forest, graduate
of Yale's Sheffield Scientific School, whose name was often mentioned
with that of Marconi following the introduction of his vacuum "Audion"
tube in 1906. This key element in the advancement of broadcasting was
duly patented and merchandised by the inadequately financed and badly
managed De Forest Radio Telephone Company. It produced no significant
response from investors or wireless interests. De Forest sought relief from
the near failure of his company and the panic of 1907 in regular experimental broadcasts, for which canned music was supplied by Columbia Records whenever promised live talent failed to appear. In 1908, De Forest
broadcast disks and cylinders from the Eiffel Tower, in Paris, to listeners
as far away as 500 miles.

On his return to New York, he began daily transmissions of Columbia
records, and on January 10, 1910, broadcast live arias sung by Enrico Caruso from the Metropolitan Opera House stage. Although of interest to other
experimenters and the operators of wireless telephone facilities, these programs had only a small public audience. Broadcasting history waited for
tragedy at sea. It was announced by twenty-one-year-old David Sarnoff,
wireless operator of Wanamaker's New York store's experimental broadcasting station. A series of dots and dashes spelled out the news of the
sinking of the S.S. *Titanic* in the darkness of April 14, 1912. Sarnoff, born
in Russia and reared on the New York's lower East Side, became an office
boy at the age of fourteen for the American Marconi office in New York,
one of the first twenty wireless stations in the United States. The fame he
won for the seventy-two hours, without sleep, of reporting news of the
terrible disaster at sea, in which 1,500 perished, brought Sarnoff the nick-
name "Wonder Boy of the Radio" and the first of a series of responsible
positions with Marconi.

Wireless telephony advanced quickly within the decade after Marconi
sent his *S* across the Atlantic. Soon known as "radio," short for "radio-
telephony," it was the nighttime plaything of thousands of American tink-
erers, who built inexpensive crystal sets, on which they listened through
earpieces for the sounds of a Marconi signal, a human voice, recorded
music, or live entertainment being sent out into the air from experimental
laboratories. War in Europe was in its second year, and the American Telephone & Telegraph Company had completed installation of the first giant
radio station in the United States, at Arlington, Virginia, when Sarnoff sent
a memorandum to his superior. "I have in mind," he wrote, "a plan of
development which would make radio a 'household utility', in the same
sense as the piano or phonograph. The idea is to bring music into the home
by wireless."

Evidently disregarding work that had already been done by De Forest and other pioneers, and citing only that attempts had failed to provide music by wires, Sarnoff envisioned a single "Radio Music Box," supplied with amplifying tubes and a loudspeaker telephone, which could be placed in the family parlor. The manufacturing cost of such a box, complete with a receiving antenna, he estimated to be around seventy-five dollars if made in large quantities. Its acceptance by a mere seven percent of all American families would mean a gross business of about $75 million.

Sarnoff's visionary 1916 memorandum was regarded as frivolous and went into a Marconi file cabinet. Along with other communication companies, Marconi concentrated on the development of high-powered equipment for military use. When America declared war on April 6, 1917, the 6,000 professional and amateur radio stations were closed down or turned over to the navy. Many of the professional operators, scientists, and 100,000 radio hobbyist members of the American Radio Relay League, dedicated to the progress of wireless broadcasting, were taken into the armed forces. Radio patents were expropriated, and experimentation was subject to control by the Navy Department. The Radio Music Box was an idea whose time was postponed.

Immediately after President Woodrow Wilson lifted all wartime restrictions, business in radio equipment and parts began to boom, lifting gross receipts from near $1 million in 1914 to more than $8 million in 1919. Had it not been for the determination of certain Washington officials to prevent the largest wartime supplier, the British-owned and -operated Marconi Company, from continuing its hold over international wireless broadcasting, the electric companies might never have taken the course that led inevitably to the realization of Sarnoff's Radio Music Box. First with private support and then with semiofficial approval from the federal government that assured against antitrust complications, the General Electric Company formed the Radio Corporation of America in October 1919. Equipment manufactured by GE would be sold and operated by RCA, under a plan to provide competitive international communication. All patents were mutually cross-licensed. American Marconi, which was dissolved, and its forty land stations were acquired by GE in a stock transfer and turned over to the new corporation. With them came David Sarnoff, in an upper-management position. A series of additional deals and swaps followed, interlocking many other manufacturers and suppliers. Within eighteen months, the leading operator of ship-to-shore wireless installations, the United Fruit Company, joined A T & T, General Electric, Westinghouse, and others in a vast patent-pooling and cross-licensing arrangement, in which the telephone interests had major control.

Licensed transmitters were slow to return to the air, and then most of them only beamed out voice and Victrola music. The best known operated in the Pittsburgh area and was located near plants owned by its licensee

Westinghouse Electric. On November 2, 1920, broadcasting from a shack atop the main Westinghouse building, station KDKA sent out what is generally regarded as the first scheduled news-and-music program. Returns in the 1920 presidential election were supplied by a local newspaper and read during the intervals in a concert of recorded music. The response from those who heard the broadcast, over sets mostly assembled from parts, gave Westinghouse the signal that a market existed for a home radio receiver. So production was started. To promote public demand for the Aeriola, Jr., a tiny crystal set with earphones, for $25; the Aeriola, Sr., with a single vacuum tube and powered by dry batteries, for $60; and the table-cabinet Aeriola Grand, with built-in loudspeaker and several tubes, driven by wet battery, for $125, the KDKA staff was enlarged and put to work to create suitable and attractive programs. Listeners within a thousand-mile area (farther when weather conditions were favorable), could soon hear the newest popular recordings, supplied by a nearby shop in return for mention on the air; the latest sports scores; play-by-play baseball and football; boxing championships reported from ringside; regular remote Sunday-morning church services; market and farm reports; and a weekly live old-time barn dance.

Sales of the Aeriolas mounted, and other manufacturers—Atwater Kent, Philco, Zenith, and Grisby-Grunow—followed Westinghouse into the marketplace. Only RCA evinced little interest in the manufacture of receivers. During negotiations leading to the formation of the radio-telegraph-telephone giant, Sarnoff resurrected his 1916 memorandum and presented it to his new board of directors. The board appropriated $2,000 for the development of a receiver, called the Radiola, possibly as a gesture of confidence in Sarnoff, but the board was reluctant to go further.

Thirty-one stations were granted licenses by the Department of Commerce in 1921; 576 in the next year, when between 500,000 and a million sets were in use. One tenth of these were assembled by the "hams," who spent $50 million for parts, and $60 million was spent for factory-assembled receivers. American broadcasting had become a strange composite of ownership in two years: 231 radio and electric-equipment makers; 70 newspapers and other publications; 65 educational institutions; 30 department stores; and assorted auto-supply dealers, churches, municipal institutions, banks, railroads, and a single laundry company, all of whom footed the bills for installation and operating expenses. Only the performing talent was free.

Most license holders viewed station ownership as an indirect source of monetary returns. Almost all programing was musical, most of it what was regarded as the "best of standard good music," provided without charge by record companies, music schools, professional and amateur musicians and soloists, and music publishers who had stumbled on another vehicle for offering their wares to the public.

Bandleader Vincent Lopez was the first to appear with an orchestra on radio, when he led a studio recital from station WJZ, Newark, New Jersey, in November 1921. In the days when the ether was free of the extraneous noise and interference that pollutes it today, broadcasts could be heard for hundreds of miles. Lopez and other musicians found that radio gave them free advertising and brought dancers who had heard them on the air to the hotels, cabarets, and night clubs where they played regularly. New fans were recruited and local record stores had to stock additional disks whenever the Coon-Sanders Nighthawks, Abe Lyman's Californians, the Ted Weems Orchestra, Ted Lewis, Ray Miller, Jean Goldkette, Isham Jones, or one of a hundred other regionally or nationally known bandleaders appeared on the air, generally from places whose owners had paid all costs for the installation of remote sending equipment in return for the free publicity.

Most license-holders did not conceive of the special use for commercial advertising that lay ahead for the medium they controlled. There was general opposition to A T & T's announcement in February 1922 that it intended to engage in "toll" broadcasting. Having won the sole right to use its long lines and transmitters for direct commercial purposes, by virtue of the agreement to take part in the operation of RCA, the A T & T management was ready to do exactly that. Sarnoff, whose vision of the future was unique, suggested later that year that a separate broadcasting company be formed, subsidized by the payment of two percent of the gross from receiver sales. In August, A T & T began to broadcast, using the free amateur talents of employees, over station WEAF, in New York. The first toll-paying "sponsor" was heard on August 28, 1922, after paying fifty dollars for a ten-minute "afternoon talk" to sell cooperative apartments being constructed in the borough of Queens. Only a few advertisers took advantage of the WEAF microphones at first, but by mid-1923 their number had grown sufficiently to bring the telephone giant and a few other Metropolitan-area broadcasters into a legal confrontation with a most unlikely foe—the music business.

As early as February 1922, details of the daily "music by wireless" concerts, which appeared in newspapers across the country, caused both the Music Publishers Protective Association and the American Society of Composers, Authors and Publishers to fear that the new invention's use of canned music would lessen the sale of phonograph recordings in a short time. Many leading musical-comedy people were broadcasting solos and ensembles from their hit shows without payment. Operatic and concert soloists were succumbing to the lure of free advertising in return for a few arias or simple instrumental pieces. Dealers were unable to keep up with the demand for radio parts sweeping the country; orders were backed up for half a year. The Woolworth stores' supply of ten-cent components, which produced a complete crystal set for $1.50, was exhausted soon after it was placed on a counter.

Already in a prolonged legal battle with motion-picture-theater owners, and hoping to fix a new yearly rate of $250 for unlicensed vaudeville theaters, ASCAP met with representatives of the leading radio interests to advise them of the federal laws regarding public performance of copyrighted music. Negotiations continued throughout the summer of 1922, after ASCAP had granted permission to use its catalogue on a day-to-day basis to stations owned by the large electric companies. The only stipulation was the announcement that the music was performed through the courtesy of the society and the copyright owners.

A conference in September at ASCAP's New York office, arranged by Claude Mills, brought together representatives of GE, A T & T, Westinghouse, RCA, the Department of Commerce, some publishers of standard music not affiliated with the society, and other interested parties. Mills began by reminding the group that ASCAP controlled 90 percent of all music, and that among its members were all the important popular and musical-theater writers and a majority of those who composed modern serious works. Responding to the argument that radio did a favor for the music business by popularizing its property, he argued that it did not. Ninety percent of that function was carried on by vaudeville artists, concert singers, song pluggers sent by the publishers to various functions and gatherings, and by operatic performances and musical comedies. Radio, records, piano rolls, even the boy in the street whistling a new tune were contributing factors only. He proposed a minimum fee of five dollars a day from radio stations, with final figures to be based on potential audiences. Those representing radio returned some time later to reject the suggestion on the ground that no station except WEAF intended to ask for money for the use of its facilities. The others were in an experimental stage, and the talent was not paid.

Mills, Nathan Burkan, and J. C. Rosenthal, ASCAP's general manager, were determined to guard the rights of composers, authors, and publishers and immediately instituted a legal action. They sought to confirm that a radio performance was a performance for profit and thus to establish ASCAP's right to collect fees. Shortly afterwards, applications for ASCAP licenses were sent out, accompanied by a letter that fixed the costs at from $250 to $5,000 yearly, the exact amount to be based on transmitting power, location, size of audience, and profits from the sale of radio apparatus.

In November, *Variety* floated the rumor that the MPPA planned to install its own broadcasting station, in New York's Times Square area. Transmission equipment intended for use on a battleship had been purchased from government surplus, for $4,000, and the association was prepared to set aside time each day for song plugging by publisher members. The fantastic array of musical artists working along the "Great White Way" would provide other programing. Sarnoff, meanwhile, continued with the installation of two 100-foot-high towers on a building just four blocks from the MPPA building. He was in the position to send out signals through RCA's new property, station WJZ, which was being moved from its New Jersey site.

Once on the air, Sarnoff had the world's most powerful radio station at his disposal and became a serious rival to A T & T, which was connecting a few stations in the northeast to build a small chain of toll broadcasters. The first regularly scheduled program sent out on that regional network was "Roxy and His Gang," which used talent from the Capitol Theatre staff.

Restricted by the government's ban on "direct" advertising and A T & T's exclusive rights to use its transmitters and long-distance lines for commercial purposes, many stations used direct action or subterfuges to get along without the telephone company's facilities. Sarnoff arranged for a Western Union cable to connect WJZ with Broadway theaters and leading New York hotels. Interviews, dance music, and coverage of banquets and social events went over this line from eleven in the morning until late evening.

The radio manufacturers considered any cost of operation to be a general public-relations and advertising expense aimed at potential customers and not connected with "direct" advertising. Their regular transmissions created an audience of over 20 million persons in 1923–24 and were responsible for the sale of two million receiving sets. Other commercial interests used broadcasting for a similar purpose. The makers of batteries powering most of the 500 different types of receivers introduced before 1926 hung onto the skirts of the electric giants. So, too, did motor oil and gasoline companies, white-goods makers and others, all taking advantage of the "indirect" advertising policy. Singing groups were sent on tours of independent stations, and covered thousands of miles and dozens of facilities in the course of a single season. Paid by "sponsors," the Ray-O-Vac Twins, the Eveready Music Makers, the Mono Motor Oil Twins, the Moxie Minute Men, May and Tag the Washing Machine Twins, and the Happiness Boys became national celebrities after months of radio appearances on key stations. They were matched in popularity by song-plugger–vocalists, assigned by music publishers, who were not identified with the broadcasts in order to assist local broadcasters in this experimental period. Among them were: Little Jack Little, the Whispering Pianist Art Gillham, Ford and Glenn, Billy Baskette, J. Russell Robinson, the Radio Franks, and Wendell Hall, the "Red Headed Music Maker," whose "It Ain't Gonna Rain No Mo'" sold millions of copies of sheet music and recordings as the result of unrelenting plugging on the air by its ukulele-playing composer. Operating expenses for the average station were less than $50,000 in 1924, due in great measure to the policy of putting only free talent on the air. However, a small number whose income was reported to be near the million mark were beginning to pay performers, generally at least ten dollars for an appearance.

Two court decisions affected the future of broadcasting: the ASCAP victory in an action against the operators of a Newark station, which sustained the society's claim that the least vestige of advertising on the air infringed the public-performance right; and the settlement in an action against Marcus Loew and his New York station WHN by A T & T, which opened the way for commercial broadcasting after the plaintiff agreed to permit the use of its long lines and transmitters for that purpose. Before New Year's Day 1925, several hundred stations were selling time for "indirect advertising," which provided only discreet identification of the sponsor with the program. ASCAP income from 199 radio licenses was $130,000, up from the previous year's $35,000 but far from the million predicted when the drive to collect from broadcasters began in the summer of 1922. It was proving to be a hard and bitter fight and divided the music business when publishers joined the tax-free (non-ASCAP) movement in order to get time on the air for their music. Another dimension was added when the MPPA initiated its own campaign to remove the two-cent compulsory license fee for mechanically reproduced music from the copyright law.

The secondary issue created an unexpected union of many of ASCAP's traditional music-user antagonists: the motion-picture industry and exhibitors, hotel and other entertainment people, and the record and piano-roll manufacturers who wanted to keep the status quo at the very least. In the course of proposed copyright revision, broadcasters had the opportunity to get special legislation favoring their cause introduced by congressmen and attached to copyright bills. In the end, compulsory licensing continued in force, and all radio-industry-sponsored bills failed of passage. In the course of the fighting, a new lobbying group was born—the National Association of Broadcasters.

Made up of highly independent entities, the radio business was divided in its approach to a solution of the music-licensing problem. Some station owners insisted on government action to curb ASCAP's "monopolistic practices." The Federal Trade Commission in 1922 had given the society a clean bill of health, as did a Justice Department conclusion four years later that grounds for action against ASCAP did not exist. Other broadcasters proposed a different course—the creation of a strong, industry-supported alternate source of music similar to the tax-free libraries currently serving many motion-picture exhibitors, hotels, theaters, and some Chicago radio stations. Meanwhile, during the period prior to ASCAP's revitalization in 1920, most leading Tin Pan Alley popular-music houses had supplied vaudeville with non-ASCAP music, effectively stunting the society's growth.

These two courses were joined in April 1923 by the activation of the National Association of Broadcasters in Chicago during a meeting of broadcasters representing Midwestern stations. Paul B. Klugh, founder of the Music Industries Chamber of Commerce and recently retired from the piano-roll industry, where he had been a leader in its fight against music publishers, was hired as executive secretary for the new group. One of his earliest suggestions was that broadcasters hire Claude Mills away from the MPPA and put him in charge of the organization's Tax-Free Music Bureau. Mills insisted that the NAB get industrywide support before he would accept the position. It was slow in coming, particularly from GE, A T & T, Westinghouse, and RCA, and so were lost the services of a man who became one of broadcasting's most commanding antagonists.

Members of Chicago's Associated Independent (non-ASCAP) Music Publishers provided broadcasters with many of their popular songs during the next twelve months. Among the fifty or more important houses allied with the NAB's Tax-Free Music Bureau, whose catalogues of thousands of titles circulated among broadcaster members, were the Chicago firms owned by Will Rossiter, first of the city's Tin Pan Alley-like music men, F. B. Haviland, Milton Weil, Denton & Haskins, and Carrie Jacobs Bond. Many of them had joined the broadcasters in the hope of having their songs used in moving pictures, following the admission of the Motion Picture Theatre Owners of America as a Class B member of the NAB. Equally important, though only for a time, during this early period, was a decision by the MPA to allow the use, without charge, of their standard and concert music for broadcasting. Carl Fischer, G. Schirmer, the Ditson and Church companies, and several other music houses were involved in this. America's most important serious music was added to the ASCAP repertory only after its directors and the executive committee gave these music houses four places on the society's board, two for publishers and two for composers, as well as free licenses to Carnegie and Aeolian halls, the Metropolitan Opera House, and other major concert-music auditoriums.

The defection of Henry Waterson, and his important Waterson, Berlin & Snyder catalogue, from ASCAP and an antitrust suit filed by that veteran firm in April 1924, asking for restraint of the society's interference with radio performances of his music, provided broadcasters with telling new arguments during Congressional hearings. A man whose vision of the music business went far beyond song plugging, Waterson had been one of the first music publishers to enter the record business with any success. Between 1911 and 1919, 1,300 titles were issued on his ten-cent 5½-inch Little Wonder records. Even after Irving Berlin left the company to form his own soon after the war, Waterson remained one of the most important men in the business and openly opposed ASCAP's plan to increase income by licensing radio use. He announced that he would harness radio scientifically as a exploitation medium and grant temporary permission to use specific songs without charge while his song pluggers were boosting them. He filed his lawsuit only after ASCAP refused to release him from a membership agreement. Forming two subsidiary non-ASCAP houses, he offered seventy copyrighted pieces to all broadcasters. Whereas other publishers worked on a handful of songs at a time, he sent out five teams of song pluggers, all of whom were recording artists for his Cameo Records Company, to work on those seventy tunes. From June 1923 to the summer of 1925, the Radio Franks, Little Jack Little, and other Waterson employees visited stations in thirty carefully selected cities. Their work provided him with record and sheet-music sales of individual songs that did not reach hit proportions but in the aggregate matched them and at considerably less expense than an all-out campaign would have cost. The most farseeing of Tin Pan Alley publishers, Leo Feist, who remained a loyal ASCAP member, used Waterson's strategy in 1924, sending out song-plugging teams with all-new material to key stations known to have started radio hits. He had a similar rate of success.

When his contract with ASCAP ended in 1926, Waterson had already lost interest in the music business and was concentrating on the record business and radio-receiver manufacture. Some years before he returned to the ASCAP fold, in 1928, the antitrust suit died, though it continued to be mentioned in anti-ASCAP testimony at Washington hearings.

At the leading NAB spokesman during those hearings, Paul Klugh found a worthy adversary in the new ASCAP president, Gene Buck. Trained at the Detroit Art Academy, Buck had been staff illustrator for the Jerome Remick Company, where he created 5,000 colored pictorial music covers before losing part of his sight. In New York in 1907, he had found employment painting the moonlight, apple trees, and canoes that figured on most sheet music of the time. His first hit song, "Daddy Has a Sweetheart and Mother Is Her Name," was written when he was twenty-five. Its success attracted Florenz Ziegfeld, who signed him to write lyrics for most of the twenty succeeding editions of the *Follies,* as well as for the *Midnight Frolics,* which Buck originated.

The heavy use of music on broadcasts over A T & T's WEAF and a network of a dozen northeastern stations at ten dollars a minute threw a new light on broadcasters' pleas for free music. The Eveready Hour, A & P Gypsies, Cliquot Club Eskimos, Ipana Troubadors, Silvertown Cord Orchestra and its Silver Masked tenor, and the other musical programs used professional musicians who had grown up with the popular-music business and were friendly with the song pluggers. RCA's introduction of a new and much-improved "superheterodyne" receiver in 1924 created a new, affluent audience which demanded more professional entertainment on a regular basis from the medium that was approaching $800 million in gross income from all sources. Victor's new series of programs to sell records of high-class popular and standard music was already showing the importance of radio performances in pushing music sales.

The Washington hearings that began in February 1925 for a new copyright law, prepared by the registrar of copyrights, Thorwald Solberg, in association with all owners of intellectual property, immediately polarized most music users. Its main features extended copyright protection for the lifetime of an author plus fifty years, retained public-performance licensing (removing only the "for profit" language), and abandoned the two-cent royalty limit on phonograph records and piano rolls. For the first time,

A T & T and RCA cooperated with the NAB to fight the proposed changes. Nathan Burkan and Claude Mills repeated the statesmanlike presentations they had twice made already on ASCAP's behalf in Washington. Buck introduced not only leading dramatists, novelists, and other authors, but also a group of songwriters whose income had been reduced 40 percent by what he said was broadcasters' use of their works. In six weeks it became evident that radio would have to pay for music, and any copyright revision was dead for a time.

Many radio men began to concede that those who owned a commodity that occupied between 60 and 70 percent of all air time should be compensated. That judgment gained greater advocacy after the Supreme Court upheld several new decisions in ASCAP's favor. Having concluded at last that the public would pay for its programs by means of commercial advertising, Secretary of Commerce Herbert Hoover brought both groups together at the annual National Radio Conference in November 1925. Claude Mills introduced a new phrase—"blanket licensing"—which gave total access to the ASCAP repertories but allowed the society to restrict specified selections on written notice. In passing, he also mentioned a "per-piece" concept for the first time, a specter that in time rose to haunt the music business. The NAB turned to Congress to fix a "just" rate, but after a bill to that purpose was saddled with exemptions for film exhibitors, hotels, dance academies, and others, it was permanently stalled. It was clearly evident that the adversaries would have to negotiate an understanding on their own.

With some exceptions, radio was still in the experimental stage it had been in when ASCAP abandoned free licenses and let loose regional representatives, who retained one third of collections made within fifty miles of their offices and half from those beyond. Regarding transmissions as either a public service or a means to build good will for the principal source of their income, the majority of stations continued to refuse to pay for music and performing talent. In all, about 200 stations over which sponsored broadcasts were being aired had signed contracts with ASCAP that had no standard by which to determine fees other than the dollar-a-watt basis. Among them was RCA, which had a special license calling for payment of twenty-dollars an hour; the more advantageous five-year contract on which Sarnoff had insisted was denied. Thus a single five-times-a-week program now cost in excess of the society's top fee of $5,000, paid by A T & T's WEAF. Many advertisers were now paying A T & T $2,600 for an hour on its basic thirteen-station network, producing a total of $750,000 from time sales in 1925.

Still the victim of A T & T's monopoly, RCA maintained an indirect advertising policy for the seven stations that made up a network connected by Western Union telegraph lines. Because A T & T or sponsors paid musicians and artists, Sarnoff found himself obliged to do the same, and his board of directors seriously considered other methods to finance operations. Sarnoff had recently completed construction of the first experimental 50,000-watt transmitter, in spite of warnings that it would interfere with reception throughout the northeast. Proving to be a good neighbor in the sky, this forerunner of things to come played an important role in the RCA board's conclusions.

The drawn-out, complex, and secret struggle between the broadcast and the telephone components of the industry was formally resolved in the summer of 1926 by means of a plan suggested by RCA's board. A T & T removed itself from broadcasting to concentrate on its principal business—communications. Its station licenses were abandoned, and the flagship WEAF operation was sold to RCA for one million dollars. A ten-year contract was executed giving access to A T & T's long lines, for a minimum million-dollar annual fee, to the new National Broadcasting Company, in which RCA held a half-interest, GE 30 percent, and Westinghouse the balance. In the midst of these negotiations, Mills announced on behalf of ASCAP that because broadcasters were now "willing within their limitations to pay fair and reasonable amounts for the right to use music," peace with the radio trust was a reality. For the first time, the society's income approached that mythical million-dollar mark, half from motion-picture exhibitors and more than a quarter from 322 commercial broadcast licensees.

The abandonment of the "superstation" concept of broadcasting, embodied in WEAF and WJZ, with their ancilary networks, in favor of national network radio was introduced by a gala program of varied dance music by Vincent Lopez, George Olsen, B. A. Rolfe, and Ben Bernie on the night of November 15, 1926. An estimated 12 million people tuned in to a network of stations extending as far west as Kansas City. The National Broadcasting Company had spent $50,000 on the program, half of it for talent, but, as it pointed out several days later, advertising would thenceforth pay for the elaborate programs to come. Thus, NBC was engaged in the direct-advertising business.

The path to that decision had been smoothed by the successful outcome of a suit challenging the secretary of Commerce's right to assign wavelengths and power, and to regulate the industry. As broadcasting waited in the resultant uncertainty for a new official regulatory and licensing agency, without government approval NBC put together two networks of predominantly clear-channel 50,000-watt stations. From New York, WEAF fed the fifteen-station Red Network, which offered sponsored programs of conservative music and entertainment; WJZ fed the ten-station Blue Network, on which, amid educational talks and cultural presentations, future stars served an on-the-air apprenticeship while waiting for a call to the more prestigious and prosperous sister operation. From the Blue emerged many of what *Variety* tagged "the new school of entertainment, running more to the popular tune." Stations on both networks were paid fifty dollars for each hour of sponsored time carried and charged forty-five dollars for "sustaining," or unsponsored, programs supplied by the networks.

The few dozen faithful who gathered at the NAB's fourth annual convention in September 1926 participated in heated discussions about looming federal regulation and the changes inherent in RCA's proposed paid-advertising network scheme. The ASCAP situation had evidently been placed on a back burner, for only a few present agreed to support a new radio-program service whose offerings would rely on tax-free musical content and be made available to the industry. Arthur Judson, the manager of the Philadelphia Orchestra and owner of a small concert-artist booking agency, was employed as director of the proposed Judson Radio Program Corporation. A few days after the Blue and Red networks were launched, Judson and his backers met with Sarnoff to offer the bureau's services in signing talent and in building programs. The discussion grew heated. Sarnoff rejected the offer, because NBC had opened its own artists' bureau; Judson, with no experience in broadcasting, promised to build a rival network of his own.

The United Independent Broadcasters network was formed soon after, with the third-ranking New York area station, WOR, as flagship. Representatives scoured the nation seeking stations that would take ten hours of program time weekly for $500. A dozen accepted this seeming bargain and awaited the brilliant programing promised by Judson. Several likely sponsors—the Victor Company, Paramount Pictures, and the Atwater-Kent Company, which was already spending a million dollars a year to advertise its radio receivers—were approached, with little success. Only Louis Sterling, alarmed by rumors of an impending NBC-Victor merger, agreed to become involved. With talent assembled by Judson, the network went on the air on September 19, 1927, and lost $100,000 the first month. Sterling pulled out, despite the unpaid advertising being offered by the network. After a series of temporary injections of venture capital, the network was taken over and became the Columbia Broadcasting System. With an eye to a future in which television might be important, Paramount Pictures immediately turned over a block of its own stock for a forty-nine percent interest in CBS.

The Radio Act of 1927 made only a few changes in the 1912 legislation written to regulate wireless communication between merchant ships and land. All existing licensing and regulation of individual wireless and broadcasting systems that followed had been based on its provisions. The new legislation mentioned neither network broadcasting nor paid radio advertising, nor did it create a new regulatory commission. Only a series of short-term extensions by Congress maintained the life of an agency regarded as being composed of "jellyfish" afraid of the big broadcasters. Under these circumstances, there was little action except for a temporary halt to the proliferation of stations. The number of licensed facilities was then 732, only ten of which made any profit in 1927. During that year, NBC spent six million dollars on programming and collected nearly four million from advertisers for program time and talent. With no expense except that for a radio set and having available the best free entertainment it had ever been offered, the American public flooded Washington with protests every time any change in the broadcasting structure was proposed. Usually this was done at the urging of local stations. Nourished by regulatory inaction on the part of an underfunded and understaffed commission, commercial broadcasting thrived.

RCA shrugged off a four-year-long investigation into its monopolistic control of patents by licensing a few dozen competing radio and equipment makers. It received seven and a half percent of their gross sales, in return for their access to the patents. From this arrangement came a quarter of the corporation's 1927 income. At that time there was a 24 percent saturation of receivers in American homes, which grew as 3.281 million sets, worth $650 million, were sold the next year, and 4.428 million in 1929. Network-created programming continued to be of a solidly conservative nature, with heavy emphasis on "good" music, half of it what is today's war horse, semiclassical, and classical, which occupied nearly seventy percent of program time. Blunt, direct advertising was confined to the predinner hours. Restrained "good-will" announcements were offered after 7:00 P.M., the time for recreation; they were read by announcers garbed in mandatory formal evening clothes. Many were testimonials from highly regarded Americans proclaiming the virtues of a sponsor's product.

At the end of 1928, regular coast-to-coast broadcasting was a reality, with the hookup of sixty-nine NBC affiliates. It could be heard on over 80 percent of the 11 million receivers in 9.6 million American homes. Previews, presidential speeches, and championship prize fights had been offered, and in September the Lucky Strike cigarette company sponsored the first experimental national program series, featuring its new headline attraction, B. A. Rolfe and his thirty-five-piece orchestra, which had four arrangers, each paid $3,750 a week. In getting away from the usual nighttime dramatic series or classical and semiclassical music, Lucky Strike was also experimenting with audience response. Rolfe was instructed to play only dance music, in contemporary jazz or waltz tempo; no concert interludes were wanted. The company remained a major sponsor for many years with programs of up-tempo popular music that culminated in the famous "Your Hit Parade." Most of the sixty four other NBC sponsors continued to offer concerts of standard music that urban audiences were believed to prefer, with the advertiser's name mentioned at the start, the middle, and the end of each broadcast. Jazz and dance music was principally relegated to the after-11:00 P.M. remote broadcasts from hotels, dance halls, and night clubs.

With the $10 million paid to it by commercial sponsors in 1928 promising to increase by at least half in the next year, NBC expanded its radio and electric patents-connected interests. Sarnoff had already engineered deals through Joseph Kennedy for control of the Keith-Albee vaudeville holdings, which led to the creation of RKO and the introduction of RCA Photophone into talking motion-picture studios and theaters. Now the RCA board approved his plan to consolidate the manufacture of all radio sets and equipment into a single corporate entity. Sarnoff was elected president of the unified RCA Victor Company, and for 6.5 million shares of new RCA common stock, GE and Westinghouse turned over all manufacturing rights for radio equipment, phonographs, sound-picture technology, and many white goods.

Wall Street suffered its most severe stock-market crash just as the final contracts were being approved. Many companies failed, and others appeared ready to go under, but RCA, undisputed leader of what was now the nation's fourth-largest business, remained in a position to carry out Sarnoff's plan to maintain domination over every phase of the entertainment business. When RCA went into the music business in the winter of 1929, its stock was beginning to edge up, after its plunge of twenty points in October. For more than a year, private offers had been made by RCA for ten important music houses, at a rumored $20 million, but Warner won out, with its $8.5 million offer for the Max Dreyfus music holdings.

At year-end, when many companies were retrenching and investment money was drying up, E. Claude Mills, who had recently resigned from the MPPA and ASCAP, announced that his new employer, the Radio Corporation of America, was forming an additional subsidiary, Radio Music Company. Capitalized at $6.6 million, it had already purchased Leo Feist and also Carl Fischer, the standard music house. Each was guaranteed its average annual profit of the past five years. In addition, Feist received between three and four million dollars' worth of Radio Music stock, Fischer half that sum. Mills sought to allay fears that RCA's entry into the music business was a move to reduce ASCAP's monopoly in order to get a more attractive licensing arrangement. As president of Radio Music, he hoped only "to restore sanity and harmony to contemporary musical composition and to strike a death blow at the tedious and inane ro-de-o-do school of music." He promised there would be no boycotting by NBC of music published by competing firms.

Unconvinced, ASCAP pointed out that its contracts with the songwriters published by Feist and Fischer had been extended to run through 1935, that this music would continue to be licensed by the society until then. NBC was pressed to renegotiate its yearly blanket licenses, and in February 1930 the five stations from which network programs originated agreed to pay more. The two New York stations, each already paying $25,000, accepted a 50 percent increase, and most of the other seventy-two NBC affiliates doubled their payments of between $3,500 and $10,000. Fees for non-ASCAP music were negotiated with the publisher, and then charged to the sponsor. In addition to his functions at Radio Music, Mills became involved in bargaining for NBC's music licenses and played a role in increasing ASCAP's income from broadcasters to $800,000, out of a total of two million, which remained the high-water mark for the next five years.

The listening audience continued to grow in 1930, but only one out of every seven stations made money, and profits of the three networks fell below expectations for the year. Dialect comedy of the sort featured on the variety stage for many years, popular singers, and syncopating bands edged out the bland musical programs that had predominated since NBC's formation. Attracted by these changes, 51 million persons tuned in nightly from 12 million homes. The vast majority listened to NBC's coast-to-coast broadcasts of "Amos 'n' Andy" five times a week, to hear a minstrel-show comedy in comic-strip stories; the first of the great crooners, Rudy Vallee, singing and leading his Connecticut Yankees Orchestra for Fleishman's Yeast on Thursday nights; and "The Rise of the Goldbergs," a five-night-a-week sentimental saga of upwardly mobile Jewish-Americans whose Yiddishisms and malaprop dialogue enchanted what was essentially a white, Protestant audience. Dance bands were in great demand by sponsors; Guy Lombardo broadcast one night a week for a cigar company, and Paul Whiteman for a paint manufacturer.

Advertising agencies played a leading role in this change of program content. Commercial time was completely sold for both NBC networks and the CBS operation, which now was a chain of about sixty stations from coast to coast. An hour of peak broadcasting time, between 7:00 and 11:00 P.M., cost approximately $10,000, out of which the network rebated a 15 percent commission to the agency for negotiating the sale of time. The hard-sell commercial became more prevalent, and soon CBS became the first to permit mention of the price of a product. The networks began to look to advertisers and their agencies to provide and pay for all entertainment. For this, the agencies collected an additional 15 percent commission, so that a sponsor spending $7,000 on talent really paid the network $5,950 for it, the balance going to his agency.

When they could not afford network time rates or wished to tap the Pacific Coast audience during its after-dinner hours (network programs from the East Coast began at four o'clock in the afternoon in California), national and regional advertisers used the "electrical transcription." This medium for canned voice and music had emerged from the sixteen-inch recordings and large 33⅓-speed turntable developed in connection with ERPI's sound-on-disk talking-picture process, which was refined for radio use by engineers at station KNX in Los Angeles, working with Paramount Pictures. Freeman Gosden and Charles Correll, white harmony singers who became black-dialect comedians, first demonstrated the marketability of electrically transcribed programs with their "Sam 'n' Henry" series. After two years on the air in Chicago, the pair began to syndicate recorded five-minute segments of their on-the-air comic strip to Midwestern stations. Their success was such that NBC signed them for $100,000 a year. Their new "Amos 'n' Andy'' series went on the air over the junior Blue Network late at night in the summer of 1929 for Pepsodent toothpaste. In the fall, they were moved, to open the nightly peak advertising period at 7:00 P.M. over the top-ranked Red Network, and became the highest-paid entertainers in the world.

Variety was slightly short of the mark in December 1930 when it predicted that $11 million would be spent during the next year on electrically transcribed commercial programs. Chevrolet, Chrysler, the National Refining Company, Majestic and Grigsby-Grunow Radio, and other advertisers improvised temporary networks by shipping recorded programs, complete with commercial announcements, around the country to stations with more than 1,000 watts of power for simultaneous broadcast at specified intervals. The same year, transcriptions were accepted by all three networks for "spot" advertising; they were played during the regular hour and half-hour breaks that were originally intended only for station identification.

These added sources of revenue notwithstanding, during 1930 commercial radio spent $250,000 more on operating expenses than was taken in from advertising. Millions were spent on nonpaying public service, religious, and political broadcasts, as well as for land-wire leases. RCA was A T & T's best customer, paying three million dollars to connect its two chains of affiliated stations. In the antitrust action, charging industrywide restraint of trade, filed in May 1930, both user and supplier and other subsidiaries were named as co-defendants. The government sought a total reorganization of the manufacture of radio sets and equipment. RCA, whose 20 percent share of all receiver sales provided its real profits, was deemed to control the business through exclusive ownership of significant patents. The Justice Department asked that GE and Westinghouse dispose of their holdings in RCA. This and restoration of free access to patents would create vigorous competition with the industry giant, whose profits in 1930 were more than $5.5 million.

In December 1931, A T & T made its peace with Washington, agreeing to cancel all cross-licensing arrangements with RCA. The final disposition of other charges awaited the conclusion of negotiations looking toward a consent decree and settlement.

Of more concern to broadcasting's smaller fry was ASCAP's announced intention to raise license fees, which represented less than two percent of their 1930 gross receipts. Profits were, in the main, nonexistent.

CHAPTER 9

A Glut of Movie Music

The Roaring Twenties was a decade during which relations between publishers and songwriters, never completely amicable in the past except when surefire-hit writers or production-music composers were involved, deteriorated into an angry fight over business relationships and share of profits. The million-copy sellers of Tin Pan Alley's golden days—Ernest Ball, Teddy Morse, Harry Von Tilzer, Charles K. Harris, and their peers—were dead, dying, or in the final days of occasional creativity. Those who struggled to keep abreast of a world in which social and cultural values seemed to change daily took to the vaudeville circuits, to play their sentimental old-time hits or accompany headliners, for whom they dashed off special material. The music business continued to foster the notion that "popular songwriting is the most highly overpaid form of writing in the world," as *Variety*'s music editor, Abel Green, wrote and seconded. When a song could not be bought outright, publishers offered contracts with a maximum "2 and 33" royalty. These gave the songwriters as much as a two-cent royalty on sheet-music sales and up to one third of phonograph record royalties, terms that were generally regarded by the industry as overmagnanimous. Only Feist and Max Dreyfus were more generous, and were considered radical for this abuse of custom. Between three and five collaborators shared in royalties, some acknowledged on the sheet-music cover, others getting a percentage for "cooperative contributions." These ranged from a gratuity in return for boosting the song on stage or radio to making a merely good song "truly commercial." Toward the end of the decade, a hit song earned from $5,000 to $10,000 in royalties, but paying performers and bandleaders in order to obtain public performance reduced the writer's share to only a fraction.

In this era of prosperity, the secular-music business was the most obvious element in the general revolt against the cultured tradition that had dominated the nation for a century. Except on network radio in its formative years, the "high-class" influence of past years, ranging from Foster to Sousa, was gone, giving way to syncopated jazz music written for fast dancing and popular songs. Changing technology—the improved talking machine, wireless radio, the talking picture—moved audiences from around the parlor piano to comfortable seats within earshot of the Victrola, the radio, and the movie-theater loudspeaker.

The decade heard a constant stream of complaint from popular-music publishers that the major users of their music were responsible for their declining profits. Yet record and piano-roll royalties averaged about $2 million a year; sales of printed music remained around $15 million annually; and income from licensing the public performance of music through ASCAP rose from about $250,000 in 1921 to nearly $2 million in the year 1930.

The run-of-the-mill staff songwriters (usually also required to plug their company's current candidates for success) were the ones who had just cause for discontent. Only a Gus Kahn, Irving Berlin, or Walter Donaldson could count on as much as $150,000 in royalties in a good year. They were far from the norm. Kahn's string of postwar hits put him in the position to work with only the most successful composers, at higher royalties, and to reject cutting in others on his copyrights. Berlin, who wrote both words and music, became his own publisher. Donaldson provided the successful Berlin firm with million-copy hits whenever its talented owner did not.

The compromise in 1920 that ended the production-music writers' control of ASCAP was arranged in order to bring tax-free music houses back as licensees and thus strengthen the society as a collection agency. As a further token of good will, the writers planned to assign all performing rights to ASCAP for ninety-nine years. This altruism the publishers did not share. They voted instead to keep assignments on a five-year, renewable basis. When the Music Publishers Protective Association moved its headquarters next to ASCAP and used the same telephone switchboard, most songwriters regarded its Claude Mills as a watchdog on behalf of the few important music publishers. Both prosecutor and judge in matters dealing with payment of cash inducements to vaudeville performers, Mills remained true to his major supporters when a group of small publishers presented evidence that the large firms were spending between $1,000 and $2,000 in this practice and he took no action.

Recognizing the need for solidarity, Irving Berlin and other important songwriters reactivated the Lyric Writers and Composers Protective League in early 1921. Its principal demand was a new contract raising the songwriters' royalty by 50 percent, to three cents a copy. This was considered exorbitant by the publishers. A standard contract more favorable to songwriters had also been the aim of an earlier organization, in 1907, the Words and Music Club, to which only "recognized writers" were admitted. When the music firms refused to budge on any issue, the group had degenerated into a social group. In 1921, the publishers agreed to several minor changes, but they refused to accept the royalty increase because the chain stores were asking for twenty-five-cent sheet music, to replace the new publications that cost thirty, thirty-five, and forty cents. At a league meeting in May 1921, songwriters questioned the publisher's role in the modern music business. Attention was drawn to the $150,000 in profits recently realized by Frederick Knight Logan, the arranger-composer and also publisher of "The Missouri Waltz." Arguing that artists should not associate themselves with organized labor, Victor Herbert frustrated a proposed strike against the music business, in which the American Federation of Musicians was also to take part. He and other production-music writers were rewarded for their stand by a three-cent sheet-music royalty. The other writers got nothing new. Eventually, the league, too, became a fraternal group, the Songwriters, which held a series of Sunday-evening benefits to create a building and burial fund.

The music publishers were wary of taking the lead in enforcing the right of public performance for profit when it threatened their sources of exploitation. They argued that vaudeville, still a leading arena for popularizing new songs, was covered by the dramatic rights they themselves controlled and was not responsible to ASCAP. Nearly two years passed before the thirty-eight MPPA houses agreed to print the warning "All Rights Reserved Including Public Performance for Profit" on all printed music. Several firms by-passed that responsibility by forming new companies not affiliated with ASCAP. Shapiro, Bernstein, for instance, founded Skidmore Music, which published the 1923 national hit "Yes, We Have No bananas." Saul Bornstein, business manager for Irving Berlin, formed an auxiliary firm to publish race and jazz songs.

Operating costs were half of ASCAP's expenses in the early years. Legal fees rose as court actions increased, the home office staff grew, and regional representatives who collected locally often cost more than they brought in. As income rose, however, pressure mounted to have ASCAP classify authors and composers and allot performance royalties on that basis. In fixing the status of a writer, the "number, nature and character" of his catalogue, the "popularity and vogue" for his work, and the length of his association with ASCAP should be taken into account. Classification was handled by volunteers after 1920, as before, but the reorganization had been possible only after the new publisher members insisted that provision be made for two thirds of their directors to determine the share to be paid to the music companies. The cabals and cliques that followed created a self-perpetuating board. In the next three years, the largest quarterly payment to a writer member was $291 and that to a publisher $1,390, a normal disparity resulting from the larger author and composer membership. The writer classification committees had great difficulty in assigning members to the A, B, and C categories. Victor Herbert suggested putting all the money into a single pot and dividing it equally. Others expressed concern about recognition of the contributions old-timers had made in ASCAP's formative years. The youngest pointed to their hits.

A serious examination of ASCAP's business practices followed a meeting of all sales and field representatives in May 1923. It persuaded a majority of the board that income was not increasing as it should be and that strong central management was needed to oversee all operations. A three-man advisory committee was named: Nathan Burkan's protégé J. C. Rosenthal, who remained as general manager in charge of legal affairs and daily operations; founding member Silvio Hein, a writer, who was named traveling secretary; and E. Claude Mills, the publishers' nominee. Rosenthal received $13,000 a year, and the others, $10,000 each. This raised Mills's guaranteed annual income to $30,000, in addition to the 10 percent he received from all new income he brought into the MPPA treasury.

Late in 1923, Gene Buck was elected president of ASCAP, without pay, to replace the society's first head, the British-born George Maxwell, who had never become a naturalized citizen and consequently, it was said, was never eligible to govern such an American organization as ASCAP. At the end of his first year, Buck announced the largest quarterly distribution in ASCAP's history so far: $80,000, from an annual income of $600,000, a 25 percent increase over the previous year. The deal he had just worked out with the MPPA to remove the music its members published from the tax-free category it had announced in 1923 brought in fifty-three "name" standard-music composers. Among them were Carrie Jacobs Bond, Charles Wakefield Cadman, Bainbridge Crist, Lily Strickland, Clara Edwards, Mischa Elman, Edwin Franko Goldman, Percy Grainger, Fritz Kreisler, Albert Spaulding, Serge Rachmaninoff, Oley Speaks (who was promptly named one of the two "classical composer" directors Buck had promised the publishers), Caro Roma, and the estate of Ethelbert Nevin. They had in common either that some of their compositions had entered the repertory favored by the superstations or that they performed regularly on radio. Their publishers immediately were elected to the Class A group and paid in four figures.

In the following five years, Burkan, Buck, and Mills represented ASCAP in the tangled morass of litigation and Washington lobbying that threatened the organization's existence. Having grown comfortable in his role as official spokesman for the music publishers, Mills assigned himself a similar chore for the society. From his desk in the combined MPPA-ASCAP operation, during appearances in the courtroom and at Washington hearings or speaking with newspapermen, the one-legged Westerner continually provided good copy for reporters. Though it was never built, the five-million-dollar ASCAP skyscraper that Mills casually proposed received wide coverage. So, too, did his account of personally weeding out blue material from manuscripts submitted by MPPA members for clearance. Speaking as a voice of reason, which won him the esteem of opponents as well as offers of high office, Mills's arguments created a favorable public image for publishers and songwriters and made him the supreme expert on the music business in the trade press and the august *New York Times.*

Mechanical royalties, printed-music sales, and steadily rising ASCAP income were ignored; instead, at every opportunity Mills and the music men he represented hammered on radio's excessive use of popular songs and the resulting general decline in royalties. The disappointing sheet-music sales of "I Love You" from *Little Jessie James,* Victor Herbert's "A Kiss in the Dark," and the Gus Kahn–Isham Jones "The One I Love Belongs to Somebody Else" were ascribed to radio's overuse. The success of "It Ain't Gonna Rain No Mo," published by a tax-free house and plugged incessantly on radio, was considered an example of a quirk in American minds that made them thrive on overfamiliarity. The overnight success of Irving Berlin's "All Alone" after John McCormack sang it on an eight-station hookup failed to change the prevailing judgment that radio killed music. Even so, the most aggressive houses rededicated their efforts to securing on-the-air play.

In its 1924 year-end summary of the music business, *Variety* suggested that the day of the million-copy seller was gone, that true success was now measured by a sale of 500,000 to 800,000. With retail prices of twenty-five and thirty cents for popular songs, financial returns were greater even if overhead had grown. Modern promotion techniques permitted a song to be made into a hit, but only with a tremendous outlay of money and great care taken in its selection.

The business revealed its flexibility by grabbing hold of the ukulele craze that followed the success of "It Ain't Gonna Rain No Mo." Americans were first exposed to that simple-to-master, four-string Portuguese-Hawaiian hybrid in vaudeville. Native islanders had appeared with an authentic Hawaiian steel guitar and fretted its strings with a bone, bottle neck, or knife to produce a jazzy and tremuluous sound. Every record company signed steel-guitar virtuosos—Fred Ferara, Sol Hoopii, the Hanapi Trio, the Bird of Paradise Trio, among others. For the thousands of amateur "uke strummers," who doted on Tin Pan Alley's version of true "down home" island music, publishers included ukulele arrangements on all sheet music and issued folios containing twelve to twenty songs arranged for the instrument.

Radio, meanwhile, clearly was changing the profile of the average sheet-music buyer. Gone was the ragtime performer who had purchased great quantities of Tin Pan Alley's product just prior to the jazz age. The young women who tried out new songs by playing on the piano the few bars printed on the back of all sheet music and then ordered them from New York no longer were the social center of attention. They were replaced by the bobbed-hair, short-skirted, gum-chewing flappers who dialed around the radio frequencies looking for a new song to learn. Wailing saxophones and male vocalists made the singing orchestras a national rage.

Through their radio appearances and phonograph records, Ben Bernie, Isham Jones, Fred Waring, the Coon-Sanders, and Paul Whiteman were among the earliest favorites. Leo Feist signed the most popular bandleaders, including Whiteman, as "musical advisors," and they rarely went wrong with a new Feist song. As soon as Whiteman had his first smash hit, on the Victor label, the publisher promised him $10,000 a year to "tinker with" manuscripts before he recorded them. Feist songs and Whiteman were synonymous on *Variety*'s chart of record hits: "I Never Knew," "Wang Wang Blues," "My Man," "Sweet Lady," "Stumbling," "Three O'Clock in the Morning," "My Wonderful One," "Linger Awhile," "I Miss My Swiss." Whiteman became Victor's most popular bandleader. Eleven official Whiteman bands in New York, seventeen on the road, and forty more around the country played only arrangements Whiteman recorded or had in his working library.

If bandleaders were the key to making hit songs, it was Tin Pan Alley's true golden boys, the writers of production songs, who enriched the coffers of the most prosperous firms, in particular those belonging to the Dreyfus brothers, Max and Louis. The various companies they owned or backed formed the most valuable music-business property in the late 1920s. Max Dreyfus believed that, although nobody could tell if a song might become a hit, "it *would* become one if you worked to sell it." With that precept as a guide, the Dreyfuses made a major power of Harms and its several subsidiaries. Born near Baden, Germany, in 1874, Max arrived in America at fourteen to seek riches as a pianist and composer. Louis, younger by three years, followed him in the early 1890s. By then Max was taking down and making viable songs out of melodies sung or hummed or whistled by musical illiterates, among them Paul Dresser, whose innate gift depended on men like Dreyfus. Max, chief plugger at Howley, Haviland & Dresser, was resigned to demonstrating music after his most commercial piano piece, "Cupid's Garden," proved to be only a minor success. Realizing that he would never be a great composer, he decided to be a rich publisher and to concentrate on America's vernacular art music, written for the musical theater.

He worked for the Witmarks and then joined Tom Harms, owner of the T. B. Harms Company, who had snatched away from William Pond the monopoly of New York theater-music copyrights, which the former publisher of Stephen Foster had been amassing since the Civil War. When Harms died in 1906, Dreyfus, with backing from relatives and some London music houses, had already acquired a large interest in the business. New money came from Jerome Kern, not yet twenty, who had first worked for Stern and Marks demonstrating songs for twelve dollars a week.

Because of Harms's hold on Broadway musical comedy, Dreyfus had little difficulty in arranging the interpolation of Kern songs into hit productions in New York and London, to which the young writer was sent for seasoning. Sometime near the end of 1904, after Kern had returned, T. B. Harms moved into new quarters on West 45th Street. Kern became a major owner, in association with the Dreyfus brothers, and the firm devoted itself principally to publication of music by Kern. A parallel company, Harms, Inc., owned entirely by the Dreyfus family, was formed. In the early 1920s, it purchased British Chappell's American outlet and formed Chappell-Harms, as a repository for nonproduction music.

Max and Louis Dreyfus were among the founders of ASCAP and had remained loyal during the difficult period prior to 1920 when the popular-music houses were providing tax-free music to the world. They did not join the MPPA, asserting that because the warning "This Number Is Fully Protected by Copyright and Restricted to the Above-Mentioned Production," which appeared in their advertising and on their printed music, was respected by the vaudeville business, they were not involved in the evil practices that the MPPA had been formed to curb.

Kern's wartime successes, the Princess Theatre shows *Very Good Eddie, Leave It to Jane, Oh, Boy,* and *Oh, Lady, Lady,* and Ziegfeld's 1920 production of *Sally* made the composer the best paid of the day and his publishers the people theatrical producers turned to for the best song-writing talent. Kern's success (his income from stage-performance royalties, in which Dreyfus shared, was regularly over $3,000 a week at the time) signaled the advent of a new kind of theater music and inspired young composers who in turn attracted his publisher's attention. Max Dreyfus's usually unerring instinct for discerning genuine talent became the keystone of his giant music empire. Early, he believed that a young Czech pianist and composer had the makings of a second Victor Herbert and was instrumental in getting him a Broadway show, the score for which went to another house. Ten years later, Rudolf Friml came under the Dreyfus banner, with *Rose Marie, The Vagabond King,* and *The Three Musketeers.* Impressed with George Gershwin's spirit, Dreyfus paid the nineteen-year-old rehearsal pianist to do nothing but sit at a piano and write music. Vincent Youmans was a young Wall Street broker who had written a single song when Dreyfus took him on as staff writer and song demonstrator and began to teach him how to write for the stage. Eventually, every important Broadway-musical writer was published by Harms. Max Dreyfus did not like "Manhattan" when Richard Rodgers and Lorenz Hart played it for him as college students. Then, when it became a hit for E. B. Marks, Dreyfus complained that he had never been given a real chance to judge the song's merits. From that point on, every Rodgers and Hart score had his personal attention.

Sustained by profits from almost all the successful Broadway musicals, the Dreyfus brothers completed their conquest of the production-music field. Producers with whom they were allied made it clear that if one of the writing team selected to work on a new production was under contract to another house, he would be replaced at once unless Harms got the score. The reason was simple. Producers were paid "supplementary producers' royalties" on each piece of music and recording sold, an arrangement known in the Dreyfus office as "graft contracts." The practice was common. In 1917, when the Shubert brothers signed Sigmund Romberg and Rida Johnson Young to write the libretto, words, and music for *Maytime,* originally a German production, they assigned publication rights to G. Schirmer on condition that they be paid five cents per copy and 50 percent of all record royalties.

Max Dreyfus was known as a prodigious gambler, ready to advance up to $15,000 for the music to a show his writers were assigned to create. The money was usually enough to take care of a producer's initial costs, including rehearsal fees, orchestrations, which alone could cost up to $2,000 for a single production, and scenery. Because of Dreyfus's ability to read a score as easily as he might a penny dreadful, and the superb job of exploitation his professional staff assured, producers expected one or two hit songs from any production with which he was connected. An average of twenty-one songs were generally written for a musical show, many of them the ensemble and chorus numbers to fill gaps in the action or carry the plot along. Most were printed and on sale in the theater lobby. Harms's writers received more than the usual 2 and 33 royalty, and statements were issued to them every quarter rather than the customary twice a year. Kern got eight cents a copy and half of all mechanicals, part of which he shared with his lyricist.

Important changes began to take place on Broadway. In order to sell the printed songs from a show, as Victor Herbert said, "they must have words that are independent of the play—that is, on some general theme and attractive to the person who has not seen the play. I think that this may have had its effect in weaning us away from comic opera in which lyrics are woven into the plot and are part of it."

The Ziegfeld production of *Sunny* in 1925, starring the ballerina–stage dancer Marilyn Miller, marked another change. It grossed more than $40,000 a week, three percent of which went to Kern, which was about a tenth of the $10,000 Miller was paid, and deserved. War and the influence of Ruth St. Denis and Isidora Duncan on modern dancing had established that art form as a principal feature of contemporary stage musicals. The average back-line chorus girl had had ballet training and was a better dancer than were most principals before the war. The Totem Pole Dance in Friml's *Rose Marie* and the ensemble dancing in *Sky High, Top Hole,* and *Big Boy* were examples of the change. With it, a new demand was placed on the musical-comedy composer: the skill to compose and orchestrate complex dance music. Dreyfus solved the problem by adding the brilliant, classically trained Robert Russell Bennett to his staff and made him responsible for all theater-music arrangements and head of the firm's music staff.

At Dreyfus's insistence, ASCAP, in 1925, invoked for the first time a clause in its radio contracts allowing for the restriction of specific music on written notice. Broadway producers had been delighted when the early stations broadcast songs, dramatic segments, or sometimes an entire production with dialogue and music, but they complained when these cut down ticket sales on the road, where productions usually recouped losses from the New York run. Arthur Hammerstein, head of the Producers and Managers Association, instituted a drive to obtain a larger share of publisher royalties and a part of the ASCAP fees. The PMA threatened to take over all rights, including those for publication and sale of new production music, and ask for a half share in the money broadcasters paid ASCAP. A serious disruption of property rights was avoided when Mills signed letters from ASCAP to all stations announcing the restriction of six songs from *Rose Marie,* citing declining sheet-music and record sales. The restriction policy was difficult to enforce, but music publishers, Harms in particular, invoked in often, cutting off fifty songs from eight productions with a single letter. It was later extended to nonproduction music, beginning with Chappell-Harms's imported hit "Valencia," which was restricted to one use a week per station. Song restriction remained a source of contention between broadcasters and ASCAP for some time. The efficacy of ASCAP's restriction letters is questionable. The failure rate for Broadway musicals remained constant at around 45 percent between 1923–24, before restrictions were instituted, and 1927–28, when commercial broadcasting developed. To a great degree, radio was influential in popularizing the relatively sophisticated popular music of the theater, especially on the late-night broadcasts that made this "quality music" known to listeners who could not afford the theater.

Wearing his MPPA hat, Mills fought a parallel battle to reduce the "playing to death" of his members' copyrighted popular music. It was obvious after the successful series of Victor broadcasts in the first quarter of 1925 that radio had learned how to use the network concept of programing to build audiences. Even the most obstinate music men felt that a readjustment must be made, that the business had to live with reduced sales. Harms was the first publisher to increase the wholesale price of production music, to twenty cents for a forty-cent retail cost. This was after Feist and others raised their popular-song wholesale rate to twenty-three cents for thirty cents retail. No matter what its classification, a printed sheet of music cost one and a half cents, six cents for a four-page song, to which a two-cent royalty was added. Under Phil Kornheiser, general manager, the Feist staff was experimenting with mapping out air plugs and regulating weekly radio performances. The MPPA then adopted a rule that cut down the number of free orchestrations and limited them to a "blue list" of bandleaders. These were moves to regulate the speed with which radio killed a song.

Summertime's usual music-business off-season failed to materialize in 1925 for Shapiro, Bernstein, whose greatest successes came from novelty songs. In August, the firm had a nearly $200,000 turnover and shipped more than one million copies of "Collegiate," "Alabammy Bound," and a piece that promised to sell well, "The Prisoner's Song." The industry was by then reconciled to sales of 400,000 copies for a hit, but this hillbilly song was destined for much more. Written by Guy Massey, "The Prisoner's Song" was recorded first for Victor by his cousin Vernon Dalhart in July 1924 and later on several dozen other labels during its two-year reign at the top of the best-seller lists. A Texan trained for the concert and opera stage, Dalhart took his stage name from two counties back home. After small success as a singer of serious music, he began to make records in 1915, specializing in coon songs, for which his accent was eminently suited. Nathaniel Shilkret, supervisor of the Victor recording session, took Massey's penciled lyric from Dalhart and, recalling the melody he had sung in an audition, wrote down the music and provided some additional verses. The song was released on the back of a new version of Dalhart's current Edison release "The Wreck of the Old 97." Because Ralph Peer had not yet introduced the copyright-assignment scheme to Victor, Dalhart, soon after the record was shipped, copyrighted it as his own work and then sold publishing rights in Massey's name to Shapiro, Bernstein for the standard 2 and 33 royalty.

With little or no effort by Victor or the publisher, "The Prisoner's Song" became a gold mine for all concerned and one of the best-selling vocal records and songs of all time. Dalhart collected more than $85,000 from Shapiro, Bernstein, five percent of which he paid Massey until his death. Tin Pan Alley was flooded with follow-up songs, at least a hundred of them. Even the most likely, "The Prisoner's Sweetheart," "The Prisoner's Wife," and "The Girl at the Prison Gates," failed. Nor did Dalhart or any other singer of old-time hillbilly songs attain equal sales for a single selection until years after World War II.

No music house had a windfall to equal "The Prisoner's Song," but business turned a corner with Victor's introduction of the Orthophonic Victrola line and Brunswick's better-sounding new Panatrope. The direct-advertising radio stations looked to music from the old masters and the standard houses' better output. Playing in cafés, hotels, and motion-picture theaters, the popular syncopating orchestras and their singing entertainers plugged new popular songs over the air after 11:00 P.M., a time when the "right" audience was not expected to be listening.

The Feist business had learned to fine-tune radio plugging. Kornheiser and his professional men concentrated on important radio bands, and when demand followed a few carefully selected performances, sheet music was rushed to stores around the country. A few of the old music companies had almost succumbed to such changing ways: Fred Fisher and Harry Von Tilzer went into backruptcy and paid off ten cents on the dollar before reopening, and M. Witmark & Sons turned to an attorney to pull the old house from disaster. Good times and the success of the Witmark Black and White Library of operatic and standard music had spoiled that company. With twenty-four branch offices, operated by high-priced men, overhead had gone out of control. The firm had two of 1924's big hits, "I'm Heading South" and "California, Here I Come," but it operated at a loss. Al Jolson, who had the power to select the publisher for any song he featured (which also meant that he had been cut in on the deal) had handed the latter song to the Witmarks. Because he was singing it nightly in a Shubert show, the song should have gone to Harms or Shapiro, Bernstein, but Jolson was bigger than the music business. Still, a financial collapse of the Witmark firm was avoided chiefly because of Sigmund Romberg's loyalty to the people who, when he needed financial support during the war, gave him a twelve-year contract that guaranteed him $7,500 a year. Romberg continued to resist all attempts by the Shubert management, who produced his hits *The Desert Song, My Maryland,* and *The New Moon,* as well as Max Dreyfus's offer of a $50,000 bonus, to leave the Witmarks.

With their credit restored and the operation tightened, the Witmarks bought the Arthur W. Tams Music Library, their most important competitor in the music-rental field. The combined Tams-Witmark Library became the largest source of musical-comedy and operatic music for amateur productions.

In late 1926, Paul Whiteman severed his connection with the Feist company to devote himself to the publication of "futuristic" music by his favorite composers and songwriters and the arranger-composers for his large concert jazz band and dance orchestra. His associate in this venture was Jack Robbins, a second-generation music man who had started in the business in 1919 with his uncle Maurice Richmond. Richmond, born in eastern Europe, had formed his first music-publishing company as an adjunct to the sheet-music jobbing and supply business he started before the war. He added to it the F. A. Mills and Howley, Haviland & Dresser copyrights. When his nephew joined the business, the firm's name was changed to Richmond-Robbins Music Corp., and when the two parted the following year, Richmond kept the jobbing company and gave Robbins many of the copyrights. Richmond's purchase of the E. T. Paull Music Company gave him its oversized sheet music, which had covers lithographed in five brilliant colors illustrating such violent action as "The Midnight Fire Alarm," described by the music. The firm's name was changed to Paull-Pioneer Music.

An intrepid and inveterate ballroom dancer, who mastered each new terpsichorean distortion of the human frame as it appeared, Robbins was one of the first to court the up-and-coming bandleaders; at his insistence, Calvin Child, of the Victor Talking Machine Company, signed Paul Whiteman to an exclusive Victrola recording contract. Robbins also saw the eventual commercial value of the scores being written for the screen and bought the music of Erno Rapee, Hugo Reisenfeld, Domenico Savino, and Nathanial Shilkret for his company, Robbins-Engel, then Robbins-Whiteman and later Robbins Music Corp., which sold its "symphonic syncopated" music scores and choral arrangements to schools and bands. Robbins Music was formed in partnership with Domenico Savino, an Italian-born composer, conductor, and music editor, who had an 11 percent share, and with the production manager, Steve Levitz, the sales manager, Bernie Prager, and Jack Bregman, who had smaller interests.

In addition to symphonic-jazz compositions and arrangements commissioned by Whiteman, Robbins-Whiteman published Abel Green's *Inside Story on How to Write Popular Songs*. *Variety*'s music editor was frank in dealing with the prevailing state of the music business in 1927. He emphasized that a connection with Whiteman, Fred Waring, Paul Ash, Vincent Lopez, George Olsen, Abe Lyman, or any of the other famous baton wielders was imperative. Their "plans in editing and suggestions," together with regular broadcasts of a song from one to three times a week and appearances in person at night clubs, hotels, presentation movie houses, and vaudeville theaters were essential in making a hit. It was logical that they should be "compensated with royalty interests" of one half, one third, or one quarter and also credited on the title page. They could be approached; most important bandleaders considered it a poor week when they were cut in on only twelve to fifteen songs.

The average hit brought its writers and those cut in between $5,000 and $10,000, but the business dealt in much larger sums. Irving Berlin, Inc., spent $750,000 annually for operating expenses and, as a result, Berlin's name was the only one known to the average sheet-music buyer. Songs by others were sold by radio song plugging, live performances by their bandleader collaborators, and their illustrated title pages.

Astute publishers built up a catalogue of popular songs running the gamut from ballad to comedy song, from love song to nonsense ditty, from tango to foxtrot. For this purpose, they depended mostly on staff writers, who were paid between $100 and $200 weekly, which was charged off against royalties until recouped. The average staff writer's existence was not easy; he was often written out in ten years and then had to resort to selling his titles and ideas to those who had replaced him, for fees ranging from $25 to $50.

All was far from serene in the music business and in ASCAP in the late spring of 1927. The summer slump, when staffs were laid off, had come early, propelled by a series of natural disasters and by uncontrolled expansion of installment buying that syphoned off leisure-time spending. About 2,000 automobile-financing agencies supported the making of cars, the nation's number-one industry. Music sales had dropped in the chain stores, once the most important outlet but now reduced to sixty-three operations. The year's biggest seller, Berlin's "Russian Lullaby," was not yet above the 200,000 mark, a far cry from normal, when most good songs matched that figure.

In order to raise the ASCAP ratings of his supporters at the MPPA, coincidentally the publishers of the year's most popular songs—Berlin, Feist, Remick, and Shapiro, Bernstein—Mills instituted a special four-week survey of radio performances. The society's fifty regional representatives, located in twenty-two places around the country, were responsible for the findings. They did not use printed music lists, but, instead, personal recognition of music they heard on the radio. On the basis of their findings, a new class of writers, AA, was formed to supercede the A group, and its members were awarded an additional $10,000 for performances. Publishers not elevated in any class—E. B. Marks, the reorganized Von Tilzer firm, Charles K. Harris, Schirmer, and Sam Fox—argued that, because of their general ignorance of the repertory, local representatives could not recognize and report on old-time songs and standard music, which formed the bulk of radio and motion-picture-house use. Half of the society's income was coming from the latter source.

An anti-Mills faction had existed ever since the MPPA chairman was forced on them by Pat Casey and the vaudeville trust in 1919. Max Dreyfus had never joined the association and Waterson, the Witmarks, Marks and others had resigned, displeased with Mills's ego. Abel Green entered the lists, writing that the MPPA had lost sight of its purpose—the elimination of payment to singers—and worked only for the benefit of a "favored few." Mills's close association with Berlin's general manager, Saul Bornstein, was cited, and that music man's "sewing up" of one or more of the important "disk selectors" employed by the record makers. Bornstein and some other leading MPPA houses had set up dummy corporations, Green alleged, in order to evade the organization's rules against paying singers and song plugging on the radio.

Green also drew attention to the emergence of Harms as the foremost publisher of the day. It was an open secret that the firm promoted nonproduction songs by paying leading vaudeville and stage acts and singers for quick exploitation of potential popular hits. Mills used his position, Green claimed, only to increase his ASCAP-MPPA salaries, now $37,500, and by his unilaterial actions effectively displaced J. C. Rosenthal as ASCAP's general manager. Unperturbed, Mills continued negotiations for picture-synchronization rights with Western Electric's ERPI and concluded a five-year agreement that guaranteed the MPPA $100,000 for the first year and $150,000 for the second, for an expected grand total of one million. These collections were based on taxing a maximum of two million sound-theater seats. In addition, fees would be paid for each song synchronized. ASCAP, the sole custodian of performing rights in screen theaters, had not been party to the negotiations, but in a jubilant Christmas-season statement Mills noted that authors and composers would share in this additional income through separate agreements with their publishers. Royalties separate from ASCAP's regular allocations would be distributed on the basis of size of catalogue.

Mills was castigated by *Variety* for his inept handling of the National Association of Orchestra Directors affair. In February 1927, the music-business attorney Julian T. Abeles was named "Czar of Jazz" by this band-leaders' organization, at an annual salary of $25,000. His announced intention to regulate the "stealing" of top-flight players by member dance bands, to forbid performance of songs with blue lyrics, and in general to work for the purification of American popular music by leading members in a fight against the publishers' exploitation of second-rate works was immediately attacked by Mills. As head of the MPPA, he charged that the NAOD was an attempt by its founders (Paul Whiteman, Mal Hallett, Irving Aaronson, Ernie Golden, Jacques Renard, Johnny Hamp, Roger Wolfe Kahn, Sam Lanin, Vincent Lopez, George Olsen, B. A. Rolfe, Fred Rich, Ben Selvin, and Fred Waring) to monopolize the cut-in business and work at cross-plugging songs of which members were co-owners. The new czar formally denied that this was the group's intention and charged that music publishers were behind Tin Pan Alley's corrupt practices. A $100,000 anti-trust suit against the NAOD and its members was filed on behalf of songwriter and publisher Fred Fisher. It alleged that because of their radio and phonograph outlets, the bandleaders controlled American popular music and dictated what was heard and what was boycotted. All mention of the suit disappeared from the press following the NAOD's Sunday-night concert in April 1927 for the benefit of a new benevolent fund, at which Fisher's song "Dardanella" was performed. The lawsuit was evidently dropped after Fisher sold his entire holdings to publisher Jack Mills for $15,000 in 1929 and went to Hollywood to write for the film business. The NAOD disappeared shortly after the April concert, bowing to pressure from the music publishers, with whom most of the bandleaders had $10,000-a-year contracts as advisers and songwriters.

Mills's unilateral and often autocratic actions at ASCAP brought about a public confrontation with young songwriters, dissident new writers, and Class B and C publishers in April 1928. His planned elevation of Berlin, Feist, Remick, and Shapiro, Bernstein, plus Harms, to the AA category was stopped after open opposition by those publishers who would be set back one or two classifications to make up the additional $40,000 intended for his friends, who were already receiving $32,000 a year. ASCAP's membership had grown to ninety-two publishers and 600 writers. Class A writers were to receive $1,000 a quarter, Class B $500, Class C $250, and Class D $125, a 50 percent reduction for each group.

As the prospect of three million dollars in collections by 1930 loomed, demands were presented, at the first general business meeting of ASCAP in ten years, for specific information about operations that represented 20 percent of income, distribution, the classification process, and for an itemized list of expenditures. Among these were twenty-two-dollar charges for each cuspidor in the new ASCAP headquarters on Broadway, on the site of the restaurant involved in *Herbert* v. *Shanley*. Jack Yellen, a successful young songwriter who had recently become a publisher, offered a resolution calling for information about these payments. Mills responded that Yellen was a radical and a Trotskyite. Questions were raised about the MPPA chairman's negotiations with Vitaphone and RCA that would bring more than $100,000 to the publishers, rather than to ASCAP. This was done, it was suggested, in order to protect his salary. The bitter argument was terminated with an agreement to meet again in three weeks, when Yellen's motion would be acted upon.

During this temporary truce, there was the most serious discussion of the society and its business since its formative days. A national survey had been sent to ASCAP's 16,000 licensees, asking for regular reports on current music use, on the basis of which all classifications would be made. The 25 percent response revealed that the music houses with branch offices around the country dominated: Feist; Berlin; Harms; Shapiro, Bernstein; and Remick. It was argued that Marks, Belwin Music, Sam Fox, Witmark, Robbins, Fischer, and Schirmer, whose standard and motion-picture music was most in demand for screen synchronization and therefore responsible for a major part of annual income, should be ranked with the five Class A firms. The new and successful De Sylva, Brown & Henderson was another victim of the survey. Together with other recently formed houses, these songwriter-publishers believed that the old school of music men who were active in the early days deserved special consideration, but that young new blood should have an active role in operations as well as a larger allowance of total income.

Many reforms were proposed at the next session, among them open annual meetings, a standard songwriters' contract, changes in the voting procedure to end the self-perpetuating board, and a permanent Class B category for authors and composers who had been members for more than ten years and had written themselves out. The last was ratified in June, and forty-five veteran songwriters were placed in various permanent categories and guaranteed from $3,000 to $7,500, computed on past income. The remaining proposals were shelved in the interest of unity after leaders of the dissenting group were persuaded to divert their energies to the passage of a favorable revised copyright bill.

After years of hearings, the House Patents Committee had approved a bill for presentation to the full House that permitted the "divisibility," or assignment, of various rights vested in copyright and eliminated the two-cent-royalty clause. If it passed, record makers would pay whatever rate was negotiated for the first release of a song. *Variety* speculated on the possibility that the major music firms might take advantage of this provision and, with their large reserves, go into the business and distribute the first recording of a song themselves. The bill made little progress, however, and died, but the possibility of its passage had succeeded temporarily in unifying publishers and songwriters.

The sudden economic impact of talking pictures was an equal factor in the temporary suspension of ancient antagonisms. "Charmaine" from *The Big Parade* and "Diane" from *Seventh Heaven* had each sold more than a million copies of a small West coast publisher and had swollen the pictures' receipts. The nations' new number-one and -two songs were at their heels: Feist's "Laugh Clown Laugh," which began to take off once it was associated with the Lon Chaney silent film of the same name, and "Ramona," written to exploit that movie, which went on to become the company's biggest seller of all time. Even the great Irving Berlin found his own new number-one tune, "Roses of Yesterday," smothered by the surprising and spontaneous demand for two picture songs published by his company, "There's a Rainbow 'Round My Shoulder," from Jolson's talking picture *The Singing Fool*, and "I Loved You Then," the theme song for MGM's *Our Dancing Daughters*.

In the course of a single year, Hollywood changed its attitude toward the value of popular music in promoting its products, and some segments of the music business were made aware of the awesome power of the talking picture and its weekly audience of 70 million to catapult songs into success. Green had often proclaimed, "If the song isn't there, the picture can't help it," but many second-rate songs were selling in great quantity. It was possible for a music man to print dance orchestrations of a movie song for distribution to radio bands and picture-house stage bands and organists, then sit back and wait for the screen to work for him at little other expense or effort.

William Fox was the first in Hollywood to make an alliance with a leading Tin Pan Alley house. He made an agreement for De Sylva, Brown & Henderson to be the outlet for his picture music. A new subsidiary, Crawford Music Corp., was formed, with Bobby Crawford, the publisher's general manager, as president, and Erno Rapee was put in charge of all creative activity. Contracts were signed for the services of the major art composers Oley Speaks, Charles Wakefield Cadman, Lily Strickland, Geoffrey O'Hara, and Frank Grey. The Paris Salabert catalogue, of 2,000 copyrights, was bought to form a reservoir of music suitable for Fox films.

De Sylva, Brown & Henderson had an unexpected hit in a second *Singing Fool* song, "Sonny Boy," written in an hour after a telephone call from Jolson, whose name was added as co-writer. Coupled with "There's a Rainbow 'Round My Shoulder," Jolson's recording of "Sonny Boy" for Brunswick sold over a million copies, for each of which he was paid a 10 percent royalty. Within six months, "Sonny Boy" sold over a million sheet-music copies and threatened to better the sales of "Ramona." Contrary to music-business belief, sales fell immediately when its use on radio was restricted, and rose dramatically once the restriction was withdrawn.

In the comparatively brief period of two years, Buddy De Sylva, a California college-graduate, small-time bandleader, and special material writer; Lew Brown, born in Russia, brought up on New York's East Side, who had left high school to write song lyrics; and composer Ray Henderson, trained at the Chicago Conservatory of Music and once a thirty-five-dollar-a-week Feist song plugger, set a new Broadway record for success. On New Year's Day 1929, four of their musical comedies: *Follow Through, Good News, Three Cheers, Hold Everything,* and a musical revue, *George White's Scandals* (on which Henderson replaced George Gershwin), were running simultaneously on the Great White Way. Fox took the team to his Hollywood studio in 1929. There they wrote four hits for one of the earliest musical-comedy talkies, *Sunny Side Up.*

The first original movie musical, *Broadway Melody,* was released by MGM in 1929, with songs that went into Robbins Music's catalogue. A 51 percent interest in the business had been picked up from Jack Robbins, at a time when he needed cash, through a loan of $75,000 at interest, leaving him a 26 percent share, with the balance held by three of his employees. Robbins's venture with Whiteman into futuristic music had not been particularly successful. However, his catalogue of original motion-picture thematic music, compiled by Domenico Savino and the firm's growing body of popular music offered MGM a medium for exploiting new screen musicals, as well as a hedge against successful commercial sound-and-picture broadcasting. Operating with a minimum of expense and no professional staff except himself, Robbins took advantage of the MGM chain of theaters. He put uniformed pages in the lobbies to sell sheet music and recordings of songs from *Broadway Melody.* Much of the credit for the award of the Academy of Motion Picture Arts and Sciences' first Oscar to a screen musical was due to its hit songs, "You Were Meant for Me" and the title song. Under his MGM contract, he retained all copyrights in his own name.

The music division of Warner Brothers, operated by Jack Warner's son Lou, and E. H. "Buddy" Morris, the son of Warner's chief of foreign sales, anticipated a problem within three years, when ASCAP's per-seat contract with movie houses and MPPA's agreement with ERPI would expire simultaneously. Rather than expose itself to the tender mercies of those monopolies, Warner decided to control all music copyrights used in its talking pictures.

Hollywood was already signing up important songwriters' guaranteeing salaries that ranged from $12,500 to $35,000 a year; $1,000 a week for

Rodgers and Hart or De Sylva, Brown and Henderson, who were regarded
as the most outstanding songwriters on any movie lot.

Abel Green wrote in *Variety,* July 2, 1929:

> Never before in the history of Tin Pan Alley has the average songwriter
> enjoyed such affluence and influence. . . . [Many] are content to collect weekly
> and let it go at that, although in natural sequence these same hacks will strike
> on a hit by the law of averages, especially in view of the screen's power to
> carry mediocre song material to hitdom, providing the picture is strong. . . .
> Songwriters at first rebelled against the competitive racket of making some 10
> to 12 teams write for the same situation, having the supervising music man
> select one, discard the others, but they quickly found out that it served the
> twofold purpose of making them work where they might otherwise be idle and
> also it gave them a surplus of material easily adaptable for other pictures.
> Even if it's a girl-name song, any facile lyricist can switch the monikers or
> substitute a new title and development, providing the tune is worthy of reten-
> tion.

Early in 1929, writers on the Warner lot were told that copyrights would
henceforth be assigned to the film company and put into the Witmark catalogue. *Variety* viewed this as leading to the inevitable disintegration of
ASCAP. Once a catalogue of a sufficient number of copyrights made Warner independent of existing music-licensing organizations, the company could
grant performing rights to exhibitors without charge, and force competitors
to pay whatever the traffic would bear for synchronization licenses. Anticipating such a strategy, ASCAP had already persuaded songwriter members
to extend their membership contracts for an additional two years, to coin-
cide with the expiration of the original MPPA-ERPI agreement.

The root of the picture industry's problem lay in the nature of American
music firms' agreements with foreign publishers. Each European music house
granted rights only for the United States and Canada, reserving all others.
Thus, when an ERPI license was negotiated, the film company had, in
addition, to obtain one in each foreign country, generally paying a much
higher sum than in the United States. Until American publishers were in a
position to obtain world-wide synchronization rights, the movie companies
would have to control all new copyrights, own all the synchronization rights,
or suffer smaller profits from growing foreign markets.

Warner Brothers' purchase of the Witmark business, which had resigned
from the MPPA, and the impending conclusion of its deal to buy all of the
Dreyfus music holdings clearly indicated, *Variety* editorialized, that this
important music user had little use for the established music business, and,
indeed, intended to pull it down. The independent study of Harms's books,
paid for by Warner, showed that Max Dreyfus got five times his ASCAP
income by selling synchronization rights on his own, at rates higher than
MPPA's $100 for full use and $50 for partial use. Clearly Dreyfus had been
wise in refusing to become an MPPA member.

Rather than pay cash, Warner floated the $8.5 million paid for Harms by listing 140,374 additional shares of stock on the New York Stock Exchange. It took over all assets and copyrights in the summer of 1929. The principal firms involved were Harms and Chappell-Harms, De Sylva, Brown & Henderson, Remick Music, Green & Stept, Famous Music, T. B. Harms (Jerome Kern's company), and George Gershwin's New World Music, publisher of all his music. A new corporate entity was formed in Delaware to handle the merger, Music Publishers Holding Company, and an advisory board was formed to supervise the business. Max Dreyfus, who shared four million dollars from the sale with his brother Louis; Harms's Bobby Crawford, recipient of one million and Henry Spitzer, Lou Warner, and Buddy Morris were among the board members.

Anticipating the worst while preliminary Warner-Harms discussions were in progress, and hearing rumors of a vast takeover of music companies by RCA, Mills journeyed to Los Angeles in April 1929—publicly, to meet with ASCAP songwriters and plead for mutual action against the moving-picture companies that threatened to drive ASCAP out of business; privately, with the hope of negotiating new synchronization fees with these enemies of the music business. The movie men refused to talk with Mills; instead, they directed him to meet with their legal counsel in New York for a discussion of already "exorbitant" fees. The trade papers cited one producer who had been asked by the MPPA to pay more for synchronization rights in a single foreign country than he would receive for all exhibition rights there.

The bitter antagonism felt by writers that had dominated the ASCAP meeting a year earlier surfaced again when Mills addressed seventy West Coast authors and composers during a dinner meeting. Forecasting a total annual royalty of four million dollars in three years, he urged that public-performance rights be reserved in any proposed contract, especially with those "worst offenders," the Warners. He was quickly interrupted with a matter of more concern to the writers: discrimination by Class A members of the East Coast committees against West Coast writers in lower classes and their movie hits. The meeting degenerated into an impassioned protest against Mills and his function at ASCAP.

A generally disregarded problem was taking shape for ASCAP and its members around the country at the same time, one whose ramifications would involve the society in years of lobbying for the correction of yet another copyright inequity. The threat was present in many tearooms, restaurants, grill rooms, dance halls, and other public places where live musicians were being displaced by large, electrically powered mechanical record players, some of which used large disks capable of playing a half hour of music. During the 1909 copyright hearings, a leading publisher had testified that the so-called penny parlor and penny vaudeville, where one could hear the newest recorded song for a penny or a nickel, were "of first assistance as an advertising medium." None of the other music men there or their lawyers complained, even though a corporation capitalized at half a million dollars was building up a chain of such places around the country. On a single day an estimated 200,000 persons crowded into them and spent at least ten cents each. Virtually any city with more than 10,000 inhabitants could support one of these poor man's music halls, whose mechanical music-reproduction machines were specifically exempted by the 1909 act. The coin-in-the-slot phonograph industry had not used disks until 1908, when the first automatic coin machines went on sale and coin-operated Peerless Player Pianos replaced recorded music with paper music rolls. The mechanical record player was still in an early stage of development when it disappeared from circulation in 1910. It returned in 1927, when the Automatic Musical Instrument Company replaced its own mechanical player pianos with the Selective Phonograph, which offered twenty recorded selections. In three years, 12,000 of them were in use. AMI was followed by Seburg, Wurlitzer, Homer Capehart, and the Mills Novelty Company, the most sophisticated of whose machines offered ten- and twelve-inch disks and used the turn-over record changer developed by Columbia.

Hollywood's unexpected and regular compensation to songwriters gave those who had moved west a new sense of the value of their work and to those who stayed in the East a new fear that their ASCAP ratings would fall if those "hack writers" in California were ever able to take control of the society. There had been intermittent attempts to form a New York-based counterpart to the MPPA; all of them foundered on the publishers' unconcealed opposition. The most recent of these, the Songwriters, had been dormant for several years when its secretary, Leo Woods, invited all of the city's 200 authors and composers to a free dinner on April 19, 1929. A general tone of unease persisted on that occasion. Earl Carroll presided, and Gene Buck was guest of honor. A ways and means committee was appointed to work toward the creation of a new association and the correction of present and potential abuses. ASCAP president Buck was named chairman of a committee representing the entire range of those present. It was directed to prepare a new standard contract, with a minimum guaranteed salary, improved accounting methods, elimination of all cut ins, and the obligation of the publisher to work on a new song within six months of buying it or to return it to the writer. About 750 professional songwriters had been accepted for membership in ASCAP, and it was agreed that a similar requirement of being a professional obtain for admission to the new group, in order to keep out the "hordes of amateurs." Little was accomplished, however, over the next two years, a period of disorientation, during which the film industry made a sudden turnabout in its conception of the value of popular songwriters.

That confusion was reflected by the record companies. When Hollywood created a glut of as many as six or eight songs in a single production, it led to a superabundance of recorded movie music, which sold pictures but not recordings. A Hollywood-connected publisher could no longer assure record makers that a specific song in a forthcoming film would be the plugged hit. Frequently, in the completed film, it was cut off at sixteen or twenty-four bars or completely eliminated. Another problem was the picture people's predilection for songs longer than the customary thirty-two bars, which confused sheet-music buyers and added pages and printing costs to the completed product. Max Dreyfus, then also a consultant at Warner, summed it up best: "Picture people don't take advice, they give orders."

Louis Dreyfus, meanwhile, was in London. With part of the four million dollars the brothers had received for their catalogues, he had purchased a controlling interest in the venerable British firm Chappell & Co. As a new director of Chappell, Max Dreyfus was an important figure in negotiations with the British Performing Rights Society, which led to the first payment made from England to ASCAP. The same arrangement followed with the Canadian performing-rights body, and three ASCAP officials were added to its official board, solely to deal with matters pertaining to both organizations.

Finally succumbing to the series of offers from ASCAP-licensed music users, Claude Mills resigned from both ASCAP and the MPPA to become head of RCA-NBC's Radio Music Corp., capitalized at six million dollars through floating additional RCA stock. Few in ASCAP mourned his passing, but Mills's years of experience served his new master well in connection with music-licensing negotiations and the purchase of the music catalogues of Feist, Fischer, Boosey & Hawkes, Enoch et Cie., Oxford University Press, and several popular-song houses. He was also the chief target for the Warner companies' complaints that NBC boycotted their catalogues in favor of those controlled by Radio Music. The success of "The Maine Stein Song" was a particular case in point. An old copyright that Carl Fischer had long forgotten, the college song was published in a new edition "arranged by Rudy Vallee." The bandleader featured it on all his NBC network broadcasts and in a few months, on the strength of his plugging on the air and an RCA Victor record, the song sold a half-million copies. NBC's reported suggestion to artists on commercial programs and to band-leaders heard on remote broadcasts that they favor Radio Music copyrights brought threats from Warner to restrict 3,000 of their songs if the order was not rescinded. Confusion and stalemate followed.

Three important changes in the Copyright Act were introduced in early 1930, but had little support from music-business figures. As a result, passage was doomed for American membership in the Berne Convention, which would have brought harmony to international copyright protection; for elimination of the compulsory licensing clause and the two-cent royalty; and for an amendment to permit divisibility of rights so that individual copyright privileges could be assigned separately. Enactment of the last provision might have foreclosed a later attempt to render ASCAP impotent.

For a time, it did appear that the popular-music business had at last found the most potent force yet for promoting and merchandising its products. Before the advent of talking pictures, it had taken four months to place a song with the 100 leading big-time vaudeville acts, who would give it the widest possible exposure. Afterward, 100 Jolsons, Chevaliers, Ramon Navarros, or Lawrence Tibbetts provided the same sort of plugging for a song in the first week of a picture's exhibition. There was a 150,000-copy sale edge for a forty-cent picture song over the twenty-five- or thirty-cent straight pop hit, which might at best sell 250,000 copies.

Radio artists and bandleaders who were paid or cut in by movie-affiliated publishers unfailingly made full identification with a current movie of the songs they sang, a form of unpaid advertising the networks sought to reduce. Commercial programs were made up at least a month in advance, and all scripts were approved by network officials, who consequently deleted any mention of new pictures. It was more difficult to restrain the fast-talking bandleaders on remote broadcasts. They were usually paid ten dollars or more for each performance of an orchestration made especially for them. With 250 new songs, 90 percent of them for films, being worked on at a time and twenty-two first-string song pluggers peddling their publishers' new material, cash on the line for air play and a cut-in contract were the only way to do business. Publishers complained about having to pay for performances, but they approved a new MPPA regulation reducing the mandatory $1,500 fine for it to $250, "in order to make it easier to uncover bribery," and continue to work closely with radio stars. Morton Downey and Rudy Vallee were favorites, and not just because they saved money by reciprocity in plugging songs on which either was cut in.

In an earlier summer slump than usual, one far more serious, the stock market crash of the previous fall caught up with the popular-music business. Wholesale orders were 75 percent below normal. Radio's restriction of free advertising for new pictures raised the stakes for plugs so high that even the biggest firms expected to be in the red until winter. Some companies were paying pluggers on a commission basis: five dollars for a network plug, two and a half for a remote performance. An unexpected product of the poor times was a reemergence of bootleg five- and ten-cent song sheets containing the words only of current hits whose melodies were drilled into the heads of listeners until sheet music was unnecessary.

The record business suffered, too, a victim of overproduction and tumbling sales, and competition from the British-owned Durium records, which sold for fifteen cents at newsstands. Durium's single-side flexible disks were pressed in initial quantities of 210,000 and paid a royalty of about $4,000 to the publishers, equal to the amount earned from the combined sales of eleven other disks. A Victor hit disk sold between 50,000 and 75,000 copies; the two other majors, Columbia and Brunswick, averaged 10,000.

The surplus of material, but dearth of true hits, from the Warner Brothers' song-writing stable, which had been working on a twenty-four-hour basis, was responsible for an edict that songs would be used only in purely musical features, and only five teams were offered contract renewal.

In June 1930, John G. Paine, the successor to Claude Mills at the MPPA, called a meeting of the publishers to discuss the business slump. There was little agreement about the reasons for it. The only outsider present, Abel Green, who thought, with the publishers, that radio killed songs as quickly as it made them, urged that ASCAP control and regulate radio performances by restricting songs as Max Dreyfus had been doing successfully for the past five years. One thing was learned, Green concluded, "the suspicion that Radio, through its own publishing interests, was endeavoring to create its own library of songs in order to be rid of royalty obligations, is immediately disproved." Not enough sufficiently worthy material could possibly be turned out to fill radio's needs. The MPPA made no effort to curb air play; it merely instituted a fee of fifty cents per song per station when electrically transcribed commercial programs were broadcast, which was to be paid to the association for distribution to the appropriate publishers.

Fall was nearing when *Variety* discerned a strong comeback for old music, a result of Hollywood's reduction of synchronized music and songs. Picture producers who had stirred up the destructive flood of new and often worthless songs and forced them on the market to promote their releases no longer called the tune in New York. The tide had turned almost overnight, and five of September's big songs were pop material. Finding that its new music holdings were not making profits, Warner permitted their Harms and Witmark firms to operate in the traditional flamboyant Tin Pan Alley manner. The songwriters' hegira to Hollywood was slowly reversing, and it was noted that the quality of new material being submitted in New York for publication was a cut above that of the recent past.

In a roundup of happenings in 1929, *Variety* had called the talking picture Tin Pan Alley's savior, preserving what "threatened to become a doddering product of the show business." Twelve months later, Abel Green wrote that the music business was now back to normal, "or at least that phase of normalcy of the pre–theme song days. No more fitting 'em to match the profile of the heroine. Songs were [now] written in the same vein as the pre-gold rush of 1929 Hollywood style."

It was also a year that mourned the passing of Leo Feist, at the age of sixty-one. An invalid for many years, Feist had kept in touch with the music business by listening to his secretary read the dailies and the trade papers, particularly *Variety*. Edgar Bitner, who ran the Feist operation in its founder's absence, was a Tin Pan Alley pioneer who, with Julius P.

Witmark and Nathan Burkan, was one of ASCAP's honorary pioneer members. As a sideline, he founded *Metronome* magazine, which his son, Edgar, took over after his death.

In an obituary story about Feist, *Variety* noted that one of the most remarkable men in or out of show business was gone, a man possessed of an idealism that impressed "what is perhaps the most cynical of all trades or professions."

PART THREE

1931–1940

CHAPTER 10

The Fall and Rise
of the Record Business

In his article "The Rise and Fall of the Phonograph," in the *American Mercury* of September 1932, Dane York traced the decline of the phonograph-recording business as a self-contained industry to the year 1925, when retail sales tumbled by almost half from the 1921 high of $106 million. It was also the year the Victor Talking Machine Company failed to pay stockholder dividends for the first time since 1901, and Eldridge Johnson, founder and chief executive, seriously contemplated the disposition of all his holdings in the world's largest record company. Although he regretted it until his death, Johnson's decision to do so the following year was a wise one, for sales in general continued to slip, eventually dropping by 60 percent in in a single year, to $16.9 million in 1931.

The new block-square facility RCA had built in Los Angeles in connection with its sound-on-film Photophone process contained recording studios, but they remained mostly unused. Victor's entire distribution system was merged with RCA's product-merchandising operation, and the Camden factory ceased all manufacture of radio-phonograph combinations to concentrate strictly on the Radiola. On June 16, 1931, an official order cut recording down to a single wax take per selection, unless it was defective. As soon as contracts expired, the most expensive artists were dropped by Victor, as they were by Columbia and Brunswick, its two major competitors. Johnny Marvin, who had given the company the year's best-selling vocal recording, "Little White Lies," which sold 40,000 copies—contrasted with a hit's 350,000 a few years earlier—worked on a session-to-session basis and was paid per recording in lieu of royalties on sales. Louis Armstrong's highly individual interpretations of Tin Pan Alley's major plug tunes, which made near classics of the music, sold more for Columbia than the combined output of his closest rivals on the label, Guy Lombardo and Ted Lewis.

Vocalists topped Brunswick's sales lists—Bing Crosby, the Boswell Sisters, and the Mills Brothers—whose recordings were made under the supervision of Jack Kapp, now in charge of the money-losing operation that Warner Brothers was ready to unload for a minimal sum.

The national newspaper and magazine advertising which had kept consumers apprised for years of new weekly Victor issues was dropped and replaced with stickers on music-store windows and pamphlets describing new products that retailers sent to their local mailing lists. In early 1932, a series of transcribed radio programs was introduced over 200 stations, with time costs shared equally by the company and local dealers. Each week, a sixteen-inch transcription was mailed out containing excerpts from the latest releases and giving the name and address of the local dealer. The 10 percent increase in sales claimed after a month on the air actually represented only a few thousand records. The company's only extravagance was the $60,000 spent to buy back the unexpired and substantial contract with which Columbia had lured away Paul Whiteman in 1928.

Among the few artists retained on a year-to-year contract basis at Victor was Jimmie Rodgers, the hillbilly singer whose record sales had slipped dramatically from the accumulated 350,000 for each new release in the 1928–1930 period. Ralph Peer, his recording manager and music publisher, who remained in charge of Victor's field recordings of hillbilly and race music, was instrumental in retaining Rodgers, even though his own position was in serious jeopardy. Fellow recording supervisors were jealous of the partnership he enjoyed with Victor through the music house he had formed, Southern Music Publishing Company, and they kept away from him new and unpublished selections they recorded, in spite of the understanding that all such copyrights should pass to Southern Music. Eli Oberstein had become a special enemy. Peer had brought him from the OKeh bookkeeping department to Victor's sales accounting group in order to have someone on staff to protect his complicated interests. In the face of rumors accusing him of various white-collar crimes and petty expense-account cheating, Peer clung on tenaciously and continued to build his catalogue with copyrights from his recording sessions in Memphis, Dallas, San Antonio, and Chicago.

Conditions in the British record business were much like those in America. The two major manufacturers, the Gramophone Company–His Master's Voice (HMV) and Columbia suffered a joint decline of 90 percent in profits during fiscal 1930–31 and were forced to merge in order to stay afloat. Under Louis Sterling's guidance, Columbia had already acquired virtual control of European machine and recording manufacture. In 1925, he had purchased important interests in the Carl Lindstrom Company of Berlin and the Transoceanic Trading Company of Amsterdam, a merger involving many millions that brought him factories in France, Germany, Italy, Austria, Spain, Sweden, Switzerland, and Argentina, to add to the

Columbia plant in Bridgeport, Connecticut. The companies involved were consolidated into a holding company known as Columbia International, capitalized at five million dollars. Three years later, Sterling increased the scope of this musical League of Nations with acquisition of Pathé Frères, the owner of major Far Eastern phonograph and record subsidiaries.

In March 1931, Sterling's international phonograph combine was joined with Gramophone-HMV to form Electrical & Musical Industries, whose fifty factories operated in nineteen different countries and had only Deutsche Gramophon–Polydor for competition. David Sarnoff was elected to the EMI board to represent the Radio Corporation of America, traditionally HMV's American cousin and owner of basic patents that continued to affect the international talking-machine business. This connection was severed in 1935, when RCA Victor surrendered all interests in EMI for $10 million in cash, leaving the latter without any American affiliation, Sterling having disposed of Columbia several weeks after EMI became operative. That move had been made chiefly because federal antitrust action against RCA could threaten others involved with the American giant in the radio receiver and transmitting business. Grigsby-Grunow, manufacturers of Majestic radios, washing machines, and refrigerators, become proprietors of Columbia Records in America, purchasing it at a bargain price.

During Grigsby-Grunow's brief tenure as owner, Columbia introduced its superior all–royal blue records, a product improvement that failed to attract any new business. Times were desperate, and Americans, whose income fell with each new economic catastrophe, had turned to radio for their entertainment. Columbia's fifty-five-dollar Radiograph record-playing attachment went begging, along with Victor's new long-playing disks. The increasing use of quarter-hour radio programs recorded on electrical transcriptions had persuaded some Victor executives that a resurgence of consumer interest might be stimulated by fifteen-minute-long recorded musical and comedy material. Despite official policy to concentrate only on the development of improved radio sets, Victor engineers and furniture designers produced a fifteen-minute disk for home use and handsomely encased equipment with which to play it. Inertia and fear of reprimand for having run counter to orders slowed introduction of the new technology and provided the Erwin-Wasey advertising agency with an opportunity in the summer of 1931 to be first on the market with a double-faced recording bearing five minutes of the newest hit songs on each side, which could be played on standard Victrolas and cost only fifteen cents. The patent holder for the composition materials of which these disks were made, the Durium Products Company had failed to delight Tin Pan Alley in the summer of 1930 with guaranteed sales of 250,000 of each new Hit of the Week release. When past-due royalties mounted to $141,410.39 by early 1931, many music houses sued, and sent the company into bankruptcy. Erwin-Wasey was the highest bidder at the receivers' sale, and resumed release of new five-

minute Hit of the Week records, featuring some former Victor artists—
Gene Austin, Morton Downey, and Rudy Vallee, among others. These
enjoyed an average sale of 60,000 copies each.

Goaded into action by the new competition, Victor finally introduced
longer-playing records, ones that provided three or four times as much music.
Raymond Scoey, the chief recording engineer at Victor, and his assistants
had doubled the number of grooves on a new compound called Victrolac,
which was flexible, like the Durium material, and cut down playing speed
to the 33⅓ revolutions per minute used for electrical transcriptions. Unfortunately, RCA's pricing policy prevailed, and an overpriced line of ornate
combination radios and two-speed record players went into production. They
cost from $247.50 to $1,000. The first ten- and twelve-inch releases went
on sale in mid-October: Leopold Stokowski and the Philadelphia Orchestra,
reduced to sixty players in the interest of economy, playing Beethoven's
Fifth Symphony, and Leo Reisman's "complete score" for the Broadway
musical revue *The Band Wagon,* which featured Adele and Fred Astaire.
Prices at retail ranged from $1.50 for the Reisman to $4.50 for classical
items that had cost $2.00 a record in the 78-rpm form and usually had sold
only about 500 sets of four or five disks. Columbia announced its entry into
the race, with long-playing disks and compatible machines expected to go
on sale the following spring. Enthusiasm for long-playing records waned
quickly once the public rejected the expenditure of large sums for two-
speed machines. By the autumn of 1932, any reminder of this innovation,
expected to turn the business around, had disappeared from music stores
and record shops.

The general apathy prevailing at all record companies around Christmastime of 1932 reflected the 40 percent decline in a single year, to sales of
$11 million at retail from total production of 10 million disks: American
Record Company–Brunswick, 6 million; RCA Victor, 3 million; the balance spread among Columbia and lesser firms. Warner Brothers had finally
disposed of its Brunswick phonograph and record holdings to American
Record, the major purveyor of twenty-five-cent and three-for-a-dollar records to the chain stores and mail-order-catalogue business. Sears, Roebuck,
the most important of the latter, was catering chiefly to the old and important middle-American market for hillbilly music, the "hick disk" business,
as *Variety* dubbed it, which had tripled since 1930.

Now second to American Record, Victor cut down on all field and out-
of-town recording and tightened its fiscal belt further by bringing a few
authentic, working hillbillies to the New York and Camden studios. Now
that he was in full charge of Victor's race and hillbilly catalogues, Oberstein's determination to remove Peer from any connection with the company
was obvious to all. Still, when Jimmie Rodgers, the best-selling hillbilly
artist of all, came in for his yearly recording sessions in response to an
offer of $2,500 for a maximum of ten sides, Ralph Peer selected his songs,

supervised all activity, and copyrighted all music. Hostilities between the two former friends came to an unexpected conclusion in September when Sarnoff learned the terms of RCA Victor's deal with Peer. Justice Department attorneys were active at RCA headquarters, seeking anything that might legally discredit the corporate giant, and Sarnoff was determined to avoid any such possibility. Orders were received by Victor to dispose of Southern Music to Peer. He continued, however, to enjoy a favored near-insider's relationship with RCA Victor throughout the years during which he built his music holdings and turned the parent company into an important ASCAP member. He also became a leader in the Music Publishers Protective Association and was a major factor in 1941's "music war."

RCA Victor's negotiations with the F. W. Woolworth Company to provide a line of cheap records nearly foundered. The latter insisted that, having never sold any but miniature disks in the past, it would introduce full-sized recordings only if they were priced no higher than twenty cents. Several other manufacturers were ready to fill Woolworth's projected annual distribution, in its 1,800 stores, of 12 million records at that price. Victor disposed of all rivals in August 1932 by introducing eight-inch popular-dance-music records made specifically for the chain, to sell for a dime. The following month, regular ten-inch Victor Electradisks went on sale at the same price. When demand warranted and distribution of the fifteen-cent Hit of the Week releases was terminated, the price was raised to the agreed-upon twenty cents.

Recorded music was beginning to be heard with greater frequency over the approximately 600 radio stations (80 percent of the total number) not affiliated with the three national networks in the early 1930s. Many of them still looked for their music to live performers and electrical transcriptions. Live talent was paid only a few dollars, or often nothing at all. An electrical-transcription service cost between $40 and $150 a week, depending on a station's transmitting power, and provided only eight fifteen-minute programs, hardly enough to fill a day. Consequently, these broadcasters began to buy records at local stores at list price, or get them without charge in return for frequent mention. Durium had been the only manufacturer to mail new releases to stations, sending two copies of each and hoping they would be used often. No other major company had yet followed this worthy practice.

At the request of the Music Publishers Protective Association, in January 1933, RCA Victor, Columbia, and Brunswick began to print the legend "Not Licensed for Radio Broadcast" on every new pressing. A flood of mail from concerned members to the National Association of Broadcasters followed. They were assured that the warning meant nothing, that property rights ended once a record was sold across the counter, a legal opinion vigorously opposed by manufacturers and many leading artists, particularly Paul Whiteman and Fred Waring. The latter's talented aggregation of musicians, vocalists, and entertainers, known as the "Pennsylvanians," had been recording for Victor since 1924 and was negotiating for a new contract that would reserve the use of Waring disks by broadcasters. The bandleader was vociferous with his complaints that small stations regularly aired sponsored programs which used his name and featured only his recordings, failing to identify them as mechanical reproductions. The result was that listeners believed Waring and his musicians were live and in the studio. This harmed his prospects of being signed for network broadcasts by a national advertiser. So he refused to come into a recording studio until his property rights were affirmed by legal action. Few bandleaders followed him, but they did continue to insist that the meager royalties from record sales failed to compensate for the depreciation of their value to network broadcasting. Music publishers were generally sympathetic, but they pointed out that they could not join in legal action against broadcasters because an ASCAP license gave stations the right to perform music in any form without restriction as to means. In point of fact, ASCAP did not pay for recorded or electrically transcribed performances.

Tin Pan Alley was having problems of its own with the phonograph industry and many of its artists. For years, music publishers had paid between thirty-five and seventy-five dollars for the special orchestrations bandleaders prepared for recording sessions. The average hit disk now sold around 3,500 copies in the first three months of its popularity and an additional 1,500 before it disappeared three months later. The publisher received just enough royalties to pay for the arrangement, an expense they now refused to shoulder. Only the money invested by Harms in an arrangement of Cole Porter's "Night and Day" for Leo Reisman had paid a dividend, around $400 from 45,000 copies.

A survey taken in 1933 concluded that half a million record players were available in the United States, almost all housed in combination units whose radio receivers were most often in use for network broadcasts. Following the stock market collapse, the sale of classical albums had fallen to an average of 500 copies, but with the optimism that followed the first hundred days of Franklin Roosevelt's presidency, an interest in recorded art music began to revive, and that figure jumped to 2,000 albums. Responding to this new consumer demand, Columbia raised the price of its Master Works by 50 percent, to $1.50, which was still less than the two- and three-dollar Red Seal price, from which Victor refused to budge, come depression or prosperity.

Sales of popular hits in the twenty-five-cent lines had fallen from 50,000 to 5,000 in an eighteen-month period, so expenses were cut even nearer the bone. Bandleaders were hired to record four numbers in four individual takes and paid just enough to cover union scale. There was little or no royalty share. Production costs for Victor's new Bluebird Records, an offshoot of the disks pressed for the Woolworth stores, were the same as those for the more expensive black labels, and sales were less than half, a profit ratio evidently not worth the effort. Observing Victor's failure to take over the cheap-record market, Columbia scuttled its own plans to bring out a low-cost series on a revived OKeh label. All three major companies seriously considered cutting prices of their top-of-the-line popular products to fifty-five cents or two for a dollar. They also adopt devices to encourage customer interest—for instance, Columbia's royal-blue records, drawings of the artists on the label, and bandleader and singer autographs incised into the record.

Newly infused with enthusiasm, brought to the recently improved facilities at Camden by a new record-division manager, Edward "Ted" Wallerstein, Victor's management approved a promotion and advertising budget to revive the record-buying habit in Americans. Wallerstein was just over forty, and had been in the business for a dozen years, since 1922 at Brunswick-Balke-Collender. His firm belief that the bottom had been reached spurred Victor's decision to spend $350,000 on advertising and $200,000 to ensure the cooperation of retail dealers of the RCA radio line, which had enjoyed a comfortable share of the $300 million spent in 1933 for receivers.

With Ralph Peer's departure, Fred Erdman, in charge of all recording for Victor, found another music man with broad experience in both race music and popular-song-and-dance bands, one who was also reputed to have made more recordings than all other studio supervisors combined. He was Irving Mills, born in 1894, a flamboyant, fast-talking figure on the Manhattan music scene since just after the war. He had begun as a songwriter and dance-hall singer and became a talent scout and producer for cheap-label manufacturers. With his older brother Jack's $500 and a catalogue of three new copyrighted songs, the two found some garment manufacturers from Philadelphia, ready to take a fling in the music business, who put up the additional $4,500 needed to form Mills Music, on July 1, 1919. Jack Mills had been a song plugger for Waterson, Berlin & Snyder in Philadelphia and professional manager in New York for McCarthy & Fisher. Irving Mills was the outside man; he bought outright for a few dollars music offered by the out-of-work songwriters who frequented record-company offices, or the manuscripts of uncopyrighted new material written by musicians at recording sessions Mills supervised for every three-for-a-dollar label in New York. Typical of such groups was the Hotsy-Totsy Boys, originally comprised of Irving Mills; Mills Music's professional manager, Jimmy McHugh; Sammy Fain, a pianist, singer, and songwriter; and Gene Austin, a singer from Texas who made history with his recording of "My Blue Heaven."

Irving Mills's predilection for Negro jazz brought about his most successful connection, as manager and booker of Edward Kennedy "Duke" Ellington, a young black enigmatically blithe spirit, whose six-piece 1924 band played in the basement of a Mid-town New York building. The group matured into an ensemble of consummate master players, who became the instrument for which Ellington wrote more than 5,000 compositions. The body of Ellington's work brought the accolade from Igor Stravinsky that he was one of the greatest living composers. Mills was instrumental in obtaining Ellington's earliest recording dates, before moving him into a "jungle music" period, written to satisfy the demands of speakeasy and night-club operators, who were profiting from white America's infatuation with the Negro. The venues in which Ellington appeared were decorated to re-create an African habitat peopled with jungle princesses and ferocious cannibal kings. Through connections with the bootlegging underworld in 1927, Mills booked the Ellington band into one of Manhattan's most prestigious night spots, the Cotton Club, in Harlem. There, twenty beautiful black showgirls and a cast of other black entertainers appeared in a series of extravagant floor shows, set to music by Jimmy McHugh and his lyricist, Dorothy Fields. The Cotton Club's owners installed remote-broadcasting wires, giving Ellington and his expanded orchestra the opportunity to be heard coast to coast, which introduced the bandleader's instrumental music and popular songs, most of them with special lyrics by Mills. A corporation was formed to handle Ellington's business affairs and copyrights; 90 percent of the stock was divided between Ellington and Mills; 10 percent went to the attorney who wrote the contract.

In the early 1930s, when Victor started to drop even its most popular band artists as an economy measure, Mills shuttled Ellington, who was by then among the company's five best-selling orchestra leaders, around to the seventy-five cent and three-for-a-dollar companies to record under many pseudonyms. As the most successful booker of black talent, Mills continued to hold a monopoly in that field when RCA Victor offered him a year's contract to build up a profit-making talent roster. He had dealt in the hyperbole of newspaper publicity for most of his life, and now directed his personal press agent to encourage newspapers and magazines to review new Victor popular records, which would be provided without charge. As a result of Mill's urging, this sort of promotion became the company's single means of general press relations and exploitation for more than a decade.

In the final quarter of 1933, the unexpected success of the recording of a hillbilly song, "The Last Roundup", with sales of 100,000 copies on all labels, signaled a small upturn in industry income the following year, the first since the 1929 gross of $75 million. The new technical recording techniques responsible for that upturn included an effort to meet the challenge of sharp and clean-cut master disks from England and a daring new course being considered by Jack Kapp, general manager of Brunswick. RCA Victor had issued a number of imported British HMV masters, of music by the Ray Noble ochestra, whose superior sound qualities rapidly became the talk of the trade. Record supervisors called on their British associates to learn the secret. It lay merely in the oversize studio used for Noble's disks, a mammoth sound stage on a film lot. It was a far cry from the usual small recording rooms in America, with their bare cement walls, unfelicitous hardwood floors, and meager wall drapings, which combined to frustrate any improved quality that might have come from the recently developed directional microphones suspended overhead from booms. A press agent said that Noble's practice was to place his men at the far end of the studio. By the time the sound reached microphones at the near end, it had acquired the distinctive quality for which a small army of American record buyers was spending money. Victor, Columbia, and Brunswick were soon engaged in a veritable musical comedy of searching for sufficient space in which to reproduce the British sound and spotting musicians in outside halls, inside men's rooms, and all over. Brunswick was the first to solve the problem. Its musical director, Victor Young, began to record in a Los Angeles motion-picture studio, acquired from a bankrupt customer by Herbert Yates, the majority stockholder in Brunswick's new parent company, American Record.

It was Yates's intention to use British financing for the purchase of Columbia Records and its licensed Western Electric recording equipment from the creditors of the bankrupt Grigsby-Grunow Company—so that he could go into the electrical-transcription business—that started the move of the record business in a new direction. Throughout the worst years of worldwide economic instability, the British Decca Record Company had prospered, under the management of its stockbroker founder, E. R. "Ted" Lewis, with a successful line of two-shilling (fifty-cent) and one-shilling-sixpence recordings. As the British and European distributor of the subsidiary Brunswick and Melotone labels, it had also become the chief source of profits for American Record. Ready to buy a 50 percent interest in Yates's option to purchase Columbia Records from the Grigsby-Grunow creditors, Lewis went to the United States in May 1934. Prior to his trip, the purchase price of $750,000 had been agreed upon, together with the assumption of $200,000 in liabilities and past-due bills, principally for leaseholds on deteriorating property in downtown New York, where Columbia's headquarters was housed. It was anticipated that Kapp, who had brought American Record–Brunswick to the top place in the business, would head Columbia under the new ownership.

The urbane Lewis and the freewheeling Hollywood buccaneer Yates, owner of Consolidated Film Laboratories, who was building an empire by acquiring film companies unable to pay their processing bills, made a strained partnership, which soon dissolved. Yates planned to scrap Columbia's Bridgeport plant and remove the pressing equipment to his plant in Scranton, Pennsylvania, where most twenty-five-cent and three-for-a-dollar disks were manufactured. The decision was opposed by both Lewis and Kapp. The Englishman offered to buy Yates out of Brunswick instead, but found the $750,000 asking price too steep and went back to London. As rumors flew that he would soon return to build his own American company in partnership with Kapp, Yates accepted his general manager's resignation.

One of the Depression period's two most innovative and successful record men (Oberstein of Victor was the other), Jack Kapp was in his mid-thirties and had already spent half his life making and selling recorded music. As a young boy, he had accompanied his father, a salesman for the Chicago branch of Columbia, in a buggy to take and deliver orders from retail shops, and at the age of fourteen was a part-time shipping clerk for the company. After graduation from high school, he became a full-time worker in the order department, where he demonstrated a determination to get ahead with the prodigious feat of memorizing the titles and numbers of every selection in the firm's catalogue, nearly 5,000 items. When Brunswick bought the Vocalion Company in 1925, Kapp was hired to run its race-music division out of Chicago, where he and a younger brother, David, also operated a record and mail-order business catering to middle-class and minority customers, a market that made him familiar with what he considered to be the best gauge for determining the sales potential of recorded music. His insistence in 1928 that Brunswick record and release, on a single disk, Al Jolson's versions of "Sonny Boy" and "There's a Rainbow 'Round My Shoulder" and its subsequent million-copy sale were responsible for his assignment to supervise the entire operation. He quickly became known in the trade as a "man of no taste, so corny he's good," but he built up a stable of best-selling artists: Bing Crosby, Mae West, the Mills Brothers, Ted Lewis, Isham Jones, the Casa Loma Orchestra, Guy Lombardo and his Royal Canadians, the Dorsey brothers. The trade credited Brunswick's success to Kapp's operating principle that the quality of a record and artist coupled with ear-catching, easy-to-remember melody—and not plugging on the air—resulted in sales of both disks and sheet music.

A series of complicated business transactions took place as Kapp assembled a complete recording, mechandising, and distributing operation that could compete with Victor or American Record–Brunswick, based on the investment of $250,000 by Lewis. He had already prepared by ensuring the services of nearly the entire Brunswich artist roster through personal contracts with him, rather than his employer, for all future recording work. Warner Brothers was given a one fifth interest in the new venture through one of its wholly owned subsidiaries, the Brunswick Radio Company (acquired in the purchase of Brunswick, Balke, Collender holdings), in return for a $60,000 note and sole use of the facilities and all recording equipment owned by yet another Warner company, United Research, for an annual royalty of ten dollars. Through supplemental agreements in 1937, Brunswick Radio exchanged 5,000 shares of common stock, on a one-for-five basis, for another 25,000 Decca shares, and took an additional 7,500 in payment of the balance of the old note for United Research. Title to the equipment was then turned over outright to Kapp. Herman Starr, Warner's music division vice-president, and for a brief time in 1931 head of business affairs at Brunswick Records, who had engineered the several transfers, surrendered to Brunswick Radio without any consideration an additional 1,357 shares of Decca stock held in his own name since 1934, the first year of his tenure on the recording company's board of directors.

Lewis was named chairman and Kapp president of American Decca Records, and the first studio sessions were scheduled almost immediately. *Variety* reported that Decca disks would be sold for twenty-five cents, because Kapp was known for his conviction that cheap records of high quality made by top artists could outsell the seventy-five-cent Victor, Brunswick, and Columbia products. The price was actually fixed at thirty-five cents each or three for one dollar. Decca's entire first three months' production proved to be inferior and was immediately rejected by Kapp's potentially best customers, the operators of coin record players. The old pressing plant in New Jersey Kapp had taken over from United Research turned out warped, improperly grooved, off-center recordings, which, in addition, proved to be a minor fraction of an inch too large to fit into the disk-cradling mechanism that was then standard on automatic phonographs. Only Lewis's infusion of an additional $400,000 saved the day.

As Kapp and Decca went through such operational difficulties, Yates went ahead with his plans to merge Brunswick and Columbia and close the Bridgeport plant. He sent all pressing and processing work to his Scranton factory, notorious for second-rate work. Stripped of almost the entire artist line-up, Brunswick's executives scurried about for talent. Irving Mills, his Victor contract soon to expire, was brought in to assist in procuring bands, vocalists, and instrumentalists in numbers sufficient to satisfy the needs of American Record's various subsidiary companies: Banner, Cameo, Conqueror (made exclusively for Sears, Roebuck), Melotone, Pathé, Perfect, OKeh, Romeo, and Vocalion, a few of which were temporarily withdrawn from the market while the quest for artists proceeded. To guard against future mass departure of talent, Yates and American Record instituted a new artist-acquisition policy, under which all contracts were made directly with the recording company, not through the executive in charge of bookings. At the age of fifty-seven, the talking-machine business had found a more modern way in which to operate.

In September 1934, RCA Victor announced a new and inexpensive record-player attachment, its Duo, Junior, to sell for $16.50, a price more consistent with the times. Easily attached to any radio set, the quality it produced was directly related to that produced by the receiver with which it was connected. Within the year, competing inexpensive record attachments were attracting a new and chiefly youthful market for dance records, one whose tastes were shaped by name bands heard on late-evening broadcasts from hotels and dance halls across the country. This audience, which soon accounted for 40 percent of sales, was looking for accompaniment to a new kind of energetic dancing, known as "swing."

There were few swing musicians among the founders of the new Society of American Recording Artists, formed in California in late 1934. Its distinguished leaders were Al Jolson, chairman of a board that included Fred Astaire, Eddie Cantor, Ben Bernie, Vincent Lopez, Jeanette MacDonald, Gene Austin, Mary Garden, Lucrezia Bori, Jack Benny, and Nathaniel Shilkret. Contracts asking for five to fifteen cents, depending on the station's power, for each use of recorded music were dispatched to the existing 614 commercial broadcasters. Of these, an estimated 400, with a thousand watts or less, regularly used recorded music. Few stations took the matter seriously; they questioned the validity of SARA's power and planned to wait for a court decision.

After they had learned how to run recorded music through control amplifiers in the mid-1920s, broadcasters took the microphones away from in front of a Victrola and offered a more lifelike sound. The vast majority of "one lungers" not affiliated with the networks and dependent on regional or local sponsors for revenue then began to use recorded sound with ever greater frequency. Small stations in such major listening areas as New York, Chicago, and Los Angeles played as much as eighteen hours a day of canned dance and vocal music. Preliminary needle hiss and silence between disks were covered with speech and commercial announcements, but they neglected to identify the source of entertainment, in spite of a Federal Radio Commission rule requiring it.

More prosperous operators also used electrical transcriptions to supplement live or record shows, and thereby incurred the wrath of various locals of the American Federation of Musicians. Correctly anticipating that canned music would finally eliminate the employment of live musicians, AFM leaders, chiefly James C. Petrillo of the Chicago local, forced the radio industry to employ union musicians even to manipulate turntables. When the new Rossevelt administration sought to stimulate economic recovery by forcing codes of business practice and regulated wage scales in various industries, the musicians' union lobbied without success to prevent any use of commercial disks by radio.

Martin Block, whose facile tongue soon successfully defeated all record hiss or needle noise and made the time between records exciting with spell-binding monologues and irresistible advertising pitches, was hired by WNEW in New York as an announcer at twenty dollars a week. Among his duties was keeping listeners turned in when the station's live news-bulletin coverage of the trial of the Lindbergh baby's kidnapper was halted during recesses or technical difficulties. On February 3, 1935, Block introduced listeners to "Make Believe Ballroom," an imaginary, crystal-chandeliered dance palace, where he engaged in an imaginary conversation with Decca's bandleader artist Clyde McCoy between spins of his latest platters. Because

WNEW owned no recordings, Block had purchased them from the nearby Liberty Music Store. When he suggested that his program would be an ideal regular morning and evening feature, he was told to find a sponsor. In a few days, he had a new large supply of records and a client, the maker of Retardo weight-reducing tablets, who had agreed to pay $129.50 for six quarter-hour broadcasts a week, after a test campaign warranted the expense. Block paid ten dollars of his own money for the first broadcast. The following morning, his honey-tongued pitch—"Ladies, does your husband kiss you when he comes home at night? . . . Maybe, just maybe, you've added an extra curve or two. Now here's a simple way . . ." was heard, and it brought 600 orders for Retardo. In two weeks, WNEW raised Block's salary by five dollars, and his sponsor was giving him 10 percent of all mail orders generated by the broadcasts. Within four months, four million New York–area listeners were tuning in to Block's twice-a-day three-and-a-half-hour segments of music by name bandleaders and singers "brought to you by the courtesy of" sponsors who increased his annual income to over $60,000 by World War II. In addition, he received a percentage of all advertising revenue produced by his programs and was the star of an electrically transcribed and syndicated "Make Believe Ballroom" show.

Actually, the program was copied from one Block had heard in Southern California, "The World's Largest Make Believe Ballroom," hosted by Los Angeles announcer Al Jarvis, who also had played phonograph records and talked between them. America's new "Super Radio Salesman" and the premier "record-jockey," had gone to the West Coast from New York with his wife and child in 1930 after an unremarkable career as a street vendor and sidewalk pitchman. There, Block hawked razor blades, announced motorcycle races, sold trade-paper advertising and vacuum cleaners, and sometimes panned for gold, before he went to work for a Tijuana radio station. He was discharged for interrupting Pepsodent toothpaste commercials with announcements he had sold to local merchants without his employer's knowledge. A short stint with a Los Angeles station preceded his return to New York. Block was by no means the first man to air recorded music, but his style and the persuasive ad-libbed commercials he perfected made the business of spinning platters on the air a respectable one for several decades.

Decca owed much of its survival in the early years to Block, who regularly introduced new popular releases in the key New York market. Jack Kapp disapproved from the start, and remained adamant in opposition to radio's use of his products for years. It was only one of many problems besetting the new recording enterprise. Contending that Victor, Columbia, and Brunswick were conspiring to keep his records off retail counters, Kapp instituted a million-dollar suit, charging restraint of trade and naming all three and their managements as defendants. Pretrial postponements and a series of objections on technical grounds occupied the court for many months, but Kapp's action frustrated Brunswick's plan to open a price-cutting war with the regular release of twenty-five-cent disks by Crosby, Lombardo, and other artists he had brought to Decca.

Many of these were among the record, radio, and film stars who formed another new organization, the National Association of Performing Artists in June, seeking to "curb promiscuous broadcasting" of their commercial recordings. A new form of bootleg disk had recently appeared: off-the-air waxings by electrical transcription of broadcasts by name performers, bandleaders, and vocalists from which all advertising and announcements were excised. These generally contained material that had not yet been cut for commercial release, and thus provided small stations with sufficient new selections to broadcast all-Paul Whiteman, all-Bing Crosby, or all-Fred Waring programs, for example, sponsored by druggists, used-car dealers, and other local merchants. Although the conditions and terms of his original 1923 contract with Victor ($250 a side) were still in effect in his newest agreement with the manufacturer, Waring had not been in a recording studio during the past three years. As a result, the popular Ford Motor Company network show, for which he received $12,500 a program, had become a prized target for transcription pirates. This motivated him to take a lead in organizing NAPA. Unlike the now-defunct West Coast SARA group, Waring and his associates worked with ASCAP to amend the copyright laws, but they also were determined to proceed with immediate legal action to test existing legislation. A suit brought by Waring and NAPA against a Pennsylvania recording studio that was selling pirated disks of his music brought an immediate injunction, but radio station WDAS, Philadelphia, NAPA's next target was ready to go to the Supreme Court to win. The association's attorneys charged the station with unauthorized use of Waring recordings and asked for an injunction, but no damages, because the orchestra leader had divested himself of all rights under his Victor contract. The WDAS lawyers argued that the only thing Waring brought to the records other than his name were the special orchestrations he purchased from arrangers, and that any equity in these was also granted to the manufacturer.

In early 1936, a Philadelphia court found for Waring, declaring that his "unique and individual interpretation of musical compositions is important and increases the sale of recordings and compositions. During the past decade he has created a good will and reputation in the mind of the public by the expenditure of upwards of $300,000 as well as by his unusual creative and interpretative talent." The injunction sought as relief was granted, but was stayed on an appeal that dragged through the courts.

Musicians who recorded for the electrical-transcription companies signed away all rights under a "work for hire" contract and were outside the scope of NAPA's concerns. But of interest was the new business in libraries of popular dance-music selections, recorded for radio use only. The West Coast–

based Standard Radio Library, C. P. MacGregor Services, and the RCA-NBC Thesaurus Library appeared soon after the pioneer World Broadcasting Service was established. Victor went into the field only after an employee pointed out that the obsolete Vitaphone sound-on-disk recording presses and playback equipment (worth $16,000 each), being sold to Japan as scrap iron by the Camden factory, could be retrieved for the manufacture of electrical transcriptions. The owners of a recording studio since the takeover of Arthur Judson's Columbia Phonograph Broadcasting System, CBS had contemplated going into the transcription business for several years. Negotiations for the purchase of the Columbia label in 1938 were carried on initially for the unannounced purpose of obtaining its sixteen-inch transcription presses and equipment, not to engage in the classical-music business envisioned by Judson. By 1936, at least 350 stations made yearly contracts with one or more of the four services, each of which permitted only a single station in a market area to use their music, in order to preserve exclusivity.

The first completely recorded radio program of any kind was the inspiration, in the late 1920s, of Raymond Soat, program director for a small station, who had thus solved his problem of selecting individual records, reading commercial announcements between them, and acting as keeper of the turntable and engineer. He had petitioned the Federal Radio Commission to call the recordings he used, in order to coordinate all these functions, "electrical transcriptions," in order to differentiate them from "mechanically reproduced" commercial disks, held in low esteem by large-power stations.

Sensing a potential demand for mass-produced transcribed programs, a group of entrepreneurs and electrical engineers, headed by Percy L. Deutsch, had formed the World Broadcasting System in 1929. Licenses were secured from Western Electric for the exclusive use and sale of sound-on-disk recording and reproducing technology developed for the movie business by Electrical Research Products. World then began to merchandise improved sixteen-inch transcriptions, 33⅓-speed turntables, and high quality amplifiers through ownership of cross-licensed patents with ERPI. When the film industry discarded all ERPI technology in favor of RCA's sound-on-film Photophone process, and royalties from the recording business declined, ERPI went into the transcription business, with a minority interest in World Broadcasting. World improved an old recording process by adapting it for use on a light plastic substance. This in combination with an extremely light pickup reduced surface noise greatly and permitted 200 to 5,000 playings in place of the average "for home use only" disk's 100 to 250. In addition, World transcriptions' "wide range" provided greater fidelity and extended audible sound to a range of 30 to 10,000 cycles. By 1936, more than a million dollars in profit had accrued to ERPI from World and other makers of transcribed programs and music libraries.

From the beginning of the decade, small advertisers aiming at a limited regional market used transcriptions to sell their products, as did national sponsors whose advertising budgets ran into the millions. Wanting more coverage than the usual fifty-station NBC and CBS networks could provide, Ford, Chevrolet, and the Coca-Cola distributors bought fifteen-minute transcribed programs, which enabled them to use two or more stations in a single market over ad-hoc hookups of as many as 400 stations. Coca-Cola's "Refreshment Time with Singin' Sam," which featured good old songs and new tunes, was only one of the early dealer-cooperative series; it ran over several hundred stations for many years.

World boasted in its advertising and promotion for the library service that an electrical transcription cut down to two the eighty operations that took place between the performance in front of a microphone to the actual playing of phonograph records over the air, between dropping a sapphire stylus onto a wax recording blank, and dropping a diamond stylus onto the flexible transparent surface of one of World's Vinylite sixteen-inch electrical transcriptions, which produced the same "loud, clear, and sweet" sound Thomas Edison had claimed for his first tinfoil talking machine.

The transcription business added to Tin Pan Alley's income through licensing agreements, forged by the MPPA, that called for the payment by radio stations or advertisers of a fee for each performance of music copyrighted by its members. In 1935, the MPPA collected $200,000, at the rates of twenty-five cents per performance and fifty cents for performance of a song whose use on networks had been restricted by the publisher. To simplify bookkeeping, the libraries worked out a new arrangement with MPPA: they paid fifteen dollars a year for each song recorded, regardless of the number of times it would be aired, to a maximum of 200 transcriptions manufactured.

Decca weathered its near-disastrous first year only after Kapp found his best customer to be, as few in the business had anticipated, the coin-operated music-machine business. He began to tailor his product to meet the demands of this market, which took 40 percent of all recordings for its 150,000 jukeboxes in 1936. Undercutting competition, he supplied disks to the coin machines at twenty-one cents each, lower than either RCA Victor or Brunswick could afford for their thirty-five-cent lines.

The jukebox, as this re-creation of Edison's original penny-parlor talking machine with earphones and wax cylinders became known, got that name from its great popularity in the South, where people went "jukin' " when in search of inexpensive entertainment, and where half of all coin machines were located. It had been modernized and electrified in the years just before the Great Depression. In 1931, *Variety* reported that music boxes located in speakeasies, ice-cream parlors, restaurants, and cafés were doing a million-dollar-a-year business in a seven-state Midwestern area. Three companies collected half a share of coins from five-, ten-, and twenty-five-cent machines, each priced according to location and clientele. The jukeboxes became the poor man's chief source of public entertainment after repeal of the Prohibition Act in 1933 made neighborhood saloons and beer parlors a rival of movie theaters. Record sales had always succumbed to Tin Pan Alley's traditional summer slump, but the coin machines' demand kept manufacturers busy, since operators changed records every two or three weeks, bicycling them from location to location. Almost half of Decca's total early production was intended for the South, mostly recordings of hillbilly and down-home black music. The East took 35 percent and the West 20. It was these last two markets that made Bing Crosby a national favorite. Sales averaged 20,000 copies for his top hits, but that was not near the potential that the market had revealed in the sale of 150,000 copies of a bawdy, "sophisticated" song, "Sweet Violets," recorded for Vocalion by Gladys Bentley, used principally in coin machines. In October 1936, Eli Oberstein, elevated to full charge of all RCA Victor recording, reported that his company's business had risen over 300 percent in the past year. Two-thirds of the increase had occurred during the summer. Thereafter the company had been selling 1.220 million disks a month, 700,000 of them the cheap Bluebird line and 400,000 on black label, of which Fats Waller was the best seller. An average sale of 300,000 copies a month of Red Seal disks was expected by Christmastime as the demand for classical music enjoyed a resurgence. Arturo Toscanini had been persuaded to return to the recording studios; the start-and-stop recording technique had driven him away seven years earlier. His new albums of Wagner, Beethoven, Brahms, and Rossini sold 25,000 sets by year's end, and the company's valuable friends the music critics heralded a new age for the classical-disk business.

In the electrified jukeboxes' early years, before the sale of spirituous beverages was legal, record manufacturers, ready to do anything to move stock, reduced prices for disks bought in quantity. Now that the coin machines were consuming almost half of all production, price cutting became the rule. Decca cornered the market by meeting and bettering all competition. Victor, in particular, continued to lose money on its cheap records, which only sometimes produced the .0075-cent per-disk profit margin Kapp was willing to live with. Cutting corners by reducing manufacturing costs and general expenses, he paid a publisher royalty of less than the now standard one and a half cents on thirty-five-cent disks, reported sales rather than the *"manufactured* and sold" number called for in the 1909 Copyright Act, and omitted reports on those delivered to coin-machine distributors. He also took the 10 percent breakage discount, which was now excused by the MPPA only as a reward for prompt monthly payments. To curb a payment scheme spreading through the industry, several new requirements were introduced by the MPPA, among them a fifty-day limit on credit and quarterly rather than monthly reports. The MPPA board directed John Paine, its chief operating head, to create a separate mechanical-licensing office to deal with all companies on an equal basis. Herbert Yates, of American Record, who had lost $110,000 to Decca on his twenty-five- and thirty-five-cent disks, had suggested an industrywide fifty-cent price floor, which he believed would allow everybody to operate profitably. He now encouraged the MPPA in its reforms. Only after he got out of the business did the extent of his defalcations and distorted reports to the MPPA become public knowledge.

The five major manufacturers of coin music machines—AMI (Automatic Musical Instrument Company), Homer Capehart, the Wurlitzer Company, Rockola, and Mills Novelty—continued to improve their jukeboxes, increasing the number of records each held from the eight of the early 1930s to twenty-four in 1937. Operators complained when new machines were installed to replace still-operable ones on a take-it-or-leave-it basis, without their consent. They argued that generally only three or four popular hits got the majority of play, the remainder bringing in only an occasional nickel; therefore, an increased number of selections was unnecessary. This logical argument was disregarded. When local legislation put an end to the manufacturers' control of slot machines, candy derricks, and other such devices, organized crime moved into the business and changed not only the usual 50-50 split of all proceeds after the monthly space rental charge was deducted to a 72–25 division from the first coin; it also took over control of all record supplies. From the start, Decca had permitted a full return policy for all jukebox records, crediting them against future sales. The overabundance of discarded but often brand-new or still-playable disks on all labels that followed led to dumping in large cities. Alert record fans sought out their local jukebox supplier for bargains, and in New York City one retail chain regularly bought a million copies of the excess at a time and then sold them at nine, seventeen, and twenty-five cents, depending on the condition and the original price.

The first "album" containing several recordings of popular music by a particular artist or group or built around a central theme was released by RCA Victor in the summer of 1936. It was the "Bix Beiderbecke Memorial Album," six ten-inch disks plus a twelve-page booklet containing extensive historical annotation. As early as 1906, the Victor Talking Machine Company had sold storage "albums" that fitted into space provided in cabinet Victrolas, and in 1909 a complete Tchaikovsky *Nutcracker Suite* was issued in a four-disk container by the German-based Odeon Company, the first to issue double-faced records.

Claiming unhappiness with the way his artists were being handled and American Record's apparent unwillingness to move with the times, as Kapp was doing, Irving Mills had offered to join Decca in early 1935 as supervisor of all dance recordings and bring along all the bands and vocalists he controlled. After he had lectured Kapp and the Decca staff on his expertise in recognizing musical talent and on selection of material for recording, the offer was declined. Kapp told his people not to use any music or talent associated with the Mills management agency. Because Mills was correct in his self-estimation, however, Brunswick, Vocalion, OKeh and Perfect recordings made under his direction sold well, and when his contract expired, he was signed to another, for $60,000 a year. The agreement made him the only recording-artist contractor in the business and guaranteed 120 recordings over a year. The records he produced appeared with the legend "For home use only," and all American Record contracts with him and his artists ceded only the right to release the disks for that purpose, reserving all other property rights to Mills personally.

Mills had always expected to go into the record business himself one day and in late 1936 made no secret of that intention. It was generally known that he had discussed the matter with Jack Kapp, offering to guarantee $52,000 a year against royalties for distribution of his new products. Rather than add to Kapp's major share of the business, Yates and American Record more than met that proposal. Mills's new seventy-five-cent Master and thirty-five-cent Variety records appeared in March 1937, and sold surprisingly well in the first month. Mills had further ambitions, for an international affiliation. In London, the record business was dominated by EMI and British Decca, which had recently effected a working agreement and now effectively controlled Phonograph Performance, Ltd. This new licensor of all British music on the air and in the theater and other public places had collected more than $300,000 in the first half of the year alone. But rather than deal with this monopoly, Mills negotiated with Boosey & Hawks, music publishers and instrument dealers, to establish a European manufacturing, distribution, and selling organization to handle his Master and Variety releases. This intrusion of competition into a controlled market was thwarted by the power of EMI, to which American Record was committed. Unsuccessful in his hope to obtain a European outlet, Mills returned home. There, he was retained as an executive and consultant, with his own recording unit and artists and orchestras as in the past, but all of his new releases now appeared on either the Brunswick or Vocalion label.

RCA Victor, American Record–Brunswick, and Decca prepared to take one step further Mills's plan to sell records for home use only to prevent their use by radio. Kapp had complicated the entire issue of property rights in records earlier in 1937 by intervening in a lawsuit brought, for an unauthorized performance, against WHN, in New York, by one of his artists, Frank Crumit, and NAPA. Claiming that Crumit had already been sufficiently compensated by Decca for making the record, Kapp argued that if a performing license was to be issued and fees collected, it was the function of the manufacturer to do so. Other firms concurred, hoping to make clear to NAPA that the recording companies created "the musical art which evolves in the form of records" by employing a staff of technical and musical experts to arrange the music and to supervise and direct the final performance. With approval of the American Federation of Musicians, in August manufacturers began to print the legend "The use of this record has been licensed under specific patents. The resale of this record except for home use is prohibited" on each record. On behalf of the music publishers, Harry Fox, general manager of the MPPA, informed the manufacturers that they had no authority to do this, under terms of the mechanical licenses issued by the association, that they were presuming on the copyright owners' privileges. He pointed out that the transcription companies paid fifteen dollars per copyright for 200 recordings, a larger royalty than the disk makers' usual one and a half and two cents, for which they received implicit permission to allow their products to be performed on radio. The MPPA did not intend to give an unfair competitive advantage to the makers of "for home use only" records. He added, however, that the publishers had no desire to frustrate any move by the manufacturers to protect their wares from free use over the air. American Record–Brunswick, Decca, and RCA Victor continued plans to license broadcasters and added an amplified restricted-use notice on all record envelopes.

The MPPA's response was the first probe of record-company account books in history. It was based on a claim that evidence had recently been been found that most manufacturers allowed unlimited return privileges to jukebox operators and suppliers and treated such dealings as rentals rather than outright sales. Searches by MPPA's accountants had revealed special deals with recording companies made by certain publishers and incomplete or inaccurate royalty accounting. Victor, the most honest of all the manufacturers in reporting, tightened its control over distribution to jukeboxes and notified all dealers and distributors that they could no longer supply broadcasters with records, either at the discounts they had been offering or at retail prices, on pain of losing their franchise. The most tangible and lasting reform to stem from the investigation was the formation of a central MPPA mechanical-licensing bureau with standard and uniform contracts, supervised by Harry Fox.

Finding themselves victims of equally inaccurate weekly sales reports from the manufacturers, *Variety*'s editors abruptly dropped the periodical's recently restored weekly popularity charts in March 1938. The corporate embroidery of sales figures was excused on grounds that cutthroat competition in the jukebox market, where people relied on *Variety*'s figures when stocking their machines, had necessitated the rigged statistics, which were based on advance orders for new releases rather than on accumulated sales, as in the past. The magazine's ban on this type of chart stood for years.

All three companies constituting America's entire record business in 1938 were eager to capture a lion's share of the automatic-music-machine field, which now accounted for 60 percent of all purchases, three-fourths of them Kapp's releases. In order to change the ratio, RCA Victor was ready to lose a penny or two per sale, and in the summer instructed the Bluebird people to concentrate on that market. Fats Waller, long a best-selling artist on the seventy-five-cent label, was moved over to the cheaper one. A Canadian who sounded uncannily like Bing Crosby was signed, and Artie Shaw was moved over from Brunswick to tap the youthful swing market, in which the Big Apple, Little Peach, Buffalo Leap, Shag, and other vivacious dances prevailed and Benny Goodman ruled. On the basis of sales of 800,000 disks a month to the jukeboxes, it was believed that Kapp cleared a profit of 1.8 cents from each thirty-five-cent disk, so Bluebird executives slashed their wholesale price to eighteen cents, a cut Kapp was not able to match and remain in business. Sales of Bluebird disks in 1938 were a few hundred thousand copies shy of the 4.1 million black labels, but twice those of the Red Seals.

Even though he had maintained his higher wholesale cost to jukeboxes, Kapp still ruled the thirty-five-cent record world, with sales of 12 million disks in 1938, 95 percent of them his lowest-priced products. A trio of girl singers, the Andrews Sisters, who were hired to replace the Boswell Sisters when they chose show business and the joys of life in New Orleans, had given him a smash hit with "Bei Mir Bist Du Schön" and were following it up with "The Beer Barrel Polka." Ella Fitzgerald, a teen-age black singer with a gift for singing with a swing, made hit after hit. And there was always Bing Crosby, the old reliable, who refused to leave Decca even when offered $3,000 a recorded side to do so. Kapp had always believed in melody, as the placard hanging around the neck of a wooden cigar-store Indian in his office lobby affirmed with its query "Where's the Melody?" Some Victor executives doubted the future of that "rhythmic hodge-podge" called "swing" and expressed a hope that melody would come back. Although sales of records by Benny Goodman were always substantially above the 5,000 that had been regarded as a hit only a few years back, they argued, only two of his platters had sold in great quantities, "Stompin' at the Savoy" and "Don't Be That Way." In the future, *Variety* editorialized, "records will have to let the fans know what they are playing and keep within recognition distance of the melody as originally conceived." There was, it believed, a scarcity of good song material. "Slick clikeroos" like the score for Walt Disney's full-length color cartoon *Snow White and the Seven Dwarfs* were no longer coming out. That one was a mainstay for the entire business throughout 1938, eventually selling more than 1.5 million copies on all labels and more than 800,000 pieces of printed music. The "general apathy was solely among the writers and not the public," *Variety* explained.

Blithely unaware of any shortages of suitable material, the coin-machine trade grew at a rate of 25 percent above that of 1937. A conservative estimate by the Wurlitzer Company, supplier of three quarters of all automatic music machines, held that no more than 175,000 existed in the United States; this conclusion was based on the fact that there were less than 170,000 liquor licenses, and "the selling of drinks is almost synonymous with the mechanical talking machine.'' More informed sources put the figure at 225,000, and ASCAP and the MPPA remained convinced that nearly half a million were in use, including several hundred thousand reconditioned machines that were still capable of nabbing nickels.

Whatever the number, it was owing to them that Decca was moving up on the world's greatest record company, a success that did not go unnoticed by Victor's leading black-label artists. Guy Lombardo, itching to jump to Decca, had been persuaded by his network-radio sponsors to stay with the more expensive line, because it lent greater prestige. After refusing to go on Victor's cheaper Bluebird label, Paul Whiteman, who had been the company's most reliable artist in point of sales for a decade, looked to Kapp to provide the exploitation and merchandising the veteran company could not. Bing Crosby was satisfied to ''make a good waxing'' for Decca and gross between $35,000 and $40,000 a year from a guarantee and royalty contract, much less than his annual take from motion pictures and network radio.

Ironically, the most effective and aggressive merchandising in the business was being done for classical recordings, where a profit of 10 to 20 percent now prevailed. It was directed by Victor's advertising vice-president, Thomas F. Joyce, whose efforts were responsible for the distribution of 150,000 record players to the public in a single year. On March 15, 1938, the Victor Record Society was launched; membership cost six dollars a year plus an initial purchase of eight dollars' worth of recordings. Built on the highly successful Book-of-the-Month Club concept and expected to bring in 120,000 members and an initial $8.3 million in disk sales, the society sent new subcribers a record-playing attachment, valued at $14.95, that could be plugged into any radio receiver; *The Music America Loves Best*, an illustrated monthly magazine devoted to both classical and popular music, *The Victor Society Preview;* and ''correspondence privileges,'' giving them access to Victor's director of music. The expenditure of an additional sixty dollars annually, slightly more than a dollar a week, provided a dividend of $1.50 in Victor products for each fifteen-dollar outlay, a premium for which the local dealer paid. An all-out publicity and promotion campaign was instituted, using streamers, displays, broadsides, direct-mail solicitation, and time on ''RCA Magic Key,'' a radio program heard six nights a week over nine NBC stations.

The society's activities were supplemented by a scheme involving the company's custom recordings service. Nathan Hurwitz, a Brooklyn entrepreneur and expert in advertising and mail-order promotion, was franchising a plan to build newspaper circulation by giving away low-cost classical-music albums for $2.99 each and coupons clipped from participating papers. A no-frills record player was available for three dollars and a pledge to buy all ten advertised albums. Hurwitz's Publishers Service Company disposed of more than 300,000 albums (over a million disks) in the winter of 1938–39. They were manufactured by Victor from previously unreleased masters or ones cut from the active catalogue.

Kapp expanded his quality music line with the introduction of twelve-inch one-dollar recordings, drawn exclusively from British Decca and masters leased from small companies in Europe and Latin America. With reciprocal access to the HMV portion of EMI, Victor offered principally European classical music. As had been true under former owners, the Columbia Master Works albums released by American Record–Brunswick were pressed from imported masters of principally foreign performers and music.

RCA Victor's monopoly of classical music, and an evident disdain for many leading American artists and conductors, led directly to the acquisition of the American Record Company by the Columbia Broadcasting System in late 1938. The move was suggested by the concert impresario Arthur Judson, and came at a time when CBS was ready to move into the electrical-transcription business, an area in which the Radio Corporation of America was a major factor. Judson had been largely responsible for the creation of the original CBS network in 1927 and, as the second-largest stockholder, remained on its board after a controlling interest was transferred to a group of Philadelphia investors headed by the Paley and Levy families. Judson's principal occupation was the management of a concert-booking bureau and of both the Philadelphia and the New York Philharmonic symphony orchestras. In the darkest days of the Depression, a coalition of independent concert managers, at Judson's suggestion, formed the Columbia Concerts Corporation, with William S. Paley as chairman of the board, representing the majority stockholder, CBS, and Judson as president. Because most managers preferred to represent artists from whose bookings they collected a percentage of income for every performance, rather than conductors, whose services were recompensed by salary, Judson and the new coalition represented almost every important symphony conductor in the United States, as well as many distinguished instrumentalists. When many of his artists complained that the lack of exploitation implicit in a recording contract handicapped them in securing international bookings, Judson set about to remedy the lack. He suggested to fellow directors and Paley that a recording company controlled by CBS could have exclusive access to its talent roster and become a major competitor of NBC and its Artists' Bureau, which handled concert artists as well as popular performers.

Originally, CBS intended only to retrieve the Columbia name by purchasing that record company. It soon succumbed to Yates's irresistible asking price of $700,000 for American Record, with all its assets and properties, a modest figure dictated by a year during which sales were about six million disks, one fifth of the total market. With the company came the Bridgeport factory where electrical transcriptions could readily be produced and Brunswick's new and remodeled studios, one of them large enough to accommodate a symphony orchestra. Edward Wallerstein was lured away from RCA Victor to become president and given authority to develop a recorded classical repertory at prices that would attract those buyers of serious music thought to be 30 percent of the entire market. The latest developments in recording technology were introduced into Columbia's studios, including Millertape, which was being used on an experimental basis.

An army engineer, who had been in charge of building the 1.350-million-watt station in France that had sent the first radio message around the world, in 1918, James A. Miller had also organized the Vitavox Company in Hollywood, one of the first to record sound on motion pictures, which was sold to Warner Brothers. His experiments with improved sound reproduction led to a new system for engraving sound impulses on a special film, named after him, which produced the highest-fidelity recording on tape prior to the 1950s. Cutting and editing of speech or music, impossible on wax-based masters, was easily accomplished on Millertape—celluloid strips of 2,000 feet on which thirty minutes of sound could be recorded. The British Broadcasting Corporation began to use it in 1935, and electrically transcribed commercial programs reproduced from Millertape masters became fairly common on the Continent. With it, a radio show could be pieced together from different takes, much as movies were put together by film editors. Retouchers could eliminate words and correct lisps and mistakes. Kay Kyser's dance orchestra was recorded in February 1939 on Millertape as well as on the aluminum recording blanks, coated with many layers of acetate varnish, that were standard in the Columbia studios.

Having won an outstanding victory in its fight to increase the employment of union musicians by broadcasters, the AFM resumed the war on canned music. New licensing agreements were approved at the musicians' annual convention in 1938, and were accepted by RCA Victor, Columbia, and Decca soon after. Before a recording session could take place, it had to be registered with the local AFM chapter, and union representatives looked in to verify the presence of paid-up members or that of union musicians in a number equal to non–card bearers. The AFM also threatened, for the first time, to remove its license to major companies when officials of the black musicians local in Chicago complained that only nonunion musicians were hired to make race recordings and that the stand-by provision in the AFM agreement with the record company was being ignored. Chicago and New York were the two centers for black music recording, and the artist-and-repertory men employed to supervise recordings worked along the lines of the first Peer contract with Victor: they bought all rights for a small sum, kept the publishing rights, and paid only a small or no mechanical royalty. Fearing a walkout by white musicians, Victor and Decca immediately complied with AFM regulations, a manifestation of power that surprised many in the business.

Working for almost a year through the symphony conductors he represented, Judson secured the services of several American orchestras for Columbia. When the European war put an end to all nonessential recording there, the battle for American classical-music talent between Columbia and Victor concluded only after almost every top-rated conductor and his orchestra were signed.

To implement the "good music equals public service" programing used by the networks to win over the custodians of public taste and appease the Federal Communications Commission, CBS had already increased time on the air devoted to educational programing during unsold periods. Now more emphasis was placed on serious music. CBS's most highly regarded cultural broadcast was the weekly Sunday afternoon concert by the New York Philharmonic, which joined Columbia Records when its RCA Victor contract shortly expired. In anticipation of that event, NBC had organized its own symphony orchestra, under Arturo Toscanini, raiding both European and American orchestras to obtain the best first-chair players. Until the broadcasters' association censured the scheme as a violation of its code, RCA Victor offered free Red Seal disks and a transcribed "Music You Want When You Want It" series to radio stations around the country. The Community Concerts division of Columbia Concerts Corporation, in which CBS owned 55 percent of all stock, took a full session of classical-music concerts to 375 American cities and towns. This competition for his attention exposed the classical-music lover, hence prospective record buyer, to more music by Bach, Brahms, Beethoven, and other masters, and an occasional dollop of contemporary American music, than he had ever heard before on the air or in an auditorium.

Popular music was not neglected by Wallerstein and his hard-working employees, many of whom were inspired by their involvement with a management that intended to change the character of a business they loved. American Record's stable of contract artists was purged; only those whose prospects appeared bright were retained. Reacting to Columbia's aggressive product exploitation, contract bandleaders cross-plugged each other's latest releases on commercial and sustaining broadcasts. A nighttime network program featured a different Columbia "Young Man with a Band" every week, and the CBS "Saturday Night Swing Club" regularly offered live previews of new Columbia and Vocalion releases. Columbia talent scouts and recording executives raided the Victor roster for swing and dance bands and popular vocalists whose contracts were about to expire, and became regular habitués of dance halls, night clubs, gin mills, and 52nd Street swing joints to hear tomorrow's talent.

The already hectic business faced the prospect of added turmoil with the addition of a new entrant: Eli Oberstein and his United States Record Corp. When Ralph Peer left Victor to concentrate on the music-publishing company he planned to build into another Tin Pan Alley giant, Oberstein had taken over recording of all race and hillbilly music. As times worsened in the depressed rural South, where Peer's artists had sold best, all such releases were cut back, and Victor's recording staff was regularly reduced until only Oberstein was left to supervise all the studio work. He remained in that spot, except for a brief interim as manager of some Harms companies. Never profiligate with corporate funds where compensation was concerned, Victor paid him only $6,000 throughout the late 1930s, according to the recorded reminiscences of Steven Sholes. Oberstein's life style demanded a much higher income, which allegedly came from a share in the cut ins, under-the-desk deals, bribery, and participation in music-business speculation at an insider's privileged price—all of which were regarded as normal practices at the time.

The success of Benny Goodman, Tommy Dorsey, Larry Clinton, Glenn Miller, and others he had brought to the company gave Oberstein the reputation of being second only to Jack Kapp as a shrewd judge of talent, as well as complete mastery of recording-studio techniques. In early 1938, it came as a surprise when Frank Walker, in one of his first official moves, fired Oberstein without any public explanation, replacing him with Leonard Joy, an Oberstein assistant. Following Wallerstein's departure for Columbia, Walker had been moved from the custom-record service, which included supervision of all electrical-transcription manufacture, to head the entire Victor operation.

Oberstein's immediate announcement of a new recording company was reminiscent of Kapp's action on his departure from Brunswick in 1934, when he took with him the cream of the company's artists. With an assured minimum order for one million disks a month from a syndicate of investors that controlled 150,000 jukeboxes, Oberstein overnight became a factor in the realignment of recording firms that was taking place. But his United States Record Corp. was foredoomed to disaster. His declaration that Tommy Dorsey—whose recordings of "Marie" and "Song of India" had each sold more than 150,000 copies without benefit of any music-publisher or Victor promotion—Artie Shaw, Glenn Miller, Sammy Kaye, and other artists would also leave the company proved inaccurate. Dorsey was retained with a new long-term Victor contract and a $60,000 guarantee, and others were kept by similar attractive terms. Columbia stepped into the confusion and signed Benny Goodman, an addition in which the company's jazz and swing talent scout John Hammond played an important role. Several of Goodman's key musicians in the famous Carnegie Hall Concert group also joined Columbia, with newly formed orchestras, among them the trumpet player Harry James.

Oberstein's original backers proved to be involved in organized gambling and other underworld activities and scurried into the shadows when their participation was revealed, taking with them the chain of machines on which the venture depended. Other investors came and went as the products of a man regarded as infallible failed to sell in substantial quantities. Oberstein's only major success was "She Had to Lose It at the Astor," which became a hit on the coin machines because of its suggestive lyrics. Bitter legal actions involving Oberstein and RCA (the latter changing misappropriation of corporate funds by its former employee) titillated the music business for weeks. United States Record slid into bankruptcy.

The recording business was further complicated by a surprise announcement in the late summer of 1939 that the Brunswick label would be retired, and henceforth all its new releases would appear under a Columbia imprint and sell for fifty cents. This created an immediate problem for RCA Victor. Under its agreement with Benny Goodman that old releases could not be marketed at a price lower than that offered by any other manufacturer, it was impossible to move his records to the thirty-five-cent Bluebird line as planned.

In less than a year, the price cut brought Columbia's sales back to those of 1927. Even in competition with Decca, new releases sold so well that many artists were moved up from the lower-priced Vocalion catalogue. Total Columbia sales in December 1939 were up almost 600 percent over the previous year and for all of the year up by an average of 350 percent.

With the best-selling single record of the year, "The Beer Barrel Polka," done by a Czechoslovak brass band and selling for seventy-five cents, Victor reported total income up by a substantial 700 percent over the 1933 low mark. Decca's 90 percent share of all jukebox sales was responsible for total production of 13 million disks in 1939, and a total pretax income of around four million dollars. It was the best year the record and music business had enjoyed since 1929; $750,000 was paid in mechanical royalties. The major publishing firms once again assigned song pluggers to maintain regular contact with the record manufacturers, a practice abandoned when sales plummeted in 1932.

The progress was made without the questionable benefit of the promotion of new releases by radio stations. The still untangled complex web of property rights in commercial records had bogged down in the process of appeal to higher courts. Many broadcasters were reluctant to face the possibility of liability for payment to the manufacturers or to the artists, or possibly both. Caution on the part of high-powered broadcasting facilities increased dependence on staff musicians and vocal performers or on the transcribed libraries. Radio's worst fears were confirmed in July 1939, when Judge Vincent L. Leibell, of the federal court in New York, found for Paul Whiteman in his action against radio station WNEW. The National Association of Performing Artists saw it as a triumph in the long fight by artists to establish control over their mechanically reproduced music. Counsel for RCA, however, immediately claimed that NAPA was now effectively eliminated from the licensing picture by the ruling, which put that right firmly into the manufacturers' hands. After advising all recording artists that it intended to share licensing revenue with them, Victor had joined the Whiteman lawsuit, in order to obtain a ruling that would exclude performers from licensing their rights personally. Leibell found for the manufacturer in that regard, ruling that Whiteman was privileged to reserve broadcast rights provided the company agreed, but that he could license use only in conjunction with RCA Victor.

Victor promptly went ahead with plans to license broadcasters, and was followed at once by Columbia and Decca. An immediate outcry from broadcasters followed the announcement of a scale of fees for air play that ranged from $100 to $300 per month. Stations in the top grade using the product of all three manufacturers were confronted with monthly fees of $900, in addition to their payments to ASCAP and the transcribed library services.

Many people believed that the record companies were really more interested in terminating all radio-station use of records than in collecting fees. Few stations signed licenses, and more turned to the transcription companies, World, NBC Thesaurus, and Standard, which had been joined during the past several years by Associated (part of the Muzak operation), LangWorth, and McGregor. The quality of transcriptions was superior to that of commercial recordings or the over-the-air sound of network programs, which, because of telephone-line transmission, was cut off at 5,000 cycles. Wide-range recording and transmitting equipment and other higher-fidelity technology could be found in 544 of the nation's 761 commercial stations, with an on-the-air frequency-range reproduction extended to 10,000 cycles, 2,000 more than the most improved commercial disks.

The transcription business had demonstrated the commercial viability of a truer and more faithful reproduction of music and speech for home use, one that eventually contributed to a return to the prosperity the record business had enjoyed in the years before 1921. Improved amplification, speakers, and record-playing components capable of reproducing the extended range were available in fully assembled but expensive units. Capehart offered a super-deluxe jukebox for the home, with a record changer that accommodated both ten- and twelve-inch disks. These were sold by franchised dealers, usually the most exclusive music store in each territory. Housed in handsome, less garish pieces of furniture, combination radio-phonographs assembled by small independent factories delivered high fidelity at a more modest price than the Capehart. Most Americans, however, had not been exposed to or were not aware of the miracle of purer reproduced sound already possible, but were content with the comparatively antiquated modern record machine, over which the latest releases sounded better than ever.

Almost every day the general and trade press reported a new boom in the record business, bringing back memories of the World War I period, when 125 million disks were sold in a single year. Glenn Miller's recording of "Tuxedo Junction" sold 115,000 copies in its first week on the counters, a sensational response to the bandleader's constant prerelease plugging on his radio programs. "Wee" Bonnie Baker's revival of the old favorite "Oh, Johnny," with the Orrin Tucker band, went over the 400,000 mark and with other versions amassed a million-copy sale, just under "The Beer Barrel Polka." The Curtis company, publishers of the *Saturday Evening Post, Ladies' Home Journal,* and *Country Gentleman,* established a record-distributing subsidiary to supply its 60,000 newsstands. The American News Company, which had already installed sheet-music racks around the country, announced plans for its own twenty-five-cent record company, a project in which Eli Oberstein was involved briefly. Leading specialty music stores came into the business with their own dollar disks, aimed at their smart, sophisticated clientele. It appeared that everybody ready to buy a twelve-dollar license from the MPPA was preparing to join the twenty-eight record makers already licensed by the American Federation of Musicians, all but three of them recently formed.

Columbia's price cut on all popular records had been responsible in great measure for this resurgence of optimism. In March 1940, Columbia invaded the classical market with a new Master Work line of two-dollar disks by American orchestras (one of CBS's original purposes) seventy-five-cent and dollar concert and operatic music recorded from European masters. Within the month, Victor's long supremacy in that field was suffering a serious sales blow, not only from Columbia but also from Decca, whose red-label dollar disks purposely imitated the Red Seal and offered many of the same artists RCA Victor had imported for years from HMV. Price cutting followed price cutting, and new seventy-five-cent and dollar Victor recordings of such hallowed names as Caruso, Paderewski, Jeritza, Kreisler, and Gigli went on sale. The trade awaited a general price reduction for the entire RCA Victor output. It came in August, fifteen days after the upstart Columbia management dealt the final blow when all Master Works disks were reduced to a dollar each and Beethoven's "Pastoral" Symphony, including the album, could be had for $5.50.

As Wallerstein had anticipated, every company benefited, and orders generally rose 200 to 1,000 percent, promising a 100-million record-sale year. After the reduction of its top-of-the-line records, Victor enjoyed an unprecedented buying spree; dollar volume from the Red Seals increased more than seven times in a month. Columbia crowed about a 1,500 percent increase in Master Works sales and a general 400 percent increase in dollar volume over the period before the price war started.

The remarkable change was explained by a *New York Times* editorial of September 18, 1940, which found it a dramatic example of "surviving individualism in a mass production age," made possible only by radio. "By turning the wireless knob a person now may command the services of the very greatest talent. . . . But a hunger may rise in the soul for something by Bach played by Stokowski or Toscanini when the men are not available.

Then comes the family phonograph. Or a man may be a glutton and insist
on two encores of the third movement of Beethoven's Fifth. . . . The phonograph on the family table will repeat as often as the neighbors can stand
it.''

For years, American opinion molders, including the *Times* and the record
companies, had praised radio when it offered a fairly limited classical-music
fare, and condemned it for gross overuse of popular products. Judge Leibell
appeared to have given the manufacturers power to curb that surfeit. Ruling
on the appeal in *Waring* v. *WDAS,* the Pennsylvania Supreme Court had
recently affirmed the artist's right to prevent unauthorized performance of
his music. In December 1940, the United States Supreme Court refused to
review a subsequent reversal of the Pennsylvania decision. In effect, property rights ended with the sale of a record. Broadcasters could no longer be
constrained from using music recorded ''for home use only.''

The golden age of the disk jockey was about to begin.

CHAPTER 11

Music in Motion Pictures

When speaking to the press and public groups in the early 1930s, Will H. Hays, president of the Motion Picture Producers and Distributors of America, Hollywood's self-inflicted guardian of morality and ambassador to the political world, described the industry that provided his annual $600,000 budget as the fifth-largest American business, with an estimated audience of 115 million. The statistics were a typical promoter's sham to gloss over the true facts. Attendance actually had fallen by 40 percent in a few months, principally because of interior films, and Hollywood was in the first year of a decline that continued until 1934. Significant improvements in the vital process of recording speech on film made production less time-consuming and expensive. For the next several years, however, Warner Brothers clung to the sound-on-disk process that had made the company a leader in pushing films into the sound era. Having learned early that it was no longer feasible to make pictures only for Hollywood, Warner committed itself to a policy of less art and more box office, and managed to lose only $30 million in operating costs during the next four years, while competitors went into bankruptcy. The gangster movie was the company's salvation. Cheap to make and peopled with Broadway actors not yet well known enough to command the salaries of established stars, these brawling, gunfire-ridden reels of excessive violence reigned at the box office in the early thirties.

In the industrywide wave of reducing costs and cutting corners wherever possible, much like that affecting most American business, Warner, which had spent nine million dollars to buy a major share of Tin Pan Alley, turned the operation of its music holdings over to the former owners. Songwriters imported from the East were sent back on the expiration of their contracts, and the studio music staff was cut down to a single person, Leo Forbstein, who was responsible for all film scoring and hired musicians or songwriters only when the need arose. Hollywood had come to think of popular songs as only something to use in comedy scenes; other sequences were accompanied by bits and snatches from old releases or music written by the few trained composers still on salary, men like Alfred Newman at United Artists and Max Steiner at RKO. They wrote the lyrics, too, made the orchestrations, and conducted the final recording sessions.

The year 1931 was not distinguished for music in pictures. Only "Reaching for the Moon," written by Irving Berlin for a Douglas Fairbanks feature, made any perceptible bid for popularity. The year's top-grossing films included a single musical, *The Smiling Lieutenant,* starring Maurice Chevalier, who had become one of Paramount's top box-office favorites after his Continental charm and bewitching French accent had first been displayed on the American screen two years earlier. Paramount still maintained a large music department, with a staff of thirty-six that included eight New York songwriters and a French lyricist-translator for the international market, which provided 40 percent of all rentals. Despite a drop from the 143 songwriters under contract to all companies during the musical talkies' short-lived heyday to fewer than 20 in 1931, several hundred songs were used, generally acquired directly from the music publishers. The business had turned half circle since 1929, when music reigned and a film was rarely released without a title song and original popular music. The elaborate musical picture with vast choruses of dancers and singers, like those in Broadway productions, was no longer affordable, and the Academy of Motion Picture Arts and Sciences, formed by the moguls to forestall the organization of a screen actors' union, had yet to regard popular music as worthy of its Oscars.

Jack Robbins, Tin Pan Alley's perennial stormy petrel, was in the forefront of those who found fault with Hollywood's penny-pinching way of "spotting" songs in feature releases: selecting a piece haphazardly or having one written on the spot, and then recording it, all in a single day. His own contract songwriters, Nacio Herb Brown and Arthur Freed, were products of a studio music department, men who had written major commercial hits for musical films but now could not obtain a writing assignment. His crusade for the use of songs in movies was regarded as futile by the New York music business, especially in light of the recent sale of the De Sylva, Brown & Henderson business back to the original owners. The company had been taken over in 1929 for a reported three million dollars, 10 percent in cash and the balance in Warner stock, which was immediately sold at the prevailing high prices. The new transaction was on a strict stock-transfer basis and initiated a desperate struggle to raise cash in order to buy the $350,000 of Warner securities demanded in exchange.

The first of a series of recurring shifts of executive stance on the role of popular music in movies took place in late 1932, when the ratio of production costs to income left a wide gap compared with those of 1929. Four million dollars had been saved by lowering expenditures for story material and film rights to Broadway legitimate and musical properties, and another $18 million by lending stars, contract players, writers, and directors to other studios. The imposition of a 10 percent federal tax on theater tickets that cost more than forty cents forced admission prices down to as little as a dime, and was responsible for the introduction of double features, bank and dish nights, Screeno and Bingo games. MGM set a limit of $200,000 on new productions, but found that costs had doubled by the time they were ready for release. Moreover, like the other major studios, MGM found it difficult to maintain the necessary fifty-two features a year to keep its screen and vaudeville theater chains from going dark.

As the picture business had done since Thomas Edison signed the first Broadway star to make a silent movie, the industry turned to the currently most popular entertainment medium—network radio—for entertainers with guaranteed appeal. Bing Crosby, Kate Smith, the Mills Brothers, the Boswell Sisters, and some others with top-ranking radio programs went west to make *The Big Broadcast,* the first of many successful movies starring on-the-air personalities. After the final international distribution fees were counted up, Al Jolson's 1929 singing-talking picture *The Singing Fool* was found to have grossed five million dollars, a result not lost on Warner Brothers, where new sound-on-film equipment was being installed to replace the Vitaphone process. Faced with impending receivership, Warner now pinned its future to the type of movie that had provided a springboard for Vitaphone. Plans were announced for two productions in which songs would be important to the plot and not dragged in, as in the past. United Artists, Fox, Paramount, and MGM also planned musicals, along the same lines, with no chorus appearing from nowhere and with no symphony-size orchestra to accompany a radio star vocalizing in the shower. Only Chevalier's naughty operetta-flavored Paramount musicals had been consistently popular, but Warner went again to the Broadway and Tin Pan Alley songwriters for its songs. Harry Warren and Al Dubin were teamed to write the music for *42nd Street,* a low-budget film with a Cinderella plot set in Manhattan show business. The studio's modest production plans were dashed by the unexpected genius of Busby Berkeley, who was the last dance director with Broadway experience not yet signed by any studio. Berkeley, who did not know even the basic positions of classic stage dance, possessed a hitherto-unrevealed and incomparable sense of the camera's potential for providing views of dancing ensembles that could never be seen in the confines of a legitimate theater. It was coupled with a gift for telling a fast-moving story within the limitations of song-and-dance situations, to which music and choreography added the natural movements that bore his own stamp. Production costs mounted with each bold venture by Berkeley into new film dimensions, first in *42nd Street* and then in the *Gold Diggers* series, *Footlights Parade, Dames,* and other successes: sets with as many as three orchestras and hundreds of dancing boys and girls in geometric patterns unfolding to music; the use of a single camera as a personal eye to replace the multiple setups favored by less adventurous directors; the monorail camera crane; costumes that gave a near-nude effect; spectacular dancing and swimming scenes; a waterfall built indoors at a cost of $97,000. Profits from these spectaculars sustained Warner during another periodic economic dip, and Berkeley was permitted excesses long after audiences and the industry had turned to the personality musical, featuring stage and radio entertainers and slim opera divas.

The first of the former was RKO's 1933 *Flying Down to Rio,* with Fred Astaire and Ginger Rogers, in which dancing was integral to the plot line, and audiences were exposed to the monster camera's-eye view of sophisticated ballroom dancing. Although Astaire claimed humbly that he only "put his feet in the air and moved around them," the eloquence of his dancing with Rogers and several other partners in a series of successful miniature musicals raised screen dance and music to a level of perfection and public appeal seldom enjoyed by other forms. In 1934, film music was first recognized by the Motion Picture Academy, with Oscars for "The Continental" from Astaire's *The Gay Divorcee* and the score for *One Night of Love,* starring Grace Moore, a Metropolitan Opera star. More to the point for the music business, quality screen songs also sold sheet music: those from *42nd Street* and *Gold Diggers* had a combined sale of 400,000 copies, and "Who's Afraid of the Big Bad Wolf?" from a Walt Disney cartoon two-reeler, *Three Little Pigs,* sold roughly the same number.

Strenuous song-plugging activity in New York, still the center of network broadcasting, was essential to the success of both the songs and the movies from which they came. Bing Crosby and Dick Powell, a Warner contract player featured in singing musicals, were recognized as the best movie-song hit makers; Crosby's continued plugging of numbers from his films never resulted in less than a "semi-hit," and "Love in Bloom" was a 500,000-copy seller. Rudy Vallee's reputation as a music publisher's best single source of exploitation was still intact after five years of broadcasting, and Kate Smith, the "Songbird of the South," who had risen from small-time vaudeville to the Palace and musical comedy, ranked close behind him.

Having given up song writing after the dissolution of the team of De Sylva, Brown, and Henderson over arguments about their individual talents, Buddy De Sylva, now producing movies in Hollywood, was among the first to recognize that the system of restricting the use of songs on the networks (a policy surviving from the days when all production songs were barred from vaudeville) was foolish. He had learned under a master of promotion, Max Dreyfus, who used the ASCAP lists of restricted-production songs to regulate radio's use of his copyrights. De Sylva argued that nighttime programs for which commercial sponsors paid thousands each week could be used to create advance interest in songs and at far less expense. Whenever a singing star or bandleader announced the picture's title (which could be insured by under-the-table subsidies), the public's interest was stimulated. Despite the large sales of some movie songs, the profits that accrued were a minor consideration when compared with the potential box-office returns. De Sylva recommended selective plugging at the national level at least two weeks in advance of national release, followed by concentrated mass exploitation during first-, second-, and third-class runs.

In approving double-feature presentations, against which the major studios had fought since their introduction, the government-mandated National Recovery Act's code of Hollywood business practices created a demand for secondary, low-budget features from about 10,000 of the country's screen theaters and led to the organization of independent shoestring operators specializing in action pictures. From these came the earliest singing-cowboy movies, initially with the interpolation of popular hillbilly and old-time songs and then with a style of music with roots in Tin Pan Alley and vaudeville, like Jimmie Rodgers's hit recordings. A hillbilly cowboy singer, discovered by Jack and Dave Kapp and recorded for one of Herbert Yates's three-for-a-dollar companies, was suggested for a role in a musical Western produced by a bankrupt company Yates had acquired. In Gene Autry and, after him, Roy Rogers and lesser luminaries, the image of the pure and unblemished cowboy was fixed, the composite of ideal country-folk values, and their songs became part of the country-and-western music that flowed like an underground stream waiting until it could run free in the sunshine years later.

Paramount survived a complete takeover by its Wall Street backers chiefly with products less pure than the clean-cut independent cowboy movies. Mae West, whose sultry invitation to "c'mon up and see me sometime" was responsible for nearly six million dollars in rentals from three pictures in which she sang the joys of dalliance, provided the company's margin of profit. Because of her saucy innuendoes and a general loosening of morality in the musicals that followed, perceived chiefly by the church-affiliated Legion of Decency and its supporters, the blacklisting of specific movies and actors ran rampant. Projects were scrapped, stories were rewritten, and, in the interest of an improved general moral tone, most studio heads turned to properties suitable for the family trade. Jerome Kern's simon-pure Broadway hits were reproduced for the screen, Victor Herbert's *Babes in Toyland* was revived, Maurice Chevalier and Jeanette MacDonald appeared in a purged version of *The Merry Widow* by Rodgers and Hart, and the year's biggest box-office draw was a five-year-old girl, Shirley Temple, who succeeded West as the year's top star.

With producers demanding radio performances for title songs or any connected with a current release, paying for play grew to such proportions that the Music Publishers Protective Association initiated the most drastic reforms in its history to purge the business of "its greatest evil." To enforce the new regulations, Lew Diamond, head of Paramount's Famous Music firm and an official of the publishers' group, promised to out-bribe all comers, from a $100,000 payoff budget. This was clearly a violation of the music-business NRA code and would also cut independent publishers out of the fight for radio performance. In order to forestall a trek to Washington for relief through the Federal Trade Commission, Diamond withdrew his threat, and payola returned.

Herman Starr, Warner Brothers' vice-president of music operations, regularly shifted all rights in movie scores to less active firms in order to improve their ASCAP ratings, which, owing to recent changes in classification standards, were based on network-radio performances. Determined to enforce Jack Warner's directive that his music holdings must provide at least a million dollars annually by 1936, Starr was preparing to withdraw from ASCAP unless performance royalties increased significantly. Throughout 1935, company employees concentrated on radio plugs to ensure that Warner copyrights represented at least 40 percent of all the music used by network radio. The competition for higher ASCAP payments was intense in a year when eight of the ten most-performed songs, thirty of the top fifty, came from movies. Sixteen of the eighty-four musicals and feature pictures with songs produced in 1934 were made by Warner Brothers, and twenty-five of the 100 songs most played on the networks were Warner publications.

A new sense of the value of music had permeated Hollywood in a single year. There was a 100 percent increase in the creation of original music, not only for musicals and features with songs, but also for expensive dramatic productions. Radio's lavish use of the old classical repertory over a decade had burned out that once-universal source, and classically trained and experienced screen composers were hunted with a fervor equaling that for a prospective movie queen. Dr. Erich Wolfgang Korngold, a former Viennese child prodigy, whose opera *Die Tote Stadt* was an international sensation when he was twenty-four, joined the staff at Warner. The trade papers were full of references to other musical stars—Stokowski, Anthiel, Toch, Janssen. After years of experience in man-of-all-work assignments, Max Steiner, Alfred Newman, Nathaniel Shilkret, Herbert Stothart and other veterans were now regarded as their equals in music departments that had doubled in size almost overnight. Warner, employed a full symphony orchestra, under Leo Forbstein's direction, on a full-time basis, and other studios had agreements for the exclusive services of the best remaining West Coast musicians. 20th Century-Fox was experimenting with film cutters who had training in music, as well as film synchronization, to supervise music tracks.

Busby Berkeley was king of the Warner lot, where he was engaged in what many believe to be his masterpiece, *The Gold Diggers of 1935;* its song "Lullaby of Broadway" won the Academy Award for best song that year. The six to eight weeks of rehearsal and free hand with expenses allowed to Berkeley had a serious economic effect at other studios. Their dance directors began to scorn a chorus line of only sixteen or eighteen dancers (Berkeley had as many as 500 chorines available), and producers insisted on at least one vast musical production number in each new release. Costs mounted, too, as rentals for these extravaganzas began to slip. The public became jaded with overhead shots, and such well-publicized routines as Berkeley's hundred grand pianos played by glamorous showgirls elicited little favorable response from critics or ticket buyers. The answer for many studios was the small-scale, intimate feature with music. The Sigmund Romberg–Oscar Hammerstein II song for such a film "When I Grow Too Old to Dream" was the most played composition on network radio in 1935 and had a sheet-music sale of 600,000, markedly contributing to the picture's success in third- and fourth-run houses.

Great strides in the development of color photography and processing and radical improvements in sound recording and theater amplification, coupled with royalty cuts by RCA Photophone and Vitaphone in their battle for control of the market, were responsible for the improved quality of Hollywood productions that began in 1936. The budget for 500 new features from the majors was $200 million, and nearly half that was planned by independents, who spent between $20,000 and $40,000 on six-reelers made in less than a week. The first Technicolor musical, *The Dancing Pirate*, with a score by Rodgers and Hart, was not a box-office success, but it did offer a vision of the possibilities in a swing away from black and white to the richness of great paintings.

In a land where income was the chief indication of the quality of work, songwriters were beginning to attain greater financial compensation than in the golden days of 1929. The team of Harry Warren and Al Dubin, responsible for the music in most Berkeley films, was signed to a $3,000-a-week contract; Harold Arlen and E. Y. Harburg, newcomers to the Warner lot, received $2,500 a week each; and Irving Berlin, the nonpareil, was paid a flat fee of $75,000 for a film score, as well as a percentage of gross receipts.

General wisdom had it that a successful film song added significantly to box-office returns and that radio play was an essential factor, a relationship Herman Starr preferred to ignore. Believing that the Warner copyrights were vital to the automobile makers, grocery chains, patent-medicine dispensers, and the manufacturers of cosmetics, household wares, and toothpaste who used musical programs to attract audiences, he took the position that his music rights were worth more than he could ever receive through continued affiliation with ASCAP. On January 1, 1936, the entire Warner music catalogue was pulled out of the society and off the air. Overtures had been made to the networks and individual sponsors for separate music licenses, but none had shown any interest. Without his chief source of income—the royalties from air play—and having disregarded the correlation of radio promotion to sheet-music sales, the secondary source of income, Starr was forced to plead for the best deal possible. In the summer of 1936, Warner Brothers' music interests returned to ASCAP.

Sixty-three of New York's top songwriters had moved west during the Warner boycott, half of them under contract, the others working on a free-lance basis. Among them were Kern, Berlin, Hammerstein, Rodgers and Hart, Cole Porter, and Harold Arlen. Their absence was a major factor in the dearth on Broadway of successful musical comedies and revues. With the largest song-writing staff on any lot by then, MGM purchased the Feist music-publishing business for $400,000. Its holdings were second only to Warner's after that. Starr, who had earlier sent out signals to broadcasters that the entire Warner catalogue could be had for two million dollars, was soon caught up in the splurge of film musicals and began to negotiate for the remaining Chappell properties.

Studio heads, after reading *Variety*'s list of the twenty-five songs most played on the air, picked up their phones to berate their East Coast music men. Under their whips, Tin Pan Alley music men drove their own professional staffs, and during 1936 and for the next half-dozen years film songs were generally at the top of the chart and held a majority of the twenty-four other positions. Irving Berlin, alone among publishers associated with film companies, questioned the validity of the promotion represented by the *Variety* list. Admitting that he enjoyed seeing his songs predominant (in a single week, his music for the Astaire movie *Follow the Fleet* had a total of 131 radio plugs), he argued that songs could easily be forced onto the list, which provided at best only a synthetic form of promotion for the music, and he questioned whether popular music really played a part in adding to the box-office grosses of movies. The eternal maverick Jack Robbins disagreed. He had been responsible for MGM's acquisition of the Feist business, as well as the recent purchases of Miller Music, which had been subsidized, until his death, by W. H. Woodin, president of American Car & Foundry and secretary of Commerce in the Roosevelt Cabinet, who poured nearly $400,000 into the business as an outlet for his compositions. Robbins found producers to be self-appointed experts in the potential value of a song, though as a rule they had no musical training or experience. Louis B. Mayer, head of MGM, who could not sing it, had once demanded that the song "You Are My Lucky Star" be cut from the picture it was written for. Robbins believed that, rather than shoulder music publishers with the financial responsibility for the coast-to-coast exploitation asked in connection with each new film, a company should be prepared to pour out a quarter of a million dollars a year for advertising and promotion. Hollywood was not prepared for that, and music men continued to bury the sums spent for subsidies under other expenses. But overplugging was driving the independent music houses out of business, reducing, as it did, the opportunities for air play. Because ASCAP distributions were based mainly on network play, the independents' income from this source was similarly reduced. They turned to Washington. Confronted with an investigation by the Federal Trade Commission in response, the movie-affiliated publishers resorted, as had others in 1917, to a corrective code of trade regulations. The attempt a decade earlier to curb excessive payments to vaudeville artists had been responsible for the formation of the Music Publishers Protective Association. Now, investigation by the FTC, and the MPPA chairman's own admissions, revealed that the old practice of paying for plugs was still industrywide, and that many firms spent more for that purpose than could be retrieved from sheet-music sales or ASCAP royalties. Responding to steady pressure from the West Coast, film-company music houses continued to dominate *Variety*'s weekly list, by the use of "money, gift, bonus, refund, rebate, royalty, service, favor, and other things or acts of value," as the new code catalogued the practices. Subscription to the new rules by a majority of MPPA members was sufficient to call off further FTC investigation, but in 1937, the thirteen music houses owned by or connected with Hollywood interests continued to share 65 percent of the ASCAP publisher distributions, as they did for the next decade.

The swing to Technicolor features was growing, and expansion planned for the 1937–38 season was the most ambitious since pre-Depression days. Admission prices tended upward. Hollywood's new prestige in show business was affirmed by the networks' move to California of 90 percent of all prime-time shows. When exhibitors complained about the glut of new releases, MGM was the first to reduce its annual schedule, to twenty-six A pictures a year, but it increased the sums spent on their production and improved quality in general.

It was again a year for songwriters and composers, the greatest film-musical season in history, with plans for $750,000 and million-dollar productions. It had become routine to involve the music head in all discussions, from the preliminary stages. Stories were written with greater concern for the involvement of music and songs in the flow of action. West Coast tunesmiths truly earned their weekly $750 to $1,000 checks, by writing "situation songs" that pleased the producer while keeping an eye on their AA ASCAP ratings rather than on print sales. Their songs had lost all the traditional, simplistic elements that appealed to the typical sheet-music buyer—a mythical woman in the Midwest—and that put songs in the Tin Pan Alley mold—"Vieni, Vieni," "Boo Hoo," "A Chapel in the Moonlight," "When My Dreamboat Comes Home"—among the year's best sellers. Constant demands for advance publicity in connection with a forthcoming picture, whose songs the trade-wise Easterners knew to be unsalable, were temporarily halted when professional managers and company heads were moved to California to coordinate the selection, spotting, and promotion of all new songs. A number of expensive new film musicals were probably saved by the inclusion of songs immediately recognized by the new liaison men as "commercial."

No one in the two-billion-dollar film industry yet dreamed of the astounding sums that would accrue from television, but as early as 1935 a few of the major companies did concern themselves with future royalties from a medium still in its experimental stages. That year also, ASCAP mailed a new five-year extension agreement to all its members that included television rights. The earliest American development of image-with-sound transmitted by wireless telephony was undertaken in 1919 by Vladimir Zworykin, a Russian refugee from the Bolshevik revolution employed in the Westinghouse laboratories at Schenectady, New York. His crude working model was displayed there five years later, at a time when other scientists were simultaneously at work on electronic tubes and scanning systems. Zvorykin conducted the first public demonstration of a television set in 1927, and daily experimental broadcasts emanated from Westinghouse's Schenectady studios in the following year. Radio stations throughout the country began to apply to the Federal Radio Commission for experimental television licenses, and Paramount's participation in CBS in 1929 was predicated on the belief that the time for picture-casting was just around the corner. The soundness of that judgment appeared to be confirmed in 1935—long after Paramount had retrieved its CBS investment—when David Sarnoff announced that RCA-NBC was ready to spend a million dollars on over-the-air demonstrations. Zvorykin had gone to his fellow Russian immigrant just prior to the Wall Street crash and persuaded the already enthusiastic Sarnoff that only $100,000 lay between experimental and full-development stages. Six years and much money later, a television station was erected atop the Empire State Building in New York, from which programs were regularly telecast within a fifty-mile range.

The movie business had witnessed the growth of broadcasting into a multimillion-dollar business, much of which depended on the use of their music, licensed for a fee regarded as completely unrealistic and out of proportion to radio's profits. The broadcasters did not intend to perpetuate that inequity. Hollywood-affiliated ASCAP publishers held that any use of music by telecasting would be similar to synchronization of music on film and therefore outside the society's scope; a separate license would be required, which only the publisher could offer. The six major ASCAP houses refused to sign any ASCAP document that referred to television, and a revised version omitting the word was distributed. Thus was the ground prepared for future battles over television performing rights, which plagued ASCAP with internal dissension and brought music licensing to the brink of economic disaster in a period when television broadcasting grew into a $400-billion business.

The MPPA's most recent code of practice was two years old in 1939, and five Hollywood–New York music-house combines—Warner Harms,

MGM Robbins/Feist Miller, 20th Century-Fox/Movietone/Berlin, Paramount Famous, and RKO Chappell/Gershwin—collected the lion's share of all ASCAP publisher distributions. The MPPA itself protested to the Federal Trade Commission that, in addition to the "fabulous sums" paid for airing their music, the companies lured bandleaders with promises to make and distribute short commercial films of their bands in actual performances. Over the protests of picture music publishers, ASCAP cast about for months before a majority was formed to change the current means of paying publishers. A notable decline in film songs on the most-played lists followed.

Hollywood, representing a total investment of $2.5 billion and operating in a market of 80 million American consumers, with the cost for a single production ranging from under $100,000 to more than $2 million and profits anywhere from 10 to 100 percent, depending on public response, offered an economic anomaly to its conservative Wall Street backers. Its complex and unusual practice of amortizing production costs against rental income and writing all expenses off in a year frustrated college-trained businessmen sent from New York to oversee investments. Among the few verities they understood was the viability of romantic musical dramas and comedies with songs of high quality. The traditional screen musical had seen its day, and Al Jolson was reckoned a has-been. The year's two most profitable features were Walt Disney's *Snow White and the Seven Dwarfs,* bringing in a $6.5 million gross in the first year, and *Alexander's Ragtime Band,* the first in a series of films with Irving Berlin songs, both old and new. Close behind was *Hurricane,* whose success was ensured by the song "Moon of Manakoora" and the abbreviated sarong worn by its singer, Dorothy Lamour. Herbert Yates's Republic Pictures, home of "class" Westerns, was budgeting large sums for "musical oaters," cowboy films with music starring Gene Autry and Roy Rogers. Responding to the change from rootin'-tootin' action pictures to the cowpoke troubadour, audiences of women had grown beyond any expectation.

The story became the thing with which to win the dollars of a music-conscious public. People turned out in great numbers for such epics as *Gone With the Wind,* which had a memorable musical main theme. Billboards advertised the three-million-dollar Technicolor production *The Wizard of Oz,* Walt Disney's *Pinocchio,* a revival of Victor Herbert's *Sweethearts,* with new songs interpolated, and screen biographies of Herbert, Lillian Russell, the Tin Pan Alley pioneer Gus Edwards, George M. Cohan, Florenz Ziegfeld, and Stephen Foster.

The boom in record sales added to the song plugger's list of people to see the bandleaders and vocal artists under contract to record manufacturers. Making no secret of their contempt for the Hollywood masterminds' judgments, they suffered in public when blamed for the failure of a film on whose music they had worked. It often became necessary to force a plug tune on a bandleader in the name of friendship, funded by payola. The New

York musicians' union banned mention of film credits on sustaining programs if the pay scale for commercial shows was not observed, and many bandleaders used these programs to feature material they themselves published—swing instrumentals and novelty tunes—or dug into old catalogues for songs overlooked, leading to such surprising revivals as that of "Begin the Beguine," or made modern swing adaptations of themes from the classics. To keep producers content, recording supervisors were paid to wax all the songs from a forthcoming movie release, and thus preserved music that often was best forgotten.

Government figures released in late 1940 put an end to the decade-long assertion that the picture industry was America's fifth-largest business. With $2.5 billion invested in theaters, studios, and distribution, and another billion overseas, it was, in fact, the thirty-fourth. The myth stemmed from a misquotation of remarks made by the British publisher Lord Northcliffe, who had called the motion picture the "fifth estate"; it was transformed into the "fifth industry" by Will Hays, among others. In only one year, 1937, did gross income exceed expenses, but 1940 promised to be a profitable year. Attendance at the country's 19,000 wired theaters, more than half owned by private individuals, had flattened out at 80 million in the past year, with women outnumbering men three to one. Admission prices had peaked at an average of thirty cents in 1929, then fell to twenty cents in 1933–34, and were now rising to twenty-five cents. Optimism was leavened by government imposition of an additional 10 percent tax in the second half of 1940 and the possibility of involvement in the European war, which had drastically cut income from foreign sources. There was also the uncertainty caused by the consent-decree settlement in the antitrust suit brought against Paramount, Loew's-MGM, RKO, Warner Brothers, and 20th Century-Fox by the Department of Justice. Block booking of a season's entire production was outlawed, and exhibitors could see new releases in advance, rather than accept them sight unseen, as in the past. Film makers could no longer pass off inferior products along with pictures much in demand. The possibility also loomed that the major studios would have to divest themselves of the 20 percent of all theaters they owned, which provided 54 percent of their total revenues because of the special financial advantages offered to these picture houses.

Equally important for the future was the prospect of another kind of war at home, one between ASCAP and the broadcasters, who had, surprisingly, united against the new contract with increased rates being offered to all stations. All of show business laughed at suggestions that the independent, alternative licensing organization, whose doors opened in February 1940, would be capable of substituting for the glorious ASCAP repertory of more than a million copyrights. The lesson of 1936, the Warner war with radio, was forgotten, with consequences that were to shake every aspect of popular entertainment.

CHAPTER 12

Popular Music and Radio

After a temporary early setback, the steady economic growth of radio broadcasting throughout the 1930s, and its increasing importance to show business, was paralleled by the quick advance of news about it from the back pages of *Variety*, chief chronicler of popular entertainment. In 1930, a few columns devoted to general industry news, gossip, and reviews of new programs followed such ephemera as "Foreign Show News," "Times Square Chatter," and "Literati," with only "Music," "Outdoors," and "Obituaries" after them. When the decade ended, "Pictures" and "Radio" shared the publication's front half and first page. These two major sources of Americans' favorite entertainment had much in common in seeking the widest audiences, who paid an average of twenty cents to see movies, but got radio programs without charge, though they were expected to spend a substantial portion of their income for products advertised on the air. Sensitive only to box-office figures and time-sales billings, they catered to the most homogenized tastes. Each placed much dependence on music to attract customers, and both were in frequent dispute with ASCAP. All three were under continual government scrutiny, but only radio, in theory and sometimes in fact, was under the supervision of a federal agency.

Picture returns went into four years of constant decline beginning in late 1930, whereas network income rose in 1931. NBC and CBS enjoyed a combined gross of $35.7 million that year. However, the industry's total expenses exceeded total income by $237,000, and half of all stations operated in the red, taking in an average of $3,000 from all sources.

Initially regarding network radio as only a temporary phenomenon, whose future was in doubt, major advertising agencies ventured into on-the-air advertising only at the insistence of clients who thought radio might be a better way to sell their products. Magazine advertising, which produced 15 to 20 percent commissions for space buyers, was still the major source of agency profit, and every effort was made to discourage the use of radio. This hesitancy produced the individual time broker and station representative, who purchased blocks of time and then dealt directly with sponsors. They were so successful that radio departments were formed by the advertising agencies in order to take advantage of the commissions offered by the networks on time charges, production costs, and talent.

At its start, when programing was on a hit-or-miss experimental basis, with audience mail the only measure of response, NBC created most of the nighttime shows it offered. Reacting to the new importance of radio to advertisers, the agencies began to take ever greater control of program content, holding over network officials' heads the alternative of electrically transcribed broadcasts, over which they already had full power. In 1931, all but three of the 702 stations in America were equipped with the Vitaphone–Western Electric turntables and amplifiers, capable of reproducing the standard sixteen-inch, 33⅓-speed disks. The holdouts were NBC's two New York flagships, WEAF and WJZ, and an affiliate in Rochester, New York. These followed the company's policy against the use of recorded sounds, either on transcriptions or on records made for use in the home.

Because of the time difference, "Amos 'n' Andy" and all other popular network programs were heard on the West Coast at 5:00 and 6:00 P.M., too early for the family audience. Two live broadcasts daily, with mounting relay charges, became too expensive, so programs were recorded for one-time use only in better time periods. With a choice between the entire national market at any time desired and those fewer than 100 stations connected in the chain operations, some sponsors opted for the cost-saving broader market offered by "radio disks." Many important clients, even RCA's own Victor Record company, chose transcriptions as the most effective medium to carry their messages. Seventy-five national sponsors went on the air with electrical transcriptions, an increase of 175 percent in a two-year period.

To remove the potential threat of dissolution by government action, General Electric and Westinghouse entered into a consent-decree settlement of the antitrust action against them, A T & T, and RCA. Their stock in RCA was disposed of, and all cross-licensing agreements among the four giants were voided. NBC and all its stations, the radio-connected manufacturing divisions, and other communication facilities were turned over to David Sarnoff's administration. Only RCA's control over the patents on radio tubes was found to be in violation of antitrust laws. Now free to concentrate on the realization of his dream to make radio the principal medium for home entertainment, Sarnoff directed the formation of West Coast NBC auxiliary networks and moved some national program production to San Francisco.

With almost complete rule over sponsored network programs, the advertising agencies, which found it in their best interest to respond to "what the public wants," instituted the use of surveys, charts, and graphs as the basis on which to build radio shows. Listeners were no longer satisfied with those once-reigning stars radio had created, so the agencies sought out the best-known names of Broadway and big-time vaudeville. George Burns and Gracie Allen were teamed with Guy Lombardo's orchestra, Eddie Cantor began a series of scripted comedy shows, and other headliners made the move from variety to the broadcast studio. In September 1932, Rudy Vallee moved the brightest stars of the Palace to his hour-long Fleischman's Yeast "Rudy Vallee Varieties" on NBC. Performers who did not care to be recorded on transcriptions became a part of the commercial advertising that was integrated into live programs. Products once peddled in sonorous tones, with copy written for the eye rather than the ear, became the butt of comedy stars. Dramatized commercials provided a new relief from monotony, and sales increased when network officials reluctantly permitted mention of product prices. Purveyors of food, drugs, toiletries, and tobacco, all of whose products sold for less than fifty cents, became the largest time buyers on network radio, spending $39 million in the 1932–33 season.

In the face of hard times for most independent broadcasters, the networks' prosperity had created dissension within the industry. It was exacerbated by the latest resolution of radio's decade-long war with ASCAP. Tin Pan Alley and the society were also plagued by the problems that faced all American business. Sheet-music profits and record royalties were seriously depressed, and music publishers and songwriters depended on their ASCAP distributions to survive. ASCAP had successfully thwarted the passage of an amendment to the Copyright Act that would have freed the use of musical works of any license fees. Armed with this and other court decisions in its favor, the society entered into negotiations with the National Association of Broadcasters for a new agreement, hoping to double or triple annual earnings over the $833,000 in sustaining fees paid by all broadcasters in 1931. A new document, tendered with NAB approval, called for a fixed fee on the use of music by individual stations on sustaining (commercial-free) programs, and three percent of receipts from time sales in 1933, with annual increments to five percent in the final year, 1935. Several deadlines for ratification by the industry were set and passed, while cries of "monopoly" were heard from broadcasters, and petitions were made to the government for dissolution of ASCAP.

A new antagonist entered the scene in the person of Oscar Schuette, who was retained by the NAB to coordinate negotiations with ASCAP and handle all government and public-relations aspects of the situation. He had been so effective in an earlier battle by independent radio-receiver manufacturers against RCA control of tube patents that the corporation itself recommended Schuette to the broadcasters' association. Schuette advocated and pursued a waiting policy, hoping to force more acceptable terms on ASCAP.

A second committee, assigned to negotiate the networks' contract, made up of a CBS and an NBC executive and an independent station manager to represent the affiliates, finally arrived at an agreement. It was quickly approved by the NAB and ASCAP and signed by the chains and most of their affiliated stations.

Public discussion of the independent stations' differences with ASCAP was barred by new NAB officials at the November 1932 annual convention. The dissidents were urged, for the time being, to accept the proffered licenses in order to avoid mass infringement suits. Oscar Schuette was appointed the director of copyright activities for the NAB and given a free rein in any action involving ASCAP. Convention proceedings were given over mostly to the issue of the amount, $8 and $10 million annually, paid to A T & T for line charges, 60 percent of it by the networks, and to the welter of legal, technical, and economic problems facing an industry threatened by the presence of a new president, Franklin Delano Roosevelt, thought by many to be antibroadcasters.

With the opening, in early 1933, of the RCA–Rockefeller family's $250-million Midtown New York real estate development, Rockefeller Center, built around the NBC headquarters and main studios, *Variety* moved its coverage of broadcasting up to a spot immediately ahead of ''Vaudeville,'' which the radio chains had supplanted as a national institution. One of the front-page headlines soon after, NO DEPRESH FOR RADIO, was correct as far as the networks were concerned. Engaged in developing a mass medium for the nation, they had created the chief soapbox on which American business could make its honey-coated appeals to the broad base of consumers, 60 million listeners, among whom unemployment had risen to 25 percent of the work force. Eleven of the twelve top-rated radio shows advertised products made to sell for less than a dollar, and on the twelfth Al Jolson plugged the merits of General Motors' lowest-priced Chevrolet automobile.

The NAB's strategy in 1933 to effect relief from the music-trust monopoly was dedicated, almost entirely, to winning a per-program system of payment to copyright owners, which had been introduced by Claude Mills during discussions with broadcasters in the mid-1920s. With Schuette as its president, the Radio Program Foundation was activated, to demonstrate the viability of such a licensing process, as well as to build a source of tax-free music for radio, supplied by songwriters and composers not affiliated with ASCAP. One of the purposes outlined in the RPF's charter was to ''own stock in, lend money to, and otherwise assist'' independent publishers. Some music-publishing veterans of the 1923 NAB v. ASCAP music war took advantage of the offer—publishers in Chicago and New York and the prestigious former ASCAP member G. Ricordi of Milan (which was long represented in America by George Maxwell, the society's first president).

Schuette's enthusiasm and promises were not sufficient to produce a single hit song or earn enough performances of the RPF library, and the project died within the year for lack of support, only 10 percent of the NAB membership contributing.

The networks and large stations were simultaneously engaged in a struggle with American newspaper publishers for the right to broadcast "news." In its formative years, radio was regarded as a source of amusing items, but as sets in use increased, many papers began to carry daily program listings and radio columns, in return for which stations read from the daily papers, properly crediting the sources. Later, some installed wire-service tickers to provide a wider range of news. Declines in advertising revenue, coupled with radio's Election Day coverage of the Hoover-Roosevelt race for the presidency and the on-the-spot broadcasts reporting an attempt on the new president's life, which killed the afternoon extra editions, led many papers to remove all program logs except as paid advertising. The wire services, Associated Press, United Press, and International News Service, allowed only local independent stations to use their tickers, on a for-pay basis. NBC and CBS opened their own news-gathering departments, the latter on a more ambitious scale, employing local correspondents around the United States and gaining access to foreign news services. Fearful of losing even its ineffectual relations with the press, NBC was the first to capitulate to the publishers' demands; it reduced the activities of its news department, sweeping CBS along with it. A truce was arranged, and a Press-Radio Bureau was formed, with permission from the publishers' association, to be used only in connection with nonsponsored broadcasting. The networks' news departments were scrapped. When newspaper advertising revenues began to grow again, and more news publishers acquired their own broadcasting facilities, the constraints imposed on network news loosened, the tension decreased, and program listing returned to many newspapers. Except on the local level, however, news and commentary did not form an important aspect of broadcasting for several years. Some eight hours of news and commentary were regularly scheduled on the networks each week in 1934, doubling in 1940, but only after shortwave news broadcasts and the war in Europe attracted that 70 percent of all Americans who believed that radio news was more accurate than that in newspapers.

The NAB conventioneers were mainly not correct in their apprehension in November 1932 of President Roosevelt's view of broadcasting, mastery of which he immediately asserted with the first of his "fireside chats." Talking directly to the people about momentous events facing the nation, he continued to use the medium as his chief means of communication throughout the twelve years of his administration. In imprinting his own stamp on the government, he originally called for the creation of a single commission to regulate communication by telephone and broadcasting. The Federal Radio Commission, formed in 1927 as a temporary body, was seven

years old and the good friend of broadcasters, affirming that relationship
with the statement that "any plan to eliminate the use of radio facilities for
commercial advertising purposes will, if adopted, destroy the present system of broadcasting." The declaration came in response to pleas from groups
of educators and representatives of cultural organizations for the allocation
of one fourth of all time on the air to nonprofit educational, religious, and
other public-service broadcasts, which would truly represent the operation
"in the public interest" called for in the commission's mandate. During
public hearings conducted by the commission, radio shared with Hollywood
clamorous attacks on their "creeping degeneracy," by the Legion of Decency and other church-associated organizations. The new Congress came
up with a compromise bill, substantially duplicating the 1927 act but with
a few minor provisions endorsed by the broadcasters. It became law on
July 1, 1934, and the seven-man Federal Communications Commission replaced the FRC. The public-service protagonists were mollified by a requirement that the new commission study the allocation of fixed percent-
ages of time to nonprofit groups. The FCC, like the former commission,
was provided with a single restraint: the power to reject renewal applications after three years, on the basis of findings from public hearings. Broadcasters were already governed by two sets of regulations, their own NAB
Code of Ethics and Practices, adopted in 1929, and the NRA Code, imposed by the federal government. Both dealt with many familiar trade abuses:
manipulation of rate cards; monopolistic and discriminative practices; payment of gratuities for song plugging on the air; blue-sky claims. Both were
abused by various elements in the business.

The firm hold of NBC and CBS on chain broadcasting was loosened in
1934 by the formation of several small networks. Eight-, ten-, and twelve-
station hookups, involving major NBC affiliates, were formed to handle
transcribed commercial programs and spot advertising on a cooperative basis; and MBS, the Mutual Broadcasting System, owned by the *Chicago
Tribune,* was established. NBC addressed the challenge by introducing a
station-relations department to deal with unhappy affiliates, added a music-
library service to its electrical-transcription division, and went into the now
important national spot-advertising business on behalf of its affiliates.

MBS remained a four-station network for two years—the *Tribune*'s local
station, WGN; Macy's WOR in New York; and stations in Detroit and
Cincinnati. In 1936, twenty-three stations in New England and ten in California were affiliated with it; the total was forty-five the next year. Mutual
paid all stations their regular commercial rates, deducting only a small sales
commission, advertising-agency fees, and wire charges. Programs were created by originating stations or by sponsors and their agencies, the network
itself owning no studios or transmitting facilities. It was in fact no more
than a business office with sales and station-relations representatives.

The ASCAP situation had taken second place to the newspaper-radio problem, but there was much activity behind the scenes and on a local level, where broadcasters in thirty states were instrumental in the introduction of legislation against music licensing. The NAB brought in a new attorney to handle the copyright situation, Newton D. Baker, Cabinet member in Wilson's administration and a powerful figure in Democratic Party circles. His connections were responsible for a Department of Justice investigation of ASCAP, the second major examination of the society since the mid-1920s, when it had been given a clean bill of health. It resulted in an antitrust suit against the society's officers, all its members, and other music-business organizations. Eleven pages of the complaint were devoted to a listing of the defendants' names. ASCAP filed an answer in late 1934. The NAB and its members were confident that a decision would be reached before September 1, 1935, when the current three-year contract was to expire.

Complaints by NBC and CBS affiliates about the excessive share of ASCAP royalties they were asked to pay and the meager compensation payments they received from the networks threatened to split the NAB at its next annual meeting. They were little mollified by announcements in January 1935 of new affiliation rates. NBC abandoned any charge for sustaining programs, for which it had been collecting $1,500 per station each month in return for several hours of free evening time. Compensation to affiliates was boosted on the basis of a sliding-scale percentage of time rates, increased to 25 percent by NBC and 22 percent by CBS. Under previous contracts, the networks had grossed $42 million in 1934, of which affiliates received less than half, and spot and local advertising garnered them an additional $30 million. Altogether, radio paid ASCAP approximately $850,000.

A number of events in 1935 added a new perspective to the use of music on radio, and to its future course as well: a new program rating service; George Washington Hill's determination to have his own way on his own radio programs; the resignation from ASCAP of the Warner Brothers' music businesses; and Martin Block's introduction of "Make Believe Ballroom."

Block's influence was not felt immediately. Only jukeboxes provided a truly varied fare of recorded music. That heard over most radio stations was a bland homogenization of Hollywood songs and those in the familiar Tin Pan Alley hit pattern, as well as the ever reliable music favored in the early days. The selection of popular music was left mostly to the orchestra leader or guest singing talent. Format music programing was anticipated only on Lucky Strike's "Your Hit Parade," broadcast over the NBC Red Network on Saturdays, beginning in September 1935. It was the creation of the American Tobacco Company's flamboyant president, George Washington Hill, who was known for programs that were "the noisiest on the air." Immortalized in the 1950s' novel *The Hucksters,* Hill was one of the first to enforce a formula, or music format, on orchestra leaders. His budget to advertise Luckies in 1931 was nearly $20 million, a sum of such significance to NBC that its executives mildly suffered his brash, boorish behavior and joined him at Saturday-morning rehearsals to test the "foxtrotability" of every selection programmed. *Variety,* in 1931, quoted from Hill's music formula:

> The program shall consist of songs that made Broadway Broadway. Not songs that are making Broadway Broadway, but the songs that made Broadway Broadway. People like to hear things their ears are attuned to, not new numbers. Songs that have so rung in the public ear that they mean something, recall something, start with a background of pleasant familiarity. Occasionally a new song may be used, but only when it has been presented first as a part of a Saturday program and is reviewed by the executive group at a Saturday dress rehearsal.
>
> Only the chorus of such songs shall be played. That is to say, the characteristically familiar melody content, not the introductory part. . . . There shall be no extravagant, bizarre, involved arrangements—"no pigs squealing under the fence." . . . The opening and closing numbers must be particularly stirring and rousing. Consideration must be given to contrasts particularly where the specialties are introduced. As they should constitute the soft element of the program, the numbers following must be particularly lively, and snappy. . . .

Variety, was not impressed with the premiere of "Your Hit Parade," doubting that Hill could capture a large audience with "an ordinary aggregation of musicians, [forty, under Lennie Hayton's direction] and warblers [five soloists and two vocal groups] and whip them into something extraordinary." As for the week's fifteen top hits, the paper declared: "If Lucky plans on playing 'em according to the actual standings it will have to do lots of repeating each week. They don't turn over in the music business that fast."

Program ratings, the measurement of listener preference and share of audience that determines program content on both radio and television today, advanced in 1935 from the "listener preference" letters of the twenties. The first of the twelve methods current in 1935 was the Crossley Report, which was introduced by the American statistician Archibald M. Crossley and adopted by the Cooperative Analysis of Broadcasters, an association of advertising agencies and national advertisers. Relying on a group of listeners' memories to determine which programs they had heard the previous day, Crossley used a telephone recall check. Coincidental telephone checking had been introduced by the Clark-Hooper Service, later Hooper Rating Reports, in 1934; the next year it became the official survey of the CAB. Experiments began in 1939 with the Nielsen Audimeter Survey—meters attached to radio sets that recorded the exact length of time various stations were tuned in. The A. C. Nielsen organization had developed the Audimeters to supplement survey methods employed in connection with its three-million-dollar business in statistical checking of food and drug inventories in retail outlets.

Until the broadcasting industry itself adopted other means, the networks operated on the principle that radio coverage could be measured like magazine circulation, and based all time rates on the 21 million sets in homes, a figure representing all the radio receivers believed to be in working order. The size of an audience for a network program was reckoned to be the accumulated number of sets within range of each participating station's transmitter. The result was that advertisers spent three fourths of their radio budgets on one third of all stations. Local rate cards employed the same measurement, and cutthroat competition among the stations within a market induced rate cutting and dissension. Newspaper publishers were quick to jump on the statistical inconsistencies in the networks' claims, followed by advertisers and their agencies, and the validity of radio's claim to be the better advertising medium was in serious jeopardy until it, too, based rates on quantitative studies.

The NAB convention in July 1935 set a new record for attendance; more than 400 broadcasters met to discuss the economic consequences of the networks' bombshell announcement of an extension of the five percent ASCAP rate for five years. The society had insisted on collection from owned-and-operated network stations on the basis of card rates, but compromised when NBC accepted an increase in the sustaining-fee payments from flagship stations in New York, from $15,000 to $25,000 a year beginning in 1936.

Many independents had been meeting with Claude Mills to discuss a change to "payment at the source" licensing of all network broadcasts, and they believed the society was ready to negotiate a new formula based on that principle. The government's antitrust suit had gone to trial, but was adjourned after nine days at the government's request. At that point, the assistant attorney general handling the case joined the NAB staff. Network representatives argued that the suit had been inadequately prepared and would probably be lost, in which event far more onerous terms would be demanded.

A complicating issue was Warner's announcement of its resignation from ASCAP. In the final days of 1935, NAB officials and members desperately negotiated for the improvement of a contract proposed by Warner, asking for 40 percent of the ASCAP sustaining rate and 2 percent of gross receipts. The latter figure was grudgingly reduced, but at the new year between 20 and 40 percent of the total ASCAP repertory, depending on whose statistics were accurate, was not available to most American radio stations. In the next six months, until the Warner catalogue was restored to ASCAP, most of the music of Gershwin, Rodgers and Hart, Herbert, Romberg, the songs from Warner's lavish musical film hits and those of many leading songwriters, Broadway composers, and lyricists were not heard on the air. More to the point, there was little complaint from listeners about the omission.

A more than coincidental factor in the film company's defection was Jack Warner's hope to diversify his holdings and acquire control of a third national radio network. When his offer to purchase the Mutual Broadcasting System, for more than one million dollars, was finally rejected in April 1936, plans were stepped up for the activation of Muzak-wired radio, to compete with network radio, once Interstate Commerce Commission permission was granted. Muzak already offered eighteen hours of commercial-free recorded music on three channels: dance and popular music; light classical; "better" instrumental and vocal, familiar standard, and palm-court music; and news broadcasts on the hour, interspersed with cultural and religious programs and symphonic music. Carried to subscribers on telephone wires, Muzak programs were recorded on celluloid Millertape, and the resulting wide-range high-fidelity sound was superior to any on radio. Sixty-five percent of all homes in Belgium and Holland were already wired for entertainment, and wired radio was spreading on the Continent and in England.

The first patented plan to provide music, news, and entertainment to that half of all American homes already wired for electricity had been proposed to the mammoth public-utilities holding company North American in 1922 by General George Owen Squier, chief army signal officer during World War I. His scheme to use electric-power lines to transmit programs directly into homes and offices was immediately acquired by North American, and a subsidiary was formed, Wired Radio. A license to ride piggyback on power lines was contained, and plans were shaped for a nationwide broadcasting network. Large-scale experiments and irregular local service were interrupted by the Depression. They were resumed in 1934 when the Muzak Corporation was formed in New York and began to lease popular and dance music to night clubs, cafés, hotels, and restaurants. Among the parent Wired Radio's board members in 1935 were two financial figures associated with the moving-picture business: Wadill Catchings, a member of the Warner board, and Harris Connick, Kuhn, Loeb's original representative in Hollywood.

The veteran bandleader and recording artist Ben Selvin, who was a music supervisor for Brunswick under Warner's ownership, headed the Muzak recording operation in ERPI-Warner Vitaphone's former New York studios. Many of the artists he used were under contract to Columbia and Brunswick, but they worked for him on condition that their names not be used. Muzak had an open-end agreement with ASCAP, but depended for much of its music on Associated Music Publishers, a holding company for non-ASCAP music, chiefly standard classical and operatic selections published by French, German, and Viennese houses.

In 1938, when Muzak was unable to secure permission from the FCC to compete with the networks, it concentrated on special music services designed for offices and factories, as well as the home audience, under Warner Brothers' majority ownership, and a new transcribed-music library service for radio was instituted using the AMP label.

Ten years after its inception in 1927, network broadcasting enjoyed a $55-million year, and the price for a single affiliated station was at a new high: the $1.2 million paid by CBS for the Los Angeles KNX operation, to serve as the principal point of nighttime programing. An increased emphasis on improved relations with affiliates, following the findings of an independent business consulting service urging it to do so, was responsible for a change in the method of compensating NBC stations for time used on chain broadcasts. A new, more equitable, though not completely satisfactory, contrast was accepted by the affiliates. It extended the term for cancellation privileges, guaranteed sixteen day and night hours a week for local commercial broadcasts, and continued to absorb line charges. CBS affiliates remained under the standard contract introduced in the early 1930s, without the local-station option time. One quarter of all stations were owned by newspaper interests, but the war with news publishers was at an end. Sponsors spent $22 million for network talent, and half that for electrically transcribed advertising and entertainment. Following the impact on small stations of WNEW's successful "Milkman's Matinee" programs from midnight to dawn, all-night record shows became a new attraction for night workers and the wakeful.

Anticipating the next confrontation with ASCAP, the NAB formed yet another tax-free catalogue, the Bureau of Copyrights, to replace the bankrupt Radio Program Foundation. No complete listing of active musical compositions yet existed, most broadcasters being unaware of what percentage of the music they used was licensed. The bureau embarked on a program of recording an initial 100 hours of tax-free music for sale to radio stations, and special arrangements of non-ASCAP music were made. But the project foundered late in 1937, owing to the recession that began in the autumn and to the American Federation of Musicians' new demands for more jobs for members.

Local action in Chicago had already increased the number of stand-by union members to the number of those used on any commercial recording or electrical transcription played over a Chicago station. An ultimatum from the AFM in the summer of 1937, asking for the implementation of a similar stand-by practice by all stations and the guarantee of a minimum allocation of an additional $2.5 million for the employment of union musicians in the studios, came as a shock. A series of meetings between NBC and CBS and the AFM produced a tentative agreement that at least $1.5 million of this would come from the networks and their affiliates. The ill will generated by the earlier "sellout" to the songwriters and publishers still rankled, as did the networks' continuing refusal to consider the concept of taxation, or "clearance," at the source, which would make the networks responsible for obtaining licenses and paying fees for network programs broadcast by affiliates.

The firebrand of the AFM, James Caesar Petrillo, president of the Chicago local and a member of the national executive board, was the chief goad in the drive for more money from radio. Possessed of a modest command of the English language, the result of only a few years in the Chicago public schools, he had a storehouse of expletives. He had learned the trumpet as a child, but had abandoned the four-piece neighborhood band he formed at fourteen to open a cigar store, and later operated a saloon. In 1918, he joined the violence-ridden all-white Chicago AFM Local 10, and was elected its president eight years later. His years in that office were notable for strides made on behalf of his constituents, a successful strike against Chicago theaters, the first contract with an American radio station, establishment of peace with the city's hotels, and support of the local Democratic Party.

He burst on the national labor scene at the 1937 AFM convention, leading a fight against "canned music." He virtually dictated the threat that all AFM musicians would walk out on August 17 if broadcasters did not accept the group's new terms. The record manufacturers had already been persuaded by a walkout threat to print a more stringent warning against use on the air of commercial disks, and now engaged in discussions that brought an agreement guaranteeing the employment of union musicians and union-approved talent only.

Broadcasters again split into factions: one, representing the new National Independent Broadcasters group, ready for a fight to the finish; the other wanting to make the best deal possible. The second body was made up of network representatives and many of the most important affiliates, united in a belief that a strike would cause great loss of income and alienate not only a Washington administration viewed as prolabor, but also sponsors with similar beliefs. A new coalition—the Independent Radio Network Affiliates—was activated inside the NAB. It assumed sole responsibility for dealing with a union determined to ensure the employment of its 3,000 members at wages of twenty-five to forty dollars a week, estimated to total $5.5 million annually, almost twice the total paid to ASCAP.

Network officials made it plain to the IRNA that they would not stand for a strike. Sensing a new feeling of appeasement, the union agreed to a series of extensions that postponed the strike until, in October 1938, a final contract was ratified by a majority of stations. Terms for network affiliates were based on a percentage of time sales, which on the basis of 1937 revenue amounted to a general five and a half percent. A group representing 388 independent stations that used electrical transcriptions and commercial records dealt separately with the AFM, and by October, 162 of them had agreed to contracts with locals in their cities. Approximately 200 small stations, whose average income in 1937 was under $20,000, were exempted from any obligation to employ live union musicians.

The lives of an already problem-laden NAB board and staff were further complicated in 1937 by an appeal from members for help in dealing with the Society of European Stage Authors and Composers, which sold music licenses. This group was owned and operated by Paul Heinecke, a European who had represented German and Austrian music firms in the United States during the 1920s and then organized them into a holding company, Associated Music Publishers, which he sold to North American's wired-radio division in 1929 for a reputed $250,000. SESAC had been formed two years later to handle music licensing for various foreign publishers not affiliated with ASCAP. Heinecke's first important radio deal was made in 1932 when Sydney M. Kaye, a young CBS attorney, and other network executives settled an infringement suit against CBS by negotiating a fifty-cents-per-performance arrangement with SESAC, calling for a minimum annual fee of more than $52,000. SESAC's victory in a 1936 action, against a New York hotel, that established the right to collect when loudspeakers in hotel rooms came under the purview of the law on performing rights solidified Heinecke's position. As their representative, he split all radio and mechanical-license collections with music publishers on a fifty-fifty basis, collecting an estimated $100,000 dollars for himself in 1937. Wild reports of his income prompted some leading broadcasters to suggest publicly that they should float a stock issue of between $10 and $20 million for the purpose of buying into the music business, and thereby profit from an industry into which they were pouring several million dollars to ASCAP alone.

SESAC's new contentiousness, impending failure of the Bureau of Copyrights and, with it, the NAB recorded music library, and the negotiations with the AFM represented to many IRNA members situations from which they should withdraw at once. The networks and some more pragmatic broadcasters, wishing to maintain a show of industry solidarity, suggested a reorganization of the NAB, with new directors and staff, and a paid full-time president. A search began at once for candidates for that post, someone with clout in Washington and proper regard for the industry's more powerful elements.

The recession that temporarily blocked a national recovery began in late 1937. For the first time in its history, modern radio suffered nationwide declining time sales. Automobile companies, tire makers, suppliers of auto accessories, manufacturers of laundry soaps and cleansers— the largest network time buyers—reduced or canceled advertising on the chains and moved to local stations. Those affiliates who had signed with the AFM were required to add paid professional musicians and other talent, something new for most of them. The responsibility for producing daytime musical shows shifted from the owned-and-operated stations in New York, Chicago, San Francisco, and Los Angeles to the affiliates, some of whom soon had staff orchestras of as many as fifteen musicians. Given the opportunity for the first time to show their skills to a national audience, local program directors and musical talent raised the general quality of daytime shows from the sloppy levels to which they had fallen. NBC alone added forty-five programs from affiliates to its regular schedule, and national advertisers looked for programs and performers in the once-derided hinterland.

Many American broadcasters were still asking for moratoriums on past-due bills and salary checks in June 1938, when the NAB's hunt for a paid president ended. He was an attorney, Neville Miller, once provost of Princeton University, mayor of Louisville during the recent catastrophic flood, when his use of radio to reach the outside world for help brought him to national attention.

The new NAB board instructed Miller to make resolution of the ASCAP problem his first order of business. They authorized him to enter into immediate talks with the society, and directed a committee representing national and regional networks, station affiliates, and large and small independent stations from all parts of the country to advise and assist him. John Paine, ASCAP general manager, and Claude Mills, who was serving the society chiefly as a roving ambassador to broadcasters, reminded Miller and the committee members that any new license would hinge on higher rates of payment, probably at the expense of the networks. At one point, Mills mentioned a 15 percent music charge, the same as that refunded to advertising agencies in commissions.

Nearly half a hundred bills and resolutions affecting broadcasting were presented during the 75th Congress, in 1937–1938. Proposals called for more strenuous censorship of program content on the networks, an increase in public-service programs by all stations, more evidence of self-regulation, and amendments to the 1934 Communications Act that would curb the existing monopoly situation in national and regional chain radio. Music licensing was removed for the moment from Miller's attention when the FCC announced new hearings. After a series of aborted starts, an investigation of all networks began in November with David Sarnoff. In a typically statesmanlike manner, part teacher, part defender of the medium for whose present structure and position he was so markedly responsible, he sought to avert government regulation with the theme of his prepared statement: "Self-regulation is the democratic way for American broadcasting." This provided a battle cry for the industry, number-one problem for the NAB—the preparation of a new code governing standards—and a new chore for Miller— selling it to sponsors, opinionmakers, legislators, and 722 broadcast licensees. The industry had paid little attention to the earlier codes, in 1928 and 1929, neither of which had any real teeth. The 1933 NRA code had been ruled unconstitutional by the Supreme Court a few years after its adoption. A few voices rose in opposition to the new document framed by the NAB, which among its provisions sought to draw the line between controversial and noncontroversial content. They spoke in solemn measure, arguing that radio should never worry about majority points of view or taste, that anything new was by its nature controversial. The Bill of Rights, one said, demanded concern for minority opinion and taste. This issue was to surface again two decades later.

There were technological developments in the latter part of the 1930s, too, ones that would also shake the structure of the networks and all radio: television and frequency modulation (FM)—the static-free transmission of sound to which radio is inextricably bound. RCA-NBC continued to maintain the lead taken when it built the first modern television transmitting station in 1935, two years before CBS did. With it began the development of an experimental program service and manufacture of a limited number of RCA television sets, to be "deployed at strategic points of observation." Competition increased from other radio companies and laboratories—Zenith, Philco, GE, the Allen B. Dumont Laboratories, and the Farnsworth Company. Sarnoff welcomed their presence in the field, since RCA was required by a consent decree to license its patents on a royalty basis to competitors. RCA technology was essential to the manufacture of all television sets, and thus kept the electronic giant abreast of new approaches to the final mastery of the medium once regarded as "Sarnoff's folly." Shortly before his appearance at the FCC hearings, he had announced the technical feasibility of television in the home and the inauguration of a limited "radiovision" service in the New York market, to begin with public demonstrations at the 1939 World's Fair.

Static-free reproduction of sound to accompany image, transmitted over ultrahigh frequencies, was imperative, and Sarnoff, ready to spend as much as one million dollars to obtain his patents for FM broadcasting, began negotiations with Edwin H. Armstrong. Armstrong had earned his first million from RCA in 1922 from the sale of an important patent, promptly married his friend Sarnoff's secretary, and returned to the laboratory inspired by Sarnoff's suggestion that "a little black box to eliminate static" could bring in the same sum. It was ready ten years later—not a small box, but a patented new system of broader-range frequency-modulated signal transmission through upper frequencies. It was immediately moved to RCA facilities atop the Empire State Building. The revolutionary sound was first sent from there to a point seventy miles away in 1934. But because of RCA's concentration on television and Sarnoff's now-certain realization that FM would make obsolete overnight the present structure of broadcasting and slow the development of television by preempting ultrahigh frequencies, he ended further collaboration with Armstrong, who was asked to remove his apparatus, to make room for telecasting.

Armstrong persevered, and eventually received permission from the FCC to build a 50,000-watt FM station in New Jersey, which went on the air in the late winter of 1939. In twelve months, the mass production of FM sets was in full swing at GE and other manufacturers, and the FCC was deluged with 150 applications for FM stations. In October 1940, FM was given the go-ahead signal by the commission, and a new technology seriously threatened entrenched amplitude modulation (AM).

Variety hailed the broadcasters' ratification of a new code of practices, at their June NAB convention, as a historically significant decision, one demonstrating that they "have become progressively more responsive to public opinion . . . and reasonably consistent in observing their own rules." The press was barred from several sessions but did learn of other issues discussed: the probability of a nationwide AFM strike by mid-January; an adverse decision in a lawsuit challenging radio's right to play disks made "for home use"; and the need to call an emergency meeting of the entire industry in September, to discuss the formation of a new music-licensing organization, if ASCAP did not cease its "run-around" tactics.

ASCAP's president, Gene Buck, who had taken negotiations into his own hands, was not present when the NAB Copyright Committee came to New York to meet with him in early August. It was informed by Paine that a new contract had not yet been framed. A war of press releases began: radio seeking to portray itself as engaged in a fight with a "city slicker" ready to foreclose the mortgage, and the society depicting the broadcasters as greedy monsters who were employing scare tactics to build up a war spirit preliminary to bargaining.

The traditionally splintered radio business was united on at least one issue, and knew exactly what it was after. Even the most combative elements no longer wanted a per-use contract, having found it too expensive and time consuming (much to the relief of Claude Mills, who had first broached it in the mid-1920s, but now was amenable to a per-program method of payment). Except for the stations owned by NBC and CBS, payment at the network source was regarded as mandatory, royalties to be paid only for local programs on which ASCAP music was performed.

Neville Miller began extended meetings with Sydney Kaye, a member of the CBS law firm headed by Paley's personal attorney, Ralph Colin. Regarded as a leading authority in the field, Kaye had been made available to the NAB to advise on copyright matters. In 1935, when both NBC and CBS were considering the consequences of a renewal of the favorable ASCAP contract, he had submitted a plan proposing the creation of a reservoir of non-ASCAP music, which would have the effect of placing radio in a position of trading equality with the society, and which would eventually create the most important source of music, relegating ASCAP to a secondary position. In addition to securing rights to music controlled by societies other than ASCAP—SESAC, AMP, and approximately 150 small independent firms—Kaye urged that inducements be offered to a few conspicuous American composers to let their ASCAP contracts terminate, and that they be given direct, favorable compensation for the use of their works on radio. They could retain all publishing, stage-performance, and other property rights. The plan had been pigeonholed after contracts were renewed. Now Miller and the NAB committee asked for a similar proposal, brought up-to-date, for consideration at the special NAB meeting.

The new, fifteen-page Kaye blueprint for building an alternate source of music was a masterful and tidy outline for NAB's future course. In it, he revealed a new and better knowledge of the music business, whose success and profits depended almost entirely on an ability to control network plugging of selected songs. The extent of that control was illustrated in information made public in 1940. Thirteen music firms affiliated with Hollywood interests completely dominated Tin Pan Alley and "Your Hit Parade," receiving 60 percent of the $2.5 million paid to the 165 ASCAP publisher members in 1939. A study of ASCAP research, on the basis of which distributions were made in 1938, showed that 368 selections received 47.1 percent of air play, and, altogether, 2,500 selections furnished 83 percent of all performances on NBC's Blue and Red and the CBS networks.

Kaye urged the industry to bear in mind that because the proposed organization would be a money-spending, rather than money-making, company, no dividends would accrue, and he suggested initial broadcaster pledges of up to $1.75 million to get it off the ground. Funding would be raised by an SEC-approved sale of 100,000 shares of capital stock, at five dollars, of Broadcast Music Incorporated, one dollar of which would constitute capital; the balance, surplus. Each investing broadcaster would receive stock in the amount nearest 25 percent of the sum paid to ASCAP in 1937 (the only year in which a survey of total expenditure on music was undertaken). License fees would be equal to 40 percent of ASCAP payments. No provision was made for network payment at the source, and one fifth of the BMI stock was allocated to NBC and CBS. Both agreed to maintain a unified front and not make a deal with ASCAP without their affiliates' approval. An April 1, 1940, deadline was set for implementation of the project and the start of BMI operations, provided that at least $400,000 had been raised from stock sales. The plan was unanimously approved at the Chicago meeting in September. Kaye believed, as did many others there, that if ASCAP saw a show of strength and resistance, it would modify its demands, and that an additional five-year term would be accepted.

A coast-to-coast survey of ASCAP's relations with radio was published by *Variety* on October 18, 1939. It painted an industrywide perception of the society as an organization that felt nothing but ill will toward broadcasters and was "working one huge squeeze play whose only virtue seems to be that it is legal." The reporter found that ASCAP had failed in everyday public and customer relations. Even the newspaper-owned stations, which got lower rates than others, found that discount a Machiavellian scheme to sunder solidarity, one they would not support. There was real enthusiasm for BMI everywhere but at the network-owned stations, whose managements awaited word from New York before making public statements.

ASCAP responded to the *Variety* piece with a new users' relations department, staffed by pleasant young men, whose principal function was to be the handshaking the society had so long neglected. Broadcasters who asked these representatives about progress toward new terms were told that ASCAP would do away with all sustaining fees and apply the payment-at-the-source principle to all stations, network or not. Estimates of ASCAP income for 1939 only exacerbated the situation. A total of $6.9 million was anticipated, $4.3 from radio.

Armed with a new line, IRNA officials assured all that NBC was no longer wavering, and CBS was more anxious than ever to win the fight. Privately, both tended toward a settlement that involved a specific sum, which they would in turn allocate among their affiliates. When official reports of network income were issued, enthusiasm waned for even that compromise. Out of estimated gross industry sales of $165 million, NBC had made $45.2 million in 1939, and CBS, as always second, but gaining, had the best single month in network history in November, and had collected $35.5 million in annual time sales. ASCAP income from radio, of which the networks paid about 20 percent, had risen from $757,450 in 1932 to $5.9 million in 1937, and had then dropped to $3.8 million the following year. It increased by 12 percent, to $4.3 million, in 1939.

The war in Europe and the possibility of America's involvement, plus the uncertain general business economy, were expected to reduce radio revenues in 1940 by half. The recent AFM situation had been resolved only with the added expenditure of more than three million dollars, which was certain to increase after new talks with the union. The cost of developing television, to which the networks were committed, and FM, as well as rising pay scales, made inevitable by the proliferation of craft and labor unions, could not possibly be adequately covered by anticipated revenues. Buoyed by the first general boom in a decade in sheet-music and record sales, music men looked for the same in music licensing, and talked about a 100 percent increase. The latest Crossley-CAB ratings gave them good reason for optimism. National spot business looked good, and there was an increase as high as 13 percent in some markets. Network evening ratings had jumped more than a third over 1938–39.

Although Kaye and Miller and the NAB staff had done yeoman work, meeting with people from 400 stations, only one quarter of the million dollars pledged had come in by January 1940. BMI opened an office in February, with rented furniture and a staff of four, hired on a temporary basis.

The first adverse publicity for ASCAP came on George Washington's Birthday, when Gene Buck was arrested for extradition from Phoenix on a warrant telegraphed from Montana. Several station owners there had complained that Buck and eleven others, including NBC and CBS officials, were obtaining money from broadcasters under false pretenses, and they had taken the matter to a small-town judge. Ever the showman, Buck took advantage of the comedy and played to a national public gallery with such effect that he and his negotiating committee were able to keep the broadcasters off balance, and then withheld the new contract for a month.

When it came, just before BMI's self-imposed deadline of April 1, the manner of its presentation solidified the radio business to an unexpected degree, a tactical misstep that cost the society dearly, and the repercussions lasted for years. Rather than deal with radio's designated agent, ASCAP did not invite Miller, and, surprisingly, Mills was not present. Hoping once again to split the industry, Buck called in representatives of the three networks, several major affiliates, and one independent. John Paine read them the new contract provisions.

Radio was divided into four categories: some 300 stations whose gross billings were under $50,000 would pay 3 percent of sales receipts, less agency and other deductions, and a one-dollar a month sustaining fee; an intermediate group of about 255 stations that grossed between $50,000 and $250,000 annually would pay 4 percent and a sustaining fee reduced by twenty-five percent; the large network stations would pay the present 5 percent charge; and, for the first time, regional and national chains would be charged 7½ percent. The duration of the proposed agreement was not yet fixed.

When Paine completed his reading, Edward Klauber, executive vice-president for CBS, rose to say that only the NAB would negotiate for his organization, and then walked out. Others followed, one pausing to say in a loud voice to Oscar Hammerstein II that broadcasters would grind the society into the dust. Hammerstein's fervent recitals of the incident, years after, were still marked by the feeling of contempt for broadcasters it roused in him. A letter castigating Klauber's behavior as "unbecoming a gentleman, and completely discourteous" was hand-delivered to Paley. Furious, he rejected "ASCAP's attempt to split our industry into hostile camps," and wrote that he agreed with his vice-president, who would continue to represent CBS in all business affairs. Throughout the next year, Paley and Klauber were BMI's most ardent champions.

The CBS representative's unceremonious departure provided Buck with the opportunity to bring into play a public-relations strategy that had been successful for broadcasting—making targets for personal attacks out of leading players in the game. Klauber and Miller, whose status Buck challenged, asking whether he represented the stations or the rich networks, bore the brunt in the next barrage of news releases. Hazy arithmetic was employed by both sides, ASCAP saying that 540 stations would pay between 20 and 50 percent less than in 1939, the networks countering with claims that they were being asked to pay an additional $3.25 million. *Variety* calculated that, using 1939 as a sample year, ASCAP would have collected $7.1 million, instead of $4.3 million, if the new system had applied, $4.125 million from the networks, which would have to add this to the nearly $28 million spent for technical, program, sales-promotion, and general administrative expenses.

With such millions at stake, the support of the small stations, who represented 49 percent of all licensees, was essential for industrywide support of BMI. An experienced supersalesman, former California broadcaster, and proverbial modern Renaissance man was brought to New York to serve as director of station relations. He was Carl Haverlin, who led BMI as president in later years and brought it to a position of international dominance of the music world. The son of a mining engineer, he had spent four years of his childhood in Mexico, and his little formal education was gotten in Arizona and California, where he came into contact with American folk music and the common man's vernacular songs. After flunking out of high school, he went on tour as a vaudeville dancer, and acquired an increasingly wide education in local libraries and secondhand bookstores. The first of many careers in broadcasting began in the early 1920s at KFI, a leading Los Angeles station. As announcer, station promotion man, time salesman, sales and station manager, he was at the heart of the station's successes, among them the first radio performance of the entire Shakespearean canon and the initiation, in 1926, of Standard Oil of California's vaunted classical-music broadcasts. In the radio booth at the 1929 New Year's Day Rose Bowl football game, he took the microphone from a suddenly ailing Graham MacNamee, and described the famous "wrong-way sprint," when California captain Roy Riegels ran to his goal line by mistake, as "running backwards," which was forever after ascribed to the more famous sports announcer.

Leaving KFI in 1936, Haverlin moved, with his growing family, to the California desert, to write for the pulp action and detective magazines. When he returned to Los Angeles in 1938, he worked as a salesman for a local transcription service. He came to Kaye's attention when his employer wrote an open letter attacking the BMI plan, and the attorney soon learned of Haverlin's reputation among broadcasters for an exceedingly wide vocabulary and a readiness to conjure up mental images and articulate them in magnificent speeches that persuaded reluctant customers. Haverlin could be had for a small salary, and he was at once regarded as the logical candidate to sell the new organization to holdouts at all levels of the business.

The task was a formidable one. Half of the network stations and nearly two thirds of the independents had not yet closed ranks. Among them was a hard core of broadcasters who were still smarting from earlier network surrenders to ASCAP. Haverlin's work on the road, spreading the gospel and ameliorating old enmities, raised the number of subscribing stations and brought in more than 85 percent of the industry's time-sales income. His efforts were substantially assisted by the ASCAP mailing to all stations of the new contract. In it, the term was for five years, but television rights were excluded, as was any reference to either a per-piece or per-program alternative.

In the light of later developments, it was a blunder by ASCAP to offer a per-piece arrangement to stations in Montana and Washington, where state laws, instigated by broadcasters, prohibited the society from intrastate business. Radio operators in other states, who had been seeking this relief for years, were angry and signed with BMI.

At the next convention, Haverlin and other BMI executives explained their sliding-scale license charges, ranging from one and a half to two and a half percent of revenues above $100,000, to which the networks were asked to add half a percent of their time sales. Haverlin's arsenal included regular updated reports of progress.

An experienced music man of stature, capable of managing the BMI operation, and not afraid of repercussions from the music business should it fail, was hard to find. Neville Miller, president of the NAB, became BMI president, also, but because he was unable to be on the scene every day, Kaye was elected operating head and attorney. For general manager, Kaye chose Merritt Tompkins, former head of Schirmer, and most recently president of the AMP.

BMI's staff and the flow of printed sheet music and arrangements for various instrumental and vocal combinations were constantly increased. Though Tompkins's experience had been primarily in classical and foreign concert music, under his direction BMI was soon releasing one new popular song a day, and twenty-five new arrangements of public-domain, non-ASCAP musical numbers a week. With the support and a promise of suitable financial backing from CBS, which was also interested in acquiring a major ASCAP firm, and support from NBC, negotiations were conducted to purchase the MGM Big Three music catalogues for $4.5 million. Robbins, Feist, and Miller copyrights provided one seventh of all ASCAP music used in 1939, and could keep radio going for at least three months. Only a warning from songwriters published by the Big Three that their rights were nontransferable from ASCAP, and the possibility that MGM might be named a co-defendant in a rumored federal indictment against ASCAP frustrated the deal.

By September, BMI had 220 full-time employees, including all the available union arrangers, copyists, autographers, and proofreaders in New York, who turned out fourteen printed popular songs and thirty-five arrangements of BMI-licensed familiar public-domain music each week. In addition to regular new releases of transcribed selections in the BMI Bonus Library, made available without charge of subscribing stations, 400,000 units of printed music were shipped to them each month, together with vast quantities of music from thirty affiliated publishers. These included Ricordi, of Milan, some American standard-music houses, and the M. M. Cole Company, of Chicago, a former SESAC affiliate and a leading publisher of hillbilly and cowboy music, available in cheap folio editions that sold in the Midwest and South and were promoted at Saturday-night barn dances and on transcribed hillbilly-music shows.

Before the year ended, BMI cracked a tenuous ASCAP-publisher front and executed long-term contracts with Ralph Peer and Edward B. Marks. The latter was a veteran music man and a founder of Tin Pan Alley. Each of them had regularly petitioned ASCAP for a reclassification of ratings, but without getting any relief. Their copyrights proved to be crucial to BMI's survival during its first year, Peer's because of the Latin-American popular music he provided, and Marks's because it answered pleas by advertising agencies for recognizable music suitable for their network programs.

When he left RCA Victor in 1932 as the sole owner of Southern Music Publishing Company, a business formed in association with the Victor Talking Machine Company for its race and hillbilly songs, Ralph Peer left behind a favored-nation licensing understanding with the recording firm and began the world-wide expansion of his Peer International Corporation. He opened offices in England and on the Continent, in South Africa, Latin America, and Canada. In the United States, he owned a number of ASCAP companies, among them the Charles K. Harris catalogue, and was a director and officer of the MPPA. His first international foray was in 1930 in Mexico, where Southern and Peer International gained control of a major catalogue of native popular and classical music for exploitation locally and around the world. Nine years later, in association with Don Emilio Aczcarraga, a leading financier and owner of major broadcasting properties, Peer formed Promotora Hispana Americana de Musica, in which he held a 49 percent interest, and Aczcarraga 35 percent. Peer also held the majority interest in the American Performing Rights Association, an enterprise that owned rights to a large catalogue of Latin-American compositions, including music from Cuba and other Caribbean countries. ASCAP refused to deal with either organization, because of their private ownership and profit-making nature, leaving Peer only SESAC or the new BMI to license his music in the United States. When rumors of Peer's negotiations with BMI reached ASCAP, a representative was dispatched to deal with Latin-American publishers and songwriters, only to learn that Peer had scooped up the cream of the lot. These and his Southern Music catalogue made Peer's copyrights a formidible source of music suitable to many stations, as well as for jukeboxes, now a major force in promoting new music.

BMI's continuing efforts to ally itself with a dissident but well-established ASCAP house that owned a substantial catalogue of past hits culminated in late 1940 with the signing of the E. B. Marks music business for five years, with a guarantee of $225,000 annually, and $25,000 to attorney Julian Abeles, who masterminded the deal. The networks' financing of this reflected their apprehension about the effect a switch from almost all ASCAP music to the BMI repertory would have on sponsors and advertising agencies, and the name bandleaders on commercial and late-night broadcasts.

Because the Warner music blackout in 1936 had demonstrably produced little complaint from listeners, most sponsors, other than George Washington Hill, reluctantly agreed to go along with the networks. The tobacco magnate, who threatened to take "Your Hit Parade" off the air unless BMI could guarantee familiar music, regarded that Marks acquisition as a personal victory, and promised to hold the line until the end of March 1941, playing only "the ten most popular songs available to radio." After several unsuccessful attempts to bring in the FCC or the Justice Department to knock heads together, and after BMI had bought a million-dollar infringement-suit insurance policy to protect itself and advertisers and their agencies, the most intractable Madison Avenue men went along with the sponsors who paid their commissions.

Remembering their experience in late 1935, when they prepared for a Warner music companies' strike with a gradual tapering off of music from those catalogues, the networks required, first, a reduction of ASCAP music by degrees on sustaining programs, and threatened to cut off remote pickups of bands that failed to comply. There was grudging acceptance until bandleaders found they could make more money plugging their own music and opened small publishing companies, licensed through BMI. By October, ASCAP music was reduced from 80 percent on sustaining programs and 76 percent on commercial broadcasts to 25 percent and 31 percent respectively.

Kaye's blueprint contained only a brief mention of compensation to songwriters and composers. Reference was made to original music "created by employees of the corporation," the work-for-hire principle that was then being tested in the courts in the "Come Josephine in My Flying Machine" case. Kaye thought that composers would be better off if they "received no compensation for performing rights, provided they received a fairer share of the revenue incidental to music publication and to the sale of mechanical rights."

Contracts with BMI's thirty affiliated publishers, who at the start were paid only an annual guaranteed sum, did not obligate them to pay their authors and composers for performing rights, though it was expected they would. As for the songwriters and composers whose music BMI published itself, the share of publication and recording rights was more generous than that in general practice. They were paid one penny per performance, either live or recorded, per station, based on a new system devised by Paul A. Lazarsfeld, of the Columbia University Office of Radio Research. It involved monthly examination of 60,000 hours of program logs listing all music, supplied to BMI by 150 stations in all parts of the country, as required in their contracts with the licensing body. One striking difference from the ASCAP method was payment for recorded performances, on both transcriptions and commercial disks, something the society did not do until the early 1950s. This gave a decided advantage to BMI in a new world in which "canned music" began to dominate time on the air.

On the day after Christmas in 1940, spokesmen for the Justice Department announced that it was entering the music war, and would add the NAB, BMI, NBC, CBS, and "possibly some others not yet specified," to the list of defendants in a criminal antitrust action in Wisconsin. Thurmond Arnold, the new assistant attorney general in charge of the antitrust division, was already furious with ASCAP for its "foot-dragging" in signing the consent decree for which the society had asked, to settle the revived action instituted in 1934. Denouncing the "ASCAP welchers and double-crossers," according to *Variety*, Arnold insisted that ASCAP meet every one of the six points raised in the 1934 complaint, rather than only the few covered by the proposed decree. In a recent book, *The Bottlenecks of Business*, the former Yale law professor had argued that "when copyright owners, each engaged in selling articles on which he holds valid copyrights, agree with each other to sell or distribute their copyrighted articles upon the same terms and conditions, such agreements and concert of action is outside any privileges conferred by the copyright law, and the resulting restraint of trade, if unreasonable, is prohibited by the Sherman Act."

While expressing surprise that they and their associates were to be indicted, both Gene Buck and Neville Miller praised Arnold for his intention to investigate their opponents. An invasion by network presidents, their most important assistants, and BMI board members swept into Washington on January 27, to meet with the NAB president. In the afternoon, Kaye visited the Justice Department, where he met with Arnold and his staff, but learned only that the preliminary investigation was not yet complete, that others would be indicted in short order, and that Arnold regarded BMI as a substitution of one monopoly for another.

There was little for the visitors to Washington to do, except to close ranks and hope for the best. On reflection, any last-minute compromise with ASCAP, renewing the present form of licensing, which the government appeared to regard as a violation of antitrust laws, would put them into additional jeopardy. Unlike 1935, radio was now prepared to take all possible precautions to avoid infringements. The society had set up listening posts in major centers to record as many as sixteen hours of broadcasting to document illegal use of its music. Of the million-dollar protection policy, a $30,000 premium check had already been cashed. A total of 660 stations, out of the 796 commercial facilities, were signed to BMI. Among the last-minute stragglers were members of the National Independent Broadcasters, who voted en masse to support BMI, despite the lure of ASCAP contracts offering lower rates. Others, antinetwork to the death, intended to perform only ASCAP music. Some were already to be all-night oases of Tin Pan Alley and Hollywood music with midnight-to-dawn broadcasts, and to cash in on the situation.

The last week of December was the first without any ASCAP music on the networks and their affiliates. RCA Victor and Columbia Records, owned by the networks, were printing legends affirming the ASCAP or BMI status of each selection on all new releases, and small new companies were doing the same. Guy Lombardo and other name bandleaders were prepared to go on the air on New Year's night with tax-free arrangements of "Auld Lang Syne."

The ASCAP v. radio music war was beginning in earnest.

CHAPTER 13

ASCAP versus the Broadcasters

There was general pessimism all along Tin Pan Alley as music publishers faced the prospect that popular sheet music had seen its day, that the business could no longer survive in its present state. A year or two earlier, the biggest song hits had sold between 500,000 and a million copies of sheet music. By 1931 the sale of 200,000 was extraordinary. Sold wholesale for between eighteen and twenty cents to music stores, retail dealers, jobbers, and syndicate stores, in equal proportion, four pages of printed music still cost about a nickle to produce, but few firms had more than a single hit in a year. Business was down everywhere. Kresge's, the largest outlet in America, since Woolworth had closed down its sheet-music departments, reported a 25 percent drop in sales, along with a 65 percent decline in three-for-a-dollar dance disks. The major record companies began laying off their most expensive artists when the sale of the most popular disks began to slip under the 40,000 mark. The chief source of income for members of the Music Publishers Protective Association was from mechanical licensing—the twenty-five cents collected by the association for four minutes of radio play on electrical transcriptions. After a strict rationing of free orchestrations, the sale of printed dance arrangements tripled, wiping out, for most large houses, losses from the operations of their professional departments.

Song pluggers, piano players, counter boys and girls were being fired and branch offices reduced to those in Chicago and Los Angeles. In New York, only those bands that were on the air with a sponsored show or at least five times a week on sustaining programs were sent free music. On the West Coast, the twelve top bands, out of sixty working in the area, got free music; the others received only orchestrations with some parts removed, so that a complete copy would have to be bought.

For the first time, bandleaders headed for the long-shunned hinterland, traveling in large buses to cut expenses. They played one-night stands at dollar-a-couple ballrooms, on a straight percentage of receipts, with or without guarantee. Many were ready to play free of charge, hoping one engagement might lead to others.

Many music men believed that the spreading practice of cutting in band-leaders as the authors of new songs, in return for plugging on the air, was a poison that was destroying the business. Long an industry plague, this generally condoned form of bribery was assuming proportions greater than existed in the mid-1920s, when ASCAP and the MPPA invoked curbs, which proved no cure. More than 300 new songs were constantly involved in the process, creating great confusion among sheet-music buyers, whose leisure-time expenditures had been drastically reduced. The most popular bandleaders and singing stars were rich and independent, beyond such control as Albee and Murdock once imposed by banning all non-MPPA music. They called their own tunes, from which they collected royalties in addition to a weekly payment, and regarded both as part of the trade. In the past year, Rudy Vallee, proud that he had collected $75,000 in sheet-music and mechanical royalties, was cut in on seventy-five new songs, Guy Lombardo on sixty-five, Vincent Lopez on forty. In the case of the current hit "I'm Gonna Get You," two rival West Coast bandleaders were listed among its authors, neither having seen the music before an advance copy was shown to him. One of the most frequent "collaborators," Ben Bernie, won a breach-of-contract suit by demonstrating in court that he could neither read nor write music.

A controversial resolution aimed at the practice, calling for a fine of half a year's ASCAP distribution, was unanimously approved at the annual meeting in March 1931. With their chief sources of revenue—sheet music and record royalties—about to be unimportant by-products, publishers deeply involved in the payoffs rushed to make deals with new artists and band-leaders before the regulation became effective later in the year. For Class A publishers, the penalty would amount to $20,000; for top-rated writers, about $2,500. Six months passed before the first formal charge was made; it was against Roy Turk and Fred Ahlert, who cut in Bing Crosby on their new song "When the Blue of the Night Meets the Gold of the Day," in order to get the crooner to use it for the theme song of his CBS show.

Turk and Ahlert were among the AA ASCAP writers who joined Billy Rose, Sigmund Romberg, Harry Warren, and others in a fraternal group formed two years earlier to serve as a counterbalance to the publishers' association. There was some disagreement about restoring the division of performing rights to the two-to-one writer-publisher ratio abandoned in 1921, but everyone was united behind the idea of a uniform songwriters' contract and a closed shop for members of the Songwriters. The publishers had recently cut all sheet-music royalties to a penny a copy, citing the reduction to a 16½-cent maximum wholesale price forced on them by Kresge's and the jobbers. A new Songwriters Protective Association emerged from the deliberations. It opened its rolls to ASCAP members who agreed to join for life. In August 1931, Billy Rose was elected president of the SPA, and his friend Arthur Garfield Hays, attorney for the Authors' League, was hired to guide the group in framing a suitable new contract. It was expected to change the order of things and put songwriters on the same footing as authors and dramatists, who could hold copyrights in their own names throughout the two terms of protection, for fifty-six years. The SPA hoped to push through a clarification of who owned the small rights, in favor of songwriters, who could then license each of them: publication, mechanical reproduction, public performance. To demonstrate their concern for the future of ASCAP, all SPA members, 100 of them by the end of 1931, were ready to grant the last right to the society for life. The MPPA would not make a similar offer.

The very mention of a possible affiliation with the American Federation of Labor, which was discussed with its president, William Green, stiffened the publishers' opposition to the SPA. Lobbying in Washington, where Rose had many contacts, produced the introduction of an amendment to the Copyright Act that would make it, like the patent laws, call for registration in the name of the creator. As practical men, the SPA leaders were forced to agree with those voices of caution among the membership who believed that the SPA might have gone too far. Demands were modified, and ASCAP was asked to arbitrate.

While meetings between the SPA and the MPPA continued, the half-dozen New York music houses that published almost all the hits demonstrated their control of the business as an object lesson to the "presumptuous" songwriters. Though there was little profit in foreign songs, now that ASCAP income provided most of a firm's funds, the first agreement between ASCAP and the British Performing Rights Society, to run for three years beginning on January 1, 1930, called for a blanket payment of $15,000 a year to the British music business. Most of the American firms that published European songs shared performing rights with their foreign partners, at best a minuscule portion of the small sums paid to the licensing societies. Nevertheless, in the first half of 1932, these six music houses selected imported songs for their number-one plugs. Radio and movie crooners found these "different" popular songs to their liking and were cut in on most. Almost single-handed, Rudy Vallee plugged the British "Goodnight, Sweetheart" into a half-million-copy hit.

After seven months, a "standard uniform popular songwriters' contract" was ready for distribution, having won the approval of both ASCAP and the MPPA at the board level. The agreement did not establish any minimum royalty from sheet-music sales; instead, it called for individual negotiation. A minimum 33⅓ share of mechanical and foreign rights was fixed, as well as of "receipts from any other source or right now known or which may hereafter come into existence." Its vague language permitted publishers to withhold any share of the rapidly mounting radio transcription disk fees collected by the MPPA on behalf of its members, or from the talking-picture synchronization fees. The first of these was regarded as a "grant right," and not as the double taxation on broadcast performances it might otherwise be described. The contract introduced regular accounting periods and gave the writers the right to have an accountant examine the publishers' books. It did not deal with the issue on which Romberg and others intended to stand firm: Who owns the small rights?

The death of ASCAP's general manager, J. C. Rosenthal, in late December 1931, created a vacuum in management that was filled, at the behest of his publisher friends, by Claude Mills. NBC's six-million-dollar venture into the music business, with the purchase of eight ASCAP music companies, had proved to be less profitable than Warner's $10-million purchase, and both were engaged in ridding themselves of all or part of these properties and employees. Mills had been a principal in the network's music operation, but when the subsidiaries were sold back to their original owners, at a substantial loss, he was asked to remain as a consultant to NBC until his contract ran out. Over the protests of songwriters, who remembered his role in arranging their capitulation to the publishers in 1920, he was brought back to ASCAP at a salary of $50,000 a year from ASCAP and set to work on what he regarded as the first order of business: changes in the method of distribution and of license-fee collections—along lines he had unsuccessfully tried to introduce in 1928.

The society's latest try to rectify injustices had been made the previous April, when the publisher payment ratios were rearranged and a new double-letter classification was added to the top three classes. The amount of payment to each class was also changed. Storms of protest and pleas for reclassification came from all but those in Classes AA and A. Jack Robbins was the loudest. He was the only large publisher to have been punished for a violation of the cut-in rules; his income was reduced by 75 percent when he was moved from Class A to Class D. He also claimed discrimination, because MGM, which held the majority interest in his business, would not join ASCAP as a publisher member. Irving Berlin resumed his continuing unsuccessful efforts to gain recognition as both an author and a composer, and Edward Marks, owner of a catalogue of music dating back to the 1890s, got no response to his request for a higher rating.

In the summer of 1932, Robbins took his cause to the courts, filing an antitrust suit against ASCAP, which for the first time made public the workings of publisher classification and exposed the extent of control of the board of directors by motion-picture interests. By voting together, Warner Brothers, Paramount, the music houses of Irving Berlin and the Santley brothers, which had agreements with Universal Pictures, and Max Dreyfus's half-dozen firms that represented major Broadway production writers were in a position to dominate the society, or, if they chose, to split away and form their own licensing collection agency. Soon after, Robbins was voted a return to Class A and retroactive royalties, and the suit was dropped. Mills's proposal for a new payment system, which would distribute 70 percent of all money on the basis of use by customers, was temporarily shelved, as was a campaign to increase license fees from motion-picture theater operators for the first time since 1917.

A year earlier, Gene Buck, the ASCAP president, had warned that to press for higher fees from radio would only lead to legislation harmful to ASCAP. Rosenthal, who was excusing the delinquencies of broadcasters near bankruptcy, also urged caution. Now that it was obvious that income from radio would fall below the 1931 levels, and most songwriters and small publishers could no longer rely on their ASCAP money for support, the time had come for an increase from the business that killed music through repeated use. A modest one of 25 percent, to $1.25 million a year, was proposed, and, of course, rejected by the National Association of Broadcasters.

Anticipating a fight to the finish with ASCAP, the NAB made plans for another tax-free library of music to take the place of the society's copyrights if the need arose. There were many in the music business who welcomed the prospect of a war with radio, whose concentrated use of a small body of hit songs was killing them off within a few months. They were ready for a showdown and a return to the old ways of song plugging in theaters, dance halls, vaudeville houses, and restaurants, which could, they predicted create substantial hits and prolong their lives.

Claude Mills was assigned to meet with former network colleagues and began discussions with executives from CBS, NBC, and an independent affiliated station. Edward Klauber of CBS handled the final negotiations. Seeking to hasten a settlement, the network representatives suggested that the chains would cooperate provided some recognition was made of their vast expenditures for the development of radio through furnishing sustaining programs to their affiliates and for experimental work not reimbursed by their affiliates. It was proposed that, rather than tax the networks "at the source," ASCAP collect its royalties from the income by all local stations, including their owned-and-operated facilities.

With Mills, Klauber forged an agreement, to expire at the end of 1935, calling for fees that would rise annually from three to five percent of all commercial time sales, less specified deductions, over the next three years. The networks' first contracts with ASCAP contained what was to become known as the "twilight zone exclusion," which allowed the chains to escape from any ASCAP fees for commercial programs other than those by their owned-and-operated stations. Unaware of the full ramifications of this provision, the ASCAP board approved the agreement, and members of the society hailed a contract that was expected to bring in at least three times the 1931 collections from broadcasting in purely "sustaining fees."

What Klauber achieved with Mills's cooperation was an agreement that eliminated the network's gross income from licensing fees and focused instead on proceeds collected directly by the radio stations. It was generally anticipated that the chains would receive around $40 million in 1933, the first year the new contracts would be in force, and the other broadcasters an additional $35 million. However, the networks' $40 million was immediately reduced by $6 million because the affiliates were paid only 15 percent of all time sales from sponsors for network programs. For example, a half hour on NBC's basic Blue Network, fourteen stations, was sold for $2,556. Instead of three percent of that, the ASCAP fees would be three percent of $350, or fourteen times the twenty-five dollars each Blue Network station was credited with by NBC.

As for the remaining $41 million, on which the society's expectations were based—$6 million paid to stations, plus the $35 million earned by local stations on their own—that figure was reduced to $25,840,000 after approved exemptions, deductions, and discounts amounting to more than 40 percent, which included the cost of station representatives and advertising-agency commissions, cash-payment discounts, and political and other music-license-free programs. Three percent of this remaining figure was $775,000, to which there was then added approximately $660,000 in sustaining fees, a grand estimated total of $1,435,000.

Within a few weeks, *Variety* said that the music business had been "outsmarted by broadcasters," and some network affiliates complained that they had "been exploited" by CBS and NBC. NBC affiliates among the latter were charging from $150 to more than $550 for an hour of locally sponsored time for, generally, electrically transcribed programs. When they were connected to the network, however, they received no more than $50 an hour. No option on their time was paid for by NBC, and when sponsors wished to include NBC affiliates in specific markets or regions along the network, separate agreements had to be made to ensure the coverage, the advertising sponsor being billed for any difference. Because of William Paley's determination to create a network that would rank one day above both NBC chains, the situation was different at CBS. It offered sustaining programing without charge of all affiliates (those of NBC paid $50 an hour for such feeds) in return for a confirmed option on any part of an affiliate's time on the air. All income from CBS network broadcasts was shared with the participating stations after expenses had been subtracted, based on a schedule that varied from station to station but in every case left the major portion of income to the network.

By 1940, according to the Mutual Broadcasting System's *White Paper* of May 23, 1941, twilight-zone income, "that portion of network receipts which is not paid over to affiliate stations or credited to the network's own stations, but is retained by the networks,'' represented about $34 million out of an estimated total of slightly more than $60.8 million of net network time sales, and of slightly less than $129 million of the entire industry's total net time sales.

ASCAP's public image was deemed to be so poor during the early 1930s, even by the society's own directors, that negotiations were held to secure the services of John D. Rockefeller's public-relations expert, Ivy Lee. Rather than complicate his position by such formidible competition, Claude Mills recommended the acceptance of a suggestion made by a newspaper-owned station manager that his owner and other press lords might be inclined to treat the society better on their pages if they were offered more advantageous contracts than other broadcasters. The most-favored-nation agreement prepared for newspaper stations provided Oscar Schuette and the NAB with yet another opportunity to point out publicly ASCAP's traditional discriminatory practices. Nevertheless, nearly 250 stations had signed with ASCAP, accepting the various terms offered, by Christmas of 1932.

Heavy drains on ASCAP reserves, made in the third quarter of 1932 by publishers and writers who applied for relief, had brought the society to a desperate point. The finance committee, made up of men of substantial wealth, among them Jerome Kern, Otto Harbach, and Louis Bernstein, who handled the society's investment portfolio of more than a million dollars invested in blue-chip securities, had themselves suffered a dramatic decline in their fortunes and were reluctant to recommend that ASCAP sell at a loss, but conditions indicated it should.

Surprisingly, even after *Variety* made public their error in accepting the networks' exclusion of their own time-sales income, the ASCAP directors did not blame Mills for the blunder. He was put in charge of streamlining the society's operating systems and methods, which absorbed thirty-two cents of every dollar taken in. A committee studying reclassification, made up only of Class AA and A publishers, recommended that income from radio be set aside in a separate fund to be divided among writers and publishers only on the basis of performances. The proposal was immediately adopted by the very same men who had made it and stood to gain the most from it.

After months of planning, in the summer of 1932 the thirteen leading music publishers, who brought out 60 percent of all new songs (Shapiro, Bernstein; Irving Berlin; Remick; Donaldson; Douglas & Gumble; Leo Feist; De Sylva, Brown & Henderson; Harms; Witmark; Santley, Ager, Yellen & Bornstein, Famous; Mills Music), banned together to merge their distribution and bookkeeping departments into a single cooperative entity, the Music Dealers Service. They hoped to save what they regarded as a fast-sinking business by controlling distribution, fixing prices, and acting in restraint of trade, even as their forgotten ancestors, the Board of Music Trade, had done throughout half of the nineteenth century. Many of them believed that the middleman-jobber had outlived his usefulness, and considered methods to freeze him out of handling printed popular, standard, and production music by servicing the retailer directly, at the jobber's prices. Some important wholesalers, who were also music publishers, would be eliminated— Lyon & Healy in Chicago, Sherman, Clay of San Francisco, and the Jenkins Company of Kansas City—all of whom had been responsible for extending the lines of distribution for Tin Pan Alley throughout the country, from its earliest days. So, too, would be Richmond, Mayer Music Supply and the Plaza Music Company, New York's most important wholesalers, who distributed hit songs only in order to sell their own publications of reprinted noncopyright music.

Each member firm invested $1,000 in the MDS, but for the time being it was expected to operate on the proceeds from a penny added to wholesale prices. A twenty-five-cent was printed on all copies of popular, two-page songs. The wholesale price was fixed at fifteen cents, providing a uniform 40 percent margin of profit to retailers. Harms's production songs and imported stage music went for thirty-five cents at retail, the price the company had always demanded, as did similar publications by other houses. Fifty-cent orchestrations were sold wholesale for 37½ cents, and the new "prestige" seventy-five-cent arrangements for forty-five cents. A ticket for a vacation in Florida was given to any large retailer who agreed to deal only with the MDS. To remove any doubt about its future, Maurice Richmond, of Richmond, Mayer, was brought in as general manager.

No increase in sheet-music sales was immediately evident, but in less than ninety days Richmond's former partner, Max Mayer, filed a $1.125-million antitrust action against the MDS and the twenty-two publishing firms it represented, charging that they had combined and conspired unlawfully to control the sheet-music business, and had sought to eliminate him as a competitor. Troubling already muddied waters at the MPPA, John Paine, Mills's successor as chairman of the board, was also named a defendant, described as the organizer, representative, and agent for the MDS.

Immediately after *Mayer* v. *MDS et al.* finally went to trial, in March 1934, attorneys for the Warner firms and Irving Berlin's company approached Mayer with an offer to settle the matter in his favor in return for a cash payment and the promise to dissolve the MDS and restore the jobber-publisher relationship to its former state. Stunned by this unexpected development, other firms scurried to join them, offering an average settlement of $7,500 each. On the ninth day of the trial, only three publishers, representing less than 10 percent of the MDS's business, remained to fight the action. The jury was released, and both sides agreed that the judge's decision would be binding, without any chance of appeal. His ruling came as the trial's second surprise, giving MDS only a tainted bill of health. The judge found the uniformity of wholesale prices disturbing, tending to support the belief that some form of understanding existed, but the plaintiff had not produced proof of its actual existence. Though he lost the suit, Mayer was victorious in hastening the dissolution of the MDS. Richmond immediately began organizing his own jobbing business to take over MDS's functions.

In 1933, ASCAP was forced to cancel the annual dinner instituted in 1914, and rented a large hotel room for an open meeting, putting the $4,000 to $5,000 saved into the fund for relief loans to members. Writer and publisher checks for the first quarter were higher than they had been a year earlier, though only with a supplementary disbursement. They were smaller, however, than for the last quarter of 1932, a year when $1.8 million was collected, half of it from radio, but $100,000 less than for 1931. Broadcasters' right by contract to delay payments for forty-five days was cited as a reason for the smaller checks. Not until the end of 1933 did a 10 to 15 percent increase become evident.

At the annual meeting, it was suggested by newcomers to ASCAP that the organization change its name to the American Society of Publishers, because of their self-perpetuating control. Writers who had recently joined flayed their own classification committee for the way in which it determined ratings, always giving preference to the no-longer-productive old-timers. The constant stream of complaint led finally to the creation, late in 1933, of a writer review board, elected by popular vote. Many now believed that the SPA could do a better job of representing songwriters than the society. Sigmund Romberg and his fellow officers were to pursue the introduction of an amendment to the copyright law that would permit splitting a copyright and assigning of individual rights.

Hard times were getting harder. A number of the syndicate stores on which the publishers depended for large sales were forced to shut down. Record royalties were at the lowest point ever, but synchronization fees turned out to be higher, due to the $825,000 settlement of the "bootleg seat" tax against ERPI, which had omitted to account for their number as screen theaters proliferated before the Depression.

Looking for a more prosaic and homey song to suit the times, the public was making hits of "Goodnight, Little Girl," "Just a Little Street Where Old Friends Meet," and "The Valley of the Moon," all of which sold more than 350,000 copies, rivaling the sale of the best song written in the past ten years—"Stormy Weather"—and a hillbilly song, "The Last Roundup," which went over the half-million mark. But the sale of 5,000 copies a day was not required for Class AA publishers to break even, and their guaranteed $35,000 ASCAP income could not stop drastic reductions of personnel and expenses.

Under the new system, predicated on the number of performances, ASCAP found the foreign societies clamoring for money. Accustomed to a total census of all music performed by licensees, and not just that by radio, the

French society, for example, wanted a 500 percent increase from the $20,000 a year it was receiving, a sum ASCAP could not afford.

In spite of *Variety*'s continued insistence that Mills, with his honey-toned drawl, to which, one wag had it, a person could waltz, was too much a hayseed for ASCAP's sophisticated customers, Ivy Lee's polished Wall Street public-relations techniques proved to be even more out of place. Mills was asked to take on more of the office operations and began to pay attention to the problems of the younger writer members. To placate those who complained, with justification, that they were discriminated against in favor of older members with permanent A, B, C, or D rank, a special fund of $12,500 was set aside each quarter. It was distributed among the writers of the ten most-played songs for that period, which first were listed on a regular weekly basis by *Variety* on September 5, 1933. Coincidentally, the West Coast radio bandleader Meredith Willson introduced a precursor to "Your Hit Parade" when he played *Variety*'s top ten songs on weekly broadcasts from San Francisco. Out-of-work songwriters and song pluggers were hired to monitor establishments that refused to take out an ASCAP license.

Mills's long and close relationship with some music publishers and his recent concern for songwriters did little to spare him their wrath when a report was completed on the society's first year under the contract he had predicted would bring in two million dollars. It showed only a $300,000 gain, and that the networks had paid on only 18 percent of time sales. His explanation, that the Depression was reducing radio income generally, was contested, and the board remembered that he had advised it to reject an early offer by broadcasters to guarantee $250,000 more than in the previous year, while maintaining a higher sustaining fee than in the new pact. Tempers were defused for a time by Mills's announcement of pending negotiations with A T & T to use its ERPI subsidiary, to do what it did for the MPPA, and collect from all radio stations. ERPI would perform the job for a 25 percent commission, less than the thirty-five cents out of every dollar currently spent. The proposition died when A T & T removed itself from consideration on the ground that such an association might conflict with other corporate interests. The music business, however, was reminded of Claude Mills's easy access to the business world, where rumors flew that a Justice Department probe of ASCAP was being instigated by Newton D. Baker, the new NAB counsel and a prominent figure in the Democratic Party, then in power.

Mills established amicable relations with Baker immediately and then with Baker's assistant and successor at the NAB. Both were apprised of Mills's bottom line, that ASCAP would dissolve itself if it had to, under government pressure, leaving the networks and broadcasters the inevitable chaos in copyright that would follow. In discussing the situation with NBC officials, who considered dissolution of ASCAP the last thing they wanted,

Mills was assured that they would not support the NAB's tax-free bureau, and might be amenable to maintaining a 5 percent rate throughout the decade, possibly with some taxation at the network source.

Along with other established businesses, Tin Pan Alley was required to submit a code governing their trade practices, wage scales, and other affairs, intended to eliminate unfair competition, a chore that was taken up by John Paine and the MPPA. A tentative covenant was sent to Washington, over the protests of member publishers who claimed that it went beyond the intention of the 1933 National Industrial Recovery Act and would "not only squeeze the business dry of all friendly intercourse with the exploiters of music but seriously hamper individual initiative," according to *Variety*. "Friendly intercourse" was presumably that involved in securing radio performances or in "greasing" sheet-music pluggers employed by the major chain stores and the largest retailers. Not even after the NRA and its blue eagle were declared unconstitutional could publishers agree on regulations that might control paying for plugs.

Of more immediate concern to Tin Pan Alley was the interest shown by the SPA and Hollywood-connected music houses in revising ASCAP's Articles of Association. Writers wanted an assurance written into them that they would share equally with the publishers in all music rights. Determined to get a new classification to ensure them a larger share of distributions, the Warner music group indicated that it might not renew with ASCAP in 1935, when the present affiliation agreements ended. It was felt in Hollywood that it might be cheaper to license all Warner music separately, or else buy time on the air to promote new film songs and screen musicals, than to operate expensive music companies under the present structure. Whatever the future, Warner would not countenance a change to the "tenants in common" language the SPA demanded.

During the winter of 1933–34, Sigmund Romberg wrote a long, confidential memorandum to the SPA officers and council, dealing with ASCAP's difficulties. He proposed a number of changes in the articles, in return for which SPA writers would sign renewals of membership to ensure survival of ASCAP for at least the next five years. Essentially, he wanted changes that would remove the restrictions imposed on the writer by the Copyright Act of 1909. As to who owned the small rights, the recognition of which first made it possible for ASCAP to exist and operate, he urged support of an amendment to the Copyright Act introduced by William Sirovich, of New York, which provided that "the author or composer may, to the extent of his ownership, license all or any part of the rights of such author or composer."

When the memorandum was offered to the ASCAP board, there was such opposition from publishers that any significant changes were postponed. A temporary palliative was offered by the institution of separate classification review boards, elected by popular vote, whose findings would be final.

The publisher of many of the best-known SPA members, Max Dreyfus was prominent among the financial backers of the lobby working to kill the Sirovich bill. Ironically, a tribute to him, written by Gene Buck, appeared in the SPA *Bulletin* in which Romberg's prescription for restoring ASCAP to good health first appeared in print. "One of the most outstanding music publishers in the history of American music," Buck called him, "primarily because he sensed the fundamental necessity of inspiring faith and confidence in the composer and author and realizing that his firm could only be as good as his writers." After the defeat of the Sirovich bill, the SPA council gave much thought to the possibility that ASCAP might be dissolved and they would have to step in and take over its licensing function on behalf of the writers. More than 500 authors and composers and most small music houses were ready to renew their ASCAP affiliation for five years, but the large publishing firms, chiefly the Warner group, held out, fearing the vague promises in the agreement to effect changes in ASCAP's distribution process and the compromise in the small-rights impasse being urged on them by their own most successful authors and composers.

Meantime, the eighteen-year-old war conducted by the MPPA over the payment of gratuities to performers went on. John Paine was given the power of attorney to act for MPPA members and immediately to levy a fine of $1,000 on the first occasion a publisher was found giving payments or free orchestrations to bandleaders. A $200 fine was exacted for each succeeding offense. One third of the money collected went to the informant; the remainder was for the operation of the association. The large movie-connected houses found little in the MPPA to warrant their participation and continued to remain outside the group. A new point system was introduced at ASCAP, removing the AAA classification enjoyed only by Harms, and the AA for the other major publishers. A performance on NBC or CBS was credited with one point; every use in a major motion picture, with one quarter. In the third quarter of 1934, Harms topped the list, with 681 points; Berlin was second, with 610. Jerome Kern, majority owner of the Warner firm that published his music, agreed to unlimited use of the songs from his latest Broadway production. For years he had insisted on the restriction of all new music for six months, but, having observed how the widespread plugging of his "Smoke Gets in Your Eyes" made a hit of *Roberta* despite unfavorable notices, he had become an avid reader of *Variety*'s most-played list. The song was seventh on the year's recapitulation of network plugs, and ninth of the ten songs that received one tenth of all performances on NBC and CBS and were published by houses owned or associated with Hollywood.

When the *Mayer* v. *MDS* lawsuit was settled, the plaintiff, Max Mayer, had turned over to the Federal Trade Commission the evidence purporting to prove the interlocking interests of ASCAP, the MPPA, and the MDS. The split between the networks and their affiliates and the majority of the business, initially springing from economic differences, now extended to fixed opposing positions on music licensing. The chains feared dissolution of ASCAP, though each felt the society was in technical violation of the law, but most members of the NAB wanted it put out of business. In response to countless complaints from broadcasters, the Justice Department's antitrust division engaged in an investigation of ASCAP that began in 1933.

On August 31, 1934, a formal complaint was filed in the New York District Court, charging ASCAP, all its 778 writers and 102 publishers, the MPPA, and the MDS with having interlocking directorates and agreements in a conspiracy to monopolize the music business. A perpetual injunction was sought to terminate agreements between the defendants and also with record companies and broadcasters. The MPPA board resigned immediately, but was replaced by other officers of the dominant member firms who remained on the ASCAP board.

The rush to trial was attributed by Tin Pan Alley and its lawyers to the approaching NAB convention, at which, as always, ASCAP would be the principal topic of discussion, and a possible conflicting action by the 15,000 motion-picture owners just before the expiration of their ASCAP contracts. After having postponed it several times, to keep the board united, ASCAP offered a new seat-tax agreement for the first time since 1917, which was expected to bring in as much as an additional four million dollars.

The first effect of the government suit was the hasty compromise with the theater operators, arranged by Buck and Mills, which called for only a 50 percent increase in fees and much less in actual income. This was followed by a forty-two page reply to charges. Just before New Year's Day 1935, the society's veteran legal adviser, Nathan Burkan, went on a vacation, leaving behind an ASCAP management and board confident of the successful outcome of the trial, though faced with mounting problems on the Warner front.

After a game of golf with William Paley of CBS, Harry Warner, the operating head of the giant film company built by him and his brothers, was determined to make at least a million-dollar annual profit from the music business. Commenting of CBS's most recent balance sheet, Paley had attributed much of its profits to musical programs like that he had created starring Bing Crosby. The task of increasing Warner's ASCAP income was given to Herman Starr, Warner Brothers treasurer, who came to the business in 1920 as an accountant and, when the company was incorporated in 1923, was elected a director and assistant treasurer. Three years later, he organized the first Warner companies in Europe. In 1926, he moved to First National Pictures, as president and director, but when it was merged with Warner four years later, he became a vice-president of the combined firms. He was made president of the recording, radio-set manufacturing, and music division of Brunswick, Balke, Collender when it was acquired in 1930. Starr put Jack Kapp in charge of recording activities. After Herbert Yates's purchase of the entire Brunswick record business, he was elected president of the remaining Brunswick Radio Corporation, a Warner subsidiary until 1942, when it was sold to Kapp. It is doubtful that Kapp would have been able to build the new Decca Record Company without Starr's support and the access he provided to Brunswick's rusting pressing equipment, old-fashioned though it was. A testy, domineering man, remembered by those surviving songwriters who dealt with him as possessing a long memory where enemies were concerned, Starr instructed Warner representatives on the ASCAP board, among them Buddy Morris, the operating head of the Music Publishers Holding Corp., that they should proceed on the assumption that Warner would pull out of the society at the end of 1935 unless its share of publisher distributions was greatly increased.

An intensive drive was launched to obtain at least part of the renewal rights of songs written in the years 1910 through 1913, so that Warner could claim their performing rights, and an employee was settled in Washington to comb the copyright registration files. To increase the use of Warner musical comedies and operettas, fees for radio use were substantially reduced. This use fell under Warner's grand rights, never yet defined by the courts, though the music business claimed that the performance of three or more selections from a stage work, with some of the dialogue and narration tying the songs together constituted a grand right. This was not covered by any ASCAP license or agreement. Without any variation, the same principle was applied in licensing electrical transcriptions—the twenty-five cents for four minutes of radio use.

Mills, Buck, and a majority of the ASCAP board members made strenuous efforts to keep the Warner firms, offering to compromise on the renewal contract, removing Mills as the sole and final arbitrator of differences over publisher-distribution values, and conveying their belief that the SPA would eventually be brought into the fold on the "tenants in common" argument. Starr would not budge, and because they believed that ASCAP might be dissolved should he prevail, most publishers signed the five-year renewals. The film publishers did not, even though all television rights were excluded, because they insisted that grand, and not small, rights were involved. Starr's resolve was strengthened by a sound defeat at the annual meeting of an amendment to the by-laws instituting elections by popular vote. It was sponsored by the Warner firms and supported by Hollywood songwriters, many of whom had what appeared to them to be a permanent B rating.

Mills and Buck then went to Los Angeles to placate the writers and lure back Jerome Kern, who had resigned from the ASCAP board to protest the defeat. While there, the pair met with Harry Warner, who told them that he would leave the society unless ASCAP distributions were based completely on performances, as was done by the British society. It was evident that the die had already been cast. To obtain the million dollars a year he wanted, Warner required $2.5 million annually: $1 million for writers, $250,000 for collection expenses, and the balance for profit, clearly more than the entire $2 million being collected for 1935, of which Warner would get $360,000, with an additional $40,000 from the MPPA for electrical transcriptions. The movie magnate did not mention that he was also talking to Paley about a sale to CBS of all Warner's music houses. There was substance to rumors from Washington that Warner lawyers were seeking a separate consent decree for the company in the antitrust suit against ASCAP, in order to begin separate music licensing. To that end, negotiations were instituted with the two major networks to license the Warner catalogue, which represented 40 percent of the ASCAP repertory and 80 percent of all Broadway musicals written in the last several decades. Starr made clear that there would be no last-minute reconciliation without a victory, when he took over from Morris on the ASCAP board and immediately demanded an accounting of all income, expenses, and royalty distributions since 1925, down to Mills's expense accounts.

At the semiannual membership meeting in October, Burkan warned that, in his opinion, 70 percent of the writers on Hollywood payrolls had contracts that signed away all rights, including that of public performance. Only Berlin, Kern, Romberg, and Youmans were in a position to reserve both grand and small rights. Although a standard clause in producer-songwriter contracts recognized that the performance right was subject to an agreement with ASCAP, Burkan said, when the present affiliation agreement expired, producers could regain ownership of the right and add it to the mechanical rights they already controlled. The issue had not been tested in an American court, but in a single case in England the court found for the writer. The Hollywood contracts were subject to the publishers' membership in ASCAP, an advantage on which Starr based his right to withdraw.

While Mills was conferring with the NAB about a new contract to begin in 1936, he was also negotiating with the networks. The revelation of their decision to renew with ASCAP, at a steady 5 percent for five more years, came as a bombshell to most broadcasters. The sudden recess of the government suit after only nine days made it clear that the case was on shaky ground, and that it was only a matter of time before it would be dropped. With only Warner as an alternative, and succumbing to pressures from the IRNA, many broadcasters signed, reluctantly. Diehards, however, took advantage of the ninety-day provisional contract offer by Warner, and began to exclude ASCAP music, in order to force Mills to come up with an acceptable per-piece arrangement.

The entire Warner group resigned officially in early December, leaving other film publishers in a quandary about their own future action. A final olive branch was held out to them by ASCAP with the installation of a new method of payment: a 50 percent distribution based on performances, and the balance based on availability-seniority. The holdout firms were told privately that without them the society would have to turn over everything to the songwriters and the SPA. That possibility was too dreadful to contemplate, and a united writer and publisher front existed on New Year's Day. Despite his earlier judgment, Burkan was ready to defend the networks in case of infringement suits, now proceeding on the theory that Warner's music was licensed by ASCAP through the songwriters.

Pay for air play was taking its dreadful toll in 1936 of publishers and songwriters. Not new to the business, of either classical or vernacular music, payola was omnipresent and international. In England, a standard price of two pounds prevailed for the introductory performance of a song on the BBC, and one pound for each subsequent playing. It was customary, too, for a publisher to pay all musical and talent costs when his music was recorded. In the United States, neither the MPPA, the FTC, nor organized contact men—once known as "song pluggers"—were able to halt its pervasion of Tin Pan Alley. It cost at least $1,000 to start a song on its way to the top of the *Variety* list, or to the number-one spot on "Your Hit Parade." The star vocalists on radio and the big bandleaders with commercial shows had their own private arrangements with the music houses— being cut in on songs as co-writers and getting free baseball or football tickets or lavish gifts of clothing, liquor, women, and, always, free orchestrations. When the New York musicians' union levied a charge of three dollars per man for remote broadcasts, the tab was usually picked up by a publisher with music to peddle. A special arrangement cost twenty-five dollars, only five of which went to the man who did the work; the leader pocketed the difference. Song pluggers, whose stock in trade traditionally was the good will, personality, and (often synthetic) enthusiasm they brought to their work, became singers on predinnertime sustaining popular-music programs, or got out of the business, or served as messengers, carrying professional copies, orchestrations, and money to bandleaders. Fearful they might be replaced by envelopes, in late 1935 175 working pluggers banded together for mutual support and solace. They were careful to explain to their employers that Professional Music Men was a fraternal organization, with no trade-union implications.

The hysteria extended to Hollywood, where film producers and songwriters imported from the Broadway theater and Tin Pan Alley poured over the latest *Variety* lists, and, when not satisfied, belabored their New York outlets with complaints about the poor showings. They told everyone that overplugging killed songs, but the best songwriters began to place high-stake wagers on the progress up the chart of competing songs, using *Variety* as the sole arbiter of the success, if not the quality, of their music. Under that publication's scoring system in 1936, even a recognizable strain of a song was reckoned as a complete plug, and scheming music firms paid a bandleader to feature a number of songs in a "medley," which added the same number of points to their weekly score.

Starr fired all his song pluggers at the end of December and resorted to the use of mailed requests to his 167 licensed customers, asking them to play songs from new Warner Brothers musicals whenever convenient. To take advantage of the absence of these MPHC pluggers, a new wave of extraordinarily expanded song plugging began, reducing the possibility of complaints from radio listeners about the music-licensing situation. The rush to get on *Variety*'s lists produced an overnight hit, smacking of the days in 1923 when "Yes We Have No Bananas" was king, for Santley, Joy, Select, the music house in which Bing Crosby had an interest, and which got all the songs from his movie musicals. After only two weeks, orders for 300,000 copies of "The Music Goes 'Round and 'Round" poured in, and, after sales jumped over the 600,000-copy mark, three motion-picture companies bought it for forthcoming musicals.

When Starr announced a reduction from the twenty-five- and fifty-cent fees per radio use of transcribed songs to two cents only for mechanical rights, some advertising agencies and music libraries concentrated on his music. There was immediate panic among publishers, because the practice of charging for both performing and mechanical rights in connection with transcriptions might be declared illegal. Matters became even more complicated when, in a suit defending against alleged infringement of Warner copyrights, CBS followed Burkan's lead and questioned the total ownership of all privileges of copyright by music publishers, including that of public performance. Warner's return to ASCAP was made a major priority.

The vast majority of independent stations had held back from renewing ASCAP contracts. Hoping to change their minds, the society floated several rumors: ASCAP was about to go out of business and turn its affairs over to the SPA; it was providing the money for some large music houses to buy Warner Brothers out of the music business; Claude Mills was moving over to NBC to take charge of music-rights acquisition. Things were not going well for Starr, who was able to collect only $25,000 a month from NAB stations and those commercial broadcasters who had taken out licenses for fear of copyright suits. He did manage to eke out several thousand dollars of profit monthly from sheet-music sales and recording royalties paid on old songs. Warner's $170,000 share of the record $935,000 taken in by ASCAP for the first quarter of 1936 was divided among loyal publishers, but most Warner writers turned their checks over to the ASCAP relief fund.

Maintaining the policy of genial cooperation Burkan recommended, ASCAP opened its files for the first time, to employees of the NAB, who compiled the first title index to ASCAP music, preparatory to building another tax-free library. The certainty of Warner's return and the death of Nathan Burkan marked the end of ASCAP's conciliatory policy.

The society's first and, thus far, only chief legal counsel, Burkan had begun practice in music copyright law for his first client, Victor Herbert, and then for the composer's publishers, the Witmarks. His clientele eventually extended into all branches of show business and included Charlie Chaplin, Florenz Ziegfeld, Mae West, Al Jolson, United Artists, Columbia, Paramount, MGM, and the MPPA, as well as ASCAP. He was, in addition, a member of the council for the notorious Tammany Democratic political club in New York City, where he served as a power behind the throne and had access to Congress and the White House. He succeeded in controlling the various factions that arose within ASCAP and the MPPA as no man other than Mills, on occasion, was able to do. A quarter of a century after his death, his portrait that hung on the walls of ASCAP's New York headquarters and the old-fashioned furniture from his office there were sent to the Songwriters' Hall of Fame in New York City.

Mills dangled revision of the ASCAP network contract as bait for Starr, whose vacant place on the board was not yet filled, interrupting the Warner music head's sudden renewal of negotiations with NBC and CBS for a ten-year contract recognizing payment at the source. This panic-inspired move by the networks was stimulated by a concern, now that Burkan was gone, that they would have to shoulder responsibility for all legal costs and a possible two-million-dollar judgment against them for copyright violations. By signing with Warner, they would have an effective hedge against any future ASCAP increases, know exactly what their expenses would be during a time of accelerated technological development and union demands, and repair, in time for the next NAB convention, the rift within the radio industry. Simultaneously, CBS and its law firm, Rosenberg, Goldmark and Colin, with which Sydney Kaye was associated, were pulling out of a group called the American Grand Rights Association. It had proposed to license the Russian music catalogue Arthur Judson had acquired from Amtorg, the Soviet trading group, and other non-ASCAP European music.

With backing from Gene Buck and at the suggestion of Max Dreyfus, Mills secretly went over Starr's head and sent Sigmund Romberg and Jerome Kern to Harry Warner to promote a network contract with a 10 percent share of all commercial income at the source, predicated on a reunited ASCAP. Publisher distribution had jumped 25 percent in a single quarter, and writers were clamoring for change. Many in classes AA and A could not hear their old songs on the networks, and their new ones suffered from slipshod exploitation. On being told, Starr was furious, and developed the deep personal hatred of Mills that eventually led to the latter's ouster from ASCAP's inner circles. There was also great pressure on Warner from his producers, who told him either to get back into ASCAP or give up making film musicals. Many songwriters on the lot refused to remain, and Gershwin, Porter, Kern, Rodgers and Hart, Oscar Hammerstein II, and Otto Harbach were switching to the Chappell Company, Max and Louis Dreyfus's chief interest now that Warner's option on it had expired.

On August 4, Warner's music was back on the networks. All seven of its companies were restored to membership in ASCAP, with the loss of only one year's seniority, and began major drives to get their songs to the top of the most-played list. Infringement suits against the networks and other stations, asking for four million dollars in damages, were withdrawn immediately. Before making the move, Warner attorneys secured approval by the Justice Department, to preclude its being used as grounds for a resumption of the recessed federal suit. The government's acquiescence surprised many music-business lawyers, who felt that peace within ASCAP only added strength to charges of monopoly. There was considerable joy in September after the government prosecutor refused to speculate when the trial would be resumed. Kaye, CBS's outside counsel for copyright affairs, began to travel again to Washington on behalf of the NAB to press the Justice Department for relief.

Warner started a frenzied drive to get on the *Variety* lists and those of two newcomers: the semiofficial *Accurate Report,* which was used by ASCAP bookkeepers; and the regular Sunday feature in the *New York Enquirer,* a show-business newspaper and racing form owned by the Annenberg family, which placed a new focus on Tin Pan Alley's chief preoccupation, landing plugs. The first was put out by the Accurate Recording Service, the property of the chief sheet-music buyer for the Music Dealers Service and her brothers. It tabulated in detail daily performances on radio stations in New York and Chicago. It was sold on a monthly subscription basis only to music-business insiders, and on it were based battle plans in the war for plugs. The *Enquirer* listed the previous week's "action," in numerical order of plugs, accompanied by a column, garlanded with racetrack jargon, that detailed the efforts of New York's contact crew. Until wisdom and the memory of the MDS fiasco prevailed, for several months the MPPA pondered a proposal to put the *Accurate Report* out of business in order to restrict its confidential material to the association's thirty members. Further control was planned by extended coverage of stations in such important cities as Cincinnati, Kansas City, and Los Angeles, using local branch-office employees to gather information that would be made public only when and if the publishers desired.

ASCAP's new point system, with its heavy concentration on radio plugs, was proving to be an economic boon to writers and publishers in the top brackets. Payments to Class AA writers jumped by 25 percent in the last quarter of 1936. The large publishers looked forward to as much as $200,000 each a year, out of an anticipated $2.5-million annual distribution, offsetting the inroads made on sheet-music sales, which had declined by 70 percent since 1927. Music publishers were reluctant to make public any information about their business that they could not control, chiefly because music dealers might use it as a basis for placing sheet-music orders. Lucky Strike's "Your Hit Parade" was regarded as particularly damaging. A sudden drop in a song's rating usually brought a rush of order cancellations, and dealers were wary of the rush to the top brought on by a "drive week," when there was an increased concentration of work on a song that they and the wholesalers firmly believed would be a "dog," or unsalable. Protests were regularly made to the show's producers, who made a series of grudging compromises, beginning with ratings for only the top three songs, playing the remaining twelve leaders without any comment on their status. A running war between the MPPA and Lucky Strike went on for years, always over the effect "Your Hit Parade" ratings had on sheet-music sales. From time to time, the basic criteria were modified, but the emphasis was always on sheet-music sales, record sales, network performances, and requests to bandleaders. Knowing well, from their own experience with radio plugs and sales figures, how manipulable the criteria were, the music publishers were never completely happy with the program, even when it went their way, as it usually did. If song ratings had to be made, they preferred *Variety*'s lists. Though not amenable to an MPPA demand that it drop the Most Played on Radio list, the publication instituted a 15 Best Sheet Music Sellers list, based on information supplied by the publishers themselves.

Johnny O'Connor, the *Variety* advertising salesman who had been so instrumental in the formation of the MPPA, was the manager of Fred Waring's orchestra and music business during World War I, as well as head of the new Words & Music publishing firm. It had been formed with an initial investment of $25,000 each by Waring, Paul Whiteman, and Guy Lombardo, and other bandleaders were being asked to participate in its ownership. O'Connor negotiated the purchase, for $22,000, of an ASCAP music house in order to get its Class B rating, which he intended to push several grades higher by a fairer treatment of songwriters than generally prevailed. When he offered to share all rights equally with his writers, some in the trade pointed to the unfair competition inherent in the very nature of Words & Music's ownership. Waring, Whiteman, and Lombardo were on nighttime radio thirty times a week and, with the cooperation of other leaders who might invest in the company, could become a new and formidable force in song plugging that would disrupt the existing balance. However, O'Connor's special stature among music men as a founder of the MPPA won him the presidency of the organization in his first year as a publisher himself.

Throughout 1937, praiseworthy but ineffective attempts were made to change what was publicly branded Tin Pan Alley's "unhealthy condition." It was recognized that most problems sprang from the performance-right distribution system introduced in January 1936 in order to keep the society united after Warner's departure. In removing the authority to determine how much each publisher would receive from the self-perpetuating publisher half of the ASCAP board, the society had, in effect, turned it over to the most free-spending music firms and the radio bandleaders. Radio's position was solidified as the only vehicle that could bring a song to a mass public with sufficient performances to make or break it, a development that soon worked against the society's interest. To guarantee that distributions were made on a mathematical basis, the determination of the performance and seniority factors on which 70 percent of them were based now rested in the hands of ASCAP bookkeepers, who rated all broadcast performances equally, whether a complete three-minute interpretation of words and music or one of the eighteen works whose melodies only were played on some fifteen-minute remote dance-band pickup late at night.

The repeal of Prohibition and a slowly rising economy were creating a dance-band business estimated by *Variety,* in December 1937, to represent $40 million in bookings alone in that year, made through thirty licensed booking agencies in New York and Chicago. Across America, 18,000 musicians regularly traveled, playing in drinking places and for dancing. As always, most bandleaders were shrewd businessmen, with an eye for the dollar, and the music business was big business for those at the top. Along with the major music firms that could afford the expenses, the chief beneficiaries of ASCAP's changed system were those generally small and recently purchased new publishing houses that established close personal relations with, or were owned by, bandleaders. Words & Music stood alone among the bandleader-owned firms, showing no evidence of logrolling among its owners by way of reciprocal plugs, a lapse credited by many for the firm's weaker showing than O'Connor had expected. There were at least twenty orchestra leaders on the air who had some interest in or financial involvement with a publishing house. The "give and take" business extended to late-afternoon sustaining programs featuring vocalists, on the network payrolls for twenty-five dollars a week, whose performances were as important to music publishers as those on expensive coast-to-coast programs. Many of their singing coaches and the station-employed musicians who accompanied them had private understandings with music firms, another element in the industrywide practice that *Variety* began to call "payola" in late 1938. The networks sought to curb it by reducing the number of times a song might be played between 5:00 P.M. and 1:00 A.M., only to learn that they had little control over the remote shows. Now that others were treading on once-private turf, and with the promise of strengthened antibribery provisions in a proposed new MPPA code of practices, two of the three dominant ASCAP publishers—Warner's and Max Dreyfus's firms—finally joined the organization, leaving only MGM outside. Contact men jumped into the situation and organized an association of professional men, threatening to resign their jobs if their employers subsidized performances.

The Accurate Reporting Service refused to count any but full vocal and instrumental choruses, ending those "eight bars at a time" renditions. *Variety* introduced a new Breakdown of Network Plugs chart, indicating how many were on commercial broadcasts and how many were vocal interpretations. In 1938, this became a complete tabulation, Network Plugs, 8 A.M. to 1 P.M. and offered advance information, on which forthcoming ASCAP royalties could be anticipated. To keep cheating orchestra leaders out, requirements for admission were tightened by ASCAP, and works offered for registration in the society's catalogue were scrutinized to avoid cut ins.

There was no way, however, to bring the advertising agencies into line. The insistence of these "program makers," who controlled all prime-time commercial programs, on using only those songs at the top of the list removed any incentive for radio artists to seek out new or special material, and a relative handful of songs dominated time on the air and the music heard by most Americans. George Washington Hill was made the scapegoat for this. "Your Hit Parade," *Variety* observed in April 1938, had made "the weekly breakdown of network plugs the absolute and dominating fetish that it is today." The tobacco man's music-format control had been refined since the program's introduction, but his insistence on "numbers full of rhythm, full of shoulder shake, full of dance," remained in full force. Hollywood's concentration on songs that could be played only in slow tempo moved Hill to give the program's musical director instructions to play shorter versions and to give almost half of program time to the "specials," Hill's kind of music, which rarely got to the top of *Variety*'s lists.

At a meeting of publishers in the spring of 1938, with a wider representation of members than in the past, Gene Buck was directed for the second time that year to appoint a committee to find ways and means to improve the distribution guidelines. For one thing, 84 percent of the crucial availability points went to publishers represented on the board, as did 70 percent of the seniority factor. At year-end, the new publisher reclassification committee, whose members had leaked the news that it was prepared to administer drastic cuts in ratings, collapsed under great pressure from the film-owned houses and avoided any meaningful changes, leaving them to the next committee charged with that responsibility.

With little hope, under current circumstances in Washington, for a successful outcome of the government suit (which a few broadcasters recognized as a valuable asset, though only as long as it remained a sword dangling over the society's head), the independents-dominated NAB was not ready again to be forced by the networks and the IRNA into a compromise of the music-licensing problem with ASCAP. At its prodding, anti-ASCAP activity at the state legislative level grew to its highest in a decade, culminating in bills in thirty-four states by 1939. Freed of managerial duties, and now chairman without vote of a special all-publisher administrative committee, Claude Mills was on the road, lending his slick "good old boy" image to lobbyists and lawyers who needed it to persuade Middle American skeptics of ASCAP's probity and respectable Wasp management. He was replaced by his successor at the MPPA, John Paine, who modernized the collection procedures and instituted an auditing department whose representatives were empowered under terms of the standard ASCAP contracts to inspect the books of delinquent customers or those suspected of being such. As the second former MPPA head to hold the office, Paine was viewed with only slightly less suspicion by songwriters among ASCAP's founding members.

Under Paine's direction the examination of radio broadcasts was increased toward an eventual goal of 25,000 live programs on the networks and their affiliates. Despite this and a number of other relatively minor changes, 64 percent of publisher distribution continued to go to the 13 houses affiliated with Hollywood interests.

Having twice benefited from division among broadcaster groups, ASCAP was determined to avoid or postpone dissension in its own ranks. Until a new ten-year contract with radio, at higher rates, was in effect, little more than lip service was paid to the drastic reforms advocated by a voluble minority of writers and publishers, most of them without any Hollywood connection. Every effort was made to force compromises. Believing, after intimations from Washington, that the government might shelve the suit, and with its collection and distribution systems, though not without fault, working to the satisfaction of most members, ASCAP was able to produce a dramatic show of approval in the renewal of membership affiliation agreements, which were to run for ten years, beginning January 1, 1941. The grant of television rights was again excluded out of deference to the film-music publishers, whose owners insisted. Officers and the board handled the business of a new SPA standard writers agreement with exemplary circumspection, forcing a compromise whenever necessary to enforce the feeling of good will they wished to maintain. The new SPA contract called for no less than a minimum equal distribution of mechanical, synchronization, and foreign receipts. The touchy question raised by Sigmund Romberg in the blueprint for reform of ASCAP remained unanswered, and the "tenants in common" language was skillfully evaded. Songwriters were given more voice in merchandising their music: bulk deals could not be made without their consent; their approval was needed to license television performances, the use of a song title, and certain synchronization uses; and the publisher was required to issue statements on a quarterly basis, on pain of cancellation by the writer.

Only Claude Mills mentioned BMI, and then in passing, at the annual ASCAP dinner on April 21, 1940, marking the society's twenty-sixth year. The verbal brickbats *Variety* delighted in reporting were missing from this gathering of 600 authors, composers, and publishers, a record turnout. In a two-hour speech, Buck hailed the recent rapprochement between the SPA and the MPPA, after years of bickering, as a symbol of the united front "that eliminates any strife in the ranks of capital and labor in the industry," striking a note of solidarity against radio that ran throughout the evening. No one present, nor most music-business veterans, took seriously the broadcasters' latest attempt to build an alternative pool of music. To many, it was only another of countless similar unsuccessful ventures. The genesis of the first viable tax-free non-ASCAP library, during World War I, offered by publishers now prominent in the society to hotels, night clubs, and vaudeville theaters in order to bring the songwriters in ASCAP to heel, had generally been forgotten. As yet unperceived, blunders in strategy and misplays of tactics eventually brought defeat for the society, and with it the seeds of a revolution in the entire music-business structure.

Tin Pan Alley had enjoyed its best year in a decade, and an even better one lay ahead. Sheet-music sales had gone over the 15-million-copy mark, an increase in 25 percent in a single year. Annual record sales neared the 70-million-unit mark, with more than $750,000 distributed by the MPPA for 1939's mechanical royalties. With all the professional songwriters and music publishers already in ASCAP's ranks, it was difficult to believe that Broadcast Music Incorporated could compete.

When Neville Miller, the reorganized-NAB's president, met with John Paine in April 1939, it was to inform the latter that he wanted two things. Claude Mills had already informed the industry in conciliatory speeches that the society did not wish to live with radio "like bulldogs," but it did want more money. A trial balloon sent up by him a month earlier at an NAB district meeting in Florida had reminded his listeners that they were not reluctant to pay a 15 percent commission to advertising agencies, and he asked why such a sum should not also be paid to the people who wrote the music on which the business depended. Miller's requests to Paine were for a per-piece license and at-the-source collection from NBC and CBS that would provide a reduction in music fees to all other levels. There was no response for months. ASCAP publisher board members were opposed to the per-piece concept, having been soured on such an arrangement for radio by Mills's similar arrangement, on behalf of the MPPA, with the talking-picture business in the late 1920s. Although it did meet, in part, Miller's request for collection at the source, the first document introduced at the aborted March 21, 1940, conference in ASCAP's New York headquarters, actually stiffened recently growing industrywide determination. The in-house auditing and collection service introduced by Paine had taken a toll, because of fancied or real "imperious" demands on many stations by representatives in the field. Now that they were convinced that ASCAP would not again compromise in their favor on the at-the-source collection, the networks, too, were ready for a fight to the finish.

The domineering presence of Herman Starr on the ASCAP board for a

second time and his appointment by Buck as chairman of the Radio Negotiating Committee were the keys to the unyielding behavior of that group.
Starr made no secret of his "embittering" recollections of the first six months
of 1936, when he sought to get Columbia and NBC to accept a Warner
music license. The revenge for Mills's call on Harry Warner in April 1936,
which by-passed Starr, came after a meeting of the society's Radio Negotiating Committee, prior to the March 21 conference. Mills was shown, for
the first time, the new at-the-source network-licensing provision, which had
none of the deductions customarily allowed to radio stations. After a quick
mental calculation, Mills said that he did not believe that NBC or CBS
would pay the approximately six million dollars asked, particularly with
after-tax income of three and two and a half million respectively in 1939.
After he said, according to his later statement, that the broadcasters would
reject the proposal and "stand by their rejection to the bitter end," he was
removed from any further participation in the radio negotiations. Shortly
after, his resignation was requested, as of December 31, 1940, and granted.

The society did not enjoy the benefits Claude Mills had expected when
he made the special deal with newspaper-owned stations. Only their competitors, usually papers with smaller circulation and less local prestige, played
up the ASCAP cause. The decision to take the issue to the public was a
mistake, all in all, with such staged incidents as the burning of radios in
the streets to symbolize public protest. The public had little interest in a
battle over millions between two groups, foreign to it, one a well-off songwriters' union, as the possibility grew of America's involvement in the
European war, in which radio listeners might be asked to stake their lives
and that of their children.

A grandiose scheme was moving toward fruition under the direction of
attorney Julian Abeles. MGM intended either to realize a five-million-dollar
net profit from the $75,000 it had lent Jack Robbins at interest years before
for a majority share in Robbins Music, through a sale to BMI, or to obtain
from ASCAP in increased royalties the $500,000 it cost each year to oper-
ate the Big Three. The only one of the society's most important publishers
to withhold the renewal of its affiliation, MGM played a cat-and-mouse
game with ASCAP. It had started in 1939, and continued, to represent the
constant threat of the society's dissolution, possibly at the end of 1940.
When BMI opened its doors, Abeles began negotiating on behalf of the Big
Three with Sydney Kaye for their sale for seven million dollars. This was
whittled down to $3.35 million, which William Paley agreed to advance on
behalf of CBS, but he backed away when MGM would not guarantee in-
demnification for all copyright infringement, coincidentally with the government's renewed antitrust suit against ASCAP. For a brief period, MGM
considered licensing the entire scores for new films on a grand-right basis,
a plan that was dropped when it appeared that BMI itself might raise the
$3.35 million.

The E. B. Marks deal with BMI, also arranged through Abeles, brought to an end MGM's expectation of being the first film company to have the advantage of exploitation by radio's own music pool. The veteran music man Marks, too, made his decision to leave ASCAP on the anticipation of "BMI's power to make hits with the cooperation of broadcasters." Marks Music collected around $85,000 from the society annually, which paid all business expenses and left a profit to the family partners. Under the BMI contract, which guaranteed $225,000 annually ($25,000 to Abeles), there was no need for Marks to spend money for promotion, and the firm's income would increase several fold. Bookkeeping expenses were cut down because BMI agreed to set up a special royalty accounting system to take care of Marks's writers, most of whose music was owned outright, or through the general work-for-hire arrangement that was currently being tested in the New York courts. Most of Marks's songwriters had given him their music before being accepted for membership in ASCAP. A total of 15,000 copyrights were involved, embracing the music of twenty-eight subsidiaries, many of them belonging to Mexican, Cuban, and Argentine performing-rights societies, with which BMI had, or soon would have, agreements for broadcast use as their arrangements with ASCAP expired. Because BMI was eager to provide the sort of music some important advertisers wanted, it gave up any indemnification against copyright infringement in the case of Marks, which had been partially responsible for the collapse of the MGM negotiations. NBC and CBS agreed to assume responsibility for the entire $1.7 million involved in the Marks transaction, sharing it on an aliquot basis with their owned-and-operated stations.

Only after the Marks negotiations were concluded did Abeles begin to dicker with the ASCAP board for its best counteroffer to his demand for a guaranteed $500,000 each year to Robbins, Feist & Miller. The board had already rejected an additional $15,000 to Marks annually, on which the retention of that catalogue depended, and now looked to other Hollywood studios to put pressure on MGM. It came from the industry's songwriters and film-musical screenwriters, who threatened a sit-down strike that hastened MGM's return at the last minute. However, the society had to make one compromise, an agreement to return television rights in the Robbins, Feist & Miller catalogues to Loew's.

The intra-industry rift, on which the ASCAP Radio Negotiating Committee counted to break a solidly united front at the last minute, did not happen. As *Variety* cautioned ASCAP, a general feeling of ill will toward it pervaded all levels of broadcasting in 1939, which became more intense once the society introduced the new contracts. The field work done by Miller, Kaye, and their staff, particularly Carl Haverlin, in selling BMI was responsible for an industry united behind the new organization. A sophisticated and learned man, though not formally educated, Haverlin presented an image of one whom radio people could trust. The adroitness of his arguments on behalf of the creation of a successful BMI and his tenacity in beating the backwoods to bring in reluctant stock buyer–licenses were crucial to the solidarity against ASCAP when the contract in force expired at the stroke of midnight, December 31, 1940.

Of more serious effect on the established music business was the government's renewed activity, beginning in 1939 under Thurmond Arnold, which eventually legitimatized ASCAP, with internal reforms, and ensured its existence by curbing the monopolistic and discriminatory practices that threatened its survival. On joining the Justice Department, after teaching at the Yale Law School, and determined to activate the government's trust-busting activities, Arnold became interested in the suit against ASCAP after members of Congress showed great interest, responding to the urging of constituent radio-station owners. Anti-ASCAP legislation existed in most states. The networks, who had never favored the suit, had changed their minds when they realized that ASCAP was intransigent in the matter of payment at the source, and were agitating for a renewal of government interest, pressing the cause through their Washington representatives and friends. In May 1939, at Arnold's direction, a move to dismiss *United States* v. *ASCAP* was dropped.

With newspaper coverage of the issue growing, and opinions rendered in several appeal courts that ASCAP was a "price-fixing monopoly," Arnold, now head of the antitrust division, moved toward a settlement by consent decree, in order to remove the matter from the path of important antitrust cases with which he was more concerned. A dissenting opinion by Supreme Court Justice Hugo L. Black found the society "a price-fixing combination . . . which wields the power of life and death on every business . . . dependent on copyrighted musical compositions for existence." In late May 1940, subpoenas were sought to permit access to hitherto-unexamined ASCAP files and records, orders that could be obtained only in a criminal action. The subpoenas were granted, over objection by ASCAP counsel Louis Frolich. Using lists so obtained of all members and the society's 33,000 customers, including radio stations, a set of twenty-five questions in connection with ASCAP practices and methods of operation was sent out over Arnold's signature. Washington insiders predicted that a grand jury would be impaneled in a few weeks to hear evidence against the society.

When it was suggested to Frolich shortly after Thanksgiving that a good deal could be worked out for ASCAP in a consent decree, Starr, in his capacity as head of the Radio Negotiating Committee, and with assent by Buck, the only one with whom Starr consulted, sent his personal attorney, Milton Diamond, to Washington to negotiate the terms. Frolich was omitted from any participation.

Variety reported that the compromise offered by Arnold embodied "an agreement to license performances on a per-piece basis, with abolition of the blanket fee, a different basis for splitting the ASCAP take so that new members might receive fatter checks, limiting the organization to the function of police work in order to detect infringement, insuring the right of individual bargaining by writers and composers, lowering of the membership eligibility bars, and to a more democratic form of control.''

By bringing these quasi-voluntary reforms to ASCAP, the government felt that the broadcasters had no reason to refuse to deal with the society. If, however, they continued to use only BMI and non-ASCAP music, it would prove that radio was engaged in a conspiracy to restrain competition. Because ASCAP had violated the law, Arnold said, he did not intend to allow broadcasters to do the same thing. One monopoly would not be substituted for another.

Acting as semiofficial spokesman for the Hollywood-owned publishers, Starr shrugged off the prospect of admitting a criminal action on a nolo contendere plea by signing the consent decree on Arnold's terms. Accompanied by a partner, Charles Poletti, the lieutenant governor of New York State, Diamond completed "the best deal possible for ASCAP" with Arnold and his staff in Washington, who were proceeding on the belief that he and Poletti were empowered to act for ASCAP. Final papers were to be signed in New York on December 24, in the federal court. An open break followed between the anti-Hollywood faction and Starr and the major publishing houses. It was stimulated by Frolich, for one, who advised the board to have no part of the decree. The matter was left up to Gene Buck, who directed that word should be sent to Washington that ASCAP did not intend to sign the consent decree.

Arnold was preparing for the trip to New York when he got the news. On the day after Christmas, a press officer for the Justice Department announced that an action would be filed in Wisconsin, pressing eight criminal charges against ASCAP, BMI, CBS, NBC, and other parties to be named. Each one expressed its innocence while applauding the government's charges against opponents. There would be no temporary truce in the ASCAP v. radio music war.

PART FOUR

1941–1953

CHAPTER 14

On the Road to New Technology and an Expanded Industry

The struggle between broadcasters and the American Society of Composers, Authors and Publishers appeared to have little immediate effect on the recording business. However, its economic consequences were destined to change not only the character of all popular music, but also the very structure of the music industry.

With the exception of RCA Victor, whose warehouses bulged with imported German wax and shellac from India, most of the other fifty or so record firms had abandoned the old method of cutting on wax-based masters, and, instead, used acetate blanks, painted over an aluminum base. Because of a growing scarcity of aluminum, other materials were tested—copper, brass, zinc, plastic, and some alloys—and all were found both unsuitable and increasingly difficult to obtain, in anticipation of the country's possible entrance into the European war. Strikes, government priorities, and shipping problems regularly beset most firms, forcing Columbia and Decca to curtail recording for several weeks at a time. With the largest manufacturing facilities in the business, Victor kept up with orders and speeded up work on additions to a secondary plant in Cincinnati, whose production was expected to match that of the Camden factory's 25- to 30-million annual 78-rpm output. Government work at Victor's original plant officially was the production of cartridge pouches, but in reality most of it dealt with military preparedness or secret research and development. With Camden's best workers thus engaged, the quality of the Red Seal albums was affected. Labels were often misprinted, records were mismatched, and delivery was generally four months behind. To shore up sagging Red Seal sales, in the autumn of 1941 Victor began one of its most ambitious and expensive advertising campaigns, to stimulate "the growth of good music in America." Tied in with promotion of a new "Magic Brain" turntable, a two-for-a-dollar sale began of selected orchestral, instrumental, and art-song disks, on which the artists agreed to forgo their customary 10 percent royalty. Like the turntable in the Capehart jukebox company's $1,000 unit, designed for the discriminating private consumer, the Magic Brain was equipped with two separate tone arms, one above and one below, with sapphire needles, capable of playing both sides of up to 10 or 12 assorted records relatively instantaneously. Sold for $425, the Magic Brain was hailed in advertising as one of the past decade's most revolutionary innovations, bringing the performance of extended works nearer concert-hall reality.

The business, in spite of the difficulties besetting it, had its best year since the high-water mark of 1921, producing 130 million records, 15 percent above the number twenty years before. Certain that drastic curtailment of their most important supplies would follow the Japanese surprise attack on Pearl Harbor and the immediate declaration of war by the United States on Japan and, later, Germany, Columbia and Decca rushed the installation of new presses that had been waiting for sufficient space and stepped up production. In April 1942, a month after the manufacture of all radio receivers and phonographs for personal use was terminated by the War Production Board, the annual production of records was fixed at the 1940 level of about 50 million units, and prices were frozen at the December 1941 levels. A few months later, Victor curtailed production of the Red Seal records that had brought the company its reputation for quality soon after their introduction, in 1903, when the Australian soprano Ada Crossley recorded four art songs with piano accompaniment. From that time to the present, however, the company depended on the sale of popular recordings for the profits that allowed it to make Red Seal records available to the public. Only the best-selling Red Seals in the catalogue now remained available.

The consumption of records by the coin-machine jukebox operators, chiefly responsible for the dramatic turnaround of the business following repeal of Prohibition in 1933, dropped almost overnight from the 40 percent of 1940. It happened not because suddenly there were fewer machines, but because they had stimulated a great surge of popular-disk sales in the retail shops. Glenn Miller's "Chattanooga Choo Choo," a leading jukebox "nickle-nabber," became the biggest-selling Victor popular disk of all time in 1942, after quickly overtaking the Gene Austin 1927 rendition of "My Blue Heaven." However, Miller's total sales were surpassed by both the Dorsey brothers: Tommy, on the seventy-five-cent black label, usually sold several hundred thousand copies of his hits; Jimmy, on Decca, where his thirty-five-cent coupling of "Green Eyes" and "Amapola," with sales of 850,000 already accumulated, was dipping into the company's shellac allotment and about to pass the Miller classic. Second in sales for the first time, Columbia had only one vocalist, Kate Smith, among its top five sellers; the others were the dance bands led by Harry James, Kay Kyser, Benny Goodman, and Charlie Spivak. The sale of five million copies of assorted hits by that reliable, spectacular, and steady seller Bing Crosby, which ran the gamut from "White Christmas" to "You Are My Sunshine," put Decca in third place among the major manufacturers. It was the only company that owned its production and distribution facilities.

Columbia's and Victor's communications-industry owners, CBS and RCA-NBC, had already engaged in controversy with Petrillo and his 140,000 disciplined and obedient American Federation of Musicians members on several occasions during the 1930s. Now it was time again for them and Decca to deal with this man to whom it had been demonstrated on numerous occasions that he held the power of economic life or death over any business that employed live musicians. Speaking to the AFM's annual convention in May 1942, Petrillo announced that the present contract with manufacturers would terminate on August 1, giving only a month's period of grace, rather than the year he had allowed broadcasters during the late 1930s. No union member would enter a recording studio in the United States or Canada until his demands were met. Record men had expected the threat and stockpiled against it, hoping to continue issuing records until the White House intervened in the interest of the war effort. Government restrictions were reducing the number of units that could be manufactured, and a sizable store of unreleased or previously rejected masters was available. Using Ralph Peer's Latin-American music-business connections, Victor made an unsatisfactory attempt to release some songs that had unexpectedly appeared on radio, recording them in Cuba. Local vocalists were meticulously taught the English words they did not comprehend, but most of these masters were finally put into storage. An attempt to use Mexican studios was out of the question once its musicians' union announced that such strikebreaking would not be countenanced. The studios in London owned by EMI, Victor's overseas distributor, had been appropriated for war production, and recording elsewhere in Europe was not possible.

Unprecedented sales and desperate, last-minute recording sessions in the first quarter, before government restrictions and production ceilings were imposed, enabled Victor to finish 1942 with 56 million units sold; Columbia sold 39 million, and Decca 35 million, for a second 130-million total annual sale.

The times clearly were not propitious for a new company to join the dozens of small independent firms struggling to stay alive, as the founders of the new Los Angeles–based Capitol Records soon learned. Distribution and production were controlled by the major companies, or by free-lance companies dependent on them for business. The government's regulations had created a black market in shellac and other essential materials. Capitol had been formed just after Pearl Harbor, when Glenn Wallichs, the owner of a record-and-radio store, who also had a small custom-recording service for audition disks and air checks, decided to make commercial records with his friend the songwriter Johnny Mercer. During a lunch with Buddy De

Sylva, executive producer at Paramount Pictures and once a successful Broadway musical lyricist, Mercer expounded on the profits possible with such enthusiasm that De Sylva offered to support the venture with an investment of $25,000. When the company's future was in doubt the next spring, De Sylva was a tower of strength, agreeing to serve as president; Mercer was in full charge of recording and song selection and Wallichs handled all other production and business details. Originally incorporated as Liberty Records, the name was quickly changed to Capitol. An arrangement was made with the MacGregor electrical-transcription business to share its pressing facilities to turn out the small initial order Wallichs anticipated, on a royalty basis. The first sides, two incipient jukebox hits, Mercer singing his own "Strip Polka" and the unknown Ella Mae Morse doing the "Cow Cow Boogie," were ready on July 1.

Petrillo's month of grace proved to be a blessing for Capitol. It gave Mercer an opportunity to work day and night to build up a supply of masters, which lasted throughout the next fifteen months. To do this, Wallichs was constantly called on by MacGregor to bring in sufficient scrap records to meet the quota of reclaimed shellac that all record makers had to produce before an order could be filled. Mercer and Wallichs depended chiefly on disk-jockey friends acquired over the last seven years to build public demand for their new releases. Armed, at first, with acetate pressings and, later, Vinylite disks, the pair made the rounds of the area's record-playing stations, and then began to mail copies to the cream of the nation's platter spinners, some several dozen out of all the employees of the 500 stations that depended on Petrillo's reviled "canned music" for survival. Among these were a few large, high-power stations, usually owned by newspapers, that in the noon-to-five period broadcast news bulletins five minutes before every hour from their owners' city rooms, and top name brands and singers during the rest of the period.

Capitol was the first record company to service disk jockeys on a regular basis with free releases. Victor and Columbia, waiting in 1940 for a Supreme Court ruling, were prepared to charge for radio use of their products. Unexpectedly, the court let stand a lower-court decision that said that when a record was purchased at its list price, all property rights belonged to the buyer. Jack Kapp was famous for the fervor of his determination to prevent broadcasters from using his records by any legal stratagem his attorney, Milton Diamond, might devise. The only records mailed without charge by the three majors were sent to music editors and record reviewers for general newspapers and magazines, and the entertainment and music trade papers.

In the first year of their strike, union musicians lost four million dollars in wages from the record makers, but their former employers were prospering, selling anything offered on their reduced schedules. Half-million- and million-copy sellers were common; name bandleaders reaped more royalties from disk sales than any artist except Crosby. Orders for a half-million copies of Glenn Miller's "Old Black Magic" came in the first week after its release. Harry James, the former Benny Goodman trumpet star, was second in sales only to Crosby, who had just signed a five-year contract with Decca guaranteeing "Der Bingle," as the Germans called him, a million dollars. In the first half of 1943, when James sold 3.5 million disks, Columbia, to which he was under contract, exceeded any other manufacturer's previous six-month sales figures. Victor presses were busy, on overtime, turning out records as well as special orders for the Office of War Information—Records for Our Fighting Men and V-Disks, produced by the Special Services division of the army.

The first monthly batch of 100,000 twelve-inch unbreakable V-Disks was shipped out in September 1943, one tenth for domestic distribution, the balance borne around the world by bombers and transport planes to American military personnel. Petrillo gave his permission for their production, and the initial release contained air checks of Bing Crosby, Dinah Shore, Kate Smith, and Rudy Vallee singing on their network commercial broadcasts. Within a year production was doubled. Two million V-Disks were shipped in 1944, and twice that annually before the war ended. The V-Disks project was organized by Captain Robert Vincent, a former Edison consultant and Victor engineer, who headed a staff that included Sergeants Morty Palitz of Columbia, Steve Sholes and Walter Heebner of Victor, Tony Janik, a Columbia engineer, and, later, George Simon, a music critic, professional drummer, and former editor of *Metronome,* a jazz magazine. Between 13,000 and 14,000 waterproof containers were sent out each month, containing twenty double-faced platters, packed with 100 needles. They provided four hours of recorded entertainment. Initially, one third of each shipment was made up of newly recorded music; the balance was taken from air checks, existing masters made available by all companies except Decca, which refused to cooperate, and motion-picture sound tracks. After surveys were taken of armed forces' preferences, the ratio changed to 86 percent new material, 70 percent of it popular music, the balance divided among classical, hillbilly, and race music, and specialized entertainment recorded under the supervision of the V-Disk staff. The pressings were made by Victor at the start, but later also by Columbia, Muzak, and World, the transcription company Kapp had acquired in early 1943 for $750,000.

The Decca chief made his purchase at a comparatively bargain price not only to secure additional shellac but also in anticipation of a settlement of the musicians' strike being arranged by Milton Diamond, who was also chief counsel to Petrillo and the AFM. When it came, it broke the major manufacturers' hitherto united front and gave Decca an almost year-long advantage, because Victor and Columbia continued to believe that the government would take action to curb the insolent labor leader. Herman Starr, owner of a quarter interest in Decca, was instrumental, with Diamond, in forging a contract that permitted Kapp to release any music previously or thereafter recorded by World, provided the musicians were paid additionally at full union scale.

Samuel Rosenbaum, the real estate speculator and patron of the Philadelphia Orchestra was, as had been predicted, a key figure in the capitulation to Petrillo's demands. The musicians' leader had stood firm even after President Roosevelt pleaded for an end to the strike and legislators threatened federal action. Rosenbaum, a former owner of a CBS radio station affiliate and organizer of the Independent Radio Network Affiliates, had been instrumental in ending the prewar radio-AFM controversy, to Petrillo's advantage, and had become a trusted friend and adviser to the labor chief. That the radio industry was not included in the 1942 ban, while all other employers of musicians were, was attributed to Rosenbaum's influence with Petrillo.

The first move to the bargaining table by any music user came within six months of the strike, when the owner of Ringling Brothers–Barnum & Bailey Circus accepted an increased pay scale for his musicians, from $47.50 to $50 for whites, from $26.50 to $30.50 for blacks. Other tent shows and carnivals fell into line. The Decca break and, with it, agreements by some new small independent labels came in the fall of 1943. When Victor at last began to run out of existing materials in its vaults, and found unsuitable the a cappella vocal accompaniments it and Columbia had been forced to order to record new talent and songs, its executives seriously considered meeting with Petrillo. Their decision was also influenced by Decca's five-to-one advantage in jukeboxes, as well as the dent in their monopoly being made by Capitol Records, which had recently enlarged its production and distribution chains in the East. In addition, the government appeared ready to relax further its restrictions on the use of shellac, a move that would increase the scarcity by making the additional supplies available to the new competition. When rationing first began, the manufacturers were allowed to keep possession of shellac stocks already on hand. Monthly directives were issued as to what amount of that could be used, in a 20-to-80 percent combination with shellac bought from government warehouses. The price of shellac, like that of all other black market items, floated, but that supplied from government sources remained fixed at thirty-six cents a pound, to which a mandatory twelve cents was added for processing, something the companies could do themselves for a penny a pound. Vinylite, the best substance yet developed for a record surface, was never available, because it was used for waterproofing raincoats and for other war materials. The transcription companies made do with stock on hand. Because Vinylite was 95 percent salvageable, customers had to return one Vinylite disk for each new one.

The key feature of the new musicians' contract—in addition to better working conditions and pay, along the lines of the Decca agreement but without its permission to reissue electrically transcribed selections—was the establishment of the Performance Trust Fund, to provide money to out-of-work musicians. It was subsidized by a fixed fee for each musical recording made by union musicians sold, half a cent for thirty-five-cent records, up to two cents for each two-dollar disk, and five cents for those priced higher. The AFM planned to use all collections for fostering and maintaining musical talent and culture and music appreciation by furnishing live music, without charge to the public, performed by paid unemployed symphony musicians, bands, or other instrumental musical combinations.

A number of new devices to improve sound recording and playback were developed for military use during the war, among them wire and tape recording and reproducing machines, and a 16-rpm recording machine with disks capable of playing many hours of music. W. L. Camp, chief engineer of the Armour Research Foundation, was responsible for the wire recorder. It had a reusable five-dollar spool of 11,700 feet of wire capable of holding nearly seven hours of sound. Portable wire recorders were used by the military and radio correspondents on various fronts. The latter used them for playback to world-wide audiences, with such success that more than 100 applications were filed for a license from the patent holder, General Electric, to manufacture them after the war. A machine using 320-foot loops of tape, treated with chemicals to withstand the rigors of extreme weather conditions, was demonstrated by its inventor, Jay Fonda, of the Fonda Corporation of New York. It recorded eight hours at a time, and recording and playback styli moved automatically along sixty tracks on each inch-wide tape, above a pliant felt base, at forty feet a second. Dr. U. L. DiGhilini's recording and playback machine, demonstrated in June 1945, did not cut disks the same way the record companies did, but embossed the music on blank masters. Running at sixteen rpm, the slow-playing records offered slightly more than two hours on a twelve-inch disk, and over five on a sixteen-inch disk.

The real future for recorded sound was first revealed to American civilians by the head of the Russians' Radio Berlin in September 1945. He showed a group of visiting radio executives a bulky captured German Magnetophon, whose fourteen-inch reels reproduced symphonic works on magnetic tape with such fidelity of sound they could not be distinguished from the real thing. They were far superior to any commercial disk or the best electrical transcription known in the United States. The machine was an improved model of the original dictating machine offered for sale in 1935 by Allgemeinische Elektrische Gesellschaft and I. G. Farben, to which General Electric held American rights under the cartel arrangement through which they divided the world's markets. All these advances notwithstanding, even the most open-minded record men were convinced that music on wire or tape, or any form other than that already in use, was at least five years away from the market.

At the beginning of 1945, the business looked forward to a sales boom that would see a total annual output of 600 million records. This optimism was shared by the owners of those 103 other labels of all kinds who had paid $100 to register with the Performance Trust Fund, most of whom were selling only between 2,000 and 5,000 copies of each new disk. Two of the new firms, specializing in popular music, were regarded as having the potential to take their place among the majors: Majestic Records and the MGM-Lion Company. The former was owned by the Majestic Radio business, whose proprietors intended to take advantage of a built-in distribution system—the receiver and parts dealers who did business with Majestic—to put 500,000 new records on the market each month. Studios, a pressing plant, and a backlog of masters were purchased from Eli Oberstein, who had resurrected his bankrupt Hit and Classic labels during the war, to produce bootleg records cut in Mexico and new releases made under an AFM contract in the United States. The former playboy mayor of New York City, James J. Walker, was installed as Majestic's president, at $40,000 a year. The veteran record maker Ben Selvin, whose name already appeared on nearly 9,000 individual dance recordings, took Oberstein's place when his new partner-employers found his flamboyant music-business style too rich for their conservative operation.

Just before the musicians' strike, Louis B. Mayer, head of MGM, allocated $500,000 to the formation of a record business, but Petrillo and wartime scarcities shelved the project. Jack Robbins established a Lion label during the interim, using Oberstein's studios and pressing plant. He took the first thousand records, to exploit his new songs, and the remainder were marketed by Oberstein. Once essential materials were available, Loew's, the MGM parent company, signed Frank Walker, formerly of RCA Victor, to be operating head of a new company. The veteran record man had been chafing under enforced retirement when the offer to join MGM was made. In the record business since just after World War I, Walker had been in charge of a rapidly sinking Columbia Records Company in 1923 when he signed and recorded Bessie Smith. She was the label's challenge to the black blues queens who had moved the business into the early rhythm-and-blues field. For a number of years during the 1920s, Walker had been Ralph Peer's chief rival in field recording of both hillbilly and black music and artists. At RCA Victor during the 1930s, he had been in charge of its custom-recording division, active in the introduction of the thirty-five-cent Bluebird label, and in full charge of the company's popular-music activities at the time Oberstein left. In the game of musical chairs that characterized the shifting of both executive and musical talent from one label to another throughout the following years, Oberstein unexpectedly returned as chief of artists and repertory for Victor, after having been unceremoniously dumped eight years earlier.

The expectation of the entrenched companies that they could, after the war ended, begin immediately retooling and expanding their factories was dashed by labor unrest. Strikes, particularly in the steel industry, by workers whose wages had remained fixed under government control, delayed the production of new equipment and materials for construction. A series of settlements began only in late 1945. Even the most conservative in the business believed that the released flood of pent-up demand would greatly improve conditions, but nobody was ready for the doubling of sales that took place, to $89 million and 350 million records, all but 50 million released by Columbia, Decca, Victor, and Capitol. Once they were ready to begin deliveries, Columbia, Victor, and Decca discovered an almost overnight switch by record buyers from dance music to a veritable mania for singers, like those with which Capitol and a few smaller new independents had become an important presence. The disk jockeys, whom Mercer and Wallichs courted with promotion techniques the others would not adopt, were responsible. They had been the first to discern that a large portion of the radio audience was no longer happy with the same old music, played in the same old way by the same orchestras, and catered instead to the new taste by programing records by Frank Sinatra, Margaret Whiting, Nat "King" Cole (a former race-music performer), Dick Haymes, Mel Tormé, Eddy Howard, Georgia Gibbs, Helen Forrest, Peggy Lee, and Perry Como, who alone enjoyed a sale of 10 million disks that year.

Strengthened by the proceeds of an eight-million-dollar stock sale on Wall Street, Capitol improved its manufacturing and distribution facilities by the purchase of the old Scranton, Pennsylvania, pressing plant that had been supplying most small labels since World War I. New independents throughout the East and Midwest were not harmed by this loss. Thirty-two pressing plants were now operating across the nation, providing that additional 50 million records sold by the independents in 1946. A portion of these were the products of small firms, some of them specializing in jazz, hillbilly, and race music, who had done well during the war when the majors could not or would not fill orders. They charged about a dollar for their records, even when relatively unknown new talent was used, and won air play by making new releases available to the 462 small 250-watt stations whose owners could not afford electrically-transcribed programs, which cost five dollars each and did not use the sort of music local audiences wanted. Many of these small firms had become music publishers, recording only their own copyrights, written by the artists, the owner, or his assistants, in order to save the copyright law's mandatory two cents for each side sold. As talent in specialized fields had been feeling since Ralph Peer's earliest days, the musicians and singers they recorded were happy to get the publicity that accrued from a phonograph recording and willing to forgo royalties for the opportunity. Once these small firms learned that the new licensing organization, BMI, was offering to pay as much as $250 per side for the air-play rights, many used that money to build and operate a catalogue.

A major problem for these new firms, once materials were available and the cost of a pressing had fallen from more than thirty-five cents to about eighteen or nineteen was having an efficient distribution system, on a scale larger than that available during the war. East Coast and Midwestern pressing plants added a three-cents-per-record charge to ship to West Coast customers, a departure from traditional custom. With 210 record makers now licensed by the AFM, six leading eastern independents formed their own distribution chain for key cities, offering a full return privilege as an inducement to jobbers and retail dealers. Accustomed to a five percent return policy after six months, and with nothing to lose, many local suppliers placed large orders, and then returned them once the majors began to crowd out this unwelcome competition.

Another problem was the copying of an up-and-coming release by an artist on one of the Big Four labels. The New York-based National label anticipated a nationwide best seller in its initial version of "Open the Door, Richard," by Dusty Fletcher, a black vaudeville performer who had used it in a piece of comic musical business in black-only theaters for years. Fourteen versions appeared, five of them on major labels, the rest on those of various new independents. The song became number one on *Billboard*'s Honor Roll of Hits in early 1947, principally because of the Decca version, made by Louis Jordan, a veteran race artist whose records were beginning to cross over regularly to the long-all-white hit charts. The West Coast Exclusive firm was fortunate, because its black-ghetto race release "The Honeydripper" was considered by the large companies to be too heavily race-music inflected and too suggestive to record. Joe Liggins's recording of the song sold a million copies for Exclusive and made it the leading independent race-record company of the postwar years.

Aware of growing challenges to their control of distribution, the majors made some moves to solidify their position. New men, who had grown up during the Depression and been exposed to records by disk jockeys and jukeboxes, were coming into positions of power. Still firmly convinced that classical music was the key to industry success, Edward Wallerstein went to Europe to negotiate with foreign manufacturers for distribution. Columbia's prewar arrangement with EMI was still in effect, and the giant was retooling, getting ready to return to its earlier dominance. Wallerstein learned, however, from investors who sought to compete with EMI, that an appetite for American popular music had developed because of the omnipresence of American armed forces radio programs, the V-Disks every GI seemed to have, and the live American bands and singing talent.

Columbia's first annual dealer convention concentrated on the company's popular product. The 420 important retailers and jobbers, whose expenses were fully paid by Columbia, were indoctrinated in the company's new "Let's beat 'em all" policy during two days of sales pitches and told about forthcoming single releases and album collections (one of which, Harry

James's reissued wartime hits, had advance orders for 300,000), records made exclusively for children, and upcoming classical records. Entertainment was provided by the hit makers: Frank Sinatra, Frankie Carle, a piano stylist who sold seven million disks that year, Dinah Shore, Gene Autry, and Lily Pons and André Kostelanetz. While in Cincinnati, the assembled throng was shown the new Columbia pressing plant, a reconditioned war materiél factory, capable of raising the company's output to that of Victor. With greater funds Columbia went one step further than Capitol in the station-service field, opening an in-house department for publicity and promotion. It bought time on radio stations, on 537 within a year, at a cost of $70,000 a month, for a transcribed show featuring America's best-known disk jockey, Martin Block, who introduced new releases supplied by the local distributor or retailers. When Block became a million-dollar-a-year network disk jockey a few years later, transcribed material was sent to local "deejays," who were allowed to select their own music, only occasionally being instructed to feature specific Columbia releases, in the conviction that a Columbia product was always better.

As Columbia and others increased cooperation with platter spinners, Decca and Victor fought the practice. Angry because many small stations programed sponsored all-Crosby record shows, Jack Kapp offered to license the entire package of Crosby's 275 sides for $750,000, to be sold as an exclusive package in single markets, complete with transcribed introductions and comments recorded by the singer. The proposal foundered when it was faced with immediate litigation in those forty-seven states where common-law rights did not prevail. Kapp turned next to the Federal Trade Commission to protect his product. That government body failed to accommodate him, and Crosby signed a contract with Philco, maker of electronic equipment and white goods, for $30,000 a week for an hour-long transcribed show for the ABC network, which was expected to keep small stations and disk jockeys from intruding further into Kapp's domain. Victor strengthened its warning to distributors and franchised retailers against providing free copies to stations, or sale to them at either wholesale or retail price.

Faced with vigorous competition from the majors, and with pressings of improved quality and expanding distribution, many independents began to specialize in fields of music that most majors neglected, usually for lack of creative sympathy at the executive level: the hillbilly and western music with which Capitol was making a dent in the market; and the race-record business that was offering many young white consumers, and some white artists seeking suitable material, a vital and exciting kind of music. It was rooted in country blues, the new kind of vaudeville blues made popular by Louis Jordan and his admirers, and in gospel music, jazz, and swing, reflecting the changing life of urban black communities, which would radically change the popular culture and vernacular music of the world. A four-month sales slump in 1946 hit even the most successful independents. Shellac was up to eighty cents a pound, and the promise by radio manufacturers to concentrate on the production of radio-phonograph combinations was upset by the failure of the Office of Price Administration to reduce ceiling prices on tubes and other components. The expected flood of machines did not occur. Many retail stores, particularly in the South and Midwest, where hillbilly and race music were most popular, stocked only the fifty-cent disks of Victor, Columbia, and Decca, and omitted the secondary labels, whose prices of seventy-five cents and up had held, in anticipation of an increase by the majors. Jukebox play was seriously affected as well, the result of a grain shortage that cut down production of beer and resulted in fewer nickels in the slot. Having already broken their pledge to the OPA immediately after Pearl Harbor to hold the production of thirty-five-cent disks at prewar levels, in late 1946 the majors increased by one dime the price of the fifty-cent lines, which had become the largest selling but was no longer producing any profit because of higher production costs.

The cancellation of all wage and price controls, except on rent, in late 1946, brought on rapid inflation, which had mixed effects on the record business. Freed of all restraint, the majors' popular disks went up to seventy-five cents, classical music to one dollar, but the Commerce Department predicted a 400-million-disk year. As in most other industries, it was the small, underfinanced independents that suffered most, pricing themselves into bankruptcy or absorption by more successful competitors. Columbia and Victor expanded the scope of their album catalogues, and embarked on an ambitious program of recording full-length performances of operas. After dipping into the world's largest storehouse of "the music America wants most," Victor offered transparent Vinylite pressings of the hallowed Red Seals at a premium price of $3.50, which only the most fanatic record buyers would pay. Decca matched the extraordinary success of the pioneering original-cast album of *Oklahoma!* (fast nearing one million sales at five dollars a set), with the first album by a popular artist, a compilation of the songs from *The Al Jolson Story,* sung by its hero, for $3.95.

Kapp had retrieved full ownership of Decca by buying back the remaining 25 percent owned by Warner Brothers. A revolving credit line of four million dollars, available from the Boston First National Bank at one half percent interest, which rose to three and a half when the money was put to use, freed him to make his company, unencumbered by control by a large corporation such as RCA and CBS, the only true independent of all the prewar major firms. His records were distributed in Britain and Europe by British Decca, and he was ready to make new arrangements elsewhere. Following many months of economic and production setbacks, MGM Records, financed by three million dollars from Loew's concluded an agreement with EMI for world-wide distribution of recordings by Hollywood personalities and sound-track music. Capitol began overtures to South

American distributors, content with lower expectations. In the first fallow period since its initial success, Capitol emerged from mid-year economic uncertainty with three hit recordings, which put it back on its feet, two of them hillbilly flavored and a race hit: Tex Williams's western swing-and-talking-blues-influenced "Smoke, Smoke, Smoke That Cigarette"; an outrageous rural parody of a torch song, "Tim-tay-shun," by Red Ingle and a Spike Jones alumnus with a vocal chorus by Jo Stafford, in a hillbilly diva role; and Nellie Lutcher's "Hurry on Down," the product of years in black saloons and night spots.

Ted Lewis, the British co-founder of Decca, returned to the American market after a seven-year absence with a new label, London Records, a subsidiary of British Decca. Though he continued to handle Kapp's records in Europe, his departure from participation in the American business had not been happy, and it did not allow for reciprocal distribution of his product in the United States. During the war, the Royal Air Force had commissioned him to produce a series of training records for navigators in the battle against German submarines. They were recorded by a new process, developed by British Decca's chief sound engineer, Arthur Haddy, known as "Full Frequency Range Recording." The first examples of this major advancement in the science of sound recording, which gave response from 30 to 14,000 cycles per second, went on sale to the British public after the war. When civilian freight traffic between India and England was resumed, the Decca laboratories were in a position to mass-produce FFRR records with unprecedented high-shellac content that made the most delicate overtones audible to the human ear and with none of the "sandpaper scratch" present on too many American disks.. The first imported FFRR album, Stravinsky's *Petrouchka,* and with it a new, inexpensive record player that demonstrated all its superior qualities, went on sale in the United States in the summer of 1946. After forming the London Gramophone Corp. of New York, Lewis announced release of the first block of 10,000 popular and classical 78-rpm disks six months later. Most of London's British artists were familiar to American soldiers, who had seen and heard them during the war.

The sudden, almost overnight, success of a number of new independents, whose million-copy sales moved them out of the ranks of companies content to make a small profit on an average sale of 35,000, was due to the attention of the country's disk jockeys. They were responsible for the combined sale of four million records of "Near You," written and recorded by Francis Craig for Bullet Records, of Nashville; the Harmonicats' "Peg o' My Heart," recorded by Vitacoustics, of Chicago; and Jack Owens's rendition of his own "How Soon" on the Los Angeles Tower label. It cost them an average of $300 for advance shellac copies, and three times that for Vinylite pressings, sent to about 1,000 platter spinners believed to be central to making a hit. Together with a few up-to-date independents, Capitol, Columbia, and Decca (which had finally succumbed after years of Kapp's opposition) were adding promotion men to their payrolls, who were charged with visiting deejays to secure their friendship and air play. *Variety* gave the new confraternity of radio personalities its highest accolade, a weekly chart measuring the popularity of songs and recorded talent as reflected by the "most-requested" records reported by a pool of nearly 100 disk jockeys. Each of them was identified by name when his nominations were printed. Feeling that "entirely too much accent" was placed on the publication's chart of songs that enjoyed most performances on prime-time network radio, *Variety* added that "more valuable to the music [business] . . . would be an early insight into what new disks the public wants."

The most important disk jockeys no longer merely slapped a disk onto a turntable after making some critical or laudatory remarks about the song or the artist. Considerable thought was given to format and pacing. Special nights were set aside for specific programs: all-request shows, all-new-release segments, shows devoted to a single vocalist or orchestra, just old songs—the predecessor of the "golden oldies" concept. There was much to be said for that body of industry thought which believed that local disk-jockey programs had driven live network programs starring Crosby, Sinatra, and Shore off the air. Their loyal fans no longer had to wait for a single half hour each week to hear their idols, but got their fill from the record shows.

The National Association of Disk Jockeys was created by a press agent to promote a new Universal moving picture, *Something in the Wind,* in the summer of 1947. The starring actress, Deanna Durbin, played a disk jockey in it, working for a small radio station. The get-together of eighty of the country's top deejays in Chicago, under the film company's auspices, with all traveling and entertainment expenses paid, surprised its sponsor when the assembled group elected Barry Gray of New York to be president and named other officers. The country was divided into nine districts, to be organized locally after being chartered by the national body. Paul Whiteman, Tommy Dorsey, and some other respected performers who were signed by the networks at high salaries to be coast-to-coast disk jockeys were not asked to join the association. However, their presence in that capacity enhanced the importance of the radio performer who "presents and comments on popular phonograph records," as the dictionaries began to define *disk jockey.*

The platter spinners did "represent big radio income," as *Variety*'s Ben Bodec wrote in an analysis of their place in broadcasting. "A goodly percentage of them have moved into upper-income brackets. They have to a widening degree community standing. They have become an integral part of local broadcasting. They carry economic weight with the advertisers. The only way their ranks could be seriously decimated in the next years would be for Congress to amend the copyright law so as to curb their use of records. That eventuality is hard to imagine."

Petrillo had given up all thought of such legislative correction by an unfriendly Congress that had castigated him for being, it said, a racketeer. He turned his attention to the welfare of his constituents, which, he argued, should be funded by contributions from the recording business. To that end, he announced, months before it would take place, that another ban on recording by AFM members would take effect on January 1, 1948. The Taft-Hartley Act, which proscribed such an action, as well as other current labor practices, was passed over President Harry Truman's veto in June. Victor, Columbia, and Decca were confident that the act would be upheld by the Supreme Court and so adopted a more leisurely pace of prestrike recording than they had in 1942. But fearing the worst, the three Capitol partners studied an attractive offer from the American Broadcasting Company: to buy control of the company and its transcription business in return for a similar amount of ABC stock. Differing over what action to take, Mercer and De Sylva resigned their $100,000-a-year directorships in the summer and left Wallichs in full charge of Capitol's business affairs. The deal fell through when neither side could agree on the dollar value of the other's securities.

Once Columbia and Victor were convinced that Petrillo was in earnest, they invested two million dollars in a down-to-the-wire frenzy of record cutting, and produced 2,000 masters, made at an average cost of $1,000 each. The rush was due in part to a provision in their contracts with the AFM that, in the event of a strike, all existing artist contracts were no longer valid—after which, a bidding war for talent would certainly follow. There was also a clause in the Taft-Hartley Act that made the payment of royalties to the Performance Trust Fund illegal after June 1, 1947, when the union leader began his struggle to the death against the record companies, with the possibility that their radio-network owners could be involved. Only Decca was better prepared; it had an existing store of unreleased masters and the World Transcription Library, to which Petrillo gave it unlimited access under the 1943 settlement.

When sales were finally tabulated, 1947 proved to have exceeded 1921, the industry's previous best effort. It was a $214.4-million year at retail; 3.4 million record players of all kinds were produced. The Big Four issued 300 million popular and classical records, and possibly another 75 million were released by the rest of the industry. There was no way for the business but up, it thought, once Petrillo was beaten.

A year passed before union musicians returned to the studios, twelve months that witnessed a magnificent leap into the future for recording techniques and equipment, opening the modern age of the art. The announcement in February 1948 that the ABC Radio Network was going "all-tape" for nighttime programing drew new attention to the changes that had taken place since American troops first stumbled across the Magnetophon during their liberation of occupied Europe. Though the Signal Corps had immediately confiscated every machine found for secret research and development, some were dismantled to be smuggled home, piece by piece, as souvenirs of war, and had been brought to the attention of civilian radio and electronics experimenters. Once the secret was out, a number of laboratories began a race to produce and patent an improved Magnetophon, and develop compatible magnetized plastic tape. Bing Crosby received national publicity in 1946 when, in order to have more time for golf, he switched from the tedious job of doing live shows, which took three or four days a week out of his life, to ones recorded on tape and then rerecorded on acetate transcriptions, a process that was completed in one or two days. The tape his production crew used was 3M, a product of the Minnesota Mining & Manufacturing Company, and the recorder was an Ampex, made by an electronics firm that was Bing Crosby Enterprises' major competitor in the development of radio and video tapes. Crosby's announcement broke the ice, and the networks ordered Ampex recorders, to replace wire recorders and the studios for recording and editing purposes.

A Telegraphone, the earliest device to transform sound into electrical impulses and then, by reversing the process, to convert it back into sound, was patented in the United States in 1900 by a Dane, Valdemar Poulsen. A few were sold for commercial use, but were discarded when more modern business machines took their place. The development of the Magnetophon in Germany in the early 1930s led to the introduction of iron-oxide-coated tape and then plastic-based reels, discovered in 1944 at the studios of Radio Luxembourg. With the enormous profits from its highly successful gummed-cellophane tapes at its disposal, 3M experimented with the type of tape used for the Magnetophon. Its technicians produced an improved, similar material, capable of recording 15,000 cycles per second at a speed of an even seven and one half inches per second, a decided advance over the 10,000 cps at thirty inches per second of the German reels.

Despite the intriguing possibilities inherent in tape, other matters demanded the attention of executives at some of the large companies. At first, the recording strike appeared to have little effect, and the regular release schedules were maintained. Then sales began to fall. The surprisingly great demand for recorded music a few months before appeared to have dulled the imagination and daring of the heads of most major labels, in spite of challenges from such progressive new firms as London and Mercury. Formed the year before by a booking agent and the son of a plastics manufacturer, Mercury had immediate assets: its own pressing plant and an amazing ability to raise cash when needed. On short notice, it purchased the now-bankrupt Majestic operation and its nearly 2,000 masters, 140 of them unreleased, and then sold many of them and all excess presses and machinery to other manufacturers. In order to promote its first best-selling performer, the company created the artist promotional concert tour, working with local retailers, who sold tickets, for from $1 to $2.50, to their customers for singer

Frankie Laine's twelve one-nighters through the Midwest. The older executives at Victor, and to some extent at Columbia, continued to sit on top of hundreds of unreleased masters, many made without concern for appeal or commercial worth in the rush to stockpile during 1947's last weeks. Their subordinates in charge of artists and repertory and sales had become more conservative than the industry in the darkest days of the Depression; they were reluctant to chance their reputation on new sounds or more advanced musical arrangements and were puzzled by the success of songs produced by writers and publishers outside the Tin Pan Alley, Broadway, Hollywood establishment. They continued to depend for artistic and creative sources and cooperation in exploiting their merchandise on their oldest music-publisher allies. In general, judgments were confined to affirming those of their competitors by imitating rather than outdoing them, and the result was too large an output, too startlingly alike.

Eli Oberstein was made the first of many scapegoats at Victor, and was replaced with the decisions-by-committee of product and merchandising department heads who had ruled twenty years before. A ''disk test'' was introduced to seek out new talent, not only for the popular line, but for the race, hillbilly, and jazz output. Various microphone setups were used for these auditions, but the songs were tried-and-true material. A few compromises were made: one, a recognition that the disk jockeys on about 1,200 radio stations influenced 85 percent of all popular record sales. Last of the original Big Three to make the move, Victor instituted a massive revision of its promotion policy and sent some 2,800 program directors, music librarians, and disk jockeys, at 850 stations, Vinylite pressings of all new releases except the Red Seal packages. But as soon as the high cost of this daring move was apparent, the responsibility for delivery of free disks was shifted to regional distributors and dealers, who were charged at wholesale for promotional materials.

The first impetus to move Victor out of its creative lethargy came from David Sarnoff, chairman of the parent, RCA. He was given an advance performance of new long-playing Columbia records, much like those Victor had brought out in 1931, played on a new compatible machine with a lighter pickup and head than that of the earlier 33-speed Victor player. After he nodded polite approval, he issued a directive to his technicians to devise a similar record and player, but at a different speed.

Late in 1947, Edward Wallerstein had been moved to the post of chief operating officer of Columbia Records. He had never lost his faith in concert music and was a fervent supporter of the development at the CBS laboratories of long-playing microgroove records and players. They were ideally suited to the classical music he loved, as did the inventors, Peter Goldmark and William Bachman, and their fellow chamber-music-playing co-workers. After many months of work, they had created a recording head capable of tripling the eighty-five grooves to an inch of standard records and appropriate lightweight, high-fidelity pickup, amplifier, and 33-speed players, which bettered London's new records and portable phonograph. A symphonic or concert work no longer had to be played with those annoying breaks between records demanded by the bulky and heavy twelve-inch 78-speed disks. In anticipation of Columbia's long-playing records, Waller-stein had ordered his staff to record all classical works on sixteen-inch tran-scriptions and, once Columbia added tape machines, on them as well.

Wallerstein's eagerness to share the miracle brought on the demonstration for Sarnoff, along with a few Columbia executives who did not share his enthusiasm for the importance of serious music in relation to the popular product. To gain their support, the decision was made to extend the im-proved technology to all Columbia releases. It was Wallerstein's original intention to demonstrate the complete long-playing package publicly for the first time at the annual dealers' meeting in August, but the trade press got wind of it by accident, so a general press conference was held on June 18. A beaming Wallerstein stood between a fifteen-inch stack of 101 LP albums and eight feet of the same music on 78s as he extolled the virtues of Col-umbia's latest accomplishment. It was indeed the "revolutionary new prod-uct" the press was promised in publicity releases, but not all of those pres-ent were convinced. Some pointed out that the purchase of special equipment on which to play the microgroove disks might be an economic drawback, and that the industry was congenitally fearful of breaking with tradition.

Other than an announcement some months later that a new 33-speed RCA portable player was available for $166 (which could not accommodate the new Columbia disks), there was no word from Radio City or Camden. Columbia intensified consumer research and cancelled all promotion of 78-speed popular disks, including the weekly transcribed disk-jockey show. The Cincinnati plant was shut down, preparatory to its sale, and all existing 78-speed presses were put on the secondhand market. The first long-playing releases, fourteen classical and popular ten- and twelve-inch disks, were announced in September. Among them were a *La Bohème* by the Metro-politan Opera company; the Philadelphia and Cleveland orchestras; Dinah Shore and Buddy Clarke in duets; Victor Borge, the Danish pianist-comedian; Kay Kyser; and the Charioteers, black singers who could sound comforta-bly white. The records were priced at $3.95 and $4.85. After four months on the market, Columbia reported that several hundred thousand plug-in LP players, built by Philco, and 1.25 million LPs had been sold. Only Mer-cury, of the new major firms, took advantage of Columbia's offer to press its classical microgroove records on a licensing basis. The Chicago com-pany had recently completed arrangements, through a European agent, to distribute Telefunken records in America.

The American record industry's international-licensing situation was thrown into a state of confusion following the announcement in August of a gov-ernment action seeking to end an alleged conspiracy and disk cartel scheme.

The defendants included the giant EMI and both the British and the American Decca companies. The complaint charged that they had divided the world's record markets among themselves, in order to control the manufacture, sale, and licensing of phonograph recordings. EMI was the majority partner, and, the Justice Department charged, beginning in 1934 the three had allocated all of the Americas to Kapp and American Decca; Australia, New Zealand, and the Far East to EMI; the rest of the world to Lewis and British Decca. However, as EMI grew stronger it had begun to dominate. The government asked for cancellation of all existing contracts, an injunction against restraint of trade, and an order to cease all price fixing by the three defendants. This left the matter of international representation of American firms activated since 1934 wide open. Columbia was already negotiating with Philips of the Netherlands, and Capitol waited only for the government to confirm an agreement with Telefunken, made through its headquarters in Berlin, that would supercede the Mercury-Telefunken arrangement. When it was approved, Capitol, for the first time, had outlets throughout Europe, with the exception of Russia, and soon after in Africa, through EMI, also with government permission.

With its EMI agreement under fire, the Decca management, headed by Milton Rackmill, president since Kapp's death, in March 1949, concluded a reciprocal deal with Deutsche Grammophon, the last European major without an American connection. Decca became the German firm's representative in the United States and Canada, and gave Deutsche Grammophon its German, Austrian, and Norwegian rights.

Victor's backlog of useful masters was nearing depletion when David Sarnoff became personally involved in talks with the AFM, just before Thanksgiving. He was alone in his readiness to end the strike, but was quickly joined by representatives of a reluctant Columbia, who feared that their major rival would get an advantage by surrendering. In the weeks that followed, the Justice and Labor departments argued over responsibility for approval of the peace plan, whose acceptability under the Taft-Hartley Act might be questionable. With an end in sight, most manufacturers other than Columbia and Victor went back to their recording studios, which had been used only for unsatisfactory a cappella or vocal sessions with harmonica accompaniment. After eleven and a half months, the Labor Department approved a settlement that was substantially the same as the one terminated on the previous New Year's Day. Only one new element was added: the appointment of an impartial trustee to oversee distribution of record royalties. Petrillo's former antagonist and now friend Samuel Rosenbaum was the agreed-on choice as administrator, at a salary of $25,000.

Victor won the race to bring out the first release under the new agreement—Perry Como's version of "Far Away Places," backed by Truman's alleged favorite, "The Missouri Waltz." Disk jockeys in the New York and Philadelphia areas had acetate copies within twelve hours, and the song's publisher used air freight to get it into the hands of platter spinners in Chicago and on the West Coast a half day later.

The battle of speeds preoccupied manufacturers and angered consumers for most of 1949. Then a new challenge was hurled into the seething feud between Sarnoff and Paley, which had become more bitter following RCA's victory in the fight for the right to manufacture approved color cameras and receivers and program color television. Sarnoff gave permission to Victor's management to leak news to distributors that a new 45-speed disk would go on sale the following spring. This further disrupted the marketplace. The new speed formulation was the result of Sarnoff's instructions, immediately following the demonstration of Columbia's LPs, for his engineers to come up with a new record at any other speed. They brought out of storage a player modeled after one created in 1938 by Philco, which had made the 45-speed player for Muzak, when the wired-music, electrical-transcription company contemplated going into the commercial record business. Victor had begun its own experiments with a 45-speed machine, up to testing these "Madame X" models, as they were known for purposes of secrecy. A shortage of Vinylite and the company's success with traditional 78-speed records and phonographs halted further planning to market the new machine after the war.

Record sales were falling by 25 percent below the level of 1948 when the 45-speed system was finally introduced, with much fanfare, as "the first integrated program of records and player planning in the 70 year history of the business." The new seven-inch disks of unbreakable Vinylite—forty-five cents for popular selections, ninety-five cents for Red Seal—could be played on only two record changers: "the world's fastest," a plug-in machine priced at $24.95 and a self-contained three-tube model that sold for $39.95. Columbia immediately reduced the price of its player attachment to $9.95, and marketed a Microconverter which enabled a 78-speed turntable to play 33-speed LPs. With a center hole much larger than the new 33s or the standard 78s, the new equipment needed a converter insert in order to be played on the same turntable.

Victory in this competition rested on several factors: the number of new players that could be sold (Columbia sold its as a loss leader with a number of cut-rate LPs); the degree to which records at the new speeds would be accepted by radio-station disk jockeys and jukebox operators; and how many of the other major manufacturers would install suitable presses and adopt one of the new speeds. The manufacturers of phonograph players and radio-phonograph combinations, except for RCA, made a Solomon-like decision and used both. Capitol was the first major to jump on board the 45 bandwagon, a move made necessary by the inadequacy of the Scranton plant's twelve-inch presses to accommodate Telefunken's 78-rpm classical-music masters. For access to Victor's twelve-inch presses, Capitol enthusiastically endorsed the 45s.

The increasing presence of tape reels and recorders in many large studios, and the reduction in production costs thus afforded, presaged an era of more faithful reproduction and new sounds on commercial records. Columbia was the first of the majors to benefit, redubbing all old material and recording new sessions on improved plastic tape, on which a range of 20 to 20,000 cps was possible, wider than the 80 to 5,000 cps of mass-produced phonographs. In the early 1920s, the range of sound on commercial records was 200 to 3,200 cps; after the advent of electric recording, it went from 120 to 4,200, and reached from 70 to as high as 8,000 just before the war.

The easy manipulability of 3M tape gave Victor one of the year's few million-copy sellers, Vaughan Monroe's "Riders in the Sky," with the echo-chamber effect that did more than anything to sell Americans on the 45-rpm concept. At the same time, one of the first guitarists to use an electrified instrument, Les Paul, experimented with overdubbing on tape, a process that had been used on Edison cylinders as a studio trick in the late 1890s. Paul also raised the state of the art to twenty-four tape tracks at a time; most studio engineers were then delighted with two- or three-track layering. Using electrified instruments and multiple tracking, the guitarist-inventor created a series of successful records for Capitol in 1949 and 1950. Tape made it possible not only to rerecord existing music and produce superior doctored masters, but also to record popular music over several sessions. At the first, the instrumentalists laid down their music, and in later sessions, using earphones to hear what had already been recorded, vocal soloists and groups overdubbed their voices. Engineers then made the two performances compatible for a final master.

Columbia had spent two million dollars and Victor five million to promote and merchandise their new systems before a three-speed formulation was accepted even by the most demanding discophiles. Victor's Extended Play classical 45 disks had not been generally accepted by them. Even the world's fastest record changer required a break in the movements of an extended work. In December, Victor indicated that it might be ready to resolve the dilemma; it demonstrated a new line of three-speed machines at a furniture-show preview, promising them for delivery in the spring of 1950. Victor was willing to go along with a classical repertory on 33s, but it held out for its own favorite creation as the medium for all nonclassical music.

Record sales continued to drop and inventories to pile up. Confused by the different speeds and bored by records that usually seemed without character or individuality unless they had novel production stunts, choral effects, or used bleached black rhythm-and-blues music or hillbilly tunes from the country-and-western field, many Americans were turning to television. During 1949, there was a 400 percent increase in the production of television receivers.

Nowhere was the dearth of experienced talent made more obvious than in the fact that only one out of every twenty-five popular releases enjoyed some measure of success in the record stores. There were no more than twenty qualified men at work for the major labels. The committee system of choosing material, instituted by Victor after World War I and recently restored, clearly was not practical, and a single autocrat in complete charge of making such decisions—such as Ralph Peer, Jack Kapp, or Eli Oberstein in their glory years—could not cope with the multiplicity of material offered for consideration. About 200 new songs were offered each week by the established large publishers alone, and another hundred by songwriters. Fewer than a dozen got any serious attention. It cost a major publisher between $25,000 and $30,000 for promotion and exploitation of a song that eventually got near the top of *Variety*'s Most Played on the Networks list. No longer certain of their ability to pick hit songs, publishers offered six to twelve manuscripts at a time to the record companies, hoping that lightning might strike and keep them out of the red. When a song was accepted, the exclusive right to record it was confirmed, a guarantee that no other company would see the words or music until its release to the public. Speed was called for to "cover" a rival's potential hit, a gift for which Mitch Miller, of Columbia, revealed a magnificent flair. Two days after Decca's first version of "Tzena, Tzena," by the Weavers, was released, with English words to the familiar Yiddish melody written by Gordon Jenkins, a Decca A & R man, Miller was on the market with a Columbia release. It had taken him twelve hours after the Jenkins disk was out to prove the validity of his reputation as "Cut 'em, press 'em, ship 'em" Miller.

Talent raiding, characteristic of the dance-band business in the 1920s, went on at all large manufacturers. Hugo Winterhalter, one of the best arrangers and record supervisors, was enticed from Columbia to Victor with a contract promising him $20,000 a year and a 5 percent royalty for each disk with which he was associated, the standard fee paid to best-selling artists. In his most successful years at Victor, prior to the war, Oberstein averaged an annual $6,000, and he was responsible for all black-label and Bluebird records. Mannie Sachs, a member of one of the Philadelphia families that had invested in CBS when the Paley family took control of the network, moved from his job at Columbia Records to take charge of RCA's popular-record division, at a salary rumored to be between $50,000 and $75,000. Sachs was frank to say that he relied on the judgment of a ten-year-old niece when selecting songs to record, which few in the business believed. Hoping that some of the expertise for which the trade paper *Billboard* was famous would rub off on Victor employees, Sachs hired its managing editor, Joe Csida, to run Victor's popular artists-and-repertory department. At Columbia, the urbane classical composer and near-Renaissance man Goddard Lieberson, was elevated from responsibility for the Master Works catalogue to full charge of the company's entire recorded output. Immediately, he lured an old friend and fellow student, Mitch Miller, away from Mercury with an offer of $40,000 a year to take over the popular-music department. The bearded, cigar-smoking, often profane Miller was an accomplished concert oboist with experience in the symphony hall and the broadcast studio. His ability to create hit records, possessed of a so-called new sound, had moved Mercury into the ranks of the majors, alongside Victor, Columbia, Decca/Coral, Capitol, MGM, and London.

The owners of the independents, who had learned that specialization was the key to profit, took full charge of choosing material themselves, or gave on-the-job training to underpaid young employees in love with music and the record business. Their market was still a small one, but they had found that by making deals with local jukebox operators, who were willing to guarantee a minimum purchase of likely releases, they could at least break even if sales went over 10,000 units. A combination of six or seven large operators with a string of machines could, when they chose, easily guarantee that number. Additional sales were clear profit.

Now that the name bands and their remote and commercial radio plugs were no longer crucial to promoting a song, the publishers' contact men, assigned to deal with disk jockeys, had great difficulty in getting past a radio-station receptionist. But a select group of young men with experience in the record-promotion business had valuable personal relationships with influential deejays. While a press agent, contacting disk jockeys on behalf of Dinah Shore, Frank Sinatra, and others, Howard S. Richmond won the ears of some of the country's most important platter spinners. In the spring of 1950, he purchased several thousand copies set aside for disk jockeys of the Weavers' version of "Goodnight Irene," which he mailed from his own small independent music house to 1,500 disk jockeys around the country. Because of well-established contacts with these men, who received at least a hundred likely candidates each week, his song got attention and much air play. After only three live performances on prime-time network radio, in the first month Richmond sold 250,000 printed copies of the song and a half-million recordings.

Once they resolved public confusion over their rival claims to superior new products, Columbia and Victor enjoyed better sales with new, high-quality, unbreakable disks. The surfaces of 33s and 45s were considerably improved because of a new thermal engraving process that used a heated stylus and provided a quieter record, without the high-frequency hiss present in the early 78s. Their combined sales accounted for nearly one third of 1949's $172 million retail gross, and represented 50 percent of the sale of conventional 78s. LPs and 45s, which originally were pressed only by the Columbia and Victor custom-service departments, were pouring off presses installed in new and vastly expanded factories across the country. Discount selling, the acceptance of the 33 as standard by several hundred new record companies that specialized in classical music, and a growing audience reflected a broadening of what once was regarded as a small but steady connoisseur market. A new element was the popularity of the hitherto neglected original-cast, complete-score musical, LPs of which shared the display bins in discount record stores.

The father of discount selling in the record business, Sam Goody, of New York, originally got into the game before World War II when he added used records, bought from southern coin-machine operators, to his novelty and magic-trick business in a store near the financial district. Moving uptown in the late 1940s, to sell only classical, original-cast-, and high-quality popular-music LPs, Goody applied a merchandising principle common to the novelty products he once carried: he sold new LPs at a 30 percent discount. The $3.98 ten-inch Columbia collection of hits by Rosemary Clooney, Guy Mitchell, Tony Bennett, or the seemingly fading idol of American women, Frank Sinatra, which Goody sold for $2.80, actually cost him $1.85, giving him a profit of almost one dollar. Ballyhoo, an inventory of 300,000 LPs, and an overhead strictly maintained at 15 percent made Goody the talk of the business, and inevitably led to litigation, instituted by Columbia.

The company had smiled on his price-cutting tactics when he pushed its wares in large-scale advertising that offered a free Microconverter to any customer who purchased twenty-five dollars' worth of LPs. But once the Columbia distributorship in Philadelphia, owned by a few CBS stockholders, was found guilty of price fixing and restraint of trade, the company began to fight price cutting in states where price-fixing legislation prevailed. Several attempts had already been made to stop Goody. He was refused a special 10 percent return privilege, offered to dealers who held the price line, and denied the extra credit granted to a few favored major outlets. Columbia suffered a serious defeat in a hearing before a New York Supreme Court referee, who ruled that the state's Fair Trade Act was intended to protect the trademark, name, and good will of the manufacturer and could not be applied to record price discounting. Columbia and Victor had opened themselves up to price cutting, he pointed out, when they unloaded old 78-rpm albums on dealers at discounts up to 60 percent, but denied the offer to Goody.

The ruling had an immediate effect on discounting in large metropolitan centers, where Sam Goody's operation and selling policies were copied. A boycott by Columbia and Victor of these operations followed quickly, but was countered by Goody with transshipping. It was customary in the record business to allocate new record releases, as well as radios, phonographs, and television sets, on the basis of past sales. Many distributors and dealers were often left overstocked with items that did not sell and could not be returned until six months after receipt. With sufficient cash in hand, Goody had little difficulty in finding dealers who were happy to take the money and transship to him LPs and 45s at a 40 to 50 percent discount, in order to maintain their quotas. He could still enjoy a 4 percent profit, a little below the 6 to 7 percent earned by Columbia and Victor. They had waited

almost a decade to crack down on him and other discounters, which gave
them sufficient time to become indispensable to consumers in their territory,
and to build a devoted following for classical music and the outpouring of
original-cast albums.

From the cylinder's earliest days, stage performers had been brought into
recording studios to preserve songs from current musical productions on
wax, but until Jack Kapp recorded *Oklahoma!* in 1943 there had been no
complete recording of a musical made by an original cast exactly as performed in the theater. Kapp's success with the first Rodgers and Hammerstein show, followed by successful albums of *Bloomer Girl, Carmen Jones,*
the revival of *A Connecticut Yankee,* and other current Broadway shows
whose producers gave him recording rights, attracted the other majors. It
became the general practice to advance a musical's producer several thousands for first-rejection rights, in return for which, and a royalty up to 10
percent on all sales, the original cast was made available for recording
sessions. Spirited bidding became the rule, even though an album often did
not return the costs of production, though the show was a box-office hit.
Tape and the long-playing records offered a more commercial medium for
musical comedies, permitted the addition of what had previously been
throwaway material, and enlarged the market for cast albums.

Shortly after assuming his position at Victor, Mannie Sachs added a new
financial dimension to the business of recording musical comedies when he
agreed, on RCA's behalf, to put up the entire $250,000 backing for the
Irving Berlin–Lindsay and Crouse musical *Call Me Madam,* which went
into rehearsal in the spring of 1950. Berlin, his co-writers, the director, and
Ethel Merman, the star, agreed to a 20 percent temporary reduction in their
royalties, until Victor's investment was recouped, after which the usual
author and performer royalties would be restored. However, because Merman was under contract to Decca, which refused permission, she could not
make the album for Victor. In her place, one of Sachs's trophies from the
Columbia roster, at $100,000 a year, Dinah Shore, sang the role of the
"hostess with the mostes'." Decca covered with an album of its own, starring Merman. Neither recording was a success, though Columbia LPs of
Gentlemen Prefer Blondes, Kiss Me Kate, and *South Pacific* were at the top
of the year's best-selling lists. Yet Sachs had introduced a new gambit to
the game of ever-higher advances. In order to get the new Cole Porter
show, *Out of This World,* Columbia agreed to a $25,000 advance for first-
refusal rights and a 15 percent royalty on all sales to the producers. It was
not one of Porter's hits.

The market was witnessing the world-wide popularity of a type of song
far removed from Porter's production numbers, but not unlike Berlin's earlier hits, when *Out of the World* folded. The biggest popular hit in twenty
years, "Tennessee Waltz," sung by Patti Page in a duet with herself, thanks
to the wonders of tape and overdubbing, had already sold two million copies,

and an additional 2.2 million sung by others. The barriers had broken down between the "classy music" of Broadway and Hollywood and that scornfully defined as "hillbilly." It was now becoming known as "country and western" out of deference to its devotees. They were lining up to buy a million records of "Chattanoogie Shoe Shine Boy," "Cold, Cold Heart," "Slow Poke," and other hits that crossed over to "Your Hit Parade." Over a third of the year's popular-record sales were soon country-and-western hits. Tennessee Ernie Ford, Red Foley, Ernest Tubb, Hank Williams, and Little Jimmy Dickens generally averaged more than three quarters of a million disks. The "Tennessee Plowboy," Eddy Arnold, generally went over a million, and was one of Victor's most advertised artists. Sales were not confined to rural areas, but spread to a myriad of fans in urban centers, who spent freely. Hank Williams got $150,000 in record royalties alone, from platters made by country and popular performers. Roy Acuff, half owner of Acuff-Rose, the publisher of "Tennessee Waltz," paid $48,000 in income taxes for 1951. Nearly half of all pop single Decca records sold that year—many of them to jukeboxes, consumers of one out of every five disks made—were rooted in country music. Columbia announced that country-and-western records represented 40 percent of all 78-rpm sales in this, the best year in its history. *Variety* attributed much of this increase to the twelve-to-twenty-year-olds, with their preference for new artists, new sounds, and every new kind of song. Evidently adults shared their tastes and enthusiasms, as witnessed by the success of this music on jukeboxes, whose consumers generally were above the age of consent.

Black America"'s "race music"—officially rhythm and blues, or R & B, once *Billboard* adopted the phrase for its charts in June 1949—was enjoying a growth paralleling that of country and western, or C & W, without its commercial returns. That the differences between northern city blues and the rural blues enjoyed for so many years in the South had disappeared was evident, insofar as the record industry was concerned, in the popularity of the disciples of the Father of R & B, Louis Jordan. Vocal artists accompanied by a small instrumental group took the place of Jordan's recordings. Promoters in the South and Midwest took advantage of the fact that two R & B artists could be had for the price of a single white "name" performer, and began to feature rhythm-and-blues shows. Occasionally a few whites could be found, too, attracted by the publicity on black radio stations.

By 1951, rhythm-and-blues soloists and groups were big draws in a circuit that embraced Atlanta, Kansas City, St. Louis, Houston, and Oakland. A top R & B attraction now cost as much as $5,000 for a one-night stand, between $1,800 and $2,500 in small towns. Labels specializing in rhythm and blues—Atlantic, Savoy, King, Imperial, Apollo, Aladdin—were tasting the wonder of an occasional half-million or better seller. Each had its own publishing company, formed to avoid paying song royalties or to take advantage of contracts offered by BMI. Money was laid out only for promotion, or sometimes to make deals with distributors and retailers. Only the best-selling artists received a royalty.

R & B distributors, in turn, put the most important local deejay on their payrolls, for between twenty-five and fifty dollars a month, gave them boxes of free records if they owned a retail store, or paid a royalty on each disk sold within the listening area. Expenses of this type were passed back to the manufacturer, who gave a higher discount, a cash subsidy, or one free record for every three ordered.

As aware of the economic significance of R & B music as the major companies, now that whites accounted for as much as 40 percent of the earlier all-black radio audiences, many local stations added at least one deejay to play that kind of music, preferably done by white artists who covered the hits. After using market research to learn how the independents had built a market that accounted for more sales than those of hot jazz, Latin, and international music combined, many of the major companies opened a "race," "sepia," or "ebony" department. The trick, they learned, lay in adopting the marketing pattern of the independents, which, like their own to sell popular records, called for harnessing the power of disk jockeys, particularly those catering to the 13 million blacks.

Existing contracts with their distributors and major retailers stood in their way, however. There was also the fear of interference by the FTC should word get out. So subsidiary labels were formed to handle the rhythm-and-blues lines—OKeh by Columbia, Coral and, later, Brunswick by Decca—each with independent distribution and promotion. In spite of them, the independents continued to prosper. New black talent and their agents tended to prefer labels to which their favorite artists were signed, owners who were compatible, and artists-and-repertory men and musical directors who were already familiar with R & B's folkways.

In order to compete, the majors were forced to change some of their traditional ways of doing business, particularly their return policy. Because the new distributors and retailers had no previous experience with them, did not know their often unfamiliar talent, and feared being left with unsold inventories, they insisted on a 100 percent return privilege. Panicked by declining sales in 1951, after new releases glutted the market, some majors shipped out as many as 100,000 copies of a new release by an unknown performer to major retailers, on a guaranteed 100 percent return basis, hoping that they would push the record. With the cost to the manufacturer of pressing, packaging, and shipping at around twenty cents, the loss could be considerable when a record was unsuccessful and returns piled up in warehouses. The manufacturer was taking all the risk, the retailer none.

Mannie Sachs, given a free hand to sign musical talent with a potential for television, offered huge guarantees against future royalties to Perry Como, Vaughn Monroe, Dinah Shore, and Milton Berle to sign long-term contracts. The singers found a place on television programs broadcast between

7:00 and 8:00 P.M. and won enthusiastic response from viewers and sponsors. Like the radio broadcasts on which they had first won fame, their telecasts were little more than a radio program played in front of a camera, with pieces of visual business. Changing musical styles, viewer satiation, and consumer boredom eventually made many of Sachs's deals completely unprofitable, but the immense amounts offered to established stars spoiled any new performer with whom Sachs negotiated. Mario Lanza, who was a piano mover a few years before he signed with Victor in the late 1940s, enjoyed a million-dollar income in 1951: $224,000 from appearances on NBC, $220,000 from concerts, and $150,000 a picture from MGM. As a Victor classical artist, he also received a 10 percent royalty on sales of his $1.29 records, paid because the Red Seals were not supposed to sell as well as popular records, on which the 5 percent royalty was general. His Victor income in 1951, half a million dollars, included money from the sale of 1.6 million copies of "Be My Love," the only Victor Red Seal thus far to get into the jukeboxes.

Lanza's impressive royalty statements and those of other newcomers (Les Paul sold six million disks in 1951, and Patti Page earned royalties of $180,000 from nine successive hits since "Tennessee Waltz") annoyed many executives, who believed that talent was dispensable. They demanded a revised standard recording contract. The document called for a 2½ percent royalty on retail price, with a 10 percent return or breakage privilege. The artist was also asked to pay all costs for a recording session, taken out of royalties. A popular disk cost between $750 and $1,000 for studio time, musicians, arrangers, and other expenses, which could be recouped only with the sale of 50,000 records. All costs were accrued on the artist's statement, and every unsuccessful recording ate up previous royalties, making most artists economic peons to the manufacturers. Like R & B performers, they looked to the proceeds from concerts and personal appearances for most of their income. Local disk jockeys became more important than ever to the recording artist, playing their new releases on the air and promoting live performances.

The new role disk jockeys had assumed in the entertainment business provided fodder to nationally syndicated gossip columnists, who delighted in carrying items about payola, especially in those cities that could make an overnight hit—Boston, Philadelphia, Detroit, Cincinnati, and Chicago. The large and faithful audiences commanded by deejays in these cities symbolized their power over a new record or artist. Promotion men, working for manufacturers, music publishers, or disk talent, applied great pressures on these radio personalities, dispensing gifts or buying time on their stations. In a fashion similar to that in 1916, when it was responsible for the formation of the MPPA, *Variety* took up the matter in a series of editorials that continued throughout the 1950s. It blamed the publishers for building the disk jockey, "the music biz's Frankenstein," up to a position where some were paid more than the U.S. President. The solution lay, *Variety* concluded, in a revision of the Copyright Act that would end free use of recorded music by broadcasters and coin operators.

Though not publicly stated as a reason, free records to disk jockeys, payola, and Sam Goody's discounting were among the many issues that brought about the formation of the record manufacturers' most important postwar trade association and lobbying group. The Recording Industry Association of America was established in September 1951, a nonprofit corporation chartered in the state of New York. It was officially designed to deal with legislation, the allocation of materials, preparation of industry statistics, and such matters as the government's request the previous December for a voluntary price cutback. Fortunately for the manufacturers, it came just after they had boosted prices generally, in fear of a Vinylite shortage due to the military action in Korea, and they continued to hold the new line. More recently, a 10 percent excise tax had been added on all records manufactured.

The first suggestion for the RIAA had come from the head of the independent Allegro label, Paul Puner, during the war of the speeds, when, according to *Fortune,* he asked for a body that could bring reason to that "probably unnecessary and certainly wretched controversy." His pleas went unheeded, but official frowns from the price-control agency and a possible scandal involving payments to disk jockeys spurred the companies to action. Milton Rackmill, of Decca, Frank Walker, of MGM, and Capitol's president, Glenn Wallichs, took the lead in forming the association. Within a few weeks, they were joined by Columbia's new president, James Conkling, at thirty-five the industry's youngest chief executive, and Paul Barkmeier, of Victor. With all the Big Seven on the board, the RIAA spoke for the thirty-two most important manufacturers in the business, representing at least 85 percent of the dollar volume. The organization was funded by membership dues ranging from $10,000 for the major firms to a minimum of $25.

At this time, about 800 record companies were registered with the AFM and the Performance Trust Fund, but fewer than forty-five did an annual business in excess of $20,000. In his annual report, Rosenbaum stated that 300 were about to go out of business and would probably be joined by an additional 300.

In the early 1950s, EMI faced serious competition in its own back yard. Victor was making new arrangements for international distribution when its contract with EMI expired in 1957. The well-financed Philips, Europe's largest electronics manufacturer, bought out French Polydor, and, ready to distribute America's Columbia, moved into England to begin inroads to a market long dominated by EMI and British Decca. American independents got the opportunity for distribution in Europe that they had been denied for years by the new combines. A consent decree, signed in New York in

December 1952, dissolved the last vestige of EMI's cartel agreement in the United States and permitted Decca to make its masters available for sale or lease to any foreign distributor if EMI did not accept them within ninety days after release. Within a year, EMI was doing business in the United States through the resuscitated Angel label, owned in partnership with Dario Soria, the former head of Cetra-Soria, distributor of complete recordings of Italian operas with La Scala casts. The Angel label—a winged cherub reclining on a disk and using a quilled feather as a recording stylus—was the oldest record trademark in Europe, dating back to 1898. From the start, EMI-Angel was hailed by critics and record buyers for the imposing array of performers and artists it made available in the United States, from HMV, British Columbia, Parlophone, Pathé, Odeon, and their subsidiary labels. Angel used a wooden dowel to reinforce the stiff spine Victor had introduced in 1952 for its long-playing albums, a touch of extra care that, with the elaborate artwork and cellophane wrapping of its premium releases, justified their higher price.

Retired from CBS, Wallerstein could view with personal satisfaction the dramatic showing of classical records during the early 1950s—a sale of $37.8 million, representing about 20 percent of total industry volume, which rose to almost 35 percent in 1952, an all-time high. The mail-order services of Sam Goody and other discounters bringing concert music even to the hinterlands, accounted for an estimated 80 percent of all classical sales. The twin miracles of tape technology and long-playing recordings, and the spreading availability of high-fidelity playback components, had taken on a more solid substance with the formation of independent labels that specialized in generally unrecorded repertory. The Haydn Society, Remington, Urania, Vox, Westminster, and other small companies went to Europe to record music that had never been available to Americans in recorded form. In August 1949, the first issue of the Schwann catalogue of long-playing music listed eleven labels; by the end of 1952, there were 160. In 1949, a classically oriented company could buy a professional Ampex tape machine for $1,000 or $2,000 and with an additional $8,000 put enough recordings on the market to realize a small profit. With increasing costs and more discriminating customers, who no longer automatically bought every new independent release, recording shifted to Europe, where engineers and musicians worked for less than U.S. union scales. The stakes to get into the game had been raised to between $30,000 and $50,000. The break-even point for a work performed by a small European orchestra of sixty-nine pieces, but manufactured in the United States by union labor, was 2,000 units. The same recording by American musicians in an American studio had to sell more than 5,000 copies.

Freed from a dangerous position in the antitrust EMI-cartel suit, Decca moved into a period of aggressive expansion, with an eye toward diversification, by entering into production of television programs. Its new president, Milton Rackmill, saw the film industry as being in the same position as the record business in 1929, when radio seriously affected sales. Many manufacturers believed then that the end of their world was at hand, and doubted any future for the business. They had been proved wrong. Radio became their most important ally in promoting new products. Rackmill believed that a marriage between theatrical film production and television was inevitable, and he moved toward the purchase of a substantial portion of Universal Pictures for $3.75 million. First, he hastened the departure of Dave Kapp, the last important Decca stockholder to think along record-business-only lines, who might oppose expansion into other fields. (On the lookout for a man with experience, Victor promptly took on Kapp to run its popular-music division.) Rackmill improved Decca's cash position by borrowing four million dollars from the Boston First National Bank, on the basis of his holdings in Universal, and issuing six-year 3% percent notes. Universal stepped up production of three television series, at a cost of $20,000 a segment, to be sold as a package of twenty-six programs. The profits lay, Rackmill believed, not in selling the films, but in residual rights, which might not be realized for three to five years, but would continue as long as a series remained in use. J. Arthur Rank, the leading British film producer, and the owner of a large block of Universal common stock, opposed Rackmill's takeover. Using credit based on the recent cash acquisition, Decca bought out Rank, raising its share of the film company to 43.3 percent. As president of both Decca and Universal, Rackmill set about trimming studio costs to realize what he perceived to be the future of motion pictures on television. The record operation was strengthened in the Orient by an agreement with Japanese Teichiku, whose record production was limited because of its shortage of American Vinylite, unlike its competitors, Victor Company of Japan and Japanese Columbia, which accounted for 11 million sales in 1952.

The first official breakdown of industry figures, issued as one of the RIAA's initial public statements, reported a $200 million national gross sale of 186 million disks in 1951, purchased by the owners of nearly 22 million record players of all types, or one in every three families. The figure represented a dramatic jump from the 8 million disks in 1946, when only 78-rpm records were available. The traditional pre-1939 largest market for singles, the nation's 550,000 jukeboxes, now accounted for only about one tenth of total production. The new versions, which could hold as many as 100 or more records, were adapted to the 45 speed and were of considerable assistance in gaining public acceptance for that tangible product of Sarnoff's pique. For the first time, production of 45s surpassed 33-rpm records, almost doubling their sale. Popular disks represented about half of the total output; classical, 18.9 percent; country and western, 13.2; children's, 10.2; rhythm and blues, 5.7; international, 1.1; Latin-American, 1.0, and hot jazz .8 percent.

The undisputed king of artists-and-repertory men in 1952, Mitch Miller, and Columbia's popular-music A & R staff were responsible for the label's industry lead, the company's best showing of all time. The secret of Miller's success and that of his new sound was essentially a preoccupation with treating the popular product as if it were classical music, and the introduction of musical instruments and vocal effects for which tape seemed to have been created. He looked for the best possible sound balance by shifting microphones around the studio, hoping to add that extra dimension of realism most earlier disks had failed to attain. The favorable profit situation for which Miller was chiefly responsible helped to underwrite the expansion of the CBS television network and the development of a CBS color receiver, which also expanded the smoldering feud between Paley and Sarnoff.

Notable among the statistics reported by the RIAA for 1951 was that of children's record sales, predominantly 78s. The last stronghold of obsolescent technology, the children's room, where one found an inexpensive portable player or the old family Victrola was being invaded by 45s. Their garishly illustrated and elaborate heavy-paper jackets attracted children, who then demanded their own 45-speed players. Six million "kiddie players" were sold in 1952. Coincidentally, the growth of public music education, beginning at the kindergarten level, created a demand for low-cost musical instruments, which was satisfied by easy-to-learn chord instruments, particularly the ukulele and guitar. Once a young child got its fingers properly calloused and learned a few chords, the number of songs it could perform acceptably on the guitar was surprising. A lot of the music came directly from the major companies' recent popular releases, written by tunesmiths whose songs were prominent on "Your Hit Parade." Seeking to get their share of the children's market, approaching $15 million in annual sales, many A & R men used top artists to record material written for across-the-board tastes, from the kiddie disk to the million-copy pop seller.

While the twelve-to-twenty record buyers were developing into the industry's best customers, their parents forced the established music business to pay attention to something of their own, songs that came to the city from the southern and western hills. Many adults were first exposed to C & W music during the war, heard on PX jukeboxes or over armed forces radio and from the broad cross-section of Americans with whom they comingled. Regional differences faded fast, and country music acquired a new populist character, a Middle-American vernacular form, often like that of Tin Pan Alley's songs before the war. It was recorded with the same devices—echo chambers, multiple recording, accented rhythms, all the instruments of the modern dance or television orchestra—which appealed to the young. Its subject matter, taken from everyday adult life and now aimed at the popular market, revealed the influence of postwar urban America. More to the point for the record industry, the appeal of country-and-western music extended to preadults and to children.

C & W had its own cohort of disk jockeys, a few hundred of whom gathered in Nashville just before Thanksgiving in 1953, with visitors from New York, Chicago, Los Angeles, and other centers of the music business, to celebrate the anniversary of the Grand Ole Opry, the true home of hillbilly music. The Country and Western Disk Jockeys Association was formed, to work for the advancement of a type of music whose commercial viability was becoming more apparent each day. Some of the big-city music men present feared that the association would hamper their effort to fight payola to platter spinners. Others believed it would expedite their service to disk jockeys.

Not even the RIAA was in a position to compile an accurate list of disk jockeys employed by radio broadcasters. The figure 2,000 bandied about since the middle 1940s, included program directors and managers, music librarians, and some staff announcers who occasionally handled a disk show, as well as the 700 deejays who were on the air regularly. Those on little 250-watt "one lungers" were paid as little as twenty-five dollars a week. All of them, however, fought to get on the manufacturers' free lists. A smart record-company promotion man concentrated on about 100 "real song breakers," men with national reputations as effective song boosters, who could sense a hit after hearing a song a few times. These were the disk jockeys who regularly received some form of payola in the early 1950s, paid on behalf of record companies, music publishers, or artists. It came in the form of something as innocent as a dinner, a Christmas gift, or presents for the children, or as blatantly outright as a commercial bribe, such as a down payment on a car, the car itself, or its value in cash. Generally, it depended on the power of the station or on the size of its audience in relation to record sales. Bill Randle, who worked for a Cincinnati station and was regarded throughout the industry as one of the most powerful record spinners of the era and a man of honor, told *Variety* in 1952 that the most important of his confreres, no more than 100 real disk jockeys employed on a contract or fee basis for doing specific record shows, really controlled the popular-music business. Without their concentrated action, no song could become a major song and no artist could remain a major artist, nor could a new name be made. However, Randle said, in discussing "good songs and bad songs, good singers and bad singers, good groups and bad groups: there is no such thing in the music business. There are varying degrees of quality . . . but these are not be be confused with commercial acceptability. . . . The fact that a great song or artist will command a public of its own and will have meaning in the society is highly important to American culture, but has nothing to do with the music business."

The world of rhythm and blues was subject to the same value judgments. It had remained in economic isolation until the independents made it sufficiently attractive for the major manufacturers to get into the field. In spite of them, in 1953 R & B was still outside the white-dominated music business, just as black radio was still looking in from the outside at commercial radio. None of the black disk jockeys employed by the Negro (the term "black" was not yet fashionable) stations was counted among Randle's significant 100, nor among the record-promotion men's important targets.

In the years after 1942, the income of the average black family had tripled, while that of a white family had doubled. In New York, the city with the sixth-largest black population, one third of the residents of its leading black ghetto—Harlem—left to settle in other parts of the city, and high-priced staples and luxury items were purchased by blacks in greater quantities than by any comparable population group in the city, according to *Billboard* in January 1954. At least four New York radio stations were targeted at this market, and 260 throughout the country, as television forced nonnetwork radio into some form of specialized programing.

Economic improvement brought with it an increase of black disk jockeys, from a few to over 700, who were joined by some alert pop, white, record spinners (among them, Alan Freed, in Cincinnati; Ken Elliott, in New Orleans; Bob Smith ["Wolfman Jack"] in Shreveport; "Symphony Sid" Torin, in Boston and later New York; Dick Hugg and Hunter Hancock, on the West Coast; Zenas Sears, in Atlanta; Gene Nobles, in Nashville) who, by early summer 1951, had observed the interest of the major manufacturers and switched to R & B. Quickly, they were deluged with larger black audiences, along with preadult whites just discovering rhythm and blues, and with more sponsors. In 1953, the first few advertisers, all large companies, found television becoming too expensive, and blacks not yet the owners of TV sets in great quantity. The platter-spinning route seemed to be the best way to reach this expanding market. Listeners responded most favorably to the products of the Aladdin, Apollo, Atlantic, Herald, King, Savoy, and Specialty labels. Hit disks by Ruth Brown, the Clovers, the Ravens, the Five Royales, the Orioles, Amos Milburn, Edna McGriff, Faye Adams, and Little Esther rarely sold fewer than 150,000 copies, and the Clovers had already sold two million disks of a single hit. Brown's value to the owners of Atlanta Records was affirmed by the contract the company gave this only female vocalist on their roster; it guaranteed $100,000 over the next five years.

In an eighty-page brochure, *The 50 Year Story of RCA Victor Records* put out in 1953 to celebrate the company's anniversary and the diamond jubilee of Edison's talking machine, the house Eldridge Johnson had built freely admitted that popular records made for "the Coney Island crowd" underwrote all losses from the celebrated Red Seal catalogue. Victor's total sales since 1902 were approaching two billion units, including 325 million Red Seals, the booklet reported, one billion since 1946. During a meeting with department heads in December, Mannie Sachs told them that a 15 percent increase from the year's $200 million loomed for 1954. He based his conclusion on three factors: the entrance, on a large scale, of chain stores, supermarkets, and major department stores into the retail record business, particularly with children's records and LPs; the steady growth of the major record-buying group, teen-agers; and the high-fidelity boom.

The improved sound that came from the usurpation of FM frequencies for telecasting plus the introduction of binaural and stereophonic sound into moving-picture theaters, in connection with Cinerama, Wide Screen, and 3D features, were influential in creating great interest in high fidelity. Once an affluent adult record buyer heard what a record actually held, he succumbed to a virus descended from the bug that had put a crystal set in every boy's hands in the early years of commercial broadcasting. The new electronics fans had already spent several hundred millions on turntables, amplifier, and speaker components—as high as $1,350 for assembled units in handsome cabinets. Exhibitors at the fifth annual Audio Fair, in 1953, predicted they would spend at least $200 million in the next twelve months, looking for sound that would satisfy their "golden ears." Every one of them was a heavy buyer of LPs, as much to demonstrate the superiority of his "system" as to show the quality of the music on his records.

Like the makers of raw film stock, who sold cameras almost at wholesale price in order to stimulate its purchase, Victor and Columbia put their excellent record players on the market at favorable prices. Only a superior machine could reveal the full glory of London FFRR, Victory New Orthophonic, Capitol Full Dimensional, Columbia Variable Pitch, and the other registered trade names the manufacturers used for their improved noise-free, unbreakable, vinyl plastic records. Columbia had added a third speaker to the 360 Sound player introduced the year before, giving it a binaural effect. Victor mass-produced high-quality components that originally were intended for radio-station use, and was ready to bring them "into five times as many American homes as now have hi fi."

Even cheap-radio-set makers entered this once-specialized business and did a strong selling job to take high fidelity out of the hands of discophiles and audiophiles and put it into the homes of anybody ready to spend $100 for a "hi-fi machine."

The major manufacturers kept pace with the research and development of improved tape-recording capability, and some of them debated over whether to release prerecorded tapes of new classical LPs. One million wire and tape-recording machines had been sold since 1946, and many of them were now antiquated. Ampex offered a low-price machine for home use, and its eastern distributor, Audio-Visual, announced a new library of 160 prerecorded tapes, copied on new high-speed duplicating machinery from Remington masters. Citing the possibility of overnight obsolescence of a major portion of their Red Seal and Master Works catalogues, Victor and Columbia decided to delay their entrance into the taped-music field. The memory of the marketplace's disruption during the battle of the speeds lay at the root of this decision.

There was little response from the A & R, sales, and executive offices of Columbia and Victor when a $150-million civil antitrust suit was announced on November 9. Speaking for songwriters as a class, the thirty-three plaintiffs alleged that CBS and RCA, with their recording companies, and a host of other defendants, including the major radio and television networks, were responsible for the present condition of the music business. The defendants were engaged, the complaint stated, in a conspiracy to create a monopoly in the production, exploitation, and use of music, favoring that available from the broadcaster-owned music organization, BMI, through which most R & B and C & W hits were licensed. After a flurry of denials by Mitch Miller, Mannie Sachs, and other major record executives that no such discrimination existed, and protests that the manufacturers' sole function was to give the public what it wanted, the record industry settled back to see what line of public relations and legal defense would be pursued by the principal defendants. Two of them, CBS and RCA, had their radio and television networks at stake.

Buried in the welter of trade-paper news of the record business were several items whose consequences or implications proved to be as noteworthy as the lawsuit:

In Memphis, a young truck driver and repairman for an electric company, Elvis Aaron Presley, got up enough courage in late 1953 to enter the storefront offices of the Memphis Recording Service, a small custom studio, to make a personal acetate record for his mother.

Two white Philadelphia songwriters, Max Freedman and James De-Knight, who was the co-writer of the 1945 pseudo-hillbilly hit "Sioux City Sue," persuaded a small rhythm-and-blues recording company to cut a master of their song "Rock Around the Clock." Neither the performer, Sunny Dae, nor the record received any measurable jukebox or air play.

Todd Storz was looking for a way to control the selection of music by disc-jockey employees of his radio station, KOWH, in Omaha, when he watched customers drop nickels into the jukebox of a tavern near his office. The frequency with which certain current hit songs were selected impressed him and inspired the creation of the prototype for "top 40 programing." George Washington Hill's "Your Hit Parade" formula was taken one step forward into the world of record exploitation by radio.

Speaking at the Grand Ol' Op'ry celebration in Nashville, Carl Haverlin, the president of BMI, told the audience of deejays and music men of his conviction that "in seeking its own level . . . an amalgamation of musical styles has begun, and it will end with American music finding its own unique character."

CHAPTER 15

Mass Entertainment and the Music Business

The international hostilities into which the United States found itself hurled on December 7, 1941, did not last as long as the revolution that had brought it independence, nor was there such a great outpouring of popular music inspired by the conflict as had occurred during the War Between the States, the nation's "singingest" war. With the memory of George M. Cohan's "Over There" made more vivid by a current film biography of the song-and-dance man, officials of the Office of War Information, charged with overseeing morale, urged Tin Pan Alley to set people to singing and to build up hatred of the enemy and a determination to win the war. Having been a participant in the ASCAP–radio war as a CBS executive, William B. Lewis, head of OWI's Radio Section, believed that if the American people "were exposed to enough worthy war songs on radio . . . some of them would . . . drive away such drivel" as was being played there. The airwaves, he complained, were full of "Goodby, Mama, I'm Off to Yokohama," "Remember Pearl Harbor," and a new contender for novelty-song honors, "Send a Great Big Salami to Your Boyfriend in the Army (And He'll Bring Home the Bacon to You)."

Yet, as Sigmund Romberg pointed out, this was not a "marching war," or one like that fought in the trenches of Europe in 1918. Unlike the home front, where motorized vehicles languished because of gasoline rationing and rubber shortages, and the buses on which name bands had been traveling were confiscated for the war effort, everything used by the armed forces was mechanized, and the march rhythm sought by the OWI was out of place. Those people who chose music for recordings, soon the preferred medium, or selected and performed songs on network programs, quickly became aware that their audience—the young women at home who awaited the return of loved ones, and those two or three out of every four civilians who worked to support men in combat—responded best to sentimental ballads and novelty songs. During its four-year course, the war was brought home in such songs as "Praise the Lord and Pass the Ammunition," "White Christmas," "Johnny Doughboy Found a Rose in Ireland," "I'll Be Seeing You," "As Time Goes By," "Don't Sit Under the Apple Tree" and in the novelties "Der Fuerher's Face," "Pistol Packin' Mama," "The G.I. Jive." The nearest thing to a real old-fashioned sentimental war song to achieve popularity was "There's a Star-Spangled Banner Waving Somewhere," which found its greatest audience among the nation's blue-collar working people and rural Americans whose notions of patriotism, duty to country, and values were still rooted in the frontier culture of the nineteenth century. The song sold an astonishing 1.025 million copies in little more than a year. Other war-associated songs that sold over a half-million copies of sheet music were: "The Army Air Corps" (800,000), "The White Cliffs of Dover" (650,000), "Comin' In on a Wing and a Prayer" (600,000), "Praise the Lord and Pass the Ammunition" (575,000), and "When the Lights Go On Again All Over the World" (525,000).

Under government controls, there was little change in costs or standard of living, until the restraints were lifted in late 1945. Heavy taxes on luxury items and entertainment, the government's war bond campaigns, and gas rationing kept Americans at home, and were factors in the return of sheet-music sales to proportions of the golden days. At a retail price of thirty-five cents, they doubled, to approach a range of 800,000 to one million, despite the early paper shortage, aggravated by government restrictions. At the start, these were based on 1941 figures, when most of the major old-line firms were off the air because of the ASCAP strike. In 1942, 22 million pieces of music were sold, 40 million in 1943, then slipping back to 25 million in 1944, because of the record ban instituted by the American Federation of Musicians.

Walter Douglas, president of the Music Publishers Protective Association, was chiefly responsible for the growth of profits from this old source of music publishing, which rose from $275,000 in 1942 to $750,000 annually after the war, all of it shared only by members of the association. Sheet music was one of the oldest music-business trade items. Its antecedents were the Elizabethan broadside ballads, which carried only the words of the most popular current songs, with appropriate music indicated under the title and description of the contents. The song sheet was also a lineal descendant of the songsters on which American printers from colonial times depended for ready cash when business was slack. Trade in unlicensed song sheets grew to large proportions immediately after World War I, which was a source of annoyance to the MPPA and the American Society of Composers, Authors and Publishers, because these nickel and dime items cut directly into sheet-music sales. For a time, ASCAP fought the song pirates, but eventually it left the task to the MPPA, chiefly because this was income in which authors and composers did not share. Only after the pirates were stopped by injunctions and heavy payments for damages did the MPPA become licensor for song-lyric reprinting in the two legitimate song-sheet magazines, *The Hit Parader* and *Song Hits*. Because these publications would reprint only MPPA-licensed lyrics, Broadcast Music Inc. was obliged to fund competing magazines.

Another important factor in the modern distribution chain, the music-rack business, had successfully replaced the five-and-ten-cent and syndicate stores after wholesale prices rose above the six-cent level that had made it possible for Frank Woolworth and his rivals to sell millions of ten-cent copies of hit songs prior to the 1920s. In early 1940, the MPPA entered into a formal agreement with the Hearst Corporation's International Circulation Co., which guaranteed the placement of metal display racks for sheet music in about 500 locations in newspaper shops and near newsstands. Following approval by Walter Douglas and Larry Richmond, head of the Music Dealers Service, two copies of each new song that found a place among the top twenty sellers were automatically put into each music rack. In four years, 13,000 racks were installed around the country, in barbershops, stationery stores, and other outlets that had never before carried sheet music. Each rack displayed between fifteen and twenty of the best-selling songs, guaranteeing an initial total order of 93,000 copies, and bringing in much more than the $5,000 to $20,000 it cost to promote a song into a top spot on "Your Hit Parade."

The return of prosperity to the printed-music business during the war years, paralleling that enjoyed in the late 1920s, was surpassed only by the economic gains enjoyed by ASCAP. Despite dire predictions of eventual disaster, made during the contretemps with broadcasters and the government, distributions to members nearly tripled during the war years, from the $2.8 million in 1941 to $7.3 million in 1945. There was a growing conviction along Tin Pan Alley that 1946 would see a $10 million gross from a combination of record and sheet-music royalties and the ASCAP distributions.

It had been a perilous journey, beset with a variety of suddenly emerging problems, which had threatened what was to become the industry's largest single assured source of income. For several weeks in early 1941, there was a complete absence of ASCAP music from the air, except on some 200 independent stations that programed phonograph records and electrical transcriptions, and some others that chose not to go along with the two major networks. *Variety* found that "having gone over the falls in a barrel, the industry has finally faced the one thing it always feared, and found that ASCAP music is not indispensible." There was no significant public clamor for its return, except in sporadic instances where loyal members stimulated letters of protest to broadcasters and the FCC. The bottom dropped out of sheet-music sales for all ASCAP-affiliated music houses. In 1940, they had sold a total 16 million copies, at the rate of about 300,000 a week. Now the turnover dropped to 120,000 a month. Realizing that the networks would hold out for months, and stripped of their principal medium for plugging, the large firms shut down their hit-making machinery to wait out the dispute. There was only slight solace in the evident limitations of a repertory drawn entirely from BMI and public-domain non-ASCAP sources.

Thurmond Arnold, assistant attorney general, did not intend to let much time pass before a settlement of the fight between ASCAP, BMI, and the broadcasters. Having been reassured by both personal and corporate counsel that the case against them was without merit, William Paley and David Sarnoff met with members of the boards of BMI, the National Association of Broadcasters, and the Independent Radio Network Affiliates in Washington, in early January 1941, but could not agree on a course of action. Paley and his chief assistant, Edward Klauber, adamantly opposed the 7½ percent network fee to which Arnold and ASCAP appeared wedded. Sarnoff and the NBC contingent believed that a favorable decree could be arranged, one that would do little damage to the existing radio-industry structure and would permit BMI's continued operation. With counsel for CBS, Sydney Kaye and Geoffrey Goldmark, and the NAB president, Neville Miller, they started days of negotiation with government lawyers. The consent decree that emerged was signed at once by the NAB board on behalf of BMI, terminating the grand-jury action against the broadcasters. Among other provisions, it gave music users a choice of blanket, per-program, or per-use access to BMI's repertory; required payment at the source from the networks; and was conditional on the acceptance and signing of a similar order by ASCAP. The per-program and per-use provisions were included only after attorneys for the Mutual Broadcasting Company insisted, those representing the NAB and the networks apparently forgetting an issue for which they had argued since the early 1930s. A year of grace was permitted in order to revise network-affiliate contracts to reflect the payment-at-the-source requirement.

Reactions to the sort of decree they also would be asked to approve varied among ASCAP writers and publishers. Hollywood and its representatives on the board favored the blanket-license concept, regarding a per-performance provision as one that would affect screen-theater licensing. Small publishers thought the per-piece concept gave them more of a competitive edge in the fight for air play. Many of the top-classed production writers and concert-music composers resented the government's treatment of the society as just another labor union, and were concerned about language that treated all ASCAP music on an equal basis, regardless of its artistic value or merit.

All elements of the business, however, were agreed on the permanence of BMI's existence as a source of competitive music licensing. The networks had already invested four million dollars in BMI and its future to which smaller publisher affiliates had also contributed.

Annoyed when Louis Schwartz, ASCAP's counsel, accompanied by Herman Finkelstein, a young associate recently assigned to the ASCAP account, returned to Washington in late January to resume discussion of the settlement, members of the antitrust division prepared a criminal information charging the society with violations of the Sherman Act and other offenses. Schwartz was well known to them; he had counseled his client Columbia Pictures to reject the consent decree forged in an antitrust action against the movie industry, still not settled.

Thinking in ASCAP's New York offices went through some major changes following the new charges. Herman Starr's inflexible antinetwork attitude, which had infected his fellow members on the negotiating committee, was rejected for a more conciliatory policy. Claude Mills's resignation was shelved, and the veteran negotiator was restored to his place on the executive management committee.

Arnold had been blunt. In plain language, he had said:

ASCAP is charged with exploiting composers by preventing them from selling their music except on terms dictated by a self-perpetuating board of directors. That board has had power arbitrarily to determine on what basis various members of ASCAP shall share in the royalties from ASCAP selections. In addition to discriminating against composers, ASCAP has begun using its monopoly powers to charge the users of music for songs they do not play. This is done by compelling the user to pay a percentage of his gross receipts on programs where other music is used or where no music is used. By this method, anyone who does not belong to ASCAP is excluded from the market. These practices we consider not only illegal, but unjustifiable on any ground of fair dealing. Our proceeding is aimed only to compel ASCAP to stop these abuses. It does not desire to prevent ASCAP from protecting the copyright privileges of its members.

A new, outside, counsel, Charles Poletti, was instructed to hold firm to two positions in dealing with Arnold's men: first, the need to revise the language that would effectively strip the society of its discretionary power to pool and distribute income; second, the need to insist on network payment at the source for music. Surrender on the first would be a veritable act of suicide, which would reduce ASCAP merely to a policing organization; the second was needed in order to increase revenues, and to correct an old abuse.

On his return from Washington with an acceptable consent decree, in which he had prevailed on both points, Poletti assured a meeting, in February 1941, of 700 ASCAP songwriters that the society was emerging from its antitrust difficulties a stronger organization than ever. He stressed that ratification of the revised decree, to which the board had already agreed, would ensure the government's blessing and give ASCAP a cachet of respectability and legitimacy never enjoyed before. A voice vote was unanimous in support.

Over a series of objections by the NAB, the consent decree was approved by Judge Henry Goddard, of the federal court in New York, on March 4, 1941. This dismissed a six-year-old civil action, aborted in 1935, though it left for resolution the Justice Department's criminal case. Henceforth, any new contracts into which the society entered required the approval of the New York court, to which complaints and applications for enforcement or modification of the decree must be brought.

Variety, on February 26, 1941, printed the complete decree, together with a comparison between the reforms and past conditions. First among the changes was the clause barring ASCAP from sole, or exclusive, right to the works of members, freeing them for direct licensing. In effect, ASCAP had returned to the 1914–20 condition, when most firms licensed directly, which led, according to *Variety,* to "so much chiseling that it was decided to relieve them of the right and to invest the exclusive rights with ASCAP." However, direct licensing could be done only with the society's permission, and all fees were paid to it for distribution. Other significant changes enjoined the discrimination of the past in prices and terms between similarly situated music users; gave broadcasters and other users a choice among blanket, per-program, and per-piece licenses; ended the self-perpetuating board by giving all members a voice in electing it; removed the requirement that a candidate for admission must show evidence of five published works—one now being sufficient; and based royalty allocations on the "number, nature, character and prestige of a member's works, the seniority of a member's works, and popularity and vogue of such works." The last would prove to be the most troublesome and lead to further consent decrees. It was, as *Variety* pointed out, at least in regard to publisher classification, the method abandoned in 1935. Since that time publishers had been paid on a "more scientific, or mathematic formula": 50 percent for performances, 30 percent for availability, or value of each catalogue, and 20 percent for seniority. As matters now stood, those writers whose high ratings were under fire from less well-placed authors and composers were protected.

It took fifty-five minutes for Judge F. Ryan Duffy, who was regarded as one of ASCAP's leading legislative enemies during his years as a U.S. senator, to settle the government's criminal action. Pleas of nolo contendere were accepted from Mills, Paine, twenty-three directors, and thirteen members, and a total fine of $35,250 exacted, to be paid in cash. Before accepting the pleas entered on their behalf by Poletti, Duffy said that he was making an exception to his usual practice of refusing such a plea, because a guilty plea made the defendants liable to civil damage suits and, in an antitrust case, imprisonment for a year or fines of up to $5,000, or both, could be imposed. With the decision that no moral turpitude existed on the defendants' part to require a prison term, Duffy found guilty individually each of the ASCAP representatives present. Among them were the most powerful publishers in the society: Max Dreyfus, who had been a director of ASCAP since 1916, Louis Bernstein, Saul Bornstein, Herman Starr, and Gustave Schirmer. After a week of worry about the consequences of their pleas, the ASCAP defendants were heartened when the charges were declared to involve a misdemeanor, not a felony.

The payment-at-the-source clause in the consent decree, for which Poletti and ASCAP had persevered in supporting, presented a giant stumbling block in the way to quick peace in the music war. It provided CBS and NBC an opportunity to drag their feet for months before a final settlement was made in November. This twilight-zone issue had already been resolved in the case of BMI, which was also obliged to license networks at the source. BMI's new contract, which became effective on April 1, 1941, called for a flat fee from both chains of 1½ percent of income, less certain deductions. Before a compromise could be effected between the 7½ percent originally asked by the society and BMI's lower figure, the network affiliates had to be persuaded that a new ASCAP agreement was not putting the same load on their shoulders as had been carried since 1932.

The respite that followed, before ASCAP offered acceptable terms, was a particular boon to the two major networks. Observers in Washington daily predicted that some extreme Justice Department and FCC actions were due at any moment on several fronts: the monopoly represented by newspaper ownership of broadcasting facilities; multiple-station ownership by individuals and corporations; the vertical integration implicit in the ownership by both CBS and NBC of recording and transcription companies, and of artists bureaus, as well as their involvement in BMI; and, most significant, the results of the three-year-old FCC monopoly inquiry into network ownership of stations and their contracts with affiliates.

While unproductive network meetings with ASCAP were in progress, the Mutual Broadcasting System, an independent cooperative alliance of stations, began its own negotiations, looking for an agreement that would enable it to use ASCAP music immediately and still benefit from any gains made later by the two major chains. The society welcomed the overture, believing it would give bargaining leverage in dealing with CBS and NBC. Mutual's executives, who had agitated for an investigation of network operations, were especially pleased with the plight of their major competition when the FCC released the formal monopoly report in early May and turned it over to the Justice Department for further implementation. Six of the proposed new regulations dealt with practices and arrangements between the chains and their affiliates; two, concentrating on the networks themselves, touched tangentially on the current and future music business. RCA's dual ownership of the Red and Blue networks was cited as serious restricting competition, and led finally to the divestiture and sale of the latter, which as the American Broadcasting Company owned one of the major record operations of the 1960s. The second matter was each network's artists bureau, which gave the network dual roles as employer and agent of musical and program-building talent and control of who recorded for their record companies. This was considered to be "a serious conflict of [fiduciary] interest." Before the year was out, this issue was resolved to the satisfaction of both the FCC and the Department of Justice. NBC's artists bureau was sold to a partnership of several leading independent booking agents and managers, the National Concerts and Artists Corporation. CBS's sale of its talent agency to the Chicago-based Music Corporation of America, gave MCA the first step up on its climb to such domination of the entertainment, record, and television business that it was eventually forced, by government intervention, to divest itself of the original talent agency in order to remain the leading supplier of television programing in the 1970s and 1980s and the owner of several major record labels. Formed in 1924 by the Chicago band-booker Billy Stein, who was joined several years later by his optometrist and part-time dance-band pianist brother, Jules, MCA was already a leading agent and booker for singers, dance bands, actors, and comedians when the FCC spurred CBS to the sale, which added creative writing, directing, and producing radio talent to the stable MCA was handling. The Columbia Concerts Corporation, the leading representative of concert and classical-music artists, in which William Paley held a large interest, was completely separated from CBS and purchased by Arthur Judson, the man responsible for the formation of the chain in 1927, and, a decade later, for CBS's acquisition of the American Record Company.

The fruit of the Mutual Broadcasting System negotiations with ASCAP was made public coincidentally with the release of the FCC monopoly report. The agreement quickly caused cries of "treason" from both the NAB and the other networks, because it broke the industry's hitherto united front. Claude Mills's public statement that the new terms represented the best ASCAP would offer further exacerbated intra-industry tensions. The agreement, subject to approval by the MBS affiliates, was to run until 1949 and called for a three to 3½ percent fee, less deductions, for all network and single-station commercial programs. ASCAP had held out for slightly higher rates until the last moment, tendering the new fees only after Mutual agreed to drop its insistence on outside arbitration in case of a bargaining impasse in further negotiations.

In spite of strenuous lobbying by the NAB and the exertion of various pressures by CBS and NBC, the majority of MBS affiliates approved the agreement in early May, and ASCAP music went out over a network for the first time since January 1. The music business was not prepared for this turn of events. Only a small number of new ASCAP songs were ready for intense plugging, and few of the dance bands that played for the important remote broadcasts after eleven o'clock had a sufficient number of ASCAP arrangements ready. Under the song pluggers' union rules, free arrangements could not be provided to them. Several weeks passed before the latest ASCAP repertory made an important impact on Mutual's broadcasts.

During the annual NAB convention, held in May, at which the MBS "sellout" was a chief topic of conversation, Sydney Kaye fired up industry support for BMI by announcing, during a session *Variety* described as bordering "on the evangelical," that BMI would reduce its rates by one third. Local-station fees, which ranged from 1 to 2½ percent, were cut to ½ to 1 percent. Though CBS and NBC remained at the previously announced one and a half percent rate, Kaye did not discuss the actual basis of accounting in the twilight zone that was permitted to the two chains, which involved the difference between what they received from advertisers and what they paid out to the affiliates. BMI's rate for per-program licensing, which, in the face of reduced music costs because of the AFM strike, did not seem as ideal as it once had, ran from 3 percent of time costs for stations with an income below $50,000 to 5 percent for all others. Accepting his audience's plaudits for the "brilliantly operated and richly successful" organization he represented, Kaye reported that it had spent $1.8 million in its first year, and that the new contracts would bring in nearly $2 million for its second. BMI intended to surpass present accomplishments.

Nearly one quarter of BMI's projected income, after expenses, for 1941–42, a minimum of $250,000, was earmarked for the E. B. Marks catalogue, which had the highest cost-per performance rate for any of its music, and was causing a severe strain on cash outlay. Of this, $225,000 went to the publisher, and $25,000 to his attorney, Julian Abeles, who had engineered the transfer of 15,000 copyrights from ASCAP. Ironically, had the society increased Marks's annual payment by $15,000, bringing it to $100,000 a year, the publisher would have remained with ASCAP. A substantial portion of the Marks's catalogue, between 5,000 and 6,000 songs, was not under BMI license. The exact status of these was in doubt, awaiting a declaratory ruling by the courts. It was Marks's contention that these songs were not owned by their writers—many of whom were now among ASCAP's most prominent authors—because they had been sold to the publisher under the usual pre-1930s contract, which turned over to him full proprietary rights. Most major publishers feared any court clarification of this practice. If the writers won, there was the possibility that they would take over control of ASCAP, throw out the publishers, and divide all collections among authors and composers only. If, as many eminent music-business attorneys believed, the court upheld Marks's position, songwriters would realize that they shared ASCAP income only on the sufferance of the publishers, would withdraw from the society when their contracts expired, and would support a strengthened Songwriters Protective Association. Through it, they could control all the small rights—publication, mechanical reproduction, and performance. In either event, the music business as constituted would suffer drastic consequences.

In June 1941, Marks and BMI brought suit against ASCAP in the New York Supreme Court. They hoped to resolve the question most ASCAP publishers had avoided for years, the true ownership of small rights, particularly that of public performance for profit. The plaintiffs maintained that Marks owned all rights in the three songs selected for the case. They had been written and copyrighted in Marks's name before their writers joined ASCAP, and they were not linked specifically to the society, as was true in the modern SPA contract, which provided for a fifty-fifty division of performance royalties.

The ASCAP answer, filed almost one year after all technical arguments had been overruled, bowed to the major publisher directors and avoided any assertion of ownership or conclusion of law, leaving that to the court. Had the society done otherwise, the publishers contended, it would be used against them in any future lawsuit, brought by songwriters, over the issue of small-rights ownership. The SPA lost in its desire that the defense should be based on the argument that the writers vested rights in ASCAP, or that they did so with publishers as joint tenants in common, which the MPPA and its members had resisted since Romberg first broached the issue in his long, confidential memorandum to songwriters written almost a decade earlier. Three years passed, during which some unsuccessful attempts were made to settle the issue out of court, before the declaratory judgment sought by BMI was delivered.

Meantime, riding on the crest of a wave of industry admiration, "the man who licked ASCAP," Sydney Kaye, was retained by a group of newspaper-owned radio stations to concoct the strategy for their forthcoming appearances at FCC hearings on their broadcast operations and practices. Kaye was instrumental in his new clients' victory in January 1944, when, after three years of enquiry, the FCC decided not to adopt a general rule on the issue. All future applications made by newspaper interests for licenses and renewals would be treated on an individual basis.

Shortly after the first papers were filed in *Marks* v. *ASCAP,* the society itself looked to the courts for assistance in concluding the music war. A calculated leak said that ASCAP had retained special counsel to handle a $20-million antitrust and conspiracy lawsuit against CBS, NBC, BMI, and the NAB, and possibly network sponsors as well. Special counsel was David Podell, who had made a fortune as a courtroom trust buster since his victory in the *Mayer* v. *Music Dealers Service* case in 1934, and now was a dollar-a-year adviser to Thurmond Arnold and his staff. Within a fortnight, counteroffers to the Mutual agreement were in the hands of a new ASCAP Radio Committee. The proposals offered between 2 percent (CBS) and two and a half (NBC) of net receipts after agency commissions, time-sales fees, line charges, and various other expenses. An immediate reaction by the Radio Committee to reject the offers was quickly tempered by instructions to speed up settlement, which came from Hollywood through financial men to the management of its music-publishing firms.

With the major houses losing at least $40,000 a month, and business at a complete standstill because of ASCAP's absence from the networks, total losses for the music divisions of Hollywood studios, including potential profits and lost performing rights, had already passed beyond the two-million-dollar mark. It took another six months after peace came before control of the song-plugging mechanism could be retrieved from BMI firms and the networks. The consent decree was signed by the Big Five studios. Its terms reduced block booking to a package of five or six features at a time, making it necessary to sweeten every package with at least one presold production. This was usually based on a best-selling book or a Broadway play or musical comedy whose hit songs had already gained some currency and been recorded. Because they could add new songs, Hollywood was producing musicals on a scale like that following the introduction of the talking picture. For half a year, however, air play had been denied to songs from these potential blockbusters, most of which were being held in the can awaiting a settlement of the contract dispute. Hollywood was taking a new look at its ASCAP connection, particularly in light of the consent decree just signed. Taking advantage of its new nonexclusive provision, which allowed separate licensing, many of the large studios were engaged in getting performance rights from their staff songwriters, or employing them on writer-for-hire contracts. Now, in order to get all those important radio plugs that brought in audiences, the studios were preparing to license their music either without charge or through BMI.

For that purpose, BMI was setting up its own subsidiary publishing house, Radiotunes, and offering subsidies to encourage new music companies owned by the film studios. Anxious to get the songs from his new cartoon feature, *Dumbo,* on the air, Walt Disney insisted that Irving Berlin, Inc., the AS-CAP house that usually published Disney music, either clear them through BMI or license them without charge. If the Berlin firm would not agree, Disney was ready to open his own BMI house. In the interests of the war effort and to secure air play for the new music, including the revived 1917 production song "God Bless America," Berlin had himself made them available for broadcasting without any charge. West Coast songwriters, too, were plaguing the ASCAP headquarters office to do something to get their songs played in order to stop the studios from giving their music away free.

As acting ASCAP president, Louis Bernstein took up the cause of the film companies and got an affirmative vote from the Radio Committee, only Herman Starr dissenting, the memory of his 1936 rejection by the networks still vivid to him. CBS had passed the negotiating lead to NBC, whose representatives had always been more compatible with music men, and was amenable to ASCAP's most recent compromise offer. Made in late July 1941, it called for 2.75 percent from the networks, and 2.25 percent from affiliates. In addition, stations were given the opportunity for the first time to pay only for the ASCAP music they used, on a per-program basis. The charge was 8 percent of program time costs for those using ASCAP music and 2 percent for ASCAP music used for themes or as background.

Despite what certainly was a substantial financial victory for the networks and for them, many NBC and CBS affiliates opposed any agreement. They felt that BMI was supplying sufficient music for their purposes, and were ready to postpone approval of a new offer for as long as possible in order to continue saving on their ASCAP fees. The two chains found themselves perched on a tightrope of prospective litigation. Off the record, ASCAP officials told them that, if approval was not forthcoming quickly, the society would disband under protest, and leave broadcasters to the chaos of negotiating individually with separate copyright owners for each composition they wished to program. If that happened, the antitrust suit against them would be filed immediately, with an added charge of conspiracy to destroy the society. Due to clever public relations, which portrayed ASCAP as a collection of wealthy songwriters and Hollywood-based movie-tycoon music owners, public opinion had generally been on the networks' side in early 1941. Now it was shifting, principally because of the series of investigations and public hearings being held in Washington.

Quite suddenly, the NAB officially announced an end of the music war in late October, and NBC, CBS, and a majority of their affiliates signed the contracts. The publishers were ready this time, and ASCAP music returned to the air almost immediately. However, it took many months of enlightened customer relations and salesmanship before it was broadcast on the majority of radio facilities. Looking for victory in what was recognized by the best informed as a defeat, the ASCAP board and executive management pointed to the vindication of its stand on payment at the network source, which the Justice Department had also supported. Joint CBS-NBC billings were projected at $80 million for the next year, which, in the face of that "2.75% of net receipts from sponsors after deductions" called for in the agreement, represented a vast jackpot. In 1940, NBC had paid ASCAP $410,000, CBS $384,000. The increase in income anticipated as a result of payment at the source would be substantial, if not astronomical.

Ben Bodec wrote in *Variety,* in January 1942, that the networks had actually "out-foxed ASCAP, preserving the twilight zone on music licensing payment, but in a different form." A rebate of each affiliate's share of ASCAP fees was deducted by the networks from their payments for local participation. "In the case of the Blue Network," Bodec explained, "the deductions can amount to as much as 85% of the gross billings, so that the amount turned over to ASCAP by NBC on a particular program could be

even less than the fees that NBC has deducted from the Blue affiliate involved . . . if the network rate on say, PQW, is $100 the Blue would be
required to pay ASCAP only on the basis of $15.'' He continued:

> The rate that NBC would pay that same Blue station is $30. The station is
> committed to permit the network to deduct 2.75% from the $30 as its share
> of the fee going to ASCAP. That deduction would amount to 55¢. The Blue's
> residue figures in this illustrative instance as $15. The ASCAP network fee of
> 2.75% applied to the $15 figures 41¢. Out of this arithmetical operation there
> may be derived the observation that whereas NBC has deducted 55¢ from the
> station's money, the network itself is obligated to pay ASCAP only 41¢ on
> this particular bit of business, leaving the network a profit of 14¢.
> In the case of the NBC-Red and Columbia the results would be somewhat
> different. With the frequency discount limited to 25%, the most that either
> network could deduct from the billings is 65%. Assuming that same station
> PQW were on either of these webs and rated at $100 per hour, the taxable
> residue would be $35. The ASCAP network fee of 2.75% applied to $35 to
> 96¢. Under the circumstances the network's own disbursement for ASCAP
> music would be 41¢ while the station's figured at 55¢. Broken down into
> percentages, the station would be paying ASCAP on the basis of 2.75% while
> the network would be paying its share on the basis of between 1.8 and 2%.

Unless ASCAP called for new rates and new language before January 1,
1949, the agreement would automatically extend after January 1, 1950. In
addition, the society had capitulated on the arbitration issue, but any fees
arrived at through such a procedure could not be reduced by a penny.

The understanding also called for ASCAP's best offices in disposing of
a $1.2-million antitrust suit, brought in March 1941 by fourteen songwri-
ters, charging NBC, CBS, BMI, and the NAB with a conspiracy to destroy
the society, thereby damaging the plaintiffs financially. Among them was a
future ASCAP president, Stanley Adams, the head of this group of militant
young SPA members. At the urging of Podell and some ASCAP publishers,
the plaintiffs agreed to accept $15,000 toward legal fees in settlement. Adams,
an attorney, had been the president of a short-lived small bloc of writers
known as the Forum for Songwriters, who were dissatisfied with the consent decree and attempted unsuccessfully to make sweeping changes in the
board's composition.

The conclusion of the music war in November was a victory of which
the networks were proud, though officials at each were reluctant to discuss
in detail the twilight zone and its problems. Instead, they pointed with pride
to BMI's accomplishment, promising to support the organization until 1949,
if only as an insurance policy. BMI was, after all, they said, responsible
for a saving of at least $10 million over the next nine years.

Within four weeks after their return to the air, ASCAP publishers were
responsible for all but one of the twenty-four most-played numbers over a
seven-day period. Clearly, Sydney Kaye and the BMI stockholders would

never again have air play all to themselves, as had been true during the music blackout. BMI, as a publisher, brought out only one of the year's song hits, as measured by Tin Pan Alley's major criterion for success, sheet-music sales. It was "I Don't Want to Set the World on Fire," and was disparagingly dismissed as "one of those accidents" that never would have happened "under normal circumstances." Written several years before, it had been performed by minor New York black bands, but never with the air play it finally won because of the ASCAP blackout. Two other major BMI hit songs, "You and I" and "The Hut Sut Song," were products of one-man publishing operations, free of the large overhead and expenses of a professional company, and they realized a profit of sixteen and a half cents on every copy of sheet-music sold. Twenty songs enjoyed a combined sale of 4.7 million copies, of which BMI's share was about 500,000. Moreover, with ASCAP back in business, many of the successful new BMI-affiliated companies were flirting with the society.

The poor showing made by BMI as a full-service music publisher moved its six-man board of directors to get a future course for it exclusively as a licensing agency. Its principal duty would be to encourage the formation of additional independently owned companies to join the fifty-five truly professional music houses that had come under the BMI banner in 1941. A sore point with them, however, and with many others among the several hundred part-time smaller ventures, was BMI's payment system. It was based on the program logs sent in at least once a year by all of BMI's broadcast licensees. These were broken down into nine "sample groups," with similar characteristics, determined by such factors as affiliation, power, share of market, time on the air. The number of performances of a sample group was used to compute the total number of performances on all licensed stations.

The original two-cents-per-performance payment to publishers (out of which they were expected to pay their writers) was doubled in time for the second-quarter distribution in 1941, when three million performances were logged and $200,000 paid to affiliated publishers, the most successful dozen of which received between $2,000 and $4,000. There was disappointment, particularly in view of the large sums BMI stockholders had regularly paid ASCAP in the past. The payment system continued to go through refining, and payments were increased, often in relation to the importance of complaining parties, or their potential for securing performances on the networks and affiliated stations. BMI then embarked on a program to actively recruit professional managers and key contact men employed by the large ASCAP houses. Salaries beginning at $18,000 a year and going as high as $60,000 were offered, the amount depending on judgments made by BMI's still amateur executive staff. Several name bandleaders formed partnerships with song pluggers, who then entered into affiliation with BMI, and received cash advances based on the guarantee of a number of network performances, or the regular accretion of recorded music. While network performances remained the key ingredient in creating hit songs, this form of advance-payment agreement grew.

The reforms imposed on ASCAP by the consent decree opened a Pandora's box of complaints from writers and small publisher members, providing ammunition for factional confrontations that continued for years. The self-perpetuating board of directors, which the government expected to be removed from power, was replaced with many of the same faces, chosen by the new weighted vote called for in the decree, based on income, that left little opportunity for newcomers. Due to the heavy call on the treasury during the confrontation with radio, and despite the fact that the "hatchet men" of the new Ways and Means Committee trimmed $600,000 from operating expenses, the society's 1941 debits exceeded the $4.2 million in income by $800,000. More cuts, aimed at a still tighter operation, were on the way, including the retirement of Claude Mills, who, with fluency in Spanish, was abroad, dealing with the South American societies, among whom BMI was making serious inroads. Mills's salary had already been reduced by $15,000, from the $50,000 he had received in the 1930s, and additional slashes were being administered to all other top-management executives. There was growing discontent among the publisher directors with Gene Buck and his long grip on the president's chair, since 1931, which was fanned to full heat by Herman Starr, Louis Bernstein, and Saul Bornstein, who were bitter about Buck's conduct of the antitrust suit, his engaging outside counsel without consulting the board, and his responsibility for their guilty pleas in connection with the criminal suit. After winning over five writer directors, to secure the two thirds approval necessary to implement action, they succeeded in ousting Buck in April, with the promise of a $25,000 annual pension.

Deems Taylor, composer of symphonic music and a network radio personality, was chosen as the new president, without salary, principally because of his prestige as a public figure and the type of music he wrote. Soon after, Mills was retired by the board with the promise of a year's salary, to be paid weekly, provided he did not engage in any association inimical to ASCAP.

There had been no change in the basic structure of publisher distribution standards since 1935: the 50, 30, 20 percent division based on performances, availability (size, character, and continuing popularity of catalogues) and seniority (length of membership in the society). Required to do so by the consent decree, the publisher-directors began an overhaul of the royalty classifications. A 10 percent increase for performance was made for use by the network and New York City and Chicago flagship stations, availability remained fixed, and seniority was cut to 15 percent. By a majority, the weighted-vote principle was approved. For publishers, it was based on ASCAP income in the preceding year, one vote for every $500 or fraction thereof, and for authors and composers, one vote for every $20 effectively installing a new self-perpetuating board, favoring the highest-paid members.

The plan selected by the twelve writer-directors for distribution among their peers was based on a proposal drawn up in 1941 by the songwriters Fred Ahlert, later a president of the society, and Edgar Leslie, and approved to go into effect in 1944. It set up fourteen classes of writers, ranging from AA to 4. Payments to the upper half were based on an application of 70 percent for "efficiency," meaning the "value" of each catalogue to the society as determined by the bookkeeping department, 15 percent for seniority, and 15 percent for performances. Under the new contract with broadcasters, stations were required to furnish on request a list of all musical selections performed during a period of not more than three months each year. But because 55 percent of the publisher distribution was based on network performances only, and broadcasters were slow in sending in the reports, this form of logging performances was dropped, and the tabulations were based instead on daily network reports of all musical performances, supplemented by the Accurate and Peatman reports, sent daily to subscribers.

Despite many attempts by both the MPPA and the song pluggers' chief organization, the Music Publishers Contact Employees, to scuttle the Accurate Reporting Service, it had continued to survive. During the music blackout, the Accurate sheet had dropped tabulation of BMI music, a gap that was filled by BMI's subsidization of the *Peatman Report*, which covered all performances, regardless of licensing affiliation. Its operator, Dr. John Gray Peatman, of the City College, New York, believed that a more sophisticated approach should be taken in assessing the worth of radio air play. His particular *bête noir* was "Your Hit Parade," whose method of gathering and collating information for each week's Top 15 he found both inadequate and inaccurate. Music publishers, he argued, traditionally limited themselves to a hit-or-miss promotion pattern, making money on hits, losing it on others. A professor of psychology, he believed that the music business would operate with greater economy and effectiveness if its merchandising was based on an understanding of the "social psychology of popular music," which he was willing to impart as a function of his service. The old-line music men remained content with the old trial-and-error technique, however.

In preparation for the new writer distribution system, all members were sent photostatic reprints of their copyrights listed with ASCAP, and were asked to make corrections and add anything that had been omitted. The Ahlert-Leslie plan called for modernization of the ASCAP bookkeeping department, on which the documentation of 70 percent of writer distribution depended. Advanced IBM machines were ordered, and when finally delivered several years later—after delays caused by wartime material shortages and production problems—they were immediately requisitioned by the government. Full-scale testing of the plan, which was the subject of major disputes among various writer factions, was started only in 1945, when the borrowed equipment was returned. One group was led by deposed president Gene Buck and made up of many AA writers and others in the top classes. Their music was not performed as often as that of the younger, more productive composers and authors, who had to work their way up from the fixed-income lower classifications but found it difficult because that system was controlled by the majority weighted vote of the top classes.

An FCC survey made in April 1942 to determine the possible effect of the recording ban and projected AFM strike showed that the radio industry's appetite for music had increased to the point where about three quarters of all time was filled, either partially or entirely, with musical presentations. The average station operated 112 hours a week, 86 of them devoted to musical programs. Forty-three percent of that time was filled with recorded music, and 33.7 percent with live. More than half the time on non-network stations offered "canned music," either popular recordings or electrical transcriptions.

This attention to music to attract listeners increased. In the year 1944, $383.9 million was spent to buy time on the air, the highest in the industry's twenty-five-year history. Local advertising sales had risen from the previous year's $78.2 million to $105 million, indicating a growing home market and an audience for locally originated programs, the majority of them depending on recorded music. Network income had increased by 25 percent in a single year, jumping to nearly $185 million. The combined performing-rights income paid to ASCAP and BMI was more than $7.5 million, a major share of it coming from NBC and CBS, more than half of it paid by affiliated stations because of the "Chinese bookkeeping" in the twilight zone practiced by the chains, of which few of them were aware.

In August 1945, *Variety* reported that, once a comparison of figures under the Ahlert-Leslie plan was made, the "real scrap will probably begin," with the possibility that more emphasis would be placed on performances, rather than on the prevailing factors that favored veteran songwriters. Payment to them had been rising; the AA class received $20,000 in 1945, a figure that dropped by approximately 25 percent for each of the eight classes below them. A revised writer-payment method was adopted in April 1946. For the first time, all writers in the fixed-annual-royalty classes began to receive distributions related to ASCAP income, figuring on a point basis, which gave an opportunity to move up the economic scale. It was common gossip in New York and Hollywood that the move was made only to stop this growing group, made up almost entirely of younger songwriters, from swinging to BMI. There was also Sydney Kaye's latest protestation to some trade-press reporters than his board of directors was ready to study a proposed plan to distribute performance royalties to writers of BMI-licensed songs for the first time.

The initial rationale for ASCAP's sudden turnabout to recognition of younger songwriters proved to be more substantial than that of the BMI threat, in spite of the fact that BMI was steadily attaining more importance as a licensing organization but with a significant repertory of recorded music. It was waging a continuing struggle to achieve recognition of its position and respectability among the international music-business community. Performance rates had again been increased, to four cents for local performances, and five cents per station for network air play. The number of bandleader-owned music firms had trebled during 1945, to about forty; they gave contracts that guaranteed from $1,500 to $40,000 a year, and asked for a minimum of 250 network performances in return and a specified number of phonograph recordings. The established ASCAP music publishers complained about such arrangements, which reduced their opportunity for network performances as well as new recordings of their copyrights. A variation on this type of publisher contract, which paid forty-eight dollars for each network shot, and matched the forty dollars that a major ASCAP publisher received for similar network play reached an absurd height in the case of Bradley Music Company. A sponsored seven-night-a-week program on the ABC network, from 12:30 to 1:00 A.M., featured as many as eighteen of Bradley's largely unfamiliar songs each evening. The average orchestra could not, even by speeding up the tempo, perform more than ten numbers in the course of such a broadcast. The average of $3,200 that Bradley collected from BMI for each week's play seriously tested the future of the forty-eight-dollar contracts, until the networks cracked down on the scheme, and the program was canceled by ABC. BMI bought its way out of the Bradley contract for $35,000 and the publisher's pledge not to go back into the music business for a year. Simultaneously, BMI paid a standard $250 for each recorded side of copyrighted music to recording artists and small disk companies specializing in serious works and hillbilly, race, and other popular music. Publishers whose only distribution medium was mechanically reproduced music, rather than the traditional printed page, brought it an important body of music, of considerable interest to that half of all American radio stations that subsisted on recorded music for their programing.

For nearly two decades, ASCAP had been honoring the agreement made in 1924 with the majority of standard (art song and serious music) publishing companies not to license opera houses and concert and recital halls; that was left to these publishers. However, the society acquired from them control of performing rights to their much-used catalogues of old classical music and thematic music for piano, organ, and pit orchestra that was omnipresent in screen theaters. A year before, in 1923, speaking for the Music

Publishers Association, to which most standard publishers belonged, Merritt E. Tompkins (then of G. Schirmer; since 1940, general manager of BMI) had announced the availability to radio of the world's best music without charge. In order to foreclose this important source of music at a time when the NAB was beginning to assemble a major repertory of tax-free music for broadcasters, ASCAP had offered, in perpetuity, four places on its board of directors. Two of these were for publisher representatives and two for composers selected by the publishers. As result of this arrangement, popular parlor music and ballads from the late nineteenth and early twentieth centuries, best-selling music from the catalogues of the Ditson companies, G. Schirmer, John Church, Boosey, and other firms, was added to ASCAP's essentially popular- and production-music repertory.

BMI made successful overtures in late 1940 to the American Composers Alliance and its pioneering publisher arm, Arrow Press, and an agreement with the Associated Music Publishers for broadcast rights to the music of leading European serious-music houses, including Breitkopf & Härtel, Schott, Universal Edition, and Boosey & Hawkes—most of whom had figured in the tax-free catalogues of the early 1920s. These brought BMI both an effective public-relations cachet and an important repertory of music. Rumors that BMI was about to purchase AMP, made more credible by the independent legal work Sydney Kaye was performing for the transcription company/licensing agency, had raised the possibility that BMI might soon extend its licensing activities into the concert field.

Acting on behalf of the ACA, Aaron Copland, its president, had attempted without success to win ASCAP membership for both the organization and himself. The society showed little interest, because of its understanding with its standard-music publishing affiliates. Its agreements with European performing-rights societies did not include licensing rights to serious or symphonic music, leaving those to the American agents for the original publishers.

In a telegram to Gene Buck on December 4, 1940, sent coincidentally with the public announcement of an agreement between BMI and ACA, Copland said that he had been trying "in vain for genuine consideration of the needs and problems of composers of serious music. Neither you nor the ASCAP committee which is nominally supposed to be considering this problem had been interested enough even to respond to our telegrams, no less to arrange an appointment for such discussion." It was ASCAP's public position that once the society began to license this music, a serious problem would arise with women's clubs and musical organizations, which would charge that imposition of fees "tended to stifle the development of audiences for serious music in America." Consequently, Copland and the members of ACA licensed their music through BMI on a short-term basis.

At the urging of some publisher directors who also dealt in serious music and many among the one third of its composer members (200 of them in the New York area alone), and owing to BMI's active courting of Copland and his associates, a major change was made by ASCAP. ACA was paid to undertake a survey of serious American music, and a special fund of $5,000 was allocated to promote it, so that at least one American work would be performed in every concert. The first announcement that ASCAP intended to license concert halls was made in February 1943, after financial projections indicated potential annual collections of nearly $150,000 a year, once negotiations with symphony-orchestra managers and concert-hall operaters were concluded.

Looking to expand its repertory of serious music before embarking on the licensing program, ASCAP opened a series of conferences with representatives of European performing-rights societies. The first was with the British Performing Rights Society, which had been formed around the same time as ASCAP, in 1914, but, unlike it, dealt in nondramatic public performances of both serious and popular music.

On April 1, 1914, two years after British Copyright Act had gone into effect granting to the creators of original literary, dramatic, musical, and artistic work the rights of publication, performance in public, reproduction in any form, including mechanical, and authorization of other persons to do these acts, thirty-nine British publishers and composers formed the Performing Rights Society. Because of the war, which began a few months later, little progress was made until early 1919, when licenses were offered for the first time to variety houses and theaters, their fees based on the number of musicians in each orchestra. Believing that this would lead to a reduction in the employment of its members, the British Musicians' Union organized a boycott against all PRS music. The majority of popular-music publishing houses resigned, taking their writers with them. The society continued to function, on a less ambitious scale, dealing in nonpopular music, but in 1925 began to aid the formation of similar societies in various parts of the Empire. Peace was made with the popular-music companies and their songwriters in 1926, when they were offered representation on the PRS board and a share in license fees, a move that soon doubled membership. Now a more effective and viable body, PRS had increased its membership to around 1,000, and its licensees to 11,500.

The initial agreement between PRS and ASCAP, one of the latter's first with any foreign society, was made in 1929, for three years, with an annual lump-sum payment of $15,000. PRS paid ASCAP half the money ascertained to be due for performances of the music it controlled. The other half was distributed to British co-publishers of American music, which they again split equally with their partners in the United States, giving the latter 75 percent of what PRS actually paid for the music.

In 1932, as their agreement was about to expire, PRS negotiated a new understanding, one that properly recognized and compensated performances of British music in the United States. Because ASCAP did not distribute its income solely on the basis of performances, after a study of the daily logs of music used on American networks, PRS representatives proposed the payment of 6 percent of ASCAP collections or, as an alternative, royalties based on actual network use, ascertained from the program logs. The second course would bring in about $60,000, four times the existing payment. ASCAP opted for the second proposal, and PRS regularly received about 4 percent of the society's collections, after expenses, although it did not yet collect fees for its concert-music repertory.

A tentative agreement with the French society, SACEM, for its concert music, was similarly negotiated, through the Office of the Alien Property Custodian, a State Department bureau that handled all business dealings for copyright owners in Nazi-occupied Europe. This concert music had previously been licensed in the United States through the American branch of Elkan-Vogel Music, of Paris. The new contract and one for the music of the Spanish society were signed by John Paine, the ASCAP general manager, and Herman Finklestein, ASCAP's resident counsel since December 1942, during a visit to Europe in the spring of 1945. Each was for five years on a straight per-performance payment basis, with no advances or guarantees. ASCAP had thus acquired a valuable concert-music repertory, and was ready to compete effectively with BMI and AMP. It began formal licensing of concert halls and symphony orchestras on January 1, 1945.

Despite their cordiality to the foreign-born representatives BMI had dispatched to deal with them, officials of both PRS and SACEM viewed the members of the broadcaster-owned organization as "buccaneers" who represented music users and not authors and composers. They proved to be invaluable in furthering ASCAP's determination to frustrate BMI's inroads in Europe and Latin America. Encouraged by PRS and SACEM, the two Brazilian societies were the first to defect from BMI, and, in the fall of 1945, representatives of the European organizations joined Paine and Finkelstein in persuading the Argentine writer and publisher group, SADIAC, to return to the ASCAP fold and agree to reciprocal representation. BMI's offer to triple its original $15,000 guarantee was met by ASCAP, and ended the threat by the Europeans to boycott Argentine music internationally through the international confederation of publishers and composers, CISAC. By making it clear that it would no longer remain isolated in the United States, but would, instead, actively seek out foreign licensing societies, ASCAP won CISAC's support in effecting liaisons with its members.

By the summer of 1945, ASCAP had collected about $20,000 from American concert halls, far from the anticipated $150,000 gross predicted a few years before. No method of distributing this income had been devised, but some of the one fourth of ASCAP membership recognized as "serious composers" (although they continued to be classified with popular-music writers, usually in the bottom six ranks) suggested adoption of a multiple-payment factor for concert and symphonic music. With the Ahlert-

Leslie plan still in the experimental stage, this proposal was shunted aside, pending adoption of a new popular-writer payment scheme.

Finkelstein and Paine had found talking points against BMI, during their international dealings, in the annual rebates made by BMI to broadcast licensees. This reduction of fees, made because BMI had operated at less than the maximum called for in its contracts, was first announced by Kaye during the crucial NAB meeting in June 1941, when BMI's future appeared to be in jeopardy in the face of MBS's defection from the broadcasters' closed ranks. This payback became an annual practice, 30 percent for the year ending July 31, 1943, and then 37 percent, beginning with the $750,000 returned for fiscal 1944. The BMI board continued to be made up of working broadcasters only, and its president remained the incumbent head of the NAB. Neville Miller, no longer viewed as the small stations' friend, was deposed in 1944. He was replaced by J. Harold Ryan, of the Storer stations, who was followed in 1945 by Justin Miller, formerly judge of the United States Court of Appeals for the District of Columbia.

ASCAP's income continued to increase, rising to $8.891 million in 1945; AA writers received $20,000 and the major music firms got from $150,000 to $200,000. A $10-million year was anticipated for 1946. In spite of that, the society's defeat at the hands of the NAB and BMI still rankled. Intercession of the *Marks* v. *ASCAP* suit, seeking clarification of the "joint tenants in common" issue that had been a major goal of Romberg and the SPA in the 1930s, was regarded as yet another example of duplicitous conduct on the part of Sydney Kaye and the BMI board.

In the interest of maintaining a stable ASCAP, the SPA had joined that action alongside the defendant society, with its own counterclaims. Developments during Claude Mills's short tenure as general manager of the SPA made it patently clear that not only major publishers had tremendous influence over the ASCAP board, but leading SPA officials and councilors as well.

Shortly after his enforced retirement from ASCAP became official Mills had been named to the newly created SPA post, serving without compensation during the period that his ASCAP salary remained in effect. In addition, he was a member of the board of United Artists Films, as Charlie Chaplin's representative. Sigmund Romberg, again president of the SPA, explained that with negotiations for a new publishers' contract still several years in the future, Mills would establish reciprocal relations with songwriter groups in Great Britain and other English-speaking countries, as well in Latin America, with which he was familiar.

It was soon evident to his old colleagues at the MPPA that Mills still possessed the boundless ambition and enormous vitality that had made him so valuable to them during the 1920s. He was no longer content to remain in limbo, a retired veteran of the music wars. He now intended to build the SPA into an organization of such power that in the approaching MPPA negotiations it would have sufficient bargaining strength to retrieve many of the privileges that authors and composers had surrendered during the past half century. His first communication to the SPA's 2,000 members, urging them to withhold television rights in future contracts, threatened to disturb the unwritten agreement prevailing among the ASCAP writer and publisher directors that any resolution of their ownership of these rights and its extent remain unspecified until conditions warranted otherwise.

The full details of Mills's master plan for the SPA emerged only after he received his last check from ASCAP and was free to disturb the waters further. Many of its details were known to the inner councils of the SPA, some of whom were publishers or under sweetheart contracts, with special privileges, to large Hollywood-owned publishing firms. Addressing a West Coast SPA meeting in May 1943, Mills said that among the reforms he intended to introduce were these: songwriters would retain control of copyrights, rather than convey them to publishers; they would receive two thirds of all performance and synchronization rights, rather than the fifty-fifty division for which he had been responsible in 1920; and all contracts would have to receive SPA approval before they were signed. With the details made public, some MPPA members initiated a campaign to raise doubt about the future for songwriters, many of whom were beginning to act as if those gains were already a matter of fact. Mills was charged with "trying to upset the ASCAP applecart," at a time when matters there "were at their smoothest." If Mills and his followers persisted, they warned, there would be a boycott of all music by SPA members, and the publishers would look to nonaffiliated, more grateful writers for new material. They were particularly indignant about Mills's suggestion that songwriters get half of the half-million dollars paid for lyric reprint rights by the three best-selling song-lyric magazines. Bidding for exclusive rights, these now legitimate businesses—Lyle Engel, Charlton, and D. S. Publishing—were so competitive that each major MPPA music house cleared $60,000 yearly.

Romberg, the SPA president, hailed Mills's proposals as "constructive, far-reaching, [which] if carried to a successful conclusion, will establish revolutionary improvements in the songwriters' bargaining position." Unwilling to have the SPA "revert to inactivity," Romberg said he was "ready to go to war." A recent Supreme Court decision had found that a writer had the right to dispose of his renewal privilege at any time he chose, and withhold it from the initial agreement. In addition, ASCAP's anticipated victory in the Marks case, in which the SPA was also appearing with the defense, would, it was felt, only strengthen the writers' position.

To finance the revitalized SPA, Romberg called for the tripling of annual dues, which would raise those of AA writers to $200, only about 1 percent of their performance royalties. But it was from this group that the greatest protest came, fed by publishers who whispered that the increase was a ruse to give Mills a large salary. A contingent of five SPA councilors, all of whom were also ASCAP directors, who opposed Mills's plan went behind Romberg's back and negotiated a way to end the expected "strike in the music business." During a special ASCAP board meeting in July 1943, by unanimous vote, the directors agreed to halt the checkoff system for SPA dues, which had been in effect for the past ten years. By a similar unanimous vote, those present also agreed to an extension of ASCAP membership for an additional fifteen years, ending in 1965. Thereby, no matter what the outcome of the Marks suit was or what reforms the SPA won in a new MPPA contract, all its members, now comitted to the society for twenty-two years, would have to share ASCAP royalties on the fifty-fifty basis until then. Within three months, the extension agreement was approved by votes representing 82.4 percent of the previous quarter's writer payments, and 80.2 of the publishers'. In January 1944, Mills resigned his post as the SPA general manager and went to California, where he was a music-business consultant to broadcasters, once did a disk-jockey program for one of his clients, and engaged in the real estate business until his death, in 1959, at the age of seventy-seven. The SPA made no decision to replace him, and returned to that inaction about which Romberg had complained.

Clarification of the ownership of music on television returned to the limbo in which it had been resting, only to reappear as a secondary issue in early 1945 after an appellate court held that *Marks* v. *ASCAP* should proceed. The presiding judge in that action, Ferdinand Pecora, had asked all parties to negotiate a settlement. This was rejected by the ASCAP board when BMI offered to license the disputed songs and some 3,000 others in the Marks catalogue on the same basis as it did music written by members of the society. In a behind-the-scenes dispute, Herman Finkelstein argued against that settlement, and emerged as the strong man in the society's legal future.

Edward Marks did not himself appear as a party in the action, and BMI, handling the plaintiff's case and bearing all expenses, argued that once a writer assigned his copyright to a publisher, the later could then assign administration of any portion of the copyright privileges to a third party, and the writer could not. ASCAP's position was that, as a member of the society for many years, Edward B. Marks Music Co. had never disputed its writers' grant of the administration of public performing rights to ASCAP, and in accepting the equal division of license fees with them could not now assign their entire administration to BMI on behalf of all parties.

Pecora's verdict, on May 1, 1945, in *Variety's* words, "threw a bombshell into the music business," giving ASCAP "what's deemed as the most important victory it has ever won in court." In sustaining the society's role, it stated that the relationship between a songwriter and a publisher was "basically a joint venture for the commercial exploitation of the performing rights to the songs." The publisher's title to a copyright was "subordinate to the joint venture," the publisher holding title "to that end that the exploitation of the songs might be more advantageously achieved. He is in this respect merely a trustee of ASCAP and its [writer] members." Marks was faulted for having negotiated with BMI without consulting his writers to obtain their consent, and the million dollars he got from BMI was said to represent a breach of contract. With the Marks understanding soon up for renewal or the exercise of an option to buy the entire catalogue for a second million, Pecora deplored BMI's conduct, but said, "It is certainly not the duty of the court to give such counsel in the form of a declaratory judgement, to parties contemplating business ventures."

Many of the younger and more progressive SPA members found Pecora's surprise ruling proof that, for the first time, a court had judged them to be the sole owners of performing rights. In the event that this might be true, and seriously affect not only television licensing, but also control of their vast music catalogues, MGM, 20th Century-Fox, and others involved in the ownership of music houses seriously considered maneuvering an immediate appeal. Many music-business attorneys thought that the decision could be upset if Marks was in a position to prove that he had "worked the copy-rights" by licensing them for recording, publishing, and merchandising sheet music, and other printed music.

Shortly after the Pecora decision, a group of leading Hollywood film-score composers formed their own protective organization, the Screen Composers Association, and began to agitate for participation in the income ASCAP was collecting from screen theaters. The staff songwriters employed by the studios had little voice in ASCAP's operation until the consent decree strengthened their position by its requirement that at least 80 percent of the writer vote, based on recent distributions, was necessary to pass changes. But because their music was used principally in film theaters, performances that were not counted in establishing classifications, the screen composers were given the lowest ratings. While Claude Mills was in Hollywood in 1944 boosting his plan to build the SPA into a more powerful body, he made a telling impression on this West Coast group. His enthusiasm had led to the formation of the SCA. Max Steiner was president, and the board included Adolph Deutsch, Daniele Amfitheatroff, Franz Waxman, Robert Dolan, Victor Young, Herbert Stothart, and others. One of the members, David Raskin, enjoyed a popular hit with his music for the film *Laura*, which, with lyrics by Johnny Mercer, was widely performed on the networks, building up its lyricist's rating in ASCAP but doing little for its composer, who had just been admitted.

Hollywood's moguls were well aware of the artistic urgency for integrating carefully crafted music into their dramatic films, even though it rarely brought in the large additional grosses that came from a popular hit song written for a musical movie. The $300,000 paid for the use of Cole Porter's songs in his film biography, *Night and Day*, was a record until Irving Berlin's new contract with Paramount was signed. It brought him a flat $250,000 for twenty songs, three of them new, plus 12½ percent of all gross receipts above two million from Bing Crosby's feature movie *Blue Skies*.

Studios made one of three deals to get a new song score. Berlin, Porter, Kern, and several others were able to hold onto the copyrights and turn them over to their own music companies or to publishers to whom they were under exclusive contract. There also were arrangements for the outright sale of the music to the film company, or a flat-fee payment plus a share in sheet-music and record royalties. In both cases, the copyright was vested in the studio's name and then turned over to a subsidiary music house for handling, from which the company received a sheet-music royalty of between two and six cents (depending on whether the income was shared with the writers), and half the publisher's record income. Often the entire cost of a musical score was recouped from the profits of a single hit song.

In 1946, Bing Crosby's current favorite song-writing team, Johnny Burke (words) and Jimmy Van Heusen (music), broke new ground. Under their new five-year contract with Paramount Pictures, they retained all rights to the music, which was licensed to the studio for one-time use only for $75,000 a picture. Burke and Van Heusen paid only a one-cent sheet-music royalty to Paramount and no income from mechanical licensing.

A serious difference of opinion divided the ASCAP publisher ranks over whether music should be licensed to television as a grand right through the Harry Fox Agency of the MPPA or as a small right, available through ASCAP. The society's plea to publishers for a grant of television rights was met by an affirmative response from more than 80 percent, but not from the MGM music firms. The assent had come only after a compromise was made, changing a vital clause in the original proposal, that authors and composers would retain the right to restrict the use of their music on television, a privilege that had previously been granted only to a few top composers. The Hollywood-owned companies objected and in the spring of 1946 won.

The significance of this surrender was not lost on the Screen Composers Association. Leonard Zissu, a New York attorney, who had been retained to deal with the ASCAP management and board, resumed the argument that his clients should receive a share of collections from movie-house owners and operators. Now that ASCAP had moved into new fields and was licensing concert halls and symphony orchestras on behalf of serious music composers, the day was not far distant when it would license television for the use of feature films, of which SCA members' music was a vital ingredient. The screen composers were urged to be patient, until after ASCAP had accumulated all television rights and devised a new method of collection from that burgeoning industry.

During the following twelve months, Zissu and the SCA readied a new course of action in the fight to obtain a greater share of the approximately $1.25 million ASCAP collected annually from film houses, as well as an improved standard contract between the producers and the screen composers. They wanted such income divided, as in Britain, solely among those who were responsible for it, not, as with ASCAP, where it was dumped into a single pool, a substantial portion of which was allocated on the basis of radio-network performances. Only one third of the SCA's approximately 100 members had been admitted to ASCAP, despite the new consent decree and its reforms. Max Steiner, SCA's president, and the composer of music for 187 feature films, was being paid only $175 per quarter by ASCAP in 1946, which he got chiefly for popular songs taken from his original instrumental music.

As for the agreement with studios, the SCA asked for the retention by the composers of all rights other than synchronization use, except when the film makers' own music firms worked on the music or issued it in printed form. In addition, the proposed document forbade the use of music in more than one feature movie without full compensation each time. Shortly before the SCA board gave Zissu approval to proceed on this new course, in late 1947, developments in a new power struggle among members of ASCAP's executive management hierarchy rendered the matter meaningless. This infighting was over who would succeed John Paine as general manager of the society, following his sudden death late in April 1947.

Paine had been born in 1890, in Pennsylvania, and studied law at George Washington University before he joined the Victor Talking Machine Company, at the age of twenty-three, where he first handled copyright clearances and then supervised all artists' contracts. He left Victor when talking-picture technology made necessary negotiation for synchronization rights. He served Warner Brothers' Vitaphone Company for a year, and then succeeded Claude Mills as ASCAP's general manager in 1929. His frequent visits abroad, as ASCAP became more involved with foreign licensing organizations, led to his election as head of the Authors and Composers Federation of CISAC in 1946. This international confederation of societies, headquartered in Paris, and dedicated to protection of all intellectual property, had been formed in June 1926 by representatives, from eighteen separate bodies of the publishers and authors of dramatic works. Two years later, societies representing the creators of music were admitted, and in 1932 CISAC's doors were opened to mechanical-rights collection agencies, boosting the number of member groups to forty-six. Soon after, literary societies were admitted. When Hitler invaded Poland in August 1939, Saul Bornstein, of the Irving Berlin firm, and an ASCAP official, was serving as vice-president of CISAC, the first American to be elected to any major office in it. The organization then represented groups in twenty-nine countries. After six years of war, during which CISAC was relatively inoperative, it was reorganized, Paine was elected to head the music-creators' federation, and its fifteenth meeting, the first since 1939, was the first to be held in the United States.

UNESCO was a major presence at sessions in October 1946, at the Library of Congress, made available through the good offices of Deems Taylor, ASCAP's president. John Paine's speech of welcome contained severe criticism of BMI, as an example of "new philosophies [that threaten] to recreate the authors' serfdom that existed in the past." Little actual business was transacted during these meetings, chiefly because of a hotel strike that shut down the capital. However, the government was assailed by several foreign speakers as "a nation out of step with the new world," for its failure to change a copyright law that allowed free use of music in coin machines.

After intense pressure from BMI, as well as by representatives of the Music Machine Operators Association, the government filed a civil action through the Justice Department in June 1947. The complaint charged that ASCAP's exclusive licenses with members of CISAC constituted a monopoly, creating an international cartel. The society, it was charged, had conspired with similar societies in all the principal nations to prevent other licensing bodies from having access to their music. Made aware of the action a week before it was filed, ASCAP had unsuccessfully attempted to persuade CISAC to remove a regulation in its bylaws forbidding any member body from doing business with a society in another country that did not itself belong to the confederation. This rule made it impossible for any CISAC member to deal with BMI, but officials of the organization refused to change the regulation.

Even before ASCAP filed a reply to the government's charges, it prepared to make resignation from CISAC the first matter of business at the confederation's first full-scale postwar meeting, in London later in June. The resignation was accepted with regret, but CISAC refused to budge from its position. Negotiations between ASCAP and the Justice Department then began, looking for a consent decree that would resolve the business to the government's satisfaction. ASCAP said it was ready to sign a decree that would wipe out any exclusive agreements with foreign societies, but refused to do so unless BMI was required to do the same.

In March 1948, ASCAP filed its formal answer, in which it charged that BMI had been formed to crush the free enterprise that ASCAP represented, and now threatened to use "the same tactics to embrace the entire world . . . to destroy" CISAC and its members, and make the world's composers and authors "subservient to the American broadcasting industry." BMI, ASCAP charged, was seeking to destroy the competitive system in which "each work rises to its natural level" and replace it with a "controlled market under which those who yield to the American broadcasting industry will have their works brought to the attention of the American public [and those] who refuse to yield will submit to the disappearance of their works from the American scene." Rather than a competitor, BMI was "the creature of an industry on which authors, composers and publishers must rely for their existence." Unless BMI was made a joint defendant, ASCAP argued that the complaint should be dismissed by the court. Judge Simon Rifkind, before whom the case was being heard in New York, struck down ASCAP's bid to bring BMI into the action and ordered the suit to continue.

There had been a number of significant developments between the time of the CISAC meeting in Washington and the autumn of 1948, when the government was ready to pursue a revised ASCAP consent decree. They took place not only in the continuing fight between the society and the broadcasting industry, personified by BMI, but in the popular-music business itself, and in the relationship between ASCAP and its writer and publisher members and ASCAP and its film-theater–owner customers.

Once the music war of 1941 ended, BMI's easy access to network commercial and remote programs ended. When measured by the statistics that Tin Pan Alley best understood, BMI's showing as a music publisher was so poor that it would drive any less well-financed operation out of business. That of its most aggressive publisher-affiliates, who competed with the major ASCAP houses on traditional terms, was little better, despite the various financial and supportive incentives offered to them. In 1945, only one BMI-licensed song appeared among the twenty most-played songs of the year, and four among the top thirty-five sheet-music sellers. The following year, BMI published the single non-ASCAP song on Peatman's recapitulation of 1946's most-performed songs. Plugged by the professional staff BMI continued to maintain, in spite of a consistent lack of accomplishment, BMI's "Laughing on the Outside" was its first best seller since 1941. In 1947, four BMI-licensed songs achieved a place among Peatman's thirty-five and five among the thirty-five best sellers, followed in 1948 by two in each category.

These poor showings were due, in some part, to a change made, in response to demands by the major ASCAP publishers, in the traditional way of measuring success as represented by the number of "plugs" secured on New York radio stations and reported in alphabetical order by the Accurate Reporting Service and in *Variety*. The once-official Accurate sheet was finally replaced by Peatman's surveys, which, ironically, had been introduced and financed by BMI in 1940 when Accurate refused to report its performances. The change came as the result of a series of meetings of ASCAP publishers, called by Paine, in order to end "certain music industry evils." The most recent estimate of money paid by Tin Pan Alley in payola was half a million dollars. With the replacement, the emphasis on radio plugs was for "quality" rather than quantity, because Peatman based his findings on "audience coverage," which was greatest during prime-time network hours, rather than the daytime sustaining shows and after eleven-o'clock big-band remotes, on both of which payola, paid by ASCAP and BMI firms, had been running rampant. The effect was most serious on new or small publishers, who had been having a field day on sustaining time and remote shows. Prime-time programers now rejected songs that did not appear on the Peatman lists, on which they could not get without already having had those evening performances.

With its share of radio music use hovering around 10 percent, contrasted with ASCAP's 80 to 85 percent, and the cost to broadcasters for its music, on an actual performance basis, far above that of its competitors, BMI began, according to *Billboard*, "to say it with flowers," in the form of service to its best-paying customers, giving them "everything for free, but music." A staff of five representatives, all former broadcasters, was on the road constantly, visiting stations to offer suggestions and listen to gripes. Stations were "bombarded with catalogs, brochures, bulletins, indexes, lists, copyright info, clearance data, ready-to-use radio scripts" (715 hours a year, compared with ASCAP's 78 hours) once the society began to play the same game. In addition, ASCAP's traveling auditors, who had the right, under contract, to inspect a licensee's books, were asked to perform the same functions as BMI's field men. BMI also regularly mailed out two complementary orchestrations of new songs to stations employing live talent and about a dozen hillbilly orchestrations monthly, sent to some 350 stations that programed country-and-western music.

In order to stem any potential movement among broadcasters to dump BMI on the termination of its contracts in 1949, because another music war was not possible, Sydney Kaye played on ASCAP's reluctance to disclose its plans when its agreement expired at the same time. That contract would be renewed automatically for nine years provided an increase was not asked. If one was, however, the option was canceled, and if the two parties could not agree on new terms, arbitration would follow. The society had traditionally shunned arbitration, but offered it as an added inducement to end the 1941 impasse, with the proviso that any new rate would not be lower than the one in effect. Nevertheless, raising the possibility of a second ASCAP boycott, Kaye proclaimed that "BMI will be ready!" He reminded audiences of network program directors, regional meetings of broadcasters, and the NAB membership at its annual conventions that BMI had made it possible to effect vast savings. To dismantle it now would permit ASCAP to restore its "stranglehold." This confusing logic was particularly effective with station owners who usually dealt with ASCAP remotely, through its auditors. BMI enjoyed the loyalty of these and other small-station owners who paid it at the lowest rates, but used its catalogue of country music, and, in a few cases, rhythm-and-blues music, almost exclusively. At the October 1946 NAB convention, Kaye openly pleaded for new discussions looking toward another nine-year contract with BMI, so as to be ready in the event of an adverse finding by an arbitration panel.

ASCAP's difficulty in making an early announcement about its future intentions sprang from the continuing failure of its publisher constituency to agree on how, and for how much, to license music on television. More than 80 percent of the membership had assigned representation of these rights to the society, until December 31, 1948, with only MGM's music firms holding out. The major film studios continued to have ambivalent feelings about giving NBC, CBS, ABC, and other television-station owners the right to use their feature films through an ASCAP contract. GM and 20th Century-Fox were both anxious to get into the business, and Paramount's interests in the new medium verged on those of a monopoly, into which the government was looking. The first of the Big Seven movie companies to show an interest in television, Paramount had bought and sold stock in CBS before 1931, and now owned several stations and a half-interest in the Allen D. Dumont Laboratories. Forced to play a waiting game until the Hollywood giants made up their minds, ASCAP formed a separate Television Negotiation Committee to meet with the networks and other parties.

Speaking at ASCAP's 1947 membership meeting in New York, John Paine told an audience that included among its invited guests the largest turnout of network attorneys and executives ever to attend such a function that the $6 million out of a gross income of $9.9 million paid by radio for 1946 was one reason ASCAP would not seek a higher rate after 1949. That sum was the most broadcasters had ever paid the society, even under the higher rates prevailing before 1941. Income from the screen theaters was only $1.5 million, and music-business insiders were certain that the society would soon be asking for more from this source, to change what was a disproportionate share of total income. About $7.5 million had been distributed among 1,850 writers and 301 publishers in 1946, Paine reported. There were no speeches that night, only conviviality, but the point was clear: ASCAP was still the predominant music-licensing body with which broadcasters had to do business.

With the major burden of the networks' music fees on the backs of their affiliates, the chains were satisfied with the status quo. Further, they wished no more contention with ASCAP, having become increasingly uncomfortable with the charges of conspiracy to destroy it being made by ASCAP in the pending international-cartel antitrust action involving CISAC, allegations being used to good advantage by broadcasting's enemies in Washington. Also, many upper-echelon executives privately questioned the propriety of continuing the NAB-BMI-broadcasting link, from which NBC and CBS had just extricated themselves, at least in part, by resigning from the NAB. That move was credited to the widening breach between the big-city broadcasters and the grass-roots majority, which usually failed to side with the chains on major issues, an attitude that had traditionally been an NAB problem.

It was precisely that large group which welcomed a figure well known to them as BMI's first full-time, paid president, Carl Haverlin, beginning in June 1947. Haverlin, whose persuasive salesmanship and familiarity with leaders of the independent and local broadcasters had swelled BMI's stockholder ranks in 1940, had remained on the BMI board when he went to the Mutual network. As an additional symbol of BMI's independence, Judge Justin Miller relinquished the BMI presidency, since 1940 an unpaid function of NAB's president, and became the company's board chairman. In the reshuffling of titles that followed, Kaye became vice-president and general counsel, so that he would have more time for his private law practice, much of it dealing with CBS matters.

Haverlin was introduced in his new capacity to NBC flagship program directors at a luncheon in May, at which he urged them and all broadcasters to pay more attention to BMI music, so that ASCAP's grip on the industry might be weakened. Following his remarks, Roy Harlow, the head of BMI's station-relations group scored broadcasters for an increasing drift toward disk-jockey programing, a "laxity" he found troubling and a symbol of the industry's increasing evasion of its programing responsibilities. It was an ironic comment, particularly in the face of BMI's growing strength in recorded music of all types, and the increasing use of that repertory by non-network local and independent stations.

A few weeks later, Haverlin announced a change of policy, saying that BMI would operate more actively as a publisher, but would not disturb the work of its Tin Pan Alley affiliates in their pursuit of success. In August, negotiations were concluded for a takeover of Associated Music Publishers' remaining capital stock, and all publishing and performing rights for a group of fifteen music houses in Germany, France, England, Hungary, and Holland who published the music of Richard Strauss, Stravinsky, Sibelius, Hindemith, and Britten, among others. Soon after, the British house of Boosey & Hawkes resigned from the AMP, to join the PRS, taking with it Britten's music and that of other major British composers, but the acquisition still represented another saving for stations that used concert music. It was also a valuable gain in the company's international position, particularly in the face of CISAC's alleged boycott.

Meetings between ASCAP's Radio Committee and broadcasters continued through the summer. In September, at the annual NAB convention, Theodore Streibert, of Mutual, and head of radio's negotiating committee, assured the meeting that ASCAP did not intend to ask for increased fees from radio, but wanted only to clean up some minor accounting details. Many present were then surprised by Streibert's recommendation that the NAB divorce itself from BMI, because the time had come for it "to stand on its own feet." Such a move, he pointed out, could only ensure "more kindly business relations" with all other music licensors. It was the first time that such a suggestion was made publicly, and by a leading broadcaster.

There immediately was considerable maneuvering before an announcement, while the convention was still in progress, that NBC, CBS, ABC, and Mutual were ready to extend their present BMI contracts until 1959, to run concurrently with any new ASCAP agreement. The reason given for this unexpected decision was that, because of Streibert's assurance that the society would not ask for an increase, the networks felt that BMI should follow suit. Unlike ASCAP, which charged one dollar a year for television rights, BMI had granted them to all stations in its initial contracts, on the same terms as for radio—a percentage of revenue received from the sale of time on the air—a pattern the networks wanted ASCAP to offer.

In November, BMI took advantage of the network support and wrote to all its broadcasting licensees, asking for a similar extension to 1959. Haverlin pointed out that, under existing circumstances, it was impossible for BMI to enter into contracts with songwriters and music publishers for longer than twenty-eight months, while ASCAP was under no such restraint. A favorable response from over 800 stations within a month was indicative of the high regard in which Haverlin was held.

The networks' move was not guided by charity or concern for the industry. ASCAP's current assignments of television rights ran only through 1948. Because of pressure from the AA Broadway musical-production writers, as well as a threat from the Screen Composers Association that it might unite with the Screen Writers Guild, the ASCAP board intended to license television in the future on a year-to-year basis, no matter at what rate, until the medium developed its own music programing patterns. Both the production writers, who were watching fees climb steadily for the use of their music in films, and the screen composers, who wanted to retain rights in their music after exhibition in movie houses, believed that television would become Hollywood's major competitor. They were all reluctant to give away their performing rights for fees that might quickly become inadequate.

In addition, the networks feared the results of the rapidly widening confrontation between ASCAP and the country's independent film-theater owners, sparked by the announcement in late March 1947 that the society was about to open a drive to increase taxes on movie-house seats. That income had been $1.335 million in 1946, and was based on an annual fee of ten cents a seat in houses with a capacity of fewer than 900; fifteen cents for those between 900 and 1,600; and twenty cents for more seats. ASCAP officials said that this figure was out of all proportion to the six million dollars being paid by radio, and that it was time for an increase. Within a few weeks, a long-dormant antitrust suit, initiated in 1942, was resumed by 164 independent theater-owner plaintiffs. The action, *Alden-Rochelle* v. *ASCAP*, sought triple damages and an injunction restraining the society from charging for music-performance rights.

Antagonism had existed between theater owners and ASCAP from the beginning, and had increased in intensity after the advent of talking pictures in 1927, when control over the music heard in movie houses passed from the operators to the studios. In 1937, Claude Mills made an attempt to calm the situation by opening discussions with the Motion Picture Producers Association of America. His proposal for "clearance at the source," with all ASCAP fees from film houses to be borne by the Hollywood studio suppliers, was quickly rejected by the MPPAA. More than a third of the publishers' participation in ASCAP dividends was then being paid to subsidiaries owned or controlled by major motion-picture producers. In 1947, that figure amounted to $1.432 million, at a time when many major studios, faced with the prospect of complete divestiture of their theater chains, were further expanding their ownership of music-publishing companies, and had no objection to raising the rates ASCAP charged independent theater operators. MGM was approaching Warner's predominance, and was expecting to acquire the Von Tilzer family catalogues and the Bregman, Vocco & Conn firm. Shapiro, Bernstein had joined in partnership with Columbia Pictures and Jack Kapp, of Decca Records, to form Mood Music, to publish all the studio's musicals, beginning with *The Jolson Story*. (The Decca album of songs from that film was the first to sell one million copies.) Central to all these mergers and partnerships was television's coming of age.

Immediately after losing an early motion to dismiss the Alden-Rochelle suit in April 1947, ASCAP met with the motion-picture companies to ask them to assume the seat tax, as Mills had urged in 1937, and to tack those fees onto rental charges. John Paine's premature death ended the talks, during which the studios had shown little interest in the suggestion.

In the lull that followed, Haverlin wrote to all independent broadcasting licensees, asking them to extend the existing BMI contract so that it would expire concurrently with the networks' agreements in 1959, together with ASCAP's still-to-be-formulated contract. He pointed out that under the existing circumstances it was impossible for BMI to enter into contracts with music publishers and songwriters for longer than twenty-eight months, whereas ASCAP was under no such restraint. Within a month, 800 stations had agreed; by year-end, nearly 1,000.

No immediate move was made to nominate a new ASCAP general manager, which had been the publishers' exclusive privilege since 1920. Instead, Fred Ahlert and Stanley Adams, songwriter directors, and the publishers Lester Santley, an MPPA official, and Herman Starr constituted a management committee. Paine's duties were temporarily divided among Herman Finklestein, the society's house general counsel, Richard Murray, recently brought in by Paine to handle the theater-seat licensing, Herman Greenberg, another Paine assistant, and George Hoffman, who dealt with finances. In an immediate three-way rivalry, between Finkelstein, Murray, and Greenberg, to take Paine's place, the last named made a bold bid for publisher support and the job. He recommended an immediate 300 percent increase in seat taxes, to which Finkelstein objected, warning that it would backfire and cause litigation and government intervention. He proved to be correct on both counts. Alden-Rochelle was to begin trial in the spring of 1948. Action by the Justice Department came later.

The music business to which BMI returned, with Haverlin's presidency, as a competitive publisher, after an absence of six years, was undergoing one of the dramatic changes that continued to characterize its history, owing this time to its influence as a licensing organization. After sixteen years, the record industry had matched and bettered its previous all-time high sales mark—the $105.6 million retail ($47.8 million wholesale) made in 1921—with $214.4 million retail ($97 million wholesale) earned during 1947. There were an estimated 200 record companies registered with the American Federation of Musicians, plus uncounted independents, most of them in the business because of BMI's economic support. The logical medium for promoting and exploiting these new companies' products was the independent radio stations, none of them affiliated with networks and all turning to records being supplied by the newcomers.

In a forecast of the future made in late 1948, FCC Chairman Wayne Coy predicted that there would soon be 3,100 AM stations in operation and 1,100 FM facilities. Seventy million radio sets were already in use in 37.5 million households, representing a 94 percent saturation. According to Nielsen statisticians, each family tuned in four hours and nineteen minutes each day, an increase of more than one hour since 1940–41. Coy added that the expected competition from television's 100 stations now in operation could not possibly reach more than one eighth of those homes for another two years.

The growth of music publishing and its income from public performance matched that of the recording industry and broadcasting. ASCAP had 300 publisher members, and BMI counted nearly 1,000 publisher affiliates on its roster. The vast majority of the latter were small operations, associated with minor recording ventures, which published their music on phonograph recordings. The combined license fees paid to ASCAP and BMI by broadcasters in the years 1941 through 1947 came to nearly $52 million, $39.6 million to the former, and $12.3 million to BMI. Approximately 75 percent of the society's collections was distributed to writer and publisher members; 58 percent of BMI's income to affiliated publishers, foreign societies, and writer-publishers who licensed their works through the broadcaster-owned organization. The average sheet-music sale of a hit song, long the publishers' major source of income, was about 350,000 copies. There were exceptions, however, songs that appeared to signal a return to the days when a million-copy seller was common: "To Each His Own," "Near You," "A Tree in the Meadow," "Nature Boy," "Now Is the Hour," each of which sold a million copies of sheet music and millions of recordings. These and similar successes reflected the influence and importance of new independent record companies, new recording techniques, new artists, and new songwriters. They had another thing in common, all of them were "made" by disk jockeys. In the influential New York City market, ninety-three disk jockeys were broadcasting over nineteen local stations, with 106 programs each week, sending out 400 hours of usually recently recorded music. Thirty-nine platter spinners flourished in the number-two music city, Chicago, and similar conditions existed in other major markets, giving James Caesar Petrillo, of the American Federation of Musicians, cause to pull his constitutents out of the recording studios for a second time, all through 1948.

Disk jockeys had become such an influential factor that, in September 1947, *Variety* instituted a full-page weekly chart measuring the popularity of songs and recorded talent as reflected in regular reports from a pool of nearly 100 disk spinners employed by major stations around the United States. The *Peatman Report,* which emphasized live network air play and quality of performance, rather than number of plugs, was relegated to a minor position in the publication.

The AFM strike was responsible for a slump in record sales for most of 1948, beginning in March, with retail sales down to $172 million. However, Capitol Records, the first of the large firms actively to court the disk jockeys, became a major power that year, owing to their response to its product. They made hits out of Nat Cole's "Nature Boy," Margaret Whiting's "A Tree in the Meadow," Peggy Lee's "Mañana," and Pee Wee Hunt's "12th Street Rag," which was taken out of Capitol's transcription library for commercial release. Surveys indicated that disk-jockey air play now motivated 85 percent of all record sales.

Throughout Haverlin's first year as president, BMI enjoyed little prominence on *Variety's* disk-jockey chart or its Peatman survey, as either a licensing organization or a music publisher. Fully committed to securing industrywide renewal of BMI's contract until 1959, and maintaining that support, he created a new "muscle-flexing" statistical base to emphasize the company's apparently increasing share of the popular-music business. Employing the imagination of a classic "snake-oil" salesman, he added findings from *Billboard's* race charts and its former folk lists, now "country and western," to a mix of his own devising. As demonstrated by these figures, BMI's position in the marketplace appeared to advance steadily, even though its share of network performances, measured by the Peatman survey, remained consistently around 10 percent for many years, To increase BMI's representation on *Billboard* charts, employees hunted down unaffiliated publishers and record companies, once they had appeared in that trade paper. Telegrams were speeded off pointing out that BMI paid for recorded performances of the music it licensed and that association with the company could be arranged immediately. BMI's offer of a cash advance against earnings, credited against a base of four cents for each local air play, was an unexpected largesse that was quickly accepted by almost all of those to whom it was offered.

Haverlin's own musical tastes and his willingness to engage in new experiences did much to improve morale at BMI. During his years in West Coast radio, he had developed the catholic tastes that began when he occasionally served as announcer on remote broadcasts by white and black entertainers and orchestras in the Los Angeles area. Though not a musician, he had learned to play the music of "Darktown Strutters' Ball" and a few other popular songs on the piano. He had learned "Darktown Strutters' Ball" from its creator, Shelton Brooks, while working on the same bill in vaudeville before World War I. BMI employees were infected with his enthusiasms for new rhythm-and-blues and country music and modern serious music.

The proliferation of radio stations since 1941, with the resultant increase in the number of performances of music it licensed, created a financial problem for BMI as the 1940s drew to a close. Its income from broadcasters had doubled, from the $1.8 million of 1941 to around $3.5 million in 1949. At the same time, the number of publishers to whom it had guaranteed advanced payments against performance income went from 25 at the end of the 1942–43 fiscal year to 125 for fiscal 1949–50, nearly all of them firms whose music was chiefly available on recordings and initially played on nonnetwork local stations. With the disk-jockey charts being the current key to the true value of a performance, BMI dropped its forty-eight-dollar "payment-by-plug" agreements in favor of recorded air play in major markets. The basic payment for local-station performances had been raised in 1942 to four cents, and to six cents per station for network performances. Although eighty-three new publisher affiliates joined BMI during 1949, most received contracts on a straight performance basis, the "open-door" policy with which BMI had gone into business in 1940. This had partially closed when BMI gave substantial financial encouragement to promising new music ventures. The opportunity for veteran Tin Pan Alley music men to go into business for themselves with BMI firms had shrunk in the face of the increasing success of the major BMI firms—Hill & Range Songs, Duchess Music, Acuff-Rose Publications, and a few others—the bandleader-owned houses that relied on contracts with the large record manufacturers, and the new firms being formed by manufacturers of country and rhythm-and-blues disks, in California, New York, New Jersey, Tennessee, Ohio, Illinois, the Southwest, and other areas where the new music business was taking root.

The change was fruitful, and for the first time in nine years BMI-licensed music was prominent on all the best-selling sheet-music and record charts, representing activity in all categories of popular music. This excellent showing, which was most significantly reflected in the air play on local stations, had little effect on BMI's income. That was fixed by contracts whose terms went back to 1940 and had been extended through 1959. Little of its music was used by the radio networks or on the increasingly popular new sound-and-picture medium, where, it was said "television was putting music back twenty years into the vaudeville pit.'' Such popular programs as Milton Berle's *Texaco Star Theatre,* Dumont's *Original Amateur Hour,* and Ed Sullivan's *Toast of the Town* depended on traditional theatrical routines and its ASCAP music. ASCAP's income from all sources, $11 million in 1949, was nearly three times that of BMI, and it truly mirrored the use of its repertory by the best-paying broadcasters—the networks and their affiliates.

During the middle of his third year in office, Haverlin's task was made easier by the increasing intrusion of the public's newly acquired taste for the music in which his company dominated, and the first intimations of Tin Pan Alley's final decline. As Abel Green wrote in *Variety* on January 6, 1950, "the Lindy set, content to rest on its ASCAP laurels, has found itself eclipsed time after time by the BMI upstarts. Too late have the ASCAPers realized that the cornballs and the European-flavored ballads are fundamentally good songs, good if only because a large segment of the American public prefers them. . . . BMI has achieved under peacetime business methods what it couldn't do under extraordinary pressure and drives ten years ago . . . [and has] started to dominate the 'Hit Parade' and the top sellers week after week.''

The most dramatic example of the reality of the new Music Street U.S.A., challenging New York City's long reign, and the BMI-affiliated publishers who were building that road, came in early 1951 with ''The Tennessee Waltz,'' the most successful song in twenty years. It was not BMI's first great hit out of the country-music world. There had been ''Smoke! Smoke! Smoke!,'' ''Bouquet of Roses,'' ''Cool Water,'' ''I Love You So Much It Hurts Me,'' ''Candy Kisses,'' ''I'm So Lonesome I Could Cry,'' ''Jealous Heart,'' ''Room Full of Roses,'' ''Slippin' Around,'' ''Someday,'' and ''Chattanoogie Shoe Shine Boy,'' none of which reached the multimillion-copy sheet-music and record sales around the world of ''The Tennessee Waltz.'' The song was published by Acuff-Rose Publications, which did business from a street-level, storefront office located in a suburb of Nashville. The company was owned by Fred Rose and Roy Acuff, the King of the Hillbillies, who lent his name to the venture, leaving the funding to Rose. A successful popular songwriter during the 1920s, when he became a favorite of Paul Whiteman, Rose was elected to ASCAP in 1928 on the basis of his hit songs ''Honest and Truly,'' '' 'Deed I Do,'' ''Red Hot Mama,'' and others, and had Class 4 rating by 1934, with an annual royalty of $200. He was not particularly successful as a pop-song writer in the late 1930s. In Nashville, he did a daily music program over station WSM, and came into contact with the hillbilly artists and songwriters who starred on its weekend broadcast of ''Grand Ol' Op'ry.'' Loyal to his friends at ASCAP, Rose traveled to New York in 1943 to offer John Paine an opportunity to ''lock up'' hillbilly music and songwriters, by funding a Rose-operated ASCAP firm working out of Nashville, which would be the first country-music publishing house located there. He was turned down, principally because the society did not pay for the nonnetwork live and recorded performances that were all Rose could promise. He then went to BMI, where he received an advance of $2,500. By 1947, when his company's annual income from BMI had doubled, Rose had built up a roster of songwriter-performers that included Pee Wee King and Redd Stewart, writers of "The Tennessee Waltz," and Hiram Hank Williams, with whom Fred Rose formed one of the most successful music-publisher–editor–collaborator and songwriter relationships in the history of American popular music. Acuff-Rose's returns from BMI for radio performances grew steadily throughout the late 1940s, rising to nearly $130,000 with the success of "The Tennessee Waltz," though they were still less than the $200,000 a year that leading ASCAP publishers received from the society that year.

BMI saw almost all of the big-city writers to whom it had first given opportunity leave to join ASCAP, chiefly because it had been wrong in an expectation that its publisher affiliates would share performing-rights income with them. During these years, it had regularly announced that a writer-payment plan was under consideration, but not until August 1949 did it make a tentative step toward that goal. In the next twelve months, twenty writers were signed by BMI as affiliated writers, for terms averaging seven years, with a sliding scale of payment and a $400 maximum annual guarantee, based on the number of performances expected from each. It was hoped that by the end of their contracts these writers would have achieved parity with ASCAP members who had similar success and air play. However, since a BB ASCAP writer earned $10,000 a year and those in AA double that, BMI did not expect even its most successful writers to achieve such royalties without a substantial surge in its income. The society, meanwhile, was fearful for its future, plagued as it was by the pending negotiations for radio and television contract renewals, the impasse between the MPPA and the SPA over a new agreement, and resumption of the *Alden-Rochelle* v. *ASCAP* action.

A historic decision in that case, with potentially disastrous consequences, found that the society's theater-licensing practices constituted a monopoly operating in restraint of trade. On July 20, 1948, federal court judge Vincent H. Leibell ordered ASCAP immediately to divest itself of all public-performance rights dealing with motion-picture exhibition, and return them to the original copyright owners. In addition, he restrained the society from obtaining those rights from its writer members and from refusing to permit these members to grant them to film producers directly, as it had been doing for years.

Although the SPA had not intervened in the case, in October 1948 one of its leading members, Milton Ager, represented by the association's general counsel, John Schulman, asked Judge Leibell to reverse himself and permit ASCAP to represent composers and songwriters in licensing screen-theater performances. Failing that, Ager pleaded that such rights revert to the songwriters rather than the publishers. Schulman was paid for his work in this action through a special fund of between $30,000 and $40,000 raised by SPA members on the basis of their ASCAP ratings. The secrecy involved in establishing this fund, and its future implications, puzzled many MPPA members, most of whom had been meeting with Schulman over a new standard songwriters contract ever since the previous document's expiration at the end of 1946. Ager's plea, made on behalf of all songwriters as a class, frightened the publishers, most of whom saw only sinister implications in it. The pending SPA contract already provided that writers were to receive 50 percent of income from all licensing rights, which would include any that might be sold individually in the future. Herman Starr attempted to mend the widening breach between publishers and songwriters, arguing that it was injurious to ASCAP. A meeting, arranged by Starr, between leading SPA members and publishers ended abruptly when the former asked that they be given a "proprietary interest" in copyrights for the future, co-administration of all rights. The request was viewed as part of a secret blueprint drawn by the SPA to win control of both ASCAP and the music business. It was rejected. Max Dreyfus, publisher of the Ager compositions in question, promptly joined the action on behalf of all publishers.

The Ager and Dreyfus motions and an ASCAP brief arguing that the divestiture of theater-performance rights was not in the public interest, and reminding the court that the attorney general had not sought such relief in the 1940 consent decree, postponed any clear resolution of the matter. Leibell denied all motions and directed ASCAP to permit licensing of performing rights to motion-picture producers concurrently with licensing of recording rights, the fee for the former to be added to production costs and recouped through licensing of the motion pictures that made use of ASCAP music.

Most important to broadcasters and movie companies, Leibell's decision raised the possibility that composers and songwriters might capture the right to deal directly with them, leading to other reforms that the SPA had been seeking since its formation, and thus lead to the destruction of ASCAP. Neither wanted this solution. It would create many small groups of copyright owners, from whom performance licenses would have to be obtained individually, with bookkeeping and negotiating costs far in excess of the fees now being paid to ASCAP. Wise heads at ASCAP, counseled by Robert P. Patterson, former secretary of war and head of the New York Bar Association, decided against an appeal of the Leibell decision, and met with the Justice Department to seek a modification of the 1941 consent decree that would offset Alden-Rochelle's effects.

CHAPTER 16

ASCAP and BMI Face the Reality of Television

It was evident to some ASCAP members that the time had come to take a good look at themselves and the society. Alden-Rochelle should never have been allowed to take place. The distressing decision in the case, the SPA's aggressive role, and other potentially serious developments were the result. As Abel Green wrote in *Variety* in December 1948, "The curious secrecy about some of the legal negotiations through the years have made every [ASCAP] faction's lawyers wonder what somebody might be getting—or getting away with. Thus, Judge Leibell has done one affirmative thing for ASCAPers. The talk about what 'they' did up at ASCAP has prompted the shirkers into workers."

Little public mention was made by ASCAP that it had paid $160,000 in damages to the plaintiffs for dropping a collateral action, together with $75,000 to their attorneys.

ASCAP's negotiations with the major film studios to recoup the $1.25 million in theater-licensing fees, cut off by the Leibell decision, began after March 1950, when a second, amended, consent decree was entered, ending the judge's freeze on such collections. The decree gave either ASCAP or individual copyright owners the right to be paid at the source by film companies. Since April 1948, the studios had continued to negotiate with publishers for synchronization licenses, coupling them with permission to perform the works publicly, payment for which would be made when a blanket license was negotiated by the society with the entire film industry. A sizable sum was already due, $150,000 from a single company, but though the consent decree cleared the way, and ASCAP could take the matter to a federal court for settlement, Hollywood continued to drag its heels.

ASCAP reportedly was asking for a half-million dollars annually from Warner, MGM, Paramount, and 20th Century-Fox, and the same sum from all other companies and independent producers. Because the consent decree called for a resolution of the matter no later than March 4, 1952, the film industry was in no rush to make up for ASCAP's losses. So matters remained suspended through 1951. In the spring of that year, a new issue was raised when the studios suggested that a blanket license for public exhibition include television fed to theaters. Convinced that future income from commercial television would soon be larger than from radio (it was doubling over 1950's one million), the ASCAP negotiating committee rejected the proposal and disbanded. In September, less than six months from the deadline, ASCAP indicated that, without an agreement, it would be forced to divorce itself of all film-performance rights.

With the coaxial cable from New York to the West Coast nearing completion, there was a firm belief in the video business that at least 80 percent of all programs would, out of economic necessity, have to be on film for the near future, that it would become the electrical transcription or taped-network program of television. Only the twenty or thirty largest corporations could afford to sponsor programs featuring big-name stars, whose talent fees were between $50,000 and $60,000 an hour, and time rates that were expected to jump to $90,000 an hour when the networks were enlarged from coast to coast. As with network radio, advertisers willing to spend that kind of money wanted to reach families during evening prime time, which was subject to a three-hour time difference between New York and Los Angeles, and only programs on film could resolve that variance. Network affiliates would also prefer film, because their largest income came from "hitchhiking," the sale of local advertising before and after network broadcasts.

More to the point for Hollywood, big-screen television in movie houses was an immediate reality. Theatre Network Television, owned by the Theatre Operators' Association, was already offering sports events on closed circuit, and was attracting as many as 250,000 to a single telecast, transmitted to a chain of screen theaters. TNT was also ready to go into the production of special programs, from the stage of the Metropolitan Opera House, for example, and to television business and sales meetings and major fund-raising social occasions.

Faced with the prospect of such competition, the major film companies offered ASCAP token amounts totaling about half a million dollars. The sum represented less than .05 percent of motion-picture theaters' annual income of $1 billion in ticket admissions alone. Against this, ASCAP collected a combined fifty times more on the basis of dollar revenue from broadcasting that it was ready to accept from Hollywood. The society feared that radio and television broadcasters would raise the issue of discrimination over such a settlement and go to court for lower fees. It was effectively extricated from such a prospect when BMI, owned by the networks and radio stations, offered its music without charge to theater exhibitors.

Consequently, in early March 1952, in time to meet the Justice Department's order, ASCAP and the major studios forged the language of a blanket license settlement, representing about $500,000 annually, plus $1.4 million for retroactive performance fees covering the previous two years. Apparently, however, only Universal Pictures actually signed the agreement. In August 1952, ASCAP began billing theater exhibitors on a monthly basis for the use of recorded music during intermissions. Fees based on theater size ranged from fifteen to forty-eight dollars for an enclosed theater, and from thirty-six to sixty dollars for drive-in houses. BMI followed immediately, with fees considerably lower than those its rival charged.

Such scant collections from a major music user were of little interest to the songwriter and publisher associations, between whom a state of armed peace continued. Symptomatic of that were the extended negotiations that had taken place from mid-1946 to the summer of 1948 to frame a third new standard songwriters contract, and the resistance and maneuvering by some music houses to block any settlement. In September 1946, after eight months of work by an SPA committee, proposed terms for a document to replace the one that would expire at year-end were presented to the MPPA and to Herman Starr, who represented such powerful non-MPPA firms as his own Harms, Witmark, Remick, and the Paramount interests. It was generally understood that the provisions, which were kept from the press by all parties, called for a full half-share of the standard two-cent royalty on recordings, regardless of any compromise publishers might make with the record manufacturers. In addition, the SPA was understood to be asking for a sliding-scale sheet-music royalty. These and other proposals were rejected out of hand by the publishers, who announced they would offer a counteragreement. Starr was quoted as saying, "We'll work out what we think is fair terms, and the writers can take it or leave it." The possibility of strike by the songwriters was discounted. The publishers believed that those who were under contract to the studios would never walk out, for fear of being replaced by members of the aggressive new generation of songsmiths, who had not yet developed loyalties to either the SPA or ASCAP.

The existing contract was renewed on a monthly basis, and MPPA representatives met regularly to work out a mutually satisfactory new one. Several major sticking points were slowly overcome. For much of 1947, Tin Pan Alley witnessed the most serious slump in sheet-music sales in fifteen years, even though a handful of songs, among them "Nature Boy," which had been recorded by Nat Cole, and the Australian "Now Is the Hour," approached the million-copy mark. Name dance bands, the foundation stone of any record company's catalogue since before World War I, were being supplanted on disks and on the radio networks by romantic male singers—Sinatra, Dick Haymes, Cole, Perry Como, Frankie Laine, Vic Damone—whose hits were responsible in great measure for the recording industry's best year since 1921. All that a new song required to make its mark was a good recording. The established practice of releasing a recording only after the publisher pronounced himself ready to work on the song was coming to an end. Scheduled release dates were consistently jumped by manufacturers, disrupting the music houses' plans. Younger songwriters had found an open door at the record companies, particularly to the most successful A & R men. With a release assured, they could make a better financial arrangement than had prevailed in the past, and could then publish the song themselves, using an established house to handle distribution of the sheet music.

Early in negotiations that came to an end in the summer of 1948, the SPA had won the option of a straight minimum three-cent royalty on all sheet sales or a sliding-scale payment, beginning with two and a half cents for the first 100,000 copies, going to a maximum of five cents for all copies in excess of 500,000. In addition, the publisher was required to pay a minimum royalty of 10 percent on any and all printed music, other than sheet copies, sold domestically. Gradually, other gains were made by the SPA. Within a year after he acquired a new work, the publisher was obliged to issue piano copies, and to secure a recording or issue a dance orchestration, or else return the copyright and pay a minimum penalty of $250. After the initial copyright period of twenty-eight years, all rights, including those abroad, were returned to the writer, all new contracts became valid only after approval by the SPA. As had been true since the early 1930s, only ASCAP was specifically designated as custodian of performing rights for SPA members, making it impossible for songwriters published through BMI publishers to join.

The SPA's success in achieving a new contract with publishers, to run for ten years, until 1957, emphasized its coming of age as a force in the music business and swelled its ranks to 1,800 members, 1,000 of them established ASCAP authors and composers, the balance young newcomers waiting to be accepted by the society. By the summer of 1950, 289 publishers had accepted the new terms, with only a few firms owned by Hollywood studios holding out until ASCAP's status was cleared by the amended consent decree that had stemmed from the Alden-Rochelle action. Of equal concern to the film companies were the protracted negotiations with network-affiliated television stations. Under the terms of the SPA contract, ASCAP could not license television rights until they were assigned to the society by the publishers, who had first to obtain permission to do so from composers and authors representing at least 80 percent of the total ASCAP distribution for 1947. Many of the major writers—Berlin, Kern, Porter, Romberg— with important Broadway musical productions to their credit seriously weighed the possibility of licensing their music themselves on a dramatic-use basis, rather than through ASCAP.

During the many months that ASCAP negotiated with an NAB committee for the resolution of a new television contract, the dollar-a-year fee remained in effect, but stations had to clear every piece of music in advance with the society for every single performance. ASCAP retained the right to revoke this license on thirty days' notice any time a majority of its membership wished, or to impose restrictions on the use of ASCAP music in connection with dramatic shows. In October 1949, the ASCAP board decided that the time had come for television to begin paying for music just as radio was doing. Fred Ahlert, the fourth president in ASCAP's history, began the campaign with a letter to all members, asking for permission to negotiate a ten-year contract with the television industry. The progress of television within the past year, he wrote, could only be described as "in leaps and bounds," and therefore "in the interest of good customer and public relations it has become imperative for us to arrive at a license agreement with [television], commensurate with our contribution as quickly as we can." The medium's progress had truly been spectacular. Orders for new receivers were up 400 percent, equipping one million households with sets to view such new miracles of programing as the live *Your Show of Shows*, starring Sid Caesar and Imogene Coca.

The response from the membership was generally favorable, though the major production writers still maintained that their music was worth more than ASCAP could ever collect. That longtime holdout the MGM-Loew's group finally assented also. After nearly a year of bargaining, NBC, CBS, and ABC signed a five-year blanket license agreement, retroactive to January 1, 1948, on behalf of their fourteen owned-and-operated stations. The terms were roughly about 10 percent more than those for radio, or 2.75 percent of billings, less deductions, and 2.25 of the affiliates' gross. A new 25 percent deduction was added to subsidize the cost of the coaxial cable to the West Coast, which was to be reduced by small increments over the next five years.

Several problems remained for ASCAP and Ahlert, among them extension for an additional three years of the present licensing assignment by writers and publishers, and a per-program contract that would satisfy the vast majority of independent station owners who had refused to go along with the networks. They had found the costs too high, and invoked the Leibell decision, questioning whether ASCAP had the right to collect fees from them for the use of motion pictures. The networks had agreed to pay for movies, not wishing to upset the ASCAP structure, on the specific stipulation that copyright owners would not be paid "at the source," as a number of music firms were doing.

The All-Industry Television Committee, appointed by the NAB to deal with the situation, was funded by contributions from telecasters, who intended to take the matter to court. In March 1951, after finding itself unable to agree to satisfactory terms, ASCAP mailed all television stations a contract of its own making. It proposed an 8.5 percent commercial rate and a 2 percent sustaining charge for stations doing an annual business under

$150,000, and 9.5 percent and 2.5 percent for those with grosses of more than $300,000 annually. Because ASCAP based the fees on a one-time advertising-card rate, rather than on actual station income, which was subject to the customary discounts, the offer represented a 100 percent increase over the AM radio rate, with a 300 percent increase for those stations doing the most business. Simon Rifkind was retained by the committee to resolve the case under the terms of the amended ASCAP consent decree, which enabled music users to take their complaints to the New York court for resolution. Former judge Rifkind had ruled against ASCAP and CISAC in the case involving the international cartelization of music licensing, which led directly to the 1950 amended consent decree. Acting on behalf of all independent television stations, in July 1951, he asked the U.S. district court in New York to set a fair music rate. The matter lay dormant for the next two years, with all ASCAP television licenses in limbo, pending a unanimous expression that the agreements were fair and equitable by all television licensees.

The society's parallel discussions with the All-Industry Radio Committee foundered on the rocks of cooperative network programs, those that emanated from the networks as sustaining broadcasts, but on which affiliated stations sold time to local sponsors. ASCAP insisted that these programs were commercial shows, to be paid for by local stations at the higher network rate. The stations argued that they should be considered purely local commercial broadcasts. The NAB Radio Committee pursued the matter until May 1953, when ASCAP accepted its position and agreed to a 2.25 percent rate for cooperative programs over stations with a blanket license, and 8 percent for those using a per-program formula.

The amended consent decree that came out of months of meetings during 1950 covered far more than CISAC's international cartel, the ramifications of Judge Leibell's findings, and the continuous complaints from broadcasters. It tackled the ASCAP distribution system, grumblings about which were pouring in from members, particularly the group known as "the young Turks." They opposed any method that favored those highly rated old-guard writers whose songs had gone out of style and use. Most of the younger writers had entered the business with BMI-affiliated firms, because they could not get into ASCAP, and they wanted a formula that placed maximum emphasis on the current use of their music.

Early in the discussions, it became obvious to Sigmund Timberg, chief of the Justice Department's antitrust judgments enforcement section, and to his assistants, that the revision of ASCAP's writer classification and distribution system was a matter of first concern. The old system called for fourteen classes, ranging from AA to 4, and alloted less than 15 percent of total income for performances. Shortly after the radio-music war, the board had promised an improved formula, based on a plan proposed by Ahlert and Edgar Leslie, which would allow 20 percent for performances during the first year, to be increased gradually. Unfortunately, though the veteran songwriters' proposal had been accepted, it was never implemented.

Timberg's staff found a suitable pattern for change in the current publishers' distribution plan, which had been functioning satisfactorily since the Depression. It alloted 55 percent for performances, 30 for availability, and 15 for seniority. The suggestion of such a division to authors and composers split the society into many warring camps, with about 250 charter members or their heirs, whose income had been fixed twenty years earlier, at one extreme and writers whose songs enjoyed current popularity at the other.

One of the directives in the amended consent decree curtailing ASCAP's scope and structure, which was filed by the Justice Department on March 14, 1950, and approved by the society soon after, required that future distribution be made "on a basis which gives primary consideration to the performance of the compositions of members as indicated by objective surveys of performances . . . periodically made by or for ASCAP." How this was to be accomplished was left to the society. Other provisions were more precise. Judge Leibell was upheld in every particular regarding motion-picture music licensing. BMI was provided with an open door to the international music-licensing world because ASCAP could no longer enter into exclusive contracts with foreign societies. Judge Pecora's decision in *Marks v. ASCAP* was validated. Although an ASCAP member could withdraw his catalogue on proper notice, he could not license his music until all existing ASCAP contracts with music users terminated. All groups of similarly situated music users were entitled to uniform rates, with the right to take any dispute to a federal court for final determination. In order properly to democratize ASCAP, the decree did away with the self-perpetuating board of twenty-four member-directors, eight of whom were elected annually on a rotating basis, by requiring election of the entire board every one or two years. Membership eligibility was liberalized so that songwriters who had had at least one work "regularly published," or a firm whose musical publications had been distributed for a year, could join the society on a "non-participating or otherwise" basis. All methods of classifying members for purposes of distributing license income were to be made known. In sum, while ASCAP's practices and activities might, taken together, represent restraint of trade or monopoly in violation of the Sherman Act, the decree permitted court regulation of those that appeared to be in the public interest.

The new writer distribution plan was unveiled at ASCAP's annual business meeting on April 25, 1950, and elaborated upon by Ahlert, whose term would expire the following day. He spoke after the formal presentation of the annual financial report, which revealed that, due to the loss of half a million dollars because of the Leibell decision, income for 1949 was $10.6 million, rather than the anticipated $11 million plus. The board was confident that the loss would be more than covered by direct licensing of the film studios, permitted by the decree, by licensing of screen theaters that played live and recorded intermission music, and from railroad and airline terminals where ASCAP's repertory was used for background music. Waxing enthusiastic, Ahlert predicted that television's recent growth would mean an additional million dollars for 1950, though the medium had provided only a few thousand dollars two years earlier and $400,000 in 1949.

After the terms of the amended decree had been detailed, the new distribution plan was revealed. Quarterly payments would begin in October, calculated on three factors; the most important was a performance average for the years 1945 to 1949, which would account for 60 percent of the distribution. One fifth of this, or 12 percent of total writer money, was to be set aside for allocation to the composers of works in the standard- and concert-music fields, whose performances could not be measured by the society's logging operation. Twenty percent would be determined on the basis of current performances during the past year, and the final fifth by a combined seniority and availability factor. Ahlert promised there would be no radical changes in income, because the society's promising fiscal future would more than offset any drop to a lower category.

ASCAP's thirty-six-year-old classification system would be replaced by an IBM machine-calculated number formula, which would base 60 percent of the writers' money (30 percent of ASCAP disposable income) on five-year performance averaging that calculated writers' ratings. These would be graduated by increments of twenty-five points, from one for Class 4 writers to between 775 and 1,000 for those in AA. Promotion or demotion would be automatic, with safeguards against too rapid a fall. On the other hand, a writer with between 500 and 1,000 points could jump by 200 points at a time; one with between 100 and 500, by 100. A special category, ranging from 1,050 to 1,500 points, was established for a handful of the society's most illustrious writers—Berlin, Porter, Rodgers, Harbach, Hammerstein, and the Gershwin estate.

To augment the new system and satisfy provisions of the decree, as well as to compete with BMI's growing position in country, rhythm-and-blues, and other specialty music, the ASCAP board installed a new logging program. Network performances continued to receive most attention, but an effort was made to catch ASCAP music on stations that concentrated on recorded music, which had been lost in the previous mix. A group of independent stations in ten key markets were logged daily for three hours, on a rotating basis. ASCAP field men taped these stations, excised any identification, and sent the information to the society's New York headquarters for analysis. The additional information was expected to reduce the current performance point value, now between six and a half and seven cents, by only a fraction. Performances were evaluated on a point basis: one point for a network shot; one tenth of a point for theme songs and jingles. Only if a theme song was an established standard song did it receive a full credit. Concert works of more than five minutes and choral pieces of more than thirty minutes received six points per performance. The Screen Composers Association had made frequent protestations to the Justice Department, asking for recognition of its members' contributions; as a result, background music used in motion pictures was credited with one tenth of a point for each performance.

The task of mollifying a majority of the writers, once their checks were received in late October, would fall to ASCAP's new president. The functions of that office had increased greatly because a new general manager had not yet been named. The publishers, headed by Herman Starr, Max Dreyfus, and Saul Bourne (formerly Bornstein), were happy with Ahlert and ready to vote him back into office for a third term, despite the recently adopted two-terms-only resolution. The songwriter half of the board was adamantly opposed, and insisted on anybody but Ahlert. A compromise was effected with the election of the seventy-seven-year-old Otto Harbach.

In that confused period following Judge Leibell's decision, the SPA— now nearly twenty years old and an important presence because 289 publishers were using its most recently revised basic contract—was growing more aggressive in the new role it had cast for itself: spokesman for all authors and composers. The SPA's chief attorney, John Schulman, was a familiar figure wherever issues regarding songwriters' rights were involved—in Washington, in courtrooms, and during the arbitration proceedings the SPA encouraged. In September 1950, the SPA attempted, without success, to introduce a new secondary standard renewal contract, with increased rates and guarantees, for songs entering the second twenty-eight years of copyright protection. Prior to the institution of the SPA uniform contract in 1932, the major old-line publishers had insisted on the right to renew all copyrights in their own names, with the prior consent of all writers involved. Acceding to SPA terms, most publishers were prepared to offer a renewal contract that raised the mechanical rate from the 1920s' one-third share to a half, and sheet-music royalties from the former standard two cents to four or five. However, in the case of such valuable standard song as "That Old Gang of Mine" (Billy Rose–Mort Dixon–Ray Henderson), the original publisher, Bourne Music, took advantage of the original contract and retained the copyright. Billy Rose, a founding member of the SPA, took the matter into his own hands and, with John Schulman as attorney, brought suit to recover the copyright, on the ground that the transfer of a right was not binding unless an adequate consideration had been given to secure it.

While the case was waiting for a place on the court calendar, the SPA prepared for the celebration of its anniversary and counseled its members on problems stemming from the most recent ASCAP checks they had received. Harbach, to whom most complaints were presented, had intended to stay in office as president for just one year, until all wrinkles in the new system were shaken out. Although the new plan was designed "to boost the little fellow,'' it had succeeded only ''in lifting the big fellow into the stratosphere,'' as Harbach wrote to all members in late October. Nearly three out of every ten of ASCAP's 2,000-plus members had received a smaller check. The income of twenty AA writers, however, had doubled, rising well above the previous ceiling of $4,500 a quarter. Because they wrote both words and music, with which they were credited for the first time, Irving Berlin and Cole Porter headed the special new elite group in earnings. At 1,500 points, Berlin received three times his previous AA check, and Porter, just behind him, doubled his last quarter's earnings.

When the 60-20-20 plan had been submitted to the government, it was neither approved nor disapproved, but was, instead, subjected to a three-year test period. With no marked difference in the second new quarter distribution, the writer board members sought some means to cushion the drop in income, which most seriously affected the middle-rank ASCAP constituency. The young Turks, led by the comparatively junior songwriters Redd Evans and Pinky Herman, fought the proposed revision of seniority and availability suggested by some directors. They insisted on a change in an interpretation of the decree that placed undue emphasis on seniority, and an end to the cushioning of the special top class. They also demanded a reform of ASCAP in that section of the new decree calling for the open election of directors by all members. For years, the board had been a closed corporation, with directors consistently selected from among the society's top brackets and working only for the benefit of their peers. Given a voice in the process for the first time, and hoping to win at least a handful of new directors to represent them and the lower grades, the young Turks and their adherents concentrated on a write-in voting campaign, which proved fruitless. Except for one director who declined to run again, the election was a clean sweep for the incumbents. Harbach, the only candidate agreeable to all parties, was reelected president. His continuing problem, amelioration of the chaos following installation of the 60-20-20 plan, was not to be resolved until the Justice Department again intervened.

At the end of a year of dispute and dissension, it was plain that under the new system the 100 highest-rated ASCAP writers would continue to receive 56 percent of the income, the most serious result of the government's insistence that performances remain paramount in determining royalty payments. A number of alternate interpretations of the basic formula were considered by the classification committee, but with little hope that the government would approve any. Its intervention had brought writer distribution closer to the 55-30-15 formula used by the publishers since 1935, with the greatest emphasis on live prime-time commercial radio, and now television, air play. A growing sentiment took form among tiring rank-and-file members that the controversy between those who argued for the importance of their seniority in ASCAP and the supporters of concentration on current performances would ultimately fade, because no more satisfactory plan than that in use could be found.

The publishers, who had taken no public stand, suddenly found themselves confronted in early 1952 with a crisis of their own, which threatened to overturn their distribution plan: 55 percent for performances, 30 for availability, and 15 for seniority. Ralph Peer was the first publisher to take advantage of the appeal machinery insisted upon by Timberg and his staff. He sent a representative to appeal before a newly organized classification arbitration panel on behalf of the major ASCAP holding, Southern Music. The committee—an ASCAP publisher, an ASCAP writer, and an outside expert—found for Peer, raising Southern's availability from 250 to 450 points, a position among the society's forty leading publishers. It also recommended a broad revision of the availability ratings of all publisher members, with an eye to evolving a new formula for computing their standings. The decision and the recommendation revived a proposal that many of the large firms had long advocated, a straight 100 percent performance payoff, or at least an increase of the performance factor to the 60 percent level of the writer system. With appeals to the arbitration panel piling up, and the seventeen-year publisher distribution scheme apparently falling apart, AS-CAP's executive committee and legal department, under the direction of Herman Finkelstein, worked to prepare a new system that would be acceptable to the younger publishers.

As anticipated, there was no serious disruption of the status quo. The new system, devised to measure the important publisher availability factor, became effective with the October 1952 distribution. It rated the availability of every song more than two years old, by the use of IBM machines, on the basis of its radio and television performances during the previous five years, or eight quarters. This was hailed as a milestone of the society's history. For the first time, the value of each work was reckoned in terms publishers understood. Performance, availability, and seniority were retained. Any impact from a change in measuring seniority was cushioned by a guarantee that income could not fall below 80 percent the first year, 70 the second, and 60 the third. Under the new plan, whose major emphasis remained on old copyrights, the powerhouse firms—Harms, with the highest previous availability rating, 11,000 points, MGM's Big Three, and Max Dreyfus's Chappell group—continued to take the lion's share of distribution. Middle-sized firms viewed the new system as an opportunity to grow by securing more air play. Only the standard-music houses and new small companies suffered. Without a 100 percent current performance payoff that recognized recent hits, the latter could not increase their availability ratings or their ASCAP earnings until their copyrights went beyond the eight-quarter limitation.

Damaged by distribution that effectively allocated 85 percent of all payments on the basis of broadcast performances, which their music houses had difficulty in securing, the standard-music publishers had two options. They could fight for an increase in the value of performances of classical, standard, and art music by broadcasters, as well as in public concerts, or they could form BMI-affiliated companies. Many of their best-known younger composers, among them William Schuman, Norman Dello Joio, Roger Sessions, and Walter Piston, had moved to BMI, where Carl Haverlin was ready to give financial support to modern concert music and those who created it. During the war Aaron Copland resigned to join ASCAP, but the American Composers Alliance had moved back to BMI after a short association with ASCAP. When ACA's contract had come up for renewal in 1950, Haverlin proved to its negotiating committee that he was, in the words of Otto Luening, who was one of them, a man who "knew the difference between long-term projects and speculation with short-term results. He understood that time was needed to launch and to make accessible and popular certain kinds of music and he gave us all the support that he could get out of his board of directors throughout the years of his office." BMI took over all performance licensing on behalf of ACA and paid its members, as well as other modern composers, advance guarantees against earnings, generally out of all proportion to actual collections. The ACA library of manuscript scores and parts and its Composers Facsimile Editions were moved to the BMI premises. Tapes and recordings of ACA members' works were sent to radio stations and the conductors of symphony orchestras. Recordings of ACA and other BMI-licensed music were subsidized, as were live performances, including the first public concert in the United States of taped music. Conducted by Leopold Stokowski, it was held at the Museum of Modern Art on October 28, 1952, and inspired *Time* to observe that "the twentieth-century instrument is the record machine—a phonograph or tape recorder." These projects all served to assist Haverlin in his campaign to secure an improved national public image for BMI, through increased involvement in and support of minority music.

In pursuing that ambition, and because of the competition engendered for the services of composers of "serious" American music, higher income could be expected. But as ASCAP's collections from symphony orchestras and concert-hall managers and local impresarios demonstrated, there was so little profit in licensing them that any figures reported publicly were highly exaggerated. The society collected directly from the country's symphony orchestras for blanket access to its music on a descending scale, beginning at $1,000 a year, down to inconsequential fees from lesser-known organizations. The two major concert-artist management corporations, one owned by CBS, and many of the other's artists under contract to NBC before the FCC ordered their divestiture, collected a fee of 1 percent on behalf of ASCAP from performers and local entrepreneurs. Using their best efforts, together they did not realize more than $12,000 for the 1951–52 season. BMI did not yet license either symphony orchestras or concert halls.

With so small a return, few performances of large-scale works on radio, and none on television, ASCAP attempted to subsidize its serious composers, who in 1943 had represented one out of every four writer members, by dipping into the availability fund to compensate for the "cultural importance" of their music. When 85 percent of distribution was measured by performance, under the first revised plan in 1950, and the value of works between thirty-six and forty minutes in length was fixed at sixteen points, the society's serious composers found their checks smaller than ever. In October 1952, the value of such "unique and prestigious" works was raised to forty-four points, the total distribution available to them was fixed at $35,000 a quarter. When the annual guarantees offered by BMI to several ASCAP members surpassed the society's fixed budget, few resisted BMI's blandishments. The raiding proceeded with certain success, and Starr and Dreyfus were asked to intervene and promise any potential defectors substantial guarantees against all income, including their ASCAP checks, in order to keep remaining eminent composers in the society. A large number of ASCAP publishers shared the attitude of an unidentified Tin Pan Alleyite who was quoted in *Billboard:* "We must encourage American composers of the type of Leroy Anderson and the late George Gershwin, etc., but to hell with those longhairs who write compositions for the oboe."

The second modified ASCAP writer-payment plan was accepted by the Justice Department in June 1952 with its usual "we do not disapprove" statement. The proposal was the handiwork of a committee headed by Stanley Adams, with suggestions from several perennial stormy petrels, one of them Hans Lengsfelder, a Viennese composer who had joined the society in 1942. After winning success with a few popular hits, some of which he published in part himself, he became a leading spokesman for the small publisher and new authors and composers in the society.

The Adams committee plan changed the 60-20-20 three-fund allocation to a four-fund formula. The 60 percent performance factor was split into equal parts, a sustaining fund and an availability fund. The remaining 40 percent was divided equally into current performance and accumulated earnings funds. Writers had the option of either a ten- or a five-year-basis for the sustained performance rating, and availability was cushioned against a drop in income, remaining fixed for five years, which in effect placed major emphasis on old music.

With at least half the membership expected to receive higher payments under the new play—those in the lowest classifications to gain the most on a percentage basis—ASCAP authors and composers on both coasts approved the scheme without opposition. Irving Berlin was hailed for accepting an annual reduction of $5,000 from the $72,000 he had been receiving each year since October 1950, "as a contribution to the general welfare of ASCAP."

Rather than reduce the income of the special top writers, and some in the AA group, the new distribution method actually increased their take beyond expectation. Berlin received $87,000 for 1952, during only one quarter of which the revised plan was in effect. Cole Porter was immediately behind him with $78,000. Four estates, those of Jerome Kern, George Gershwin, Gus Kahn, and Lorenz Hart, and Rodgers, Hammerstein, Harry Warren, and Ira Gershwin received between $40,000 and $44,000 each. Johnny Mercer, Jimmy Van Heusen, Dorothy Fields, Jimmy McHugh, Johnny Burke, Arthur Schwartz, Frank Loesser, Jule Styne, Leo Robin, Harold Arlen, the estates of Walter Donaldson and Sigmund Romberg, and a few others were paid between $23,000 and $26,000 for 1952.

In October 1952, speaking to the West Coast membership in the third term of his presidency, a tiring Harbach predicted that the society's income for 1952 would reach an all-time high of about $15 million, four of that from television, and would certainly make forthcoming writer and publisher checks larger. In spite of his wish to retire, or probably because of an expressed desire for a younger man by the same important writers who had voted Ahlert out and him in, which irked Harbach, he agreed to accept a third one-year term. Regarded by most of the membership as indispensable, particularly because the society had not yet found a successor to John Paine as general manager, Harbach was considered the best man to present a persuasive case on behalf of ASCAP in Washington, where hearings were being held to change the law so that the operators of jukeboxes would pay for the music they used. Only Stanley Adams and Oscar Hammerstein II had been considered to succeed Harbach, but Dreyfus was still not persuaded that Adams was the man. On the crest of a wave of success in his collaboration with Richard Rodgers, which had already produced *Oklahoma!, Carousel, South Pacific,* and *The King and I,* the veteran lyricist and librettist Hammerstein was not ready to give up writing.

During copyright hearings in connection with a revision of the law in 1909, music publishers had shown little interest in having the coin-operated phonograph business made liable for payment when it used recorded copyrighted music, unless admission was charged. Committee reports, accompanying the completed legislation, made reference to statements by some publishers that the machines were a chief means for promoting their music and should not be touched. The coin-operated music industry was enjoying a boom that had begun in the early 1890s. The precursor of the modern jukebox could then be found in greatest number in the nation's penny vaudevilles, where the latest musical cylinders were offered. The first of these emporiums, with nearly 100 ear-tube-equipped Edison Penny Coin Slot Machines, was opened on Union Square in New York, operated by a corporation capitalized at $500,000, which eventually built up a chain of thirteen additional locations around the country. On a single holiday, an estimated 200,000 people crowded into these fourteen vaudevilles and spent at least ten cents apiece. Any city of more than 10,000 inhabitants could support such a business, and it spread rapidly, yielding substantial profits to the owners. The automatic-phonograph industry did not use disks until 1908, when the first automatic coin players went on sale, but by that time the nickel-in-the-slot Peerless Player Piano was beginning to replace recorded music with that of the paper music roll. Within a year or two, the end came for the coin-slot automatic-phonograph business, but it returned in the early 1930s, when desperate economic times brought back the poor man's concert hall.

Spearheaded by ASCAP, the popular-music business waged an unrelenting campaign to change the 1909 copyright law in several particulars, chiefly compulsory licensing and the two-cent record royalty. Beginning in 1926, these matters got out of various Congressional committees only twice, reaching the House floor in 1930 and that of the Senate in 1935, only to be tabled. In 1940, ASCAP was active in support of a pending bill that was expected to yield a fee of five dollars a month from every jukebox in America. The struggling BMI promptly offered its music to all coin-machine operators without charge and urged their cooperation in fighting the society's "practical monopoly of popular music." For years after, a friendly relationship continued between the coin operators' trade association, the Music Operators of America, and BMI.

During the 80th Congress, Representative Hugh Scott, of Pennsylvania, made a strenuous but unsuccessful try to end the jukebox exemption and obtain passage of his "Interpretation Bill," which proposed copyrighting of recorded versions of previously copyrighted musical works. During the same session, another Pennsylvania legislator, Congressman Carroll Kearns, tried, without success, to have phonograph records labeled either "For Commercial Use" or "For Home Use Only."

In the 1951–52 Congress, Scott again introduced a bill removing the jukebox exemption, only to have its place on the agenda taken away by the Kefauver-Bryson bill, which exempted the owner of a single jukebox, but required all others to obtain a license and pay a weekly penny royalty on every copyrighted work inserted into their machines. The MOA spokesmen suggested that "it was false and misleading to assert that jukeboxes do not pay for the music they use." Coin operators were, in fact, the largest single users of phonograph records, purchasing about 15 percent, or 50 million disks, annually. The top twenty-two songs of the period December 1950 to September 1951 had sold 53, 535, 551 records and received $1.003 million in royalties. The best-selling "Tennessee Waltz" sold 4,225,000 disks and received $79,580 in copyright fees. "Mule Train," with 2,663,303 records sold, received $53,183 in royalties, and "Some Enchanted Evening," sold 2,565,514 records and got $51,205 in royalties.

Testifying on behalf of the record manufacturers against the bill in a written statement, Mitch Miller incurred even greater enmity from old-line music companies by telling the committee that the coin-machine operators were chiefly responsible for making those songs into hits. His bold assertion that "some of the most successful" songwriters by-passed the music companies and went directly to the record companies to place their material negated much of the MPPA's testimony regarding the important role of the music publisher.

Despite appearances by a formidable group of ASCAP supporters, testimony by and about the music business was so contradictory that the committee reached no conclusion. Bryson filed only a minority report recommending the legislation, which died in late 1952.

With Otto Harbach ineligible and unwilling to serve for another term, in April 1953 a younger man took his place as ASCAP president: Stanley Adams, forty-five, an attorney before he became a working songwriter in the early 1930s. As a writer-director since 1944, he had built a reputation as a dedicated committee worker, ready to take on the most onerous chores, and a shrewd negotiator. His participation in the 1941 antitrust lawsuit and his activity in organizing the still-shadowy Songwriters of America, put him in the forefront of the reformers. The most powerful publisher members of the ASCAP board, Starr and Dreyfus, had switched their support to Adams in time for him to be voted in by unanimous acclamation. In a further reshuffling of the board, Louis Bernstein, a major MPPA official, was named vice-president, sharing the office with Fred Ahlert.

Ahlert, who had become a familiar figure to Washington legislators during previous copyright hearings, was put in charge of the presentation to the Senate Sub-Committee on Copyrights, to which the battle against the coin-machine business had shifted. In July, while music-business proponents were testifying on behalf of a bill similar to Kefauver-Bryson, Sydney Kaye of BMI threw what *Variety* dubbed "a Kaye-bomb" into the proceedings by joining ASCAP in the copyright fight. This marked the first time since BMI's formation that it took an active stand in support of any ASCAP position, and it broke its long cooperative association with the MOA. No new bill emerged from the deliberations.

The sudden reversal of BMI's position on jukebox exemption was due to the equally dramatic reversal of BMI and ASCAP in their position on the nation's coin music machines. In a December issue of *Cash Box,* a trade paper originally intended for the coin operators, but becoming a successful competitor of both *Billboard* and *Variety* because of its increased music coverage, a poll of all subscribers put BMI music in an 81.8/18.2 percent position over the ASCAP repertory in the pop, country-and-western, and rhythm-and-blues categories currently most popular on America's jukeboxes.

Such an astonishing share of the market was first forecast in October

1951, when BMI-licensed music took the first three places on *Billboard*'s "Honor Roll of Hits," as well as the sixth and ninth positions, its best showing since 1941. Most significant was the fact that four of the five were "legitimate pop songs," firm evidence, according to *Billboard,* that BMI publishers "could hustle and promote in the same league with top ASCAP pubbers, particularly in view of the new position radio deejays play in the current pattern of exploitation." The number-one song, "Because of You," was a revival of a 1941 BMI copyright; in second place was Hill & Range Songs' "I Get Ideas," set to the music of the old Argentine tango "Adios, Muchachos"; Acuff-Rose's Hank Williams's country hit "Cold Cold Heart" was third, now a Mitch Miller triumph in Tony Bennett's version, which had already sold over a million records. The other two were the William Saroyan–Ross Bagdasarian (his nephew) "dirty old Armenian man" song urging all pretty young women to "Come On-A-My House," sung by Rosemary Clooney and produced by Miller, and "It Is No Sin," written by two Philadelphia writers and popularized by the local Four Aces quartet on a master they paid for themselves, which, in turn, was purchased by Decca. Since January, BMI had tasted the fruits of success with "The Tennessee Waltz," "The Thing," "The Rovin' Kind," "Goodnight, Irene," and "On Top of Old Smoky," the last four published by Howard Richmond.

In the annual letter to stockholders, Haverlin noted that the company had paid $2.6 million in performing rights, from an income of $4.8 million, representing an increase in payments to publishers of $400,000 over the previous year. BMI had also made one of its annual rebates to all broadcast licensees, a 25 percent reduction during the last three months of the fiscal year. The strong relation with broadcaster customers was due in great part, Haverlin wrote, to the nationwide program clinics that had begun in the mid-1940s with demonstration in New York of a model music library, conceived by the company's station-relations staff as an educational service to station managers. In 1947, soon after he joined the company, Haverlin changed the emphasis of this promotional activity to programing and programers, with BMI-subsidized meetings in some major markets. Following invitations from many state broadcaster associations, some created for the occasion by Haverlin's friends in radio, BMI covered thirty-five states annually, with a road company of four specialist speakers, including a BMI executive, which joined local panels to discuss the latest developments in programing and strategy to cope with the looming specter of television, before an audience of local broadcasters. Taking over a natural function that the National Association of Radio and Television Broadcasters (the NAB brought into the television age) had overlooked, the clinics proved so popular and effective that Haverlin was offered, but finally declined, a better-paying position as president of the NARTB.

ASCAP executives and its board looked with suspicion on the clinics, muttering darkly that they were gatherings where broadcasters, determined to destroy the society, plotted together to push BMI music into popularity and ASCAP music into oblivion. ASCAP, too, had continued to ignore that large and vocal body of grass-roots broadcasters whose programing held up the mirror to changing American musical tastes. Throughout 1951, the society's problems were numerous and proliferating. Hollywood appeared determined to let the blanket licensing of motion pictures hang until ASCAP accepted a token payment. Authors and composers were arraying themselves on separate sides over the issue of equitable distribution, and the SPA was making its bold bid to take over the role of spokeman for songwriters. In the face of an ongoing mysterious government investigation of the music business, whose true goal was uncertain, the ruling block of motion-picture-owned publishers feared that the studios might be forced to divest themselves of their music interests, as they had been of their theater chains. The All-Industry Television Committee had dug in its heels, refusing to accept the most recent ASCAP per-program proposal, and, as provided in the consent decree, asked the district court in New York to set a fair fee. The annual membership gatherings and every ASCAP board meeting were interrupted by complaints about the foothold BMI and its publishers were getting on the leading music trade-paper charts. Since 1949, there had been few weeks when a BMI song was not among the top ten hits, and recently its share had jumped to a steady three out of ten.

Two efforts by ASCAP's membership to correct at least some of the society's problems were taking shape. The first was an offshoot of the short-lived Forum for Songwriters, in 1941, and the action by fourteen songwriters against the networks, BMI, and the NAB, charging them with conspiracy to destroy ASCAP. Stanley Adams had been at the head of this militant group of young ASCAP writers. It was at the insistence of leading publishers, who had promised to dispose of the action as part of the price for an end to the ASCAP-radio war, that Adams, Paul Cunningham, and other leaders of the plaintiffs agreed to accept $15,000 toward legal fees.

The music business first became aware in the late spring of 1951 of activity by Adams and other former plaintiffs in the 1941 action to do something about BMI. First identifying their organization as the Guild, or League, of American Songwriters, later the Songwriters of America, a steering committee, whose members preferred to remain unknown for the time being, solicited contributions to a $250,000 fund from the 100 ASCAP writers whose income from the society aggregated one million dollars. The money was to be used to fight not only BMI but also the "unfair treatment by publishers, record company domination of the song business, payola, artist favoritism, moving picture company power in the music industry, and the closing of avenues for the display and performance of a song." Publishers were not asked to support the organization, because "a canoe with both writers and publishers is sure to rock." The group's attorney was Robert Daru, who, as chief counsel to a Senate committee in the early 1930s, had conducted an investigation into underworld activity in American business, and had represented the plaintiffs in their 1941 suit against BMI.

Spokesmen for the organization were quick to point out that the fund was being collected to defray legal expenses, including any for an appearance before the Supreme Court, and that neither ASCAP nor the SPA was involved, though known to be sympathetic. By October, the fund had grown to $300,000, helped by a checkoff contribution of 5 percent of ASCAP writer royalties, and Daru had been displaced by John Schulman. With most of its anticipated funding in hand, in late 1951 the group announced that action would await the outcome of a complaint against BMI filed with the Justice Department during the summer.

That petition was made in connection with an appearance by ASCAP, in August 1951, before the New York district court, responding to a demand by the All-Industry Television Committee for a fair rate from the society. ASCAP asked Judge Henry W. Goddard to approve the terms it had offered in March to the committee, which represented fifty-six stations, or about half of those in the industry. ASCAP had already stopped accepting interim payments from the litigants, a move agreed upon in a pact made early in 1950, which called for eventual payments retroactive to January 1, 1949. In the meantime, a lump sum, based on each station's income, was being put into escrow each month.

Simultaneously with its plea, ASCAP filed a 100-page document, known as the Harbach Affidavit, asking for new language in the amended order of 1950. It argued that broadcasters would "skim off" the society's "gems" and devote the remainder of their programing to the BMI repertory. If the plea was granted, the society could refuse a per-program license to any radio or television station that had a blanket BMI license. The claim was made that otherwise BMI had an unfair competitive advantage. Remembering that the society had been told in early 1941 that "when BMI became big enough to hurt ASCAP" the government would step in and change things, legal counsel and the board anticipated an early favorable action.

The Harbach Affidavit was passed to the Justice Department, and a lengthy investigative process began, which eventually produced a lengthy request for information on eighty-six points. Disturbed by the inaction, in March 1952 ASCAP reminded the public and the press of its plea for relief by filing a formal request for an investigation of the charges incorporated in the affidavit, essentially that BMI operated as a combination in restraint of trade through its relations with the broadcasting industry, which made BMI, in effect, its creature. Paul Ackerman of *Billboard,* who had been covering the BMI-ASCAP situation since its genesis, wrote in April that while ASCAP "has endeavored to set itself up solidly in TV, and while it has been fighting to re-establish itself in films, it has been constantly losing ground on another front—promotion . . . it has steadfastly refused to promote itself to music users. The result has been that BMI . . . has run the latter a very fast race. BMI, of course, is a wholly-owned corporation, the structure of which permits money to be freely expended for promotion. ASCAP has always taken the position that such funds as are collected must be distributed to the membership.''

Rising economic stakes and the changing balance of power in the electronic entertainment business were major factors in the continuing strained relations between broadcasters and ASCAP throughout this period. Almost overnight, the value of television as a source of income to the society had grown to undreamed-of proportions. In early 1946, television had not yet become a big business, and ASCAP was content with its dollar-a-year arrangements with stations. Anybody with the modest sum of $272,500 could buy all the equipment needed to go into television, according to a promotion pamphlet designed by Dumont Laboratories' sales department to sell the Paramount subsidiary's transmitting technology. In thirty months, the sales pitch continued, the station owner would make a net operating profit before taxes of $47,983.97, or 17.6 percent of his capital investment. Critics argued that profits should run even higher, because advertising time rates had been increased. The constantly rising valuation placed on the Blue Network, after the Supreme Court upheld an FCC order to RCA to divest itself of its second network, dramatically illustrated the profits being made in broadcasting.

To comply with the court's ruling, NBC had formed a separate corporation, the Blue Network, Inc., which owned WJZ, New York, WENR, Chicago, and KCO, San Francisco, and then sold it to the Life Saver King, Edward Noble. The sale was finally approved in the fall of 1942, provided Noble disposed of radio station WMCA in New York, which he had acquired for $850,000 but which was now worth over $1.5 million. During the protracted negotiations, the Blue Network not only showed no loss for the first time, but also made a million-dollar profit, which went to Noble. He changed the network's name to the American Broadcasting Company after recouping a fifth of his investment in the first year of operation. Because of the boom in building new radio stations after the government lifted its wartime freeze on new construction, ABC grew from 195 affiliates in 1945 to 282 five years later. One reason for its success was the presence on the schedule of Bing Crosby, who had helped to build CBS into a major network before moving to NBC in the early 1930s; he now became ABC's most important personality and introduced the taped radio program to broadcasting. Taping resulted in considerable savings for ABC, which otherwise would have paid overtime to talent and engineers for repeat broadcasts to the West Coast. With tape simplifying recorded broadcasts, ABC was the first network to adopt disk-jockey programing on a national basis, in 1947, followed reluctantly by CBS and NBC.

In 1950, with a television network of thirteen stations, ABC ran a poor fourth to its rivals, NBC, CBS, and Dumont, the last of which had a network of fifty-two affiliates, making it second to NBC. However, ABC had become, and remained, a target of vital importance for motion-picture companies that wanted to get into the new picture-and-sound medium. In late 1948, 20th Century-Fox offered $15 million for the ABC radio and television networks, the latter including owned-and-operated facilities in New York, Chicago, Detroit, Los Angeles, and San Francisco. The deal fell through only because the film company would not meet Noble's asking price of $21 million. CBS began negotiations in the spring of 1951 to acquire the ABC network for $26 million, so that it could add the Chicago, Detroit, and San Francisco television stations to the only two video facilities it actually owned, New York's WCBS-TV and KNXT-TV in San Francisco, the cornerstones of its operation. William Paley intended to sell off the ABC radio network, now with about $35 million in billings, and its New York and Los Angeles television stations, to parties unknown, for $20 million. Because of its complexity, the CBS-ABC transaction broke down, but offers followed at once, from United Paramount Theaters and International Telephone and Telegraph, to purchase Noble's holdings. The ITT offer was withdrawn. The Paramount negotiation terminated when Noble insisted that he receive sufficient UPT common stock to give him a major controlling interest.

UPT officials, principally Leonard H. Goldenson, did not want to let ABC get away. A graduate of Harvard Law School, who joined Paramount soon after receiving his degree, Goldenson became head of its theater chain in 1938, at the age of thirty-two. The Supreme Court ruling in *U.S.* v. *Paramount et al.*, which ended the control of Hollywood by the Big Five and their satellites convinced Goldenson that the film industry's future lay with television. Historically, Paramount had been the earliest of the studios to turn an eye on the technology in which Vladimir Zworykin pioneered. It lent money to Paley in 1928 to swing his purchase of CBS, but only in order to gain a foothold in the broadcasting business. When *U.S.* v. *Paramount* was filed in late 1945, Paramount was already well on its way to building a vast empire. It had a 50 percent interest in the Dumont Laboratories, owned television stations in Chicago and Los Angeles, had already filed applications for other stations on behalf of a wholly owned subsidiary, and owned a major interest in British theater-television patents. The consent decree had put an end to block booking and severed the film companies from ownership of vast theater-chain monopolies, with which they had stifled all competition. Remaining were their production facilities.

Long before the January 1, 1950, deadline for disencumbering itself of all theater holdings, Paramount Pictures split into two distinct corporate entities—Paramount Pictures Corporation and United Paramount Theaters—which Goldenson continued to head. Paramount films were sold to its former outlets through a theater-by-theater arrangement. Any question as to UPT's right to acquire television facilities was cleared with the FCC immediately after the Supreme Court ruling, and Goldenson prepared to buy ABC. Within three years of the separation, he had bought and sold theatrical real estate worth $50 million, in order to raise the $25 million asked by Noble for a merger of UPT and ABC, as American Broadcasting–Paramount Theaters, which was consummated in 1953, with Goldenson as president.

During the years preceding the union, the television business had gone from a loss of $25 million in its first big year, 1949, with total revenues of $34 million, to a $41.6-million profit in 1951. Serving only sixty-three markets through 108 stations, television was doing half the business of AM radio, which had 1,200 markets served by more than 2,000 stations. The profits in television, however, were going to the local stations, and not to the networks. In 1951, NBC and CBS just managed to get into the black, and in 1952 they showed their first profit from video, a net of one million for NBC, slightly less for CBS. A single independent station, either NBC's affiliate WTMJ-TV, in Milwaukee, or the Paramount-owned WBKB-TV, the CBS affiliate in Chicago, showed profits the same year matching those of the entire NBC and CBS television operations. Ninety-four of the 108 television stations telecasting in 1952 reported profits, and, of them, seventeen, mostly network-owned and operated, averaged a one-million-dollar gain. None of the forty stations in a single market suffered a loss, profits averaging $654,000. Although the four networks' profits were relatively small, $9.9 million in all, they and their owned-and-operated stations accounted for 55 percent of total time sales, or $180 million. ASCAP's collections from television in 1952 came chiefly from the networks, fees from the independent stations still being put into escrow. The networks collected at least half their ASCAP fees from affiliates, who, because of complicated bookkeeping practices, were not yet aware of the extent of that contribution of its existence.

Income from television more than made up ASCAP's loss of $1.3 million in theater-seat collections, part of which was also recouped by the payment of about $600,000 a year by the studios for at-the-source licensing. The producer-distributors were learning not only how to live with television, but also that this potential enemy was a medium to which Hollywood could make a lucrative contribution. A tentative collaboration began in late 1952 when Paramount, Columbia, and United Artists activated their television subsidiaries and began making half-hour filmed series. Four years earlier, when the picture business were suffering from a postwar recession and the video-station business beginning its climb, Columbia had formed Screen Gems, to make filmed commercials for national television sponsors. After more than 200 were made during the next two years, Screen Gems in 1951 sold its first made-for-video package, to Du Pont: seven half-hour historical dramas for *Cavalcade of America*. In the spring of 1952, Screen Gems introduced feature-motion-picture budgeting to television and agreed to sell a thirty-minute anthology package, featuring film stars who had not yet been seen on the video screen, to Ford for $20,000 a unit, a one-third reduction of its production costs. As the studios had been doing for years, Columbia expected to get back the other $10,000 and more from rerun distribution. The success of the *Ford Theatre* put Screen Gems in the forefront of TV film production and syndication, with packaged shows that continued to be sold around the world for years.

In July 1952, *Variety* reported that the production of films for video, ranging from commercials to package shows, had become a $100-million enterprise. Twenty-two percent of all network shows were now on film, and informed thinking was that the figure would grow to 75 percent for the same reasons that a majority of radio programs had been forced to go on tape or electrical transcription.

Three percent of that $100-million business was for libraries of three-minute musical programs, designed for the television disk jockey. The largest libraries, United Television Programs, with 1,300 filmed musical subjects, and Official Films, which had 1,200 subjects in its *Music Hall Varieties* series, charged a minimum of $300 a month to stations for a basic library of about 400 three-minute features. A small New York firm filmed young Broadway and night-club performers to be lip-synched with the latest popular record releases.

Hollywood producer-distributors watched and waited after Herbert Yates's Republic Pictures, the first of them to take the jump, leased a library of 104 Western action features to major-market stations. WCBS-TV paid $200,000 to show the movies exclusively in the New York market, and others followed that lead. The impact of Westerns had already been demonstrated, when, in 1948, William Boyd bought back control of his *Hopalong Cassidy* movies and sold them to NBC. Cut from their original feature length, they served as hour and half-hour programs, making Boyd so independently wealthy, from the sale of subsidiary rights to clothing, gadgets, and gimmicks spawned by the character, that he financed a new package of fifty-two half-hour Cassidy pictures for local syndication.

Fearful that movie exhibitors would immediately boycott all products of the first major studio to cooperate with television, the top eight studios sat on their treasures. The negatives for 4,057 full-length movies and 6,000 one- and two-reel shorts made between 1935 and 1945 represented a potential quarter-billion-dollar income from television. Walt Disney, whose new releases were bid for with reckless abandon, turned down a million-dollar offer for television rights to a package of cartoon shorts. Most Disney movies were in color, and his caution was correct in view of the ceaseless competition going on between RCA and CBS to introduce the first successful color-television programs. Time was on the side of the studios. Six hundred hours of new feature movies filled up only one tenth of a vast empty belly that was eating up more entertainment than any other medium ever known to man.

Years of failure to placate Hollywood's background-music writers and their Screen Composers Association with enough financial recognition of their contributions to ASCAP's repertory were crucial to BMI's success in gaining an early advantage in the control of music used on video film. ASCAP's revised payment system credited the performance of music written expressly as background with 1/1,000th of a point, whereas a popular song, ordered expressly for the film or selected from past standards, got full credit. With its flexible payment structure, and free of Justice Department supervision, BMI was in a position to offer attractive guarantees to film composers and producers for television rights. At the urging of Robert Burton's office, BMI publishers began to secure the rights to music on such highly popular shows as *Kukla, Fran and Ollie, This Is Your Life,* and *Howdy Doody.* Several important cue and bridge libraries opened BMI houses, and many leading video production companies formed "file-cabinet" music firms, into which all rights to background music were placed, secured from their composers on a work-for-hire basis. BMI compensated these composers by guaranteeing a flat annual fee until machinery could be set up to gauge the value and count the use of background music on video films and feature movies used on television.

In June 1953, a new BMI office was opened in Hollywood to deal specifically with producers and screen composers. Some months before, 150 movie, radio, and television composers, most of them in ASCAP, had formed a rival Composers Guild of America. Plans were made by its founder, Leith Stevens, to form an eastern branch.

While license fees from television climbed, soon to overtake those from radio as both ASCAP's and BMI's major source of income, in spite of the medium's relatively small use of their catalogues, the fortunes of network radio were waning. The days of fortune and glory for the NBC, CBS, and ABC chains, whose profits subsidized the more glamorous and potentially more profitable world of television, slowly slipped away to local stations, whose major offering was recorded music. Network radio income began to erode, particularly in the markets where the 108 video facilities operated.

Meanwhile, new AM and FM stations were springing up, leading some to expect that FM broadcasting, with its more faithful reproduction of music, would capture most of the new audience being conditioned by disk jockeys to recorded musical entertainment. A ruling by the FCC in June 1945, when forty-six commercial FM stations were on the air and 430 FM applications waited for approval, moved frequency broadcasting into a higher-frequency band, for which neither transmitters nor receivers were available. Pent-up wartime demand for new AM receivers and sending equipment, plus RCA's concentration on black-and-white television sets for home use, had put production of FM technology on the back burner. During this transitional period, FM stations already on the air had obtained temporary permission to operate on the lower band, in order to serve the "interest, convenience and necessity" of owners of equipment already in use. "Simulcasting" of AM programs by FM stations proved to be both felicitous and inexpensive for station owners, who no longer needed separate temporary transmitters while waiting for the completion of new facilities.

The initial breakthrough of FM-receiver manufacture in 1949, with 1.5 million sets produced, failed to meet the demand stimulated by new interest in high fidelity for the home. At least 7.5 million FM sets were in use by early 1951, but the shortage persisted. Commercial FM broadcasting appeared to stabilize at around 700 stations, few of them expected to survive the next five years, when 30 million television receivers would lure audiences away from sound-only listening.

Those daytime FM operations that shared in a $1.5-million advertising gross in 1950 made their profits from investments in Transit Radio, which carried music and advertising on local transportation; Storecast, which beamed recorded music and advertising into supermarkets and large stores; and Muzak, or Functional Radio, which provided background music for factories, restaurants, hotels, and offices.

During radio's adolescence, advertisers had pushed their agencies to buy time on the air. Now, major advertisers were again doing the same on television. NBC-TV had become the largest single advertising medium in the country, grossing $126 million for time charges and programs, more than *Life*, the most successful print publication, which did an annual business of $94 million in space and production charges.

With only 108 stations offering time, every evening segment on the four television networks was sold before the 1951–52 season opened, and the chains had had the opportunity to select only those sponsors who were willing to pay for high-quality programing. Because network radio was the only place in broadcasting left for sponsors who could not find a place on the picture tube, vigorous competition to sell them time enforced drastic cuts in talent and production fees and major discounts in time rates, which hastened the death of a medium that offered only the same face as in the past. Rather than provide adequate replacements for the Jack Benny, Bob Hope, Edgar Bergen–Charlie McCarthy, Amos 'n' Andy, and Fibber McGee and Molly shows, the networks simply reduced their asking prices. There was a common feeling that network radio could no longer better what local stations were offering—certainly not the news and music that made them profitable. Wire services brought them news from around the world, and the successful introduction of LPs and 45s made all kinds of music available to even the lowliest 250-watter and its disk jockeys.

As troubled by the direction toward which America's record spinners appeared to be heading for the 1950s as ASCAP was by BMI's growing share of the music, Tin Pan Alley's old-guard publishers found a ray of hope in television's need for better-quality music, now that its programing was acquiring more maturity. Disk-jockey broadcasts on 50,000-watt stations around the country, with their ceaseless repetition of a small number of new songs, had effectively destroyed the value of those late-night dance-band remote plugs that had once made songs into hits. With more network affiliates running disk-jockey shows and fewer picking up broadcasts from remote spots, ASCAP overhauled its after-11:00 P.M. payment schedule and reduced the value of a remote-band plug. Publishers now received ten cents per song per station, or between $2.40 and $4.50 for a twenty-four-to-forty-five-station network, pittances that could not possibly offset the cost of contacting bandleaders, let along such payola as cut ins.

The music business began to look to television for its salvation when comics who had started in vaudeville and were transforming that medium into the most popular video fare began digging into the past for the songs and the special material they had once offered at the Palace. Television producers, loath to use songs that had not already proven their audience appeal, were setting the most lavish production numbers on the high-rated Milton Berle, Perry Como, and Dinah Shore shows to great standards of the past. By the winter of 1950–51, all but twenty-three of the Music Publishers Contact Employees 550 members were gainfully employed at their craft. Almost overnight a television plug had become worth ten times a radio shot. The days of no deals, no returns on standards songs disappeared, and salesmen were given a free hand in arranging special discounts, depending on the size of an order. It still cost a few cents to print a piece of popular music, and the highest profits came from the fifty- to sixty-cent standards, even with the higher royalties that went to production writers. The old music being featured on television became the bread and butter of Tin Pan Alley. Except for "The Tennessee Waltz," few of the new popular hits were selling as they might have in the old days. "They Try to Tell Us We're Too Young," second only to Acuff-Rose's success, had trouble getting over the half-million mark. It was not that the retail outlets were not there. During the past ten years, there had been a 418 percent increase in music sales, to $337 million for 1948, and the number of stores carrying printed music and phonograph records had doubled, according to the Census Bureau, even if they concentrated on the latter. California, New York, Illinois, Pennsylvania, and Michigan, areas with the most television coverage, led in music sales, accounting for almost half.

Warner Brothers, Max Dreyfus, the Big Three, and Paramount Music used television exploitation to create new markets. Soon they were doing a $2.5-million gross business in a field that formerly had been monopolized by the standard classical music houses. With knowledgeable and accommodating field salesmen, and imaginative advertising in magazines directed at public-school educators, they changed the song material used in elementary schools from the Bach, Beethoven, and Brahms that Victor's Red Seal division had done so much to make acceptable, to the standard songs they were plugging on television, published in choral, band, and symphonic arrangements suitable for five-to-eighteen-year-olds.

Rumors of sheet-music price fixing by jobbers sparked the first government investigation into printed-music pricing in twenty years, bringing back memories of the Max Meyer–Music Dealers Service lawsuit of the early 1930s. Herman Starr and G. Schirmer had refused to do business with Jenkins Music, of Kansas City, a major jobber-retailer, because of its discounting policy. Information about similar discriminatory practices and accounts of price cutting by other jobbers followed the first indication of the Justice Department's interest. Within a few months, the focus of government attention appeared to have shifted to the connection between the film industry and the music business. The books of Paramount–Famous Music, the Big Three, and Shapiro, Bernstein, connected with Columbia Pictures and Decca Records in Mood Music, were examined by federal investigators without any clue as to the purpose of the inspections. Concurrently, the antitrust action that had been filed in March 1950 by E. H. "Buddy" Morris against Warner, Loew's, 20th Century-Fox, Paramount, Universal, and fourteen publishing companies was winding toward final settlement, which came in September 1952. Morris had asked for triple damages, amounting to six million dollars and an order restraining the defendants from monopolizing the publication of movie music and songs and conspiring to fix prices and limit competition. The complaint pointed out that by such conspiracy the defendants "succeeded in establishing control of at least 60% of all compositions" used in motion pictures. That control became possible once the five major film studios took over their "captive affiliates": Witmark, Remick, Harms, New World, and Atlas, owned entirely by Warner; Robbins, Feist, Miller, in which Loew's had a 51 percent interest, 20th Century-Fox holding the remainder; Harry Warren Music, 51 percent owned by Loew's, the balance by Warren; Shubert and Advanced Music, of which Warner owned half; Fox's Movietone Music, and some others.

Morris's out-of-court victory changed the process about which he had complained. The new arrangement, which ran for five years, enabled any publisher to bid for publication rights during a sixty-day period, provided the writer and producer had not already come to a publishing understanding. Under the old practice a studio peremptorily assigned all rights to one of its own affiliates. Few writers still had exclusive pacts with film companies, preferring to free-lance, but the settlement opened up the situation for small independent firms like Morris's, which had traditionally been Hollywood's victims.

The five major studios had already written off the importance of a music-publishing apparatus as a prime vehicle for building up box-office receipts. A Peatman survey of the most performed songs in the 1942–52 period suggested a serious decline in the number of hit songs coming from films and the Broadway stage. Their place among top songs of the year had dropped from 80 percent of them in 1942 and 1943 to 70 percent the following year, and then to an average of 40 percent for the succeeding seven years. Tin Pan Alley blamed songwriters for this or attributed it to the changing whims of producers and directors. A song no longer was spotted several times in a feature movie, and at best received only a single full chorus treatment, hardly enough to boost it into a hit. Audiences no longer walked into screen theaters whistling the song that had brought them to the box office.

With the first copyright term of many compositions nearing expiration and the SPA fighting to overturn the traditional renewal process, in June 1951 Warner dickered for the sale of its music-holding operation, MPHC. The move was part of a program to raise cash in order to purchase company stock in the open market and maintain slipping per-share profits. Between three and a half and four million was being asked, but Warner insisted on retaining first-refusal synchronization rights to the entire catalogue. Among the bidders was the Allegheny Corporation, with which it was rumored Herman Starr had struck a secret understanding. When he found that most songwriters in the MPHC stable were ready to turn over their second-term renewal rights without protest, he advised his superiors to take the company off the market. With the final divorce of its screen theaters imminent, Loew's simplified the structure of its subsidiary music holdings by buying out all but one of the four remaining original partners in Robbins Music, paying a half-million dollars for their combined 17 percent share. Five years earlier, Loew's had paid Jack Robbins $673,000, so that he could pay all federal and New York State taxes and still retain half a million dollars for his 26 percent interest in the entire Robbins, Feist & Miller catalogue. At the time, Tin Pan Alley estimated the worth at between eight and ten million dollars, and worried about the deflationary aspects of the transaction. Clearly, it had not affected the growing value of music companies.

The doubling of home record players between 1945 and 1950, half of the more than 25 million capable of playing all three speeds, was the final blow in toppling the old-time professional manager and his minions from their place in the exploitation process and in elevating A & R men to the seats of power. At their right hands were the most influential disk jockeys, who now were the first to be "romanced" by publishers. Once the deejays pushed a record and it was moving up on the charts, the publishers resorted to the second line of plugging, the live radio and television performers. Though they ruled the roost now, the A & R men had no better record of success than those whom they had displaced. In the first half of 1952, the six major manufacturers—Columbia, Capitol, Mercury, RCA Victor, Decca, MGM—released 788 recordings of copyrighted music, only 66 of which appeared on *Billboard*'s best-seller charts. Mitch Miller, who chose all music for the current industry leader, Columbia, was the most successful, with 12 percent of all hits. Ten publishers supplied 44 percent of all combined pop, country-and-western and rhythm-and-blues recorded material.

Because human instinct tends to seek out winners, these publishers scrambled for the attention and favor of the most successful A & R men, giving them the first look and a promise of exclusive first-release rights to all promising material. Often months passed before the promised disk came out, and then it might be by a slipping artist or an untried one. The day had passed when a top-rated songwriter demonstrated a song for the professional manager and walked out with an advance of $1,000 or better because everybody was certain that it was a hit. Only major houses, with solid cash reserves, were now in a position to hand out $200 advances on a large scale, hoping that the law of averages would work in their favor. Smaller firms had to be content with the leavings, and took new songs on a consignment basis, to peddle to the record companies before a modest advance was made. More sophisticated young writers went directly to their favorite A & R men, and when their material was taken, it often was on condition that it go to a publisher of the A & R man's choice, chosen either because of personal friendship or by the traditional under-the-desk arrangement that had been typical of the business since the 1920s and probably before.

Veteran music men chafed under a system that relegated them to the role of money men, responsible only for funding the new exploitation chain. Because their contracts with the MPCE union precluded them from employing record-promotion men and they needed songpluggers to work the television performers, they paid for promotion under the table or through the recording artist. After Martin Block and other disk jockeys had become so important that they needed personal treatment, independent promotion men emerged, often former press agents, such as Barney McDevitt, Mel Adams, Henry Okun, Jack Egan, and Jim McCarthy, who made certain that disks sent by artist or publisher would not be lost in the shuffle, but would get on the air.

The most successful graduate from the record-promotion men's ranks, Howard S. "Howie" Richmond, of the Richmond and Robbins music families, had worked for recording artists before he began to promote recordings of material he himself published. He was already the personal friend of a number of key deejays and maintained steady correspondence and telephone contact to keep them aware of his latest assignments. He had broken into the publishing business when he took a test pressing of Phil Harris's RCA Victor recording of "The Thing" to BMI and got enough expense and traveling money to put it on the charts in major cities. This almost instantaneous success as a publisher was not a unique occurrence, and would not have been possible without his disk-jockey friends. Though it took a few years, by 1953 such veterans as Starr were persuaded that the record-promotion man was, for purposes of boosting a recorded tune, superior to the old-fashioned song plugger. "If you have a tune the public wants it soon shows up," he told *Variety* in September 1953. "If it's not in the groove, nothing will help, no matter how you knock yourself out and no matter how many plugs you land." Like Starr's, most major old-line music firms had already reduced their professional departments to a minimum and closed them down in the cities where vaudeville circuits once headquartered. Many of the old professional managers were now operating their own music companies, affiliated with BMI, or had left the business entirely.

The guaranteed-advance contract, keyed to securing recordings and local performances, that BMI continued to offer publishers had been regarded by ASCAP and Starr as a minor problem so long as the performances of BMI music were negligible and its showing on trade-paper charts insignificant. During its early years, BMI contracts offered to publishers with substantial catalogues were handled by Sydney Kaye or Merritt Tompkins, the company's first general manager and a veteran of the standard classical-music world. Several other employees handled arrangements with smaller firms dealing chiefly in recorded copyrights, and were assigned to the task on the basis of their particular expertise. Gradually, all primary responsibility for most new contracts with popular-music publishers was shifted to a young house counsel, Robert J. Burton, who joined BMI in January 1941. Born in 1914 in New York, he had received his degree from Columbia Law School in 1937 and then joined the law firm headed by Arthur Garfield Hays, who had been a lawyer, without compensation, for the SPA in its formative years. In 1943, Burton was named director of publisher relations for BMI, and the following year an assistant secretary to the board of directors.

No set criteria had yet been developed by BMI for handling advances of guarantees to new affiliates. Decisions were made by Burton on the basis of an applicant's past experience in the music business or his access to promising non-ASCAP songwriters. Most contracts were for five years, renewable only if BMI agreed, and all carried a sixty-day cancellation clause. Conservatism was enforced by the BMI board, a product of its anticipation that BMI might be mothballed at any moment, its activities terminated by a majority of its stockholders.

One of Carl Haverlin's initial acts as BMI president was to put Burton in charge of repertory accumulation, as vice-president for publisher relations. With Haverlin's full confidence, Burton immediately placed more emphasis in his negotiations on productivity than on activity, or number of copyrights. Failing to best ASCAP music men at their own game, he soon abandoned his unproductive strategy of paying forty-eight dollars for a network performance. Soon after *Variety* shifted from the Peatman survey, with its synthetic popularity based on prime-time network air play, to a full-page disk-jockey popularity chart, Burton sought out music men with access to the key record-spinners who worked on large stations in major cities. Their request programs more truly reflected changing public response to new music, as well as the growing importance of the BMI catalogue he was building. Small publishers were given contracts that focused on disk-jockey performances. They received as much as $40,000 a year, larger ones up to and over $100,000.

Following the annual stockholders' meeting in October 1952, Burton was put in charge of BMI's new combined publisher and writer activities, and the former director of publisher relations, Robert B. Sour, was elected a vice-president. A Princeton graduate, whose father had been a friend of Kaye's, he wrote popular music as a hobby while working on Wall Street, turning professional in the late 1920s, when he wrote the American words for "Body and Soul." His application for membership in ASCAP was rejected, despite seconding by Johnny Green, the composer of "Body and Soul." During the Depression, Sour was on the staff of the Federal Works Theater, which he left to join BMI in February 1940 as lyric editor and staff lyricist. BMI's first published song, "We Could Make Such Beautiful Music," was a Sour collaboration, as were "Practice Makes Perfect," "Walkin' By the River," and "I See a Million People," other early BMI hits. As director of writer relations in the late 1940s, Sour was an active proponent of a writer payment plan and was put in charge of the program when it was adopted in 1949. His assistant in the writer department was the veteran song plugger George Marlo, former president of the MPCE and a storied character in the music business.

With a larger and more able staff, which gave him opportunity to expand his activities, Burton took on a much more active role in the operation of BMI Canada, the subsidiary formed in conjunction with the Canadian Association of Broadcasters during the 1941 music war. He was made its general manager in 1947. His early education in France and his fluency in the language worked to BMI's advantage. Under his direction, BMI Canada had a roster of 120 affiliated composers and 27 publishers, and a catalogue of 5,000 works, one third of them in French.

BMI's own writer-affiliation program was similarly productive, with 115 composers and lyricists under contract in the winter of 1952. Not all affiliated writers at that time had yearly guarantees, but those who did received amounts varying between $250 and $3,000. During the past year, BMI contract writers had amassed 2.5 million performances, but their share of royalties was not yet in proportion to that paid publishers. The following year, for example, BMI paid only $72,325 to its writers, but $3.4 million to the publishers. There were, in addition, many songwriters who were under contract to BMI publishers on either an exclusive or a song-to-song basis. They received their performance fees, if at all, directly from the publishers, who racked up the majority of BMI performances and were responsible for a reported four to one performance advantage over ASCAP on independent stations. There, programing was predominantly recorded music and regular news summaries, the latter usually taken from the wire-service ticker and read immediately. An increased portion of the music they played came from the independent record companies, whose copyright-owning subsidiaries affiliated with BMI as quickly as possible, for the four-cent-a-station royalty. The policy of paying for recorded air play, which was instituted in 1940, reaped dividends its designer, Sydney Kaye, had never envisioned. After analyzing a single *BMI Record Bulletin,* which was mailed each week to all stations, *Variety* found that 175 out of the 275 records listed were products of independent labels, and half of all titles were published by the desk-drawer copyright arms, created specifically to control the music they used as well as to collect performance money from BMI. Most independent record companies concentrated on the rhythm-and-blues field, a market that had recently shown renewed activity.

In many cases, part of a BMI publisher's advance or guarantee, which could be as much as $100,000, went to prime the independents' pumps. Publishers used it to wheel and deal with the smaller labels. They paid for recording sessions, accepted reduced mechanical royalties, and picked up the tab for exploitation by disk-jockey or local-distributor payola, all with the expectation that the more local performances BMI logged, the surer one could be that his annual guarantee would be renewed.

When, for the first time since 1941, BMI songs captured the first five places on "Your Hit Parade," in March 1952, many young ASCAP publishers and songwriters, who felt they were not being paid what they ought to get even under the revised distribution scheme, took a new look at association with BMI. A number of publishers who had started out with AS-CAP had been successful in the early 1940s had already opened BMI affiliates. Others followed, and by 1952 it was difficult to name a younger ASCAP publisher board member who had no sort of affiliation with the rival organization. One aspirant to the ASCAP directorate, Buddy Morris, had to purge himself of all connections with BMI in order to get on the board. Morris had been one of the first ASCAP music men to join BMI, having come into possession of one of its earliest country hits, "Pistol Packin' Mama," in 1943.

Under pressure from dissidents, ASCAP, in 1950, began expanded spot-check logging of independent stations. Its philosophy had always been to "follow the dollar," and because the vast proportion of its revenue came from major networks, the emphasis had remained on their programing. In early 1953, John Peatman, of the Audience Research Institute, was brought in to take charge of the society's logging operation. He added 170 local stations to the year-round logging of the networks made by the society from a complete recapitulation of all music played from sign-on to sign-off, provided by the chains. Performance credits of one point for each popular song were multiplied by the number of stations carrying each performance. Seventy local stations, scattered around the country and representing about

100,000 hours of programing each quarter, were logged regularly on a spot-check basis. The remaining hundred stations, from ten regional areas, were logged on a rotating basis for two and a half hours a day. Every performance on the seventy fixed stations received a full performance credit, and a song logged on one of the rotating sample received seven and a half credits. Television was logged on a similar principle—the four networks on a census basis, and three selected local stations each day, with a performance receiving three points.

The attraction of BMI's logging system, based entirely on broadcast performances, even to publisher members of ASCAP, was brought home in March 1953 with the consummation of a contract between the society's seventeenth-highest-rated music house—Santly, Joy—and BMI, in connection with a new BMI-affiliated publishing company. Joseph Csida, former editor of *Billboard* and once head of A & R for RCA Victor, was a principal in the new firm, Trinity Music, with George Joy and his son Eddie. Their new contract represented the latest thinking of BMI and Robert Burton on the matter of plugs: that forty performances on large stations, scattered around the country, represented more value than a network shot over forty affiliates. As Abel Green pointed out in *Variety,* BMI had come to this conclusion because "cut-ins, payola, and other angles could put some tune up in fallacious high brackets via a series of blanket network performances and it would still not achieve the desired saturation that comes from the multiplicity of local originations."

Trinity received a "unique incentive advance" of $55,000 for the first year, to be paid off at premium performance rates, higher than BMI's basic four- and six-cent fees. The second year's advance would be exactly what had been earned in the first; the third, that earned in the second; and so on for five years. A series of performance plateaus was established, and as each was reached, the premium air-play rate dropped to a lower one.

The Santly, Joy deal put a new spotlight on BMI's logging operation, which except for rates had not changed since it was first put in place in 1940. One tenth of all stations in the United States, about 325, representing a cross-section of every type of broadcasting facility, were logged each quarter. The networks were logged, as by ASCAP, on a census basis, using the same material furnished by the chains to the society. Every network performance was credited with a minimum of seventy-five points, regardless of how many stations were hooked up, unless the number was higher, in which case an additional credit was added for each. Television logging covered all of the current stations every quarter, and performance payments were made on the same four- and six-cent basis as on radio. Because BMI logging picked up 150,000 performances on average for a hit song, an aggressive firm like Hill & Range could pile up two million performances in a year, producing a quarter-million-dollar payment from BMI. Early in 1953, ASCAP asked to examine the logs sent to BMI by local stations, which listed every selection used regardless of licensing affiliation. After being refused, the society adopted the position that disk jockeys on local stations were directed by their employers to favor BMI music, or did so because BMI was "owned by the industry," having advertised for years, on all promotional material, "If it's BMI, it's your's."

BMI's consistently flamboyant broadcast customer-relations program, directed by Haverlin, was having a marked effect on ASCAP's controlling publisher group, which made belated efforts to catch up with the rival's gains. It was feared that such projects as the *TV Sketch Book,* containing short skits built around "Pin-Up Hits," informational material prepared expressly for disk jockeys, and a growing presence in the modern American concert-music world would have a serious effect in 1959 when contracts with radio and television expired.

However, a new fire was breaking out, one that the old guard would never extinguish and that changed the entire course of American music. The large ASCAP music houses had finally succeeded in breaking through the A & R men's "iron curtain," and were going directly to radio and TV live plugs to demonstrate the latest ballad or imported novelty song they had found. According to the Peatman survey of the most-played songs on radio and television in the year ending June 31, 1953, the new medium was crowding out network radio as a publisher's most effective plugging medium. The survey's top song, "I Believe," an ASCAP song, received 15,738 performance points on radio, but 18,601 on television. Radio was no longer responsible for the largest sheet sales. Thirteen of the year's best sellers did not appear among the thirty-five most-played songs. The steady decline in music sales had not abated. The day of the multimillion seller faded with the amazing success of "The Tennessee Waltz." A publisher had to be content with a half-million sale at best, after months of plugging on radio and television, and his $20,000 from a million-record seller was shared with songwriters.

Both small and large music companies made drastic reductions in overhead and operating expenses. The retail price for a new popular song was increased from forty to fifty cents, long the regular price for a movie or production song, and from twenty-three to twenty-five cents for jobbers and thirty-five cents for dealers. Most publishers adopted a "no return" policy on new songs until they showed some activity on the trade-paper charts. Howard Richmond's firms issued about 100 songs in 1953, six of which attained a "return" privilege. The other ninety-four sold an average of 200 copies. Publishers saved money on arranging and engraving dance-band arrangements of current hits by buying the completed product from their overseas sub-publishers. The sale of orchestrations was still big business in England and Continental Europe, where publishers continued to concentrate on live performances by dance orchestras to promote their music. With that source of once-important income almost gone in the United States, American firms sold off foreign rights with the stipulation that they could import orchestrations at 60 percent off retail price. Smaller firms reduced overhead by lowering their sales and assigning selling rights to agents on a 10 to 15 percent basis, leaving themselves free to get new records and radio performances, which were becoming their chief source of income.

The first accurate estimate of printed music sales in the United States was commissioned in 1952 by the Music Publishers Association, to be submitted to a Congressional committee in connection with a requested reduction of postal rates. Sixteen percent of the $30 million income from printed music sales, an estimated 15 percent of the record industry's total annual gross, came from popular sheet music. The remaining $25.2 million was from standard classical, religious, and educational music. Twenty-one percent of all popular sheet sales were made in retail stores, the balance in syndicate stores or from racks and by mail. The five or six major firms operated on a fairly stable basis, led by the MPHC, with its pillow of $1.2 million in ASCAP royalties, supplemented by an important share of the new millions it, Chappell, the Big Three, and Paramount reaped from educational folios, band instruction books, and choral and solo arrangements of their great standard songs.

At the major record companies, only Columbia's Mitch Miller still had complete control of pop music—what was cut, who recorded it, and when it was released. At most other companies authority was diffused, and many executives had the same uncertain perception of the future as Herman Starr and his peers. They were content to satisfy the demands of the "typical teen-age record buyer," a female who spent as much as fifteen dollars a week to buy every new release by Perry, Bing, Vaughan, Dinah, Eddie, Frankie, Nat.

Under the noses of the established music and record businesses, during 1953, $15 million worth of rhythm-and-blues records was sold, equal to the industry's entire sales fifteen years earlier. It was the product of about seventy-five manufacturers, among them RCA Victor, Columbia, Decca, and Mercury, who covered the field with almost exact musical duplications of the real thing. Any legal barrier to the practice was removed by the courts in 1951 with a decision in the "Little Bird Told Me" case. The initial recorded version of the Harvey Brooks song was released in 1947 by "sepia" star Paula Watson on the Supreme label, and was covered by the white chanteuse Evelyn Knight on a Decca arrangement, copied Watson's phrasing exactly, and confused even musical experts. Supreme sued, but lost in a verdict that declared musical arrangments were not copyrighted property and therefore not subject to the law's protection.

For the original source, one looked to the products of the R & B independents—Atlantic, Savoy, Peacock, Duke, Alladin, Chess-Checker, Imperial, and Herald—whose best-selling releases featured the Earl Bostic band, the Dominos, Tiny Bradshaw, the Orioles, Ruth Brown, Dinah Washington, and every new artist who broke out on the national charts. Jukebox operators in locations that attracted a white teen-age trade were the first to notice their growing appetite for black R & B, and then local record retailers caught on, though at first they had difficulty in keeping up with the demand, because most companies went into that business for an all-black market only. Hitherto, only white pop-music disk jockeys, in the north responded to this latest expression of white-youth taste, by spotting R & B disks between those by white radio and television plugs and the cover versions of R & B hits. In the South, where black radio was a growing business, the white audience that eavesdropped represented between 20 and 30 percent of all listeners.

The tremendous potential white ticket-buying audience for live black rhythm-and-blues shows, which for many years had been confined to segregated theaters and night clubs, was first made known to white show business by a Cleveland disk jockey of Welsh-Lithuanian descent. A significant factor in his appeal was a hoarse voice, aggravated by complications following an operation for throat polyps and black-sounding enough to fool most listeners. After years as a classical-music and record-request disk jockey, in 1951 Alan Freed switched to rhythm and blues on the insistence of a new sponsor, a Cleveland record-store operator into whose shop young whites crowded to buy the latest R & B releases.

Freed and his associates in a new dance promotion scheme attracted national attention and almost spent some time in the city jail after a near-riot in connection with an R & B dance in March 1952, whose featured performers included some of the most popular and talented R & B artists in America—Charles Brown, the Dominos with Clyde McPhatter, the Orioles, the Moonglows, and the orchestras of Tiny Grimes and Jimmy Forrest. Eighteen thousand tickets had been sold to fans of Freed's "Rock 'n' Roll House Party" radio show, but the Cleveland Arena held only 10,000. Charges against Freed and his partners were dropped, but the national publicity attracted an audience to his radio show that grew larger and more devoted. Freed also brought this audience the genuine musical article in sold-out dances featuring the newest black stars, and packed regional dance halls with audiences that were never less than one third white.

This growing market was one reason for the 25 percent drop in the output of the six major manufacturers in 1953 to 2,190 popular releases, during a year when 59,371 musical compositions were copyrighted. Ninety popular records appeared on *Billboard*'s best-seller charts in 1953, but only seventy-two were released by RCA Victor, Capitol, Mercury, Columbia, MGM, and Decca, in that order. The balance came from well-financed new independents, reach to compete with the leaders. Because of smaller output, the majors' success rate rose from 1952's 2.3 to 3.3, or one hit out of every thirty releases.

Network television's increasing emphasis on those familiar standing songs that festooned the ASCAP catalogue persuaded the society's ruling hierarchy that there would be no complications in negotiating with the chains for a new contract, holding to the same figures for another four years, to the end of 1957. All members were asked for and assigned their video rights to run concurrently. Most of the rank-and-file membership took little notice of a situation that potentially was crucial to their future financial well-being. The per-program litigants remained adamant in their position not to accept the proffered new license, expecting Judge Goddard to rule in their favor once ASCAP's motion to amend the 1950 ASCAP consent decree was finally disposed of and pretrial examinations were begun.

To speed matters up and end hostilities between the society and the broadcasters, in the person of BMI, and to disengaged itself from involvement in any private antitrust action against its rival, ASCAP, suddenly and surprisingly, withdrew the motions supported by the Harbach affidavit. However, the formal request for a Justice Department investigation of BMI, filed in March 1952, remained in effect.

The stratagem had little impact on the networks or on the independent plaintiff stations, whose number had increased to seventy-nine. The networks met with ASCAP and argued that the original television licenses had been drawn up when the medium was in an undeveloped state and broadcasters were unaware that the figures demanded could represent a $10-million payment. They suggested a substantial reduction in the new agreement. By the end of the year, there was a possibility that the networks would again lock out ASCAP music and fill in the gap with the BMI repertory, or else would petition Goddard for a new, lower, rate, while continuing to use the society's music. In most foreign countries, music fees were higher than those in America, which shook the chains' resolve to leave the decision to a judge. Another possibility the networks found unacceptable was a proposal to change the base on which ASCAP fees were computed—to net income, instead of gross receipts. This would mean that financial records might become available to the competition, as well as to the affiliates, who, without their knowledge, were bearing most of the networks' ASCAP television load.

The new ASCAP president, Stanley Adams, found the same internal problems when he took office in April 1953. The young Turks complained, Hans Lengsfelder complained, and so did those songwriters whose music was used chiefly by disk jockeys on large independent stations, usually about the foundation stone of ASCAP distribution—the logging operation, with all its alleged inequities. The continuing attraction of BMI's logging practices, its gains in the concert-music field, and its larger share of the trade-press charts made it difficult for Adams to provide a form of pension for veteran writers by basing their payments on the length of their association with ASCAP. At the autumn membership meeting, he predicted that, with more money coming in each month, income in excess of $18 million was expected for 1953. Yet ASCAP had relaxed admission standards in order to compete with BMI for promising new talent, and 800 new members had joined since the beginning of the year. Therefore, with 3,200 authors and composers now in the society, there would be no meaningful increase in the quarterly checks.

The autocratic attitude toward the general membership of the ruling bloc of publisher-directors, and of those writer-directors and officers who owed their positions to them, was exemplified by Herman Starr's remarks at the meeting. Stricken by the untimely death of former president Fred Ahlert, he insisted on the award of a $25,000 pension to Ahlert's widow. The board approved this without any public discussion, contrary to ASCAP's bylaws.

Unable to reform the society from within and frustrated, not only by BMI's seeming control of what was played on the air, but also by doubts about their own ability to write what the public appeared to want, many ASCAP members became eager recruits to the ranks of the Songwriters of America. The cause was just, and they would share in the bonanza of $150 million that lay waiting for a decision by a jury of men like them, who had had enough of BMI's "garbage" and wanted the return of the kind of music they had written.

The television negotiations and the hearing before Goddard moved to the sidelines on November 8, 1953, when a group of thirty-three ASCAP songwriters filed a $150-million civil antitrust suit on behalf of 3,000 composers and authors, charging a radio–television–recording-company conspiracy, centered upon BMI. NBC, CBS, ABC, and Mutual, RCA Victor and Columbia Records, the NARTB, and a number of other corporations and individuals, including BMI's directors and executives, were charged with conspiring "to dominate and control the market for the use and exploitation of musical compositions." The actual complainants included only one of those involved in the 1941 antitrust action, Paul Cunningham. ASCAP president Adams, his associate in that action and in the Songwriters of America, was absent from the complaint. Other plaintiffs included Arthur Schwartz, the leading complainant, Ira Gershwin, Dorothy Fields, Virgil Thomson, Samuel Barber, Alan Lerner, the current SPA president, Charles Tobias, Milton Ager, and Edgar Leslie.

The press conference in the Waldorf-Astoria Hotel on November 9, at which *Schwartz* v. *BMI* was made public, included an explanation of the matter by John Schulman, attorney for the plaintiffs and counsel to SPA. The complainants had been united by a common desire to destroy BMI's giant subsidy scheme, he told the assembled press. It was financed by the broadcasting industry and pitted 1,300 BMI-affiliated publishers against a mere 600 ASCAP houses, who were not financed by anything but private capital, in a battle for air play, to the detriment and financial damage of ASCAP's song-writing membership.

A few weeks later, *Variety* reported a press interview in which Schwartz argued that broadcasters were in a position to "turn the plugs on and off at will . . . it's no longer a case where a song can fail or succeed on its merits, because the public is denied the opportunity to judge for itself . . . when a writer comes to an ASCAP publisher, who also has a BMI affiliate, he'll suggest that 'if you collaborate with a BMI writer we'll handle it via our BMI firm,' which can only prove indubitably that the BMI affiliation is more positively lucrative [due] to the subsidies from the number of BMI plugs over BMI-affiliated stations and networks."

Starr saw greater worth in ASCAP's repertory than in BMI's "flash-in-the-pan" jukebox hits. "Quality," he said, "is what lasts and what pays off. At the moment BMI is hot . . . but the music business is everything, and dominantly it's ASCAP income. This is the prime source of income and not the byproduct as when Nathan Burkan helped found the Society."

With more experience in the music business than Starr, Max Dreyfus was content to leave everything to "the brain trusters around the Brill Building and in Lindy's," the gathering places of those who supported the Songwriters of America in their war on the new music business.

The Schwartz suit came as no surprise to BMI, but did stun its executives and board because the long-pending issue was finally joined in the uncertain arena of trial by jury. Calling the complaint a "rehash of charges ASCAP has been making for years, and has never been able to substantiate," Carl Haverlin pledged a fight to victory. Shortly before Thanksgiving Day, with Robert Burton and others, he traveled to Nashville, the first visit to Tin Pan Valley, USA that most of them had ever made. During radio station WSM's second annual Country and Western Disk Jockeys Festival week, Burton presented Citation of Achievement certificates to the writers and publishers of twenty-four outstanding country-music songs of 1953. This presentation was without the big-city hotel glitter of BMI's second annual Popular Music Awards black-tie dinner just before Christmas. Five of the fifteen songs honored there came out of Nashville or were influenced by country music.

The day before the dinner, BMI won its first victory in *Schwartz v. BMI:* the right to examine ten of the thirty-three plaintiffs in pretrial proceedings. The ten were directed by the court to answer specific questions put by BMI counsel, seeking to link ASCAP to them and the action.

Abel Green's annual review of 1953's significant industry events emphasized that the publishers were not involved in the songwriters' suit, but he hinted that they might be pleased if control of the business was taken out of the hands of the record manufacturers and restored to the publishers. A veteran of Tin Pan Alley told Green: "Everybody but the music publisher, who used to be pretty good at that, nowadays picks songs. And don't tell me that in the final analysis the public really picks 'em. We . . . used to have a pretty good concept of quality and values in songs that we published. . . . Today, we don't dare publish a song until some artist perhaps likes it, or when the whim of an A&R genius decides it should be done. . . . A record should be a by-product of publishing; not the sparkplug of songwriting and publishing.''

PART FIVE

1954–1966

CHAPTER 17

From Monaural to Stereophonic Sound

When all the figures for 1953 were finally in and analyzed by the Recording Industry Association of America, it was confirmed that the previous all-time sales high of $204 million, in 1947, had been surpassed. Resistance to the new 33⅓- and 45-speed disks continued, each earning only 20 percent of all sales, with the soon-to-be obsolete 78-speed records accounting for $90 million in sales. In spite of the recent technological advances in recording and record players, only one out of every five American households owned a phonograph. The remaining 80 percent continued to resist the staid blandishments of record-company advertising and the increase of new distribution networks. At its best, the industry produced only one hit out of every thirty releases, and its costs could be recouped only by a sale of at least 40,000, which few new offerings enjoyed. The high costs of recording, about $2,000 for a session using twenty-five men that produced four numbers, as well as costs for pressing, packaging, promotion, and distribution were leading to ever higher break-even points. A major hit did, however, provide returns far in excess of those in the past, for both manufacturer and performer. Jo Stafford had just achieved 25 million sales since she began recording in 1937. The young singer Eddie Fisher, attracting the same sort of teen-age female audience that Sinatra once fascinated, had sold five million records in a year. Out of the limelight for several years, Sinatra had just come up with his first hit of the decade, "Young at Heart." RCA Victor and Columbia, to each of which he had once been under contract, dug through files for his hits and unreleased masters to take advantage of a comeback of which few in the industry had believed the singer capable.

The threat that James C. Petrillo and his American Federation of Musicians long represented had become blunted by time. The possibility of a third walkout from the recording studios, scheduled to begin on January 1,

1954, came to an end with a settlement that a more affluent industry shrugged off. Musicians' wages were increased by 20 percent, and an increase was made in the royalty paid to the union's Music Performance Trust Fund. Although more than 1,500 manufacturers were licensed by the AFM in 1954, only 250 actually contributed to the fund, and an uncounted number of new independents, which employed both union and nonunion musicians, did not.

Television had become the favored medium for "breaking" a new release. "Young at Heart" was launched on the *Colgate Comedy Hour,* but only because Capitol executives and the song's publisher persuaded Sinatra to introduce it after he had publicly canceled his appearance. Mercury held up release of Patti Page's "Cross Over the Bridge" until Ed Sullivan found a place for the singer on his *Toast of the Town* program. Decca waited for Bing Crosby to introduce "Y'All Come" on his TV debut. Despite an immediate rush of orders following Crosby's appearance, sales of his disk were disappointing, lending support to the charge that, because Decca had not delivered a best seller in months, it was time for Milton Rackmill to step down as company president. A courtroom fight and a major stockholder-proxy battle were already in full swing, the consequences of his purchase of Universal Pictures, beginning with 26 percent of its outstanding stock, which by early 1954 had risen to a 72.5 percent. During 1954, profits of nearly two million dollars from Universal accrued, sustaining Decca through a fallow period in its twentieth-anniversary year, which ended with the success of a number of Universal sound-track albums, some hits by the Four Aces and Kitty Kallen, and "Rock Around the Clock," "Shake, Rattle and Roll," and "Dim, Dim the Lights" by Bill Haley and the Comets. In a year that was characterized by the major success of "white balladry," as Arnold Shaw described it in his *Honkers and Shouters,* Haley provided the first examples of commercial white rock 'n' roll, abetted by Milt Gabler, the Decca A & R man assigned to handle him. Few of the Comets could read music and, as Gabler told Shaw, he taught them the shuffle rhythms of Louis Jordan's Tympani Five, whom he had produced during the 1940s. "You know, dotted eighth notes and sixteenths, and we'd build on it. I'd sing Jordan riffs to the group that would be picked up by the electric guitars and tenor sax. . . . They got a sound that had the drive of the Tympani Five and the color of country and western. Rockabilly was what it was called back then." A spurt in Decca sales and continuing substantial profits from Universal played their part, and Rackmill prevailed in both courtroom and board room.

The most optimistic people in the business looked forward to a "fatter platter" year in 1955, despite increasing talk of an economic decline. Columbia increased its production by about 35 percent with a million-dollar plant in Indiana and the installation of advanced automatic-injection-molding equipment in its three factories. Edison and other pioneers had experimented with master molds for both cylinders and flat disks, and an injection-molding process was introduced in the early 1930s to make such plastic items as buttons and combs. The industry had, however, continued mostly to use compression molding. In this process, a doughy mass known as a "biscuit" was compressed into final shape by "stampers," which produced no more than 1,000 units before serious deterioration of quality became evident. In the new system, polystyrene pellets, dropped from a hopper atop pressing machines, were forced in heated-liquid from between a pair of stampers whose life was virtually indefinite, a process that provided greater speed of production as well as superior disks. Each double-cavity injection-molding machine was capable of producing 200 seven-inch records, 90 ten-inch LPs or 78s, or 70 twelve-inch LPs of the highest quality every hour.

In order to help overstocked stores whose credit was extended to the limit, as well as to launch a surprise attack on RCA Victor and the discounters, early in 1954 Columbia announced a temporary 25 percent reduction by offering one classical LP at half list price for each disk purchased at full cost. RCA Victor countered with a greater reduction—30 percent off all Red Seal LPs. None of the other manufacturers followed. When the battle ended on March 1, and original prices were restored, it was estimated that a loss of nearly a million dollars had been sustained by the two companies. The discounters had won. They had found themselves in a better position than ever to load up on transshipped material, on which they enjoyed discounts of as much as 50 percent from retailers who had been oversold.

A breakdown in communication with Chicago-area retail dealers was responsible for the temporary abandonment in the summer of 1954 of the earliest attempt by a major manufacturer to extend the distribution network with mail-order merchandising. The unbreakable LP, light in weight and easy to ship through the mails, had brought a number of imaginative persons to the fringes of the industry. Among these were the operators of Music Treasures of the World and its subsidiaries, the Children's Record Guild and Young People's Records, and Concert Hall Records' Musical Masterpiece Society. During the previous autumn, Columbia successfully tested its Family Record Club in the Ohio market, with franchised dealers directly involved after mail-order promotion brought customers into the stores. Based on the Book-of-the-Month Club plan, the program offered one free recording for every three purchased from local dealers, a 25 percent discount on the four disks. The dividend LP was supplied by Columbia without charge, so that each retailer got his full profit on all sales. Columbia also offered phonographs at the same 25 percent discount to club members who agreed to buy a requisite number of records each year. Because the Chicago retailers had not been made aware of the project prior to its introduction into their territory, they accused the company of competing with them unfairly as did the discounters. Their protests forced Columbia to withdraw the record-player discount first and then to shelve the entire plan.

During this argument, the inventor of the direct-mail book club entered the fray. Harry Scherman, of the Book-of-the-Month Club, began a test run of its Music Appreciation Record Club. Initially, it produced its own records, but beginning in early 1955 it purchased them from Angel Records' catalogue. The club's 200,000 members were offered first Debussy's "La Mer" on one side of a twelve-inch recording; on the other was a spoken analysis of the work, with musical passages performed by an orchestra conducted by Thomas Scherman, son of the BMOC's founder. Angel defended its participation by explaining to dealers that the club price of $3.60 a disk could not hurt them, but would instead bring them new customers for Angel's "thrift" releases of classical music, at $3.48, or its de-luxe factory-wrapped package, with music on both sides and detailed notes enclosed, at $4.98.

Directly after the Metropolitan Opera Company's contract with Columbia expired in June 1955, principally because the Met could not guarantee the availability of its leading performers, who were already under exclusive contract to competing record firms, Scherman announced the formation of the BMOC's Metropolitan Opera Club. There were sufficient second- and third-rank soloists to provide more than acceptable operatic records and to permit the club to offer six packages a year.

The record clubs had a total membership of one million subscribers in 1955 and an annual sale of $20 million. A dozen clubs existed, four of them of major importance, doing about 15 percent of the entire LP business and responsible for a third of all classical-music record sales. Most operated on far smaller production budgets than the majors and recorded in Europe, where costs were considerably lower.

RCA Victor and Columbia adopted slightly different tactics to combat the record clubs' threat to their sales volume and to add customers unaccustomed to buying from retailers, whose number had leveled off at 7,000 in the past decade. Many of these concentrated on the more than 12 million teen-agers, who had seven million dollars to spend, and carried records only as a sideline had a very limited inventory and were located in large cities. With three quarters of the nation without a place for young people to buy records, their newest means of gratification, or for adults to have an opportunity to sample the growing glories of the LP catalogues, RCA Victor added local white-goods appliance retailers to the distribution network, supplementing their radio and phonograph-combination sales with a coupon plan, first called the Personal Music Service. Any one of 400 LPs could be purchased with coupons gotten from the local appliance stores; the records were shipped by mail from RCA Victor's Indiana branch. The name was changed to the SRO (Save on Records) program, which was extended to all retail dealers. A $3.98 coupon book entitled the purchaser to three free bonus records each year and the option to buy up to three LPs each month from popular, classical, and jazz lists at a dollar discount. By means of this scheme and others instituted by competitors, the number of retail outlets carrying records rose to 17,000 by late 1957. According to Census Bureau figures, however, only 2,889 of these were "establishments primarily selling phonograph records and albums," doing a $140-million annual business.

In what was called by *Variety* "the most controversial move in the disk industry since 'the battle of the speeds,' " Columbia moved into the record-club arena once more in the late summer of 1955, but with a proposal that gave record retailers a guaranteed share in profits from the members they recruited. Expected to sign four out of every five members, 6,200 dealers were promised that the company would "bring members into your store, sell the records and the Club plan, ship the records, collect the money, and send you your share of the profits," 20 percent of the gross price of each club selection. Within a few months, 88 percent of all Columbia dealers had agreed to cooperate. It was quickly evident that the project was attracting new customers to the LP market, its reason for being. The vast majority of the initial 409,000 who joined were not regular record buyers, at least one third of them not having bought one in the previous half-year.

The Crowell-Collier organization, publishers of *Collier's* and *Woman's Home Companion,* which had embarked on a program of diversification, beginning with a purchase of radio and television stations, established a record-industry connection in September 1956 by buying the Concert Hall Society and its four record clubs. Begun in 1946 by David and Samuel Josefowitz, the society went into the direct-mail-order business four years later with the first of its clubs. The combined catalogues of the Musical Masterpiece, Chamber Music, Jazztone, and Opera societies eventually included more than 1,000 recordings. They had 600,000 subscribers.

Not until early 1956 did RCA Victor join the record-club bandwagon. By then, legions of new customers were responsible for an average sale of 50,000 copies of every club selection and had increased the sale of a hit LP to more than 100,000 copies, a number rare prior to Columbia Record Club's formation. RCA Victor joined with the Book-of-the-Month Company to form the RCA Victor Society of Great Music, to be operated by BOMC. Like Columbia, Victor placated angry dealers by giving them a 20 percent commission on all memberships they secured, thus ensuring the purchase of six classical music selections annually. Attracted by the offer of Toscanini's complete Beethoven symphonies, some 200,000 members joined within three weeks after the first announcement was published. This thirty-five-dollar item was available to members for $3.98, creating a response that prompted Victor to open the Popular Album Club and look forward to a million subscribers to its two clubs within a year. This optimism was shared by Capitol and other labels that opened their own clubs during the late 1950s.

Reader's Digest, which eventually became the largest mail-order record packager, tested the market in March 1960 in conjunction with RCA Victor, prior to entering the business. An album of twelve newly recorded classical Reader's Digest–RCA Victor LPs by European artists, many of whom were also featured on the $1.98 Camden label, was offered to several million *Digest* subscribers for sixteen dollars, with stereo versions available for an additional two dollars. After selling a quarter of a million albums in the United States and 1.5 million world-wide, the publication began its club, creating and merchandising disks produced especially for the project.

The record-club business had indeed boomed. Columbia alone had 1.3 million members, who spent $30.3 million in 1959, and, with Capitol and RCA Victor, accounted for 90 percent of the mail-order record business.

Stimulated by the acceptance of the Extended Play 45 four-selection package and the multimillion-dollar market for LPs created by the record-club movement, the packaged and prerecorded-music industry began to focus exclusively on the middle-class white adult market. These packages were responsible by early 1955 for 40 percent of total sales volume, or around $80 million. Just before World War II, 78-speed albums of jazz, Broadway songs, singing personalities, and vocal and instumental recitals had enjoyed modest but satisfactory returns. The surprisingly large demand during the war and immediately after for Jack Kapp's original-cast albums of Broadway shows, in which he was the first to specialize, caught the attention of other majors, who entered vigorously into this facet of the trade.

The earliest LP and 45 packages had standard passe-partoute designs or modest and inexpensively decorated covers, with the most economical of liner notes. The imagination of artists and designers was first recruited to attract adults looking for recordings suitable for their young offspring. With the increase in the postwar birthrate, Golden Records (a subsidiary of Simon & Schuster), Peter Pan, Cricket Records (owned by Pickwick Records), the Children's Record Guild, and the Big Four built records for youngsters into a fifteen-million-dollar annual enterprise. On discovering that their franchised dealers regarded these as a seasonal Christmas item and neglected to display them at other times, the majors finally reduced or completely abandoned their activities in this field.

Adults who had succumbed to the blandishments of advertising that promised high-quality recordings and high-fidelity record players became the prime customers for the boxed sets, multiple-color artwork, and even leather-bound packages that poured from the majors and the most prosperous independents, and often ended as record-club selections. The emphasis was no longer on classical music, but on the widest variety of recorded entertainment ever known to the industry, which was often distributed as a "loss leader" in order to enhance the value of the entire line or its poorest-selling part. Columbia offered the Literary Series, with great writers reading from their works; it sold for $100 and served as a club dividend. Surprisingly, these packages sometimes turned into runaway best sellers. "Bing," Decca's multi-record anthology of the most important Crosby hits, with the singer talking about the records, sold for $27.50 in vast quantities. The unexpectedly large demand for the 90,000 Limited Edition of Glenn Miller recordings issued by RCA Victor created a black market for the album and stimulated a second volume of Miller releases, 170,000 sets, selling for twenty-five dollars each. The "jazzak" mood-music packages issued by Capitol, beginning with Jackie Gleason's "Music for Lovers Only," released in LP and EP form, were among the greatest sellers to the new "grown-up" music market. They came at a time when hits were not breaking in such proliferation as in the past for that West Coast major.

Popular twelve-inch "sampler" LPs and EPs were issued at ninety-eight cents to increase sales in the popular-adult and classical fields. Among them were Columbia's "I Like Jazz," the Victor Ep "Listener's Digest" condensed-version albums of a dozen classical war-horses, and its "Arias— Acted and Sung" series of operatic selections. Victor was going all out to create a two-speed market, to make its 45-speed patented technology the industry's standard for all popular singles and the 45 EP and 33 LP standard for albums. It began killing off production of the 78-speed disks with which it had dominated the industry for decades. It did this by an increase in 78 prices and a rise in the dealer discount on them and on all 45s, from the traditional 38 percent to 42 percent, ascribing the jump to mounting production costs. More than 200 million 45s had been sold in the previous five years, and Victor intended to increase that share of sales to three out of every four units sold in another five years.

On January 1, 1955, Victor unveiled its Operation TNT. The price of all 45s was set at eighty-nine cents; that of 78s was raised to ninety-eight cents; that for all LPs was reduced by one-third. The move was designed, the company announced, to make recordings a mass consumer item, by simplifying the existing twenty-one different prices. Victor also expected to raise "deteriorating" morale at the dealer level, where at least 100 stores had gone out of business in recent months because of competition from the discounters. There would no longer be so great a price differential between them. Consumers who dealt with discounters might come back, attracted by the increased number of competing retailers. The other majors were reluctantly obliged to conform to Victor's new schedule, even if they did fail to enjoy its 100 percent increase in classical-music sales, a predictable response to a half-million-dollar advertising campaign.

The singles business did not appear to have been affected by these changes. Decca was riding high with the greatest showing since Kapp's death. Mercury was doing well, as was Dot, a newcomer beginning to appear on top-ten charts with regularity. The business had gone, as *Variety* said, "R&B

crazy." It was engaged in a massive splurge of covering hits produced on smaller labels, which continued for the next several years. Perry Como revealed that he could snap his fingers with the best of them on his cover version of Gene and Eunice's "Ko Ko Mo," one of the many fruits of a Chicago federal judge's decision in the "Little Bird Told Me" action. Other examples of this legitimized piracy included versions by white artists on major labels of the original R & B hits "Earth Angel," "Sincerely," "Ain't That a Shame," "Dance with Me Henry," "Tweedle Dee," "Maybelline," "Bo Diddley," "Long Tall Sally," and "Two Hearts, Two Kisses," recorded by the Crew Cuts, the McGuires, Pat Boone, Georgia Gibbs, the Fontane Sisters, Jim Lowe, Joe Reisman, and Frank Sinatra, who was looking for an R & B cross-over hit.

In January 1955, *Billboard* celebrated the sixth anniversary of its decision to drop the words *sepia, Hot in Harlem,* and *race* as descriptives and adopt the phrase "Rhythm and Blues" in their place. In the course of those six years, the field had burst through old barriers and was no longer the disk business's stepchild. With the exception of Capitol and MGM, which returned late to the field (although the latter had continued to issue Ivory Joe Hunter records) the major firms were all heavily into R & B, on both main and subsidiary labels, attempting to compete with now-entrenched independents. Atlantic led that pack, with one third of the year's top-selling R & B disks. Rhythm and blues had become a $25-million annual business, $15 million from recordings, which rose to $25 million in 1955 (more than one tenth of that year's total sales). The independents' 1940s' distribution problem, caused by dependence on a half-dozen firms to handle their $1.10 singles lines, was cured. Some now had their own sales staffs and promotion men. Atlantic, Savoy, Chess, and some others had gone into the packaged-music field and were issuing LPs and EPs by their best-selling black artists. Record-company owners who once were happy to turn their copyrights over to established popular-music firms in a position to assure cover records of their hits now insisted on a full two-cent statutory mechanical fee for them. Desk-drawer publishing had become a thing of the past at the major R & B firms. Progressive Music, Atlantic's publishing arm, was among the top-ten BMI performance earners in 1955. It had a staff of contact men to visit radio stations that programed for both black and white audiences.

In addition to the inherent appeal of R & B music, several factors contributed to its escape from the ghetto to the national white-pop-hit charts: the fantastic popularity in 1955 of the motion picture *Blackboard Jungle,* which introduced Haley's "Rock Around the Clock" to the world's youth, making the song, Frank Zappa suggested later, "the Teen-Age national anthem"; the increased number of cover versions of R & B hits, made with white talent that was more acceptable to a large audience; and the presence on the national scene of R & B's Barnum, Alan Freed, who had moved from Cleveland to the big time of New York City. While serving as the leading Pied Piper disk jockey for American youth, he became the favorite whipping boy of newspapers, magazines, and white parents, all deploring the intrusion of black music, with its sexual innuendos, into the once-placid American popular-music business, dominated by whites.

Rock 'n' roll, as Freed had named the new music, awaited someone to do for it what Caruso had done for the Victrola, Crosby and Sinatra for the great American ballad, and Benny Goodman for the swing movement: a figure who, with his music, would emerge larger than life from the small speaker of a record player or a portable radio. He was found in what might have been thought the unlikeliest of places, but that was, on sober reflection, exactly the right spot—the stage of Nashville's Ryman Auditorium, a former revival tabernacle, from which the Grand Ole Opry was broadcast. And he was Elvis Presley.

The Palace Theatre of country-and-western music, the Opry had brought an average weekend audience of 5,000 to Nashville, or six million persons from all over North America, since November 1925, when it first went on the air. Distinguished from pure "hillbilly" music, such best-selling examples of C & W music as "The Tennessee Waltz," "Jambalaya," "Cold Cold Heart," "Don't Let the Stars Get in Your Eyes," and "Crying in the Chapel" were doing about 15 percent of the industry volume, mostly from singles. Personal appearances by country singers, promoted by the sale and radio play of their records, accounted for an annual take of more than $50 million, earned in at least 3,000 locations in the United States and Canada.

The success and influence of country music on other forms had enforced changes on it, even "down home." The once-prominent fiddle was supplemented with guitars, mandolins, and the dance-band bass fiddle, used for percussive effects. As rhythm and blues surreptitiously intruded into country music, and country music into it, bringing electric instruments and the drums that the Western swing bands first introduced, a hybrid form of both, known as "rockabilly," had emerged, generally to the scorn of devotees of the old-time hillbilly music with which Elvis Presley grew up. Presley was, like his peers who also frequented juke joints along the lower Mississippi, familiar with blues and R & B records made by Arthur Crudup, Jackie Brenston, B. B. King, Little Walter Jacobs, Bobby Bland, Howlin' Wolf, Little Junior Parker, and others who recorded for Sam Phillips in Memphis, Chicago-based Chess, RCA Victor's Bluebird line, Modern-RPM in Los Angeles, and Houston's Peacock label. At the start, there had been the white, finger-snapping, Blackwood Brothers, accompanied by piano and tambourines, and the Statesmen Quartet, and it was from all these that Presley was shaped.

When Presley first went into Phillips's Memphis recording studio in late 1953 to make a four-dollar acetete of two currently popular songs as a gift for his mother's birthday, he tried to sound like Dean Martin, one of a spate of Sinatra-imitating Italian crooners. After trying a variety of other styles, Presley, a year later, made his first commercial release, a combination of country and R & B music: Crudup's "That's All Right, Mama" and "Blue Moon of Old Kentucky," which bluegrass musician Bill Monroe had written and first recorded. The formula was ideal and was maintained throughout Presley's stay on Phillips's Sun label, which ended in October 1955.

Presley had gone to Nashville for the Country and Western Disk Jockey's Festival held in connection with the anniversary of the Grand Ole Opry, and found himself a major center of attention. Colonel Tom Parker, who had successfully managed Eddy Arnold through a remarkable career, guiding him to the RCA Victor roster of artists and "Red Seal merchandising," had advised Presley to sign with any manufacturer that would meet terms set by Sam Phillips for his contract and his Sun masters. Columbia had already refused to go over $25,000 for any singer, and there was nobody at Victor ready to go higher, in spite of the urging of Steve Sholes, head of C & W recording. The Aberbach brothers, Jean and Julian, majority owners of the BMI-affiliated Hill & Range Songs, as well as of several ASCAP houses, put together the package that brought Presley to RCA Victor. According to Arnold Shaw, in *The Rocking '50s,* the recording company "ostensibly put up $25,000 for Presley's recording contract while the Aberbach brothers paid $15,000 for publishing rights and the purchase of Hi Lo Music," owner of several songs Presley had recorded for Sun Records. Hill & Range Songs also wound up with the administration of Presley's BMI-affiliated Elvis Presley Music Corp., as well as his ASCAP company, Gladys Music, through which the majority of songs he recorded were published. The young singer's contract with RCA Victor was for only two years, with a one-year option, which few in the company expected to be exercised.

Within a year, Presley's unexpected sales enforced changes in both the original contract and Victor's sales operation. He had sold well over 10 million disks, among them five million-copy sellers, "Heartbreak Hotel," "Blue Suede Shoes," "Hound Dog," "Love Me Tender," and "Don't Be Cruel." Seven reissued singles, originally made for Phillips on the Sun label, were each selling at the rate of 12,000 copies a day. The initial 300,000-copy sale of his first LP, "Elvis Presley," had broken the previous record of 200,000 copies sold of Mario Lanza's "Student Prince" and the "Selections from the Glen Miller Story" album. The young singer, described by one New York City newspaper critic as unable "to sing a lick, [making] up for vocal shortcomings with the wierdest and plainly planned, suggestive animation, short of an aborigine's mating dance," was responsible for two thirds of Victor's entire singles output. In order to keep up with demand, for the first time in its history the company was obliged to pay other manufacturers to press its disks.

Income tax demands compelled a restructuring of Presley's original contract. A new one was negotiated guaranteeing him $1,000 a week for twenty years. It was reminiscent of the similar arrangement made with Al Jolson by Jack Kapp in the 1940s, but that was for only a five-year term. The $430,000 in royalties Presley had already earned were spread out, and the original contract was extended to five years, with an option for another five.

Colonel Tom Parker, the laconic impresario of mysterious origin, who was now in full charge of the twenty-one-year-old rock 'n' roller's business affairs, on a 75-25 percent basis, with 10 percent off the top going to the William Morris office, had made Presley a millionaire in just nine months. In addition to the income from records, an estimated $250,000 came from Hollywood deals, starting with $100,000 for the soon-to-be-released *Love Me Tender,* and an agreement with Paramount Pictures involving a guarantee that eventually rose to more than a million dollars per movie. In spite of Presley's failure in his first Las Vegas appearance, (a "female Al Jolson" was rushed in to take his place after a few performances), Parker had contracts in hand guaranteeing at least another $250,000 for personal appearance. In addition, performance, mechanical, and sheet-music royalties piled up at the Presley music firms owned jointly with the Aberbachs.

Record sales in general rose by about $100 million in 1956 over the previous year's $227 million, and some major film companies looked to the record business to improve their earnings reports. The number of million-plus single sellers had risen steadily since the previous summer, and several more attractive independent operations appeared among the companies responsible for the twenty-five most popular records in early 1956, only a few of which were out-and-out rock 'n' roll. EMI had recently acquired Capitol, which had enjoyed a 33 percent increase in profits and had sold an estimated 5.75 million singles of only three songs in a few months.

The largest sales increase in 1955 had been in LP records, with only a minor increase in 45s, and a significant decline in 78s, to which, principally, customers for rhythm-and-blues and country-and-western music continued to cling. Because the old-fashioned 78 record represented one fourth of all sales, but less than 20 percent of dollar volume, and its production costs were climbing, manufacturers were slowly phasing it out and forcing the independents to do the same by increasing its manufacturing costs, while making those for 45s more attractive. The prevailing factory cost to an independent record company, one without its own pressing facilities, was around 15 cents for a 45 single, which was then sold to a distributor for about thirty-three and a half cents, out of which came the one-and-a-half- (generally unusual) to four-cent mechanical royalty. In the event the recording artist was to receive 4½ percent of the eighty-nine cent retail price that became standard following RCA's Operation TNT, it was paid only after advances and costs for studio time, musicians, engineers, and so on had been recouped. The general markup from distributor to retail dealer was twenty cents, but in the case of distributors handling twenty to thirty consistently "hot" companies with major performers this would be increased to as much as twenty-eight and a half cents a disk. It was the distributor who realized the largest profit from a hit record, between $60,000 and $85,000 on a 300,000-copy seller.

The increase in the sale of LPs was initially attributed to those important disk jockeys who were paying them more attention then in the past and played all of the cuts until their listeners fastened on one or two tracks. The manufacturers' mailing lists for free records included about 1,800 disk jockeys, compared with the fifty or so of a few years before, because there was more profit in promoting an LP than a single. The same $4,000 it cost for a session of singles, out of which one hit might come, would pay for an LP that eventually returned all costs, something few singles ever did.

The film industry's connection with the music business dated back to the late 1920s, when Tin Pan Alley was literally picked up and moved to Hollywood. Throughout the 1930s, the plugging of movie songs on network-radio programs by film industry–owned music houses served as the chief means for motion-picture exploitation. The first marriage between movie making and record manufacture was born after the war out of the allocation by Louis B. Mayer of $500,000 for the development of an MGM-connected record company. Milton Rackmill's logical plan to create a studio–record-company combine bore fruit with Decca's purchase, on credit from the First Boston Bank, of Universal Studios in 1950, providing the means to make movies sell records and records sell movies with great profit. The third broadcasting network's plan to join RCA-NBC and CBS in the record business came to a conclusion only after a long and unsuccessful search for a money-making operation—Dot or Cadence, for example—with its own management and distribution network. In June 1955, ABC-Paramount launched the new company, with a Boston record distributor, Sam Clark, as president. His first job was to set up a distribution chain for Mickey Mouse Records. Mickey's creator, Walt Disney, the first major studio head to go into feature television production, had sold ABC-Paramount Television the *Disneyland* and *Zorro* series, giving the network an opportunity to get into the television game alongside the big boys, NBC and CBS. Disney also got a nationwide medium for the promotion of his amusement park, in which ABC-Paramount had invested $500,000 and guaranteed loans up to $4.5 million for a 34.48 percent share. Mickey Mouse Records used the young talent that appeared on Disney television shows, produced independently and distributed temporarily by ABC-Paramount.

Clark was having difficulty lining up experienced management and distributors. The situation was saved by his innovative venture into the marketing of smaller labels that retained their own identity, charging them a low fee to cover financing, promotion, and exploitation, with ABC-Paramount participating in the profits. In 1959, when annual sales had jumped to about six million dollars, and the distribution chain included a number of successful independent labels, ABC-Paramount paid three million for Grand Award Records. The label had been started in 1954 by the veteran bandleader and recording artist Enoch Light and currently had a three-and-a-half-million annual gross. The package included Light's services and his new Command label, whose three intriguing "ping-pong" LPs were making converts to stereo out of a public long accustomed to monaural recorded music.

ABC-Paramount's inability to secure the services of experienced music and record men, many of whom had developed their own successful record companies, pointed up the dearth of qualified executives and creative personnel. The sales departments did not suffer from a lack of applicants, usually college graduates, but they were reluctant to go out on the road as field men and gain experience or to accept the low scale of compensation that prevailed for junior employees. For years, the best executives had come up through the ranks, often starting in retail stores or distribution companies, where they became familiar with the entire line. Retail clerks therefore looked on their jobs as temporary stopgaps that would lead to an executive position with one of the major labels.

The dramatic shift, after the war, of responsibility for choosing the music to be recorded from publishers, who promised to make every song selected their "number-one plug," to company personnel had given new importance to those trained musicians who served as staff musical directors and artists-and-repertory men. Gordon Jenkins, Hugo Winterhalter, Percy Faith, the Hugo Peretti and Luigi Creatore team, Henri René, Archie Bleyer, who had been one of the best-paid writers of stock arrangements, Don Costa, Billy Vaughn, and Sid Feller, who became head of A & R at ABC-Paramount, created arrangements of the songs they supervised or assigned the work to qualified staffers or free-lance arrangers. With the increase of singles output and then that of LPs of ten to twelve selections, a modern A & R chief had nearly a hundred appointments to telephone conversations a day in connection with proposed material, was in charge of the promotion of his work, and was responsible for the happiness of all artists under contract, as well as auditioning or negotiating with new talent. Mitch Miller of Columbia, who selected or passed on 95 percent of all popular single releases, had two men in charge of all popular LPs and several additional individuals responsible for C & W and R & B products. In turn, he reported to Columbia's president, James Conkling, who was replaced on his resignation in June 1956, by Goddard Lieberson, Miller's classmate at the Eastman School of Music and a CBS employee since before the war.

The Mutual Broadcasting System, which fed its affiliates fifty minutes of music and ten minutes of news each hour in 1955, was the last radio chain to get into the record business. After acquiring RKO Pictures in 1955 for $25 million, the new owner of MBS, General Teleradio Pictures, a division of the General Tire & Rubber Company, purchased a quarter-interest in the year-old Unique Record Company. It proved to be the least successful merger between the motion-picture industry and broadcasting and recording businesses, and was deactivated in October 1957.

The value of music holdings to a film company was underlined by Loew's annual report for 1956, which showed that the company had kept out of the red because its music-publishing–record operation earned $2.2 million before taxes, $645,000 of it from MGM Records, which was now producing 22 million units annually in its own factories. The label had operated since 1946, with an investment to date of $2.3 million, which had been depreciated to $1.2 million; net income to date was $3.5 million. MGM Records continued to provide significantly important exploitation for Loew's film products in the form of sound-track LPs, every cent off whose profits from sales added to the parent company's balance sheet.

The race to obtain the services of Dot Records' "young genius" president, Randy Wood, who had recently transferred his headquarters to Los Angeles, was won by Paramount Pictures in early 1957. During 1956, Dot had enjoyed a 12-to-14 percent share of the singles market, with sales of six million dollars, and had fourteen singles on the year's top-seller charts, matching the performance of RCA Victor. Wood had been operating an appliance repair shop in a Nashville suburb in 1946 when he bought several thousand 78-rpm race records, which he sold on a disk-jockey program at six for a dollar by mail. With $1,000 from the profits of his "world's largest mail order record shop," he formed Dot Records in 1951 and concentrated on the production of country records with some success. As orders for R & B recordings continued to surpass those for his own product, he started covering rhythm-and-blues hits by records of the young white Ivy League–educated singer Pat Boone. Wood's reported insistence that publishers of any song he covered permit the distribution of up to 70,000 royalty-free records for disk-jockey promotion was cited as one reason that Boone's cover records became major hits, second only to Presley's sale of 20 million singles in 1957, with Como third at seven million. The screen composer Dimitri Tiomkin, writer of Boone's first noncover hit, the film title song "Friendly Persuasion," wanted Como to record it on the original sound track, expecting it also to be released by RCA Victor. Finding the $50,000 that Como's agent asked too high, Tiomkin settled for Boone at $5,000, giving Dot and Wood a smash LP and a multimillion-selling single. The two million in cash and substantial block of Paramount stock paid for Dot Records, as well as a place for Wood on the company's board, was recouped within five years. In his first year under the studio's banner, Wood doubled his singles sales and increased those of Dot's LP product by five times, for a $10-million year. The record company that had been bought as an investment, not an exploitation department, proved to be a costworthy purchase, though it continued to operate as if independently owned.

Paramount's good fortune with Dot, and that of Leonard Goldenson and

ABC-Paramount with hits from a number of new performers, including fourteen-year-old Paul Anka, whose first record sold over a million copies, prompted the operating heads of major studios without a record-company affiliation—Warner Brothers, United Artists, 20th Century-Fox, and Columbia—to take a more serious look at the disk industry. Except for United Artists, all had major music-publishing affiliations, but none had yet been able to strike an agreement with either of the two currently attractive independent labels, Liberty and Imperial. With a successful stable of young singers, and the most talented Presley imitator, Eddie Cochran, Liberty ranked among the twenty-five leading companies, a standing that rose immediately in the Christmas season of 1958. Ross Bagdasarian, co-writer of "Come On-A-My House," used the name David Seville on his single "The Chipmunk Song," which manipulated magnetic tape to create three lovable rodents. He and Liberty eventually sold 12 million copies and another million dollars' worth of licensed Chipmunk items.

Imperial's three-million gross in the first six months of 1957 represented the best earnings picture since Lou Chudd, its president, formed the business in 1947. Once producer of the "Let's Dance" network-radio program, which propelled Benny Goodman to fame, Chudd took half of the $20,000 he had saved during the war to record Latin-American music, from which he realized an immediate 50 percent profit, which was used to cover topten hits of 1948 in Spanish-language versions for the large Mexican-American audience in the southwest. Imperial made $400,000 that year, with a 25 percent profit return. Chudd next went into the square-dance-music business, and then into country and western, children's records, and, finally, rhythm and blues, always with success. In 1950, he signed a young black New Orleans pianist-singer, Fats Domino, who eventually moved with Presley across once-impenetrable barriers onto the pop charts with a suddenly commercial and immensely danceable rock-'n'-roll style that appealed to both adults and the dominant youth audience. When Chudd eventually disposed of Imperial to United Artists in the early 1960s, Domino had sold 30 million disks, eighteen of them Gold Record award winners. With the UA sale came a young white teen-age "soft" rock-'n'-roller, Rick Nelson, the son of Ozzie and Harriet Nelson, whose family adventures made a successful transition from radio to network television in the middle 1950s. Chudd had stolen Nelson from Verve Records, for which he had made his debut with a cover version of one of Domino's hits. After coming up with two Gold records in 1957, Nelson, who proved to be the most successful West Coast teen idol, was rewarded by Chudd with a five-year contract, guaranteeing him $1,000 a week. This was in addition to the 4½ percent royalty he already got, which was now based on sales in excess of $1.155 million.

United Artists had moved into the record business in October 1957, starting from scratch with two subsidiaries, UA Records Corporation and UA

Music Corporation, the latter a desk-drawer operation with about fifty copyrights. Negotiations to acquire one of the top ten ASCAP houses, Mills Music, for around four million, ten times Mills's annual income from performances, had fallen through. Irving Mills, one of the firm's owners, said that there was a million-and-a-half-dollar difference between UA's offer and the asking price. He lamented that too many people sought to buy music holdings with future profits, rather than pay full price.

Having been completely reorganized in the early 1950s, United Artists was unlike all other motion-picture companies. It had no production facilities or studio; it financed independent productions in return for all distribution rights and a share of profits, paid under one of several formulas. The same policy was expected to obtain in the record business. "Cross promotion" offered independent film makers and recording artists the benefits of United Artists' "cross advantages." It was a type of arrangement already in effect between Frank Sinatra and Capitol Records. The singer's Essex Productions controlled the masters for all his albums and left the distribution, advertising, and promotion to Capitol.

While building a production and management staff, in its first year United Artists leased masters made outside the company, chiefly jazz products and sound tracks leased from producers of films it distributed. It had one of the 175 hits in the first three quarters of 1958. With an offer of complete financing and a half-share in all profits after costs were recouped, the company attracted tested independent songwriter-producers, on a production-to-production basis, who brought the company into the rock-'n'-roll business. With more than 150 United Artists international offices to promote soundtrack recordings of its movies, a goal of $10 million within two years was set by the management of the record division.

In February 1958, 20th Century-Fox chose one of Randy Wood's lieutenants to head its new subsidiary, 20th Century Records, which it, like United Artists, intended to develop from the ground up, having been unable to purchase an already established company with its own manufacturing and distribution operations. Columbia Pictures, which had unsuccessfully attempted a merger with Lou Chudd, established its own disk division in June, using the name Colpix, its own conflicting with the long-established CBS Columbia label. Almost simultaneously, Warner Brothers crystallized plans to enter the recording and electronics business, its second foray into the world of recorded sound. The initial venture had been an economic disaster, coming just before the 1930s depression, when Warner purchased the American Brunswick label, only to sell it twenty months later at a significant loss. Ironically, there was talk of a new economic recession as the announcement was made, but Jack L. Warner intended not to fail again. James Conkling, former president of Columbia Records, was brought in as president, with a three-year contract at $52,000 a year plus a percentage of net profits. Warner owned-and-operated sales offices in forty-five countries around the world were expected to provide the label with built-in distribution outlets, the most serious necessity for a new enterprise, but only three company-owned branches, in New York, Chicago, and Los Angeles, filled that function. Five independent distributors were eventually added.

Jack Warner originally conceived of his record company as a source of added exposure for the artists under contract to his movie company. Record stars were also made out off some personalities in twelve productions appearing on ABC-TV, among them the nonsinger Ed "Kookie" Byrnes, whose "Kookie, Lend Me Your Comb," got to *Billboard*'s number-three spot, and Connie Stevens, the Warner lot's ingenue for all seasons. The successful ABC-TV series *Maverick, Bourbon Street Beat, 77 Sunset Strip,* and other top-rated programs provided a cache of sound-track LPs, which delighted their most ardent followers.

The rosy financial picture painted by Loew's, on the basis of earnings by its record and music-publishing arms, proved the truth of Wood's prediction, after a year in Hollywood, that "the way the picture business is going, the record and music business may well surpass it for revenue." The $5.52 million earned by MGM Records, the Big Three music houses, and WMGM Radio in New York City was in excess of the $3.97 earned by Loew's American and Canadian picture houses, providing a profit before taxes of $1.314 million, which more than offset the serious loss of $7.8 million from motion-picture production and distribution.

Capitol's success with the *Oklahoma!, Carousel,* and *The King and I* motion-picture sound tracks and Decca's with those from *Around the World in Eighty Days, The Glenn Miller Story,* and *The Benny Goodman Story* (each of which sold well in excess of 100,000 copies, a gross to the manufacturer of a quarter-million dollars) sparked the industry's interest in marketing movie and Broadway show music. Spirited bidding for rights put the studios and the theatrical producers in a position to enforce higher royalty fees and more and more supplementary mood music, jazz, and vocal LP albums, as well as single recordings of songs from each score. The profits ratio in Hollywood was cracked with the failure of the elaborate sound-track LP of Cecil B. De Mille's *Ten Commandments.* After spirited bidding by all the majors, Wood had spent more than $40,000 to rerecord the music in order to make it a suitably commercial album. Not until the best-selling sound-track LP of all time, Rodgers and Hammerstein's *Sound of Music,* which went over the seven-million mark, did Hollywood reach the money spent by American consumers on Broadway original-cast albums.

All LP production costs were rising; those for the now-mandatory four-color artwork were up 60 percent, to $600. With a profit of fifty-one cents from a $3.98 popular-music LP, and a net of twenty-one cents after all expenses, including 2½ percent of the retail price to the AFM Trust Fund, the standard twenty-four cents to publishers, twenty cents to the artists, and a forty-cent excise tax, record men wondered whether sound-track LPs were not worth more to the studios than to the manufacturers. The new practice of limited engagements in selected first-run screen theaters, on a reserved-seat basis, reduced the effect of concentrated air play immediately after the initial LP release. Hollywood no longer released its major productions during the winter, scheduling them instead for summer release to attract audiences whose favorite television programs were off the air and the record business was in its traditional slump. By the time all the major studios had opened their own disk firms, the bottom of the feature-film sound-track business could be seen. This left only the rock-'n'-roll and pop-singles business to keep figures on annual reports in the black. Between January 1 and September 31, 1958, thirty-five sound-track LPs were released by the entire industry. Only six appeared even once on *Billboard*'s Best Selling Pop Album chart, five of them from musicals: Presley's "Loving You" and "King Creole"; "Gigi," a sleeper that went over the million-copy mark; "South Pacific"; and "The Singing Idol," starring Tommy Sands, one of the more palatable of Presley clones.

Both the motion-picture and the recording-industry studios faced their regular quinary problem with organized labor in 1958: a strike by members of the American Federation of Musicians. James C. Petrillo, the feisty trumpet player from Chicago, was no longer president of the union, having just stepped down, after nineteen consecutive terms, in favor of Herman D. Kennin, a Portland, Oregon, attorney and professional musician, who had been an ASCAP field representative. When Kennin took office, a West Coast group of dissident AFM members was in the sixteenth week of a wildcat strike against the motion-picture and television production companies. Among the strikers were the 303 contracted musicians, who earned $2.7 million a year from the film industry and now demanded a $12 million wage increase and other benefits. Because of their absence from the movie lots, new productions and TV series were sent to Mexico for musical scoring, where they cost as much as in Hollywood but came back with far less audience appeal.

After a vote by the strikers in favor of the new Musicians Guild of America, the NLRB recognized the guild as the sole bargaining agent with the motion-picture and television production industry and negotiations began for new contracts. A determinant factor in the industry's decision to deal with the dissidents was the fact that the music in pre-1948 movies sold to television, and that in new television productions, had mostly been performed by the strikers. Their legal representatives questioned to which union the mandatory five percent musicians' royalties from these sales belonged, an issue Hollywood preferred to evade. The proposed thirty-nine-month agreement, which guaranteed thirty-nine weeks of work annually at higher salaries, were accepted. The payment of contributions to the Music Performance Trust Fund was eliminated, but not the 5 percent musicians' residuals from TV sales. Sound-track LPs were vitally affected, because the

AFM contract with the manufacturers did not permit the latter to handle recordings made in the United States by non-AFM musicians.

The recording business faced another stroke-of-midnight walkout at the end of 1958, but did not stockpile new masters in anticipation, as it had in 1942 and in 1947, regarding such a move as pointless. It was difficult enough to record sufficient good music in the best of circumstances, and the industry generally believed that the AFM would avoid a showdown this time because of competition from the Musicians Guild.

A less bristling man than Petrillo, Kennin showed his skill at bargaining and his statesmanship by achieving the largest gain ever for recording musicians in a new five-year contract—an increase in wages of from 30 to 47 percent. The payment of 20 percent of a musician's scale to the Music Performance Trust Fund was discontinued, and a pension fund was instituted instead. Lower recording rates were fixed for established symphony groups, and the basic payment by the manufacturers to the trust fund was increased by 1½ percent.

National AFM pressure on local unions to stop segregation of black musicians had been inaugurated by Kennin soon after his election. It was now stepped up as part of a national AFL-CIO drive to put an end to discrimination. Some of the black locals, which had been formed before the AFM itself, fought the order, claiming that they could elect their own black officers and bring their own delegations to the annual conventions under the old system. Extreme vigilance was exerted to ensure that members of all races received the same pay scale, an imbalance that had long been one of organized labor's most blatant imperfections.

The proposed sales of post-1948 motion pictures to the television business precipitated a new conflict between the AFM and the MGA, each threatening to take action unless its members got their share of all 5 percent residual royalties from the transactions. During this impasse, most producers put the money in escrow. The MGA became more active in negotiating contracts with California-based record companies, for which most of their members worked. Among these were Sinatra's Essex Productions which produced and owned the masters of all his post-1958 recordings, and Verve Records. A new agreement gave a 30 percent increase over current AFM scale, and, for the first time, a musician doubling on instruments would receive compensation for each.

The logical solution to the fight between the AFM and the MGA was compromise, which Kennin effected in September 1961. The Musicians build was dissolved, and its members, who had been expelled from the AFM, were reinstated with full rights. A new contract with the record manufacturers, which was approved by a united membership in 1964, improved working conditions and increased compensation and fringe benefits. Recording-session musicians would now participate in the proceeds from the sale of records, whose total gross at retail had risen to $698 million in 1963, a large portion of which came from original-cast LP albums.

The battle for musical rights had grown to large proportions since the lackadaisical days when Jack Kapp introduced the original-cast album to the music business after paying the Theatre Guild a few thousand dollars for the right to record *Oklahoma!* It had gone to a new extreme in 1951 when Mannie Sachs invested $250,000 on behalf of RCA Victor in the Irving Berlin musical *Call Me Madam,* whose chief attraction to audiences was Ethel Merman, and the song "I Like Ike," inspired by the Republican Party's candidate for the presidency, Dwight D. Eisenhower.

The box-office success of *South Pacific,* whose 78-rpm albums and LPs grossed $9.25 million, followed by sales of 1.5 million sound-track LPs, put such eminent teams as Rogers and Hammerstein in a position to reserve all recording rights to their original-cast albums and to negotiate directly with the record makers. Their own publishing companies, generally formed in partnership with Max Dreyfus and Chappell Music, demanded an initial outlay in 1958 of between $50,000 and $100,000, as well as either all or partial funding of theatrical-production expenses for a share of royalties, toward the recording of a cast album, several popular- and jazz-version LPs, and a certain number of single versions of songs from the production made by artists the writers selected.

Goddard Lieberson's faith in *My Fair Lady,* from the time he read the book and heard the music, was such that he persuaded the CBS board to invest $360,000, the entire cost of mounting the production, for a 40 percent share. It gave the corporation initial returns in excess of two million dollars in the first two years from a record that cost $22,000 to make. CBS also received an option to produce a television version of *My Fair Lady* on its network, following the permanent closing of the first Broadway production, which took place on September 29,1962, after grossing $20,257,000. During the run, CBS bought Lerner and Loewe's 30 percent share of *My Fair Lady* royalties outright for two million, increasing its interest to 70 percent. CBS then sold movie rights to Warner Brothers for $5.5 million and a 47½ percent share of earned income over $20 million from distribution.

Finding that record companies were profiting more than they were from recorded versions of their Broadway musicals, Rodgers and Hammerstein, who provided backing themselves for their stage productions, formed their own record company to produce the cast album for *Flower Drum Song.* Acting as their exclusive distributor, Columbia Records paid them not only the standard twenty-four-cent publisher-writer mechanical royalty on each album sold, but also the manufacturer's share. *Flower Drum Song* sold only 300,000 copies, proving that even the most famous theater musical team and the most innovative major record label could be wrong. Reputations were restored with *The Sound of Music,* whose cast album Rodgers and Hammerstein also produced, for distribution by Columbia Records. It sold more than a million copies, adding to *Variety*'s estimate that the pair had earned royalties from original-cast 78-rpm and LP albums in excess of $75 million since 1943.

During the 1958–59 theatrical season, record companies had invested several million dollars in the theater, receiving in return fourteen original-cast albums, from both musical and spoken features. However, only four of the musicals were regarded as hits with any chance of paying back the investment. The structure of theatrical financing had undergone major changes. One was that the music conglomerates and their heads of A & R were taking the place of the Prohibition era sugar daddy and the Tin Pan Alley music houses that usually provided the necessary backing for a stage musical. After CBS advanced the entire $480,000 to back 1959–60's Lerner and Loewe musical *Camelot,* in return for a 40 percent share of receipts after expenses, Columbia Records still had to bid against RCA Victor for the album rights, and won only after it agreed to pay more than the standard 10 percent of the LP selling price to the producers, Lerner, Loewe, and Moss Hart. Tax accountants had ruled against a Lerner-Loewe record-production firm, so four cents was added to the standard twenty-four-cent publisher's royalty, the highest yet paid.

In the light of a loss of a half a million dollars in LPs, EPs, and singles of stage music that rested on warehouse shelves or were remaindered to jobbers and discounters, Victor's readiness to bid for album rights was surprising. When caution took over again, Meredith Willson's *Unsinkable Molly Brown* went to Capitol, where profits from *The Music Man* and *Fiorello* recordings subsidized the $220,000 asked. Nine singles of songs from the Willson musical, an unusual number, were promised, as well as the author-composer's right to restrict air performances of all *Molly Brown* music for three weeks after the Broadway premiere.

As the success of *My Fair Lady* proved, Lieberson knew better than anyone how to record musicals. He treated them, not as a duplication of the stage performance, but as something that had been designed specifically for the recording studio and an audience in armchairs. After sitting through twelve hours in a Columbia studio while his new musical *Mr. President* was being recorded, Irving Berlin said that Lieberson had "gotten values into the album that you don't get in the theater, which gives an album a personality of its own. Hearing the show being recorded is like watching a movie script being written and shot at the same time."

In order to get the *Mr. President* rights, Lieberson had agreed to match the 17 percent producer's royalty introduced by Capitol into the bidding wars the year before, for *No Strings,* a musical play for which Rodgers wrote both words and music. Moreover, the intense competition with RCA Victor, Capitol, and Sinatra's Reprise Records helped push up the producer's royalty. Columbia agreed also to lend the musical's five producers $200,000, to be used to settle an income tax matter for one of them. Lieberson branded such dealings as "verging on hysteria," adding, "for a producer to ask a record company for money is immoral, for a record company to give it is ignorance." The cost to produce a cast album had quadrupled since *My Fair Lady* opened, and Lieberson thought something had to give, particularly the inordinate producer's share. Musicians, the cast, which received a full week's salary, engineers, studio time, and other pertinent expenses were all higher, running between $35,000 and $50,000, with another $20,000 for supplementary LPs and singles. Then there was the $20,000 for cover art and special photography and packaging design, and such promotion as the mass distribution of a free special three-inch disk of music from *Camelot* that helped bring in $1.2 million in orders for 200,000 LPs prior to the show's opening.

The possibility of hitting another *My Fair Lady* gold mine lured other manufacturers into fighting for cast-album rights, but it also helped Columbia accept errors of judgment and losses from a string of box-office failures in the 1961–62 season, on which it had invested $1.5 million. On the other hand, Columbia did have six of the seven Gold Record cast LPs, each of which made in excess of one million dollars, and were sure to be record-club selections. The madness Lieberson deplored continued. In the summer of 1963, five major companies, or their parent organizations, had invested nearly three million dollars in forthcoming Broadway productions. ABC-Paramount advanced a million for three musicals, all of which failed; Columbia, half a million for two box-office "bombs." The record business had drawn back from the 17 percent royalty, but the mad search for gold from the theater went on. It achieved only a 10 percent success rate. Some of the losses were recouped through record clubs or special sales to discounters and rack jobbers for that loyal group of consumers who bought virtually everything connected with Broadway. Cast albums were highly recyclable, even box-office failures, and were regularly reissued in new packaging or rerecorded in enhanced stereo sound.

With the 10 percent producer's royalty restored, with box-office prices beginning to climb over the once-taboo ten-dollar limit, and with music a more integral part of a musical comedy, a venture into the theater was regarded as a more reasonable investment, at its best recoupable in six months or so. When the federal excise tax on recordings was finally revoked in 1965, and half of that bonanza passed along to the consumer, cast-album profits and those of all other LPs rose by the other half. Record sales and home phonographs had both doubled since the *My Fair Lady* LP was released, which eventually sold six million units, a figure no other cast or sound-track album surpassed until the filming of *The Sound of Music,* whose sound-track LP came out in 1966. It was an international success even in that 90 percent of film markets where the movie had not yet played. In Lebanon, for example, where the average sale of an American LP was

400 copies, and *My Fair Lady* doubled that number, *The Sound of Music* sold 4,000 units.

The halcyon days of the 1920s', to which Tin Pan Alley still fondly pointed, when 611 musicals had been produced, were a faint memory. During the decade beginning with the 1955–56 season, only 131 musicals were staged, and only one, *Fiddler on the Roof,* was among acknowledged box-office hits, one of eight in the 1965–66 season. A collaboration between two giants of the modern theater, Alan Jay Lerner and Richard Rodgers, *Do I Hear a Waltz?,* had the shortest run of any Rodgers' musical since the war. Goddard Lieberson was now chairman of the newly organized CBS-Columbia group, charged with diversifying the corporation's holdings. He still supervised the production of cast albums, however, though investment in the musical theater was decided by Clive Davis, an attorney who had handled the FTC suit against the Columbia Record Club. As vice-president and general manager of CBS Records, Davis was responsible for the loss of a sizable investment in the production of *Superman,* and had supported putting $450,000 into *The Apple Tree,* by *Fiddler*'s writers, Jerry Bock and Sheldon Harnick. It proved to be a failure at the box office and in the record stores. Those disasters brought about a $100,000 limit on all theatrical adventures, a small figure in view of the doubling of record-industry volume since 1959, when the business was entering a new golden age, whose potential many believed would not be reached in the immediate future.

Except for a slight dip in 1954, there had been a steady upward progression of retail sales since the beginning of the decade, according to RIAA figures (later revised upward):

1951	$191,000,000
1952	$202,000,000
1953	$205,000,000
1954	$195,000,000
1955	$227,000,000
1956	$331,000,000
1957	$400,000,000
1958	$438,000,000
1959	$514,000,000

Approximately 100 singles were issued each week in the late 1950s, enough for a disk jockey on the air sixteen hours a day to play each just once, without touching anything issued in the past. It was a glut that the country's nearly 700 distributors found difficult to handle. Increased by 30 percent in the last five years of the decade, they included manufacturer-owned branches belonging to RCA Victor, Columbia, Decca, Capitol, Mercury, and King, and did one third of their business in New York, New Jersey, Detroit, Cleveland, and Philadelphia. Because of the recent success of independents, who sold three out of every five 45-rpm singles, there had been a surprisingly small mortality rate among distributors.

Overproduction of singles created a serious problem for retailers, too, who were offered 1,200 new releases each quarter, only between 5 and 10 percent of which sold in measurably significant quantity, that is, between 100,000 and more than one million copies. Sixty percent of all releases sold from 2,000 to 3,000; 20 percent, up to 25,000; 10 percent over 50,000 or more, according to *Billboard* in 1958. At the end of 1957, the Big Four increased the price of their 45s from eighty-nine to ninety-eight cents, offering distributors a three-month, 100 percent return privilege for 45s only. Now that three singles cost the same as a popular LP, the majors, who had 54 percent of all popular-music sales, expected the independents to be hurt severely. Instead, production by 600 companies reached a peak in 1958, a total of 5,249 releases, 1,000 more than in 1955, and 11 percent higher than in 1957. Twenty-four percent of the 283 sides on the most important *Billboard* charts in 1958 came from the Big Four, the remaining 76 percent belonging to independents, including Dot, Roulette, Cadence, Atlantic, Imperial, Sun, Chess, and Liberty, all of which had five or more of the total. It was one-stop operators, discounters, and rack jobbers who played a major part in bringing the industry nearer to the half-million gross that the most optimistic had predicted at the beginning of the decade.

With the proliferation of record labels following the introduction of the LP and the 45, it was difficult for the average jukebox owner to keep up with the hits his customers wanted. The one-stop store, which had come into existence before the war, originally catering exclusively to the coin-machine trade, was operating in every major city by the early 1950s. Several hundred of them were of significant size and had an ample stock of current hits and promising 78s and 45s, on all labels, which sold for five cents above the distributor's price. Within a few years, the one-stops had become, in *Billboard*'s words, "the fulcrum of the entire pop singles setup." Both manufacturers and independents offered them giveaways of a free disk for every one ordered, a flexible return policy, and rapid delivery. The one-stop was a convenience not only to jukebox owners but also to local retailers, who, willing to pay the premium nickel for ready access and simplified bookkeeping, got half their singles from them. Their music-business know-how was invaluable.

RCA Victor's Operation TNT, one of whose purposes was to create confusion in the discount-record market, once price-fixing court cases against Sam Goody had failed, proved to be the making of many cut-rate record stores. The value of transshipped classical-music overstock, for which discounters had an ample supply of ready cash, was made evident by Goody's success in 1955, when he sold four million dollars' worth. His nondiscount competitors were convinced that there was something to be said for his explanation that, though he lost on each sale, he made it up in volume.

Some five years later, Sam Goody, Inc. filed for reorganization under the Bankruptcy Act, owing three million dollars to some 200 creditors, mainly record companies, distributors, and major retailers from whom much of the stock had been transshipped. A plan to pay off forty-eight cents on the dollar over the next ten years was approved. It included a unique provision that tied in future LP prices, increasing the value of Goody's inventory as they rose, and thus his payments on the indebtedness. The business finally went public in 1966, when it had an annual income approaching eight million dollars, with a 25 percent increase projected for the next year. Goody's seven retail outlets in the New York and Philadelphia areas, an audio store, a Long Island warehouse, and stock had a net worth of $3.1 million; liabilities were $1.3 million.

All other measures having failed to curb the transshipping of LPs, which had become their most serious problem, a group of retailers, meeting in Chicago in July 1958, formed the National Association of Record Dealers. They hoped to create a national "fighting force" of retailers who would also counter the inroads being made by the major manufacturers' record clubs and by rack jobbers. The first rack operation in the United States, offering the top fifteen hits on both 78s and 45s in syndicated, variety, drug, and self-service food stores, was the creation in 1952 of Elliot Wexler, of Philadelphia. He enjoyed a sub-distributor's status with some record companies, including Columbia (where his brother, Paul, headed the sales department), which entitled him to the same 10 percent discount as the one-stops. Each location that installed one of his four-and-a-half-foot metal racks paid five cents above the distributors' price for the records displayed.

Record racks were not new to the business; they dated back at least to the "Hit of the Week" operation in the early 1930s. Sheet-music racks, licensed by the Music Publishers Protective Association through the Music Dealers Service, both before and after the war, provided MPPA members with profits from a guaranteed first order that alone underwrote all production and promotion costs. When sheet-music rack distribution finally dwindled to only a Hearst connection in 1959, the MDS listed liabilities of half a million dollars. The rise of rock-'n'-roll had cut severely into sheet-music sales, facing MDS with bankruptcy. The convenience of racks to customers provided an opportunity for financial returns, which Wexler was the first to recognize.

The average small retailer, who carried items other than records, and expected current hit disks to bring in trade, was loud in protesting Wexler's racks, but rarely with the awareness that they represented the beginning of a merchandising revolution that would someday swallow him up. Bell Records, a division of the Pocket Book reprint operation, followed Wexler in the business, placing about 180,000 racks carrying its own twenty-five-cent seven-inch 45-rpm cover versions of current hits alongside twenty-five-cent book reprints. A few major labels cooperated with Bell and supplied selected releases in specially prepared sleeves. Columbia, RCA Victor, and Decca started their own quasi-independent 45 labels, free of price control, for sale on racks. Only Columbia cooperated with Wexler, allowing him 15 percent above the standard sub-distributor's discount. Seeking to get the same treatment from the others, Wexler brought an unsuccessful suit against Capitol and Decca, charging them with conspiracy to put his racks out of business by discriminatory trade practices. Caught in a morass of litigation, after a year of operation Wexler closed up his Music Merchants business.

Joe and David Handleman, of Detroit, major supplier of drug and beauty items to chain stores, had already established their first record-rack installations throughout the Midwest. With a distribution chain to regular customers already in place, they could subsist on the usual 10 percent discount allowed to sub-distributors, making up the difference with great volume. As orders grew large enough, they were in a position to by-pass local distributors and deal directly with the manufacturers, at a larger discount. They established the policy, which quickly became standard, of fully servicing the racks with top hits and some standard items, in return taking all operating and inventory risk and giving a smaller share of profits than retailers usually received.

RCA Victor was the first of the majors to recognize the sales potential in chain drugstores' and food supermarkets' displaying record racks close to check-out counters, where impulse buying was normal. Followed by Decca, Victor instituted regular training seminars for rack jobbers, showing them how disks were made, packaged, shipped, and merchandised. Adopting Angel's practice of encasing its de-lux classical LPs in cellophane, Victor and Columbia bagged their $1.98 Camden and Harmony LPs in factory-sealed polystyrene, at a cost of two cents a unit, an accommodation to rack jobbers, who recognized that it preserved the disks, minimized wear, and increased sales. Camden and Harmony releases began to appear in four-color jackets, with liner notes, made for rack locations, which accounted for 16 to 18 percent of all LP sales by 1960. The budget LP market, disks selling for $1.49, was controlled by four independent manufacturers: Remington Records; Tops Records, of California; Miller International; and Pickwick Sales of New York, which started in 1947 with a children's record line and now dominated the cheap LP market. Miller, which had started doing business in a former luncheonette, rented for seventy-five dollars a month, now grossed five million a year from its Somerset and Stereo-Fidelity labels, and was housed in seven buildings in a suburban Philadelphia industrial park. Miller and all the other budget-line manufacturers had changed to stereo or were soon going to.

Nearly twenty years had passed since a demonstration in April 1940 of practical true stereophonic recording, made by Western Electric–Bell Laboratories technicians, for a black-tie audience at Carregie Hall in New York. Two hours of stereo music had come over three speakers, hidden, as was all the equipment on stage, behind an immense screen. Music by Leoppold Stokowski and the Philadelphia Orchestra and the Mormon Tabernacle Choir, and the dramatic presentation of a scene from Eugene O'Neil's *Emperor Jones,* starring Paul Robeson, had been recorded on three different tracks on a single continuous reel of film tape, with a fourth track to regulate volume in order to avoid distortion. The three tracks were fed through separate amplifiers to the speakers, which were spread across the stage to provide width and depth to the music, lending the illusion that the sound actually traveled just as it did when performed by live musicians.

A decade before, a British engineer at EMI, where work on two-channel sound had already started, secured the patent for a practical two-channel disk, using both hill-and-dale and lateral recording. Five years later, scientists at Bell Laboratories experimented with two-channel stereo, using a similar process. The sound track for Walt Disney's *Fantasia,* released in the late 1930s, gave movie audiences a hint of what stereophonic music could sound like, but it was upstaged by some of the cartoonist's most lovable characters. Emory Cook, of Stamford, Connecticut, who made high-fidelity records for the connoisseur market, brought out a binaural record in 1952, with two separate but continuous grooves, one for each channel, played by two pickups attached to a single arm, a technical triumph but a commercial failure whose operation few laymen could master.

There were many studio technicians who believed that the future for the best high-fidelity reproduction and true stereophonic sound rested with packaged prerecorded magnetic tape. A million or more recorder-playback units had already been sold, one quarter of them in 1953, the majority for home use and of generally inferior quality. Capitol was the first of the large manufacturers to get into the taped background-music business. It transferred its entire transcription library of 3,000 selections to tape for leasing to banks, factories, and restaurants through its Magnetronics subsidiary. To counter that invasion of its territory, Muzak, which had cornered the wired background-music field, made ready to transfer its own library of 7,000 titles to magnetic tape for similar use. Announcing a library of seventeen packaged prerecorded music tapes and a new line of machines, RCA Victor joined the small group of generally independent tape packagers, among them A-V, Concertapes, Tempo Tapes, Hack Swain, and Audiosphere, whose chief problem was, like that of the flat-disk companies, the matter of speed.

No standard had been established, and existing machines ran from 3¾ inches per second to 7½, 15, and 30, with sound quality generally related to playing speed. Though the market was limited by the number of playback machines in use, the 3M Company's series of price cuts during 1955 of raw magnetic tape brought the cost of reel-to-reel prerecorded music tapes nearer the possibility of mass production. So did the experimentation by Columbia and RCA Victor with less-expensive tape machines. Working with Bell & Howell, makers of motion-picture equipment, Columbia developed tape machines utilizing the company's latest speaker assembly, the K, for Kilosphere, a candy-bar-size unit that provided "the equivalent of 2,000 minute loudspeakers, capable of relaying frequencies up to 20,000 cycles-per-second." The table-model Columbia–B & H tape recorder with a K speaker listed for $229.50, and a portable unit for $20 more. A competing RCA plant was opened in Ohio in 1956 to produce stereo tape machines and tapes. High-quality stereo tape machines that sold for $600 and more soon had serious competition from Victor's latest, which sold for just under $300. Despite their stabilized high prices—as much as $14.95 for classical music—RCA Victor's prerecorded tapes and the lower-priced playback machine presented a challenge to the industry, particularly in light of the impending single-groove stereo flat disk.

In April 1954, British EMI had launched the HMV Stereosonic label, and in early 1957, British Decca entered the stereophonic-disk field with a rival multichannel recording technology, after test recordings made by Ted Heath and his orchestra demonstrated its immediate commercial feasibility. This progress nagged at RCA Victor officials, who took the problem of a single-groove stereo record to the Westrex Company, a subsidiary of Western Electric–A T & T. Westrex handed the chore to laboratory technicians already familiar with sound motion pictures and disk recording. An inexpensive but not yet fully developed stereo cutting head and compatible single reproducing stylus had already been submitted to Victor by a West Coast engineer. They combined the vertical hill-and-dale and the lateral cutting techniques employed before the war in Britain and America. Being the most practical and logical, it was, with certain modifications in the angle of the head, developed by Westrex and demonstrated in August 1957 to Victor executives.

Sidney Frey, head of Audio Fidelity Records, was present at a second Westrex demonstration, a few months later, to the Audio Engineering Society in New York. He saw an opportunity to get national publicity for his small independent specialty label by jumping on the stereo express while it waited for a signal to start, and he ordered masters for a stereo LP from Westrex, using the already-released "Railroad Sounds" for one side and music by the Dukes of Dixieland on the other. The first practical American stereo disk was ready to be demonstrated by audio and record dealers, but they had no machine on which to play it. The lack was soon remedied by the growing availability of stereo reproducing components and the production by the Electro-Voice Company, followed by Fairchild Industries, of cartridges capable of reproducing Frey's stereo LP. Quick to take advantage of the impending revolution in recorded sound, Frey rushed out four additional stereo LPs, "Lionel Hampton," "Leon Berry on the Giant Wurlitzer," "Bagpipes and Drums," and "Mardi Gras Time with the Dukes of Dixieland."

The Westrex process that produced Frey's first American stereo LPs soon became known to the trade as the 45/45 system, because the heads inscribed sound into a single groove at a 45-degree angle to each other. British Decca's stereo recording heads, already producing London Records for export to the United States, functioned differently, as did those that produced Columbia's initial stereo recordings, introduced in March. These were designed to create compatibility between stereo disks and monaural disks, and make use of record players already sold. The speed dilemma was solved by the Recording Industry Association of America, which operated with tremendous energy for an organization whose two most important members were at odds over the future course of the business. RIAA recommended industrywide acceptance of the 45/45 stereo. The logjam was broken, but only a trickle of stereo-disk sales followed initially. The audio component and phonograph industry went into full stereo production, and by autumn every record firm was cutting all sessions in both monophonic and stereophonic sound. Even with their slow start, stereo disks accounted for six percent of the year's half-billion-dollar gross.

RCA's introduction of a new packaged tape encouraged proponents of stereo tape as the ideal medium for recorded sound; they predicted that the market would double within the next three years, with at least five million playback-recorder units in home use. The new prerecorded Victor single-reel stereo tapes were encased in a plastic cartridge approximately the size of a paperback book and could be loaded into an automatic player as easily as a flat disk onto a turntable. The speed of the cartridges was reduced from 7½ to 3¾ inches per second, and the width of the tape from one half to one quarter inches. Each tape carried four tracks rather than the earlier two, offering twice the music, and prices were reduced substantially, from the previous $3.95-to-$18.95 range to between $4.95 and $9.95, comparing favorably with stereo disks. RCA offered the new technology to the industry without cost, an offer of which several manufacturers took quick advantage. The noticeably improved sound quality of the new Victor cartridges came from a change in the recording studios—a switch to triple-track tape, which produced a better-balanced final result. Various sections of each recording group were picked up through one of three microphones, which fed into the same number of tape decks. This fixed a soloist into his natural place in the aural spectrum. Bell Sound, 3M, Motorola, and Pentron began production of similar cartridges, and made life easier for the rank amateur by eliminating problems attendant on threading tape around capstans and onto reels. Columbia provided recorded tape masters and space in the CBS laboratories in Connecticut to 3M and Revere-Wollensak for their joint experimental work on a new cartridge automatic-changer system. The final result, a single-speed reel and playback, was not launched until late 1962.

The inroad stereo tape cartridges might have made during the lull in late 1958 and early 1959, when consumers were making up their minds about the expenditure of about $500 to change over to stereo disks, was thwarted by Ampex Corporations' fight to make its own 7½-inches-per-second open-reel tape the industry standard. The new battle of speeds that followed, between Ampex and RCA, only confused consumers further and helped turn them to the two-channel record and player at a time when their future was in doubt. The smaller-than-expected 10 percent increase in retail record sales during 1958 (after an average 27 percent annual jump during the preceding three years) was attributed to the decline in singles sales and consumer indecision stemming from the stereo dilemma. Production costs for stereo disks ran much higher than for monaural records, and their rejection rate by quality control was out of all proportion to the profits they returned.

Chiefly because it could not produce sufficient cartridge players to meet the demand, RCA Victor added a line of prerecorded 7½-ips tape reels in July 1960. The monopoly in raw-tape manufacture enjoyed by 3M and its smaller competitors Reeves Soundproof and Audio Devices, an EMI-Capitol subsidiary, had been broken earlier in the year with the opening of an RCA tape plant in Indiana. The new facility was capable of producing two billion feet of tape in the first year, with a potential two-million-dollar wholesale gross, Victor's first four-track stereo reels were packed in de-luxe Pliofilm wrap and priced from $7.95 for popular music to $8.95 for Broadway shows and classical music. The addition of another half-million tape-deck players for home use strengthened a market that was taking second place to the stereo-disk business.

Most of the confusion had been set aside when the "hype" for stereo music moved out of the record industry and into other spheres. A few radio stations transmitted stereo music, one channel on AM and the other on FM. A growing number of "good music" FM facilities, aware of its attraction to the high-income listeners sponsors looked for, added regular broadcasting-in stereo programing. Consumers Union, a nonprofit product-research organization, whose 800,000 middle- and upper-class subscriber families looked to it for purchasing recommendations, devoted considerable space to audio components. A favorable report on the Shure cartridge sent the small company's earnings skyrocketing, and other manufacturers benefited similarly from Consumers Union's approval. More than 2,500 chain-store outlets joined the boom when Newberry, Woolworth, Kress, and J. C. Penny added low-price stereo players, bearing their own names, to their stock, having a significant effect on rack jobbers.

Double-channel broadcasting over AM and FM outlets and multiplexing—transmitting two signals on a single channel—which was already used to send music into subscriber supermarkets, stores, and business offices, were factors in the speeded-up programs by major manufacturers to re-record the classical repertoire in stereophonic sound. So, too, were "gim-mick" demonstration records, which provided an illusion of a speeding train crossing the living room, a place in the center of the Indianapolis

Speedway, the noises of a tropical rain forest, or the "bouncing brass" that "ping-ponged" melodies from side to side. The most successful of these were Enoch Light's "Persuasive Percussion" and "Provocative Percussion" on the Command label. Light did not intend his records to become the background music that too many LPs now were, but, rather, "sounds that involved the listener in the substance of the music." He used expensive thirty-five-millimeter film tape for his master recordings, rather than magnetic tape, to produce LPs that were the first to provide greater definition and wider range of sound.

Manipulated stereophony had much to do with generating a wider interest in stereo technology, whose sales increased by 21 percent in 1959, 26 percent in 1960, and 30 percent in 1961, a period when total gross record sales at retail were $480,000,000 for 1960 and $513,000,000 for 1961, according to RIAA figures, later revised upward. The retooling of home-entertainment units from monaural to stereophonic sound progressed in a comparably upward manner. The cry no longer was for hi-fi but for stereo, and by New Year's Day 1961, 7 million of the 30 million phonographs in American homes were capable of playing stereo disks. Poor man's stereo hit the supermarkets in mid-1960, when Pickwick Records, the largest rack supplier, developed a "compatible fidelity" processed disk that retailed for $1.98, rather than the standard $3.98 of the major labels.

The 32 percent drop in single-disk sales during 1959 was felt most by independent labels, which generally concentrated on singles and had not built up the across-the-board lines of music of the major companies. A ninety-eight-cent single offered two songs for a total playing time of between five and six minutes, whereas a $3.98 LP offered twelve tunes and forty minutes of music. The majority of America's 4,500 disk jockeys adhered to a Top 40 established-hit-only program format, enforced on them by the station manager or owner. They played the same handful of hit singles over and over again, so that teen-age buyers often tired of the songs before getting into the record stores. Except for superhits, the sales of a successful song had tumbled from the million copies or more of a few years earlier to about 200,000. Dealers, too, concentrated on the ten top hits and ignored most of the 125 new singles released each week. The odds for a hit single dropped under the one-out-of-ten range. Eight lost money, and the remaining one barely repaid production and exploitation costs. The initial cost of promotion for a newly formed independent was chiefly the $400 for 5,000 singles, out of which came copies to send to those record spinners who still selected their own music. The hope was that a hit might break out in a few key cities and stimulate distributor and dealer interest, which could be served quickly from the 5,000-copy reserve. Because of the explosion of releases and the drop in sales, distributors had adopted a conservative wait-and-see attitude toward both the major independents and the new companies before taking on new releases. Eighty-eight labels made all the places on the *Billboard* 1959 Hot 100 chart, but only one out of every three was the product of a recently formed firm.

It was economically most practical for the ten companies that did half of the total record business to abandon the now old-fashioned singles recording projects and continue their massive LP release programs, which provided the major portion of 1960's total output of 4,000 LP packages. Whenever a track from one showed any sign of promise, it was quickly released as a single, public taste rather than manufacturer judgment having marked it for special attention. That was the case with the Kingston Trio's "Tom Dooley," Marty Robbins's "El Paso," Percy Faith's "Theme from *A Summer Place*," the Mormon Tabernacle Choir's stirring rendition of "The Battle Hymn of the Republic," Johnny Mathis's "Misty," "Greenfields" by the Brothers Four, Bobby Darin's "Mack the Knife," and the "Peter Gunn Theme" by Henry Mancini—singles that jumped out of albums and contributed to the large companies' hold on record sales. All of them won the RIAA's Gold Record award.

During the year, Columbia emerged for the first time with the major share of the business, 21 percent, followed by RCA Victor, Capitol, and Decca. Lieberson ascribed the success to the Columbia Record Club, which had more than one million members, who provided the more than $30 million sales gross, for which the company spent $5.5 million on advertising. The proliferation of the mass mail-order business, as well as that of record racks, which were now in 15,000 supermarkets alone, forced the closing of specialty- and department-store record counters and speeded the doom of the small stores, which had dropped to less than 6,000 in the past several years. Their sales had increased, but dollar volume was down considerably because of various sales strategies on the part of manufacturers, rack jobbers, and discounters. To push their rival speeds and increase sales of new packaged music, Columbia and RCA Victor offered discounts to the country's 600 distributor and all retail dealers, ranging between 10 and 20 percent above the standard 38 percent, but forcing profits down by a fifth. The changes were the result of a decision to cut the cost of singles and hold the line on manufacturer-established packaged-music prices.

Hoping to restore vitality and inject new interest in the singles business, Lieberson proposed the gradual restoration of a one-speed industry through the introduction of new singles. He hoped that it would attract mature buyers who had given up on singles in favor of LPs and were responsible for the acceptance of stereo, which now had an 80 percent share of sales. Columbia's Stereo Seven—seven-inch, 33-speed disks—and Victor's Compact 33 singles were introduced almost simultaneously during 1960, followed the next year by Capitol and Mercury. Many trade insiders were certain that it would take between two and five years to switch the teen-age market away from 45s, which, coupled with the shortage of an inexpensive automatic 33-speed singles player, discouraged promotion of the compact disk. The picture for 45s brightened dramatically throughout 1961, rising from 182 million units sold that year to 210 million the next. The Atlantic-Atco-Stax/Volt group, the last a Memphis-based black "soul"-music company, whose distribution Atlantic had taken on, enjoyed a 45 percent increase in singles sales. London Records' Felsted distribution group, encompassing twenty-seven independent labels, and RCA Victor, with a roster of new hitherto-unknown artists, almost matched Atlantic's success. Thirty-three-speed compact disks drifted further away from public acceptance once Goody, Korvette's, and the majority of 3,000 discount stores that handled records cut the price of 45s from ninety-eight cents to seventy-seven cents.

The consequence of such an act of economic buccaneering was the subject of considerable discussion in the RIAA's inner circles. The organization had, from its start, seen itself as the voice of the major manufacturers, who remained its nucleus. And it continued to be the avowed instrument for carrying out two basic functions: "to promote the best interests of the phonograph record industry; and, to gather from its members and to disseminate in lawful and appropriate ways information relevant to the industry." When, in the late 1950s, Congress resumed its debate on revision of the 1909 Copyright Act, the RIAA found the mission whose pursuit would occupy it for the next several decades. Ancillary to that would be a war on record pirates, which had already been declared by another trade association.

Until it found its true purpose, the RIAA had been involved in a number of projects, which had varying degrees of success. Its campaign in the mid-1950s to remove the 10 percent excise tax on retail record sales floundered from the beginning. The tax had originally been passed in 1917 to support the war effort, was repealed in 1921, reinstituted early in the Depression by the Hoover administration, repealed a second time in 1938, and became law again in 1941. Though its application to other products was repealed once more, it remained in effect in connection with recordings until 1965. When President Lyndon Johnson did sign legislation enabling the repeal that year, it was with the expectation that the savings would reach consumers. Downward adjustments were made reluctantly, for, as the RIAA claimed, the net profits after taxes for record manufacturers had fallen from 6.8 percent in 1957 to 1.7 in 1964, giving the record buyer value "far beyond economic wisdom." List prices, a fiction in most instances, were cut and proportionate reductions made in dealer-distributor costs. In the first general price cut in more than a decade, a majority of the industry reduced list prices on LPs by twenty cents and by four cents for 45-rpm singles, passing less than half of the savings along to the consumer.

Variety's suggestion in February 1954 that it be supplied by the RIAA with official record-sales figures and all other components for a new chart to be published in conjunction with the paper's revived war on payola was scuttled by the manufacturers' reluctance to reveal figures that might conflict with those on royalty statements. The next year, $25,000 was spent to educate a group of retailers in the techniques of self-service operations. The project was abandoned once it became obvious that the rack jobbers were far ahead of the retail industry in that connection. Over a period of years, plans were regularly discussed, and shelved, for an annual affair at which official awards would be presented for the best-selling records, artists, and so on.

The Gold Record award to the manufacturer and the artist for the sale of a million single records, which brought the RIAA its least controversial publicity, was first given in February 1958. Arrangements were completed with a firm of public accountants to examine sales figures and reports available only at the record companies, and then to certify the accuracy of a million-sales claim. The RIAA's fee for this service, together with two gold plaques, was $350. To spur the use of the RIAA seal and its certification of million-copy sellers by nonmembers, the fee was reduced several times, finally to $150 in 1960, with an extra $50 charge for each additional plaque, though the sale of a half-million LPs was deemed sufficient for Gold award by that time. To afford recognition to multi-LP collections, the criterion was revised again in 1961, and called for a minimum factory billing of one million dollars, rather than the sale of 500,000 LPs. The regular flow of press releases reporting each quarter's awards served as the staple for the trade and general press, and made the RIAA generally better known.

CHAPTER 18

Growth to a Four-Billion-Dollar Business

The Recording Industry Association of America's fight on record counterfeiters accelerated in 1961, stimulated by the activities of ARMADA—the rival American Record Manufacturers and Distributors Association—among whose associate members were some of the major labels. Forgery of a single record, including the label and printed sleeve, which had grown more sophisticated and prosperous, was moving to LPs. The RIAA was present as a witness at state and national deliberations to outlaw the practice, and played a role in the passage in October 1962 of a federal act providing criminal penalties for trafficking in disks bearing counterfeit labels.

Open war, which dragged on until 1976, between the RIAA and the music publishers represented by the MPPA over the issue of compulsory licensing broke out violently in 1963. In a 102-page report that had taken more than a year to prepare, the RIAA warned that to repeal compulsory licensing "blithely ignored" a fifty-year practice that had become the foundation of the current half-billion-dollar music business. Payments to the Harry Fox Agency of the MPPA, which collected royalties from record companies on behalf of three quarters of all music publishers, had risen from $4.4 million in 1955 to $13.1 million in 1961. Programing of phonograph records supplied by RIAA members, which had accounted for 46.9 percent of all time on the air in 1953, now occupied 79.7 percent on a far greater number of AM stations. The RIAA was in favor only of a provision calling for criminal penalties for counterfeiting phonograph records.

In a talk to the National Association of Broadcasters in April 1964, Henry Brief, recently appointed the RIAA's executive secretary, confided that in a $758-million business, the manufacturers for whom he spoke were investing $68.7 million yearly to create new products, at an average cost of $2,500 for a single and $15,000 for an LP album. New legislation was being discussed in Congress to increase mechanical-royalty rates paid to writers and publishers by 50 percent. It would, he contended, also increase the cost to the manufacturers of a single by two cents and of an LP by twelve, which, he maintained, would increase royalty income to nine times the record industry's entire profit.

An all-star delegation of record-company presidents, including Lieberson of Columbia, Alan Livingstone of Capitol, and David Kapp, representing his Kapp label, testified before the House of Representatives' copyright subcommittee in June 1965. They were accompanied by Thurmond Arnold, now special Washington counsel for the RIAA, which represented three fourths of all record companies, and a Harvard economics professor, John D. Glover. Glover stated that whereas the disk industry's profits after taxes had fallen from $6.1 million in 1960 to $4 million in 1964, royalties paid to copyright owners had risen from $17.4 million to $25.2 million in the same period. Clearly, he argued, the statutory rate should not be raised, but, rather, reduced. Capitol Records, Livingstone testified, was the number-one company in terms of retail sales in 1964, but had realized only a 3.3 percent net profit from sales. Pointing to the value of a copyright in contrast to that of its recordings, he cited the example of the song "Autumn Leaves," which was published by a Capitol subsidiary, Ardmore Music. Between 1950 and 1953, it had earned $479,879 from all sources in the United States. Thirteen years after the song was first recorded, it earned $21,000 in record royalties and $8,400 for broadcast performances in the past year. The first record of "Autumn Leaves," made by the Capitol artist Jo Stafford, sold 18,926 copies, not enough to pay its production and merchandising costs.

The issue of payment by broadcasters for their use of records on the air was raised by Livingstone, who intended to make that industry, whose members were already complaining about the fees they paid to the performing-rights organizations, a record-business tool in this case. It was inequitable, he said, that the record companies, the performers, and the arrangers did not receive a single penny from air performances of their work. With the injection of that notion, a new and confusing ingredient entered the issue of copyright revision.

In October, the House Judiciary Committee passed a 149-page copyright-revision proposal, which, among other provisions, extended copyright protection to the life of the holder plus fifty years, imposed a nineteen-dollar license fee on each jukebox, and raised the mechanical fee to either two and a half cents for each work or half a cent per minute of playing time or fraction thereof. It appeared highly unlikely that full House and Senate approval would come before the end of 1967, which gave the RIAA, the Music Operators of America, and other lobbying groups time to force changes in the legislation.

Prior to his resignation in 1955 from Columbia Records and the RIAA,

of which he was also president, James Conkling had been a persistent proponent of a record-industry awards night, one that would celebrate the business and its artists. Two years after he had retired to California, the Hollywood Beautification Committee added five representatives of the recording
industry to the panel of advisers responsible for selecting artists and actors
whose names would be inscribed on the sidewalks of Hollywood Boule-
vard. At first they used the yardstick of record sales to select musicians and
singers for the honor, which the RIAA also used, but then they noted that
many artists they believed should be honored did not enjoy large sales.
Charges were made on both coasts that hit records were frequently the result of a conspiracy involving the country's disk jockeys.

Out of these conflicting currents the National Academy of Recording Arts
and Sciences was formed, to reward artistic creativity in the recording field,
not in sidewalk cement, and with a significant symbol. Casting about for a
man of stature, NARAS chose Conkling as temporary chairman. His thinking had changed somewhat; he now believed that recognition of achievement should spring from creative people themselves, rather than from the
recording industry's sales figures. Sixteen people involved in making records attended the first membership meeting, on June 25, 1957. An executive secretary was employed, who was empowered to step up formation of
NARAS chapters around the country. With assistance from the RIAA, a
New York chapter was formed the following February.

The first NARAS awards were presented in May 1958 in Los Angeles,
to Frank Sinatra, Ella Fitzgerald, Henry Mancini, Count Basie, Domenico
Mondugno (the singer of the Song of the Year—"Nel Blu Dipinto di Blue"),
and others, choices strongly reflective of a bias for West Coast music and
against the Top 10, and representing elitist standards. Presley, Mathis, Anka,
the Everly Brothers, and others who had dominated the sales lists through
the year were ignored, which happened also in succeeding awards. A metal
replica of a talking machine on a wooden base, for which the NARAS
became best known to the public, was presented to the winners. A composite based on the Victrola and early Edison and Columbia record players,
the award was named by a woman from New Orleans, who won twenty-
four LP records for recommending that it be known as a "Grammy" because it was "a replica of the old-fashioned gramophone."

The announcement of nominations for the 1960 Grammys evoked a public letter of complaint from Goddard Lieberson questioning the manner of
selection, which he said could not "provide a true measurement of artistic
merit or give any indication of the record industry's accomplishment in the
classical, jazz or popular fields . . . the omission of so many internationally famous artists and the casual inclusion of so much obviously partisan
material demonstrated the inadequacy of a voting system which provides
such results." The letter and similar expressions of dissatisfaction from
East Coast executives, artists, and critics began an annual reassessment of

nominating practices and voting procedures to extend the categories. Beginning with twenty-eight in 1958, there were thirty-four awards in 1959, thirty-nine in 1960, forty in 1961, thirty-nine in 1962, forty-two in 1963, forty-seven in 1964, forty-seven in 1965, and forty-two in 1966. A formal voting process was taking shape, starting with an initial list of several thousand selections suggested by record companies and voting members. These recommendations were screened to ensure eligibility, correct any errors, and make certain that nominations appeared in the proper categories. Committees of qualified members who were experts in various fields, trade-paper and general-magazine critics, local chapter governors, and national trustees participated in the process that led to the printing of the final ballot. These were processed by an international accounting firm and made public at the annual Grammy Awards presentations, which were first shown on television in November 1959. The national exposure that television brought made necessary recognition of a changing record scene, which often followed public taste belatedly.

The first national meeting of Los Angeles and New York trustees took place in October 1960, out of which came major changes in the award process. The following March, George Simon, musician, critic, and member of the World War II V-Disk production team, was appointed executive director of the New York chapter. A Chicago chapter was formed in July 1961, and the first NARAS constitution was ratified by all chapters that August. Christine Farnon, the secretary of Capitol Records' president, Alan Livingstone, who had been a loyal volunteer worker throughout the NARAS's earliest years, moved into the salaried executive director's office, in Los Angeles, beginning an association that eventually saw her named executive director of the national office.

Failing since 1959 to recruit sufficient applicants to be granted a NARAS charter, members of the Nashville music community organized a local chapter in 1964, the first year that country-and-western artists received Grammys, an honor not yet granted Presley. Rhythm-and-blues was recognized in only one category, whereas country music appeared in six, a discrimination that was not repeated on the next year's ballot. Because so many different tastes and cultural attitudes were involved, and the awards continued to be based on artistic achievement as perceived by NARAS' 2,000 members, and not on record sales or other measures of public acceptance, the trustees were required to tinker with procedures every year. The actions they took reflected a collective conscience, born out of the hope that the NARAS would eventually catch up with what was really going on in an incredibly fast-changing world.

Cutthroat competition, rather than the need for improving their industry's image, brought about the formation of a number of record-business merchandising-related associations in 1959, the most effective of them being ARMADA and NARM, the rack jobbers' National Association of Record

Merchandisers. Both faced problems created by the larger record firms, which, wishing to move old and new records, cut prices, offered special discounts to favored accounts and free records to disk jockeys, jammed the market with tie-ins, and by-passed rack jobbers to do business with "dumpers." These small-time entrepreneurs bought up large quantities of discontinued records for little more than their production cost and resold their booty at a large discount to retailers, who returned the shipments to distributors and were credited with the regular discount. Eventually, at ARMADA's insistence, some of the majors foiled the dumpers by scrapping deleted stock at substantial losses or selling it through special mail-order-only programs.

Initially, free records, or freebies, were new releases furnished to radio stations or important disk jockeys by record companies, artists, distributors, and publishers in return for preferential treatment on the air. Now it was the retailer who might receive free boxes of a hot release in return for substantial orders. When the going was hard a one-for-three, one-for-six, or as much as a 15-for-100 policy was instituted to push an entire line or the existing LP catalogue.

Premium or tie-in records had existed earlier, but came into the big time in 1957 when RCA Victor, in cooperation with Kellogg, Proctor & Gamble, and H. J. Heinz, issued them in vast quantities. The promotion for Crest toothpaste involved five-million packages containing coupons that offered a twenty-five-cent EP sampler of new releases, introduced by Tony Martin, who appealed to the young housewives Proctor & Gamble was after. A surprising 10 percent mail response for the price-liquidating sampler, which cost about twenty-five cents to produce, attracted other manufacturers, ready to spend substantial sums on advertising, as well as several of the major labels. Columbia used deleted repertory for its premium records; RCA Victor promoted new releases. Premium tie-ins became such a large business that record companies opened special departments to take care of it exclusively, and several specialty-record firms were formed to handle business the majors rejected. High volume and low-cost-per-unit premiums gave sponsors an item whose true value was usually three or four times what the consumer paid and would repeat the advertiser's message in millions of homes long after a campaign in print would be forgotten. Annually, the Goodyear Tire & Rubber Company distributed three million copies of a Christmas-song LP for one dollar, available through 60,000 dealers and franchise holders. The immediate response in 1963 was so great that all advertising in connection with the LP was canceled a month before Christmas. Many advertising agencies and national merchandisers had similar successful premium tie-ins.

With significant budget-LP catalogues, RCA Victor, Columbia, and Warner Brothers were among the initial twelve manufacturers that joined the NARM in 1958 as associate members. Supermarkets and self-service and five-and-ten-cent stores were selling one out of every three LPs supplied by rack-jobber NARM members. Women shoppers were the low-cost and budget LPs' best customers, with children a major stimulus.

Rack merchandisers, including 45 NARM members, 60 percent of whom each did over a million dollars in annual business, serviced 18,500 outlets that made half of all rack sales, representing 27.4 percent of 1961's $513-million gross volume. The following year, with their rack customers increased to 24,000 outlets, the NARM's member companies increased their total sales gross by 25 percent. No longer concentrating only on rack jobbing, they were becoming the largest single factor in record retailing. The biggest NARM members now owned retail record departments in locations they once only serviced, and had spread out with installations in post exchanges. A few, like the country's largest rack jobber, the Handleman Company, acquired major distributorships or formed distribution pools, leaving the role of the NARM's major constituents in the national distribution apparatus in serious question at a time when the FTC was actively involved in a study of record-business practices. The request in early 1963 by some NARM rack-jobber members to be treated by associate-member manufacturers no longer as sub-distributors, but as full distributors with the prevailing discount privilege, was refused. Instead, CBS Records initiated a price-stabilization policy shortly after. Anticipating that a reduction of about twenty cents on LPs and prerecorded tapes would put all retail dealers on an equal footing with discounters and rack jobbers, CBS fixed wholesale prices to them on a round-the-year basis. The role of a sub-distributor, vis-à-vis wholesale and retail sales, was reappraised, leading to consternation in many NARM members. Almost every important record company, including RCA Victor, established similar stabilized year-round price policies.

Initially, ARMADA was ignored by the major labels, possibly because it was far more vocal in calling for industry reforms than the RIAA, which represented only three of every ten record companies. Without their own RIAA, many leading independents found a home in ARMADA. Rack jobbing, the one-stops, disk counterfeiting, the existing price structure, freebies, transshipping, the brewing payola scandal, and other problems occupied 200 independent labels and distributors who serviced retail outlets NARM members did not. They had gathered to form the association in 1959. Twenty million of the $100 million single-disk gross went for bootleg records with counterfeit labels, depriving the federal government of two million dollars in excise taxes. ARMADA, not the RIAA, took the lead in a fight against record pirates, beginning in state legislatures, and soon after in Washington. The importance to the members of this course of action rested on sheer economics. By eliminating such costs as production expenses, royalties, and excise taxes, disk pirates realized a profit of about one dollar from selling, for $1.50, counterfeits of LPs that were high on trade-paper charts, thus cutting deeply into both the manufacturers' and the authorized distributors' returns. Piracy especially affected ARMADA's large manufacturer members—United Artists, Cameo-Parkway, Vee-Jay, ABC-Paramount, Atlantic, and London, among others—its major victims in the early 1960s.

The major retailing operations owned by NARM members, with ready access to the large manufacturers, dealt directly with them, by-passing ARMADA-affiliated distributors. The preferential treatment thus accorded was clearly in violation of the Wright-Patman Act, and a matter ARMADA did not intend to let lie. Speaking at the NARM's fifth annual convention, in July 1963, Earl Kintner, former FTC chairman and now ARMADA's special Washington counsel, warned the industry that if it did not clean up   · its own house the government would, and that his client would accept either. Responding to the pressure exerted on it by ARMADA, in September the FTC and Congressman James Roosevelt called for a record-industry trade-practice conference, after which the FTC would issue rules.

During the 1930s, the FTC had cooperated with the MPPA to draft a code of ethics for payment of gratuities to orchestra leaders and other performers, a practice becoming known then in Tin Pan Alley as "payola." Whatever reforms the document was expected to effect vanished quickly in a milieu where evasion of regulation was a high art. Well aware that payola flourished in spite of its intercession, the FTC took no official action and washed its hands of further involvement.

The record industry came under serious government scrutiny in 1955, when a New York grand jury served subpoenas on the Big Four manufacturers and a few smaller companies in connection with a Justice Department investigation. The documents requested were expected to provide evidence of the shipment of free records to radio stations, unfair dealings with independent distributors, discriminatory LP price practices, price cutting, and other such matters. Nothing came of the probe, but it was clear that many industry practices were questionable, at best skirting current legislation, and that if evidence of antitrust violation was adduced, indictments would be handed down.

In a sudden reaction to the House subcommittee hearings on deceitful practices in radio and television, as well as to the disk-jockey-payola scandal scheduled for investigation in early 1960, the FTC made a three-week probe of record-distributor relationships with disk jockeys. The Eisenhower administration was in its last year of power, and the regulatory agencies, in particular, sought to establish a good record of accomplishment. Earl Kintner, then FTC chairman, had just won White House approval of a supplemental budget, increasing to $2.2 million the share of the agency's annual $7-million budget channeled into the "policing of advertising and other deceptive commercial practices."

At the conclusion of its hurried investigation, on December 3, 1959, the FTC rushed out the first nine of the eventual hundred or more complaints against record manufacturers and their distributors. Most charged violation of Section Five, of the act that established the FTC, by paying disk jockeys to favor "certain" recordings and play them as often as six to ten times a day, thus giving the defendants "the capacity to suppress competition and to divert trade unfairly from competition through deceptive advertising." Neither the RIAA nor the world's largest record companies had ever sought action by the FTC to clean up their business. As though stricken by a sudden revelation of truth, RCA Victor now saw the complaint against it as "taken to assure the highest standards for the record industry . . . in the best interests of the people, the artists, record distributors and retailers, and the entire industry."

The consent order framed by RCA and the FTC became a model for all succeeding settlements made to terminate the complaints without the un-pleasantness of public hearings. There was no admission of guilt, only the promise never to do again what had not been admitted. By the time a new chairman was appointed to succeed Kintner, eighty-two complaints and ninety consent orders, involving every major label, had been issued, and, in the words of a commission press release, "successfully attacked this evil at its source." The new FTC head promised no let-up by the agency in its ad-ministration of antitrust laws.

The record-club business, which continued to account for more then 15 percent of industry volume, by selling LPs to consumer members at prices lower than to retailers, had been the subject of unsuccessful legal actions by retailer groups. Another was instituted by the FTC in the summer of 1962, invoking the now-dreaded Section Five against CBS and the Colum-bia Record Club, alleging monopolistic practices, illegal suppression of competition, and deceptive advertising. At the heart of the complaint were Columbia's exclusive agreements with Verve, Mercury, Warner Brothers, Kapp, Cameo-Parkway, and other companies, which gave CBS the special privilege of merchandising, through its club, records made from their mas-ters. The RCA Victor Club, which was operated by *Reader's Digest,* and Capitol's mail-order business, which together accounted for 40 percent of the record-club business—Columbia having half of the business—were not cited in the action, because they sold only their own recordings.

A Columbia Record Club member paid on average $2.14 for an LP, exclusive of handling and mailing charges, after pledging to buy twelve popular LPs in the course of a year. The dealer cost of an LP ran between $2.47 and $2.12, the latter only during periods of special promotion or discount deals. In 1960, the FTC reported, after extended examination of the CBS's financial records, Columbia's total sales were over $54 million in a ten-month period, with $30.4 million from the club's 1.3 million mem-bers. The retail-dealer advertising budget in that period was $2.1 million, that for club advertising and promotion $5.5 million.

During the second round of FTC hearings, in 1963, following public examinations around the country, Columbia credited the record-club movement for a gross-volume increase every year since 1955, when the Columbia club was introduced. In addition, the increase in high-fidelity units, a steady 2 percent annually prior to 1954, had grown at a 14 percent rate each year since, because of record-club promotion.

More than a year after the hearings were concluded, an FTC examiner cleared CBS of all charges, having found that the Columbia Record Club did not discriminate against retail dealers. That clubs had not damaged the industry, he added, was manifest in its rapid expansion to 1964, when 200 of an estimated 2,750 companies produced records on a regular basis. The examiner's recommendations were rejected by the FTC general counsel, who began a new set of hearings and court appearances, which led to a final FTC consent order in 1971. This ended Columbia's exclusive access to the products of nonaffiliated record companies.

ARMADA's continuing determination to do something about industry inequities had been aired publicly several weeks before the findings in the CBS complaint were announced. Appearing at a hearing conducted by the House Subcommittee on Small Business, chaired by James Roosevelt, Amos Heilicher, president of ARMADA, outlined the dual distribution and vertical integration abuses besetting both independent distributors and retail dealers, for which, ARMADA contended, CBS, RCA Victor, and other major firms were responsible. The congressmen had been examining practices in a number of presumably stable industries in which one or two companies dominated production and distribution, possibly in violation of fair-trade legislation by encroaching on smaller companies' business affairs. Heilicher told the subcommittee that a handful of companies dominated operations in the record business, "from manufacture down through the retail level," out of which many evils had sprung. The absence of well-defined functional levels of distribution, he added, "had given rise to a variety of free-wheeling predatory tactics that must be seen to be believed."

During several hours of contentious debate before the FTC the following spring, in which representatives of all segments of the industry participated, the draft of rules of trade practice prepared by FTC staff members was torn apart and then rewritten. The final FTC Trade Practice Rules for the record business went into effect in November 1964. Essentially a restatement of the existing Wright-Patman and Clayton acts, the document was less comprehensive than ARMADA had hoped, but it did deal to some extent with the rampant dual-distribution and vertical-integration situation. Retailers were granted more protection, and such lesser fry as one-stops and rack jobbers were barred from receiving functional discounts. There was no real change in the vertically integrated structure of the largest companies. Without exception, record companies were restrained from deceptive practices and discriminatory price-differential practices. A supplementary Guide Against Deceptive Practices, issued the following January, added additional prohibitions. No one was entirely pleased. The new rules appeared to have little effect on economic concentration in the business. MGM Records completed the acquisition of additional major distributorships on both coasts. The Handleman Company continued to increase its ownership of Midwestern distribution outlets, giving it "almost irresistible powers in bargaining with suppliers," as Roosevelt complained to the FTC. Freed by the FTC examiner's preliminary ruling in the Columbia Record Club complaint, RCA Victor bought back direct control of the Victor Record Clubs from *Reader's Digest.*

The American record business in the mid-1960s was a far cry from the six-million-dollar affair dominated by a single manufacturer belonging to a vast holding company whose international ramifications were subject to government scrutiny. The simple distribution system—manufacturer-retailer-consumer—that had existed had been extended into a circuitous pattern whose components were at one another's throats. The business was no longer a segmented affair, isolated by geography, but had become a vast interconnected international complex.

The earliest harbinger of this change had come in January 1955, with the announcement that the vast Electric & Musical Industries combine was acquiring ownership of Capitol Records, the first international negotiation to get control of an American record firm. The British holding company, which controlled the manufacture of radio, phonograph, and television equipment, home appliance and electronic components, in addition to ownership of the HMV, British Columbia, American Angel, Parlophone, Marconiphone, Pathé, and Regal-Zonophone labels, concluded arrangements with Capitol's majority stockholders—Glenn Wallichs, Johnny Mercer, and the estate of Buddy De Sylva—to acquire their 248,435 common shares at $17.50 each. The price was $4.50 above the market selling figure at the time of the announcement. Of the trio that had organized Capitol in 1942, with the investment of under $25,000, only Wallichs remained with the organization. To complete the negotiation, EMI had to purchase two thirds of the remaining 476,230 outstanding Capitol shares by March 14, 1955, at the same figure, representing a total investment in one of the Big Four American disk companies of $8.5 million. The purchase of additional Capitol shares was financed by an issue to current EMI shareholders of three million second-preference shares at $2.80 each.

Now that the sun no longer set on the Capitol label, long-placid international waters were roiled as the eyes of other major U.S. companies looked to existing and possibly new European connections. EMI had been cautious and highly selective in forging links with the postwar American record business, which appeared to be, in the words of an old British popular song, turning its own world "upside down." It picked up the distribution of MGM Records in the late 1940s, specifically for the film company's important sound-track record library, and King Records of Cincinnati, for some country-

and-western hits, which had become popular with England's blue-collar workers.

Recordings of American origin accounted for about one third of Europe's purchases, and the combined total of 75 million disks sold in Great Britain and West Germany in 1954 represented a third of the American market. The high price of records in Europe (twice that in the United States), antiquated production machinery, and bigger publisher royalties mitigated against increased sales. In France, publishers' mechanical fees were double those in the United States; in England they were 6½ percent of the retail price.

Mannie Sachs, who was in full charge of all RCA Victor records, and George Marek, who headed the company's A & R department, were ready to improve these conditions. They began with the introduction of the 45-speed disk and player in England. During visits there and to RCA plants on the Continent, they completed a reciprocal distribution agreement with Sir Edward Lewis, of British Decca, effective in 1957, when Victor's fifty-year liaison with EMI-HMV terminated. Lewis intended to maintain his London label in America, but he gave RCA access to its concert-music artists, of whom there were enough for both. Similar distribution arrangements were made simultaneously with Telefunken, to inaugurate Teldec Records in West Germany, and Musikvertrieb of Switzerland, thus providing the RCA Victor logo world-wide visibility for the first time. Contracts already existed with other independent European record makers and distributors. Victor of Japan, formerly owned jointly with RCA, handled all distribution in the Far East.

The state-controlled Russian record industry had not been penetrated by RCA, but rights to Soviet music tapes for North America had been assigned in 1950 to the American popular-music publisher Lou Levy, under a contract with the Soviet Trade Agency. In 1956, EMI got European and Asian rights to all music recorded in Russia, for distribution by its foreign affiliates. American Decca, whose founder, Jack Kapp, had acquired rights for the United States to eastern European and Spanish- and French-language music prior to the war, renewed a long-term pact with Deutsche Grammophon for both its classical-music repertory and popular music from its Polydor division.

The competition engendered by RCA International's new major presence in the European market and the rapid spread of record clubs in Britain— British Decca's Ace of Clubs, the Encore and Concert Classics series, and the World Record Club, the country's largest—and later in Germany led to an average 25 percent reduction in the cost of European disks. The clubs handled only records withdrawn from domestic and American catalogues, whose production costs had long since been written off. They could still make a profit at a reduced price. Without disclosing the fact, for fear of further irritating retail dealers, EMI purchased a three-quarter interest in the

World Record Club, hoping to expand local consumer markets. When the ownership was made public, EMI explained to the dealers, "the very backbone of our industry," that its sales to them had doubled despite the success of its clubs. The first German Schallplattenring, or record club, was started by Bertelsmann, a leading German book publisher that also managed the country's largest book club. Record clubs introduced many Europeans to the new American artists, among them Elvis Presley, who was, in England, Italy, and France, as in America, soon the hottest disk performer, billed as the "man who sings like Marilyn Monroe walks." Another favorite was Bill Haley, who was brought to public attention in Europe by the performance in the film *The Blackboard Jungle* of "Rock Around the Clock," a recording that outsold those of the beloved Edith Piaf for nearly a year. In Britain, Pat Boone's white-buck–shoe cover version of "Tutti Frutti" sold a half-million disks in three months. America's share of recorded music in England rose from fifty-two of the Top 100 in 1952 to seventy-two four years later; twenty-seven to forty-one in Germany; and twenty-one to twenty-nine in France.

RCA speeded up the termination of its contract with EMI in the late spring of 1957, in order to activate the partnership with British Decca and introduce the RCA Victor label in Great Britain. A fierce competition developed among existing local companies and between Victor's pressing plants and the entire European record business. The RCA-EMI divorce enabled Angel Records to increase its distribution of classical music in the American market and Capitol to augment its classical catalogue when most HMV concert-music masters were made available to it for the United States. A corporate reorganization followed at EMI, and the existing Angel stock was sold to Capitol, giving it control in early 1958 of a classical line that could successfully compete with both RCA Victor and Columbia. Under the leadership of Dario Soria, founder of Angel, in 1953, and its president, Angel had created a catalogue of 500 titles and had sold four million LPs. He introduced the concept of separate packaging—a de-luxe, wrapped LP with extensive liner notes, sold at a premium price, and a simple and less expensive plan album in a cardboard sleeve. Dario Soria sold the remaining quarter-interest in Angel to Capitol and, after resigning completely, joined Victor as a consultant-producer.

The introduction in the winter of 1957–58 of Philips NV's new Fontana label, using, predominantly, Columbia masters, boosted the company's European sales, despite the tremendous local popularity of Presley and Harry Belafonte, whose "Mary's Boy Child" sold 1.4 million disks in England alone during the Christmas season. However, dissension among Philips's management left Columbia behind its major rival.

A vast expansion of the European record business, possibly equaling that in the United States, and affecting American firms already doing business there on a reciprocal basis, was expected to be one result of the activation of the European Common Market in 1958. The original members—France, Germany, Italy, and the Benelux countries—agreed, among other reforms, to lower and finally eliminate tariff walls between themselves, a major factor in the high cost of many commodities, regardless of their country of origin. LPs were, for instance, three times higher than in America. The "one world" ideology implicit in the ECM would eliminate inefficient and limited record production, imposed by geography and tariffs, and lead to large and efficient modern plants, where sufficient LPs could be produced to meet the entire continent's demand at a standard retail price.

Bias against American music was then manifesting itself. In England, the Songwriters' Guild, a counterpart of the American SPA, actively sought to enforce a drastic reduction in the use of American music and recordings on the BBC, where it occupied two thirds of all musical programing. West Germany's radio networks censored Elvis Presley songs and the theme from the motion picture *Exodus*, as "offensive to German culture." To save money, or for reasons of nationalism, some German music publishers would not pay the usual $500 to $3,000 advance for the rights to publish American hits unless the original publisher secured a German-language recording by a major artist. In France a 45 percent ceiling was imposed on the broadcasting of foreign recorded music on the state radio network, and a union of French authors and composers lobbied to increase the quota restriction. Unless it was curbed, such discrimination against American music and records could have serious effects.

Reciprocity of a kind suddenly flourished. Doris Day made an LP in four languages; Nat Cole, a package of French hits; Johnny Cash, a German version of his American successes. American popularity charts recorded a sudden new vogue for foreign artists and music; Bert Kaempfert's "Wonderland by Night," the Lawrence Welk version of "Calcutta," "Sailor" by the German singer Lolita, and Jorgen Ingmann's "Apache" crowded into the Top Five category.

The purchase of Mercury Records and its pressing plants in late 1961, for cash and stock worth about three million dollars, by American Consolidated Electronics Industries on behalf of its owner, Philips's Incandescent Lamp-works Holding Company, represented the second foray into the American record business by a major European combine. Philips's recent earlier bid of $10 million for Dot Records had been rejected by ABC-Paramount. The Mercury purchase was a reaction to Columbia's sudden cancellation of their reciprocal understanding, which left Philips without any connection in the United States, and an early move by that American telecommunications giant to establish itself as its own label in the international record business. The success of RCA International, with thirty-three associated or licensed company affiliates around the world, was another factor in Philips's purchase, as was Great Britain's impending admission into the European Common Market. American manufacturers had recognized that a connection with the ECM through manufacturing and distribution facilities in any of the member countries would enable them to avoid surplus import duties and sell their merchandise in Europe at prices comparable to those at home. The opening of the RCA Italian motion-picture–sound track and commercial-disk-recording studios in Rome, with adjacent custom-record manufacturing facilities, built at a cost of half a million dollars, marked one of the earliest effects of the Common Market on the international record industry, of which the United States had a 56 percent share. Excluding the Iron Curtain countries, Europe represented one quarter of all record-sales volume: the United Kingdom and West Germany, 6 percent each; France, 4 percent; Italy, 3 percent; the Benelux and other countries, a combined 4 percent. Two percent of all disks manufactured were sold in Australia, New Zealand, and the Asian and African nations.

The formation of a Dutch affiliate, in January 1963, to press and distribute CBS records in the Benelux countries came just before Columbia Records International formally opened its Paris headquarters and introduced Disques CBS in France. The $125,000 paid for a half-interest in an active German firm was expected to provide CRI with a five percent share of that market by the end of the year. There already were wholly owned CRI branches in Latin America, Canada, Japan, Greece, Italy, and Great Britain, where Philips temporarily marketed the CBS label. CRI had additional plans to set up new wholly owned or affiliated record firms throughout the world, to present local talent on locally made disks for local consumption, as well as to sell LPs and singles made from American masters. Masters had already been distributed of Mitch Miller singing along in Japanese, Steve Lawrence and Edie Gorme in Spanish and Italian, Barbra Streisand in German, Jerry Vale in Tagalog for the Philippine trade, and Andy Williams in French, Spanish, German and Italian.

To supplement the home country's music-publishing business, fourteen CRI-owned music firms were to be opened in major countries. Speaking at a music-business seminar in March 1963, Nat Shapiro, A & R director for CRI, discussed the world's record business from the perspective of an executive just returned from abroad. Though it represented about one percent of all record sales in the world, the Australia–New Zealand sphere was the highest per-capita market in the world, with American products outselling those from Britain. Germany was the largest market for singles, with an average sale of a million copies for a domestic hit, but only 100,000 for imported hits recorded by leading American artists, although their German-language versions did better. Singles outsold LPs and EPs in Italy and England. Italian versions of rock-'n'-roll hits sold between 250,000 and one million. EP 45s were preferred in France, where there was no singles market and American hits were rare. International record piracy thrived in Hong Kong and Taiwan, where several hits on a single record sold for a dollar.

In spite of efforts by the Songwriters' Guild of Great Britain since 1958
to force a reduction of U.S. disks on the BBC, programing preferences
there still favored music from abroad. Sixty-eight percent of all popular
music played by the BBC was foreign, 59 percent American. The denizens
of Denmark Street, London's Tin Pan Alley, shared with their American
counterparts an apparent inability to master the kind of rock-'n'-roll music
sung by Presley and Haley, which topped British hit charts almost immediately after their records' first appearance in London stores. Being number
one in Great Britain, however, was based on different sales figures, often
needing only the sale of 40,000 units.

Beginning in 1962, the tide turned in the international popularity war.
Twenty-four British records appeared on the best-selling lists in fourteen
countries, and Acker Bilk's "Stranger on the Shore" was voted the year's
best instrumental by 2,000 American disk jockeys. Presley now found it
difficult to get into the Top 10, his "One Broken Heart for Sale" never
rising above number eleven. Making the same kind of music that had propelled the Americans Buddy Holly, Little Richard, Bobby Vee, the Everly
Brothers, and Duane Eddy to the top in their country, British artists and
songwriters pushed Presley to one side. British record producers were evolving
their own "British sound" out of American recording techniques and were
putting it to good use on the international front.

Sir Edward Lewis was not pleased with the treatment his American subsidiary, Capitol, gave EMI-produced records in the United States, his largest export market. The chaotic state of affairs in that land of "profitless
prosperity," with its rack jobbers, discount houses, record clubs, and gimmicks, troubled him. He had recently terminated negotiations for a merger
with Paramount Pictures. One example of Capitol's neglect involved the
Beatles, a rock-'n'-roll group from Liverpool, who had four singles, an EP,
and an LP on the hit charts, which had a combined total sale of more than
three million units by November 1963. But Capitol did not indicate any
interest in exercising an option to release the British masters in America.
The Capitol executives, instead, expected great things from the newest U.S.
musical fad, "beach music," and its best proponent, the Beach Boys.

Early in 1963, an American international clearing house for record masters, Transglobal, of New York, had obtained rights to several Beatles disks
and had leased the masters to Vee Jay Records, of Chicago, a black-owned
R & B label. Vee Jay put out two singles and got no indication of interest
in the trade press. Having received no payment from Vee Jay, Transglobal
terminated their agreement and returned all rights to EMI. Disregarding the
cancellation, Vee Jay released an LP, "Introducing the Beatles," again
producing no chart activity.

Responding in January 1964 to what he described as "pressure . . . too
great for us to hold back any more," Alan Livingstone announced the immediate release of a Beatles single, "I Want to Hold Your Hand," with a

$50,000 exploitation budget. It sold a million copies in three weeks. Several months before Capitol began to promote them, the Beatles had effectively crossed the Atlantic from England.

The journey of John Lennon, Paul McCartney, Ringo Starr, and George Harrison from total obscurity on the river Mersey to world-wide acclaim and massive record sales had started in 1960 in Hamburg's St. Pauli district, where American rock 'n' roll was offered alongside exotic sexual attractions. Called the "Beatles," after Buddy Holly's Crickets, they played all night and made one recording, which inspired a Liverpool department-store record manager for the largest disk retailer in the North Country, Brian Epstein, to seek them out, become their manager, and tell all who would listen that they would become "bigger than Elvis." Decca, Pye, HMV, and Philips turned him down. Then George Martin, in charge of A & R at Parlophone, offered a contract for four sides in the next twelve months, and a one-cent royalty on each single. The Beatles "were very lucky," as Peter Brown and Steven Gains wrote in *The Love You Make.*

> Their alchemy with George Martin synthesized real gold. Although Martin's role in the production of their records changed over the years, he was always their primary conduit, the intermediary who transposed their inarticulate ideas into music. None of the Beatles could read or write music, although Paul was to teach himself. They had no knowledge or command of any instruments except those they already played, and they knew nothing whatsoever about how records were made or the capabilities of the recording studio. . . . The Beatles' first songs were recorded on four-track recorders in monaural, compared with the sixteen- and thirty-two-track overdubbings of later years. In any event, Martin was to become the interpretive vessel through which they were presented to the world.

Martin was lucky, too, on the day he and Epstein signed the contract. Parlophone's sales were slipping, and it was rumored that Martin might lose his position with the vast EMI complex.

The Beatles were selling records world-wide at a monthly rate of $1.2 million when they arrived in New York City in January 1964 to begin a two-week tour with two performances at Carnegie Hall, which were sold out within hours after the tickets were put on sale. Epstein demanded and got $7,000 against 60 percent of the gross, a fee that left the promoter without a cent until $25,000 was taken in at the box office. United Artists' press representatives were all over the house, because the company had distributed the Beatles' first movie, *A Hard Day's Night,* for which the group was paid $50,000 plus 7½ percent of the receipts after production and distribution costs. UA did not expect much from the film, but tremendous sales of its sound track were certain.

Beatlemania, American style, was exposed for the first time to a national audience over CBS television the Sunday before the tour began, on the *Ed Sullivan Hour,* as screaming teen-age girls drowned out the music with shrieks and moans of excitement. Representing 6 percent of the total American population, 11 million young girls spent 56.3 percent of the entire $650 million paid for recorded music in 1963, buying an average of fifty-five singles and twenty-two LPs. There was something about the group from Liverpool, with their pageboy haircuts and neat clothing, prescribed for them by Epstein, that immediately increased the female teen-agers' expenditures for records, particularly LPs. As George Marek explained, "A phenomenon like the Beatles helps to bring people into record stores. Children are bringing in their parents, who buy other types of music. Everybody benefits." The initial Beatle LP, "Meet the Beatles," outsold their first single, 3.6 million to 3.4 million, the first time an album had sold more than its single counterpart, in both units and dollars. During all of 1963, only two singles had sold more than one million copies in the United States, "Hey Paula," by Paul and Paula, and "Sugar Shack," by Jimmy Gilmer and the Fireballs. The sales of "Meet the Beatles" quickly surpassed the two previous major LP sellers, "The First Family," a spoof of the Kennedys, and the cast album of *My Fair Lady*.

Fifty million American dollars in orders for Beatle T-shirts, wigs, dolls, books, and novelty items ran neck and neck for a time with those for their Capitol records, which, even on a round-the-clock basis, strained the company's pressing facilities. As Victor had been forced to do in order to fill orders for Presley disks, Capitol farmed out orders to competitors. The company also took a radical step into the tangled jungle of record merchandising and instituted a uniform 49 percent discount off list price on all its records to all dealers, one-stops, rack jobbers, and sub-distributors who screamed for Beatle records.

Paul Revere's midnight warning that the British were coming was heard again in 1964. Led by the Beatles, whose every new release automatically hit the number-one position and eventually quadrupled Capitol's annual revenue, perhaps fifty British groups made their way across the Atlantic and were enthusiastically welcomed by record executives who wanted a share of the action and were ready to advance enormous sums against distribution rights. Being of varying quality and appeal, they enjoyed varying degrees of success, none of them approaching the $80,000- to $90,000-a-day business done by the Beatles on their second American tour.

With a generally scruffy presence, the Rolling Stones, best of the diverging stream of British rock 'n' rollers, whose chief inspiration was American rhythm and blues, were a far cry from the clean-cut physical impression Epstein had fostered for the Beatles in their first incarnation. The Stones came, not out of Presley, but out of black performers Chuck Berry, Muddy Waters, Bo Diddley, and Elmore James. Dick Rowe, British Decca's head of A & R and the first to turn down Brian Epstein, looked for a counterpart to the Beatles and found one in the Stones and their calculatedly created image of rebellious musicians whom parents would love to hate. A reverse of the Beatles' rock-'n'-roll coin, they cleared the way for pure rhythm-and-blues–oriented British rock musicians and added another dimension to American popular music.

The earthy, crudely artistic, black heritage on which the Rolling Stones built their act and their music did not motivate the formation of Motown Records by Berry Gordy, Jr. His original purpose was to provide a safer and smoother kind of R & B, one that sounded as nearly white as it did black and would have no problem crossing over on the trade-paper charts, one to which white teenagers and young adults could dance. The record shop he opened in a black section of his native city, Detroit, in 1953, after two years in the army, featured modern jazz music, from the innovative bop of Charlie Parker to the progressive swing of Stan Kenton. However, the neighborhood customers who came in wanted the latest Fats Domino or Ruth Brown release, and Berry, whose small capital was invested entirely in his jazz stock, went out of business and into work at a Ford assembly plant. It was there that he began to write songs in his head, influenced by the commercial rhythm-and-blues music he now knew more about. The songs wanted to get out, and Gordy embarked on a different career in the music business, beginning as a striving independent record producer using local talent to make masters for two sides of a 45-rpm single. The market was in New York, where he learned the bitter lesson that changed his life. A white publisher who was also a record-master middleman, to whom he sold one master and all rights for a promised 5 percent producer's royalty, rejected Gordy's offer to give him the other master, whose copyright Gordy would keep, for a writer-publisher's share of royalties. Put in simple, and racist, terms, Gordy was told that the music business was no place for a pushy black man from Detroit.

With a stake of $700 from members of his family, and a shove from a young Detroit songwriter, William "Smokey" Robinson, Gordy formed Motown Records in 1959, and put all its copyrights into his fully owned Jobete Music Company, a name based on those of his children, Hazel Joy, Berry, and Terry. Motown talent came cheap, not dreaming of asking for money when its signed with Gordy, content with what he offered—a total of $250,000 in advances in the first five years. Working for Ford had taught him that "getting it right" was what it was all about, and Gordy was a stern taskmaster, insisting that a take be done over and over until it was "right." Every record had to be a hit, he later recalled, "because we couldn't afford any flops." Motown had its first two cross-over Top 10 hits in 1961, five the next year, eleven in 1965, and fourteen in 1966. By 1967, seven of every ten releases that produced Motown's $21-million gross that year were sold to the white buyers he had targeted in the beginning.

The success of Motown's "colored sound," as it was known in England, created further cross-pollination of that country's music. A Motown Revue package of Gordy artists—the Supremes, Temptations, Stevie Wonder, and

Martha and the Vandellas—was the first to tour the British Isles, in 1965. Each was a product of Motown's International Talent Management training school, contract artists who had been trained to walk, talk, sit, rise, learned table manners, had their hair and clothes styled by staff experts, and were taught how to fill out tax returns.

A & M Records, the other and equally successful newcomer independent of the 1960s, which like Motown remained in the hands of its founders throughout the swallowing of other companies by conglomerates and major manufacturers in the 1970s and 1980s, began with a single hit in 1962. Regarded at first as a one-shot phenomenon, A & M aimed at an audience not yet staked out by others, the buyers of easy-to-listen-to instrumental music with a beat that could, to the untutored ear pass for rock 'n' roll, offend no one, and appeal to adults. The A of the firm name, trumpet player Herb Alpert, had written a few successful songs before he went into business with the M, Herb Moss, an East coast record promotion man transplanted to California. Their first single, "The Lonely Bull," introduced two trumpets in harmony with a Mexican mariachi sound and appropriate bullfight noises to 700,000 record buyers in 1962. A & M's gross sales jumped by 12,000 percent, from $600,000 in 1964 to $7.6 million the next year, chiefly from the sale of Alpert's group, the Tijuana Brass, whose five LPs sold 5.3 million and its 45-rpm singles 2.5 million. With a fixed limit for many years of $10,000 for the production of the group's LPs, and less for other artists, Alpert-Moss records offered music that successfully crossed the growing chasm between teen-agers and adults. In 1966, when the Beatles, with "Beatles '65" and "Beatles VI," sold more LPs than anyone, the Tijuana Brass was second, with 13 million copies of their five LPs.

Constant rumors floated that overexposure on the movie screen had washed up the now grand old man of rock 'n' roll, Elvis Presley, but he continued to be RCA Victor's largest single source of income. His original contract, negotiated in 1955, had been extended through 1975, and he had racked up the sale of an additional 28 million singles during 1965, to raise his total sales to $150 million. The glut of Presley movies, which were consistently among the ten top pictures of the year, cost between $1.5 to $2 million to produce, and brought the singer $1.5 million in salary and a full half-share of all profits above that figure.

It was no longer rock 'n' roll or rhythm and blues on the charts. Folkrock and Bob Dylan made strong inroads with their message songs, which moved others, too, to deal with controversial subjects long left untouched by the pre-Presley and Beatles music business. Dylan's records and sheet music sold so well that the oldest, and very conservative, music-publishing combine, Warner Brothers' MPHC, bought his catalogue of seventy-eight songs and worked on them with such effect that eight reached the top of the charts. Protest songs had destroyed old shibboleths and the recording industry's self-imposed strictures on a song's content and its playing time.

Because of the great demand for Dylan's songs, which usually ran four or five minutes, much more than the 120 seconds preferred by disk jockeys and Top 40 stations, they were played again and again, and not only Dylan's own performances, but also best-selling versions by new folk-rock groups.

The success in 1965 of new independent specialist record firms and the influence of independent producers with their own stables of performers had brought about a broadening of the major labels' output. A billion-dollar volume was the next obstacle to surmount. Records were now slanted toward age brackets and tastes. At one end were hit-making artists who aimed at the youth market: Beatles, Rolling Stones, Presley, Yardbirds, Dave Clark Five, Righteous Brothers, Beach Boys, Gary Lewis and the Playboys, Sonny and Cher, Herman's Hermits, the Lovin' Spoonful, Dylan and the Byrds. In the middle of the road, with their safe music, were Motown's Supremes, Four Tops and Marvin Gaye, Tijuana Brass, Roger Miller, Bert Kaempfert, Four Seasons, the group Peter, Paul, and Mary, New Christy Minstrels. And at the extreme, adult-slanted, end were Frank Sinatra, Barbra Streisand, Nat Cole, Andy Williams, Dean Martin, Nancy Wilson, Robert Goulet, Jerry Vale.

The earliest independent record producers were jazz fans of the World War II period, who paid union musicians to make four sides at a session, released the music on their own labels, and sold their wares to local retailers or by direct mail, or, in special instances, got one of the country's privately owned distributors to handle their records. A proliferation of record companies followed, and the introduction of less-expensive magnetic-tape recording on portable equipment brought new entrepreneurs into the business. They wanted only a good return on a small investment, and depended on acquiescent artists and songwriters to provide the material they sold. Without any special musical training or interests, these new businessmen looked for young persons who were infatuated with rhythm and blues or rock 'n' roll, and put them on the payroll for indecently modest wages, to do a multitude of chores, including production of records.

The teen-aged white team of Jerry Lieber and Mike Stoller began in the early 1950s by teaching their songs to singers who had never learned to read music, and then gradually took over other aspects of making a record. Presley's earth-shattering "Hound Dog" was a cover record of an earlier Lieber-Stoller production on which they did everything. It brought the team to the attention of conservative major firms who were seeking to get in on RCA Victor's unexpected rock-'n'-roll success. In 1959, when they were twenty-five, Lieber and Stoller had ten RIAA Gold Record awards, and were enjoying profits from sale of 27 million singles, many of which they had both written and produced. Like other successful independent producers, they leased masters to both majors and independents on a two-or three-percent override basis, or eight percent of retail price, from which their artists also received a share. The A & R man's job, which Mitch Miller had glamorized by his personality and success, was taken over slowly by Hugo (Peretti) and Luigi (Creatore), Doc Pomus and Mort Shuman, Al Nevins and Don Kirshner, among others, who were resented by the veterans they displaced.

The most successful independent production operation in New York, next to the Lieber-Stoller combination, was formed by Nevins, the guitarist for the Three Suns, a successful cocktail-lounge trio, with Kirshner, a thwarted basketball player and Bobby Darin's first partner in the music business, who had immediate access to the most popular young performers and a gift for inspiring creativity. In 1958, when Darin's records were climbing up the charts, and new management handled him, Kirshner and Nevins formed Aldon Music. Nevins was a veteran of the days when the major Tin Pan Alley publishers hired staff writers to turn out new material on demand. Now, in the age of rock 'n' roll, when the young spoke better to their peers than had the songwriters of other generations, Nevins moved Aldon Music and its stable of writers into the Brill Building, the camp of new music's enemies. Aldon's doors were open to any young talent ready to audition and work hard. Gradually, a stable of the potentially best songwriters in the New York area could be found on the Nevins-Kirshner payroll, producing what become known as "Brill Building Pop." Among those Kirshner cajoled or forced to deliver popular hit songs were Carole King and Gerry Goffin, Barry Mann and Cynthia Weill, Neil Sedaka and Howard Greenfield, Jeff Barry and Ellie Greenwich, Jack Keller, Charlie Koppelman and Don Rubin. Their average age was under twenty-five, and they provided Aldon Music with more than 300 recorded copyrights and 200 chart hits.

Rather than send slapdash piano-vocal demonstration tapes or records of his writers' material for consideration, Kirshner invested in high-quality production, using an orchestra to play from arrangements that presented the songs as he thought they should be done. His "demo" singers were of the caliber of Tony Orlando, whose Aldon tapes won him his first recording contract. Kirshner's ability to produce master tapes that could be put on the market as they were led to the formations of two record companies, adding to the value of a budding music empire, for which Columbia Pictures paid about $2.5 million in March 1963. The package included the future services of all contract songwriters, the Aldon copyrights, and Kirshner as full-time operating head at $75,000 a year, to supervise Colpix Records and other music and film-production subsidiaries owned by the studio. Ready to relax after years in the music business, Nevins served as consultant.

Living in a milieu where the pressure of producing thousands of new single disks and LPs every year stretched the capabilities of existing personnel, the major manufacturers were anxious to comply with the wishes of consistently successful artists who wished to form their own production teams and lease finished master tapes, leaving the full responsibility for sales, distribution, and promotion to the record company. Bing Crosby, Pat Boone, Louis Prima, Keely Smith, and Stan Kenton had such arrangements in the early 1960s. Frank Sinatra, no longer satisfied with his Capitol contract, in spite of the reborn success the company had created for him, formed the Reprise Records label as a subsidiary of his umbrella corporation, Sinatra Enterprises. The Reprise products were intended for the middle-of-the-road market, and there was to be no compromise with rock 'n' roll, that "martial music of every side-burned juvenile delinquent on the face of the earth," as Sinatra deplored publicly at every occasion. As soon as they were free of the encumbrance of existing contracts, Sinatra's adult-market-oriented singer friends signed with Reprise, creating, eventually, a roster of sixty-two contract artists.

Harry Belafonte formed a production company of his own, with distribution through RCA victor, in 1961. The following year, after Bobby Darin was brought into Capital after Sinatra's contract expired, he formed his own unit, too. Soon after switching to RCA Victor, Paul Anka prevented the possibility of competing with himself on the budget-LP racks by paying ABC-Paramount $250,000 for all master tapes, copyrights, and the right to reissue his old recordings. A $1.5-million restraint-of-trade suit filed by Sinatra and Reprise against Capital in September 1962 had inspired the transaction. Sinatra's complaint charged that EMI-Capitol had damaged the sale of his new Reprise releases by dumping twenty-one of his old LPs on the market to selected dealers, on a buy-one-get-one-free offer. The suit was dismissed on grounds of improper venue and lack of jurisdiction.

The Screen Gems–Columbia publishing combine, which included Aldon Music, published 173 songs, recorded on thirty-seven different labels, in Kirshner's first year as president. Twelve of them sold more than a quarter of a million. The accomplishment was duly noted in Columbia Pictures' financial report, whose other figures, except those for the Screen Gems television production unit, were far less impressive. Poor times for the feature-movie business were being mitigated by profits from record and music subsidiaries. Sales of Dot Records loomed larger each year, and MGM Records' recent purchase of the Verve catalogue for nearly three million dollars added one of the world's largest jazz repertories and some best-selling vocal and comedy artists. The lesson was not lost on the management of the Warner label's parent company.

In its first four years, Warner Brothers Records continued to lose several million dollars annually. Long accustomed to an already fully integrated manufacturing and merchandising operation, on the order of Capitol and Columbia, over which he had presided, James Conkling, the Warner president, could not create a miracle by duplicating either overnight. Warner considered shutting down, but was dissuaded when a hoard of unpaid distributors' accounts was discovered. In 1961, Conkling was replaced by a former associate at Columbia, John K. "Mike" Maitland. Conditions and sales reports gradually improved. The new vogue for comedy LPs made stars of Bob Newhart and his "button-down mind," the parodist-singer Allan Sherman, and black comedian Bill Cosby, who in one period accounted for nearly half of all Warner LP sales. Warner's new white singing trio, Peter, Paul, and Mary, used Dylan songs and other message material to precipitate the international popularity of folk-rock and sold 13 million LP units over the next eight years. The addition of Reprise's contract artists to Warner's existing roster of twenty-eight complicated matters, but it did bring in the Latin-beat folk-rock singer Trini Lopez, Sinatra's daughter Nancy, and his boon companion Dean Martin, who struck gold in the country-ballad field.

The union of Warner with Reprise in 1963 sprang not from a desire to become more deeply involved in a business that had already stung the studio, but to shore up sagging feature distribution figures with a guaranteed box-office attraction. Involved in the merger were four new Warner feature movies starring Sinatra, all of which proved to be failures in the theaters but continued to appear on local television, and Reprise's impressive library of master tapes, worth between three and four million dollars. The singer got a total of $22 million in a capital-gains arrangement, including twenty-two unissued Warner Brothers Records shares, which gave him a one-third share in the new company and of profits from labels that might be acquired in the future. Jack L. Warner, president of the company, denied that the merger represented his decision to make Sinatra his "heir-apparent." Warner-Reprise's fortunes went on an upswing, but in the autumn of 1963, Columbia still led on the 100 Best-Selling LPs chart, with a share of slightly over 20 percent. Capitol was second with eighteen records; RCA Victor third with a dozen; Warner-Reprise had eleven; Paramount-Dot, eight; Decca-Coral-Brunswick, seven; Liberty-Dolton and MGM-Verve, each six; Mercury-Philips-Smash, five; and ABC-Paramount and Roulette Records, four each.

The displacement of certain American artists from their long domination of the international hit lists by British groups made some British producers a newly valuable commodity on a world-wide scale. CBS went to London to sign Mickey Most, one of England's "golden boy" producers, to a three-year contract, for $250,000, that ensured his services for immediate call. Still in his twenties, within a nine-month period and with little previous recording experience, Most has supervised the hits recorded by the Animals, Herman's Hermits, and the Nashville Teens. Andrew Loog Oldham, who produced the Rolling Stones, was put in full charge of the Decca subsidiary label on which the group was now released. Polydor Records, the British affiliate with which Deutsche Grammophon had returned to the British record business, pouring in $6.5 million for expansion and modernization, snatched The Who group away from other bidders by giving their young Australian producer-manager, Robert Stigwood, his own label and an independent producer's override royalty. The taping-leasing arrangement the deal introduced was to become standard internationally. With the permission of their employers, George Martin and three A & R men at EMI and Decca formed a cooperative, which licensed all tapes recorded by talent the four turned up. Subsidized by a $750,000 advance from EMI, the group built the AIR studio to handle their large recorded output on their own label.

When NBC-TV planned to build a vast advance audience for a new comedy series through cross-promotion of recordings by the Beatles-like quartet of actors who starred in the programs, Don Kirshner was brought in to direct the project. Columbia Pictures' original label, Colpix, had been deactivated for lack of success, leaving Screen Gems–Columbia Music open to an affiliation with RCA Victor. The latter's sales of the ever-reliable Presley and the company's strong country-music division were more than satisfactory, but it had not yet broken into the hyperactive youth market with any profit. Kirshner's genius for digging up new artists and material proved irresistible to yet another new head of RCA's record operations, Norman Racusin. Sixty of the songs Kirshner had selected for exploitation in the previous twelve months had landed in the Top 10, and ten of them achieved the number-one slot.

The television series *The Monkees,* starring the first successful "bubblegum group," was calculatedly created to attract the principal consumers of that confection—young females between the ages of nine and twelve. Believed to be in search of their own new singing idols, they would, it was anticipated, prove their devotion by buying the Monkees' records and products advertised by the program's sponsors. Their older sisters had preempted the Beatles, just as an earlier generation had taken Presley and his records to its heart. For slightly less than two years, before the mercurial bubble gummers chose new idols, the Monkees were more than equal to the challenge. Their first single, "Last Train from Clarksville," published and produced by Kirshner, as were all Monkees' songs and records, was issued on a new Colgems label, and distributed by RCA Victor. It hit the number-one spot, with over a million sales, in time for the Monkees' first telecast. It had sold more than three million units by the end of 1966, as advance orders for more than a million copies of a second LP were coming in. Because only one of the Monkees was a musician, and the others had to be taught, staff musicians made the early Monkees' records, accompanying the group's singing. Gradually, as they became acceptably expert, the four young performers made records and appeared in public concerts, from which most of their income came. Their contract with Screen Gems Television, owners of the package, called for the payment of only $500 an episode.

As that Mount Everest of the American recording industry, a billion-dollar annual gross, was nearing conquest, Philips and RCA became locked in a battle of tape systems, whose outcome brought the business to a crossroads, with possible disaster ahead. The stalement between Ampex and RCA in the late 1950s over tape speed and mode had been resolved; the former's reel-to-reel configuration was now standard for high-quality sound and reproduction in recording studios and among sophisticated audiophiles and musical amateurs. Victor's predilection for the tape cartridge was rooted in a corporate judgment that, as the transistor radio had made clear, record buyers were no longer chained to the living room. The future lay in entertainment as mobile as the consumer. The total market for duplicated prerecorded tapes had not yet reached the potential envisioned for it by RCA, CBS, Capitol, and others, but automobile owners, it was thought, would expand it almost five times, to nearly half a billion dollars in 1970.

Four years before the RCA four-track reel-to-reel 3¾ ips cartridges were placed on sale, the Cleveland inventor George Eash had developed his own continuous-play tape cartridge, which offered 600 feet of stereo music at a speed of seven inches per second. These were sold for seventy-five dollars and could be plugged into a home system. Eash told *Billboard,* in March 1966, that "the tape was guided across the playback heads by a capstan and pinchwheel assembly," and was based on the old continuous-loop principle. "The problem was in getting a quantity of tape to go around that would not bind or stop. I concentrated on developing a hub and reel shape plus utilization of a lubricant to allow the tape to slide freely over its adjacent layer." With an eye on its use as an automobile accessory, the flamboyant Midwestern entrepreneur Earl "Madman" Muntz began work improving this Fidelipac in 1958, and met Eash in Chicago in 1961. With $35,000 in capital and a $100,000 loan, he opened his Muntz Stereo-Pac headquarters in California in 1963. Eash functioned as a consultant and assisted in improving Fidelipac, receiving royalties for his basic patents.

Muntz salespersons usually were pretty young women dressed in red shorts and other gaudy clothing. They took orders for the installation of a hang-on four-track cartridge playback, which was heard through a car radio speaker; it cost from $225 up for a unit. The Muntz library of taped music grew as the cost of loading a continuous tape fell from thirty-five cents to a nickel. Franchise operations and Stereo-Pak distribution centers expanded into Texas and Florida, and a plant was opened in Tokyo. By 1965, Muntz was anticipating a retail gross of $18 million to $20 million.

William Lear, inventor of the car radio, developer of the Lear Jet, and a Los Angeles area Muntz distributor, doubled the playing time of the Muntz cartridge by increasing the tracks to eight, which the Fidelipac could not accommodate. Limited production of a patented Lear Stereo 8 playback unit began in a section of his airplane factory, and improved cartridges were supplied by RCA Victor. After studying a prototype, Ford Motor Company agreed to install Stereo 8 playbacks as optional units in its 1966 line of higher-priced automobiles at a cost of about $180. A contract was awarded to the Motorola Radio Company, to which Lear had assigned his first car radio, for the manufacture of all Lear radio-tape units. Most leading car makers opted for Stereo 8; General Motors, Chrysler, and American Motors announced that they would include the Lear tape player, in their 1967 models.

Lear tape components designed to be attached to existing stereo phonograph systems went on sale in time for the 1966 Christmas season, simultaneously with Philips's compact cartridge system, distributed through Mercury Records. The twin spools, encased in what Philips called a "cassette," used one-eighth-inch-wide tape, which played at 1⅞ ips, miniaturization far beyond that in earlier tape cartridges. Unlike the Stereo 8 and the Muntz Pak the Philips players permitted both playback *and* recording, and were available in home units as well as for automobiles.

The original cassette deck had been introduced in Germany in 1962, and the following year in the United States by Norelco, Philips's North American Electric Company. Intended only as a pocket dictating machine, the first Philips Carry-Corder had against it sound quality inferior to that of the average stereo disk, as well as tape hiss, which was not fully erased until the introduction of the Dolby Noise Reduction System in 1970. A new international battle in the record business developed quickly. German Grundig and Telefunken obtained international rights to the Lear Jet–RCA Stereo 8, while Philips effected agreements for the manufacture and distribution of cassettes in thirty countries, involving General Electric, Revere-Wollensak, EMI, Sony, Hitachi, Columbia, and Victor. New American companies were organized to supply an anticipated five million four- and eight-track stereo tape units by the end of 1967, but Lear enjoyed the exclusive advantage of a $60-million advertising program, subsidized by the major car manufacturers.

Television's switch to all color, starting in the 1965–66 season, meant larger profits for the film companies, whose vaults were packed high with Technicolor movies, waiting only for the networks' highest bids. It was a lure that could no longer be resisted by the major studios, whose giant real estate holdings caused them to look for diversification. 20th Century-Fox's profits from land were a case in point. In 1940, the company paid $217,000 for 2,300 acres in Malibu on which to build outdoor sets and additional production facilities. In 1962, an offer of $5 million for the land was turned down, and with good reason. Alcoa's booming $500-million Century City development was on 260 acres in the Westwood section of Los Angles for which $25 million, after taxes, was paid to the film company. 20th Century-Fox withheld a small parcel of land on which oil wells were operating, to be turned over when they ran dry, and also secured a ninety-nine-year lease on seventy-five choice acres in the center of Century City on which to build a giant residential project.

Milton Rackmill's purchase in 1950 of a substantial interest in Universal Pictures for $3.75 million, proved to a similar problem. During a period of internal reorganization and diversification, the Music Corporation of America—by then the largest talent agency in the world—paid $11.25 million in cash for the Universal-International lot, also the largest in the world; its 367 acres were ideal for the action television series being produced by an MCA subsidiary, Revue Productions. Universal retained a portion of the main facilities for ten years, at an annual one-million-dollar rental fee. Additional sound stages were built for Revue and rental to other film makers. Now both a landlord and a producer, MCA retained a larger share of the $150 million spent by the networks for television film production in 1961–62 than did its competitors. With cash from the MCA purchase, Universal produced a few select big movies, rather than the quickies for which it was famous, and in 1960 shared consolidated gross sales of $85 million with Decca, owner of 87 percent of Universal stock.

Those holdings served as the basic leverage for a proposed exchange of stock that would merge Decca-Universal, as separate divisions, with MCA, whose future was now recognized to be in providing the television industry with moving pictures. In 1961, Decca-Universal had grossed $90.5 million and MCA $82.1 million. The initial plan, announced in April 1962, was to exchange one share of Decca capital stock for one new MCA preferred voting stock and a third of a share of MCA common stock. Opponents of the merger argued that Decca was contributing 47 percent of its earnings to acquire 24 percent of the combined operations, whereas MCA would hold 76 percent in exchange for the balance of combined earnings. Nevertheless, after approval by the SEC, stockholders of both companies approved the merger, taking several months to do so, a period during which MCA stock fell about forty-five points, in anticipation of government intervention.

A month after the MCA–Decca-Universal merger was consummated, the Justice Department filed a suit, charging MCA with violation of the antitrust laws. It was quickly settled by MCA's surrender of franchises to operate as talent representative issued by the various craft and talent unions. Overnight, with its MCA Artists dissolved, 1,400 entertainers of great magnitude in the United States and England had no agent to represent them, and a wild scramble ensued. In the consent decree, MCA was forbidden, for a period of seven years, to acquire any major film or television production company or any recording operation without permission from the Justice Department.

The growth of Revue Productions and Universal-International Pictures continued, stimulated by a market whose total 1967 budget for video series and feature-movie production for the networks was in excess of $200 million. In a single week in October 1966, ABC and CBS spent $93 million for 102 post-1948 movies. Paramount Pictures' $127-million gross in 1965, including profits from Dot Record Company and music-publishing houses, caught the fancy of executives of the Gulf & Western Corporation, whose sales of automotive parts and military hardware alone exceeded the studio's entire revenue. Charles Bludhorn, the G & W chairman, was determined to effect a merger with the studio, whose major real estate holdings could serve as collateral for immediate cash. Paramount's large library of feature movies, many of them in color, was another good-as-gold asset. G & W already owned 18.5 percent of outstanding Paramount stock. The merger was consummated in October 1966, on an exchange-of-stock basis. A fourth G & W division was formed, devoted exclusively to leisure-time products. It took over immediate control of the Paramount record and music-publishing activities.

The increasing interest in the film industry by big business set off a 40 percent increase in the price of stock offered for sale by the eleven companies listed on the New York and American stock exchanges. Television-network stock rose only 10 percent. News of a takeover of Warner Brothers and its subsidiaries caused its stock to register a 51 percent gain in a four-week period. Warner's record-business holdings, almost bankrupt, rose to a place among the world's giant manufacturers in November 1966, through a merger with Seven Arts Corporation. The entire negotiation occupied eighteen days. A prime mover in the transaction was the reclusive Boston banker Serge Semenenko, executive vice-president of First National Bank of Boston, who boasted that in the thirty years he and his institution had financed the motion-picture industry, to the extent of three billion dollars in revolving credit, not a penny had been lost. In 1959, First Boston had extended $10 million in credit, later increased to $40 million, toward the formation and operation of Seven Arts, an independent production and distribution company, which now owned the single largest catalogue of feature movies not yet licensed to television, whose estimated potential value was around $100 million.

Jack Warner, in his late seventies, was ready to remove himself from day-to-day production on a gradual basis after completing shooting of his current project, *My Fair Lady*. Approximately 4.8 million shares of Warner Brothers stock was outstanding, 1.6 million owned by him. Seven Arts got effective control of the company when a consortium of banks guaranteed the purchase of his massive bloc of stock, for twenty dollars a share. Among the assets acquired by Seven Arts were the Burbank studios and adjacent real estate, whose worth was incalculable.

Variety reported in January 1967 that Frank Sinatra was furious that his old friend Jack Warner had not given him a chance to buy Warner stock at the same twenty-dollar price paid by Seven Arts. It was said that friends were ready to back him in buying the film company. Shortly after, he sold part of his one-third control of Reprise Records, leaving him a 20 percent share in all profits. The money involved in that sale was not made public, but the company's earnings were a matter of public record. Profits had risen steadily in the past three years, from $33,339 to $1,301,721 in 1966, representing an eightfold increase in Reprise's total net worth since 1964.

During the Warner/7 Arts negotiations, an agreement in principle, leading to a merger, was concluded between the Transamerica Corporation, a holding company with insurance, car-financing, and small manufacturing interests, and United Artists, then the most successful American picture distributor, and owner of UA Records, the most successful manufacturer of sound-track LPs. In the past six years UA had distributed six feature movies that earned more than $25 million each in world-wide rental fees. It also hed exclusive rights to the James Bond 007 pictures and the three Beatles movies. A similar merger with the Consolidated Foods complex had been proposed earlier in 1966, but had fallen through because of opposition from stockholders on both sides. With Transamerica's $2.5 billion in assets to finance new feature pictures, the film-distribution company could enlarge and diversify the operation of a leisure-time music division.

"The times they are a-changin'," Bob Dylan sang. And so they were.

CHAPTER 19

ASCAP versus BMI

The time had long since passed when entertainers in search of new material they could live with during a year on the vaudeville circuit beat their way to the concentration of music houses on West 28th Street, then on West 46th Street, and now in the Brill Building and 1650 Broadway, around the corner. The hegira had been in eternal search of the centers of song exploitation, which in the mid-1950s were New York's television and radio networks. It was no longer necessary to have large offices with rows of piano rooms where songwriters could work or demonstrate the newest songs. The trade in free professional copies was mostly a thing of the past. New songs now were taken directly to the A & R men, who had taken the place of the music publisher and his general manager in determining what would be recorded and promoted. Next in importance to the record-company executives were the disk jockeys and radio stations, which had become the primary conduits of exposure to the public.

It was radio's use of music, plus that of the fast-growing video medium, that gave music publishers their single largest source of monetary returns. Only Herman Starr, head of Warner Brothers' Music Publishers Holding Corporation, who was secure in the certainty that the combine would continue to receive the largest single annual ASCAP payment (over $1.5 million), could maintain that sheet music was "still the barometer of music publishing," completely ignoring the collapse of printed sheet-music sales. The MPHC had extended the operation of its school-band division, published new junior-high-school music textbooks, started a department for the accordion market Lawrence Welk stimulated, stolen a march on others in the growing chord-organ field, and increased its activity in amateur-theatricals production with special editions of Victor Herbert operettas and newly commissioned series for the youth market. The song "Secret Love," from a

Warner movie, sung and recorded by Doris Day, had to wait half a year before concentrated plugging by MPHC's professional staff pushed it onto the million-sales chart, a period during which only 200,000 printed copies were sold.

"Without ASCAP's performance revenue I couldn't survive," Irving Berlin told *Variety* in October 1954. "Without those quarterly remittances from a performing rights society like ASCAP I would have to close shop and see my 30-year-old organization go down the drain because sheet music and records, and revenues from foreign affiliates, no longer can keep a publisher going."

ASCAP made its quarterly payments for 1953 on the basis of 19 million performances for writers and 16 million for publishers, paying eight cents per air play to the former and twenty-four cents to the latter. Twenty percent of ASCAP's writer royalties was based on performances. Current performances accounted for 55 percent of the publishers' distribution, availability—performances of songs more than two years old—for 30, and seniority for 15. In 1954, writers of an ASCAP hit earned between $4,000 and $5,000 from performances and might look forward to an additional $20,000 over many consecutive years of membership. The publisher of such a song got between $12,000 and $15,000 from ASCAP, as well as deferred cumulative-distribution royalties.

At BMI, where all affiliated publishers, but only writers in the company's writer plan, shared in the bulk of distributions, measured by broadcast performances, publishers received six cents for each performance on a network and four cents for those on independent stations. None of the additional factors taken into account by ASCAP were recognized. A song whose performances were mostly those of its recordings earned approximately $6,000 from BMI, whereas one that enjoyed both live network and recorded air play received more than $15,000.

Television was taking ever larger bites out of the networks' production budgets and such once-reigning network stars as Amos 'n' Andy, Edgar Bergen and Charlie McCarthy, and Red Skelton worked off their long-term contracts by doubling as record spinners on the thirty-four hours each week devoted to recorded music. Many of the dozen or so nationally syndicated transcribed programs starring "name" personalities as disk jockeys were written so that recordings of the local subscribing station's choice could be interpolated. In New York and on the West Coast, nearly 600 union song pluggers pitched material to network program directors, advertising-agency men, and artists. Television alone remained open to them as the quickest route to a song's success, but it remained one to which only the largest music houses had access, and for which top stars formed their own publishing companies. Without television, and in the face of several dozen new releases each week from the major labels alone, smaller publishers had to rely on the stars of the last live daily radio-network musical program,

"The Breakfast Club," in Chicago, or the fifty leading deejays in major markets.

The popular-music business played the angles as it never had before. Vocalists who had been cut in on a song insisted on singing it on their TV programs, whether it was destined for success or not, and further ruined prospects for a true hit. Successful young publishers used their BMI royalties to break the gentlemen's code among ASCAP publishers, which observed proprietary interests in copyright renewals that had existed for years. In such a deal, the established price was between seven and ten times the song's ASCAP earnings. But where such transactions had been concluded when the songs were first written "for hire," the publisher already had all rights. Paying larger sums than usual for even a share in an important copyright, the BMI publishers built up future availability and seniority rights in the society. The ASCAP inner circle fought this breach of traditional courtesy by ruling that the holder of a reviewed copyright could not share in earnings for five years, the money, instead, being paid to the original publisher. Tin Pan Alley was no longer the tight little energetic island on West 28th Street, and ASCAP publishers sat back on their performance royalties while newcomers searched for new material with a willingness to sample even the most exotic in order to satisfy a demand from the major labels that was more voracious than ever. The several thousand new releases that had to make it within a few weeks or disappear, and the 35,000 demonstration records made in 1956, which cost from sixty or eighty-five dollars to several hundred dollars a song, added to the hit-or-miss situation generally prevailing throughout the new record and music-publishing business.

The increased sales of packaged albums, accounting for more than one fifth of all volume in 1956 further removed the need for an A & R man to guess right. It took between twelve and sixteen tunes to fill both sides of a twelve-inch LP. Now spending more money for recorded entertainment than ever, the public was receptive to music of all types, lending credence to the idea that anybody could make it in a business that continued to enjoy an annual 20 to 25 percent rate of expansion. With that came a change in the general attitude of publishers toward their standard songs, for which, only a few years before, no effort was made to secure new recordings. A check to one publisher from the Harry Fox Agency of the Music Publishers Protective Association for $28,000 in such "accidental" royalties did much to compensate for the fall of sheet-music sales to rock bottom. Songs that were number two or three on "Your Hit Parade" sold fewer than 10,000 sheet copies, the number one around 15,000. Cole Porter's "True Love," from the film *High Society,* was a glaring exception, going over the half-million mark at a time when most publishers refused to supply the sheet-music racks with an initial order of 75,000 copies, fearful they would be buried by the returns. Only the sales of printed educational music continued to grow, at a steady 20 percent rate, and choral and band arrangements of

standard songs from the MPHC, MGM Big Three, and Mills Music catalogues, leaders in this field, more than offset the failure to become involved
in the rock-'n'-roll business.

Conditions at ASCAP, meanwhile, and as usual, were far from serene.
The first year of Stanley Adams's presidency was marked by a public-relations
triumph when for the first time an ASCAP president met the President of
the United States, at a Washington function where Irving Berlin sang new
lyrics for "I Like Ike." By playing a key role in the 1953–54 negotiations
with television broadcasters, Adams had won the confidence of even the
most skeptical publisher directors and his reelection to a second term was
regarded as certain. A committee consisting of Adams, Herman Starr, Max
Dreyfus, Oscar Hammerstein, and Herman Finkelstein was writing the final
details of a new television agreement. Bowing to the arguments of the All-
Industry Committee, they reduced license rates from independent broadcasters to 10 percent below those prevailing in radio on both blanket and
per-program contracts. The networks would enjoy a similar reduction in
every year in which their income did not fall below that in 1953. The new
licenses would run for four years, rather than the customary five, so that
they would expire a year before the radio licenses.

Except for the still-smoldering fire ignited by Hans Lengsfelder and his
group of dissidents, pressing for a revision of the distribution system to
benefit the lower-bracket members, the society entered a new era of internal
good feeling with the celebration of ASCAP's fortieth anniversary in early
1954. Three or four of the top publishers formed a solid block of support
and voted Adams in again as ASCAP's chief executive, leaving the rest of
the membership little voice.

In general, the membership looked with favor on the society's operations, though there were some unhappy older members, whose performances and, consequently, income had fallen off. They wished ASCAP to
protect them by disregarding all elements, other than seniority, of the four-
fund distribution plan put into place by the 1950 consent order. With receipts for 1954 heading toward another new high, Adams assured his constituents that "the youth of the society is helping to replenish our shelves
with the vitamins of new members to offset the possible malnutrition of
public domain material," words of comfort that failed to satisfy those Starr
called "rabble rousers."

In order to end the collaboration between BMI and ASCAP members,
often writing under assumed names, which many contended had built up
their rival's share of the market, in April 1955 ASCAP relinquished all
rights to such works of joint authorship. Having won approval in the amended
consent decree to gain access to music written by ASCAP members on such
a nonexclusive basis, in May 1952 BMI had withdrawn its long-standing
appeal in *Marks* v. *ASCAP*. Simultaneously, the $200,000 annual guarantee
paid to Marks since 1941 was reduced and a new understanding was ex-

tended until 1959. The million-dollar option to buy the Marks catalogue was voided. Such a work as Marks's "Glow Worm," with new lyrics by ASCAP's Johnny Mercer, precipitated ASCAP's decision. It was licensed through both organizations on a nonexclusive basis, Mercer receiving 70 percent of what the society paid a collaborative work by two members. With the joint-authorship alternative removed, BMI began to pay all writers, regardless of affiliation. A BMI co-author was given the full three- and two-cent writer's share, with the understanding he would divide it with his collaborator. A number of outstanding compositions were added to the BMI repertory by this means, contributing to the increased resolve of many among the ASCAP leadership to dispose of BMI by whatever means possible.

At the October 1955 membership meeting, Lengsfelder, proponent of distribution based on a straight 100 percent current-performance basis, found new support from young writers who asked the society to enlarge the logging procedures and increase the recognition of current pop, R & B, and country hits songs. Until the amended decree, only the networks had been logged from sign on to sign off. One hundred regional nonaffiliated stations were then added and covered on a rotational sampling basis for two and a half hours a day. The new, improved logging plan presented by Adams in response increased the local sample base by over half and air play credit by a quarter. The points assigned to publishers and writers for performances on a sustaining network show were reduced considerably, and other reforms were also made.

By diminishing the value of such performances, ASCAP hoped to attract those smaller publishers whose records dominated air time on independent stations and provided the type of performance that enhanced BMI's value to broadcasters. But ASCAP could not really match BMI's payments in this area; the publisher of a "record" hit that received little or no play on the network shows got $15,000 from BMI and, because of the logging method, very little from the society. Eighty percent of ASCAP distribution of income from radio was based on network performances, divided equally between commercial and sustaining use, and only a number that crossed the charts into all divisions and was played substantially on the networks earned any significant ASCAP royalties. Those damaged by the society's operating methods vowed to "take it to Washington" for a day of final reckoning. Among them would be those publishers outside the inner sanctum that moved and shook the society.

The recent sales of pre-1948 motion pictures to television made other changes in the improved logging plan of even more importance to the publishers specializing in background film music, whose value had been raised only a fraction. Fred Fox, son of the founder of the Sam Fox Publishing Company in Cincinnati early in silent-picture days, offered his full support to that cause. The Fox firm was one of the ten largest in ASCAP in terms of catalogue, but was not represented on the board, a victim of the practice that weighed voting power in accordance with earning power. One who earned ten times as much as another had ten times as many votes. The California-based Screen Composers Association was similarly affected and took up arms over what it, too, considered to be a woefully inadequate voting and logging system. Several veteran SCA background-music composers looked into the legality of the use on television of films with their music made prior to 1940, when the studios first included television-use clauses in their contracts.

Adams, having served the maximum three terms, in his presentation to members of ASCAP's new president, Paul Cunningham, reported that the society would distribute more than $20 million in 1956, one tenth of it from European societies. Cunningham, a veteran ASCAP public-relations and lobbying operative in Washington, where he was much involved in pending copyright legislation, made good use of the self-imposed ceiling on their ratings made my Berlin, Rodgers, Hammerstein, and others, and won an ovation for them. He also urged an immediate return to agreements extending television rights through 1961, so that an ASCAP salesman "would have a full sample case when he goes out to sell the broadcasters."

With the Walt Disney music company leading the opposition to the revised payment system on the West Coast, and Lengsfelder, with assistance from Sam Fox, in the East, *Variety* was correct in observing, in December 1956, that an ASCAP storm was blowing from coast to coast. A hastily prepared revision superceding the 1954 Adams plan was considered by the opposition to be an attempt to confuse the members. The first small fruits from trips to Washington by Lengsfelder and other ASCAP writers and publishers appeared in early 1957 with word that the Justice Department was once again investigating and that the matter might again be considered by the House Small Business subcommittee.

A major complaint to Washington centered on the weighted-vote issue: a writer got one vote for every twenty dollars he earned. This gave sovereignty over the society to the major publishing houses that had the most prolific writers under contract. The high point of a meeting in early 1957, at which this issue was discussed, was Oscar Hammerstein's observation that there could never be an equal voting system in the society. "There is no reason why a man who owns a thousand copyrights should only have the same voting power as the man who owns one copyright," he said. He concluded with the promise that if he and other top writers were forced out, "the devil would take the hindmost."

The statement was cheered by Arthur Schwartz, who followed with an account of a recent meeting during which he had killed a series of pro-BMI articles that would have damaged ASCAP in a leading New York City newspaper. Born at the turn of the century, he had had a long and successful career as a composer on Broadway and in Hollywood, which had begun in 1929 with the *First Little Show*. A graduate of New York University and

Columbia Law School, he had practiced law successfully before devoting himself to composition. Among his great standards were "Something to Remember You By," "Dancing in the Dark," "Alone Together," "By Myself," and, most recently, "That's Entertainment," written with his longtime collaborator, Howard Dietz, for the MGM musical film *The Band Wagon.*

His wholehearted dedication to the cause of the Songwriters of America and their $150-million lawsuit against BMI had been precipitated by an RCA Victor executive's rejection for recording of some songs from the Schwartz–Dorothy fields 1951 musical *A Tree Grows in Brooklyn.* Though it ran for 270 performances, the show had failed to recoup the original investment.

The material he was shown by the activists preparing the lawsuit began with that collected for the 1941 action against the networks by Stanley Adams, Paul Cunningham, and twelve other young ASCAP members. That suit had been settled by the networks with a $15,000 payment to the plaintiffs for their expenses. These documents plus others amassed since formed the basis for *Schwartz* v. *BMI.* Many of them referred to BMI president Carl Haverlin's program to maintain the support of BMI stockholders and other broadcasters during a period when BMI's share of performances was a fraction of ASCAP's. A major document was the so-called Haverlin "five year-plan," "Your Stake in BMI," offered to the NAB convention in 1948. It pointed out that the company had saved the radio industry some $67 million over the contract proposed by ASCAP in late 1940. Haverlin proposed a drive by all stations to achieve an average of 12,000 performances per station in 1953, a goal that the Songwriters of America thought had been surpassed. It was generally believed by ASCAP publishers and some songwriters, Schwartz included, that there was an inherent preference for BMI music and against ASCAP's, arising from the ownership of BMI stock by broadcasters, a situation emphasized in its promotion and advertising during the early years. The prime thrust of *Schwartz* v. *BMI* was to prosecute "an action against BMI, the interlocking radio and television broadcasters, and networks, which control it, those recording companies which are a part of it, and all those others who have directly, and indirectly injured writers by placing American music in a strait jacket manipulated through BMI." The "statement of endorsement and support" was signed by Schwartz and thirty-two other plaintiffs: Ira Gershwin, John Jacob Loeb, Dorothy Fields, Virgil Thomson, Douglas Moore, Gian Carlo Menotti, Samuel Barber, Randall Thompson, Milton Ager, Walter Bishop, Paul Cunningham, Mack David, Milton Drake, James Kimball Gannon, L. Wolfe Gilbert, George Graff, Alex Kramer, Jack Lawrence, Alan Jay Lerner, Edgar Leslie, Jerry Livingstone, George W. Meyer, Joseph Meyer, Vic Mizzy, Charles Tobias, Leonard Whitcup, Joan Whitney, Don Raye, Jack Yellen, Victor Young, Robert MacGimsey, and William Grant Still.

BMI's original strategy was to establish a direct link between the preparation and filing of the action and ASCAP, the Songwriters Protective Association, and the Songwriters of America, whose steering committee was made up entirely of past and present SPA officials and councillors. For the next two years, there was little action other than pretrial examinations of defendants and plaintiffs, and all potential co-conspirators at the network-owned record companies. The legal maneuvering that followed included filing to dismiss the suit because many of the claims were barred by the statute of limitations, and a general denial of all charges by BMI.

Coming on the heels of the industry's general acceptance of a new standard songwriters contract, lasting until 1957, the close relationship between the SPA and the SOA was solidified by the former's plan to widen its membership base and extend its importance in the business, while reducing that of the MPPA. SPA membership dues were raised in 1955, the second increase since the organization was formed in 1930. Twenty-five hundred songwriters were members, among them more than 200 BMI writers, and at least one quarter had some sort of occupational tie to the radio and television field. Significant revisions of the existing contract were planned, all of them to the publishers' disadvantage. A new minimum writer's record royalty was scheduled, beginning at a penny, regardless of any deal made by the publisher with the record company, a too frequent occurrence in the rhythm-and-blues and country-music business. The SPA also intended to improve the lot of its BMI members by getting them the same benefits enjoyed by ASCAP songwriters. Under consideration was a petition to the National Labor Relations Board for a certification of the SPA as the official bargaining agent for all songwriters.

In the center of a troubled and changing business, BMI pursued the course laid out for it in the early 1940s, acquiring repertory and expanding its use. The Performing Society of Britain, largest and last of the international licensing bodies to do so, concluded a reciprocal understanding with BMI for the representation of one another's publishers, an affiliation that further increased the BMI catalogue. BMI now had more than 9,000 writer members, to whom royalties were paid. Annual guarantees to BMI publishers, about which the Schwartz plaintiffs complained at every opportunity, were now used only to keep major firms from going over to ASCAP.

Confronted by problems stemming from growth, Robert Sour, in charge of publisher relations, created two new classes of BMI music companies. The first got the standard rate of four and six cents, plus a 25 percent bonus, offered originally to successful country-music houses whose performances were predominantly on local stations and were not given guarantees by ASCAP. The second class of companies, instituted in August 1955, were paid full logging royalties plus an additional 38 percent, offered in lieu of a guarantee to record companies with publishing arms. The ramifications of the Schwartz case had made BMI more cautious in giving a guarantee to such companies, which might be regarded as an inducement to record only BMI songs. In no case was a guarantee offered to the early rock-'n'-roll houses, not because BMI wished to pay less for the music, but because it came from outside established channels and was the product of individuals who might have a hit or two on their own labels and then go out of business.

Other things were also taking place that lent credibility to many of the plaintiffs' charges. There had always been a certain amount of diversification in the entertainment business, generally of a relatively minor nature. Now, independent radio broadcasters and their employees, television-film syndicators, and talent managers and their clients formed music companies. Publishers manufactured and distributed records and managed talent. Motion-picture studios with television interests looked for companies to acquire. Broadcasting networks backed Broadway shows.

Then, almost overnight, the focus of BMI's concern was diverted to a single individual—Congressman Emanuel Celler, chairman of the House Judiciary Committee and one of ASCAP's best friends. He had chosen the broadcasting networks for his ticket to the U.S. Senate and ordered new hearings, into monopolistic network practices, by the Antitrust Subcommittee, in New York. A hitherto unexpected element entered the probe with the surprising announcement that the involvement of radio and television networks in music publishing and promotion would be addressed on the third day, September 17, 1956.

Accompanied by John Schulman, attorney for both the SPA and the SOA, the recent past president of ASCAP, Stanley Adams, set the tone for the rhetoric that would follow over the next several days, during which a public preview would also be given of evidence, exhibits, and pretrial testimony gathered for the antitrust suit. Being "arbiters of the audible and viceroys of the visual," Adams said, the networks "have sought to and do control the faucets through which music flows." The committee's counsel took an openly anti-BMI line of questioning, citing the material provided by Schwartz and the SPA.

A press conference during the first day's noon recess, sponsored by the SPA and stage-managed by Schwartz, featured Oscar Hammerstein, who read a statement, later entered into the record by Celler, blasting the networks as "an intolerable combination of forces which is handicapping and will eventually stifle the creative musical talent of America unless all composers have an equal chance to be heard."

Carl Haverlin appeared after lunch to deny that BMI was "an instrument of the broadcasting industry." The networks, he said, owned less than 20 percent of BMI, whose stock was also owned by 600 stations across the country. In response to a query, he did admit that the majority of BMI's fourteen directors were from network-affiliated stations. As to the faucet

Adams had invoked, he offered statistics showing that 75 percent of the songs played on radio and television stations were licensed by ASCAP, 15 percent by BMI. Any study of broadcast performances would find a three-, four-, or five-to-one ratio in favor of ASCAP music. Furthermore, he said, the $22 million paid to ASCAP in the past year was three times the amount paid to BMI. "I never encountered anything like it," one congressman observed. "Each side claims the other side does more business."

The multimillionaire founder of the SPA, and one-time songwriter, Billy Rose, provided front-page copy for newspapers in observations such as: "It's the current climate on radio and TV which makes Elvis Presley and his animal posturing possible. When ASCAP songwriters were permitted to be heard, Al Jolson, Nora Bayes, and Eddie Cantor were our big salesman of songs. Today . . . not only are most of the BMI songs junk, but in many cases they are obscene junk, pretty much on a level with dirty comic magazines."

Pointing out that if they did not like them, broadcasters now had the opportunity to have their ASCAP rates fixed by the court, the society's general counsel, Herman Finkelstein, told the committee that there was no longer any justification for BMI to continue under broadcaster ownership. He did not believe, he concluded, that broadcasters would dare to take ASCAP music off the air when the current contracts expired the following year, for fear of massive public protest. Before moving on to the hearing's original purpose, the chairman, Celler, said that in his opinion action by the Justice Department against BMI was inevitable.

Voluntary statements in the following days by both CBS president Frank Stanton and Robert Sarnoff, president of NBC, that they "would take another look" at their holdings in BMI, provided the lawsuit that had been pending for the past three years was dropped, were received enthusiastically by Celler. A spokesman for the SPA, on the other hand, found the offers just not good enough. Even the divestiture of BMI stock by the entire broadcasting industry would "not give sufficient relief to songwriters."

The part of the hearing that received the most public attention was a telegram sent by Frank Sinatra and read into the record by Celler. It was intended to redress, in part, old grievances against Mitch Miller, who had been in charge of CBS recording when the singer's contract was not renewed and when he owed more than $100,000 to the company for back studio-session costs. Before Miller went to Columbia, in 1950, Sinatra wired, he had had freedom in selecting material, "which I may modestly say resulted in a modicum of success for me. Suddenly, Mr. Miller, by design or coincidence, began to present many, many inferior songs all curiously bearing the BMI label." Sinatra had taken his talents to Capitol Records, which had no broadcasting connections. Now that his success was established, once again, he omitted to mention that the song responsible, "Young at Heart,'' was licensed by BMI. Miller sent documents to the committee verifying that during Sinatra's three-year association with him, the singer recorded fifty-seven selections, five of which were BMI songs.

Celler's antipathy toward BMI and the music business remained fixed after the hearing. During several subsequent appearances on television and radio, arranged by press agents for the SPA, he continued to vent his fury on BMI. Moreover, his publicly voiced misperception of contemporary popular music, in particular rock 'n' roll, seemed to come from a generally deeply rooted Puritanism and fear of the black man in the American psyche, naïve, as with Celler, or mean-spiritedly vicious, as when it drove members of the local White Citizens' Council to beat Nat Cole seriously after a concert in Birmingham. Crudely written letters about his love for "nigger music" assailed the editor of *Billboard,* Paul Ackerman. Both Catholic and Protestant clergymen asked the police to censor the lyrics broadcast over local stations, in particular R & B material. Riots following screenings of *The Blackboard Jungle,* in which Bill Haley sang "Rock Around the Clock" (an ASCAP song), gave additional credence to the proposition expounded by Billy Rose that such music appealed only to "the zoot-suiter and the juvenile delinquent." The most politically liberal among the SPA membership had little compunction in turning the wave of racial hatred, masked by concern for the nation's youth, against BMI, the monopolist of rock-'n'-roll and rhythm-and-blues music.

As for BMI, from the beginning it had "cleared" songs offered for licensing, in order to guard against plagiarism of ASCAP music, as called for in the giant insurance policy it took out in 1940. Gradually, the function of censor of lyrics was added, to satisfy the demands of continuity acceptance or censoring departments at the four networks. Coincidentally with *Variety's* well-publicized war against "leer-ics" in 1955, BMI, as a self-protective measure, appointed teams of employees with the proper religious and educational backgrounds to screen questionable lyrics. Sinatra's disdain for BMI increased when the words of one of his new records, "From the Bottom to the Top," were put on its "Play With Caution" list, sent to all licensees. Because of BMI's intervention, these innocent words of "Shake, Rattle and Roll," "you wear low dresses, the sun comes shinin' through/ I can't believe my eyes, all of this belongs to you," were changed to the less-provocative "you wear your dresses, your hair done up so nice/ you look so warm, but your heart is cold as ice."

In a *Billboard* editorial in April 1955, Ackerman wrote: "Rhythm and blues struck the big time not because of obscene lyrics. It did it through the musical talent of its A & R men and artists. . . . It ill behooves pop publishers, mechanical men, and artists to demean R & B, and it is unfortunate that some will cease only after they latch on to an R & B hit." R & B and rock 'n' roll were crosses that BMI continued to bear, often to the embarrassment of its network stockholders, and they provided Schwartz and the SPA with vulnerable targets for attack.

The motion-picture and communications industries' expansion, beginning in the mid-1950s, into the record business made the ownership of established music firms an equally attractive investment. Lawrence Welk paid $175,000 out of the annual $4 million his "champagne music" brought in to buy the Harry von Tilzer Music Company, a Tin Pan Alley pioneer. The purchase marked the birth of a Welk empire, which eventually included the T. B. Harms catalogue and other companies that owned music of the kind Welk continued to perform despite changing styles and tastes. Rumors circulated through the business of a sale of Warner Brothers' MPHC subsidiary and of Mills Music, another of the half-dozen largest ASCAP houses. Both fell through. MGM's Big Three bought the British B. Feldman music interests, including seven subsidiary firms on the Continent, for about $225,000. That transaction was followed by a merger of Robbins, Feist & Miller with the British firm Francis, Day & Hunter, formed in the 1880s, which had branches throughout Europe. The Howard S. Richmond operation, which continued to provide BMI with many hits, but was also active in ASCAP, expanded in a major way in Europe and Latin America. Richmond worked on the principle that placing music with his own self-contained foreign subsidiaries in a position to collect royalties at the source was more remunerative than assigning the American copyrights to a single European publisher, who then sub-licensed it throughout the world outside the United States. Hill & Range Songs, one of BMI's top ten publisher affiliates, concentrated on acquiring copyrights as well as catalogues, sometimes on a split basis with other publishers, and increased its position in both societies. Among its buys were shares in the renewals of the Buddy De Sylva and Ernest R. Ball catalogues of major ASCAP standards.

The Aberbachs' repeated breach of the gentlemen's code among ASCAP publishers respecting copyright-renewal rights further exacerbated relationships between leading young BMI and old-line MPPA-ASCAP executives. A purportedly nonpartisan, though leaning toward BMI, organization, the Association of Independent Music Publishers, was formed in late 1957. The officers included Hill & Range's Jean Aberbach, Joe Csida, Ralph Peer, Howard Richmond, and Edgar Burton. The plea was made that "time to be heard" had come for the association's members, because charges being made by the SPA against BMI were also detrimental to them. The organization lasted for only a short time before its most important members were absorbed into the MPPA and the ownership of both ASCAP and BMI firms moved them out of the conflict.

Many older, larger-than-life, music men were no longer active or had died, At eighty-six, Max Dreyfus was in poor health. Gustave Schirmer, who had been with the firm his father formed in the 1860s since 1911, retired at the age of sixty-one. The veteran publisher Saul Bourne (formerly Bornstein), a co-founder of the second Irving Berlin publishing company, long ASCAP's treasurer, and a power in the councils of the MPPA, died at the age of seventy-three. The fifty-six-year-old Mannie Sachs, in charge of NBC's radio and television programing, who treated the powerhouse publishers with the respect they thought they deserved and as uncomfortable as they were with the direction being taken by popular music, died.

It was no longer the quality of a song that counted, but its sound on recordings. Immediately after the short-lived resurrection of the sheet-music business in 1957, and the tremendous sales of "Tammy" and "Around the World in Eighty Days," that market collapsed again. The number-one song of 1958, "Volare," sold fewer than 250,000 printed copies. Most new hits could not sell the initial order for the sheet-music racks, which the leading print jobber, the Music Dealers Service, still handled. There were two schools of thought about the decline, one holding that rock 'n' roll was responsible, the other that the racks had only prolonged the life of sheet copies in the postwar era of concentration on recorded music. MDS went bankrupt in 1959, with more than half a million dollars owed to publishers.

Changes in the record business also affected the old-line houses' relations with recording artists and A & R men. The vast number of one-hit artists and one-shot record companies rendered the exclusive recording contract obsolete and made it difficult to maintain a profitable working arrangement with either. Sixty percent of the records played by the Top 40 stations came from independently produced masters, whose "spontaneous sound," according to Pat Ballard, an ASCAP writer, was "a reckless disavowal of the old rules, and [had] enough dissonance to appeal to the youthful record buyers who feel more at home with sounds that aren't parlor-perfect."

The stalemate in 1956 between ASCAP and every major studio, except Universal, in securing blanket licenses for the use of copyrighted music on film—one consequence of the Leibell decision—was another factor that split, even wider, the organized songwriters represented by the SPA and the MPPA publishers. Some MPPA members, whose music was prominent in the pre-1948 material being sold to television, by-passed ASCAP and licensed directly on a per-song basis, causing Universal to cancel its ASCAP contract and reduce the use of music covered by it. Maintaining that reruns on TV constituted a new use and required a new license, the Harry Fox Agency of the MPPA passed the problem to the videofilm distributors and syndicators, who were ready to negotiate so that lawsuits would not disturb their relations with telecasters.

The SPA contract due to expire at the end of 1956 was extended by mutual agreement with 204 publishers, and in considering reforms, the association planned to assume the duties of both the Fox Agency and ASCAP and collect performance money from the motion-picture and television industries. SPA's counsel, John Schulman, argued that "writers should get their money without having it pass through anyone else's hands . . . it isn't fair for music publishers to have the use of a writer's money." In July 1955, the SPA had tested the waters in Hollywood by offering licenses to some studios, but quickly learned that it needed the support of the Composers Guild, the only body certified by the National Labor Relations Board to represent background-music composers who worked for the studios. Since the guild's formation in 1953, as a more militant group than the Screen Composers Association, the lot of its members had improved, because of television's growing use of filmed program material.

The older and more conservative SCA had continued to flourish since its formation in the 1940s. During the celebration of its tenth anniversary in 1955, film producer Dore Schary hailed its major accomplishment: prior to its organization, a composer might net $300 a year, but he now earned $15,000. The SCA was foremost among those protesting ASCAP's proposed change in the distribution formulas affecting background music, warning that BMI already was the "biggest threat . . . in the background music field" and that unless proper consideration was given its members, more of them would desert to the enemy. The guild, on the other hand, was in the forefront of the AFM's fight to impose a tariff on imported prerecorded music, whose use on television had tripled, saving producers between $3,000 and $5,000 on each series episode. The libraries were made available to the videofilm makers almost without charge, because of the resulting ASCAP and BMI performance income.

When Leith Stevens, president of the guild, now the Composers and Lyricists Guild of America, claimed that his organization was also the only representative of those working within the broadcasting industry, the SPA and the guild asked the NLRB to certify one of them in that capacity. With the exception of those employed by the networks, screen-music composers and arrangers were regarded as contractors working for hire and therefore had no Social Security or unemployment-insurance benefits. Led by Arthur Schwartz and Deems Taylor, some SPA authors had joined the guild in anticipation of a merger of the two or the absorption of the guild by the SPA. When the CLGA insisted on preserving its autonomy, despite the NLRB's recommendation of a merger with the SPA, the latter body joined the networks and proposed a dismissal of the guild's petition, and then resumed the fight to administer film-performance money.

With a film-performance collection agency of its own in mind, the MPPA moved quickly. Following a conference between John Schulman and Sydney Wattenberg, attorney for the MPPA, a new agency was formed to license jointly the public-exhibition rights of motion pictures, as distinguished from those in the home, taking them away from ASCAP. Operated by Schulman and Wattenberg through their law offices, the agency would fix rates and charge a 10 percent collection fee, almost three times that asked by the Fox Agency. The plan had the full support of Herman Starr and a few others, but most publishers objected because it gave songwriters and composers an equal role in fixing license fees. The reason for support of the agency plan was the presence of film-company men on the ASCAP board, an obstacle to the negotiation of a satisfactory contract between the society and the film studios. It was said that ASCAP would also be in a stronger position legally if it gave up film performing rights. However, if it also gave these up for television, its hold on the industry would be greatly reduced, as would income to ASCAP members.

When the CLGA began negotiations for a new contract with the Motion Picture Producers Association in 1958, the SPA revived talks of a merger. The proposal was quickly withdrawn after influential Hollywood-based songwriters insisted that the CLGA was only a trade union, whereas the SPA was a bargaining agent dealing with publishers on behalf of creative people. The release of pre-1948 motion pictures continued to enrich the networks as well as the studios, the latter maintaining that music rights in a motion picture, for all types of performances, including those on television, were vested in the film producers. The publishers held that a performance right differed from the synchronization or film-recording right for which the Fox Agency was paid, and that an ASCAP license was conditioned on and subject to the clearance of all other rights. Clearly the issue needed clarification by a federal court, at the behest of either the former SPA (as of 1958, the American Guild of Authors and Composers) and its militant new president, Burton Lane, or the MPPA. Three test cases on behalf of MPPA members were brought for declaratory judgment, all stating that motion pictures may not be used for television without a new license from the publisher. The actions were based on the theory that motion-picture synchronization rights were granted only for theatrical exhibition, and that the rerecording of the pictures for television use required a new synchronization license in any event. In potential for cost to television, the suits were the most important actions yet brought in the copyright field, since they involved stations in direct payments to the publishers in addition to their ASCAP payments. Without comment, the actions were withdrawn soon after, leaving in doubt ASCAP's right to collect from television for the use of feature motion pictures originally made for theatrical showing. One explanation for the move was that the major studio-owned music houses did not wish to disturb conditions that were bringing Hollywood millions of dollars annually.

Except for the failure to add the CLGA's 300 members to its ranks, much that took place in 1957–59 was viewed as a victory for the SPA and its public-relations front, the SOA. Unremitting militancy against BMI won newspaper headlines and inspired action in Washington expected to speed up the networks' divestiture of their holdings in BMI as well as of their record companies. When it became obvious that most MPPA members did not intend to give the songwriters an inch more of control of their copyrights by adopting the Schulman-Wattenberg movie-music clearing house, the SPA moved to another course to whittle down the publishers' control. In a poll of SPA members, a majority accepted a new centralized collection agency to deal directly with the publishers in all areas except performance royalties. The first rumor of this intention infuriated publishers.

The change in May 1958 from Songwriters Protective Association to American Guild of Authors and Composers was explained by Lane as due to the addition, because of his and Schwartz's recruiting drives, of serious music composers and their publishers to the fold. Because the AGAC insisted on meeting with the publishers before putting its demands on paper, and because the latter seemed unwilling to discuss mutual problems, it was not until November that the writers began to draft a new contract to replace the several-times-extended 1946 document. The Chappell group, to which Lane was under exclusive contract, had never used an SPA contract. Herman Starr, who had in the past, replaced it with one of his own early in 1957. Authorized to do so by about 850 members, in February 1958 the AGAC prepared to make the initial distribution of collections 5 percent, minus a fee, from approximately 1,500 publishers, to most of whom the whole business was distasteful. Now embarked on an effectively aggressive course, Lane and the AGAC councillors agreed to an indefinite extension of the existing songwriters' contract and prepared to enforce reforms by their own direct means.

The death in February 1957 of Gene Buck, ASCAP's president from 1924 to 1941, brought a temporary halt to dissension within ASCAP. To reinforce this cease-fire, the services of the American Arbitration Association were secured as a last resort for writer members after all appeals within ASCAP were exhausted. To broaden the local radio logging base, the society's consultant, Dr. John Peatman, took all taping of radio stations out of the hands of the twenty-two branch offices and gave it to thirteen auditors under his direction; only a few were to know what stations would be monitored. The change was made to assuage some smaller publishers, who had received lower payments for the first quarter of 1957 because of revised performance credits for sustaining radio shows and because they had been asked to refund money to the society, whose distributions now neared five million dollars a quarter. A problem not as easily resolved was the fact that, except for the powerhouse publishers, 80 percent of the ASCAP publishers had some form of affiliation with BMI and were arguing for the repeal of the 1955 ruling that ended collaboration between ASCAP and BMI writers.

The limitation set by ASCAP in 1955 restricting the value of a theme-song performance, no matter how many times it was played on the same program, was responsible for the first public disclosure in a dozen years of what top-rated composers were paid. The theme song for Arthur Godfrey's ninety-minute radio-television network program, "Seems Like Old Times," was played twelve times a day for five days a week. Its writers, Carmen Lombardo and John Jacob Loeb, had earned $80,000 since Godfrey started using the song in 1950 to 1955; they contended in a suit against ASCAP that the sum should have been larger. Their argument was that each of the daily nine segments was sponsored by a different advertiser, necessitating a new accounting of the number of actual performances the song had received in the last ten years. Among the figures entered as evidence was Irving Berlin's income from the society: $101,000 in 1954; $100,000, 1955; $102,000, 1956; and $55,750 for the first half of 1957. Cole Porter's income in 1954 was $65,000; 1955, $65,750; 1957, $71,500; and for the first six months of 1957, $37,750. Hoagy Carmichael's earnings were $22,000 in 1954; $26,500, 1955; $27,750, 1956; and for the first six months of 1957, $13,250. Among other disclosures were these: Richard Rodgers and Oscar Hammerstein got between $65,000 and $75,000 a year; there was a broad second level of top musical-comedy composers and lyricists who got around $50,000 annually; the "third level" of composers, as one ASCAP witness described them, including Frank Loesser and the estate of Sigmund Romberg, was paid between $25,000 and $30,000 a year. Lombardo and Loeb lost their case, but the revelations of payments to the top writers further aggravated those younger members whose currently popular hits enjoyed a substantial number of performances, but whose checks never showed this.

All these matters to one side, ASCAP was about to engage in another of the encounters with telecasters that have continued to bedevil it periodically through the years. It had taken the television industry four and a half years and $100,000 in expenses before the ASCAP contract due to expire at the end of 1957 was accepted; such expenses now accounted for half of the society's total income of over $20 million. The All-Industry Television Committee deputized to hammer out a new agreement was confronted with the probability that the charges made by plaintiffs in the Schwartz case—that BMI writers dominated the current hit charts—might be used by the networks against ASCAP, while BMI continued to concede that ASCAP controlled the bulk of broadcast performances. While Finkelstein and Hammerstein sought to disassociate ASCAP from the lawsuit, its own president, Paul Cunningham, was one of the plaintiffs. The chief stumbling block to a quick agreement was the $150 million antitrust action.

Under terms of the 1950 consent order, broadcasters had the right to ask the court to fix rates, but they now feared that these might be increased, because it had been admitted that ASCAP licensed 80 percent of the music on TV networks but was paid on the ratio of only two to one over BMI. Late in December 1957, the negotiators wired their more than 250 subscribers that ASCAP was willing to renew for four years at the same rates only if a substantial majority of stations accepted. Within a few weeks, a substantial majority of the committee's 250 supporters agreed, and with them 150 other stations that had refused to finance the negotiations but were willing to partake of their fruits.

Television's hold over American audiences betokened a continuing increase in ASCAP income from the industry, which had already risen from a negligible amount after the war to more than $10 million in 1957. As TV prospered, the rise in ASCAP distributions was spectacular. In 1954, the cost to a sponsor for thirty-nine half hour programs was about $1.25 million; for such top-rated shows as Jackie Gleason's and Sid Caesar's the cost was nearly $100,000 an episode, which led to multiple or rotating sponsors. During the first post-freeze year, when 215 new stations joined the existing 108, industry profits rose more than 41 percent, to $78.5 million, $18 million of that to the networks and their sixteen owned-and-operated stations. The business of producing and distributing videofilm to the networks and for syndication was moving into the big time, with gross sales of $130 million. Four companies—Ziv, NBC Film Division, CBS Television Film Sales, and MCA–TV/Revue—accounted for $25 million. Most of their competitors lost money.

Cost was no longer the object to a dozen prime-time sponsors by the 1955–56 season. The accent remained on live programing, sending its price to the networks for the season to a half-billion dollars. The Danish pianist-comedian Victor Borge was paid more by CBS-TV for two one-man shows than he made from a two-year run on Broadway, presenting virtually the same material. The ever-upward surge in costs was driven even higher by the introduction of the ninety-minute spectacular. The financial picture for syndicators brightened as well, the most successful concentrating on production for national sponsorship rather than for regional or local markets.

General Tire & Rubber's sale, for $15 million, of 740 RKO-Radio A and B feature productions, bought from Howard Hughes, Warner's sale of its entire library of pre-1948 pictures, and MGM's pending sale of its entire library, estimated to be worth about $110 million, opened the floodgates and put Hollywood into television. The picture tube was no longer beneath Hollywood's dignity, and, as David Sarnoff had prophesied, the medium was becoming "just another distribution arm for the picture business." Another half-recognized element of the business, away from the networks, was national spot advertising by the same blue-chip sponsors that fed the chains; it appeared during and between syndicated programs and feature movies on independent stations and accounted for half of the $307-million gross billings in the last quarter of 1955. Motion pictures accounted for 13 percent of all American television programing in 1956, a total of 73-million home-hours each week. The public was offered 4,169 movies each week, a figure that rose after the MGM, Warner, and other sales were completed. Competition by the videofilm producers for a share of air time was so intense that thirty-nine out of every forty pilot programs for projected series could not be sold.

With spots unexpectedly open on the Jackie Gleason program and CBS' vaunted *Playhouse 90* and sponsor cancellations on *I Love Lucy*, it appeared in the spring of 1957 that the "great man" era of Gleason, Caesar, Berle, Ball, and the comedians who had sold television sets over the years was ending. It had crested in 1956, when ABC-TV exchanged three million dollars of ABC-Paramount stock for a 40 percent share of Frank Sinatra's Kent Production Company in order to obtain the singer's services for three years. Sinatra was also guaranteed $250,000 a year, and the network budgeted nine million for 117 episodes of a musical-dramatic series starring him. In addition to that show, the 1957–58 season began with almost two-dozen programs that plundered Tin Pan Alley's vaults. In a season entirely bereft of any new program ideas or concepts, the comedians made way for affable singing personalities who could handle a half hour of prime time with more talent than merely performing their current and past record hits. Perry Como knocked Gleason's *Honeymooners* from the Nielsen ratings, and Dinah Shore's Southern charm mowed down the opposition. Before winter arrived, *Variety* reckoned that television had "a sore throat," with Sinatra in trouble. Only Como and Shore remained when the season ended, the latter with one of the most expensive shows yet offered. Singers Gisele MacKenzie, Polly Bergen, Guy Mitchell, Pat Boone, Patrice Munsel, Patti Page, and Rosemary Clooney, among others, followed Sinatra's drama and musical-variety program off the tube. The great screen musicals of the past, part of the pre-1948 packages, failed also. More than any other type of movie, they showed the age of their plots and their music, which was keyed to an earlier time. Clearly, television was not a medium to which people looked for their popular music on a regular basis, as they did with radio deejays. There were exceptions, such as the appearances of Elvis Presley, Bill Haley, and other rock-'n'-roll stars, but the youth market did not control the TV-set dial as it did the record player.

ASCAP would not admit it publicly, but television's dependence on the society was essentially for the background music written for the screen and the standard songs on which adults doted. The ten most popular syndicated strip series, most of them reruns from radio and television, that kept local audiences tuned in to local stations ran a gamut, from Liberace and his candelabra-bedecked piano to the *Four Star Playhouse* anthology, known in syndication as *Star Performance*. Since being taken off the networks they had grossed $8.5 million in syndication sales, and contributed greatly to the typical local video operation in 1957, which showed an average profit of $170,000 before taxes, compared with $50,000 two years before.

The eleven personalities responsible for the largest time sales since the advent of the television networks were: Arthur Godfrey, $150 million from a career in TV that began in 1948 with *Talent Scouts;* Ed Sullivan, gossip columnist turned vaudeville host, $80 million; Perry Como, $65 million, beginning with his five-times-a-week *Chesterfield Supper Club* program in

1948; Dave Garroway, $60 million, mostly from eight years as anchorman on the *Today* show; Garry Moore, $59 million; Art Linkletter, $57 million; Milton Berle, tied with Lucille Ball–Desi Arnaz, $46 million; Ralph Edwards, $44 million from *This Is Your Life* and *Truth or Consequences;* Groucho Marx, $40 million; followed by Goodson-Todman's *What's My Line?*, $35 million.

The last major technological revolution in television—from the kinescope copies of a live show, made by filming from the monitor and ready in three hours, to high-fidelity videotape in color, ready to be played back immediately on the same machine—was in the wings. Color tape was first demonstrated publicly in July 1955 by Bing Crosby Enterprises, which, like RCA, had been experimenting with magnetic tape for TV since 1951. The Crosby tape was not yet ready to replace live programing, but the demonstration by the Ampex Corporation of a black-and-white tape recorder to broadcasters at the 1956 NAB convention persuaded most of those who saw it that the time was now. Tape on television was to have an even more significant effect on the medium than it had on radio. By-passing the time-zone problem, tape solved the delayed broadcast for both. TV tape went further; it got rid of the kinescope machinery and made possible easy files of fourteen-inch spindles of two-inch high-quality tape that could be used again and again. Overnight, stock of the engineer-manufacturer Alexander Poniatoff's Ampex Corporation jumped skyward as orders for the first model poured in. Soon after, Crosby Enterprises got out of the videotape business, selling all inventory and equipment to 3M. In April 1957, Ampex announced that a compatible Video Tape Recorder would be ready in less than two years. The problem of interchangeability—playing a tape recorded on one machine on a different one—was solved, making it possible to tape a show in New York and ship it anywhere for local broadcast. The cost of the earliest black-and-white VTR fell to $45,000 a unit. Shortly after, Ampex exchanged patents with RCA, which controlled the most significant advances in color videotape, and the two electronic companies got control of the most important TV-tape patents and their manufacture.

The death knell was sounded in October 1958 for live black-and-white programing, and an all-color future was inevitable. A four-year-old civil antitrust action charging RCA with monopoly of radio and television patents was settled by a consent order. More than 12,000 patents were put in a pool that was available to the entire industry on a reasonable royalty basis. Paramount Pictures moved into videotape by merging its 75-percent Telemeter Magnetics, manufacturer of dictating machines and supplies, with Ampex under the latter's name. The transaction increased the value of Paramount's holdings in Telemeter, which had been acquired for $700,000 to $12 million.

The 1959 National Association of Broadcasters convention was once again the locale for the introduction of new RCA color and black-and-white VTRs, prompting the prediction by John L. Burns, RCA's president, that the 1959–60 season would be the year of color television. New models with simplified operation made it possible for persons without an advanced degree in electrical engineering to fine-tune a colorcast. The Ampex Videotape Cruiser, introduced at the same time, took the VTR out of the studio and enabled it to do anything a movie camera could. The first Ampex traveling unit was self-powered, and used the new long-distance Zoomer Universal lenses. It could be set up anywhere and could shoot while moving at high speed on the open road.

Including feature movies, which had to be transferred to film tape to be shown over the air, most network programing moved nearer the all-tape era. During the 1959–60 season, $150 million worth of taped shows occupied 70 percent of all nighttime programing. For the first time, television's total revenues went over the billion-dollar mark, but profits were down because of increased operating costs, imposed by the new technology and a jump in the cost of packaged programs.

Radio's soaring expenses provided the same mixed financial picture. Industry profits had declined in 1958 by 31 percent, to $37 million, while revenue rose only 1 percent, to $535 million, approximately half that of television. Profits had continued to rise in the past several years as the number of commercial AM stations increased from 2,603 in 1953 to 3,197. The four national networks and three regional networks were no longer breaking even, as they had in 1957.

People tuning in at different times on different days, the car radio, disk jockeys, and the transistor radio were responsible for the remarkable success of many local stations in the face of saturation by profitable commercial television. The hour and half-hour commercial network radio programs were the first to go, victims of the five-minute newscast between periods of recorded music. There were four times more car radios in operation than 1943's eight million. In 1947, a team of Bell Laboratories physicists—John Bardeen, Walter Brattain, and William Schockley—had found a smaller and more energy-efficient replacement for the vacuum tube in the tiny transistor. Zenith engineers used it the following year to build a truly portable radio receiver. Advances in the United States and Japan in the further miniaturization of components produced ever-smaller and more efficient battery-powered radios, known as "transistor sets," which became the teen-agers' delight. They made available anywhere the local-station deejays, with the newest pop hits and rock-'n'-roll record releases.

Rather than concentrate on 50,000-watt stations, once the kingpins of the marketplace, the biggest-spending local radio advertisers—car dealers, supermarkets, grocery chains, and department stores—used lower-powered stations, which outpulled the network affiliates with music and news, for their saturation campaigns. ABC and CBS managed to retain a loyal daytime following with personality-variety programing and soap operas. NBC went in for a daytime music-and-news format, with live dance bands around midday. A period of stabilization in audience share for the networks occurred in 1957, when, for the first time in the network TV era, they did not lose any money, although they did not make any either. Owing to rising operating costs, nighttime network television turned into a mass-entertainment medium, ridding itself of the music, news, and public-service elements borrowed from radio in the early days of development. It left the entire music and national news field open for the taking.

Local radio-station owners resented the fact that they paid about 10 percent more than television stations did to ASCAP in 1958, a situation brought about five years earlier when the All-Industry Television Committee and the networks convinced the society that television's booming expansion would provide ASCAP with more money in the future and hence justified a reduction from the existing "radio plus 10 percent" to "radio minus 10 percent." The seventeen-man Radio Committee wanted a substantial decrease in the rates it paid to ASCAP, as well as those to BMI. Particularly adamant were the stations that employed a Top 40 format, which used more BMI music than ASCAP, and provided BMI in late 1958 with a third of all local radio performances, double the number a decade earlier.

The committee did not have the confidence of all broadcasters, having made what seemed to many inordinate demands on ASCAP and exaggerated promises to the industry. A one-year renewal on the old terms tendered by ASCAP had already been signed by the networks and many stations. There were also a substantial number of stations that had come into the industry since the contract in place was forged; these had signed separate five-year contracts, expiring on various dates between 1960 and 1964. Four choices were open to the industry: contest the fee in the U.S. Southern District Court in New York, which administered the consent decree; get a five-year contract under the existing most-favored-nation clause; sign a one-year renewal; or take out a blanket commercial and a per-program sustaining license. By this last device, stations could save $1.2 million without any risk at all. There were commercial announcements on practically every program using music, so that there were no sustaining broadcasts, which permitted a saving of the entire sustaining fee, based on a percentage of each station's gross and said to represent 12 percent of the society's total radio revenue. The committee chose the first of the alternatives, and for the first time prepared to ask a court to fix rates in the matter for more than 600 stations. ASCAP had refused to drop its radio rate from 2.25 percent to the 2.05 percent enjoyed by television, arguing that because of the prevailing music and news policy, the society's repertory played a more important role than it had in 1941, when the contract was written.

With preliminary sparring over and talks at an impasse, the committee filed a petition in March 1959 asking Federal Judge Sylvester J. Ryan to fix "reasonable fees." More than 3,000 stations had renewed their BMI licenses on the old basis, and the judge ordered the society to renew an interim contract. In June, a new rate scale was announced, reducing radio payments by approximately $800,000, a general 9 percent decrease. The society insisted, however, that stations that had already signed would be held to the old rates for the term of their contracts. At the prompting of the Justice Department, which had come under pressure from Congress, a final settlement was made in January 1960, coincident with a third consent order, which reorganized ASCAP practices in order to avert new antitrust action. The terms obtained by the committee were extended to all radio stations.

The solidly entrenched old-line music houses and their songwriter allies were to lose far more than the $800,000 gained annually by radio broadcasters. Actions taken by Hans Lengsfelder and his dissident supporters in New York and Washington were about to produce results. In late 1957, Lengsfelder had brought a suit against ASCAP, attacking the weighted vote as unfair to smaller publisher and writer members. Since 1942, he charged, voting control had been vested in less than 5 percent of the writer members and 15 percent of the publishers. Representative James Roosevelt held four days of hearings in March 1958. The first witness, Herman Finkelstein, explained ASCAP's workings, stating proudly that there was little or no rock 'n' roll in its catalogue. He was followed by Oscar Hammerstein, as representative of the board of directors. He defended his colleagues and affirmed his statement, made to a meeting of the ASCAP membership in 1957, that ASCAP "was not a United States, it is more like United States Steel. Do not think that people who own a whole lot of property in this, and many copyrights, are going to take one vote, the same vote as the man who owns one copyright." Ralph Peer, on behalf of his ASCAP firms, representatives of the Walt Disney Music Company, G. Ricordi, and others, attacked the weighted voting system, ASCAP's performance surveys and logging procedures, the distribution formulas, the maintenance and availability of minutes and directives, and an appeals process that discouraged appeals.

In May, the subcommittee issued a report of its conclusions and directed the Justice Department to take whatever steps were necessary to remedy the problems presented by witnesses in order "to effectuate the terms and spirit of the consent decree of March 14, 1950." Negotiations between the Antitrust Division and the society began in June to write a consent decree that would avoid further hearings and litigation.

President Paul Cunningham's remarks to the October 1958 membership meeting in Chicago that changes were to be expected in the distribution concluded with a hint that they would be at Washington's direction. During the following week, Paul Ackerman of *Billboard* learned that "ASCAP would like to settle out of court if entrenched interests could maintain control." It was said that the biggest copyright owners "would resign in the event of a drastic change in the weighted vote." Cunningham's offhand remarks raised the possibility that an 80 percent performance factor would force major changes in the operation of large firms, with or without motion-picture and Broadway connections.

Redd Evans, one of the dissidents responsible for the amended 1950 consent order, appeared at the October ASCAP meeting to serve as chief spokesman for the Lengsfelder-Fox coalition. His request to Finkelstein to bring the membership up to date on Washington matters was refused. It was already common knowledge that ASCAP had hired one of the country's top antitrust attorneys, Arthur Dean, for a reported fee of $350,000. Dean's constant presence at the Justice Department inspired persistent rumors that a resolution was at hand, since the large publishers would make tremendous sacrifices to rule out court action. Congressman Roosevelt, in January 1959, began the first of a series of public demands on the Justice Department to take immediate corrective action. The sticking point was the weighted vote; progress was reported on all other aspects of the case. At last, new terms for settlement were discussed with the dissidents, who learned that the government did not see eye to eye with them on the matter of a straight-performance pay system. After more months and much public exasperation, ASCAP and the Justice Department reached a tentative agreement on an amended consent order. Final hearings were announced for October 1959.

A 4 percent increase in ASCAP income, to another record high, $28.4 million, for 1958 was confirmed at the spring 1959 meeting by the society's new president, Stanley Adams. As *Variety* had noted, ASCAP needed a half-billion dollars in the bank at a nominal 4 percent interest to achieve such an annual income. In 1959, it climbed to $30 million.

Objecting to what they viewed as the greatly watered-down provisions of the revised consent order, some ASCAP writers prepared for the October hearings before Judge Ryan, ASCAP's legal overseer. Weighted voting had been retained, but was modified so that no writer or publisher would have more than 100 votes. All subsidiaries of major publishers were regarded as individual members, and the order limited any increase in the votes of the top ten publishers to no more than one tenth of their current votes. Writers had the option of either a 100 percent current-performance base or a "four-fund" mixed base, which would continue the 20-30-30-20 ratings for current performance, five-year performance average, recognized works (formerly "availability,") and seniority. Four-fund writers could switch over to straight performance royalties at the end of any fiscal year, but those paid on that basis had to wait two years before making a switch to the other option. The publishers' 15 percent seniority factor would be phased out over the next five years, leaving a formula of 70 percent for performances and 30 percent for recognized works. Payments for performances of concert or classical music were raised, and credits for background music, themes, cues, jingles were raised from 100 to 1 to 10 to 1.

Some young members, the Current Writers Group headed by Hal David, a contemporary-popular lyricist, objected particularly to the new "recognized works" pool of songs more than one year old. They would not receive a penny for a new song until four distribution quarters passed, especially troubling in a world where the popularity of a song dropped so quickly and older songs continued to receive larger payments than new ones. Other critics maintained that, in spite of the imposition of a 41 percent vote limitation, large companies still controlled the board. There were reservations too, about the chance to give smaller publishers a place among the directors by allowing a group that controlled one twelfth of the total vote the right to elect one member, which might end secret balloting.

Arthur Dean gave lengthy and complicated explanations of the proposed order but turned questions around to emphasize the possibility that if the order was not approved a long and expensive suit would follow. In the 1950 decree, the society had agreed that the government could apply for any modification of it, including the dissolution of ASCAP. In arguing for unanimous approval of the consent decree, Adams gave an unexpected blessing to rock 'n' roll for the first time when he remarked that "the equities of all must be protected—old and new writers, rhythm and blues writers, rock and roll, country and western and pop."

Among the reforms proposed was the provision that ASCAP employ an independent outside expert, named by the court and paid by the society, to design a scientific performance measurement system. ASCAP had consistently refused to use the logs, also sent to BMI, arguing that the conspiracy to favor their rival's music extended to them. Prior to the Roosevelt hearings, Joel Dean, a Columbia University professor and statistician, had replaced Peatman and started an overhaul of the logging procedures. His plan substantially increased the local radio sample and placed it on a more scientifically random basis. An annual total of 25 million performances was anticipated, on the basis of which all writer and publisher payments were to be calculated. Network television accounted for between 41 and 43 percent of the total under the new plan; local TV, between 16 and 19; network radio, between 4 and 6; and local radio, between 34 and 36. The total logging of ABC, CBS, and NBC television networks continued as in the past.

Judge Ryan's hearings provided a field day for the legal profession. ASCAP would not confirm that a million dollars had already been spent for legal fees. An outstanding music-business attorney, Lee Eastman, represented the Current Writers Group, whose members had produced 35 percent of the society's hits in the past year. Charles Horsky, an outstanding antitrust lawyer and a Nuremburg trials prosecutor, appeared for the Evans-

Lengsfelder-Fox group. The American Arbitration Association had recently found for Fox in a matter dealing with the duration of such works as his "Cornish Rhapsody." The AAA panel found that ASCAP had punished the publisher after he attempted to obtain more performance money for works over four minutes in playing time by reducing what he had already received. Responding to a plea by the dissidents that there had not been unanimous approval of the order by members, Ryan delayed approval and asked for an early vote by the entire ASCAP membership. If objections from within ASCAP did not permit him to approve the revised consent order, an antitrust suit by the government would immediately follow, he said. In the argumentation that followed, Horsky attacked the lack of democratic procedures in ASCAP and suggested a division of the publishers into three bodies based on earnings, each having the right to elect four directors. Eastman found the recognized works performance fund discriminatory against currently active writers and asked for its withdrawal and a full 100 percent performance payment.

Once 2,960 writers voted for the order and 1,285 against, and 654 publishers for and 440 against, Judge Ryan signed the second amended ASCAP consent decree, finding it a fair compromise. Two unemployed New York political stalwarts, former Supreme Court Justice John E. McGeehan and former Senator Irving M. Ives were appointed by Ryan to serve as impartial advisers to oversee the distribution of ASCAP royalties. It marked the first introduction of outsiders, other than government personnel, to the society's operation.

Concurrent with the conclusion of the Ryan proceeding, a House committee embarked on a probe into allegedly widespread record-company payola to disk jockeys, the result of lobbying by Burton Lane and the SPA. They and their supporters hoped to force the divestiture of BMI by the broadcasting industry and to obtain a large cash settlement in the Schwartz case.

In November 1956, John Schulman, attorney for the SPA and the SOA, approached a representative of NBC to set up settlement talks with a third-party arbitrator. There had already been a tentative bid by the networks to pay damages to ASCAP as part of the pending television contract negotiation. NBC could not escape responsibility for having created BMI, "a cancer on the music industry," Schulman said. He was certain that his clients had enough power to make the society ratify anything to which they agreed in order to dispose of the lawsuit. The matter never got beyond the talking stage at this time, but it did hint at the networks' hope to get rid of it as expeditiously as possible. One of their fears stemmed from the fact that BMI was paid one third as much as ASCAP for 10 to 15 percent of the performances. ASCAP could argue in the contract talks that the networks' ownership of BMI gave BMI preferential rates and money that otherwise would go to the society. The defense that the networks and other broad-casters paid what they did in order to maintain competition and prevent monopoly might not be enough.

When BMI had added the first Rhythm and Blues Award Luncheon in February 1957 to its annual popular and country award presentations, it brought the immediate complaint from an NBC executive that the company had taken a poor public-relations stand in light of the generally rampant anti–R & B public attitude. It was suggested that RCA consider dropping the lucrative Elvis Presley contract that was bringing in millions.

BMI's seventeenth anniversary in February found the company with the greatest number of popular hits in its history, six of "Your Hit Parade's" top seven and thirty-four of *Variety's* forty-five "Top Record Talent and Tunes" selections, including the first ten. The upsurge of success troubled ASCAP, whose only hope, should BMI continue to increase its share of the market, lay in the possibility that its per-performance costs might bankrupt it. It was a possibility BMI had recognized and for which it sought a cure by discouraging new contracts with guarantees against future earnings.

While awaiting the wholesale indictment of BMI and the networks they expected in the Celler Committee report, Schulman, with Arthur Schwartz, Otto Harbach, Dorothy Fields, Stanley Adams, and other SPA members, was actively seeking a new forum for complaints in Washington. A brief charging that a combination of all the leading broadcasters and the largest recording companies conspired to gain full control of the country's music and that legislative action was needed was handed to Senator Warren G. Magnuson, chairman of the Commerce Committee, which had jurisdiction over the broadcasting industry. With dogged persistence, the SPA scattered copies of the brief among chairmen and leading members of other commit-tees. BMI songwriter members of the SPA protested vehemently but use-lessly. Though the standard SPA contract contained an exemption for AS-CAP performance payments, it did not apply to any rival organization. BMI had never been able to induce the SPA to include similar provisions for BMI. But because only membership in the SPA permitted them to collab-orate with its members, BMI writers had remained in the organization, hop-ing to effect reforms from within. A compromise was promised that would satisfy both ASCAP and BMI writers, but the standard contract was not amended.

The Celler report was not issued until June 1957. It was generally soft on the networks, but it recommended that the Justice Department undertake "complete and extensive investigation of the music field, to determine whether the antitrust laws have been or are being violated." Most of its initial ver-sion, recommending immediate action against BMI by the Justice Depart-ment and investigation of Columbia's and Victor's preference for BMI mu-sic and the power of the broadcasters to turn ASCAP music off, was omitted.

So, too, was significant information supplied after the hearing by BMI. The general impression that Celler was predisposed against BMI was strengthened when a staff-prepared news release summarizing the report stated that the committee urged an investigation "to determine whether the antitrust laws have been or are being violated by BMI." The last two words did not appear in the printed report.

Passages from the Celler findings favorable to the SPA's war on BMI and the networks were cited during a press conference in New York, at which Arthur Schwartz and others repeated the charges made in the lawsuit and commended Celler's efforts. As in the past, the general tenor was that the top ten songs were junk for which the BMI-network monopoly was responsible. Bing Crosby, a member of ASCAP who received $5,000 a year from the society, of the SPA, and admittedly cut in on the songs that made him eligible for membership in both, joined the fray with a telegram to Magnuson in which he called the caliber of currently popular songs deplorable. "I think it is the result of pressures exerted by BMI," he concluded.

The focus of this and other propaganda activity and lobbying in Washington—the $150-million antitrust suit brought by thirty-three ASCAP members—had ground on relentlessly for forty-two months. A special master was appointed to reduce the heated tensions that surfaced during pretrial examinations, which covered more than 20,000 pages. The special master's decision to permit BMI and other defendants to examine performance cards of 250,000 ASCAP songs from 1934 to the present served only to prolong the trial. With little prospect that ASCAP would budge on the matter, it was expected that the suit would remain in the pretrial examination stage for a year or more and that only a special dispensation of the court would start actual trial proceedings sooner.

Schwartz and other SPA officials found a shortcut, which they expected would resolve the case as well as the networks' divestiture of their record companies, in the June 3, 1957, decision of the Supreme Court in *United States* v. *General Motors–Du Pont*. It said that a corporation may not own stock in another corporation that supplied it with material if in so doing it caused "probable" lessening of competition or a tendency to monopoly. Although the relationship between GM and Du Pont was that of customer and supplier, the latter owned 23 percent of outstanding GM stock. According to the SPA, this paralleled the stock ownership by broadcasting companies in music-publishing and recording companies.

Presumably at the behest of the SPA, a bill was drafted that would prohibit the granting or holding of a license for a radio or television station by any person or corporation engaged directly or indirectly in publishing music or manufacturing or selling musical recordings. George Smathers, Senator from Florida, agreed to introduce the bill and did so on August 21, 1957. Senator John F. Kennedy had already inserted into the *Congressional Re-*

cord of August 12 an anti-BMI column written for *Newsday*. It urged that BMI be probed, quoted Crosby, and used some of the material that was being widely distributed by Schwartz, the SPA, and the SOA.

In introducing his bill, Smathers said that BMI had subsidized "hundreds of publishing firms [and] today this musical empire consists of 2,000 such firms." Joining in the colloquy on the Senate floor, Barry Goldwater, acting on information supplied by Hoagy Carmichael, agreed that "the airways of this country have been flooded with bad music since BMI was formed." Synchronized attacks on BMI in the next several days included a column by Oscar Hammerstein in the *New York Herald Tribune* of August 26, 1957, in which he wrote that "once [broadcasters] became owners of songs, they acquired an interest beyond giving the best music to the people. It became important to them to give *their* music to the people.

The high cost of meeting the SPA's constant attacks and forays into legislative circles, mounting legal fees, and steadily increasing performances of its music forced BMI to draw back on its expenses, beginning late in 1957. BMI's radio-broadcaster program clinics, for many years the centerpiece of Carl Haverlin's station-relations program, were suspended. The Chicago and Los Angeles song-plugging branches of the company's music-publishing operation were closed down. Clerical staffs were reduced. Sale of the BMI publishing department, which had shown small or no profit in eighteen years, was considered.

Robert Burton was promoted to the newly created position of vice-president in charge of domestic performing-rights administration. Robert Sour was moved to take charge of writer relations and deal with nearly 4,000 songwriter affiliates. Theodora Zavin, a graduate of the Columbia Law School who had joined the company in 1952, took Sour's place as assistant vice-president in charge of publisher relations.

From the start, BMI had paid distributions on a local- and network-station performance basis. To build up a repertory of music in the ten months before the 1941 music war started, the company had made many fixed-guarantee contracts, ranging from six-figure advances down to $24,000 and $12,000 annual guarantees to lesser publishers. After the 1954 crisis, when more performances than expected were logged, arrangements for logging plus 25 percent or 38 percent were made. At the bottom of its publisher roster were about a thousand firms that got the standard four- and six-cent contracts, among them houses that had failed to earn earlier guarantees or had been cut down during regular reappraisals of their activity. With more and more publishers applying for affiliation, more record company–publishing houses in the marketplace each year, and a larger share of hit songs in all fields of music, BMI's problem in 1958 was its success. The difference between income and outgo was shrinking to a dangerous point. Zavin was charged with reversing the situation and correcting inequities. The cost-per-performance to BMI in 1953 ranged from 47.1 cents, paid to a Hollywood-

Broadway publisher whose contract called for $30,000, to 4.1 cents, paid
to a country-and-western publisher who received $9,600 that year but had
five times more performances.

BMI's guarantee contracts had first come under scrutiny during the Celler
hearings, when the renewal, in 1949, of an agreement with Hill & Range
Songs, owned by the Aberbach family, was addressed. It had been brought
to the committee counsel's attention by plaintiffs in *Schwartz* v. *BMI*. Jean
Aberbach, recognized by the music business as one of the most profession-
ally astute in it, was born in Europe, where he started working in 1926 for
publishers in Berlin and Paris and as a representative of the major British
music house, Campbell, Connelly. He had also become a member of the
Italian music society and enjoyed success as a popular songwriter. At some
point during World War II, the Aberbach family came to the United States.
Between 1945 and 1948, Jean worked as the American representative of
Salabert, of Paris, and was responsible for the success in the United States
of its "Symphony," and for Max Dreyfus, of Chappell Music, as West
Coast representative, placing Chappell music in feature motion pictures.
Both relationships were terminated in 1948 when he joined Hill & Range
as a full-time employee to negotiate contracts with country-and-western
songwriters to form their own companies and affiliate them with Hill &
Range. By means of the affiliated companies, the Aberbachs had built up
BMI's leading publisher combine of country-and-western music firms.

Hill & Range had originally been formed in 1945 by four stockholders,
brother Julian and father Adolph Aberbach, Milton Blink, and Gerald King,
both of Standard Radio Transcription Service. The original catalogue consisted of music already cleared through BMI that had been recorded for and
assigned to Standard and then transferred to Hill & Range. By the time of
the 1949 renewal, the Aberbachs had formed three ASCAP companies, and
it was those that were referred to in a clause in the document that permitted
them to operate the firms but did not permit them to exploit songs published
through the ASCAP firms. BMI had inserted the restriction at the demand
of its directors, who felt that a protective provision would ensure the Aberbachs' best efforts. The contract also called for a $100,000 annual guaran-
tee, and $250 for each copyrighted song recorded by any of a number of
major labels, up to a maximum of $75,000 yearly. By 1956, Hill & Range
was the seventh-highest-paid BMI publisher affiliate. The "anti-ASCAP "
clause, which BMI insisted at the Celler hearings had never been invoked,
came under particularly heavy questioning and was used by Schwartz in the
charges he made publicly through the press.

In a letter written to the Celler committee on October 18, 1956, Jean
Aberbach said that though three ASCAP firms were mentioned during the
hearings, only one of them was important. Among other firms they owned
in 1956 was Ross Jungnickel, one of the oldest and most respected firms in
ASCAP, Reg Connelly, Rosarita Music, and Charles N. Daniels. "As a

result of the efforts of this group the ASCAP income rose from $850 a quarter in 1949 to $66,000 this year. . . . This dramatic growth . . . under the well-known difficulties of a young publisher to get any money at all out of ASCAP within the short period of five years is, I am sure, unparalleled. . . . I am informed that . . . our group has emerged as the one showing the highest rate of growth during the years in question.''

Similar restrictive clauses appeared in BMI contracts with other major companies affiliated with both organizations. They called for quotas of ASCAP songs vis-à-vis BMI music; agreement not to render any services, directly or indirectly, to a non-BMI firm; payment of the salary of a professional manager to devote full activity to the BMI house; money for special exploitation that would not be deemed to be payment for performances. All the restrictions were put into the record of the hearings.

With an eye to both budgetary and public-relations problems, Zavin eventually established a new method for computing guarantees, basing them on an average of performances in three years multiplied by ten cents. If a publisher had consecutive performances of 600,000, 800,000, and one million, a total for the period of 2.4 million, or an average of 800,000 performances per year, he was guaranteed $80,000 in the next year. Most new publishers did not receive guarantees, except for such an exceptionally successful operation as Nevins–Kirshner Aldon music. Guaranteed publishers were dropped each year, but the bulk of BMI's most important firms, around fifty, continued to receive guarantees.

Senator Smathers assured his broadcaster constituents that the sole target of his bill was the networks and their recording business. He did not intend to destroy BMI, which, he believed, should be allowed to maintain competition with ASCAP. The statement did not satisfy Schwartz or Finkelstein, who continued to insist publicly that there should be complete divestiture of BMI by all broadcasters. Smathers insisted on public hearings. They were announced for March 1958 by Senator John O. Pastore, chairman of the Communications subcommittee, as part of an over-all investigation of the networks. Schwartz and Hammerstein were among the witnesses the first day, March 11, the latter commuting from the House Office Building, where he was appearing as a witness for ASCAP at Roosevelt's hearings. Both assailed the frightening power of the broadcasting business ''over the entire music industry and over the listening habits of the American public.'' Hill & Range's 1949 contract was cited as an example of that power. The author of a recent best-selling exposé of Madison Avenue's advertising and selling techniques, Vance Packard, was introduced and identified himself as an ''expert in the manipulation of American musical taste.'' He asserted that a ''gross degradation in the quality of music supplied to the public over the airwaves'' was taking place, due to the use of the ''cheapest types of music'' available through BMI, hillbilly and rock 'n' roll, a mistake that returned to haunt Packard and infuriate Schwartz.

Senator Albert Gore, of Tennessee, read a telegram from his state's governor, Frank Clement in response to Packard. Clement found Packard's "remarks to the effect that the only reason broadcasters are interested in country music is that it is cheap financially and intellectually . . . a gratuitous insult to thousands of our fellow Tennesseans both in and out of the field of country music." An amateur country fiddler himself, Gore concluded his appearance by saying, "The area where springs this music in the mountains of Tennessee is characterized by people of pioneer stock. Some of the people there still speak English of the Elizabethan age. The language of the music expresses the hopes and aspirations of these people. I would not like to see all country music branded intellectually cheap." Speaking to no one in particular, Schwartz snapped, "If you attack country music you attack southern womanhood, I see."

It was not the first time country music, Tennessee, and BMI's involvement with both came to the aid of the beleaguered licensing organization. A few months earlier, Wesley Rose, son of the co-founder of music publisher Acuff-Rose, in Nashville, told a reporter for the city's *Tennessean:* "BMI was a Godsend to country music . . . with the advent of BMI we were able to open a firm in Nashville and others followed–and that exposed the writers—who couldn't reach New York, to a publishing contact close to home . . . and this has given something new and fresh to the country and the world."

Politicians had recognized the advantages to be gained from the new national interest in country-and-western music. Presidential nominee Adlai Stevenson had made the principal address at the annual memorial to Jimmie Rodgers in May 1954, and young Tennessee Representative Howard Baker had offered a joint resolution calling for a week-long celebration of country music that summer.

For a time, Nashville's claim to fame as the major network origination point for country music was challenged by *Ozark Jubilee* on KWTO and KWTV in Springfield, Missouri, which sent out weekly television and radio programs to the ABC network, most country-minded of the chains. In this brief period when the networks included country music among their varied musical fare, ABC also presented the *Midwestern Hayride* from Chicago and the "Pee Wee King Show"; Tennessee Ernie Ford was on both CBS-TV and AM radio; and *Grand Ole Opry* was an NBC radio and television feature. Other radio programs and syndicated videofilm series sent the message of Hank Williams, Roy Acuff, Ernest Tubb, Red Foley, Eddy Arnold, and Kitty Wells to a nationwide audience. In that most sophisticated of cities, New York, country-music sales accounted for 10 percent of revenue, but were limited to a handful of name artists.

Veteran country-music publishers complained that artists, record men, station executives, and professional sidemen were going into competition with them. It was difficult to get an artist to record a song in which he did not have some sort of interest, which discouraged new songwriters. The major source of income was radio-performance money from BMI, and to get it one had to give a special rate to the recording company, pay for all exploitation, and make all the other now-standard cut-ins. This led publishers to establish their own labels and go into artist management.

Nashville's struggle to take charge of country music's destiny began with the first Country Music Carnival and Summer Festival of America's Music, sponsored by the Country Music Disk Jockeys Association, in Springfield, Missouri, in the summer of 1956. The tide swung quickly that November when Governor Clement rose to the defense of a battered BMI, still suffering from its public punishment at the hands of Emanuel Celler. Astonished by the "weird testimony" offered by Billy Rose, equating country music with "dirty comic magazines," Clement wired Celler that he was ready to appear before the Congressmen and "tell them the truth." Labeling the hearings part of a "scheme of a small inside group in New York and California to gain complete control of the music business," he lashed out at the "plot to stifle competition and country music" by the New York monopolists who "for so many years had prevented free enterprise in the American music industry."

In a violent reaction to the sudden Elvis Presley phenomenon, then sweeping the world, some country-music executives had called for a boycott of his records on the air, to negate any effect of the "bastardization" of white American musical tradition. The more progressive and realistic looked instead for equally dynamic performers with a more palatable rock-'n'-roll style, one that could coalesce with those middle-of-the-road ingredients in modern country music that had been attracting national audiences since just after the war. Out of the hunt emerged the "Nashville sound," of "countrypolitan music" that caused the purists to weep when rockabilly fused with "Your Hit Parade" and crossed over to the Hot 100.

Nashville now faced problems. Early in 1958, the CMDJA met in its fourth national convention and voted to establish national headquarters in Kansas City, Missouri, where a new community-financed municipal auditorium had quickly become a stopping-off place for leading country performers, and the city's commercial establishment was ready to lend financial support. One of the association's first moves was to begin efforts to protect the name Country Music Spectacular, used for the organization's annual show at the close of each convention. With a membership of 250, the group looked for another 750 members, all professional country disk jockeys, and planned for a giant fund-raising drive to support its efforts. Without explanation, a week later the entire CMDJA board of directors resigned, to join in the formation of a nonprofit lobbying group, the Country Music Association chartered in Tennessee. There were rumors that the divorce from the CMDJA was the result of Nashville's desire to move away from such close cooperation with disk jockeys, who, as a class, were becoming associated with corrupt programing and "deplorable" music.

Governor Clement's appearance before the Pastore subcommittee came on April 17, in the second round of hearings. Fourteen witnesses had preceded him, among them John Schulman, all in support of the Smathers bill. Schulman was reported by *Variety* to have "recovered a considerable amount of the ground lost" by Schwartz, Packard, Hammerstein, and other witnesses. Hammering away at the fact that the Communications Act of 1933 contained rules of conduct for broadcasters, Shulman held that the proposed amendment to it was merely another rule to protect the public interest.

The man who had drafted the blueprint for BMI, Sydney M. Kaye, now its chairman of the board and a member of the law firm representing BMI, was the first to speak against the legislation, on April 15. He began with a history of BMI and its development in the past eighteen years, calling the episodes in those years cited by Schwartz and others as proof of a conspiracy "so irrelevant, so trivial, so easily susceptible of explanation, that they lack not only individual but cumulative probative force." He concluded by saying, "It is clear to me that the only guilt of which the proponents complain is the guilt of competition. . . ."

Gene Autry, singing movie cowboy, stockholder in BMI, and owner of major broadcasting, real estate, and baseball interests, was among those following Kaye. It had been easier for him to get an invitation to the White House, he said, than to get into ASCAP, of which he had been a member since 1939. Logically, the BMI executives staging the flow of opposition followed Autry with representatives of the Nashville music world, Clement, Eddy Arnold, and Pee Wee King, writer of "The Tennessee Waltz." The governor's extended testimony made the point that in giving writers and publishers of country music the opportunity denied them by ASCAP, BMI made it possible for Nashville to become "one of the major music capitals of the world."

After twenty-four witnesses for BMI were heard, Schulman asked for three days for rebuttal, rather than the one scheduled, and was refused. "There is no gainsaying the polish of the BMI performance," *Variety* reported. "It was designed as a counter-balance against the ASCAP testimony—lawyer against lawyer, publisher against publisher, composer against composer, singer against singer." BMI had also presented broadcasters and spokesmen for state associations, including operators of small radio stations, "to avoid any charge they were representing the powerful web interests."

They were also, to a man, constituents of every member of the Senate Commerce Committee. The witness from Florida, Mae Boren Axton, writer of "Heartbreak Hotel" and a schoolteacher, opened the third session, on May 6, and surprised the senators, because the author of the song that had introduced Presley to their children was a well-dressed mother of two. William Schuman, president of the Juilliard School of Music and a BMI composer; Lew Chudd, president of Imperial Records and of three BMI-affiliated music firms; Murray Kaufman, one of the most famous rock-'n'-roll deejays; and seven others were followed by Robert Burton, of BMI. His summation concentrated on the public-service programs that Carl Haverlin had initiated to shore up the company's image.

Several weeks later, the motion-picture industry, whose major studios were becoming more heavily involved with the recording and music business, sent its representatives to oppose the bill. In the present state of the movie business, "which is known to all," Paul Raiborn, of Paramount Pictures, said, "adjunct sources of income," such as Paramount's Los Angeles station, KTLA, Dot Records, and two ASCAP music subsidiaries, were vital to his company's existence. Omar Elder, general counsel for ABC, said the bill would force his company to divest itself of all owned-and-operated radio and television stations and two music-publishing companies, one in ASCAP, one in BMI, because it owned 3,334 of BMI's total issue of 73,864 shares of stock.

After witnesses representing the Motion Picture Association and the Columbia and RCA Victor record companies were heard, Pastore announced a recess until July. Smathers had shown little more interest in his bill than two appearances in the hearing room, and Gore promised a floor fight if it ever got out of committee. The possibility of Celler's threat becoming action, unless broadcasters cleaned their own houses by divesting themselves of BMI, seemed most remote.

Only Pastore, of the legislators, was present when Schulman read a twenty-four-page statement, to frequent interruptions by the chairman, and submitted a 110-page printed addition to his previous testimony. When he spoke disparagingly of the current hit "Yakety Yak," Pastore told him that his own daughter had bought a copy and that it was what young people wanted. The type of legislation Schulman and Schwartz were after, Pastore said, was bad legislation, which would throw "every Tom, Dick, and Harry into the soup," while the songwriters really wanted to get CBS and NBC and their stations. "The little fellow in Rhode Island [Pastore's home state] is trying to make a living . . . you are making him an awful, mean, nasty man because he belongs to the broadcasters' association [the NAB]. . . . I know what your problem is and I think I know what you are getting at, [but] your bill is reaching out to 4,000 little fellows."

Before bringing the hearing to an end, he said that he had made his own "freedom of the music on the air" test by calling local radio stations to fill a request for the performance of the ASCAP song "Louise," his daughter's name, on her birthday. He had not identified himself, and all the stations had complied.

In direct contrast to his action at the Schulman sessions two weeks earlier, Pastore rarely interrupted Judge Samuel Rosenman when he spoke in surrebuttal of the testimony offered on July 15. Formerly an assistant to President Franklin Roosevelt and with a record of distinguished public service, Rosenman was magisterial in speaking. "Never in my experience have I seen such sweeping charges made against so many people with such flimsy evidence. . . . They have made the most slanderous kind of charges against a whole industry . . . and they have failed to substantiate these charges with the slightest shred of evidence."

The record of the hearings was sent for comment to the comptroller general, the Justice Department, the FCC, FTC, and the SEC, from none of which came any request for further information. Apparently the Smathers bill would have heavy sailing.

The ruling in March 1958, by the special master for *Schwartz* v *BMI,* giving the defendants access to 225,000 ASCAP cards, for which all had fought for more than a year, seemed a token of further good things to come. The first true court test in the now five-year-old action, a motion to dismiss filed in March, was not expected to be ruled on for some time. The brief pleaded that, because the songwriter plaintiffs neither published nor licensed their music themselves, they were not directly engaged in any activity that could be injured by an alleged conspiracy, and the suit should be dismissed.

All pretrial examination was suspended until, the following November, when Judge Edward Weinfeld, of the New York federal court was free to resume his involvement and deal with the dismissal motion. Both sides hailed his ruling in December. It struck down the principal charge—that BMI and the broadcasters were engaged in a conspiracy against ASCAP—and upheld their contention that the society alone was the proper party to sue in the matter, not the songwriters. However, Weinfeld affirmed the plaintiffs' rights to bring a suit claiming that the publishers of some 5,200 of their copyrights, all affiliated with both ASCAP and BMI, had been induced by BMI to discriminate against their music. Once again the possibility of an early trial dimmed.

Attorneys for the defendants believed that it would take at least two years to prepare defenses under the new circumstances, because the 300 publishers with whom the plaintiffs had placed their songs would now have to be examined. There were already 23,000 pages of testimony, 11,000 exhibits of 55,000 pages, and 3,000 pages of answers to interrogatories.

With the shelving of the Smathers bill more certain, the networks began to divest themselves of stock in BMI, though neither the Justice Department nor the FCC had found any reason for them to do so. The negotiations with ASCAP for a radio license were at a dead end, but BMI renewed all existing contracts with 3,300 radio stations for five years, and with the television industry on the old basis, a sliding scale from 1.2 percent of gross income to .75, depending on a station's revenue. NBC and ABC signed five-year blanket licenses for television and three-year renewals for their radio networks; Mutual, for five years; and CBS, a three-year TV pact. For the first time in BMI's history, a network—CBS—asked for a per-program pact, to pay only when BMI music was used, rather than one calling for fees based on a percentage of all income. BMI's per-program contracts ranged from 2.25 percent of income from a program using its music, to 4 percent for income at the level CBS earned. In addition, like the few other per-program licensees, CBS was expected to pay .72 percent of time-card rates for sustaining programs.

In April, CBS honored Frank Stanton's pledge to Celler to "take a hard look" at its relationship with BMI. Many senior network executives had long been unhappy about their corporate association with BMI, the spawner of unsavory rock 'n' roll. There was also concern that BMI would be deeply involved in the brewing payola scandal and would drag its stockholders into the mess. During the previous year, the networks had withdrawn their representatives on the BMI board, all of whom had ceased attending BMI's annual award dinners once they began to include the writers and publishers of rhythm-and-blues and country music. Believing that the hearings had shown there was no merit to the Schwartz charges, CBS was the first to act. At its request, BMI bought back 7,012 shares, representing 8.9 percent of all outstanding stock, for around $35,000, or $5 a share, the price originally paid in 1940. NBC followed in September, receiving $21,320 for its 5.8 percent. ABC sold back its 4.5 percent interest a few years later. The largest remaining stockholders were: General Teleradio, 4,600 shares; Crosley Broadcasting and Westinghouse, about 2,500 each; WJY Detroit, 1,375; and Storer Broadcasting, almost 1,000 shares. Some of BMI's officers welcomed the sales, believing that, freed of the possibility of further antitrust actions, they would now have an opportunity to operate with less caution. Sydney Kaye had told the Pastore committee that if broadcasters did sell all their stock, and BMI became an association of publishers and writers like ASCAP, competition between the two would ultimately cease, leaving one the monopoly. If BMI ownership dwindled to a few stockholders, the profit margin would prevail, and any interest in competition with ASCAP or in increasing the catalogue would disappear. *Variety,* in September 1959, felt that "whatever the networks' moves, there is little likelihood that the indie stations, which have stock in BMI, will similarly drop out. The indies regard BMI as an 'insurance policy' against the return of a music licensing monopoly."

The divorces had little effect on BMI's precarious financial situation. Annual income from licensees was around seven million dollars, out of which two million, or about half that paid to publishers, went to 4,000 writers affiliated under the Robert Sour plan. A bonus-payment guarantee for writers who consistently showed high performances over a three-year period was in effect, adding about 50 percent to the four and two cents paid all BMI writers for network and local performances. Several hundred song-writers participated in the bonus plan, some of them earning around $3,500 a year, a larger number getting between $1,000 and $2,000. The American Composers Alliance—writers of contemporary concert music—had a separate understanding with BMI, and received an annual guarantee out of which the ACA paid for performances of its music. Unlike ASCAP, which paid its members for overseas performances only in England, Sweden, and Canada, BMI deducted 10 percent for the administration of income from all foreign societies and then paid its writers the balance on a nation-by-nation basis. Film composers benefited particularly under this arrangement. Most music-performance fees in many countries came from screen theaters and were passed on to BMI for distribution.

Increased payments to BMI writers enforced an overhaul of all guarantee contracts negotiated with music houses that no longer contributed their anticipated share of air play. This took some years to untangle.

There were few publishers who mourned the passing of "Your Hit Parade" on April 24, 1959, dead, its fans insisted, at the hands of rock 'n' roll and a changing music business. Sheet music, too, was perishing from the extraordinary popularity of the phonograph recording aimed at the youth market. Once the "Lucky Strike Hit Parade," the program was last sponsored by Hit Parade cigarettes, the final merchandising scheme to prolong the life of a program that went on the air in 1935 and shaped the tastes of the American public for popular music over two decades.

At the same time, the latest and most serious effort yet was taking shape to collect for the performances of recorded music from the operators of coin music machines, which, with "Your Hit Parade" had been responsible for the revitalization of the record industry and the music business. In 1959, a half-million coin-operated jukeboxes consumed forty-seven million disks, bought at a discount from one-stops or supplied free by record companies or their distributors or as payola to feature certain selections in preference to others. The more than $442 million generated was usually split equally between the jukebox owners and the owners of taverns, soda shops, and other teen-age hangouts, restaurants, diners, and other places where the machines were located. The honored division was already changing in many places, to a front-money or minimum-guarantee system: a sixty-forty split, with the operator getting the larger share, or even an eighty-twenty split. Half of all operators earned less than $5,000, but, based solely on jukebox revenue, 29 percent of them had incomes of from $5,000 to $10,000, and another 10 percent were in the $10,000 to $15,000 bracket. Eleven percent got more than $15,000. Location owners supplemented this income with earnings from games, cigarette machines, kiddie rides, and food-and-drink machines manufactured by Seeburg, Wurlizter, Bally, AMI, and Keeney, who also made the 75,000 jukeboxes sold in 1959 at a "conservative" price of $1,000 each.

Celler's compromise, in July 1959, to get passed the first copyright law requiring coin-machine operators to pay a collective annual royalty of $2.5 million to the performing-rights societies, for distribution to authors and composers, was halted by the unwillingness of the industry trade association, the Music Operators of America, to commit its membership to the plan. Legislation to remove the coin-machine exemption mandated in the 1909 Copyright Act had been introduced in every Congress since 1926, and had failed to obtain majority approval when it did get out of committee.

In 1955, when such a bill was still in the hearing stage, a number of senators urged the MOA to enter into discussion with the licensing societies and effect a compromise. Capitol Hill's intervention stemmed from the Senate's ratification of the Universal Copyright Convention, which made the United States a participant in a world-wide copyright convention for the first time. Almost every other nation with coin machines had compulsory legislation that required them to be licensed. The fees, based on a percentage of receipts, ranged from a minimum of $14 in Italy to $198 in Sweden.

The UCC represented a significant advance in the United States, freeing, as it did, authors, publishers, and other copyright holders from dependence on the International Copyright Union for the protection of their works around the world, with the exception of China. The new convention gave nationals of all signatory countries equal protection under each other's domestic law. Although it did not deal with jukebox-royalty exemption, the UCC authorized the creation of an international commission to study the question.

Legislation introduced in Congress to remove the exemption emphasized the need for a fact-finding commission. Failure to create such a commission would be, according to *Variety*, verification of the "blunt truth that the jukebox lobby in Washington is stronger than that of ASCAP." In its own survey of the coin-machine business that year, *Billboard* found that the American public played 28 million tunes a day on the nation's 450,000 machines, each of which had a capacity of between 80 and 120 selections, and consumed nearly 80 million disks a year.

In Lester Velie's article "Racket in the Juke Box" in the November 1955 issue of *Reader's Digest,* the celebrated crime reporter asserted that the mobster "who owned a piece of an artist" could dictate the use of that performer's records on the machines he controlled. In Chicago, Velie wrote, Capone gangsters boasted that they had pushed 400,000 records by one protégé, and the city's Crime Commission reported a new wrinkle in the business. Gangsters took over the management of a singer and booked him into night clubs in Las Vegas and Chicago. Guest appearances on television were forced, giving the performer a build-up that resulted in three record releases. Operators were told to give these the number-one or -two position on their machines, and the Capone hoodlums boasted that they had turned those records into best-sellers. The Chicago criminal establishment also offered ASCAP the passage of a bill removing the copyright exemption if they got back a 20 percent share of the take, a proposition Herman Finkelstein reported to the Justice Department. Velie concluded that the big-city mobs that contributed heavily to Congressional campaigns were really responsible for stalling all jukebox legislation.

In the face of this and other adverse publicity, the MOA retained one of the country's leading accounting firms to conduct the fact-finding study that had been urged. A questionnaire prepared by the accounting firm Price, Waterhouse and sent to all MOA members asked for these figures: number of machines in operation, operators' total share of collections in 1955, total expenses less salaries, total value of jukeboxes and other equipment, and total record purchases in 1955—information never before officially collected.

The Velie article and grand-jury investigations of alleged racketeering in the jukebox industry were responsible for the introduction of a bill in 1956 proposing an annual fifty-two-dollar tax on every machine. It served only to tighten the MOA's ranks, which, according to its president, George Miller, had saved operators millions of dollars in the past six years, "if nothing else." A grass-roots lobbying campaign was initiated by the newly formed National Tax Council, organized by the MOA to lead local operators in their fight against a jukebox tax. A performing-rights society sponsored by the MOA was formed to handle the copyrights used by a new recording company funded by the MOA. It was to release only one or two records a month initially, but would be ready if there was a nationwide boycott of all ASCAP and BMI music.

With the indictment filed by a Chicago grand jury charging the country's largest coin-machine manufacturer, the J. P. Seeburg Company, maker of 40 percent of all coin-operated phonographs, with violation of the Sherman Act, the first break, although an illusory one, came in the jukebox situation. Seeburg, which soon negotiated for a consent order to dispose of the indictment, entered into licensing agreements with ASCAP and BMI for a new jukebox background service for supermarkets, hotels, offices, and other locations. ASCAP received three dollars a month and BMI sixty cents for each machine, which contained 200 45-rpm disks with three selections on a side, a total of 1,200 musical works.

Seeburg's problem had no effect on the MOA. Its officers and legal representatives bluntly informed the Senate that they would not "contemplate industry suicide" by agreeing to pay for music. The performance societies had "nothing to offer, nothing to compromise, and nothing to sacrifice. There is no benefit or boon they can confer on us."

If changes were to be made in the Copyright Act of 1909 to bring it up to date with current technology, they would be part of an omnibus copyright-revision bill, which had the full support of the Copyright Office of the Library of Congress. Such a bill would be based on several studies commissioned by the Register of Copyrights, Abraham L. Kaminstein. The first of these was written by Harry G. Henn, dean of Cornell University Law School, and was released in October 1957. It called for two changes in the act affecting phonograph records: elimination of the compulsory-licensing provision or, at least, elimination of the statutory two-cent rate; and clarification of such provisions as they affected new forms of recording—tape, wire, motion-picture sound tracks, kinescope, and any other. Conflicting views on the first change found BMI's Sydney Kaye in opposition to the MPPA, the SPA, and ASCAP. In defense of compulsory licensing as it stood, he maintained that without it most songwriters would hand over exclusive rights to the first record company that offered to cut their music, leading to a loss of the diversity of recordings and destruction of smaller record companies.

A second study, by William Harris, attorney for the Copyright Office, dealt with performance royalties and damages for unlicensed performances, posing questions over which Kaye and Finkelstein again disagreed. The study asked whether the present penalties ($250 to $5,000) should be retained, eliminated, altered, or left to a court's discretion; whether multiple infringements should be lumped together, or treated separately; whether innocent or secondary interests—infringers, printers, stores, dealers—should be absolved of responsibility. Finkelstein was keeping the $250 minimum, for without it the performing right was valueless. Kaye wanted a revision of the "unduly harsh" provisions now that innocent "multiple and evanescent" infringements took place, and proposed the elimination of all fixed damages, leaving them to a court's discretion on a case-by-case basis.

None of the other studies dealt with the jukebox exemption. That issue was in the hands of the Senate Judiciary Committee on Patents and Copyrights, which was considering a bill offered by its chairman, Joseph C. O'Mahoney. Hearings were scheduled for early 1958. They came at a time when more dirty linen of the music business was being aired, during the Roosevelt committee probe into ASCAP's distribution and voting practices and in testimony for and against the Smathers bill. The jukebox-exemption hearings came and went in April without incident, after which the O'Mahoney bill was passed by the entire Senate Judiciary Committee and sent on its way through the legislative process, only to be stopped in its tacks when the Senate adjourned too early to consider it. As to the issue of whether the jukeboxes were important in the exploitation of songs, the accompanying report said that "the evidence indicates that in certain instances, the jukebox does popularize music, that on the whole this is a very minor gain to the composer and author in the over-all picture. As a matter of fact, disk jockeys, TV and radio programs are the biggest medium for the popularizing of musical compositions."

The Hearst newspaper chain began a series of articles in October 1958 revealing the "inside workings of the juke box empire," a three-billion-dollar industry that faced a probe by the Senate Rackets—or Improper Activities in the Labor or Management Field—Committee, headed by Senator John L. McClellan. The Justice Department had brought antitrust proceedings against major coin-machine manufacturers, including Seeburg, and had ordered them to stop placing limitations on distribution territories and the right of purchase or resale. The FTC had investigated the jukebox business from manufacturer to coin deposit, and various grand juries were probing the industry. Much of the information contained in the Hearst articles came from a little-known 224-page report, "The Juke Box Racket," prepared by Virgil Peterson, chairman of the Chicago Crime Commission, in 1954.

Herman Finkelstein had explained to the Hearst investigators that he had indeed gone to Chicago to meet with operators, who he had assumed could speak for at least 100,000 machines, and who seemed to be respectable. The deal had fallen through, he told them, when the operators wanted a ten-year contract, and the society was prohibited by its consent decree from offering one for more than five. The entire meeting was detailed to the Justice Department by Finkelstein and ASCAP's president, Stanley Adams.

Other topics covered in the Hearst series went into detail about "The singer who auditioned in a chicken market and went to Las Vegas," "Who is the New York Juke King, the Horatio Alger story of the juke box industry," "Vito Genovese, King of the Rackets, the name that spreads fear," and "The mysterious lucrative distributorship whose list of stockholders has included a gambler, two ex-convicts, and an Appalachin '65 Mafia mobster with powerful underworld connections."

The music industry welcomed the McClellan rackets hearings on the jukebox business and its alleged infiltration by organized crime, seeing it as the final tool needed to prod a discredited MOA into accepting a licensing deal. Over a three-week period, the committee heard about mob domination in New York, New Jersey, Illinois, Louisiana, Ohio, Michigan, Florida, and Indiana; gangster connections with some singers; counterfeiting of hit records; the use of unions to bring reluctant customers into line; underworld warfare; death threats; and other violations of the law—accompanied by frequent interjections of recourse to the Fifth Amendment. One unhappy subpoenaed witness said that when it was all over "the boys will be back doing business at the same old stand."

The final report said that the majority of operators were "honest, hardworking citizens," who had been the victims of an "astounding number of racketeers, posing as both businessmen and union officials." There was no rush by legislators to push through a bill after the hearings concluded, nor did the MOA offer its sword in surrender. A patchwork bill replaced O'Mahoney's original proposal, with a provision to double record royalties for disks sold to jukeboxes, from two to four cents. In March, the powerful chairman of the House Judiciary Committee introduced in the House for the first time since 1952 a bill to remove the jukebox exemption from the law. "Everytime the composers of America have petitioned the Congress to remedy this rank injustice,'' Emanuel Celler said, ''the jukebox interests have pleaded poverty and good citizenship and have attacked the composers as being greedy and bad citizens. This farce of the poor but honest jukebox interests is about played out.''

With a public-relations problem of monstrous proportions, the MOA revived the languishing Price, Waterhouse questionnaire, using failure to complete final figures as an excuse to delay House action for a few months. Every element of the world of copyright revision was on hand in June when hearings on the Celler bill started. They learned quickly that ASCAP's problems in Washington, where a revised consent order to reform the society had been in the making for more than a year, provided already unfriendly committee members with ammunition against the legislation. As Jay Lewis wrote in *Variety*, the Celler bill was ''variously depicted as a way of stopping 'legalized piracy,' and a way of destroying small business, helping monopoly, spreading unemployment, and, even, promoting juvenile delinquency.'' William Miller, a New Yorker representing the district where the Wurlitzer Company had its main factory, likened ASCAP to the Teamsters' union, and said its members had nothing to say about the society's operation.

The Price, Waterhouse survey, introduced late in the hearings, was based on a sample of 1,285 usable replies and represented a total of 75,756 machines, which produced revenues of $33.4 million to the operators from their half-share. Revenues left after expenses for each operator were an aggregate of $5,871. Assuming an average of sixty-four cents for a record, the 1,285 operators spent $5.5 million to keep their machines stocked with an average of 114 new records per machine annually.

ASCAP countered with its own recent survey of members' income. The annual average per writer was $2,321; 88 percent of the membership received less than $5,000 in 1958; only 244 earned between $5,000 and $10,000; and only 7 percent, or 310, received more than $10,000 in royalties from the society. Kaye said on behalf of BMI writers that they got an average of under $500, a ''meaningless'' figure because of the enormous variation in songwriters' income, obtained by dividing total money paid out to writers by the number of affiliates under contract.

Failure to agree on an acceptable bill prompted Celler to offer himself as a mediator between the MOA and jukebox manufacturers on one side and the proponents of termination of the jukebox exemption on the other. His compromise called for a five-dollar royalty per jukebox, the fees to be collected by three trustees, who would distribute the money on the basis of performances of ASCAP and BMI music on the machines. One trustee was to be appointed by the attorney general, one by the licensing organizations, and one by the MOA. The music industry supported the compromise. The MOA asked for a delay until its meeting in May 1960, to get its members' approval.

CHAPTER 20

Payola Problems and Rate Wars

Such suspense as there was in regard to the MOA's final action was dissipated by developments on the AGAC-BMI front late in 1959. The previous year, a New York grand jury had seen the first intimations of quiz-show "rigging" on network television, particularly the *Twenty One* show, on which contestants were allegedly provided with answers to questions they would be asked on camera. Among legislators looking for issues that would assure constituents back home of their concern for keeping the nation on a straight moral path was Arkansas' Representative Oren Harris, chairman of the Special Subcommittee on Legislative Oversight. During hearings in the autumn, his committee had learned that, not only *Twenty One,* but also *The $64,000 Question* and *The $64,000 Challenge* had been fixed by their producers, sometimes at the direction of the programs' sponsors. There was the possibility that if the committee dug deeper, a dozen more quiz shows would be in jeopardy, with more national publicity accruing to Harris and his colleagues.

A serious debate took place at the same time among other legislators on whether the FCC or the FTC already had the authority to prevent fradulent programing and whether the Harris hearings were necessary. BMI's newest nemesis, Burton Lane, president of the American Guild of Authors and Composers, had already dispatched letters to the FCC and the FTC, without result, and on November 6 he came in person, at the end of the Harris hearings, to deliver information about "the commercial bribery that has become a prime factor in determining what music is played on many broadcast programs." The material offered to the committee was essentially a rehash of quotations from news stories, a few of them recent, but predominantly from the late 1940s to 1954. It was all reminiscent of testimony during the Smathers hearings, but was apparently new to Harris, who placed it on the record and directed his staff to look into charges that disk jockeys were being bribed to plug songs on their shows.

In a letter sent a few days later to the FCC chairman, Lane asked the commission to require station owners to get rid of their conflicting music-business interests or have their licenses to operate revoked. Payola, he wrote, was "merely a symptom of a disease. The disease itself is the involvement of the entire broadcasting industry, networks and local stations, in a deliberate and successful distortion of music programing for their own financial gain."

Ignored by Lane, perhaps because it involved ASCAP publishers with whom AGAC members did business, was the multimillion-dollar television payola business, already well publicized in the pages of *Variety* and *Billboard*. The rapid growth of television had created "videola" in the mid-1950s, when income from public performances put program producers into a position to ask for money before they selected music. In one case, reported in *Variety,* a producer asked for $5,000 before he gave a publisher all rights to the theme song for a projected video series. When a change in ASCAP's distribution system reduced the value of theme songs and increased by three times that of a network feature-song television performance, while also lowering radio-network air-play payments, the pitch became, according to *Variety,* "If I don't play your tune, it'll be somebody else's. If you want the plug you gotta give one-third of the publisher's share and cut me in as co-writer. There'll be more than enough money to go around." Videola on prime-time programs was not yet rampant, because the accent on them was on standard songs, and the big publishers did not have to play with cut ins. The Harris investigation had not touched on videola on the five-day-a-week morning and afternoon strip shows. At about seventy dollars in ASCAP royalties for each performance of a song recognizable to monitors, it could earn $350 a week. The fifteen pieces of music usually performed on such shows offered a potential bonanza of $4,250 weekly to the publisher who could lock in all the music used. Originally, guests on quiz shows were introduced by a drum roll or fanfare, but when the publishers showed some producers how they could get a share of important money, videola spread.

The Justice Department was aware that in 1958 six million dollars was distributed by ASCAP for background music and theme songs. That year, twelve songs earned more performance credits than the entire catalogue of Irving Berlin, the highest-paid writer in ASCAP. A new figure had entered the scene: the broker representing TV producers with vacancies on their programs. "Some of the indie producers like Barry & Enright [producers of *Twenty One*] saw the gravy potential in tv music and set up their own publishing company," Herm Schonfeld wrote in *Variety.* "Barry & Enright's Melody Music Co. reportedly earns about $100,000 annually from ASCAP. One small ASCAP publisher, who was getting about $6,000 a year, jumped to $80,000 after getting hep to the tv angle.'' Some of the biggest ASCAP houses had the least compunction about getting such money from television. Of the 272 selections used on twenty-one shows in a single week in September 1959, 192 were owned by Warner Brothers. MPHC music on *Beat the Clock* during the same week accounted for nearly $5,000, predicated on ASCAP distribution procedures, or a quarter-million dollars a year from this show alone.

Max Dreyfus and Louis Bernstein attacked Herman Starr, of MPHC, at an ASCAP board meeting because of his high-flying song plugging, which cut them off from more money from television. This was the first time such giants had fought one another openly over ASCAP money. As they did, the membership was voting on the amended consent order. Harris committee investigators were questioning disk jockeys around the country in connection with hearings to begin next February to determine the extent of corrupt practices on local radio stations.

Local independent broadcasting had boomed since the year of panic, 1954, when all industry billings fell. Soap operas and other daytime network radio fare had little appeal for the growing youth market and a nation on the go in automobiles. "New Radio" was born, in a direct line from WNEW in New York, where Martin Block had introduced modern professional disk-jockeying in March 1935. With libraries of electrical transcriptions or 78-speed disks worth $100,000 or more in some cases, stations were at first reluctant to go along with the 45s supplied to major stations without charge, and to the smaller ones at a low nominal fee. A group of New York stations, including WNEW, made a last fight against the new technology, citing problems in tracking and cuing on 45s. With the promise of regular shipments of free 45s—325,000 in July 1954 alone—and a two-week priority mailing of new 45 releases, the boycott was ended and most stations were brought into line. Columbia made the switch to 45s easier by standardizing the sound level of deejay copies, followed by its competitors, a move that contributed to the 300,000 recorded performances taking place daily on independent AM stations in 1955. The average station received thirty new 45s a week, selected to conform to its programing policy. Middle- and large-size stations tended to give deejays more freedom of selection than ever, matching that confidence with higher wages.

New York City platter spinners, whose salaries started between $25,000 and $30,000, earned a combined total of more than a million dollars. Top men in Chicago, Washington, Pittsburgh, and Detroit started at $35,000 a year. Bill Randle, of WERE, Cleveland, probably the highest-paid deejay in America at the time, was believed to own a piece of the station and did a Saturday show on the CBS flagship station in New York. His instinct for American tastes and his well-earned reputation as a hit maker got him preferential treatment from the major labels, "first play" on new releases.

It was general knowledge in the industry in 1955 that payola flourished, but few admitted to taking any. Martin Block was an exception, explaining that the ten dollars that came along from a publisher with a new record was like a headwaiter's tip to get a ringside table at a night club. Alan Freed admitted accepting gifts, according to *Cue,* but "not in front. If I've helped somebody, I'll accept a nice gift, but I wouldn't take a dime to plug a record. I'd be a fool to. I'd be giving up control of my program."

Randle, Bloch, and Freed, and their peers were exceptions; the majority of disk jockeys were salaried staff announcers in the mid-1950s. Their main natural gift "is gab," Bernard Asbell told the readers of *Harper's Magazine.* If a deejay "can demonstrate . . . that he can deliver a commercial with conviction and that, between commercials, he has the talent for thinking on the tip of his tongue—about anything, so long as he doesn't stop—he has the qualifications which get the job as staff announcer. . . . His acceptability as a musical judge is taken for granted." The salary usually is small, but there are compensations. "The stars and their managers lavishly intoxicate the disk jockey, literally, by a binge of cocktail parties, and figuratively, by personal visits, full-page ads in the trade papers (I owe all my good fortune to the deejays of America—thank you one and all) and by endless quantities of endearing mail (it's people like you that make people like me like people like you). The teen-agers, too, write him adulatory letters, phone him to request songs, and turn out in sighing droves whenever he appears in person to open a new supermarket." He became the enthusiastic supporter of whatever this audience wanted to hear.

It was precisely to control such enthusiasm that Top 40 programing was invented, credited to Robert "Todd" Storz. He began the Storz chain of stations in 1949 by buying KOWH, Omaha, for $60,000; in 1953, he added WTIX, New Orleans, to the young and growing Mid-Continent Broadcasting Corporation group. Looking for a format that would give his first station some individuality among the hundreds within its signal area that also relied on a music-and-news policy, he found part of the answer in the great popularity of some hit records in an Omaha beer-tavern jukebox. Having grown up with "Your Hit Parade" 's concentration on a few top tunes, he transferred the idea to KOWH in 1951 and to WTIX in 1953. In the twenty-four-hour "Hit Parade" format, the music was pop hits, with a careful, small infusion of white R & B cover disks. There was no ad-libbing, introductions were short and to the point, label credit was never given, nor was there any hint of enthusiasm for any particular piece of music. It was all upbeat hoopla. Advertising jingles and musical station breaks prevailed, as did gimmicks to attract telephone response from listeners, and prize contests to keep them tuned in constantly, with enough public-service announcements between to keep an FCC examiner satisfied.

Gordon McClendon was the first to copy the Storz formula, and then came the Bartell, Plough, and Westinghouse stations, the latter pulling out of the NBC network to present just music and news and public-service announcements. Payola on their stations was curbed, they made all the money, and they owned the number-one local station in every local rating period. In fiscal 1956, a year before William Buckley, the Conservative pundit, bought KOWH for $800,000, and maintained its Top 40 policy, Mid-Continent enjoyed billings of $3.5 million. Plough copyrighted and licensed its program and production book, which chiefly took into account surveys of leading local record dealers and were in turn distributed in quantities of from 18,000 to 100,000 copies in each city the Plough group served. A Plough station used only about 100 records at a time, assorted in tempo, out of which the emphasis was placed on forty, played all day long, intermixed with a few standard and upcoming numbers.

Surveys of record popularity were in great vogue, giving the networks an opportunity to try for an audience apparently lost forever. ABC came up with a "Hit Preview of the Week" feature, in which a potential hit was introduced each week, after being chosen by producers, singers, musical directors, and air personalities on seven live ABC musical-variety programs. Each tune selected was guaranteed twenty plays during the following week. Mutual augmented its "America's Top Tunes" service with "The Big Decision," which spotlighted a panel review and forecast of possibilities for new records. One potential hit was selected weekly by a group made up of a teen-ager, a Mutual deejay, a jukebox operator, and a dealer.

The dependence on lists had its inevitable backlash. Mitch Miller said that Top 40 was turning radio stations into "automated disk jockeys." An MGM executive complained that the concentration on single record sales, which teen-agers dominated, ignored the adults, whose purchases of LPs represented 65 percent of the business. Adults were tuning out Top 40 stations, he said, and turning to television. Not every radio station in the country was tied to a Top 40 format, but one fourth were bound by station-management directives, and half of all the deejays attending the first annual Pop Music Disk Jockey Festival, in Kansas City in March 1958, indicated that the Top whatever record lists were the most important factor in their selecting the music they played.

Nashville's annual Country Music Disk Jockeys' Festival had served Todd Storz as model for the Kansas City meeting, sponsored by the Storz stations. It was attended by 1,700 persons, who listened to such diverse discussions as "What the Deejay Can Do for the National Advertiser at the Local Level," "Can Album Music Bring the Deejay Listeners?," "Increasing Income and Prestige Through Related Outside Activities," "Is the Main Requisite of the Deejay Today the Ability to Count Up to 40?" and a speech by Mitch Miller, "The Great Abdication."

Columbia Records A & R chief received the only ovation from the disk jockeys present after he said, with one eye on station owners and managers present:

> You carefully built yourself into the monarchs of radio and abdicated your programing to the corner record shop, to the eight to 14-year olds, to the pre-shave crowds that make up 12% of the country's population and zero percent

of its buying power. It must be more than a coincidence that single record buying went into a decline at the very time the number of stations that program Top 40 climbed to a new high. . . . I'm not asking you to snuff the musical life of these kids and their followers. I am asking you to put new life into radio; I'm asking you to take radio away from the lists and give it back to the people. I'm asking you to give up lazy programing—to play music for every age group and taste. The by-product of such a move will be aesthetic, and you can take pride in the public service. But principally you'll be doing it for your pocketbooks by insuring a broader, healthier audience, and guaranteeing advertisers who are seeking that audience a fair share for their money.

Separate from but coincident with the attack against BMI, and tangentially Top 40, being made at the same time in Washington at the Smathers bill hearings, there appeared a trend away from rock 'n' roll by many advertisers and their agencies. Hoping for maximum value for their advertising dollar, they looked to the adult market, and many moved to the all-album stations. Disturbances at rock-'n'-roll shows contributed to this move, particularly a riot during a concert in Boston, for which Alan Freed was indicted, on charges of inciting the destruction of private property. It became a time of record banning. In reaction to the Miller speech, Storz barred all Columbia releases. After the riot, some stations barred all rock-'n'-roll music. Freed moved from the number-one New York City station, an independent, to ABC's flagship there. But since ABC-TV already had the top-rated national TV disk-jockey show, *American Bandstand*, with Dick Clark, he had to content himself with a video dance program on a local independent station.

Clark, the most successful television deejay in history, did not start *Philadelphia Bandstand*, as it was originally known, with a format of rock-'n'-roll records to which the kids could dance, guest stars lip-synching their disks, and little talk. When the program's creator, Bob Horn, was discharged by WFIL-TV, Philadelphia, a property of the Annenberg family's Triangle Publications, Clark substituted for him temporarily. Soon his well-scrubbed, low-keyed, all-American-boy personality helped the program surpass all previous ratings, and he stayed on. A graduate of Syracuse University, he had come to WFIL in 1952, at the age of twenty-three, to work as a news announcer. In August 1957, *American Bandstand* went on the network for ninety minutes each day. Within two years, it was being broadcast by 101 affiliates to an audience of 20 million. It was that coverage that brought record artists to Philadelphia at their own expense. Because of program policy, they were invariably white in the early years, miming their disks for scale when they accepted only top dollar to appear on the Ed Sullivan, Perry Como, or Steve Allen programs.

Clark did not always "make" a record just because he played it on the *Bandstand*. Generally, he used the local time, just before the program went on the network, to test new releases by reactions from his live audience; he rarely played a new release nationally unless it was recorded by a truly hot act. Manufacturers and distributors fed him sales figures and other statistics to maintain the myth they helped create that Clark was the most powerful of the country's 10,000 deejays and could make a rock-'n'-roll hit merely by playing it a few times. In fact, Clark was onto the wrong version of "Tequila" for several weeks before the studio audience let him know his error. But the legend persisted, and in 1959 his personal holdings in the music business, including shares in publishing firms, a pressing plant, and other interests, were substantial.

Instead of disappearing because of the adverse national publicity, Top 40 and its lists came into even wider use. National advertisers whose products appealed to the younger market took over printing of the tip-sheet lists that Plough distributed as local promotion. Record stores displayed the lists and mailed them to their best customers. Manufacturers stepped up new weekly releases to between 80 and 125 disks. Thus more records had fewer chances of being played. As *Billboard* wrote in July 1958: "The manufacturer, the distributor, the music publisher and the artist all put pressure upon the disk jockey to expose their product. And the jockey, faced with a constant stream of new records . . . programs the few he can, selecting them either by actual listening, by the librarian's list [responsible for an estimated 95 percent of all music selections on the air], by guess work, by the competition, or *by being influenced*."

It was no wonder that payola grew so fast. Some of it was masked. The "pre-test record plan" offered by seven West Coast stations promised eight daily plugs per station in a ten-day period for $1,200. A Detroit station promoted a "Sound Special," one plug an hour for a week; charge, $800. An "Album of the Week" promotion guaranteed distributors 114 plays a week for six weeks at $350 a week. When the CBS Radio network reduced its program schedule, effective January 1, 1959, from ninety hours a week to about fifty, paying the stations with free programs in place of cash in order to get into the black, some 200 affiliates were left with twenty hours a week to fill. Music and news were their best answer.

The increased urgency to fill more and more time with music divided most station programing into formats of either Top 40 or Top LPs, and more chart-programing formula radio than ever. It also put a premium on the best record spinners, music programers, and librarians. A problem was created as well for the record companies, which did not intend to leave the center of attention to Columbia Records at Todd Storz's Second Annual Radio Programing Seminar and Pop Music Disk Jockey Festival, May 29–31. The site had been moved from Kansas City to more spacious accommodations in Miami, sufficient to house and entertain the 4,000 deejays who came, some with their families and others ready for whatever favors the record makers would bestow. The emphasis of the forums was on formula radio, pro and con, but fewer than 150 attended them. The other thousands recuperated from the effects of an endless round of parties, free meals, entertainment, and other pleasures supplied by the record companies. There was no Mitch Miller this year to galvanize the assembled and blast station owners. A meeting to form a national disk-jockey association attracted about sixty persons, half of them from the music business.

In a debate over "Network Radio vs Independent Radio," Matthew Culligan, of NBC, asked for a truce between the two because the open warfare debased the value of radio as an advertising medium. Defending formula radio and the independents, Gordon McClendon complained about the networks' "dubious sales techniques," in particular the recently released surveys intended to show that only teen-agers listened to the independent stations. He urged experimentation with program formats, like the "good music" station he was testing as well as all-sports, all-talk, all-news, all–soap opera, and other specialized operations. When the convention ended, *Time* characterized the meeting as devoted chiefly to "Booze, Broads, and Bribes."

With Bill Galvin, a programing consultant from San Francisco whose free "Lucky Lager Top 60" tip sheet was mailed to stations across the country, as organizing spirit, a second try was made in July to form an association of disk jockeys and music programers. The new Disk Jockey Association, with a board of directors of fifty-six, representing six geographic regions, and a membership by August of 1,000, all with at least two years of professional experience, made its first order of business a national campaign to enhance the status of members as good citizens and professional entertainers.

In connection with the second Storz convention, *Broadcasting* magazine had assigned a team of reporters to investigate exactly how big payola was in connection with records. The final report, in August 1958, was accompanied by an editorial, which said in part:

> Readers . . . . can hardly fail to reach the conclusion that the opportunities for payola are abundant. It is also obvious that some personnel sucumb to the blandishments of pay-for-play promoters. But there is no evidence that the practice is anywhere near as widespread as the nagging rumor would make it seem. To the contrary, there is much evidence that music policies, record-selection systems and other controls employed at many major stations constitute a barrier which can be surmounted only with ingenuity if at all.
>
> No general investigation, however, no matter what the findings can do the job that needs doing on payola. The task can only be finished by the stations themselves. Each management should undertake a thorough investigation of its own. If payola is found, it should be eliminated and safeguards erected against recurrence. Programing responsibility belongs to the stations, so too does commercial responsibility. Management cannot shirk one, and it should not wish to have diluted the profits that go with the other.

There was no citation of this editorial or the payola report in the AGAC's memorandum to the Harris committee, which was, instead, replete with quotations from *Variety* and *Billboard,* and record-company memorandums going back to the 1940s. However, as Burton Lane and the AGAC boasted later, it did divert the committee's attention from further exploration of television rigging to the music business and, expectedly, BMI. Responding to reports that Dick Clark was to be the first subject of investigation by the committee, BMI had examined its own records and notified all stations that it no longer licensed some songs purportedly co-written and published by the producer of Clark's television programs. Soon after, ABC had announced that Clark had agreed to divest himself of all possible conflicts of interest insofar as his television connections were involved. Alan Freed, whose local ABC station billings of $200,000 contrasted poorly with the *Bandstand*'s $12 million, had been dropped from his nightly rock-'n'-roll deejay program on WABC-AM. The FTC had then begun its hurried investigation of corrupt practices by record companies involving disk jockeys. Simultaneously, the FCC, to which Burton Lane and AGAC had also dispatched a memorandum of complaint, invited "comments, suggestions, information and other data which will be useful to the Commission" in its forthcoming inquiry into network TV and radio programing and commercial practices.

The commission also sent a notice to the 5,326 broadcast licensees that their right to remain on the air would be in serious jeopardy if evidence was found that any station or its personnel were guilty of accepting payola in any form.

The impact of payola's national exposure was expected by many in the music business to speed rock 'n' roll's demise and bring a return to sweet music, big-band sounds, and other instrumental music. Rock 'n' roll was already on the way out, a representative of ABC announced even as sponsors renewed for another thirteen weeks of "American Bandstand." In some markets, only one of twelve stations played current hits; the others played albums of sweet music and singles. In other markets, a current-hits format kept stations in their customary number-one situation. Records were bought at full retail price, and the hundreds of free items from record firms were sent back. The small independent companies suffered most, since they were no longer able to get their disks auditioned.

It was revealed early in the hearings that the seminar in Miami had cost the Storz stations and eighteen record companies $117,665, a small price with which to corrupt American radio. The bills ranged from $41.69 to London Records to $11,485 to Dot Records.

Paul Ackerman, of *Billboard,* appeared before the committee as an invited guest, to provide both a historical perspective and an insider's point of view on the music business and its long involvement with pay-for-play. "Much of the investigation of the music business has centered around the so-called singles record business, which is a small part of the total record business," he said. "The singles' business is a declining one and in December [1959] represented only 20% of the industry's dollar volume [or over $40 million]. . . . Long play records currently account for approximately 80% of the total dollar volume.''

It was, he continued, the very abundance of products, resulting from the great explosion during the past twenty years of music-publishing firms, songwriters, record companies, and radio stations, that had effectively removed control of hit-making from Tin Pan Alley and put it into the hands of local radio programers and record manufacturers. A major-market station or disk jockey received more than 1,000 LPs annually and more than 5,000 45-rpm singles, representing a total of at least 20,000 individual selections. Competition for exposure from this surfeit to mass audiences had become extreme, and with it had come all types of payola.

The hearings adduced findings from 335 jockeys that they had been paid $263,245 as "consultant fees" in the recent past. Almost all of them were in major cities, and their influence was great on small-fry deejays, who, like the industry employing them, had a tendency to follow the leader. One witness who admitted that he had taken cash and other favors protested that he had in no way been influenced, that he was given the money by record companies in the hope that "something good would happen." A random remark by another witness that he had been paid to favor one label's version of a Tchaikovsky symphony over another's elicited the comment that the committee was not intersted in anything but pay-for play in relation to "bad" music. A third said that payola was "the American way." It appeared to some cynical spectators that he was indeed correct, for testimony already heard by the committee eventually led to the resignation of the FCC chairman, a commissioner, and an assistant to the President, whose pressures on the FTC brought about his downfall. Eisenhower, however, who commented publicly on disk-jockey payola, did not equate it with pay for political favor, even though it involved several of his own appointees.

Dick Clark's name was mentioned in testimony on a number of occasions, but his appearance was delayed until late April, more than two months after the hearings began. It started with a closed session, made possible by a House rule providing for one when testimony might tend to defame, degrade, or incriminate a witness. When America's most influential disk jockey testified under oath that he had never received payola, he added that he felt "convicted and condemned" before he had had an opportunity to tell his story. Much of it was drawn from documents submitted by his attorneys, confirming that he had made half a million dollars in twenty-seven months from music publishing, talent representation, record manufacturing, pressing, and distributing, before he disposed of all these interests in November 1959 at the recommendation of ABC.

In circumstances much like Clark's, Alan Freed testified in an executive session that he had been paid $40,000 a year by WABC-AM but had given back $30,000 of it to advertise his rock-'n'-roll shows. Representative John

Moss added, "I would like to say Mr. Freed, in my opinion, is one of the few completely truthful men we've had before us in open or executive session."

The upshot of the hearings was that Congress amended the Communications Act of 1934, and outlawed all pay-for-play, with a year's jail term and a maximum fine of $10,000 for convicted offenders. History's best appraisal of the deliberations may have been written by Bernard Schwartz, who had served as committee counsel but was dismissed in early 1959 in an argument over the direction the investigations were taking, namely, a certain reluctance to investigate political and government payola. Before the disk-jockey hearing began, he wrote in late 1959, in the *New York Post:* "What the country does not realize . . . is that improprieties other than those committed by 'disk jockeys and others who testified' have thus far remained buried in the Harris Committee's files. Those fully aware of the material involved know we are really deceiving ourselves to believe that the Congressmen carried out anything like the really thorough investigation of the federal agencies that is so urgently needed."

The second prong of the Songwriters of America and the AGAC's attack on BMI was revealed at the January 7, 1960, session of the FCC's inquiry into network and radio programing and practices. Appearing on behalf of the guild, Burton Lane repeated much of the testimony heard at the Smathers hearings and again urged the divestiture of BMI stock by its remaining stockholders. Owners of stations were as guilty as their disk jockeys in the matter of payola, he said, which faded into insignificance in the face of profits derived by the networks from the record business. On being asked whether the ownership of radio stations by such AGAC members as Bing Crosby, Frank Sinatra, and Pat Boone did not constitute a similar problem and should be prohibited, he responded, "That's a new thought. If it resulted in a conflict of interest, yes."

At a star-studded press conference following Lane's appearance, the Broadway stage star Helen Hayes, appearing in the role of an indignant mother, authors Pearl Buck and Howard Lindsay, and ASCAP members Otto Harbach, Jimmy McHugh, Rodgers and Hammerstein, and Arthur Schwartz, who was now chairman of the society's executive committee, joined Lane. They renewed charges that the giant payola of a $10-million slush fund was being used to foist rock 'n' roll and BMI music on the public. The plea made in an AGAC petition to the FCC asking it to force the divestiture of BMI stock by the industry was strongly supported by all the celebrities present.

Four days later, at another session of the FCC inquiry, ASCAP made its first public attack on BMI since the 1951 Harbach affidavit. A ten-month-long suit by 800 radio stations to get a 9 percent decrease in license fees had just been settled to their advantage, and the consent order reorganizing ASCAP affairs had been signed a few days earlier by Judge Sylvester J.

Ryan, who had also been appointed overseer of the society. It was the fourth such decree imposed on ASCAP since 1941. Appearing with the society's general counsel, Herman Finkelstein, its president, Stanley Adams, made a statement that referred to the "creation and collective ownership of BMI by the broadcasting industry at large and the incentive thus created for broadcasters to perform BMI music not on its comparative merits, but because BMI is operated for the exclusive benefit of owners of radio and TV stations." He added that the artificial ratings for songs created by BMI manipulation could be substantially reduced if the FCC acted to prevent further payola.

When Finkelstein was reminded by a commissioner that the divorce from BMI he suggested had been considered by the Pastore committee, the general counsel responded that he had not followed those preceedings. Adams did not, he readily admitted, know how Top 10 tunes were selected, but he did credit the presence of ASCAP songs among them to "sheer merit, breaking through the BMI barrier." Under further examination, he said he was not prepared to be more specific in his charges and was directed to compile and supply the commission with any specific information on payola the society might have. "Put Up or Shut Up on Charges BMI Promotes Payola," *Variety* described it in a headline.

Sydney Kaye, who was present during the Adams and Finkelstein testimony, requested an opportunity to answer and was asked to return on January 24. Coincidentally, an account of rock 'n' roll's international popularity outside areas where payola allegedly prevailed had appeared in the *New York Times* on the day of Adams's appearance. One of the largest Soviet black-market rings, specializing in rock-'n'-roll music, recorded on exposed X-ray film, had been broken by the authorities. Seven-inch 78-speed disks were copied from foreign shortwave broadcasts or from records brought into the country by tourists. They were sold in the giant Russian department store GUM, or sent by mail to customers outside Moscow.

In addition to a printed statement rebutting point by point the charges made by Lane, Adams, and Finkelstein, on January 24 Kaye spent a long afternoon of oral testimony and cross-examination. BMI music had ranked lower on charts reflecting broadcaster–disk-jockey choice than on those based on retail record sales, he argued. The performance of BMI music had been higher in 1957 than in 1958, one of the two years when payola was alleged to have been at its peak. He then addressed the current videola situation at ASCAP. "Under ASCAP's system, the emphasis on background music is accelerated by the exaggerated advantages given to even a few seconds' use of an old established hit accompanying the closing of a door, which will yield as much as if an artist had featured the same song in a full performance on the same program." And in 1957 some 42.5 percent of all ASCAP's payments were based on TV network performances. As to the charge that broadcasters plugged BMI songs because they had made an investment, that was a fantastic dream. It could easily be ascertained that BMI was held in greater esteem because it "did not systematically insult, vilify, and attack its customers," Kaye asserted.

Seven weeks later—a period during which the Harris payola hearings went on—ASCAP filed a supplementary statement to Stanley Adams's "strongly confirming" that "the practice of payola payments to disk jockeys goes much deeper than a few isolated cases." On the basis of testimony already presented or complaints made by the FTC, 53 percent, or 146 of the 277 records that had reached the Top 50 in popularity during 1958 were released by companies already charged with being involved in the payment of payola. Further, ASCAP believed that the commission's proposed "disclosure" rule, seeking to curb payola, and other proposed FCC rules did not go far enough. The disclosure rule, which took the form of a routine statement that "This performance is a paid performance," would be meaningless to the public. In its place, ASCAP proposed two new rules against payola and another aimed at BMI, barring broadcasters from owning part or all of a performing-rights organization.

Although the commission had already drafted stiffer rules of its own, Celler introduced his own bill, "modeled after one recommended by ASCAP, which would in itself discourage payola by imposing criminal sanctions." It would bring to an abrupt end a number of means of exploitation that songwriters, including ASCAP members, had always considered legitimate. For example, a person who permitted himself to be interviewed by a disk jockey in order to induce him to play that person's latest record was making a payment in service; this would be prohibited by the Celler bill. An Ed Sullivan salute to ASCAP, which involved many member songwriters who knew that their works would be performed, also represented the type of payment in services to be proscribed.

The FCC ruling, issued in March, prohibiting radio stations from playing free records unless an announcement was made that they had been obtained without cost, and that stations had to purchase the records used on their broadcasts, was a burning issue not only for broadcasters, but also for the smaller record companies. Under it, only established labels and artists could be heard. It would become almost impossible for a new artist to get his records played. Broadcasters protested that few stations were in a position to spend the $10,000 to $20,000 it would cost to stock new releases, figures that represented the difference for many small stations between profit and loss. The National Association of Broadcasters maintained that the Celler bill went far beyond the intent of the 1934 Communications Act, and its enforcement would substantially reduce the amount of music the country heard. Payola was commercial bribery and should be so handled by the enactment of a commercial bribery statute. A compromise bill offered months later by Oren Harris, exempted stations from making the disclosure required by the FCC and spelled out requirements for the use of free records. In the final bill, payola remained a criminal offense, quiz-show fraud was forbidden, application procedures were revised, and deals among station applicants were limited. Station fines were reduced to $1,000 a day, and the proposal to give the FCC authority to suspend licenses was eliminated.

Eisenhower signed the bill weeks after the 86th Congress came to an end in September. The session had also passed legislation of particular benefit to music publishers and record companies. Fourth-class "cultural material" postal mailing privileges were extended to sound recordings, including popular releases, but a bill to remove entertainment expenses from their tax-deductable status, a frequent dodge to cover payola payments, was defeated. The highly unpopular Supreme Court decision in the "Moonlight and Roses" case—that the executor of a deceased songwriter could assign the copyright-renewal term where there was no surviving widow or child—added pressure for the revamping of the 1909 Copyright Act.

The renewed petition of Fred Fox and other dissidents, to the Supreme Court in March 1960, to intervene on their behalf in *United States* v *ASCAP,* together with Kaye's emphasis in public on videola involving some leading ASCAP publishers, attracted new attention to corrupt practices within the society. The FCC had withheld the license renewal of a Florida station owned by the producers of *Twenty One* and *Tic Tac Dough,* whose ASCAP house had broken into the twenty best-paid publishers on the basis of performances of music on their own television shows. With approval from the Justice Department, a new rule was put into effect curbing "incentives for artificial stimulation of performance payoff" on network programs for "unusual use of theme and background music." The across-the-board daytime programs and half-hour shows using the ASCAP maximum of fifteen songs were particularly affected, as were those old-line powerhouse publishers who monopolized the shows with under-the-desk arrangements. Max Dreyfus, leader of the fight among board members against videola, who had engaged in a confrontation over the matter with Herman Starr, walked out of a meeting at which the salary of Starr's protégé Stanley Adams was raised from $25,000 to $40,000. Only Starr's enforced retirement from the chairmanship of any ASCAP committee mollified Dreyfus and brought him back.

The Supreme Court's decision to hear the Fox case brought ASCAP and the dissidents before that body for the first time, and speeded up other internal reforms. The performance payment for current hit songs was increased, a move to appease the Current Writers Committee. A song whose current performances equaled those of the society's top fifty songs over the past five years was immediately granted "recognized work" status and eligibility for the 30 percent share of the four funds. An improvement in distributions was also made for concert, choral, and symphonic works. Having expected the October 1960 distributions to be larger as the result of the changes, the CWC held a protest meeting when they were not, at which some said that it "was time to join BMI." A number of prominent screen composers, all members of the CLGA, had already made the jump. Adams explained to the meeting that there was $400,000 less money to distribute and another factor was the 5 percent contribution set aside for the new special awards fund for serious music writers who did not get many performances. The protesters then discussed the possibility of amendments to the consent order to repair the inequities.

On seeing in the October statements the result of their own decision to accept the four-fund reforms, rather than opt for full performance payments, many of ASCAP's 117 highest-paid members questioned the value of that sacrifice, made to trickle a share of their royalties down to the lower classes.

AGAC's councillors met to consider intervening on behalf of the younger writers, but decided to let the matter rest inside ASCAP. The guild had problems with veteran members over a proposal to make participation mandatory in the AGAC collection agency They complained that AGAC was cutting itself in on songs written years before the old SPA was formed. However, a majority of members, 1,360 out of 1,630, agreed, and the agency moved ahead.

Many leading publishers also protested the inequities of the first distribution under the new consent decree made in October. It covered the period in which Starr and some others had made their largest deals with television producers, musical directors, and others, which had precipitated the government intervention. The dissident publishers' group was led by Mickey Scopp, general manager for the MGM Big Three, and Max Dreyfus, whose combined loss under the new system came to half a million dollars. Threats were made at board meetings that, unless a remedy was forthcoming, major publisher defections from ASCAP might follow. BMI's increased competition, underlined by the resignation from the society of a group of important film-score and background composers on January 1, 1961, tempted many of the oldest publisher members.

Loyal dissident writers and publishers looked instead to a restructured board, now possible because of the change in weighted voting that reduced the maximum number of votes for a single member to 100. The change was also expected to remove the possibility of a relatively small group's controlling the election of the whole board. In the case of Irving Berlin, prior to the change his ratio of votes to that of the lowest-rated members was 9,000 to one. There were no new faces on the board that took office in 1961 except that of E. H. Morris, one of only two top-ten ASCAP publishers never yet to have been elected a member. The first director to be affiliated with both societies, he soon sold his BMI operation, losing annual earnings of only around $110,000, contrasted with the half-million he collected each year from ASCAP.

The society won more breathing space in May when the Supreme Court upheld the new consent decree, following the submission of detailed briefs by Sam Fox Music and other dissident smaller publishers, in opposition to ASCAP and the Justice Department. Fox and the other petitioners asked for the right to intervene in the amended decree in order to correct further an inadequate performance survey and unfairly weighted voting, as well as the dubious weighting of questionable performance credits. The Justice Department asserted that the amended order was not yet a finished product and that many changes in ASCAP had already been fashioned and others were in preparation. In an eight-man vote, one justice abstaining, the Supreme Court decided not to review the dissidents' pleas and returned the matter to the Justice Department and ASCAP. Fred Fox and his colleagues announced their determination to continue the crusade.

ASCAP and Herman Finkelstein focused next on BMI and its practice of giving long-term contracts and substantial cash guarantees to screen composers whose music was used widely on television. That practice was forbidden to the society, it was alleged, because the consent order required ASCAP to distribute royalties solely on the basis of earned performances. The NAB and its All-Industry Television Committee were preparing for immediate negotiations for a new license, to take effect at the end of 1961. Finkelstein believed that ASCAP had in its favor the fact that the industry's own licensing body gave more money for music on television, and the telecasters were not paying enough to ASCAP.

The society's income had gone up seven percent in 1960, to $32.3 million. Total membership was 5,229 writers and 1,727 publishers. The radio negotiations had been completed, though with a 9 percent cut. An executive was hired to deal with writers on the West Coast, one of ASCAP's major problems. There, the most serious complaint from film composers was the fractional payments for themes, bridges, cues, and background music, compared with BMI's currently far superior payments to both writers and publishers of such material. There were agreements with only six BMI publishers providing that if the publisher had rights to the theme and 60 percent of the background music, and the program appeared for a specified minimum number of times during the year, he was guaranteed a maximum of $5,000. As the payments to publishers of music used on television increased greatly, these contracts became meaningless. TV music publishers then were given an advance from BMI based on an estimate of what they would earn in the following year. If the advance was not met, the excess was carried over to the next year. It was in connection with this that Arthur Dean was again retained as special counsel to institute legal action against BMI for what ASCAP felt were improper activities in connection with television music. The proposed suit would have no connection with the Schwartz case, by then nearly nine years old.

The scope of damages in that $150-million action had been limited in

March 1960. In ruling against Judge Weinfeld's decision to give BMI access to half a million ASCAP performance cards, Sylvester J. Ryan, chief judge of the federal court and overseer of the society under the amended consent decree, permitted the defendants to examine the performance records of only twenty-five ASCAP members, none of them plaintiffs. He also limited the damages sought by the thirty-three plaintiffs to those actually suffered by them.

The Harris committee staff report on two years of hearings appeared in December 1960, a 265-page document of which only nine pages were devoted to "Payola and Songplugging by Disk Jockeys and Others." Contrary to the expectations of Burton Lane, AGAC, and ASCAP, the only reference to BMI was in a section, about half a page long, in connection with ABC's ownership of a record company and music firms, as well as the ownership of BMI by the broadcasters.

In testimony in 1958 to the Pastore committee, John Schulman had demonstrated that BMI had licensed more than half of the music for television film in 1953, 1954, and 1956. In spite of that warning, ASCAP had continued to neglect its West Coast screen composers in favor of the powerhouse publishers, composers, and authors whose weighted block voting controlled the directors. AGAC's fight with the CLGA widened the breach between the organizations and their members, a situation the 1960 consent order failed to mend. West Coast composers continued to look about for the best financial deal they could get and began a move to BMI, which also made payments for the performance in all foreign countries of motion pictures for which they had composed the background music. By the start of 1961, several dozen important ASCAP CLGA members had joined BMI.

The use of taped library musical material was giving way on the more prestigious dramatic and comedy shows to that of live music, written by men who had to score more music for a half-hour program than they did for a feature movie. The precedent-setting agreement with the AFM by MCA's Revue Productions to use only live music on all future videofilms speeded the demise of the libraries. So, too, did the forty-month contract signed in November 1961 by the AFM and the Motion Picture Producers Association. Under it, all films produced in the United States and Canada had to be scored there, and all "canned music" was banned. At the same time, the CLGA completed negotiations with the motion-picture and TV producers for a new four-year agreement that guaranteed members of the guild minimum weekly compensation. Composers and lyricists under contract to film and television studios got a minimum of $325 a week, and those employed on a temporary basis got $350 a week to start. They were also covered by all existing pension and health plans. There were about 300 screen and video composers at work in Hollywood and on the East Coast, but few of them were under contract to a movie studio. The Screen Composers Association had 120 members, thirty of whom were regularly employed. Roughly nineteen videofilm series were in production in 1960, some of them using a single composer and his assistants to write all the music.

Representative Celler's rekindled ire, fanned higher by the pleas of ASCAP to do something about BMI and television music, was vented on the Justice Department and the FCC in June 1961. The projected acquisition by BMI of all music for the entire Goodson & Todman production schedule, *The Price Is Right, Play Your Hunch, Say When, Number Please,* and others, was the final stroke, particularly when the producers removed all ASCAP music and replaced it with only BMI-licensed material. With revenues from TV the largest single source of ASCAP income, and with television programing precluding any increase in the use of standard popular songs, because of the switch to taped comedy, adventure, and dramatic series, the society was fearful of the pending independent-TV-station negotiations. According to the telecasters' survey, the average percentage of local TV-station time devoted to feature music had declined from 6.3 percent in 1953 to 3.7 in 1961.

During a two-day hearing by the House Antitrust Subcommittee, Celler demanded to know from FCC Chairman Newton Minow whether the commission was ready to require the divorce from BMI of every broadcasting licensee. The following day he asked Lee Loevinger, chief of the Justice Department's Antitrust Division, why the department had been foot-dragging on recommendations made after the hearings in New York in 1956. Neither Minow nor Loevinger was ready to bow the knee to the House subcommittee chairman, but both were aware of his power. Yet they were careful not to agree with his charges against BMI and broadcasters; nor did they promise any action against either. Loevinger stated that he was not persuaded that legal action was necessary against BMI, that in fact there had been a weakening, rather than a strengthening, of the case against BMI now that CBS and NBC had pulled out of it.

"Broadcast Music, Inc. appeared reasonably safe from antitrust threats posed against show business activities by the Kennedy Administration," *Variety* wrote after that session. "This despite vigorous blandishments from House Judiciary Chairman Emanuel Celler who leveled one of his harshest assaults on BMI." With its bid through Celler to separate BMI from broadcasters fruitless, ASCAP turned to the independent telecasters, with a final offer it believed could not be refused.

The society had been mending some fences. New writer and publisher adviser committees were established, including in them some of ASCAP's severest internal critics. Writer performance credits were increased by the simple expedient of stabilizing the total number of credited performances at 25 million a year, regardless of the number actually surveyed. Writers and publishers were asked to extend the assignment of their television rights through 1966. A half-million-dollar "prestige melon" was divided among authors and composers whose music had "unique prestige value for which adequate compensation would not be otherwise received" and for music not surveyed by the new monitoring method devised by Joel Dean Associates. The payments were restricted to composers of serious music who received less than $25,000 from the society and to popular-music writers with performance earnings of less than $15,000.

A key publisher-director, Mickey Scopp, of the Big Three, called for exploratory talks between ASCAP and BMI. He felt that federal action would resolve the issue of whether broadcasters could operate as both buyers and sellers of music. He hoped for a peaceful settlement rather than recourse to the courts.

Former Judge John E. McGeehan, the new special adviser to ASCAP, appointed by Judge Ryan, echoed Scopp's plea for peace through government intervention once again when he told the membership in November: "Until your competitors are made to observe the rules of the game, ASCAP is at a disadvantage and penalized for obeying the law. You can't have a double standard of conduct. The spirit of fair play should reign. I've looked into your adversary and I want you to act and bring this to the attention of the lawmakers." Unfortunately, Arthur Schwartz, Burton Lane, and the society itself had gone to the Washington well once too often.

There had not been a resolution as yet of another matter vital to the society: whether it had the right to license movies of any kind to television, a subject Hollywood preferred to leave untouched. The action filed late in the 1950s was dropped without explanation, but several new suits involving the issue were pending in the courts: three filed by Jerry Vogel Music company; *Sam Fox Publishing Co.* v. *National Telefilm Associates and 20th Century-Fox,* for the latter of which Sam Fox Music acted as co-publisher for its Movietone Music subsidiary; and *E. B. Marks* v. *20th Century-Fox.* All challenged the film studios' right to sell moving pictures to television without their permission to use the musical compositions synchronized with them.

These actions caught the attention of the legal representatives of the All-Industry Television Committee, supported financially by about 300 stations and chaired by Hamilton Shea, of WSVA-TV, Harrisonburg, Virginia, owned by the Shenandoah Broadcasting group. In October, a Shenandoah committee asked Judge Ryan to grant independent television stations at-the-source clearance of all rights to music licensed by the society and played in the feature films and syndicated programs they had purchased or were renting, a form of programing that now represented 75 percent of all local-station time on the air. The court was also asked to determine "reasonable fees" and set interim rates, reducing present fees by one quarter.

This proposed form of clearance was different from that devised by ASCAP and the networks in their prewar radio licenses, which had carried over into TV licensing. To achieve it, film and taped-program producers would acquire synchronization *and* performance rights to the music they selected. The costs would be included in the final package price of every program or series rented or sold to local stations. In an accompanying affidavit, Shea said that because music "was 'in the can' after it had been recorded and produced," stations buying prerecorded material were given no choice about the music involved or what they paid for it. In another affidavit, counsel for Shenandoah explained that "the producer often arranges to be the 'publisher' of the original music he selects, and thus is able to share in the monies ASCAP collects from television and disburses to its members." If the producer paid the composer up to the same amount he got now through his ASCAP membership, "the total music costs would be substantially lower since the composer receives only 50% of the tv performing right revenues distributed by ASCAP. The other 50% is paid to the publisher, who in most instances is the producer himself."

Pending a decision by Ryan, TV licenses were extended automatically past their December 31, 1961, expiration, for both independent stations and the networks, which were conducting their own negotiations. After a firm statement by Ryan that he could not rule on clearance at the source because of the ASCAP consent decree, the negotiations made little progress until March 5, when an offer described as "Judge Ryan's idea all the way through" was thrown on the table by ASCAP. In it television stations could get a 17 percent reduction, about $2.2 million a year, for ten years, and the networks one of about 10 percent against revenues exceeding those in 1961, in return for their complete divorce from ownership of BMI stock or control of the organization. BMI would have to submit itself to the same sort of consent order as that signed by the society in 1950, which moved all rate-fixing negotiations and disputes to Ryan for resolution.

Because the proposal would require the approval of a majority of BMI stockholders, *Broadcasting* wrote in an editorial that "some broadcasters believe that BMI has become a boondoggle that could stand to be trimmed of fat under a reorganization. Some think there would be no loss to broadcasting if BMI went out of business. Most of those with doubts about BMI lack full information about BMI's recent operations, and that is a gap they ought to try to fill before coming to a final judgement."

The vivid memories of misinterpreted documents introduced in the Schwartz case, material dealing with BMI's muscle-flexing advertising, claims of success, and business practices, introduced in the Celler and Pastore hearings had persuaded BMI's attorneys and its board to be cautious about releasing potentially damaging statistical information. But after some vital information was leaked to *Broadcasting,* an official stricture not to fight the matter in public was withdrawn and a full-scale information program was launched. *Variety, Billboard, Cash Box,* and, especially, *Broadcasting* spread the message to the industry, most of the television part of which had already decided that the saving of ASCAP fees was more important than support of the present BMI structure. It became widely known that ASCAP and BMI supplied music to radio and TV on an almost equal basis. BMI had music in eleven of the top fifteen Nielsen-rated television shows, and in thirteen of the twenty most-performed syndicated film series. ASCAP had a two-to-one lead in the performance of feature music on the networks, and a five-to-four share of background music. Out of the $46 million spent for music in the last year, ASCAP was paid $33.1 million, or 72 percent; BMI, $12.7 million, or 28 percent.

The hottest issue in music licensing since 1941 split the industry, and caused enmity among station owners and attorneys that lasted for years. Those independent broadcasters who looked on BMI as an insurance policy against the rebirth of an ASCAP monopoly saw the Shenandoah members and supporters as traitors ready to throw them to the wolves. BMI's station-relations staff spent days on the road, hoping to reap the benefits of years of work among the country's small broadcasters. It seemed touch and go for BMI.

There was a ray of good news amidst the pessimism. In a confidential letter to all plaintiffs and supporters of the Schwartz case, John Schulman wrote about the "good possibility of settlement," and with it the necessity for a "compromise on the question of the amount payable by the defendants even to the point where the cost of the suit will not be entirely recouped." the letter disillusioned most of those diehards who continued to allot 2 to 5 percent of their annual ASCAP royalties to support the action, a total since it was started of nearly three million dollars.

News much more favorable to BMI came at the end of March, when the openly disunited Shenandoah committee succumbed to the united front of radio-station BMI stockholders and rejected the ASCAP-Ryan offer as unworkable. The decision was announced to tumultuous approval at the NAB convention a few days later. All talk about television licensing returned to the Ryan court, where a long fight seemed inevitable. With the Schwartz case seemingly grinding to an end, BMI, no longer concerned about being a sacrificial lamb, returned to its fundamental function—the music business.

After a confused initial period, the music and record industries found the new rules dealing with them in Section 317 of the amended Communications Act easier to cope with than had been anticipated. Musicasters, as the disk jockeys called themselves in the aftermath of the payola hearings, identified both label and artist of the records they played. "Promotion" records were known as "audition" records, more clearly defining their purpose. Some stations accepted free copies, but most broadcasters bought new disks and LPs at wholesale prices from local distributors. After a decline of 45-rpm singles' sales during 1959, when they dropped to a gross of $39 million, down 25 percent from 1954, pop single disks enjoyed a new surge of popularity. It was signaled by the return in March 1960 from army service abroad of Elvis Presley, whose new single "Are You Lonesome Tonight" brought several million people back to the record counters. Hit singles by Jim Reeves, the Everly Brothers, Johnny Preston, Mark Dinning, Brenda Lee, Connie Francis, Chubby Checker, and a host of artists new to the public once again showed the music business that new vocal talent was not established with albums, which denied the concentrated air play a hit needed.

Two tokens of days past or disappearing could be found in Martin Block's retirement on October 29, 1960, and the demise of the last of the air-play "sheets," the *Accurate Report,* some months later. Block's departure from the air was, as the pioneer deejay said, an indication that rock 'n' roll was not about to go away in favor of the kind of music he had continued to program throughout the Presley mania, as witness the country's continued demand for the Big Beat in spite of the payola disclosures. The other victim of changing times, Martin Alexander's Accurate Reporting Service, almost the last of the daily records of air plugs, had listed the number of remote band shots, network plays, and other radio performances since the 1930s. The *Accurate Report* had been distributed on a daily basis since the mid-1930s to music publishers, advertising agencies, the MPPA, ASCAP, and BMI, among others, for $77.25 a month, until the cost of monitoring radio stations in New York, Chicago, and Los Angeles became too great to sustain, especially with the competition from John Peatman's *Peatman Report* prepared and merchandised on the same basis.

Major investors with Wall Street connections and other entrepreneurs had discovered that there was no buy to match that of an ASCAP publishing company with a substantial catalogue of copyrights. With a guaranteed minimum return of 10 percent from such a firm, the initial purchase price could be amortized within a decade, after which everything was profit. Potential buyers continued to sniff around Mills Music, with offers in the four-million-dollar range. A unique public auction in the New York Surrogates Court disposed of three Saul Bourne firms, with their $300,000 yearly ASCAP payments, for $3.45 million. Originally a partner with Max Winslow and Irving Berlin in the first Irving Berlin music house, Sol Bornstein (Bourne after 1947) had a falling out with Berlin in the 1940s over their deceased partner's share and assets. Berlin took his own copyrights, leaving the remainder to Bornstein, who opened Bourne Music.

It was not just a matter of pre-1940 standards to the new breed of investors interested in the music business. Youngsters who grew up with "Earth Angel," "Don't Be Cruel," "Hearts of Stone," "Lovey Dovey," and "Fever" were now adult, looking for their own evergreen memories. "Oldie" and "Golden Oldie" programing had found its place alongside the Top 40 hits, broadening the base of the music heard on most stations. In order to break into formula radio, some independent record labels found a way to by-pass the payola statutes by purchasing blocks of time on selected stations to "break" new hits. It was there that "twist music" got its first chance to become the most important new development in the rock-'n'-roll business since Presley. Hank Ballard had recorded the original "Twist" in 1958, and in 1961 Chubby Checker dusted off the cobwebs and recorded it on a Philadelphia label. From there, it spread, after exposure on radio, to New York's Peppermint Lounge and eventually even to the White House. Checker's price for a club date jumped from $500 to $2,500, and *Variety* found the Twist to be the most effective night-spot audience-builder since the repeal of Prohibition.

Most old-line music firms were frustrated by the fragmentation of radio programing in the early 1960s, along with the shifting of programing responsibility. It had been presaged by the controversy between Big Beat and sweet "good" music, when time salesmen found some question among advertisers about whether the basic top 40 audience was actually in a financial position to buy hard goods. They had committed themselves to the good-music stations. The paragon of such operations was New York's WPAT-AM, over which 250 advertisers ran campaigns in 1961–62, paying a premium nighttime rate, when all other stations had reduced their's. In three transactions since 1956, the price of WPAT jumped from $600,000 to between four and five million dollars.

Small-market stations had the option to switch from specialized radio—Top 40, easy listening, albums only—to a general format, a potpourri of everything. In larger markets, competition between stations was rife and the specialized format continued: talk-music, aimed at an audience that tolerated music but had a greater interest in news; special features, interviews; news only; classical and semiclassical music; popular music, for an audience that occasionally tolerated rock 'n' roll in their definition of popular music; Big Beat; and, at the lowest end, background music.

The growth of FM stations in 1961 and the increased use of FM multiplex stereocasting encouraged the advent of softer sounds. In New York City, WINS, long the top rocker, switched to the "pretty music" of pop standards, celebrating the move by playing sixty-six hours of nothing but Sinatra records. The station's programing was anchored on a group of artists—Sinatra, Ella Fitzgerald, Glenn Miller, Johnny Mathis, Connie Francis, Judy Garland, Nat Cole, Jimmy and Tommy Dorsey, Doris Day, and Perry Como, the latter alone having managed to live through all of television's changes. Within a few days, the Sinatra sound was the biggest thing in radio since the Twist, and stations around the country switched to it. Some attributed this and other changes to a desire to please the FCC, which was now, under Newton Minow's direction, more responsive to the public. Actually, the motivation was economic, based on studies showing that automobile manufacturers, the airlines, and food advertisers—the three largest groups of radio sponsors in 1962—had embarked on their own undeclared boycott of Top 40 radio.

But the lure of the Big Beat was irresistible and rock-'n'-roll–station ratings held their place at the top of the Nielsen and Pulse studies. WINS asked public pardon for its Sinatra heresy and returned to the fold with a slightly "less raucous sound." Other stations switched to all-talk and then back. It was evident that the only real formula for success in radio appeared to be constant experimentation with program directors as well as with formats, a situation as confusing to the broadcasters as to the music men who sought to service them.

Judge Ryan's adverse ruling in September 1962 in connection with the request for clearance at the source of all filmed programing had come as no surprise. It confirmed his frequent public assertions that he could not issue such a license because the government consent order did not contain a provision for one. Speaking for ASCAP, Finkelstein reaffirmed its contention that the present form of licensing should not be tampered with, that, instead, rates should be restored to their 1954 level by effecting a 20 percent increase, a view exactly contrary to that of the telecasters. In an informal meeting of all parties in the rate-fixing procedure, as well as representatives of both sides in the Schwartz suit, called at Ryan's suggestion, he repeated his feeling, expressed on many occasions, that the basic problems facing those present could be solved by the regulation of some BMI practices. Principally, these were the advances to writers and publishers. Judge Rosenman offered a three-point policy statement on behalf of BMI, in lieu of any divestiture, which Finkelstein rejected. The Shenandoah committee had recourse now only to the Supreme Court, in the form of a petition to reverse the Ryan decision. The papers were filed in December. A hearing once again denied the petition several weeks later, on the same grounds—that the society was not required to accept a license that was neither permitted nor prohibited by the various consent orders governing its operation.

At ASCAP membership meetings on both coasts in 1962, copyright law was a subject of considerable interest, especially the removal of the jukebox exemption, which could add to the society's income, now more than $33 million, and the duration of copyright protection. Stanley Adams's frequent public comments that "public domain is the chief competition of ASCAP" were based on the impending and relentless termination of copyright protection for works written more than fifty-six years earlier.

The economic importance of copyright in the American business world was underlined in a special report by the Copyright Office, which estimated that contributions to the gross national product in the form of wages, rents, interest, and profits by institutions based on and using copyrighted materials were surpassed only by those of the automobile business and the railroads. In 1954, the year on which the study was based, the copyright industries had accounted for $6.1 billion out of a total $299.7 billion national income, more than banking, mining, and public utilities.

The 227-page report and recommendation by the register of copyrights, submitted to Congress on July 10, 1961, urged a radical overhaul of the

1909 act. It asked for a twenty-year extension of the maximum copyright term; elimination of compulsory licensing; statutory protection for works as soon as they were registered or made public; enactment of separate legislation in the meantime to remove the jukebox exemption; protection of choreographic works as well as the principle of protection against record piracy; a provision making copyrights divisible, so that parts of a work could be assigned separately; lifting of the ceiling on damages; and some minor recommendations affecting music. It was generally agreed on Capitol Hill that any enactment of these proposals was a long way off.

Representative Celler immediately launched a package of interim legislation. One proposal would add five years to the life of an estimated 47,000 works, the vast majority musical. "ASCAP's best friend" attacked his old adversaries the jukebox operators with proposed legislation to remove the jukebox exemption and impose coin-machine license fees of from five to twenty-five dollars. New friends at ARMADA, American Record Manufacturers and Distributors Association, whom he had recently addressed at their annual convention, also had something to cheer: a bill to make record counterfeiting a criminal offense, with penalties up to $10,000 and jail terms up to ten years.

Surprise opposition to the proposed extension of copyright came from the Justice Department. Attorney General Robert Kennedy wrote that "copyrights and patents are forms of monopolies and should not be extended for periods longer than those now provided in law. Considering this from the viewpoint of the public, which is interested in the early passing of copyrighted material into the public domain, it would seem unwise to extend further the copyright monopoly."

An amended bill reducing extension to three years passing the House and the Senate, and was signed by President John Kennedy in September. The Celler legislation did not fare as well. An ensemble of supporters, headed by ARMADA, with the RIAA in a supporting role, testified to the impact of record piracy. It was estimated that piracy drained at least $20 million from the manufacturers. The large chain-store operations, Sears and Woolworth, were alleged to be the pirates' best customers, buying in lots of 10,000 to 20,000 copies of an item at a time. Unfortunately, the manufacturers and the publishers split over the bill's provisions. The RIAA favored the criminal-punishment clause, which made it a felony, rather than a misdemeanor, to counterfeit disks. The MPPA wanted the bill to allow the recovery of full damages for copyright infringement. The watered-down legislation that emerged, finally, was the country's first legislation against record counterfeiting, but, with the damages clause missing, it promised little relief to copyright owners.

In the face of continuing bad publicity in the daily press and consumer magazines for the jukebox business, surprisingly, the Music Operators of America and its friends were able to delay passage of two Celler bills through the full Congress. A second compromise had been introduced; it permitted coin operators to negotiate license fees after a mandatory five-year licensing period during which fees ranged between five and twenty-five dollars a machine. The affair dragged over to the next Congress.

Umbrage taken by the Arkansas Congressional delegation following the appointment of a Tennessee attorney, E. William Henry, to head the FCC, was one of many motives for the adoption of copyright revision in the Senate, led by Arkansas' John L. McClellan, chairman of the Subcommittee on Patents, Trade Marks and Copyrights. An incumbent Democratic member of the commission, John S. Cross, of Arkansas, had been slated for the post and his being passed over had an impact on White House relations with Congress for months to come.

The new FCC chairman was a close colleague of John Hooker, Jr., leader of a Nashville-based group of young liberals who were attempting to get control of the state's Democratic Party machine and put Hooker in the governor's mansion. The task was one for which the support of country-music artists, songwriters, and publishers was essential, those who had over the years been of great support to BMI.

Since its formation in 1958, the Country Music Association had grown into an institution of national importance. The initial board included Ernest Tubb, representing artists; Cracker Jim Brooker, disk jockeys; Wesley Rose, the chairman, music publishers; Ken Nelson, of Capitol, record companies; Walter Kilpatrick, radio and TV stations; Charlie Lamb, the trade press. Robert Burton, of BMI, was director-at-large.

A statement by Steve Sholes, the man who had brought Elvis Presley to RCA Victor Records and was currently director of its A & R department, read at the Country Music Festival that year, had it that old-fashioned country records had disappeared from the record stores and the manufacturers' lists. "Television has had its impact, musical tastes have been broadened, perhaps not for the better, but that's the way it is." Yet, a quarter of a million dollars a year was made by Johnny Cash, a twenty-six-year-old singer-guitarist-songwriter, who had been lured away from Sam Phillips's Sun Records. Cash had sold six million disks for Sun, with "I Walk the Line," "Ballad of a Teen-age Queen," "Folsom Prison Blues," and other hits making for him between $1,500 and $2,000 a night against a 60 percent guarantee from more than a hundred dates a year. He had opened both ASCAP and BMI firms, a sign that he had crossed over to the pop charts, for which hits were beginning to pour out of "Tin Pan Valley"—Nashville—the capital of country music. There, its new prestige could be seen in the presence at CMA's first meeting of hundreds of record and music-business executives, among them the urbane Goddard Lieberson, of Columbia. CMA had 500 members, who paid ten dollars a year, and it desperately needed more. BMI's first invitation-only, black-tie Country Award Dinner was held at the same time but separate from all official functions.

The money in country music provided an avenue for national advertisers to reach an important new market. A Pulse study in late 1959 showed that, unlike the R & B or foreign-language audience, country-music followers had not yet been completely catalogued. However, of the 11,000 questioned in eighteen markets, 3.5 percent earned more than $10,000 and 40 percent above $7,500 annually. Nearly 45 percent of all the pop singles made the following year came from Nashville, the product of the new Nashville sound, whose main feature was its spontaneity. It was relayed from musician to musician, each making a contribution, as the "head-arranged" accompaniment for an artist, never written down, grew and was completed. When asked if he could read music, one Nashville sideman replied, "Sure. But not enough to hurt my playing."

Thirty-six percent of the country's 3,327 AM stations devoted some of their time on the air to country music in 1961, the year the first immortals, Jimmie Rodgers, Hank Williams, and Fred Rose, were elected to the CMA Hall of Fame, and bust plaques of them were on exhibit temporarily at a Nashville museum. The Grand Ole Opry played Carnegie Hall, and country music enjoyed its greatest international popularity yet in Europe, where American soldiers bought records in PXs and listened with the locals to country music over Radio Luxembourg and Armed Forces Radio.

The following year, Ray Charles, the "Genius of R & B," introduced country music to whatever part of the world had not yet been bitten by its bug in two LPs, "Modern Sounds in Country Music," volumes 1 and 2. Country music accounted for half of all recordings that originated in Nashville. Seventy TV stations employed live country talent, and ninety-seven AM stations were on a full-time country-music schedule. Victor's Record Club, operated by the *Reader's Digest* music division, opened a country-music monthly record subscription service. ASCAP opened its first small office in Nashville, where BMI was negotiating for property.

ASCAP's move into Nashville was another step in the plan of younger ASCAP directors and concerned publishers to develop a new and more favorable contemporary image for the society, both in the music business and among its members and customers. The electronic computing machinery installed in the New York headquarters was expected to speed up distributions and reduce complaints from members while negotiations to effect other changes were being pursued with the Justice Department. The five-year averaging on which the four-fund system was based, covering the period when videola was prevalent among the highest circles and some new publishers, was a major point of discontent. So, too, were the special awards, which the Current Writers Committee believed were better spent to attract the new songwriters who were going to BMI.

On October 1, 1963, changes in the ASCAP distribution system to improve the lot of younger members went into effect. Writers who had chosen the 100-percent-performance option could now cancel it immediately. The recognized-works base was cut from 30 percent to 20; the difference was applied to the average performance fund, raising that to 40 percent. Seniority, the continuity-of-membership factor, was now based on a ten-year, rather than five-year, average. The former limitations on average-performance and recognized-works ratings were removed to allow an increase in royalties immediately, rather than over a two-year period. Credits for theme, bridge, and background music were increased. Stanley Adams and his new special assistant, George Hoffman, promoted from comptroller, prepared for the celebration of the society's fiftieth anniversary.

When an appeals court would not reverse the Ryan ruling against clearance at the source, the Shenandoah committee embarked on a tangential course of action, which led again to the Supreme Court after a year of legal sparring in lower courts. It was now suggested that independent telecasters pay only for music used on their locally originated telecasts. The producers of feature movies and syndicated programs that occupied 68 percent of non-network time were expected to deal directly with ASCAP for other rights. Music on network programs was already covered by interim ASCAP contracts. In June 1964, the Supreme Court again refused to review adverse findings against Shenandoah. The 346 stations represented by the committee were told that the fight would continue.

Three years of concurrent negotiations between the TV networks and ASCAP ended in December 1964 when a compromise five-year contract was signed with CBS, NBC, and ABC. The 2.05 percent network rate was maintained, and a fee of 1.9 percent was fixed for owned-and-operated stations. The networks would also pay 2 percent on all revenue above that earned in the base year of 1963; their owned-and-operated stations, 1.325 percent.

ASCAP's income and that of the networks and their fifteen stations had continued to grow during the most recent war over music rates. The year 1961 was a $1.3-billion year for television. The networks earned $675 million, with profits of $87 million. Eighty percent of all VHF stations showed a profit, over $400,000 for more than one third. The fifty-minute program hour was refined to its tightest, leaving six of the other ten minutes for commercials, the remainder for station breaks—promotion, billboards, station identification, and trailers of between five seconds and one minute for forthcoming programs. Pay television, or "tollvision," for which ASCAP had negotiated experimental licenses, boosted signals through local community antenna systems into about one million homes, with a potential audience of some three and a half million viewers. TelePrompter, the largest CATV operation, owned fifteen systems, worth about $15 million. TelePrompter's most recent closed-circuit heavyweight fight had attracted about 150,000 ticket buyers.

Pretaping made possible by advanced VTRs brought about the refinement of the specials-variety-personality programs, whose leisurely paced production patterns provided a new medium for previously unavailable guests. Aided by 11,000 feature motion pictures, which were a staple of programing in 1963, purchased from Hollywood for well over $400 million, television's gross revenues went above $2 billion. The networks and their stations had an income of $1.1 billion and profits of $136 million.

A record income was reported for that year by ASCAP: $37.8 million, an estimated $32 million of which came from broadcasters, one third from radio, whose rate of return on investment had declined from 13.3 percent in 1958 to 10.1 in 1962, according to FCC data. In its argument for an increase from television, ASCAP stated that the television stations' rate of return had increased from 21.1 percent in 1957 to 32.9 in 1962.

The All-Industry Radio Committee's announcement that it, too, wanted a reduction in the new contract that would take effect at the beginning of 1964 came at a time when independent radio was almost entirely music and news. The Big Beat and the Big Sound predominated from coast to coast, the first from forty-five-rpm singles and the other from LP albums, which had cliché Nelson Riddle, Henry Mancini, Percy Faith, Sy Zentner, Billy May, Hugo Winterhalter, and Billy Vaughn arrangements. AP and UPI tickers continued to provide the world's news, read on small operations, rewritten and read by station news departments. The FCC was kept happy with public-service announcements sent out by government agencies and public charities, selling enlistment in the armed forces, government bonds, security against the atom bomb, Easter Seals, the March of Dimes, and other philanthropies.

And there were the eternal jingles, set to the golden oldies of the past decade, which lent stations formerly connected to a network a musical identification all their own. Broadcasters spent $3.5 million on jingles in 1962. Music publishers got up to $50,000 for the use of a hallowed standard by Cole Porter in a nationwide advertising campaign, and anywhere from $750 for a current hit to be used on a regional-or local-market schedule. A handful of 50,000-watters insisted on a musical personality of their own, and bought exclusive jingle promotion and program-aid packages for between $15,000 and $30,000. Probably the most successful of the pop-music independents was WNEW-AM in New York, which grossed $33 million in the five-year period ending in 1961, well worth the $25 million asking price, and was known for the individuality of its station-break jingles and musicaster introduction themes.

In their last negotiation was the society, resulting in the 1959–63 contract, radio broadcasters won a reduction of around 9 percent. Now they found it difficult to get representatives of ASCAP to sit still in order to extract from them an ever larger reduction. The first meetings, three months before the present contracts expiration, were fruitless, and in March 1964 the committee applied to Judge Ryan, asking him to fix a $7.7-million ceiling on radio rates for the first year of a new contract, a 22 percent reduction from the 1962 level and 10 percent below that when talks had started for the 1959–63 agreement. Two very different pictures of the situation in radio in the late 1950s were offered to Ryan in arguments. One had it that reduction had been part of a "Marshall Plan" to infuse money into a "very sick industry" that was now on its economic feet and in a position to pay the society its just due. The committee, on the other hand, denied that "compassion," and insisted on a significant additional reduction on the grounds that radio profits were declining and with them the use of the ASCAP repertory. Trade-paper-chart studies were offered in evidence to show the decreasing ASCAP presence among the top-rated songs, from 94 percent in 1948 to 25 percent in 1963. BMI, which wanted an increase for that reason, had agreed to a one-year extension of its contract with radio broadcasters expiring in March 1964. When the ASCAP negotiations with the committee were concluded, BMI was ready to press the fight for more money from radio. Counsel for ASCAP attributed the change, if true, to a conspiracy to use more BMI music and reduce that of ASCAP.

At the same time, Judge Ryan was petitioned by CBS-Radio to approve an ASCAP per-program arrangement like that concluded by the network with BMI. As ground for approval, CBS offered its increase of air time devoted to public service and the decline in the use of music. The Justice Department filed a contempt suit against the society for its failure to accede to the CBS demand, as required in all consent orders since 1941. In spite of this and other pressures, CBS's demand remained stalled in the name of negotiation. No effort was made by Ryan to speed up the matter.

In March, Metromedia, a BMI stockholder and the owner of stations spun off from the old Dumont Television chain as well as ten AM and FM stations, including WNEW, complained to Judge Ryan. The society would not respond to a Metromedia request for a contract based on net rather than gross income. Metromedia was spending half a million dollars a year on a thirty-five-man news department at WNEW AM and FM, but under present circumstances could deduct only the charges for news-service tickers. The company paid ASCAP $200,000 for 1963, and offered to pay one million on the spot for a five-year license on the new terms. ASCAP refused the proposition, its counsel said, because "we might prefer to take a percentage of the gross, but don't know what kind of Pandora's box the Metromedia request might open."

The first formal ASCAP offer to the radio stations came in late April. It increased rates by 22 percent, exactly the reduction sought by the committee. The increase was expected to come from an ascending commercial fee, rising in increments of $50,000, from 2.125 percent to 2.75 above $150,000. Network and station per-program contracts remained at the same fees, but were conditioned on a modification along the lines of the current television per-program agreements, with certain definitions updated. It was estimated by the committee's economist that they would cost more than the present blanket access licenses. For example, because of the great reduction in music use CBS would pay sixty dollars for a song that had cost the network ten dollars five years before.

A new round of meetings of all parties was called by Ryan to discuss a compromise settlement, for ten years, of all issues, including the Schwartz case, CBS-Radio's per-program request, bids for reasonable licenses, and other pending litigation. The judge's complicated package of solutions, which did not include BMI's divestiture, was immediately regarded as irresistibly attractive, However, all negotiations to implement the plan came to a standstill on December 10, 1964. A civil antitrust suit was filed against BMI by the Justice Department. The action came as a surprise. It was known that the FTC had been investigating both BMI and the Society of European Stage Authors and Composers, the latter because of complaints from Southern broadcasters.

Remaining undisturbed on the sidelines during the years of bitter confrontation between broadcasters and ASCAP, the SESAC had lived a relatively untroubled life. The third licensing body in terms of income, it was the second to be organized, in 1931, by Paul Heinecke, a European-born representative of major classical-music publishers on the Continent. He and his family retained full ownership of the organization. In 1959, in the case of *Affiliated Music Enterprises, Inc.* v. the *Society of European Stage Authors and Composers,* Judge Ryan had dismissed the lawsuit but had said that SESAC's "classic pooling of rights and sharing of revenue" violated the antitrust laws, particularly Section One of the Sherman Act.

Pressure in the early 1960s from Southern radio stations first brought members of the Senate and the All Industry Radio Committee into the SESAC situation. Legislation was introduced in Washington to require all licensing organizations to identify their music on phonograph-record labels, an industrywide practice dating back to the 1941 music war. The committee mailed questionnaires to all stations, asking for details about the most persistant complaints against SESAC—the lack of a catalogue, the extent to which its music was used, alleged coercion against stations—and a full report on all payments to SESAC since 1953. In response to similar complaints, the FTC began its own investigation, and the Senate Small Business Committee embarked on a probe of SESAC. All of the investigations ended the following year when SESAC agreed to publish a catalogue of the compositions it licensed, so that broadcasters could determine whether they needed a license from the company.

Unlike ASCAP and BMI, SESAC did not function under a consent decree and represented only publishers, sharing all mechanical, synchronization, and performing-rights revenues with them on a fifty-fifty basis, after the deduction of operating expenses. The original group of foreign publishers had been enlarged in the years since 1931 by the addition of American firms, and now numbered about 320, of which some 200 were subsidiaries of about sixty companies, with a total repertory of approximately 150,000 works. As had been true of ASCAP until 1942, there was no printed catalogue of all the music SESAC licensed. A list of affiliated publishers was sent on request, with the suggestion that catalogues could be obtained directly from them.

SESAC's broadcasting license fees were not based on income, but on a variety of factors: station location, size of the community it served, hours on the air, and time-card rates. Thanks to the government's action in 1950 against the international cartelization of the foreign performing-rights field, formerly monopolized in America by ASCAP, SESAC had reciprocal commitments with twenty-four overseas performing-rights and/or mechanical-rights bodies.

SESAC was best known to the broadcasting business for its station-relations field staff, second only to that of BMI, and its LP Program Service. Musical-production aids, minute-long recorded instrumentals, and a library of music by well-known artists were sold as various packages to approximately 300 radio and television stations. The SESAC 45 Repertory Samplers of music in the basic library of 100 LPs were sent on request to all prospective clients.

The SESAC contemporary American repertory in 1963 was essentially gospel, folk, and religious music, which failed to turn up on the trade-paper charts until a Nashville office was opened early the next year to give it an opportunity to break into the country-music business. From time to time previously, a SESAC work, usually of foreign origin, had broken into best-selling lists, but there was never a major American popular-music firm among its affiliates, and the organization remained almost unknown outside the music business.

Of more interest was the quickening recognition of music catalogues and copyrights as highly profitable investments. For years, the value of copyrights had been kept low by a serious threat to the music business of confiscatory taxation, which could put many companies out of business. A ruling by the Treasury Department in the 1950s held that all royalty receipts from copyrights constituted personal holding-company income whenever they represented 80 percent or more of total revenues. With the decline in sheet-music sales and in their profit return of several hundred percent, mechanical royalties began to exceed 80 percent of gross revenue by the early 1950s, leaving some publishers liable to a surtax of 75 percent on the first $2,000 and 85 percent income over that. A bill to relieve the situation took years to get through Congress, finally reaching President Eisenhower's desk in 1960. The removal of this threat to the solvency of a music company strengthened outsiders' interest in the business and speeded up the traffic in catalogues and copyrights.

During 1963 through 1965, millions of dollars passed through the hands of parties involved in major sales. The Aberbachs purchased Progressive

Music, Atlantic Records' publishing division, and the Duane Eddy and Paul Cohen firms, for a total of $1.3 million. Bobby Darin bought Trinity Music, the former Csida-Joy-Burton company, for a half-million dollars. Paul Anka bought back all his copyrights, master tapes, and reissue rights from ABC-Paramount for a sum in excess of $200,000. Gene Autry sold most of his music holdings, for a six-figure sum. A one-third interest in Bregman-Vocco & Conn was bought by E. H. Morris for an undisclosed amount believed to be around $500,000, in anticipation of the purchase of the remaining shares. Lawrence Welk continued to make inconspicuous purchases of ASCAP and BMI firms, building a publishing empire. BMI sold its last owned-and-operated music house, Associated Music Publishers, which specialized in contemporary American and foreign concert music, to G. Schirmer, a power on the ASCAP board of directors. Lew Chudd's catalogue of 2,300 master tapes and 6,000 copyrights was sold to Liberty Records for more than two million dollars. ABC-Paramount's purchase of the M. M. Cole business, one of BMI's earliest affiliates, which had more than 5,000 country-and-western copyrights, picked up over a forty-year period, left RCA Victor alone among the Big Five manufacturers without a publishing subsidiary. Four Star Television expanded into the record and music business by buying Sherman and Devorzon Music and Valiant Records.

Regarded as the most significant sales during this period were those of the Leeds and Duchess music businesses to MCA and Mills Music to Utilities & Industries Management Corp. of New York City, a $42-million public-utilities holding company that had been doing business for seventy-five years.

After seeking unsuccessfully to buy E. B. Marks once BMI's option on it was returned, MCA took the first step in a plan to build a music-business empire equal to Warner Brothers' MPHC or MGM-Loew's Big Three. For a price reportedly more than $4.2 million, it bought out the interests of veteran music man Lou Levy in Leeds Music (ASCAP) and Duchess Music (BMI), together with subsidiaries in Canada, England, and Australia, and the United States representation of AmRuss's catalogue of modern Russian concert music. In the course of a show-business career that had begun in 1933 when he won a prize in New York City's famous Harvest Moon Ball, Levy had come into the publishing business in the mid-1930s with Leeds Music. Through a close connection with Decca Records and Jack Kapp, he got access to the songs written by Sammy Cahn and Saul Chaplin, which were frequently recorded on the Decca label, and the music of many Decca artists, among them the Andrews Sisters, whom he managed for years. In addition to Duchess Music, formed in the 1940s, Levy owned nearly two dozen other catalogues, including one formerly belonging to Clarence Williams, a pioneering black A & R producer of race music; and the Wabash and Mayo catalogues, into which much early rhythm-and-blues music of the 1930s and 1940s, recorded on Decca's Sepia label and RCA Victor's

Bluebird label, was placed. With a keen eye for the international market, Levy picked up the American rights to many songs that became American hits, as well as two of the Beatles' earliest successes, "I Want to Hold Your Hand" and "P.S. I Love You." The sale to MCA also included a contract for Levy's exclusive services as a director of MCA and operating head of MCA-Leeds Music.

The financing for the Mills Music sale was far more complicated than that for the Levy firms. Since the late 1950s, there had been recurrent reports of the sale of the company to various interests. The usual offer included a reasonable down payment, with amortization of the remainder spread over a period of years. In the words of the tax attorney who set the pattern for the Mills sale, it was "subject to a major participation in the annual proceeds resulting from performances, mechanical and other uses of the copyrights included in the Mills catalogs. This participation will be offered for direct subscription by shareholders of Utilities & Industries Corp. The present owners of Mills Music will realize $5 million from the transaction." In 1964, Mills Music had gross receipts of $1.4 million, including $530,379 from ASCAP and from Canada, double those of a decade before.

Jack Mills, president of Mills Music, held a 51 percent controlling interest in the company, his brother Irving 39 percent, and the firm's attorney, Sam Buzzell, 10 percent. During the years, Mills had bought up many old companies, some for as little as $300, and had built up a catalogue of 25,000 copyrights by the time of the sale. Among them were Joseph Daly Music, Gus Edwards Music, Gotham-Attucks—the first all-black-owned popular-music firm—Kalmar, Puck & Abrahams, Keit Music, Theodore Morse Music, B. F. Woods Music, Vandersloot Music, and Waterson Berlin & Snyder. The last-named company, stripped of its Berlin and many other valuable copyrights, was bought by Mills at auction after Henry Waterson went into bankruptcy in the 1920s. Jack Mills had also built up a wholly owned group of overseas subsidiaries in Brazil, Mexico, Canada, England, Spain, France, Germany, and the Benelux countries.

After $500,000 was put down for an option to buy, a public offering of 277,712 shares of Mills Music, worth $4.5 million, was fully subscribed within a few days, at a unit price of $6.50 a share. The balance of $2.25 million was raised through bank loans. A week later, Mills stock was selling at around $17 a share. U & I's attempt to get a place on the ASCAP board was rebuffed when the membership failed to reelect Jack Mills to the directorship he had held for years.

During the copyright sales' boom, a number of music-business giants died: Louis Bernstein at eighty eight, Max Dreyfus at ninety, and Herman Starr, outliving any attempt to put him out to pasture at MPHC, at sixty six. Six days prior to Dreyfus's death, Chappell's London office burned down; the loss was more than a million dollars. Louis Dreyfus was now in full charge of the world-wide music empire, whose centerpiece, Chappell

Music, had been purchased in the late 1920s with proceeds from brother Max's sale of his earlier music holdings to Warner Brothers.

Irving Berlin's "White Christmas" continued to be the most valuable single copyright yet known. In the twenty-two years since 1942, when it was written as one of a package of anniversary and holiday songs for the Paramount movie *Holiday Inn,* the song had become an unexpected success. It had sold 40-million recordings and 5,587,730 printed copies, including sheet music. Since that success, the Beatles and their completely original body of recorded copyrights had brought a change in the economic character of the business. When 1.2 million shares of stock, worth twenty-eight cents each but offered at $1.09, in Northern Songs, the publishing company owned by John Lennon, Paul McCartney, Brian Epstein, and Dick James Music, went on sale in February 1965, Richard Rosenthal, the financier president of U & I's Mills Music, remarked that Mills owned valuable standard songs, whereas Northern had a catalogue that was "considerably more recent, if not more transient."

Northern Songs was formed in 1963, with Lennon and McCartney each owning 20 percent of the company; Brian Epstein and his Nemperor Holdings, 10 percent; Dick James Music, which had a ten-year managerial contract, 50 percent. The company's chief assets in 1965 were fifty-six Beatles copyrights and a contract for six new Lennon and McCartney songs a year for ten years. Actually, the songwriters had assigned their music to Maclen Music, a wholly owned American subsidiary, which assigned all future copyrights to Northern. Seventy-five percent of Dick James Music was owned by James, a one-time band and session singer, and the balance by his friend and accountant, Charles Silver. James and Silver also had pieces of other companies, formed with Epstein, pop star Gerry Marsden, and some American record companies, producing assets reported to be worth $12 million dollars in just a few years.

After the public offering of Northern Songs shares was closed, Lennon and McCartney owned 30 percent of the stock, worth about $640,000; Epstein, 7.5; and James and Silver 37.5. The small balance of 1.6 percent was divided between George Harrison and Ringo Starr. At the close of fiscal 1965, Northern Songs showed pretax profits of $1.7 million, and paid a 37.5 percent dividend. Three years later, during a fight by outside interests to get control of Northern, nearly five million dollars was offered for any outstanding shares from the 1965 sale.

Only one American publisher had shown any interest in the Beatles and their songs prior to their 1964 tour of America. He was the veteran Tin Pan Alley song plugger George Pincus, who had gone into business for himself in the 1950s. In 1962, he had opened a London branch, Ambassador Music, placing one of his sons, Lee, in charge, Pincus had little competition from rival American publishers. Only a handful of them had established working arrangements with the English rock-'n'-roll music business.

Even before the formation of Northern Songs, Pincus, who was a walking compendium of stories about the American music scene and the giants in it for whom he had worked, had found an audience and a soul mate in Dick James. Through his good offices, a Pincus copyright, "A Taste of Honey," was one of the few nonoriginal songs the Beatles ever recorded. In 1963, James made a deal with Pincus for the American rights to a half-dozen Lennon-McCartney copyrights, including "She Loves You," which was number one early in 1964, but had failed to impress the Capitol executives.

The affiliation with BMI of Northern-Maclen Music and other Dick James properties prior to the start of the Beatles' popularity in America was one of a series of business coups that brought virtual equality with ASCAP in terms of air play and prestige, if not in income from music users. The key to this success was the youth market, 20 million teen-agers with $10 billion to spend and a special affinity for BMI's music. Attributing BMI's continuing success, not to this, but to the conspiracy and questionable practices charged in the ten-year-old and dormant Schwartz lawsuit, ASCAP's management and some of its board shifted their complaints from courts and hearing rooms to the Justice Department, expecting, at the very least, an amended BMI consent order.

Carl Haverlin's sixteen years as president of BMI came to an end in 1963, at a time when BMI's roster of writers and composers included 6,871 names and there were 5,603 affiliated publishers. *Billboard,* in December, marked Haverlin's retirement in an editorial, saying in part, "few would deny that our industry today is at once more competitive and more truly a part of the national heritage than ever before. It is indeed a distinguished ornament, a treasure to the fabric of the nation. Much of this development was brought into focus by what may be termed the Haverlin Era—during which period Carl Haverlin, with a large measure of insight and graciousness, guided the destiny of BMI."

The departure of the networks, through divestiture and resignation of their representatives as directors, had shifted the balance of power on the BMI board to directors associated with important station groups and successful independent broadcaster stockholders. As major executives with corporate experience, the directors intended to bring a more businesslike administration to the BMI operation. Much control shifted to a newly formed executive committee.

Haverlin's predilection for music of all kinds, from the 1953 rhythm-and-blues hit "Shake a Hand" to that of Edgard Varèse, Charles Ives, Harry Partch, and Alan Hovhaness, had often been perceived as unseemly or whimsical by the new breed of matter-of-fact broadcaster executives on the BMI board. He had been the only businessman present at a meeting called by the Ford Foundation in 1951 to foster performances of modern American concert music; he had offered both support and action. Several

concerts subsidized by BMI followed, including Leopold Stokowski's introduction of electronic music, and in 1953, one at which a Carnegie Hall
audience that included sixty United Nations representatives heard the first
full concert of all-Canadian music in the United States. Haverlin plucked
Oliver Daniel, a concert-music program director and producer at CBS, away
from his part-time management of the American Composers Alliance to
head BMI's new Concert Music Department in 1954. Daniel was immediately instrumental in bringing Charles Ives into BMI, as well as other important composers, and in the formation of Composers Recordings, a commercial record label of which the ACA was the majority stockholder. In the
ACA Bulletin, the association's president at the time, Avery Claflin, wrote:

> The broadcasting and record-playing business being what they are today, the
> composer gets his great initial opportunity, not by being performed, not by
> being published, but by being recorded. Once a record is available, it inevi-
> tably gets around to the esthetically curious, the non-commercial broadcasters
> (and even some commercial ones), and the leaders of college and other non-
> profit groups . . . in this manner audience familiarity gradually can be built
> up and a composition makes its way more on merit than caprice.

A survey of broadcasting stations made in 1954 disclosed that 78 percent
of them aired some concert music. The 175,000 LPs of concert music being
supplied to stations by large manufacturers without charge or for a small
fee were worth one million dollars at retail. The radio stations serving as
the chief medium for bringing serious modern and classical music to Americans were small competition to the two giant concert bureaus—Columbia
Artist Management and National Concert & Artist Corp.—both spin-offs of
the divestiture of the CBS and NBC artist bureaus, forced by the FCC in
the early days of World War II. The two new bureaus allocated to one
another the 1,200 American cities, where their Community Concerts and
Civic Concerts subsidiaries provided music by the 200 artists each managed. Their practices were not only monopolistic; they also determined what
live music American concertgoers would hear. A government antitrust suit
against them was brought in 1951 in response to complaints from smaller
independent managers. It ended with a consent decree in 1955, after which
the concert management and performance business was ostensibly open to
all competitors and the future of modern American music was considerably
enhanced.

BMI's activities in this connection, plus the proselytizing of radio, played
a part in the "massive unstopping of the American ear," according to *Time*
in 1957, to hear the widest breadth of live and recorded music ever available. In 1958, more than 4,000 pieces of American music were performed
by American orchestras, and a thousand recordings of American music could
be purchased. For the first time, it might be possible for a gifted American
composer to make a living by devoting the major portion of his time to his

music. The publication of a score and parts for a modern concert work was feasible, because thirteen public performances paid for costs and connected expenses. Among those benefiting from this improvement were the winners of prizes given in another project Haverlin created, BMI's Student Composers Awards, initiated in 1951, out of which came many future Pulitzer Prize winners. Ironically, one of the first orders of business following Haverlin's retirement was the disposition of the AMP, the BMI subsidiary that served as publisher for many new concert compositions.

A sense of urgency to shift part of the load of performing-rights payments to other music users, out of fairness to broadcasters, was also evident. The Beatles' sold-out closed-circuit telecast, shown in 100 theaters in March 1964, provided a unique opportunity to enforce a new policy. A 1 percent share of the gross take from all promoters was enforced for access to the BMI repertory, to be divided equally among the writers and publishers of music performed, after a modest collection fee was withheld by BMI. The old, modest policy had been instituted in 1947, under which BMI's share of the market was almost nonexistent. The new policy was extended to cover all venues—concert halls, arenas, auditoriums, and college campuses, the last of which accounted for half of all nonbroadcast live music in the United States, but paid nothing for the right to perform it.

In order to build up a significant catalogue of standard songs from the musical theater and feature motion pictures, BMI inaugurated a new writer-distribution policy, which tripled payments for them. A similar system for concert music was already in place, and had led to serious competition with ASCAP for composers of modern music. Screen-music composers benefited particularly as BMI amassed the greatest collection of new movie scores since its formation. So, too, did popular-song writers who supplied feature songs for 1964's beach-party movies, the Elvis Presley pictures, and other youth-oriented features.

A group of veteran Hollywood composers and independent smaller publishers had retained counsel to ascertain why synchronization arrangements, with reduced rates, continued to be made between studio-owned music firms and the major production companies, a price-fixing situation that affected them vitally. Most publishers paid a share of the synchronization fees to composers but neglected to share any additional performance royalties. Acting on the complaint of 132 CLGA-ASCAP members, the Justice Department recommended to the society that it base all payments for screen music on its duration, a suggestion counter to the demand of guild members that their music be treated on a par with feature songs. The government intervention did lead to further reforms in the distribution process, however, as well as to BMI's bonus payments for theater and movie feature songs.

The winner by 1964 of four Oscars for the best song written for a feature motion picture, Henry Mancini was a contemporary bridge between the music of Erno Rapee, Erich Korngold, and Dimitri Tiomkin and that of

Earle Hagen, Jerry Goldsmith, and Quincy Jones. He was equally capable of satisfying the technical and artistic requirements of a studio sound stage and an RCA Victor recording session. A big-band pianist and arranger during the late 1940s, he had started at Universal in 1952 by writing the score for an Abbott and Costello movie. After achieving recognition, he found himself in a position to hold on to half of each new copyright, which, in the past, he had been obliged to assign to studio-owned publishing houses. His royalties from Paramount's Famous Music for *Breakfast at Tiffany's* were more than $230,000, including those from Andy Williams's hit single and the album "Moon River." The film sound tracks he recorded from *Breakfast at Tiffany's, The Days of Wine and Roses, Hatari, Charade,* and *The Pink Panther* sold millions of copies, though they were actually recreations that included material that had been cut, and were made in a recording studio. The original music had been considered too episodic for the LP market. Few screen composers were in Mancini's position in 1964, when he was able to stop working for videofilm producers and to take one out of every ten assignments offered.

The failure of the motion-picture and television producers to recognize the Composers and Lyricists Guild of America as the bargaining agent for its 400 members raised the possibility of a strike by all screen composers and copyists some time in 1964. The guild had already gone to the NLRB, only to get the ruling that the power of videofilm producers was "insufficient to establish an employer-employee relationship," and that "all composers in the unit sought are independent contractors." The fight to win recognition and a contract took thirteen months, during which the producers negotiated with other more powerful guilds and craft unions. At a fundraising concert in Hollywood Bowl in September 1964, sixty Academy Award–winning works and 310 nominations from the pens of CLGA members were performed, with fourteen of the best-known CLGA members conducting their own music. The two-year contract that was approved by the producers' association in June 1965 recognized the guild and set a base of $325 a week for composers under contract and $350 for those employed temporarily; covered all guild members by the industry health and welfare plan; gave composers and lyricists a year's option to buy back any music or songs that had not been used, following a five-year period of grace; affirmed the guild members' right to collect their share of performance royalties through the societies with which they were affiliated; and provided some other major benefits. A few months later, a similar pact was signed by the Society of Independent Producers.

The perseverance of Fred Fox and the Sam Fox Music Company to seek payment from motion-picture companies for the use of music originally written for the screen but then sold to television was rewarded in July 1964. An out-of-court settlement offered by 20th Century-Fox was accepted, paying Fox Music $100,000 over a ten-year period by increasing payments to it already agreed upon for acting as selling and licensing agent for the film company's own Movietone Music. Other suits had been filed, unsuccessfully, over the years to resolve the issue, but Fred Fox had persisted, winning this Pyrrhic victory when the studio avoided a definitive court decision on whether or not film producers could deal with television by offering the compromise. The film industry had resolved the post-1960 situation in this respect by including in all contracts with composers and lyricists permission from them to use their music in theaters and all other media.

When ASCAP's friend in court, Judge Ryan, failed to include the divestiture of BMI in the package of compromises he suggested early in 1964, the society embarked on its own campaign of public attack on BMI. Formal expressions of the differences between ASCAP and BMI were made by Stanley Adams at membership meetings and during the celebration of the society's 50th anniversary. The standard line ran: ASCAP was made up of composers and publishers, BMI was owned by broadcasters, who subsidized "a vast supply of music, much of it inferior," and attempted to dictate public taste; unlike the society, BMI "would not bind itself to a distribution formula which is published to the world"; BMI did not allow its members to elect the board of directors; BMI continued to "subsidize selected writers, publishers, recording companies, producers, and their employees," and the time had come for the "liberation of BMI writers and publishers from the broadcaster domination that now exists."

With assurances by the Justice Department that presumably all was well, BMI went on with its business. The increased payments for feature music from motion pictures and theatrical productions had their salutary effects. BMI music was in seventy-two of the ninety-two prime-time TV programs scheduled for the 1964–65 season, much of it the work of former ASCAP writers who had switched affiliation to take advantage of the more attractive royalty system. The writers who created the scores for half-hour network programs averaged about $12,000 in BMI royalties.

The Justice Department's antitrust suit filed against BMI on December 10, 1964, offered the possibility that the government would itself put an end to BMI and the practices with which it was making ASCAP a second-class competitor. The complaint demanded that the broadcasters who owned BMI stock divest themselves of all holdings. Only one of that group of 517 was named, as representative of all and a co-defendant, RKO General, the largest remaining single stockholder after the networks' departure from BMI.

Nearly one year into his presidency of BMI, Robert Burton reminded the press that the company had been formed in 1939 to "combat what the [Justice] Department itself recognized as a complete monopoly by ASCAP. Every broadcaster has licenses from both BMI and from ASCAP and pays substantially more money to ASCAP. ASCAP is still the dominant performing rights organization and gets about two-thirds of all money paid for performing rights." Of the more than $40 million paid in performance fees for fiscal 1963–64, ASCAP had collected \$35 million and BMI \$14 million. Closer to the situation than the general press, *Variety* pointed out that the statistics accompanying the charges closely resembled those in the complaint in the Schwartz case. "The vast amount of research done in behalf of the ASCAP songwriters' suit against BMI, which fizzled out in inconclusive pretrial rulings in the New York Federal Court, have been made available to the Justice Department."

ASCAP would not comment on the suit, but a spokesman did say that there was no reason to believe that the government action was in any way inspired by the society. "They are surely capable of gathering their own information and making their own judgements." There was a theory, however, that unfiled actions rejected or put on hold by the Kennedy administration were activated by those who sought to show themselves to be Lyndon Johnson men. Among the unnamed defendants, but a party to the action because it owned stock in BMI, was the Austin-based Texas Broadcasting Corp., formerly the LBJ Co., owned by Mrs. Lyndon B. Johnson.

A general denial of all charges was made by BMI and RKO General in March 1965, as was a motion to dismiss the suit, which served only to postpone its resolution for at least a year.

A new strategy for the All-Industry Television Committee, agreed upon prior to the government suit, was outlined in documents filed with Judge Ryan in January 1965. They pleaded that no reasonable rate could be agreed upon by the committee unless it had access to ASCAP's full financial and other pertinent records dating back to the first television license. The fact that publishers had nothing to do with the background or incidental music that formed nine tenths of all local-station programing but got half of AS-CAP's net income was the central point in the new argument. An 80 percent increase in station payments to ASCAP, against a 33 percent rise in audiences in the 1957–64 period was offered as additional evidence that the present fees were "becoming increasingly unreasonable and excessive." Because the negotiations had been pending since 1961, longer than those with radio stations, they were now given precedence by the court, with the approval of ASCAP. The society was ordered to turn over various unspecified data as requested, but it delayed delivery by asking for similar information from the 365 stations that supported the committee financially.

ASCAP's income continued to soar—\$41 million for 1964 and \$42.7 million in 1965. Every one of the dually affiliated major publishers—the Big Three, Shapiro-Bernstein (whose BMI house had been opened in Nashville to get in on the country-music boom), MCA-Leeds, and Schirmer Music—were reelected to the ASCAP board in the annual membership voting. Clearly the "Big 15" dictated the publisher make-up of the board. Because the dually affiliated publisher issue was evidently ineradicable, Hans Lengsfelder and other veteran dissidents focused on the sampling of local-radio-station performances, on which a substantial portion of the society's income was expended. Stanley Adams reminded Lengsfelder that the changes he and his associates suggested in order to improve the fortunes of the small writer and publisher would cost additional millions of dollars. With 9,112 writers and 2,785 publishers sharing the 1964 distribution of $32.2 million, many members had received smaller checks and would oppose any changes made at such costs.

Additional sweeping changes in the distribution system and its criteria were approved in September 1965. Payments were speeded up to bring them nearer to the performance period on which they were based. With elimination of the recognized-works fund, publisher distributions would be based entirely on performances by 1968. The last lingering vestiges of videola were attacked, by crackdowns on the manipulation by members of network logging reports for across-the-board afternoon programs and a reduction in the value of authentic performances. Payments for music on nighttime strip shows were increased. A 20 percent reduction was introduced in the distribution to those at the top.

The entrance of the giant tape holding company, Minnesota Mining & Manufacturing, late in 1965, into the background-music business brought the American Guild of Authors and Composers again into conflict with large ASCAP publishers. The latter had negotiated with 3M for performing and mechanical rights, by-passing the Fox Agency and AGAC's own collection agency, thus violating, the guild charged, the 1948 Songwriters of America agreement. AGAC's collection agency, founded six years before, over the MPPA's protests, now collected two million dollars a year for 2,200 members. One quarter of the sum was recovered after surprise audits of publishers' books, which were permitted by the uniform songwriters contract.

A new 1⅞-speed, four-track, monaural tape machine, capable of playing twenty-six hours of 700 selections continuously was being merchandised by 3M. It was sold for around $430 to homes and commercial establishments. A standard background-music service contract had been negotiated with BMI for its entire repertory, but BMI publishers were expected to deal with the mechanical licensing. Most ASCAP publishers rejected the 3M proposal, but MCA-Leeds; Bourne; Shapiro, Bernstein; and a few other majors granted a license on the basis of a two-cents-per-tune annual payment for performances and a mechanical fee of three cents. AGAC argued that publishers who signed such bulk or block licenses without each writer's approval were violating the 1948 pact.

In January, the AGAC's president, Burton Lane, had startled the publishers with a proposal that the new contract, now two years in preparation, require all new copyrights to be taken out in the songwriter's name, a common practice in book publishing and for musical-theater writers. Lane said: "Under the new contract, the writer grants the music publisher the right to publish and license his material for records and other entertainment usage.

Since the music publisher is given the legal license to market the material, he is protected. He can secure recordings, collect monies, publicize and exploit, without any hindrance to his publisher's prerogative.'' Other proposed conditions were intended to further strengthen the rights of writers. An "option agreement" would require a music publisher to obtain a recording within six months, or pay a $250 advance for six months' extension. Contracts would be operative only after a first recording was secured.

Many of the proposed changes were eventually accepted, but the publishers held firm against the transfer of ownership of a song to the author and composer. To the present day, the writer "assigns, transfers, and delivers to the publisher . . . the right to secure copyright therein throughout the entire world.'' The 3M licensing arrangement remained in effect, accepted by most publishers, its validity based on a provision in the ASCAP consent order granting publishers a nonexclusive right to licenses performances.

The sudden death of BMI's second paid president, Robert Burton, in March 1965, shocked even old-line ASCAP publishers, who in the 1950s had considered offering him a major position with the society in order to remove him as a threat. The largest delegation to attend his funeral came from Nashville, where he had been a beloved figure, well known as one of country music's most ardent supporters. In recognition of this, *Billboard* had named him "Country Man of the Year" in 1964. Shortly before his election as BMI president, Burton was named to head the fund-raising committee for the CMA Hall of Fame and Museum. Plans were made for an elaborate building on Music Row. ASCAP and SESAC, both now visible presences in the city, were among the earliest contributors to the building fund.

The isolation of country music was long gone. At one point, executives of WSM had said that the station broadcast country music on Saturday nights, but "good music" the rest of the week. Now the Grand Ole Opry radio show was heard in 300 markets. Taped syndicated country-music video shows were spreading around the United States and crossing the oceans to Europe, South Africa, and the Far East. CMA's 1965 survey found 208 radio stations programming country music full-time compared with 97 two years before. The association now had 1,100 members and 111 supporting organizations. The Hall of Fame and Museum were nearing reality because of a unique LP merchandising scheme. Permission was granted by record companies, publishers, and artists, who waived all royalties, for the production of two LP albums to benefit the museum. An independent record merchandiser guaranteed $85,000 and a twelve-cent royalty on all sales. The first LP, for two dollars, sold more than one million copies, but it never got on the charts, a new occurrence in record history. When its sales went over four million units, the second LP was released, with equal success.

When ground was broken in the spring of 1966 for the $500,000 Country

Music Hall of Fame and Museum, BMI was already at home in its own building next door. Nashville then rivaled New York and Los Angeles as a music-business center, with ten recording studios, twenty-six record labels, 850 professional songwriters, amateurs ready everywhere to find fame in country music, and all three licensing organizations.

While the board and executive committee of BMI searched for a new chief executive, Sydney Kaye took charge. The first legal action was one against promoters of the Beatles' and other live and closed-circuit concerts, who had failed to take out the BMI license requiring 1 percent of gross admissions, introduced by Burton. Following BMI, ASCAP stepped up its own drive to collect for live concerts on an approximately similar basis. Credits were increased simultaneously by fifteen times for the performance of works in concert and symphony halls.

BMI's announcement that things had gone well on television, the 1965–66 season being the best in its history, came simultaneously with the election by the BMI board of Robert Sour as president in October. The revolt by popular-music concert promoters was cut short when the company adopted ASCAP's traditional seating-capacity formula for concert licensing. The payment formula, introduced the year before, for feature-picture songs was reduced by a third. The $1.08 per-station royalty for a TV network performance fell to 72 cents, and that on a local station from 72 cents to 48 cents. Feature-song performances on nonprime-time television were cut by one third. Sour said in an interview that he and BMI looked forward to parity between its writers and publishers in the near future, the equal sharing of all performance money.

In succeeding weeks, the publishers' share for performances on stations paying BMI less than $1,000 a year was reduced. The company had sustained a pretax loss of $1.7 million for the year ending June 31, 1965, and with performances climbing steadily, and disheartening results from studies of income received for the same songs by ASCAP and BMI publishers, the organization faced a problem of considerable proportions.

Approximately 7,000 publishers were already affiliated with BMI and sixty new ones were added every month. Few publisher contracts were terminated, rarely more than 100 a year, and then only because the publisher could not be located, there had been no activity for a number of years, or the publisher was engaged in illegal activities. Only seven publishers affiliated with BMI which were primarily engaged in the popular-music business had five-year guarantee contracts. Among them were E. B. Marks, Hill & Range, Peer, the Richmond organization, and Acuff-Rose (which alone generally exceeded its guarantees). BMI also had one-year guarantee contracts with twenty-seven other publishers, which ranged from $5,000 to $375,000, and totaled $1.6 million, representing 18.5 percent of the total BMI domestic publisher distribution and accounted for 19 percent of the company's logged air play. The amount of a guarantee was computed by averaging a publisher's performances over a three-year period and multiplying by ten cents, so that guarantees exceeded logged earnings.

Thirty-seven publishers of jazz, gospel, concert, and other music considered by BMI to be of cultural importance and deserving of support made up a third class of guarantee publishers. These had contracts for between $1,000 and $10,000 (higher in the case of a few larger concert-music houses) and received a total of $403,000 in 1965, or 4 percent of the entire distribution to publishers.

A bonus-payment category of publisher affiliates was created in order to decrease the number of guarantee publishers, a result of the phasing-out of ASCAP's credit for recognized works. Eligibility for bonus payments and the rates paid were determined by the number of performances logged in the prior year. These contracts generally ran for a year, after which they were reevaluated, and the publisher was shifted to a class appropriate to his previous performance totals. After logging 250,000 performances in the last four quarters, a publisher was paid a bonus, or overage, of 25 percent on each logged performance for the next year. The publisher who got 400,000 performances in a single year received a 50 percent overage for the following year. After the first full year under this arrangement, publishers had to have 300,000 performances for logging-plus-50 percent and about 150,000 for logging-plus-25 percent. The Beatles' Maclen firm and Presley Music were among the eighty-eight publishers in the first class during 1965, and there were sixty-six publishers in the second, the two groups being paid a combined total in 1964–65 of about $2.5 million. Approximately sixty publishers had contracts for advances against estimated earnings, representing $1.65 million in this period. Such contracts were based on estimates of the publisher's potential earnings in terms of previous earnings history, or, sometimes, on current trade-paper-chart performance. Most advances were earned during the year, or, if proved overly optimistic, recouped in the following year.

Of the 9,000 writers affiliated with BMI in early 1965, all but about 400 were paid at standard rates called for in the BMI writer contract. The others had contracts that provided advances or guarantees in direct relation to predictable earnings showings. BMI had no bonus system for writers comparable to that compensating publishers. There were few straight guarantee agreements. Out of the approximately 400 writer affiliates, 187 had three-year contracts that paid them a guarantee equal to 150 percent of earnings logged during the preceding year, ranging from less than $1,000 to more than $30,000. These totaled about one quarter of all BMI writer distributions in fiscal 1965, or $4.1 million. Fifty-seven jazz composers and twenty-eight composers of concert music, who were treated alike by BMI, had guarantee contracts for varying periods of time, for a total amount of $166,096.

Fifty-three composers of television theme and/or background music had agreements of up to five years that amounted to $669,000, which contrasted with total TV writer earnings of about one million. With twelve and a half hours of prime TV network time a week and ten daytime programs, Earle Hagen was BMI's highest-paid video-film composer, responsible for the music on the top-rated *Andy Griffith, Dick Van Dyke, Gomer Pyle,* and *I Spy* shows.

At the end of 1965, an initial 10 percent cut in the value of performances over a three-year spread was instituted, part of a program to retrench that was the result of increasing high cost per use of the BMI repertory by radio and television broadcasters. In extending the BMI radio pact for another year, from March 11, 1964, Robert Burton had written that his company did so without prejudice to its claim for more money from radio, and that the extension could be terminated by either party on three months' notice. Robert Sour's letter to the Radio Committee of December 8, 1965, reminded it of that privilege and asked for "all possible speed and diligence" in negotiating an increase. The rates in effect since 1941, when BMI's first and only contract was drawn, ranged from 1.2 percent for a station with income over $100,000 to .72 percent for those at the bottom, minus specified deductions—sales and agency commissions, and time, frequency, and volume discounts. Radio's pretax profits for 1965 were $72.8 million. The four radio networks showed an operating loss of one million, but their owned-and-operated stations had revenues of around $36 million. Ninety-one radio stations had incomes of more than one million dollars.

After a breathing time, during which no more progress was made and an offer to arbitrate the rates BMI intended to ask, using the services of the American Arbitration Association, was refused, BMI sent a three-month cancellation notice to all stations. It had been hinted to the company that the committee would recommend a 20 percent increase, provided the contract was for a long period. BMI accepted the suggestion in the proposed contract accompanying each termination notice. The final agreement, approved by the committee in June 1966, raised BMI's blanket license rate by 12.5 percent, the first raise in twenty-six years, during the last twenty of which the average radio station trebled the use of BMI music.

At the end of November, the government officially abandoned its attempt to force 517 stockholders to give up their stock in BMI, but did order some changes in the company's practices, none of them of sufficient substance to harm its operation or structure. BMI was barred from recording or printing and distributing music, and prohibited from entering into a contract for more than five years. Affiliated writers and publishers were allowed to issue nonexclusive licenses. The type of contract BMI had made with Hill & Range in 1949, which enjoined a publisher from doing business with another licensing organization, was also prohibited. BMI could not force other parties to record or perform any stated quota of music to which it had the performing rights. Many of the provisions were identical to those of the

1941 decree, but, as Sour said in a public statement, "compliance with other provisions of the order could not hamper BMI in any way."

ASCAP declared its intention to intervene in *United States* v. *BMI* during the mandatory thirty-day waiting period before the decree was entered, and asked for an evidentiary hearing, which would, in effect, try the Schwartz lawsuit. The society's principal claim was that the settlement was not in the public interest because it approved the broadcasters' ownership of a music licensing organization. In January, a federal court judge affirmed the consent decree and ruled against ASCAP's plea, as well as one by AGAC, using as precedent another music-business proceeding, in which the Supreme Court ruled against the Sam Fox Music petition to intervene in the 1950 amended consent order in *United States* v. *ASCAP*. According to *Variety*, the society was hoist by its own petard.

During the past several years, many things on other fronts had not gone as well as the society's management and board wished. The most recent Celler bill to repeal the jukebox exemption languished in the House Rules Committee. The Music Operators of America had thrown up a roadblock earlier in the year by proposing an increase in mechanical rates to be paid by operators in lieu of any license from the performing-rights organizations. ASCAP and BMI objected, as did the Recording Industry Association of America, coming out for the first time in public in opposition to the jukebox industry. That group's antipathy to ASCAP in particular, as the personification of its potential oppressors, had been reflected in the statements of many legislators during the Rules Committee hearings, as had the general misinformation about the music industry and ASCAP on the part of Congress.

The blue-ribbon Copyright Revision Panel assembled in the summer of 1963 to assist the Copyright Office in formulating omnibus revision legislation was a witness to the disparate interests of creators, owners, and users. The RIAA tore into proponents of either the removal of compulsory licensing or a higher statutory rate. The MPPA was for either or both. Music and book publishers fought any reversion of a copyright to the creator of the work after twenty-five years. The MPPA protested that its members lived off the old standards and needed more than a quarter-century hold on their property. The strongest opposition to extension of the life of copyright came from the National Association of Broadcasters and the networks. Students, professors, librarians, and the entire educational establishment, all of them photoduplicators of copyrighted music without payment, appeared to regard themselves as different—a privileged class that should not be hampered in its work by consideration of the protection of intellectual property.

The panel's work and final recommendations were introduced in both houses the following summer, with the certain knowledge that Congress would adjourn without taking action. Compulsory licensing would be retained, and the mechanical rate would go from two to three cents, or one cent per minute of play, whichever was greater. Strengthened civil and criminal penalties against record piracy were established, and the jukebox exemption was to be removed. The copyright term would be extended to the span of the author's life and fifty years. After a period of thirty-five years, authors of their heirs could, with two years' notice, transfer a copyright. The exemption of payment for a ''not-for-profit'' performance was revoked, and only in-school use, educational radio or television broadcasts, and performances where no admission was charged or the money went to education, churches, or charities would be exempt. An ad-hoc committee on copyright revision of twenty-four educational groups immediately opposed the bills, specifically the elimination of the not-for-profit limitation and the limitation on fair use of copyrighted materials, printed music among them, which was intended to harness photoduplication and distribution.

The RIAA's appearance in opposition was indicative of the schism between users and creators. Everyone, as *Variety* reported in June 1965, was in favor of new copyright legislation, as long as he did not have to pay for it, and Congress was treading most carefully in the face of organized national opposition from educators. After 163 witnesses had provided 2,300 pages of testimony and 1,600 pages of written documents, the House Copyright Subcommittee had concluded its 1965 hearings and was ready to start the whole business all over again in January. The Senate had been less active on copyright, finally squeezing it in during three days of hearings before the session came to an end. There were few positive results. The MOA had yielded slightly and was ready to discuss again the possibility of an extra two-cent charge for each new recording put into a coin-operated machine. The Copyright Office had toyed with the notion of a performance royalty for the use of recordings on radio, then decided not to push it in the face of new opposition from the broadcasters.

The following year, the House subcommittee wrote a mammoth and much altered new revision bill. The chief new provisions affecting the music business contained some compromises. The term of copyright remained the author's lifetime plus fifty years. The jukebox operators were faced with a tax of about nineteen dollars on each machine. The statutory mechanical rate was raised by only a half penny, two and a half cents or a half cent for each minute of playing time, whichever amount was larger.

Time was again too short to get the bill through the complicated legislative processes, and the game would have to begin again in January 1967. As Abraham L. Kaminstein, the father of revision, warned its supporters, they would do well to go ahead with what they were offered in the proposed bill. ''To see the job through,'' he warned, ''I think it is up to you to go forward on the truly significant issues and the matters that are aimed at strengthening rather than weakening the bill. . . . I do remind you that we have a deadline of December 31, 1967. This is the date when all renewal copyrights that were extended by the interim expansion acts of 1963 and 1965 will expire."

In 1965, the Supreme Court's refusal to hear Metromedia's appeal for a blanket license on the terms fixed by the station group was one of ASCAP's few victories on the broadcasting front. The informal agreement made with the TV networks late in 1964 again bogged down in argument. In a compromise early in 1966, ASCAP offered a fixed-annual-payment contract to them, to extend over five years, replacing the long-established arrangement of a percentage of time sales, created by Claude Mills in the early 1930s in collaboration with Edward Klauber of CBS. No specific amounts were made public, but court records later showed that CBS had paid $3.9 million to the society and later agreed to pay $546,790 more. The proposed flat-fee contract applied only to the networks; their owned-and-operated stations continued to pay by the revised 1964 formula. CBS's principal problem and that of NBC, which had conditionally accepted the proposal, was how to explain the new arrangement to the affiliated stations. Their regular contributions of 50 percent and more of the networks' ASCAP fees remained buried in the language of the 1941 contract formula and were not generally known outside the networks' bookkeeping and executive departments. Under the proposed simplified new method for compensation by the networks, which reduced complicated accounting, the affiliates would learn the facts sooner or later. The immediate implementation of the flat-fee proposal was postponed, and the revised percentage agreements between the society and the TV networks continued in force.

Caught up in seemingly interminable legal proceedings, the TV-station committee considered accepting the new reduced network owned-and-operated-station formula: 1.94 percent on money equal to that earned in 1963, 1.325 on revenues above that. But it then decided to remain on its course toward a "reasonable rate." In the eight years starting in 1957, television-station fees to ASCAP had risen 76 percent, up to $11.3 million in 1964. Judge Ryan suggested that the stations and ASCAP quickly work out something "to eliminate auditing and constant friction," a calculated reference to the flat-fee deal, before his mandatory retirement as chief judge of the New York federal court in October 1966. That occasion came and went, 1966 passed into history, and Ryan remained in charge of all ASCAP matters in the purview of the consent orders.

The newest changes in the ASCAP distribution gave the society ammunition in 1966 to fight BMI for the new writers of hit songs, by putting, in Stanley Adams's words "more performance money into the pocket of new writers and giving them their money sooner." The amended consent order had been reinterpreted to give ASCAP the right to hand out cash advances to writers, based on their current activity as indicated on the trade-paper charts, the BMI practice that the society had so long fought to end. New members could start immediately on the 100 percent current-performance system of payment, and change to four-fund performance averaging after several years, during which these were counted. Performances of BMI-licensed works brought over to ASCAP, which had taken place in the prior nine months, were counted in the ASCAP surveys, giving dual payment from the societies.

When he officially announced ASCAP's income for 1966, $52.6 million, Adams, president of the society for the eighth consecutive term, took advantage of the occasion to brand the new BMI consent decree as "the greatest invitation to payola that exists anywhere." This statement came when many believed there was a thawing of the long cold war between the two organizations.

Some months earlier, in May 1966, the Music Publishers Protective Association, center of the old-boy network of ASCAP publishers, formed in 1917 at the insistence of the Albee vaudeville trust to curb payola being paid by the very music companies that became its members, had changed its name. Just as SPA officials had felt in 1958, that the "protective" in its name represented a shoddy period of American history, the MPPA was no longer comfortable with their name and changed it to the National Music Publishers Association.

Of more immediacy to the new NMPA than copyright or piracy was the overbearing presence of the Harry Fox Agency, which for many years had cast a shadow over the MPPA. Though Fox was an employee, he operated from a separate office adjacent to that of the MPPA and had outright autonomy, won for him by the association's legal counsel in a series of actions against record companies deficient in forwarding mechanical royalties. The agency now represented more than 2,300 publishers, including all major houses except MCA-Leeds and those in the MPHC, whereas the NMPA had a membership of fifty, some of whom were often delinquent in paying their dues.

Early in 1927, Claude Mills, then chairman of the MPPA board, had devised its synchronization licensing contract and collection apparatus, making himself responsible for all transactions involving the Warner Brothers Vitaphone system in the United States and Canada at a 10 percent agent's commission. Eventually, he took over the collection of mechanical fees, for the smaller commission of 5 percent. John Paine replaced Mills in 1929 and made an MPPA clerk, Harry Fox, his assistant. Then in his early thirties, Fox was also responsible for handling the quarters and fifty-cent pieces sent in by radio stations and advertising agencies for each use of an electrically transcribed popular or production song. When he became head of the agency, it took his name.

The phonograph industry's postwar resurgence raised the Fox Agency's collections to five million dollars a year, half of it from the then Big Five manufacturers—Columbia, RCA Victor, Decca, Capitol, and Mercury. Within four years, collections doubled, and a branch was opened on the West Coast. Fox and Al Berman, his assistant, extended the business internationally, representing licensing societies in England, France, and Sweden on a reciprocal basis. In spite of all NMPA initiatives to enforce an understanding of its relationship to the Fox Agency, Harry Fox's autocratic control continued until his death in 1969, when the agency was separately incorporated as the Harry Fox Agency, a wholly owned subsidiary of the NMPA, with Berman at its head.

The buying and selling of copyrights and catalogues continued on a stepped-up pace in 1966, the third year of the Beatles' supremacy. E. H. Morris sold back his one-third interest to Bregman, Vocco & Conn for more than he had paid two years before to the late Rocco Vocco's family with the expectation that he would also pick up the remaining shares within a few years. Morris had been a silent founding partner in Bregman, Vocco & Conn when it was formed in 1938, investing $25,000. In 1943, he sold out for a few thousand dollars. Music executive Jack Bregman had been a pupil of the late Jack Robbins at the Big Three, in which he remained the only private partner in 1966, with a 4.6 percent interest after refusing all offers to sell out. Vocco headed the Leo Feist branch in Chicago and worked for the MPHC before becoming a partner in the firm bearing his name. Chester Conn was a successful songwriter-songplugger for Vocco in Chicago and then a Robbins employee under Bregman. The Morris sale was a prelude to 20th Century-Fox's purchase of the firm a few months later, for $4.5 million. An important part of the company's catalogue was the copyrights for the music in twenty-five musicals made by 20th Century-Fox during the war years. Had Morris retained his share of the company, he would have realized a profit of more than a million dollars.

The Aberbach brothers were the winners in spirited bidding for the twenty-seven-year-old ASCAP member Joy Music and some subsidiaries. The Joys, father and son, held out for two million dollars "on the barrelhead," which was paid by the Aberbachs in a transaction completed over twenty-four hours. The Joy Music takeover sweetened an arrangement Hill & Range Songs made with NBC-TV for a jointly owned television-music firm.

The purchase of a half-interest in the late Max Dreyfus's American Jubilee Music and New World Music in Britain by the British Associated Television Corp. was influenced by the growing interrelationship of the world-wide video business and the music industry. Publishers in America recognized the importance of access to a medium that offered the greatest promotion of their product, and video film makers were cognizant of the millions paid by television for music. Lew Grade, head of Associated Television, had first come into contact with popular music as a Charleston dancer in British variety, the poor man's theater in his adopted country. More recently, he had learned of the contemporary value of popular music through the sale of video series to CBS-TV network. After buying rights to the

Secret Agent television package, CBS at once threw out the original British theme music and substituted an American song, which became an immediate commercial hit and more than repaid the network's investment in the series. Associated Television was also a large stockholder in the British Pye Record Company, which Grade now perceived as a testing ground for the potential of all original music and songs written for his television series and specials.

The Europeans were getting into the American music business, and not only as rock-'n'-roll performers.

PART SIX

1967–1970

CHAPTER 21

Copyright Revision or Not?

That "knight without fear and without blemish" of the American Society of Composers, Authors and Publishers, Emanuel Celler, the man with the most seniority in Congress during the 1960s and chairman of the House Judiciary Committee for many years, suffered one of his major legislative setbacks on a Sunday morning in April 1967. It came at the hands of 7,000 persons who were not present at a conference in the Library of Congress, those "sturdy and vociferous small entrepreneurs," as the *Washington Post* described them, "who provide the taverns and way stations of American life with entertainment by jukeboxes." The meeting had been arranged to save at least part of the copyright legislation, which would be doomed otherwise.

The omnibus 1965 copyright revision bill had been reintroduced in Congress early in 1967. In April, it was reported out of the full Judiciary Committee, with Celler's blessing, and it appeared that it would have no difficulty in sailing through both houses. The Democratic leadership and the Republican House Policy Committee had both endorsed the legislation despite its several highly controversial provisions: payment for the use of copyrighted material by educational radio and television stations; a royalty for artists as well as manufacturers for the use of recorded music; payment of royalties for the first time by the young cable television industry for programs taken off the air and sent to subscribers over telephone lines; and a tax of about nineteen dollars on every jukebox, representing a total of around $10 million in collections if reports were true that half a million coin record players actually were in operation.

Pointing out during debate by the full House that Sweden charged from $20 to $198 per machine, Brazil $24 to $30, and Spain $30 to $90, Celler thundered: "Yet these people [the coin operators] want to go scot free and

493

pay nothing to the men who give their lives, their blood, their sweat and their tears to making these songs. The jukebox would be a junkbox without the song." Shortly after, pro-jukebox forces sought vainly to send the bill back to committee, but found surprising support in the 252 to 126 vote that defeated the proposal.

The unexpectedly large number of "yes" votes shocked Abraham Kaminstein, Register of Copyrights, who had been fighting to revise the Copyright Law for the past twelve years, as it did Herman Finkelstein, of AS-CAP, the prime proponent of the nineteen-dollar tax, and other music-business observers. "By mid-afternoon," the *Washington Post* observed, "they had the answer. It was turning into one of those Rube Goldberg days that the legislative titans find too painful to recall. The 'autocratic' jukebox lobby was being metamorphosed on the floor of the House into the last bastion of free expression for the little man. The Leadership Establishment was breaking up into quarreling sects."

Affronted because he had not been consulted, the chairman of the House Commerce Committee belatedly made it clear that he did not intend to let the cable TV business be taken out of his jurisdiction. In response to that and a series of other complaints supporting either the CATV interests or responding to pressures from the National Association of Broadcasters, the industry's lobbyists for restraint of cable television, patchwork amendments were offered, and Celler moved to withdraw the bill for the time being. In an off-the-floor negotiation, he agreed to drop the CATV section. It remained, however, for some move to effect a compromise to save the jukebox tax.

The Library of Congress conference involved three attorneys representing the jukebox business and the Music Operators of America's chief lobbyist, Nicholas Allen. On the government side were two lawyers and Kaminstein, with three associates. Representatives of ASCAP or any other music business or copyright interest had not been invited. The coin-machine people conceded that the time had come to make some payment for the use of music, but they felt that nineteen dollars was not reasonable. Kaminstein had come prepared to suggest an eleven-dollar figure, but, instead, accepted Allen's promise to make an offer on behalf of the MOA the following day.

It was not Kaminstein, but Celler who was blamed for the "Library of Congress surrender" by a majority of the copyright interests, including officials of BMI. It was their conviction that, through Celler, ASCAP was ready to sacrifice most of the nineteen-dollar jukebox license in order to save the "life plus fifty years" copyright provision, protection most vital to the society in preserving its repertory for future negotiations with music users.

The entire bill, including the revised jukebox amendment, was passed by the House with a near-unanimous vote and sent to the Senate and the hands of John McClellan, chairman of the Subcommittee on Patents, Trademarks and Copyrights. Even as the bill arrived, he was chairing a hearing on a proposition to give artists the same copyright protection for their recorded performances as that enjoyed by composers and publishers. The bandleader Stan Kenton, president of the National Committee for the Recording Arts, was among those who testified. The NCRA was not unlike Fred Waring's pre-World War II (National Association of Phonograph Artists, a loosely organized group of recording artists who asked to be paid when their music was used by broadcasters. Unlike the NCRA, NAPA had not enjoyed the financial backing of the manufacturers. The new artists' organization asked for the enactment of a law that would permit the record companies to copyright new recordings in their names and collect royalties when recorded music was played commercially on radio, television, and jukeboxes. The money collected was to be divided equally between the manufacturers and the artists, much in the manner in which ASCAP and BMI distributed their collections.

Alan Livingston, at the time president of Capitol Records, had first introduced the possibility of charging broadcasters for the use of recorded music in June 1965, when he was part of a delegation from the Recording Industry Association of America testifying against proposed copyright revision. This ploy to hold up or postpone enactment of the increased mechanical-recording rate was intended to bring broadcasters and their national association into active opposition to the bill. It proved to be immediately successful. Despite an increase of more than 50 percent in radio profits in the mid-1960s, the NAB objected to the "double payment" for music and regarded ASCAP and BMI fees as more than sufficient.

The recording industry, on the other hand, the expected recipient of half of all performers' license fees, excused the new taxation on the ground that it would aid "good music." As part of his prepared testimony for the 1965 hearing, according to Mitch Miller, in *Music Journal,* Livingston argued, with questionable candor, that "if performance fees were to go to the record company and the recording artist, the frantic concentration on rock-and-roll in the search for fast and large sales and quick return would stop. Sales are the only means of profit for the performer and record companies right now, so all music must be designed for the mass record-buying market. Let us be compensated for the use of our records on the air and we can record for the benefit of the vast listening audience who want good music."

The Register of Copyrights responded soon after to Livingston's proposal: "There is no doubt in my mind that recorded performances represent 'the writing of the author' in the Constitutional sense, and are as creative and worthy of copyright protection as translations, arrangements, or any class of derivative work. I also believe that the contributions of the record producer to a great many sound recordings also represent true 'authorship' and are just as entitled to protection as motion pictures and photographs."

Kaminstein never did go beyond that statement in working for recognition of the performance right, believing that it would, as expected by the RIAA, create a vast protest movement in opposition and hold up revision indefinitely. The NAB's massive campaign against Livingston's suggestion pleaded that radio was already paying 20 percent of its pretax profits to ASCAP and BMI, and that another $20 million to the artists and the manufacturers would double that percentage, placing "the burden on those least able to afford it—the small stations." In response, Kenton claimed that approximately 73 percent of all radio air time consisted of recorded music and produced 81 percent of all radio's income.

Nothing changed McClellan's determination that a new copyright bill would not emerge from his committee before the Supreme Court decided whether cable television should pay copyright royalties for the movies offered to its clients. The court had on its docket the case of *Fortnightly* v. *United Artists Television,* the plaintiff being a small West Virginia cable operation which sought a final ruling that CATV systems, Fortnightly's in particular, did not violate the Copyright Act when they imported distant signals for their subscribers. Lower courts had already ruled twice against Fortnightly, decisions which seriously affected the future of CATV as constituted. The Supreme Court reversed those rulings, McClellan could push through a provision calling for a minimum copyright fee from cable.

When the winter of 1967–68 passed and no action appeared to be forthcoming, Kaminstein asked to be allowed to present to the Senate committee his views on the situation, as well as those of a small group of copyright interests, chiefly the Authors' League and Broadcast Music, Inc. He urged that a temporary, "bare bones" revision bill, minus the most controversial provisions, be introduced. If something was not done, he said, the cause of copyright would lose the interest of Congress and set it back another several decades. The Authors' League was not interested specifically in the controversial life-plus-fifty-years provision, because most books enjoyed their great income in the first years of copyright. And now that the jukebox people had agreed to the eight-dollar compromise, which would also be part of the pared-down legislation, Sydney Kaye, of BMI, asserted that ASCAP's refusal to support the Kaminstein compromise was keeping an additional four million dollars or more from both ASCAP and BMI writers during each year of the society's stubbornness.

In public testimony in April 1968, Kaminstein pleaded his case, suggesting three alternatives: that writers, publishers, and Congress wait until next year; that the bill wait for the resolution of *Fortnightly* by the Supreme Court, and then the omnibus revision be pushed through; that Congress immediately pass the bare-bones revision. McClellan asked his committee to wait for the court. So revision of the 1909 Copyright Act was sidetracked for another six years, until 1974.

The Supreme Court's reversal in *Fortnightly* later in 1968 gave CATV a free hand in carrying copyrighted material without permission or payment, and, with revision apparently out of the way, McClellan held off any action affecting the cable business. Instead, five months after the FCC had been granted jurisdiction over cable by the *Fortnightly* ruling, it adopted an interim-procedures rule requiring cable to get permission from copyright owners to use their property. During the next four years, no such consent was asked or granted, and in this period of contradictory rulings from the Supreme Court and the FCC, CATV went its own way in the use of protected materials. Congress, in the meantime, regularly passed two-year copyright extensions to protect musical and literary properties that otherwise would have lost their protection and gone into the public domain.

CHAPTER 22

The Music-Licensing Wars

The now more than twenty-five-year-old antagonism between ASCAP and BMI had been further inflamed by the latter's successes in 1967, despite the terms of the latest consent order it had signed, which were expected to have exactly the contrary effect. BMI music totted up a 78 percent share of *Billboard*'s Hot 100 chart, 92 percent of its Top Country Hits, 100 percent of the Top R & B Hits, and 48 percent of the top Easy Listening Singles. In March of the year the three-year-old lawsuit to achieve "reasonable rates" was concluded, ASCAP accepted a 6.25-percent rate cut from radio stations, whereas its rival received a 12.5 percent increase from the same negotiating body, the All-Industry Radio Licensing Committee. The saving to broadcasters was estimated to be around $800,000, but because radio income was rising at an annual 8 percent rate, the society might in the future be even a bit ahead. Only because of ASCAP's sharply declining share of time on the air had the reduction been granted, a matter the society's board and executives intended to change. Precluded, as it long had been, from making payments to its members ahead of distributions, the sort of advances to publishers and writers on which most of BMI's success was believed to be based, ASCAP put into place a full 100 percent performance payment on a new member's joining, with the option of changing to the four-fund distribution system three years later. Funding was plentiful; ASCAP's income for 1966 was $52.7 million: $45.7 from domestic licensing revenue; $6 million from foreign collections; the balance from interest and dues.

As Stanley Adams, once again elected president of the society, explained: "Writers, at the end of three years, can elect to join the four fund system where performance fees are averaged over a five-year period. The first three years are counted in these averages, so that, in effect, he gets paid twice. For a new writer, ASCAP multiplies his first quarter of credits by four, paying him on a yearly basis.''

The enticement had been successful. Playing as well on the fact that ASCAP was run by publishers and writers who, unlike BMI's broadcaster-affiliated directors, were motivated to get the largest amount of money from licensees, the society made its first real inroads in Nashville, and elected Wesley Rose of Acuff-Rose Music to the board of directors. ASCAP's Nashville membership grew significantly.

Late in 1967, Adams proposed on behalf of his board that money be paid in advance to publishers in amounts of up to $20,000 a year, and that 2 percent of the entire publisher distribution be paid to firms that had achieved major positions on the trade-paper charts. The society had always maintained that BMI's advances and guarantees were unlawful. Learning from the new BMI decree that the Justice Department did not agree, by making no reference to the practice, ASCAP now was making changes in its own operating procedures.

BMI's fourth paid president in twenty-one years, Edward M. Cramer, took office at the end of March 1968, replacing Robert Sour, who became vice-chairman of the board. Cramer, a lawyer, had first become involved with BMI in 1953, when the Schwartz lawsuit was filed. For the next seven years he was active in many of the company's legal involvements. In 1960, he was retained by BMI's president, Carl Haverlin, as special counsel.

The new president was immediately confronted by a growing financial dilemma: BMI's music was being used with more and more frequency, but its income remained fixed while its distributions kept rising. Cramer had to prepare for emergency negotiations to effect an increase in radio license fees at the very time that the All-Industry TV Committee successfully concluded its lawsuit against ASCAP, winning a $53-million saving over the ten-year life of a new contract with the society. The old fee of 2.05 percent of station revenue was reduced to 2 percent of average industry income for the years 1964–65 and 1 percent of income over that. The sustaining fee, which had brought in about $2.4 million from telecasters, was cut by one third.

Cramer's insistence, in a letter to all radio licensees, that BMI was entitled to higher rates from them was quickly characterized as "foolhardy." Further meetings with the Radio Committee were broken off when new terms were announced calling for an increase in the maximum rate for all stations with receipts in excess of $100,000, from the present 1.35 percent to 1.79. As in the past, BMI did not ask for any sustaining fee. The committee argued that under the most recent contract BMI's income from radio had already jumped by about half in just two years, from $5.7 million in 1965 to $8.5 million in fiscal 1968. Countering that the increase was due to a similar increase in radio's revenues during that period, Cramer suggested arbitration, a proposal traditionally opposed by broadcasters. Terms were finally reached at the end of 1968. They raised BMI's fees 10 percent in the first year, to 26 percent over five years for all stations earning in excess of $80,000. This would increase BMI income by $820,000 the first year and $2.1 million in the fifth.

In a letter to all broadcasters, the committee reported that when discussions began with BMI in March "we were reluctant to recommend any increase in music costs [but] we finally concluded that an increase was justified not only because BMI is today furnishing more music than any other music-licensing organization, but also because your cost for using BMI music will be at least 25% less than the current sums you will be paying ASCAP during the term of the current ASCAP contract." *Variety* hailed the settlement as "an important victory" for Cramer personally, because of his insistence "upon a tough stance against the radio broadcasters [which] was upheld by BMI's board of directors, all of whom are broadcasters."

Additional changes in the ASCAP distribution policy, expected to improve the society's competitive position in popular music, were approved by Judge Sylvester Ryan in February 1969. Performance credits for ASCAP members regularly associated with across-the-board network programs were reduced, because they could, when they chose, rig the music logs. Among other changes approved by ASCAP's legal overseer were the formalization of cash advances to new publisher members in amounts up to $20,000, based on trade-paper charts, similar to those already being made to songwriters; an increase in credits for concert works of more than four minutes' playing time; and the reduction by 20 percent over two years in the amount flowing down from writers in classes above 1,000 points. The immediate effect of these changes was the resignation of another bloc of productive BMI writers and their publishers, about which BMI again complained to the Justice Department, again without receiving any relief.

Nearly a year after it had been announced in the summer of 1968, the new ASCAP contract with independent television stations was mailed, having been held up by a dispute over whether it should be extended to stations that owed money to the society. Court papers were made public at the same time showing that both CBS-TV and NBC-TV had agreed to make additional cash payments to ASCAP for the years 1964 through 1968; these waited only for Judge Ryan's approval of a similar flat-fee payment for 1969. The rationale for this new method of payment was the changes, beginning in the mid-1960s, in the manner in which sponsors bought network time. A single advertiser no longer purchased an entire program, but bought time in minutes; the fees included both time and program charges. Such shows as *Laugh In, Mission Impossible,* and *Mayberry RFD* got $65,000 for a minute. Hence the proposed change from the time-honored percentage of advertising revenue to the fixed rate, which had the additional advantage to networks of knowing in advance what the cost of ASCAP music would be, as well as reduced record-keeping and the elimination of ASCAP auditing. The proposal called for CBS to add $4.2 million to the $23.7 it had already paid through 1968, and $5.68 million for 1969. NBC agreed to add $3 million to the $22.9 million already paid for 1963 through 1968, and $5.68 million for the next year. Negotiations with ABC-TV along the same lines were under way.

Contending that, like ASCAP, it had contracts calling for a percentage of income, BMI asked for a correction of the underpayment to which the networks had admitted. With a network-TV rate of about half that of AS-CAP, BMI reckoned it was owed around $3.5 million by the two chains. Interestingly, the "Chinese bookkeeping" used in the past by the networks to hide their affiliates' payments of a share of music fees had been abandoned, to a degree, and CBS affiliates were notified that their share of the extra payment would be about one quarter of the total sum.

CBS proved to be particularly difficult in negotiations dealing with the underpayment, because of what its officials dubbed BMI's "impossibly high demands." In late October, BMI sent a notice of termination of license to the network. The argument ended just before Christmas, when CBS dropped a bomb whose repercussions would be felt by the music business well into the next decade. In similar letters sent to both licensing bodies, CBS asked for a new form of licensing, a per-use arrangement, "under which the amounts to be paid are based on the actual use of copyrighted music." A CBS-TV vice-president wrote, "we are quite prepared to consider a rate structure reflecting the relative values of different uses of music. For example, you might wish to offer per-minute rates, based on the time of day during which the music is performed (and thus on the size and character of the potential audience) and also to the different uses to which the music is put—feature performance, background performances, and performances in commercial announcements."

In ASCAP's case, such a request, combined with the termination of network contracts at year-end, demanded a sixty-day period of negotiation and, failing an understanding, an appeal to the federal court for resolution. BMI, on the other hand, had already given notice of termination of any right to play its music as of New Year's Day. CBS asked ASCAP and BMI for an extension of the contracts on an interim basis. At the same time, the network filed complaints charging both organizations with antitrust violations and asking the court to direct both to grant CBS the per-use licenses requested. The defendants were charged with ignoring the demand and insisting that CBS take the only types of agreements they offered, a blanket or a per-program license.

The increasingly strange brew that saw BMI pitted against its major founding parent was further muddied on February 3, when BMI filed an antitrust suit of its own. Both networks were accused of joining ASCAP in a "contract, combination or conspiracy" to restore the society to the position of monopoly it had enjoyed in the autumn of 1939, the period in which BMI was founded. Asking for nearly $60 million in triple damages, BMI charged that the TV chains had discriminated against it by paying ASCAP substantially more than warranted. The extra money was going to the society so that it could continue to "induce" BMI writers and publishers to move to ASCAP. One of the examples cited of this conspiracy was the "double compensation" paid to BMI affiliates. Royalty payments were made to former BMI writers and publishers for performances in the nine months preceding their move to the society, regardless of whether they had already been paid by BMI.

In April, NBC-TV took another tack in its fight to reduce music fees; it withdrew its request for a new ASCAP blanket license. Claiming that it did not care for the "right to use ASCAP's millions of copyrights" when they were not needed, it asked for the right to play only 2,217 specified songs licensed by the society and "certain background music libraries." It offered $762,000 a year for this bundle of copyrights, rather than the more than six million ASCAP wanted for a single year's blanket license. Network research had unearthed figures indicating that performances of ASCAP music on NBC-TV had declined almost 67 percent between 1965–66 and 1968–69, those of ASCAP background music by nearly 20 percent. In an affidavit filed with the petition, it was stated that if any interim fee fixed by Judge Ryan while the matter was in negotiation was disproportionate to that paid BMI "it could well be, as BMI contends in its lawsuit, that ASCAP will be able to raid BMI of its members and drive it from business."

A brief filed by the Justice Department shortly after NBC's request pointed out that under its consent decree ASCAP could be ordered to accede. The court was reminded that movie studios had always dealt in individual songs, without asking for court intervention, and that the law of the marketplace could operate in television equally well.

A similar application for a limited-repertory license from BMI, involving about 2,700 selections, was filed by NBC in the court presided over by Judge Morris Lasker, to which both the CBS and BMI antitrust actions had been submitted. In papers accompanying its new proposals to ASCAP and BMI, NBC explained that it intended to deal with program packagers for rights to the background music they controlled, as well as with individual members of both societies for music outside the limited-access arrangements.

BMI tightened its pressure on the third network next, hoping to bring at least ABC-TV into line, and terminated its license. A six-million-dollar infringement action was put on record simultaneously against NBC-TV. With both licensing organizations and all three networks at one another's throats in the courts, it appeared to veteran broadcasters that the situation was as bad as that in the late 1930s, when the ASCAP–radio-music war was in the making.

Rather than pursue the wait-and-see policy of 1940, the society took a bold action in the television-network standstill at the end of May, and filed a sweeping counterattack in the New York federal court. It asked for the revocation of all owned-and-operated station licenses and, in the most vitriolic language used against them since 1940, charged NBC and CBS with a conspiracy to restrain trade and to corner all television programing by creating "a monopoly of program material and access to television facilities," particularly in prime time. Although BMI was not cited as a defendant, its history was detailed as a prime example of the networks' power to depress the price of music by systematically favoring and promoting the BMI repertory in increasingly larger proportions. The FCC had recently ruled that major-market stations were barred, beginning in September 1971, from programing more than three hours of network offerings in the 7:00–10:00 P.M. period, but ASCAP wanted more drastic control. It asked the court to enjoin both CBS and NBC from "hereafter producing, selling, purchasing, distributing, licensing, syndicating, or otherwise having any interest in or control over any television program other than news and public affairs programs in connection with the operation of their television networks."

The compromise payment proposed by Judge Ryan to CBS and NBC—$4.3 million for 1970, to be paid at the rate of $360,000 each month for access to the ASCAP catalogue while their requests for limited licensing were pending—brought BMI once more to the court for relief. Judge Lasker, who was to hear BMI's conspiracy suit against ASCAP, CBS, and NBC, was asked to grant preliminary injunctive relief, requiring CBS to pay 70 percent of the rate the networks agreed on in response to the Ryan suggestion. Though without a BMI license, CBS continued to use its music, as many as 190 selections a week, lending support to BMI's charge that serious competitive injury followed the loss of some of its principal affiliates to ASCAP.

The bidding for BMI's songwriters and publishers that escalated soon after the society's most recent amended consent order was publicly manifested in a series of trade-paper advertisements, which ASCAP threatened to "repeat as many as 11,000 times." Their message was, in general: The difference between ASCAP and BMI is simple—publishers and writers own ASCAP; broadcasters own BMI. The more money you get, the less money the broadcasters keep, and vice versa. In a case like that, self-interest usually dictates which choice will be made. You know what you made at BMI. We have a computer, it tells us what you would have made with ASCAP. You can figure out to the penny what each of us pays.

The two systems of performance payment had been at the heart of the fight since the early 1940s, *Broadcasting* said, in February 1972:

> ASCAP officials have derided what they say is a system that pays one writer in a particular category more than another writer in the same category. BMI claims that ASCAP makes it very hard for writers who are on ASCAP's "four fund plan"—a system of payments that takes membership and recognized

works into account and spreads payments over a longer period than would straight current-performance payments—to leave because they forfeit money they would have received from the fund in the future.

ASCAP claims that it splits payments equally between publishers and writers while BMI gives more to publishers. In fact, BMI pays equally to publisher and writer except in one category: publishers get more for performances on radio stations which pay more than $3,000 in licensing fees. BMI accuses ASCAP of offering large advances and guarantees to prominent BMI writers to woo them away, a practice BMI had freely admitted using in the past.

Both organizations have systems of payment that grant bonuses for hits and take into account length of membership. Both will offer a prominent writer an advance to sign. A writer cannot get out of either society without losing payments on copyrights from the organization he leaves. Both now have "open door policies" concerning membership, as BMI has had from the beginning. And both, under consent decrees, allow writers and publishers to make independent licensing contracts for their works.

It was the last provision that CBS now intended to take advantage of. In a lengthy memorandum, filed in opposition to BMI's request for an annual fee representing 70 percent as much as it paid ASCAP, CBS raised the possibility of negotiating with BMI writers and publishers and paying them on the basis of BMI's readily accessible royalty schedule. It called for a basic rate of seventy-two cents to both writer and publisher for every feature use during evening hours, or $288 for nighttime feature use on a 200-station network. On such a basis, CBS would have paid $800,00 for BMI music in 1970, half that called for by its contract. BMI's president said in response that this would "greatly magnify ASCAP's present competitive advantage over BMI." The BMI payment schedule, he continued, "does not reflect either the amounts received from the television networks or the amounts paid by BMI to its affiliates." Rather, it was a minimum-rate schedule, published long before the company could possibly know exactly how much money would be available for distribution.

NBC's bid for a license limited to 2,217 ASCAP selections and some music in several tape and record libraries was rejected by Judge Ryan near the end of 1970. He ruled that the consent decrees did not require the society to issue anything but a blanket license to a television network. Their language called for licenses for "any, all or some" of the ASCAP repertory, and involved "mechanics for setting appropriate license fees, not for establishing the scope of a license. The real issue [is] not one of broad antitrust policy, but the much more limited inquiry as to whether a license to the largest and most influential network in the U.S. of a limited number of ASCAP selections is required by terms of the consent decree. We find that it is not." Ryan also reminded all parties that he had ruled against earlier All-Industry Committee applications for a similar type of limited access and been upheld on appeal.

During its continuing rancorous dispute with the networks, BMI had slightly better luck with the independent TV stations. The permanent All-Industry

Committee, reconstituted from a former ad-hoc body in April 1970, had met at once with BMI to push through a new contract, whose terms substantially reduced the company's present nine-million-dollar income from all independent TV stations. If BMI did not accept the proposition, the committee claimed, its constituents would lose over $50 million in the next ten years, a figure representing more than half of the estimated savings written into the recently completed contract with ASCAP, the result of eight years of negotiation.

A compromise settlement tied BMI's rate to the pending ASCAP contract with independent TV stations, and simultaneously brought the two organizations closer to economic parity in this field, for the first time. In an agreement that would expire with the ASCAP contract at the end of 1978, each station paid BMI fees equal to 58 percent of its payments to the society. This was not specified in the document, but had that effect. The combined saving achieved by the committee meant that stations actually paid $60 million less than they would have under previous agreements, but it did represent an increase for BMI, being a compromise between the 70 percent asked by BMI and the committee's initial lower offer. BMI's first victory in the network disputes came at the same time—a fixed-dollar contract with ABC-TV, at an undisclosed figure, but reported to be one quarter more than the network had ever paid before.

Many informed broadcasting insiders thought that all the public contentiousness between the networks and the music societies was merely to make a record for future litigation. They believed that peace was possible if a series of realistic compromises could be worked out. There was no foundation, they maintained, to the theory that the networks actually intended to destroy the performance societies, which might be possible with any industrywide reduced or limited-license structure. The NBC limited-access proposal, for example, would bring the society $785,000 for 2,217 selections, whereas under the flat-fee blanket contract ASCAP received nearly $6 million from the network in 1969. As attractive as such a prospect might seem, the networks were conscious of the possibility of an antitrust conspiracy action brought by both societies, which would certainly lead to government intervention and their possible dissolution.

The theory went further. Faced with mounting music fees, of which they could see no end under the present payment structure, and which had included disbursements over and above terms of contracts of more than $20 million to ASCAP in the 1960s, the networks made their demands for limited licenses in order to halt the escalation. If a long-term cap could be placed on music costs, the networks would abandon their suits to change the licensing formula. In such an event, BMI and ASCAP might agree to more "reasonable" fees from the networks, provided that blanket licensing remained in effect, and that BMI's share of the market was properly reflected in its income.

It appeared that part of such a scenario was about to be played out. Both

CBS and NBC accepted the Ryan proposal for a compromise $4.3-million interim annual ASCAP fee while their suits for limited licenses were in court. CBS continued, however, to be openly antagonistic and unbending toward the child it had helped to father, refusing to swerve from the demand that its BMI fees be based on a per-use formula, paid at BMI's published rates. The network budged only after Judge Lasker ordered it to pay BMI an annual $1.6 million for blanket access to its music. Retroactive to the beginning of the year, the sum was the same as had been paid for 1969, the largest BMI had ever received from CBS. BMI's copyright-infringement suits against the network, totaling about $10 million at the minimum $250 penalty, were dismissed with prejudice. Both parties were given the opportunity, once every year, to seek a rate adjustment ''on the basis of changed circumstances,'' until the per-use issue was resolved.

CHAPTER 23

Big Money Invades the Music Business

Contrary to an industrywide certainty that the record business would, because of rock music, pass the one-billion-dollar list-price mark sometime prior to 1970 was a frequent complaint of most responsible disk executives that they remained the victims of that "profitless prosperity" first discerned during the 1950s. A study of 1964's figures revealed that the combined net profit from sales of $758 million had been 1.7 percent, and the consolidated return on net worth, 3.8 percent. When final figures for 1967 were released late in 1968, they showed that business had already passed the billion-mark. So the grumbling focused on competition from prerecorded tapes, in all their configurations. Stereo and tape sales had been $234 million, compared with disks' $1.124 billion, and by 1972 was to be $541 million to $1.383 billion. About 70 percent of the 7,300 stereo and monaural singles released in 1967 failed to recover initial costs, and 60 percent of the 3,700 LPs, made for between $15,000 and $20,000, failed similarly. Electronic gadgetry, the innovations of the Beatles and other rock performers, and free-spending independent producers financed by some of the larger manufacturers were regarded as responsible for the steadily climbing cost of a recording session.

Rack jobbers, and the department and discount stores they serviced, whose principal customers were upwardly mobile suburban consumers, had succeeded by 1967 in driving down the standard price of a popular stereo LP to as little as two dollars. Only twenty-three singles had sold over a million copies that year, and only fifty-eight LPs had sales in excess of one million dollars, qualifying them for the RIAA's Gold Record award.

The monaural record, either 33- or 45-speed or LP, which now accounted for less than half of all dollar volume, was ready to follow the 78 single into oblivion. To get it there, the price of all monaural records was raised in mid-1967 to that of its stereo counterparts, in the hope that consumers would switch in greater number to the more modern technology. The move had its elements of daring, since prices had generally been lowered in the past decade. When Columbia and RCA reduced the list price of their basic popular LP lines from $4.85 to $3.95 in 1955, the industry had followed. It had done the same in the mid-1960s, when the federal excise tax was removed, reducing the price to $3.79. Now, however, consumers did not respond as expected, owing to the poor products they were offered. In order to create an all-stereo industry, many companies had started to issue "compatible stereo" recordings, which could be played on either monaural or stereophonic equipment. Others offered "electronically re-processed" or "enhanced" stereo disks, which actually were from slightly doctored monaural masters. In all cases, they were vastly inferior in sound and fidelity to the original product, a failing easily discerned by record buyers, who had been exposed to true stereo and were learning to appreciate it. It was generally recognized that an increase in stereo LP prices was inevitable, because of spiraling prices generally and a tight profit squeeze in the record business in particular, but an almost unnatural caution ruled for the time being. At the start of 1969, RCA blazed the trail, closely followed by Columbia and some others, and increased prices to their 1966 level, before removal of excise taxes had obliged them to make cuts. They had no compunction in adding extra markups for the first time on LPs made by best-selling artists, who would soon be known as "superstars."

The rush of amalgamations and mergers in the early 1960s was a mere ripple when contrasted with those being made by big venture capital in the last years of the decade. The music industry appealed to capital, Robert K. Lifton, of Transcontinental Investing, said, because it was a leisure-time business and catered to the youth market, a pool of Americans representing almost half of the population, whose spending power was growing steadily. More important was that the existing structures of the business were breaking and newer and better ones were needed to replace them. Therefore, music publishers were becoming record manufacturers, and record companies sought to add music publishers to their holdings. The field was ripe for the entry of outside interests. Having observed a steady near 10 percent annual increase in retail sales over a decade from an industry that was becoming more internationalized, major investment advisers put out the word that the recording business was a promising field in which to invest. Five major manufacturers controlled more than half the market—Columbia, Warner–7 Arts, RCA Victor, Capitol-EMI, and MGM. Thirty-five percent was divided among nearly 100 smaller competitors, and the remaining 10 percent or so was shared by hundreds of others, which also enjoyed good profits. A new period of industry expansion was at hand.

Neil Bogart, soon to be America's "bubble-gum king," was twenty-five when he started his Buddah label, as a subsidiary of the small Kama Sutra firm. Financed by $105,000 in loans from record distributors, he had three quick hits—"Simon Says," "Yummy, Yummy," and "Green Tambourine." The first record company to use concentrated television advertising and promotion, Buddah enjoyed pretax earnings of $1.4 million in its first year of operation, out of a gross revenue of $5.8 million.

With $75,000 advanced by ABC Records, which also contracted to sell and distribute his products, Lou Adler began to record a soft-rock Los Angeles group, the Mamas and the Papas. Their first release for his Dunhill Records made more than four million dollars. ABC Records then paid him between a semiofficial two million dollars and a rumored five million for the singing group, Dunhill Productions, and its label. Sales of the combined ABC-Dunhill operation went up 150 percent.

Most big-business investors did not recognize that new record companies failed more frequently than they enjoyed success. A single 45 had to sell 11,200 copies to break even, and if it did not, the manufacturer took a loss. This happened, according to Henry Brief, the RIAA's executive director, to 74 percent of all 45s put on sale in 1968–69, and 61 percent of all popular LPs, which had to sell a minimum of 7,800 copies to recoup their initial cost.

In a late 1969 issue of *The Bulletin of the American Guild of Authors & Composers,* the AGAC delineated the new trend in ownership of record companies and, coincidentally, music publishers' catalogues, by holding companies. Twelve of these were examined, and, with them, 110 music houses and 59 recording companies, as well as tape-manufacturing companies, rack jobbers, and record distributors, all of which formed the new web of financial involvement by giant outside interests.

The Warner/7 Arts group had been among the first to expand in the music business on a large scale, adding Atlantic Records in 1967. With this purchase came its owned-and-operated music firms—Cotillion, Pronto, and Walden—but not its first publishing operation, Progressive Music, which had been sold to Hill & Range Songs in 1964 for $500,000. Some $17 million in cash and stock was involved in the sale which brought Warner one of the last major independents.

Atlantic was formed in 1948 by Ahmet Ertegun, the urbane jazz- and blues-loving son of a former Turkish ambassador to the United States, and Herb Abramson, a jazz-record collector and qualified dental surgeon, who had abandoned that profession for the postwar recording studios. In the early 1950s, when the major manufacturers began to cover Atlantic's R & B hits, recorded by the Chords, Laverne Baker, Ruth Brown, and Joe Turner, the company had no distribution apparatus of its own with which to challenge them. Later, Ertegun, his brother Nesuhi—brought in to build up the label's jazz catalogue—and Jerry Wexler, a former reporter for *Billboard* and then record promotion man for the Big Three group, raised $300,000 to buy out Abramson.

The firm's cover-version and distribution situation went through changes in the late-1950s when Jerry Lieber and Mike Stoller and other young rock-'n'-roll producers moved in under Atlantic's banner and were responsible for crossover rock hits by the Coasters, the Drifters, Bobby Darin, and others. At the time of the sale to Warner, Atlantic was doing an annual gross of $20 million, based on the popularity of Aretha Franklin, Sonny and Cher, Wilson Pickett, Vanilla Fudge, Buffalo Springfield, and Memphis-based record companies whose products it distributed. In addition, Atlantic released music by the English group Cream and the Australian BeeGees, both acquired from the British branch of Polydor Records, to which Ertegun had switched licensing rights for the United Kingdom. The Erteguns and Wexler signed multiyear employment contracts with Warner and operated Atlantic as an independent division, with its own distribution, artists, and international licensees, much as Warner and Reprise had been doing.

The web of Warner/7 Arts ownership became highly complicated in this period and for some time to come. National General, owner of 278 screen theaters in twenty-three states, a savings-and-loan association—the Great American Holding Company—and fruit-packaging and popcorn factories, and with control of the book publisher Grosset & Dunlap, proposed to buy a controlling interest in Warner/7 Arts. National General already owned $1.5 million of its convertible debentures and an option to buy the film company and all subsidiary music properties. But because National General also owned a substantial number of film theaters, the Justice Department indicated its opposition to the purchase.

This provided Steven J. Ross, head of Kinney National Service, with an opportunity to expand into the leisure-time communications field. He had already built his father-in-law's chain of funeral parlors into one of the country's most productive privately owned conglomerates, with car-rental, airport-concession, and office-cleaning services. To these, he added two companies in 1968: National Periodical Publications, a large publisher of comic magazines, including *Mad,* and national distributor of paperbacks and magazines; and Ashley-Famous, a giant agency. Each of these mergers had involved an exchange of $17 million in corporate stock.

After buying the option to purchase Warner/7 Arts and its $1.5 million in convertible debentures, for $6 million in cash and Kinney stock, Ross began acquiring Warner common-stock purchase warrants, 400,000 of them by March 1969, including 100,000 common shares sold by Frank Sinatra and his associates. At the time, the Warner/Reprise and Atlantic group provided 69 percent of the year's first-quarter profits. The merger was consummated by summer for between $350 and $400 million, based on the price of 40 million new shares of common stock and 5 million preferred shares, issued for the occasion. To avoid antitrust problems, Ashley-Famous was sold. Elektra Records, begun during the classical and folk vogue of the

1950s, but now heavily involved in rock, with The Doors, was added to the roster later that year, bought for $10 million, and in 1973 Asylum Records was added and eventually amalgamated with Elektra. Warner Communications was formed in the early 1970s as the parent company for this empire of motion-picture and television production facilities and the record and music group. Only some banks and real estate holdings and the Kinney Corporation itself were excluded from WCI. Within two years, the record group almost owned one quarter of *Billboard*'s best-seller charts, with Atlantic contributing almost the same share of all profits. Warner Communications' earnings before taxes increased by more than 25 percent over the preceding year, from $171 million to $215 million. The music operations had already brought in a nearly 50 percent increase in those earnings since 1970.

Transamerica, a San Francisco insurance company, operator of Trans International Airlines, and owner of Transamerica Fund Sales and the Transamerica Computer Company, purchased United Artists Pictures and its subsidiary music interests, including United Artists and Unart Records, for an undisclosed sum in 1967. A year later, it paid in excess of $25 million in an exchange of 500,000 shares of its common stock for Liberty Records, which had been formed in 1955 to record rock-'n'-roll performers in the Los Angeles area. With Liberty came its subsidiaries, the former Lou Chudd label and its masters, the jazz-oriented Blue Note Records, a tape-duplicating plant, and several music companies.

With holdings in real estate and a rubber company (and not to be confused with Transamerica), Transcontinental Investing diversified by forming the $12-million Transcontinental Music Corp. The company was financed by seven million in unsecured loans from banks around the country, the balance in a fifteen-year loan from Prudential Life Insurance Company. The parent company's head, Robert Lifton, recognizing early that most record companies were not strong enough financially to sustain their own nationwide distribution chain, bought several record wholesalers and formed Transcontinental Distributing Corp. It became the largest single-record and tape distribution operation in the United States, and a $73-million business in 1967. With control of 20 percent of all rack-jobber business, representing the same percentage of retail sales, Transcontinental Distributing amassed control of more than half of the entire record-distribution business.

Transcontinental Music bought major control of several independent record-production companies, and paid $3.5 million for an 80 percent interest in Mike Curb's Sidewalk Productions, which specialized in sound-track music. Desperate for distribution outlets, the movie-business executives of MGM, parent of cash-poor MGM Records, signed an agreement with Lifton that gave Transcontinental Distributing exclusive control of the record company. Curb was immediately installed as a vice-president of MGM-Loew and president of MGM Records, with a stock interest, and managed, through great flair for producing middle-of-the road recordings, to weather the financial crash of 1970.

Beginning with aerial cameras, Viewlex had become the most important American company engaged in the manufacture of audio-visual equipment for military and commercial use in the 1960s, and moved into supplying electronic missile-control subsystems for the Vietnam War. Viewlex's diversification into music-business properties began with the purchase of record-plating, pressing, and label-printing plants. It then moved to the financial backing and eventual buyout, in 1968–70, of several new and immediately successful independent record companies—Kama Sutra, Cobblestone, and Buddah.

Electrical & Musical Industries, whose economic fortunes in the record business had continued to skyrocket with Beatlemania, was slowly losing its lead as the world's largest and most prosperous manufacturer of disks and allied products in the late 1960s to American Columbia Records. Without the Beatles' knowledge, their discoverer and manager, Brian Epstein, had extended their contract with EMI, which expired at the end of 1967, for nine years, obtaining a $25-million advance, which included accrued royalties, against a 17.5 percent royalty, from Capitol Records, but only 15 percent on all EMI singles that sold over 100,000 copies and LPs selling over 30,000 units. Epstein's NEMS Agency now collected its own 25 percent share of Beatles' royalties directly from the manufacturers. The Beatles had already reaped twenty-two Gold Records from the RIAA in America, the most recent for "Strawberry Fields," which "went gold" before it was released. It was estimated in a press release announcing the renewal that they had sold 180-million units in total world sales. The new British 50 percent purchase tax placed a burden on English buyers, which, added to EMI's world-wide switch to stereo, accompanied by an exchange with dealers and distributors on all monaural disks, and the expansion and automation of manufacturing and engineering facilities, was responsible for a general reduction of EMI dividends.

Regardless of continuing demand for Beatles records, followed by that for releases by the Beach Boys, before they left to join Warner Records, Capitol Records' sales had declined from their all-time high in fiscal 1968, reducing dividends from the previous year's $1.20 on sales of $120 million, to 34 cents. Capitol had taken over control of one of the major tape manufacturers, Audio Devices, maker of AudioPak cartridges, in which it had long held a minority interest. A program of corporate reorganization put Audio Devices and Capitol Records in control of a new entity, Capitol Industries, in which EMI owned majority control. The Capitol Record Club, on which nearly five million dollars had been spent in 1966 for advertising and promotion, was renamed the Capitol Direct Merchandising Corp. Operations were further enlarged in this period of general industry expansion with the purchase of one of the largest rack jobbers, which quickly turned into a money-losing venture. So, too, was the Record Club, sold in 1968 to Westinghouse to shore up its own Longines Symphonette Society mail-order operation. Alan Livingston, Capitol's president since 1961, resigned in a rift over policy. He was followed by two presidents in several months, one of whom, Stanley M. Gortikov, became president of the RIAA following his departure from Capitol in 1971. When the Beatles broke up that year, the company's fortunes reversed completely. It went from an $8-million profit in 1970 to an $8-million loss the next year.

A new president, Bhaskar Menon, who had been trained in the EMI-Gramophone Company of India, pulled Capitol into the black by 1973, prerecorded AudioPak tapes accounting for more than half of all volume. The A & R staff of thirty and artists roster of 247 were pruned drastically. More helpful, the track record of nine failures out of every ten releases was reversed, by such artists as Pink Floyd, Grand Funk Railroad, Helen Reddy, Merle Haggard, Buck Owens, and Anne Murray.

With the European Common Market, of which Great Britain was not yet a partner, having come into force on January 1, 1968, a new element of competition was introduced into the European record business. Already forced to deal in devaluated English pounds while it sought to maintain its hold on a rapidly more turbulent music business, EMI had to watch the acquisition by two of its international competitors of one of the oldest and most important catalogues of American and British musical-theater and popular-music copyrights. Using North American Philips as their agent, Philips Phonographic Industries, of the Netherlands, and Siemens, owner of Deutsche Grammophon Records, paid $42.5 million in June 1968 for the British and American Chappell companies. With them came major real estate holdings in England and around the world and some of the choicest theater properties in London.

Rumor of a Chappell sale had circulated ever since the death in 1966 of Louis Dreyfus, managing head of the venerable music houses, but it had been delayed while attorneys for Morgan Guaranty Trust Company dealt with the intricacies of international inheritance taxes. A bid of $40 million by CBS had earlier been rejected by Dreyfus. A number of firm offers were tendered to Morgan Guaranty, including one by ATV of London, the domain of Lew Grade, and others by Metromedia, the American radio-TV, supermarket, and billboard combine, and by Columbia Pictures.

The Chappell trustees and the Jerome Kern estate held on the T. B. Harms catalogue, formed by Max Dreyfus and the composer in 1905 to control Kern's copyrights. In order to maintain the firm's high ASCAP rating during Kern's fallow periods and after his death, Dreyfus had occasionally transferred copyrights of hit songs from other Chappell-controlled houses to T. B. Harms. With permission from the Kern family and that of the late Oscar Hammerstein II, frequent collaborator with the composer, Harms was sold in 1970 to the Lawrence Welk Group, for $3.2 million.

Philips and Siemens, two of Europe's largest electric-goods conglomerates, had formed a partnership in 1963 by exchanging 50 percent of their stock, but they continued to maintain separate manufacturing and sales divisions for all their products, including those of their recording companies, Polydor and Deutsche Grammophon. With the Common Market a reality, they combined some of their British record-sales offices and signed a contract with the Robert Stigwood Organization to promote some of their popular artists. Stigwood was an expatriate Australian manager of rock artists, among them the heavy-rock groups The Who and Cream, whose records proved to be equally successful in the United States. The first to introduce leased taping to England, Stigwood paid all recording and production costs for the master tapes made by groups he managed and then sold the finished product for a royalty of 15 percent or more. With a partner, David Shaw, a British speculator, Stigwood obtained from Brian Epstein an option to buy a 51 percent interest in his NEMS artist-management agency, of which the Beatles owned 10 percent, for a future payment of $12.5 million, a little more than half of the $20 million offered some months earlier by an American entertainment conglomerate.

Stigwood moved his business into the NEMS offices, along with his own stable of recording musicians. On first hearing a young Australian trio, the Bee Gees, he immediately signed them paying them $2,500 for 51 percent of their publishing rights. His option to buy NEMS was never exercised, because of his inability to raise the money and the death of Epstein. Under the terms of Epstein's will, his mother inherited 70 percent of the company, which had been renamed Nemperor Holdings, and his brother, Clive, got 20 percent. To help pay the large death duties, Clive negotiated the sale of his mother's share, with its quarter-interest in all Beatles' royalties, to the British Triumph Investment Trust, for around two million dollars, after giving the Beatles an opportunity to match the bid. In a financially intricate turnover of Nemperor, Triumph got back its money and a share of several millions of EMI royalties, frozen in a legal fight that pitted Paul McCartney against John Lennon and the other Beatles, plus 5 percent of all future earnings by the group through 1976. An offshoot of the differences that divided the Beatles and led to their final separation was the purchase, for $2.5 million in 1969, of Northern Songs and Maclen Music in the United States by Lew Grade and ATV, despite all McCartney's and Lennon's attempts to keep the companies.

EMI's biggest moneymakers, the Beatles, had become unresponsive, even to the American press, which adored them. In announcing publicly the first sketchy details of their new tax-saving dodge, Apple Corps, Ltd., in 1968, McCartney and Lennon had been purposely vague about particulars. Apple was a corporation set up to deal in films, music, electronics, and merchandising, each related to their primary business, and thus not suspect to tax men. The company would be operated for several years and then sold to the public. The new Apple label, on which all future Beatle releases would appear, gave world rights to EMI and American manufacture and distribution to Capitol Records. Royalties were on the terms renegotiated by Epstein in 1967.

A new manager, whose presence eventually led to a final and lasting break between McCartney and Lennon, was brought in to handle Apple's business affairs. He was an American, Allen Klein, who had represented a number of artists in the United States. He held an important block of MGM stock and was involved in the several proxy fights that beset the company in the late 1960s. The Beatles admired him for the tough deal he had worked out with British Decca for a renewal of the Rolling Stones' contract. As their agent, Klein had wangled a bonus advance of $1.25 million.

In early 1968, he bought the foundering Cameo-Parkway label, home studio of "Philadelphia schlock" in the late 1950s, paying around half a million dollars for a majority interest. He was, as ever, shrewd in his dealings with Sir John Lockwood, head of EMI, in the second rewriting of the Beatles' contract in 1969. The new terms raised LP royalties from thirty-nine cents to fifty-eight cents through 1972, and then to seventy-two cents until the end of 1975, when the agreement would expire. The average American royalty to major artists was 10 percent, but Capitol was happy to pay the Beatles 25 because they continued to account for at least half its sales. The right to release old Beatles' material, unavailable under the existing contract, was leased to EMI, and a tidal wave of repackaged albums followed, for which an eager new market waited. Klein's price for the gains was one fourth of all the increases he could get.

Continuing on the momentum of its long reputation as the world's largest record company (no longer accurate), RCA's profit margins during the mid-1960s generally ran below those of the parent organization, one of the few American conglomerates matching the largest in Europe. The record company continued to offer a balanced and homogenized repertory that put little emphasis on the changing world of contemporary progressive rock, which was becoming responsible for half of the record business. The man who had carried RCA into the modern era in spite of itself, Elvis Presley, had become a film idol, whose sound-track LPs attracted new members to the company's record club. Then in 1969, his "Suspicious Minds" and "In the Ghetto" reminded old fans who had deserted him for Peter, Paul and Mary or Trini Lopez of the glories Presley had revealed and also let several younger generations learn what all the excitement had been about and why he should still be known as the King of Rock 'n' Roll. The union of popular music with country that would provide RCA with one third of all sales by 1973 was still to come.

Owing to the war in Vietnam and the space program, RCA had become a major beneficiary of federal monies, which, on the annual balance sheet, it lumped under "Electronics–Consumer Products and Services," together with the record division's profits or losses. In 1972, when RCA released 453 new LPs and 318 singles, it was rumored to be responsible for slightly more than $200 million of the corporation's $400-billion annual gross.

The jump in Columbia Records' sale of rock records from 15 percent of the total market to 60 in the five-year period ending in 1969 was due in great measure to the presence of the head of its record division, Clive Davis, at the first of the giant rock festivals, held in Monterey, California, in June 1967. Among the underground figures surfacing there for scrutiny by the big-time record business was, Davis later told *Billboard*'s seventh annual International Radio Programing Forum, a "strutting shouting, vibrant, soul-searching belter, Janis Joplin, who took the place by storm. . . ."

> And there was the Electric Flag, an exciting new group that used brass to complement the dynamic drumming of Buddy Miles and the great guitar of Mike Bloomfield. These artists plus Jimi Hendrix, Steve Miller, The Who, Quicksilver Messenger [Service]—they all heralded a new trend in music: loud amplification and instrumental virtuosity involving lengthy passages. It is the artists who create trends in music, not executives of record companies. But executives can spot them and I was lucky to be there for this one.

The previous year, two Warner-Reprise executives, Joe Smith and Mo Ostin, had been lucky, too, in hearing a hard 1950s' rock-'n'-roll-inspired band, The Grateful Dead, in San Francisco's Haight-Ashbury district, where acid rock prevailed. The group was immediately signed, for an advance of $10,000—$3,500 to put their names on the contract, the balance against their first 10,000 units sold. At the end of two years, with three LPs released, the group owed $120,000, most of it for recording costs, and it was five years before they were completely out of debt to the company. It proved to be invaluable experience for Warner executives. "We learned," Smith told *Rolling Stone* in 1971, "that there were other ways to sell records, like sponsoring a free concert in Detroit. We learned you don't have to be on Top 40 radio, that there's a whole market in underground FM. We learned that posters mean something, that billboards mean something. . . . I grew up learning there was another way to live, there was another way to make records, another way to sell records, there was another kind of music."

Without intending to alert competition too quickly, Davis signed new talent representing what he believed was the best of the new revolution in music. Beginning in early 1968, Columbia's steady releases of its new contemporary rock stars set new sales' records—Blood, Sweat & Tears' second album sold 3.8 million; Santana's *Abraxas* sold 3.5 million LPs; each new album of Chicago sold well into seven figures.

The Warner-Reprise/Atlantic group worked hard to match Columbia's success, sharing a major portion of each week's *Billboard* Hot 100 chart, and had well over 100 LPs that sold more than a million copies each in the 1968–70 period.

When the superstar groups began to disband, the market turned to singer-songwriters whose music reflected the new life style of many of their fans. But having found themselves in on the beginning of a new kind of music and new ways to sell it, Columbia and Warner had boosted their revenues to peaks that held even when the general business economy slipped in the early 1970s.

CHAPTER 24

FM and Top 40 Radio

Come the hell of another disk-jockey scandal or the high water of editorial complaints about the quality of the recorded music they played, American radio stations had developed an immutable affinity for Top 40 programing. With recorded popular music still filling the vast majority of time on the air, rock-'n'-roll music was turning out to have a viability that even the stoutest defender of Elvis Presley never imagined. Much to the consternation of its most outspoken enemies, it provided stations with top ratings, no matter what type of music their competitors programed. The brief period in 1961 when frequency modulation was seen as the best antidote to rock 'n' roll had passed. The approval of FM stereo broadcasting by the FCC, making possible the use of high-quality stereophonic recordings of good music, had little effect, chiefly because 60 percent of the 990 FM stations then on the air had duplicated the programing of the AM facilities with which they were connected. Advertisers were provided with an extra share of audience for which they did not pay, and hi-fi bugs got a few hours of the static-free "fine music" that FM meant, but neither made a difference in the over-all picture.

Simultaneous AM/FM programing came to an end on October 15, 1965, when all jointly owned AM/FM stations in markets of more than 100,000 in population were required by the FCC to program nonduplicated music at least half of their time on the air. In the interest of operating economies, the most prosperous AM broadcasters put their FM operations on a noncommercial basis, giving listeners the kind of music they appeared to want and making Mantovani and the Hollywood Strings the earliest legatees of separation. The FCC order had been made with the hope that it would create a diversity of programing. But those 10,000-watt FM stations that adopted a stereo rock-'n'-roll format selected their music only from the top of the trade papers' pop-music charts, a formula exactly like that of their Top 40 AM radio competition for the rock audience.

The FM audience was growing faster than advertising revenues, coincidentally with the disappearance of talk from its programs. At the end of 1966, FM advertising revenues were at the $32-million mark, far from local AM times sales of $580 million and a national spot-advertising business of $285 million, all aimed at the eighteen-to-forty-five-year-old audience AM had staked out for its own. Much to the chagrin of a business that issued 11,000 new records a year—7,700 singles and the balance LPs that Top 40 stations would not touch—AM played only from a list of thirty hit singles each week, with a few "specials" thrown in.

Tom Donahue, a disk jockey who was program director of KMPX-FM in 1967 and was later known as the Father of FM Radio, believed that Top 40 radio was dead. Due to the separation ruling the previous year, FM radio had moved from the classical music with which it had first attracted discriminating audio buffs to the same programing that AM radio offered. An NAB survey of FM programs, issued in March 1967, found that at least one quarter of all stations had changed their formats in the past year, and that 61 percent now played middle-of-the road music; 16 percent offered easy listening; 7 percent, classical music; 5 percent, county music; 4 percent, rock 'n' roll, often in slicked-up stereo instrumental versions; 3 percent, light classical; 3 percent, Broadway-Hollywood music. The target audience was the thirty-five-to-fifty age group, with twenty to thirty-five secondary. As Leonard Marcus wrote in *High Fidelity*, "It's clear that FM is no longer a medium primarily for the elite. The medium may still retain, even perfect, its sonic quality, but the message is just medium."

A huge, shaggy hulk of a man, "Big Daddy" Tom Donahue had moved to California in 1960, together with some other East Coast expatriates who, like him, had been victims of the payola hearings. He went to work for KYA, San Francisco, playing the rhythm-and-blues hits of the 1950s, which had somehow been ignored by California deejays. A new owner gave him and other disk jockeys from the East wider latitude over music selection, and KYA, stripped, by Donahue's order, of jingles, that indispensable element of 1950s' Top 40 radio, became "Boss of the Bay," using a highly varied "Boss Top 40" format. After leaving, to become a concert promoter, Donahue was the first to bring the Beatles to San Francisco. He incurred a BMI lawsuit for failing to get a license, and later ran his own small independent label. Later yet, he got the eight-to-midnight slot on a mostly foreign-language station, KMPX-FM, San Francisco, in April 1967, and in six months turned its music policy around. He experimented with contemporary music programing, playing rock 'n' roll, folk, traditional and city blues, raga, electronic music, and some jazz and classical. "It could have been done in any market," Donahue explained to Ralph Gleason, of the *San Francisco Chronicle*, who had found in the new KMPX a radio station parallel to the underground press. "People are tired of being yelled at and the new music has so much more to offer than just the best selling singles. . . . Top 40 radio doesn't reflect it . . . we're just not playing hippie music for hippies, we're offering an alternative. Nobody is told what to play. We're just appealing to people who have hip taste." And because he was tired of "looking at all those old men through the glass who don't like the music," Donahue staffed KMPX with an all-women engineering unit.

The revolution in music propelled the world of FM radio, using album cuts too long for AM Top 40, songs whose contents troubled the establishment, and musical forms that refused to submit to clichés, from a handful of stations in the late 1960s to a 12 percent share of the 100 top facilities in the country. Free-form progressive-rock underground radio concentrated on more music, fewer hard-sell commercials, and used no jingles, games, or noisy gimmicks. The majority of the time was bought by record companies, enabling stations to switch from wall-to-wall easy listening or classical music to the fresh morality and stark reality of music aimed at the fifteen-to-twenty-nine male market. Boasting of "telling it like it is," free-form radio kept faith with its audience, and FM listeners remained loyal because additional advertising contracts that would mean less music and more interruptions each hour were rejected out of hand. In the early 1970s, however, concerned practitioners of the new medium, Donahue among them, correctly perceived that because their progressive radio was no longer as unique and good as when it started, it would disappear or be co-opted by commercial AM radio.

PART SEVEN

1971–1976

CHAPTER 25

Continued Fighting Over Licensing

A change in the chairmanship of the All-Industry Television Committee in 1971 brought onstage a new player, one who would rattle the structure of music licensing and put in doubt the permanency of ASCAP and BMI income, on which sheet-music publishers had relied ever since the collapse of their empires. He was Leslie Arries of WBEN (later WIVW) AM-FM-TV, of Buffalo, New York, under whose leadership an operating fund was launched, by assessing each supporter an initial $160,000, to be used to effect a real decrease in broadcasters' payments to the licensing societies.

BMI's financial position had changed greatly since the period five years before when it faced a major deficit. With income from 6,472 radio stations, 680 TV stations, the networks, and some 15,000 nonbroadcast licensees, revenues for fiscal 1971 were $36.3 million, and retained earnings at year-end $3.1 million. Its gains were not limited to the United States. Through reciprocal agreements with twenty-nine foreign societies, BMI licensed 70 percent of the foreign songs that became American hits. In the past decade, royalties from these bodies had increased by more than 300 percent, and BMI's most recent annual foreign collection, $3.4 million in 1968, represented one third of all money sent from abroad for American music.

There was other good news as well. *Schwartz* v. *BMI*, the $150-million antitrust suit filed in 1953, died on June 23, 1971. Judge Sidney Sugarman, of the New York federal district court, dismissed it with prejudice and without any financial settlement by the defendants. As recently as 1964, when Robert Burton assumed the BMI presidency, talks had been conducted among the various interested parties on a settlement of around half a million dollars. Now that seven of the original plaintiffs had died, and no substitutes had been named for them, twenty-three of the remaining twenty-six agreed by affidavit to the dismissal. None of the remaining three, among them

Alan Jay Lerner, who had resigned from ASCAP to join BMI, had prosecuted the action since 1961 or shown any interest in it.

The TV networks' determination to reduce their payments for music appeared to have little effect on ASCAP, whose income continued its annual climb, from $62.2 million in 1971 to $89.6 in 1975. Raids on BMI writers and publishers had accelerated after the ASCAP board voted in December 1971 to allow members to be paid for their collaborations with BMI writers. A boycott against the practice had begun in April 1955, when the society abandoned all its rights to works of "joint authorship." A new victory was won a few months later when ninety-seven writers from the Motown songwriting pool resigned from BMI to join ASCAP, together with their publisher, Motown Music, the Berry Gordy–owned firm that had affiliated with BMI when he formed his own record company. The Motown writers, among them Stevie Wonder, Ashford and Simpson, and Smokey Robinson, joined former BMI writers Rod Stewart, Frank Zappa, Carole King, and Neil Diamond, who had made similar moves in response to ASCAP's higher financial guarantees.

When negotiations began for a new contract to replace the eight-year-old ASCAP agreement with independent radio stations, the Radio Committee adopted the television networks' strategy. The society hoped for a renewal of the 2 percent blanket fee. The committee demanded a substantial reduction from the $18.3 million being paid in 1971, and offered statistical evidence to show that although ASCAP radio fees had gone up 70 percent since 1963, its share of radio air play was down from 60 percent to 36. The drop was due chiefly to the change in American popular music following the Beatles' invasion and, with it, a return to rock 'n' roll, in which BMI predominated. After a strained ten months of argument and hearings in federal court, a new contract was approved by Judge Ryan. A fee of 1.725 percent over a five-year period brought ASCAP's radio rates nearer BMI's, which had been established in 1968 on a stair-step formula that would reach 1.7 percent when the contract expired in 1973. Putting the best face on the compromise, the committee pointed out that it represented savings of $2.4 million annually, a far cry from the 50 percent reduction that had been demanded when negotiations began and which were expected to bring radio fees into line with independent TV's one percent rate.

The anticipated spirit of practical compromise had yet to show itself in the television arena; it was particularly stopped by the continuing refusal by CBS to terminate its per-use suit and accept blanket licensing. Motions by NBC and ABC for summary dismissal of BMI's two-year old conspiracy, breach-of-contract, and antitrust suit against ASCAP and the networks were denied by Judge Lasker. So, too, was a petition to dismiss BMI's fraud charges, made in a separate case. ABC-TV had been made a codefendant in both matters, once it settled a back-payment problem with ASCAP in May 1970. However, Lasker did grant the ABC motion to sever the antitrust claim from other charges made against it by BMI, saying "it would be unfair at this point to permit BMI to gain access to ABC's and NBC's books and documents and thereby perhaps allow BMI to achieve a competitive advantage." He also assented to pleas that the antitrust case be tried before the contract and fraud claims.

The politically vindictive civil antitrust suit filed by the Justice Department on April 15, 1972, against the three networks, in many aspects mirrored that brought in 1970 by ASCAP. It sought to prohibit ABC, CBS, and NBC from engaging in the production of any television programs. It went further, however, than the society's complaint had, and dealt, not only with prime time, but with daytime productions as well. It sought also to prohibit the chains from securing a vested interest by providing financial backing to programs they purchased. The suit asked that nothing more than "first-run right of exhibition" could be acquired, stripping the networks of the right to spread initial costs over reruns.

The case had been prepared two years earlier, based on figures for 1967. Actually, however, the matter had had its birth in 1963, when the FCC barred as anticompetitive those segments of a station's programing over which affiliated stations had given up control to the networks as option time. In 1965, the Justice Department and the FCC had started an investigation into the covert ownership by network officials of companies from which they purchased television programs. It had become well known throughout the industry that a program in which the networks did not have a half-interest had little or no chance of getting on prime time, making it impossible for the independent production companies to compete. Preparation of the complaint began then, and led first to the prime-time access rule, in May 1970, as a holding action until the completed document was filed. Once it was, the case dragged. A motion in November 1974, to dismiss the action, on grounds that it had been motivated by political spite against the networks, was won, but "without prejudice," leaving to any new Justice Department an opportunity to bring the business up again. The networks asked the Supreme Court to preclude that possibility, but were denied. NBC then offered to settle, and signed a consent decree that would not be effective until ABC and CBS accepted a similar order, which they declined to do until 1980. They agreed then with NBC to limit the amount of prime-time programing each could produce in the next ten years.

Peace between NBC and BMI came in 1973, when the network accepted a three-year blanket contract, believed to call for double the $1.3-million interim settlement reached by compromise in June 1971. With the signing, NBC was removed as a defendant in the various BMI suits, and its application for a limited BMI copyright license was rescinded.

With that problem out of the way, the All-Industry Radio Committee offered another. It had never before heard complaints about BMI from broadcasters, but now things changed. In the past ten years, BMI's local radio income had almost tripled, from $3 million in 1963 to $15.5 million, and its rates had been increased on five occasions, rising from 1.07 percent to 1.7. Broadcasters wanted this constant escalation to stop, or at least to slow down. There was no justification, in the eyes of the committee, once it had been prodded by its constituents, for BMI's radio fees to continue at a rate 85 percent as high as that of ASCAP, when that for television was only 59 percent as high. ASCAP's current 50 percent share of *Billboard*'s Hot 100 charts, after so many fallow years, and its successful raiding program, as in the case of Motown, BMI's most successful publisher affiliate in the last several years, betokened the possibility of changing fortune.

A new bargaining ingredient was thrown down by BMI for inclusion in a four-year license extension, maintaining the 1.7 percent fee but promising lower rates in its final year, 1977. An experimental "incremental" formula, modeled after that introduced recently by the society, would go into place for 1977, using nonnetwork time sales in 1974 as the base on which the final year's rates would be established. Anything earned then above that figure would be taxed at an 0.85 percent rate, that below at the 1.7 percent rate. The new feature was hailed by the committee as an important achievement, because of the savings it was expected to effect.

After many months of recess, declared following several weeks in which the CBS per-use case had proceeded, *CBS* v. *ASCAP, BMI et al.* was resumed in late 1973. The delay had been occasioned by federal guidelines giving precedence to criminal cases. The battle to reduce television operating costs by destroying the blanket-license concept resumed with summaries by both sides of what had taken place in the courtroom prior to the recess. Essentially, counsel for CBS concentrated on the issue of restraint of trade and the lack of a mechanism for direct licensing of music copyrights. The court was urged to direct writers and publishers affiliated with both societies to cooperate in setting up such an apparatus or else be held in violation of antitrust laws. Both ASCAP and BMI attorneys argued that, because no network, including CBS, had ever attempted to deal directly with writers and publishers since 1929, when CBS first accepted a blanket license from ASCAP, or 1946, when its first blanket television license was signed, no demonstrable need existed now for the per-use contract demanded. After several weeks of additional testimony, the trial concluded, early in 1974.

Twenty months later, Judge Lasker dismissed the CBS complaint on the merits in a 107-page decision, finding that the network had not proved that ASCAP and BMI were guilty of restaint of trade, and that CBS had failed to demonstrate that there were indeed "significant obstacles to direct licensing" negotiations with writer and publisher members of both societies.

> Nor had it been established by credible evidence that copyright owners would refuse to deal directly with CBS if it called upon them to do so. To the contrary, there is impressive proof that copyright owners would wait at CBS' door if the network announced plans to drop its blanket license. . . .

Neither the history of the relationship between the parties nor the events leading to this action remotely suggest that CBS had been compelled to take a blanket license it did not want. Indeed, CBS does not even appear to have seriously considered alternatives to the blanket license prior to the commencement of the suit. . . .

In sum, CBS thought very little indeed about revising its licensing practices prior to [its] "demand" letter to ASCAP and BMI. . . . The evidence described hardly supports CBS' contention that it had been compelled to take a blanket license. To the contrary, it suggests that CBS did not even view music listening as a business problem until immediately prior to the suit.

In short, the Judge found, it was not until BMI made an attempt in 1969 to achieve parity with ASCAP in the matter of additional payments by the networks for prior years that CBS rushed to the courts. While CBS attorneys believed that the Lasker ruling was appealable as a matter of right, others felt that since the countersuits filed by ASCAP and BMI had not yet been tried, there could be no final judgment. It would be at the Appeals Court's discretion whether the decision was reviewed. CBS quickly filed a notice of appeal.

CHAPTER 26

Industry Associations
Play Their Part

With the largest single source of music-business income, that from public-performance licensing, temporarily removed from the threat of destruction by the termination of all blanket licensing, income continued to grow for both BMI and ASCAP. Because of inflation, the erosion of the American dollar in relation to many foreign currencies, and the increasing appetite abroad for American popular music in jukeboxes and imported musical talking pictures, payments from the foreign societies had risen by 10 percent in 1974, to a gross of more than $18 million. Of this, $12.3 million went to ASCAP, which had sent $5.9 million abroad for the year; $6 million went to BMI, whose international distributions for 1974 came to $3.2 million; and $125,000 was collected by SESAC, the Society of European Stage Authors and Composers, only recently involved in reciprocal foreign licensing, with ten such arrangements in place. Playing for these increasingly large stakes, ASCAP and BMI quickened the competition for European writers and publishers and their music. The society won by several days in the race to be the first to sign reciprocal agreements with the Soviet Union's licensing body, VAAP, following meetings and presentations in Russia during the summer of 1974 by both American organizations. The door was now almost opened, beginning on January 1, 1975, to true international reciprocal copyright protection. Two years before, the USSR had become a signatory to the Universal Copyright Convention, leaving only China of the major powers still not a member.

Western Hemisphere publishing rights to the full spectrum of Soviet music, including the catalogue of AmRuss, whose association with Leeds Music had expired, were assigned soon after to Macmillan, for a guarantee of $100,000 annually over the life of a ten-year contract. Then the largest and most diversified book and magazine publisher and distributor, producer of educational materials, and owner of the Brentano book stores, the Berlitz, Katherine Gibbs, and LaSalle Extension schools, the company had moved into the concert-music business in 1969, after acquiring 25 percent of the 4,476 outstanding shares in the Schirmer Family Trust. A 51 percent control of the family's 107-year-old publishing business, G. Schirmer & Sons, was then purchased, for a little more than eight million dollars. The sale also included full ownership of Associated Music Publishers, which Schirmer had bought from BMI in 1965. It was the major American publishing outlet for native contemporary-music composer-members of ASCAP and BMI.

The competition between ASCAP and BMI for repertory had occasionally verged on the adolescent in self-serving advertisements and public-relations statements. Many in the music business, however, had become aware that the vendettas of the past were best forgotten, for insofar as the societies were concerned, when one was wounded the other often bled. The CBS application for per-use licensing, NBC's demand for limited access to copyrighted music, and the extended and expensive legal defenses that followed had wedded the two, despite themselves, into an awareness that they must and could live together. Acceptance of the fact was difficult for veteran executives and members of the society, with their bitter memories of the 1940 music war, as well as the lawsuits, Congressional hearings, and vitriolic attacks of the 1950s. The increasing economic significance of performance royalties was emphasized by the verity that the organizations' joint distributions had outgrown the combined profits from printed-music sales and mechanical fees and were rapidly increasing. The retirement in 1974 of Herman Finkelstein, ASCAP's veteran general counsel, and that of Sydney Kaye from BMI presaged an uncertain relaxation of tensions. The Aiken case, in which the owner of a carry-out restaurant threatened to overthrow the law on which all nonbroadcast licensing activities of both were based, served as an important unifying agent.

The 1931 Jewell-LaSalle case, in which ASCAP prevailed at the Supreme Court level, had established the legal precedent for the licensing of hotels, restaurants, department stores, and other places where music was played over multiple speakers. Attorneys for Aiken in the suit for infringement brought by ASCAP and based on the restaurant owner's failure to secure a five-dollar-a-month license for the five speakers in his establishment that relayed radio music to his customers from a single receiver, argued in the lower court that radio music was already cleared for performance under the 1909 Copyright Act. They lost. Another case based on Jewell-LaSalle, involving the $2.1 million collected by ASCAP from such wired music operators as Muzak, was in the lower courts simultaneously. Having charged publicly many times that ASCAP fees were exorbitant, the giant background-music organization took a more than incidental interest in Aiken and gave the restaurant owner its support, hoping that the case would be appealed. It was, and was reversed, the court finding a similarity to

Fortnightly and *TelePromter,* in which the Supreme Court had each time ruled that signals transmitted by cable TV merely extended audience reach and therefore did not constitute a performance.

Both ASCAP and Muzak sustained a serious economic loss when the Supreme Court declared in Aiken that radio music was free, removing the reason for background-music services to deal with the former and with establishment owners who wished to set up their own music programing with the latter. Jewell-LaSalle, in the dissenting opinion of Chief Justice Warren Burger, had been "sidestepped." The court majority found that to require Aiken and other small businessmen with radio and television sets on their premises—bars and beauty shoppes, cafeterias and car washes, dentists' offices and drive-ins—to take out music licenses "would result in a regime of copyright law that would both be wholly unenforceable and highly inequitable." Even if such a vast licensing procedure was viable, "it would unfairly enrich copyright holders who would reap from an untold number every time a single song was played on the radio."

The decision underscored once again the need for omnibus copyright revision, based on an awareness of advancing technology and recent experience. A bill being considered in Congress stated that the exemption allowed a single radio or television set in small establishments did not apply where broadcast music was "further transmitted to the public [reaching] substantial audiences." After nearly a decade of frustration, the music industry and the societies were confronted with the realization that a united coalition of forces, stripped of past enmities, was necessary in order to effect the passage of revision before the next Congress recessed. Otherwise they would have to learn to live under the 1909 act for years to come.

Another of the rifts that had been a continuing plague, the one between songwriters organized in the American Guild of Authors and Composers and the publishers represented by the National Music Publishers Association, was also on its way to mending. In 1967, after serving as president of the AGAC for ten years, Burton Lane had stepped down for Edward Eliscu, a Broadway and Hollywood lyricist, whose principal collaborators had been Vincent Youmans, Vernon Duke, and Billy Rose, one of the guild's founders. Membership in the guild was at an all-time high, 2,400, and collections in the royalty plan Lane had instituted in 1959 hit a high of three million dollars, at which they remained for many years.

Eliscu encouraged a more collegial relationship with BMI writers, adding to the standard AGAC popular songwriters' contract the line "this agreement is subject to any agreements between the writer and Broadcast Music, Inc." Prior to this change, AGAC contracts and those for the Songwriters Protective Association sanctioned only relationships between members and ASCAP firms. Next, Eliscu opened the guild's door to all writers and publishers, regardless of what societies they were affiliated with, thus acquiring members from ten licensing organizations around the world. A new system for dues payments was instituted in 1972, classifying members according to their royalty income. When Eliscu was succeeded as president in 1973 by the composer Ervin Drake, he confessed his frustration at being unable, after lobbying for three years, to win a fight for a proper reward to the secondary lyric writer, the one who wrote words in English for foreign songs. At the 1970 meeting of the Confederation of International Societies of Authors and Composers, Eliscu had won a statement of intention and support calling for payment to the secondary writer in any territory other than that controlled by a subpublisher. It had not been implemented. The fight for this right continued under Drake, still without success, until AGAC succeeded in 1974 in persuading ASCAP to change its royalty statements so that foreign performances could be counted on an itemized song-by-song, country-by-country basis. Unlike BMI, which did provide such information, ASCAP had traditionally lumped all foreign-writer earnings into a single dollar amount. The change was expected to goad the foreign societies to do the same. AGAC's Catalog Administration Plan, instituted in 1972 to supply administrative services to the growing number of writer-publisher operations, for a small percentage of their income, was also moving ahead. And, having learned the political advantages inherent in an alliance with a major grass-roots association, under Drake AGAC established close ties with the Nashville Songwriters Association International, which became a potent lobbying force in copyright proceedings.

The SPA and the AGAC's former West Coast affiliate the Composers and Lyricists Guild, first felt shock waves from the CBS per-use suit near the end of 1972. Next to the American Federation of Musicians the most important labor union dealing with music, the CLGA still had been unable to obtain a renewal of its original two-year contract with the picture studios and the Association of Motion Picture and Television Producers. The agreement had established base pay, guaranteed health and welfare benefits, and affirmed the right of members to collect performance royalties through the societies. Early in 1972, a $300-million antitrust suit was filed in the New York federal court against the three TV networks and eight major studios. It charged a conspiracy in restraint of trade, because the defendants had all agreed to sign a new contract that would not allow the plaintiffs to retain ownership of music they had written for the defendants. The plaintiffs were headed by Elmer Bernstein, president of CLGA, Percy Faith, Henry Mancini, Nelson Riddle, and there were 128 other composers and lyricists. They also complained that because of existing conditions in Hollywood they were precluded from performing their own recent TV feature and movie music in public. The suit asked that the defendants be stripped of the right in previous contracts to assign music to their own publishing companies. In September, CBS severed itself from the lawsuit by returning to those plaintiffs who had been employed by the network the rights to music written for past programs and offering to negotiate future contracts that left these rights to the plaintiffs.

The patience of other defendants was rewarded in June 1974 when the suit was dismissed. The judge ruled that the matter was a labor dispute, more properly within the jurisdiction of the National Labor Relations Board, which had given the CLGA its status as a union. The decision added that on three occasions in the 1960s the plaintiffs had negotiated their contracts with film and television producers through their union, the CLGA. The protest of those much-in-demand composers Bernstein, Mancini, and Riddle that they had always negotiated individually with producers, using expensive agents and legal representatives, failed to persuade the judge otherwise.

Motion-picture and television-feature sound tracks had lost their appeal to record-club members almost immediately after the great studio hunt began for rock-'n'-roll songwriters and performers. There were no sound track or TV program-music albums on the Top 10 LPs of the Year charts from 1971 until 1976 except for 1974, when "American Graffiti," a collection of rock-'n'-roll golden oldies, used to great advantage in the highly successful movie of the same name, made the number-one position, and proved to be so successful that a double LP of more of the same was issued. The combination of superstars Barbara Streisand and Kris Kristofferson in the feature film *A Star Is Born* was preserved on an LP that went on sale in time for Christmas 1976; its sales were in excess of three million dollars by summer. In addition, more than 100 cover versions of the picture's theme song, "The Love Theme . . . Evergreen," were recorded. The movie sound track was back. The producers of *A Star Is Born* had employed only the crossover marketing that had shaped post-Depression Tin Pan Alley.

A sound-track LP with "Rocky Theme," which also appeared as a single, vividly duplicating the series of crescendo effects of the final scene in the movie *Rocky,* did much to sell that low-budget picture to audiences and help it win the Motion Picture Academy's Oscar as the year's best movie in 1976. When Bill Conti, composer of the score, had seen the final rushes, the dramatic musical effects he had expected in the finale had been lost. Believing they could be retrieved by reshooting and rescoring, he had persuaded the producers to spend an additional $50,000. The gamble more than paid off.

Scores by Conti, John Williams's work for *Jaws,* Leonard Rosenman's for *Barry Lyndon,* Jerry Goldsmith's for many successful box-office hits, and work by others had persuaded some producers to permit screen composers greater participation in production, often from the start of shooting through to the finished print. The fees for those members of the CLGA most wanted by producers now climbed over the $25,000 that only a Mancini, Riddle, LeGrand, or Barry had previously obtained, to as much as

$50,000 a film. They also got a share in publishing through their own company; a producer's percentage of the LP list price; and a two to three percent royalty for rerecording the music in a recording studio. The price for doing what had once been hackwork scores for NBC's *Movie of the Week* rose from $5,000 to $10,000, as did the quality of the music. Top film composers insisted on clauses in their contracts that required a 50 percent reuse charge when a production was sold overseas for theatrical exhibition. Insofar as these men were concerned, the CLGA's functions were no longer necessary, and when the lawsuit was settled in the late 1970s, it made little difference despite a compromise surrender of their right to exploit film music in the event the studios or producers did not.

Screen music written by composers of an earlier generation, men who had usually worked for hire, had found its way into the catalogues of Mills Music in late 1969, when it merged with one of the earliest silent motion-picture background-music companies, Belwin. Formed by Max Winkler in 1918, Belwin had published the biggest-selling silent-movie theme song of the 1920s, "Charmaine," originally "Valse Thematique," written by Erno Rapee. Lew Pollack wrote lyrics for it in 1926, for the promotion of the feature film *What Price Glory*. Belwin had also published massive compilations of public-domain and original music for the screen-theater organists, pianists, and small instrumental combinations or large pit orchestras. The company had become one of the most important publishers of educational music materials, sheet music, and folios, and served as the American representative for many foreign houses, renting and selling the music of Ricordi, Novello, Salabert, Casa Musicale Sonzogno, Hans Sikorski, and others. The transfer of Mills's ownership from the public-service holding company, Utilities & Industries Management Corp., which had bought it in 1965 for around five million dollars, to the new Belwin-Mills Publishing Corp., involved turning over 47 percent of Belwin-Mills's stock to U & I in exchange for its 100 percent interest in Mills Music. Then 53 percent of Belwin-Mills was transferred to the Winkler family, in exchange for all its Belwin stock.

As the tendency grew in music publishing to use one of a small group of well-established companies with first-class printing and distributing facilities for the printed-music portion of their business, E. B. Marks contracted, in 1973, with Belwin-Mills for the latter to be its exclusive representative for all printed products. MCA–Leeds/Duchess entered into a joint venture around the same time with Mills Music, by then a Belwin-Mills division. Mills agreed to promote, warehouse, and ship all already-printed MCA publications and to assume editorial responsibility for new ones. The acquisition of the Kalmus reprint catalogue of more than 6,000 titles in 1976 added 48,000 active titles to the Belwin-Mills repertory and an additional 40,000 from agency commitments.

These and other transfers of copyrights had been painstakingly worked out over a period of months, for only those music houses owned by record companies with major foreign publishing and subpublishing connections were in a position to act with speed in the following years. The Polydor Records division of Phonogram International, the recently activated combination of Philips and Deutsche Grammophon interests, made its bow in the United States in the summer of 1970. An autonomous unit, like all Phonogram companies, and without a pressing plant or distribution facility of its own, Polydor arranged for distribution through United Artists. Two years later, Mercury Records Productions and its associated labels, including American Philips, in all of which a 35 percent interest had been acquired in 1965 by North American Philips (Norelco), were transferred to the Phonogram group. The transfer included Norelco's 49 percent interest in Chappell Music, for a reported $30 million, thus giving Phonogram complete control of the giant music operation. The true complexity of Philips's North American holdings was made public in 1974 in connection with the Dutch combine's projected takeover, through Norelco, of Magnavox for about $150 million, in order for Philips to move into the American videodisk, blank-tape, and video-cassette/recorder and audio business. Sixty-one percent of Norelco was owned by the United States Philips Trust and the balance by a European holding company that controled Philips N.V., the thirteenth largest international company, with revenues of $8.1 billion in 1973.

Phonogram's next move in building up an American record business was almost a year in the making. After losing six million dollars in 1968 and again in 1969, MGM Records' financial picture had improved under its new president, twenty-nine-year-old Mike Curb. For several years, he and the record division enjoyed an autonomy previously denied to anyone by Metro-Goldwyn-Mayer's ruling hierarchy. They produced a string of successful soft rock, middle-of-the-road, and bubble-gum hits. One of their most successful groups, the Osmond family, broke the Beatles' record-winning streak and received ten RIAA Gold Record awards in a single year. Curb stayed on for a year after Phonogram bought MGM Records in 1972, for an undisclosed sum, decorating his wall with another multimillion-selling record, Donny Osmond's "Puppy Love," before he sold his share of MGM stock to Phonogram and withdrew.

Metro-Goldwyn-Mayer had also sold its vast British-based Affiliated Music Publishing group to Phonogram in 1972, receiving $10 million. It insisted on retaining ownership of Robbins, Feist & Miller, finally disposing of it to the United Artists/Transamerica in 1974, during another of the financial crises that regularly plagued the company.

Having broadened its American base, Phonogram moved to consolidate the manufacture and distribution of its products. The result was that it moved higher in the reigning order of the domestic record business, into the company of WCI, Columbia, RCA, MCA, and Capitol-EMI.

Many of the long-established publishing companies had not yet recovered from cultural and economic shocks sustained during the 1960s. For years, they had depended on their established contract writers for hit songs and those B sides that backed them on singles and filled LPs to support one or two hits. Most of these writers had not been able to cope with rock 'n' roll and faded into inactivity. While the old-line houses sat back on their AS-CAP and, occasionally, BMI income and the mechanical royalties from old standard songs that were rerecorded from time to time, they awaited the return of "good music." In doing so, they had missed the opportunity, in the late 1940s and early 1950s, when new technology was making it possible for almost anybody to get into the record business, to use their not inconsiderable financial resources to form their own record companies.

Now it was the record companies that were taking over, making it truer each day, as Stanley Gortikov of the RIAA told a copyright revision hearing in 1975, that, though publishers had once performed many creative marketing functions, in recent years they had become "heavily administrative and clerical; they are largely service entities, conduits for the processing of income and paper transactions. They don't promote as they used to. They don't employ field representatives as they used to. They don't create demand as they used to. These functions have necessarily been taken over by the recording companies."

In the new state of amity that prevailed between the NMPA and the AGAC, fostered by the exigencies of forcing through omnibus copyright revision, Ervin Drake, president of the AGAC, embraced both old-line and new publishers. "We view publishers," he said, "as our partners in a sense that is best expressed by the word 'symbiosis.' It is true that a publisher's work may not begin 'til our work is complete; but in the large sense, our work is not complete until they exercise their functions properly as publishers."

Sam Trust, president of American ATV Music, recommended to the plethora of writer-artists untutored in the complexities of the business, which increased every day, that they allow "a knowledgable publisher to protect" their interests. He recommended co-publishing deals, in which the publisher shares ownership.

Negotiation with a superstar, or one regarded as certain to acquire such eminent status within the foreseeable future, designed to acquire co-publishing rights, involved the outlay of more cash than ever before in the music business. Front money was being pushed ever higher by the major manufacturers in the bidding for talent. There were certain drawbacks however. In the early 1970s, when LPs still sold for the $4.98 reintroduced in 1969, standard artist royalties averaged around 7.5 percent. There was little risk for Columbia in the $50,000 Clive Davis paid to sign the Electric Flag, with Buddy Miles and Mike Bloomfield, in 1967. Half of it was immediately written off toward the cost of recording, which was exacted from the top of artists' royalties until completely retrieved. With a profit of around seventy-five cents from each LP unit, the entire $50,000 was more than recouped from the sale of 70,000 copies, with promotion and advertising costs still be be absorbed. However, as Joe Smith of Warner said in *Rolling Stone* in 1971, "the group still does not have its advance money back because they're recovering it at a lesser rate than we [the record company] are. . . . At 100,000 albums they've paid back their advance and recording costs, and from then on they're making money. But only 10 to 15 percent of the albums sell that well."

Artist guarantees, if not their royalties, grew after 1967, when Brian Epstein renegotiated the Beatles' contract with EMI. Some leading San Francisco acid-rock groups got $250,000 in front. Donovon, balladeer of the flower children, was paid $100,000 on signing with Columbia/Epic in 1965, and a guaranteed $20,000 a year until 1970, a period during which he delivered "Sunshine Superman," "Mellow Yellow," "There Is a Mountain," and "Hurdy Gurdy," all RIAA Gold Record awards.

Clive Davis's negotiations to sign Janis Joplin, who had made a stunning impression on him at the 1967 Monterey Pop Festival, were far more expensive and complicated, and took a year to become final. The Texas belter was part of the Big Brother and the Holding Company troupe, which was already signed by Mainstream Records, a minor independent label. In order to get them and her, Davis bought off Mainstream for $200,000, half of which was charged as an advance to Big Brother, together with a two percent override on Columbia's first two LPs. Luckily, one of them held Joplin's first hit, "Piece of My Heart." Blood, Sweat & Tears joined Columbia for a mere $25,000 advance, to which a loan of $10,000 was added just before their second album went into production. It included three Gold singles and sold four million units. Davis's four- to eight-million-dollar contract with Neil Diamond, as it was reported in the trade press, was the second he negotiated with the songwriter-singer. The first had been in 1968, when Diamond was ready to break away from the small Bang label on which he had started the climb to superstardom. Davis's offer was immediately topped by MCA Records, a $250,000 guarantee on behalf of its UNI label and the promise of a motion-picture appearance. Five years later, when some time was still left on Diamond's MCA contract, his representatives let both Columbia and Warner know that he was looking for a new record connection. Davis suggested a $2.5-million contract, $250,000 an LP for ten albums, the highest offer he had yet made. Warner countered with a $4-million package, $400,000 an album for a total of ten. Preferring to join Columbia, Diamond signed with Davis, but on the terms that Warner had proposed.

This record-setting arrangement was surpassed in 1974 by one put together by MCA to effect the renewal of Elton John's contract. All six of his LP releases had sold more than a million units, "gone platinum," as it was known after 1976, when the RIAA introduced a new super award to recognize the explosion of sales then taking place. A new Rocket Records label had already been created for John and his protégés, so MCA offered him the highest recording-artist guarantee yet known, in excess of eight million. It called for one million dollars each for a half-dozen new LPs during the five-year life of the contract, as well as $1.40 royalty on every $6.98 album. John's next three LPs went platinum, and his tenth album, "Captain Fantastic and the Brown Dirt Cowboy," was number one "with a bullet" in the trade papers the first week it went on sale, having moved 1.4 million units in the preceding four days.

The contract for exclusive song-writing services that John and his lyricist partner Bernie Taupin had signed with Dick James Music Ltd. in 1967 was soon to expire. Under its terms, he had received an initial fifty pounds advance and a weekly fifteen pounds guarantee against the 20 percent author's share of royalties alloted him in the agreement, and seventeen-year-old Taupin, three years his junior, was paid ten pounds each week. The following year, Dick James Music took over management of Elton John as a performer for 30 percent of all income. These figures and others were first made public in papers filed with the British High Court in 1985 relative to a lawsuit that asked for the return of 137 songs written by the team and turned over between 1967 and 1975 to Dick James Music, whose property they would otherwise remain until fifty years after the death of both members of the team. The papers also stated that adjustments had been made in 1970 that gave John 40 percent and then 60 percent of his mechanical royalties and reduced the management fee to 20 percent.

Superstars' sales were now in the millions, rather than the hundreds of thousands of the 1960s, and their relationships with record companies and music publishers had reversed, putting them in the driver's seat. A 16 to 18 percent royalty prevailed for them, guaranteed by contracts that had become increasingly complex and had pages and pages of riders. These documents covered anything from record-club royalties (generally half those from retail sales), control over advertising and promotion budgets, the number of review copies to be distributed, the color of promotion T-shirts and satin jackets, control over LP cover artwork, to guaranteed tape-version distribution.

The $650 million from eight-track and cassette tape sales in 1974 accounted for, roughly, more than one quarter of the industry's total $2.2 billion revenue that year. However, while between 10 and 20 percent was subtracted before royalties from gross tape sales, a packaging charge on them might run between 25 and 50 percent. Clever attorneys learned to insist on a fixed packaging charge in terms of cents per unit rather than a percentage.

The energy crisis in late 1973 had an immediate and serious effect on those record manufacturers who did not own pressing plants, as well as on new performers. There was a shortage of polyvinyl chloride, made from petroleum, from which both records and tapes were manufactured. Custom pressing was immediately canceled by the large manufacturers, and some small firms were driven out of business. There was also a general reduction of new releases by independents. To avoid rising production costs occasioned by the shortage, new and untried talents were offered the release of one single, and as much as a year was used to determine whether to exercise an option. If album deals were offered, an advance against earnings was paid only after delivery of the finished tapes. New talents thus looked more to established music firms for co-publishing deals, and co-ownership by as many as a half-dozen corporations, most of them owned by members of the group, became routine.

Superstars were, by definition, above such mundane considerations as an international shortage of petroleum. Their guarantees continued to set new levels of economic reward and personal privilege. Eight months before his contracts with EMI and Capitol-EMI as a member of the Beatles were to expire, at the end of 1975, Paul McCartney renewed agreements with both for his exclusive services until 1978 for an undisclosed amount. The press speculated that the Elton John figures had been bettered, and McCartney's guarantee was in excess of eight million dollars. The agreement called for one album a year by McCartney and his new group, Wings, whose third release, "Band on the Run," put out in late 1973, sold more than six million copies, matching the success of the Beatles' biggest album and their last, "Let It Be." Deferring to McCartney's demand, EMI and Capitol released new Wings' songs throughout the world, not as Apple productions, but on a label bearing the old Capitol logo, under which the most successful Beatles' records had been merchandised.

For much of the 1970s, about two thirds of the income of ATV Music came from Lennon-McCartney songs, without regard to which of the two had actually written them. Sir Lew Grade's music company, built on the rocks of Northern Songs and Maclen Music, lost all McCartney songs written after his exclusive contract with ATV expired in 1973. When Wings first began recording, and the ATV contracts were still in effect, many of the songs were credited to Mr. and Mrs. Paul McCartney, which would reduce world-wide royalties on the new material. Grade instituted a court action for breach of contract, claiming that Linda McCartney was incapable of writing music; he lost. From that point on, all new McCartney songs were published by MPL Communications, owned by Paul and his wife.

In 1974, ATV became the co-publisher throughout the world of all new songs written by John Lennon. The arrangement resulted from a settlement of Lennon's earlier charge that ATV had defrauded him of about nine million in royalties, filed as a counterclaim to ATV's own million-dollar suit against Lennon and his wife, Yoko Ono, for "unlawfully abridging" Maclen's contract with Lennon. Albums of music co-written by John and Yoko and performed by them, but crediting a half-share of the music to Lenono

Music, appeared on the Apple label and were a chief reason for the legal action.

The Beatles were finally and for all time broken up. George Harrison had his own label, Dark House, issued by A & M, and Ringo Starr was appearing on Polydor releases.

It fell to Stevie Wonder, Berry Gordy's blind *Wunderkind* discovery, who had matured into a true genius of studio-recorded music, to establish a new ceiling on record-company guarantees. Soon after the new McCartney-EMI contracts were signed, Wonder accepted a $14-million offer from Motown Records. He had won nine Grammy awards in the last two years, his six most recent LPs had each sold more than 500,000 copies, and he was the recipient of thirteen RIAA Gold Record awards. The new seven-year contract was to become effective as soon as Wonder delivered a two-LP "concept" album, "Songs in the Key of Life," on which he was working as composer, producer, engineer-mixer, singing artist and performer on the assemblage of electronic instruments he had mastered. The new agreement paid him a royalty of 20 percent on the retail price of all future albums, and reaffirmed the complete artistic control over his recordings that he had won on reaching his twenty-first birthday, as well as ownership of all original Wonder compositions used in his albums. "Songs in the Key of Life" was delivered to Motown in May 1976, and a check for the $14 million was handed to Wonder.

Like Stevie Wonder, the superstars now were in a position to insist that their music go to their own publishing houses, which generally were administered or operated on a co-publishing basis by well-established firms with a substantial catalogue of their own copyrights. One significant exception was Paul McCartney, whose MPL Communications, formed in 1973, was directed by his father-in-law, the experienced entertainment-business attorney Lee Eastman. Using royalties paid by ATV for old Lennon-McCartney songs and those paid to MPL for subsequent McCartney music, Eastman built the new company into an entity of major proportions. All Buddy Holly copyrights, among McCartney's favorite music, were acquired first, followed by others that were not only rock-'n'-roll music, but also hit songs dating back to the 1940s and 1950s. In 1976, Eastman made another major buy, E. H. Morris Music, the property of his old friend and client Buddy Morris, for nine million dollars. The company, which owned the scores of many successful stage musicals of the past three decades, remained a separate, wholly owned entity. McCartney's quarter interest in Apple Corps was another MPL asset. The only one of the Beatles not to have consented to be represented by Allen Klein in 1969, McCartney applied for and won court appointment of a receiver for his share of Apple. When the other Beatles sued Klein, in 1973, charging mishandling of their interests, Klein countersued for breach of contract, and also instituted a $42-million action against McCartney, claiming that he had induced the other three to bring the action. The matter ended in McCartney's favor three years later, but Lennon, Starr, and Harrison paid $4.2 million to settle the affair. Apple Records, the nexus of the action, had closed its doors in May 1975.

Such splintering of what had once been a highly concentrated business, controlled in the United States by a handful of firms, into hundreds of entities, each working with older firms, had given the NMPA new importance and a far larger base of prospective members. The association was doing exemplary work in Washington, directing activities there for itself and for major songwriter organizations in a unified fight for copyright revision. The appearance of NMPA and Harry Fox Agency attorneys on behalf of publisher plaintiffs in record-piracy cases had led to the passage in 1971 of legislation that broadened the scope of relief for copyright owners. Modern technology had provided a new tool for the printed-music pirate's workshop, the photocopying machine, and the NMPA was in the forefront of a drive to educate unwitting violators of copyright owners' rights and to establish "fair use" guidelines for educators and libraries.

The NMPA had been active in 1954 in getting the United States to adhere to the Universal Copyright Convention, and its representatives were part of the U.S. delegation to the 1971 UCC revision conference. In performing the functions of a trade association, the NMPA had been active in securing the amendment of tax laws that discriminated against music publishers and in the extension of preferential postal rates to printed music and records. The association's membership had tripled in six years, to 120 members representing music interests in eighteen states and encompassing all contemporary expressions of vernacular music. The board of directors was expanded to eighteen members and included representatives of Motown-Jobete Music and Acuff-Rose Publications, exhibiting a diversity of taste its MPPA founders would have found offensive.

The first "official" survey of the retail volume of printed-music sales was undertaken by the NMPA in 1971, in cooperation with the Music Publishers Association of the United States (the direct descendant of the nineteenth-century Board of Music Trade), the Church Music Publishers Association, and the International Gospel Music Association. Only the sale of hymnals was uncounted. During the ensuing four years, sales rose at an average rate of nearly 20 percent, from $120.1 million to $197.8 million in 1975, a period during which the average retail price of sheet music increased by one third, from $1.00 to $1.50, and the wholesale price from forty-two to sixty-seven cents. Throughout this period, songwriter royalties had remained constant, between four and eight cents.

Considering the difference in the value of the American dollar in the six decades since World War I, when songs sold millions of ten-cent copies, the NMPA's figures accurately mirrored the decline and fall of the full-service music house, from its eminence in the days before recordings cost more than five dollars and enjoyed an annual sales of fewer than 100-million units, as they had in 1920. Music-publishing revenues had, in four years, dropped below those the year before, and a further fall of between 12 and 15 percent was anticipated for 1976.

The publishing of sheet music, the "single" of printed music, and the folio, containing from twelve to forty songs and comparable to the LP album, had become the monopoly of several large companies: the youngest, formed in 1971, Screen Gems–Columbia Publications, owned by Columbia Pictures; Charles Hansen Publications; Warner Brothers Music; and the oldest, Big Three Music, owned by United Artists. Working out of fully equipped and self-contained printing and production facilities housed in Florida, with staffs of professional arrangers, Screen Gems and Hansen did about two thirds of their industry's $140-million annual retail gross in 1975. Unless it was already licensed or sublicensed to them, each time a new song appeared on the trade papers' Top 100 singles charts the companies went into action, using the telephone to offer their services to publishers, record companies, or the artist-songwriters. They discussed the possibility of printing sheet music at once, or, in the case of stars and superstars, the publication of a "personality folio," containing the newest hit with other songs they had recorded or with which they were associated. Distribution of both forms was handled in Screen Gems' case by regional jobbers who dealt with the estimated 4,000 music stores that carried printed items, and with the music departments of record and department stores. Rack jobbers took care of the outlets they traditionally had dealt with—department, chain, discount, and individual retail stores. Mail-order business was handled by the printing companies themselves. Hansen had its own distributing chain—seven jobbing and/or retailing companies scattered around the country, which handled only Hansen merchandise. In addition, Hansen owned twenty-four retail music stores and additional concessions in strategic markets.

Sheet music was still purchased mostly because of the accessibility of its melody. A song with a memorable tune sold as many as 100,000 copies, though "The Way We Were," the Oscar-winning song in 1973, sold three times that number in the initial stages of its popularity. A personality, or celebrity, folio or a collection of songs by a well-known performer or group sold from 10,000 to 50,000 copies. There was a super-selling folio, Carole King's *Tapestry,* which contained all the songs from her eight-million-copy LP seller of the same name.

Only the recession-depression the country went through in 1974–75 precluded an immediate widening of the market into the educational field, which eventually proved to be printed music's biggest consumer. Whether or not the 94th Congress finally agreed on copyright revision, the sheet-music folio business had to update and make more aggressive its merchandising and expand its distribution apparatus. With the number of titles on an LP now reduced from twelve to ten, the record business was less of a promotional influence on sheet music. Such a tried-and-true booster of sheet music as Andy Williams, whose albums contained both melodic new songs and standards of years gone by, had been cut from three LPs a year to only one. The Top 40 stations had squeezed their play lists again, down to twenty songs. The future of music publishing lay in the laps of record-company presidents or in the hands of Congressional legislators.

CHAPTER 27

The "Seven Dirty Words" Case and MOR Music

An estimated 400 of the 2,700 FM stations on the air in 1972, including those on college campuses, claimed to be programing progressive-rock music. However, the major record companies attached importance to only a half-dozen. Jac Holzman, of Warner-owned Elektra, found that because underground radio was essentially being financed by the leading manufacturers through advertising schedules and other support, it tried "to give everybody a taste." The airwaves had become glutted with mediocre music in the process. FM stations were using imported records given them by promotion men. "Until FM can begin to create new artists out of its own professional capabilities, I will be disappointed in the medium," Holzman told *Record World* in 1971. "Why not use [their] time to expose creatively new material which, in the opinion of the station's music staff, makes a musical contribution? I'm asking FM radio to go a bit more out on a limb than they have in the past."

Top 40 radio, unlike underground FM, was not confronted with the threat of government censorship, which, under several communication acts, the FCC was forbidden to exercise. Since the first broadcast of popular music, there had been varying degrees of protest over its content. Soon after Elvis Presley rotated his pelvis within full view of a national television audience, complaints moved to the content of rock-'n'-roll music, a discontent that network TV and Top 40 radio sought to defuse by internal censorship. The Rolling Stones had nearly been replaced by a trained-seal act on the *Ed Sullivan Show* after it was learned that they intended to sing their current hit, "Let's Spend the Night Together." A compromise was hastily struck for the sake of ratings and a coast-to-coast plug, and the group sang it on camera as "Let's Spend Some Time Together."

With the war accelerating in Southeast Asia and social protest growing, the gap between generations widened, and was nowhere more apparent than in the recorded music played on FM radio. Songs were no longer about love, as they had been in the Coolidge-to-Eisenhower pop-music era. While the electronic media relied on censorship to alleviate pressure from adults on their programing, underground, freewheeling FM broadcasters and disk jockeys made a Freedom Hall of the air, claiming it to be a place open to any recording, regardless of content.

In response to many protests about rock-'n'-roll "thrill" lyrics and songs about smoking pot or going on LSD trips, in the summer of 1967 the FCC was forced to admit that it was powerless to do anything. Recent Supreme Court decisions affecting questionable motion pictures, magazines, and books made the commissioners apprehensive about going on record with their consequent decision not to engage in censorship of questionable song lyrics.

Upon prodding from a new Nixon-appointed FCC chairman, as well as from the White House, which feared that "smut and indecent language" would grow without action by the commission, a public notice was issued in March 1971 calling attention to various complaints about song lyrics, which some feared promoted the use of illegal drugs, and warning broadcasters that they were responsible for the meaning of the words they broadcast. Almost immediately, such hits as the Beatles' "With a Little Help from My Friends" were removed from play lists. Fearing that they might have been understood, the commissioners issued a second notice, a month later, asserting that they did not intend to ban the playing of drug-oriented music; instead, they expected broadcasters to make discretion a part of their licensed responsibilities. When the FCC refused to accept a proposed program policy offered by Yale University in its application for an FM license, on the grounds that it was "abstract" in dealing with lyric screening, the matter went to the U.S. Court of Appeals in Washington for a rehearing and a clarification of the commissioners' language. In March 1973, the court refused to take any action in the matter.

After playing an LP that contained a questionable four-letter word not usually heard on the air, a notoriously antiwar Norfolk, Virginia, FM disk jockey was indicted, for having uttered "obscene, indecent and profane language, which language is not included in the indictment as the same would defile the records of this [federal district] court." Quickly, the Norfolk U.S. attorney was authorized by the Justice Department to call off the government's prosecution, on the ground that the disk jockey had not made the management of his station aware of the word used on the LP.

The "seven dirty words" case began its slow march to the Supreme Court in October 1973, when a New York City parent complained to the FCC that his son had been exposed to foul language when a George Carlin monologue, recorded on the LP "George Carlin, Occupation: Foole" was broadcast over publicly supported FM station WBAI. The seven words, four nouns and three verbs, were terms for "sexual or excretory activities and organs." Ignoring the statute forbidding it to censor radio communications, the FCC sought to establish standards for regulating obscenity on the air and censured WBAI for irresponsibility. An FCC order banned the seven words from the air.

Nearly four years passed before the U.S. Court of Appeals in Washington overturned the FCC's "dirty word ruling," finding it too broad and carrying the commission "beyond protection of the public interest into the forbidden realms of censorship." If taken to an extreme, the judges found, the order could prohibit the broadcast of Shakespeare's *Tempest* or *Two Gentlemen of Verona,* or some passages from the Bible.

In an atmosphere of lowering standards, which might invite FCC intervention into every programing and advertising facet of an increasingly prosperous industry's operations, the National Association of Broadcasters board of directors voted to support WBAI. They knew full well what could be lost if the court found against the station. It did so, in July 1978, saying that the FCC had properly exercised its right to regulate and punish a broadcast of indecent material. In light of the strenuous campaign of over-all deregulation of government-controlled industries being pursued by the Carter administration, it was generally considered doubtful, and correctly so, that the ruling would have any meaningful effect.

Although there were many music and program directors around the country capable of doing as Holzman urged in 1971, owners of many AM and FM operations continued to look to the program counselors and the taped-show producers to perform all programing functions. Bill Drake, the best known and most successful of the former, had worked as a program director in the San Francisco market during the early 1960s, with Tom Donahue on his staff. It was there that Drake first refined and modernized Todd Storz's now stale Top 40 formula by creating a format with more music, less talk, and fewer commercials. It was on this that Donahue later grounded his revolutionary free-form FM programing.

Ever ready to take any advertising revenues offered them, the Top 40 stations continued to reduce music time on the air in the interest of profits. Responding to growing complaints from the public, in mid-decade the NAB finally took action and imposed a self-governing policy on its members; it reduced commercial announcements to a maximum of eighteen minutes every hour. Soon after he became program director of KHJ Los Angeles, in May 1965, Drake reduced spots further, to twelve an hour. He also created a twenty-twenty news policy (twenty minutes past and before the hour), and held his disk jockeys to a tight eight seconds for introducing each record. His play lists included only thirty-three current hit singles, based on *Billboard's* Hot 100 and reports from local record dealers, as well as three "hit-bound singles," chosen by Drake, and later by assistants. The pool of

400 "golden oldies" that was available for fillers occupied almost every minute of weekend air time, when everybody in the Los Angeles area was either on the road or on the beach.

With radio-station owner Gene Chenault as his partner, to run the business side, Drake and Drake-Chenault Enterprises became far-famed in the business in 1968, the year of its formation, as a take-charge program consultancy. It seemed certain to raise ratings when RKO-General took Drake on to supervise the operation of its thirteen AM and FM stations. His regular fee for personal service became $100,000 plus a monthly retainer. Drake-Chenault's major division, American Independent Radio, was formed to supply taped programing to stations in medium- and smaller-size markets, which did much to eliminate the use of local deejays. AIR's initial package was "Hitparade" made available only to fully automated stations, followed by "Super Gold Rock 'n' Roll" and programs that appealed to various social and age groups, among them "Great American Country," "Supersoul," "Classic Gold," "Contempo 200," and "300," and a fifty-hour "History of Rock 'n' Roll." Each basic library offered an initial fifty one-hour tape reels, to which additional reels were added regularly, all produced and distributed by a Drake-Chenault unit. The cost for packages ranged in 1976, from $550 to $5,000 a month, depending on the size of the market. AIR's total income in 1980 was an estimated three million dollars.

The oldest and most successful of the syndicated FM rock-concert tape packages, "The King Biscuit Flower Hour," went on the air in 1972 and within three years was being sent to six million people every second Sunday night over 175 stations, all in top markets. In the case of a Rolling Stones concert, the audience was estimated to be nine million people. Booking agencies, managers, and the record companies' promotion people fought to get their major artists on the taped live remotes and their new releases on programs. A number of broadcasts were also issued as live albums. "The King Biscuit Flower Hour" required at least twenty to thirty promotion spots for the program each week.

The syndicated taped-program business would not have been feasible without the automated facilities installed in many of the country's 2,000 FM stations in 1970 in order to multi-plex music and provide background music services. Automation gave several bonuses: it made a 250-watt station sound like its 50,000-watt competitors; it paved the way for phasing out the two-dollar-an-hour disk jockey; and it added to profits by reducing the number of engineers to the one who took care of the equipment and did other household chores. The tape cartridges, or "carts," used in an automated operation were much like the standard eight-track commercial product, but were driven at 7.5 inches per second, instead of the standard 3.75. In the early stages of tape-cartridge use in radio, disk jockeys inserted each one into the player separately and waited for the appropriate moment to set it spinning. Technological improvements moved the player out of the manual stage, with, first, a carousel accommodating twenty-four carts, and then a stacking-rack mechanism with several variations. Governed by its computer, an automated broadcast used only pretaped music, commercials, station identification, telephone calls, disk-jockey banter, time announcements, and other business, all of which appeared to give the spontaneity of a completely live operation. By 1977, such a system cost more than $1,000 a month to rent; it could be purchased for $20,000 to $70,000.

Those stations that could not afford or did not care to pay for the services of a programing consultant had the trade-paper charts and the mimeographed newsletters to help them revise each week's play lists. The first trade paper to print a music chart, *Billboard,* was held in the highest regard by station managements; later arrivals in the field, *Variety, Cash Box,* and *Record World,* were soon close behind. Second only to *Billboard* in esteem, Bill Gavin's *Record Report* was an offshoot of his *Lucky Lager Dance Time* weekly lists, produced by the McCann-Erickson advertising agency, and first issued to western record stations as a promotional medium for the beer. The *Gavin Record Report* was begun as a private enterprise in 1958. Initially, it dealt with Top 40 records; then the five-page weekly added all major fields of popular music, offering "Smash of the Week," "Hot Shots," "Sleepers to Watch," "Hit Bound," and other predictions, based on the editor's expert judgment. Gavin was instrumental in turning stations to formats other than Top 40. Under pressure from him and others, a search began for a format that would hold the twenty-five-to-forty-nine audience, one that had grown up on rock music and was ready for more "adult" fare. In the early 1970s, middle-of-the-road music grabbed that share of the audience and, with Top 40 and rock and album-oriented rock (the latest jargon for commercial album-cut radio), held more than half of all listeners.

Prior to the advent of rock 'n' roll, the recording industry had concentrated on a homogenized product that offended few. In the postwar era, it produced such best-selling vocal artists on singles as Frank Sinatra, Patti Page, Peggy Lee, and Tony Bennett, whose average sales looked anemic later, when Presley and the Beatles turned the business around. Those MOR vocal stars were being replaced by those who had sales of millions of albums. Among the new MOR favorites were Jim Nabors, whose singles sold about 50,000 copies, but whose albums quadrupled Sinatra's sales; Neil Diamond; Petula Clark; Bread; Neil Young: the Jackson Five, with ten-year-old Michael Jackson as a central attraction; and Carole King.

Broadcasting magazine printed in 1972 a formula for the success of "assembling and running a big-time, mainstream MOR (homogenized music) station."

Walk into a major market with the license to a 50kw AM station in your hand. Hire a morning man who is a bit uninhibited and not afraid to do anything to get attention. Find nine to ten men for your news department. Buy a helicopter for traffic reports (a fixed-wing aircraft is OK, but often can't get off the ground in bad weather). Hire a former Top 40 program director or jock with a good knowledge of old rock and roll but who still remembers a few Wayne King hits. Pick up at least one of the ball clubs in town, preferably football (and be careful about buying football and baseball for the same year, the schedules overlap). After your key personality's air shift each day, book him into every fair, civic luncheon, garden show and charity fund-raiser in town. And resign yourself to carrying close to 18 minutes of commercials an hour to support all of these operations which your audience will soon be demanding that you maintain and probably expand.

CHAPTER 28

Configurations, Payola, and Soul Music

The improved qualities of prerecorded music tape, which was fast making MOR and other successful formats both practicable and profitable, was one result of the public's growing interest in magnetic recording tape and players. In an excess of enthusiasm, the tape industry predicted that total retail tape sales would climb over one billion dollars by 1975 and represent more than 40 percent of all estimated record sales. If it succeeded in that, the industry that had begun massive improvements in products, merchandising, and promotion only in the mid-1960s would in one decade match the economic progress the record business had needed nearly ninety years to achieve. Professional audio equipment now operated with nearly perfect fidelity at several speeds and could record up to twenty-four tracks on two-inch tape. Equipment for the home, sale of which had jumped from $159 million in 1965 to more than $800 million seven years later, encompassed all configurations, four- and eight-track cartridges, reel-to-reel tapes, and the Philips cassette, whose manufacture had been leased to GE, Revere-Wollensak in the United States, and Sony, Hitachi, Victor, and Columbia.

The cassette's inherent mechanical drawbacks precluded its immediate acceptance by consumers, and the Lear eight-track system remained the product of choice for Americans well into the early 1970s. Possessed of longer playing time and a fully automatic operation, the eight-track offered complete compatability for use in both home and automobile, with all the features that duplicated the sound quality of a high-fidelity record machine. Among the cassette's early failings was its often erratic 1⅞ = ips speed and poor frequency response, which failed to deliver better than passable sound. It was considered, in its early stages, to be incapable of dealing with the high vibration and voltage variations of an automobile's electrical system, but both were conquered by the Lear system, which eventually accounted for 90 percent of all factory automobile installations. By the time eight-track became responsible for four fifths of all prerecorded music sales and the cassette for the remaining 20 percent, more than twenty-four million Lear players were in use, in cars and in homes.

Eight-tract technology continued to improve, and in May 1970 RCA Records, the first major manufacturer with a large catalogue of cartridge music, introduced the revolutionary discrete four-channel, eight-track compatible sound system for car and home use, developed in association with Motorola. High-fidelity aficionados were the first to buy the four-channel phonograph cartridge and special compatible four-channel equipment to play the QuadraDisc, the name RCA bestowed on its new offspring. Sony-Columbia soon unveiled its SQ "Matrix" quadraphonic records, Sansui a QS disk and player, and other manufacturers several new quad conformations, a reminder of the "battle of the speeds" of the late 1940s. Special decoders were usually required, but the standard stereo record cartridge generally sufficed. In each case, however, two additional speakers were needed to bring listeners the magic of sound from all quarters of a room. RCA's QuadraDiscs sold for $6.98 each, owing to the more expensive special compounds called for by the records, masters that were cut at half-speed, and a pressing cycle of forty seconds, several times that for standard disks.

Anticipating an all-quadraphonic industry within five to seven years, to be preceded by RCA's announcement that it was on the brink of phasing out stereo completely, Warner jumped on the discrete quadraphonic bandwagon in 1973 and made ready to go into production for distribution in the United States, Canada, and Japan. Unfortunately, the public failed to share the enthusiasm of hi-fi devotees, who had been primarily responsible for establishing both the LP and stereo. Quadraphonic represented just too much electronic gear for most average consumers, and both discrete and matrix disks disappeared from advertising and the record stores. There remained only the memory of them as one of the greatest fiascos the business had suffered, equaled only by that of the 3⅞-inch Pocket Disc singles, which had been introduced and promoted in 1968 by Philco-Ford. These were simultaneous releases of Warner-Reprise, ABC, Capitol, and other licensed singles masters that could be played on any 33-speed machine and cost forty-nine cents each. With their jackets removed, several dozen Pocket Discs were supposed to fit into a hip pocket. Within the year, they disappeared under the tide of consumer interest in tape equipment, including an improved cassette and a price cut for its record/playback deck, completely different from the eight-track machine, which allowed only the latter function. The new cassette player was superior to the stereo cartridge machine in another respect: a built-in fast forward and reverse that could select any specific band within seconds. Eight-track cartridges played through to the end before a desired selection could be picked out.

It was the American physicist Ray Dolby who made the cassette the winner in the battle of configurations that took place during most of the 1970s. He transformed it from a gadget to a serious hi-fi component with his revolutionary miniaturized B-type noise-reduction unit. Tape hiss and other noises had always been annoying factors for both audio and video tape. Beginning in 1949, when he was still a teen-ager, Dolby was employed by Ampex, and there built his first noise-reduction circuit, for a videotape recorder. Following further education in the United States and at Cambridge University, he worked for several years in India and then, in 1965, returned to London, and opened his first laboratory, where he started work on a professional noise-reduction unit for multitrack recording work. His A-type system, with low-level differential noise reduction, was demonstrated to leading British record manufacturers, beginning with British Decca, which bought up most of his early production. It made a successful debut in America in 1966, after which Dolby started work on the application of his invention to the eight-track cartridge and the cassette. A new B-type circuit, demonstrated in 1970–71, permitted recording engineers to make favorable contrasts between the cassette and the master tape, leading to its adoption by Decca in England and then by RCA in the United States, all of whose cassette production was completely Dolbyized, beginning with the use of the A unit at the recording stage. By late 1972, Dolby had licensing agreements for the B with virtually every large manufacturer in the world except Philips, which had been the first, in 1964, to put out a miniaturized twin-reel system inside a plastic cassette. For a time, Philips promoted its own Dynamic Noise Limiter, which was available only in Norelco-Philips players, but finally it succumbed to the superior qualities of Dolby's invention.

In 1975, sales of tapes of all types accounted for 29 percent of all pre-recorded music sales, most for use on 101 million eight-track units. Over a nine-year period, cassettes had jumped from sales of $6 million, in 1967, to a high of $102 million, in 1972, fell back, but then began a quick comeback two years later. The future for cassettes was highly predictable after the sale in 1975 of 150 million units of blank tapes, an indication of the growing practice of taping music off the air or from borrowed albums.

When disk sales and the number of new releases showed a decline in 1971, it had been the consumers' growing interest in taped music that increased total industry revenues. Writing in *Record World,* the record and music-business consultant Murray Ross pointed out many of the inherent industry problems, which made it the "most under-developed of any billion dollar business in America." All sales were on a consignment basis, with a ninety-day collection cycle, and a return factor, for either exchange or cash, that could be as high as 100 percent. The product's obsolescence began the first day of its exposure for sale. Eighty-one percent of all single releases and 77 percent of all popular albums failed to make a penny of profit. Yet new LPs were being released at the rate of 100 a week, and the number of new taped cartridges and cassettes was up by more than 50 percent, to 4,469 for 1971.

During the past two decades, the integrated rack jobbers had gradually expanded their role in the business, adding wholesale distribution and the operation of one-stop retail and self-service discount locations, bringing them control of nearly 80 percent of the business by the early 1970s. For many years they had serviced the independent labels by delivering copies of new releases to local radio-station program directors and librarians. Now, because of the multiplicity of label stock, often running to more than 100, they could no longer offer the promotional activities most independents needed. The advent of free-form FM had given birth to a new kind of company promotion man, an employee who dealt only with LPs and particular cuts on them. The change made clear, as Ross advocated, that the major manufacturers must undertake the sophisticated, unified advertising, promotion, and marketing practices of producers of more mundane consumer products.

RCA Records was the first, in 1969, to introduce "dual" or "multiple" distribution by restoring to its merchandising chain the company-owned or-franchised distribution facilities that had prevailed in the pre–rack-jobber era. In the next several years, the other eight companies, which had 70 percent of the LP and tape business and half of all singles sales in 1972, made the same return to the past. Only A & M and Motown of the important record firms continued to work exclusively through independent distributors, whose share of the market continued to be around one third for some years to come.

Dual distribution was a blow to rack jobbers. It could be compensated for only by an increase in suggested retail prices, which did come in 1973, when the medium LP price was raised to $5.98. The manufacturers had tested public reaction to an increase by charging premium prices for monster hits. "Jesus Christ Superstar," which sold nearly four million LP and tape units had a suggested $12.00 retail price, and the two-record Neil Diamond "Hot August Night" retailed for $9.98. The day of the $6.98 double LP had arrived, giving people more music for the money but preparing them for yet another increase. Suggested prices remained the farce that rack jobbers and discounters had made of them. Raising their prices to accommodate an increase, rack suppliers paid $3 and charged $3.40 for a $5.98 middle-line album, which was sold for $3.98. The manufacturers' branches paid 5 percent less wholesale than the independent distributors—between $2.86 and $2.90—and sold the middle-line LP for $3.35. The difference was only a few pennies, but it was pennies the business had been built on, and on pennies it would continue to operate.

Recording costs were up by 200 percent. Studio charges had risen from $70 to $120 an hour. The tape that used to be $50 a carton was now $90.

The pre-Presley royalty of four to five percent no longer existed; a 10 percent royalty was general. In some cases an artist got as much as 14 percent; so a nine percent deal was looked upon as a triumph. Quadraphonic appeared to be, more and more, a failure, a debacle subsidized by the general increase in late 1974 to $6.98 for most new album releases and catalogue items, and $1.29 for singles.

Most industry stock prices had tumbled during the Wall Street near-disaster in 1970–71, resulting in a serious loss of investor interest in the business. However, improved earnings reports for 1972, particularly those from CBS and Warner, numbers one and two, turned market analysts around. CBS tape and disk sales for the year were reported to be $340 million, with rock music accounting for over half. Gaining rapidly on its most important competition, Warner Communications reported increased earnings of 25 percent over 1971 and gross sales of $215 million.

An incipient payola scandal affecting the executive suites of several major labels cast a pall over this increasingly rosy picture. It had been heralded by the surprise announcement from CBS early in the summer of 1973 that Clive Davis, president of the reconstituted CBS Records Group since 1971, had been summarily dismissed, and a civil action charging him with improper use of company funds was being filed. Several months before, federal attorneys of the Strike Force Against Organized Crime, working with a federal grand jury in Newark, New Jersey, had asked CBS questions about one of Davis's assistants, and it was this inquiry that had apparently led to his dismissal.

Overnight, the record business became the subject of concentrated attention in regard to alleged payola, the drug traffic, and links to organized crime. Reports that the FCC was investigating dozens of payola complaints were confirmed by a commission spokesman, who added that those of any substance were being turned over to the Justice Department and the Strike Force. Goddard Lieberson, the Columbia record executive who had once served as its driving force and then been shunted to a senior vice-presidency, was named to take Davis's place.

A horrendous picture of payola practices within the business was painted by the press, involving airline tickets purchased with company funds and then turned over to disk jockeys or dummy companies owned by staff promotion men, to be returned for cash; payments to trade papers and weekly tip sheets to ensure the breaking out of selected new releases; and the old business of boxes of new products sent to disk jockeys, to be exchanged for cash by local distributors or sold at substantial discounts to local retailers.

As had the MPPA in the 1930s when confronted with a potentially broadening scandal, the RIAA made public a code of self-regulatory business practices. It had been framed by the twenty record-company presidents who made up the RIAA board, and it called for company action on the part of the fifty-five member manufacturing firms as well as by non-RIAA firms; established standards of conduct for employees at all levels; and urged broadcasters to initiate their own parallel internal investigations and to take other remedial actions.

Seeing an opportunity to increase ratings, the CBS vice-president in charge of television news took it upon himself to assign a news team to cover the scandal, beginning what would turn out to be a year of investigation.

Another matter meriting examination was the racism inherent in the charges. Payola, the *New York Times* said parenthetically, in reporting on the workings of the recording industry and Clive Davis's appearance before the Newark grand jury, was "said to be in force mainly among disk jockeys whose music is aimed mainly at the black community. Most of these stations are white-owned. Their disk jockeys, most of whom are black, traditionally are paid less than their white counterparts at rock 'Top 40' and middle-of-the-road music stations."

As recently as 1958, when some seventy radio stations in the United States aimed their programing exclusively to a black audience, there was some justice to complaints that the majority were a "cheap insult" to the race to which they catered. Owned by absentee landlords or operators of chains that had the same sound, the same-sounding deejays, and the same programing, as many middle- and upper-class blacks charged, they offered the "trash of lowdown music" and religious exhortation to ghetto listeners. With the increase in civil-rights action, more sophisticated black audiences emerged, staying tuned during the day to black stations that programed to meet the needs of the communities they were pledged to serve and switching at night to television.

The word *soul* was emerging in the ghettos to signify what was considered best in the stultifying character of black life there. The rhythm-and-blues companies grabbed the word quickly to describe their music, and Aretha Franklin, an Atlantic artist, appeared on the cover of *Time* as an exemplar of soul. R & B or soul artists drew sell-out white audiences, who also purchased records, in the millions, cut by Jimi Hendricks, Stevie Wonder, Carla Thomas, Otis Redding, Roberta Flack, Sly and the Family Stone, the Supremes, the Chambers Brothers, Gladys Knight and the Pips, or by white artists, most often British, who sounded black. Not until their records hit the Top 10, however, did any of them appear on the white Top 40 station play lists.

The crossover traffic grew, and by 1972 the importance of soul stations as the best vehicle for getting on Top 40 radio was made clear by the presence there of three R & B records out of every ten played. It had become a trade truism that one needed black radio just to get on a Top 40 radio station. The success of Atlantic, to some extent Motown, and the Memphis-based Stax group, which had a 10 percent share of the soul market, made it possible for them to broaden their lines and move into the lucrative pastures where CBS dominated—pop, middle-of-the-road, and, sometimes, musical theater.

A study of the "soul music environment," made for CBS Records by the Harvard Graduate School of Business, bluntly told the company that it was "perceived as an ultra-rich, ultra-white giant which has for the most part chosen to snub blacks in the business. . . . CBS knows little about black consumers, soul artists, and black professionals in the music and record business . . . a successfully expanded soul program would strengthen [CBS's] dominant position on the 'Hot 100' to the point of making it practically invincible."

Responding to the recommendations made by Harvard, CBS embarked on a pioneering course of action in the black music field. A new soul-music division was created; black music production was expanded by the signing of black artists and the initiation of manufacturing and distribution arrangements with existing independent soul-music firms, among them Brunswick and Dakar Records; and a public-relations effort was set into motion to improve the corporation's image in the black community. Six million dollars was advanced against royalties to Stax Records when it turned over its distribution to CBS, an arrangement that was expected to increase the CBS share of soul to 15 percent within five years. The Philadelphia song-writing and record-production team of Kenny Gamble and Leon Huff, together with their Philadelphia International and Gamble Records operation, was added to the CBS Records Group.

By 1973, the year of the payola revelations, the presence of CBS in the soul-music market had manifested itself in a series of hits made by Gamble and Huff and others by the company's own staff. CBS-TV picked up syndication rights for *Soul Train,* the television program most sought after by black artists for national exposure. In the first year of carrying out the Harvard recommendations, CBS achieved the final objective, regarded as possible only by 1977: a 15 percent share of the black music business.

Clive Davis had waited nearly a year for vindication before private negotiations were concluded, in June 1974, for his services as consultant to the recording and music operation of Columbia Pictures Industries. During that time, he dictated an autobiography into the cassette player that had formerly auditioned new talent or played proposed new releases on the CBS label. There had been no movement in the civil case brought against him by his former employer, and rumors had floated that he would become president of several new record companies, formed by American Express, Sony, and a cooperative venture formed by Bob Dylan, the Beatles, and Paul Simon.

Davis's initial function at Columbia Pictures was to supervise the operation of one of its subsidiaries, Bell Records. Columbia had paid $1.5 million in cash and stock for the then singles-oriented Bell label in 1969, thus buying a major independent company that merchandised only records made by independent producers. Initially, Bell had done so because it could not afford an A & R staff. But with success, its owner and founder, Larry Uttal, was free to concentrate on promotion, marketing, and merchandising of music that came from such diverse places as Memphis, Philadelphia, Pensacola, Dallas, Chicago, New Orleans, Nashville, and Los Angeles. Uttal also had time to build up a network of distributors throughout the United States that matched those of the major companies. With the proliferation of bubble-gum music, he moved nearer to the middle of the road with a line of singles by David Cassidy, the Partridge Family, Tony Orlando and Dawn, the Fifth Dimension, and two new finds, Barry Manilow and a Scottish clone of the Beatles, the Bay City Rollers. Such a record of success was not lost on EMI, which was seeking to broaden its base of activity in America. An offer of equal equity interest in a new United States EMI label, with multimillion-dollar financing, was made to Uttal, who resigned his Bell presidency to begin the groundwork for the new Private Stock–EMI firm. Davis was brought in to replace Uttal.

The Bell name was dropped in favor of a new Arista logo, and the company added black jazz and progressive-rock/jazz lines to its already successful singles and LP products. By June 1975, Arista could boast of an increase of three million dollars in profits. It had also garnered eighth place on *Billboard*'s annual chart of corporate share of singles and LP sales.

The Trouble with Rock, the product of the CBS-TV investigative news team's year-long search for the truth about the record business, finally appeared in August 1974. The first half hour was an upbeat filmed documentary that could have been made by the RIAA, depicting rock's appeal to the young and asserting that it had become a two-billion-dollar industry, grossing more than the motion-picture business. The failure of the second portion to document or substantiate any charges of drugs and payola as central to creating hit records rested essentially on the use of discharged employees and others in the business who made nonspecific allegations but continued to attack the whole industry. The CBS vice-president in charge of TV news who ordered the report had been moved to another post, and many of those now in charge of the news division were admittedly embarrassed by the final result. If there was truth to the charges carried in the press during 1973, it would have to wait to be revealed in the federal courts.

On June 14, 1975, the Justice Department announced the indictment, on eighty-six counts, of nineteen persons, four of them record-company presidents: Gamble and Huff, of Philadelphia International Records, and the president of Brunswick and Dakar Records, Nat Tarnapol, all of whose soul music was manufactured and distributed by CBS Records. All three were charged with conspiracy, interstate travel to commit bribery, mail fraud, wire fraud, income tax evasion, and failure to file income tax returns. There was no mention of drugs in any of the indictments. Clive Davis, the fourth president to be indicted, was charged only with personal tax evasion, with a comment by the U.S. District Attorney that "there are no charges of payments by him to others in the recording industry or any charges that he received money or benefits other than from his employer." Columbia Pictures was quick to give Davis a vote of confidence, stating that it fully intended to maintain their ties.

Fewer marked on the racial bias running through the indictments, which called to justice only people dealing with soul music. Rather, now that the indictments were public, the business worried about the difficulty of getting anything but giant hits by superstars played on radio.

Davis was found guilty of only one of six counts of evasion, involving $2,700 in taxes and $8,000 of undeclared income, received for traveling expenses. He paid a $10,000 fine. Tarnapol and four other Brunswick/Dakar employees were found guilty, a verdict that was overturned by the Court of Appeals in 1977. The Philadelphia International defendants pleaded nolo contendere to all charges and were fined $45,000. Gamble had read a statement during the short trial in which he admitted that he had made gifts of clothing, money, and airplane tickets to disk jockeys, but denied that he had done anything wrong by those gifts, intending only to get more air play for his releases.

The indictments had been handed down by grand juries in three cities, New York, Philadelphia, and Los Angeles, signifying the scope of an investigation the Justice Department promised would continue unrelentingly and extend to other music markets. Under pressure from the black, nonvoting U.S. representative for the District of Columbia, Walter Fauntroy, the Internal Revenue Service admitted reluctantly that a special Project Sound had been active for several years, looking into tax returns in the record industry and focusing on evidence of payola. The FCC had provided personnel to work on the payola indictments with the Newark U.S. district attorney, who made a public promise that "it was only the beginning" of a probe that would continue, and that immunity awaited any disk jockeys who were ready to come forth and tell all.

There was yet another government investigation in mid-1975, looking into the financial affairs of Capitol Records and its owner, FMI. It was precipitated by a class-action antitrust suit involving securities fraud, brought by a former Capitol employee. Prior to the opening of the suit, a Los Angeles Grand Jury had subpoenaed Capitol's financial records. Soon after, a tender offer by EMI to acquire additional stock in the company raised its share of ownership from 70 to 97 percent. Now below their requirements, Capitol stock was delisted by the American and Pacific Coast exchanges. Combined with a decline in sales and a fall in earnings, the lawsuit and grand jury probe seriously damaged Capitol's financial standing. Its stock had recently gone through a dizzying roller-coaster ride after rumors spread that its financial report had been doctored, driving down its shares from fifty-six dollars in November 1969 to twelve the next August, and six a year later. It was during this time that Beatles' LPs, including "Abbey Road," and Glen Campbell's hits accounted for nearly half of all sales.

With the Beatles about to break up, the plaintiffs in the stockholders' suit contended, Capitol had followed the road to success being traveled by Columbia and Warner Brothers and squandered its profits on hard-rock acts. Betting on "wrong performers," it lost close to eight million and found itself with almost 20 million unsalable records and tapes. To push its records, Capitol, it was said, gave million of dollars in discounts to record dealers in the form of cooperative advertising rebates never used for advertising. The company also appealed to dealers not to return records before key financial reporting dates.

The presiding judge appeared to accept the Capitol-EMI defense that the transfer of "interim reserve" funds into sales columns, which it acknowledged doing, followed generally accepted accounting standards. The Securities and Exchange Commission sent one of its top accountants to testify to the contrary.

EMI's petition to dismiss the case against it because there was no evidence that it had acted in bad faith was accepted, leaving only Capitol and its executives as defendants. In 1978, the court found that Capitol Industries–EMI had not violated the securities law and that those minority stockholders who had brought the action were not entitled to financial relief. Following an appeal by them, in 1980 an appeals court panel affirmed the decision, finding the charges to lack merit. Capitol was vindicated, after almost six years.

Its sense of shock blunted by the Watergate disclosures and President Nixon's resignation, the American public showed little interest in the payola trials. Consequently, that they had dealt almost exclusively with soul music escaped public notice. Black music was actually thriving, having won over many of the major manufacturers, first because of its power to affect Top 40 programing, and then because of the major boost it got with the emergence of disco music in clubs, lofts, and night spots. Audiences found temporary thrills in a musical eroticism that now pulsated to the sensual and strict tempo of 125 beats every minute. Dancing to flashing lights and special electrical effects, long the province of the Broadway theater, and an overwhelming sound, disco patrons became the star performers they had dreamed of being. Neil Bogart, president of Casablanca Records and soon to become known as a pioneer of "sex rock" because of the disco music he promoted, beginning with Donna Summer's seventeen-minute "Love to Love You Baby," observed that people were "tired of guitarists playing to their own amplifiers . . . they needed mood music . . . they wanted to be the star."

Disco records were cheap to manufacture, for most of the performers worked for scale rather than the guarantee or advance arrangements demanded by rock players. A relatively simple lead sheet was prepared by the producer, who usually wrote both words and music and owned the copyright. Computerized rhythm machines laid down the initial bass drum and bass guitar tracks, almost always to 125 beats a minute, and in successive sessions the other tracks were made by masses of sound synthesizers, conventional and electrical instruments, piled over one another to be mixed and balanced finally by the producer, the disks' ultimate creator, before the final vocal track was recorded. One of disco's earliest national hits, the George McCrae single, "Rock Me Baby," which jumped to number one on both popular and R & B charts, was recorded by T. K. Records of Florida while McCrae waited for his wife to finish her own session for the company. Harry Stone, owner of T. K., was a distributor who had started his own label. It was disco exposure that built up his business, as it did for the producers of Gloria Gaynor's "Never Can Say Goodbye," the first master to be mixed specifically for discos, Millie Jackson, the Hues Corporation, and Barry White and the Love Unlimited Orchestra, the earliest disco-record superstars.

Disco-record companies and their distributors noticed that within a few weeks after the initial release of new disks they began to sell all around the country and without benefit of marketing, advertising, or air play. Such unusual public acceptance was due to one thing alone, the popularity of their product in the disco clubs. Once radio latched on to disco, the gap narrowed from the two to four months it took disco records to get from the discotheques to music stations in 1973 and 1974, to a few weeks by 1975. New superstar disco deejays were responsible; with their inborn sense of programing, they provided music for dancers for several hours at a stretch without pausing. Superb cuing and the use of special mixers connected each selection to a unit played from a tape desk and twin turntables through separate theater-sized speakers with separate amplifiers for bass and treble. No longer a record show, it had become a sound-and-light spectacular, augmented by color organs that translated sound into light and computerized light units with built-in "psychological crowd control." Disco sailed through the 1974 recession unfazed, attracting good-time crowds to the 1,500 discotheques known to exist around the country.

When number-one disco hits stretched beyond their original three-minute length into quarter-hour performances, through the use of tape loops, a Latin record manufacturer, the Cayre Corporation, introduced twelve-inch disco records on its Salsoul label. Impressed by the speed with which Salsoul caught on, a number of record executives predicted that the twelve-inch singles, played at a speed of 33⅓ (there were 45 disco records, too), would ultimately replace the seven-inch single. Casablanca, Atlantic, and CBS Records were leaders in the movement, marketing big singles with two disco-length performances remixed for dancing, and with rhythm tracks boosted to maintain disco's straight-ahead beat and grooves wider apart than usual to accommodate the 2,000-watt amplifiers favored by dance clubs.

At the start, the records were used only for promotion and were shipped almost exclusively to disco jockeys. When they went on public sale, the big singles were priced at $2.98, but they sold for anywhere from $1.79 to full cost. Long after disco had run its course, the twelve-inch single maintained a place in the business as the medium for what minimalist composer Philip Glass called "the final stage of the composition." New versions of popular hits were made by dubbing, echoing, tape manipulation, and the use of as many as four kinds of "reverb," among other new wonders of the studio. A new "mini"-album market of punched-up tracks was developed, which made their way into the Hot 100, such as Bruce Springsteen's "Dancing in the USA" and "Cover Me" and Cyndi Lauper's "Girls Just Want to Have Fun."

Control of what was played in the pace-setting discos in major American cities was in the hands of the owner-operators of "disco pools," ostensibly cooperatives, with as many as 200 to 300 members, each of whom paid fees of twenty-five to thirty-five dollars a month. Organized along racial lines in many cases, the pools made it simpler for record companies to deal with the growing business of disco record spinning by serving as a point of focus to which all promotional materials and advance releases were sent, out of which disk-jockey copies were chosen by the pool operators for distribution to members for test marketing. In a position to make or break a new recording, pool owners were courted by the record companies' aspiring disco artists and their managers, as well as by songwriters, music publishers, and distributors. Only when the disco beat was appropriated by the white music power structure in 1977 did the pools' power wane.

Discotheques and disco pools had provided the record companies with a way to save money in test-marketing new talent and new releases without the great expense of using finished singles and LPs. Apparently following Murray Ross's suggestion, and using the services of Harvard's Business School, the Wharton School of Business, and similar sources to modernize their operations, the major labels slowly developed new business practices. As Walter Yetnikoff, risen from the company's legal department to succeed Goddard Lieberson as president of the CBS Records Group, told *Business Week:* "Things are considerably different . . . today. Now every album that goes out has a complete marketing plan—with details on advertising, displays, discounts for the trade, personal appearances by the artists, sales targets, and national and regional breakdowns."

The record business had faced a year beset by problems. Months after W. T. Grant Stores, a major outlet for the biggest labels, closed its doors, all ABC record and tape profits were wiped out, because of the vast bills unpaid by the giant chain-store operation. In August 1974, ABC Records had surprised the industry with the first step in a major growth program—the purchase of all Gulf & Western's record operations, for a reported $55 million. The sale included the Paramount label—which would be phased out because G & W still owned the name—as well as Dot, Neighborhood, and Blue Thumb records. Though ABC's contract with United Artists Music Publishing was soon to expire, none of the assets of Famous Music, Paramount Pictures' forty-two-year-old publishing arm, were involved in the transaction. Some time later, announcement was made of ABC's acquisition of Word, a major religious communications business that produced and distributed white gospel records, tapes, books, sheet music, songbooks, multimedia instructional materials, owned a magazine and retail bookstores, and had consolidated revenues in excess of $14.5 million annually. Included in Word's assets was the revival-music publishing company founded by the early-twentieth-century evangelist Homer Rodeheaver. Approximately 300,000 shares of ABC common stock were exchanged for Word's outstanding common and preferred stock and warrants. The incumbent management was retained.

In the course of an interview months later, Larry Utall told *Record World:* "During the halcyon days of the 1960s the virility, excitement and growth of the record industry made our business the darling of Wall Street. It became a conglomerate dominated era in which bottom line orientation had a stultifying effect on the development and growth of our most basic raw materials—creativity."

The industry had grown at a steady six-to-eight percent rate annually from 1960 through 1965. Then, in an accelerating economy, the introduction and growth of tape led to an increase of 17 to 18 percent. In the eyes of the financial community, the quality of corporate management in the industry had not improved since then. Business failures, the inability of too many companies to show consistent growth patterns, and the lack of verifiable industry sales figures soured Wall Street. The RIAA's annual survey of record revenues came under serious question in 1975 following the release of *Survey of Financial Reporting and Accounting Developments in the Entertainment Business,* made by the accounting firm of Price, Waterhouse.

The study indicated that revenues of the eight major companies should produce a figure higher than reported by the RIAA, a difference resulting from the inclusion of income from music publishing, manufacturing, retailing, distribution, and other sources. The RIAA's $2.2 billion for 1974 was based on list figures. But, as *Cash Box* reported in February 1976, when calculated "at the manufacturers' selling price to their distributors (both independent and company-owned) the record business appears to be an $850-950 million industry, less than half the $2.2 billion published figure." The RIAA's explanation was that the $2.2 billion was based on figures submitted by the 85 to 90 percent of the industry affiliated with it; the balance had been projected by a committee. Compiled on a calender-year basis, the total figure was reached by deducting returns from the sales/shipped figures.

Cash Box continued: "Which figures are more accurate is hard to determine. The RIAA reflects industry sales at an unrealistic list price level, presumably to make the number larger than it should be. And yet when record retailing and manufacturing, music publishing and domestic revenue from international deals are added in, the overall record industry is a multi-billion dollar industry. But how many multis will remain hard to determine until more accurate sales statistics are made available.''

To create "better trust in the eyes of the investing public," as a WEA executive explained, Warner Communications and CBS, the industry giants, disclosed more information in annual corporate reports about their record/music operations. Using Price, Waterhouse's measure of income to reveal the extent of their earnings, CBS reported an income of $484.3 million and Warner $313.8, a combined total increase of $350 million over previous divisional earnings. On the basis of other, now more detailed annual reports, expressed in millions of dollars these two were followed by ABC, with $157.4; MCA, $137.0; Capitol Industries–EMI, $120.2; Transamerica-UA/MGM, $98.7; Columbia Pictures Industries, $30.1; and 20th Century–Fox Film Corp., $17.9. As had been its practice for years, RCA, the thirty-fourth largest industrial entity in *Fortune*'s 500 list of top corporations, did not separate record/music earnings from its $4.8 billion income for 1975.

CHAPTER 29

A New Copyright Bill at Last

The piracy or counterfeiting of printed music had been one of the music publishers' paramount problems from the day that mass duplication of music first became practicable. With the cheap-book explosion in the mid-1870s, which nearly wrecked the book trade, counterfeiting became a national business. It was centered in Canada, where the copyright laws were vague. On at least two occasions, in 1882 and three years later, publishers circularized dealers and the trade, calling attention to Canadian reprints being offered openly for "extraordinary and tempting" prices. A reward of forty dollars was offered for any information leading to the conviction of persons engaged in the business. The practice remained rampant despite the offer, even after new copyright regulations called for the active intervention of U.S. postal authorities in the war against counterfeiters of printed music.

The MPPA and its attorney, Julian Abeles, were foremost in action against both printed-music and record bootlegging during the 1950s and 1960s, generally on the theory of unfair competition in the absence of appropriate copyright protection. Abeles usually recovered around $200, when the true obligation was more likely to be $2,000. However, his activities succeeded in getting a law passed that established the guilt of the retail merchandiser of pirated materials. The first federal anticounterfeiting legislation was passed in 1962; it established a fine of not more than $10,000 and imprisonment for no more than a year for any persons who "transports, receives, sells or offers for sale in interstate or foreign commerce, knowingly and with fraudulent intent, counterfeited records." A second offense called for the fine of not more than $25,000 and a prison term of not more than two years. Apparently, however, no action was ever filed under this law.

In 1972, after active lobbying, principally by the NMPA, amendments to the 1962 legislation provided uniform federal protection for the first time, including both civil and criminal remedies against record piracy, and established federal copyright in sound recordings made following ratification on February 15, 1972, to be effective for the succeeding two-year period. The Criminal Division of the Justice Department was empowered to bring action, but the bill reduced piracy to a misdemeanor, with penalties of one year in prison and/or fines of between $100 and $10,000. Both the music business and the Justice Department found the revised provisions totally ineffective. The bill did not make stronger America's position at a convention in Geneva later in the year, at which an international treaty was ratified outlawing counterfeited and pirated sound recordings. The United States became a full party to it in March 1974.

The greater public acceptance of music cartridges and cassettes provided counterfeiters with access to a new technology that was not only inexpensive (one could go into prerecorded tape piracy for under $10,000), but also far simpler to handle than that involving disks, piracy of which represented an annual $50-million loss in 1970. The same year, a Senate committee was later told, nearly 20,000 units were manufactured every day, siphoning off $100 million, one fifth of all legitimate taped-music sales. It was an America on the move that was responsible for the surge in prerecorded tape piracy; cartridges and cassettes could be bought in gasoline stations, truck stops, highway rest areas, convenience stores, and other outlets that had never carried legitimately recorded music.

Omnibus copyright revision and its scheduled increase in mechanical rates for record companies, apparently stalled in House and Senate committees, gave the RIAA an opportunity to take on a new function: working for stronger antipiracy legislation on both national and state levels and using that already on the books to better advantage by seeking retroactive protection for recordings made prior to the February 15, 1972, starting date. NMPA involvement had been sidetracked by a new problem: the move by one company to legitimize its counterfeiting business by filing a first notice of intent to record, as was called for by the compulsory licensing provisions of the 1909 act. The gambit failed in 1972 when an appeals court ruled that compulsory licensing was not available when disks or tapes were manufactured without the express permission of copyright owners. A test, by pirates, in the Supreme Court, of a California anticounterfeiting statute, one of fourteen on the books in various states, failed when a majority of the justices upheld the right of states to enact their own antipiracy bills.

By 1974, thanks to its allies the National Association of Record Merchandisers and the Country Music Association, the RIAA was able to report that, in the war against professional counterfeiting, now doing an estimated $200-million annual business, the tide was turning. New federal and state legislation, several landmark court decisions, and an increase in the involvement of government forces in prosecuting piracy, with stiffer fines and more severe sentences, were responsible. The NMPA had won its own victory in affirmative decisions in three more appeals court cases that declared that pirates could not hide behind the existing copyright laws by paying mechanical royalties to music publishers. An amendment to the 1909 law signed by the President at the end of 1974 stiffened earlier federal penalties: the first offense was made a misdemeanor; fines were raised to $25,000 and to as much as $50,000 for a second offense.

There were many political and legal roadblocks to a copyright revision package. The federal court ruling that dismissed the CBS case against TelePrompter for infringement of copyrighted programs over its CATV system was, like that in *Fortnightly*, intended to put the propriety of using distant signals on cable into the lap of Congress. The CATV lobby had already agreed to accept liability under the proposed bills; the FCC had, after years, produced regulations governing cable TV acceptable to all sides; intra- and inter-industry differences between cable and commercial television had been ironed out to the relative satisfaction of all parties; and the way to passage of revision of the law, at least as it affected cable, was assured. But then Judge Constance Baker Motley's ruling in *CBS* v. *TelePrompter* had destroyed that delicate balance. She had found that a cable pickup was only an extension of the ability to view the original broadcast, a ruling with which the Supreme Court concurred in 1974, finding that cable systems were not liable when carrying any broadcast signals, under the meaning of the 1909 Copyright Act.

Hearings on the newest Senate revision bill extended through 1974. The educational and library interests agreed to exempt "musical works" in an amendment extending permission for photocopying scholarly materials. A Copyright Royalty Tribunal was suggested by Senator McClellan, to serve as a forum for statutory rate-change petitions. It was also agreed that 15 percent of the royalties being paid by cable TV for all copyright materials would be allocated for distribution to the music-copyright interests. Following the Supreme Court's decision in *TelePrompter,* this faced serious opposition. A ceiling of three cents, or 0.75 cents per minute of play, on mechanical royalties was approved. The Music Operators of America extended their eight-dollar compromise royalty on each jukebox, recalling that a twenty-dollar royalty had nearly been passed in 1967.

As anticipated, a major bone of contention was the amendment calling for a record-performance royalty that had been first introduced in 1967. Owing to masterly lobbying by the broadcasters, the bill's terms were reduced by half from the initial 2 percent of all advertising receipts by stations making more than $200,000 annually.

Speaking for the RIAA, its president, Stanley Gortikov, argued that the performance-royalty provision represented the only money issue in the bill to offer any gain in income for the record makers. "Publishers will profit from the mechanical license fee gains, and broadcasters will raise their income base through new cable television income. But our industry will only pay out funds unless we secure this performance right." The senators from Tennessee and other centers of recording were strong supporters on this issue; those with major backing from broadcasters or friendly to the jukebox interests were against it.

The Senate's version of copyright revision was passed in November 1974, without the record-performance provision. But the 93rd Congress ended with no action by the House. The division of thought about copyright prevailing in the House was made clear the following May by some members who openly commented that the "disseminators," the users of copyrighted materials, had more than amply fulfilled the intent of the Constitution. "In any clash between authors and disseminators to the public," one said, "the public wins."

The several times rejected performers'-right amendment was again introduced in both houses, but with more moderate terms, to assuage the complaints of broadcasters. As in the past, it was expected to serve as a roadblock to progress, stirring up the radio people as well as the jukebox association and the wired-music services, both of which were being asked to pay twice as much of their gross receipts as were the broadcasters. Chances of the amendment's passage this time were regarded as better than ever. Lobbyists for the artists' unions and the AFL-CIO were working in support of the American Federation of Musicians, which had traditionally backed Stan Kenton and his National Committee for the Recording Arts.

An amendment introduced by Senator Charles Mathias, one of the copyright interests' best advocates, called for the application of the statutory licensing principle to public broadcasting in connection with all copyrighted materials, including music. A new proposal by McClellan raised jukebox license fees to $19.70 per machine from the eight dollars that had come out of the Library of Congress meeting in 1967. Remembering its defeat then, ASCAP was ready to stay with the eight-dollar fee, subject to review in the future by the Copyright Royalty Tribunal. BMI wanted to keep both Congress and the Tribunal out of the matter and rely on the marketplace to originate an appropriate rate. Whatever compromise the NMPA might have effected between the publishers of books, sheet music, and other printed works and the school libraries and others to work out regulated photocopying had broken down when an appeals court opened the door under the fair-use section of the 1909 act.

The power of organized broadcasters to scuttle the entire revision process was demonstrated at a Senate committee hearing on the performance-royalty bill. Although she supported the concept wholeheartedly, Register of Copyrights Barbara Ringer urged that the "killer provision" be dropped at once, leaving it for study as a separate piece of legislation, chiefly because of potential powerful opposition from the NAB and its members. Nevertheless, Gortikov attacked the broadcasters, demonstrating with charts that, although 75 percent of their programing time was devoted to recorded music, they provided "zero sales benefit" from that. The vast majority of new releases never got any air play at all, and the Top 40 stations added only five or six new songs a week to their play lists, out of more than 900 new recordings each week. The sales life of 56 percent of the records they did play was already over. Record manufacturers, he said, paid far more money to advertise their product on the air than they asked the industry to pay. They spent nearly $65 million in this fashion in 1974; yet less than five million was expected to come out of the amendment if it was passed.

The war over rates, which involved the largest sum of actual cash in the proposed revision, began now. Proposed as an inflation adjustment, the suggested increase from two cents to three cents per side would, in Gortikov's works, impose "the burden of an additional $50 million in annual royalty fees." The elaborate economic studies introduced by the RIAA showed an increase in mechanical fees in the seven-year period ending with 1972 from $41 million to $78.2 million. The reduction proposed in record-performance royalties from broadcasters, to one percent, from the original two, would, he complained, deprive the recording industry of "a meaningful source of new income . . . while suffering" the added burden of a 50 percent increase in mechanical fees.

Citing the risk of losses taken by the manufacturers, the RIAA offered insight into problems currently affecting its constituents. Using figures for 1972, the most recent available, it demonstrated that, to break even, a 45 single had to sell about 46,000 units, but that four out of every five singles failed to reach that point. About 60 percent of all releases sold less than 10,000 copies. The break-even point had risen dramatically since 1963, when only 11,200 45 singles had to be sold. The break-even point for LPs in 1972 was about 61,000 units. Some 23 percent of all releases did that or better; the remainder sold 20,000 copies or less. In 1963, the sale of only 7,800 LPs had been necessary to break even.

Ninety-five percent of all classical LPs never recovered the original investment in their production, and about 79 percent of prerecorded popular tapes did not have sufficient sales to do so. Since 1969, record returns from distributors and dealers had risen to about 21 percent of all sales, with enormous dollar losses—$311 million in 1974.

"The record-by-record odds against success are especially difficult for the smaller or newer company, which can produce only a few releases a year," the RIAA study concluded. "An increase in statutory rates, if not passed on, would raise the breakeven point and the odds against success for all record companies still higher. . . . There is not, and has not been, any significant amount of bargaining or *real* negotiation about these rates. Any statutory rates would become the norm."

The executive vice-president of the NMPA, Leonard Feist, who appeared in behalf of the AGAC, recalled that in the three times over the past ten years he sat in Congressional hearings dealing with revision, he had heard the record interests make the same dire predictions of doom. As to the RIAA presentation, he said that it overlooked two facts. The proposed royalty was only a ceiling which increased the range for bargaining, and not the rate actually paid, which was currently 1.62 cents. At hearings ten years earlier, the RIAA had predicted that a one-cent raise in the ceiling would push the manufacturers to raise the price of a $3.98 LP with its twelve songs by twelve cents. What had happened since then, without any change in the law, was that the price of LP albums had been increased by three dollars or more, to $6.98 and up, and the number of songs had been dropped to ten. What the NMPA and the AGAC wanted, Feist said, was to create a ceiling with the same purchasing power as the 2½ cents suggested by the Register of Copyrights in 1964. Since then the Consumer Price Index had gone up by more than 70 percent. Therefore, the NMPA and the AGAC asked for a new ceiling of four cents.

In the interest of achieving unanimity with the Senate, as well as to get the whole business out of the way, the House committee began to match, word for word, its draft with that passed by the Senate in the last days of the 93rd Congress. The performers' royalty had been put over until the 95th Congress and a new Copyright Office study ordered in anticipation. Responding to advice from the Justice Department that the Senate-created Copyright Royalty Tribunal represented a violation of the separation of powers, the committee wrote new language making it a regulatory commission, funded by Congress, with members appointed by the President.

Long before these and other changes had been agreed upon the Senate Judiciary Committee on Copyrights completed work on its updated version of the bill that had been passed in 1973. Subjected to intense pressure from the RIAA, particularly that by the respected Consumers Federation of America, which had been enlisted by the record companies, a majority of the Senate committee turned the clock for songwriters and publishers back to 1967 insofar as record royalties were involved. In a letter delivered to all committee members the morning of a scheduled vote on mechanical rates, the Consumers Federation urged them to hold the line against "bloated royalties" and restore the 2½-cent rate agreed upon eight years earlier. When the bill emerged for a vote the following February, all provisions were unchanged except the performers' royalty provision, which was excised. The "no surprise" legislation was passed unanimously.

The House bill was expected to be ready for a vote in September. The late September date was expected to create a sense of urgency that would make Congressmen anxious for its passage more congenial about last-minute differences. Pressures anticipated from the AFL-CIO, the musicians' union, and the various artists' guilds for the performance royalty failed to materialize. A majority of the committee killed the amendment during the summer, chiefly because they thought its inclusion would lead only to the bill's final defeat.

Among other provisions dealing with music in the final House bill were: elimination of the "for profit" restriction of public performance, with specific exemptions for educational and other nonprofit uses; copyright protection extended to life plus fifty years; "fair use" guidelines for the duplication of copyrighted materials, including the exemption of music from the new right of public libraries to make copies under certain circumstances; overthrow of the Supreme Court's *Fortnightly* and *TelePrompter* decisions, with cable television now liable for compulsory licensing; the creation of a new regulatory body, the Copyright Royalty Tribunal, to review royalty rates regularly in connection with compulsory licensing of recordings, jukeboxes, public broadcasting, and cable TV; and an eight-dollar jukebox tax per machine.

Immediately after the House voted, 216 to 7, in favor of the revised bill, both copyright committees began a series of meetings to reconcile the difference between their versions. The result was essentially the bill passed by the House, with only a few minor changes, one of them a 2.75-cent mechanical rate, or a limitation of 5 cents per minute of playing time.

This struggle to change U.S. copyright law ended, after a twenty-year fight, on October 19, 1976, when President Ford signed the omnibus copyright revision bill, which would become effective on January 1, 1978.

PART EIGHT

1977–1980

CHAPTER 30

The U.S. Supreme Court and Licensing

The temporary pause in legal actions between CBS and BMI following Judge Morris Lasker's decision dismissing the network's antitrust complaint and suit for a per-use license gave BMI a new opportunity to plead "undue hardship" unless a final judgment was entered soon. The company's reserves had eroded during double-digit inflation, while CBS enjoyed record earnings and profits, and its television network used BMI music for $1.7 million a year, well below the $4.3 interim rate paid to ASCAP. In pleading for a final judgment in *CBS* v. *ASCAP, BMI et al.,* BMI also asked for an expeditious retroactive adjustment of its interim fees. Basing proof of its right to additional income from CBS on studies of the use of its music on all the networks, BMI expected any adjustment to produce in excess of $10 million. Though he commiserated with BMI on the fact that it had been frozen in its position for the past five years—and continued to be for some years to come—Lasker rejected the petition, because the matter was now before the Court of Appeals.

Meanwhile, BMI continued to reach new levels in the use of its repertory. It licensed sixty of the one hundred most played songs on American radio in 1975, music in 68 percent of the leading film box-office earners, and thirty-four of the fifty-three RIAA Gold singles during its fiscal year, ending June 30, 1976. During a year when ASCAP's domestic revenues were in excess of $80 million, BMI had paid out $45.6 million of the $56 million taken in.

The anticipated installation of state-of-the art computer technology made it possible for BMI to promise a new bonus-payment system that would give additional royalties to songs whose performances exceeded certain established plateaus, and pay, for the first time, for all music used on local syndicated television shows. The sampling system on which payments had been based in the past was discarded, replaced by a total census of all synchronized music on independent TV, made possible through access to material provided by *TV Guide*. The new payment plan, effective in the summer of 1977, doubled the minimum half-cent rate for popular songs on local FM and that for concert music from four cents a minute; increased royalties from four to six cents for popular music played on AM stations that paid BMI more than $4,000 a year; instituted a new bonus song plan; and vastly increased television music rates. Payments for popular songs performed on Group A television stations (those on the air between 7:00 and 11:00 P.M. or on variety shows made expressly for showing before 1:00 A.M.), were increased from thirty-six cents to $2.25 per station hooked to a TV network; and from twenty-five cents to $1.25 on Group B stations.

The new plan represented a fundamental shift in BMI policy, moving from the catalogue bonus system of the past, which had attracted many publishers to its ranks, to one based on the company's new philosophy that "songs with many performances [as opposed to catalogues with many performances] were of more help in persuading licensees to acquire and use the repertoire." Under the new scheme, songs with more than 25,000 feature performances, as reflected by BMI's newest logging machinery, were paid at 1½ times the basic rate; those with from 100,000 to 499,000 performances, twice the basic rate; from 500,000 to 999,999, 3.8 times. Simultaneously, BMI also reduced its 10 percent collection fee on foreign income to five percent. Some time later, ASCAP began to deduct three percent from foreign remittances for performing the same function.

The possibility of future legal entanglements involving its fully owned and operated Canadian subsidiary, BMI Canada, in connection with growing Canadian chauvinism regarding the ownership of national business enterprises by foreigners was removed in 1976. Granting full autonomy to the company, BMI transferred all issued stock to a nonprofit foundation, for which the Royal Trust Company acted as trustee.

ASCAP's new and more realistic competitive policy toward BMI, including the payment of advances to new members, was bearing fruit. The society's share of *Billboard*'s Hot 100 charts jumped from 12 percent in 1972 to nearly half, a victory for which ASCAP had to write off, in a single year, advances of $507,000 already made to promising writers and publishers who failed to deliver hits. The ninth amendment since 1960 of the provisions of the 1950 consent order was made in 1976. The often revised system had particular attraction to young writers. They had had their choice on joining of being paid on a current-performance basis or spreading out the four-fund royalties that had been established for the benefit of older members. The amendment provided that only new members could start with the more attractive current-performance payoff and switch to the four-fund system after three years.

The windfall of four million dollars in license income distributed in early

1976, covering network air play between 1964 and 1970, released to ASCAP by the court, came from an escrow account that had been built up during its almost-ten-year-long dispute with the networks. Music on the owned-and-operated stations had declined almost to the vanishing point; it was used only in commercials and for occasional bridges and themes. The improving economy, coming after many advertisers had been forced to reduce operating expenses during a two-year national recession, found many of them still moving away from TV and over to radio, where rates were substantially more attractive. The twenty-four hour all-news format on network stations generally made for top local ratings and increased profits. Six of the CBS-owned stations offered straight news all day and night, and NBC had developed a syndicated fifty-minute hourly all-news service, charging from $750 to $15,000 to affiliates it had once paid to carry its news broadcasts. All-news was about fifteen years old, having been introduced in 1951 over the Mexican border station XTRA by the Texas broadcaster Gordon McClendon, who was also one of the leading exponents of early Top 40 music shows. McClendon's rip-and-read operation intermixed advertising with wire-service reports. The phenomenon was explained by Columbia University professor William Woods as a ''quick and easy way of keeping informed.'' With their changes in radio content as leverage, the networks drove down their ASCAP fees by as much as 70 percent: from $180,000 to $50,000 for CBS Radio, and from $42,000 to $20,000 annually for Mutual.

This reduction stirred new dreams of a further cut in their ASCAP payments among independent radio-station owners. Citing a greater use of the BMI repertory, they had already won an estimated $2.4 million reduction from $18.3 million in fees to the society. Their annual 1.72 percent ASCAP rate was just a bit higher than BMI's 1.7 percent fee, revised in 1973 to include the new incremental revenue feature. While the all-news format challenged them for top ratings in local markets, that vast majority of independent broadcasters who continued to concentrate on Top 40 rock, MOR, and country music in that order grabbed off nearly two thirds of all music time.

Now the representative of 2,200 stations, the All-Industry Radio Committee went to the bargaining table early in 1977 ready to insist on a new 1.3 percent rate, a reduction of nearly 25 percent, which would lop about $5 million off their annual ASCAP fees. An experienced and wary adversary, well aware that it was about to be asked for a substantial cut, ASCAP jumped the gun at the initial meeting and made the proposal to increase rates by 16 percent. If it was accepted, the figure would add at least $3 million in the first year to local stations' payments, which were in the $22-million range each year.

At the rate-fixing procedure in the New York federal court held later that year, ASCAP raised the possibility of new antitrust violations by BMI. It made strong objection to the presence on the BMI board of broadcasters only. Their manipulation of BMI and its rate structure had been responsible, ASCAP claimed, for the reduction of license fees by all three societies, from 2.9 percent in 1971 to 2.6 in 1975.

Eighteen months after this stalemate began, it was ended by the court's approval of a new five-year contract between ASCAP and independent radio, which would expire on December 31, 1982. The 1.725 percent rate remained in force, but concessions by the society in many other areas, including an increase from 5 to 15 percent of the standard optional deductions that most stations took, put the stations in a position to save $6.5 million to $8 million during the life of the agreement.

Similarly deadlocked negotiations between BMI and the Radio Committee for their new five-year contract took twenty-seven months to conclude. The result was a document that lifted the rate back to 1.7 percent for stations with income over $100,000 a year, the same rate as that before the new incremental provision of 1977. Like ASCAP, BMI lifted the optional standard deduction to the 17 to 18 percent range and simplified some reporting procedures.

The CBS petition filed late in 1975, asking the Court of Appeals to reverse the Lasker decision made shortly before the per-use suit was dismissed on its merits, was reaffirmed in August 1977, and the lower court was asked to vacate its findings. Judge Lasker was ordered to require ASCAP and BMI to offer the type of license for which CBS continued to ask. There was some solace for the defendants in the part of the opinion by Appeals Court Judge Murray Gurfein striking down the CBS contention that the licensing organizations were monopolies in violation of the Sherman Act. Otherwise, it was all bad news. The per-program option offered by both societies was found to be merely another form of blanket license, Gurfein wrote, because neither allowed "a licensee to pay only for those compositions it actually uses." Further, he added, there was no merit in Lasker's opinion that because CBS had a right to negotiate with individual copyright owners this constituted an alternative to blanket licensing. ASCAP's position that blanket licensing was essential to the marketplace was declared invalid. In its present form, the judge held, blanket licensing was price fixing, and with respect to the television networks could not serve as a "market necessity" defense. All rulings in regard to ASCAP, he noted in a footnote, were to be "taken to include BMI, unless the context clearly indicates otherwise." The appeals process now was invoked by the music organizations, and supporting briefs were prepared for submission to the Supreme Court.

The Gurfein decision was hailed by the All-Industry Television Committee and particularly its chairman, Leslie Arries, who found in it some guiding principles for his continuing fight to reduce the money being paid to the licensing bodies. As early as 1972, when he was named chairman, he had told an NAB meeting of independent TV station owners and their managers that they should take another look at the traditional method of paying for music with a percentage of gross revenues. Like CBS, he said, they should seek a per-use license, with which they would pay only for what went out over their transmitters. He made special reference to Judge Gurfein's conclusion that blanket licensing amounted to a price-fixing arrangement among copyright holders, and was therefore unlawful.

Arries's regular presentations at NAB conventions in the years that followed were complete with charts and graphs showing the discrepancy between money paid for music by the networks and by independent stations. The 1976 figures, for example, showed the differences to be $18.5 million from the networks, much of which was paid by affiliates because of the twilight-zone bookkeeping reimbursement, and $48 million from local TV stations.

Briefs filed by ASCAP and BMI early in 1978 called for a hearing by the Supreme Court on their appeal for a ruling that blanket licensing did not constitute an unlawful practice. Again denying that it engaged in price fixing, the society urged an immediate review. "The time is now," ASCAP pleaded, "not years from now after federal courts all over the country have been inundated with plenary lawsuits and counterclaims in infringement actions, in which users assert that the unavailability of an ASCAP 'per use' license devised to meet their particular needs entitles them to use copyrighted music for nothing." Pointing to the intrinsic differences in the structure and operation of the defendants, BMI reminded the court that "every governmental body which has looked carefully into the facts in recent years has concluded that blanket licensing is a reasonable and lawful response to the unique problems of licensing music performance rights."

Following twelve months during which only one meeting was held to discuss the matter, the ghost of the Shenandoah Committee's demand for clearance-at-the source licensing was summoned up by a new All-Industry Television Committee in December 1978. A class antitrust action was filed in the New York federal court by five local TV entities on behalf of the 700 independent U.S. television stations. The fifteen owned by the three networks were not party to the action. The papers alleged that ASCAP and BMI, with their members and affiliates, had structured a music-licensing system that unfairly set prices for performing rights, and required the plaintiff licensees to pay for all compositions represented by the two organizations whether or not they wanted to use them. As a result, the complaint continued, local TV stations were proportionately paying more to ASCAP and BMI than any other group of music users.

Although the networks provided about two thirds of their affiliates' programing, and syndicated and local programs the balance, the plaintiffs were paying two and a half times as much as the networks did. Arries submitted an accompanying affidavit to substantiate the claim. In the 1972–77 period, CBS, of which his Buffalo station, now WIBV, was an affiliate, paid

ASCAP and BMI on average $66,580 a year for the music used on two thirds of WIBV's programing. WIBV paid the societies $130,000 annually to license music for the remaining one third, and also paid CBS $33,000 a year to reimburse 50 percent of the network's music-licensing payments. A similar situation existed at all other network-affiliated stations.

Asking for an injunction against continuance of blanket licensing, the plaintiffs also sought a halt to the "practice of 'splitting' performance and synchronization rights for pre-recorded television programs," which would make feasible the "clearance at the source licensing by TV packagers" that was at the heart of their action. What quickly proved to be a serious economic blow to the licensing societies—the request that the court issue a temporary restraining order and place in escrow 20 percent of all plaintiffs' payments to ASCAP and BMI—was granted, as were temporary extensions of all licenses.

This unexpected reversal of attitude on the part of independent TV station owners and managers toward BMI, whose relations with its biggest-paying customers had always been regarded as exemplary, was explained by some veteran broadcasters as due to changes in the company's station-relations policy, which had brought it closer to that of ASCAP. For years, the society had continued to be regarded as the enemy of broadcasters, and its later acknowledged failure to reverse that image remained a burden. As the men Carl Haverlin had recruited for BMI's station-relations department retired, they had been replaced by younger employees almost all of whom were without any experience or familiarity with upper-level station management and ownership. In recent years, the function of the department had become that of a collector of bills past due, and fraternization between it and broadcasters was discouraged. Consequently, such a fire as the "Buffalo station case," which would have been extinguished early in the game in Haverlin's regime, had burst into a major conflagration.

Arguments were heard by the Supreme Court in January 1979. The Justice Department had filed a brief that urged such a course, suggesting that the legality of blanket licenses could be tested under a "rule of reason" and emphasizing the benefits to both copyright holders and music users of the present system of licensing. The deputy solicitor general, who appeared at the petitioners' request and as amicus on behalf of the government, told the court that blanket licensing tended to lower prices and provided real economic benefits. No one else could sell what ASCAP and BMI did, and to accept the CBS arguments would turn the antitrust laws into a redundancy.

The attorney representing ASCAP pointed out that CBS had never approached any member of ASCAP for an individual license, proving that its case was predicated on conjecture and speculation. CBS actually had an extraordinary range of options open to it, he argued; it could deal with individual copyright holders, negotiate with ASCAP for a per-program blanket license, or have the federal court that supervised the society's negotiations with its licensees establish a reasonable fee.

In BMI's presentation, its attorney said that the issue was whether offering a blanket license really constituted a violation of the Sherman Act. Judge Gurfein had assumed that copyright holders would prefer the blanket license as the medium of choice in performance to individual bargaining. This assumption, she argued, was unwarranted. Testimony offered Gurfein had clearly demonstrated that individual licenses could be had for the asking.

Responding to ASCAP's contention that CBS had never attempted to deal with individuals for a license, the CBS attorney said that the network had no obligation to do so, and then asked rhetorically whether the victim of price fixing was obligated to approach one of the price fixers before going to the courts for relief. CBS, he pointed out, was not dealing "with economic pygmies when we look at the music publishing companies."

In final rebuttal, ASCAP urged the court, should it reverse the Gurfein decision, not to order a remand, thus serving notice that antitrust litigation could not be endless.

The eight-to-one Supreme Court ruling announced three months later overturned Gurfein, holding that the laws against price fixing were not automatically violated by the blanket licensing offered by ASCAP and BMI. Because years of experience with that form of music contract, Justice Byron R. White wrote for the majority, "plainly enough indicate that over the years and in the face of available alternatives, the blanket license has provided an acceptable mechanism for at least a large part of the market for performing rights to copyrighted musical compositions, we cannot agree that it should automatically be declared illegal in all of its many manifestations. Rather, when attacked, it should be subjected to a more discriminating examination under the rule of reason. It may not ultimately survive the attacks, but that is not the issue before us today."

CBS was determined not to drop its pursuit of per-use licensing, and in August 1980 petitioned the Supreme Court for a rehearing. The network had stopped all payments to ASCAP when Gurfein announced his decision, but had resumed them earlier in the year, paying nearly nine million dollars in back fees plus interest. A retroactive adjustment waited for final disposition of the case, as did that for BMI, to which CBS had been paying the ordered $1.7 million annually, and, in 1979, had added a temporary additional adjustment of $900,000 a year, ordered by the Lasker court.

At the urging of the solicitor general, the Supreme Court denied CBS's petition, effectively putting an end to the network's lawsuit. The recommendation to deny a rehearing stressed that a narrowly defined issue was involved and to hear it again would stimulate fears that the matter might reverberate eternally. The final resolution of back payments from CBS-TV to BMI, including accrued interest and adjustments for inflation involving many millions, was finally made, but only after protracted negotiations and appeals to the courts.

Two other significant developments had taken place at the licensing societies during 1980, one of them stemming directly from the TV stations' lawsuit. After twenty years in office, Stanley Adams stepped down from the ASCAP presidency, to be replaced by Hal David, a lyricist who had won twenty Gold Record awards as a record producer, as well as songwriter. He had been one of the Young Turk group in 1960, serving as co-chairman of the movement to make the society's distribution system more equitable for the writers of contemporary hit songs. Yielding reluctantly to urging by both publishers and writers that he step into the president's office, David did so because he "wanted to make sure ASCAP was in the late 1980s."

Also during 1980, BMI saw the first concerted effort in its history by some of its stockholders to put candidates of their choice, and not the usual self-perpetuating slate, on the company's board. Taking advantage of the cumulative voting system, Leslie Arries collected sufficient proxies to elect two representatives of the Buffalo case plaintiffs, unaware that he had more than enough to name four. This turn of events had been completely unanticipated by either the BMI management or members of the board, including those whose companies were among the plaintiffs.

CHAPTER 31

The Copyright Royalty Tribunal

The completely revised Copyright Act was less than a year away from being the law of the land, and the Copyright Office had the staggering burden of preparing for its implementation. New rules needed be drawn up and clarified, regulations interpreted, and a system set up for licensing jukeboxes, logging their performances, and collecting license payments. The RIAA and the NMPA were actively lobbying for new mechanical rates, and a new attempt was being made to legitimize performance royalty, in connection with which the Copyright Office had been instructed by Congress to prepare an economic study.

There was, as well, the activation of the Copyright Royalty Tribunal. It was late in 1977 before the five appointments to it were made. Each carried an annual salary of $42,000. Thomas Brennan, MaryLou Burg, Douglas Coulter, Frances Garcia, and Clarence Jones were named by the White House and quickly confirmed by the Senate. The group, following the President's expressed wishes, represented women, Hispanics, and blacks.

An organizational meeting took place in December, at which the new commissioners voted to study the impact of home taping, which Senator McClellan had called the principal "unfinished copyright issue." A series of educational presentations by copyright owners and users was made later, at which each explained their structure, functions, and position on public-broadcasting rates and jukebox regulations. The next order of business was to push ahead on compulsory licensing of music by public broadcasters, fees that had already been privately negotiated by the licensing societies and those dealing with synchronization and mechanical rights by the Harry Fox Agency.

A slightly modified licensing bill was introduced in the House in June 1977. In addition to existing provisions, including a 1 percent tax on radio stations, it would require jukebox operators to add an additional dollar to the eight dollar per machine they paid, beginning on January 1. In preparation for the Copyright Office report dealing with the subject, the register of copyrights set up two sets of hearings, at which opponents and proponents could state their cases. The arguments remained much the same. The broadcasters continued to say that if the recording artist is entitled to more money, let the record companies pay for it. The money performers get is directly owing to radio-station air play, they held. The RIAA took a new tack in one respect. "If the stations are so successful in expanding our market," Stanley Gortikov asked, "why do 77 percent of our popular recordings fail to recover costs and only 6 percent do really well? Radio plays only the winners that attract advertisers."

Alan Livingston, the new president of 20th Century-Fox's Entertainment Group, disparaged further the value of air play as a record promotion vehicle in an affluent world where people heard recorded music in many places and bought "what they want to own whether they hear it first on radio, on a jukebox, in a discotheque, or elsewhere." As the hearing ended, Gortikov vowed that he and other interested groups—the AFM, the American Guild of Musical Artists, and the American Federation of Television & Radio Artists—would go to Congress "for a showdown on the basis of raw political power" if the Copyright Office's final report was unfavorable to their interests.

The economic report commissioned by the Copyright Office from a private Washington study group found that broadcasters could pay a recorded-music use license "without any significant impact" and would pass fees along to sponsors. Any economic jolt from the $10 million expected to flow after passage of the bill was difficult to estimate, the report continued. Using industry figures, the study concluded that the number of companies engaged in making records on a full-time basis had risen from 287 in 1967 to 507 ten years later. Only a fraction of the union musicians engaged in the business made a living wage, a third earning $7,000 or less; only about one tenth earned more than $25,000. "Clearly," the report stated, "musicians who do receive sales and performance royalties are in the minority, and in some cases the extreme minority. Most performers are not in a strong enough position to bargain with record companies for a sales royalty." For those who were, all production, studio, and other costs had to be repaid before any royalty was received. Moreover, production costs had become so high that most records never reached the break-even point.

Two new disk performance bills were introduced during the next Congress, 1979–80. Broadcasters appearing in opposition to both bills offered a new survey of stations, estimating the commercial time value of free air play for recordings at between $150,000 and $490,000 a week, depending on market size. "Why do record companies spend so much money on radio promotion and radio advertising if we're not selling records for them?"

they asked. A speech made by Stan Cornyn, of Warner Communications, in which he asked what would happen "the day radio died," went into the record. Responding to his own question, he had told his audience of record merchandisers that "if it weren't for radio, half of us in the record companies would have to give up our Mercedes Benz leases."

In answer to a Congressman's objection that only big recording stars would be the bill's principal beneficiaries, the manufacturers promised that all royalties would be shared equally by all musicians and vocalists on a recording. For example, if a star singer was accompanied by five musicians and three backup singers, the royalty would be divided nine ways, after, of course, the manufacturer's half had been extracted.

Opposition was based in part on the ground that the record companies should not share in any way. A series of changes introduced in May 1980 would exempt many of the smaller-earning stations, public broadcasters, other nonprofit bodies, and small businessmen who used their own recordings. These changes were sufficient to stall legislation throughout the session. In the Senate, too, nothing was accomplished. As for the manufacturers, they were confronted with the problem of securing from the Congress protection against the growing business of illegal home taping.

The multimillion-dollar receipts from eight-dollar jukebox licenses—fought by the Amusement and Music Operators Association and coveted for years by ASCAP, the NMPA, and other copyright holders—which, with cable television fears, were expected to be between $10 and $13 million in the first year, did not materialize. In 1978, the Copyright Office collected about $1.1 million from 144,468 coin machines, and in the next year, $107 million from about a thousand fewer. The money represented license fees from fewer than half the machines known to be in operation. The only compulsory-license royalties collected by the Copyright Office, those from cable and jukeboxes, were invested at interest to await distribution by the Copyright Royalty Tribunal. Agreements between ASCAP and BMI about the division of this income were difficult to achieve; there was constant bickering over the size of shares. In excess of a million dollars was paid by the Public Broadcasting Service and National Public Radio for 1978–79.

The Tribunal conducted hearings at the end of 1980 to determine what royalty-rate adjustments should be made. No increase was ordered in jukebox fees for 1981, but beginning in 1982 the eight-dollar tax was increased to twenty-five dollars, to fifty dollars for 1984, and subjected to a cost-of-living adjustment in 1987. The AMOA argued that the industry was going downhill. At its peak, in the 1950s, there had been 700,000 jukeboxes in the United States, with four manufacturers—Wurlitzer, Seeburg, Rockola, and Rowe—controlling production. Machines were replaced at the rate of 70,000 each year. Wurlitzer went out of the business in 1974, and total output of music machines fell to 25,000 a year, most of them intended for export. With the shift of public interest to discotheques, coin-operated pinball and gambling machines, pool tables, and video games, the AMOA reported in 1980 that only 300,000 were operating and that there were only between 3,000 and 5,000 jukebox operators still in business. However, among them were persons with enough political influence to induce Congressmen in the South and Midwest to introduce bills in both houses to eliminate the annual royalty and substitute a single one-time license fee of fifty dollars for each new machine and twenty-five dollars for each jukebox already in use. During discussion on the Senate floor, a complaint was registered about this "small change issue in national terms that goes on and on." In the House, a representative supporting the legislation reminded his colleagues that "there are a lot more jukebox operators in my district than there are songwriters and recording artists." One result was that ASCAP and BMI organized the Action Committee for the Arts, to lobby on Capitol Hill.

Responding to a presentation by the AMOA showing that the fifty-dollar yearly jukebox license fee represented a 525 percent increase over that originally set in the Copyright Act of 1976, the Tribunal's chairman, Brennan, who had sat through years of jukebox opposition, reminded his fellow commissioners that the eight-dollar rate was a "political compromise not based on economic evidence." Throughout their long fight, the coin operators had never shown adequate proof of economic hardship, he added. In 1958, a Senate committee report had called for $19.70 fee per machine, which, if adjusted for inflation, would now represent a figure considerably higher than that being collected.

With the permission of the Justice Department and to avoid protracted hearings, it was suggested that a compromise arrangement be worked out, which would remove any need for new legislation to take the problem out of the Tribunal's hands. An agreement in principle was finally reached in February 1985.

The 1975–76 "penny war" over mechanical rates escalated in the spring of 1980 when the Tribunal met to determine adjustments for the next seven years. During the year of hearings held by the Copyright Office on jukebox licenses, in which mechanical rates were also discussed, the NMPA unsettled the RIAA by a bold demand for an increase to 6 percent in the suggested price of disks and tapes, because the current royalty "served only to maximize the revenues of the record companies, [allowing them] to buy cheap and sell dear." The suggestion was at once labeled by the RIAA unfair, arbitrary, and damaging.

The announcement of final hearings on the subject for 1980 began a new battle of economic studies. The publishers maintained that, whereas the European royalty on records had been 8 percent throughout the past decade, the two-cents-per-song American royalty had dropped from 6 percent of the suggested $3.98 retail price to 3.4 percent of the $8.98 LP now standard. In support of the NMPA demand, the AGAC made a survey of its members and found that nearly 70 percent had averaged income from music-related sources just above the poverty line in the past five years. In view of that, the guild wanted not a 6, but an 8 percent mechanical royalty.

Once again the RIAA painted a starkly bleak picture. The industry had gone through the worst year in history in 1979, with estimated pretax losses of $208.7 million, excluding overseas revenue, out of a reported $3.7 billion total income, down from 1978's $4.1 billion. In outlining the high cost of making records, Cornyn provided another of those fascinating, though usually self-serving, glimpses into the record and music business that dotted copyright hearings. His testimony showed just what the cost had been to record manufacturers of taking over from music publishers their promotional and marketing functions. Warner Brothers Records had spent nearly $12 million on national promotion, artist development, and advertising in 1979, a 289 percent increase over 1975's $1.7 million expenditure, when only $100,000 was spent for independent promotion. The cost for outside personnel to boost air play had risen ten times since then, Warner spending more than $1.8 million for this in 1979. Album costs had increased correspondingly: those for a recording session up from $50,000-$65,000 to $125,000-$150,000; cover artwork up from $2,000 an album to $3,000-$3,500. The cost of vinyl was up 36 percent, shrink-wrapping had increased by 71 percent, and board jackets were up 53 percent.

In support of the RIAA's position that the established publishers were not doing anything to promote new songwriter-performers, or to further their careers, Cornyn testified that Warner had released 136 albums in 1979, of which more than two thirds, or ninety-one, were by singer-songwriters who received 81 percent of the company's total mechanical royalties for the year. Sixteen of them got $16 million, or 57 percent of the total. If the rate was increased to 6 percent of retail list, Cornyn said, "this extra income will go to the titans of the business, not the little songwriter starving in the attic."

To demonstrate how much of a role record manufacturers played in promoting new songwriter–recording-artist talent, Cornyn reported that Warner had spent $30,000 in advances and expenses on a new singer. There was in addition $271,723 for recording costs, advances for equipment of $11,428, cover art for $4,300, rehearsal rentals at $4,000, and a demo record for $2,700—a total of $324,151, including the initial $30,000 advance. The artist in this case did not make a successful album.

Warner made similar major investments in other new artists during the year, bringing out fifty-eight debut LPs, which sold 2.3 million units, for billable sales of $9.25 million. Without counting overhead of $2.2 million for artists' royalties, $3.25 million in unrecoverable advances, and $680,724 in mechanical fees, the company lost $1.4 million.

When the Tribunal recessed in August, in a tangled morass of contradictory figures, it asked the NMPA to gather financial data by October 1, including 1977–79 domestic and foreign income from mechanical licenses, public-performance royalties, print income and other revenue, as well as operating expenses and general administrative costs. The hastily gathered information, from nearly half of the NMPA's 204 publishing-company members, indicated that, whereas the record companies were in the most severe slump in their history, the music publishers' profits had actually increased, which could be explained by the general time-lag in transmitting record royalties. Dollar profits for the period rose by 5.17 percent in 1977, 7.04 percent in 1978, and 8.41 percent in 1979, rather than the steady 25 percent rate claimed by the RIAA. Dollar profits for those years were $9.6 million, $15.9 million, and $18.8 million. Total mechanical revenues, domestic and foreign, fell from $20.5 million in 1978 to $12.9 million in 1979; total operating costs rose from $63 million in 1977 to $77.9 million in 1979. The seventy-three singer-songwriter-controlled music companies that reported to the NMPA had received 72.3 percent of all mechanical royalties in 1977, or $14.7 million; 63.7 percent the following year; and 66.2 percent in 1979, or $12.9 million.

At the conclusion of its testimony, and cognizant of the Tribunal's readiness to approve some increase, the RIAA suggested that no adjustment be made immediately, citing the sound economic position of music publishers as the reason. Rather, the RIAA board had approved a new approach, which would use the average recommended list price of the 200 top LPs on *Billboard, Cash Box,* and *Record World* charts during the previous year to make adjustments in 1982 and again in 1985.

Two weeks before the year-end deadline for its decision, the Copyright Royalty Tribunal issued new regulations, which increased the mechanical rate to four cents, or ¾ cents per minute, whichever was larger, to become effective the following July, as well as annual inflation rate adjustments. The decision, the Tribunal explained in its report, reflected the fact "that between 1973 and 1979 sales of recorded music in the U.S. almost doubled, from $2 billion to nearly $4 billion. In our opinion, based on the evidence in this proceeding, the fortunes of the record companies, the copyright users, have been enhanced in the last decade. The evidence shows that at the same time, the fortunes of songwriters and music publishers, the copyright owners, subject to a price-fixed mechanical royalty in a period of great inflation, have dwindled."

In preparation for a decision before year-end affecting cable television, ASCAP and BMI joined the Motion Picture Association, the NAB, and several sports organizations similarly affected in order to petition the Tribunal for a 15.4 percent increase and the institution of a system that would adjust cable rates regularly on the basis of inflation. The licensing bodies, including SESAC, had been alloted a 4.5 percent share of all cable royalties, which was divided in shares approved by the Tribunal after acrimonious debate citing various claims of share of air time. CATV rates were also raised in December, by a steeper increase than had been asked, to 21 percent, reflecting the period from October 1976 to January 1, 1980. They were to remain in effect until hearings in 1985. The decision brought down the wrath of both the NAB and the National Cable Television Association, the former accusing the Tribunal of subsidizing cable by setting fees that were too low, the latter regarding it as an enemy. Both positions were stated clearly and boldly during a series of Senate and House hearings on the elimination or retention of compulsory licensing for the medium.

CHAPTER 32

Other Copyright Problems

After World War I, as a growing international market for American literary products and music had become evident, the weakness of the nation's copyright protection in relation to that of other countries was quickly made clear. Beginning in 1922, a drive was started to bring the copyright law into closer line with the Berne Convention, prevalent around the world, particularly in the protection of authors and composers for the period of their lives and fifty years thereafter.

Already deeply involved in the creation of a new tax-free music library, much of it from the public domain, with which they hoped to curb the licensing aspirations of ASCAP, attorneys for large broadcasting stations directed the opposition to anything that would give the society control of American music for a longer period. For years, they continued to play the dominant role in a series of successful fights to defeat all measures calling for revision of the 1909 Copyright Act and any intended to ratify the Berne Convention. The revision legislation that finally emerged in 1976 did bring the country closer to Berne standards, but this did not mean participation in that international copyright agreement would occur quickly. However, American book and music publishers had long before devised a back-door method of enjoying the benefits of the Berne Convention. Canada had joined the convention as an independent member, and thus created the alternative for U.S. publishers of simultaneous publication of their new works by a branch operation in Canada or a cooperative Canadian publisher. This gave copyright protection for new works under the Berne Convention in all its signatory nations.

The NMPA, like its predecessor organization, the Music Publishers Protective Association, had been in the van of the music industry's fight for copyright revision, and was instrumental in early 1978 in the formation of an international trade association of popular-music publishers. The original function of the International Federation of Popular Music Publishers was to serve as spokesman for its members in their industry's world forums and to counteract the growing image of them, spread and encouraged by the record manufacturers, as "exploiters and parasites." The fifteen publishers' associations that founded the IFPMP represented roughly 150 music companies throughout the world, with the principal exception of those in some Latin American countries. They were united by concern over the illegal duplication of recordings, as well as by the fight for increased mechanical royalties, which record companies everywhere resisted.

In England, where the royalty rate had remained at 6.25 percent since 1928, although it was 8 percent on the Continent, a massive drive mounted by songwriters and publishers to bring the rate into line had recently been defeated. Publisher members of the German performing-rights society GEMA, which also served as a mechanical-royalty collection agency, were involved in a dispute with songwriter members who were asking for a two-thirds share of record-sale royalties, rather than the present 50 percent distribution. In a move to preserve internal harmony, GEMA finally compromised in 1979 and changed the formula to a sixty-forty split favoring composers and authors, but only in this single area and on a three-year trial basis.

With a membership that had increased from seventy-two in 1974 to roughly 150 by 1977, representing more than 1,000 publishing units, the NMPA embarked that year on a public-relations campaign to celebrate the sixtieth anniversary of its founding. In association with the Copyright Office, it held a series of workshop forums around the country, to educate several thousand employees of its members and others in the intricacies of the new copyright act. A Music Publishers Forum was organized for the benefit of young newcomers to the business, to introduce them to the latest developments.

Computers were changing the nature of a publisher's administrative function, allowing executives more time to engage in creative activities and to learn the business of marketing and promotion. A full-line publisher was required to do everything, from production of demonstration cassettes of new material, to securing recorded cover versions of hit songs or ones dug out of the catalogue, to marketing elaborate printed folio collections of popular music. In some cases, the "master demo" was good enough to release and gave the publisher a producer's share of the royalties.

Conditioned by the record companies' bidding wars for their services, recording artists thought it just to accept a tremendous advance on royalties from all sources and then to insist on a relationship with a music firm on a short-term basis only. The administrative and promotional services publishers also performed entitled them to ask for and get up to half of a song's income, including that from the original release. For the publisher who agreed only to administer income, the amount usually offered was 10 percent of all revenues. On a Gold LP selling half a million copies the share might be around $14,000, for doing little more than filling in cards and forms, a job of about three hours. However, if a $20,000 advance had been paid, it become incumbent upon the publisher to work actively on promotion of the album, in order to increase sales and make the advance fully recoupable, using a means whose expenses were entirely nonrecoupable.

Often the deal included material that was not recordable beyond its creator's initial version. The publishers' influence with record companies had dwindled to almost none, unless they were associated with a hit act. As a result, the quality of songs suffered and the number of printable pieces had been reduced markedly. In the words of Marv Goodman, of ATV Music, in *High Fidelity*, "If a group is in a recording situation they don't have to worry about polishing every song. If the lyrics to it don't come out in time, it's okay, because it's going to get released, and if it doesn't get played on the air as a single, that's okay too—they'll collect royalties from its being on the album."

The future of printed music looked rosier than it had since the halcyon days of the multimillion-copy seller. Sales of $211 million in 1979 represented a 193 percent cumulative increase over the $72 million of 1967. Four-page sheet music had lost its appeal to the public, and superstar folios and songbooks were on the way up. They were displayed in department stores, chain bookshops, and on racks, places where imaginative cover and interior artwork encouraged the walk-in traffic to buy. Folios and songbooks now were in the $4.98 range, worth the price because of their consistently high production and musical qualities. Columbia's new LP-sized AlbuMusic songbook-folios, one containing the words and music of Stevie Wonder's "Songs in the Key of Life" from his best-seller Motown album, attracted buyers as much for the supersized poster insert of their composer as for the music. Most publishers had learned that it was more profitable to give up publication rights to their music on an open basis to the several specialists in printed-music marketing than to finance their own print operation. After hearing "Feelings" on an advance release, Columbia got the rights from its publisher first and brought the song out in eighteen different sheet-music arrangements, with lyrics in several languages. More than 600,000 copies were sold; royalties were in excess of $150,000.

As printed music became again a significant economic factor, piracy and infringement followed, as they had throughout the preceding four centuries of professional music publishing. The traffic in illegal "fake books," compilations of the melody and chord lines of old and new hit songs, as many as 1,000 in a single volume, had been curbed by the production of legitimate collections, properly licensed by their copyright holders. When the print pirates turned to the high-priced songbooks and folios, they opened a money-making trade on which the NMPA soon focused its attention. Infringement slackened, often because new statutes strengthened property rights.

Two actions brought by the NMPA on behalf of its members clarified some issues and established precedents that served as warnings against future infringement by organized religious groups and educational institutions, which had long considered themselves beyond the law.

A hymnal, *Songs for Worship and Fellowship,* published by the Unification Church, whose spiritual leader was the Korean evangelist Sun Myung Moon, was alleged to contain forty songs copyrighted by twenty-two publisher members of the association. After two years of legal maneuvering, the matter was settled in favor of the plaintiffs, and the church paid $40,000 and legal fees.

The other action, the first against a college for infringement of music copyrights, was filed in May 1980 by the NMPA for three of its members. Longwood College, a small institution in Virginia, was charged with "willing and intentional" violation of the copyrights of five musical works by allowing them to be photocopied without permission. During the preceding four years, the NMPA had engaged in an "intensive and expensive campaign to educate the music educators," but without effect on Longwood. After twelve months of moral and legal suasion exerted on the Commonwealth of Virginia, the college's financial supporter, the case was settled with acknowledgment by the defendants of innocent infringement and payment of damages and attorneys' fees. An advisory bulletin from Virginia's attorney general warned the Dominion's education institutions that unauthorized photocopying of copyrighted music did not fall within the fair-use exceptions of the 1976 Copyright Act. The lesson was not lost on the majority.

Elvis Presley, whose music, once deplored by the educational establishment, was now heard in marching-band arrangements on high-school playing fields and in college stadiums, provided a financial bonanza after his death for both RCA Records and the tenant of the top floor of the Brill Building—the administrator of the singer's music companies, Elvis Presley Music and Gladys Music. Once the home base of Tin Pan Alley, the Brill had moved with the times to become headquarters for many rock-'n'-roll publishers. In 1959, the Aberbach brothers, Jean and Julian, moved their offices, and those of the dozens of firms jointly owned with artists, to the Brill's eleventh, and top, floor, where the walls quickly threatened to burst as the Aberbach empire expanded.

Among the employees of the Aberbachs' latest umbrella firm, Eleventh Floor Music, was a Swiss-born nephew, Freddy Bienstock, who had started in the American music business as a counter boy for Chappell Music, and had in 1945, joined their rhythm-and-blues publishing company, St. Louis Music. After Presley's overnight success following his move from Sun Records to RCA, an arrangement helped by the Aberbachs, Bienstock assumed a major role in the singer's retinue, effectively replacing Steve Sholes, who, with the Aberbachs' financial support, had persuaded RCA executives to sign the hip-swinging singer. Presley liked to hear how his finished records would sound, and it became a function of the Aberbachs' employees to find people in New York who could imitate him and make "dubs," or demonstration records, of the songs Bienstock took to him for consideration.

In October 1966, Bienstock looked for new fields, and the Aberbachs sold him their Belinda Music Company, whose name he changed to Carlin Music soon after it became his chief base of operations in England. Among the American catalogues Carlin represented in London were those owned by Motown Records, ABC-Dunhill, the Aberbachs' Hill & Range Songs empire, and firms owned by Jerry Lieber and Mike Stoller, with whom Bienstock later went into business in America as their partner in the Hudson Bay Music combine, under whose banner twenty music firms were grouped. By utilizing American music-promotion and exploitation tactics in London and acquiring reversionary rights in British copyrights, twenty-five years after the death of their composer or lyricist, Bienstock built a Carlin Group catalogue of more than 30,000 American copyrights and 80,000 British. Since its formation in 1968, Carlin had been the top British publisher for eleven successive years, during the course of which Bienstock discovered that, whereas the record companies dictated policy in America, in Britain it was the publisher who still had the power.

In 1977, Freddy Bienstock Enterprises purchased the New York Times Music Publishing Company and its 5,000 copyrights for approximately three million dollars in cash. The *Times* had added a new division to its forty-seven subsidiaries in 1974, Tommy Valando Music, a company oriented to the Broadway musical stage, buying a major interest in it from its co-owner, Metromedia. An unabashed emulator of the late Max Dreyfus, Valando had shepherded the careers of Jerry Bock and Sheldon Harnick, writers of *Fiorello* and *Fiddler on the Roof;* John Kander and Fred Ebb, whose musical re-creation of life in pre-Hitler Berlin, *Cabaret,* had a run of 1,165 performances; Stephen Sondheim, author of both words and music for *A Little Night Music;* and other creative young musical-theater talents.

Following Presley's death, later in 1977, the unprecedented sales of his recordings contributed substantially to the profits of the Hudson Bay Group, which administered the rights to almost everything Presley had recorded since 1972; Carlin controlled the British rights to between 65 and 70 percent of the singer's earlier songs. But things were not going as well then in Britain. Redwood Music, a member of Bienstock's Carlin Group, was engaged in eight cross-actions with British music houses, whose outcome would affect the ownership of more than 40,000 popular songs written after the passage of the 1911 British copyright law. Among them were "My Wild Irish Rose," "Barney Google," "Palesteena," "Two Cigarettes in the Dark," "Dear Old Southland," "April Showers," and "Oh, You Beautiful Doll."

The 1911 act included a provision that rights assigned to publishers reverted to the estates of composers and authors twenty-five years after their death. All remaining family members or their heirs could enjoy all commercial benefits for the next quarter century. The only exception was a "collective work," usually meaning an encyclopedia, newspaper, or such multi-author work. The application to music had not been defined in the law. The reversionary provision had, however, been omitted from the United Kingdom's 1956 Copyright Act—hence Redwood's recourse to the legal process.

In February 1977, the High Court ruled that the songs in question were in fact "collective" and therefore could not revert to the estates. Redwood's only victory lay in the fact that it had true claim to the reversionary rights of any song whose words and music were written by a single individual, or to an instrumental composition. It took the decision to the House of Lords the following autumn. Eight years of litigation ended in early 1980 when the House of Lords upheld its position, finding that jointly authored songs copyrighted prior to June 1, 1957, could revert as argued by the appellant. The decision applied not only to the United Kingdom, but also to Australia, New Zealand, Canada, and South Africa, among other nations. Negotiated agreements between Redwood and the eight other litigating publishers made late in 1980 settled other issues regarding reversionary rights. By then the owner through reversion of more than 70,000 compositions, Bienstock now belonged among the ranks of the British publishers who held all the power.

In America, the record companies continued to dictate policy and practices in the music business, despite all the efforts by the NMPA to depict its own end as a high-principled entrepreneurial system, free of irregularities. M. William Krasilowsky, co-author of the standard industry reference work, *The Business of Music*, alerted *Billboard* readers to such irregularities as cut ins by recording artists and record producers; the "Chinese bookkeeping" form of accounting being practiced by some that short-changed songwriters and recording artists; the filtering of funds from international licensing by music publishers; record-plant overruns that robbed almost all copyright owners; consumer mail fraud in regard to record-club subscriptions; kickbacks to recording artists from independent studio owners; cross-collateralized advances between artist-songwriter accounts by the record companies; off-the-book sales of phantom seats for rock concerts; disk-jockey payola; and laundering of funds. He omitted to mention the growing tendency on the part of the public to make tapes instead of spending money for an LP. Whether or not the record business was crying "wolf" in its protestations that the practice would render the disk obsolete, public larceny and its cure preoccupied the industry for the next five years and longer.

CHAPTER 33

Seesawing Sales and New Ideas in the Record Business

Nowhere was the control of artists and the year's 100 best-selling LPs and singles better shown than in the pages of *Billboard*'s 1975 *Talent in Action* supplement, published on December 28, 1974. It showed that the major conglomerates—ABC, CBS, EMI, PolyGram, RCA, and Warner Communications—had a combined 81 percent share, leaving the balance to four independents—A & M, Motown, 20th Century-Fox, and United Artists. With record sales maintaining a steady growth to $2.4 billion in 1975, equivalent to all screen-theater box-office receipts, and $2.73 billion the next year, the major manufacturer were giving up long-term growth for the sake of short-term success from the sales of their superstars' share of the market. Walter Yetnikoff, of the CBS Records Group, said, "If an artist can only sell 100,000 records . . . then this company is not interested in pursuing that artist. We're looking for the major, major breakthroughs."

To back its artist-development program, CBS had invested part of its profits from $484 million in sales in 1975, which represented its 17 percent share of the market, in eighty new talents. Some were established stars, like Willie Nelson; others were newcomers, like Phoebe Snow and Boston. The band's demonstration tape had literally come in over the transom, and after expending some studio time on it, CBS sold more than 400,000 units in its first month on the market.

Supersales made for quicker recouping of investment in new performers. Studio costs for a typical rock album of more than $100,000 could be spread out more profitably over big sales. As was predicted, WEA's lead in raising the price of its front-running popular LPs to $7.98 (but sold for $5.92 in most stores) began another game of follow-the-leader, from which the manufacturers looked for an increase of forty-eight cents in wholesale-distribution profits alone. The industry's big excuse for the price increase was the high-royalty factor, which had risen to an average of 15 percent, and as much as 17 or 18 percent for superstars who had been satisfied with 10 percent a few years earlier. The jump from $6.98 to $7.98 meant thirty-five cents more in artist's royalties on a 15 percent contract, and with the average 12-cent increase in mechanical royalties that was to go into effect in 1978, forty-seven of the forty-eight-cent profit was gone. Many in the industry found the new round of dollar spending on talent suicidal.

CBS and its major rival for leadership, Warner Communications, had combined sales of $1.21 billion in 1976: $615 million for the former, whose income included sales abroad almost equal to those in the United States, and $406 million for WCI. Warner's three record divisions enjoyed a relative autonomy, which dated back to the time of their acquisition. Stock-market analysts had resumed their romance with the industry, in particular with WEA, which, in the words of one of them, constituted "a very loose show, a somewhat unstructured arrangement, where each record division doesn't have a profit or sales target. The people are not held to any quarterly or biannual estimates, they're pretty much allowed to do their own thing. That sounds like a formula for disaster, but they are monitored closely by the corporate staff. And by not thrusting administrative responsibilities on creative people, [they] keep them doing what they should be doing—developing new artists and keeping old ones selling records.'' WEA's success, like that of a few other major labels, sprang, in part, from the reintroduction of in-house producers. At all three firms, producers were assigned to handle artists only if they felt comfortable with one another, leading to a 30 percent share of chart spots, best of all the Big Six in 1976.

With its American subsidiaries, Mercury-Phonogram, Philips, MGM, and United Artists Records, acquired early in the 1970s from the Transamerica Corporation, the Dutch PolyGram Company had become sixth among the leading American record companies. Its international operations did not match this success. In the ten years since Philips and Siemens had merged, in 1963, to form it, PolyGram had moved from being a small company that did business only in Europe to being an international giant with subsidiaries in thirty-five countries, ranking behind only CBS and EMI. The transfer of control of Chappell Music from Norelco to PolyGram had strengthened its position in the world's music-publishing business. So, too, did the addition to Chappell/Intersong of a major portion of the Aberbach family's Hill & Range-controlled catalogues, not including the two Presley firms, which Chappell would continue to administer, but including many early hits from country-music firms co-owned with major recordings stars. Yet it remained for an alliance with Robert Stigwood in 1975 to propel PolyGram into its position in 1978 as the first company to enjoy world-wide music-and-entertainment sales of $1.2 billion, followed shortly after, that same year, by EMI, with sales of $1.04 billion.

After Brian Epstein died, in 1968, effectively freezing Stigwood out of any further participation in the sale of NEMS/Nemperor, the Austrailian entrepreneur diversified his activities under the name Robert Stigwood Organization. Resuming personal management of the Bee Gees, T-Rex, Procul Harum, Joe Cocker, Eric Burden, and Eric Clapton, he operated a music-publishing company that owned the copyrights of all music written by his artists, and co-produced the British version of *Hair,* which ran for five years. He also brought to the stage Tim Rice and Andrew Lloyd Webber's first two rock musicals, *Joseph and the Technicolor Dreamcoat* and *Jesus Christ Superstar,* each of which had started as a rock album and then was transferred to the concert hall, the stage, and, finally, film, the latter grossing more than $133 million by 1975 from all versions. The RSO Television Division produced features for the American *Movie of the Week* series, and the original English TV productions of *Sanford and Son* and *All in the Family.* With annual profits running high, but virtually beggared by Britain's heavy tax laws, RSO went public in 1970, only to attract little interest from investors. It was sold by its founder to PolyGram for one dollar a share, much above market value. The transaction cost PolyGram eight million dollars, from which Stigwood got one and a half million.

Early in Atlantic Records' licensing relationship with Stigwood, it formed RSO Records to handle his artists in the United States. In May 1975, when Stigwood was beginning work as co producer of a film version of the rock opera *Tommy,* Warner Communications approached him with an offer. It proposed to pay $11 million, one dollar a share, to take over the recently re-formed Robert Stigwood Organization, Ltd., in which PolyGram had a quarter interest, Stigwood and a partner a 26 percent share, and stockholders the balance. The PolyGram Group countered with the offer of a place for Stigwood on its board; a guaranteed income of $10 million from the various Stigwood music companies, which would be administered by Chappell Music; royalties from the manufacture, distribution, and marketing of all RSO-American recorded products; and the investment of five million dollars in each of the following five years for acquisition and development of screen properties. While the final papers were being prepared, Stigwood entered into a partnership with one of his American creative advisers, the former actors' agent Allan Carr, for production of a number of new films. The first would be a screen version of Broadway's longest-running musical up to that time, *Grease,* which had given more than 1,600 performances. Film rights were owned by Carr, and half of them were turned over to Stigwood as Carr's immediate contribution to their partnership.

Soon after, Stigwood became convinced that their first film production should, instead, be a version for the screen of a magazine article about blue-collar urban whites in Brooklyn and their addiction to disco dancing, their solitary form of weekend entertainment, for which they dressed in uncommon splendor to enjoy a brief starring role under a discotheque's sophisticated light show. Disco and its music had come a long way since the fly-by-night days just before the Hues Corporation and George McCrae's recordings first hit the Hot 100 charts. New York was still the hub of disco's universe, but other cities were competing to displace it. Disco had become a four-billion-dollar industry, surpassed only by professional sports. It made cross-over personalities of Donna Summer, K. C. and the Sunshine Band, Thelma Houston, the Commodores, and Gloria Gaynor. The musical expertise of disco deejays, unhampered by Top 40's three-minute limitation, had become, for the record business, what FM jockeys of the late 1960s were, changers of the status quo. In the words of Simon Frith, in *Sound Effects,* disco had also changed "the meaning of a good night out [which] had to be understood in the context of the 1970s' sexual mores. Disco was not a response [like punk] to rock itself, but challenged it directly, by the questions it asked about music and dance."

It was a filmed depiction of such nights and their consequences that intrigued Stigwood, who offered Paramount Pictures $2.5 million against profits to make *Saturday Night Fever,* starring a young talent from the Broadway stage represented by Carr, John Travolta, who had played a leading role in *Grease.* Paramount returned the $2.5 million to Stigwood Productions for distribution rights for just under a 60 percent share of the profits. Music for the film was written by the Bee Gees and published by Stigwood. To enforce his philosophy that one "built on a musical vehicle so that it got better known than the play or movie of which it was part," Stigwood hired Al Coury, Capitol's vice-president for national promotion since 1972 who had resigned to form his own company, and made him president of RSO Records. The company's first ten months saw it make an unexpectedly early contribution to PolyGram's treasury. With a sales backbone of nine collectors' LPs, reissues of Stigwood hits on Atlantic-RSO and other foreign licensees that had reverted to him, Coury concentrated on a small roster of artists, among them the Bee Gees and younger brother Andy, a newcomer to the recording studios, who all had their best year ever. Running counter to the latest industry trend, which had seen, for example, Warner's independent promotion budget grow by tenfold in just four years, Coury's first move was to build a seven-man promotion staff to handle RSO exclusively in key markets. When necessary, they were supplemented by Polydor's staff, and augmented by independent promotion men to permit maximum impact during special drives.

The world had the opportunity, beginning in the fall of 1977, to witness the start of Coury's promotion strategy, "cross-over marketing." The motion pictures had become expert in this type of promotion during the 1930s, when network air play made hits out of sound-track songs, and the frequent mention of a forthcoming song made the name known in every household long before its release date. In December, the $12.98 double-LP sound-track album of *Saturday Night Fever* was "shipped gold," with a half-million copies distributed all at once. Record buyers had become increasingly concerned with the sound quality on their purchases because of Ray Dolby's technology, which had taken another step forward in the creation of noticeably improved movie sound. When the distributors for the projected *Star Wars* movie, to which George Lucas owned all rights, became skeptical about the future of that expanded Saturday-afternoon serial feature, it was decided to open it all at once in a string of recently built widescreen theaters capable of treating it as a 70-millimeter production with six-track sound, rather than as the 35-millimeter picture with monaural sound it originally was. The young writer-director took the problem to the Dolby Laboratories. As a result, all prints were encoded by a four-channel matrix system and Dolbyized, using Type A equipment, as were at least half of the several hundred picture houses in which *Star Wars* was first shown, each equipped with the same noise-reduction encoders and equalizers to match speaker response that Dolby engineers had worked with every day of shooting in the British studios where the film was made. The effect of the noticeably improved sound was immediate and tremendous. Within the year, several dozen other features had been released with Dolby-encoded sound, among them *Saturday Night Fever* and its sound track.

In the four months before the LP's release, Coury released four singles from the album, two by the Bee Gees, an unprecedented departure from customary practice in dealing with sound-track music. Concentrated crossover marketing began when 8,000 major retailers and radio stations were sent a full-color giant poster showing John Travolta in the disco-dance position that was used on the LP cover and on all film advertising. A thirty-second trailer with the Bee Gees singing the picture's theme song, "Staying Alive," was shown simultaneously in 1,500 theaters, coinciding with the release of another Bee Gees single from the movie, "How Deep Is Your Love." Immediately after Thanksgiving, a new three-minute trailer was exhibited nationally, featuring excerpts from all four of the RSO *Saturday Night Fever* singles. Coury ordered the installation of videotape machines in major retail outlets during November and December, on which both movie trailers were shown, accompanied by footage recorded at Bee Gees concert.

In February, when all four singles were in the top ten, the first time such a feat had been accomplished since Beatles' days, Coury projected a sale of between $100 and $129 million for the package.

In the process of expanding its U.S. operation, PolyGram invested in a second recently formed company, Casablanca Records, founded and owned by Neil Bogart, the erstwhile "King of Bubble Gum Music," who had been one of the earliest to switch to disco, with its queen, Donna Summer, yet still remained the ruler of teen-age rock. Bogart had also recognized the effect of television on pre-adults and recruited groups who depended for success as much on their physical appearance as on their music. The most popular was Kiss, a rock group whose members dressed in Kabuki costume and featured a fire-breathing Fender electric/bass player, and the six-man

Street People, earliest of the "gay to straight cross-over" disco groups. A confirmed advocate of intensive promotion, by both in-house employees and outside free lancers, Bogart spent between $250,000 and $750,000 to back his touring artists with record promotion in the areas they visited. Before he died, in 1982, he had sold Casablanca to Polygram and founded yet another company, Boardwalk Entertainment, for which Harry Chapin, Joan Jett, Mac Davis, and the Captain and Tennille recorded.

RSO and Casablanca sold $300 million worth of records in 1978, just under two thirds of PolyGram's total U.S. sales. RSO released ten LPs during the year, five of which attained Gold or Platinum awards. Three sound-track albums were responsible for two out of every three PolyGram sales: "Saturday Night Fever," which sold 15 million LPs in the United States, and for which the Bee Gees received $1.20 royalty on every copy; "Grease," starring Travolta and Olivia Newton-John, 22 million units around the world; and "Sgt. Pepper's Lonely Hearts Club Band," based on a London stage musical, which sold three million copies at a list price of $15.98. These and the seven other RSO LPs earned pretax profits of $60 million for Stigwood and PolyGram. The movie *Grease* cost Paramount three million dollars to make and another three million to promote, using Coury's indisputably successful formula.

Not since the unexpected success of *Hair,* the folk-rock musical, in the late 1960s had a sound-track or musical-score LP enjoyed such mass marketing. Rivaling the success of *My Fair Lady* on recordings, it had three cast albums and fourteen songs covered by major artists in the United States alone. But not until "Aquarius/Let the Sunshine In," recorded by the MOR group Fifth Dimension, began to become a hit did *Hair*'s music and records start to sell.

For a time, the caution in making major investments in Broadway musicals that was observed at Columbia Records and other companies following the series of recorded failures in 1965–66 was abandoned for rock musicals. Then, after the quick closing of several lavish and expensively overproduced musicals written by Galt McDermott, the composer of *Hair,* classically trained record producers and budget-wary executives turned their backs on rock. Broadway was pricing itself out of the reach of the young enthusiastic audiences who filled theaters around the world to revel in rock musicals and kept "Hair" on the best-selling LP chart for 151 weeks, a success that *Godspell, Jesus Christ Superstar,* and the stage *Grease* could not match.

It was *The Wiz,* based on *The Wizard of Oz,* with a score rooted in soul music, which included one hit single, that attracted a new audience to the theater after it opened in 1975. Black families packed houses during the several years-long invasion of black musicals and revues, including an all-black company of *Hello Dolly.* Yet black-cast LPs failed to reach the best-selling charts for any appreciable measure of time.

The electronic instruments required for rock and black musicals placed an ever greater importance on the theater's amplification system and brought recording studio technology to Broadway. Miking was introduced in the 1940s in the form of sensitive foot, not body, microphones for actors who were not singers but were in leading musical-comedy roles. When strings virtually disappeared from the orchestra pit, they were replaced by saxophones and trumpets, over which it was difficult to hear singers and nonsingers. The electrician who came in only to turn on the amplification system in the 1940s, for fifty dollars an evening, was replaced by mixers entrusted with a series of amplification units, mikes, and separate speaker systems for various parts of the orchestra and the theater. Production costs went up as much as $100,000, $2,500 for weekly rental of each sound unit and $500 a week for the mixer.

A Chorus Line, which was the second Pulitzer Prize-winning Broadway musical, and still running in 1985, was Goddard Lieberson's last original-cast triumph. He often said that not since *My Fair Lady* had he felt the way he did about the Edward Kleban–Marvin Hamlisch collaboration. The LP he produced and that of *Annie* were the only cast albums since *Hair* to go Platinum.

With a solid market for only 5,000 units, except for musicals with a score including one or more popular hits, record companies abandoned the once-profitable role of angel. The music publisher who financed the purchase of scenery, paid for musical arrangements, and made "supplementary producers' royalties" had been supplanted in the 1950s by the record-company A & R head, who bid spiritedly and often carelessly to secure what might be a best-selling commodity. Neither existed any longer. Record companies were ready only to pay for recording costs and hope that the publisher would promote the LP.

Fortified with its share of a $4.1-billion business and negotiating for the British Decca and London labels, which were responsible for Decca Ltd.'s heavy losses, PolyGram instituted a ten-year program for its American music operations. Outlining it to senior executives from the company and its subsidiary firms in June 1979, Irwin Steinberg, executive vice-president of PolyGram America, looked toward the "acquisition of new fully-staffed record companies that could achieve a steady $100 million net volume annually," according to *Billboard.*

Despite a still-pending stockholders' class action, Capitol Records was generally regarded as responsible for a major contribution to the financial well-being of EMI, much of whose international record profits still came from Beatles LP albums. Not only did EMI and its international subsidiaries manufacture and distribute one fourth of all records sold in thirty-two countries, but EMI had further diversified its interests and become a leading international distributor of musical instruments; owner of the major Muzak franchise in England; operator of a chain of concert and theatrical ticket agencies and record stores; a leading talent representative; owner of the former ABC-Paramount Theatres British chain of movie houses; operator of Thames TV, Britain's leading commercial television company; and one of the world's most important suppliers of high-tech medical equipment, including electronic scanners, and military hardware. The giant conglomerate was also responsible for the introduction on an international scale of the latest British variant of rock music, recordings of "punk rock" or "new wave music" by the Sex Pistols. This group of "outrageous" English musicians, regarded as anarchistic and socially violent, paved the way for the later triumphs of the Cars, Blondie, the Police, and Cheap Trick, all of whom became successful in the late 1970s and early 1980s. The Sex Pistols were given an initial $70,000 advance, to which EMI executives added another $100,000 following the public outcry over their aggressive behavior, which forced the company to cancel its contract with them.

To expand its world-wide publishing operations, which included the old-line British giants Francis, Day & Hunter, Peter Maurice, Robbins Music of England, Keith-Prowse, and B. Feldman, and Capitol's in-house firms—Glenwood, Central Songs, and Beechwood Music—EMI bought almost the entire music-publishing divison of Columbia Pictures Industries in the summer of 1976. The transaction involved $23.5 million in cash for the operating assets of Screen Gems–Columbia Music and Colgems Music, providing Columbia Pictures with a gain after deferred taxes of approximately $15 million, which was used to reduce the picture company's outstanding debt structure. That, with its subordinated debentures, amounted to more than $222 million. Columbia's music print division, Columbia Pictures Publications, was not involved in the transfer. Expecting to reduce its obligations further, Columbia entered into an agreement with EMI Film & Theatre Corp., which advanced an additional five million dollars toward the joint production of four major films. Time Inc., publisher of *Time, Fortune, Sports Illustrated,* and owner of Home Box Office, made a similar multimillion-dollar commitment to Columbia Pictures, in return for which the TV rights to twenty already produced Columbia pictures were turned over to Home Box Office.

Now owner of the world's largest music-publishing operation, EMI was enjoying a 43 percent growth rate in sales of music and records, going from $768 million to $1.1 billion in three years. In 1979, EMI picked up United Artists Records for three million dollars, but retained the label's identity and gave it the benefit of a major branch distribution operation. In the process, country and black artists were restored to EMI's American roster. In a restructuring of U.S.-Canadian operations, EMI grouped all its record holdings in the United States under a Capitol/EMI group flag.

There had been a 21 percent increase in profits from the world-wide EMI Music in 1978, but due to unexpected losses, a drop in profits was expected in the second half of fiscal 1978–79. Lord Bernard Delfont, who had recently been installed as chief executive of EMI Ltd., immediately initiated changes to "get the company moving again." One of his first moves was to sign one of the leading MOR songwriter-entertainers, Neil Diamond, to a million-dollar contract to play the lead in a remake of *The Jazz Singer* and to write ten to fifteen original songs in collaboration with the French songwriter Gilbert Becaud. For fear of offending raised white consciousness, it was agreed that in this second talking-picture version, which Delfont expected to work the same financial miracle as the first had for Warner Brothers, there would be none of the blackface on Diamond that Al Jolson had used.

Delfont began talks with Charles Bludhorn, president of Gulf & Western, about the possibility of merging their leisure-time groups. Bludhorn had been watching massive profits from music copyrights used in the successful Paramount productions *Saturday Night Fever* and *Grease* flow into the pockets of Robert Stigwood and PolyGram. He had publicly expressed an interest in increasing Paramount Pictures' role in the entertainment industry.

The EMI-Paramount merger would involve the latter's investment of $154 million, which was based on half of EMI's estimated investments in the music business, to buy a half-interest in EMI's music holdings, with which the film company's fifty-year-old division Famous Music would be integrated. Like Screen Gems–EMI, Famous was earning annual pretax profits of $2.2 million. In September 1979, a statement from the two companies announced that the merger had been called off, for reasons unstated, leaving EMI vulnerable. Two months later, an announcement was made that Thorn Electrical Industries, a British conglomerate involved in consumer electronics, white goods, and television rentals, to which EMI had sold its radio-equipment manufacturing interests in the 1950s, had acquired EMI, Ltd., for $348 million. It was one of the largest mergers in British history. The terms of Thorn's offer were 28 of its shares, plus $116 worth of 7 percent convertible debenture shares, for every 100 shares of EMI. The merger was expected to put Thorn-EMI into a strong position in the major domestic appliance market of the 1980s—videodisks, video recorders, and video cassettes.

Just 399 years after popular music in the English language was first heard by native Americans in what is today the United States, and 101 years after Thomas Edison uttered the words "Mary had a little lamb" into his original talking machine, the prerecorded music business climbed a new Mount Everest: a $4.1 billion retail gross. The figure represented $1 billion from 137 million prerecorded cassettes; $1 billion from 133.6 million eight-track tapes; and $2.1 billion from 531.3 million recorded disk units.

Like Coleridge's albatross, payola had remained a constant and invidious force during the years it had taken to gain this peak. In early 1977, the FCC resumed hearings on payola and other improper practices. Two local independent record promoters had complained to the commission that disk jockeys on an influential black music station in Washington had received payments from them in excess of $14,000 in return for on-the-air plugging of new soul records and concerts by black artists. It was reported in Los Angeles that, preparatory to the opening of a federal grand jury hearing in February, investigators were also looking into reports that some manufacturers had talked about the application of pressure on discount record stores to end the fiction of "list price," as well as tie-in sales involving recordings by superstars and price fixing. It was also alleged that some executives had engaged in discussions, bordering on antitrust violation, to put a stop to escalating royalty rates being paid to artists. The major labels were ordered to deliver to the grand jury complete financial records for the past five years and a variety of other internal communications.

Rod McKuen, superstar of an earlier time, when the royalty offered to a major artist on cut-out records was 5 percent, brought a $60-million class-action suit against RCA Records in April 1977, claiming that the seven albums he had made for the company between 1965 and 1968 had been pressed and sold as "leftover merchandise" for a fraction of their full wholesale price. In 1971, when the alleged abuses of McKuen's contract had started, he had bought back all masters to his LPs, for $175,000, and was releasing them on his Stanyan label. If certified by the federal court, McKuen's class action would involve 359 other recording artists, 9.5 million of whose albums had similarly been distributed as "instant cutouts." RCA admitted in a written reply to having pressed the 9.5 million LPs, but asserted strongly that the payments it had made to artist, producers, and music publishers were computed on the basis of one quarter of what would have been paid if the sales had been made as wholesale merchandise. Judge Edward Weinfield, no stronger to the music business, upheld the RCA contention that the matter was a contract dispute. In denying certification as a class action, he noted that only forty-two of the 359 other recording artists cited by McKuen would be entitled to royalties of more than $10,000; the others were ineligible to participate.

The need for standardized methods of artist-royalty accounting was emphasized by a Price, Waterhouse study, which commented that there were many methods of payment and that bookkeeping methods for compensating artists were "unique to the record industry." The report found that "accounting procedures for royalty advances paid to artists which can be recouped out of future income are not uniform." The study called for reforms.

It was no wonder that contracts with superstars, many of whom produced or co-produced their own music, lacked uniformity. Bidding for them ended with contracts that involved unheard-of advances, clauses, stipulations, guarantees, and rising royalty rates. Paul Simon was offered, and signed, a contract guaranteeing him more than $13 million to leave CBS, for which he had been recording since the 1960s, and go with Warner Brothers, to make four albums. The Rolling Stones asked for and got a renewed contract by which CBS Records paid a rumored $28-million advance for their services until 1987. In contracts negotiated by his in-laws, the Eastmans, reported to guarantee $20 million, Paul McCartney renewed his agreement with EMI for all countries in the world except the United States and Canada, leaving him free to stay or not with Capitol Records. He left, signing a contract with CBS Records that guaranteed two million dollars on only the U.S. and Canadian rights for each new LP. When this was recouped, a royalty of 22 percent or $1.80 on each additional sale of his $8.98 LPs would begin. To sweeten the original proposition, Frank Music, the catalogue founded by the Broadway songwriter-publisher Frank Loesser and containing his popular and Broadway music, valued at several millions, which had been acquired by CBS, together with all rights other than grand performance rights, was thrown into the bidding. Under the CBS-McCartney deal, at least 250,000 units had to be sold before the first penny of profit was realized. But although all five of the LPs McCartney made for CBS prior to the return of his North American rights to EMI-Capitol, in late 1985, were Gold and three also Platinum, only one, "Tug of War" (1982), actually climbed to the number-one position on the trade-paper charts. McCartney's music-publishing empire continued to grow, though in 1981, ATV Music, owner of his music written with John Lennon, rejected MPL's offer of $27 million for the catalogue. When ATV Music went on public sale in 1984, MPL was a leading contender, until the firm was purchased by Michael Jackson for about $40 million.

In a surprisingly candid discussion of CBS policy in regard to new artists, contracts, and advances, as well as returns of records by distributors and retailers, Seymour L. Gartenberg, then the CBS senior vice-president of finance, told an audience of accounting executives that all artists, especially superstars, were not equal. Those in jazz and the country field always got less of everything. With a national 50-to-75 percent defective rate on superstar records, because of warping caused by inept shrink-wrapping or imperfect pressing, CBS had instituted a 20 percent exchange limit on most albums, a move followed by most of the manufacturers. This replaced the troublesome and chaotic 100 percent return privilege that had been introduced to interest the rack jobbers and to cover manufacturing mistakes now excused but that had been bringing industry wide returns of 40 percent of all shipped merchandise. Now singles and albums by new artists were 100 percent exchangeable, limited-edition packages nonexchangeable, and Christmas releases had a 50 percent limit.

CBS offered new talent only one-year contracts, with options for four more years, which if picked up required delivery of two new LPs a year. The new artists' royalty was generally between 18 and 24 percent "all in," meaning inclusion of a producer's six to eight percent. Mechanical royalties were limited by CBS to 27.5 cents on a single LP, but the rock groups' propensity for longer tracks often required the company to swallow the difference and drain the mechanical-royalties budget. There was less money for local promotion of artist tours, which, like advances and recording costs, continued to be recoupable from earned royalties.

In June 1977, after four months of hearings, an FCC administrative judge made it clear that, although the Washington black-station disk jockeys did take advantage of their position to get presents of clothing, meals, and other things, they were exonerated of the charges made by the independent soul and rock record promoters earlier in the year.

Black radio, on which the FCC appeared to be focusing its investigation, was under more guns than one. The NAB had examined the lyrics of a number of black disco hits that had crossed over to the popular charts and found many sufficiently suggestive to warn its members once again to screen all material. The Reverend Jesse Jackson, of Operation Push, met with the heads of some record companies and urged them to "assume certain moral control" over their soul releases. When the public spotlight fell on such cross-over hits as "Shake Your Booty," "Disco Lady," "Do It to My Mind," and "Love to Love You Baby," the manufacturers did take some action. CBS revised the original suggestive lyrics of a projected release and instituted a general company policy to discourage artists "from delivering offensive material by telling them we can't get it exposed." None of these gestures had any effect on the success of black music in 1977. Its sales represented approximately two thirds of the $3.5 billion retail gross that year.

The National Association of Television and Radio Announcers, composed of black broadcasting personnel, which had been formed in 1954 to deal with the problems they faced on black radio stations, was temporarily revived and then turned into BMA, the Black Music Association. Under the leadership of black-owned record-company executives, it launched a drive to obtain funds from all elements of the music business.

Black-owned or -controlled business in America, represented by its top 500 enterprises, each doing business in excess of $3.6 million annually, and led by Motown Industries, of Los Angeles, with sales in 1977 of $61.4 million, had a combined business volume for the year of $896 million. But there were few black owners of broadcasting properties among them. Of the more than 300 black-oriented stations in the United States, only sixty were owned by blacks. In 1971, the number had been six. Even a typical small-market station now cost more than a one million dollars; in the Deep South the price was around $300,000. Loans in that range for a radio property were hard to come by for blacks, because all stations did not make money. With the narrowing of space bands on the broadcasting frequencies in order to allow 125 new AM stations on the air, it was expected that conditions would improve once the economic barrier against black stations, originally built by advertising agencies that concentrated on white markets, was overcome. There long had been a tendency among blacks to invest in more tangible properties, real estate and black consumer-oriented companies, but since 1973 a growing interest in radio as a business had surfaced among black entrepreneurs.

Many successful black radio operations expanded by crossing over, adding MOR and rock programs to attract white teen-agers and adults. These groups had already been attracted to soul music by disco and funk, just as blacks had tuned in white rock-oriented stations, lured to them by black-influenced hard rock, jazz fusion, and "white soul" performers who had themselves crossed over to the R & B charts. With racially integrated sports, contemporary popular music was indeed doing, in the words of *Billboard*'s Dave Dexter, "more to eliminate discrimination than all the legislation advanced since 1976. It's a new scene, and a new and better America."

The FCC moved the payola hearings to the West Coast in mid-1977, where the most important lesson it learned was that bribery in the record business was a racially undiscriminatory business. Switching back to Washington late in the year, the commission turned from the takers to the givers, independent promotion men, whose targets were not as widespread as an industry with 8,600 AM and FM stations might indicate. A few years later, a former promotion man said privately that only 2,700 stations were important to the record companies: 468 Top 40 stations, 286 album-oriented-rock stations, 221 adult contemporary stations, and 226 country-music stations. Fewer than 200 stations concentrated on black music, and 153 on disco records.

Papers subpoenaed from some major labels tended to concentrate on the independent contractors responsible for promoting new releases and artists, to whom the dispensation of payola and other illegal inducements had been assigned. As Peter W. Bernstein explained in *Fortune*:

> Record industry executives maintain, not surprisingly, that payola is a thing of the past. Federal investigators familiar with the seamier side of the business agree, at least in the sense that the record companies are putting considerable distance between their organizations and the putative dispensing of cash for radio play. Suspicions these days—without much solid evidence—center on free-lance promotion men. Another suspicion that always hangs over the industry has to do with drugs. While it is not exactly news that performers and others in the industry use drugs, the phenomenon doesn't seem traceable to the use of corporate funds.

After five years of complete inactivity on the payola problem, a House subcommittee looked into it in 1984. After staff personnel discussed the matter with a small number of broadcasters, promotion men, and record-company executives, the information was leaked that the investigation had turned up the payment of millions of dollars for promotion, which the Communications Act did not forbid, and the whole business was dropped.

In March 1985, the New York Times rediscovered payola. A report from its Los Angeles correspondent asserted that record companies had continued to use outside promoters, who were given more than $50 million by the largest record manufacturer. "In some instances, industry sources say, managers of radio stations have agreed to add songs to their play lists in exchange for advertising payments from record companies to give an appearance of integrity." The publisher of *Radio Business Report,* an industry newsletter, told the *Times* that a "Mafia-like network" existed, control of which had been taken over by independent promoters. And Rick Sklar, former program director for WABC-AM, said he believed that the independent promoters were "largely 'money conduits' who, by making regular payments to radio executives, exercise total control over the stations' play lists."

The death in 1977 of Elvis Presley and Bing Crosby had been responsible for a growth of sales that spilled over into the following year. RCA and MCA were forced to use out-of-house presses to meet orders for reissues of material by these long-time best-selling artists. Production of four million disks a day, one fourth of them by CBS, was insufficient to meet the tremendous demand, and many releases scheduled for late 1977 and 500 new albums intended for the first half of 1978 were canceled.

According to 1978 figures, PolyGram and EMI had topped one billion dollars in world-wide music sales. The CBS Records Group was in a strong third position: $946.5 million for the year, with a 12 percent profit rate that accounted for 28.8 percent of all corporate revenues. WEA had reached $617 million, almost half of Warner Communications' total sales. Still grouped with white goods, RCA Records had enjoyed an estimated 25 percent increase in one year, to $500 million in sales; and MCA's record and music-publishing unit achieved $131.5 million in sales, a 32 percent increase. Stripped of revenues from manufacturing and excluding foreign operations, CBS Records had sales of around $500 million; Warner Records Group, $416 million; RCA Records, and estimated $200 million; Capitol-EMI, $100 million; and MCA Distributing, about $70 million. This money provided each with a sufficient financial cushion to continue bidding for stars, even though victory was occasionally Pyrrhic.

Suddenly confronted in 1979 with the beginning of another recession, the major companies stared possible disaster in the face. CBS and Warner had spent in excess of $20 million to erect new manufacturing facilities in order to meet expected large sales. Finding themselves, instead, with millions of LP returns, sent back for credit, they lowered the boom on the 100 percent return policy. There was also the problem of counterfeit LPs among the returns. Al Coury found that between 20 and 40 percent of the returns of his smash-hit LPs were illegal duplicates for which he was obligated to give credit. The same problem existed for all major labels.

After $80 million in losses over four years, because of tremendous returns and failure to produce sufficient volume to support the large in-house distribution organization, American Broadcasting Company had put its record-and-music operation on the block in 1978. Though a record sales boom was in progress, there were no bidders. MCA was able to get the initial $55-million asking price lowered, and it absorbed the properties in early 1979. The possibility of establishing ABC Records as a third independent MCA line was soon abandoned, and most of its employees were discharged. So, too, were some of the staff of ABC Music Publishing, after its 20,000 copyrights, including 1,000 catalogues, many of which were owned by songwriters-artists, were transferred to MCA Music. By the end of 1979, the MCA record-and-music unit reported an operating loss of $6.1 million, a 163 percent drop since 1978. The decline was regarded as almost matter-of-course by an industry whose leaders coped with the problem of falling demand by raising prices. More inventory risk than they cared to assume fell on the shoulders or retailers, who coped by reducing orders. The price increase meant only fifty cents, after discounts, to many consumers, but it represented an industrywide certainty that the public would accept without protest a more than 10 percent jump in list prices for recordings of their idols. There was little complaint when "Tusk," a new double LP by Fleetwood Mac, was sent to distributors with a suggested list price of $15.98. The group's previous Warner release, "Rumours," had sold nearly 12 million units, but "Tusk" sold only two million.

The principal economies effected by the major labels included the gradual discharge of more than 3,000 middle- and lower-management and factory employees, reduction in the number of promotional LPs, rationing of the T-shirts and satin jackets that once were given away by a generous hand, and a watchful eye on expense accounts.

Living on small profit margins and hoping for huge sales, the largest independent record companies were the victims of traditional distribution practices. They were forced to raise wholesale prices, while their manufacturer competitors maintained theirs, to $3.60 wholesale for a $7.98 LP, which was resold to retailers for $4.30. The manfacturers' branches meanwhile, paid $3.47 for a similar product and passed it on to retailers for $4.09. It was a fact of life for the independent record companies in 1978 that it was more profitable for them to use an independent distributor, but it was also true that rack jobbers, subdistributors, and retailers went to the manufacturer-owned branch operations for their stock.

To resolve the cash-flow problems that began to plague them in 1979 and to take advantage of the major labels' power to dominate the market, most independent record companies transferred their business to the manufacturers. They did receive less money per wholesale unit, but there was a significant cash advance against royalties, as well as a most-favored customer pressing charge, and problems with slow-paying customers were ended.

Columbia Pictures Industries solved the problem by selling its Arista Records subsidiary, whose profits were beginning to decline, to the German Bertelsmann conglomerate for $50 million, making an after-tax profit of approximately $7 million.

Elton John's Rocket Records, 20th Century-Fox Records, and A & M Records signed distribution agreements with RCA Records, a giant that had reawakened and increased its sales in the past few years and strengthened its world-wide record business. In 1976, RCA had produced more than half of its revenues from that source for the first time. The next year, it had more than forty international licensees to handle its records. It had bought German Teldec Records, entered into a joint-venture project with the Japanese Victor Company to market records and tapes, and increased production of its SelectaVision videodisk player and library in association with Matsushita of Japan. It had enjoyed its best year ever, quadrupling earnings over those of 1975. Like all the Big Six, it suffered losses in the first half of 1979, but expected to cover them with profits from its new relationship with independent record firms. Those projected for A & M alone were expected to yield a 50 percent increase in sales volume, to an over-all 13 percent share of the American market and 35 percent of the world market.

After sixteen years as the most successful independent label, during which time it produced two of the earliest "gorillas," the best-selling LPs of their time—Carole King's "Tapestry" and Peter Frampton's "Frampton Comes Alive"—A & M had made nearly $100 million in 1978. Using its profits, it began to establish its own distribution chain, but cash-flow problems later in 1979 compelled it to turn distribution over to RCA. With RCA, CBS, PolyGram, WCI, MCA, and Capitol-EMI now manufacturing and distributing 85 percent of all American recorded music, only Arista, Chrysalis, and Motown, of the important hit-making labels, were left to the independent distributors.

In 1983, RCA acquired a 50 percent interest in Arista, which had lost about $54 million that year, buying it from Bertelsmann, with which it entered into a world-wide merger in 1985. Seventy-five percent of the joint company was owned by RCA in the United States and some other countries, 51 percent by Bertelsmann in Germany, Switzerland, and Austria, and there was an equal-share arrangement elsewhere in Europe. Chrysalis signed a branch-distribution agreement with CBS in 1982, and Motown became an MCA client in 1983, giving the six manufacturers distribution rights to virtually all recorded music produced in the United States.

Although CBS's sales had increased to one billion dollars in 1979, its operating profits actually fell by 46 percent, to $51 million. Many attributed this, and the first fall in record sales in fifteen years, to blank tapes. They were being used in the home, the RIAA insisted, to take advantage of the practice of many AOR stations of playing LPs in their entirety, without interruption. When the RIAA pleaded with broadcasters to stop this practice in the interest of the rights of artists and songwriters, only a few complied.

A CBS study of home tapers in 1980 indicated that they were responsible for an annual industry loss of $700 to $800 million, or 20 percent. There were some 40 million buyers of blank tapes, up by five million in a single year, who taped more than they had in the past, either to make custom tapes or to save money. Any possibility that home taping might be reduced in the future was thwarted by Sony's introduction of its "silent disco player," the Walkman. The first of a family of compact portable stereo units, a hand-held playback-only unit with a full-size cassette, Walkman originally sold for $199.98. The technology that made the device practical was a lightweight set of headphones that produced a big stereo sound, and it came in time to take advantage of the craze for jogging, whose devotees embraced it immediately.

The threat of home taping should not have come as a surprise to the industry, many of whose members engaged in the profitable production, not only of prerecorded tapes, but also of blank reel-to-reel tapes and cassettes, for sale to radio stations, recording studios, amateur performing artists and songwriters, audio fanatics, and the general public. A Gilbert Youth Research study had shown that in 1974 36.2 percent of those interviewed were buying fewer records and spending more time on taping. Tape hardware and software manufacturers, among them Capitol-EMI and CBS Magnetics, provided high-quality sophisticated blank-tape formulations and compatible record and playback equipment. The August 1975 issue of *High Fidelity*, a property of the Leisure Division of ABC, carried articles dealing with "Everything you wanted to know about [tape] editing," "How to falsify evidence and other tape editing techniques," and "A guide to taping from radio broadcasts." Sales of prerecorded tapes in all formulations had reached the one billion-dollar mark within ten years of their introduction, and blank cassette sales grew from 150 million units in 1975 to a dollar volume of $710 million in 1978, during which 220 million Dolbyized cassettes were sold.

Foreign licensing societies were the first to call for government relief from the inroads of home taping. A German tax on hardware, rather than on blank tapes, did not cure the problem there. The British Whitford Commission's recommendations for copyright revision included one that all recording equipment should be taxed, a proposal regarded as a legislative minefield because of the estimated eight million people there engaged in home taping.

The copyright owners of motion pictures, television programs, and phonograph recordings made their first concentrated effort to secure immediate and specific government action on the home-taping problem in the late summer of 1977. There was no mention of the matter in the new copyright act.

A House subcommittee report on antipiracy laws in 1971 had failed to show any concern about home taping where no commercial gain was attached, and in the ensuing years there was no public sign of legislative interest in the situation. The Copywright Royalty Tribunal's Thomas Brennan suggested to those looking for relief that they collect statistics over the next two years to show the effects of illegal taping on the marketplace. He pointed to the "fair-use" language in the new act, in regard to making photocopies for use in education, as an opening for Congressional action. There were also legal experts who cited a provision in the new law that made home recording an infringement of copyright holders' exclusive right to duplicate.

Technologically varying versions of the videotape and the first videotape recorder—introduced by Bing Crosby Enterprises in 1951—had been tested and marketed by a number of major electronics manufacturers: Ampex, RCA, Sony, BASF, Philips, 3M, Dupont, and others. This was before the Betamax, introduced by Sony in 1975, precipitated the legal action on which relief from home taping might hinge. Avco had already taken a $40-million tax loss on its failed Cartrivision system, and Ampex had suffered an even larger failure with the Instavideo system.

In their complaint in the "Betamax case"—*Universal City Studios–Walt Disney* v. *Sony of America*—the plaintiffs held that the use of videocassette recorders in the home infringed on their motion-picture copyrights, and they asked that either the sale of VCRs be outlawed or the machines be mechanically adjusted to limit their recording capabilities. The defendants included not only Sony but also a number of California retail stores that carried the Betamax, the advertising agency that had planned the national Betamax advertising campaign, and a solitary Betamax owner. During the six weeks the case dragged through in the late winter of 1978–79, it became evident that the matter must finally be ruled upon by the Supreme Court. The chairman of Universal Studios' parent company, MCA, Lew Wasserman, referred philosophically to the underlying issue that would face Congress, if not the court: the people's right to use a VCR, an audiotape recorder, a photocopying machine. Responding to a question about the past effects of new technologies, he said, "People who constantly forecast the doom of various industries have historically been wrong." Radio did not die, he added, when television challenged it; instead it had become stronger financially. Whether the audiotape recorder would have the same effect waited for history.

In October 1979, the lower court found for the defendants, eliciting an immediate promise to appeal from the plaintiffs.

The survey of potential losses of record and tape sales due to home taping, suggested by Brennan and made for the now-allied NMPA and RIAA, and one made for the Copyright Royalty Tribunal were entered into the CRT's records at the end of 1979. Both showed that an average of 23 percent of all respondents had taped music in the past year, but that the biggest tapers were also the largest purchasers of LPs and prerecorded tapes, and that the higher the family income, the higher the incidence of taping. Unfortunately, there were statistically disparate conclusions and overstatements in the NMPA-RIAA survey, which tended to cloud its authenticity. An example was that the respondents had purchased 870.6 million LPs and tapes, whereas the RIAA's official figures showed that only 536.1 million had been sold.

Regardless of the figures, it appeared that little legally or technically could be done to stop the practice. With LP prices rising despite consumer strikes and a depressed economy, which had caused unit sales to fall 20 percent across the country, it was cheaper to tape than to buy. One out of every two U.S. households owned a cassette unit, and Americans, interested in getting the best sound quality for their dollar, were buying the latest best-selling item in audio and retail-record stores—a new premium blank cassette priced around $4.98. In a 1980 institutional study, *The Recorded Music Business—Life in the Fast Lane,* the investment house of Merrill, Lynch found that sales of blank tape would "likely continue to grow exponentially as higher record prices combined with enhanced consumers' technical capability of making high quality home records encourages such growth."

The industry was moving toward the new world of digitally encoded and recorded sound and software and hardware that promised "super hi-fi" at affordable prices by 1990. One of the innovations, actually a return to old technology, which eschewed multitrack recording techniques and put an end to tape editing, had already been rejected by the large manufacturers. The expensive technology ($12 to $17 an album) was left to independent specialist firms. Quadraphonic recording had succumbed in 1979, the victim of consumer inertia, when a new technology with massive potential for change was applied at Warner's Los Angeles studios to the remixing of Fleetwood Mac's "Tusk" LPs.

The most significant change since electrical recording and the switch from shellac 78s to vinyl 45s and LPs—computerized or digitally mastered tape-recording decks—had been developed in the United States prior to 1979 by Thomas Stockman, Jr., a Salt Lake City engineer; the 3M Company; Battelle Northwest of Columbia, Ohio; and some smaller companies. A catalogue of several hundred hybrid LPs recorded by digital methods was available in the United States by 1980, and they won critical raves for their sound and presence.

During the late 1960s, Philips had embarked on experiments in optical electronics, and it had produced its compact disk system by early 1979, offering an hour of sound, free of surface noise on a dime-thin 4½-inch reflective minidisk, whose information was played inside out by an optical laser. As many as 1.4 million pieces of computer data for each second of music were transferred through early-stage Philips compact disk players into a standard home high-fidelity reproducing system.

Soon after the introduction of the Philips' CDs, Sony joined the enterprise as a full partner, contributing enhancements to the system that led to the final Sony compact disk player, introduced in 1983, after several years of delay, during which licensing arrangements and special mechanical-royalty rates were effected throughout the world.

PART NINE

1981–1984

CHAPTER 34

Television Music Licensing

Buffalo v. *ASCAP, BMI et al.* was tried in November and December 1981 in the U.S. Southern District Court in New York, before Judge Lee Gagliardi. It was now truly a class action; all of the 750 independent television stations had refused an opportunity to get out of the suit. Evidence was introduced that provided a hitherto unavailable look into the workings of Hollywood television-film production as well as music licensing, now a business that grossed in excess of $200 million annually.

Eight companies controlled the distribution of off-the-screen and syndicated film packages, which formed the bulk of independent, nonnetwork-time programing: Viacom Enterprises, a spin-off from CBS-TV, following the FCC's order that CBS divest itself of all program-syndication and cable-TV subsidiaries in 1971; MCA/Universal; Columbia Pictures Television; Paramount Television Distribution; Warner Brothers Television Distribution; United Artists Television; 20th Century-Fox Television; and MGM Television. During 1981, these companies distributed 82 percent of all syndicated off-network reruns and 52 percent of all programs made for syndication. Almost all of the ASCAP and BMI music used in them was assigned to publishing firms owned by the corporations of which they were subsidiaries. In 1979, only 13 percent of all ASCAP and BMI publishers had received any television royalty distributions, and fewer than 8 percent enjoyed more than 75 percent of all TV performance royalties. It was a situation curiously paralleling that in ASCAP throughout the pre-World War II period, when 38 percent of the society's publisher distributions went to eight music firms, all connected with motion-picture studios.

The total music budget for a syndicated program, either network rerun or new-package show, was generally 2 percent of all production costs. New music was usually written on a work-for-hire basis under terms of the standard CLGA contract, which required the producer to clear it through either an ASCAP or a BMI publisher but to grant to the composer his share of performance royalties. Producers were not permitted to assign the TV performing rights in any manner that would revoke the composer's right to collect his share of ASCAP or BMI royalties. The right to use already existing copyrighted music was obtained from the Harry Fox Agency, which represented the synchronization and mechanical licensing of about 3,500 music publishers in 1981. In this case, too, the performance rights were separate, having been already assigned to ASCAP or BMI. It was this splitting of performing rights from the other rights on which the Buffalo attorneys concentrated, asking the court to enjoin the blanket license and allow their clients to obtain the music rights directly from syndicators, who, under the new circumstances, would obtain them "at the source" from composers and publishers.

In his decision, made public in August 1982, Judge Gagliardi found that the local-television blanket license "unreasonably" restrained trade in violation of the antitrust laws. Referring to the Supreme Court decision in *BMI* v. *CBS*, he wrote:

> Unlike CBS local television stations could not by virtue of their market power effect the transition to a reasonably practical, centralized system of direct licensing. . . . Those with the incentive to change the system lack the power, those with the power lack the incentive. The local station has no choice but to purchase access to the entire repertoires of ASCAP and BMI although the station's needs could certainly be satisfied with a far more limited selection. . . . The court accordingly holds that for the plaintiffs, direct licensing is not a realistically available marketing alternative to the blanket license.

Leslie Arries and his colleagues saw their victory as the end of blanket licensing for the vast majority of TV stations, except those that programed a large amount of music on their local shows. In such cases, it was suggested by the All-Industry Committee that a new sort of ASCAP and BMI "mini-license" could be created. Music costs could be spread across the entire marketplace, drastically reducing annual fees, which had risen to more than $80 million. The attorneys were set to work preparing for an entirely new way of dealing with the licensing societies, one that, although it might save millions a year for telecasters, would in BMI president Cramer's words "provide [them] a nightmare if the decision is not reversed." The music business, in general, regarded the Gagliardi decision as a complete misinterpretation of the Supreme Court ruling in the per-use case and felt that it would be overthrown by the appellate court.

Until that day, and after, the Buffalo case continued to pose serious economic problems for both societies. Nearly $20 million, representing the 20 percent of TV-station license fees being held in escrow, had been collected by 1980, when the complaint was amended to seek damages, and the withholding arrangement was terminated. When Gagliardi announced that he intended to defer the effective date of his final judgment until at least February 1984, he also ordered the plaintiff stations to continue paying their ASCAP and BMI fees until then, but at the 1980 levels, approximately 25 percent below the $80 million they paid in 1982. The disposition of all fees withheld would be determined by the judge in 1984, at which time he was also expected to issue an order barring both societies from collecting television performance royalties from the local stations under the blanket-licensing arrangement.

At the end of his second year as president of ASCAP, Hal David was able to report to the membership that, in spite of the pending legal action, which was taking one quarter of the society's earnings, ASCAP was headed for another banner year, with receipts approaching $160 million. His determination to get rid of "outdated ASCAP bylaws" had already been responsible for changes in the voting procedure that permitted nonvoters to control the fate of new proposals. A favorable vote of less than 1,000 had been insufficient to pass any amendment to the society's constitution, no matter how significant it was. David also changed ASCAP's criterion for popular- and country-music awards, moving them from chart activity alone to performances exclusively. The society's campaign to win Nashville writers away from BMI became more aggressive and resulted in getting such a faithful and long-time affiliate as Johnny Cash. What was called "the Nashville shootout" by *Billboard* also had an effect on SESAC, where the minimum payment to the writer and publisher of a number-one country song went from $30,000 to $50,000, and that for a number-one pop hit from $40,000 to $60,000. Subsequently, however, faced with the imposition of severe economies due to the reduction of television fees ordered by Judge Gagliardi, ASCAP and BMI suspended all cash advances and guarantees to writers and publishers. For members, which organization to remain affiliated with rested now on their view of its structure and operating practices, as well as the prestige of its membership and the extent of their involvement in its operations.

Blanket music licensing was once again in the hands of an appellate court in November 1983, when a panel of three judges heard arguments in the Buffalo case. The plaintiffs had already filed a brief complaining that the ASCAP and BMI "tapestry of sophistry, woven to confuse," sought to obscure the fact that the TV stations were paying a "super-competitive price—two and one-half times the network rate—for no visible reason other than the defendants' monopoly power to discriminate." the ASCAP plea for a reversal invoked estoppel, preventing a party from reversing a legal position already agreed to, which would bar further pursuit of the issue because the plaintiffs had been doing it for three decades and had always accepted defeat. The Buffalo counsel pointed out that 200 new stations had gone on the air since the Supreme Court ruling, and they could not be denied a hearing. BMI's attorney urged that, because the issues and the form of license were the same as in the CBS case, they should be dealt with the same way. Buffalo's chief argument was based on the plaintiffs' inability to deal directly with composers and publishers so long as blanket licensing existed, removing an incentive for them to deal in direct licensing.

At a seminar on the West Coast immediately after the appeal hearing, a CBS vice-president for music operations and business affairs spoke about the network's progress in arranging at-the-source licensing. "In negotiating with a composer," he said, according to *Variety,* "CBS agrees to pay a 'per minute' performing rights fee for each time the music is broadcast, in addition to the composer's standard fee. The stature of the composer, as well as the type of music and the way it's used in the program, determine how big the per-minute fee is." The belligerent state of relations between CBS and BMI, first made public in 1969, had not abated. New licenses for both the ABC and the NBC owned-and-operated television stations had been negotiated, but CBS had, according to BMI, "reneged" in early 1983 on a deal that provided it would pay BMI "either $1.85 million under one set of circumstances or $2 million under another set." Once again BMI filed a damage suit for infringement of copyrights by the CBS-owned stations, and the threat of a preliminary injunction to prevent the network's unlicensed use of BMI music was sufficient for CBS to accept a new blanket license agreement though the animosity continued.

Hal David was reelected to another two-year term as ASCAP president in May 1984. Reforms he supported were approved; among those dealing with classes of membership, the elimination of the "non-participating" class, to which applications had not been elected for many years. David also reported that the end was near to the deadlock in negotiations, which had started with the All-Industry Radio Committee in January 1983, for a new contract. An agreement was reached that simplified reporting procedures, but it did nothing to reduce the cumulative $80 million being paid annually to ASCAP and BMI, whose own license with radio, which had expired at the end of 1983, was temporarily extended. In fact, it was understood that ASCAP would not ask for an increase provided BMI was not given one.

ASCAP had another setback, in the New York district court responsible for overseeing its disputes with licensees. Soon after the annual membership meeting, the district judge turned down its application to modify the 1960 consent order and allow the society to reject the ABC-TV demand for a per-program license made the previous November. ASCAP maintained that to give ABC a per-program license while it still had a blanket license from BMI "would be anticompetitive because it would result in members of the Society being driven to resign and become affiliated with BMI—or face the prospect of not having their music performed on the ABC network." Its motion pictured BMI as an arm of the broadcasting industry and alleged that an ASCAP per-program license was used to discriminate against

ASCAP music in favor of that licensed by BMI. It alleged further that "BMI was engaged in various unfair methods of competition against ASCAP; it subsidized performers, publishers and broadcasters in order to encourage performances of its music and induce ASCAP writers to join BMI . . . and was attempting through various means to obtain a worldwide monopoly of performing rights.

In its memorandum of opposition to the ASCAP motion, the Justice Department stated that "if BMI acted as a tool of the networks, the networks would face the risk that many composers would respond by joining a union or guild. Indeed, many other creative artists are actively represented by such organizations. The Networks potentially could view a strong composers guild as less desirable than the status quo." For that and other reasons, it urged the court to reject the ASCAP petition. The federal court in New York did so in May, setting aside the issue of broadcaster ownership of BMI and the differences between the consent decrees signed by both organizations. The judge added in passing that the relationship between BMI and the networks had been "highly adversarial, if not tempestuous."

That element of fierce antagonism also entered the negotiation with the All-Industry Radio Committee for a new contract to replace the expired five-year agreement, which was extended regularly for three-month periods. "BMI, Radio Stations on Verge of War," a *Variety* headline read on June 27, 1984, and *Broadcasting* wrote that "the battle lines have been clearly drawn between BMI and the radio industry," in reporting the fight over a BMI rate increase, which became effective the following January. When Edward Cramer, BMI's president, had been asked for yet another contract extension, the fourth, he said he would grant it for a small increase. The suggestion was rejected, and Cramer proposed taking the matter to arbitration. When that, too, as refused, new contracts were mailed. They were for five years, raised rates by about 10 percent—" little more than one dollar a day for the average station," according to Cramer—and gave BMI the right to examine a station's program logs.

The All-Industry Committee's attorney told the press that the contract would in reality raise rates by an over-all 15 percent, and in some cases as much as 30 to 40 percent. He added that the committee was considering the institution of legal action against BMI to fight the increase as well as to settle old disputes about overpayment under former contracts. Following the intervention of the NAB and other broadcaster organizations, a truce was arranged, though many broadcasting people continued to mutter about unreasonable demands by BMI's founders. After six weeks, during which a curtain of silence was lowered, a compromise agreement was drafted. It called for a reduction to 8 percent in the rate proposed for 1985, and for negotiations "from scratch" to determine the terms of 1986 and after. It was also agreed that in case BMI and the broadcasters could not agree by themselves on new contract terms, a "formal rate-fixing procedure" would be created, presumably along the lines of the ASCAP–federal court arrangement.

Meanwhile, the appeals court upheld the licensing organizations in September, finding their blanket TV license to be legal. Options did exist, the court declared, for, "since the blanket license restrains no one from bargaining over the purchase and sale of music performance rights, it is not a restraint unless it were proven that there are no alternatives." Those that did exist included per-program licensing, already available; direct licensing from composers and publishers; and "source licensing," passed on to local stations by the producers of the syndicated programs as part of the cost of the package.

Reminding the press that "ASCAP-BMI litigation has always been characterized by decisions, reversals, and reversals of reversals," both attorneys promised that an appeal for another reversal would be made to the Supreme Court. Leslie Arries added that while he expected ASCAP and BMI to seek retroactive compensation for revenues lost during the license-fee freeze imposed by Judge Gagliardi, "the industry will not voluntarily relinquish one penny of those savings." They were significant. In addition to the $20 million in escrow, they had been at least $25 million over and above the $57 million paid by the TV stations in 1983.

With Gagliardi's freeze due to expire on November 1, 1984, BMI notified all stations that it intended to seek a "retroactive upward adjustment" of fees, and also informed them, as did ASCAP, that all existing interim arrangements would be canceled unless the stations resumed payment at the pre-1980 rates, around 1.7 percent. Charging that such an estimated 65 percent increase would cause "utter chaos" if the licensing bodies won in the end, the committee asked the court to postpone any action to raise rates until a month after the appeals process was exhausted and final order was issued.

While waiting for the court to act on an appeal for a rehearing, a consortium of thirty-two television stations that reached 45 percent of the total American viewing public was formed to finance new programing. After being shown first on the funding stations, the programs would be syndicated. Among the five group owners forming the consortium, which expected to use source licensing, were two of the original plaintiffs in the Buffalo action: Metromedia and Storer Broadcasting, neither of them any longer BMI stockholders.

In November, the Second Circuit Court of Appeals denied the plaintiffs' application for a rehearing. On February 19, 1985, the Supreme Court denied a review of that reversal. Almost simultaneously, Metromedia announced that its forthcoming syndicated show *Small Wonder* contained only music that had been cleared at the source. At the 1985 annual convention of the NAB two "#1-rated stations [that] have already successfully eliminated all ASCAP and BMI music from all locally produced programing for only a few dollars per day" gave a demonstration of how it could be done.

As Sal Chiantia, associated chairman of the NMPA, had told its annual meeting in 1984, "win or lose, licensing of television will never be the same again."

CHAPTER 35

Rates and Piracy—Unsolved Problems

Immediately after the Copyright Royalty Tribunal issued its new regulation raising the basic mechanical royalty rate to four cents, the RIAA filed an appeal, challenging the ruling and the Tribunal's right to make it. If unchecked, this delaying tactic could cost writers and publishers as much as one million dollars a week during months of protracted hearings. After the court requested that the matter be expedited, because the new rate was to become effective on July 1, 1981, a panel of three judges upheld the new mechanical rate, but it remanded the proposal to adjust rates annually. It suggested that a "reasonable mechanism [be devised] for automatic rate changes in interim years."

Months passed before the Tribunal announced, in December 1982, that it would adjust the rate in steps: on January 1, 1983, to 4¼ cents, or .08 cents a minute; on July 1, 1984, to 4.5 cents or 0.85 cents; and on January 1, 1986, to 5 cents, or .09 cents per minute, in all cases whichever was higher. During the months of pursuit of a resolution of the problem, the average suggested list price of an LP album rose sixty-one cents, to $7.75; singles, seven cents, to $1.57; and prerecorded cassettes, fifty-seven cents, to $7.69.

The absence of further opposition from the RIAA to the Tribunal's regulations was the result of a sudden "friendship" between copyright holders and users. United by the need for government intervention in the home-taping problem, the ancient antagonists—RIAA, NMPA, AGAC, and the Nashville Songwriters Association, whose lobbying support and political power had been vital during the past six years—had been forced into an alliance, into peace among themselves.

At a Senate hearing in April 1981, the new register of copyrights, David Ladd, called for repeal of compulsory licensing in the case of cable television only, a stand seconded by the MPAA, the NAB, and sports organizations, all on the ground that it was destructive of marketplace bargaining and anticompetitive, and would also rapidly be made out of date by the expected FCC deregulation of all electronic media and the advent of satellite technology. The National Cable Television Association pleaded for retention of the status quo, to which the Tribunal agreed, adding that "to consider restricting or eliminating the compulsory license with respect to cable is inconsistent if the same is not considered for the other three compulsory licenses under the statute: those for phonorecords, jukeboxes and public broadcasters."

The Tribunal was already a subject of press attention. Clarence L. James, who served as chairman during 1980, had recommended its termination. Describing it as underworked, he cited its ineffectiveness in distributing royalties. Those from cable for the years 1977 to 1980, amounting to about $41 million, were still on deposit with the Treasury, together with jukebox license fees of more than $2.1 million. In response to a Congressional request, the General Accounting Office recommended reconstruction of the Tribunal, with a single, full-time chairman and three part-time commissioners who had some experience in matters dealing with copyright and could meet for hearings when warranted; the installation of a general counsel with power to issue subpoenas, or, alternatively, disband the body, end all compulsory licensing, and transfer the responsibilities to the Commerce Department. Any of the recommendations would require Congressional action, which was not immediately forthcoming, but the Tribunal sped up distribution of the money it was holding.

The Tribunal's decision in 1984 to base cable rates for distant TV signals on a system's gross revenue each six months brought the body into trouble once more. Its action was regarded as an attempt to make national communications policy at a time when the FCC was in the process of deregulating communications.

The quickening pace of technological change in the late 1970s and early 1980s had made it clear that copyright revision would not again have the fifty-seven-year respite it had enjoyed following passage of the 1909 act. One of the many issues that was not anticipated in the 1976 act, home taping of video programs, was currently before the Supreme Court, and other applications of new technology to the home were around the corner.

A new omnibus copyright revision bill introduced in the House in May 1984 was drawn up from conclusions gathered in hearings the previous October on audio and video rentals and cable-television rulings, and those from a succeeding symposium on "future developments in telecommunications and information technologies and their possible impact on copyright laws." It proposed the exemption of home video and audio taping from copyright liability; amended the "first sale" principle of copyright law, thus giving copyright holders control over subsequent sales of their re-

corded video and audio works; overrode the Copyright Royalty Tribunal's
distant-signal royalty ruling and restored the former rates; and called for
revamping the Tribunal to three members, a general counsel, and a staff
economist.

The cable provision immediately coalesced opposition from the Motion
Picture Association, broadcasters, video retailers, and the consumer electronics industry, leaving only the cable interests to support the measure. A
"record rental bill," which gave copyright owners control over only the
rental or leasing of new recordings for the purpose of home taping was
signed by President Reagan. Reorganization of the Tribunal awaited the
next Congress. The Supreme Court's sanction of the use of videotape recorders in the home to record television programs for personal use temporarily defused the entire taping issue. And there was little time left for
action on a separate bill to change the cable rate structure.

In a report to the Library of Congress sent just as the autumn of 1984
was changing nature's colors, the register of copyrights warned that the
international piracy of copyrighted materials was a matter of urgency, with
which the Congress should deal immediately, even to the point of stronger
penal measures. However, Ladd cautioned, "excessive penalties may lead
to a shift of public attitudes away from basic respect for authors' rights to
commercial regulation of copyright products. And it may also polarize pro-
and anti-copyright positions in areas not directly related to piracy, such as
off-the-air recording, commercial lending rights and private copying."

CHAPTER 36

Continuing Difficulties for Music Publishers

Established music publishing was becoming more complicated daily in a world dominated by the recording industry, which controlled its second major source of economic reward—prerecorded music. There was no longer such a thing as a standard publishing contract, the AGAC's basic form notwithstanding. The more commercially attractive, in terms of recordability, a song, catalogue, or songwriter was, the more enticing the terms offered. Bidding was as heated as that for recording stars, and half of all songs that appeared on *Billboard*'s Hot 100 list in 1982 were co-published, occasionally by as many as half a dozen firms. When writers involved in such an arrangement teamed with writers signed to other publishers, the publishers' final shares could be reduced to a 12.5 percent royalty. The major American-based international firms concentrated on fifty-fifty deals, until the success of material written for recording by members of Fleetwood Mac, Air Supply, AC/DC, and other superstar foreign groups made it worthwhile to connect with them on any acceptable basis.

During the 1960s, a decade after the profitable business of dealing in the subpublication of foreign copyrights had died down in the United States, Europeans once more looked for American representation. Aware of the new value of their wares, they asked for shorter-term contracts—two, three, or up to ten years—and a 75 percent share, even 85 or 90, which the hungrier firms readily accepted. Many successful songwriters had come to regard the publisher, once ruler of their destiny, as a middleman, the licensor only of their creations, the merchandiser and marketer of their products.

One example of the growing breach between songwriters and publishers, the AGAC and the NMPA, was the "Who's Sorry Now" affair. The new copyright act enabled the original copyright owners of songs copyrighted before January 1, 1978, and/or their heirs to terminate all original ownership and publication rights to a work and transfer them, provided the original fifty-six-year term had expired. The newly granted nineteen-year term was still in effect. Only "derivative" works, arrangements, sound recordings, and motion pictures based on the original work were exempt from revocation. The issue was central to the pending Harry Fox Agency suit on behalf of Mills Music, original publisher of "Who's Sorry Now," and Ted Snyder Music Publishing, formed by his heirs after the songwriter's death, to which the rights to the song had been transferred. It had been recorded more than 400 times and had earned $143,000 in royalties since 1971 alone. It was these royalties, paid prior to the transfer, that the Fox Agency was asking the court to award to Mills, the directors of the NMPA having determined that to do otherwise was inimical to the basic concern of their member publishing companies. Millions of dollars were at stake for the music companies, and perhaps for the motion-picture business, if Snyder Music prevailed. Once again involved in the destiny of the music business, Judge Edward Weinfeld found for Fox and Mills in July 1982, giving Mills the right to license new releases of recordings made prior to 1978. Snyder Music and the AGAC filed appeals.

The decision of an appeals court ten months earlier, in July 1981, had reversed a lower court's finding in the Betamax case, ruling that home video taping was an infringement of copyright. The verdict inspired some Congressmen to take action and mobilized the Coalition to Save America's Music for new action on Capitol Hill. This group of nineteen music-business organizations, later twenty-seven, ranged from record manufacturers to music-trade and songwriters' associations. Further fusing ancient antagonists, it had as it co-chairmen Leonard Feist and Stanley Gortikov.

Bills had been introduced in both houses of Congress to exempt video taping when it was not for commercial use, as well as to establish it as a fair use of copyrights. Both would decriminalize the more than five million owners of videocassette recorders.

The 1 percent increase in total printed-music sales during 1982 emphasized that the year had not been a strong one for the music-publisher members of the NMPA, now 307 in number, in twenty-four states. This tremendous increase in membership, from the relative handful of the 1920s and 1930s, was a direct result of the democratization of America's popular music following World War II. The $239.1 million in sales reported in an NMPA survey, made in cooperation with the Music Publishers Association and the Church Music Publishers Association, represented all the major music houses in the United States. Less than one tenth of the 300 respondents generated more than 60 percent of all sales, 17 percent of them coming directly from consumers. It was believed that an additional $25 million might have been earned had it not been for photocopying by schools, churches, choruses, fraternal organizations, and others.

The loss to publishers and songwriters of additional millions was made public the following February at a meeting of the International Federation of Popular Music Publishers, the money going in and out of the "suspense accounts" of European mechanical societies. These were not policed by the NMPA's Harry Fox Agency, whose American clients left such work to their own foreign publishers. And because the Fox Agency did not collect on behalf of composers, when a European agency knew only the name of an American song's writer, it did not turn over the unclaimed royalties to Fox for distribution, being privileged under terms of the International Copyright Convention to return the money to the user of the composition.

More bad news for American publishers came from a reversal by an appellate court in the Fox and Mills action against Snyder Music, which now had to go to the Supreme Court.

Having, in 1981, gone through one of the worst Christmas seasons, during which six of the major film studios changed ownership or management, and with half of all movie craft-union employees out of work because production for the first two months of 1982 was half that of the preceding year, various entertainment conglomerates lumbered into an alliance, to try to wrest away some control of the home and cable-TV business. They were: Warner Communications and American Express; Fox Films, Coca-Cola/Columbia Pictures and CBS; Coca-Cola/Columbia Pictures and RCA; and Walt Disney and Westinghouse. For them, too, the fight to establish a royalty for home video taping represented a life-or-death matter, with the same millions at stake as those the recording industry was losing from home audio taping. Their lobbyists talked about a fifty-dollar fee on the sale of VCRs, and a two-dollar charge on blank videotape.

An amendment to a proposed bill in the Senate called for a tax on VCRs and blank videotapes. The amount due on each would be determined by the Copyright Royalty Tribunal and distributed after collection among all interested segments of the entertainment business. A second amendment called for a similar royalty on audio recorders and blank audiotapes.

Many countries had continued to think about a tax on recorders and tapes, but Austria was alone in enacting a law. It affected only blank tapes, and 51 percent of the collections went to charity. Germany continued to tax VCRs and hardware, up to 5 percent of their wholesale price. The losses of as much as two million dollars a day in the United Kingdom were believed to be sufficient reason for Parliament to approve the levy of a royalty on blank tape, as suggested in the 1977 Whitford Report on copyright reform. Its most ardent proponents suggested a tax of as much as $8.80 to $11 on a single blank cassette. All arguments for a tax or a royalty—depending on which side of the matter one stood—were unavailing. The government's long-awaited Green Paper was released in July 1982. Its official estimate of about $100 million a year in home-taping losses was much under that of the British Phonographic Industry's $750-million estimate. The government hesitated to suggest any tax on the public "especially since imposition of a levy would involve rough justice, with many tape users who never record copyright music having to pay. These could, for example, include organizations for the blind. Further, a levy on blank tapes could be circumvented by selling tapes with trivia recorded on them, or by obtaining them by mail-order from abroad.'' The Green Paper did agree with the British record industry that a spoiler signal, on which $100,000 had already been spent for research, was not feasible.

Those in the United States who had sat through years of hearings on revision had a sense of déjà vu when the 97th Congress packed up to go home.

After seven years of court fighting, the Sony Betamax case came to an end in January 1984, following oral argument before the Supreme Court a year earlier. The chief issues had been isolated by Sony's attorneys to ''whether all Americans, broadcasters and audiences alike, are to be denied the benefit of time-shift home television [taping for delayed viewing] because a few program owners object''; and by counsel for the film industry to ''unauthorized copying of motion pictures, that has never been permitted by copyright laws and the fact that it is now being done at home makes no difference.'' As the record companies and other holders of copyrights continued to insist, the outcome of *Universal City Studios–Disney* v. *Sony et al.* would have dire consequences if the defendants were upheld, despite the recent dramatic resurgence of music sales and profits.

The latest advances in technology affecting music and recordings, and the place of videocassette recorder/playback equipment in home entertainment threatened to change the character of how, when, and where Americans amused themselves. Cross-marketing on TV was responsible for the highest movie attendance in a quarter century, evident in the popularity of *Flashdance.* Time-shifting had increased the available viewing audience, and the sales of feature movies to the networks and cable television were booming. The refusal of consumers to pay $80 to $100 for the videocassette of a full-length movie had created a rental market in which 10,000 dealers charged from two to five dollars a night per cassette to a viewing audience of as many as 30 million persons. In some cases, the cassette of a hit movie brought in more than the ticket sales did for a marginal film. It cost about $15 to manufacture and package a movie cassette, and at $39.95 for *Flashdance,* its producers made a three-million-dollar profit from retail sales of eight million.

Senator Dennis De Concini, author of a bill to exempt home taping from copyright liability, reminded his colleagues that any royalty or tax would be passed on to the consumer. ''Generally,'' he said, ''the cost of the product is put into the price [and] it would be unfair to the consumer when you have an industry that has other ways to collect fees.''

The study *Prerecorded Home Entertainment Industry,* prepared late in 1983 by the Wall Street house of F. Eberstadt & Co., explained the recent upturn in record-industry profits by pointing to the "five mega-hit albums." Manufacturers were overcoming most of the problems that had first become evident in the late 1970s—unfavorable demographic trends, video games, how to expose new product, and poor economic conditions—but Eberstadt found that the "longterm growth outlook for traditional records and tapes is severely limited by home taping." The study suggested that future profit opportunities lay in music videos, the fastest-growing record-business product, from $40 million in sales for 1983 to a projected $1.25 billion by 1988, due to the use of the industry's distribution networks to handle all home-video companies' wares.

It all appeared both relevant and irrelevant when the Supreme Court, dealing only with the issue of time-shifting, found that home TV taping did not constitute a violation of copyright. The five-to-four decision directed the motion-picture-company plaintiffs to seek redress from Congress. "It is not our job to apply laws that have not yet been written," the majority opinion said. Senator Charles Mathias said that his copyright subcommittee would heed the explicit legislative guidance mentioned in the court's finding and carry on, but that "it would be an uphill fight." Representative Robert Kastenmeier was more pessimistic. "Candidly speaking," he told the press, "It would seem to me that Congress will not be disposed, in light of the Court's decision, to act on legislation calling for the imposition of royalties on home taping." Legislation that had the taint of anticonsumerism never had a high priority for any but the most concerned and dedicated legislators. It was generally believed that, unless extensive lobbying took place in the first weeks of February, legislation could not be expected.

An immediate and valiant effort to gain further support for a tax on recorders and tapes, as well as opposition to an amendment that would favor the jukeboxes by charging a one-time fifty-dollar license fee to play copyrighted music was made by the Songwriters Guild, formerly the AGAC. "We made a few small advances when the 1976 copyright law went into effect," the guild's president, George David Weiss, said in January 1984. "But even those advances are being eroded. We've been down to Washington to testify about our predicament but we also have to take our case to the public directly if our efforts are to be successful." The public, now the owners of nearly four million VCRs, showed little interest.

The Motion Picture Producers Association continued its lobbying work in the remaining months of the 98th Congress, seeking legislation that would place a royalty on home video recorders and blank tapes, which would be added to the retail price. It also sought to gain control for the film studios of the rental of movie videocassettes. It was pointed out to members of Congress that, several years after it was introduced, a cassette tax had finally been approved by the French National Assembly and was now on its way to the Senate. The legislation called for compensation to performing artists and producers whose works were copied from radio, television, and recordings. When Congress adjourned, only the record-rental bill had finally worked its way to the President's desk and his signature. Soon after, the Japanese tape-machine and blank-tape constituents of the country's Electronics Industries Association warned that they would brook no compromise in regard to a RIAA proposal to pay royalties on audio and video tapes and machines. A campaign fund of millions of dollars was ready to fight any U.S. legislation to that effect.

Passage of the record-rental bill, which ended the proliferation of stores engaged in the business, with consequent losses to songwriters and music publishers, had provided a note of joy. So, too, did the appellate court decision in the Buffalo case, which reversed the lower court and affirmed the validity of blanket licensing, on whose revenues, now in excess of $300 million, most publishers depended for the bulk of their income. Sheet-music sales in 1983 were 5.8 percent above the previous year, though, as the NMPA pointed out, in terms of the Consumer Price Index increase of 3.2 percent for the year, the true improvement was only 2.6 percent.

The piracy of printed music had moved through the years from the Grub Street printers' shops where it had started to more impressive environs, among them some of Chicago's Catholic churches and the University of Texas. F.E.L. Publications, of Los Angeles, which specialized in the publication and distribution of the music of its founder and head, Dennis J. Fitzpatrick, had learned in 1976 that the archdiocese of Chicago was responsible for continued illegal photocopying of F.E.L. and Fitzpatrick copyrights. The composer-publisher took his case to the federal district court, where, after eight years, a grand jury found in his favor and granted F.E.L. $3.1 million in damages. The principal portion of the settlement was to compensate the company and Fitzpatrick for the loss in business because of a ban on his music imposed by archdiocesan officials immediately after the action was filed, as well as for illegal photocopying by the Chicago Catholic churches.

In the field of higher education, where the NMPA had done yeoman work to educate the educators, many of whom were members of ASCAP and BMI and in a position to know better, the music department of the University of Texas, Austin, was discovered to be engaged in massive photocopying of copyrighted concert and choral works. In defense of the practice, the high price of printed twentieth-century music was cited. The paperback score of Richard Strauss's *Die Frau ohne Schatten* sold for $85.00 and Pierre Boulez's Second Piano Sonata for $30, according to the *New York Times.* "We are aware that the purchase of some scores may not be financially possible for many students," Leonard Feist told the *Times,* "but there are libraries, available for studying, and the institutions should have enough copies to go around. One reason that the scores have become so expensive is because of illegal photocopying. This cuts into the size of the press run, and prices must rise accordingly. Everybody suffers."

On being confronted by the NMPA, the administrators of the University of Texas acknowledged the unauthorized practice and agreed to destroy all copies already made, and to issue letters of policy to the school's music and other departments. All copying on music-department machines was put under the direct supervision of staff members. The education of heads of schools of learning continued.

The five-to-four Supreme Court decision, announced early in 1985, favoring Mills Music in the "Who's Sorry Now" case was a clear setback for the Songwriters Guild and all authors and composers in general, and a victory for the NMPA and the publishers. It restored to the original publisher the right to collect a share of income for the sale of the original and all later recordings of a song, even if the royalties were paid years later and the copyright had been transferred to another publisher. Legal circles had been surprised when the Supreme Court agreed to hear the publisher's appeal, particularly because the Second Circuit Court in New York, which had ruled in favor of the Snyder heirs, was the first federal court ever to consider the question. As had been pointed out when the case was first filed, and the Harry Fox Agency entered as amicus curiae, millions of dollars were involved and an adverse ruling would most seriously affect the publishing structure. Given that it was general practice for several courts to interpret a new law, the future could well have been years of new actions, testing the ruling in the hope of obtaining a reversal, which the songwriters and their guild would immediately contest.

CHAPTER 37

Tight Control of a Prosperous Record Business

When the major record companies began to make profits again late in 1980, it was not because of increased volume, but because they had raised prices for the fifth consecutive year. Also, an estimated 14 percent of sales was attributed to the first RIAA-NARM Give the Gift of Music promotion campaign, for which the industry spent $10 million, and the record merchandisers were charged an extra penny per unit on their invoices. The new 20 percent limit on returns for credit ended such disasters as the recent shipment to dealers of four million *Sgt. Pepper* LPs featuring the Bee Gees, Frampton, and other Stigwood clients and the necessity to take back half of them on the old 100 percent return basis. This change was responsible for the closing of uncounted small retail operators and the demise of several hundred independent distributors, all of whom found themselves suddenly saddled with records they could neither sell nor return for full credit. And there was the surprise CBS release of a budget line of former best-selling pop, rock, and country LPs, reduced from the old catalogue price of $7.98 to $5.98, which killed off more shelf items. By year-end, RCA and PolyGram just managed to repeat the profits of 1979; WEA saw an 11 percent gain in revenues, to $806 million; and the CBS Record Group had an 8 percent increase in sales, to $1.127 million.

With millions of LPs on their hands—ordered when the euphoria of 1978 led everyone to believe that a five-billion-dollar year lay just ahead for a business that was recession-proof—which were now worth twenty cents on the dollar in returns, the surviving small independent retailers and distributors found their salvation in rack jobbers, discount houses, and chain operations. They offered a 100 percent return policy on excess stock and old merchandise. The bargains were displayed as ''cheap stuff,'' ''inflation fighter

LPs,'' or "budget special values,'' and sold for $3.98, two for $5, or five for $10. They reportedly accounted for as much as 85 percent of retail sales in some major markets. Most of the purchases were made by people between the ages of twenty-five and forty-five. A majority of the sales were made in discount outlets, which had accounted for 51 percent of the overall market in 1980 but, because of the softening market in 1981, slipped to 42.3 percent.

By summertime, the retail and discount businesses expressed cautious optimism, but found reason to complain about manufacturing defects—off-center pressings, warped disks, poor quality vinyl, and marks and blemishes on record surfaces. It was disheartening for a customer to buy a $15.98 American superdisk, advertised as being pressed in limited quantities under high quality control, and find that imported Japanese LPs sold for less, surpassed the high-frequency response, and had less background and surface noise. The shrink-wrapping that RCA had introduced to merchandise its Camden budget LPs, initially produced for the rack market, was now universally used, and with it had come increasing incidence of warp and scratches.

One-stop and retail stores, as well as customers, were victims of a general "silent deletion" policy that removed hundreds of titles from the catalogues without notice. They had to return these items as overstock, rather than as deleted items, thereby reducing their allotment of defective and true overstock. Because there were so few "hot" new LPs to lure customers, records stayed on the trade-paper charts for a much longer time. By the end of 1981, Top 50 LP chart life had grown from the fifteen weeks of 1979–80 to twenty-one weeks and more, and some LPs reached, or soon would reach, their first anniversary on the *Billboard* charts. The RIAA's report of LP shipments for 1981 as down 11.5 percent from 1980's 308 million units substantiated this minor phenomenon.

Nobody was surprised when the annual Warner Communications' survey of consumer activity showed another year of declining unit sales for 1981. Walter Yetnikoff, of CBS, explained it in *Newsweek:* "People used to walk into record stores to buy one album and walk out with three. Now they just buy the one they want." The steep drop in sales, he said, was because "what we thought a couple of years ago would sell 150,000 copies might sell 50,000 now." The retailers who attended the 1982 annual meeting of the National Association of Record Merchandisers, paying $1,200 to be present, heard Warner Communications' Stan Cornyn urge a march on Washington to lobby for a legislative curb on home tapers, the only cure for the continuing slump in record sales. Eight-track cartridges were no longer an important factor, falling from their 1978 all-time high of $948 million in sales to a probable $36 million for 1982, while at the same time cassette sales went over one billion dollars. Cornyn submitted that home tapers purchased the most records, but argued that in 1980 they had spent $600 million for blank tapes and recorded $2.85 billion worth of copyrighted music.

The conventioneers also listened to accounts of the thriving business being done by independent record companies, four of whose LPs appeared on *Time*'s ten best disks of 1981. These latter-day clones of Atlantic, Sun, King, and Savoy dealt with music in which the major labels showed little interest—punk rock, salsa-reggae-disco-rock, electronic concert works, classical-music esoterica, old-time folk music, ethnic music, and "new age," the music of upwardly mobile middle-class Americans. It was on the last that Windham Hill Records concentrated, with surprising success, doubling sales every month during early 1982. Several hundred hungry independent record operations needed the sale of only 5,000 to 10,000 disks to recoup recording and initial distribution costs as well as to earn a small profit. Their artists desperately wanted exposure on a recording and neither asked for nor received an advance. Some companies successfully reissued mostly forgotten rock-'n'-roll and R & B music of the 1950s, licensing the masters from conglomerates in whose vaults they had been buried. Getting minor air play except from iconoclastic deejays or the tattered veterans of the late 1960s free-form broadcasting, this "other record" business, ready to stay with a new release for months, depended on word-of-mouth and hoped for the ultimate miracle—a major distributor taking on their line.

"Is Rock on the Rocks?" *Time* asked, pointing out that Top 40, which had always been aimed at teen-agers, was disappearing from the major markets. WABC-AM, king of that roost, had recently changed to all talk, twenty-four hours a day. Ratings were slipping everywhere for AOR stations, whose mixture of old best-selling rock LPs, timidly dosed with applications of new rock music, had carved out an audience of white adult working males, who now found the fare blank and boring. Stations with an adult-contemporary format were calling on programing consultants for something with which to tap the 80 percent of Americans who had never bought a record, phoned in a request, played Lucky Bucks, or gone to a superstar concert. The advise, according to *Time,* usually suggested that they rely on "passive research" and offer "not what listeners actually like but what they find least offensive," or "play it safe, whatever you do."

There was gnashing of teeth in the Big Six executive suites. The sale of prerecorded cassettes—usually of a quality inferior to that used in home taping—was below two billion dollars a year for the first time since 1977, though combined shipments of all prerecorded music exceeded the revenue of any other form of entertainment. Superstars continued to fail to meet the expectations of high-powered executives, who nevertheless engaged in bared-teeth bidding for the renewal of their services. CBS would not comment on reports that it had guaranteed five million dollars on each LP to Billy Joel in his latest contract. After world-wide sales in excess of 14 million for their first two albums, the newest Fleetwood Mac package, "Mirage" moved only slightly more than one million units. Declining sales meant declining advertising budgets, and one of the industry's three weekly trade papers, *Record World,* formed in 1964 after new owners took over the jukebox journal *Music Vendor,* closed its doors.

A new interloper had severed the manufacturer-to-consumer chain—the record-rental store. It was another importation from Japan, where 1,200 rental-only shops had opened in the past two years, doing business in a country where record prices were fixed at twice those in the United States. The business was spreading in America, abetted by irresistible arithmetic. One-stops sold an $8.98 LP to a dealer for $5.50. He in turn could rent it for as much as three dollars a day, and when pops, hiss, and crackle became evident, reduce the discount price to $6.49. Home tapers who did business with record-rental stores duplicated an entire album or only those cuts they wanted. The only factor mitigating against the rental stores' continued prosperity was the steadily deteriorating quality of U.S.-made albums, which were vastly inferior to the Japanese product and unable to withstand rental beyond a few times.

Looking for allies in the fight for government action or a tax on blank cassettes and tape recorders, the RIAA and its members allied themselves with their opponents of long standing—the publishers and songwriters, who had recently received a mechanical rate hike to four cents a selection—and joined the Coalition to Save America's Music. Printed-music sales had leveled off to around $240 million, an actual loss in terms of increasingly inflated dollars that brought a price increase for sheet music from $1.98 to $2.50. The publishers benefited from this increase because their royalty from the specialty printers was generally about 20 percent of the list price. The organized songwriters remained fixed to the terms of the standard AGAC contract—10 percent of the wholesale price on the first 200,000 sales, sliding up to 15 percent for sales in excess of half a million copies. On the other hand, sheet-music sales suffered because the manufacturers continued their practice of inserting or printing on a record jacket all the words sung on every vocal cut in every LP package, a practice instituted during one of the early outbursts of complaint over the contents of popular songs, but which was eventually dropped.

While the record industry waited on Congress to give it the "break" a levy on blank cassettes would provide, it instituted economies that seriously affected the smaller retailer. Pressing plants and regional offices and warehouses were closed, leaving only central facilities for direct-to-factory orders and slowing down deliveries to such an extent that, rather than wait for an album, customers taped from rented or borrowed copies. The imposition of merchandise quotas—$5,000 a year in orders by CBS—terminated many small retail operations. RCA and PolyGram increased minimum single-order quotas from $100 to sixty LPs and tapes at a time, which cost between $300 and $400. The delivery of catalogues, posters, and classical-music sales aids had already been terminated, along with visiting salesman, the industry's earliest contact between supplier and seller.

The best-selling LPs of 1982, "Asia," recorded by a new all-star rock group with the same name, and John Cougar Mellencamp's "American Fool," had neared the three-million sales mark, giving some executives the feeling that their future and that of the industry lay in new artists, whom the arch-conservative AOR stations would not touch. Warner Brothers experimented with new talents, issuing only six cuts of their music on mini-LPs that sold at reduced prices and were promoted on MTV, the Warner–American Express cable channel. Music Television showed only three-to-four-minute LP-cut music videos, a new card to play in the game of getting broadcast exposure.

The musical short made for television was not new. In 1951, Bob Horn, whose daily *Bandstand* program on a local Philadelphia station eventually became ABC-TV's *American Bandstand,* featuring Dick Clark, captured a teen-age afternoon audience with shorts made by the Snader Company featuring Peggy Lee, Nat Cole, and other Capitol Records artists. Beginning in the mid-1950s, first with mass production of sight-and-sound tape and a few years later with color tape, the 200 TV disk jockeys who hitched a ride on Dick Clark's coattails were provided, without charge, a variety of three-minute "tele-records" to accompany new releases. Made for Capitol and other labels, they cost the manufacturers $1,200 each for production and distribution to 100 stations. The medium changed very quickly from film to tape and then to the earliest videodisks, developed by Westinghouse Electric and other U.S. and Japanese companies. The French musical-video jukebox Scopitone, which featured American recording artists in three-minute performances of their hits, and ColorSonics, a similar American machine, were introduced at this time, and promised an endless source of material for TV deejays. Because of the public's great interest in feature movies and taped series, the programing of these musical shorts began to decline, and by 1967 only about seventy stations still featured them. Record companies used them in the late 1960s to give to any television station that would promise to use the service in conjunction with local personal appearances by their artists and to demonstrate new talents to local dealers and distributors.

The endearing antics of the Beatles in *A Hard Day's Night* and their other early movies and those of other British rock performers, who dabbled with movie making in studios they had purchased in order to save some income from the taxman, created the first interest in short "concept" musical films. European performers made and starred in short filmed stories based on song lyrics, for showing in discotheques on the Continent and on such British television shows as *Top of the Pops.* In 1970, the quixotic popular-music visionary Van Dyke Parks was made director of Warner Brothers' Television Film Company and charged with the production of ten-minute sixteen-millimeter promotional films starring new artists signed by the company. The cost of a musical short had been around $3,000 a few years earlier, but when expenses for Parks's department climbed over half a million dollars his services were dispensed with, and the project was reduced in scope.

Operating on tighter budgets, the video departments of other companies continued to produce promotional film clips, though their use on commercial television dropped off dramatically following the emergence of late-night rock-music shows. ABC's monthly ninety-minute *In Concert* was the first, introduced in 1972, followed by the NBC *Midnight Special* series with Wolfman Jack and Don Kirshner's syndicated *New Rock Concert* and his annual *Rock Awards* telecasts. They all presented rock stars in a concert format, which grew monotonous and eventually was responsible for their departure.

Music-related shorts made by the record companies or their artists chiefly for use in the international market were also sent to U.S. pay-television and cable systems to serve as filler. As the industry's income continued to rise, the movies became more ambitious, making stars of new performers, not because they were shown on commercial TV, but because of their effect on retailers, branch personnel, and others in the record business. There was some question about their true value as a promotional tool, and no significant relationship between their showing and actual record sales was established. However, it was generally conceded that the ''Bohemian Rhapsody'' clip made by the British heavy-metal group Queen in 1975 was directly responsible for the impressive sales of the group's debut album of the same name.

Music Television, the twenty-four-hour all-music cable service that went on line on August 1, 1981, for Warner-Amex Satellite Entertainment, was the child of a former disk jockey, twenty-eight-year-old Bob Pittman, who programed promotional clips in the same way he did records during his days on radio. Seeking an audience of from twelve to thirty-four years old, preferably to twenty-four, which had been raised on music and television, he programed MTV to allow his chosen viewers to watch as they had always watched—while doing other things. The cost of producing one of the 300 promo videos MTV used a day, four out of every five new and, as usual, sent without charge was now up to between $12,000 and $15,000. Many of them were produced by avant-garde artists who specialized in the medium, and performers were generally obliged to pay half of the production costs out of their record royalties. MTV's programing was not for family viewing, the television critic Geoffrey Stokes wrote in *Channels,* but ''a service that will repel many, if not most of the people living in the houses that receive it. On the other hand [it is] virtually irresistible to those teenagers who already flip on their sets as they used to turn on their radios, creating a new audience that will eventually treat video as a background.''

The videos found by research to be preferred by MTV's viewers were played four to five times a day, introduced with taped announcements by video-jockeys who filled in gaps on the screen with gossip about rock stars. Within a year, MTV had signed 125 sponsors for more than 200 products, who paid a modest fee of from $1,000 to $6,000 for thirty-second to two-minute spot announcements. Yet it showed a $15-million pretax loss. Once more bedeviled by a sales slump, the record companies had at last found the break that might turn the economic tide. In a late 1982 survey of retail record dealers, *Billboard* found that new acts who made their bow on MTV enjoyed an immediate 10 to 15 percent increase in sales. Mercury's Def Leppard appeared to be petering out at 100,000 units of its LP until its video clip was rushed to MTV and an additional 400,000 sales followed. Elektra-Asylum's astonishing patience with Greg Kihn during an eight-year dry spell was rewarded when MTV plugging made his "Jeopardy" a chart breaker. The story was repeated over and over. The cost of an average music video had climbed to between $35,000 and $45,000, but a superstar like Billy Joel was allowed a production budget of more than $100,00 for his "Allentown," and David Bowie spent $150,00 for "Let's Dance." Stevie Nicks was so unhappy about her $100,000 video that she made the company do another one for another $100,000. Cost was evidently not an important item, but the Wall of Voodoo's "Mexican Radio" was made for just under $15,000.

American radio's failure to program black music other than that which hit the top of *Billboard*'s pop charts was again brought under serious scrutiny because of the same lapse by MTV. Such acts as Earth, Wind & Fire, Stevie Wonder, the Commodores with Lionel Ritchie, Donna Summer, the Brothers Johnson, the Isleys, George Benson, and a few other black artists had successfully taken the cross-over route. In fact, Wonder was the first artist after Elton John to claim the number-one slot on all pop LP charts. Donna Summer had established herself as the queen not only of disco but of pop, soul, and rock, the second black woman to achieve superstardom, after Diana Ross blazed the way. In all, 116 soul LPs had fought their way into the top ten on *Billboard*'s popular-albums chart in the ten years since 1971. Michael Jackson's "Off the Wall," produced by Quincy Jones, had four Top 10 singles, only the fourth time in modern history such a feat was accomplished.

During the early 1980s, the black superstars' ranks were joined by Kool and the Gang, Marvin Gaye, Smoky Robinson, Styx, and Prince, none of whose music or that of white black-sounding performers was heard on MTV, where album-oriented-rock ruled and all other forms of popular music were shunned lest the channel lose its audience. Seven of the thirty-five best-selling albums on *Billboard*'s charts in November 1982 were by black artists, but Bob Pittman had little to do with them, pointing out in a rebuttal of charges of discrimination that Barbra Streisand was a major artist who never appeared on his channel, nor did country-music artists, show tunes, or many other currently popular songs. "You can't be all things to all people," he said. "There are going to be 100 cable television channels. You don't combine programs if you're going to be a successful channel."

The absence of black music, not only on MTV, but also on almost all AOR radio was regarded by many as "rock racism." There appeared to be little discrimination against records issued by Motown Industries, which celebrated its twenty-fifth anniversary in March of 1983, together with its 101st number-one hit. In the early 1970s, prior to the advent of disco music, soul music generally had lived alongside white pop music on Top 40 stations. But when disco knocked off Top 40 and by 1978 accounted for the major portion of all *Billboard* LP and singles charts, a backlash against that eight-billion-dollar business and black music in general followed, fostering what by 1982 became the color line drawn by AOR stations and MTV.

Black radio stations in major markets, whose listeners included an increasing number of whites, began to call their formats "urban contemporary," and the management and backers of one of them, WBLS-FM New York, tried to adapt its programs to cable television, featuring only black performers, an attempt that was aborted by economic conditions. Another cable service, Washington-based Black Entertainment Television, which did get on the air, showed only two hours a week of *Video Soul* in 1982. "The key is to support diversity," Black Entertainment's general manager, Bob Johnson, said, "but I also sympathize with MTV's program strategy. Because that's what we've done."

The Home Recording Act of 1983, introduced shortly after the 98th Congress convened, included a new provision. Rather than have the Copyright Royalty Tribunal set rates, it called for negotiations between copyright holders and the tape-equipment and software manufacturers and importers, though it left the distribution of royalties or taxes to the Tribunal. Simultaneously, bills to exempt home recording from liability were again put into the legislative hopper, as were bills calling for repeal of the "first-sale" doctrine.

A general reluctance by members of Congress to co-sponsor these bills was attributed by the music and record business to the effectiveness of the opposition's lobbying front, the Coalition for Home Recording Rights, whose chief spokesman was a former FCC chairman, Charles D. Ferris. His financial backers and chief clients in this matter included all the biggest producers of blank tape and hardware.

The spectacular sales in the first quarter of 1982 of $421 million worth of Berzerk, Defender, and, particularly, Model 2600 of Pac Man, as well as other products of Warner Communications' Atari Videogame Division, represented two thirds of the conglomerate's total profits, and more than compensated for its record- and music-publishing subsidiaries' loss of $101 million in the same period. The Warner-Amex MTV operation was still losing money, and the motion-picture division had not had a smash hit since *Superman II*.

In a five-year period, the manufacture of arcade and home video games had become a $7-billion industry, with sales of the latter expected to bring in $1.7 billion for 1982 and $3 billion the following year, by which time 15 million American homes would own video-game modules. Declaring that the video-game business still had a long way to go, Raymond Kassar, chairman of Atari, said, "The maturity level of video games will be beyond anyone's wildest dreams."

A few months later, Warner Communications' stock fell 16.75 points on the New York Stock Exchange, in anticipation of a severe loss in Atari's earnings, and its trading was temporarily halted. The stock of other video-game manufacturers also fell substantially. Orders for the latest-model Ataris had just been canceled by distributors and small retailers, together with those for new games licensed from the moves *E.T.* and *Raiders of the Lost Ark,* on which the company had staked its future. Almost overnight, fierce competition and consumer negativism toward new video-game products became responsible for a $1.1-billion loss in Warner common stock and by the second quarter of 1983 a deficit of $283.3 million. By autumn, the Warner music-publishing and record division's operating income was up 80 percent over 1982, to $14.7 million, and in time for the Christmas season Atlantic Records raised the list price for its best-selling LPs by one dollar, to $9.98, and that for the sound track from the new John Travolta and Olivia Newton-John movie by two dollars, to $10.98.

A study on which opponents of taxes on blank tape and recording decks planned to base public presentations, following its release in October 1982, found that 52 percent of the tapes made by 1,018 individuals involved in a telephone survey were not of music; tapers owned more prerecorded music than nontapers; and the $8.98 price for an LP was greatly responsible for home taping, because tapes cost half that, were less easily damaged than vinyl disks, and could be taped over. Economists in the employ of the tape manufacturers told a House subcommittee that the study proved that if a tax is levied, most of it will be paid for "taping that has nothing to do with prerecorded music"; moreover, home taping clearly has a stimulative effect on record buying, and people are making tapes to "get something they can't out in the marketplace."

Stanley Gortikov used the Commentary Page of *Billboard* to make a public rebuttal of the study and questioned whether the 55 percent of 242.2 million cassettes expected to be sold in 1982, all higher-priced premium products, ninety minutes in length, and capable of recording two full albums, would be used "to immortalize baby's first words or business dictation." He also questioned the value of copyright for music and recordings: "Do copyrighted words have economic value, and should that value translate to fair income and incentive to create?" Manufacturers and importers of blank tape and equipment "cannot reasonably expect just to *take* America's musical bounty, and give nothing in return."

Dire warnings by some record-company executives that the whole business might come tumbling down if expansion continued were ignored by many of the largest conglomerates. They continued to increase their involvement in music publishing in order to get a greater hold on the copyrights being used on cable television, videocassettes, and any technology over the horizon.

In early 1982, Warner Communications added between $10 million and $12 million in anticipated annual income with the acquisition of the 20th Century-Fox music operation, at a price of between $16 million and $18 million. The transfer also involved ownership of the picture company's film music for a term of five years. In May, Warner started negotiations to bring the United Artists music catalogue of 50,000 copyrights and the Big Three music-printing operation, both owned by Transamerica, under its banner and guarantee an additional income of $25 million to $30 million for its music division. When completed, the rumored $95-million transaction would double the size of its music catalogue and represent the largest single sale since North American Philips and others purchased Chappell Music, even after subtracting the $35 million being paid for the return from UA to Warner Brothers of some 750 of its pre-1950 feature movies and more than 300 cartoons, which it had sold in the mid-1950s. Before the sale was consummated, however, the approval of the Justice Department was required.

Walter Yetnikoff, president of CBS Records, and other company executives were reported to be among those who opposed the purchase, pointing to its inherent antitrust implications because Warner already owned the largest ASCAP house, Music Publishers Holding Corp., as well as other major catalogues. When it was clear, in late summer, that United Artists would not deliver music rights to future MGM/UA productions slated for release on videocassette, preferring to reserve them for its own Home Video Division, Warner called off the negotiations.

Confronted with growing deficits from an expansion of its book- and record-club empire into the United States, as well as unexpectedly poor sales by its American record labels, Arista and Ariola, Bertelsmann sold its four-year-old Innerworld Music Group catalogue to Chappell Music in the summer of 1982. The transaction, rumored to involve about $10 million, added some 12,000 copyrights to PolyGram's international music holdings, including works by the ASCAP president, Hal David, and by Mick Jagger, Hall and Oates, Randy Newman, Barry White, RCA's formerly owned-and-operated Sunbury and Dunbar catalogues, and Dick Clark's Sea-Lark Music and subsidiaries.

Now that Warner Communications was out of the picture, CBS Records resumed talks with the MGM/UA Entertainment Company. By the end of 1982, an agreement was arranged for CBS to acquire UA's 50,000 music copyrights for $68 million. The contract included a five-year co-publishing arrangement with MGM/UA for all music written for its future film productions and first rights to its sound-track recordings. In September 1983, the CBS Catalog Partnership was formed, in association with three insurance companies, to administer CBS Songs and subsidize the corporation's purchase of UA Music.

The year 1982 had generally been a poor one for CBS. Its operating earnings were down for all four quarters, though those of the record division, which made up 29 percent of total CBS revenues, began to edge up in the first quarter of 1983. A new giant record plant in Georgia, built for $55 million, had run well under capacity throughout the year because of poor sales by the label's superstars, and for the same reason the Terre Haute, Indiana, factory was closed down and its 1,250 employees were dismissed. The corporation's adventures in feature-film production and cable-television channels had been disastrous and were either cut back or disbanded. Other moves to reduce overhead were planned, among them disposition of the paperback book division and the latest CBS acquisition, the manufacturer of Rubik's Cube, the public vogue for which was rapidly dissipating.

The upturn in 1983 reflected sudden overnight hits, which were explained by an unexpected decline of interest in videogames as teen-agers switched their spending to LPs and prerecorded cassettes. The latter now accounted for at lest half of all sales and were at their lowest price in years, due to drastic price cutting by most companies. In a massive reduction, WEA cut the list price of 1,100 LPs and cassettes from $8.98 to $6.98. Other companies, now wary of signing talent to unrealistic contracts, sold first albums by new artists for as little as $4.98. In all of 1982, only three albums had sold more than two million units. In the first quarter of 1983, four LPs were expected to do the same or better, two of them by Michael Jackson on the CBS Epic subsidiary label, his "Thriller" album moving 60,000 units a day. In a single month, PolyGram's *Flashdance* sound-track LP went over 1.6 million in sales and RCA's "H_2O" by Hall and Oates moved toward platinum status.

Shaking off the lethargy and conservatism for which four years of sagging sales were responsible, the record industry began once more to institute changes. The latest advanced recording technology was installed to replace aging equipment, giving free rein to recording artists who had suffered in the strait-jacket of their labels' creative inertia. They now were in a position to make interesting new music, which would, of itself, stimulate sales. Out of profits of $67 million in the first half of the year, CBS gave the Rolling Stones a four-LP contract that added up to a guaranteed $28 million and included reissue rights to their fifteen most recent albums. After signing multimillion-dollar long-term contracts with Diana Ross and Kenny Rogers, that with the latter reportedly for between $20 million and $30 million for six albums over five years, the former "sleeping giant" of the

industry, RCA Records, did business with Bertelsmann, the German colleague for which it handled U.S. sales and distribution of its Arista Records. It bought a half-interest in the label, with an option to buy the remainder.

The financial fortunes of Warner Communications and the Philips-Sie-
mens combine had been buffeted by unfortunate investments made to diversify their holdings. In the summer of 1983, the two began discussions
looking toward a merger of their record companies, contingent on the purchase by Warner of Siemen's half-interest in PolyGram. Such a combined
operation showed a potential of $1.5 billion in annual sales. The plan called
for Warner Communications to transfer its record business to Warner Brothers Records, and PolyGram to Chappell. The companies would then merge
into Warner-PolyGram, which would issue new stock. The merger would
form the largest record operation in the world, with Warner owning an 80
percent interest in the American joint venture and half of that overseas, and
it would have a cumulative 25.9 percent share of the U.S. market, followed
by CBS with 23 percent; RCA, 17.9; Capitol-EMI and MCA, each 8; and
all the other major companies, 17.8. The merger would also serve to take
some of the impact on the American industry of the impending CBS compact-disk venture with Japanese Sony.

Yetnikoffs first reaction on hearing official word of the plan was to issue
a "wedding invitation" to one or more of the major U.S. companies, among
which the industry reckoned MCA and Capitol-EMI to be the most amenable. The CBS Records president's hurried trip to West Germany won
only a delay until the following spring. In the United States, Warner Communications submitted details of the plan to the Justice Department for approval. It was not immediately forthcoming, but many in the industry expected approval to be granted in light of the current appeal of deregulation
rather than trust-busting.

The importance of MTV and music videos to the superstars who enjoyed
large LP sales was confirmed by an analysis of *Billboard*'s popular-album
charts for 1983. Only six LPs had hit the number-one spot, and only three
of them had remained there for more than two weeks, the fewest since
1979. Five albums had sold a combined 28.5 million units in the United
States, all of them doing better than four million. Two of them had never
hit the number-one popular rank, but all did have repeatedly played music
videos: Michael Jackson's "Thriller," which sold 10 million copies; "Synchronicity" by the Police; "Pyromania" by Def Leppard, which never hit
the top spot (each sold five million units); the *Flashdance* sound-track accompanying what appeared to be a series of music videos interrupted by
minor plot developments (4.5 million); and David Bowie's "Let's Dance,"
the other best-selling LP not to hit number one (four million).

MTV was making small tentative gestures to remove its color line, particularly after the success of "Thriller," produced for $300,000, which

compelled Jackson's appearance on MTV. It was leavened by clips of Donna Summer and her "She Works Hard for the Money," and the young Midwestern R & B singer Prince, with "Little Red Corvette." The Black Entertainment channel had stepped up its *Video Soul* segment to fifteen hours a week. ABC-TV introduced a black-oriented after-prime-time TV production, *New York Hot Tracks,* and NBC-TV scheduled an integrated weekly, *Friday Night Videos,* paying between $1,000 and $3,000 for the clips it used. The network justified this as protection against legal actions in case the clearance and synchronization fees had not been paid. Citing traditional practices, ABC refused to pay for any music videos.

Bob Pittman continued to insist that only if music videos did not sell records would the record companies deserve to be paid for them. "We clearly sell records for them. We have a nice symbiotic relationship with the record industry, and we don't want to change it." A survey made by Coleman Research showed that viewers watched MTV longer the longer they had it, rather than only while doing other things. While the record manufacturers talked about how much to charge for music videos, now that they had determined to merchandise them to the public, Sony Video Software marketed Video 45s. These cassettes, with three or four short clips, sold for fifteen to twenty dollars a unit, but because they did not contain favorites shown on MTV and other music-video operations, they failed to sell as the company had expected.

Many of the more enterprising FM stations had created new markets for heavy-metal music during that form's resurgence in the early 1980s, as they also did for new-age groups, whose sound was considered too harsh for hard-rock AOR AM operations. Witnessing the lingering demise of AOR on AM stations, and with government deregulation, which permitted stations to become veritable jukeboxes, without any requirement to program news and public-service announcements, in late 1981 FM stations found a new format, which coincidentally also had the appeal of MTV's video jukebox. Beginning in major markets, where audiences were greater than for AM radio, they rediscovered the Top 40 format, called it contemporary hits radio, or CHR, and played hits all the time—hard and soft rock, country and pop and black music. Todd Storz's baby had gone out of style in the Vietnam War period, when post-teen-age listeners turned to FM stations, where the deejays did little talking and played album cuts. It was music that the record companies did not consider right for the bubble-gummers and teenyboppers who constituted its largest listening group. These hit-nurtured baby-boomers were in their late twenties or thirties now, the very audience CHR wanted. Men in the eighteen-to-twenty-four age bracket found CHR too soft and played little part in determining play lists.

With *Billboard*'s charts expanding to cover changing styles and tastes, and record sales and national popularity figures being fed constantly by independent promotion men employed by the major labels, CHR FM stereo was on top of hits as they broke. In less than a year, the formula was working for at least one station in each of the fifty top markets and was the hottest new trend in radio. It was the third most popular format, after contemporary and country music, among the ten most in use, all of them living in peace with music videos and all serving to boost the sales of recorded music.

During meetings with financial analysts late in 1983, Walter Yetnikoff, of CBS Records, voiced unqualified optimism about the record industry and its future, and with good reason. He cited the video-clip revolution as a source of promotion on a scale unknown in the past and an avenue to increased profits. His company was the principal beneficiary of MTV's almost mystical ability to sell both the records and the persona of the most popular CBS singer of all time, Michael Jackson, to its 18.4 million viewers. Jackson's cross-over LP "Thriller" was already the best-selling solo album in history, with world-wide sales in excess of 25 million so far. It provided CBS Records with $120 million in a twelve-month period and lifted its net income by one quarter over 1982, to $187 million. Out of royalties of two dollars from "Thriller" 's five-dollar wholesale price, Jackson invested $1.2 million in the production of a fourteen-minute videocassette of the LP, 300,000 copies of which were sold at $29.98 each in the first three months. He then went to work on a one-hour documentary, *The Making of Thriller*. It, too, sold for $29.98, and was available for bidding by the television networks. It was anticipated that Michael Jackson Inc., a holding company, would pay its board chairman in excess of $50 million by the end of 1984.

As Presley and the Beatles had done for the business in their heydays, Jackson brought customers back to the record shops, where half of all purchases of prerecorded music were of cassettes. The manufacturers welcomed this turn of affairs with enthusiasm, because it tended to reduce home taping. Then, too, a cassette cost sixty-eight cents to produce, whereas a vinyl LP cost about seventy-eight cents. A ten-cent additional profit came from savings in shipping and storage costs. The best-selling cassettes were rock, particularly heavy metal, which took on a new dimension when heard from a car tape deck, and country music, for which cassettes had replaced the eight-track cartridge that formerly accounted for 60 percent of its sales. The CBS See Red campaign in the summer of 1983, so known because of the bright-red titles on the spines of cassettes on which advertising concentrated, and the fact that some companies offered additional music tracks were other factors that contributed to the rise of cassettes in public favor.

In addition, there was a new British invasion, by artists whose LPs and cassettes enjoyed a growing share of the market—Men at Work, whose first LP ultimately sold more copies than Asia and John Cougar Mellencamp combined, thanks to MTV; the Police; Boy George, and Culture Club, which had five straight Top 10 singles; the Eurhythmics; and Duran Duran—the extent of whose presence on the American scene was driven home in June 1983 when eighteen of the Top 40 singles were of British origin, particularly owing to the extreme videogenic appeal of the artists.

The proposed Warner-PolyGram merger had touched off consideration of a similar move by RCA, which, like Warner, Philips, Sony, and its own European partner Bertelsmann, had been suffering the indigestion of over-diversification, whose result was meager dividends, fluctuating earnings, and a lack of interest on the part of investors. With new and stable management in place, in early 1984 some unprofitable units were sold, electronic military business was expanded, and the annual $100 million loss from videodisks was about to be terminated. RCA Records, which had sales of around $600 million, was in a position to seek a global tie with Bertelsmann, which itself was in process of concluding negotiations with MGM/UA, MCA, and Paramount for joint pay-cable projects in Germany.

In the years following World War II, Bertelsmann, a small religious printing business, had grown into a multinational media giant. With book- and record-club operations, and ownership of leading magazines. The firm preferred to remain involved basically with communications, and in the late 1970s moved into the American magazine business with the purchase of *Parents* and *Young Miss*. In 1980, it bought Bantam Books and a major U.S. offset-printing operation, which proved to be a misjudgment when American reading habits began to move away from paperbacks. Its Ariola-American record company and the Arista label also produced losses. Though RCA and Ariola did not share distribution in Europe, Bertelsmann's computer software division, Sonopress, made RCA records for sale on the Continent. When RCA expressed an interest in exercising its option to buy the remaining share of Arista Records, and talk about a Warner-PolyGram merger became public, negotiations began for the formation of Ariola-RCA Music in Germany, which would have a 19 percent share of the German record business, and RCA-Ariola International elsewhere.

The West German Cartel Office had already indicated its opposition to any merger that would give several companies a combined half-share of the market, and in the United States the Federal Trade Commission was seeking an injunction to block the Warner-PolyGram marriage on the grounds that it would "remove a substantial competitor and significantly increase overall concentration." The FTC maintained that the concentration levels "in this case exceed levels which courts have in the past held to establish a prima facie case of illegality under antitrust laws." Nonetheless, plans looking toward the joint RCA-Bertelsmann venture continued throughout the year, culminating with approval by the Cartel Office, in early 1985, just after RCA Records posted a 4 percent increase, to $621.8 million, in sales during the preceding year.

Warner Communications was not as fortunate in the outcome of its plans to join with PolyGram in order to take advantage of the strong international operations it did not itself have. The FTC held that the resulting reduced competition would not be cured by "new competitors," because "the volume necessary to break even in national distribution exceeds $125 million in annual sales." Independant distributors could not respond to the majors' price increases by distributing more hit records, since the best-selling artists were under contract to the majors. "Moreover, the small volume of the remaining independent distributors makes them high-cost competitors for the small amount of mainstream music they continue to distribute." Recent *Billboard* Top 200 album charts carried only two LPs distributed by independents, numbers 139 and 178.

Warner/Reprise–Elektra/Asylum–Atlantic Records had brought in profits in 1983 of $60.7 million, from sales of $755 million, but the parent corporation was in perilous straits, having lost $535 million on the Atari unit alone in the first three quarters of the year, with write-offs of between $300 and $500 million still ahead. The $875-million credit line for its cable ventures, including MTV, had barely escaped a takeover by the Australian newspaper tycoon Rupert Murdoch, who was in pursuit of the conglomerate's library of feature films and shorts, valued in the millions.

A federal judge had refused in April to block the merger, but after hearings in September, an appeals court had agreed to stop it, pending a hearing of arguments. An additional roadblock to a partnership with Philips-PolyGram was placed by Siemens's refusal to advance any further funds after learning that PolyGram had lost in excess of $200 million in the United States recently and faced a $15-million loss for the year. Siemens wanted to withdraw from the ownership of Deutsche Grammophon it had shared with Philips since 1963, 90 percent of which it returned to its partner in early 1985. After introducing the world's first VCR for home use in 1972, Philips had lost any hold it might have had on that lucrative market to Japanese manufacturers, who were making nearly half of all the sets sold. Sales of Philips's home electronics and industrial computer systems in the Common Market and other European countries were responsible for more than half of the company's $14-billion income in 1983, but then started to fall off because of American competition. A rapid turnaround in the nature of its world-wide operations had already moved Philips toward international joint-venture partnerships, among them one with Sony in connection with compact disks and software. The Warner merger would be part of a general restructuring of the PolyGram Group.

Only after an attempt to demonstrate that competition from the increasing incidence of home taping mitigated against the FTC charge that a Warner-PolyGram entity would represent a monopoly in restraint of trade did Warner Communications and Philips concede defeat. Their argument had not dissuaded the district court judge, nor the commission, whose attorneys suggested that, rather than become part of a monopoly that would control 26 percent of the U.S. record market, PolyGram, which was known to have sustained loses of $255 million in the past six years and was currently losing $300,000 a day, should seek an alliance with MCA. The increase in MCA's revenues, from $36.8 million in the first quarter of 1983 to $55.5 million for the same period in 1984, was misleading. It was actually the contribution of Motown Records, which had switched its distribution to MCA in 1983, that was responsible for that rosy picture. In fact, the company's record-and-music division showed a decline for the first quarter of 1984 of $1.4 million from 1983's January-to-March $3.5 million. MCA Records was writing off inventory and had cut thirty-seven of the forty-four popular-music acts from its roster. An alliance with PolyGram would be a more than proper move for the company.

The increase of the Warner Music Group's sales in 1984 to $817.6 million, together with the high dollar abroad, greatly reduced the possibility that Warner would soon again seek an international relationship. Its figures for 1984 were reinforced by the sale of 10 million units of Prince's "Purple Rain." The album contained music from the sound track of the screen vehicle of the same name, written, produced, and starring Prince, and made the young singer-musician the year's soul-music runner-up to all-time champion Michael Jackson.

However, the races continued to remain mostly separate in the music business and on radio, in spite of Jackson's eight Grammy awards and his twenty-five Top 10 singles and the success of Prince and Lionel Ritchie. Of the twenty-one artists enjoying much play on MTV in early 1984, none was black. Separate sales charts in *Billboard* and other music-trade publications confirmed the situation. Black bands had difficulty obtaining record-company financing for their videos, a crucial competitive factor.

The problem of rising video-clip production costs appeared to be solved by three of the Big Six in June 1984. After having determined just how much to ask from MTV for the videos they had been sending without charge, it was reported, CBS, MCA, and RCA had signed contracts with the music channel for exclusive "light rotation" rights for predetermined limited periods to selected videos, representing about 20 percent of their production. The reported $16 million paid by MTV to guarantee exclusivity—two million to MCA and to RCA over three years, eight million to CBS for two years—raised once more the question of exactly who owned the clips, since the artists paid for from half to all of the production charges out of their royalty earnings. There was also the possibility that these agreements constituted violations of the antitrust laws. Well aware of their rights in the matter, ASCAP and BMI negotiated contracts, based on income, with MTV and its for-children Nickelodeon channel for the use of their catalogues. The fees were related to the latest financial information on MTV's progress, made public in a prospectus offering 5.125 million shares of stock in the newly formed MTV Networks, Inc. It showed that MTV and Nickelodeon's combined revenue in the second quarter of 1984 was $6 million. In the first half of the year, cable operators had paid $13.741 million to carry MTV and the children's channel. The sum alloted in the prospectus for video-clip exclusivity was reported as $4.585 million, of which $925,000 would be offset by advertising time.

A suit filed in Los Angeles in September by Discovery Music Network raised the issue of illegal monopoly and "exclusive and coercive arrangements" into which MTV had "intimidated" CBS, MCA, RCA, and Polygram, the newest of the Big Six to enter into an exclusivity agreement. The announcement of plans for a twenty-four-hour Discovery music channel and those for a similar service operated by Turner Broadcasting Cable Music Channel, which claimed to have access to video clips from all the major labels, was followed by an announcement from MTV that it would mount a similar operation, VH-1, for the twenty-five-to-fifty-four-year-olds. While Discovery's suit was bogged down in pretrial discovery and examination, Turner sold MTV its music channel, which had not yet gotten off the ground, for one million dollars and $500,000 of advertising time.

Music video was also having an impact on another division of the business, children's records, which in 1951 had accounted for more than 10 percent of all sales, which was more than rhythm and blues, international, Latin-American, and hot jazz records combined had produced, according to trade-paper reports. After a dip in the mid-1950s, the market continued to grow, rising to $45 million in 1959 and $53 million the following year, principally owing to the acceptance of credit cards in places where toys and $1.98 LPs and forty-nine-cent plastic singles for children were sold. Many of the disks were inspired by characters in television cartoon series, often using their theme songs and background music. When the appeal of the first catalogue of vintage cartoon shorts—*Popeye, Looney Tunes, Tom and Jerry, Little Lulu,* and other favorites of pre-TV days—began to lessen in the late 1950s, the cartoon production companies brought out an all-color product, timed to the craze for color television sets. After a season or two, the toy and record rights to *Huckleberry Hound,* the *Flintstones, Yogi Bear, Crusader Rabbit, Quick Draw McGraw,* and other cartoon series were franchised to their sponsors or others, creating a $150-million market, which grew at a 20 percent annual rate. This franchise business was dominated for years by Disney Studios, MGM, Hanna-Barbera, De Patie–Freleng, Filmation, and some newcomers to movie cartooning, who also affiliated with the performing-rights societies. They were paid substantial royalties for the use of music created on a work-for-hire basis for Saturday-morning network shows and syndicated cartoon packages used by local TV stations on weekday afternoons.

Sales of children's records went from $87 million in 1976 to $250 million in 1982, a period during which the rock-'n'-roll generation passed on to its offspring a popular culture that was firmly rooted in the phonograph recording. Solid-state record players and cassette decks made expressly for the kiddie market were responsible for an average 4.6 percent growth in sales of prerecorded music on both disk and cassette, which included not only best-selling versions of *The Nutcracker Suite* and *Peter and the Wolf*, but music from *Sesame Street, The Wonderful World of Disney, Mary Poppins, Bambi*, and adaptations for children of *Return of the Jedi, E.T.*, even *Saturday Night Fever*, and current rock hits.

To the consternation of members of Action for Children's Television, MTV and Nickelodeon were turning many of their younger viewers away from kiddie disks to rock videos, in the process pulling down the age level of record and cassette buyers. Many of these young devotees of rock music were among the hordes that went to see Michael Jackson during the course of the Victory Tour of the United States he made with his brothers in 1984. A total of 2.33 million paid a collective $70 million gross. Yet despite the excitement of the "Victory" LP that celebrated the tour, the album sold only two million units.

After its introduction in Japan in the fall of 1983, the compact-disk player and the compact disk went on general sale in America, at between $800 and $1,200 for the player. CBS and Sony took over and jointly reopened the Terre Haute plant, which had been closed in the recent economy wave, for annual production of 10.5 million CDs. The initial small releases of compact disks included popular music, but it was classical music that appealed to the more mature consumers and provided them with the most brilliant demonstration of what was advertised as the definitive leap into the future of the talking machine. Excited by the new dimension given to their music by digital mutlitrack recording and the CD, superstar artists were quite willing to absorb the markedly higher costs involved.

Within a year, during which 2,000 CDs releases were put on the market and 4.3 million were sold, the price of a CD stabilized at around twelve dollars, and a player could be had for just below $300. Operating on a principle espoused by George Eastman—that one sold a Kodak or Brownie for as little as possible in order to sell Kodak film for as much as the market would bear—Sony demonstrated its Walkman version of a CD player, the D-5 model, small enough to be carried around, only a bit bigger than the disk it played, and capable of being plugged into a home stereo rig; it was listed at less than $300. Digital recording lived up to its fullest potential, and a U.S. representative of PolyGram, which staked much of its future on the new technology, predicted that there would be 645,000 CD units in use by the end of 1985.

When it was suffering the problem of maintaining an adequate cash flow with which to develop the compact-disk market, and unable to raise sufficient funds to buy out Siemens in early 1983 PolyGram had considered the sale of Chappell-Intersong and associated catalogues. An asking price of around $150 million was reported. Even earlier in the 1980s, when the top management team of the PolyGram Group was switched from Dutch executives to a four-man German team, it was rumored in Europe and reported in *Billboard* that Philips was considering a withdrawal from the entertainment business, "which constitutes a small share of its overall business, and, therefore, from PolyGram." Nevertheless, rumors in the United States and Britain that its publishing empire, which had annual revenues of $60 million, might be sold were regularly denied by PolyGram.

When the sale took place, in the summer of 1984, the buyers of Chappell-Intersong, with thirty-one subsidiaries in twenty-two countries and 500,000 copyrights, were headed by Freddy Bienstock and his Anglo-American Music Publishing Corp.; others were Edward B. Marks Music, Williamson Music (owned by the heirs of Richard Rodgers and Oscar Hammerstein II), and the Wall Street banking house of Wertheim & Co. Financial details were not made public, but it was believed that the purchase price had been in the $100-billion range. The dozens of publishing operations functioning under the Chappell banner included all of the Dreyfus companies, the Aberbach brothers' music houses, other companies acquired through the years, and many firms administered by Chappell on behalf of their owners.

Bienstock's first major acquisition since his purchase of New York Times Music in 1977 had been, in 1983, one of the two remaining family-owned old-line music companies, Edward B. Marks Music, bought in partnership with Williamson Music. His catalogues plus Chappell's represented perhaps the largest repository of popular-music copyrights in the world. However, it did not include music written or owned by Bienstock's former partners Jerry Lieber and Mike Stoller. Shortly after the Chappell sale, these two filed a suit charging that their agreement of separation in 1982 required Bienstock to offer them a half-share in any new acquisition he made, and that would include both Marks and Chappell. Invoking the defense of laches, or neglect, Bienstock replied late in 1984 that Lieber and Stoller had known "substantially in advance" about his commitments but had made "no effort to enforce any alleged rights to participate." The suit was settled amicably soon thereafter; Leiber and Stoller retained a working relationship with Bienstock.

Estimates by CBS Records, which had shown a high degree of accuracy in the past, indicated the the record industry had made another come back, a new high of $4.464 billion, in 1984, 17 percent over the previous year and 8 percent over the 1978 previous all-time peak. Official RIAA figures, representing only the sales of its members and none of those of small independent labels, were released in April 1985. Prerecorded cassette sales were the key to the industry's $4.37 billion gross. They were up 32 percent over the previous year, to $2.38 billion, more than half of all sales revenue. Compact-disk shipments had jumped by 625 percent in a year, representing a total dollar volume of $103.3 million, up 500 percent from 1983's $17.2 million. Total unit shipments of 697.8 million were still below those in 1978, 1979, and 1980. So, too, was the number of new album releases—

about 2,000 in 1984, 2,300 in 1983, and considerably lower than the 4,056 in 1972—indicating a steady diminution of availability to consumers of new recorded music.

The shipment of videocassettes had doubled, lending their "stimulative effect" to the sales of prerecorded music and to the popularity of superstars. The success in 1984 of Tina Turner, Prince, and Michael and the other Jacksons had lifted some of the burden from black artists and had added more than a touch of black gospel and soul music to white rock, the Hot 100, and MTV. The faith of conglomerates in the international record business, which in several cases accounted for about half of all recorded-music sales, was tested by a strong dollar overseas, leading to predictions that unless the U.S. budget and deficit were brought into line, the next year would see only a one percent increase in projected sales. Singles plus music video still made an album a big hit, successful fifty to sixty times out of the 2,000 opportunities an LP release had afforded in 1984. In the first quarter of 1985, the RIAA certified twenty Platinum albums, thirty-one Gold LPs, and five Gold singles. One nontheatrical video was certified as both Gold and Platinum in the same month, signifying sales of more than 40,000 units and cumulative retail sales in excess of $1.6 million. One was certified Gold, representing the sale of 20,000 units and $800,000 in retail sales.

CBS was the first, in 1985, to raise the list price of selected superstar albums to $9.98. If other labels followed, it might induce consumer resistance once more and put an end to the recovery. The world that lay ahead for the recorded-music business, and, in a sense, for the printed-music business as well, was essentially still in the hands of the small group that had shaped its destiny for years and had firmer control than ever of the distribution apparatus: RCA Records, now RCA Ariola International; Philips-PolyGram, until its conglomerate masters sold off their entertainment-business holdings, having already sustained a $220-million loss in the previous five years; Warner Communications, with whatever new partner its might take on in the interest of greater world-wide distribution; MCA Records, which needed a new alliance in the business; Thorn-EMI/Capitol; and the CBS Records Group, at whose heels the hounds of takeover were baying, promising to dispose of it in order to pay for the CBS Television Network.

PART TEN

1985–1996

CHAPTER 38

Anxious "Indies" In An Aggressive Marketplace

The corporate control of the musical marketplace only increased after 1984, monopolizing the choices as to which music was recorded and which artists were promoted. The retailing of music also underwent centralized control. Owner-operated "mom and pop" record stores virtually disappeared and were replaced by such chains and "superstores" as the Record Bar and Tower Records. But while record companies and retailers exerted a stranglehold on the music business, consumers began to purchase an increasingly diverse body of music. This led to the meteoric rise of black rap artists and heavy metal bands, whose records dominated the charts in this period in an unprecedented manner. Record executives capitalized on the fact that rap music appealed to more than just inner-city teenagers, and hard-rock bands expanded their audience beyond its hardcore male constituency. Motion picture producers also tapped into the youth market, adopting the crossover strategy initiated by Al Coury's merchandising of *Saturday Night Fever*. Soundtrack albums now dominated the charts, adding to the coffers of both record companies and motion picture studios. And yet the mainstream marketplace was not alone in its promotion of diverse musical forms. In part, that diversity resulted from a boom in "fringe" products available from "indie" or independent labels and distributors. Even if it was estimated in the mid-1980s that the "indies" controlled as little as five or ten percent—at most—of market sales, they enabled the inquisitive consumer to sample forms of music the majors avoided or denigrated. Furthermore, the A&R staffs of the major labels appeared to treat the "indies" as farm teams, waiting to see which of their artists found a constituency and then offering them lucrative contracts, to which a number succumbed. These many forces caused markets to expand, offering an ever-widening range of product. Even if consumer choices continued to be dictated by a small number of companies, the diversity of music and the formats on which it was recorded—what with the innovation of compact discs and digital audio technology—continued to increase.

If any music dominated the charts during the 1980s, it was movie soundtracks, r&b, and heavy metal. In 1984, ten soundtrack albums went platinum. The success of Prince's *Purple Rain* was repeated by *Footloose*: the two recordings together held the number-one chart position for more than half a year. *Footloose* generated six Top 40 singles and brought considerable attention to Dean Pitchford, who wrote both the script and the lyrics to the incorporated songs. However, in too many cases soundtracks suffered from a lack of strong creative input. Performers and writers often spared little time or effort in preparing material for films. This resulted in soundtrack albums glutted with mediocre filler or work by prominent artists that was not up to their usual high standards. Despite the often hasty lack of coordination, other soundtracks dominated the charts, including 1986's bestselling *Top Gun*, which yielded three chart-topping singles, and 1987's *Dirty Dancing* and *La Bamba*. The *Dirty Dancing* album was followed by a second release of music featured in the film and even led to a tour in the summer of 1988 by singers featured on both recordings and dancers who performed the slow grind gyrations of the early 1960s. *La Bamba*'s success proved that soundtracks need not include contemporary material, as Los Lobos' re-recording of the Ritchie Valens's 1959 hit soared to the top of the charts. It was purchased in many cases by the children and grandchildren of its original purchasers. This was also the case with the 1983 film *The Big Chill*, which led to two collections of Motown-dominated r&b of the 1960s. Still, for all the successes, many rock-dominated soundtracks failed, as did the films they promoted. For a soundtrack to be successful, the music must support the film's storyline as well as stand on its own as a coherent composition. Many in the music industry forgot that the best musical marketing tool for a film was not an album but an identifiable hit single accompanied by a frequently aired video, preferably one including enticing clips from the film. When a successful marketing strategy, good music, and a crowd-pleasing film were combined, the result was a considerable profit for all concerned.

Rhythm-and-blues performers garnered substantial sales in the 1980s. One of the principal reasons was the meteoric success of Michael Jackson's *Thriller*. It established itself as the all-time bestselling album, having racked up more than thirty million sales worldwide and held the number-one slot on the *Billboard* album charts for two years in a row. Even if *Thriller*'s success caused many to assert that Jackson's follow-up album, *Bad*, could not possibly equal its predecessor, it accumulated 2.75 million advance orders, the largest number in CBS's history. Other black performers in this period who gained wide constituencies and crossed over from one chart to another included the Pointer Sisters, Tina Turner, Kool and the Gang, Whitney Houston, Sade, and Lionel Ritchie, formerly of the

Commodores, who, in addition to contributing to soundtracks and scoring dance hits, was the top adult contemporary artist for two years, 1983 and 1984.

However, the most influential R&B format was rap music. Rap moved more units than mainstream black music and acquired a loyal audience among urban teenagers. As a chart phenomenon, rap began with the 1979 release of the Sugarhill Gang's "Rapper's Delight," and it was taken up as a commercial vehicle by Hollywood in 1984 with the release of several successful films, including *Breakin'* and *Beat Street*. Yet it was not until 1986 that the music business recognized the remarkable audience for rap with the release of Run-DMC's third album, *Raising Hell*, which peaked at number three on the pop album charts and sold three million copies. The group added to its established urban audience with the successful single "Walk This Way," a remake of the 1975 Aerosmith hit recorded in conjunction with members of that group. In 1987, Run-DMC's sales record was broken by the Beastie Boys' *Licensed to Ill*, which was the first rap album to hit number one on the pop charts. While many at the time considered rap a musically unsophisticated form, the careful listener discerned a wide range of styles among such artists as the teen-idol LL Cool J, the comic Fat Boys, the overtly political Public Enemy, and the all-woman ensemble Salt-n-Pepa. Unsophisticated or not, rap continues to be one of the bestselling forms of contemporary music and has been featured in a wide range of media, from commercials to cartoons.

Heavy metal also increased its marketability in this period. It had possessed a loyal following among young white males since the late 1960s and the early recordings of Black Sabbath and Deep Purple. Over the last two decades, heavy metal groups had consistently filled arenas with enthusiastic fans, but it was not until Bon Jovi's 1987 *Slippery When Wet*, which sold over eight million copies in the United States alone, logged 38 weeks in the top five on the Top Pop Album charts, and placed three singles in the Top Ten, that the "acceptable face of heavy metal," in *Billboard*'s words, was apparent to the public. Bon Jovi combined a hard-rock sound, memorable anthemic choruses, and stinging guitar solos with good looks. The package appealed to not only the customary leather-clad adolescent male but also an abundant number of young women. The group's success helped to lay the groundwork for more heavy metal bands to place albums in the Top 40, including Cinderella, Poison, Whitesnake, Mötley Crüe, Guns 'N' Roses, and Def Leppard.

Other musical forms fared less well during this period and seemed temporarily unable to find their ideal audience. During the course of the 1980s, country in particular appeared locked in a hard-fought effort to crossover to the pop charts and, as a result, lost sight of its roots. The success of the 1980 film *Urban Cowboy* and its soundtrack caused record producers to aim unsuccessfully at demographically expanding audiences, but traditional country fans felt something was missing. A backlash started in 1984 as a return to the genre's roots spurred the success of acts like the Judds, Ricky Skaggs, Reba McEntire, Dwight Yoakam, and George Strait. The back-to-basics movement found its most successful exemplar in Randy Travis, whose 1986 debut album, *Storms of Life*, sold over 600,000 copies.

Jazz artists, who perennially struggled to achieve wider commercial acceptance, made some headway in this period, due largely to the success of trumpeter Wynton Marsalis, whose Columbia albums contained music that reflected the jazz mainstream and appealed to a wide public. Marsalis also gained listeners by his recordings as a solo performer of the classical repertoire, which alerted many listeners unaccustomed to jazz to his name and talents, as well as those of other jazz performers—including his brother Branford, who also recorded for Columbia, both as a member of Wynton's group and as the leader of his own. When Branford accompanied rock star Sting on tour in 1985, any number of individuals probably got their first taste of masterful jazz improvisation. As the record charts attested, many of them subsequently sought out jazz releases to enlarge their awareness of what before then was to them a novel musical form.

The favorite artists of the wide audience for rock music appealed to social consciousness during this period at a number of large-scale public service events. The first, Live Aid, occurred in July of 1985. It was a massive concert staged simultaneously in London and Philadelphia and broadcast globally on television, and it raised funds to feed starving Africans suffering from a catastrophic famine. The organizer of the event, Bob Geldof, also composed a single, "Do They Know It's Christmas," which was an international hit and whose profits helped stem the hunger of many people. In September of the same year, rocker John Cougar Mellencamp and country star Willie Nelson organized Farm Aid, a live benefit concert again broadcast over national television, which raised $10 million to benefit financially strapped family farmers. Other benefit recordings were released during the 1980s on which various elements of the music business raised money for a wide range of causes. Two of particular note were "We Are The World," written by Lionel Ritchie, whose sponsor group USA for Africa raised $92 million for starving Africans, and Little Steven's "Sun City," which aimed to increase public consciousness of government repression in South Africa.

The televising of these public service events, particularly by MTV, the music video channel, indicated how much the medium continued to be one of the music industry's major marketing tools. A number of new artists, including Duran Duran, Culture Club, Cindy Lauper, and Madonna, successfully utilized video as a means of merchandising their music through striking visual imagery. However, it also became increasingly clear that merely projecting a "hot" video image, if not backed up by a substantial repertoire, could easily result in artistic burn-out. Nonetheless, many record companies relied on MTV's services, charging the cost of video production against artist royalties. Companies signed exclusive contracts with the channel in order to insure that their artists received the best chance at being in "heavy rotation" and pulling the widest possible audience. At the same time, MTV underwent organizational changes. The management that founded the channel moved on, and in 1985 it was bought by Viacom International. Ted Turner threatened in 1984 to compete with MTV by forming an alternate music video channel, but it failed to find an audience and he shut down the channel in December. It was sold to MTV, who established a new format, Video Hits One. VH-1, as it is known, was targeted to an older demographic audience of 25-to-49-year-olds; the repertoire was softer and less aggressive, including more middle-of-the-road and easy listening material than MTV. Its success in turn caused MTV to re-examine its programming. A number of the original vee-jays were fired, and the continual accusation of a racist lack of attention to black music began to be remedied as the channel incorporated more rap and dance tracks.

The success of MTV and VH-1 led to other such channels, most of them predicated on the appeal of specific genres of music targeted to a narrow niche of the national market. If MTV appealed to the urban audience with their popular show "Yo! MTV Raps," others were drawn to the all-black programming on Black Entertainment Television (BET). Country music aficionados turned to The Nashville Network (TNN). Like BET, it featured material exclusively from one musical genre—in this case a form of music rarely if ever shown on either MTV or VH-1. All these channels, however, drew upon MTV's format, for they incorporated "lifestyle" programming in addition to music videos: shows that incorporated interviews with performers (some musical and some not) proliferated as did those that highlighted cooking or sports-related activities. In the case of TNN, one also was able to view the weekly performances of the Grand Ole Opry from Opryland in Nashville, Tennessee. Lastly, one channel, "The Box," dispensed with both "lifestyle" programming and vee-jays altogether and allowed viewers to pre-select the material shown.

Video reproductions of motion pictures became a prominent consumer item during the 1980s. As ownership of VCRs increased and the rental of films took off as an even more popular means of consumption than theatrical attendance, the manufacturers of videotapes realized the foolhardiness of the exorbitant price structure for their products. They therefore continued to sell tapes to rental concerns at a premium price but soon thereafter reduced the over-the-counter cost to a reasonable rate. What became known as "sell-through" tapes took off when the Media Corporation initiated price-cutting in 1984, lowering the list price of much of their catalog to $19.95. Shortly thereafter, Paramount Pictures, which had mysteriously removed a number of films from circulation the year before, reintroduced them at premium prices with their "25 for $25" campaign. The Disney Corporation joined the bandwagon and issued a number of their classic cartoon features for $29.95. These actions resulted in the sale of fifty million units in 1985, with profits of between $1.4 and $2 billion. This did not include the mushrooming public domain market for films no longer protected by copyright statutes and therefore priced at ten dollars or less. Box-office mega-hits such as the Eddie Murphy vehicle *Beverly Hills Cop* (1984) reaped profits equal to or greater than their initial release when issued on tape at a reasonable price. As a result, in one year's time video sales more than doubled to $5 million from the purchase of 80 million units. Such profits allowed video firms to diversify, and in 1986 Vestron was the first software manufacturer to initiate a commercial film division. It also led firms to cement deals with corporate sponsors, as in the case of Paramount's *Top Gun* (1986), whose videotape began with a commercial for Pepsi-Cola. The commercial's inclusion allowed the company to sell the tape to both rental stores and individuals for $26.95 and thereby increase their profits. Furthermore, videotapes were no longer rented and sold by "mom and pop" owner-operated stores, for those same chains which had consolidated record sales began to market videotapes in large specialty outlets, outselling their competition by increasing the number of available titles and pricing them as low as possible.

The use of one media to advertise another proliferated throughout the 1980s, with music as a frequent means of enticing consumers. Popular stars were recruited to perform on commercials broadcast over television and radio and in movie theaters, and featured on billboards and in magazines. Some of the most prominent "pitchmen" included Ray Charles and Michael Jackson. Many younger people who knew nothing about Charles' long career associated him instead exclusively with the tag line "You Got The Right One, Baby, Uh-huh!" that accompanied his spots for Diet Pepsi. Another popular strategy employed by any number of advertisers was to employ classic rock songs as a supplement to their pitches. For some, this adulterated the very countercultural impulses they associated with popular music; for others, it was a familiar and successful form of appeal. The nadir of this practice was felt to be when the Beatles' song "Revolution" was licensed to accompany a Nike advertisement. Many bemoaned the commercial, but Madison Avenue had discovered an easily repeated and cost-effective system.

The consolidation of retail music marketing led to the phasing out of the sale of recorded music by department stores, as was the case with Montgomery Ward in 1984. Now the retail business was controlled by chains like Tower Records and Record Bar, the former of which began to open stores with 18,000 or more square feet packed with discounted product. These stores marketed numerous copies of a wide range of selections and swiftly attracted customers who discovered they could purchase virtually any available recording at reasonable prices. The success of chain stores was not lost on large corporations who began to purchase blocks of outlets, as did Transworld in 1985, when it bought out the owners of Record Land. Other retail chains expanded, either through the construction of new stores or acquisition of their competition. This was particularly evident in 1986 on the West Coast, where, in what became known as the "battle of California," Musicland acquired the Southern California chain Licorice Pizza from Record Bar in addition to most of the Record Bar outlets west of the Mississippi. Simultaneously, Warehouse Entertainment acquired the San Francisco–based chain Record Factory.

The marketing, production, and performance of music during this period was not free of governmental or other forms of interference. In a series of actions reminiscent of the Pastore and Celler hearings, the Parents Music Research Council (PMRC) sought to compel record companies to engage in censorship of material the council felt to be pornographic or injurious to the nation's youth. Their activities began in 1985 when the references to masturbation in Prince's song "Sugar Walls" horrified a Washington, D.C. parent. Alerted by this occurrence, the wives of a number of government officials, including then Senator Albert Gore and Reagan cabinet member Jim Baker, formed the PMRC and petitioned the national government to enact prohibitive measures so that songs like "Sugar Walls" would not be readily available to children and adolescents. Some of their recommendations included the insertion of lyric sheets with all recordings, the posting of a warning label on those recordings with "adult" content, and the admonishment of all artists to consider the effect of their lyrics upon impressionable audiences.

The group's efforts and their members' husbands' influence led to Capitol Hill hearings on the music industry in August 1985. A number of artists, including such disparate figures as Frank Zappa, heavy metal vocalist Dee Snider, and John Denver, vehemently protested what they considered an abridgment of First Amendment rights and an injudicious incursion of the central government upon the public. Despite their efforts, censorship appeared to be on the rise. In September of 1985, the San Antonio city council enacted a local ordinance that outlawed any performers whose onstage behavior they considered offensive. Retail chains took similar actions: in August of 1986 the Walmart chain refused to carry heavy metal recordings any longer, specifically objecting to the often outrageous cover art. Some musicians were more personally affected, such as Jello Biafra, lead singer of the punk band the Dead Kennedys. In 1985 he was charged with the distribution of harmful pornographic materials for his inclusion of a suggestive poster by the Swiss artist H.R. Gieger in the group's album *Frankenchrist*. Although he was exonerated in August 1987, the group had been forced to disband and Biafra was still many thousands of dollars in debt for legal fees. His acquittal indicated the degree to which what some individuals felt to be a "witch hunt" had waned, but the forces of reaction were far from eradicated from the scene.

Musicians and writers faced another threat to their livelihood from the television networks during the latter portion of the 1980s. While the resolution of the *Buffalo v. ASCAP, BMI, et al.* case by the Supreme Court denied broadcasters the right to collect payments for music "at the source," they continued to engage in legal actions to secure similar rights with the Television Source Licensing Bill. If the bill had passed, a composer or songwriter would have been required to negotiate an up-front deal with each program producer for the use of his or her material before the marketplace determined its "true" worth. In other words, if the program was a runaway success and eventually went into syndication, he or she would fail to receive any further payments other than those obtained in the initial negotiation. During negotiations over the bill, the broadcasters incorrectly argued that they had to purchase "blanket licenses" from the performance rights organizations which, they felt, owned the rights to a wide body of material, whereas the television executive or producer may be interested in only a handful of songs or pieces of music. In fact, broadcasters do not have to purchase any prescribed form of license, since all performing rights organizations offer a flexible set of options for the usage of music. The Television Source Licensing Bill never became law. However, although composers and songwriters are not legally required to negotiate up-front deals with television producers, economic circumstances force them to do so more often than not, and many individuals still fail to reap the benefits of their contributions to successful series.

Like much else in the music business, radio stations underwent consolidation in this period. Regional network chains annexed suburban stations in communities adjacent to major markets. For example, ABC paid $9 million to buy Hicks Communications' KIXX in Denton, Texas, which was transformed into Dallas's "Kiss-FM KTKS," broadcasting a Top 40 format to the metroplex area. 1985 saw an unprecedented number of acquisitions as conglomerates swallowed up major broadcasting chains: Capital Cities purchased ABC; United Stations, RKO; and Westwood One, the Mutual Broadcasting System. The Storz Broadcasting chain, associated with the Top 40 format since the 1950s, began to disband, as outlets were sold to Price Communications in 1985. Now, the manufacture, retail, and broadcast of recorded music was in the hands of an ever shrinking body of individuals.

The formats on which music is recorded and played underwent their most radical transformation since the innovation of stereo recordings. In the summer of 1983, the compact disc, or CD, entered the American marketplace as an alternative to—or, some argued, a replacement for—the stereo LP. The new format's principal selling point was its dynamic range: a CD perfectly reproduced recorded music and allowed no distortion or noise to interfere with its reception. Listening to a CD required a digital audio disk player. The small, approximately $4^1/_4$-inch plastic disc rotated within a sealed compartment. No portion of the CD's operation was visible, as all information on the disc was read by a "laser eye." The player was able to be connected to a standard preamplifier or receiver in the same manner as a cassette deck. At first, prices of both individual CDs and digital players exceeded the means of many average customers, but within three years prices lowered to the point at which CDs outsold LPs. By the end of 1987 annual domestic production of the discs had swelled to over 100 million. The LP now accounted for as little as ten percent of many retailers' sales, as the CD overtook their inventory. This resulted in a transformation of retail marketing: most record stores, in response to the demands for space to accommodate CDs, cut inventory in their "deep catalog" LPs: older but steadily moving titles, including not only classic rock albums but also slower-selling musical forms such as jazz, reggae, blues, and folk. Many in the music industry believed that as soon as CDs were accepted fully by adolescents and lower-income customers, the LP would be a thing of the past, an object sought out purely by collectors and audiophiles. This dire prediction was corroborated by the fact that little research and development was being done to improve the manufacture of turntables or the phonograph record itself.

At the same time, many record collectors who possessed an interest in the "deep catalog" items retailers dismissed from their shelves recognized the inherently archival nature of the CD format. As the disc will not deteriorate with time, older and more fragile recordings benefited from being transferred to CD. A number of record labels responded by investing in reissues or "deep catalog" items, often including alternate takes or tracks unissued on the original recording. Some, such as the L.A.-based Rhino Records, dedicated themselves almost entirely to this process, while others, like the Massachusetts firm Rykodisc, supplemented reissues with new recordings. Rhino's catalog represents the most ample evidence that a broad-based audience exists for "deep catalog" or out-of-print recordings. They struck licensing agreements with those who released rock, blues, country, jazz, punk, r&b, comedy, and all other manner of recordings. Some of their releases were in series, such as best of the blues or the 1970s or rock recordings with memorable drumming, while in other cases they packaged career or genre retrospectives into elaborate box sets with vividly illustrated booklets and other special items. Many of these reissues became bestsellers, either revitalizing dormant careers or heretofore unappreciated forms of performance and composition. When Sony Legacy's box set of all the recordings by the master blues musician Robert Johnson sold in the six figures, it was amply clear that a considerable audience existed that wanted to sample the best that had been sung or played, newly mastered on undistorted digital formats.

If the CD sent shockwaves through the music industry, the invention of digital audiotape, or DAT, promised an even more devastating potential impact. DAT allowed the consumer to reproduce the digital-quality sound previously available only on CD, and thus make unlimited copies of CDs with no loss of fidelity. DAT, like CDs, used digital coding for sound reproduction. Understandably, the music industry was horrified by the possibility of pirating albums with DAT technology. If a consumer could make a perfect copy of a CD, why would he or she buy it? Furthermore, as the record industry had invested heavily in CD technology, it was not ready or willing to see it displaced by an alternative process. Appeals for congressional protection from DAT awaited resolution, but as the Supreme Court had already decided that home taping was legal, the industry heavily invested in the Copy-Code system, whose inaudible signal placed on all CDs impaired the "illegal" recording process.

The "deep catalog" which technology threatened became the province and livelihood of the independent or "indie" record labels. In all too many cases, the majors were uninterested in signing and promoting an artist who could not reap *big* profits. As a result, they not only ignored or, at best, paid little attention to musical forms like reggae, blues, and folk music, but they also dropped once popular artists from their roster when they failed to meet the bottom line. Public awareness of this trend was aroused when Warner Brothers in 1984 dropped more than thirty artists, including new-wave performers like the Roches and Tom Verlaine as well as such perennials of the industry as Arlo Guthrie and Van Morrison. Some of them turned to independent artist-owned labels, Guthrie starting Rising Son and singer-songwriter John Prine starting Oh Boy when he was dropped by Elektra/Asylum. Artists thus received greater profits and were in complete control of their material. Many more, however, turned to the "indie" marketplace, those "little outposts of unpredictable aesthetic principle, pockets of structural resistance in the struggle for fun," as *Village Voice* critic Robert Christgau wrote. If the "indies" continued to share only a small slice of the economic pie, they undeniably added to the industry by releasing a variety of music and often committed themselves to their artists through active promotion, tour support, and continuous inclusion of their material in an active catalog. Some labels specialized in one musical genre: Alligator with blues, SST with hardcore rock, and Flying Fish with folk music, among countless others. The very plenitude of available material was overwhelming, leading even the most dedicated listener to abandon the possibility of "keeping up" with innovative music. At the same time, members of the "indie" community discerned a kind of homogenization reminiscent of the majors. A number of "indies," including the aforementioned Rhino, Enigma, and Twin/Tone, went so far as to sign distribution deals with the majors. The hope remains for many consumers that, as *New York Times* critic Jon Pareles has stated, "somewhere on another lower commercial echelon, there's still scruffy strange weird nasty obnoxious stuff, which is what indies were put on this planet to produce."

While it may not be characterized as nasty or obnoxious, certainly one of the most significant current additions to the music marketplace initiated by the "indies" was the mushrooming of international music. For years, folk music from a variety of foreign cultures was available, but never to this degree. The fusion of foreign musical styles with American popular music reached new heights, notably as a result of the success of Paul Simon's 1987 *Graceland* album. His inclusion of native South African musicians and musical forms on the record as well as his subsequent world tour with some of those players alerted many people to the dynamic range of musical expression on the African subcontinent. While some accused Simon of ransacking a foreign culture for his own benefit, it must be said that without his efforts African music would have remained an indigenous and alien phenomenon except to the musical cognoscenti. Yet African music was not alone in this new and ever-expanding field. American consumers can now readily purchase albums of Trinidadian soca, Zairean soukous, and French Caribbean zouk.

One of the labels most involved in this process was the New Jersey-based Shanachie. Started in 1973 by Richard Nevins and Dan Collins, it first released some ten records a year, selling an average of 5,000 to 10,000 copies. Now its annual list includes some forty releases, and sales average 30,000 and more. Shanachie made its name marketing a number of international forms, staring with Irish folk music, then reggae in the early 1980s, African music in 1984, in 1988 a World Beat/Ethno-Pop line, and in the 1990s a singer/songwriter division. Randall Grass, the third manager of the label, explained their choice of repertoire: "The first and most important factor is whether we're excited by the music. If we are, we'll try to find a way—unless the economics are just daunting, meaning that people involved want amounts of money that are just out of the realm of reality—to try and release it. We have, on occasion, released records that had little chance of making money just because we thought the music was great." At times, this inundation of novel and exciting music seemed a veritable tower of babble, too much product for one ear to absorb. And yet, as Robert Christgau wrote, absorbing this material was "a critical-perceptual project [that] could take decades to bear its own fruit—that is, genuinely international rock and roll. Which as far as I'm concerned is a guarantee that things will stay interesting."

As the music business entered the 1990s, it confronted a multi-billion dollar marketplace dominated by a small handful of international conglomerates, while conservative forces of censorship threatened the free flow of creation. Many were concerned that between powerful market forces that emphasized the bottom line and a regressive strain in American society that squelched controversial subject matter, the security of adventurous musicians was threatened. In 1991, six major labels—PolyGram, CBS, WEA, EMI, BMG, and MCA—accounted for 93 percent of all record sales. The market share controlled by independent labels had shrunk, as several of the most successful privately owned companies were taken over. In late 1989, PolyGram purchased Chris Blackwell's Island Records for approximately $270 million and shortly afterward added A&M Records, at a cost of $460 million, to their roster. The following March, MCA acquired the Geffen label from its owner, David Geffen, at a cost of $550 million in stock, thus making Geffen MCA's largest individual stockholder. However, he possessed restricted voting rights even though his yearly dividends amounted to approximately $7 million. All three labels acquired the benefits of corporate distribution and promotion through these takeovers, yet many in the industry wondered whether consolidation in the hands of a small number of conglomerates benefited progressive or experimental musicians. It is hard to imagine that innovative music is well served by an increasingly bottom-line mentality. At the same time, the emergence of several new labels—SBK, a pop-oriented division of Disney, Charisma (run by Virgin), DGC (a Geffen subsidiary), and a Warner-distributed company to be run by former agent and MCA Records President Irving Azoff—boded well for an expanded marketplace.

If many in the music business were wary of corporate consolidation, many more failed to respond resolutely to the accelerated censorship of musical expression. The influence of the PMRC did not abate as accusations of obscenity and endangering public safety were targeted against elements of the music community, particularly the rap and heavy metal contingents. (It did not help matters when the rap group Public Enemy was charged with anti-semitism and the heavy metal stars Guns 'N' Roses, specifically lead singer Axel Rose, made bluntly racist, sexist, and homophobic comments in song lyrics and public statements.) A number of conservative organizations and public officials proposed legislation or put into force existing laws against the sale of certain records to minors and advocated either the stickering of records as a warning to consumers or the outright banning of certain music for sale. In Florida and Alabama, record clerks were charged with violating obscenity statues by selling releases by 2 Live Crew, a raunchy rap group whose album *As Nasty As They Wanna Be* (1989) already was stickered as well as available in an edited version. The group itself was arrested for a public, adults-only performance in Florida of what a local judge deemed pornography. Finally, the FBI threatened the California-based radical rap group NWA over a song said to advocate violence against the police.

While a number of musicians and corporate executives spoke out against these threats to the First Amendment, the industry response to public pressure on the whole was vague, perhaps in the hope that the matter might blow over in time. However, as that pressure accelerated and a number of record stores refused to sell certain contested albums, the industry realized that the pressure was a threat not only to its reputation but also to its bottom line. As a result, in early 1990 the 55-member major trade organization the Recording Industry Association of America (RIAA) and the National Association of Independent Record Distributors and Manufacturers (NAIRD) capitulated and recommended the adoption of warning stickers, which they hoped would erode the threat of civic and governmental intervention and avoid passage of restrictive state and federal laws. However, using the PRMC's own figures, of the approximately

7500 albums released between January 1986 and August 1989, only 121 contained questionable lyrics and 49 of those were already stickered.

The rap community in particular faced another legal dilemma due to its use of a new technological aide: the digital sampler. This electronic keyboard allows the user to convert any musical element into a processable computer code; in effect, if one can type, one can "create" music. Rap writers used samples to incorporate portions of recordings as elements in their own work. In virtually all cases the sampled material was credited, but the technology called into question whose beats, rhythms, riffs these were. A number of suits were pursued, including the Turtles' prosecution of De La Soul, the top-selling rap group of 1989, and forced an inevitable re-examination of copyright law. Such questions as whether the fair-use law covered sampling and whether a performer's characteristics were themselves copyrightable—for example, James Brown's scream, one of the most sampled sounds in rap—remained unresolved. Singers Tom Waits and Bette Midler brought suits against advertising agencies that employed "copycat" singers and therefore stole their sound. The technological revolution insured the need for a detailed examination of the processes of creation, duplication, and imitation.

Finally, the reproduction of sound recordings went through a revolution comparable to the battle of record speeds in the 1950s. The CD took over the vinyl market. In a number of record stores vinyl now occupied a minimal portion of available floor space, and a virtual 90% drop in vinyl sales was observed. Certain formats virtually disappeared, particularly the 45-rpm single, expect in the hands of collectors. Admittedly, in 1991, the cassette tape continued to dominate the market, as thirteen cassettes were sold for every six CDs and single vinyl album, but that numerical advantage could not last long. Vinyl continued to be a collector's medium, but it was virtually marketed out of existence even though some complained that analog sound remained far preferable acoustically to digital sound. Also, until the abandonment of the elaborate jewelbox packaging in 1991, many environmentalists viewed the very display of CDs as a waste of diminishing natural resources.

CHAPTER 39

Desperately Seeking Synergy

During the last five years the course of the music business continues to be uncertain but bright. On the one hand, according to 1993 figures collected by the RIAA, music sales totaled $10 billion, an 11% rise from the previous year. Music consumers over the age of 35 spent 4.1% more than in 1992, while adults over 20 acquired 76% of all purchases. The CD continued to dominate over all other formats, with 495.4 million in unit sales, a 22% increase from 1992. If one extends the scope of sales to encompass the international arena, these figures increase exponentially. All forms of U.S.-produced entertainment, music included, constitute America's second largest net export (aerospace being the first) and bring in an annual trade surplus of more than $5 billion. American popular culture outpaces in sales and public dissemination that of any other nation and centrally determines our global economic as well as political influence. In the face of declining natural resources and social instability, the dreams and desires embodied by American entertainment permit countless individuals around the world to surmount any number of implacable obstacles. As quoted in a *Time* magazine article on our "leisure empire," television producer David Black states, "we are selling them the ultimate luxury: the fact that people do not have to live the life they're born into."

On the other hand, only the most oblivious participants in that "leisure empire" presume that the hegemony of American culture will remain uncontested. In the sphere of music, its seemingly unalterable preeminence has encountered obstacles at hand and abroad. Despite our substantial exports, forces of cultural, social and political decentralization daily erode the presumptive transferability of American music to other cultures. American cultural dominance of the world market will shrink from one third at the present time to one fifth by the year 2000. U.S. and British dominance of European sales of music already has dropped from 65% in 1985 to 45% today, while 80% of the music sold in Latin America is by Latins, and 60% of the music sold in Asia is produced by Asians. As an example of the diminution of America's cultural preeminence, take the growth of Taiwan's Rock Records. Over the last sixteen years, they became East Asia's largest independent label with estimated sales in 1995 of $85 million. Domestically, the future is similarly bleak. The six major labels who in 1990 controlled 93% of all U.S. record sales now dominate only 80.7%. This continuing downward spiral can be credited to strong showings by companies that release classical, jazz, rap, and alternative and modern rock recordings; the Disney Records soundtracks to the cartoon features *Aladdin* (1992), *The Lion King* (1994), and *Pocahontas* (1995); and Epitaph Records's breakthrough 1995 punk recording, Offspring's *Smash*.

The title of Offspring's album is just what the moguls who control the music business most fear will be done to their domination of the market—as well as what some commentators, and more than a handful of consumers, fervently hope will occur. Whatever unity American music was once thought to possess erodes year by year. The proliferation of genre-based charts in the pages of *Billboard* attests to the breakdown of the market into "niche" categories. In the case of music journalism, a long-standing chasm between what the mass public consumes and what the critical community recommends grows ever wider. The amount and degree of excoriation heaped upon some of the most successful artists of the past several years—Ace Of Base and Hootie and the Blowfish, for example—indicate either that there is no accounting for taste or that taste cultures have grown so heterogeneous that no commonalty whatsoever connects them. As Robert Christgau asserts in the 1995 *Village Voice* Pazz & Jop Critics Poll, the only response to contemporary circumstances may be to opt between decrying the balkanization of the mass public or glorying in the cornucopia of options available to it.

The music business executive, on the other hand, can ill afford to ponder either option. Pressures to reach those broadly defined audiences, withstand the diminution of foreign sales, and maintain adequate market share in the face of independent competition take the place of any conceptual daydreaming about the constitution of audiences or the artistic substance of the music he or she aims to sell to as many individuals as possible. Furthermore, the music business itself has metamorphosed as much or even more than the products it produces or the parties to whom those products are directed. The remainder of this decade will likely continue to undermine what small degree of certainty the music business possesses about markets, consumers, and the commodities that feed the system. Only time will tell whether the innovations they have proposed in recording formats, marketing plans, and corporate hierarchies will keep at bay the diminution of their once unassailable position in the "leisure empire."

Making sense of the events of the past five years as well as the pressures that will continue to consume the music industry in the 21st century requires underscoring the two most important factors in the business place at present: first, the accelerating pace of mergers and acquisitions within the "leisure empire" and the resulting "synergy" of interrelated spheres of communication, and, second, the subordination of popular music as but one of many elements in the marketing of intellectual property to the degree that its aesthetic attributes give way to its commercial viability. While American popular music has always been treated more or less as a commercial product, not an artistic form, media conglomerates increasingly view it as a means of selling other products, some musical and some not. Next, a review of the state of music retailing is required in order to illustrate how the consolidation of merchandising has effected the sales of certain genres, specifically pop, country, rock, rhythm and blues, and rap. Finally, the proliferation of the means by which music can be commodified has in turn led to a series of legal and legislative challenges to how profits from that merchandising are distributed as well as to what degree socially critical artists (particularly members of the rap community) are prohibited from making use of the commercial marketplace for the promotion of their ideas. In sum, the last five years have found the music business in the midst of a conflict between the augmentation of self-expression and the centralization of corporate autonomy whose eventual outcome remains in doubt.

The control of the media by an ever-shrinking number of organizations has been a long-standing concern. Ben Bagdikian, author of the classic study *The Media Monopoly*, observed in 1983 that fifty corporations dominated the nation's news and communications industries, only to find in 1992 that their number had shrunk to twenty and stands to fall even further to half a dozen by the year 2000. At present, only half a dozen record companies, in fact, dominate the music business. They are, according to 1995 figures, and including their corporate owner, percentage of market share, and some of their affiliated labels:

WEA (Time Warner) 26.1%
Warner Brothers, Reprise, Giant, Sire, Elektra, Atlantic, Rhino.

SONY 13.9%
Columbia, Epic.

POLYGRAM (Phillips Electronics) 13.5%
Motown, A&M, Island, Polydor, Def Jam, Deutsche Gramophone.

BMG (Bertelsman) 12.4%
RCA, Arista, Zoo, Windham Hill, Private Music, BMG Classics.

CEMA (Thorn EMI) 9.8%
EMI, Liberty, Chrysalis, Virgin, Capitol, SBK, IRS.

UNI (Seagram's) 9.7%
Geffen, GRP, Uptown, MCA Records.

Since 1991 several of these companies had merged with or were purchased by other entities in order to reap the benefits of what the "leisure empire" is fond of calling "synergy" and what others regard as nothing more nor less than "vertical integration." Simply put, those who engineer the interlocking of media and, in some cases, unaffiliated enterprises, desire to maximize the means of both production and distribution as well as take control of any or all possible outlets for the dissemination of whatever intellectual property the organization owns. In the case of music, a corporation aims not only to produce and distribute recordings but also to acquire all or a portion of the chain stores where they are sold, the magazines and newspapers in which they are advertised or written about, and the various media—radio, television, film, cable, video, laser disc, CD-Rom, and so on—in which they can be employed. In addition, despite declining market share, media companies aim to globalize their holdings by either purchasing off-shore interests or tailoring their own products to foreign customers. The ultimate aim is to capitalize upon as many venues of exploitation as possible, and few governments, domestic or foreign, appear willing either to intrude upon the process or question the social and political ramifications of its transformation of the public sphere.

1995 saw mergers and acquisitions accelerate to a near fever pitch. Some of the principal entertainment-affiliated developments included the Seagram Company's purchase of 80% of MCA for $5.7 billion, Westinghouse's acquisition of CBS for $5.4 billion, and the Disney Corporation's buyout of Capital Cities/ABC for $19 billion. At the present time, Time Warner's purchase of Turner Broadcasting ($7.5 billion) awaits final approval. To illustrate the advantages and disadvantages of these arrangements, a brief examination of Time Warner (1995 revenues $15.903 billion and losses $104 million) and its music division is in order. By acquiring Turner Broadcasting, the corporation stands to integrate into its already substantial holdings additional cable channels (TNT, TBS Superstation, CNN, The Cartoon Network, and Turner Classic Movies), film companies (New Line Cinema, Fine Line Cinema, Castle Rock Productions, and Turner Entertainment), film libraries (MGM, Warner Brothers, and United Artists), and sports organizations (Atlanta Braves and Atlanta Hawks). Each of these can be directed to advertise music or integrate Time Warner Inc. copyrights as a further means of maximizing corporate revenues. The liabilities, however, of such an all-encompassing organization range from stretching the company's assets too thinly to failing to manage the egos and interests of an ever-larger number of high-powered executives.

If the current disposition of the Warner Music Group is any indication, "synergy" devoid of collaborative management breeds chaos. During 1995, the tumultuous relationships between key executives in the organization took on the qualities of a soap opera and were widely reported by the general press. Now ousted Chairman of Time Warner's Music Division Robert Morgado drove out several of the industry's most notable participants—Robert Krasnow (head of Elektra Entertainment) and Mo Ostin (head of Warner Bros. Records)—only to have his successor, Michael Fuchs, remove new Warner Music Chair Doug Morris and in turn be fired himself before the year's end. With such upheaval, it should come as no surprise that Time Warner's third quarter earnings in 1995 dropped, with the music division losing 17%. Partisans of "synergy" argue that the key to economic survival amounts to superior product tied to guaranteed distribution, yet when those in control of intellectual property devour one another, a media conglomerate faces not "synergy" but entropy.

The lucrative advantages of corporate "synergy" can be illustrated by the increasing interrelationship between motion pictures and music as embodied by the soundtrack recording. Promotional strategies predicated upon the marketing of music in order to maximize the profitability of films (and vice versa) possess a long history reaching back to the origins of the cinema. They were perfected in recent years by such figures as Al Coury, who masterminded the 1977 "cross-over" marketing of *Saturday Night Fever* for film and record producer Robert Stigwood. In Stigwood's case, however, he only possessed a portion of but did not own the film—Paramount Pictures did. Motion picture studios are increasingly only elements of interlocking media conglomerates. The Disney Corporation, for example, replicated Coury's marketing strategy for many of their animation features and reaped profits across the board with *Aladdin* (1992), *The Lion King* (1994), and *Pocahontas* (1995), each of which featured songs by composer Alan Mencken and lyrics by Tim Rice, Stephen Schwartz, and the late Howard Ashman that were published by Disney and released on the company's record label. Other companies pursued a similar strategy, and, as a result, soundtracks were among the best-selling recordings of the last five years. Throughout this period, the #1 song, with one exception, originally appeared in a feature film: Bryan Adams's "(Everything I Do) I Do It For You" [*Robin Hood: Prince Of Thieves*, 1991], Boyz II Men's "End of the Road" [*Boomerang*, 1992], Whitney Houston's "I Will Always Love You" [*The Bodyguard*, 1993], and Coolio's "Gangsta's Paradise" [*Dangerous Minds*, 1995]. These practices reinforce the degree to which music increasingly operates as but one subordinated element of a broad-based marketing scheme. "Indeed," as Australian commentator Marcus Breen observes, "we may soon be faced with a situation where popular music is merely the adjunct to a total entertainment package within the leisure economy."

That is not to ignore the fact that popular music has always been in one sense nothing more or less than a commodity, but increasingly it is treated as an entity whose principal end is to help sell non-musical commodities.

The retailing of music has undergone a comparable centralization into the hands of fewer and fewer "mom and pop" privately owned establishments and more and more corporately owned chains. Receipts also have fluctuated, due to the shifts in the national economy as well as rises in the list price of CDs, $16.98 being the most common list price in 1992 and $20 its likely successor by the year 2000. 1991 at the same time saw unit shipping drop 11% and catalog sales fall 8%. New record stores grew at only 3%, while the most notable sales of retail stores involved the purchase by the Handleman Company of both the LIVE Entertainment-owned Leiberman Enterprises and the West Coast-based Sight & Sound stores. The following year the Blockbuster Video rental chain began to pick up record stores by acquiring the Music Plus and Sound Warehouse chains as well as portions of the worldwide Virgin Records retail division—50% of the European and Asian operations and 75% of their outlets in the United States (principally in the Northeast and mid-Atlantic). W.H. Smith of Philadelphia bought most of the Record World stores and twenty outlets from the National Record Mart chain that same year.

Record labels appeared relatively unconcerned by the takeover of the record chains but incensed by a variety of practices that eroded their profit margins. First, used CD stores proliferated and led CEMA, WEA and Sony in 1993 temporarily to pull their products from any establishment that sold second-hand CDs. Country star Garth Brooks followed suit on an individual basis, but neither the singer nor the conglomerates could dissuade customers from wanting to purchase music at the lowest possible price. A second and more intractable phenomenon also revolved around the cost of recordings and involved two different points of purchase. Discount chains such as Best Buy and Circuit City began to advertise marked-down CDs as loss-leader products in order to entice customers through the door. At the same time, record clubs continued to draw away customers through competitive prices, but cut industry profit margins to such a degree that in 1994 Virgin, MCA and Geffen dropped out of the club market altogether. The indication of sales reports that club members so desire to hear a broad range of music that they purchase more recordings at retail than non-members, did little to allay the bottom-line anxiety of both manufacturers and retailers. At the 1996 meeting of the National Association of Recording Merchandisers (NARM), a forum will be held to discuss a NARM-commissioned report that finds record club offers ("11 CDs for the price of one, with nothing more to buy, ever") devalue the recordings sold in stores and undermine any kind of level playing field for pricing CDs.

The same bodies, however, did welcome the more accurate assessment of retail sales inaugurated in 1991 with the introduction of the SOUND-

SCAN system. Instead of depending on the hit-or-miss recollections of store managers, a system fraught with unreliability and prone to fraud, SOUNDSCAN tabulates point-of-sale reports generated by the bar codes scanned at thousands of stores across the country. The *Billboard* charts, long the music industry's principal record of public popularity, also are now predicated upon SOUNDSCAN, and many believe the information they contain possesses a newfound credibility. Bruce Haring, author of a study of the music industry, is quoted in a *New York Times* article on SOUNDSCAN as saying, "Today, the only way to make a record go higher on the charts is to sell more copies." SOUNDSCAN does lead to certain liabilities. It tracks only 85% of all national points of purchase. Since few "mom and pop" record store owners can afford the average $5,000 cost of scanning devices, their customers are not fully represented by the national data. SOUNDSCAN compensates by rating a purchase at an independent store higher than that made at a chain, but the deficiency remains.

Certain artists continue to dominate the *Billboard* charts and command advances that not only stagger the imagination but in some cases seem incommensurate with the public's interest in their music. Certainly Mötley Crüe's recent sales figures fail to indicate that they will recoup the $35 million for which they re-signed with Elektra Records in 1991. The ongoing public ignominy Michael Jackson has suffered (ranging from accusations of child molestation to divorce to the recording of lyrics judged to be anti-Semitic) must make the executives at Sony wonder about the desirability of his re-signing in the same year for $50-60 million. Others appear ready and able to make good on the investment, including Michael's sister, Janet, who signed with Virgin Records for $33-50 million, and the long-popular rock group Aerosmith, who returned to their original label, Sony, for $25 million, confirming that musicians near the age of fifty can still attract and maintain a youthful audience. The six major labels remain convinced that balance sheets depend upon "superstars" and will continue to offer record-breaking contracts. At the same time, they scout the scene for new performers in order to satisfy the public's desire for novelty, even if those appetites appear easily satiated. One performer after another then fails to retain the audience attracted by his or her first or second album. Longevity appears less and less of a guarantee, although certain individuals maintained a consistent profile at the top of the charts for the past five years.

In the pop realm, a number of female performers have reigned supreme, principal among them Whitney Houston and Mariah Carey. Their music crosses over from one *Billboard* chart to another, and both women maintain a core constituency in a demographically and geographically broad audience. In addition, as earlier stated, the soundtrack theme song dominates the top of the charts, four out of the five #1 songs of the past five years having initially appeared in a film. However, the most anomalous pop success of the past five years must be the Swedish quartet Ace of Base. Formed in 1990, their 1994 album *The Sign* reaped unprecedented success in the United States. Their initial three singles all appeared on the Top Ten of the year's pop chart, the first time such a thing occurred since the Bee Gees' *Saturday Night Fever* soundtrack in 1978 and Elvis Presley's debut in 1956. Furthermore, Ace Of Base are only the second non-American, non-native English speakers to reach #1; the last time was in 1958 when Domenico Modungo recorded "Volare." The other notable feature of the pop charts of the past five years is how routinely artists cross over from one chart to another, generic distinctions seeming to possess little significance for consumers who appear to retain devotion more for artists than they do for genres.

The country charts of the past five years have been dominated by four individuals: Garth Brooks, Reba McEntire, and the duo Brooks & Dunn. While a number of other female performers (notable amongst them Pam Tillis and Tricia Yearwood) have gained in popularity, and a series of tight-jeaned hunks, pejoratively referred to by some as "hat acts," scored on the charts (the most successful including Alan Jackson, John Michael Montgomery, and Tim McGraw), these figures are the preeminent performers of the genre. McEntire has been named top female country artist by *Billboard* eleven years in a row, Brooks and Dunn the top duo for four years, and Garth Brooks's extraordinary record speaks for itself. He ranked as the top male country artist for four consecutive years and crossed over as top pop artist for several of those as well. When this initially occurred in 1992, it was the first time a male country performer achieved such dual status since Kenny Rogers in 1980 and 1981. His second album, *No Fences*, has sold thirteen million copies as of this printing; his third, *Ropin' The Wind*, four million in the first month of release; and his fourth, *The Chase*, five million in four months. The only other male figure to come anywhere close to Brooks in sales figures is Billy Ray Cyrus, whose meteoric 1992 debut single "Achy Breaky Heart" remained at the top of the pop charts for seventeen weeks.

No single figure or group has similarly dominated the rock charts. In fact, a recurrent concern of record executives is the apparent lack of longevity of many rock performers, who often appear unable to repeat success from one recording to another. Various hypotheses are offered for this phenomenon, from the fickle nature of fans to the oversaturation of performers through MTV and other venues to the lack of strong material. As an example, the San Francisco punks Green Day sold several million of their 1994 recording *Dookie*, but failed to do so again with their 1995 successor *Insomniac*. Hootie and the Blowfish's 1994 debut *Cracked Rear View* remained on the Top 200 album charts over 75 weeks and sold 8.6 million copies to date. It remains to be seen if their 1996 release, *Fairweather Johnson*, can equal that figure. At the same time, a number of established artists and groups continue to maintain strong followings. Guns N' Roses shipped four million units of their 1991 release *Use Your Illusion*

I & II, and R.E.M.'s *Out Of Time* was the worldwide #1 album of the year. Alternative rock acts found the summer Lollapalooza festival, established by Perry Farrell (leader of the defunct Jane's Addiction) in 1991, a welcome venue for self-promotion, although many in the music industry view the term "alternative" with skepticism. In their eyes, any band that sells over twenty thousand albums does not merit the attribution. A number of groups made that transition from the fringe to the mainstream during this period, including the aforementioned Offspring and Green Day, along with Pearl Jam, Soul Asylum, Stone Temple Pilots, Soundgarden, and Collective Soul.

The marketing of alternative music possesses a complex history. The existence of an annual festival like Lollapalooza dedicated to practitioners of the form, let alone the fact that the "Big 6" support it and use the occasion as a marketing forum, would come as a surprise to those who in the mid-1980s felt ignored if not vilified by the powers that be. At that time, commercial radio appeared to have little interest in any innovative material released by independent labels or the musicians themselves. Venturesome listeners therefore tuned into college broadcasters as their only resource for music that increasingly emerged from widespread pockets of regional activity. Those "scenes" generated bands associated with particular cities outside the principal entertainment compass of New York City, Los Angeles and Nashville: Athens, Georgia (R.E.M., the B52s, and Pylon), Hoboken, New Jersey (the Dbs, the Feelies, and the Individuals), Minneapolis (Hüsker Dü, the Replacements), Austin, Texas (Butthole Surfers), and Seattle and Olympia, Washington (the many artists associated with the labels Sub Pop and K). Mainstream music publications, epitomized by *Rolling Stone*, rarely connected with these groups' devoted followings, who instead turned to independently produced fanzines like *Forced Exposure, Conflict, Swellsville, the Big Takeover,* and *Motorbooty*. By 1987, however, a subtle transformation unexpectedly began to occur. College radio was recognized by the major labels as a proven marketing tool, and the newly founded weekly publication *College Music Journal* (CMJ) targeted the stations' listenership for the Big 6. At the same time, several bands either broke up (Hüsker Dü) or suffered the death of a member (the Minutemen). One group took precedence in the public consciousness during that year. Founded in 1980, R.E.M., affiliated with the independent label IRS, scored a top ten single, "The One I Love." A year later the group was signed by Warner Brothers. Self-generated communities suddenly found themselves on the social vanguard as more and more consumers joined the alternative bandwagon.

The most telling and unexpected transformation of the alternative into the mainstream was the Pacific Northwest group Nirvana. Formed in 1987, they signed to the Seattle-based Sub Pop Records a year later and released their first album, *Bleach* (recorded for $606.17) in 1989. It sold a respectable 35,000 copies and received raves from the alternative press.

Subsequent recording sessions were held, and the results were offered to the major labels. A bidding war ensued, and the David Geffen Company (DGC) won with a six figure offer. The result was the 1991 album *Nevermind*; DGC initially shipped 50,000 only to find the audience at the time for Nirvana exceeded that of virtually any other performer on the pop charts, including Michael Jackson, Garth Brooks, and the Irish superstars U2. *Nevermind* eventually sold over ten million copies and included a hit single, "Smells Like Teen Spirit." As Gina Arnold states, for a trio of "self-described 'negative creeps'—shy, weasel-faced, introverted—... it's practically impossible to imagine [them] copping any of the classic rock poses of stardom." Whether they meant to or not, their next release, *In Utero*, debuted at #1 on the album charts, as the musical and sartorial style associated with the realm of "grunge" rock became all the rage. A&R men descended upon Seattle in the hopes of uncovering the next Nirvana, while the group's lead singer, guitarist and principal writer, Kurt Cobain, struggled with his new-found stardom and lingering addictions to drugs and alcohol. Unable or unwilling to withstand the pressure, he committed suicide in April of 1994. While many pondered both the reasons for his death and the effects of his life, Gina Arnold may well have summed up both the group's impact and that of alternative rock altogether when she wrote, "the drama of Nirvana is going to be in its quiescence; in watching the fallout of the things it has symbolized, the injection of fuel into the moribund music industry, and the infusion of teen spirit into the hearts and minds of American youth."

African American popular music produced by both the rhythm and blues and rap communities continues to attract a broad audience as well as its fair share of controversy. Most of the performers in the r&b field, however, courted record buyers, not rabble rousers. As stated before, Whitney Houston, Mariah Carey, and a number of other female vocalists (Janet Jackson, Vanessa Williams, and Toni Braxton amongst them) drew large audiences, although the most notable success of the period was Houston's re-recording of the Dolly Parton-penned "I Will Always Love You," featured in the singer's 1993 film debut *The Bodyguard*. It was the best selling single ever released by a solo artist and remained #1 on the pop charts for fourteen weeks. The soundtrack album on which it appeared itself remained for twenty weeks at #1 on the albums charts and sold 20 million copies in the United States alone. Another popular r&b format during this period has been the revival of group harmony, or what some have called "neo-doo wop." Groups like Boyz II Men, Jodeci, and the female ensemble En Vogue popularized this sound. The producer-writer-performer responsible for much of the most successful African American music throughout the 1990s has been Kenneth "Babyface" Edmonds, who, in addition to his own recordings, wrote and produced hits for such artists as Whitney Houston, Paula Abdul, Bobby Brown, and Toni

Braxton. In 1995 alone, twelve of his songs hit the charts, and he was the #1 songwriter for the second year in a row.

Diverse and provocative sounds emanated from the rap community during this period. While some performers sought the limelight more than the soapbox, others used their recording contracts as a means to promote social causes or critiques of a racist society. 1991 saw the notable successes of Hammer with "U Can't Touch This" and the white performer Vanilla Ice (born Robert Van Winkle) with "Ice Ice Baby." The 1990 album on which Hammer's single appeared, *Please Hammer Don't Hurt Em*, stayed at the top of the U.S. charts for 21 weeks, and the video played in constant rotation on MTV. His follow-up, *Too Legit To Quit*, failed to repeat this achievement, stalling at #51 on the album charts. The phenomenon of Vanilla Ice was even more meteoric. His single sold fifteen million copies worldwide, but conflicting stories about his purported youth on the streets of Miami and racially derogatory comments at the 1991 MTV Video awards ceremony deflated his image altogether as a hardcore rapper, and he disappeared from the charts. Individuals who truly deserved to be labeled hardcore included Ice Cube, Ice T, 2Pac Shakur, Snoop Doggy Dog, and Dr. Dre. Their aggressive, street-savvy material, broadly characterized as "gangsta rap," met with a wide audience both within the African-American inner city and amongst music-hungry Caucasian youths. Of them, Dr. Dre had the most notable commercial success, for his 1993 album *The Chronic* is most popular hardcore rap album to date, selling over three million copies.

At the same time, the stage and recording personae of a number of these performers spilled over into their everyday lives. Several became involved in violent, even homicidal episodes and faced possible jail sentences. Snoop Doggy Dog was accused of a fatal 1993 shooting, and 2Pac Shakur of aggravated assault and the shooting of two off-duty Atlanta police officers. Both men were found innocent, but their accusers, and a number of people both within the African American and Caucasian communities, tarred all rappers with the label of "gangsta" and insinuated that the recordings they produced contributed to a climate of violence and a lack of respect for law and order. Time Warner, which owned a 50% stake in Interscope Records (the label for which both these accused individuals recorded), capitulated to public pressure spearheaded by a variety of forces, including those led by former Secretary of Education and self-styled "czar" of virtue, William Bennett. They sold off their interest in Interscope in 1995, only to have MCA Music Entertainment Group, headed by former Warner executive Doug Morris, snap the label up. A number of rap performers and their supporters argue that the music only reflects and comments upon existing conditions, but one must, in fairness, separate ideologically assertive language from the homophobia, sexism, and racism that permeates some rap lyrics. Nonetheless, the genre continues to include some of the most musically substantial and thought-provoking material to be found in all of American popular music.

Rap performers found themselves in court during the past five years for other reasons, too. In some cases, the incendiary nature of their language was felt to exceed the bounds of both good taste and the criminal statues. Specifically, rapper Ice-T's 1992 *Body Count* album contained a track, "Cop Killer," that dramatized the extermination of a corrupt public servant. Various police associations and other public officials attacked the artist for inciting murder, and Ice-T was eventually forced to remove the track from the CD only to have the album pulled the following year by its distributor, WEA. Others found themselves challenged, as was mentioned in the previous chapter, to defend the practice of "sampling" as anything other than copyright violation, if not outright thievery. In 1992, British singer-songwriter Gilbert O'Sullivan sued rapper Biz Markie for sampling his 1972 hit song "Alone Again, Naturally" in the rap "I Need A Haircut." Judge Kevin Thomas Duffy, an amateur musician in addition to a jurist, ruled in O'Sullivan's favor and declared Markie's actions tantamount to an abrogation of the biblical injunction against theft. On the other hand, when the publisher Acuff-Rose sued the group 2 Live Crew for tarnishing the reputation of the Roy Orbison song "Pretty Woman" in their rap "Oh Pretty Woman," the Supreme Court accepted the group's defense that the composition parodied but did not defame the original.

The protection of artists' and writers' rights has also met with considerable legal and legislative action during the past five years. After many years of wrangling, a Home Tape Royalty was passed in 1991 on the use of digital recording equipment. This allayed the music industry's fears that the public would employ digital audiotape in order to make copies of CDs and thereby erode their share of the market. Furthermore, a solo-copying chip was called for in order to prevent duplication on a mass scale. In 1994, another long-standing debate involving the remuneration of artists was resolved, after a twelve-year fight, with the signing of the Home Audio Recording Act. This bill stipulated that a 2% surcharge on the sale of digital audio tape recorders in addition to a 3% surcharge on blank audio tape would be placed in a fund eventually distributed to record companies, artists, music publishers and songwriters. An elaborate formula was worked out whereby the funds were split between the various bodies. Two thirds went to the performers, with 4% of that amount tagged for non-featured musicians and vocalists and the other 96% divided between record companies and featured artists in a 60:40 split; the remaining one third was split between the writers and publishers. Final signing of the Act also paved the way for manufacturers to import and market the new copy-coded digital hardware whose entry into the U.S. had been long delayed by the legislation.

The digital transmission of music over subscription services on the internet resulted in yet another piece of legislation in the form of the 1995

amendment to the Copyright codes, the Performance Right In Sound Recording Act. This applied formal intellectual property protection to any
musical works used on such systems. That same year, one of the most
widely used services, Compuserve, forged an agreement with music publishers that guaranteed the collection of royalties for the uploading and
downloading of any recordings of copyrighted songs on those on-line forums overseen by the company. Two final legislative measures await approval, one of which stands to benefit songwriters and publishers and the
other to deny them a major source of revenue. An extension of the Copyright Act from life plus fifty years to life plus seventy years remains under
review. If passed, writers' heirs could receive considerably more royalties
than is presently the case. The Fairness In Music Licensing bill, on the
other hand, would deny the need for eating and drinking establishments
to pay the performance rights societies (BMI, ASCAP, and SESAC) for
the use of any material those societies administer. The owners of those
establishments argue that music serves an incidental purpose in the selling
of food and drinks, while the performance rights societies affirm that the
use of music directly benefits the profitability of such institutions. Resolution of both issues await legislative action.

Lastly, in February of 1996 the House and Senate passed the Telecommunications Bill, certainly the most sweeping transformation of national
communications policy since the Communications Act of 1934. The bill is
predicated upon the assumption that if one increases competition by removing government restrictions, then not only will consumer prices fall but
creative new approaches to communications technologies will spring up.
Specifically, the bill determines that phone companies are free to engage
in both long-distance and local service, setting up competition between local "Baby Bells" and long-distance carriers, including AT&T, MCI, and
Sprint; cable companies can enter the phone business and their rates will,
after a three-year interim, lack any cap save what the customer will bear;
and television broadcasters are no longer restricted from owning more
than twelve stations with a maximum audience share of 25% of U.S households, that figure having been raised to 35% without any restriction on the
number of stations any broadcaster can acquire. Two further portions of
the bill provide what is tantamount to censorship of the content of communications. First, television makers will be required to include in all new
models what has been called the "V-chip," a device that allows viewers to
block out what they feel are violent or sexually objectionable shows; network executives acquiesced to this device in lieu of even more restrictive
ratings of their programming. Second, the heretofore unregulated use of
the international computer communications system, collectively referred to
as the Internet, no longer exists devoid of legal restrictions, for the Communications Decency Act criminalizes making indecent material available
to minors. The RIAA and other communications entities claim the Act
restricts civil liberties and are prepared to fight the matter in court. How-

ever, what the average person will gain from the bill remains to be seen. A number of commentators, Robert W. McChesney amongst them, wonder if the public interest is served by a process in which, during the 1993–94 campaign season alone, telecommunications industries gave almost $7 million to members of both parties. Even if the bill does not refer to music directly, the legislative support it gives to industrial consolidation helps to put the means of communication into the hands of a smaller and smaller number of organizations and encourages the "synergy" that the recording industry seeks. As McChesney states, "the extent that our society, or any society for that matter, fails to examine and debate alternative policies in communications, is the extent to which our democracy is incomplete."

As we approach the year 2000, a number of unresolved issues dominate the music industry. Will the oligopolistic dominance by the six major recording companies push out diversity of product and undermine many musicians' desire to pursue risk and novelty? Will the recordings available to the public diminish in quality even while they increase in quantity? Will the drive toward corporate "synergy" expand or contract the public's options? Will musical performances, regardless of the format in which they are purchased, become nothing more nor less than commodities, or will they retain their position as objects of very genuine if transitory pleasure around the globe? Will music continue to serve corporate purposes that are increasingly extra-musical? For many people around the globe, American popular music performs a fundamental and irreplaceable purpose in their daily lives, while for corporations it increasingly occupies a peripheral position in a broad-based agenda. May music continue to enter the lives of listeners as providentially as the coins descend from the heavens in the lyrics of the song alluded to in the title of this volume, and may the corporations, both large and small, continue to produce and promote music that augments and enriches all citizens of the globe.

Bibliography

General

Ackerman, Paul, and Lee Zhito, eds. *The Complete Report of the First International Music Industry Conference.* New York: Billboard Publishing, 1969.

Aldrich, Richard. *Concert Life in New York 1902–1923.* New York: Putnam, 1941.

Allen, Frederick Lewis. *The Big Change: America Transforms Itself, 1900–1959.* New York: Harper & Row, 1969.

———. *Only Yesterday: An Informal History of the 1920s.* New York: Harper & Row, 1964.

———. *Since Yesterday: The 1930s in America.* New York: Harper & Row, 1972.

American Society of Composers, Authors and Publishers (ASCAP). (All published by ASCAP, in New York.) *ASCAP Biographical Dictionary of Composers, Authors and Publishers,* 1948, 1966, 1980.

———. *ASCAP Grew With Music—So Will Your Business.* 1957.

———. *ASCAP in Action.* 1979–.

———. *ASCAP Journal.* 1937–.

———. *The ASCAP Story.* 1961.

———. *Chords and Dischords.* 1941.

———. *How the Public Gets Its Music: A Statement of Some of the Reasons for the Copyright Law, Its Operation and How It Benefits the Public.* 1933.

———. *Minutes of a Conference Held at 56 West 44th Street in the Offices of The ASCAP, September 20, 1922, New York City.*

———. *The Murder of Music.* 1933.

———. *Notes from ASCAP.* 1950–.

———. *Nothing Can Replace Music.* 1933.

———. "President Stanley Adams' Speech to the ASCAP Membership," March 31, 1964.

———. "Statement of ASCAP Before the National Commission on New Technological Uses of Copyrighted Works (CONTU), March 31, 1977." Mimeo.

———. *The Uses of Music and Why.* 1934.

Aptheker, Herbert, ed. *A Documentary History of the Negro People in the United States.* New York: Citadel Press, 1951.

Archer, Gleason L. *Big Business and Radio.* New York: American Historical Company, 1939.

————. *A History of Radio to 1926*. New York: American Historical Company, 1938.

Arnaz, Desi. *A Book*. New York: William Morrow, 1976.

Arnold, Elliott. *Deep in My Heart: A Story Based on the Life of Sigmund Romberg*. New York: Duell, Sloan and Pearce, 1949.

Arnold, Thurman. *The Bottlenecks of Business*. New York: Reynal and Hitchcock, 1940.

Artis, Bob. *Bluegrass*. New York: Hawthorne Books, 1975.

Austin, William. *Susanna, Jeanie, and The Old Folks at Home*. New York: Macmillan, 1975.

Autry, Gene. *The Art of Writing Songs and How to Play a Guitar*. Evanston, IL: Frontier Publishers, 1933.

Autry, Gene, with Mickey Herskowitz. *Back in the Saddle Again*. Garden City, NY: Doubleday, 1978.

Baker, David N., Lida M. Belt Holt, and Herman C. Hudson. *The Black Composer Speaks*. Metuchen, NJ: Scarecrow Books, 1977.

Baker, W. J. *A History of the Marconi Company*, London: Methuen, 1971.

Bakewell, Dennis, ed.: *The Black Experience in the United States*. Northridge, CA: San Fernando State College Foundation, 1970.

Bane, Michael. *The Outlaws: Revolution in Country Music*. New York: Country Music Magazine Press, 1978.

Banning, William Peck. *Commercial Broadcasting Pioneer: The WEAF Experiment, 1922–1925*. Cambridge, MA: Harvard University Press, 1946.

Barnes, Ken. *The Bing Crosby Years*. New York: St. Martin's Press, 1980.

Barnouw, Eric. *The Golden Web: A History of Broadcasting from 1933 to 1953*. New York: Oxford University Press, 1968.

————. *The Image Empire: A History of Broadcasting from 1953*. New York: Oxford University Press, 1970.

————. *A Tower in Babel: A History of Broadcasting to 1933*. New York: Oxford University Press, 1966.

Barzun, Jacques. *Music in American Life*. New York: Doubleday, 1956.

Baskerville, David. *Music Business Handbook*. Denver: Sherwood, 1979.

Bastin, Bruce. *Crying for the Carolines*. London: Studio Books, 1971.

Belz, Carl. *The Story of Rock*. New York: Oxford University Press, 1971.

Bennett, Lerone, Jr. *Before the Mayflower: A History of the Negro in America, 1619–1964*. Baltimore: Penguin Books, 1964.

Berkman, Paul L. *The "Rhythm and Blues" Fad: An Exploratory Study of a Popular Music Trend*. New York: Columbia University Bureau of Applied Social Research, 1955.

Bernheim, Alfred L. *The Business of the Theatre: An Economic History of the American Theatre, 1750–1932*. New York: Benjamin Blom, 1972.

Bierley, Paul E. *John Philip Sousa, American Phenomenon*. Englewood Cliffs, NJ: Prentice-Hall, 1973.

Bigsby, C. W. E., ed. *Superculture: American Popular Culture and Europe*. Bowling Green, OH: Bowling Green State University Press 1975.

The Billboard Music Year Book. 1944.

The Billboard Encyclopedia of Music. 1945–.

The Billboard International Buyers' Guide. 1980, 1982–83.

Bing Crosby on Record: A Discography. San Francisco: Mellos Music, 1950.

Black Perspective in Music. 1973–.

Blesh, Rudi. *They All Played Ragtime.* New York: Oak Publications, 1971.

Bohn, Thomas W., and Richard Strongren. *Light and Shadows: A History of Motion Pictures.* Sherman Oaks, CA: Alfred Publishing, 1975.

Bond, Carrie Jacobs. *The Roads of Melody.* New York: Appleton, 1927.

Boorstin, Daniel J. *The Americans: The Democratic Experience.* New York: Random House, 1973.

Bordman, Gerald. *The American Musical Theatre.* New York: Oxford University Press, 1978.

———. *Jerome Kern, His Life and Music.* New York: Oxford University Press, 1980.

Bowers, David. *Put Another Nickel In.* New York: Bonanza Books, 1966.

Bowker, Robert Rogers. *Copyright, Its History and the Law.* Boston: Houghton Mifflin, 1912.

Bradford, Perry. *Born with the Blues.* New York: Oak Publications, 1965.

Braun, D. Duane. *Toward a Theory of Popular Culture: The Sociology and History of American Music and Dance, 1920–1968.* Ann Arbor, MI: Ann Arbor Publishers, 1969.

Brawley, Benjamin. *A Social History of the American Negro.* New York: Collier Books, 1970.

Broadcast Music, Inc. (BMI). (All published by BMI, in New York.) *The ABC Of BMI.* 1940.

———. "BMI License Rates Have Been Reduced Since 1940: A Word from BMI." 1943.

———. "BMI Memorandum to the Committee on Interstate and Foreign Commerce, United States Senate, in Regard to the Smathers Bill." 1957.

———. "BMI Memorandum Submitted to the Federal Communications Commission Feb. 1960." 1960.

———. *BMI Newsletter.* 1943–1958.

———. *BMI 1940–1960: Twenty Years of Service to Music.* 1960.

———. *The Many Worlds of Music.* 1958–.

———. "Memorandum of the Status of BMI as of July 27, 1940." 1940.

———. *Poor Richard's Alamanac.* 1942–1943.

———. "Statement Before the National Commission on New Technological Uses of Copyrighted Works (CONTU), March 31, 1977."

———. *Your Stake in BMI.* 1948.

Broadcasting. 1931–.

Broadcasting Yearbook.

Broonzy, William, and Yannick Bruynoghe. *Big Bill's Blues.* New York: Grove Press, 1955.

Broven, John. *Walking to New Orleans: The Story of New Orleans Rhythm and Blues.* Bexhill-on-Sea: Blues Unlimited, 1974.

Brown, Les. *Television: The Business Behind the Box.* New York: Harcourt Brace Jovanovich, 1971.

Brown, Les, ed.: *The New York Times Encyclopedia of Television*. New York:
    Times Books, 1977.
Brown, Peter, and Steven Gaines. *The Love You Make: An Insider's Story of the
    Beatles*. New York: McGraw-Hill, 1983.
Brown, Sterling A. *Negro Poetry and Drama and the Negro in American Fiction*.
    New York: Atheneum, 1969.
Burton, Jack. *The Blue Book of Broadway Musicals*. Watkins Glen, NY: Century
    House, 1952.
————. *The Blue Book of Hollywood Musicals*. Watkins Glen, NY: Century House,
    1953.
————. *The Blue Book of Tin Pan Alley*. Watkins Glen, NY: Century House,
    1950.
Butcher, Margaret Just. *The Negro in American Culture*. New York: Knopf, 1967.
Butler, Tobias, and Will D. Cobb. *The Butler-Cobb Method of Successful Song-
    writing*. New York: Publishers Press, 1921.
Caesar, Irving. "A letter to writer and/or publisher members of ASCAP." Attached
    to a typescript extension of oral presentation made to the ASCAP Board of
    Directors May 22, 1969.
Cahn, Sammy. *I Should Care*. New York: Arbor House, 1974.
Calloway, Cab. *Of Minnie the Moocher and Me*. New York: Crowell, 1978.
Carmichael, Hoagy, and Stephen Longstreet. *Sometimes I Wonder*. New York: Far-
    rar, Straus & Giroux, 1966.
Caron, Paul. *The Devil's Son-in-Law: The Story of Peetie Wheatstraw and His
    Songs*. London: Studio Books, 1971.
Carpenter, Paul S. *Music, an Art and a Business*. Norman: University of Oklahoma
    Press, 1950.
Carr, Patrick. *The Illustrated History of Country Music*. New York: Doubleday,
    1980.
Cashbox. 1942–.
Castle, Irene. *Castles in the Air*. Garden City, NY: Doubleday, 1958.
Castle, Vernon and Irene. *Modern Dancing by Mr. and Mrs. Vernon Castle*. New
    York: Harper, 1914.
Chapple, Steve, and Reebee Garofalo. *Rock 'n' Roll Is Here to Pay: The History
    and Politics of the Music Industry*. Chicago: Nelson-Hall 1977.
Charles, Norman. "Social Values in American Popular Songs." Thesis. University
    of Pennsylvania. 1958.
Charles, Ray, and David Ritz. *Brother Ray: Ray Charles' Own Story*. New York:
    Dial, 1978.
Charters, Ann. *Nobody: The Story of Bert Williams*. New York: Macmillan, 1970.
Charters, Samuel. *The Bluesmen: The Story and the Music of the Men Who Made
    the Blues*. New York: Oak Publications, 1967.
————. *The Poetry of the Blues*. New York: Oak Publications, 1963.
Charters, Samuel, with Leonard Kunstadt. *Jazz: A History of the New York Scene*.
    New York: Doubleday, 1962.
Chase, Gilbert. *America's Music: From the Pilgrims to the Present*. New York:
    McGraw-Hill, 1955.
————, ed. *Music in Radio Broadcasting*. McGraw-Hill, New York: 1946.

Chilton, John. *Who's Who of Jazz: Storyville to Swing Street*. Chicago: Time-Life Books, 1978.

Christgau, Robert. *Any Old Way You Choose It: Rock and Roll and Other Pop Music*. Baltimore: Penguin Books, 1973.

Churchill, Allen. *The Great White Way: A Re-creation of Broadway's Golden Days of Theatrical Entertainment*. New York: Dutton, 1962.

———. *Remember When: A Loving Look at Days Gone By, 1900–1942*. New York: Golden Press, 1967.

Claghorn, Charles Eugene. *Biographical Dictionary of American Music*. Nyack, NY: Parker Publishing, 1973.

Clark, Dick, and Richard Robinson. *Rock, Roll and Remember*. New York: Crowell, 1976.

Clarke, Garry E. *Essays on American Music*. Westport, CT: Greenwood Press, 1977.

Clarke, Norman. *The Mighty Hippodrome*. New York: Barnes & Noble 1968.

Coad, Oral Sumner, and Edwin Mimms. *The American Stage*. New York: U.S. Publishers, 1929.

Cohan, George M. *Twenty Years on Broadway and the Years It Took to Get There*. New York: Harper, 1925.

Cohen, Nathan. "State Regulation of Musical Copyright." *Oregon Law Review*, Summer 1938.

Cohen, Norm. Liner notes for "Minstrels and Tunesmiths: The Commercial Roots of Early Country Music, 1902–1923." John Edwards Memorial Foundation LP 109.

Cohn, David L. *The Good Old Days*. New York: Simon & Schuster, 1940.

Cohn, Nik. *Rock from the Beginning*. New York: Pocket Books, 1969.

Collier, James Lincoln. *The Making of Jazz: A Comprehensive History*. New York: Dell, 1978.

Conant, Michael. *Antitrust in the Motion Picture Industry*. Berkeley: University of California Press, 1960.

Condon, Eddie, and Hank O'Neal. *Eddie Condon's Scrapbook of Jazz*. New York: St. Martin's Press, 1973.

The Congressional Record. Washington D.C. Government Printing Office, 1909–1985.

Cook, Bruce. *Listen to the Blues*. London: Robson Books, 1975.

Coon, Caroline. *The New Wave Punk Rock Explosion*. London: Orbach & Chambers, 1977.

Coon, O. Wayne. *Some Problems with Musical Public-Domain Material Under United States Copyright Law as Illustrated Mainly by the Recent Folk-Song Revival. Copyright Law Symposium Number Nineteen*. New York: Columbia University Press, 1971.

Cooper, Al, with Ben Edmonds. *Backstage Passes: Rock 'n' Roll Life in the 60s*. New York: Stein & Day, 1977.

Copyright Enactments: Laws Passed in the United States Since 1793 Relating to Copyright. Washington, D.C.: Library of Congress, 1978.

Corio, Ann, and Joseph DiNona. *This Was Burlesque*. New York: Grosset & Dunlap, 1968.

Corry, Catherine S. *The Phonograph Record Industry: An Economic Survey.* Washington, D.C.: Library of Congress Legislative Reference Service, 1965.

Coslow, Sam. *Cocktails for Two: The Many Lives of a Great Songwriter.* New Rochelle, NY: Arlington House, 1977.

Crosby, Harry Lillis. *Call Me Lucky: An Autobiography.* New York: Simon & Schuster, 1953.

———. "My Kind of Music Is Coming Back." *This Week,* April 24, 1960.

Crowther, Bosley. *The Lion's Share: The Story of an Entertainment Empire.* New York: Dutton, 1957.

Csida, Joseph, and June Bundy Csida. *American Entertainment: A Unique History of Popular Show Business.* New York: Watson-Guptill, 1978.

Cummings, Tony. *The Sound of Philadelphia.* London: Methuen, 1975.

Cuney-Hare, Maud. *Negro Musicians and Their Music.* Washington, D.C.: Associated Publishers, 1936.

Dachs, David. *Anything Goes: The World of Popular Music.* Indianapolis: Bobbs-Merrill, 1964.

———. "Thunder Over Tin Pan Alley." North American Newspaper Alliance, August 17–21, 1957.

Dalton, David, and Lennie Kaye. *Rock 100.* New York: Grosset & Dunlap, 1977.

Dance, Stanley. *The World of Duke Ellington.* New York: Scribner, 1970.

———. *The World of Earl Hines.* New York: Scribner, 1977.

Dannett, Sylvia, and Frank R. Rachel. *Down Memory Lane: Arthur Murray's Picture History of Social Dancing.* New York: Greenburg, 1954.

Davies, Hunter. *The Beatles.* New York: McGraw-Hill, 1968.

Davis, Clive, with William Willwerth. *Clive: Inside the Record Business.* New York: Morrow, 1975.

Davis, Steven. *Bob Marley.* New York: Doubleday 1985.

———. *Reggae Bloodlines: In Search of the Music and Culture of Jamaica.* New York: Anchor Books, Doubleday. 1977.

Debas, Allen G. Liner notes for "The Early Victor Herbert, from the Gay Nineties to the First World War." Smithsonian LP 30366.

DeForest, Lee. *Father of Radio: The Autobiography of Lee DeForest.* Chicago: Wilcox & Follet, 1950.

DeKoven, Anna. *A Musician and His Life.* New York: Harper, 1926.

De Long, Thomas A. *The Mighty Music Box: The Golden Age of Musical Radio.* Los Angeles: Amber Crest Books, 1980.

———. *Pops: Paul Whiteman, Kind of Jazz.* Piscataway, NJ: New Century Publishers, 1985.

Denisoff, R. Serge. *Great Day Coming: Folk Music and the American Left.* Baltimore: Penguin Books, 1973.

———. *Solid Gold: The Popular Record Industry.* New Brunswick, NJ: Transaction Books, 1975.

Denisoff, R. Serge, and Richard A. Peterson, eds. *The Sounds of Social Change: Studies In Popular Culture.* Chicago: Rand McNally, 1972.

Dennison, Sam. *Scandalize My Name: Black Imagery in American Popular Music.* New York: Garland Publishing, 1982.

Dethlefson, Ron, ed. *Edison Blue Amberol Records 1912–1914*. Brooklyn: APM Press, 1980.

―――. *Edison Blue Amberol Records 1915–1929*. Brooklyn: APM Press, 1981.

DeTurk, David A., and A. Poulin, Jr., eds. *The Folk Scene: Dimensions of the Folksong Revival*. New York: Dell, 1967.

DeWhitt, Bennie Lee. "The American Society of Composers, Authors and Publishers 1914–1938." Diss. Emory University, 1977.

Dilello, Richard. *The Longest Cocktail Party: A Personal History of Apple*. Chicago: Playboy Press, 1972.

DiMaggio, Paul, Richard A. Peterson, and Jack Esco, Jr. "Country Music: Ballad of the Silent Majority." In *The Sounds of Social Change*. See Denisoff and Peterson.

DiMeglio, John E. *Vaudeville, USA*. Bowling Green, OH: Bowling Green State University Press, 1973.

Dixon, Robert, and John Goodrich. *Recording the Blues*. London: Studio Books, 1970.

Dowd, Jerome. *The Negro in American Life*. Chicago: Century, 1926.

Dragonette, Jessica. *Faith Is a Song*. New York: David McKay, 1951.

Dranov, Paula. *The Music Publishing Business 1978–1983*. White Plains, NY: Knowledge Industry Publications, 1977.

Drew, Joan. *Singers and Sweethearts: The Women of Country Music*. New York: Doubleday, 1977.

Dubin, Al. *The Art of Songwriting*. New York: Mills Music, 1928.

Duke, Vernon. *Listen Here*. New York: Oblensky, 1963.

Dulles, Foster Rhea. *A History of Recreation: America Learns to Play*. New York: Appleton-Century-Crafts, 1965.

Dunlap, Orrin, E. *The Story of Radio*. New York: Dial, 1935.

Dunleavy, Steven. *Elvis, What Happened?* New York: Ballantine, 1977.

Dunn, Don. *The Making of "No, No Nanette."* Secaucus, NJ: Citadel Press, 1972.

Dunning, John. *Tune in Yesterday: The Ultimate Encyclopedia of Old-Time Radio, 1925–1976*. Englewood Cliffs, NJ: Prentice-Hall, 1976.

Edelman, Jacob M. *The Licensing of Radio Services in the United States 1927–1947*. Urbana: University of Illinois Press, 1950.

Ehrenberg, Lewis Allan. "Urban Night Life and the Decline of Victorianism: New York City's Restaurants and Cabarets 1890–1918." Diss. University of Michigan, 1974.

Eisen, Jonathan, ed. *The Age of Rock: Sounds of the American Cultural Revolution*. New York: Vintage Books, Random House, 1969.

―――. *The Age of Rock 2*. New York: Vintage Books, Random House, 1970.

―――. *Twenty-Minute Fandangos and Forever Changes*. New York: Vintage Books, Random House, 1971.

Emery, Lynn. *Black Dance in the United States 1619–1970*. Palo Alto, CA: National Press Books, 1972.

Engel, Lehman, *The American Musical Theatre: A Reconsideration*. New York: CBS Records, 1967.

————. *Words With Music.* New York: Macmillan, 1972.

The Entertainment Industry: A Survey of Financial Reporting and Accounting Developments in 1975. New York: Price, Waterhouse, 1976.

Erickson, Don. *Armstrong's Fight for FM Broadcasting: One Man vs. Big Business and Bureaucracy.* University, AL: University of Alabama Press, 1973.

Etzkorn, Klaus Peter. "Musical and Social Patterns of Songwriters: An Exploratory Sociological Study." Diss. Princeton University, 1959.

Escott, Colin, and Michael Hawkins. *Catalyst: The Sun Records Story.* New York: Aquarius Books, 1975.

Ewen, David. *All the Years of American Popular Music: A Comprehensive History.* Englewood Cliffs, NJ: Prentice-Hall, 1978.

————. *The Life and Death of Tin Pan Alley.* New York: Funk & Wagnalls, 1964.

————. *Great Men of Popular Music.* Englewood Cliffs, NJ: Prentice-Hall, 1970.

Federal Communications Commission. *Reports.* Washington, D.C.: GPO, 1935–.

Feist, Leonard. *Introduction to Popular Music Publishing.* New York: National Music Publishers Association, 1980.

Finkelstein, Herman. "The Composer and the Public Interest." *Law and Contemporary Problems,* Spring 1954.

————. "The Copyright Law: A Reappraisal," *University of Pennsylvania Law Review,* June 1956.

————. "Public Performance Rights in Music and Performance Rights Societies." *7 Copyright Problems Analyzed.* New York: Commercial Clearing House, 1952.

Finnis, Rob. *The Phil Spector Story.* London: Rockton, 1975.

Fisher, William Arms. *One Hundred and Fifty Years of Music Publishing in the United States, 1783–1933.* Boston: Ditson, 1933.

Fleming, Len. *Book of Information for Songwriters and Composers.* New York: Leo Feist, 1913.

————. *Dollars and Sense: A Fortune in Popular Songs.* New York: Leo Feist, 1912.

Fletcher, Tom. *The Tom Fletcher Story: 100 Years of the Negro in Show Business.* New York: Burge, 1954.

Foreman, Ronald Clifford. "Jazz and Jazz Records 1920–1932: Their Origins and the Significance for the Record. Diss. University of Illinois, 1968.

Franklin, John Hope. *From Slavery to Freedom: A History of Negro Americans.* New York: Random House, 1969.

Freedland, Michael. *Irving Berlin.* New York: Stein & Day, 1974.

————. *Jolson.* New York: Stein & Day, 1972.

Freeman, Larry. *The Melodies Linger On: Fifty Years of Popular Song.* Watkins Glen, NY: Century House, 1951.

Frith, Simon. *Sound Effects: Youth, Leisure, and the Politics of Rock 'n' Roll.* New York: Pantheon, 1981.

Fuld, James J. *American Popular Music 1875–1950.* Philadelphia: Musical Americana, 1956.

Furnas, J. C. *The Americans: A Social History of the United States.* New York: Putnam, 1969.

Gabree, John. *The World of Rock.* Greenwich, CT: Fawcett, 1968.

Gaillard, Frye. *Watermelon Wine: The Spirit of Country Music.* New York: St. Martin's, 1978.

Gaisberg, Fred. *The Music Goes Round.* New York: Macmillan, 1942.

Gammond, Peter, ed.: *Duke Ellington, His Life and Music.* New York: Roy Publishers, c. 1958.

Garland, Phyl. *The Sound of Soul.* Chicago: Regnery, 1969.

Garraty, John A. *The American Nation.* New York: Harper & Row, 1971.

Geijerstam, Claes. *Popular Music in Mexico.* Albuquerque: University of New Mexico Press, 1976.

Gelatt, Roland. *The Fabulous Phonograph, 1877–1977.* New York: Macmillan, 1977.

Gershwin, Ira. *Lyrics on Several Occasions.* New York: Knopf, 1959.

Gersohn, Frederic, ed. *Counseling Clients in the Performing Arts.* New York: Practising Law Institute, 1975.

Gilbert, Douglas. *American Vaudeville: Its Life and Times.* New York: Dover, 1963.

————. *Lost Chords: The Diverting Story of American Popular Songs.* New York: Cooper Square, 1970.

Gilbert, L. Wolfe. *Without Rhyme or Reason.* Hollywood: Vantage, 1956.

Gillespie, Dizzy, with Al Fraser. *To Be or Not to Bop: Memoirs.* New York: Doubleday, 1979.

Gillett, Charlie. *Making Tracks: Atlantic Records and the Growth of a Multi-Billion-Dollar Industry.* New York: Dutton, 1974.

————. *The Sound of the City: The Rise of Rock and Roll.* New York: Outerbridge & Dienstfrey, 1970.

Gillett, Charlie, and Simon Frith. *Rock File 3: Sources of British Hit Songs, Writers and American Hits.* London: Panther Books, 1975.

Giovannoni, David. "The Phonograph as a Mass Entertainment Medium: Its Development, Adaptation and Pervasiveness. Thesis. University of Wisconsin-Madison, 1980.

Gleason, Ralph. *Jam Session: An Anthology of Jazz.* New York: Putnam, 1958.

————. *The Jefferson Airplane and the San Francisco Sound.* New York: Ballantine, 1969.

Goldberg, Isaac. *Tin Pan Alley: A Chronicle of American Popular Music.* New York: Frederick Ungar, 1931; paper, 1970.

Goldmark, Peter. *Maverick Inventor: My Turbulent Years at CBS.* New York: Saturday Review Press, 1973.

Goldstein, Richard. *Goldstein's Greatest Hits.* New York: Tower, 1970.

————. *The Poetry of Rock.* New York: Bantam, 1969.

Goodman, Paul. *Growing Up Absurd: Problems of Youth in the Organized Society.* New York: Vintage, 1960.

Goodman, Robert Israel. "Music Copyright Associations and the Antitrust Law." *Indiana Law Journal,* Fall 1950.

Goodrich, John, and Robert M. W. Dixon. *Blues and Gospel Records, 1902–1942.* London: Storyville, 1969.

Goss, Madeleine. *Modern Music Makers: Contemporary American Composers.* New York: Dutton, 1952.

Gottlieb, Polly Rose. *The Nine Lives of Billy Rose*. New York: Crown, 1968.

Grau, Robert. *The Theatre of Science: A Volume of Progress and Achievement in the Motion Picture Art*. New York: Broadway Publishing, 1914.

Green, Abel. *Inside Stuff on How to Write Popular Songs*. New York: Paul White-man Publications, 1927.

Green, Abel, with Joe Laurie, Jr. *Show Biz: From Vaude to Video*. New York: Henry Holt, 1951.

Green, Archie. *Only a Miner: Studies in Recorded Coal-Mining Songs*. Urbana: University of Illinois Press, 1972.

Green, Douglas B. *Country Roots: The Origins of Country Music*. New York: Hawthorn Books, 1976.

Green, Stanley. Liner notes for "Ziegfeld Follies of 1919." Smithsonian LP 14272.

––––––. *The World of Musical Comedy*. New York: A. S. Barnes, 1980.

Greenfield, Jeff. *No Peace, No Place*. Gordon City, NY: Doubleday, 1973.

Grissim, John. *Country Music: White Man's Blues*. New York: Coronet, 1970.

Groia, Philip. *They All Sang on the Corner: New York City's Rhythm & Blues Vocal Groups of the 1950s*. New York: Edmond, 1973.

Groom, Bob. *The Blues Revival*. London: Studio Books, 1971.

Guralnik, Peter. *Feel Like Going Home: Portraits in Blues and Rock 'n' Roll*. New York: Outerbridge & Dienstfrey, 1971.

Guthrie, Woody, and Robert Shelton. *Born to Win*. New York: Macmillan, 1965.

Gutman, Herbert G. *The Black Family in Slavery and Freedom, 1750–1925*. New York: Pantheon, 1976.

Hackett, Alice Payne. *Sixty Years of Best Sellers*. New York: R. R. Bowker, 1956.

Hadlock, Richard. *Jazz Masters of the 20s*. New York: Macmillan, 1965.

Hamm, Charles. *Yesterdays: Popular Songs in America*. New York: Norton, 1979.

Hammond, John. *John Hammond on Record*. New York: Ridge Press, 1977.

Hampton, Benjamin A. *A History of the American Film Industry*. New York: Convici Friede, 1931.

Hansen, Barret Eugene. "Negro Popular Music 1945–1953." Thesis. University of California at Los Angeles, 1967.

Haralambos, Michael. *Right On: From Blues to Soul in Black America*. London: Eddison Press, 1974.

Harbach, Otto A. "Affidavit and Supplementary Affidavits Regarding a Conspiracy Between Broadcastors and Broadcast Music Incorporated, 1951, 1953." Typescript.

Harlow, Alvin F. *Old Wires and New Waves: The History of the Telegraph, Telephone and Wireless*. New York: Appleton-Century, 1936.

Harris, Herbert. *American Labor*. New Haven, CT: Yale University Press, 1939.

Harris, Herby, and Lucien Farrar. *How to Make Money in Music*. New York: Arco Publishing, 1978.

Harris, Sheldon. *Blues Who's Who: A Biographical Dictionary of Blues Singers*. New Rochelle, NY: Arlington House, 1979.

Harrison, Hank. *The Dead Book: A Social History of the Grateful Dead*. New York: Links Books, 1973.

Hart, Dorothy. *Thou Swell, Thou Witty*. New York: Harper & Row, 1976.

Hart, Philip. *Orpheus in the New World: The Symphony Orchestra as an American Cultural Institution.* New York: Norton, 1973.

Haskins, James. *The Cotton Club: A Pictorial and Social History of the Most Famous Symbol of the Jazz Era.* New York: Random House, 1977.

————. *Scott Joplin.* New York: Doubleday, 1978.

Hatch, James, and Omanii Abdullah. *Black Playwrights 1823–1977.* New York: R. R. Bowker, 1977.

Haverlin, Carl. "Affidavit . . . in Opposition to ASCAP's Motion for an Order Modifying Amended Final Judgment of March 14, 1950." Typescript.

Hayakawa, S. I. "Popular Songs vs. The Facts of Life." In Rosenberg, Bernard, and David Manning White, eds. *Mass Culture: The Popular Arts in America.* New York: Free Press, 1957.

Hays, Will H. *See and Hear: A Brief History of Motion Pictures and the Development of Sound.* New York: Motion Picture Producers and Distributors of America, 1929.

Heilbut, Tony. *The Gospel Sound: Good News and Bad Times.* New York: Simon & Schuster, 1971.

————. Liner notes for "Precious Lord: New Recordings of the Great Songs of Thomas A. Dorsey." Columbia LP KG 32151.

Hemphill, Paul. *Bright Lights and Country Music: The Nashville Sound.* New York: Simon & Schuster, 1970.

Henn, Harry. "The Compulsory License Provision of the U.S. Copyright Law." *Copyright Law Revision,* Washington, D.C.: Library of Congress, 1960.

Hentoff, Nat. *The Jazz Life.* New York: Dial, 1961.

Hentoff, Nat, with Albert McCarthy, eds. *Jazz: New Perspectives on the History of Jazz by 12 of the World's Foremost Critics and Scholars.* New York: Rinehart, 1959.

Herman, Pinky. *Showbiz and Me.* Lauderdale Lakes, FL: Manor Music, 1977.

Herndon, Booton. *The Sweetest Music This Side of Heaven.* New York: McGraw-Hill, 1964.

Higham, Charles. *Ziegfeld.* Chicago: Regnery, 1972.

Hirsch, Paul. *The Structure of the Popular Music Industry: The Filtering Process by Which Records Are Presented for Public Consumption.* Ann Arbor: Institute for Social Research, University of Michigan, 1970.

Hitchcock, H. Wiley. *Music in the United States: An Historical Introduction.* Englewood Cliffs, NJ: Prentice-Hall, 1969.

Hodier, Andre. *Jazz: Its Evolution and Essence.* New York: Grove Press, 1956.

Hoffman, Charles. *Sounds for Silents.* New York: Drama Book Specialists Publications, 1970.

Hopkins, Jerry. *Elvis: A Biography.* New York: Simon & Schuster, 1971.

————. *Elvis: The Final Years.* New York: St. Martin's Press, 1980.

Hornblow, Arthur. *A History of the Theatre in America, from Its Beginnings to the Present Time.* 2 vols. New York: Benjamin Blom, 1965. Reprint of 1919 ed.

Horstman, Dorothy. *Sing Your Heart Out, Country Boy.* New York: Dutton, 1975.

Howard, John Tasker. *Our American Music: A Comprehensive History from 1620 to the Present.* 4th ed. New York: Crowell, 1965.

Hubbell, Raymond. *From Nothing to Five Million a Year: The Story of ASCAP by a Founder.* Washington, D.C.: Library of Congress. Mimeo.

Hughes, Langston, and Milton Meltzer. *Black Magic: A Pictorial History of Black Entertainers in America.* New York: Bonanza, 1967.

Hurst, Jack. *Nashville's Grand Ole Opry.* New York: Abrams, 1975.

Hurst, Walter E. *The Music Industry Book.* Hollywood: Seven Arts Press, 1963.

International Research Associates. *A Guide for the Interpretation of the Musical Popularity Charts.* New York: Broadcast Music, Inc., 1956.

Jablonski, Edward. *The Encyclopedia of American Music.* New York: Doubleday, 1981.

Jacobs, Lewis. *The Rise of the American Film: A Critical History.* New York: Teachers College Press, 1939.

Jahn, Mike. *Rock: From Elvis Presley to the Rolling Stones.* New York: Times Books, 1973.

Jewell, Derek. *Duke: A Portrait of Duke Ellington.* New York: Norton, 1977.

John Edwards Memorial Foundation Quarterly. 1966–.

Johnson, E. F. Fenimore. *His Master's Voice Was Eldridge R. Johnson.* Milford, DE: State Media Press, 1974.

Johnson, James Weldon. *Along This Way: An Autobiography.* New York: Viking, 1933.

———. *Black Manhattan.* New York: Knopf, 1930.

Johnson, J. Rosamund. *Rolling Along in Song.* New York: Viking, 1934.

Jones, LeRoi. *Blues People: Negro Music in White America.* New York: Morrow, 1963.

Journal of Country Music. 1970–.

Journal of Jazz Studies. 1974–.

Jowett, Garth. *Film, the Democratic Art: A Social History of the American Film.* Boston: Little, Brown, 1976.

Kane, Henry. *How to Write a Song.* New York: Macmillan, 1962.

Karlin, Fred. *Edison Diamond Discs 50001-50651, 1912–1929.* Santa Monica, CA: Bona Fide, 1972.

Kaufmann, Helen L. *From Jehovah to Jazz: Music in America from Psalmody to the Present Day.* New York: Dodd, Mead, 1937.

Kaye, Sydney M. "A Blue-print for Broadcast Music, Inc." Prepared for the National Association of Broadcasters, September 8, 1939. Typescript.

Keil, Charles. *Urban Blues.* Chicago: University of Chicago Press, 1966.

Kenny, Nick. *How to Write, Sing and Sell Popular Songs.* New York: Hermitage Press, 1946.

Kimball, Robert, and William Bolcom. *Reminiscing with Sissle and Blake.* New York: Viking, 1973.

Kirschner, Roger. *The Music Machine.* Los Angeles: Nash Publications, 1971.

Kislan, Richard. *The Musical: A Look at the American Musical Theatre.* Englewood Cliffs, NJ: Prentice-Hall, 1980.

Knight, Arthur. *The Liveliest Art: A Panoramic History of the Movies.* New York: Macmillan, 1957.

Koenigsberg, Allan. *Edison Cylinder Records 1899–1912, with an Illustrated History of the Phonograph.* New York: Stellar Productions, 1969.

Kolodin, Irving. *The Musical Life*. New York: Knopf, 1958.

Krivine, John. *Jukebox Saturday Night*. Secaucus, NJ: Chartwell Books, 1977.

Krueger, Miles. *Showboat: The Story of a Classic American Musical*. New York: Oxford University Press, 1977.

Krummel, Donald W. "Counting Every Star, or Historical Statistics on Music Publishing in the United States." In *Interamerican Musical Research Yearbook 1974*.

Laing, Dave, ed. *The Electric Muse: The Story of Folk into Rock*. London: Methuen, 1975.

Lamb, Andrew. *Jerome Kern in Edwardian England*. Brooklyn: Institute for Studies in American Music, 1985.

Lambert, Dennis, with Ronald Zalkind. *Producing Hit Records*. New York: Schirmer, 1980.

Landau, Jon. *It's Too Late Now: A Rock 'n' Roll Journal*. San Francisco: Rolling Stone Books, 1972.

Landry, Robert J. *This Fascinating Radio Business*. Indianapolis: Bobbs-Merrill, 1956.

Lane, Burton. "Memorandum to House Special Subcommittee on Legislative Oversight Regarding Commercial Influences on the Selection and Promotion of Music for Radio and Television." October 29, 1959.

Lang, Paul Henry. *Music in Western Civilization*. New York: Norton, 1941.

Lang, Paul Henry, ed. *One Hundred Years of Music in America: A Centennial Publication on the Anniversary of G. Schirmer & Co.* New York: Grosset & Dunlap, 1960.

La Prade, Ernest. *Broadcasting Music*. New York: Stewart 1942.

Larkin, Rochelle. *Soul Music*. New York: Lancer Books, 1970.

Larrabee, Eric, and Rolf Meyersohn, eds. *Mass Leisure*. Glencoe, IL: Free Press, 1958.

Laurie, Joe, Jr. *Vaudeville, from the Honky Tonks to the Palace*. New York: Henry Holt, 1953.

Lawless, Ray M. *Folksingers and Folksongs in America: A Handbook of Biography, Bibliography and Discography*. New York: Duell, Sloan & Pearce, 1965.

Lazarsfeld, Paul F., and Frank N. Stanton, eds. *Radio Research 1941*. New York: Duell, Sloan and Pearce, 1941.

———. *Radio Research 1942–43*. New York: Duell, Sloan and Pearce, 1944.

Ledbitter, Mike. *Delta Country Blues*. Bexhill-on-Sea: Blues Unlimited, 1969.

———. *From the Bayou: The Story of Goldband Records*. Bexhill-on-Sea: Blues Unlimited, 1969.

Ledbitter, Mike, ed. *Nothing but the Blues*. London: Hanover Books, 1971.

Lederman, Minna. *The Life and Death of a Small Magazine*. Brooklyn: Institute for Studies in American Music, 1983.

Lee, Edward. *Music of the People: A Study of Popular Music in Great Britain*. London: Barrie & Jenkins, 1970.

Leiter, Robert D. *The Musicians and Petrillo*. New York: Bookman Associates, 1953.

Levine, Faye. *The Culture Barons: An Analysis of Power and Money in the Arts.* New York: Crowell, 1976.

Levine, Lawrence W. *Black Culture and Black Consciousness: Afro-American Folk Thought from Slavery to Freedom.* New York: Oxford University Press, 1977.

Levy, Lester M. *Give Me Yesterday: American History in Music 1890–1920.* Norman: University of Oklahoma Press, 1975.

———. *Grace Notes in American History: Popular Sheet Music 1820–1900.* Norman: University of Oklahoma Press, 1967.

Lichter, Paul. *Elvis in Hollywood.* New York: Simon & Schuster, 1975.

Limbacher, James L., ed: *Film Music: From Violins to Video.* Metuchen, NJ: Scarecrow Press, 1974.

Lomax, Alan. *Mister Jelly Roll.* New York: Duell, Sloan and Pearce 1950.

Lomax, John A. *Adventures of a Ballad Hunter.* New York: Macmillan, 1947.

Lombardo, Guy. *Auld Acquaintance.* Garden City, NY: Doubleday, 1976.

London, Kurt. *Film Music: A Summary of the Characteristics of Its History.* London: Faber & Faber, 1936.

Longley, Marjorie, Louis Silverstein, and Samuel A. Tower. *America's Taste 1851–1959: The Cultural Events of a Century Reported by Contemporary Observers in the Pages of the New York Times.* New York: Simon & Schuster, 1960.

Lopez, Vincent. *Lopez Speaking: My Life and How I Changed It.* Secaucus, NJ: Citadel Press, 1960.

Lowenthal, Daniel K. *Trends in the Licensing of Popular Song Hits 1940–1953.* New York: Bureau of Applied Social Research, Columbia University, 1953.

Luening, Otto. *The Odyssey of an American Composer.* New York: Scribner, 1980.

Lujack, Larry. *Super Jock: The Loud, Frantic, Nonstop World of a Radio DJ.* Chicago: Regnery, 1975.

Lydon, Michael. *Rock File: Portraits from the Rock 'n' Roll Musical Pantheon.* New York: Delta Books, Dell, 1973.

Lydon, Michael, and Ellen Mandel. *Boogie Lightning: How Music Becomes Electric.* New York: Dial, 1974.

Lyons, Eugene. *David Sarnoff: A Biography.* New York: Harper, 1966.

McCabe, John. *George M. Cohan, the Man Who Owned Broadway.* Garden City, NY: Doubleday, 1973.

McCabe, Peter, and Robert D. Schonfeld. *Apple to the Core: The Unmaking of the Beatles.* New York: Pocket Books, 1972.

McCarthy, Albert. *The Dance Band Era: The Dancing Decades from Ragtime to Swing.* London: Spring Books, 1974.

McCarthy, Albert, with Max Harrison. *Jazz on Record 1917–1967.* New York: Oak Publications, 1968.

McCarthy, Clifford, ed. *Film Composers in America: A Checklist of Their Work.* New York: Da Capo Press, 1972.

McCarthy, Todd, and Peter Flynn, eds. *Kings of the Bs: Working Within the Hollywood System: An Anthology of Film History and Criticism.* New York: Dutton, 1975.

MacDougald, Duncan, Jr. "The Popular Music Industry." In Lazarsfeld Paul F., and Frank N. Stanton, eds. *Radio Research 1941.* New York: Duell, Sloan & Pearce, 1941.

MacFarland, David Thomas. "The Development of the Top 40 Radio Format." 2 vols. Diss. University of Wisconsin, 1972.

MacKay, David R. "The National Association of Broadcasters: Its First 20 Years." Diss. Northwestern University, 1956.

MacLaughlin, M. C. "The Social World of American Popular Songs." Thesis. Cornell University, 1968.

McLean, Albert, F., Jr. *American Vaudeville as Ritual.* Lexington: University Press of Kentucky, 1965.

Malone, Bill C. *Country Music USA: A Fifty-Year History.* Austin: University of Texas Press, 1968.

————. Liner notes for the Smithsonian Collection of Classic Country Music. Washington, D.C.: Smithsonian Institution P8 #16450. 1983.

————. *Southern Music: American Music.* Lexington: University Press of Kentucky, 1979.

Malone, Bill C., with Judith McCulloh, eds: *The Stars of Country Music: Uncle Dave Macon to Johnny Rodriguez.* New York: Avon Books, 1976.

Manchester, William. *The Glory and the Dream: A Narrative History of America 1932–1972.* Boston: Little, Brown, 1972.

Mann, May. *Elvis and the Colonel.* New York: Pocket Books, 1976.

Marcus, Greil. *Mystery Train: Images of America in Rock 'n' Roll Music.* New York: Dutton, 1976.

————. *Stranded: Rock and Roll for a Desert Island.* New York: Knopf, 1979.

Marks, J. *Rock and Other Four-Letter Words.* New York: Bantam, 1968.

Marston, William Moulton, and John Henry Fuller. *F. F. Proctor: Vaudeville Pioneer.* New York: Richard A. Smith, 1943.

Marx, Samuel, and Jan Clayton. *Rodgers & Hart: A Dual Biography.* New York: Putnam, 1976.

Matlaw, Myron, ed. *American Popular Entertainment: Papers and Proceedings of the Conference on the History of American Popular Entertainment.* Westport, CT: Greenwood Press, 1979.

Mattfield, Julius. *Variety Music Cavalcade: A Musical-Historical Review 1620–1969.* 3rd ed. Englewood Cliffs, NJ: Prentice-Hall, 1971.

Mellers, Wilfrid. *Music in a New Found Land: Themes and Developments in the History of American Music.* London: Barrie & Rocklif, 1964.

Melly, George. *Revolt Into Style: The Pop Arts.* New York: Anchor Books, Doubleday, 1971.

Metronome. 1871–1956.

Meyer, Hazel. *The Gold in Tin Pan Alley.* Philadelphia: Lippincott, 1958.

Michel, Trudi. *Inside Tin Pan Alley.* New York: Frederick Fell, 1948.

Middleton, Richard. *Pop Music and the Blues: A Study of the Relationship and Its Significance.* London: Gollancz, 1972.

Millar, Bill. *The Drifters.* New York: Collier Books, 1971.

Miller, Jim, ed. *The Rolling Stone Illustrated History of Rock 'n' Roll.* New York: Rolling Stone Press/Random House, 1976.

Miller, Manfred, Klaus Kuhnke, and Peter Schulze. *Geschichte der Pop-Musik Band 1 (Bis 1947).* Bremen: Archiv für Populär Musik, 1976.

Mitchell, Loften. *Black Drama: The Story of the American Negro in the Theatre.* New York: Hawthorn Books, 1967.

Moogk, Edward B. *Roll Back the Years: A History of Canadian Recorded Sound and Its Legacy, Genesis to 1930.* Ottawa: National Library of Canada, 1975.

Moore, Grave. *You're Only Human Once.* New York: Doubleday, Doran, 1944.

Moore, Jerrold Northrup. *A Matter of Records: Fred Gaisberg and the Golden Era of the Gramophone.* New York: Taplinger, 1977.

Mordden, Ethan. *Better Foot Forward: The History of the American Musical Theatre.* New York: Grossman, 1976.

Morgenstern, Dan. Liner notes for "Souvenirs of Hot Chocolates." Smithsonian LP 14587.

Morris, Lloyd. *Not So Long Ago.* New York: Random House, 1949.

————. *Postscript to Yesterday.* New York: Random House, 1947.

Morse, Dave. *Motown and the Arrival of Black Music.* New York: Collier Books, 1972.

Mueller, John H. *The American Symphony Orchestra.* Bloomington: Indiana University Press, 1951.

Murray, Albert. *Stomping the Blues.* New York: McGraw-Hill, 1976.

Myrus, Donald. *Ballads, Blues and the Big Beat: Highlights of American Folk Singing from Leadbelly to Dylan.* New York: Macmillan, 1966.

Nanry, Charles, ed. *American Music: From Storyville to Woodstock.* New Brunswick, NJ: Transaction Books, 1972.

Nash, Roderick. *The Call of the Wild 1900–1916.* New York: Braziller, 1970.

National Association of Broadcasters (NAB). *Let's Stick to the Record.* Washington, D.C.: NAB, 1940.

————. *A Music Monopoly Is Reaching for Your Pocketbook.* Washington, D.C.: NAB, 1940.

————. *NAB Reports.* Washington, D.C.: NAB, 1933–.

————. *Portrait of a Protector.* Washington, D.C.: NAB, 1940.

National Music Publishers' Association Bulletin. 1970–.

Neale, A. D. *The Antitrust Laws of the United States of America: A Study of Competition Enforced by Law.* New York: Cambridge University Press, 1970.

Nelson, Ozzie. *Ozzie.* Englewood Cliffs, NJ: Prentice-Hall, 1973.

Nite, Norm K. *Rock On: The Illustrated Encyclopedia of Rock 'n' Roll.* New York: Crowell, 1974.

Noebel, David A. *Rhythm, Riots and Revolution.* Tulsa, OK: Christian Crusade Publications, 1966.

Oakley, Giles. *The Devil's Music: A History of the Blues.* New York: Harcourt Brace Jovanovich, 1978.

O'Connor, Eileen V. "Anti-ASCAP Legislation and Its Judicial Interpretation." *George Washington Law Review,* April 1941.

Offen, Carol. *Country Music: The Poetry.* New York: Ballantine, 1977.

Oliver, Paul. *Aspects of the Blues Tradition: A Fascinating Story of the Richest Vein of Black Music in America.* New York: Oak Publications, 1969.

————. *Blues Fell This Morning.* London: Cassell, 1960.

————. *Conversation with the Blues.* New York: Horizon Books, 1965.

————. *Savannah Syncopaters: African Retentions of the Blues*. London: Studio Books, 1970.

————. *Songsters and Saints: Vocal Tradition on Race Records*. New York: Cambridge University Press, 1984.

————. *The Story of the Blues*. New York: Chilton, 1969.

Olsson, Bengt. *Memphis Blues*. London: Studio Books, 1970.

Ord-Hume, Arthur W. J. G. *Player-Piano: The History of the Mechanical Piano*. New York: A. S. Barnes, 1970.

Ottley, Roi, and William J. Weatherby, eds. *The Negro in New York: An Informal Social History*. New York: New York Public Library, 1967.

Palmer, Robert. *Baby, That Was Rock & Roll: The Legendary Leiber & Stoller*. New York: Harcourt Brace Jovanovich, 1978.

————. *Deep Blues*. New York: Viking, 1981.

————. *The Rolling Stones*. New York: Rolling Stone Press, 1983.

Palmer, Tony. *All You Need Is Love: The Story of Popular Music*. New York: Grossman/Viking, 1976.

Parker, John W. "American Popular Music: An Emerging Field of Academic Study." Diss. University of Kentucky, 1962.

Passman, Arnold. *The Dee Jays*. New York: Macmillan, 1971.

Peacock, Alan, and Ronald Weir. *The Composer in the Market Place*. London: Faber & Faber, 1975.

Pearsall, Ronald. *Popular Music of the 20s*. London: David & Charles, 1976.

Peatman, John Gray. "Radio and Popular Music." In Lazarsfeld, Paul F., and Frank N. Stanton. *Radio Research 1942–43*. New York: Duell, Sloan and Pearce, 1944.

Perry, Dick. *Not Just a Sound: The Story of WLW*. Englewood Cliffs, NJ: Prentice-Hall, 1971.

Peterson, Lyman Ray. *Copyright in Historical Perspective*. Nashville: Vanderbilt University Press, 1968.

Peterson, Richard A. "Single-Industry Firm to Conglomerate Synergistics: Alternative Strategies for Selling Insurance and Country Music." In Blumstein, James, and Benjamin Walter, eds. *Growing Metropolis: Aspects of Development in Nashville*. Nashville: Vanderbilt University Press, 1975.

Pleasants, Henry. *The Great American Popular Singers*. New York: Simon & Schuster, 1974.

————. *Serious Music and All That Jazz*. New York: Simon & Schuster 1969.

Pollack, Bruce. *In Their Own Words: Twenty Successful Songwriters Tell How They Write Their Songs*. New York: Collier Books, 1975.

Popular Music and Society. 1972–.

Porterfield, Nolan. *Jimmie Rodgers: The Life and Times of America's Blue Yodeler*. Urbana: University of Illinois Press, 1979.

Pratt, George C. *Spellbound in Darkness: A History of the Silent Film*. Greenwich, CT: New York Graphic Society, 1973.

Progriss, Jim. *The Language of Commercial Music*. New York: Hansen Books, 1976.

Radio Daily. 1936–1965.

Ramsaye, Terry. *A Million and One Nights: A History of the Motion Pictures Through 1925*. New York: Simon & Schuster, 1964.

Randle, William McK., Jr. "History of Radio Broadcasting and Its Social and Economic Effect on the Entertainment Industry. 3 vols. Diss. Western Reserve University, 1961.

Record Industry Association of America (RIAA). *Consumer Purchasing of Records and Prerecorded Tapes in the United States: A Three-Year Report 1979, 1980, 1981*. New York: RIAA, 1983.

———. *Issues Related to Market Expansion in the Recording Industry*. New York: RIAA, 1977.

———. *A Report to the Members of the RIAA*. New York: RIAA, 1953.

Record World. 1964–1982.

The Recorded Music Industry USA. New York: Frost & Sullivan, 1973.

Redd, Lawrence N. *Rock Is Rhythm and Blues*. East Lansing: Michigan State University Press, 1974.

Reed, Oliver, and Walter L. Welch. *From Tinfoil to Stereo: The Evolution of the Phonograph*. New York: Howard Sams/Bobbs-Merrill, 1959.

Ringer, Barbara. "Copyright in the 1980's." Sixth Annual Donald C. Brace Memorial Lecture. Washington, D.C.: 1976. Mimeo.

———. "Two Hundred Years of Copyright in America." Speech to Patent, Trademark, and Copyright Section of American Bar Association, August 10, 1976.

Roach, Hildred. *Black American Music*. Boston: Crescendo, 1973.

Roberts, John Storm. *Black Music of Two Worlds*. New York: Morrow, 1972.

———. *The Latin Tinge: The Impact of Latin American Music on the United States*. New York: Oxford University Press, 1979.

Rodgers, Mrs. Jimmie. *My Husband Jimmie Rodgers*. Nashville: Country Music Foundation Press, 1975. Reprint.

Rodgers, Richard. *Musical Stages: An Autobiography*. New York: Random House, 1975.

Rodnitzky, Jerome L. *Minstrels of the Dawn: The Folk-Protest Singer as a Cultural Hero*. Chicago: Nelson-Hall, 1976.

Roehl, Harvey. *Player Piano Treasury: The Scrapbook History of the Mechanical Piano in America*. Vestal, NY: Vestal Press, 1973.

Roffman, Frederick S. Liner notes for "Naughty Marietta." Smithsonian Collection, N 026, 1981.

Rogers, Eddy, as told to Mike Hennessey. *Tin Pan Alley*. London: Robert Hale, 1964.

Rolantz, Bob. *How to Get Your Song Recorded*. New York: Watson-Guptill, 1963.

Rolling Stone. *The Rolling Stone Interviews, Vol 1*. New York: Warner Paperback Library, 1971.

———. *The Rolling Stone Interviews, Vol 2*. New York: Warner Paperback Library, 1973.

———. *The Rolling Stone Library*. New York: Warner Paperbacks, 1974.

Romberg, Sigmund. " 'ASCAP', a Free and Open Discussion of Some of Its Difficulties, Together with a Few Remedies." *The Song Writers' Quarterly Bulletin*, April 1934.

Rosenberg, Bernard, and David Manning White, eds. *Mass Culture: The Popular Arts in America*. Glencoe, IL: Free Press, 1957.

Ross, Ted. *The Art of Music Engraving and Processing*. Miami: Hansen Books, 1970.

Roth, Ernst. *The Business of Music: Reflections of a Music Publisher*. London: Cassell, 1969.

Routt, Edd, James B. McGrath, and Frederic A. Weiss. *The Radio Format Conundrum*. New York: Hastings House, 1978.

Rowe, Mike. *Chicago Breakdown*. London: Eddison Press, 1973.

Roxon, Lillian. *Rock Encyclopedia*. New York: Grosset & Dunlap, 1969.

Russell, Ross. *Jazz Style in Kansas City and the Southwest*. Berkeley: University of California Press, 1971.

Russell, Tony. *Blacks, Whites and Blues*. London: Studio, 1970.

Rust, Brian. *The American Record Label Book: From the Nineteenth Century through 1942*. New Rochelle: Arlington House, 1979.

———. *Gramophone Records of the First World War*. North Pomfret, VT: David & Charles, 1975.

———. *The Victor Master Book*. Vol. 2. Highland Park, IL: Walter C. Allen, 1965.

Sampson, Henry T. *Blacks in Blackface: A Source Book on Early Black Musical Shows*. Metuchen, NJ: Scarecrow Press, 1980.

Sanjek, Russell. *From Print to Plastic: Publishing and Promoting America's Popular Music, 1900–1980*. Brooklyn: Institute for Studies in American Music, 1983.

———. "The War on Rock." *Downbeat Music '72*. Chicago: Maher Publications, 1972.

Sarlin, Robert. *Turn It Up (I Can't Hear the Words)*. New York: Simon & Schuster, 1973.

Schicke, C. A. *Revolution in Sound: A Biography of the Recording Industry*. Boston: Little, Brown, 1974.

Schoener, Allon, ed. *Harlem on My Mind: Cultural Capitol of Black America 1900–1968*. New York: Random House, 1969.

Schuller, Gunther. *Early Jazz: Its Roots and Musical Development*. New York: Oxford University Press, 1968.

Seeger, Pete. *The Incomplete Folksinger*. New York: Simon & Schuster, 1972.

Seldes, Gilbert. *The Public Arts*. New York: Simon & Schuster, 1956.

———. *The Seven Lively Arts*. New York: Sagamore, 1957.

Shapiro, Nat, and Nat Hentoff. *Hear Me Talkin' to Ya*. New York: Rinehart, 1955.

———. *The Jazz Makers*. New York: Rinehart, 1957.

Shapiro, Nat, comp. *Popular Music: An Annotated Index of American Popular Songs, 1920–1969*. 6 vols. New York: Adrian Press, 1973.

Shaw, Arnold. *52nd Street: The Street That Never Slept*. New York: Coward, McCann, 1971.

———. *Honkers and Shouters: The Golden Years of Rhythm and Blues*. New York: Macmillan, 1978.

———. *The Lingo of Tin Pan Alley*. New York: Broadcast Music, Inc., 1960.

————. *The Rockin' 50s*. New York: Hawthorn Books, 1974.

————. *The Rock Revolution: What's Happening in Today's Music*. New York: Crowell-Collier, 1969.

————. *The World of Soul: Black America's Contribution to the Pop Music Scene*. New York: Cowles, 1970.

Shaw, Greg. *The Rolling Stone Illustrated History of Rock & Roll*. New York: Rolling Stone Press and Random House, 1976.

Shemel, Sidney, and M. William Krasilovsky. *More About This Business of Music*. New York: Billboard Publications, 1978.

————. *This Business of Music*. New York: Billboard Publications, 1964, 1971, 1977, 1979.

Short, Bobby. *Black and White Baby*. New York: Dodd, Mead, 1971.

Silver, Abner, and Robert Bruce. *How to Write and Sell a Hit Song*. Englewood Cliffs, NJ: Prentice-Hall, 1939.

Simon, George. *Simon Says: The Sights and Sounds of the Swing Era*. New Rochelle, NY: Arlington House, 1955.

————. *The Big Bands*. New York: Collier Books, 1974.

————. *The Best of the Music Makers: From Acuff to Ellington to Presley to Sinatra to Zappa & 279 of the Most Popular Performers of the Last 50 Years*. New York: Doubleday, 1979.

Simpson, George Eaton. *Black Religion in the New World*. New York: Columbia University Press, 1978.

Sklar, Rick. *Rocking America: How the All-hit Radio Stations Took Over*. New York: St. Martin's Press, 1984.

Sklar, Robert. *The Plastic Age 1917–1930*. New York: Braziller, 1970.

Slate, Sam J., and Joe Cook. *It Sounds Impossible*. New York: Macmillan, 1963.

Smith, Cecil. *Musical Comedy in America*. New York: Theatre Arts Books, 1950.

Smith, Kate. *Living in a Great Big Way*. New York: Blue Ribbon Books, 1938.

Smith, Willie the Lion, and George Hoefer, *Music on My Mind*. New York: Doubleday, 1964.

Smith-Baxter, Derrick. *Ma Rainey and the Classic Blues Singers*. London: Studio Books, 1970.

Sobel, Bernard. *Pictorial History of Vaudeville*. New York: Citadel Press, 1961.

Somma, Robert, ed. *Nobody Waved Goodbye: A Casualty Report on Rock and Roll*. New York: Outerbridge & Dienstfrey, 1971.

Song Writers' Protective Association, *Song Writers' Protective Association Prospectus*. New York: SPA, 1947.

————. *The SPA Quarterly Bulletin*. 1933–

————. *What Every Songwriter Should Know*. New York: The Songwriters' Protective Association, c. 1952.

Southern, Eileen, ed. *The Music of Black Americans*. New York: Norton, 1971. *Readings in Black American Music*, New York: Norton 1971.

Spaeth, Sigmund. *The Facts of Life in Popular Music*. New York: Whittlesey House, 1934.

————. *Fifty Years With Music*. New York: Fleet, 1959.

————. *A History of Popular Music in America*. New York: Random House, 1943.

Speck, Samuel H. *The Song Writers' Guide: A Treatise on How Popular Songs Are Written and Made Popular.* Detroit: Remick Music, 1910.

Spiegel, Irwin O., and Jay L. Cooper. *Record and Music Publishing Forms of Agreement in Current Use.* New York: Law-Arts Books, 1971.

Spitz, Robert Stephen. *The Making of Superstars: Artists and Executives of the Rock Music World.* New York: Doubleday, 1978.

Stagg, Jerry. *The Brothers Shubert.* New York: Ballantine, 1969.

Stearns, Marshall and Jean: *Jazz Dance: The Story of American Vernacular Dance.* New York: Macmillan, 1969.

Steiner, Max. *The Real Tinsel.* New York: Macmillan, 1970.

Stokes, Geoffrey. *Starmaking Machinery: Inside the Business of Rock and Roll.* New York: Vintage, Random House, 1972.

Sublette, Richard H. "A History of the American Society of Composers, Authors and Publishers' Relationship with the Broadcasters," Thesis. University of Illinois, 1962.

Suchman, Edward A. "An Invitation to Music: A Study of the Creation of New Music Listeners by Radio." In Lazarsfeld, Paul F. and Frank N. Stanton, *Radio Research 1941.* New York: Duell, Sloan and Pearce, 1941.

Sullivan, Mark. *Our Times.* Vol. 1: *The Turn of the Century;* Vol. 2: *America Finding Herself;* Vol. 3: *Pre-War America.* New York: Scribner, 1926, 1927, 1930.

Summers, Harrison B., ed. *A Thirty-Year History of Programs Carried on National Radio Networks in the United States 1926–1956.* New York: Arno Press, 1971.

Szwed, John. "Negro Music: Urban Renewal." In *Our Living Traditions,* edited by Tristram P. Coffin. New York: Basic Books, 1968.

The Talking Machine Journal. 1917–1956.

Tannenbaum, Frank. *Slave and Citizen: The Negro in America.* New York: Knopf, 1947.

Tanner, Louise. *All the Things We Were.* New York: Doubleday, 1968.

Taylor, John Russell. *The Hollywood Musical.* New York: McGraw-Hill, 1971.

Taylor, Theodore. *Jule: The Story of Composer Jule Styne.* New York: Random House, 1979.

Thomas, Bob. *King Cohn: The Life and Times of Harry Cohn.* New York: Putnam, 1967.

Thompson, Charles. *Bing: The Authorized Biography.* New York: David McKay, 1976.

Thorson, Theodore Winton. "A History of Music Publishing in Chicago." Diss. Northwestern University, 1961.

Thrasher, Fredric. *Okay for Sound: How the Screen Found Its Voice.* New York: Duell, Sloan and Pearce, 1946.

Tiomkin, Dimitri, and Prosper Buranelli. *Don't Hate Me: An Autobiography.* New York: Doubleday, 1959.

Titon, Jeff Dodd. *Early Downhome Blues: A Musical and Cultural Analysis.* Urbana: University of Illinois Press, 1977.

Toffler, Alvin. *The Culture Consumers: A Controversial Study in Culture and Affluence in America.* New York: St. Martin's Press, 1964.

Toll, Robert. *On with the Show! The First Century of Show Business in America.* New York: Oxford University Press, 1976.

Tosches, Nick. *Country: The Biggest Music in America.* New York: Stein & Day, 1977.

A Tour of the World's Record Markets 1967. London: EMI, 1967.

Townsend, Charles R. *San Antonio Rose: The Life and Music of Bob Wills.* Urbana: University of Illinois Press, 1976.

Traubner, Richard. *Operetta: A Theatrical History.* New York: Doubleday, 1983.

Tremlett, George. *The Osmond Story.* New York: Warner Books, 1975.

———. *The Rolling Stones.* New York: Warner Books, 1975.

———. *The Who.* New York: Warner Books, 1975.

Tucker, Sophie. *Some of These Days.* Garden City, NY: Doubleday, 1945.

Tuska, Jon. *The Filming of the West.* New York: Doubleday, 1976.

Vallee, Rudy. *Let the Chips Fall. . . .* New York: Stackpole Books, 1976.

Vallee, Rudy, and Gil McKean. *My Time Is Your Time.* New York: Oblensky, 1962.

Vance, Joel. *Fats, Waller, His Life and Times.* Chicago: Contemporary Books, 1977.

Variety. 1905–.

Vassal, Jacques. *Electric Children.* New York: Taplinger, 1976.

Villiers, Douglas. "Jewish Influences in 20th Century Pop Music and Entertainment." In *Jerusalem: Portraits of the Jew in the Twentieth Century.* New York: Viking, 1976.

Wakeman, Frederic. *The Hucksters.* New York: Rinehart, 1946.

Walker, Leo. *The Wonderful World of the Great Dance Bands.* New York: Doubleday, 1972.

Walker, Stanley. *The Night Club Era.* New York: Frederick Stokes, 1933.

Waller, Maurice, and Anthony Calabrese. *Fats Waller.* New York: Schirmer, 1978.

Walley, David. *No Commercial Potential: The Saga of Frank Zappa.* New York: Outerbridge & Lazard, 1972.

Warner Communications, Inc. *Annual Report.* 1974, 1975.

———. *The Prerecorded Music Market: An Industry Survey.* New York: WCI, 1978.

Waters, Edward N. *Victor Herbert: A Life in Music.* New York: Macmillan, 1955.

Waters, Ethel, with Charles Samuels. *His Eye Is on the Sparrow.* New York: Doubleday, 1951.

Weinberg, Meyer. *TV in America: The Morality of Hard Cash.* New York: Ballantine, 1962.

Westin, Helen. *Introducing the Song Sheet: A Collector's Guide to Song Sheets.* Nashville: Thomas Nelson, 1976.

Whalen, Richard J. *The Founding Father: The Story of Joseph P. Kennedy.* New York: New American Library, 1964.

Whitcomb, Ian. *After the Ball.* London: Lane/Penguin, 1972.

———. *Rock Odyssey: A Musician's Chronicle of the 60s.* Garden City, NY: Dolphin Books, Doubleday, 1983.

———. *Tin Pan Alley 1919–1939: A Pictorial History.* New York: Two Continents, 1975.

White, Llewellyn. *The American Radio: A Report on the Broadcasting Industry in the United States from the Commission on Freedom of the Press.* Chicago: University of Chicago Press, 1947.

Whiteman, Paul. *Records for the Millions.* New York: Hermitage, 1948.

Whiteman, Paul, and Mary Margaret McBride. *Jazz.* New York: J. H. Sears, 1926.

Whittinghill, Dick, and Don Page. *Did You Whittinghill This Morning.* Chicago: Regnery, 1976.

Wickes, E. M. *Writing the Popular Song.* Springfield, MA: The Home Correspondence School, 1916.

Wilder, Alec. *American Popular Song: The Great Innovators, 1900–1950.* Edited by James T. Maher. New York: Oxford University Press, 1972.

Wilk, Max. *Memory Lane, 1890–1925: The Golden Age in American Popular Music.* New York: Ballantine, 1973.

———. *They're Playing Our Song: From Jerome Kern to Stephen Sondheim.* New York: Atheneum, 1973.

Williams, Hank. *Hank Williams Tells How to Write Folk and Western Music to Sell.* Nashville, 1951.

Williams, Hank, Jr., with Michael Bane. *Living Proof: An Autobiography.* New York: Putnam, 1979.

Williams, Richard. *Out of His Head: The Sound of Phil Spector.* New York: Outerbridge & Lazard, 1972.

Winkler, Max. *A Penny from Heaven: The Autobiography of a Man Who Entered the World of Music Through the Basement and Came Out as One of the World's Greatest Music Publishers.* New York: Appleton-Century, 1951.

Witmark, Isidore, with Isidore Goldberg. *From Ragtime to Swingtime: The House of Witmark.* New York: Furman, 1939.

Woolcott, Alec. *The Story of Irving Berlin.* New York: Putnam, 1925.

Yorke, Ritchie. *The History of Rock 'n' Roll.* Toronto: Methuen/Two Continents, 1976.

———. *The Led Zeppelin.* Toronto: Methuen, 1976.

Zeidman, Irving. *The American Burlesque Show: A History.* New York: Hawthorn Books, 1967.

Congressional Hearings on the Music Business

To Provide for Recordings in Coin-Operated Machines at a Fixed Royalty Rate. Hearing before Subcommittee No. 3 of the Committee on the Judiciary, House of Representatives, Eighty-second Congress, First Session, on H.R. 5473. Serial No. 11. Washington: GPO, 1951.

Rendition of Musical Compositions on Coin-Operated Machines. Hearings, Before a Subcommittee of the Committee on the Judiciary, United States Senate, Eighty-third Congress, First Session, on S. 1106. Washington: GPO, 1954.

[The Cellar Hearings] *Monopoly Problems in Regulated Industries. Hearings before the Antitrust Subcommittee (Subcommittee No. 5) of the Committee on the Judiciary, House of Representatives, Eighty-fourth Congress, Second Session. Serial No. 22.* Washington: GPO, 1957.

Report of the Antitrust Subcommittee (Subcommittee No. 5) of the Committee on the Judiciary, House of Representatives, Eighty-fourth Congress, First Session, Pursuant to H. Res. 107 Authorizing the Committee on the Judiciary to Conduct Studies and Investigations Relating to Certain Matters within Its Jurisdiction on the Television Broadcasting Industry. Washington: GPO, 1957.

[The Smathers Bill] *Amendment to Communications Act of 1934 (Prohibiting Radio and Television Stations from Engaging in Music Publishing or Recording Business). Hearings before the Subcommittee on Communications of the Committee on Interstate and Foreign Commerce, United States Senate, Eighty-fifth Congress, Second Session, on S. 2834.* Washington: GPO, 1958.

[The Roosevelt Hearings] *Policies of American Society of Composers, Authors, and Publishers. Hearings before Subcommittee No. 5 of the Select Committee on Small Business, House of Representatives, Eighty-fifth Congress, Second Session, Pursuant to H. Res. 56.* Washington: GPO, 1958.

[The Payola Hearings] *Deceptive Practices in Radio and Television. Hearings before the Select Subcommittee on Legislative Oversight of the Committee on Interstate and Foreign Commerce, House of Representatives, Eighty-sixth Congress, Second Session.* Washington: GPO, 1960.

Copyright Law Revision. Studies Prepared for the Subcommittee on the Judiciary, United States Senate, Eighty-sixth Congress, Second Session, Pursuant to S. Res. 240. Studies 26–28. Washington: GPO, 1961.

Copyright Law Revision. Hearings Before the Subcommittee on Patents, Trademarks, and Copyrights of the Committee on the Judiciary, United States Senate, Ninetieth Congress, First Session, Pursuant to S. Res. 37 on S. 597. Washington: GPO, 1967.

Copyright Law Revision. Senate Report No. 94-473. 94th Congress, 1st Session. Calendar No. 460. 1975.

Copyright Law Revision. Hearings before the Subcommittee on Courts, Civil Liberties, and the Administration of Justice of the Committee on the Judiciary, House of Representatives, Ninety-fourth Congress, First Session, on H.R. 2223. Serial No. 36. Part 1, Part 2, Part 3. Washington: GPO, 1976.

Periodicals, with Pertinent Articles

Advertising Age.
   Robertson, Bruce. "Broadcast Changes Face of Advertising, Selling." April 30, 1980.

American Mercury.
   "Fortunes Made in Popular Songs." Oct. 1916.
   "Putting Over Popular Songs." April 1917.
   "Paul Whiteman Made Jazz Contagious." Jan. 1924.
   "Report on the Musical Industry." March 1938.
   Yark, Dane. "The Rise and Fall of the Phonograph." Sept. 1932.

American Musician.
   "Irving Berlin Gives Nine Rules for Writing Popular Music." Oct. 1920.

American Opinion.
Allen, Gary. "That Music: There's More To It Than Meets the Ear." Feb. 1969.

Atlantic Monthly.
"Industry of Music Making." Jan. 1908.
Larner, Jeremy. "What Do They Get from Rock 'n' Roll?" Aug. 1964.

Barrons.
Pacey, Margaret. "Home Box Office Inc.: Pay Television Is Finally Making the Scene." May 19, 1975.
Kagan, Paul. "Big Broadcast: Radio and Television Command Handsome Premiums." Jan. 8, 1979.

Billboard.
"ASCAP Fiftieth Anniversary Issue." April 1, 1964.
"Twenty-five Years of Tape: A History of a Powerful Communications Tool." Nov. 11, 1972.
"Music to Move to Discos." Nov. 1, 1975.
"CISAC: 50 Years of Protecting Intellectual Property Rights." Nov. 6, 1976.
"Black Music: A Genealogy of Sound." June 9, 1979.

Business Week.
"Tin Pan Alley Changes Tempo." April 16, 1930.
"Platter War: American Decca Starts Something." Nov. 10, 1934.
"Tempest in a Tune-Pot: Warner's Withdrawal from ASCAP Music Pool." Jan. 11, 1936.
"Platter Programs: Warner-ASCAP Dispute Involves Recordings for Radio." Feb. 8, 1936.
"Discord of the Air: National Association of Broadcasters Meets, but Doesn't Solve Copyright Problems." Oct. 18, 1936.
"Radio Raises Music War-Chest." Sept. 23, 1939.
"Battle Over Records." Feb. 24, 1940.
"Radio Out to Bust Music Trust: Drive to Break ASCAP's Current Tune Monopoly." March 9, 1940.
"Radio Music Battle Nears Showdown." July 6, 1940.
"ASCAP Defied." Nov. 16, 1940.
"Department of Justice Calls Tune: Big Radio Music Battle Becomes Trust Case." Jan. 4, 1941.
"ASCAP Deal Lags." May 3, 1941.
"Pax ASCAP: Final Armistice Awards Financial Victory to Radio." Oct. 18, 1941.
"Nine Year Peace." Nov. 8, 1941.
"Records Again? Senate Grilling May Force Petrillo to End Ban." Jan. 23, 1943.
"Score by Petrillo: Concludes Deal with Decca, Inc., for Extra Payments, and Musicians End 13-month Ban on Recordings." Sept. 25, 1943.
"Decca Cashes In: Meeting Petrillo's Terms Paid Dividends." March 11, 1944.

"Victory for ASCAP: Writer's Status Determines Whether Performing Rights Can Be Transferred." May 12, 1945.

"In the Groove: Sales Hit a Gold Mine." July 21, 1945.

"Petrillo Blows Hot: Disc-Making Ban Motivated by Sharp Decline in Live Jobs." Oct. 25, 1947.

"It's Music, Music, Music." July 22, 1950.

"St. Louis Station Smashes Records to End the Sway of Rock 'n' Roll." Jan. 25, 1958.

"The Record Industry Sounds a Note of Joy." Dec. 1, 1975.

"The Cable-TV Industry Gets Moving Again." Nov. 21, 1977.

"The Race to Dominate the Pay-TV Market." Oct. 2, 1978.

"Striking It Rich in Radio." Feb. 2, 1979.

Channels.

Traub, James. "Video Steps Out." June/July 1982.

Stokes, Geoffrey. "The Sound and Fury of MTV." Sept./Oct. 1982.

The Commonweal.

Hentoff, Nat. "They *Are* Playing Our Song: The Grinding Mediocre Level of Most Popular Music Today Is Due Essentially to What the Teen-agers Do Want." May 4, 1960.

Cue.

Taylor, Tim. "Disc Jockeys Rule the Airwaves." Nov. 5, 1955.

Current Literature.

"Popular Music—A Curse or a Blessing." Sept. 1912.

Current Opinion.

"Voice of the South in American Music." Sept. 1916.

"Black Music: And Its Future Transmutation into Real Art." July 1917.

"Jazz and Ragtime Are the Preludes to a Great American Music." May 1920.

"Public Music in America Today Is Petty Business." Aug. 1921.

"Secrets of Popular Songwriting." Jan. 1925.

The Economist.

"American Gramophone Records: Golden Oldies." Sept. 16, 1978.

Equity.

"The Facts of Vaudeville." Nov. 1923–March 1924.

The Etude.

"Will Ragtime Turn to Symphonic Poems." May 1920.

"What It Means to Put Over a Popular Song." March 1925.

Mills, E. C. "Protect Your Friends from This Monstrous Song Swindle." July 1925.

"Music, the Magic Carpet of Radio." Dec. 1935.

"Battle of Music." March 1941.
"Famous Composers Rally to ASCAP." March 1941.
"Publishing a Popular Song." Sept. 1946.

Forbes.
"$2 Billion Worth of Noise." July 15, 1968.
"Pay-TV: Is It a Viable Alternative?" May 1, 1978.
"The Gorillas Are Coming." July 10, 1978.
"Leisure: With home taping taking a deadly toll on the recorded music industry, retailers might end up switching to video accessories and allow records to bite the dust." Jan. 5, 1981.

Fortune.
"5,000,000 Songs Are the Commercial Heritage of ASCAP." Jan. 1933.
"Phonograph Records: From Fat to Lean and Halfway Back Again." Sept. 1939.
"Music for the Home." Oct. 1946.
"Phonograph Record Boom." Jan. 1950.
"The Money Makers of 'New Radio.' " Feb. 1958.
"Stereo Goes to Market." Aug. 1958.
"The Record Business: It's Murder." May 1961.
"The Motown Sound of Money." Sept. 1967.
"The Record Business: Rocking to the Big Money Beat." April 1979.

Forum.
Clark, Kenneth. "Why Our Popular Songs Don't Last." March 1934.

Harper's Magazine.
"The Gentle Art of Song Writing." Jan. 1910.
"What Petrillo's Up To: The Fight Against Canned Music, and a Possible Solution." Dec. 1942.
Asbell, Bernard. "Disk Jockeys and Baby Sitters." July 1957.
"Upheaval in Popular Music." May 1959.

High Fidelity.
Ackerman, Paul. "What Has Happened to Popular Music." June 1955.
Ramin, Jordan. "How to Launch a Hit Song." Aug. 1974.
Melanson, Jim. "Countdown to Monday: Charting the Top 100." May 1977.
Everett, Todd. "Automated Radio: The Future Is Upon Us." Sept. 1977.
———."The Great American Radio Ratings Rat Race." Nov. 1977.
Mayer, Ira. "Record Distribution: The Big 6 Take Over." Oct. 1979.
Rea, Steven X. "Music and Recordings in 1981: Bottom-Line Blues." Jan. 1982.
Sutherland, Sam. "The Indies Are Coming." Aug. 1982.

John Edwards Memorial Foundation Quarterly.
Green, Archie. "Graphics #39: Vernacular Music Albums." Winter 1981.

Journal of American Culture.
   Slezak, Mary. "The History of Charlton Press, Inc. and Its Song Lyric Publications." Spring 1980.

Journal of American Folklore.
   "The Hillbilly Issue." July/Sept. 1965.
   Green, Archie, "Hillbilly Music: Source and Symbol." July/Sept. 1965.
   Hellmann, John M., Jr. " 'I'm a Monkey': The Influence of Black American Blues Argot on the Rolling Stones." Oct./Dec. 1973.

Journal of Applied Psychology.
   Wiebe, G. D. "A Comparison of Various Ratings Used in Judging the Merits of Popular Songs." Feb. 1939.

Journal of Geography.
   Ford, Larry. "Geographic Factors in the Origin, Evolution and Diffusion of Rock and Roll Music." Nov. 1971.

The Journal of Popular Culture.
   Austin, Mary. "Petrillo's War." Summer 1978.
   Miller, Douglas T. "Popular Religion in the 1950s." IX, 1975.
   Crawford, David. "Gospel Songs in Court: From Rural Music to Urban Industry." Fall 1977.

Journal of the Royal Society of Arts, London.
   Wood, L. G. "The Growth and Development of the Recording Industry." Sept. 1971.

Literary Digest.
   "Ethics of Ragtime." Aug. 10, 1912.
   "To Censor Popular Songs." May 24, 1913.
   "Our $600,000,000 Music Bill." June 28, 1913.
   "Sources of Our Popular Song and Dance." Aug. 30, 1913.
   "How to Tell Good Songs from Bad." Dec. 6, 1913.
   "Canning Negro Melodies." May 27, 1916.
   "Fortune in a Popular Song." July 1, 1916.
   "Birth of Our Popular Songs." Oct. 7, 1916.
   "There's Millions in the Pop of Popular Songs." March 3, 1918.
   "Can Popular Songs Be Stamped Out." Aug. 14, 1920.
   "Organize, Not Sell, Music." June 9, 1928.
   "Radio, Friend or Foe." Nov. 3, 1928.
   "Natural History of a Song." May 3, 1930.
   "Broadcasters and Composers in a Clinch." Aug. 20, 1932.
   "How Music Is Murdered." Aug. 5, 1933.
   "Strident Song Writers Fight Duffy Copyright Bill." March 14, 1936.

Look.
"Great Rock 'n' Roll Controversy." June 26, 1956.
Schickel, Richard: "The Big Revolution in Records." April 15, 1958.
"Teen-agers Scream, Stomp and Shake for the Big Band Beat of Pop Rock."
   June 15, 1965.

Modern Music.
Copland, Aaron. "The Composers Get Wise." 4, 1940.

Music Business.
"The Story of BMI." Sept.–Nov. 1946.

Music Educators Journal.
Schwartz, Elliott. "Directions in American Composition Since the Second World
   War." Part I. Feb. 1975.
Childs, Barney. "Directions in American Composition Since the Second World
   War." Part II. March 1975.
Gary, Charles L. "A Closer Look at the New Copyright Law." Nov. 1977.

Music Trade Review.
Lux, Peter F. "When All's Said and Done, It's the Same Old Popular Song, but
   Its Dress Changed Occasionally." March 1931.

The Nation.
"Music and Monopoly: ASCAP and the Radio Industry." Dec. 4, 1940.

Nation's Business.
"Music Industry Plays Billion $ Tune." Sept. 1954.
"Country Music Makes the Bottom Line Boom." Feb. 1979.

Newsweek.
"Why a Bandleader Can't Broadcast a Song He Wrote." Jan. 11, 1936.
"Warner Publishers Give 36,000 Songs Back to Crooners." Aug. 15, 1936.
"America's Jukebox Craze: Coin Phonographs Reap Harvest." June 3, 1940.
"Radio's Battle of Music." Nov. 18, 1940.
"Dialers Face Tune Blackout as ASCAP-Radio Feud Deepens." Dec. 23, 1940.
"Peace on the Air." Nov. 10, 1941.
"Lac Bug vs. Jitterbugs." April 27, 1942.
"Czar of Platters: Petrillo Breaks Promise: Continues Ban on Musical Record-
   ings." Oct. 23, 1944.
"Covers Up: What Packaging Has Done for the Record Industry." Dec. 25,
   1944.
"Great Record Boom." Dec. 16, 1946.
"War on Wax: Behind Petrillo's Fight with the Disc Makers." Nov. 3, 1947.
"Caesar in Reverse." Dec. 8, 1947.
"Petrillo Peace." Feb. 9, 1948.
"And the Ban Played On." Dec. 27, 1948.

"White Council vs. Rock 'n' Roll." April 23, 1956.
"Rocking and Rolling." June 18, 1956.
"Golden Days: Profits on Platters." Dec. 2, 1957.
"The Folk and the Rock." Sept. 20, 1965.
"Mick Jagger and the Future of Rock." Jan. 4, 1971.
"Stars of the Cathode Church." Feb. 4, 1980.
"Record Companies Turn for the Better." Oct. 12, 1980.
"Is Rock on the Rocks?" April 19, 1982.
"The New Boom in Laser Discs." Jan. 21, 1983.
"Rocking Video: Suddenly Rock and Roll Is Here to See." April 18, 1983.
"The New Sound of Music." June 11, 1983.
"Not the Sound of Silence." Nov. 14, 1983.
"Britain Rocks in America—Again.'" Jan. 23, 1984.
"Michael Jackson, Inc." Feb. 27, 1984.
"Motown's 25 Years of Soul." May 23, 1984.

New York Daily News.
Stearn, Jess. "The Big Payola: New Tune in Tin Pan Alley." March 27–30,
    1956.
———."Rock 'n' Roll Rolls into Trouble" April 11–12, 1956.
Marsh, Dave. "The Rock 'n' Roll Recession." Sept. 30, 1979.

New York Journal-American.
Kilgallen, James L. "Irving Berlin: Fifty Years of Songs." August 5–9, 1957.
Baer, Atra. "The War of Songs." Oct. 13–16, 1957.
Horan, James, Dom Frasca, and John Mitchell. "The Fabulous 'Juke Box' Em-
    pire." Oct. 19–24, 1958.

New York Magazine.
Egan, Jack. "Breaking Records in the Record Business." March 26, 1979.
———."Hollywood vs. Sony: Betamax on Trial." June 11, 1979.
———."Pop Records Go Boom: CBS and MTV Are the Leaders." Oct. 31,
    1983.

New York Post.
Greenberg, Charles, with Peter McElroy and Bernard Schiff. "The Rock and
    Roll Story." Oct. 2–12, 1958.
Schwartz, Bernard. "The Real Payola: What the Harris Committee Pigeon-
    holed." Dec. 14–19, 1959.
Scaduto, Anthony. "The World of Rock." June 16–21, 1960.
Carr, William H. A., and Gene Grove. "Inside the Record Business." Nov. 12–
    26, 1962.

The New York Times.
"Lure of Viennese Waltz Wins Wealth for Composers." July 14, 1910.
"How Popular Song Factories Manufacture a Hit." Sept. 10, 1910.
"The Music Trust That Reigns Over Italian Opera." Jan. 8, 1911.

"Demand Royalties for French Music: SACEM Is Reestablished in New York." Jan. 12, 1911.

"New York Pays About $7,000,000 Yearly for Its Music." March 19, 1911.

"Trust for Control of Music Business: ASCAP Organized at Meeting Here." Feb. 14, 1914.

"Music Industries Chamber of Commerce Formed." Feb. 17, 1916.

"Supreme Court Rules Against Vanderbilt Hotel and Shanley's Restaurant for Playing Music by Victor Herbert." Jan. 23, 1917.

"Vaudeville Heads Accused by Board: Federal Commission Charges Managers Have Formed an Illegal Combination." May 15, 1918.

"Reciprocal Agreement for Copyrights of Musical Compositions Reached by France and U.S." May 29, 1918.

"National Association of Sheet Music Dealers Adopts Resolution to Bar German Titles and Reduce Size of Sheet Music." June 11, 1918.

"Music Publishers Sued as Trust: Irving Berlin, Leo Feist and Others Charged with Breaking Sherman Act." Aug. 4, 1920.

"Songwriters Plan Formation of Protective Association." Nov. 19, 1920.

"Music Publishers' Protective Association in Dispute with Lyric Writers and Composers Protective League Over Song Royalties." May 4, 1921.

"Chicago Songwriters Go on Strike Over Royalties." May 28, 1921.

"Tin Pan Alley: Where Popular Songs Are Manufactured." Feb. 18, 1923.

"ASCAP's J. C. Rosenthal Alleges Infringement of Copyright Law When Stations Broadcast Society's Works Without Payment of Royalties." March 22, 1923.

"50 Broadcasting Stations Begin to Negotiate with ASCAP." March 23, 1923.

"E. C. Mills Suggests Reduction in Broadcasting Stations." March 25, 1923.

"Radio Broadcasting Society Will Contest ASCAP Stand." April 12, 1923.

"ASCAP Demands Licenses from Every Commercial Station Broadcasting Copyrighted Music." April 14, 1923.

"Motion Picture Producers and Distributors of America Ready for Fight to Finish with Composers Over Copyright Fees." May 23, 1923.

"E. A. Wealti Causes Arrest for Playing 'Yes, We Have No Bananas' on Phonograph All Day." Aug. 7, 1923.

"Representatives of Broadcasting Stations Meet in Chicago: Organize National Association of Broadcasters to Press Fight to Broadcast Copyrighted Music." April 26, 1924.

"Classical Music Publishers Adopt Music Publishers' Association's Plan to Offer Radio Their Music Without Charge." May 14, 1924.

"E. C. Mills of MPPA on His Work to Censor Songs." July 6, 1924.

"ASCAP Wins Suit Requiring Movie Houses to Pay License Fees." July 18, 1924.

"Motion Picture Theater Owners Attack ASCAP 10¢ per Seat Charge for Music." Aug. 19, 1924.

"John McCormack and Lucrezia Bori Broadcast Over Eight-Station Network: Victor Talking Machine Company Produces Program." Jan. 2, 1925.

"Theatrical Managers Protective Association Will Refuse Contracts with Composers Who Do Not Retain Copyright Control." Jan. 4, 1925.

"E. C. Mills, Chairman of MPPA, Says Broadcasting Hurts Sheet Music Sales." Feb. 15, 1925.

"Passing of 'the Ragtime Queen' Causes Drop in Sheet Music Sales." Feb. 15, 1925.

Article on Methods employed by Tin Pan Alley to make songs popular. Feb. 15, 1925.

"NAB States That Radio Stations Have Concluded They Should Not Pay for Copyrighted Music." April 5, 1925.

"National Association of Broadcasters Discusses ASCAP Situation at Convention: Plans to Ask Congress to Fix Royalty Rates for Music." Sept. 17, 1925.

"E. C. Mills of MPPA and ASCAP Comments on Recent U.S. Supreme Court Decision Upholding Appeals Court Ruling That Copyright Law Applies to Broadcast Programs." Oct. 25, 1925.

"Justice Department Ends Two-Year Inquiry with Decision That ASCAP Is Not Violating Antitrust Law." Aug. 6, 1926.

"E. C. Mills Describes ASCAP's Use of Musical Scouts to Detect Radio Infringements." Sept. 5, 1926.

"E. C. Mills Believes Controversy Between Broadcasters and ASCAP Is Near Peaceful Settlement." Oct. 17, 1926.

"ASCAP Warns Members of American Hotel Association That They Must Have Licenses to Play Copyrighted Music." March 26, 1927.

"National Association of Music Merchants Urges Censorship of Suggestive Popular Songs." May 29, 1927.

"ASCAP Moves to Curtail Too Frequent Radio Play of Popular Songs." May 29, 1927.

"MPPA's Mills Signs Contract with Electric Research Products Inc., Licensors of Vitaphone and Movietone, on Behalf of Its 63 Members." Dec. 21, 1927.

"House Committee on Patents Holds Hearing on Bill to Legalize Artists' Bargaining for Compensation for Mechanical Reproduction of Works." April 4, 1928.

Article on trying out songs in Tin Pan Alley. April 8, 1928.

Article on hits in musical comedies and revues. Oct. 21, 1928.

Article on Tin Pan Alley's new methods of marketing songs. June 8, 1929.

"Bankrupt Music Publishers Blame Radio and Sound Films for Failure." Aug. 30, 1929.

"ASCAP Has Five-Year Contract with Majority of Members." Oct. 13, 1929.

"NBC-RCA Forms Own Publishing Arm." Dec. 5, 1929. Further stories on Dec. 8, 15, 1929.

"Publishers Discuss Use of Radio and Records to Stimulate Sales of Sheet Music." June 6, 1930.

Article on Tin Pan Alley's new methods of marketing. June 8, 1930.

"Some Radio Announcers Use 'Played by Permission of the Copyright Owners' to Protect Stations." March 22, 1931.

"U.S. Supreme Court Rules in Jewell-LaSalle Realty Co: Hotels Must Pay for Rebroadcasting Music to Rooms." April 14, 1931.

"ASCAP Announces New License Terms for Radio." Nov. 8, 1931.

"ASCAP President Gene Buck Denies Charges of Racketeering." Feb. 27, 1932.

Feature article on Tin Pan Alley's rise to respectability. March 27, 1932.

"ASCAP Favors 300% Increase in Radio License Fees." April 17, 1932.

"Broadcasters Hold Out for Flat Fee While ASCAP Asks Percentage for Music Use." Aug. 21, 1932.

"NAB Agrees to Pay Percentage of Annual Receipts to ASCAP." Aug. 25, 1932.

"Richmond-Mayer Music Corp. of New York and Chicago Sues Music Dealers Service for Alleged Conspiracy in Publishing and Distribution Trade." Oct. 1, 1932.

Feature article on royalties for publishers and composers. Oct. 2, 1932.

"Composers Seek Higher Fees: Broadcasters Plan Formation of Radio Program Foundation to Establish Independent Music Catalogue." July 20, 1933.

"ASCAP Lays Drop in Sales of Sheet Music and Records to Radio." July 19, 20, 1933.

"Rudy Vallee Says Radio Does Not Pay Fair Share for Use of Popular Songs." Sept. 22, 1933.

"NAB Song Reservoir Cited." Oct. 8, 1933.

"ASCAP Sued by Government on Popular Music." Aug. 31, 1934.

"Seeking to Void Music License System, Justice Department Opens Suit Charging ASCAP Violation of Antitrust Act in Popular Music Business." June 12, 1935.

"NAB Favors Per-Piece Payment for Use of Copyrighted Music." June 23, July 9, 1935.

"Warner Brothers Music Subsidiary Plans to Secede from ASCAP Because of Broadcast Royalties." Nov. 22, 1935.

"Eleven Music Companies Withdraw from ASCAP." Nov. 27, 1935.

"Expiration of Warner Brothers ASCAP Contract Forces Popular Song Hits from Air." Jan. 1, 1936.

"Independent Stations Accept Three-Month Warner Contract. Networks Not Offered Deal." Jan. 3, 1936.

"Broadcasters Protest High ASCAP Rates Because 25% of Its Music Was Withdrawn by Warner." Jan. 11, 1936.

"ASCAP May Cause Warner Brothers to Establish Its Own Nationwide Radio Chain." March 7, 1936.

"Warner Music Houses Rejoin ASCAP: All Damage Suits Dropped." Aug. 4, 1936.

Review of Warner-ASCAP fight. Aug. 9, 1936.

"ASCAP Lists Hit Songs of 1935 According to Frequency of Airplay on CBS and NBC." Sept. 2, 1936.

"ASCAP Head Gene Buck Says Radio Popularity Kills Life of Songs. Suggests Limit on Airplay of New Music." Sept. 9, 1936.

"FTC Publishes Code for Popular Music Business." March 30, 1937.

"SPA Discusses Validity of Publishers' Claim to Copyright Renewals." March 30, 1938.

Fox Sylvan. "Disks Today: New Sounds and Technology." Aug. 20, 1967.

Gelb, Arthur. "Record Companies Taking Major Role as Theatre Angels." Sept. 25, 1967.

Shepard, Richard F. "Hunt for Talent for Pop Disks Goes On." Jan. 30, 1968.

Ferretti, Fred. "Witness Details Workings of the Recording Industry." June 8, 1973.

Lichtenstein, Grace. "Some Find Rock 'n' Roll Now Rock 'n' Recession." Jan. 30, 1975.

Rockwell, John. "Latin 'Salsa' Music Gains Popularity and Recognition." May 5, 1975.

————."The Volatile Pop Field Is Bubbling." Aug. 29, 1976.

————."A Mixed Bag of Treats for a Mixed Audience." Aug. 28, 1977.

Briggs, Kenneth. "Religious Broadcasting: The Fourth Network." Jan. 29, 1978.

Brown, Les. "The Networks Cry Havoc: All the Way to the Bank." Feb. 12, 1978.

Ditlea, Steve. "Rock Sings an International Tune." June 11, 1978.

McDowell, Edward. "Record Pirates: Industry Sings the Blues." June 30, 1978.

————."Religious Networks Blossom." July 23, 1978.

Sheppard, Nathaniel, Jr. "Cities, Once Deaf to Rock, Turn On to Concert Revenues." Feb. 6, 1979.

Kirkeby, Marc. "Changing Face of Record Distribution: Cash Security Lures the Independents." Feb. 18, 1979.

Kornbluth, Jesse. "Merchandising Disco for the Masses." Feb. 18, 1979.

————."High Court Says Single Permit Fee for TV Music Is not Price Fixing." April 18, 1979.

Rockwell, John. "Decade-Old TV Music Question Still Open." April 18, 1979.

————."Digital Recording Techniques Are Already Being Widely Used in Pop Music." July 3, 1979.

White, Timothy. "The Life and Times of Reggae." July 22, 1979.

Rockwell, John. "Industry's Sales Slowing After 25 Years of Steady Growth." Aug. 8, 1979.

Holsendolph, Ernest. "Religious Broadcasts Bring Rising Revenues and Create Rivalries." Dec. 7, 1979.

Rockwell, John. "The Music Craze Was All Disco." Dec. 23, 1979.

Hollie, Pamela. "Record Industry: Big Changes." Jan. 12, 1980.

Palmer, Robert. "Rock No Longer 'Devil's Music.' " Sept. 16, 1980.

Kerr, Peter. "Music Video's Uncertain Payoff." Aug. 29, 1981.

Palmer, Robert. "New Bands on Small Labels Are the Innovators of the 80's." Sept. 6, 1981.

"Battle Looms on Decontrol of Cable TV: Copyright Fees Could Rise Sharply." March 3, 1982.

McDowell, Edwin. "A New Copyright Law Is Authors' Target." April 30, 1982.

Wills, Kendall J. "Gospel Music on the Ascent." June 27, 1982.

Holden, Stephen. "RCA Gambling on Kenny Rogers." July 28, 1982.

Palmer, Robert. "Pop Music's Heyday Said To Be Waning Amid Falling Sales." Aug. 14, 1982.

DiNardo, Robert. "Musicians vs. Tape: A Survival Battle." Aug. 22, 1982.

"Music Charges for Local TV Are Ruled Illegal: Court Bars Music Licensing System." Sept. 23, 1982.

Yarrow, Peter. "AM Stations, Hurt by FM, Are Going Stereo." Oct. 14, 1982.

Palmer, Robert. "The Pop Record Industry Is Under Electronic Siege." Oct. 28, 1982.

Palmer, Robert. "In Hard Times, Pop Music Surges with Fresh Energy." Dec. 26, 1982.

Maslin, Janet. "A Song Is No Longer Strictly a Song: Now It's a 'Video.' " Jan. 23, 1983.

"Audiodisk: Record of Future?" March 18, 1983.

Bedell, Sally. "How Copyright Fees Affect Cable TV." March 19, 1983.

Salmans, Sandra. "Sales of Records on the Rise: Hit Albums Aid Upturn." March 29, 1983.

Holland, Bernard. "Digital Compact Disks: Replacement for LPs?" March 31, 1983.

Levine, Ed. "TV Rocks with Music." May 3, 1983.

Harmetz, Aljean. "Cassettes Are Changing Movie-Audience Habits." July 11, 1983.

Rockwell, John. "Country Music Is No Small-town Affair." July 17, 1983.

O'Connor, John J. "MTV: A Success Story with a Curious Shortcoming." July 24, 1983.

Palmer, Robert. "Will Video Clips Kill Radio as a Maker of Rock's Top 10." Aug. 1, 1983.

Lacayo, Richard. "The Rock Competition Steps Up a Beat." Aug. 7, 1983.

Lohr, Steve. "Hard Hit Sony Girds for a Fight in the American Electronics Market." Aug. 14, 1983.

Levine, Ed. "Music Video Turns on the Industry." Aug. 21, 1983.

"'The Woes of the Little Guy." Aug. 21, 1983.

Palmer, Robert. "The Pop Record Business Shows Signs of Recovery." Aug. 31, 1983.

Specter, Michael J. "Rock Puts on a Three-Piece Suit." Oct. 2, 1983.

Pareles, Jon. "Copyrights, Tapes and Royalties Issue." Nov. 2, 1983.

Holden, Stephen. "Pop Music Surges Along New and Unexpected Paths." Nov. 11, 1983.

Salmans, Sandra. "What's New In Cable?" Nov. 27, 1983.

Pareles, Jon. "Pop Record Business Shows Signs of Recovery." Nov. 28, 1983.

Palmer, Robert. "Energy and Creativity Added Up to Exciting Pop." Dec. 25, 1983.

Palmer, Robert. "Songwriters Express Copyright Law Concern." Jan. 16, 1984.

Greenhouse, Linda. "Television Taping at Home Is Upheld by Supreme Court." Jan. 18, 1984.

Fantel, Hans. "50 Years Ago: The Birth of Tape." Feb. 12, 1984.

Welles, Merida. "Tower's Costly Gamble: But Will It Pay Off?" Aug. 5, 1984.

Pareles, Jon. "Rock Video, All Day and All Night." Aug. 21, 1984.

"Audio Disk Players Coming of Age." Nov. 26, 1984.

Palmer, Robert. "Pop Music Makes a Comeback and Video Helped It Out." Dec. 30, 1984.

Fantel, Hans. "Digital Sound Began To Live Up To Its Potential." Dec. 30, 1984.

Smith, Sally Bedell. "HBO Altering Its Plan After Year of Bad News." Jan. 22, 1985.

The New York Times Magazine
Wolf, S. J. "What Makes a Song: A Talk with Irving Berlin." July 28, 1940.
Miller, Mitch. "June, Moon, Swoon and KoKoMo." April 24, 1955.
Samuels, Gertrude. "Why They Rock 'n' Roll and Should They." Jan. 12, 1958.
"Global Report on Rock 'n' Roll." July 27, 1958.
Wilson, John S. "How No-talent Singers Get Talent." June 21, 1959.
Levin, Phylis Lee. "The Sound of Music." March 14, 1965.
Greenfield, Jeff. "They Changed Rock, Which Changed the Culture, Which Changed Us." Feb. 16, 1975..
Slater, Jack. "A Sense of Wonder: To Be Young, Gifted and Blind." Feb. 23, 1975.
Rockwell, John: "Rock Lives." Feb. 27, 1977.
Harmetz, Aljean. "Hollywood's Video Gamble." March 28, 1982.
Lindsay, Robert. "Home Box Office Moves in on Hollywood." June 12, 1983.

New York World-Telegram & Sun.
Fischer, Muriel. "The Music Makers." Dec. 30, 1957.

The New Yorker.
Johnston, Alva. "Czar of Song: Gene Buck." Dec. 17, 24, 1932.
"Pulse of the Public: Career of Jack Kapp." Aug. 24, 1940.

Notes of the Music Library Association.
Schultz, Lucia A. "Performing Rights Societies of the United States." March 1979.

Outlook.
Arnoth, D. G. "At the Popular Music Publishers." May 26, 1920.

The Player Monthly.
Kitchener, Frederick. "Popular Music and Its Popularity: A Study." No. 1, 1910.

Printers Ink.
Peterson, Eldridge. "Radio Quarrel with Composers Now Approaching Climax." June 28, 1940.

Publishers Weekly.
Wagner, Susan. "New Copyright Law Primer." Dec. 26, 1977; Jan. 30, 1978.

Radio Daily.
"BMII: A Story of Free Enterprise." April 17, 1950.

Record World.
"A Special Tribute to Sam Goody: 35 Years of Creative Record Retailing."
March 2, 1974.

Redbook.
Herndon, Booton. "The Battle Over the Music You Hear." Dec. 1957.

The Reporter.
Mannes, Marya. "Who Decides What Songs Are Hits?" Jan. 10, 1957.

Rolling Stone.
"Record Quality: A Pressing Problem Remains Unsolved." March 18, 1982.
"New Music Thriving on Small Labels." April 29, 1982.
"Record Executives Sing the Blues at NARM." May 13, 1982.
"Record Rental Stores Booming in US." Sept. 2, 1982.
"Record Industry Nervous as Sales Drop Fifty Percent." Sept. 30, 1982.
Letters on home taping. Oct. 28, 1982.
Connelly, Christopher. "Rock Radio: A Case of Racism?" Dec. 9, 1982.
"Video Royalty Wars?" July 7, 1983.

Sales Management.
"The Rocking Rolling Record Industry: The Tuff Generation Turned Us On."
Dec. 15, 1966.

The Saturday Evening Post.
"Trouble in Tin Pan Alley." Oct. 19, 1935.
Grevatt, Ren, and Merrill Pollack. "It All Started with Elvis." Sept. 26, 1959.
Portis, Charles. "That New Sound from Nashville." Feb. 2, 1966.
Aaronowitz, Alfred A. "Pop Music: The Most? Or Just a Mess?" July 15, 1967.

Saturday Review.
Diamond, Morris. "Following the Ban: Trust Agreement Providing Opportuni-
ties for the Playing of Live Music." Jan. 29, 1949.
Hammerstein, Oscar, II. "Some Dissonances in Tin Pan Alley: ASCAP vs. BMI."
Feb. 23, 1957.
Haverlin, Carl. "Answer to Oscar Hammerstein." March 2, 1957.
"ASCAP vs. BMI II." March 3, 1957.
"Twenty Years of Recordings." Aug. 26, 1967.
Shayon, Robert Louis. "The Copyright Dilemma." Nov. 11, 1967.
Heinsheimer, Hans W. "Music from the Conglomerates." Feb. 22, 1969.
Mariani, John. "Television Evangelism: Milking the Flock." Feb. 3, 1979.
"The Phonograph Celebrates a Birthday." July 2, 1977.

Sponsor.
"Is Radio Playing the Wrong Music?" June 27, 1955.

Television.
Land, Herman. "The Storz Bombshell." May 1957.

Time.
"U.S. vs. ASCAP." July 1, 1935.
"Merchants of Music." Aug. 10, 1935.
"Millworkers: Hollywood Songwriters." March 23, 1936.
"Phonograph Boom." Sept. 4, 1939.
"Record Price Cut: Columbia Recording Corporation." Aug. 19, 1940.
"Arnold to the Music World." Jan. 6, 1941.
"ASCAP's First Blow." Jan. 13, 1941.
"ASCAP Returns." May 19, 1941.
"Peace On Air." Aug. 11, 1941.
"Tunes Back." Nov. 10, 1941.
"Music's Moneybags: Money-Making Records." Sept. 21, 1942.
"One with the Dough: Petrillo's Contract with the Record Companies." Oct. 11,
   1943.
"Platter for the Lion: MGM in the Phonograph Record Industry." Feb. 24, 1947.
"Petrillo's Resolve." Dec. 29, 1947.
"Record Mixup." Dec. 27, 1948.
"Top Jock." Feb. 14, 1955.
"Yeh-heh-heh-heh, Baby: Rock 'n' Roll." June 18, 1956.
"Rock 'n' Roll." July 23, 1956.
"The Voice and Payola." Sept. 9, 1957.
"Rock Is Solid." Nov. 4, 1957.
"The Singing Land." Dec. 23, 1957.
"Rock 'n' Roll: The Sound of the Sixties." May 21, 1965.
"Rock 'n' Roll: The Return of the Big Beat." Aug. 15, 1969.
"Pop Records: Moguls, Money & Monsters." Feb. 17, 1973.

TV Guide.
Gunther, Max. "The Beat Doesn't Go On: Rock Musicians Are Earning Fortunes—But Not from Television." July 22, 29, 1978.

USA Today.
Baker, Rob. "Music Videos Inspire Fast, Flashy Flicks." June 6, 1983.
White, Miles. "Megahits Revive Record Industry." Dec. 14, 1983.
Heller, Karen. "Rock Channel Grabs Us Overtime." Dec. 14, 1983.
An Interview with Les Garland: "MTV's World Turns Around Rock Culture."
   Feb. 20, 1984.
Wishnik, Debra. "Registers Ringing at Record Stores." March 5, 1984.

Village Voice.
Kopkind, Andrew. "The Dialectics of Disco: Gay Music Goes Straight." Feb.
   12, 1979.
Smith, Howard, and Cathy Cox. "What's Wrong with the Record Business? 12
   Presidents Speak Out." Feb. 26, 1979.

Fergusson, Isaac. "So Much to Say: The Journey of Bob Marley." May 18, 1982.

Christgau, Robert. "Rock 'n' Roller Coaster: The Music Biz on a Joyride." Feb. 7, 1984.

Reynolds, Steve. "Rate That Tune: The PTA Would Like the Recording Industry to Label Records Containing Vulgar or Violent Lyrics." Dec. 4, 1985.

Wall Street Journal.

Penn, Stanley. "Slipping Discs: Teen-agers Cut Buying of 'Pop' Records, Slow Industry's Total Gain." Aug. 31, 1959.

"Broadcast Music, Inc. Accused of Monopoly in Popular Music Field." Dec. 11, 1964.

O'Connor, John J. "Pop Music Explosion: Rock and Roll and Bankroll." April 9, 1969.

Gottschalk, Earl. "The Sound of Money: Rock Records Spawn Fortunes and Attract Growth-Minded Firms." Jan. 13, 1970.

Schmedel, Scott R. "The Trend Buckers: Record Firms Spin to Sweetest Music They Ever Heard—The Sound of Money." April 16, 1970.

Revzin, Philip. "The Rocky Road: Record Talent Scout Studies Highs and Lows for the Bottom Line." June 15, 1976.

Wysocki, Bernard Jr. "Higher Fi?: Computerized System May Free Recordings of Distortion Problems." Jan. 3, 1979.

Drinkhall, Jim. "Are Mafia Mobsters Acquiring a Taste for Sound of Rock?" Jan. 29, 1979.

Grover, Stephen. "Record Industry May Be in Groove Again After One of Worst Slumps in Its History." July 12, 1979.

"TV Stations Win Ruling on Payments for Rights to Music." Aug. 23, 1982.

Landro, Laura. "Record Industry Finding Financial Revival in Promoting Artists on Video Music Shows." Nov. 19, 1982.

————."Video-Game Firms Face Tough Christmas As Industry Approaches a Major Shakeout." Sept. 2, 1983.

————."Movie Studios' Cut in Videocassette Prices Stirs Battle with Retailers on Video Rentals." Sept. 23, 1983.

Kneale, Kevin. "Wierder Is Better in the Red-Hot Land of Rock Videos." Oct. 17, 1983.

Western World (Brussels).

Sinatra, Frank. "The Diplomacy of Music." Nov. 1957.

Bibliography to Part Ten

Arnold, Gina. *Route 666: On The Road to Nirvana.* New York: St. Martin's Press, 1993.

Bagdikian, Ben. *The Media Monopoly.* Boston: Beacon Press, 1990.

Bernstein, Carl. "The Leisure Empire." *Time* (December 24, 1990): 56–59.

Breen, Marcus. "The End Of The World As We Know It: Popular Music's Cultural Mobility." *Cultural Studies* 9:3 (October 1995): 486–504.

Dwyer, Paula with Margaret Dawson and Dexter Roberts. "The New Music Biz." *Business Week* (January 15, 1996): 48–51.

Fried, Stephen. "Bad Vibes In Tune Town." *Vanity Fair* (February 1995): 92–99, 137–40.

Kennedy, Dan. "Merger Mania." *Boston Phoenix* (December 8, 1995): 14–8.

Lander, Mark. "The War On Warner: You're On, Mr. Fuchs." *New York Times* (June 25, 1995): C15, C20.

Landro, Laura. "Giants Talk Synergy, but Few Make It Work." *Wall Street Journal* (September 9, 1995): B1, B10.

Ledbetter, James. "Merge Overkill." *Village Voice* (January 16, 1996): 30–35.

Levy, Steven. "Now for the Free-for-All." *Newsweek* (February 12, 1996): 42–44.

Masters, Kim and Stephen Fried. "The Precarious Throne." *Vanity Fair* (October 1995): 90, 94, 96, 99, 100, 104, 106, 115–18.

McChesney, Robert. "Public Broadcasting in the Age of Communications Revolution." *Monthly Review* 47:7 (December 1995): 1–19.

———. "Telecon." *In These Times* (July 10, 1995): 14–17.

Strauss, Neil. "Are Pop Charts Manipulated?" *New York Times* (January 25, 1996): C15, C20.

Index

N.B. This index does not include Part Ten; a separate index for Part Ten will be found on p. 765

Aaronson, Irving, 104
"Abbey Road," 558
ABC, 229, 258, 281, 283, 295, 310-312, 416, 431-432, 447, 561-562, 594, 620; country music on, 427; "Hit Preview of the Week," 443
ABC-Dunhill, 509, 592
ABC Music Publishing, 608
ABC-Paramount, 312, 344-345, 347, 354, 373, 389, 471
ABC Records, 509, 560, 608
ABC-TV, 444, 501-502, 505, 524-525
Abeles, Julian T., 104, 180-181, 208-209, 259, 563
Aberbach, Adolph, 425
Aberbach, Jean, 342, 407, 425, 470-471, 489, 591-592
Aberbach, Julian, 342, 407, 425, 460-471, 489, 591-592
Abramson, Herb, 509
Abraxas, 516
ACA. *See* American Composers Alliance
Accurate Report, 202, 460
Accurate Reporting Service, 205, 266, 279
AC/DC, 627
Ace of Clubs, 377
Acid rock, 516, 536
Ackerman, Paul, 309, 406, 418, 447
Action Committee for the Arts, 584
Action for Children's Television, 652
Actors' Equity Association, 57
Acuff, Roy, 240, 288, 427
Acuff-Rose, 287, 288, 289, 307, 427, 482, 499

Aczcarraga, Don Emilio, 180
Adams, Faye, 248
Adams, Maude, 51
Adams, Mel, 319
Adams, Stanley, 263, 284, 303-304, 306, 308, 327-328, 399, 401-402, 404-405, 419-420, 422, 437, 450, 452-453, 462, 466, 478, 480, 488, 498-499, 580
"Adeste Fideles," 67
Adler, Lou, 509
Advanced Vaudeville Circuit, 58
The Adventures of Kathlyn (film), 9
Aeolian Company, 22-23, 28
Aeolian-Vocalion, 27
Aeriola, Sr., 77
Aeriola Grand, 77
Affiliated Music Enterprises, Inc. v. *Society of European Stage Authors and Composers,* 469
Affiliated Music Publishing, 534
"Afghanistan," 42
AFM. *See* American Federation of Musicians
AGAC. *See* American Guild of Authors and Composers
Ager, Milton, 289-290, 328, 402
Ahlert, Fred, 185, 266, 284, 295-299, 306, 328
Aiken case, 529, 530
"Ain't That a Shame," 340
Air Supply, 627
"Alabammy Bound," 100
Aladdin, 240, 248, 325
Albee, E. A., 53

Albee, E. F., 15, 17-19, 21, 41, 57-60
AlbuMusic, 590
Alden-Rochelle v. *ASCAP,* 283-285, 289,
    291, 294
Aldon Music, 387
Alexander's Ragtime Band, 157
"Alexander's Ragtime Band" (Berlin), 25,
    35
The Al Jolson Story, 226
"All Alone" (Berlin), 69, 95
Allegheny Corporation, 318
Allegro label, 243
Allen, Gracie, 161
Allen, Nicholas, 494
Allen B. Dumont Laboratories, 173, 281
"Allentown" (Joel), 640
Allgemeinische Elektrische Gesellschaft,
    221
All-Industry Radio Committee, 296, 417,
    467, 525, 575-576, 620-621
All-Industry Radio Licensing Committee,
    498
All-Industry Television Committee, 295,
    308-309, 412, 417, 454, 457, 479,
    499, 523, 576-577
All in the Family, 596
"Alone Together," 402
Alpert, Herb, 385
A & M, 539, 552, 594
"Amapola," 216
Ambassador Music, 473
Ambassador Orchestra, 30
AM broadcasting, 174, 285, 314; in sixties,
    518-519
American Arbitration Association, 421
American Bandstand, 444-445, 447, 638
American Biograph Company, 5, 7
American Broadcasting Company. *See* ABC
American Cash Register Company, 32
American Columbia, 67, 71
American Composers Alliance, 269-270,
    302, 432, 475
American Consolidated Electronics Indus-
    tries, 379
American Express, 629
American Federation of Musicians, 128,
    140, 169, 170, 217-218, 221, 229,
    286, 333-334, 350-351, 455, 566,
    582
American Federation of Television & Radio
    Artists, 582
"American Fool" (album), 638
"American Graffiti," 532
American Grand Rights Association, 201
American Guild of Authors and Composers,

410-411, 439-440, 447, 449, 453,
    455, 480, 485, 509, 530-531, 535,
    567-568, 624, 628; Catalog Adminis-
    tration Plan, 531
American Guild of Musical Artists, 582
American Independent Radio, 546
American Jubilee Music, 489
American News Company, 145
American Performing Rights Association,
    180
American Radio Relay League, 76
American Record–Brunswick, 120, 127,
    135-136
American Record Company, 71, 125, 133,
    135, 139, 141, 258
American Record Manufacturers and Distrib-
    utors Association, 367, 370-373, 375,
    463
American Society of Composers, Authors
    and Publishers, 12, 38-41, 43-44, 47-
    50, 54, 78-84, 88-93, 97, 108-110,
    122, 130, 152-156, 158, 161-162,
    165, 167, 169, 172, 174-181, 201,
    205-207, 209, 252, 255-263, 265-
    266, 269-271, 274-277, 279-281,
    285, 289, 291, 295, 307-308, 309,
    312, 322, 327-329, 397, 494, 496,
    498-500, 502-506, 524, 526, 529,
    531, 566, 573-574, 576-580, 584,
    586, 617-623
Ahlert-Leslie plan, 266-267
Articles of Association, 194
attempt to intervene in *United States* v.
    BMI, 485
business reforms, in twenties, 104-105
vs. BMI, in fifties–sixties, 309, 396-438
classification system, 93-94, 103-104,
    187, 193, 195, 202-203, 265-266,
    296-298
distribution plan
    in fifties, 296-298, 300-301, 401, 419-
    421
    in sixties, 452, 465-466, 480, 487-488
four-fund allocation formula, 303-304,
    419, 453, 498-499, 503-504
income
    for 1946, 281
    in early seventies, 528
    in fifties, 419
    in late forties, 288
    in sixties, 466, 479, 488
licensing, as result of 1941 agreement,
    254, 256
logging operation, 400, 420
    in fifties, 298-299, 322-323, 327

members' income, in fifties, 438
prosperity during WW II, 253
Radio Negotiating Committee, 208-210
reforms, in 1939, 210-211
restriction on radio broadcast of production music, 99
royalties, in fifties, 397
in sixties, 454, 456-457
taxing of sound-theater seats, 103, 283-
284, 289-290
and television, 440-441
in fifties, 294-296
vs. broadcasters, 158, 182-211, 588
weighted vote controversy, 418-419, 453
American Telephone & Telegraph Company,
51, 75, 78-82, 90, 160, 162, 193;
radio monopoly, 84; removal from
broadcasting business, 85
Amfitheatroff, Daniele, 275
AMI. See Automatic Musical Instrument
Company
"Amos 'n' Andy," 10, 89-90, 160, 315
Ampex Corporation, 230, 244, 249, 362,
390, 415, 551
Ampex Videotape Cruiser, 416
A & M Records, 385, 609
AmRuss, 471, 528
Amtorg, 201
Amusement and Music Operators Associa-
tion, 583-584
Andrews Sisters, 137, 471
Andy Griffith Show, 484
Angel Records, 244, 336, 358, 376, 378
Anglo-American Music Publishing Corp.,
653
Animals, 389
Anka, Paul, 347, 388, 471
Annenberg, Max, 9
Annie, 600
Antitrust suits, 250, 256, 260, 262-263, 283,
317, 328, 423, 437, 469, 475, 478,
501-502, 523-525, 531-532, 557;
against ASCAP, BMI, CBS, and
NBC, 211; against motion picture
studios, in thirties, 158; against music
business, in 1934, 196; against radio
networks, 160, 182
AOR radio, 636, 638, 641, 646
"Apache," 379
A & P Gypsies, 83
Apollo, 240, 248
Apple Corps, Ltd., 514-515, 539
Apple Records, 539-540
The Apple Tree, 355
"April Showers," 592

"Aquarius/Let the Sunshine In," 599
Ardmore Music, 368
"Are You Lonesome Tonight," 459-460
"Arias–Acted and Sung," 339
Ariola Records, 643, 648
Arista Records, 556, 609, 643, 645, 648
Arlen, Harold, 153-154, 304
ARMADA. See American Record Manufac-
turers and Distributors Association
Armat, Thomas, 4
A & R men, 345, 387, 408, 443; in fifties,
318, 319
Armour Research Foundation, 221
Armstrong, Edwin H., 173
Armstrong, Louis, 117
"The Army Air Corps," 252
Arnaz, Desi, 415
Arnold, Eddy, 240, 342, 427, 429
Arnold, Thurmond, 182, 210-211, 254-255,
260, 368
Around the World in Eighty Days, 349
"Around the World in Eighty Days," 408
Arries, Leslie, 523, 576-577, 580, 618, 622
Arrow Press, 269
Arthur W. Tams Music Library, 101
Artist fees: for black musicians, 64; Peer's
system for paying, 65; Victor's rate
for, 69
Asbell, Bernard, 442
ASCAP. See American Society of Compos-
ers, Authors and Publishers
Ash, Paul, 102
Ashford and Simpson, 524
Ashley-Famous, 510
"Asia" (album), 638
Associated Independent Music Publishers, 82
Associated Music Publishers, 168, 171, 269,
282, 471, 529
Associated Television Corp., 489-490
Association of Independent Music Publish-
ers, 407
Association of Motion Picture and Television
Producers, 531
Astaire, Adele, 120
Astaire, Fred, 120, 128, 150
A Star Is Born (film), 532
"As Time Goes By," 252
Asylum Records, 511
Atari video games, 641-642, 649
Atlantic Records, 240, 248, 325, 340, 356,
365, 373, 509-511, 554, 559, 596
Atlas, 317
A T & T, see American Telephone & Tele-
graph Company
ATV Music, 535, 538, 590, 604

ATV of London, 513-514
Atwater-Kent Company, 77, 86
Audience Research Institute, 322
Audio Devices, 362, 512
Audio Engineering Society, 360
Audio Fair, 249
Audio Fidelity Records, 360
Audion tube, 75
AudioPak, 512-513
Audiosphere, 359
Austin, Gene, 54, 69, 119, 123, 128, 216
Australia–New Zealand, record market in,
    380
Authors' League, 496
Automatic Musical Instrument Company,
    110, 134
Autopiano Company, 41
Autry, Gene, 151, 157, 225, 429, 471
"Autumn Leaves," 368
A-V, 359
Avco, 611
Axt, William, 48, 52
Axton, Mae Boren, 429

Babes in Toyland, 151
Bachman, William, 231
Background music, 359, 440, 480, 483-484
Bagdasarian, Ross, 307, 347
"Bagpipes and Drums," 360
Baker, Howard, 427
Baker, Laverne, 509
Baker, Newton D., 165, 193
Baker, "Wee" Bonnie, 145
Baline, Izzy. See Berlin, Irving
Ball, Ernest, 33, 91, 407
Ball, Lucille, 415
"Ballad of a Teen-age Queen," 464
Ballard, Hank, 461
Ballard, Pat, 408
Bambi, 652
Bandleaders; and hit songs, 96; and music
    promotion, 184-185
"Band on the Run," 538
Bands, see Dance bands
The Band Wagon, 120, 402
Bang Records, 536
Banner Records, 65, 127
Bara, Theda, 13
Barber, Samuel, 328, 402
Bardeen, John, 416
Barkmeier, Paul, 243
"Barney Google," 592
Baron, Maurice, 49
Barry, Jeff, 387

Barry & Enright, 440
Barry Lyndon (film), 532
Barrymore, John, 52
Basie, Count, 369
Baskette, Billy, 80
Battelle Northwest, 612
"The Battle Hymn of the Republic," 364
Bay City Rollers, 556
Bayes, Nora, 18, 25
BBC, American music on, 381
Beach Boys, 381, 386, 512
Beatlemania, 382-383
Beatles, 381-383, 386, 473-474, 489, 512-
    515, 519, 536, 538-539, 544, 558,
    638
"Beatles '65," 385
"Beatles VI," 385
Beat the Clock, 441
Becaud, Gilbert, 602
"Because of You," 307
Beck, Martin, 17-18
Beechwood Music, 601
Bee Gees, 519, 514, 596-599
"The Beer Barrel Polka," 137, 143, 145
"Begin the Beguine," 158
"Bei Mir Bist Du Schön," 137
Belafonte, Harry, 378, 388
Belinda Music Company, 592
Bell, Alexander Graham, 74
Bell & Howell, 359
Bell Laboratories, 66, 358-359, 416
Bell Records, 357, 555-556
"Bells on Her Fingers, Rings on Her Toes,"
    10
Bell Sound, 361
Belwin-Mills Publishing Corp., 533
Belwin Music Company, 48, 105, 533
"Be My Love," 242
Ben Hur (film), 48
Bennett, Robert Russell, 99
Bennett, Tony, 238, 307, 547
Benny, Jack, 128, 315
The Benny Goodman Story, 349
Benson, George, 640
Bentley, Gladys, 133
Bergen, Edgar, 315
Bergen, Polly, 414
Berkeley, Busby, 149-150, 152-153
Berle, Milton, 241, 288, 316, 415
Berlin, Irving, 25-26, 29, 35-36, 38, 43, 69,
    82, 92, 102, 105-106, 148, 153-154,
    157, 187, 190, 195, 198, 239, 261,
    275-276, 298, 300, 303-304, 353,
    397, 399, 412, 440, 453, 460, 473
Berliner, Emle, 28

Berman, Al, 489
Berne Convention, 111, 588
Bernhardt, Sarah, 8
Bernie, Ben, 51, 85, 96, 128, 185
Bernstein, Elmer, 531
Bernstein, Louis, 43, 190, 257, 261, 265, 306, 441, 472
Bernstein, Peter W., 606
Bertelsmann, 378, 609, 643, 645, 648
Betamax case, 611, 628, 630
Bienstock, Freddy, 591-592, 653
Big Apple (dance), 137
Big Boy, 98
The Big Broadcast, 149
Big Brother and the Holding Company, 536
The Big Parade (film), 48-49, 106
Big Three. See MGM
Bijou Theatre, 17
Bilk, Acker, 381
Billboard, 474; hit charts, 307, 350, 418, 498, 547, 635, 645, 646; Hot 100 chart, 517, 574
Binaural recording, 359
"Bing" (record set), 339
Bing Crosby Enterprises, 415
Bird of Paradise Trio, 95
The Birth of a Nation (film), 9-10, 12, 48
Bishop, Walter, 402
Bitner, Edgar, 113
"Bix Beiderbecke Memorial Album," 134
Black, Hugo L., 210
The Blackboard Jungle, 340, 378, 406
Black Entertainment Television, 641, 646
Blackface, 30
Black Label Records, 29
Black Maria, 4
Black music, 133, 222, 225, 558; Carnegie Hall concert of, in 1912, 26; censorship, in eighties, 605; discrimination against, 641, 650; in eighties, 654; in fifties, 326, 340; influence on Rolling Stones, 383-384; and MTV, 640-641, 645-646; recording, 140; in seventies, 554-555; success of, in late seventies, 605
Black musicals, 599-600
Black Music Association, 605
The Black Pirate (film), 48
Blacks: radio stations aimed at, and payola scandal, 554; as record buyers, in early 20th c., 30-31; recordings made by, 64; stereotypes of, 6; in vaudeville, 58
Blake, Eubie, 51
Bland, Bobby, 341

Blanket licensing, 84, 293, 295, 408, 487, 576-579, 618-620, 622, 632
Bleyer, Archie, 345
Blink, Milton, 425
Block, Martin, 128-129, 165, 225, 319, 441-442, 460
Block booking, 261
Blondie, 601
Blood, Sweat & Tears, 516, 536
Bloomer Girl, 239
Bloomfield, Mike, 516, 535
Bludhorn, Charles, 393, 602
Bluebird Records, 122, 133, 136-137, 222, 236, 341, 472
"Blue Moon of Old Kentucky," 342
Blue Network, 85-86, 90, 257-258, 310
Blue Note Records, 511
Blues, 30; recordings, in twenties and thirties, 64
Blue Skies (film), 276
"Blue Suede Shoes," 342
Blue Thumb records, 561
"Blue Yodel Number 1" (Rodgers), 72
BMI. See Broadcast Music Incorporated
BMI Bonus Library, 179
BMI Canada, 321, 574
BMI v. CBS, 618
Board of Music Trade, 36-37
Boardwalk Entertainment, 599
Bock, Jerry, 355, 592
Bodec, Ben, 228, 262
"Bo Diddley," 340
"Body and Soul," 321
Bogart, Neil, 508, 558, 598-599
"Bohemian Rhapsody" (album), 639
Bolero (Ravel), 72
Bond, Carrie Jacobs, 82, 94
The Bondman (film), 11
"Boo Hoo," 155
Book-of-the-Month Club, 335-337
Boone, Pat, 340, 346, 378, 388, 414
Boosey & Hawkes, 111, 135, 269, 282
Bootleg recordings, 130
Borge, Victor, 232, 413
Bori, Lucrezia, 68, 128
Bornstein, Saul, 36, 93, 103, 257, 265, 277; see also Bourne, Saul
Bostic, Earl, 325
Boston (group), 594
Boswell Sisters, 118, 149
"Bouquet of Roses," 288
Bourbon Street Beat, 349
Bourdon, Rosario, 28
Bourne, Saul, 299, 408, 460
Bourne Music, 299, 460, 480

Bowers, James F., 22
Bowie, David, 640, 645
Boyd, William, 313
Boy George, 647
Bradford, Perry, 30
Bradley Music Company, 268
Bradshaw, Tiny, 325
Brattain, Walter, 416
Bread, 547
Breakfast at Tiffany's, 477
"The Breakfast Club," 398
Bregman, Jack, 102, 489
Bregman, Vocco & Conn, 284, 471, 489
Breil, Joseph Carl, 10
Breitkopf & Härtel, 269
Brennan, Thomas, 581, 584, 611
Brenston, Jackie, 341
Brief, Henry, 367, 509
Brill Building, 387, 591
British Performing Rights Society, 111, 186
Broadcasting (magazine), 446, 458
Broadcast Music Incorporated, 175-182,
    206-210, 223, 250, 253-255, 257,
    259-262, 264, 268-269, 278-280,
    282-283, 285-287, 289, 294, 297,
    302-303, 305-310, 314, 320-323,
    327-329, 439, 444, 447, 494, 496,
    498-502, 504-506, 519, 523-526,
    529, 531, 566, 573, 575-580, 584,
    586, 617-623
  attacks on, in fifties, 423-424
  bonus-payment system, 432-433, 483,
    573-574
  business practices, in sixties, 484-485
  classification system, in fifties, 403-404
  contracts, in fifties, anti-ASCAP terms,
    425-426
  distribution system, 424-425
    in sixties, 476
    in fifties, 421-422, 431-432
  guarantee contracts, 482, 483
  income
    in early seventies, 528
    in late forties, 287-288
    in sixties, 479
  logging operation, 322-324, 327, 420
  payment policy, in late forties, 287
  performing-rights payment system, in six-
    ties, 476
  per-program contracts, 432
  radio contracts, in sixties, 484
  royalties, in fifties, 397
  Student Composers Awards, 476
  vs. ASCAP, in fifties–sixties, 396-438
Broadway: and song hits, in forties and fif-
    ties, 317-318; in twenties, 98-99

Broadway Melody, 107
Brockman, Polk, 64-65
Broekman, David, 48
Broken Blossoms (film), 48
Brooker, Cracker Jim, 464
Brooks, Harvey, 325
Brooks, Shelton, 287
Brothers Four, 364
Brothers Johnson, 640
Brown, Charles, 326
Brown, Lew, 107
Brown, Nacio Herb, 148
Brown, Peter, 382
Brown, Ruth, 248, 325, 509
Brown, Tom, 29
Brown & Henderson, 55, 108-109
Brunswick and Dakar Records, 556
Brunswick-Balke-Collender, 27
Brunswick Radio Company, 126-127
Brunswick Radio Corporation, 197
Brunswick Records, 63-64, 66, 71-72, 117-
    118, 120, 124-125, 129-130, 135,
    143, 197, 241, 348, 555; record
    sales, 113
Bryson, 306
Bubble-gum music, 390, 556
Buck, Gene, 83-84, 94, 110, 174, 176-177,
    182, 188, 195-197, 201, 205, 207-
    208, 210-211, 265, 267, 269, 411
Buck, Pearl, 449
Buckley, William, 443
Buddah Records, 508-509, 512
Buffalo Leap (dance), 137
Buffalo Springfield, 510
Buffalo v. *ASCAP, BMI et al.*, 617-620, 632
Bullet Records, 227
Burden, Eric, 596
Bureau of Copyrights, 169, 171
Burg, MaryLou, 581
Burger, Warren, 530
Burkan, Nathan, 12, 22, 37-39, 43-44, 79,
    84, 114, 196, 198-201
Burke, Johnny, 276, 304
Burns, George, 161
Burns, John L., 416
Burton, Edgar, 407
Burton, Robert, 314, 320-321, 323, 329,
    424, 430, 464, 478, 481, 484, 523
Business as Usual (musical), 27
Buzzell, Sam, 472
"By Myself," 402
Byrds, 386
Byrnes, Ed "Kookie," 349

Cabaret, 592
Cable television (CATV), 466, 530, 583;

copyright issues with, 496-497, 565, 625; licensing, 569; royalty issues, 586-587

Cadence, 344, 356

Cadman, Charles Wakefield, 94, 106

Caesar, Sid, 295, 413

Cahn, Sammy, 471

Cakewalk, 25

"Calcutta," 379

"California, Here I Come," 101

Californians, 78

Call Me Madam, 239, 352

Camden releases, 358

Camelot, 353-354

Cameo-Parkway Records, 373, 515

Cameo Records Company, 82, 127

Camerophone Company, 10

Camp, W. L., 221

Campbell, Glen, 558

Canadian Association of Broadcasters, 321

"Candy Kisses," 288

Cantor, Eddie, 51, 63, 128, 161

Capehart, Homer, 110, 134, 144

Capitol Direct Merchandising Corp., 512

Capitol-EMI, 538, 607, 609-610

Capitol Full Dimensional, 249

Capitol Industries, 512

Capitol Industries–EMI, 562

Capitol Record Club, 512-513

Capitol Records, 217-218, 220, 223, 225-229, 234, 236-237, 286, 318, 333-334, 339, 348, 358-359, 364, 368, 376, 378, 381, 388-389, 405, 488, 495, 513, 515, 557-558, 600, 638

Captain and Tennille, 599

"Captain Fantastic and the Brown Dirt Cowboy," 537

Carle, Frankie, 225

Carlin, George, 544

Carlin Music, 592

Carl Lindstrom Company, 118

Carmen Jones, 239

Carmichael, Hoagy, 412, 424

Carousel, 304, 349

Carr, Allen, 596-597

Car radio, in fifties, 416

Carroll, Earl, 110

Cars (group), 601

Carson, Fiddlin' John, 64-65

Car tape players, 391-392

Cartoons, records based on, 651

Cartrivision, 611

Caruso, Enrico, 24, 62, 75

Casablanca Records, 558-559, 598-599

Casa Loma Orchestra, 126

Case, Theodore E., 50, 52

Casey, Pat, 17, 19-21, 40-41, 43, 69

Cash, Johnny, 379, 464, 619

Cash Box, 306, 547, 561-562

Cassette tapes, 549-550; Dolbyized, 551

Cassidy, David, 556

Castle, Irene, 25-26

Castle, Vernon, 25-27

Castles in the Air (school), 26

Catchings, Wadill, 168

Catholic archdiocese of Chicago, copyright violations by, 632

CATV, see Cable television

Cavalcade of America, 312

Cayre Corporation, 559

CBS, 70, 86, 139-141, 156, 159, 162-163, 169, 173-179, 188-189, 198, 200-202, 207-208, 217, 250, 257, 259, 261-262, 281, 283, 295, 311-312, 344, 352, 374-375, 405, 416, 432, 487, 531-532, 553, 562, 573, 576-577, 594-595, 604, 607, 629, 644, 650-652; artist-development program, 594; and BMI, 620; merchandise quotas for retailers, 637

CBS Catalog Partnership, 644

CBS Magnetics, 610

CBS Radio, 468, 575; advertising, 89

CBS Record Group, 634

CBS Records, 372, 555, 559, 609, 643-645, 653

CBS Records Group, 553, 654

CBS Television Film Sales, 413

CBS-TV, 246, 500-501, 503-504, 506, 526-527, 555-556, 577-579, 617

CBS v. ASCAP, BMI et al., 526-527, 573

CBS v. Teleprompter, 565

Celler, Emanuel, 404-406, 428, 430, 432, 438, 451, 456, 463, 493-494

Celler hearings, 425, 428

Celler report, 422-423

Censorship: of music, in fifties, 406; of radio and TV, 543-544

Central Songs, 601

Century City, 392

Chambers Brothers, 554

Chandler, Anna, 25

Chaney, Lon, 13

Channels, 639

"A Chapel in the Moonlight," 155

Chapin, Harry, 599

Chaplin, Charlie, 12, 14, 201, 272

Chaplin, Saul, 471

Chappell & Co., 111

Chappell Company, 202

Chappell group, 301

Chappell-Harms, 55, 97, 109

Chappell-Intersong, 652-653
Chappell Music, 352, 425, 472-473, 513, 534, 595, 643
Charade, 477
Charioteers, 232
Charles, Ray, 465
Charles Hansen Publications, 541
"Charmaine," 52, 106, 533
"Chattanooga Choo Choo," 216
"Chattanoogie Shoe Shine Boy," 240, 288
Chauve Souris, 51
Cheap Trick, 601
Checker, Chubby, 460-461
Chenault, Gene, 546
Chess, 340-341, 356
Chess-Checker, 325
Chesterfield Supper Club, 414
Chevalier, Maurice, 148-149, 151
Chiantia, Sal, 623
Chicago (group), 516
Chicago *Daily Tribune,* 9
Child, Calvin G., 28, 30, 101
Children's Record Guild, 335, 338
Children's records, 225, 651-652; in fifties, 338; sales, in early fifties, 246
"The Chipmunk Song," 347
Chords, 509
A Chorus Line, 600
CHR. *See* Contemporary hits radio
Chrysalis, 609
Chudd, Lew, 347, 348, 430, 471
Church, John, 82, 269
Church Music Publishers Association, 540, 628
Cinématographe, 5
CISAC, 271, 277-279, 281, 296
Claflin, Avery, 475
The Clansman (Dixon), 9
Clapton, Eric, 596
Clark, Dick, 444-445, 447-448, 638
Clark, Petula, 547
Clark, Sam, 344
Clarke, Buddy, 232
Clark-Hooper Service, 166
Classical music: recordings, 133, in forties, 224-225, 231, 235, pre-WWI, 27, in thirties, 138-139, 145; sales, in early fifties, 244
"Classic Gold," 546
Clayton Act, 375
Clef Club, 26
Clement, Frank, 427-429
CLGA. *See* Composers and Lyricists Guild of America
Clinton, Larry, 142

Cliquot Club Eskimos, 83
Clooney, Rosemary, 238, 307, 414
Clovers, 248
Coalition for Home Recording Rights, 641
Coalition to Save America's Music, 628, 637
Coasters, 510
Cobblestone, 512
Coca, Imogene, 295
Coca-Cola, 629; radio advertising, 132
Cochran, Eddie, 347
Cocker, Joe, 596
Cohan, George M., 24-25, 35, 157, 251
Cohen, Paul, 471
Cohn, Harry, 36
"Cold, Cold Heart," 240, 307, 341
Cole, Nat "King," 223, 286, 293, 379, 386, 406, 461, 638
M. M. Cole Company, 180, 471
Colgate Comedy Hour, 334
Colgems Music, 390, 601
Colin, Ralph, 174
"Collegiate," 100
ColorSonics, 638
Colpix Records, 348, 387, 390
Columbia, 201, 215-217, 223-224, 228-229, 235-237, 246, 312-313, 318-319, 334-336, 364, 392, 441, 488, 508; British, 244, 376; tape recording technology, in fifties, 359-360
Columbia Artist Management, 475
Columbia Broadcasting System. *See* CBS
Columbia Concerts Corporation, 139, 141, 258
Columbia Graphophone, 27
Columbia Phonograph Broadcasting Company, 70
Columbia Phonograph Company, 4, 24-25, 62; dance recordings, 27
Columbia Pictures, 36, 317, 348, 541, 629
Columbia Pictures Industries, 555, 562, 601, 609
Columbia Pictures Publications, 601
Columbia Pictures Television, 617
Columbia Record Club, 336-337, 364, 374-375
Columbia Records, 64, 66, 71, 75, 117-120, 125, 129, 131, 141, 143, 145, 183, 231, 352-354, 371, 389, 443-445, 512, 516-517, 536; blues recordings, in early 20th c., 30; jazz recordings, in early 20th c., 29-30; Master Works, 122, 145; record sales, 113
Columbia Records International, 380
Columbia Variable Pitch, 249

Comedians, television, 414
"Come Josephine in My Flying Machine,"
181
"Come On-A-My House," 307, 347
Comets, 334
'Comin' In on a Wing and a Prayer," 252
Command, 363
Commodores, 597, 640
Como, Perry, 223, 233, 241, 293, 316, 340,
346, 414, 461
Compact disks, 612-613, 652-653
Composers and Lyricists Guild of America,
409-410, 453, 455, 477, 531-533
Composers Facsimile Editions, 302
Composers Guild of America, 314, 409
Composers Recordings, 475
Concertapes, 359
Concert Classics series, 377
Concert Hall Records' Musical Masterpiece
Society, 335
Concert halls, licensing; in fifties, 302-303;
in sixties, 482
Concert Hall Society, 337
Concert music, in fifties and sixties, 474-
475
Concerts, television, 639
Conkling, James, 243, 345, 348, 369, 388
A Connecticut Yankee, 239
Connelly, Reg, 425
Connick, Harris, 168
Conqueror Records, 127
Consolidated Foods, 395
Consolidated Music Corporation, 29, 42
Consumers Federation of America, 568
Consumers Union, 362
"Contempo 200," 546
"Contempo 300," 546
Contemporary hits radio, 646-647
Conti, Bill, 532
Cook, Emory, 359
"Cool Water," 288
Coon-Sanders Nighthawks, 78, 96
Coon songs, 6, 30, 100
Cooperative Analysis of Broadcasters, 166
Copland, Aaron, 269, 302
Copyright, 200; economic effect of, 462; and
home taping problem, 610-611; inter-
national reciprocal, 23, 528; and ra-
dio, 81; retained by motion picture
companies, 107-108; sales boom, of
sixties, 471-472
Copyright law, 294. See also Public perfor-
mance for profit
1965 revision bill, 368, 462-463, 485-486,
493, 495

1976 revision bill, 563-569, 581, 588,
627-628
1984 revision bill, 625-626
in America, 22
British, 592-593
changes, in 1930, 111-112
and coin-operated music machines, 433-
434
efforts to revise, in fifties, 304-307
infringements
efforts to oppose, in early 20th c., 37-
39
in eighties, 590-591
movie-theater owners' attack on, 50
proposed revisions
1925, 83-84
in fifties, 435-436
Sirovich's, 194-195
and song-plugging songwriters, 33
Copyright Revision Panel, in sixties, 485
Copyright Royalty Tribunal, 565-566, 568,
581-587, 624-626, 641
Coral, 241
"Cornish Rhapsody," 421
Cornyn, Stan, 583, 585, 635-636
Correll, Charles, 89
Cosby, Bill, 389
Costa, Don, 345
Cotton Club, 124
Coulter, Douglas, 581
Country and Western Disk Jockeys Associa-
tion, 247
Country and western music, 240, 246-247,
341, 376-377; see also Country music
Country blues, 225
Country music, 426-428; in fifties, 329;
growth of, in late forties, 288; in six-
ties, 464-465, 481
Country Music Association, 428, 464, 481,
564; Hall of Fame and Museum, 481-
482
Country Music Carnival and Summer Festi-
val of America's Music, 428
Country Music Disk Jockeys Association,
428
Country Music Disk Jockeys' Festival, 443
Country Music Festival, 464
Country Music Spectacular, 428
Coury, Al, 597-598, 607
The Covered Wagon (film), 48
"Cover Me," 560
Cover versions, of R & B hits, 340
"Cow Cow Boogie," 218
Coy, Wayne, 285
Craig, Francis, 227

Cramer, Edward M., 499-500, 621
Crawford, Bobby, 106, 109
Crawford Music Corp., 106
"Crazy Blues," 31
Cream, 510, 514
Creatore, Luigi, 345, 387
Crew Cuts, 340
Cricket Records, 338
Crist, Bainbridge, 94
Crosby, Bing, 69, 118, 126, 133, 137-138,
    149-150, 185, 196, 200, 217, 219,
    225, 230, 276, 310, 334, 339, 388,
    423-424, 607
Cross, John S., 464
Crossley, Ada, 216
Crossley, Archibald M., 166
Crossley Report, 166
Cross-over marketing, 597-598
"Cross Over the Bridge," 334
Crowell-Collier, 337
Crudup, Arthur, 341
Crumit, Frank, 135
Crusader Rabbit, 651
"Cry in the Chapel," 341
Csida, Joseph, 236, 323, 407
Csida-Joy-Burton, 471
Culligan, Matthew, 446
Culture Club, 647
Cunningham, Paul, 308, 328, 401-402, 412,
    418
"Cupid's Garden" (Dreyfus), 96
Curb, Mike, 511-512, 534
Current Writers Group, 420, 452, 465
Curtis Company, recording subsidiary, 145
Cut theatres, 18

"Daddy Has a Sweetheart and Mother Is Her
    Name" (Buck), 83
Dae, Sunny, 250
Dakar Records, 555
Dalhart, Vernon, 100
Dames, 149
Damone, Vic, 293
Dance bands, 293; on early records, 25-27;
    in late thirties, 204; recordings, sales
    of, 216
Dance mania, of early 20th c., 25, 29-30
Dance music: for radio, 130-131; on stage,
    98-99
"Dance with Me Henry," 340
"Dancing in the Dark," 402
"Dancing in the USA," 560
The Dancing Pirate, 153
Daniel, Oliver, 475

Daniels, Charles N., 47, 425
"Dardanella," 104
Darin, Bobby, 364, 387-388, 471, 510
Dark House, 539
"Darktown Strutters' Ball," 287
Daru, Robert, 308-309
Dave Clark Five, 386
David, Hal, 420, 580, 619-620, 643
David, Mack, 402
Davis, Clive, 355, 516, 535-536, 553-557
Davis, Mac, 599
Day, Doris, 379, 397, 461
The Days of Wine and Roses, 477
Dean, Arthur, 419-420, 454
Dean, Joel, 420
"Dear Old Southland," 592
Decca, 125-127, 129, 132-134, 136, 138,
    143, 145, 197, 215-217, 219-220,
    223, 225-226, 228-229, 233, 236-
    237, 241, 244-245, 284, 307, 317-
    318, 334, 339, 344, 358, 364, 377,
    390, 393, 471, 488; British, 135,
    226-227, 360-361, 378, 515, 551,
    600
Decca-Coral-Brunswick, 389
De Concini, Dennis, 630
" 'Deed I Do," 288
Def Leppard, 640, 645
De Forest, Lee, 50-51, 75-76
De Forest Radio Telephone Company, 75
DeKnight, James, 250
De Leath, Vaughn, 71
Delfont, Bernard, 601-602
Dello Joio, Norman, 302
De Mille, Cecil B., 13
Denmark Street, 381
Denton & Haskins, 82
De Patie-Freleng, 651
"Der Fuerher's Face," 252
The Desert Song, 101
De Sylva, Brown & Henderson, 105-106,
    148, 190
De Sylva, Buddy, 55, 107-109, 150-151,
    217-218, 229, 376, 407
Deutsch, Adolph, 275
Deutsch, Percy, 131
Deutsche Grammophon, 233, 389, 513-514,
    534, 649
Deutsche Grammophon–Polydor, 119
Dexter, Dave, 606
Diamond, Lew, 152
Diamond, Milton, 210-211, 218-219
Diamond, Neil, 524, 536, 547, 552, 602
"Diane" (Rapee), 52, 106
Dickens, Little Jimmy, 240

ick James Music Ltd., 473, 537
ickson, William K. L., 3-4
ick Van Dyke, 484
ie Tote Stadt, 152
Dietz, Howard, 402
DiGhilini, U. L., 221
Digital recording technology, 612, 652
"Dim, Dim the Lights," 334
Dinning, Mark, 460
"Disco Lady," 605
Disco music, 558-560, 596-597, 605, 641
Disco pools, 560
Discovery Music Network, 651
Disk Jockey Association, 446
Disk jockeys, 223, 310, 442; black, 248,
    605, and R & B sales, 241; country,
    428; disco superstars, 559; early,
    129; in fifties, 247, 315-316, 441;
    free releases to, 218; importance of,
    in late forties and early fifties, 242-
    243; name personalities as, 397; rec-
    ord industry relationships with, FTC
    investigation of, 373-374; and song
    hits, 286, 344, in fifties, 318, 320-
    321; and success of independents, in
    forties, 227-228
Disney, Walt, 261, 313, 344
Disneyland, 344
Disney Studios, 651
Disques CBS, 380
Ditson, Oliver, 82
Ditson Company, 269
Dixon, Mort, 299
Dixon, Thomas, 9
Do I Hear a Waltz?, 355
"Do It to My Mind," 605
Dolan, Robert, 275
Dolby, Ray, 551
Dolby technology, 598; movie sound, 598
Domino, Fats, 347
Domino Records, 65
Dominos, 325-326
Donahue, Sam, 520
Donahue, Tom, 519, 545
Donaldson, Walter, 92, 190
Don Juan (film), 48, 52
Donovan, 536
Don Q (film), 48
"Don't Be Cruel," 342, 460
"Don't Be That Way," 137
"Don't Let the Stars Get in Your Eyes,"
    341
"Don't Sit Under the Apple Tree," 252
The Doors, 511
Dorsey, Jimmy, 126, 216, 461

Dorsey, Tommy, 126, 142, 216, 228, 461
Dot Records, 339, 344, 346, 356, 379, 388,
    393, 430, 561
Double features, 151
Douglas, Walter, 252-253
Douglas & Gumble, 190
Downey, Morton, 112, 119
"Do You Ken John Peel," 67
Drake, Bill, 545-546
Drake, Ervin, 531, 535
Drake, Milton, 402
Drake-Chenault Enterprises, 546
Dresser, Paul, 96
Dreyfus, Louis, 96-97, 109, 111, 472, 513
Dreyfus, Max, 40, 55, 88, 91, 96-99, 108-
    113, 150, 187, 195, 201, 204, 257,
    290, 299, 301, 303, 306, 316, 329,
    352, 399, 407, 425, 441, 452-453,
    472, 513
Drifters, 510
Dubin, Al, 149, 153
Duchess Music, 287, 471
Duffy, F. Ryan, 256-257
Duke, Vernon, 530
Duke label, 325
Dukes of Dixieland, 360
Dumbo, 261
Dumont, 288
Dumont Laboratories, 310, 311
Duncan, Isadora, 98
Dunhill Productions, 509
Dunhill Records, 509
Duran Duran, 647
Durbin, Deanna, 228
Durium Products Company, 119
Durium Records, 72, 112, 121
"Dying Poet" (Gottschalk), 10
Dylan, Bob, 385-386

E.T., 642, 652
Earth, Wind & Fire, 640
"Earth Angel," 340, 460
Eash, George, 391
East Coast Sonoraphone Company, 54
Eastman, George, 3
Eastman, Lee, 420-421, 539
Ebb, Fred, 592
F. Eberstadt & Co., 630-631
Eddy, Duane, 471
Edison, Thomas, 3-7, 24, 48
Edison Kinetoscope Company, 10
Edison Penny Coin Slot Machines, 304
Edison phonograph company, 62, 71

Edison phonograph recordings, 24; for danc-
    ing, 27
Ed Sullivan Hour, 382-383
Ed Sullivan Show, 543
Edwards, Clara, 94
Edwards, Gus, 157
Edwards, Ralph, 415
Egan, Jack, 319
Eight-track tape, 549-550
Eisenhower, Dwight, 448
Elder, Omar, 430
Electrical and Musical Industries (EMI),
    119, 135, 224, 233, 243-244, 343,
    359, 376-378, 390, 392, 512-513,
    515, 536, 538, 556-558, 594, 600-
    602, 607
Electrical Research Products, Inc. (ERPI),
    48, 52-55, 131, 192-193
Electrical transcriptions, 89-90, 121, 128,
    130-132, 144, 160
Electric Flag, 516, 535
Electronic music, 475, 636
Electro-Voice Company, 360
Elektra Records, 510-511, 543
Eleventh Floor Music, 591
Eliscu, Edward, 530-531
Elkan-Vogel Music, 271
Ellington, Edward Kennedy "Duke," 72,
    123-124
Elliott, Ken, 248
Ellis, Seger, 71
Elman, Mischa, 94
"El Oaso," 364
Elvis Presley Music Corp., 342, 591
Emerson Records, 63
EMI, *see* Electrical and Musical Industries
EMI Film & Theatre Corp., 601
Encore series, 377
Energy crisis, of 1973, effect on recording
    industry, 537-538
England: popular music in, in sixties, 381;
    record market in, 380
Enoch et Cie, 111
Epstein, Brian, 382-383, 473, 512, 514,
    536, 595
Epstein, Clive, 514
Erdman, Fred, 123
Erlanger, Abe, 17
ERPI, *see* Electrical Research Products,
    Inc.
Ertegun, Ahmet, 509-510
Ertegun, Nesuhi, 509
Erwin-Wasey, 119-120
Essanay Company, 7, 12

Essex Productions, 348, 351
Etting, Ruth, 71
Eurhythmics, 647
Europe: attitude toward American music, in
    fifties, 379; record sales in, 380
Europe, James Reese, 26-27
European Common Market, 379-380
Evans, Redd, 300, 419
The Eveready Hour, 83
Eveready Music Makers, 80
Everly Brothers, 460
"Everybody's Doin' It" (Berlin), 25
Exclusive label, 224
Exodus, 379

F.E.L. Publications, 632
Fain, Sammy, 123
Fairbanks, Douglas, 14
Fairchild, Blair, 38
Fairchild Industries, 360
Faith, Percy, 345, 364, 467, 531
Family Record Club, 335
Famous Music, 109, 190, 477, 561, 602
Fantasia, 359
"Far Away Places," 233
Farben, I. G., 221
Farnon, Christine, 370
Farnsworth Company, 173
Farnum, William, 12
Fauntroy, Walter, 557
Federal Communications Commission
    (FCC), 164, 439-440, 464; attempt to
    censor rock broadcasts, in seventies,
    544; ban of seven dirty words on air,
    545; division of AM/FM broadcast-
    ing, 518; inquiry into TV and radio,
    449, in fifties, 447; jurisdiction over
    CATV, 497; ruling on free records
    given to broadcasters, 451
Federal Radio Commission, 163-164
Federal Trade Commission (FTC): investiga-
    tion of movie-affiliated publishers,
    155; investigation of record clubs,
    374-375; and payola, 373; and
    record-industry mergers in eighties,
    648-650
"Feelings," 590
Feist, Edgar, 114
Feist, Leo, 22, 29, 33, 35, 37-40, 43, 83,
    88, 91, 96, 100, 105, 111-114, 179,
    190
Feist, Leonard, 567-568, 628, 632
Feist business, 154, 317, 489

B. Feldman, 407, 601
Feller, Sid, 345
Ferara, Fred, 95
Ferris, Charles D., 641
'Fever,'' 460
Fibber McGee and Molly, 315
Fiddler on the Roof, 355, 592
Fidelipac, 391
Fields, Dorothy, 124, 304, 328, 402, 422
Fifth Dimension, 556, 599
Filmation, 651
Film Booking Offices of America (FBO),
    53, 60
Film music, 532-533; accompanying screen-
    ing, Zukor's production of, 10; col-
    lections of, 11; piano used for, 10-11;
    popularity of, 154
Finkelstein, Herman, 255, 271-272, 274,
    284, 301, 399, 405, 418-419, 426,
    435-437, 450, 454, 462, 494, 529
Fiorello, 353, 592
"The First Family" (LP), 383
First Little Show, 401
First National Bank of Boston, 394
First National Exhibitors' Circuit, 14
First National Pictures, 49, 55
Fischer, Carl, 82, 88, 105, 111
Fisher, Eddie, 333
Fisher, Fred, 33, 101, 104
Fitzgerald, Ella, 137, 369, 461
Fitzpatrick, Dennis J., 632
Five-and-ten-cent stores, 34
Five Royales, 248
Five Rubes, 29
Flack, Roberta, 554
Flashdance, 630, 644-645
Fleetwood Mac, 608, 626, 637
Fletcher, Dusty, 224
Flintstones, 651
The Floorwalker, 12
Flower Drum Song, 352
Flying Down to Rio, 150
FM broadcasting, 173-174, 249, 285, 314-
    315, 461, 518, 543; in eighties, 646;
    in fifties, 632; in seventies, 520, 543-
    544, 546; in sixties, 519
Foley, Red, 240, 247
Folies Bergere, 13
Folios, 590
Folk-rock, 385-386, 389
Follow the Fleet, 154
Follow Through, 107
"Folsom Prison Blues,'' 464
Fonda, Jay, 221

Fontana Records, 378
Fontane Sisters, 340
Footlights Parade, 149
Forbstein, Leo, 147, 152
Ford, Tennessee Ernie, 240, 427
Ford and Glenn, 80
Ford Theatre, 313
Foreign-language recordings, by Americans,
    379-380
Forrest, Helen, 223
Forrest, Jimmy, 326
Fortnightly v. United Artists, 496, 530, 565,
    569
42nd Street, 149-150
Forum for Songwriters, 263, 308
Foster, Stephen, 72, 157
Four Aces, 307, 334
The Four Horsemen (film), 15
The Four Horsemen of the Apocalypse
    (film), 48
Four Seasons, 386
Four Star Playhouse, 414
Four Star Television, 471
Four Tops, 386
Fox, Fred, 400, 452, 454, 477-478
Fox, Harry, 136, 488, 489
Fox, Sam, 11, 105, 454
Fox, William, 7, 8, 11-13, 52, 106
Fox-Case Movietone Newsreel, 52
Fox Films, 629
Fox trot, 26
"Frampton Comes Alive,'' 609
France, record market in, 380
Francis, Connie, 460-461
Francis, Day & Hunter, 29, 407, 601
Franklin, Aretha, 510, 554
Franklin, Ilene, 25
Frank Music, 604
Freed, Alan, 248, 326, 340-341, 442, 444,
    447-449
Freed, Arthur, 148
Freedman, Max, 250
Frey, Sidney, 360
Friday Night Videos, 646
Friedland, Anatole, 42
"Friendly Persuasion,'' 346
Friganza, Trixie, 10
Friml, Rudolf, 72, 97
Frith, Simon, 597
Frolich, Louis, 210-211
"From Nothing to Five Million a Year: The
    Story of ASCAP by a Founder,'' 39
"From the Bottom to the Top,'' 406
FTC, see Federal Trade Commission

Full Frequency Range Recording, 227
Functional Radio, 315

"The G.I. Jive," 252
Gabler, Milt, 334
Gagliardi, Lee, 617-619, 622
Gains, Steven, 382
Galvin, Bill, 446
Gamble, Kenny, 555-557
Gannon, James Kimball, 402
Garcia, Frances, 581
Garden, Mary, 128
Garland, Judy, 461
Garroway, Dave, 415
Gartenberg, Seymour, 604
Gary Lewis and the Playboys, 386
Gavin, Bill, 547
The Gay Divorcee (film), 150
Gaye, Marvin, 386, 640
Gaynor, Gloria, 559, 597
GE, see General Electric Company
GEMA, 589
Gene and Eunice, 340
General Electric Company (GE), 52-53, 76,
    82, 90, 160, 173, 221, 392
General Film Exchange, 7
Gentlemen Prefer Blondes, 239
George Melies et Cie, Paris, 7
George White's Scandals, 107
German Odeon Company, 27
Germany, record market in, 380
Gershwin, George, 97, 107, 202, 304
Gershwin, Ira, 304, 328, 402
Gershwin estate, 298
Gibb, Andy, 597
Gibbs, Georgia, 223, 340
"Gigi," 350
Gilbert, L. Wolfe, 25, 42, 402
Gillham, Whispering Art, 71, 80
Gilmer, Jimmy, and the Fireballs, 383
"The Girl at the Prison Gates," 100
"Girls Just Want to Have Fun," 560
Gladys Music, 342, 591
Glass, Philip, 560
Gleason, Jackie, 339, 413-414
Gleason, Ralph, 519
The Glenn Miller Story, 349
Glenwood Music, 601
Glover, John D., 368
"Glow Worm," 400
Gluck, Alma, 24, 65
"God Bless America," 261
Goddard, Henry W., 256, 309, 327

Godfrey, Arthur, 411-412, 414
Godspell, 599
Goetz, E. Ray, 43
Goffin, Gerry, 387
The Gold Diggers of 1935, 152
Gold Diggers series, 149-150
Golden, Ernie, 104
"Golden Oldie" programming, 460, 546
Golden Records, 338
Goldenson, Leonard H., 311-312, 346-347
Goldfish, Samuel, see Goldwyn, Samuel
Goldkette, Jean, 71, 78
Goldman, Edwin Franko, 94
Goldmark, Geoffrey, 254
Goldmark, Peter, 231
Gold Records: Blood, Sweat & Tears', 536;
    criteria and procedure of award, 366;
    Donovan's, 536; in eighties, 654;
    Fats Domino's, 347; Hal David's,
    580; Lieber-Stoller's, 386; original-
    cast albums, 354; Osmonds', 534;
    Rick Nelson's, 347; singles, in six-
    ties, 364; Stevie Wonder's, 539
Goldsmith, Jerry, 477, 532
Goldwater, Barry, 424
Goldwyn, Samuel, 13
Gomer Pyle, 484
Gone With the Wind, 157
"Goodby, Mama, I'm Off to Yokahama,"
    251
Goodman, Benny, 137, 142-143, 216, 347
Goodman, Marv, 590
Goodman, Maurice, 40, 43
Goodman, Theodosia. See Bara, Theda
Good News, 107
"Goodnight, Irene," 237, 307
"Goodnight, Little Girl," 192
"Goodnight, Sweetheart," 186
Goodson & Todman, 456
Goody, Sam, 238-239, 244
Goody's, 356-357
Gordy, Berry, Jr., 384, 524, 539
Gore, Albert, 427, 430
Gorme, Edie, 380
Gortikov, Stanley, 513, 535, 565-567, 582,
    628, 642
Gosden, Freeman, 89
Gotham-Attucks, 472
Gottschalk, Louis Ferdinand, 48
Gottschalk, Louis Moreau, 10, 48
Goulet, Robert, 386
Grade, Lew, 489-490, 513-514, 538
Graff, George, 402
Graft contracts, 98

Grainger, Percy, 94
Grammy Awards, 369-370; Stevie Wonder's, 539
Gramophone Company, 24
Gramophone Company–His Master's Voice, 62, 118
Grand Award Records, 345
Grand Funk Railroad, 513
Grand Ole Opry, 247, 288, 341, 427, 465
W. T. Grant Stores, 560
The Grateful Dead, 516
Grauman's Chinese Theatre, 59
Gray, Barry, 228
Gray, Elisha, 74
Grease, 596, 599
"Grease," 599
Grease (film), 599, 602
"Great American Country," 546
The Great Train Robbery (film), 5-6
Greed (film), 48
Green, Abel, 91, 102-103, 106, 108, 113, 288, 291, 323, 329
Green, Johnny, 321
Green, William, 186
Greenberg, Herman, 284
"Green Eyes," 216
Greenfield, Howard, 387
"Greenfields," 364
Green & Stept, 109
"Green Tambourine," 509
Greenwich, Ellie, 387
Grey, Frank, 106
Griffith, David Wark (D.W.), 8-9, 14
Grigsby-Grunow Company, 77, 119, 125
Grimes, Tiny, 326
Grofé, Ferde, 30
Grundig, 392
Gulf & Western Corporation, 393-394, 560
Gurfein, Murray, 576, 579
Gus Edwards Music, 472

Hack Swain, 359
Haddy, Arthur, 227
Hagen, Earle, 477, 484
Hager, Fred, 30, 65
Haggard, Merle, 513
Hair, 596, 599
Haley, Bill, 334, 340, 378, 406, 414
Half-in-half (dance), 26
Hall, Wendell, 80
Hall and Oates, 643-644
Hallett, Mal, 104
Hammerstein, Arthur, 99

Hammerstein, Oscar II, 153, 154, 202, 298, 304, 399, 401, 404, 412, 418, 424, 426, 429, 514
Hammond, John, 142
Hamp, Johnny, 104
Ham radio, 77
Hanapi Trio, 95
Hancock, Hunter, 248
Handleman, Joe and David, 358
Handleman Company, 372, 376
Handy, William C., 30
Hanna-Barbera, 651
Happiness Boys, 80
Herbach, Otto, 190, 202, 298-300, 304, 306, 422, 449
Harbach Affidavit, 309, 327
Harburg, E. Y., 153
A Hard Day's Night, 382, 638
Harlow, Roy, 282
Harmonicats, 227
Harmony records, 358
T. B. Harms, 96-99, 109, 301, 317, 407, 513-514
Harms, Inc., 97, 103, 105, 108-109, 190-191, 195
Harms, T. B., 29, 40, 55, 96
Harnick, Sheldon, 355, 592
Harris, Charles K., 6, 43, 91, 180
Harris, Oren, 439, 441, 451
Harris, Phil, 319
Harris, William, 436
Harrison, George, 382, 473, 539-540
Harry Fox Agency, 276, 367, 408, 488-489, 581, 618, 628-629
Harry von Tilzer Music Company, 407
Harry Warren Music, 317
Hart, Lorenz, 97, 304
Hart, Moss, 353
Hart, William S., 14
Hatari, 477
Haverlin, Carl, 178-179, 209, 250, 282-284, 286-288, 302, 307, 320, 324, 329, 402, 404, 424, 474-476, 499
Haviland, F. B., 82
Haydn Society, 244
Hayes, Helen, 449
Haymes, Dick, 223, 293
Hays, Arthur Garfield, 186, 320
Hays, Will H., 147, 158
Hays, Will Shakespeare, 50, 65
Hayton, Lennie, 166
Hearst, William Randolph, 9, 43
Hearst Corporation, International Circulation Co., 253

Hearst newspapers, series on jukeboxes, 436-437
Hearst-Selig Newsreel, 9
"Heartbreak Hotel," 342, 429
"Hearts of Stone," 460
Heath, Ted, 360
Heebner, Walter, 219
Heilicher, Amos, 375
Hein, Silvio, 37, 94
Heinecke, Paul, 171, 469
Heinesmann, Otto, 30
Hellfighters, 27
Hello Dolly, 599
Henderson, Fletcher, 72
Henderson, Ray, 107, 299
Hendrix, Jimi, 516, 554
Henn, Harry G., 436
Henry, E. William, 464
Henshaw, Annette, 71
Herald, 248, 325
Herbert, Victor, 11, 16, 22, 28, 37-39, 72, 93-95, 98, 151, 201
Herman, Pinky, 300
Herman's Hermits, 386, 389
"Hey Paula," 383
Hibbard, Charles, 65
High Class Electric Theater, Los Angeles, 5
High Fidelity, 610
High Society, 398
Hill, George Washington, 165, 166, 181, 205
Hillbilly music, 120, 124, 133, 141-142, 180, 222, 225, 227, 240, 341 (*see also* Country and western music); production of, in twenties, 64-65; recordings, in forties, 223
Hillbilly records, 72
Hill & Range Songs, 287, 307, 342, 407, 425-426, 482, 484, 489, 509, 592, 595
Hippodrome, New York, 57
Hirsch, Louis, 37, 44
"History of Rock 'n' Roll," 546
Hitachi, 392
Hitchcock, Raymond, 25
Hit of the Week records, 119-121
"Hitparade," 546
The Hit Parader, 253
HMV, 145, 244, 377, 378
HMV Stereosonic, 360
"H₂O" (Hall and Oates), 644
Hoffman, George, 284, 466
Hold Everything, 107
Holiday Hotel (film), 69
Holiday Inn (film), 473

Holly, Buddy, 539
Holmes, Oliver Wendell, 39
Holzman, Jac, 543
Home Box Office, 601
Home Recording Act of 1983, 641
Home taping, 628, 631, 635-636, 642; of commercial albums, 609-610; copyright issues with, 625; extent of, 611-612; losses from, 629; royalties on, 631; tax scheme proposed for, 629, 631
"Honest and Truly," 288
"The Honeydripper," 224
Honeymooners, 414
Hooker, John, Jr., 464
Hooper Rating Reports, 166
Hoopii, Sol, 95
Hoover, Herbert, 84
Hopalong Cassidy, 313
Hope, Bob, 315
Hope-Jones, Robert, 47
Horn, Bob, 444, 638
Horsky, Charles, 420-421
"Hot August Night," 552
Hotsy-Totsy Boys, 123
"Hound Dog," 342, 386
Houston, Thelma, 597
Hovhaness, Alan, 474
Howard, Eddy, 223
"How Deep Is Your Love," 598
Howdy Doody, 314
Howley, Haviland & Dresser, 96
Howlin' Wolf, 341
"How Soon," 227
Hubbell, Raymond, 37, 39
Huckleberry Hound, 651
The Hucksters (novel), 165
Hudson Bay Music, 592
Hues Corporation, 559, 597
Huff, Leon, 555-556
Hugg, Dick, 248
Hughes, Howard, 413
Hunt, Pee Wee, 286
Hunter, Ivory Joe, 340
"Hurdy Gurdy," 536
Hurricane, 157
"Hurry on Down," 227
Hurwitz, Nathan, 138
"The Hut Sut Song," 264

"I Believe," 324
"I Didn't Raise My Boy to Be a Soldier," 40

I Don't Want to Get Well, I'm in Love with a Beautiful Nurse,'' 40
"I Don't Want to Set the World on Fire,'' 264
'I Get Ideas,'' 307
"I Like Ike,'' 352, 399
'I Like Jazz,'' 339
'I'll Be Seeing You,'' 252
'I Loved You Then,'' 106
I Love Lucy, 414
"I Love You'' (song), 95
"I Love You So'' (Lehar), 24
"I Love You So Much It Hurts Me,'' 288
"I'm Forever Blowing Bubbles,'' 35
"I'm Gonna Get You,'' 185
"I'm Heading South,'' 101
"I Miss My Swiss Miss,'' 96
Imperial, 240, 325, 347, 356
Imported music, 186
Improved Panatrope, 68
"I'm So Lonesome I Could Cry,'' 288
"In a Little Spanish Town,'' 71
Ince, Thomas, 13-15
In Concert, 639
Independent Radio Network Affiliates (IRNA), 170-171, 176, 198, 205, 220, 254
"I Never Knew,'' 96
Ingle, Red, 227
Ingmann, Jorgen, 379
Innerworld Music Group, 643
Inside Story on How to Write Popular Songs (Green), 102
Internal Revenue Service, Project Sound, 557
International Copyright Union, 434
International Federation of Popular Music Publishers, 589, 629
International Gospel Music Association, 540
International Telephone and Telegraph, 311
"In the Ghetto,'' 515
Intolerance (film), 14
Ipana Troubadors, 83
IRNA, *see* Independent Radio Network Affiliates
The Iron Horse (film), 49
Irving Berlin, Inc., 36
"I See a Million People,'' 321
Isleys, 640
I Spy, 484
"It Ain't Gonna Rain No Mo,'' 80, 95
Italy, record market in, 380
"It Is No Sin,'' 307
"It'll Be a Hot Time for the Old Boys When the Young Men Go to War,'' 40

Ives, Charles, 474-475
Ives, Irving M., 421
"I Walk the Line,'' 464
"I Want to Hold Your Hand,'' 381, 472

Jackson, Jesse, 605
Jackson, Michael, 547, 604, 640, 644-647, 650, 652, 654
Jackson, Millie, 559
Jackson Five, 547
Jacobs, Little Walter, 341
Jagger, Mick, 643
"Jambalaya,'' 341
James, Clarence L., 625
James, Dick, 473-474
James, Harry, 142, 216, 219, 224-225
Janik, Tony, 219
"Japanese Sandman'' (Grofé), 30
Jarvis, Al, 129
Jaws (film), 532
Jazz: in early 20th c., 29-30; recordings: in early 20th c., 29, in forties, 223; in twenties and thirties, 64
The Jazz Singer, 602
The Jazz Singer (film), 52
"Jealous Heart, '' 288
Jenkins, Gordon, 236, 345
Jenkins Company, 191
Jenkins Music, 317
"Jeopardy'' (Kihn), 640
Jerry Vogel Music, 457
"Jesus Christ Superstar,'' 552
Jesus Christ Superstar, 596, 599
Jett, Joan, 599
Jewell-LaSalle case, 529-530
Jimmie Rodgers (Porterfield), 65
Jingles, 467
"Joan of Arc, They Are Calling You,'' 35
Jobete Music Company, 384
Joel, Billy, 636, 640
John, Elton, 536-537, 609
"Johnny Doughboy Found a Rose in Ireland,'' 252
"Johnny Get Your Gun,'' 35
Johnson, Bob, 641
Johnson, Eldridge, 62, 117
Johnson, Mrs. Lyndon B., 479
Jolson, Al, 25, 39, 51-52, 54-55, 66, 101, 106, 126, 128, 149, 157, 162, 201, 602
The Jolson Story, 284
Jones, Clarence, 581
Jones, Isham, 64,78, 95, 126
Jones, Quincy, 477, 640

Jones, Spike, 227
Joplin, Janis, 516, 536
Jordan, Louis, 224-225, 240, 334
Josefowitz, David and Samuel, 337
Joseph and the Technicolor Dreamcoat, 596
Joseph Daly Music, 472
Joy, Eddie, 323
Joy, George, 323
Joy, Leonard, 142
Joyce, Thomas F., 138
Joy Music, 489
Joyce, Thomas F., 138
Judith of Bethulia (film), 8
Judson, Arthur, 86, 131, 139, 141, 201
Jukeboxes, 13, 132-133, 137, 216, 226,
    237, 433, 435, 493-494, 565-566,
    581-584; copyright exemption, 304-
    307, 436-438, 462, 485; cost of, 433;
    in fifties, 356; and gangsters, allega-
    tions about, 434-437; for home use,
    144; musical-video, 638; royalty, at-
    tempts to impose in fifties, 433-434
Jungle music, 124
Jungnickel, Ross, 425
"Just a Little Street Where Old Friends
    Meet," 192

K.C. and the Sunshine Band, 597
Kaempfert, Bert, 379, 386
Kahn, Gus, 92, 95, 304
Kahn, Roger Wolfe, 51, 104
Kalem, 7, 8
Kallen, Kitty, 334
Kalmar, Puck & Abrahams, 472
Kama Sutra records, 508-509, 512
Kaminstein, Abraham L., 435, 486, 494,
    496
Kander, John, 592
Kapp, David, 126, 151, 245, 368
Kapp, Jack, 72, 118, 124, 126-127, 129-
    130, 132, 134-135, 137-138, 151,
    196-197, 218, 220, 225-226, 239,
    284, 377
Kassar, Raymond, 642
Kastenmeier, Robert, 631
Kaufman, Murray, 430
Kaye, Sammy, 142
Kaye, Sydney, 171, 174-182, 201-202, 208-
    209, 254, 259-260, 263, 267-269,
    272, 280, 282, 306, 320, 322, 429,
    432, 436, 438, 450-451, 482, 496,
    529
KCO, 310
KDKA, 77
Kearns, Carroll, 305

Kefauver-Bryson bill, 305
Keith, A. Paul, 19, 21
Keith, Benjamin Franklin, 5, 17-19
Keith-Albee, 40, 57
Keith-Albee-Orpheum, 53, 60
Keith-Albee vaudeville, 17-18
B. F. Keith Exchange, 21
Keith-Prowse, 601
Keith Vaudeville Collection Agency, 20
Keit Music, 472
Keller, Jack, 387
Kempinski, Leo, 48
Kennedy, John F., 423, 463
Kennedy, Joseph P., 53, 60, 87
Kennedy, Robert, 463
Kennin, Herman D., 350-351
Kenton, Stan, 388, 495-496, 566
Kent Production Company, 414
Kerker, Gustave, 37
Kern, Jerome, 96-97, 151, 154, 190, 195,
    197-198, 201-202, 304, 513
Keystone Kops, 14
KFI, 178
KHJ, 545
Kihn, Greg, 640
Kilpatrick, Walter, 464
Kinemacolor Company, 19
Kineto-Phone phonograph, 10
Kinetoscope, 3-5
Kinetoscope Company, 4
King, B. B., 341
King, Carole, 387, 524, 541, 547, 609
King, Gerald, 425
King, Pee Wee, 289, 429
The King and I, 304, 349
"The King Biscuit Flower Hour," 546
"King Creole," 350
The King of Kings (film), 59
King Records, 240, 248, 376
Kingston Trio, 364
Kinney National Service, 510
Kintner, Earl, 373
Kirshner, Don, 387-388, 390, 639
Kiss, 598
"A Kiss in the Dark" (Herbert), 95
Kiss Me Kate, 239
Klauber, Edward, 177, 188-189, 254, 487
Klaw, Marc, 18
Klaw & Erlanger, 8
Klein, Allen, 515, 539
Kleine, George, 8
Klugh, Paul Brown, 41, 81, 83
KMPX-FM, 519-520
Knapp, Jack, 352
Knight, Evelyn, 325

night, Gladys, and the Pips, 554
NX, 169
NXT-TV, 311
odak camera, 3
Ko Ko Mo," 340
"Kookie, Lend Me Your Comb," 349
ool and the Gang, 640
Koppelman, Charlie, 387
Korngold, Erich Wolfgang, 152, 476
Kornheiser, Phil, 99-100
Kostelanetz, André, 225
Koster & Bial, 3, 5
Koussevitzky, Serge, 72
KOWH, 250, 442-443
Kramer, Alex, 402
Krasilowsky, M. William, 593
Kreisler, Fritz, 94
Kresge's, 184
Kristofferson, Kris, 532
KTLA, 430
Kukla, Fran and Ollie, 314
KWTO, 427
KWTV, 427
KYA, 519
Kyser, Kay, 140, 216, 232

La Bohème, 232
Ladd, David, 624-626
Laemmle, Carl, 8
Laine, Frankie, 231, 293
Lamb, Charlie, 464
Lame duck (dance), 26
Lamour, Dorothy, 157
Lane, Burton, 410-411, 421, 439-440, 447,
   449, 455, 457, 480, 530
Lanin, Sam, 104
Lanza, Mario, 242
Lasker, Morris, 502-503, 506, 524, 526-
   527, 573, 576
Lasky, Jesse, 13
Lasky Feature Play Company, 13
L'Assassinat du Duc de Guise (Saint-Saëns),
   11
"Last Hope" (Gottschalk), 10
"The Last Roundup," 124, 192
"Last Train from Clarksville," 390
Latham, Woodville, 4
Latin-American music, 347
"Laugh Clown Laugh," 106
Laugh In, 500
"Laughing on the Outside," 279
Lauper, Cyndi, 560
Laura, 275
Lawrence, Jack, 402

Lawrence, Steve, 380
Lawrence Welk Group, 514
Lazarsfeld, Paul A., 181
LBJ Co., 479
Lear, William, 391
Lear car tape system, 391-392
Lear tape players, 550
Leave It to Jane, 97
Lee, Brenda, 460
Lee, Ivy, 190, 193
Lee, Peggy, 223, 286, 547, 638
Leeds Music, 471
Legion of Decency, 164
Lehar, Franz, 24
Leibell, Vincent, 143-144, 289, 290, 291,
   297
Lengsfelder, Hans, 303, 327, 399-401, 418,
   479, 480
Lennon, John, 382, 473, 514-515, 538,
   540
Lenono Music, 538-539
"Leon Berry on the Giant Wurlitzer," 360
Lerner, Alan Jay, 328, 355, 402, 524
Lerner and Loewe, 353
Leslie, Edgar, 266, 296, 328, 402
"Let It Be," 538
"Let Me Call You Sweetheart," 32
"Let's Dance," 347
"Let's Dance" (Bowie), 640, 645
"Let's Spend the Night Together," 543
Levitz, Steven, 102
Levy, Lou, 377, 471-472
Lewis, E. R. "Ted," 78, 117, 125-127
Lewis, Edward, 377, 381
Lewis, Jay, 438
Lewis, Ted, 227
Lewis, William B., 251
Liberace, 414
Liberty-Dolton, 389
Liberty Music Store, 129
Liberty Records, 347, 356, 511
Lieber, Jerry, 386, 510, 592, 653
Lieberson, Goddard, 236, 345, 352-355,
   364, 368-369, 464, 553, 560, 600
Life (magazine), 315
Lifton, Robert K., 508, 511
Liggins, Joe, 224
Light, Enoch, 345, 363
Lindsay, Howard, 449
"Linger Awhile," 96
Linkletter, Art, 415
"Lionel Hampton," 360
"Listener's Digest," 339
Little, Little Jack, 71, 80, 82
"Little Bird Told Me" case, 325, 340

Little Esther, 248
Little Jessie James, 95
"Little Log Cabin Down the Lane" (Hays),
    65
Little Lulu, 651
A Little Night Music, 592
Little Peach (dance), 137
"Little Red Corvette," 646
"Little White Lies," 117
Little Wonder Records, 82
"The Livery Stable Blues," 29
Livingston, Alan, 368, 370, 381, 495-496,
    582
Livingstone, Jerry, 402
Lloyd, Marie, 10
Lockwood, John, 515
Loeb, John Jacob, 402, 412
Loesser, Frank, 304, 604
Loevinger, Lee, 456
Loew, Marcus, 8, 15, 20, 57, 81
Loew's, 57, 61, 317-318, 346, 349
Logan, Frederick Knight, 93
Lolita (singer), 379
Lombardo, Carmen, 412
Lombardo, Guy, 89, 117, 126, 138, 161,
    183, 185, 203
London FFRR, 249
London Gramophone Corp., 227
London Records, 227, 237, 361, 365, 373
"The Lonely Bull," 385
Longines Symphonette Society, 513
"Long Tall Sally," 340
Longwood College, 591
Looney Tunes, 651
Lopez, Trini, 389, 515
Lopez, Vincent, 77-78, 85, 102, 104, 128,
    185
Lou Chudd label, 511
"Louise," 430
"Love in Bloom," 150
"Love Me Tender," 342
Love Me Tender, 343
"The Love Theme . . . Evergreen," 532
"Love to Love You Baby," 558, 605
Love Unlimited Orchestra, 559
"Lovey Dovey," 460
The Love You Make (Brown and Gains), 382
"Loving You," 350
Lovin' Spoonful, 386
Lowe, Jim, 340
LP Program Service, 470
Lucas, George, 598
Lucas, Nick, 71
Lucky Lager Dance Time, 547
Lucky Strike, 87; *see also* "Your Hit Parade"

Luening, Otto, 302
"Lullaby of Broadway," 152
Lutcher, Nellie, 227
Lyman, Abe, 78, 102
Lyon & Healy, 191
Lyric Writers and Composers Protective
    League, 43, 92

MacDonald, Jeanette, 128, 151
MacGimsey, Robert, 402
C. P. MacGregor Services, 131
MacKenzie, Gisele, 414
"Mack the Knife," 364
Maclen Music, 473, 483, 514, 538
Macmillan, 528-529
MacNamee, Graham, 178
Magic Brain turntable, 215-216
Magnavox, 534
Magnetophon, 221, 229-230
Magnetronics, 359
Magnuson, Warren G., 422-423
"The Maine Stein Song," 111
Mainstream Records, 536
Maitland, John K. "Mike," 388
Majestic Records, 222
"Make Believe Ballroom," 128-129, 165
The Making of Thriller, 647
Mamas and Papas, 509
"Mañana," 286
Mancini, Henry, 364, 369, 467, 476-477,
    531-532
"Manhattan" (Rodgers and Hart), 97
Manilow, Barry, 556
Mann, Barry, 387
Mantovani, 518
Marconi, Guglielmo, 74-75
Marconiphone, 376
Marconi Telegraph Companies, 74, 76
Marcus, Leonard, 519
"Mardi Gras Time with the Dukes of Dixie-
    land," 360
Marek, George, 377, 383
"Marie," 142
Mark, Mitchell B., 11
Marks, Edward B., 105, 180, 187, 274-275
E. B. Marks, 180, 209, 259-260, 399-400,
    482, 653
E. B. Marks v. *20th Century-Fox,* 457
Marks v. *ASCAP,* 260, 272-274, 297, 399
Marlo, George, 321
Marsden, Gerry, 473
Martha and the Vandellas, 385
Martin, Dean, 341, 386, 389
Martin, George, 382, 390

Martin, Tony, 371
Marvin, Johnny, 117
Marx, Groucho, 415
Mary Poppins, 652
'Mary's Boy Child,'' 378
Massey, Gus, 100
Master Records, 135
Mathias, Charles, 566, 631
Mathis, Johnny, 364, 461
Maurice, Peter, 601
Maverick, 349
Maxixe (dance), 26
Maxwell, George, 37-38, 94, 162
May, Billy, 467
May and Tag the Washing Machine Twins,
80
"Maybelline," 340
Mayberry RFD, 500
Mayer, Louis B., 55, 154, 222, 344
Mayer, Max, 191-192, 195
Mayer v. Music Dealers Service, 191, 195,
260
Mayhew, Stella, 25
Mayo Catalogue, 471
Maytime, 98
MCA, 471-472, 562, 607-609, 629, 650-651
MCA–Decca-Universal, 393
MCA-Leeds, 479-480, 488
MCA Records, 536, 654
MCA–Reeds/Duchess, 533
MCA–TV/Revue, 413
MCA/Universal, 617
McCarthy, Jim, 319
McCarthy & Fisher, 123
McCartney, Linda, 538
McCartney, Paul, 382, 473, 514-515, 538-
540, 604
McClellan, John, 437, 464, 494-497, 565-
566, 581
McClendon, Gordon, 442, 446, 575
McCormack, John, 68-69, 95
McCoy, Clyde, 128
McCrae, George, 559, 597
McDermott, Galt, 599
McDevitt, Barney, 319
McDonaugh, Glen, 37
McGeehan, John E., 421, 457
McGinty, 34
McGriff, Edna, 248
McGuire Sisters, 340
McHugh, Jimmy, 123-124, 304, 449
McKuen, Rod, 603
McPhatter, Clyde, 326
Mechanical royalties, 42, 624; *see also* Juke-
boxes, copyright exemption

"Meet Me Tonight in Dreamland," 32
"Meet the Beatles," 383
Mellencamp, John Cougar, 638
"Mellow Yellow," 536
"Melody in F," 10
Melotone Records, 125, 127
"Memphis Blues" (Handy), 30
Memphis Recording Service, 250
Men at Work, 647
Mendoza, David, 48, 52
Menon, Bhaskar, 513
Menotti, Gian Carlo, 402
Mercer, Johnny, 217-218, 223, 229, 275,
304, 376, 400
Mercury-Philips-Smash, 389
Mercury-Phonogram, 595
Mercury Records, 230, 232, 237, 318, 339,
364, 379, 392, 488
Mercury Records Productions, 534
Merman, Ethel, 239, 352
The Merry Widow (film), 48, 151
Merry Widow (Lehar), 24
"The Merry Widow Waltz," 34
Metro-Goldwyn-Mayer, *see* MGM
Metromedia, 468, 487, 513, 592, 622
Metronome (magazine), 114, 219
Metro Pictures Corporation, 15
Metropolitan Opera Club, 336
Metropolitan Orchestra, 25
"Mexican Radio" (video), 640
Meyer, George W., 402
Meyer, Joseph, 402
MGM, 15, 49, 149, 154-155, 187, 201,
204, 208-209, 237, 301, 316-318,
399, 413, 443, 479, 511, 595; Big
Three Music, 541; Big Three music
catalogues, 179
MGM-Lion Company, 222
MGM-Loew's, 295
MGM Records, 226, 346, 349, 376, 511-
512, 534
MGM Robbins/Feist Miller, 157
MGM Television, 617
MGM/UA, 643-644
MGM-Verve, 389
"Mickey (Pretty Mickey)" (Daniels), 47
Mickey Mouse Records, 344
Mid-Continent Broadcasting Corporation,
442-443
Midnight Frolics, 29, 83
Midnight Special (NBC-TV), 639
Midwestern Hayride, 427
The Mikado (Gilbert and Sullivan), 17
Milburn, Amos, 248
Miles, Buddy, 516, 535

Military bands, on early recordings, 25
"Milkman's Matinee," 169
Miller, George, 435
Miller, Glenn, 142, 144, 216, 219, 339, 461
Miller, James A., 140
Miller, Justin, 272, 282
Miller, Marilyn, 98
Miller, Mitch, 236-237, 246, 306-307, 318-319, 325, 345, 380, 387, 405-406, 443, 495
Miller, Neville, 172, 174-179, 182, 207, 209, 254, 272
Miller, Ray, 51, 78
Miller, Roger, 386
Miller, Steve, 516
Miller, William, 438
Miller International, 358
Miller Music, 154
Millertape, 140, 168
Mills, E. Claude, 20, 39-40, 43-44, 54, 79, 81, 84-85, 88, 92, 94-95, 103-105, 109, 111, 113, 162, 172, 174, 177, 187-190, 193, 196-197, 201, 206-208, 255, 258, 265, 272-275, 284, 487-488, 914
Mills, Irving, 123-124, 127, 134-135, 348, 472
Mills, Jack, 104, 123, 472
Mills Brothers, 118, 126, 149
Mills Music, 190, 348, 399, 407, 460, 471-473, 533, 628
Mills Novelty Company, 110, 134
Minow, Newton, 456, 461
The Miracle Worker (film), 13
"Mirage" (album), 637
Mission Impossible, 500
"The Missouri Waltz" (Logan), 93, 233
Mr. President, 353
"Misty," 364
Mitchell, Guy, 238, 414
Mix, Tom, 53
Mizzy, Vic, 402
Modern-RPM, 341
"Modern Sounds in Country Music," 465
Mondugno, Domenico, 369
The Monkees, 390
Mono Motor Oil Twins, 80
Monroe, Bill, 342
Monroe, Vaughan, 235, 241
Monterey Pop Festival, 516, 536
Mood Music, 284, 317
Moonglows, 326
"Moonlight and Roses" case, 452
"Moonlight Sonata" (Beethoven), 11

"Moon of Manakoora," 157
"Moon River," 477
Moore, Douglas, 402
Moore, Garry, 415
Moore, Grace, 150
Moret, Neil, 47
Mormon Tabernacle Choir, 364
MOR music, 547-548, 606
Morris, Buddy, 322
Morris, E. H. "Buddy," 107, 109, 197-198, 317, 453, 471
E. H. Morris Music, 489, 539
Morse, Ella Mae, 218
Morse, Teddy, 91
Moss, Herb, 385
Moss, John, 448-449
Most, Mickey, 389
Motion Picture Association, 586, 626
Motion Picture Moods for Pianists and Organists, 49
Motion Picture Patents Company, 7; demise of, 12, 14; independents' war with, 12
Motion Picture Producers and Distributors of America, 50, 147
Motion Picture Producers Associaton of America, 284
Motion pictures, *see* Movies
Motion Picture Theater Owners Association, 49-50, 82
Motley, Constance Baker, 565
Motorola Radio Company, 361, 391
Motown Industries, 605, 641
Motown Music, 524
Motown Records, 384, 539, 552, 554, 592, 594, 609, 650
Motown Revue, 384-385
Movie business: in early 20th c., 12-13; economics, in thirties, 157; in thirties, 148-149, 158
Movie companies, purchase of music companies, 55
Movie musicals, 107
Movie palace, 11
Movies, 106; advancements in, in thirties, 153; binaural and stereophonic sound, 249; block booking, 158; censorship, in twenties, 50; early maturity of, 9; in early thirties, 147; Edison's first studio for, 4; first mass market for, 5; first mass production of, 10; first score written expressly for, 11; first talking, 3; independent producers of, 7-8; music licensing, in fifties, 291-293; music-related, 638-639; music

written to accompany, 48; origin of, 3; popularity, in early 20th c., 12, 13; projector, development of, 4-5; promotion of songs through, 107-112; scoring, in sixties, 455; and song hits, in forties and fifties, 317-318; talking, development of, 50-51, 53-54; on television, 351, 393; theme songs, sales of, 52; in twenties, 49

Movie sound-track albums, 349, 532

Movie studios, and music copyrights, 276

Movie theater: ASCAP's seat tax, 103, 283-284, 289-290; early, 6; first true, 6; live musicians accompanying films in, 47; monopoly, in early 20th c., 14-15; in twenties, 59

Movietone Music, 317, 457, 478

Moving Picture World, 11

Moxie Minute Men, 80

MPAA, 625

MPHC. *See* Music Publishers Holding Corporation

MPL Communications, 538-539, 604

MPPA, *see* Music Publishers Protective Association

MPPC, *see* Motion Picture Patents Company

MTV, 638-642, 645-647, 650-652

MTV Networks, Inc., 650

Muir, Lewis, 25

"Mule Train," 305

Munsel, Patrice, 414

Muntz, Earl "Madman," 391

Murdoch, Rupert, 649

Murdock, John J., 19-20, 40-41, 57, 60

Murray, Anne, 513

Murray, Richard, 284

Musicals, 149, 152-153; Busby Berkeley, 149-150; stage: in fifties, 353, 355, in sixties, 354; and television, 414

The Music America Loves Best (magazine), 138

Music Appreciation Record Club, 335

Musicasters, 459

Music Board of Trade, 39-40

Music Corporation of America, 258, 392-393

Music Dealers Service, 190-192, 202, 253, 357, 408

"The Music Goes 'Round and 'Round," 200

Music Hall Varieties, 313

Musicians, income, in seventies, 582

Musicians Guild of America, 350-351

Music Industries Chamber of Commerce, 41, 81

Music Machine Operators Association, 278

The Music Man, 353

Music Operators of America, 305, 368, 434-435, 437-438, 463, 485, 486, 494, 565

Music Performance Trust Fund, 334, 350-351

Music publishers: first antitrust action against, 29; and jobbers, in thirties, 190-192; relations with songwriters, in twenties, 91

Music Publishers Association, 22, 36-37, 50, 628

Music Publishers Association of the United States, 540

Music Publishers' Board of Trade, 38

Music Publishers Contact Employees, 266, 316

Music Publishers Forum, 589

Music Publishers Holding Company, 109

Music Publishers Holding Corporation, 197, 318, 396, 399, 407, 441, 488, 643

Music Publishers Protective Association, 29, 40-43, 54-55, 78, 81, 92, 94, 97, 99-100, 103, 105, 110, 113, 121, 133-134, 136, 151, 155-157, 184, 186, 194-195, 201, 203, 207, 252-253, 266, 272, 290, 293, 357, 367, 403, 408-410, 455, 463, 485, 488, 563, 631; ERPI agreement, 107-108; fees from radio broadcasts, 132

Music publishing: in eighties, 589-590, 627-633; in fifties, 317, 324-325, 329-330; in late 19th c., 23; in late forties, 279; in seventies, 533-535, 540-542, 561-562; in sixties, 460, 470, 480-482

Music-rack business, 253

Music Teachers National Association, 23

Music Television, *see* MTV

Music Treasures of the World, 335

Music videos, 631, 638, 645, 650-651

Musikvertrieb, 377

Mutual Broadcasting Company, 254, 282-283, 432, 575; "America's Top Tunes," 443; "The Big Decision," 443

Mutual Broadcasting System, 164, 168, 189-190, 257, 272, 345

Muzak, 144, 168-169, 234, 315, 359, 529-530, 600

"My Blue Heaven," 54-55, 69, 123, 216

My Fair Lady, 352-355, 383, 600

My Fair Lady (film), 394

"My Man," 96

My Maryland, 101

"My Wife's Gone to the Country" (Berlin), 35
"My Wild Irish Rose," 592
"My Wonderful One," 96

NAB, *see* National Association of Broadcasters
Nabors, Jim, 547
NAPA, *see* National Association of Peforming Artists
NARAS, *see* National Academy of Recording Arts and Sciences
NARM, *see* National Association of Record Merchandisers
NARTB, *see* National Association of Radio and Television Broadcasters
Nashville: ASCAP's move into, 465; and country music, 429, 464, in fifties, 427-428; as music center, 482
Nashville Songwriters Association, 624
Nashville Songwriters Association International, 531
Nashville Teens, 389
Nashville writers, ASCAP's campaign to win over, 619
National Academy of Recording Arts and Sciences, 369-370
National Association of Broadcasters, 50, 81-84, 121, 161-163, 165, 167, 169, 171-172, 175-177, 188, 194, 196, 200, 202, 205, 207, 254, 256, 258-259, 262, 269, 280-282, 295, 367, 415, 451, 454, 485, 495-496, 545, 576, 586-587, 621, 625; Code of Ethics and Practices, 164; Tax-Free Music Bureau, 81-82
National Association of Disk Jockeys, 228
National Association of Orchestra Directors, 104
National Association of Performing Artists, 130, 135, 143
National Association of Phonograph Artists, 495
National Association of Radio and Television Broadcasters, 307
National Association of Record Dealers, 357
National Association of Record Merchandisers, 370-373, 564, 635
National Association of Television and Radio Announcers, 605
National Broadcasting Company, *see* NBC
National Cable Television Association, 587, 625

National Committee for the Recording Arts, 495, 566
National Concerts and Artists Corporation, 258, 475
National General, 510
National Independent Broadcasters, 170, 182
National Labor Relations Board, 409
National Music Publishers Association, 488-489, 530, 535, 540, 563-568, 566, 581, 584-586, 588-589, 591, 593, 623-624, 627, 629, 632-633
National Public Radio, licensing fees paid by, 583
National Vaudeville Artists, 19-20, 57, 61
"Nature Boy," 285-286, 293
NCB, 70, 85, 111, 159-169, 172-176, 179, 187-189, 200, 207-208, 257, 259, 262, 281, 283, 295, 312, 344, 416-417, 421-422, 431-432, 487, 620; Blue Network, 189, 262-263; expansion of, in twenties, 87-88; in late twenties and early thirties, 88-89
NBC Film Division, 413
NBC symphony orchestra, 141
NBC Thesaurus, 144
NBC-TV, 315, 390, 500-506, 524-525; settlement with BMI, 525
"Near You," 227, 285
Neighborhood Records, 561
Neilan, Marshall, 47
"Nel Blu Dipinto di Blue," 369
Nelson, Ken, 464
Nelson, Ozzie and Harriet, 347
Nelson, Rick, 347
Nelson, Willie, 594
Nemperor Holdings, 473, 514
NEMS, 514
NEMS/Nemperor, 596
"Never Can Say Goodbye," 559
Nevin, Ethelbert, 94
Nevins, Al, 387
New age music, 636
New Christy Minstrels, 386
Newhart, Bob, 389
Newman, Alfred, 148, 152
Newman, Randy, 643
The New Moon, 101
New Radio, 441
New Rock Concert, 639
Newton-John, Olivia, 599
New wave music, 601
New World Music, 55, 109, 317, 489
New York Enquirer, 202
New York Hot Tracks, 646

New York Philharmonic, 141
New York Times, 607; on The Birth of a Nation, 9
New York Times Music Publishing Company, 592, 653
Nichols, Red, 72
Nickelodeon, 6, 10, 650-652
Nicks, Stevie, 640
Nielsen Audimeter Survey, 166-167
"Nigger Blues," 30
Night and Day (film), 275
"Night and Day" (Porter), 122
NMPA, see National Music Publishers Association
Noble, Edward, 310-312
Noble, Ray, 124-125
Nobles, Gene, 248
Norelco, 392, 534
Normand, Mabel, 47
Northern Songs, 473-474, 514, 538
No Strings, 353
"Now Is the Hour," 285, 293
NRA, Code, 164, 172
Number Please, 456
The Nutcracker Suite, 652; Odeon album, 134
Nutting, C. V., 42

Oberstein, Eli, 118, 120, 133, 141-143, 222, 231, 236
O'Connor, George, 30
O'Connor, John J., 40
O'Connor, Johnny, 203-204
Odeon Company, 134, 244
Office of Price Administration, 226
Office of War Information, 251
Official Films, 313
"Off the Wall" (Jackson), 640
Oh, Boy, 97
"Oh, Johnny," 145
Oh, Lady, Lady, 97
"Oh, You Beautiful Doll," 592
O'Hara, Geoffrey, 106
OKeh Records, 30-31, 64-65, 123, 127, 135, 241
Oklahoma!, 226, 239, 304, 349, 352
Okun, Henry, 319
"Old Black Magic," 219
"Old Folks at Home" (Foster), 24
Oldham, Andrew Loog, 389
"Oldie" programming, 460
Oliver, King, 72
Olsen, George, 71, 85, 102, 104

O'Mahoney, Joseph C., 436
"The One I Love Belongs to Somebody Else" (Kahn & Jones), 95
One Night of Love, 150
One-stop stores, 356
Ono, Yoko, 538
"On Top of Old Smoky," 307
"Open the Door, Richard," 224
Operation Push, 605
Operation TNT, 339, 356
Orchestra, accompanying films, 11
Original Amateur Hour, 288
Original-cast albums, 226, 238-239, 349, 352-354
Original Dixie Land Jass Band, 29
"Original Dixie Land One-Step," 29
Oriole Records, 65
Orioles, 248, 325-326
Orlando, Tony, 387
Orphans of the Storm, 48
Orpheum, 17-18, 21
Orthophonic Victrola, 67, 100
Oscars, 150; first to screen musical, 107; Mancini's, 476
Osmond, Donny, 534
Osmond family, 534
Ostin, Mo, 516
Our Dancing Daughters, 106
Out of This World, 239
Overdubbing, Les Paul's advancement of, 235
"Over There" (Cohan), 35, 251
Owens, Buck, 513
Owens, Jack, 227
Oxford University Press, 111
Ozark Jubilee, 427

"P.S. I Love You," 472
Packard, Vance, 426-427, 429
Page, Patti, 239, 242, 334, 414, 547
Paine, John, 113, 133, 172, 174, 177, 191, 194-195, 206-207, 271-272, 277-279, 281, 284, 488
Palace Theatre, New York, 18, 61
"Palesteens," 592
Paley, William, 70, 177, 139, 189, 196, 198, 208, 234, 254, 258, 311
Palitz, Morty, 219
Panatrope, 100
Pantoptikon, 4
Paramount, 9-10, 49, 53, 59, 149, 151, 156, 187, 201, 560; Broadway theatre, 59; television interests, 281

Paramount-Dot, 389
Paramount Famous, 157
Paramount–Famous Music, 317
Paramount Music, 316
Paramount Pictures Corporation, 86, 148,
    311, 343, 346, 381, 393-394, 415,
    430, 602
Paramount Television Distribution, 617
Parker, Colonel Tom, 342-343
Parker, Little Junior, 341
Parks, Van Dyke, 638-639
Parlophone, 244, 376, 382
Partch, Harry, 474
Partridge Family, 556
Pasternack, Josef, 28
Pastore, John O., 426, 429-431
Pathé–De Mille Pictures, 59, 60
Pathé Frères, 7, 119, 127, 244, 376
Pathé Records, 49
Patterson, John Henry, 32
Patterson, Robert P., 290
Paul, Les, 235, 242
Paul and Paula, 383
E. T. Paull Music Company, 101
Paull-Pioneer Music, 101
Payola, 199, 204, 242, 247, 279-280, 373,
    421, 440-442, 445-448, 450-451,
    455, 488, 602-603, 605-607;
    Congressional investigation of, 447-
    449; and racism, 554, 557; in record
    industry, in seventies, 553, 556
Pay television, 466
Peacock Records, 325, 341
Peatman, John Gray, 266, 322, 411
Peatman Report, 266, 460
Peatman's surveys, 279-280, 286, 317-318,
    320, 324
Pecora, Ferdinand, 274-275
Peer, Ralph, 31, 64-65, 69-70, 72, 100,
    118, 120-121, 123, 141, 180, 217,
    222, 301, 407, 418, 482
Peer International Corporation, 180
Peerless Player Piano, 110, 305
"Pee Wee King Show," 427
"Peg o' My Heart," 227
Pennsylvanians, 122
Penny parlor, 109-110
Penny vaudeville, 109-110
Pentron, 361
Peretti, Hugo, 345, 387
Perfect Records, 127, 135
"The Perfect Song" (Breil), 10
Performance Trust Fund, 221-222, 229, 243
Performing Rights Society, 270-271
Performing Society of Britain, 403

Personality folio, 541
Personality Records, 27
Peter, Paul, and Mary, 386, 389, 515
Peter and the Wolf, 652
"Peter Gunn Theme," 364
Peter Pan Records, 338
Peterson, Virgil, 437
Petrillo, James C., 128, 170, 217-220, 229,
    286, 333, 350
Petrouchka, 227
Philadelphia Bandstand, 444
Philadelphia International Records, 556
Philadelphia Symphony Orchestra, record-
    ings for Victor, 28
Philco, 77, 173, 225
Philips, 243, 341, 378-379, 390, 513-514,
    534, 551, 595, 612-613, 649; tape
    system, 392
Philips Phonographic Industries, 513
Philips-PolyGram, 654
Philips-Siemans, 645
Phillips, Sam, 341, 464
Phonofilm Corporation, 51
Phonogram International, 534
Phonograph, Kineto-Phone, 10
Phonograph Performance Ltd., 135
Photocopying, of music, and copyright, 591,
    632
Photophone, 53, 117, 131
Piano: coin-operated, 28; used to accompany
    moving pictures, 10-11
Pianola, 16, 22-23, 29
Piano roll recordings, 28; monopoly on, 22-
    23
Pickett, Wilson, 510
Pickford, Mary, 7, 9, 14-15
Pickwick Records, 363
Pickwick Sales, 358
Pic-vaude houses, 17
"Piece of My Heart," 536
"The Pilgrims' Chorus," 10
Pincus, George, 473-474
Pincus, Lee, 473
Pink Floyd, 513
The Pink Panther, 477
Pinocchio, 157
Piracy, 486, 563, 626, 632; actions against,
    in seventies, 540; in Far East, 380;
    federal protections against, 563-565;
    fight against, in sixties, 367, 372-
    373; of printed music, 590; in sixties,
    463; of tapes, 564, 611
"Pistol Packin' Mama," 252, 322
Piston, Walter, 302
Pittman, Bob, 639-640, 646

Plantation songs, 30
Platinum records, 536-37, 600, 654
Playhouse 90, 414
Play Your Hunch, 456
Plaza Music Company, 65, 191
Plough, 442-443
Pocket Disc, 550
Podell, David, 260, 263
Poletti, Charles, 211, 255-257
Police, 601, 645, 647
Pollack, Lew, 533
Polydor Records, 389, 510, 514, 534, 539
PolyGram, 594-598, 600, 602, 607, 609,
    634, 643, 645, 649-653; merchandise
    quotas for retailers, 637
Pomus, Doc, 387
Pond, William, 96
Poniatoff, Alexander, 415
Pons, Lily, 225
Popeye, 651
Pop Music Disk Jockey Festival, 443, 445
Popular Album Club, 337
Popular music: and movie business, 47-56;
    recording, in thirties, 141; vs. "better"
    music, publication of, 23-24
Porter, Cole, 122, 154, 202, 239, 275, 298,
    300, 304, 398, 412
Porterfield, Nolan, 65
Poulsen, Valdemar, 230
Powell, Dick, 150
"Practice Makes Perfect," 321
Prager, Bernia, 102
"Praise the Lord and Pass the Ammunition,"
    252
Prerecorded Home Entertainment Industry,
    630-631
Presley, Elvis, 250, 341-343, 350, 378-379,
    381, 385-386, 414, 422, 428, 459,
    515, 543, 591-592, 607
Presley Music, 483
Press-Radio Bureau, 163
Preston, Johnny, 460
Price, Waterhouse: *Survey of Financial Re-
    porting and Accounting Developments
    in the Entertainment Business*, 561;
    survey of jukeboxes, 438
The Price Is Right, 456
Prima, Louis, 388
Prince, 640, 646, 650, 654
Prince, Charles Adams, 25
Printed music, *see* Sheet music
"The Prisoner's Song," 100
"The Prisoner's Sweetheart," 100
"The Prisoner's Wife," 100
Private Stock-EMI, 556

Procul Harum, 596
Producers and Managers Association, 99
Production music, 97-98
Professional Music Men, 199
Profitless prosperity, 381
Program counselors, 545
Progressive music, 340, 470-471, 509
Progressive rock, on radio, 543
Promotors Hispana Americana de Musica,
    180
"Provocative Percussion," 363
Pryor, Arthur, 25
Public Broadcasting Service, licensing fees
    paid by, 583
Public performance for profit: provision of
    copyright law, 37; application to ra-
    dio, 79
Publishers Service Company, 138
Puner, Paul, 243
Punk rock, 601, 636
"Puppy Love," 534
"Purple Rain" (Prince), 650
Pye Record Company, 490
"Pyromania," 645

QuadraDisc, 550
Quadraphonic recording, 550, 612
Queen, 639
Queen Elizabeth (film), 8
Quick Draw McGraw, 651
Quicksilver Messenger Service, 556
Quiz show rigging, 439
Quo Vadis (film), 8

Race music, 227 (*See also* Black music);
    Rhythm and blues recordings, 31, 64,
    72; in forties, 223, 225
Rachmaninoff, Sergei, 94
Racism: AFM's measures to end, 351; and
    condemnation of popular music, in
    fifties, 406
Rack jobbers, 357-358, 372, 634; in seven-
    ties, 552
Rackmill, Milton, 233, 243, 245, 334, 344,
    392
Racusin, Norman, 390
Radio (*see also* Underground radio):
    advertising on, 159-160;
    expenditures for, 167,
    in fifties, 315,
    in thirties, 89-90, 161, 171,
    in twenties, 79-81;
    Albee's competition with, 58;

Radio (*continued*)
  all-news stations, 575
  ASCAP licensing, 84
    in fifties, 417-418
    in seventies, 524
    in sixties, 468-469
  black-oriented, ownership of, 605
  black ownership of stations, 605-606
  BMI fees, in seventies, 524
  compensation for music played on, in late thirties, 174-175
  and copyright, 79, 82
  development of, 75-76
  double-channel broadcasting, 362
  effect on record sales, 66
  in fifties, 314, 416
  first all-recorded show, 131
  growth of, 145-146
  "Hit Parade" format, 442
  independent stations, ASCAP's spot-checking of, in fifties, 322-323
  local broadcasting, in fifties, 416-417, 441
  Loew's attitude toward, 58
  multiplexing, 362
  music broadcast on
    in early twenties, 77
    in forties, 267
  networks
    contracts with affiliates, 169
    contract with AFM, in thirties, 170-171
  news broadcasts, 163
  noncommercial, 518
  paying for play on, 151-152
  popularity of, in twenties, 63-64, 78, 87
  and popular music, 204
    in thirties, 159-183
  portable, 416
  programming
    daytime, 172
    in forties, 228
    in seventies, 547
    in sixties, 461, 467
    in thirties, 160-161
  program ratings, 166
  progressive. *See also* FM broadcasting in early seventies, 520
  promotion of recordings, in twenties, 68-69
  prospects for, in forties, 176, 285
  record companies' licensing of broadcasts, 143-144
  recorded music on, 129
    in thirties, 121
  and record promotion, 582-583
  regulation of, 85-87
    in late thirties, 172-174
    restriction of advertising for pictures, 111-112
    in sixties, 484
    and song hits, 441
    stations licensed, in 1921, 77
    taped programming, in seventies, 546
    and theater music, 99
    toll broadcasting, 78
    transistor, 416
Radio Act of 1927, 86
Radio Business Report, 607
Radio City Music Hall, 49
Radio Corporation of America, 50, 52-53, 64, 71-72, 76-78, 82, 85, 87-88, 117, 119, 160, 173, 250, 310, 380, 390, 415, 422, 508, 515-516, 562, 594, 607, 629, 634, 648, 650, 651; antitrust action against, 90; merchandise quotas for retailers, 637; radio-phonographs, 66; superheterodyne receiver, 83
Radio Franks, 80, 82
Radiograph, 119
Radio-Keith-Orpheum, *See* RKO
Radiola, 64, 77, 117
Radio Music Box, 76
Radio Music Company, 88
Radio Music Corp., 111
Radio Program Foundation, 162-163, 169
Radiotunes, 261
Raff, Norman C., 4-5
Rag (dance), 26
Raiborn, Paul, 430
Raiders of the Lost Ark, 642
"Rainbow Round My Shoulder," 54
"Ramona," 106
Randle, Bill, 247, 441-442
Rank, J. Arthur, 245
Rapee, Erno, 48-49, 52, 59, 102, 106, 476, 533
Raskin, David, 275
Ravel, Maurice, 72
Ravens, 248
Raye, Don, 402
Ray-O-Vac Twins, 80
R & B, 240
RCA, *see* Radio Corporation of America
RCA Ariola International, 654
RCA-Bertelsmann, proposed merger, 648
RCA International, 377, 379
RCA-NBC, 217
RCA-NBC Thesaurus Library, 131
RCA Photophone, 53-54, 60
RCA Records, 550, 552, 591, 603, 609, 645, 648, 654
RCA Victor, 71, 88, 121, 124-125, 129,

133, 135-136, 138-139, 142-143, 145, 183, 215, 217, 219, 222-223, 225-226, 229, 231, 235-237, 248-249, 318, 335-336, 339, 342, 353, 358, 361-362, 364-365, 371, 374, 377-378, 385, 389-392, 488. *See also* Operation TNT; Duo, Junior, 127; record club, 337-338, 374, 376, 465; tape recording technology, in fifties, 360
RCA Victor Society of Great Music, 337
"Reaching for the Moon," 148
Reader's Digest, 338
Record business, *see* Recording industry
Record clubs, 335-338, 357, 374-375; in Britain, 377; European, 378
Record distribution, 224, 552, 608
Recorded music, first public concert of, 302
Recorders, advances in, in early forties, 221
Record industry, *see* Recording industry
Recording business, *see* Recording industry
Recording industry
    artist contracts, in seventies, 535-536
    break-even points, 567
        in sixties, 509
    British, in thirties, 118
    Congressional investigation of, 375
    in eighties, 634-654
    European
        effect of Common Market, 513
        in fifties, 378-379
        in sixties, 377
    expansion, in sixties, 508
    in fifties, 316, 319, 324, 326, 333, 345, 355-356, 363-364, 373, 398-399
    in forties, 236
    FTC Trade Practice Rules for, 375
    growth, in sixties, 561
    independent companies
        in eighties, 636, 649
        in fifties, 356
        in late seventies, 608-609
        origins of, 386
        in sixties, 386
    in late forties, 285
    in late seventies, 560
    operating costs, in seventies, 552-553
    profitless prosperity, in sixties, 507
    retail gross, in seventies, 602
    Russian, 377
    sales, in sixties and seventies, 561-562
    in seventies, 551-552, 594-595
    in sixties, 364, 376, 386
    slump, in early eighties, 585-586
    in thirties, 117-146
    in twenties, 6-63

Recording Industry Association of America, 243, 245-247, 361, 365-367, 372, 463, 485-486, 496, 524, 535, 561-562, 564-565, 567-568, 581-582, 584-585, 609-610, 637, 653; code of business practices, 553-554
Record-performance royalty, 565-566
Record promotion, 287; *see also* Payola
Record-rental bill, 626, 632
Record-rental stores, 637
Record Report, 547
T. K. Records, 559
Records:
    33 RPM, 232-234, 339
    45 RPM, 234-235, 339, 343
        for children, 246
        in fifties, 338
    78 RPM, 339, 343
    advancing technology of, in early twenties, 63
    boxed sets, 338-339
    breakage discount, 63
    budget LPs, 371
        in fifties, 358
    classical, pre-WWI, 27
    counterfeited, 563. *See also* Piracy
    disco singles, 559-560
    discount sales of, 238-239, 335, 634-635
    distribution
        in forties, 224
        in late seventies, 608
    first album, 134
    free, as promotional or merchandising tools, 371, 451-452, 459
    gimmick, 362-363
    for home use only, 135-136
    improved technology for, after WWI, 66, 67
    long-playing, 119-120, 231-232
        in fifties, 338, 343-344
        in sixties, 364
    transshipping of, 357
    made by variety and music hall stars, 25
    mail-order merchandising, 244, 335
    manufacture
        compression molding, 335
        in forties, 223-224
        injection-molding process, 355
        technological advances in, 215
        in twenties, 68
    manufacturing defects, 635
    monaural, 507-508
    popular, pre-WWI, 27
    popularity surveys, 443
    premium, 371
    prices

Records (*continued*)
    in eighties, 634, 642, 644, 654
    in fifties, 335
    in forties, 226
    in seventies, 552, 594-595
    in thirties, 122-123
    production costs, 582
      in fifties, 349-350
      in seventies and eighties, 585
      in sixties, 367-368
    promotion
      in fifties, 319, 320
      and payola, 606-607
      in seventies, 598-599
      in twenties, 68, 71
    promotion costs, in seventies and eighties,
      585
    quality of, US vs. Japanese, 637
    restricted-use notice, 135-136
    returns policy, 634
      in late seventies, 604, 607
    royalty on, battle over, in early eighties,
      584-585
    sales
      in early fifties, 245
      in eighties, 635-637, 653-654
      excise tax on, 365
      in fifties, 333, 343, 355
      in late forties, 286
      and MTV, 646, 647
      pre-WWI, 27-28
      in seventies, 594, 607
      in sixties, 351-352, 507
      in twenties, 62, 112-113
    singles, 447-448
      in fifties, 363, 459
      production, in fifties, 355-356
      in sixties, 364, 365
    stereo, 508
    stereo LP, first, 360
    superstars' sales of, in seventies, 537
    tie-in, 371
    twelve-inch sampler LPs and EPs, 339
Records for Our Fighting Men, 219
Record World, 547, 637
Redding, Otis, 554
Reddy, Helen, 513
"Red Hot Mama," 288
Red Network, 85-86, 90, 257-258
Red Seal records, 24, 28, 62-63, 71, 122,
    133, 137, 145, 215-216, 225, 231,
    242, 249, 335
Redwood Music, 592-593
Reeves, Jim, 460
Reeves Soundproof, 362

"Refreshment Time with Singin' Sam," 132
Regal Records, 65
Regal-Zonophone, 376
Reger, Max, 48
Reisenfeld, Hugo, 48, 102
Reisman, Joe, 340
Reisman, Leo, 71, 120, 122
"Remember Pearl Harbor," 251
Remick, 40, 42, 55, 105, 109, 190
Remington Records, 244, 358
Renard, Jacques, 104
René, Henri, 345
Reprise Records, 388-389, 394
Republic Pictures, 157, 313
Return of the Jedi, 652
Revere-Wollensak, 361, 392
Revue Productions, 393, 455
Rhythm and blues, 240-241, 248, 339-340,
    346, 384, 422, 509; *see also* Soul
    music; and BMI, 406-407; in fifties,
    325-326
RIAA, *see* Gold Records; Platinum records;
    Recording Industry Association of
    America
Rice, Tim, 596
Rich, Fred, 104
Rich, Walter, 51
Richmond, Howard, 237, 307, 319, 324,
    407
Richmond, Larry, 253
Richmond, Maurice, 101, 191-192
Richmond, Mayer Music Supply, 191
Richmond (pub), 483
G. Ricordi, 37, 162, 180, 418, 533
Riddle, Nelson, 467, 531-532
"Ride of the Valkyries," 10
"Riders in the Sky," 235
Riegela, Roy, 178
Rifkind, Simon, 279, 296
Righteous Brothers, 386
Ring, Blanche, 10
Ringer, Barbara, 566
Ringling Brothers–Barnum & Bailey Circus,
    musicians' pay, in early forties, 220
"The Rise and Fall of the Phonograph"
    (York), 117
"The Rise of the Goldbergs," 89
Ritchie, Lionel, 640, 650
Rivoli Theatre, New York, 48
RKO, 53, 60-61, 88, 413
RKO Chappell/Gershwin, 157
RKO General, 478, 546
RKO Pictures, 345
Robbins, Feist & Miller, 209, 317, 407, 534
Robbins, Jack, 101-102, 105, 107, 148,

154, 179, 187-188, 208, 222, 318, 489
Robbins, Marty, 364
Robbins Music, 55, 102, 107, 208, 317-318, 601
Roberts, 195
Robert Stigwood Organization, 514, 596
Robin, Leo, 304
Robinson, J. Russell, 80
Robinson, William "Smoky," 384, 524, 640
Rock (dance), 26
Rockabilly, 334, 341, 428
"Rock Around the Clock," 250, 334, 340, 378, 406
Rock Awards, 639
Rockefeller Center, 162
Rocket Records, 537, 609
"Rock Me Baby," 559
Rock music: and BMI, 406-407; British groups, in sixties, 383; in early seventies, 516; popularity, in sixties, 518; production of, in seventies, 558-559; on radio, 524; thrill lyrics, in seventies, 544
Rock musicals, 599-600
Rock 'n' roll, 334, 341, 444; on radio, in sixties, 461-462; Soviet black market in, 450
Rockola, 134, 583
Rocky (film), 532
"Rocky Theme," 532
Rodeheaver, Homer, 561
Rodgers, Jimmie, 69-70, 72, 118, 120, 151, 427, 465
Rodgers, Richard, 97, 298, 304, 355, 412
Rodgers and Hammerstein, 352-353, 449
Rodgers and Hart, 108, 153-154, 202
Rogers, Ginger, 150
Rogers, Kenny, 644
Rogers, Roy, 157
Rogers, Walter B., 25
Rolfe, B. A., 13, 85, 87, 104
Rolling Stones, 383-384, 386, 389, 515, 543, 546, 604, 644
Roma, Caro, 94
Romberg, Sigmund, 98, 101, 153, 185, 192, 194, 198, 201, 206, 251, 272-274, 412
Romeo Records, 127
"Room Full of Roses," 288
Roosevelt, Franklin D., 163
Roosevelt, James, 373, 375-376, 418-419
Roosevelt, Theodore, 22
Rosarita Music, 425

Rose, Billy, 185-186, 299, 405-406, 428, 530
Rose, Fred, 288-289, 465
Rose, Wesley, 427, 464, 499
Rose Marie, 97-99
Rosenbaum, Samuel, 220, 233, 243
Rosenberg, Goldmark and Colin, 201
Rosenman, Leonard, 532
Rosenman, Samuel, 431, 462
Rosenthal, J. C., 79, 94, 103, 187-188
Rosenthal, Richard, 473
"Roses of Yesterday," 106
Ross, Diana, 640, 644
Ross, Murray, 551, 560
Ross, Steven J., 510
Rossiter, Will, 82
Roulette Records, 356, 389
"The Rovin' Kind," 307
Rowe, Dick, 383, 583
Roxy (theatre), 59
"Roxy and His Gang" (radio show), 80
Royal Canadians, 126
Royalties (*see also* Mechanical royalties): from European agencies, in eighties, 629; in fifties and sixties, 367; on music, post-WWI, 41-42; Peer's system for paying, 65; on piano word-rolls, 28-29; Price-Waterhouse study of payment system, 603; on printed music, in early 20th c., 22-23; in sixties, 368; for songwriters, in fifties, 293, 294; from TV music, 617
RSO Records, 597, 599; *see also* Robert Stigwood Organization
RSO Television Division, 596
Rubin, Don, 387
"Rumours" (album), 608
Russell, Lillian, 157
"Russian Lullaby" (Berlin), 103
Ryan, J. Harold, 272
Ryan, Sylvester J., 417, 419-21, 449-50, 455, 457, 462, 467-469, 478-479, 487, 500-506

SACEM. *See* Société des Auteurs, Compositeurs et Editeurs de Musique
Sachs, Mannie, 236, 239, 241-242, 249, 352, 377, 408
"Sailor," 379
St. Denis, Ruth, 98
"St. Louis Blues" (Handy), 30
St. Louis Music, 591
Saint-Saëns, Camille, 11

Sally, 97
Salsa-reggae-disco-rock, 636
Salesoul Records, 559
Sam Fox Moving Picture Music, 11
Sam Fox Music Company, 477
Sam Fox Publishing Co. v. *National Telefilm
    Associates and 20th Century-Fox,*
    457
Sam Fox Publishing Company, 400
Sam Goody, Inc., 357
"Sam 'n' Henry," 89
Sands, Tommy, 350
Sanford and Son, 596
Santana, 516
Santley, Ager, Yellen & Bornstein, 190
Santley, Joy, 323
Santley, Joy, Select, 200
Santley, Lester, 284
Santley brothers, 187
SARA, *see* Society of American Recording
    Artists
Sarnoff, David, 52-53, 63, 66-67, 69, 71-
    72, 75-80, 84-88, 119, 121, 156,
    160, 172-173, 231-234, 254, 413
Sarnoff, Robert, 405
Saroyan, William, 307
Saturday Night Fever, 597-598, 602, 652
"Saturday Night Fever" (album), 599
Savino, Domenico, 49, 102, 107
Savoy, 240, 248, 325, 340
Say When, 456
Scherman, Harry, 336
Scherman, Thomas, 336
Schirmer, Gustave, 39, 49, 82, 105, 257,
    317, 407, 408
Schirmer Family Trust, 529
G. Schirmer & Sons, 269, 471, 479, 529
Schockley, William, 416
Schonfeld, Herm, 440
Schools, songs used in, in fifties, 316-317
Schott, 269
Schuette, Oscar, 161-163, 190
Schulman, John, 289-290, 299, 309, 328,
    404, 408-409, 421-422, 429, 455,
    459
Schuman, William, 302, 430
Schwann catalogue, 244
Schwartz, Arthur, 304, 328, 329, 401-402,
    407, 409, 411, 422-424, 426-427,
    429, 449, 457
Schwartz, Bernard, 449
Schwartz, Louis, 255
Schwartz v. *BMI,* 39, 328-329, 402-404,
    412, 425, 431, 454-455, 459, 462,
    479, 485, 523

Scoey, Raymond, 120
Scopitone, 638
Scopp, Mickey, 453, 457
Scores, prices, in eighties, 632
Scott, Hugh, 305
Screen Composers Association, 275-277,
    283, 299, 314, 401, 409, 455-456
Screen Gems, 312-313
Screen Gems–Columbia, 388
Screen Gems–Columbia Music, 390, 601
Screen Gems–Columbia Publications, 541
Screen music, 533; royalties, 476
Screen Writers Guild, 283
Sea-Lark Music, 643
Sears, Zenas, 248
J. P. Seburg Company, 435, 437, 583
Seburg, 110
Secret Agent, 490
"Secret Love," 396
Sedaka, Neil, 387
Seeley, Blossom, 25
"Seems Like Old Times," 411-412
SelectaVision, 609
Selective Phonograph, 110
Selig Company, 7, 9
J & W Seligman, 69
Selvin, Ben, 104, 168, 222
Semenenko, Serge, 394
"Send a Great Big Salami . . . ," 251
Sennett, Mack, 14
Sepia, 471
Serial stories, 9
Serious music, licensing, in fifties, 302-303
SESAC, *see* Society of European Stage Au-
    thors and Composers
Sesame Street, 652
Sessions, Roger, 302
Seven Arts Corporation, 394
Seven dirty words case, 544-545
Seventh Heaven (film), 49, 52, 106
77 Sunset Strip, 349
Seville, David, 347
Sex Pistols, 601
Sex rock, 558
"Sgt. Pepper's Lonely Hearts Club Band,"
    599
Shag (dance), 137
"Shake, Rattle and Roll," 334, 406
"Shake a Hand," 474
"Shake Your Booty," 605
Shannon Male Quartet, 68
Shapiro, Bernstein, 29, 39, 42-43, 100, 105,
    190, 284, 317, 380, 480
Shapiro, Nat, 380
Shaw, Arnold, 334; *The Rocking '50s,* 342

Shaw, Artie, 137, 142

Shaw, David, 514

Shea, Hamilton, 457, 458

Sheet music, 253-254 (*see also* Tin Pan Alley); cover art, 32; discount sales of, 34-35; distribution, in fifties, 357; in early 20th c., 16; in fifties, 317, 396; folios, 541; merchandising and promotion, in early 20th c., 32, 42-43; sales: in early 20th c., 23, 32; in eighties, 590, 628, 632, 637; in fifties, 293, 324-325, 398, 408, 433; in seventies, 540; during WW II, 252

"She Had to Lose It at the Astor," 143

Shellac, rationing, in early forties, 220

"She Loves You," 474

Shenandoah Broadcasting, 457-459

Shenandoah committee, 466

Sherman, Allan, 389

Sherman, Clay, 191

Sherman Act, 435, 579

Sherman and Devorzon Music, 471

"She Works Hard for the Money," 646

Shilkret, Nathaniel, 28, 68, 100, 102, 128, 152

Sholes, Steve, 142, 219, 342, 464, 591

Shore, Dinah, 219, 225, 232, 239, 241, 316, 414

Short films, music-related, 638-639

Shrink wrapping, and record defects, 635

Shubert brothers, 8-9, 18, 58, 98

Shuffle Along (show), 58

Shuman, Mort, 387

Sidewalk Productions, 511

Siemens, 513-514, 649

Silver, Charles, 473

Silverman, Sime, 19-20, 37, 39-40

Silvertown Cord Orchestra, 83

Simon, George, 219, 370

Simon, Paul, 603

"Simon Says," 509

Sinatra, Frank, 223, 225, 238, 293, 333-334, 340, 348, 369, 386, 388-389, 394, 405-406, 414, 461, 510, 547

Sinatra, Nancy, 389

Sinatra Enterprises, 388

"Sincerely," 340

The Singing Fool (film), 54, 106, 149

"The Singing Idol," 350

"Sioux City Sue," 250

Sirovich, William, 194-195

Sissle, Noble, 51

Situation songs, 155

The $64,000 Challenge, 439

Skidmore Music, 93

Sklar, Rick, 607

Sky High, 98

Slides, accompanying music, 6

"Slippin' Around," 288

"Slow Poke," 240

Sly and the Family Stone, 554

Small Wonder, 622

Smathers, George, 423-424, 426, 430-431

The Smiling Lieutenant, 148

Smith, Bessie, 64, 222

Smith, Bob, 248

Smith, Joe, 516, 536

Smith, Kate, 71, 149-150, 216, 219

Smith, Keely, 388

Smith, Mamie, 30-31

"Smoke Gets in Your Eyes," 195

"Smoke! Smoke! Smoke!," 227, 288

"Snooky Ookums" (Berlin), 25

Snow, Phoebe, 594

Snow White and the Seven Dwarfs, 137, 157

Snyder, Ted, 35-36

Soat, Raymond, 131

Society of American Recording Artists, 128, 130

Society of European Stage Authors and Composers, 171, 180, 469-470, 528, 619

Society of Independent Producers, 477

Société des Auteurs, Compositeurs et Editeurs de Musique, 37-38, 271

Sodero, Cesare, 48

Solberg, Thorwald, 83

"Someday," 288

"Some Enchanted Evening," 305

Somerset Records, 358

Something in the Wind, 228

"Something to Remember You By," 402

Sondheim, Stephen, 592

Songbooks, 590

Song Hits, 253

"Song of India," 142

Song-plugging, 16, 23, 32-33, 150, 157-158, 199-200, 203, 261, 441; and radio, 80, 82-83

Songs for Worship and Fellowship (hymnal), 591

"Songs in the Key of Life," 539, 590

Songwriters

ASCAP's payments to, in fifties, 412

commercial role of, in late thirties, 206

contract

ASCAP and MPPA, in 1931, 186-187

BMI, in sixties, 483

in eighties, 627

in fifties, 293, 294

Songwriters (*continued*)
  with publishers, inequities of, 43-44
  in Hollywood, 107-108
  income, in thirties, 153
  and movie companies, in late twenties,
    55-56
  for movie studios, 147-148
  royalties, in twenties, 91-92
  as song pluggers, 33
  staff, for music publishers, 102
  young Turks, in fifties, 300, 580
Songwriters Guild, 631
Songwriters' Guild (Great Britain), 381
Songwriters of America (SOA), 306, 308,
    328, 402-404, 410, 421, 424, 449,
    480
Songwriters Protective Association, 186,
    195, 199-200, 206-207, 259-260,
    272-275, 289, 290, 293, 294, 299,
    308, 309, 318, 320, 328, 402, 404-
    411, 421-424, 453, 488, 530
Sonny and Cher, 386, 510
"Sonny Boy," 54, 106-107, 126
Sonopress, 648
Sony, 392, 611, 613, 649, 652
Soria, Dario, 244, 378
Soul music, 553-555, 558
Soul Train, 555
Sound of Music, 349
The Sound of Music, 352, 354-355
Sound-track albums, 349, 599
Sour, Robert, 321, 403, 424, 482, 484-485,
    499
Sousa, John Philip, 22, 25
Southern Music Publishing Company, 70,
    118, 121, 180, 301
South Pacific, 239, 304, 352
"South Pacific," 350
SPA, see Songwriters Protective Association
Spaulding, Albert, 94
Speaks, Oley, 94, 106
Specht, Paul, 51
Specialty label, 248
Speyer (investment firm), 69
Spitzer, Henry, 109
Spivak, Charlie, 216
Springsteen, Bruce, 560
SQ Matrix quadraphonic records, 550
The Squaw Man (film), 13
Squier, George Owen, 168
Stafford, Jo, 227, 333, 368
Standard Radio Library, 131, 144
Standard Radio Transcription Service, 425
Stanton, Frank, 405, 432
Star Performance, 414

Starr, Herman, 127, 152-154, 196-201, 207-
    208, 210-211, 219, 255, 257, 261,
    265, 284, 293, 299, 303, 306, 317-
    320, 328-329, 396, 399, 409-411,
    441, 452-453, 472
Starr, Ringo, 382, 473, 539-540
Star Wars (film), 598
Statesmen Quartet, 341
Stax Records, 554-555
"Staying Alive," 598
Steel guitar, 95
Stein, Billy, 258
Stein, Jules, 258
Steinberg, Irwin, 600
Steiner, Max, 11, 148, 152, 275, 277
Stereo-Fidelity, 358
Stereo-Pak, 391
Stereophonic recording, 358-361; sales, in
    fifties and early sixties, 363
Stereo players, 362
Stereo Seven Records, 364
Sterling, Louis, 27, 63, 67, 70, 86, 118-119
Stern and Marks, 37
Stevens, Connie, 349
Stevens, Leith, 314, 409
Stevenson, Adlai, 427
Stewart, Redd, 289
Stewart, Rod, 524
Stigwood, Robert, 389, 514, 595-597, 602
Still, William Grant, 402
Stockman, Thomas, Jr., 612
Stokes, Geoffrey, 639
Stokowski, Leopold, 28, 302, 475
Stoller, Mike, 386, 510, 592, 653
"Stompin' at the Savoy," 137
Stone, Harry, 559
Storecast, 315
Storer Broadcasting, 622
"Stormy Weather," 192
Storz, Robert "Todd," 250, 442-445, 646
Stothart, Herbert, 152, 275
Strand Theatre, New York, 11-12
"Stranger on the Shore," 381
"Strawberry Fields," 512
Street People, 599
Streibert, Theodore, 282
Streisand, Barbra, 380, 386, 532
Strickland, Lily, 94, 106
Strike Force Against Organized Crime, 553
"Strip Polka," 218
"Stumbling," 96
Styne, Jule, 304
Styx, 640
Sugarman, Sidney, 523
"Sugar Shack," 383

Sullivan, Ed, 288, 334, 414
Summer, Donna, 558, 597-598, 640
Sunbury, 643
Sunny, 98
Sunny Side Up, 107
Sun Records, 342, 356, 464
"Sunshine Superman," 536
"Super Gold Rock 'n' Roll," 546
Superman, 355
"Supersoul," 546
Superstar contracts, 603-604, 627
Supreme label, 325
Supremes, 384, 386, 554
Surprise (film), 48
"Suspicious Minds," 515
"Sweethearts," 39
Sweethearts, 157
"Sweet Lady," 96
"Sweet Violets," 133
Swing, 128, 137
Symphony orchestras, licensing, in fifties, 302-303
"Synchronicity," 645
Synchronization rights, 108-109, 277, 476
Syncopated Society Orchestra, 26

Taft-Hartley Act, 229
Talley, Thomas, 5, 14
"Tammy," 408
Tams, Arthur, 37
Tams-Witmark Library, 101
Tango (dance), 26
Tanguay, Eva, 10, 61
Tape cartridges, 361, 391; use in radio, 546-547
Tape recorders, 221; in fifties, 359-360; in sixties, 390-391
Tape recordings, 229-230, 235, 249-250; advancements, in sixties, 480; of background music, 359; car players for, 391-392; cassettes, 392, 635, 647, 653; computerized and digitally mastered, 612; by consumers, of record albums, 593; effect on record industry, 637-638; eight-track, 635; in fifties, 361-362; piracy of, 564; sales, in seventies, 537; in seventies, 549, 551; Stereo 8, 391-392; on television, 415, 416
"Tapestry," 609
Tapestry (King), 541
Tarnapol, Nat, 556-557
"A Taste of Honey," 474
Taupin, Bernie, 537

Taylor, Deems, 265, 278, 409
Technicolor, 153, 155
Ted Synder Music Publishing, 628-629
Ted Weems Orchestra, 78
Teichiku, 245
Teldec Records, 377, 609
Telefunken, 232-233, 377, 392
Telegraphone, 230
Telemeter Magnetics, 415
TelePrompter, 466, 530, 565
Television, 156, 173, 235, 241-242, 244-245. *See also* Cable television
  advertising
    in fifties, 315
    in sixties, 500-501
  ASCAP distributions from, in fifties, 413
  big-screen, in movie theatres, 292
  color, 313, 392, 415, 416
  color videotape, 415
  in fifties, 312, 414-415
  and film industry, 630
  independent stations, music fees, 504-505
  limited license proposal, 502-505
  movies on, 400, 410, 413, 457
  music, in sixties, 455-456
  music budgets, 617-618
  music fees, 524
    in sixties, 500-501
  music licensing, 274-276, 281, 283, 617-623
    in fifties, 292-293, 399
    in sixties, 454, 457-459, 466, 482, 487
  networks, limitation on prime-time programming, 525
  network stock, in sixties, 394
  payola on, 439-440
  programming
    in early fifties, 312-313
    in sixties, 466-467
  program production, in sixties, 392-393
  and song hits, in fifties, 324, 334, 397
Temple, Shirley, 151
Tempo Club orchestra, 29
Tempo Tapes, 359
Temptations, 384
Ten Commandments, 349
Tennessee Ten, 29
"The Tennessee Waltz," 239-240, 288-289, 305, 307, 316, 324, 341, 429
"Tequila," 445
Tesla, Nikola, 74
Texaco Star Theatre, 288
Texas Broadcasting Corp., 479
Texas Tommy (dance), 26
Thames TV, 601

That Creole Band, 29
"That Mesmerizing Mendelssohn Tune," 35
"That Old Gang of Mine," 299
"That Ragtime Violin" (Berlin), 35
"That's All Right, Mama," 342
"That's Entertainment," 402
Theater music, 96
Theatre Network Television, 292
Theatre Owners Booking Association, 58-59
"Theme from *A Summer Place*," 364
Theme music, 440, 483-484
Theodore Morse Music, 472
"There Is a Mountain," 536
"There's a Rainbow 'Round My Shoulder,"
    106, 126
"There's a Star-Spangled Banner Waving
    Somewhere," 252
"They Needed a Songbird in Heaven (So
    They Took Caruso Away)," 62
"They Try to Tell Us We're Too Young,"
    316
Thief of Bagdad (film), 48
"The Thing," 307, 319
This Is Your Life, 314, 415
Thomas, Carla, 554
Thompson, Fred, 53
Thompson, Randall, 402
Thomson, Virgil, 328, 402
Thorn Electrical Industries, 602
Thorn-EMI, 629
Thorn-EMI/Capitol, 654
Three Cheers, 107
Three Little Pigs (cartoon), 150
3M, 361-362, 415, 480
3M tape, 230
The Three Musketeers, 97
"Three O'Clock in the Morning," 96
Three Suns, 387
"Thriller" (Jackson), 644-645, 647
Tic Tac Dough, 452
Tijuana Brass, 385-386
"Till We Meet Again," 35
Timberg, Sigmund, 296, 301
Time Inc., 601
Time magazine, on rock music, 636
"Tim-tay-shun," 227
Tin Pan Alley, 16, 32-33, 113, 117, 122,
    132, 161, 184, 194, 203-204, 207,
    329
Tiomkin, Dimitri, 346, 476
S.S. *Titanic,* 75
Toast of the Town, 288, 334
Tobias, Charles, 328, 402
Today, 415
"To Each His Own," 285

Tom and Jerry, 651
"Tom Dooley," 364
Tommy, 596
Tommy Valando Music, 592
Tompkins, Merritt, 179, 269, 320
Tony Orlando and Dawn, 556
Top 40 programming, 250, 363, 408, 417,
    442, 445, 461, 518-519, 543, 545,
    636, 646
Top Hole, 98
Top of the Pops, 638
Tops Records, 358
Torin, Symphony Sid, 248
Torme, Mel, 223
Toscanini, Arturo, 133, 141
Tower Records, 227
"Träumerei" (Schumann), 10-11
Transamerica Corporation, 394-395, 511,
    595, 643
Transamerica-UA/MGM, 562
Transcontinental Distributing Corp., 511
Transcontinental Investing, 511
Transcontinental Music Corp., 511
Transit Radio, 315
Transglobal, 381
Transoceanic Trading Company, 118
Travolta, John, 597, 599
A Tree Grows in Brooklyn, 402
"A Tree in the Meadow," 285-286
Trentini, Emma, 48
T-Rex, 596
Triangle Film Corporation, 14
Trinity Music, 323, 471
Triumph Investment Trust, 514
Trix, Helen, 25
The Trouble with Rock, 556
"True Love," 398
Trust, Sam, 535
Truth or Consequences, 415
Tubb, Ernest, 240, 427, 464
Tucker, Orrin, 145
Tucker, Sophie, 25
"Tug of War" (McCartney), 604
Turk, Roy, 185
Turkey trot, 25
Turner, Joe, 509
Turner, Tina, 646, 654
Turner Broadcasting Cable Music Channel,
    651
"Tusk" (album), 608, 612
"Tutti Frutti," 378
"Tuxedo Junction," 144
TV Sketch Book, 324
"Tweedle Dee," 340
"12th Street Rag," 286

20th Century-Fox, 152, 311, 317, 392, 489, 562, 594
20th Century-Fox/Movietone/Berlin, 157
20th Century-Fox Records, 348, 609, 643
20th Century-Fox Television, 617
Twenty One, 439, 452
Twilight zone bookkeeping, 188-190, 262, 577
"Twist," 461
Twist (dance), 460-461
"Two Cigarettes in the Dark," 592
"Two Hearts, Two Kisses," 340
Two-step, 25
Tympani Five, 334
"Tzena, Tzena," 236

U.S. v. *Paramount et al.,* 311
UA Music Corporation, 348
UA Records Corporation, 347, 395
Ukelele, 95
Unart Records, 511
Underground radio, in sixties–seventies, 520
Unification Church, 591
Unique Record Company, 346
UNI records, 536
United Artists, 149, 201, 312, 347-348, 373, 382, 395, 511, 534, 541, 594, 643, 644
United Artists Films, 272, 511
United Artists Records, 595, 601
United Artists Television, 617
United Booking Office, 17-20, 40
United Fruit Company, 76
United Independent Broadcasters, 70, 86
United Managers Protective Association, 57
United Paramount Theaters, 311
United Research, 126
United States Record Corp., 141
United States v. *ASCAP,* 210, 452, 485
United States v. *BMI,* 485
United States v. *General Motors–Du Pont,* 423
United Television Programs, 313
Universal, 59
Universal City Studios–Disney v. *Sony et al.,* 630
Universal City Studios–Walt Disney v. *Sony of America,* 611
Universal Copyright Convention, 434, 528, 540
Universal Edition, 269
Universal-International Pictures, 393
Universal Pictures, 54, 245, 293, 334, 393
Universal Studios, 344

University of Texas, Austin, copyright violations by, 632-633
Unlicensed performances, penalties for, 436
Unsinkable Molly Brown, 353
Urania, 244
U.S.S.R., copyright reciprocity with, 528
Utilities & Industries Management Corp., 471-472, 533
Uttal, Larry, 556, 561

VAAP, 528
The Vagabond King, 97
Valando, Tommy, 592
Vale, Jerry, 380, 386
"Valencia," 99
Valentino, Rudolph, 15
Valiant Records, 471
Vallee, Rudy, 89, 112, 119, 150, 161, 185-186, 219
"The Valley of the Moon," 192
"Valse Thematique," 533
Vandersloot Music, 472
Van Heusen, Jimmy, 276, 304
Vanilla Fudge, 510
Varèse, Edgard, 474
Varieties (RKO vaudeville unit), 61
Variety, 19-20, 37-39, 41, 54-55, 59, 62, 79, 113, 320, 406, 422, 440, 547; on ASCAP-broadcaster relations, in late thirties, 175-176; Network Plugs tabulation, 205; reporting on radio, in thirties, 159; weekly song ratings list, 136, 154-155, 199-200, 202-203, 228, 286; on "Your Hit Parade," 166
Variety records, 135
Vaudeville, 16, 92-93; big-time vs. small-time, 16-17; demise of, 57-61; in early 20th c., 21; and popular music, 33; unethical management practices in, 18-19
Vaudeville blues, 30
Vaudeville Managers Association, 17-19, 40
Vaudeville Managers Protective Association, 19-21, 41, 61
Vaughn, Billy, 345, 467
V-Disks, 219, 224
Vee Jay Records, 373, 381
Velie, Lester, 434-435
Verve Records, 347, 351, 388
Very Good Eddie, 97
Viacom Enterprises, 617
Victor, 24-29, 62-72, 113, 117, 118, 119-121, 138-139, 160

Victor Military Band, 27
Victor Record Society, 138
The Victor Society Preview, 138
"Victory" (album), 652
Victory New Orthophonic, 249
Victrola, 16, 22-23, 63
Victrolac, 120
Video 45s, 646
Videocassettes, sales, in eighties, 654
Videodisks, 638
Video games, 641-642
Videola, 440, 452
Video Soul, 646
Videotape, 611; and television, 415
Video tape recorder: first, 415; home use of,
    626, 628
"Vieni, Vieni," 155
Viewlex, 512
Vincent, Robert, 219
Vinylite, 220, 226, 231, 234
Vitacoustics, 227
Vitagraph Company, 10-11
Vitaphone, 54, 131, 149, 160, 488
Vitaphone Company, 51-52
Vitascope, 3-4
Vitavox Company, 140
Viva-Tonal, 68
Vocalion Company, 126-127, 135
"Volare," 408
Von Tilzer, Harry, 91, 101, 284
Vox, 244

Wabash, 471
"Wabash Blues," 64
WABC-AM, 447-448, 636
Wah-wah mute, 64
"Waiting for the Robert E. Lee" (Gilbert
    and Muir), 25
Walk (dance), 26
Walker, Frank, 142, 222, 243
Walker, James J., 222
"Walkin' by the River," 321
Walkman, 610, 652
Waller, Fats, 133, 136-137
Wallerstein, Edward "Ted," 123, 140, 145,
    224, 231-232, 244
Wallichs, Glenn, 217-218, 223, 229, 243,
    376
Wall of Voodoo, 640
Walt Disney, 629
Walt Disney Music Company, 418
"Wang Wang Blues," 96
Waring, Fred, 71, 96, 102, 104, 121-122,
    130, 203, 495

Waring v. *WDAS,* 146
Warner, Harry, 7, 51, 196-198, 201, 208
Warner, Jack, 7, 168, 348-349, 389, 394
Warner, Lou, 107, 109
Warner, Sam, 51
Warner/7 Arts, 509-510
Warner Brothers, 51-52, 54-55, 72, 107-
    109, 111, 113, 118, 120, 126, 140,
    147, 149, 152-154, 165, 167, 187,
    194, 196-198, 200, 202, 204, 316,
    318, 348-349, 371, 394, 413, 550,
    553, 638
Warner Brothers Music, 541
Warner Brothers Records, 388-389, 585
Warner Brothers Television Distribution, 617
Warner Brothers Television Film Company,
    638
Warner Communications, 511, 562, 583,
    594-596, 629, 642-643, 645, 654;
    Atari Videogame Division, 641
Warner Harms, 156
Warner Music Group, 650
Warner-Polygram, proposed merger, 648-649
Warner Records, 536
Warner Records Group, 607
Warner-Reprise, 389, 510
Warner-Reprise/Atlantic, 516-517
Warren, Harry, 149, 153, 185, 304
Washington, Dinah, 325-326
Wasserman, Lew, 611
Waterson, Berlin & Snyder, 29, 36, 82,
    123, 472
Waterson, Henry, 36, 82-83
Watson, Paul, 325
Wattenberg, Sydney, 409
Waxman, Franz, 275
"The Way We Were," 541
WBAI, 544-545
WBEN AM-FM-TV, 523
WBKB-TV, 312
WBLS-FM, 641
WCBS-TV, 311, 313
WCI, 609
WDAS (radio), 130
WEA, 594-595, 607, 634, 644
WEAF (radio), 78, 83-85, 160
Webber, Andrew Lloyd, 596
Weber & Fields, 51
"We Could Make Such Beautiful Music,"
    321
Weil, Milton, 82
Weill, Cynthia, 387
Weinfield, Edward, 431, 603, 628
Weiss, George David, 631
Welk, Lawrence, 379, 407, 471

Wells, Kitty, 427
WENR, 310
WERE, 441
Wertheim & Co., 653
West, Mae, 126, 151, 201
Western Electric, 51-52, 54, 67
Western music, 225
Westerns, 157, 313
Westinghouse, 76-77, 82, 90, 160, 629; radio stations, 442
Westminster, 244
Westrex Company, 360
Wexler, Elliot, 357-358
Wexler, Jerry, 509-510
Wexler, Paul, 357
WFIL-TV, 444
WGN, 164
What Price Glory? (film), 49, 52, 533
What's My Line?, 415
"When I Grow Too Old to Dream," 153
"When My Dreamboat Comes Home," 155
"When the Blue of the Night Meets the Gold of the Day," 185
"When the Lights Go On Again All Over the World," 252
"Whispering" (Grofé), 430
Whitcup, Leonard, 402
White, Barry, 559, 643
White, Byron R., 579
White balladry, 334
"White Christmas" (Berlin), 69, 217, 251, 473
White Citizens' Council, 406
"The White Cliffs of Dover," 252
Whiteman, Paul, 30, 71, 89, 96, 101-102, 104, 118, 121, 138, 143-144, 203, 228, 288
White Rats, 17-21, 57, 61
Whitford, Report, 629
Whiting, Margaret, 223, 286
Whitney, Joan, 402
WHN (radio), 58, 81, 135
The Who, 389, 514, 516
"Who's Afraid of the Big Bad Wolf?," 150
"Who's Sorry Now" case, 627-628, 633
WIBV, 577-578
Williams, Andy, 380, 386, 477, 542
Williams, Bert, 8
Williams, Clarence, 471
Williams, Hank, 240, 289, 307, 427, 465
Williams, John, 532
Williams, Tex, 227
Williamson Music, 653
William Tell Overture, 10
Wills, Nat M., 25

Willson, Meredith, 193, 353
Wilson, Mortimer, 48
Wilson, Nancy, 386
Wilson, Woodrow, 76
Windham Hill Records, 636
Wings, 538
Wings (film), 53
Winkler, Max, 48, 533
WINS, 461, 462
Winslow, Max, 36, 460
Winslow's Singles, 36
Winterhalter, Hugo, 236, 345, 467
Wired radio, 168
Wireless telegraphy, 74-75
"With a Little Help from My Friends," 544
Witmark, Isidore, 37, 39, 43
Witmark, Julius P., 113-114
Witmark Black and White Library, 101
M. Witmark & Sons, 6, 22, 29, 37, 55, 101, 105, 108, 190, 317
The Wiz, 599
The Wizard of Oz, 157
WJZ (radio), 77, 79, 80, 85, 160, 310
WMCA (radio), 310
WMGM, 349
WNEW (radio), 128-129, 143, 169, 441
WNEW-AM, 467
Wolfman Jack, 248, 639
Wonder, Stevie, 384, 524, 539, 554, 590, 640
The Wonderful World of Disney, 652
"Wonderland by Night," 379
Wood, Randy, 346, 349
Woodin, W. H., 154
Woods, Leo, 110
Woods, William, 575
B. F. Woods Music, 472
F. W. Woolworth, 121
Woolworth, Frank W., 24, 34
"F. W. Woolworth March," 34
WOR (radio), 86, 164
Word, 561
Words and Music Club, 92
Words & Music, 203-204
World Broadcasting Service, 131-132, 144, 219, 220
World Record Club, 377-378
"The World's Largest Make Believe Ballroom" (radio show), 129
World Special Films, 9
World Transcription Library, 229
WPAT-AM, 461
"The Wreck of the Old 97," 100
Wright-Patman Act, 373, 375
WSB (radio), 64

WSVA-TV, 457
WTIX, 442
WTMJ-TV, 312
Wurlitzer Company, 47, 110, 134, 137, 583

XTRA, 575

"Yakety Yak," 430
"Y'All Come," 334
Yardbirds, 386
Yates, Herbert, 125-127, 133-134, 151, 157, 196-197, 313
Yellen, Jack, 105, 402
"Yes, We Have No Bananas," 93, 200
Yetnikoff, Walter, 560, 594, 635, 643, 645, 647
"Yiddle on Your Fiddle Play a Ragtime Tune" (Berlin), 35
Yogi Bear, 651
York, Dane, 117
"You and I," 264
"You Are My Lucky Star," 154
"You Are My Sunshine," 217
Youmans, Vincent, 97, 198, 530
Young, Neil, 547

Young, Rida Johnson, 98
Young, Victor, 125, 275, 402
"Young at Heart," 333-334, 405-406
Young People's Records, 335
"Your Hit Parade," 165-166, 175, 181, 203, 205, 240, 250, 266, 322, 422, 433
Your Show of Shows, 295
"You Were Meant for Me," 107
"Yummy, Yummy," 509

Zamecnik, J. S., 111
Zappa, Frank, 340, 524
Zavin, Theodora, 424, 426
Zenith, 77, 173
Zentner, Sy, 467
Ziegfeld, Florenz, 29, 83, 157, 201
Ziegfeld Follies, 8
Zissu, Leonard, 276-277
Ziv, 413
Zkor, Adolph, 8
Zorro, 344
Zukor, Adolph, 7, 10, 14-15
Zukor's Famous Players, 9
Zukor's Famous Players–Paramount Corporation, 13
Zworykin, Vladimir, 156, 311

Index
To Part Ten

ABC, 664
Abdul, Paula, 679
Ace of Base, 671, 677
"Achy Breaky Heart," 677
Acuff-Rose, 681
Adams, Bryan, 674
Aerosmith, 659, 676
Aladdin (film), 671, 674
Alligator Records, 666
"Alone Again, Naturally," 681
A&M Records, 667, 672
American Society of Composers,
    Authors, and Publishers
    (ASCAP), 682
American Telephone & Telegraph
    (AT&T), 682
Arista Records, 672
Arnold, Gina, 679
Ashman, Howard, 674
As Nasty As They Wanna Be, 668
Atlanta Braves, 673
Atlanta Hawks, 673
Atlantic Records, 672
Azoff, Irving, 668

B52s, 678
"Baby Bells," 682
"Babyface," see Kenneth Edwards
Bad, 658
Bagdikian, Ben, 672
Baker, James, 663
Beastie Boys, 659

Beatles, 662
Beat Street (film), 659
Bee Gees, 677
Bennett, William, 680
Bertelsman, 672
Best Buy, 675
Beverly Hills Cop (film), 662
Biafra, Jello, 663
Big Chill, The (film), 658
Billboard, 658, 671
Black, David, 670
Black Entertainment Television (BET),
    661
Black Sabbath, 659
Blackwell, Chris, 667
Blanket licenses, 664
Bleach, 678
Blockbuster Video, 677
BMG, 667
BMG Classics, 672
Body Count, 681
Bodyguard, The (film), 674, 679
Bon Jovi, 659
Boomerang (film), 674
"Box, The," 661
Boyz II Men, 674, 679
Braxton, Toni, 679
Breakin' (film), 659
Breen, Marcus, 674
Broadcast Music Inc. (BMI), 682
Brooks, Garth, 675, 677, 679
Brooks & Dunn, 677
Brown, Bobby, 679

Buffalo v. ASCAP, BMI, et al., 663
Butthole Surfers, 678

Capitol Cities Broadcasting, 664, 673
Capitol Records, 673
Caribbean zouk, 667
Cartoon Network, 673
Casey, Mariah, 676, 679
Castle Rock Productions, 673
CBS, 667, 673
CEMA, 673, 675
Censorship, 663, 668–69, 680–81
Charles, Ray, 662
Chase, The, 677
Christgau, Robert, 666, 667, 671
Chronic, The, 680
Chrysalis Records, 673
Cinderella, 659
Circuit City, 675
CNN, 673
Cobain, Kurt, 679
Collective Soul, 678
College Music Journal (CMJ), 678
Collins, Dan, 667
Columbia Records, 672
Commercial advertising, 662
Commodores, 659
Communications Act (1934), 682
Communications Decency Act (1996), 682
Compact Disc (CD), 664, 665, 669
Compuserve, 682
Conflict, 678
Conglomeration, 667–68, 672–74
Coolio, 674
"Cop Killer," 681
Copyright Act, 682
Country music, 659–60, 677,
Coury, Al, 657, 674
Cracked Rear View, 677
Culture Club, 660
Cyrus, Billy Ray, 677

Dangerous Minds (film), 674
David Geffen Co. (DGC), 668, 679
Dbs, 678
Dead Kennedys, 663
Deep Purple, 659
De La Soul, 669
Denver, John, 663
Deutsche Gramophone Records, 672
Def Jam Records, 672
Def Leppard, 659

Diet Pepsi, 662
Digital Audio Tape (DAT), 665
Digital sampler, 669
Dirty Dancing (film), 658
Disney Corporation, 661, 673, 674
Disney Records, 671
Dookie, 677
"Do They Know It's Christmas," 660
Dr. Dre, 680
Duffy, Judge Kevin Thomas, 681
Duran Duran, 660

Edwards, Kenneth "Babyface," 679
Elektra Records, 672, 676
Elektra/Asylum Records, 666
EMI, 667, 673
En Vogue, 679
"End of the Road," 674
Enigma Records, 666
Epic Records, 672
Epitaph Records, 671
"(Everything I Do) I Do It For You," 674

Fairness in Music Licensing bill, 682
Fairweather Johnson, 677
Farm Aid, 660
Farrell, Perry, 678
Fat Boys, 659
Feelies, 678
Fine Line Cinema, 673
Flying Fish Records, 666
Footloose (film), 658
Forced Exposure, 678
Formats of recordings, 664–65, 665–66, 669
Fuchs, Michael, 674
Fund raising, 660

Gangsta rap, 680
"Gangsta's Paradise," 674
Geffen, David, 667
Geffen Records, 673, 675
Geldof, Bob, 660
Giant Records, 672
Gieger, H.R., 663
Gore, Senator Albert, 663
Graceland, 667
Grand Ole Opry, 661
Grass, Randall, 667
Green Day, 677, 678
GRP Records, 673
Grunge rock, 679

Guns N' Roses, 659, 678
Guthrie, Arlo, 666

Hammer, 680
Handleman Company, 675
Haring, Bruce, 676
Heavy metal music, 659
Hicks Communications, 664
Home Audio Recording Act, 681
Home Tape Royalty, 681
Hootie & the Blowfish, 671, 677
Houston, Whitney, 658, 674, 676, 679
Hüsker Dü, 678

"I Need A Haircut," 681
"I Will Always Love You," 674, 679
Ice Cube, 680
Ice T, 680, 681
"Indies" (Independent record labels),
    666, 667, 677–79
Individuals, 678
Insomniac, 677
Interscope Records, 680
In Utero, 679
IRS Records, 673
Island Records, 667, 672

Jackson, Alan, 677
Jackson, Janet, 676, 679
Jackson, Michael, 658, 662, 676, 679
Jane's Addiction, 678
Jazz, 660
Jodeci, 679
Johnson, Robert, 665
Judds, 660

K Records, 678
Kiss-FM KTKS (Dallas, Texas), 664
KIXX (Denton, Texas), 664
Kool and the Gang, 658
Krasnow, Robert, 674

LL Cool J, 659
La Bamba (film), 658
Lauper, Cindy, 660
Leiberman Enterprises, 675
Liberty Records, 673
Licensed To Ill, 659
Licorice Pizza, 663

Little Steven, 660
Lion King, The (film), 671, 674
Live Aid, 660
LIVE Entertainment, 675
Lollapalooza, 678
Los Lobos, 658

Madonna, 660
Markie, Biz, 681
Marsalis, Branford, 660
Marsalis, Wynton, 660
MCA Records, 667, 673, 675
MCA Music Entertainment Group, 680
MCI, 682
McChesney, Robert, 683
McEntire, Reba, 660, 677
McGraw, Tim, 677
Media Corporation, 661
Media Monopoly, The (Bagdikian), 672
Mellencamp, John Cougar, 660
Mencken, Alan, 674
MGM, 673
Midler, Bette, 669
Minutemen, 678
Modungo, Domenico, 674, 677
Montgomery, J.M., 677
Montgomery Ward, 662
Morgado, Robert, 679
Morris, Doug, 674, 680
Morrison, Van, 666
Motley Crüe, 659, 676
Motorbooty, 678
Motown Records, 672
Musicland, 663
Music Plus, 675
Music Television (MTV), 660, 661, 677
Mutual Broadcasting System, 664

Nashville Network, The (TNN), 661
National Association of Independent
    Record Distributors and
    Manufacturers (NAIRD), 688
National Association of Record
    Manufacturers (NARM), 675
National Record Mart, 675
Nelson, Willie, 660
Nevermind, 679
Nevins, Richard, 667
New Line Cinema, 673
Nike, 662
Nirvana, 678, 679
No Fences, 677

NWA, 668

Offspring, 671, 681
Oh Boy Records, 666
"Oh Pretty Woman," 681
"One I Love, The," 678
Opryland, 661
Orbison, Roy, 681
Ostin, Mo, 674
O'Sullivan, Gilbert, 681
Out Of Time, 678

Paramount Pictures, 661
Pareles, Jon, 666
Parents Music Research Council
    (PMRC), 663, 668
Parton, Dolly, 679
Pearl Jam, 678
Pepsi-Cola, 662
Performance Right in Sound Recording
    Act, 682
Phillips Electronics, 672
Pitchford, Dean, 658
Please Hammer Don't Hurt Em, 680
Pocahontas (film), 671, 674
Pointer Sisters, 658
Poison, 659
Polydor Records, 672
Polygram, 667
Presley, Elvis, 677
"Pretty Woman," 681
Price Communications, 664
Prince, 663
Private Music, 672
Public Enemy, 659, 668
Purple Rain (film), 655
Pylon, 678

Raising Hell, 659
Rap music, 659, 680–81
"Rapper's Delight," 659
R&B, 658–9, 679–80
RCA Records, 672
Record Bar, 657, 662, 663
Record Factory, 663
Record Land, 662
Record World, 675
Recording Industry Association of
    America (RIAA), 668, 670, 682
Reissues, 665
R.E.M., 678

Replacements, 670
Reprise Records, 672
Retailing of music, 662–63, 675–76
"Revolution," 662
Rhino Records, 665, 672
Rice, Tim, 674
Rising Son Records, 666
Ritchie, Lionel, 658, 660
Roches, 666
Robin Hood: Prince of Thieves (film), 674
RKO Broadcasting, 662
Rock Records, 671
Rogers, Kenny, 677
Rolling Stone, 678
Ropin' The Wind, 677
Rose, Axel, 668
Run-DMC, 659
Rykodisc Records, 665

Sade, 658
Salt-n-Pepa, 659
Sampling, 681
Saturday Night Fever (film), 657, 674, 677
SBK, 668, 673
Schwartz, Stephen, 674
Seagram's, 673
Shanachie Records, 667
Sight & Sound, 675
The Sign, 677
Simon, Paul, 667
Sire Records, 672
Skaggs, Ricky, 660
Slippery When Wet, 659
"Smells Like Teen Spirit," 679
W.H. Smith, 675
Snider, Dee, 663
Snoop Doggy Dog, 680
Society of European Stage Authors and
    Composers (SESAC), 682
Sony, 675
Sony Legacy, 665
Soul Asylum, 678
SOUNDSCAN, 675, 676
Soundgarden, 678
Soundtracks, motion picture, 658, 674–75
Sound Warehouse, 675
Sprint, 682
SST Records, 666
Stigwood, Robert, 674
Sting, 660
Stone Temple Pilots, 678
Storms of Life, 660
Storz Broadcasting, 664

Strait, George, 660
Sub Pop Records, 678
"Sugar Walls," 663
Sugarhill Gang, 659
"Sun City," 660
Swellsville, 678
"Synergy," 673, 674

2 Live Crew, 668, 681
2Pac Shakur, 680
TBS Superstation, 673
Telecommunications bill, 682
Television Source Licensing Bill, 664
Thriller, 658
Tillis, Pam, 677
Time Magazine, 670
Time Warner, 672, 673
TNT, 673
Too Legit To Quit, 680
Top Gun (film), 658, 662
Tower Records, 657
Transworld, 662
Travis, Randy, 660
Trinidadian soca, 667
Turner, Ted, 661
Turner Broadcasting, 673
Turner Classic Movies, 673
Turner Entertainment, 673
Turner, Tina, 658
Turtles, 669
Twin/Tone Records, 666

U2, 679
UNI, 673
United Artists, 673
United Stations, 664
Uptown Records, 673
Urban Cowboy (film), 659
USA For Africa, 660

"U Can't Touch This," 680
Use Your Illusion I & II, 677

V-Chip, 682
Valens, Ritchie, 658
Vanilla Ice, 680
Verlaine, Tom, 666
Vestron, 662
Viacom, 664
Video, Music, 660–61,
Video Hits-1 (VH-1) 661
Video tape sales, 661–2
Village Voice Pazz & Jop Critics Poll, 671
Virgin Records, 673, 675, 676

Waits, Tom, 669
"Walk This Way," 659
Wallmart, 663
Warehouse Entertainment, 663
Warner Brothers (WEA), 667, 672, 675, 681
Warner Brothers Motion Pictures, 673
"We Are The World," 660
Westinghouse, 673
Westwood One Broadcasting, 664
Whitesnake, 659
Williams, Vanessa, 679
Windham Hill Records, 672
World music, 666-67

Yearwood, Tricia, 677
"Yo! MTV Raps," 661
Yoakam, Dwight, 660

Zairean soukous, 667
Zappa, Frank, 663
Zoo Records, 672

Other titles of interest

BLUES: AN ANTHOLOGY
Edited by W. C. Handy
228 pp., 14 illus.
80411-5 $15.95

BOB DYLAN: THE EARLY YEARS
A Retrospective
Edited by Craig McGregor
New preface by Nat Hentoff
424 pp., 15 illus.
80416-6 $13.95

BROTHER RAY
Ray Charles' Own Story
Updated Edition
Ray Charles and David Ritz
370 pp., 30 photos
80482-4 $13.95

CALL ME LUCKY
Bing Crosby as told to Pete Martin
New introduction by Gary Giddins
384 pp., 64 photos
80504-9 $13.95

BROWN SUGAR
Eighty Years of America's
Black Female Superstars
Donald Bogle
208 pp., 183 photos
80380-1 $15.95

CHRISTGAU'S RECORD GUIDE
The '80s
Robert Christgau
525 pp.
80582-0 $17.95

THE DA CAPO COMPANION
TO 20th-CENTURY
POPULAR MUSIC
Phil Hardy and Dave Laing
1,168 pp.
80640-1 $29.50

DIVIDED SOUL
The Life of Marvin Gaye
David Ritz
367 pp., 47 photos
80443-3 $13.95

THE FOLK MUSIC
SOURCEBOOK
Updated Edition
Larry Sandberg and Dick Weissman
288 pp., 97 photos
80360-7 $18.95

GLENN MILLER & HIS
ORCHESTRA
George T. Simon
Introduction by Bing Crosby
473 pp., over 130 photos
80129-9 $14.95

HEROES AND VILLAINS
The True Story of the Beach Boys
Steven Gaines
432 pp., 66 photos
80647-9 $14.95

I'D RATHER BE THE DEVIL
Skip James and the Blues
Stephen Calt
400 pp., 13 pp. of illus.
80579-0 $14.95

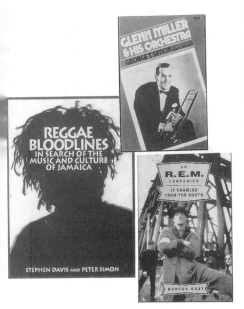

NOWHERE TO RUN
The Story of Soul Music
Gerri Hirshey
416 pp., 26 photos
80581-2 $14.95

REGGAE BLOODLINES
In Search of the Music and Culture of Jamaica
Text by Stephen Davis
Photographs by Peter Simon
224 pp., 252 photos
80496-4 $16.95

SHOWTIME AT THE APOLLO
Ted Fox
336 pp., 155 illus.
80503-0 $13.95

THE SOUND OF THE CITY
The Rise of Rock and Roll
Newly illustrated and expanded
Charlie Gillett
604 pp., 64 pp. of illus.
80683-5 $16.95

IT CRAWLED FROM THE SOUTH
An R.E.M. Companion
Marcus Gray
381 pp., 53 photos
80500-6 $16.95

JAZZ: America's Classical Music
Grover Sales
255 pp., 61 photos
80491-3 $13.95

LORETTA LYNN
Coal Miner's Daughter
Loretta Lynn with George Vecsey
236 pp., 34 photos
80680-0 $13.95

LIVE AT THE VILLAGE VANGUARD
Max Gordon
146 pp., 36 photos
80160-4 $10.95

LOUIS: The Louis Armstrong Story 1900-1971
Max Jones and John Chilton
302 pp., 50 photos
80324-0 $12.95

MUSIC IS MY MISTRESS
Edward Kennedy Ellington
522 pp., 112 photos
80033-0 $15.95

MUSICAL STAGES
An Autobiography
Richard Rodgers
New introd. by Mary Rodgers
379 pp., 145 illus.
80634-7 $14.95

NOTES AND TONES
Musician-to-Musician Interviews
Expanded Edition
Arthur Taylor
318 pp., 20 photos
80526-X $13.95